Microcomputer Applications Workbook

Microcomputer Applications Workbook

Featuring:
WordPerfect®
Lotus® 1-2-3® and Joe Spreadsheet™ (a 1-2-3® Workalike)
dBASE III PLUS®

With Software

WILSON T. PRICE

The Dryden Press
Chicago Fort Worth San Francisco Philadelphia
Montreal Toronto London Sydney Tokyo

Acquisitions Editor: David Chodoff
Production Manager: Roger Kasunic
Production Coordinator: Spectrum Publisher Services, Inc.
Interior Design: Rita Naughton
Cover Design: Marsha Cohen/Parallelogram
Part opening illustrations: Robert Andrew Parker
Photo Research: Teri Stratford
Illustrations: J & R Services
Composition: Kachina Typesetting
Printing and Binding: Arcata

Address orders:
The Dryden Press
Orlando, Florida 32887

Address editorial correspondence:
The Dryden Press
908 North Elm Street, Hinsdale, IL 60521

Printed in the United States of America

ISBN 0–03–026–397–2 Workbook with software
ISBN 0–03–026–402–2 Workbook without software
ISBN 0–03–026–394–8 with software
ISBN 0–03–026–403–0 without software

9 0 1 2 069 9 8 7 6 5 4 3 2 1

The Dryden Press
Holt, Rinehart and Winston, Inc.
Saunders College Publishing

Important: Please read this page before using the dBASE III PLUS program, a copy of which is being made available to you for use in conjunction with this Workbook pursuant to the terms of this Agreement for educational, training and/or demonstration purposes. By using the dBASE III PLUS program, you show your agreement to the terms of this license.

EXCLUSIONS OF WARRANTIES AND LIMITATIONS OF LIABILITY

THE COPY OF THE dBASE III PLUS PROGRAM MADE AVAILABLE FOR USE WITH THIS WORKBOOK IS A LIMITED FUNCTIONALITY VERSION OF dBASE III PLUS, AND IS INTENDED SOLELY FOR EDUCATIONAL, TRAINING AND DEMONSTRATION PURPOSES. ACCORDINGLY, THIS COPY OF dBASE III PLUS IS PROVIDED "AS IS," WITHOUT WARRANTY OF ANY KIND FROM ASHTON-TATE OR HOLT RINEHART & WINSTON. ASHTON-TATE AND HOLT RINEHART & WINSTON HEREBY DISCLAIM ALL WARRANTIES OF ANY KIND WITH RESPECT TO THIS LIMITED FUNCTIONALITY COPY OF dBASE III PLUS, INCLUDING WITHOUT LIMITATION THE IMPLIED WARRANTIES OF MERCHANTABILITY AND FITNESS FOR A PARTICULAR PURPOSE. NEITHER ASHTON-TATE NOR HOLT RINEHART & WINSTON SHALL BE LIABLE UNDER ANY CIRCUMSTANCES FOR CONSEQUENTIAL, INCIDENTAL, SPECIAL OR EXEMPLARY DAMAGES ARISING OUT OF THE USE OF THIS LIMITED FUNCTIONALITY COPY OF dBASE III PLUS, EVEN IF ASHTON-TATE OR HOLT RINEHART & WINSTON HAS BEEN APPRISED OF THE LIKELIHOOD OF SUCH DAMAGES OCCURRING. IN NO EVENT WILL ASHTON-TATE'S OR HOLT RINEHART & WINSTON'S LIABILITY (WHETHER BASED ON AN ACTION OR CLAIM IN CONTRACT, TORT OR OTHERWISE) ARISING OUT OF THE USE OF THIS LIMITED FUNCTIONALITY COPY OF dBASE III PLUS EXCEED THE AMOUNT PAID FOR THIS WORKBOOK.

LIMITED USE SOFTWARE LICENSE AGREEMENT

Definitions

The term "Software" as used in this agreement means the Limited Use version of dBASE III PLUS which is made available for use in conjunction with this Workbook solely for educational, training and/or demonstration purposes. The term "Software Copies" means the actual copies of all or any portion of the Software, including back-ups, updates, merged or partial copies permitted hereunder.

Permitted Uses

You may:

- Load into RAM and use the Software on a single terminal or a single workstation of a computer (or its replacement).
- Install the Software onto a permanent storage device (a hard disk drive).
- Make and maintain up to three back up copies provided they are used only for back-up purposes, and you keep possession of the back-ups. In addition, all the information appearing on the original disk labels (including copyright notice) must be copied onto the back-up labels.

This license gives you certain limited rights to use the Software and Software Copies for educational, training and/or demonstration purposes. You do not become the owner of and Ashton-Tate retains title to, all the Software and Software Copies. In addition, you agree to use reasonable efforts to protect the Software from unauthorized use, reproduction, distribution or publication.

All rights not specifically granted in this license are reserved by Ashton-Tate.

Uses Not Permitted

You may not:

- Make copies of the Software, except as permitted above.
- Rent, lease, sublicense, time-share, lend or transfer the Software, Software Copies or your rights under this license except that transfers may be made with Ashton-Tate's prior written authorization.
- Alter, decompile, disassemble, or reverse-engineer the Software.
- Remove or obscure the Ashton-Tate copyright and trademark notices.

Duration

This agreement is effective from the day you first use the Software. Your license continues for fifty years or until you return to Ashton-Tate the original disks and any back-up copies, whichever comes first.

If you breach this agreement, Ashton-Tate can terminate this license upon notifying you in writing. You will be required to return all Software Copies. Ashton-Tate can also enforce our other legal rights.

General

This agreement represents the entire understanding and agreement regarding the Software and Software Copies and supersedes any prior purchase order, communication, advertising or representation.

This license may only be modified in a written amendment signed by an authorized Ashton-Tate officer. If any provision of this agreement shall be unlawful, void, or for any reason unenforceable, it shall be deemed severable from, and shall in no way affect the validity or enforceability of the remaining provisions of this agreement. This agreement will be governed by California law.

The Limited Use Educational Version of WordPerfect 4.2 included with this Workbook is licensed to the person who purchased the book. The purchaser is free to make backup copies for his or her own archival purposes only. He or she can use the software on different computers provided the software is never used on more than one computer at a time. Under no circumstances can this software be resold.

The Limited Use Educational Version of WordPerfect 4.2 contains certain limitations:

No file larger than 50K (roughly 25 to 30 single spaced pages) can be saved to disk. Documents of any size, however, can be edited on screen.

A data file created with the Limited Use Educational Version cannot be imported into regular WordPerfect, nor can a file created in regular WordPerfect be imported into the Limited Use Educational Version.

The message "WPC" will be printed after every paragraph.

Data files of any size can be printed through parallel printer port 1 without defining a printer, but font changes and extended ASCII characters are not allowed.

One cannot use the Limited Use Educational Version's speller and thesaurus with any of one's own documents because there are only a limited number of words in the Limited Use Educational Version's speller and thesaurus. To use the thesaurus and speller in the Limited Use Educational Version, follow the instructions in the file called "readme.wp".

The help file of the Limited Use Educational Version allows the user to retrieve the function key template, but space will not allow the full help files on the Limited Use Educational Version disk.

The Limited Use Educational Version of WordPerfect 4.2 is designed for introductory word processing courses. It is not, however, meant to substitute for the regular full-featured version of WordPerfect 4.2. The full-featured version may be obtained directly from WordPerfect Corporation at a 75 percent discount by means of the enclosed order form.

Contents

Preface

The premise of this book is simple: The best way to learn is to do, so the best way to learn about computers is to "do" computers. A computer book that claims to teach you to learn by doing has to meet certain criteria:

- It must provide clear instructions on the use of specific applications on specific computers. And if those instructions are to be of any value to students, both the software and the computers must be widely used in the business world.
- It must provide abundant opportunities for hands-on practice in the form of examples, exercises, and assignments.
- It must do all this in the context of a business environment—the environment for which students want to learn computer skills in the first place.

Microcomputer Applications Workbook meets all these criteria. It provides hands-on instruction—for the IBM personal computer—on WordPerfect®; Lotus® 1–2–3® and Joe Spreadsheet™, a keystroke compatible 1–2–3 work-alike; and dBASE III PLUS®. It provides numerous hands-on examples keyed to an accompanying data disk. It provides abundant end-of-chapter exercises and assignments. Furthermore, it puts it all in a business context.

MODULAR ORGANIZATION

Microcomputer Applications Workbook is organized into the following four parts:

Part One, Getting Started (Chapter 1)

Part Two, Word Processing and Desktop Publishing (Chapters 2 and 3)

Part Three, Spreadsheets and Computer Graphics (Chapters 4, 5, and 6)

Part Four, Database Management (Chapters 7 and 8)

Part One covers using DOS and provides the student the necessary background to work with the computer. The remaining parts are application software specific with a central focus of doing. Each of these three parts starts with a part introduction that provides a generic description of the particular application area. For instance, the introduction to Part Two describes the general nature of word processing. Two chapters make up each of these parts: the first provides the basic elements to use the software (WordPerfect, 1-2-3, and dBASE III PLUS), and the second covers more advanced topics. Part Three also includes a chapter on business graphics using the graphing capabilities of Lotus 1-2-3.

"Do This Now" Sections

Student activities and learning are guided by over 100 "Do This Now" descriptions. Each defines an activity (for example, editing a document with WordPerfect) and then describes, step by step, the procedures that the student should follow to carry out the activity. These activities range from simple (such as entering text with WordPerfect) to complex (such as generating a bar graph from data of a spreadsheet). Many of these are keyed to data files included on the data disk that accompanies each copy of the book.

Available With or Without Software

Microcomputer Applications Workbook is available with limited educational versions of WordPerfect 4.2 and dBASE III PLUS, and a full-featured version of JOE spreadsheet, a keystroke compatible Lotus 1-2-3 workalike. The software comes packaged with the book.

For those of you who already have the appropriate software available in your computer labs, the text is also available without software.

Data Disk

Both versions of the text (with or without software) includes a data disk with word processing, spreadsheet, and database files keyed to examples and assignments in the text.

A Wide Variety of Assignments

Each chapter includes: review questions, objective questions, and assignments/projects.

- Review questions. At specific checkpoints in each chapter, the student is directed to complete a review question assignment at the end of the chapter. These assignments reinforce concepts encountered since the last such assignment.
- Objective questions. These questions can be assigned when the chapter is completed; they consist of matching, true/false, multiple choice, and fill-in.
- Assignments/projects. These assignments require that the student use the software described in the chapter. Each set of assignments includes a wide difficulty range with some assignments being similar to examples that the student has done in the chapter, and others requiring some careful thought and extrapolation of ideas.

Assignment Pages Designed for Easy Removal

The questions and assignments occupy over *200 pages* of the book. All of these pages are perforated so that the assignments can be removed from the book and turned in.

OTHER FEATURES

Each chapter employs a number of learning aids to help students master the material. These include:

- A list of Learning Objectives.
- A Chapter Preview containing brief descriptions of each section of the chapter.
- Boldface Key Terms throughout the text, which are also repeated in the New Terminology section.
- A New Terminology section that lists the key terms of the chapter.
- A bulleted Summary.
- Assignments, Objective Questions, and Assignments/Projects.

ACKNOWLEDGMENTS

Although only one name appears on the cover of this book, many people, including students and colleagues, have contributed to the finished product. I would like to mention first all the people who reviewed the various chapters in their many drafts. Your comments kept me in touch with the needs of those teaching and taking courses in microcomputer applications:

Wesley E. Nance	Cerritos College, California
Peter L. Irwin	Richland College, Texas
Travis D. Walker	Mineral Area College, Missouri
Kevin Holvorson	Willmar Community College, Minnesota
Steven J. Brown	Gannon University, Pennsylvania
Pat Fenton	West Valley College, California
Lister Wayne Horn	Pensacola Junior College, Florida
Richard Bernardin	Cape Cod Community College, Massachusetts
Stanley Niemczycki	El Camino College, California
Leah Rose Pietron	University of Nebraska, Omaha

Marjorie Anderson served as a developmental editor on the precursor to this book. Elise Oranges of Spectrum Publisher Services, Inc., coordinated the many pieces of the project under an especially tight schedule. Their efforts were exceptional.

Also, I must express special appreciation to David Chodoff who provided ongoing support for this book. Without David, the book may well not have been. Thanks are also due to many others at Holt and Dryden: DeVilla Williams, Butch Gemin, Roger Kasunic, Doug Chilcott, and Elaine Pascal.

To all of the people who helped make this a better book, I offer a very special "Thank you."

Wilson T. Price

PART ONE

Getting Started

INTRODUCTION TO PART ONE

Part One of this book consists of Chapter 1 describing the basic software necessary to using the computer (the disk operating system). The purpose of this introduction is to:

- Describe a simple business case study that you will use in later chapters of the book.
- Introduce the IBM Personal Computer, the computer on which software described in this book is run.

STARTING A BUSINESS

The Idea for a Business

Assume that you and an acquaintance have decided to start a small business venture. Your proposed partner might be a colleague at work who was laid off when the company retrenched, a brother or sister with an idea, or a fellow graduate who simply is not interested in starting a career by working for someone else. During your summer vacations from college, you had worked at the beach selling general casual wear such as sweatshirts, T-shirts, and shorts. Being observant, you learned from the experience. You saw what people buy, you understand the needs of the specialty shops, and you have a bold idea for marketing a new line that should appeal to impulse buying. You decide to approach your school acquaintance regarding a partnership because he studied business in college and spent his summers assisting in managing the office of his mother's small business. In that capacity, he used a computer extensively. (In addition, he has some savings that might be available for the right situation.) Here we have the right ingredients for a business venture: knowledge about the business activity, knowledge about running a business, and capital. All too often, a person with a good knowledge of a product or service will start a business and fail because he or she does not know how to run the business. Planning of expenditures, keeping accurate records of money owed, and maintaining records for tax purposes are only a few of the many information processing activities that are essential to running a business. You recognized this in selecting a partner with the necessary skills and abilities that you lack. A handshake between you and your friend is followed by a trip to the local governmental agency where the partnership papers are filed and the new company, MCT Enterprises, becomes a reality.

Defining a Business Plan

In starting your business, you must give careful consideration to the way in which you commit your resources, both money and time. Since you do not have lavish financing, you must define precisely your particular niche in the marketplace. You already know the exact products with which you wish to make your entry. After considerable discussion and weighing of various alternatives, you decide to position your company as a wholesaler selling to retail stores. One of your high-priority actions is to contract with independent sales representatives to handle your product line. With the exception of a mail order operation that you decide to pursue, you have no intention of getting into retail sales.

The careful management of your money requires many basic decisions regarding the exact way in which you plan to organize your company. For instance, some activities are best done by you and your partner and others by outside contractors. To these ends, you decide to lease a small space in an industrial park that you can use as a combination office, work area, and warehouse. From this facility, you, your partner, and a person working as a part-time pattern maker will:

- Handle all record keeping.
- Maintain your inventory of finished garments.
- Fill and ship all orders.
- Design and make all patterns for new garments to be manufactured.

All cutting and sewing will be done by an outside sewing contractor. You will place orders to your suppliers for needed fabrics and accessories, which will be shipped to and inventoried at the contractor's facility. As each sewing run is completed, the finished product will be delivered to your office/warehouse.

Data Processing Needs

Carefully analyzing your market, designing your product line, and planning your mode of operation are essential aspects of your business plan. Another critical aspect is managing data that you collect. For instance, as the result of a series of telephone calls, you may have a variety of notes relating to fabric qualities and prices from different suppliers. In this raw form, the data is of limited value. However, by arranging it into an organized form, such as tabulations by vendor, fabric type, quantity, and price, the data provides information that can be used in making decisions. The unorganized collection of facts is **data**; data that has been organized into a useful form is information. The objective of data processing is to convert data into information. To achieve the portion of your business plan devoted to electronic data processing and to expand it to all tasks you hope to computerize, you must learn about the components of a computer and the types of programs that make it work. The remainder of this introduction provides you with a basic background to computer hardware that you will be using.

THE ESSENTIALS OF A COMPUTER

About Automobiles and Computers

Virtually all of us have had some experience with automobiles. We all view our automobiles differently. For instance, a car can be seen as a status symbol or an embarrassment, a hobby or a necessary evil, a smoothly functioning machine or an unreliable piece of junk. Let us be more abstract and view the automobile from an entirely different point of view; that is, it is a machine (a piece of *hardware*) that is designed to perform a particular function—to get us from one place to another. Note that it does not allow us to do anything basic that we cannot already do ourselves. We do not need an automobile (or any other modern means of transportation) to get from New York to Boston; we can always walk. Of course, the automobile allows us to make the trip much faster (except perhaps on Labor Day weekend). As a matter of fact, we can walk to places that are impossible to drive to. For example, when is the last time you heard of someone driving to the top of Mount Everest? Overall, it is probably safe to say that the automobile certainly *extends* our ability to move from one place to another.

Now let us view the automobile as a transportation system that can be used to perform a certain function. What are the basic components of that system? One way of looking at it is to say that this system consists of two broad components: the automobile itself and the fuel that makes it run. Both are essential. Without fuel, the automobile is not much of a transportation device except for coasting from the top of a hill to the bottom. This is not to suggest that it would be *totally* useless without fuel. Indeed, with the top removed, it might make an interesting large planter box, or it could be deposited at the bottom of the ocean as an artificial reef, or it could serve any number of other creative functions. But if someone asks you which is most important, the machine or the fuel, you can answer, "One is not much good without the other."

In the event that you skipped the first section and started reading here, do not think that you accidentally picked up a book on auto mechanics. Let us consider what all of this has to do with data processing. The answer is that if, in the foregoing descriptions, *automobile* were changed to *computer hardware* and *fuel* to *software,* and a few other changes made, the statements would be completely valid (especially those about one's feelings toward one's auto).* A usable computer system consists of two basic components: the machine itself, commonly called **hardware,** and the sets of instructions that make it work, called **software.** One without the other has little value. Like the auto without fuel, the computer without software might make a good planter box or part of an artificial reef.

*An analogy is useful to get an idea across by relating something new to something that is familiar. The intent of this analogy is to emphasize the fact that hardware and software are equally necessary. However, if taken too literally, an analogy can be misleading. For instance, an automobile consumes gasoline; the computer does not consume software (it does consume electricity). Obviously, this analogy is not intended in that way.

What Can a Computer Do?

Much of what we read about computers or see about them on television tends to show them as modern marvels or technological instruments of doom. In reality, the computer itself is capable of only very elementary operations, which include:

1. *Input operations,* such as accepting information from a human-operated keyboard for entry of a customer order.
2. *Storage of data* that has been read by an input device (such as the customer order information from the keyboard) or created as a result of calculations within the computer.
3. *Basic arithmetic operations* of addition, subtraction, multiplication, and division. They are the simple functions that we can all perform ourselves such as calculating the cost of a purchased product by multiplying the unit cost of the item by the number ordered.
4. *Logical operations,* such as comparing the current inventory level of an item with a predetermined allowable minimum to determine if it is time to reorder.
5. *Output operations,* such as displaying on a screen the status of a particular customer's account based on information stored within the computer.

The computer is like the automobile. We can get from New York to Boston on foot, but the automobile is much faster (and more comfortable). The strength of the computer is that it can process information with phenomenal speed and accuracy. The computer can perform the order-processing actions of looking up a customer in the customer file, finding records for the items ordered in the inventory file, updating both files, creating a new record in the accounts receivable file, and performing all needed calculations in less time than it would take you to position a manual invoice form in a typewriter. The many amazing feats of which the computer is capable are the result of carefully planned (and often very clever) programs of instructions (software) written by people.

COMPONENTS OF THE COMPUTER

The automobile (which started this discussion) can be broken down into functional parts: the engine, the drive train, the fuel system, and so on. In a similar fashion, the computer can be broken down into the basic functional components—*input, output, processor, memory,* and *auxiliary storage*—shown in Figure P1-1. Following is a brief description of each of these components.

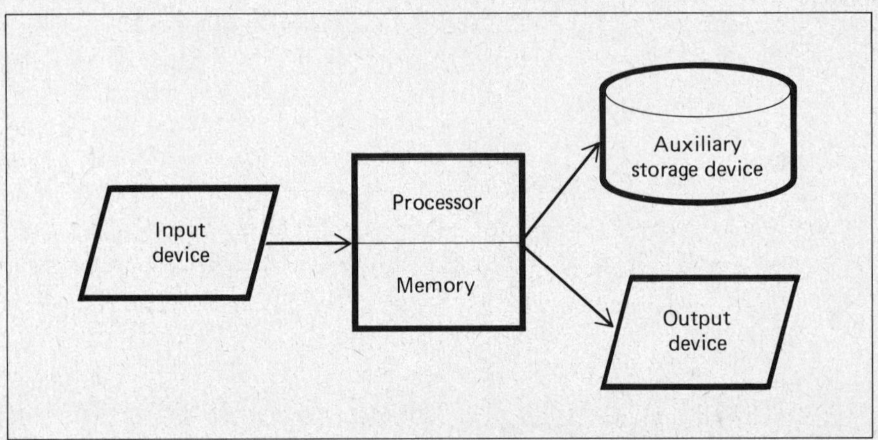

Figure P1-1
(a) The logical structure of a computer.

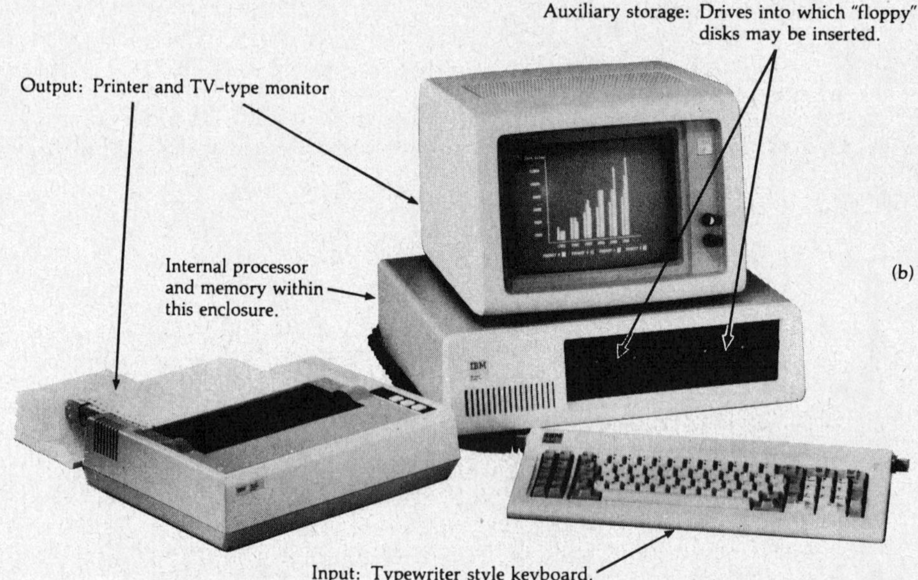

(b) The IBM Personal Computer (Courtesy of International Business Machines Corporation)

Input: The Keyboard

As the name implies, input units allow us to enter data into the computer for processing. We can see in Figure P1-1(b) that a typewriterlike keyboard is used for this purpose. In fact, entering information through the keyboard is almost exactly like typing it on an ordinary typewriter. Even though the keyboard is much like that of an ordinary typewriter, it has special keys specifically for controlling the actions of the software that you are using. These are identified in Figure P1-2 for both the original PC keyboard and the enhanced keyboard. Following are descriptions of some of the special keys; others are described in later chapters.

- Letters (uppercase and lowercase), digits, and special characters are entered as with a typewriter. After each line is entered, it is neces-

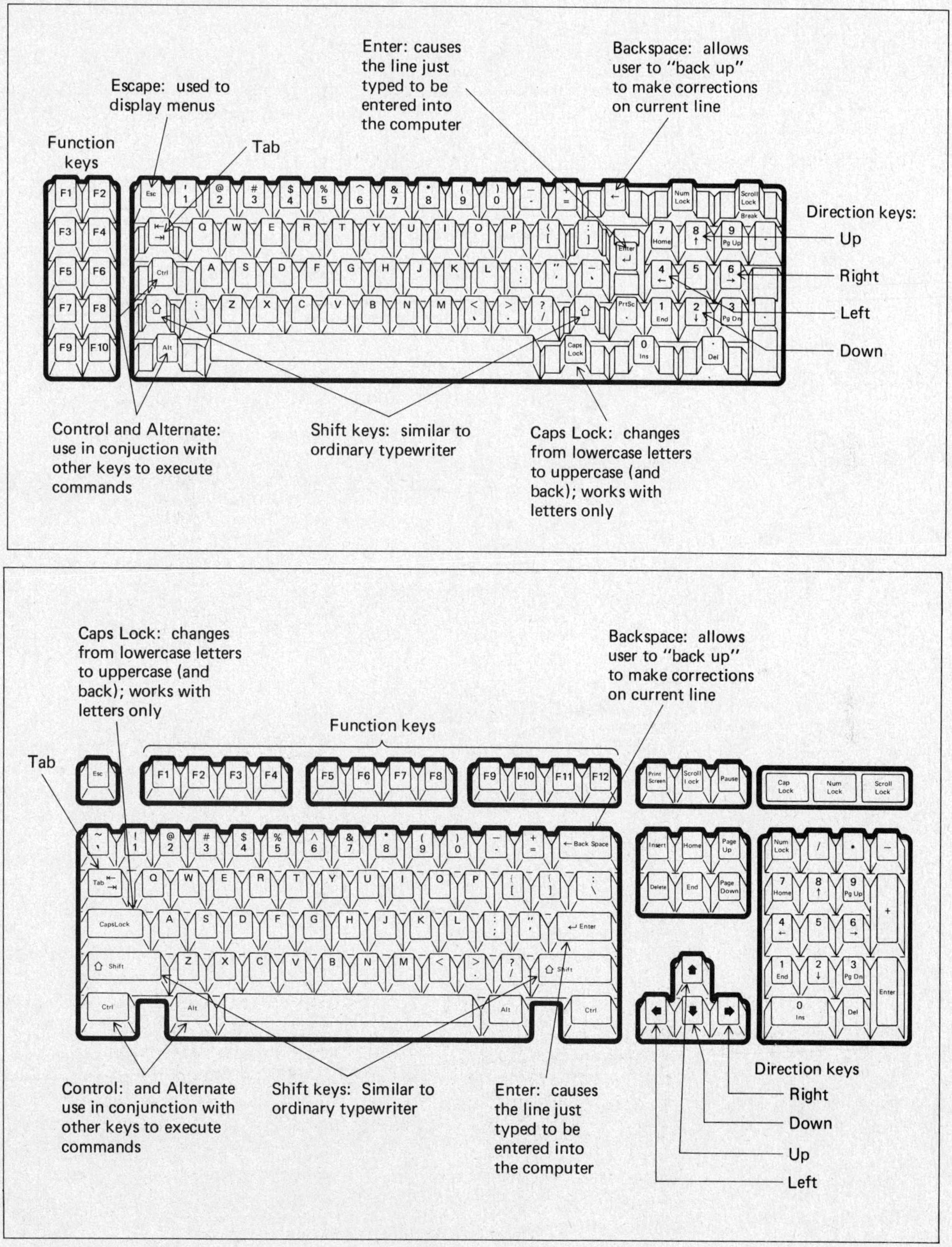

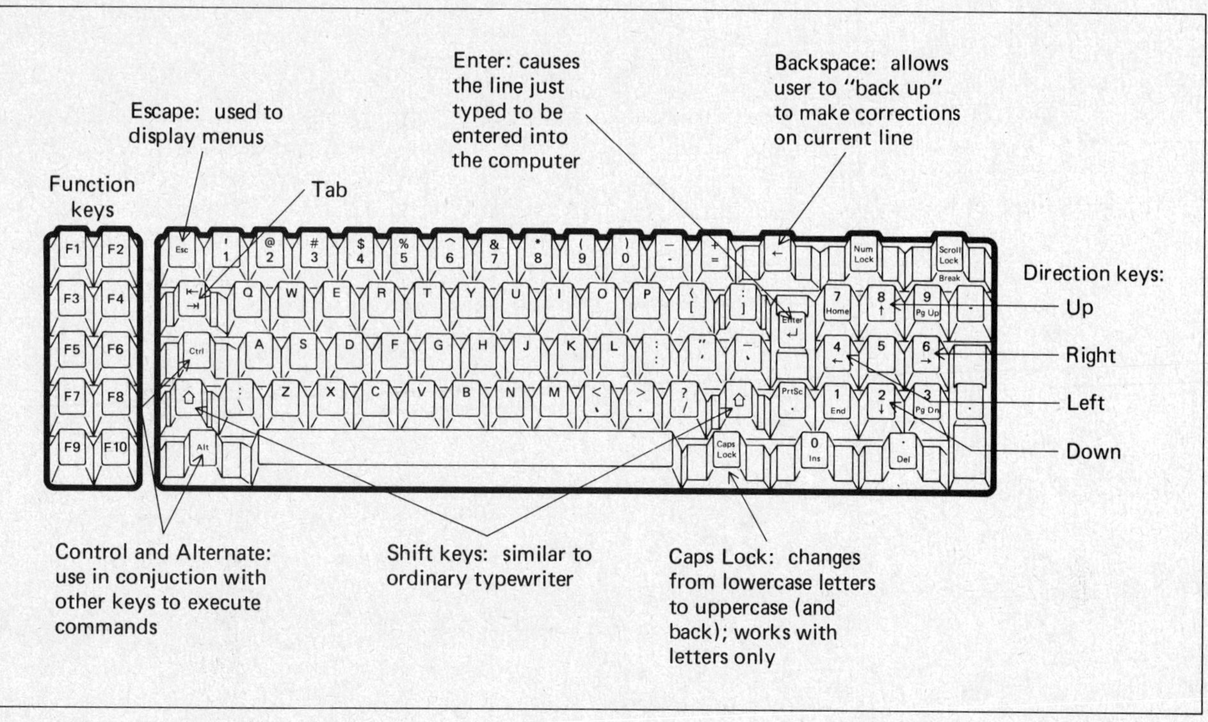

Caps Lock: changes from lowercase letters to uppercase (and back); works with letters only

Backspace: allows user to "back up" to make corrections on current line

Function keys

Tab

Control: and Alternate use in conjunction with other keys to execute commands

Shift keys: Similar to ordinary typewriter

Enter: causes the line just typed to be entered into the computer

Direction keys

Right

Down

Up

Left

Figure P1-2
(a) The IBM PC keyboard. **(b)** The 101-key enhanced keyboard.

sary to strike the **Enter key** to notify the computer to accept the line. This is identical to the return key on an electric typewriter.

- The **Caps Lock** key is similar but not identical to the shift lock on a typewriter. Striking the Caps Lock shifts to uppercase for the letter keys but not for the other keys. For instance, after you press the Caps Lock key, striking the letter G key gives you an uppercase letter, but striking the 5 key would give a 5, not the % character. Striking the Caps Lock a second time shifts back to lowercase. This key "toggles" back and forth between uppercase and lowercase; hence, it is commonly called a toggle.
- The **Shift key** works much like its counterpart on a typewriter. That is, it is activated only as long as it is held down. Depressing it gives you access to the characters on the upper part of the keys (for instance, % instead of 5). However, for letters it gives uppercase if the Caps Lock has not been activated and lowercase if it has.
- If you strike the Backspace key, the cursor will move one position to the left, erasing the character in that position in the process.
- The Control key (**Ctrl**) and the Alternate key (**Alt**), like the Shift key, do not do anything by themselves. They are always used in conjunction with another key to change the action caused by that key. The functions performed by these keys are defined within the software being used.
- Both keyboards have function keys. The original PC keyboard has ten, labeled F1 through F10, and the enhanced keyboard has twelve, labeled F1 through F12. The specific action of each is defined by the software being used.
- In using the software in this book, many actions require that you move the cursor. This is done with the group of keys with arrows pointing up, down, left, and right.

You should note that all of the character keys have automatic repeat. If you hold one of them down, the character will be entered continuously.

Output

Results of processing by the computer are made available to us through output devices. In Figure P1-1(b) we see a **monitor** and a **printer.** The monitor (which is essentially a television screen) displays results on its screen. Since it gives us no printed record, such output is commonly referred to as **soft copy.** By contrast, the output from a printer is the printed page and is called **hard copy.**

Processor

The processor is the computer's "electronic control center." Here instructions are carried out for bringing information into the system, performing computations, making decisions, and producing results.

Internal Memory

Internal memory is used for temporarily holding programs of instructions and data that are currently being operated upon. The memory of any computer is a highly organized storage area. Data can be stored anywhere in the computer's memory and retrieved in a fraction of a second. Because the speed is independent of where in memory something is stored, internal memory is designated as being random access and is commonly called RAM, meaning *random-access memory*. You will also encounter the term ROM meaning *read-only memory*. This is memory in which the contents are factory loaded with needed information or instructions that cannot be changed by the user.

In personal computers, the basic unit of memory is called the **byte.** Each byte has its own individual address and is capable of storing one character (letter, digit, or special character such as a dollar sign). Thus, in order to store the phrase

This is a line.

the computer would use exactly 15 consecutive bytes of memory. Note that in addition to the letters, this line includes three spaces and a period. Similarly, the social security number

123456789

would occupy 9 bytes but if stored with "normal" punctuation as

123-45-6789

it would occupy 11. Data of this type is called **alphanumeric** since it can consist of letters, digits, or special characters. (It is also called **character** data or **string** data.)

On the other hand, if numeric quantities are to be entered and used in calculations, they are converted to a special binary number form. Thus the numbers

187601, 8.37519, –1, 0, 652

could be entered into the computer as numeric quantities and would be converted to the special binary numeric form. With most software programs including Lotus 1-2-3 and dBASE III, the computer must be told beforehand whether given data is to be stored as numeric or alphanumeric.

One of the important features of memory is that data can be stored in it only temporarily. For instance, if we were using WordPerfect to prepare a letter, that letter would be in the computer's memory. If after printing it, we turned the computer off, or even decided to use Lotus 1-2-3, the letter would be lost from memory. Usually in addition to the printed copy, we wish to save the computer version. This is done using auxiliary storage devices.

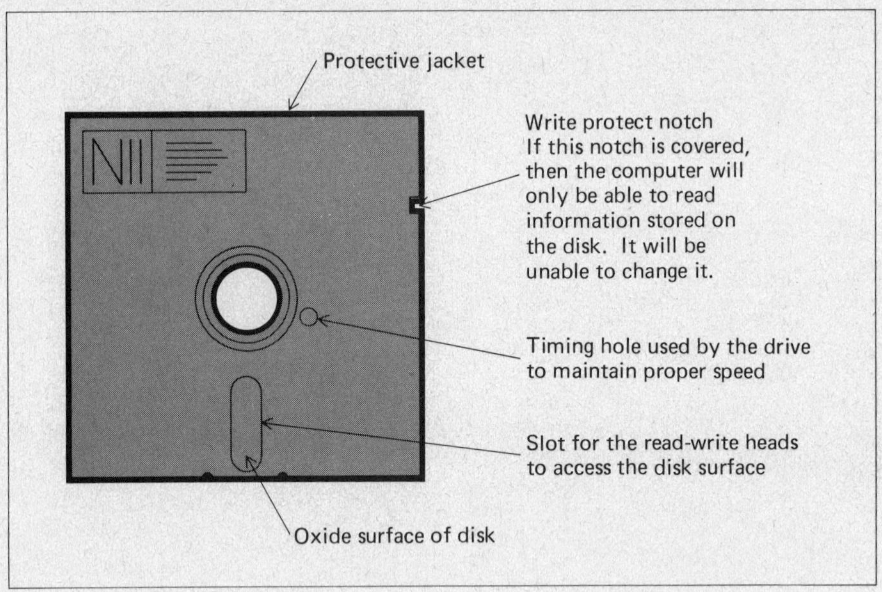

Figure P1-3
A 5 ¼-inch floppy disk.

Auxiliary Storage

Whereas internal memory holds information that is currently in use, **auxiliary storage** is used for long-term retention. This includes both software and user-generated information such as documents from WordPerfect, spreadsheets from Lotus 1-2-3, and data files from dBASE III. Auxiliary storage can best be thought of as equivalent to a large file cabinet capable of storing huge quantities of information. By far the most widely used personal computer auxiliary storage device is the **floppy disk** drive which uses the removable **floppy disk.** The physical features of the disk are shown in Figure P1-3. When inserted into a disk drive unit in the computer, the disk surface itself rotates inside the protective jacket at a rate of 300 to 400 revolutions per minute (the exact speed depends on the drive design). Notice in Figure P1-3 that one edge of the disk is notched. This is called the **write-enable notch;** a normal disk drive cannot change the contents of any disk that does not have a notch or a disk that has tape covering the notch. Thus if you have a disk that you do not want changed, cover the notch with a small self-adhesive paper (called a **write-protect** tab).

One of the important characteristics of a disk drive is its storage capacity. The disk drive most commonly encountered with the IBM PC records data on both sides of the disk (hence they are called double-sided, double-density, or DSDD). Using the disk operating system that is the primary topic of this chapter, the capacity of the DSDD disk is 360,000 bytes. The auxiliary storage capacity of a disk drive equiped computer is effectively limitless because it is a simple matter to remove one floppy disk full of information and insert another.

The word *memory* and *storage* are often used interchangeably by computer users. However, in this book, the word memory will refer exclusively to internal "working" memory.

The computer shown in Figure P1-1(b) includes two disk drives, a common configuration. The disk drive on the left is called the "A" drive and the one on the right is called the "B" drive. Technically speaking, they are referred to as drives A: and B: (the colon is included as part of the "name"). On the other hand, some machines only have one floppy drive but include a hard disk (nonremovable) with a large storage capacity, typically 50 to 100 times that of a floppy disk. The floppy drive is designated as the A drive and the hard disk as the C drive.

New Terminology

The following are important new terms introduced in this introduction; you should be familiar with each of them now because you will be using them in chapters that follow.

alphanumeric
auxiliary storage
byte
character data
floppy disk
hard copy
hardware
input
memory
monitor
printer
RAM
ROM
soft copy
software
string data
write-enable notch

Chapter 1

Using MS DOS

OBJECTIVES

The introduction to this chapter has provided you with the basic concepts of software and hardware. This chapter is designed to give you the background needed to work with the PC and to run the software systems described in the chapters that follow. When you have completed this chapter, you should be able to describe:

- The nature of the Disk Operating System (DOS) which is used with the PC.
- Controlling the computer system with DOS commands.
- Subdirectories that allow a hard disk to be "divided" into smaller working areas.

Skills in this chapter involve using DOS commands. With them you will be able to do the following:

- Inspect the contents of a disk (DIR command).
- Display the contents of a file (TYPE command).
- Initialize a new disk so that information can be stored on it (FORMAT command).
- Make a copy of a file or an entire disk (COPY and DISKCOPY commands).
- Create and use a subdirectory on a hard disk (MD and CD commands).

PREVIEW

Introduction to DOS

The operating system most commonly used with the PC is the MS DOS. DOS manages the files stored on disk; through DOS you have access to files by name stored on either disk drive of the computer.

Computer Start-up

Although read-only memory contains basic instructions to start the computer, a special DOS system disk is required to make the computer operational under DOS.

Using the Disk Operating System

You direct DOS with commands to perform such operations as deleting files and making a duplicate of a disk.

Inspecting Disk Contents

DOS maintains a directory of all files stored on a disk; you can view the contents of the directory using a variety of forms of the DIR command. The TYPE command allows you to display the contents of certain types of files directly from DOS.

General Housekeeping Functions

To use the computer intelligently, you need relatively few DOS commands. New disks are made ready with the FORMAT command; the ERASE command allows you to get rid of unwanted files; the COPY and DISKCOPY commands give you the means to make duplicates of files or an entire disk.

About Subdirectories

The large storage capacity of a hard disk requires some way of organizing stored data; subdirectories provide this capability.

INTRODUCTION TO DOS

For most of us, acquiring something new is immediately followed by the urge to try it out. Taking the time to learn how to use it properly or how it functions is often thought of as an unnecessary impediment to action. Learning something about the PC operating system falls into this same category. The urge is to get on with WordPerfect. However, without some knowledge of the operating system, situations will contine to arise in which you do not know what to do next.

MS DOS

By far the most commonly used operating system for the PC is the Disk Operating System written by Microsoft Corporation. The name is abbreviated DOS and pronounced as if it rhymed with the word boss; because it was written by Microsoft, it is commonly identified as MS DOS. The first version of DOS was identified as Version 1.0. Most software packages are written to be used with Version 2.0 or higher. The computer on which the manuscript for this book was prepared used Version 3.2 (successive releases of this version were Versions 3.0, 3.1, 3.2, 3.3, and 4.0). Each version or release provides capabilities not available with the previous version or release. When the computer is first started (described in the next section), a message appears on the screen that identifies the version of DOS. Descriptions in this chapter are relatively basic and apply to all versions of DOS.

DOS is not an item that automatically comes with the computer but is a software package that is purchased separately. The package includes a large number of programs (there are more than forty-two in DOS 3.2) that are stored on a disk called the DOS System Disk. This disk includes programs that are necessary to start the computer and use it under DOS, as well as programs that you will need for doing things such as preparing a new disk for use.

In fact, a primary focus of this book is learning by doing. You will learn about the PC operating system by using it; you will learn about each of the productivity software packages WordPerfect, Lotus 1-2-3, and dBASE III by using them. In all of these software-specific chapters, you should first read the chapter or a portion of it, making notes and asking questions as you go, and then sit down at a computer and perform each of the actions described. In working with the computer, do not be timid; you cannot damage it by making a mistake. Although there are a few ways in which you can destroy information stored on a disk, you need not be concerned that your disk will go up in smoke with the slightest wrong move. Those actions that can cause problems are called to your attention in the text, so do not allow your fear of doing something wrong interfere with your learning about the software by using it.

At the end of this chapter, you will prepare a data disk for use in the chapters that follow. All hands-on activity for this chapter is deferred until the end. In the chapters that follow, hands-on activities are an integral part of the chapter.

Naming Disk Files

In order for DOS to keep track of files stored on disk, you must give a name to each file when it is first created. For instance, a letter to Boardwalk Sales might have the name BWSALES.LTR or a customer database file might have the name CUSTOMER.DBF. The three parts of the name are described in Figure 1-1. Restrictions imposed by DOS are as follows:

1. The filename can consist of up to 8 characters.
2. The filename extension, which is optional, can consist of up to 3 characters.

Figure 1-1
Filename structure.

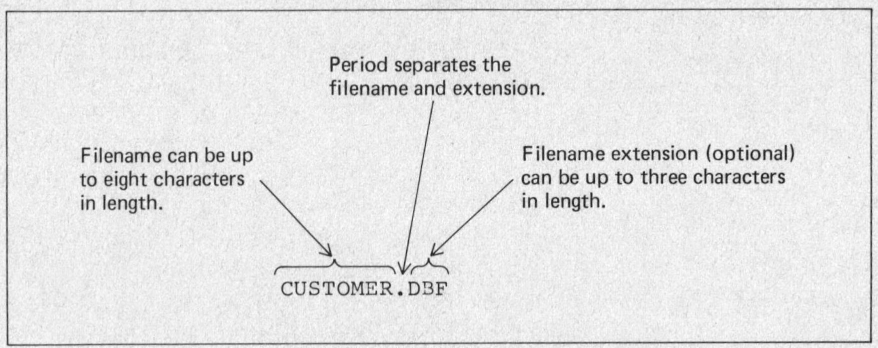

3. Any of the letters and digits can be used; there is no distinction between lowercase and uppercase. Thus, for example, the following are valid filenames.

```
X.X
x.x
LETTER.WP
MANAGER.DOC
7.SAV
```

4. Many of the special characters can also be used in forming filenames and extensions, but a number of them are not valid because they have special meaning to DOS. Some software packages restrict the use of special characters even further. However, almost all allow the use of the underscore character and the hyphen. This is convenient for separating two parts of a name (the space is not allowed). For instance, a WordPerfect-prepared contract with AR Stevens Corporation might be named:

   CON_ARS.WP or CON-ARS.WP

   To avoid any problems, avoid using special characters other than the underscore or the hyphen in creating names.

DOS manuals clearly define the single word **filename** to mean the portion of the name preceding the period. However, in common usage (including within the IBM DOS manual itself), the word *filename* is often used to indicate the entire name, including the extension. It will usually be evident from the context what is meant; remember that DOS can only find a file for you if you give it the complete name.

Although DOS allows you to select both the name and extension as needed, software packages commonly use the extension to indicate the type of file. For instance, Lotus 1-2-3 Version 2 uses the extension WK1 to indicate a worksheet file and dBASE III uses the extension DBF to represent a database file. As you will learn, when working with these software packages, you need not specify the extension if you allow the default to be used.

Drive Specification

Whenever you refer to a file, DOS requires that you specify the complete name and the drive on which it is located if the file is not on the default drive (you will learn about the default drive next). This is done by preced-

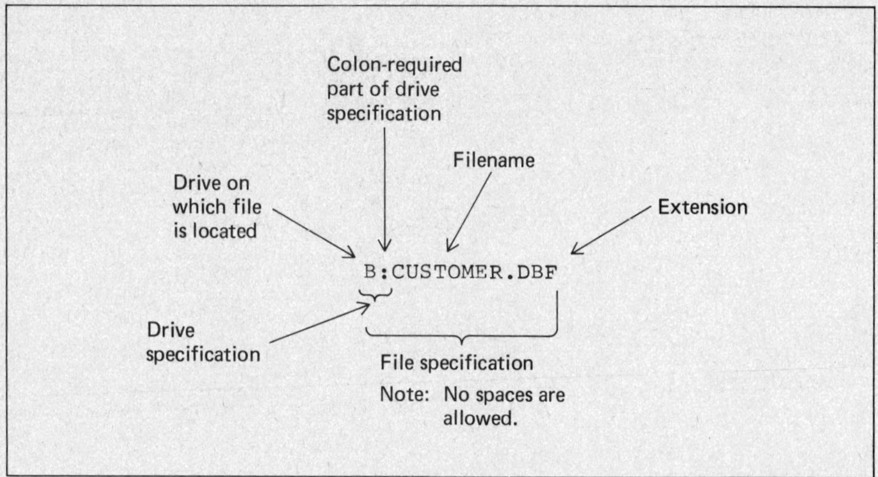

Figure 1-2
File specification structure.

ing the name by a **drive specification.** For instance, if the file CUSTOMER.DBF is on the B drive, the drive specification is B: (the letter B followed by a colon with no space between them). The complete **file specification** is B:CUSTOMER.DBF, as illustrated in Figure 1-2. Notice that no spaces are allowed within the file specification.

COMPUTER START-UP

Booting Up Under DOS

Microcomputers include two types of memory: RAM (meaning random-access memory) for general use and ROM (meaning read-only memory) with permanent contents. These permanent contents include special bootstrap start-up and hardware-test programs that allow the computer to start itself when the power is turned on. This start-up operation is called **booting up** the system; the term comes from the nature of the start-up operation in which the action is somewhat akin to "lifting yourself by the bootstraps." It includes reading needed DOS components from disk and placing them in RAM. If you are using a floppy disk computer (one with two floppy drives and no hard disk), you must have a DOS system disk. (*This is not one of the disks that came with the book;* it is one that came with DOS.) If you are using a hard disk computer, the needed DOS programs will be on the hard disk. To start the computer, follow these steps:

1. With a *floppy disk computer,* insert the DOS disk into the A drive; the read/write slot must be inserted first (see Figure P1-3) and the side with printing should face upward. Close the latch on the drive. With a *hard disk computer,* make certain the latch on the floppy drive is opened in order to force the computer to boot up from the C drive.

2. Make certain that the monitor power switch is on. In some configurations, the monitor power cord is plugged into the computer and controlled by the computer power.

3. Turn the power to the computer on.

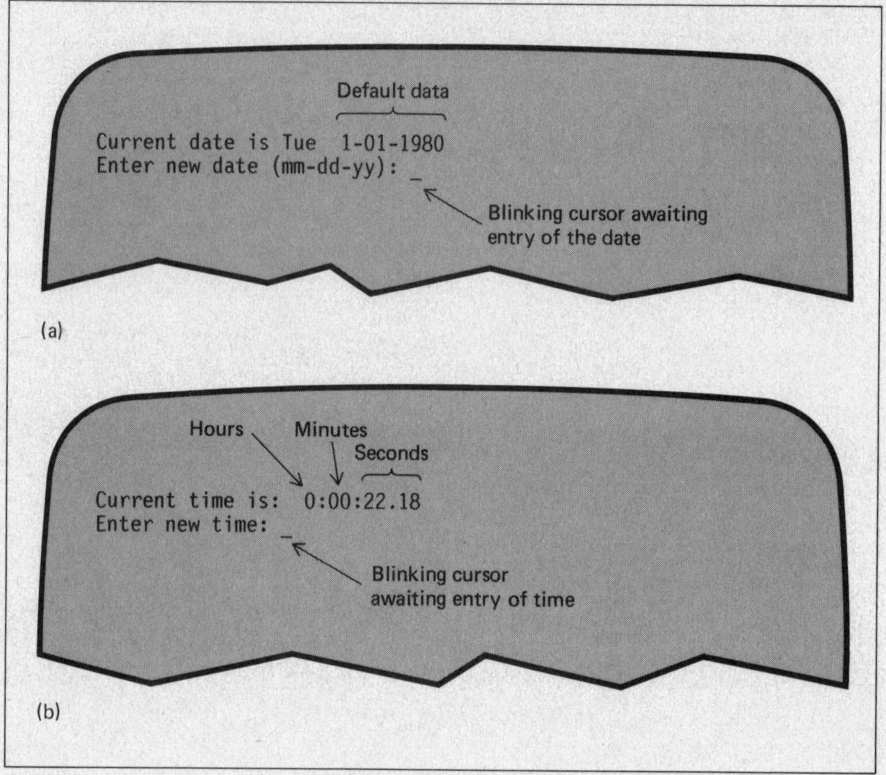

Figure 1-3
(a) Date prompt.
(b) Time prompt.

If the start-up tests find no hardware malfunctions, the A drive (or the C for a hard disk) will be activated and the needed DOS programs will be read into memory. When the operation is complete, the message shown in Figure 1-3(a) will be flashed on the screen and the system will be waiting for you to enter the date. It is important to enter the correct date because DOS attaches the date to every file that you create. In response to the date request, enter the current date in month/day/year form then strike Enter. Note that you can use either slashes or hyphens, for example, both 12/3/89 and 12-3-89 are acceptable. Next, DOS displays the message of Figure 1-3(b), then waits for you to enter the time (based on a 24-hour clock). For instance, if it is 2:35 p.m., then enter 14:35; you need not be concerned with seconds and fractions of seconds as shown in Figure 1-3. (Many computers have a battery-powered clock/calendar and the DOS disk is set up to read it automatically when booting. In this case, you will not be asked the date and time.) When the booting operation is complete, control is given to DOS. It is easy to tell that a successful booting operation has occurred by checking the screen for the following DOS display.

A> (for a floppy disk system)
C> (for a hard disk system)

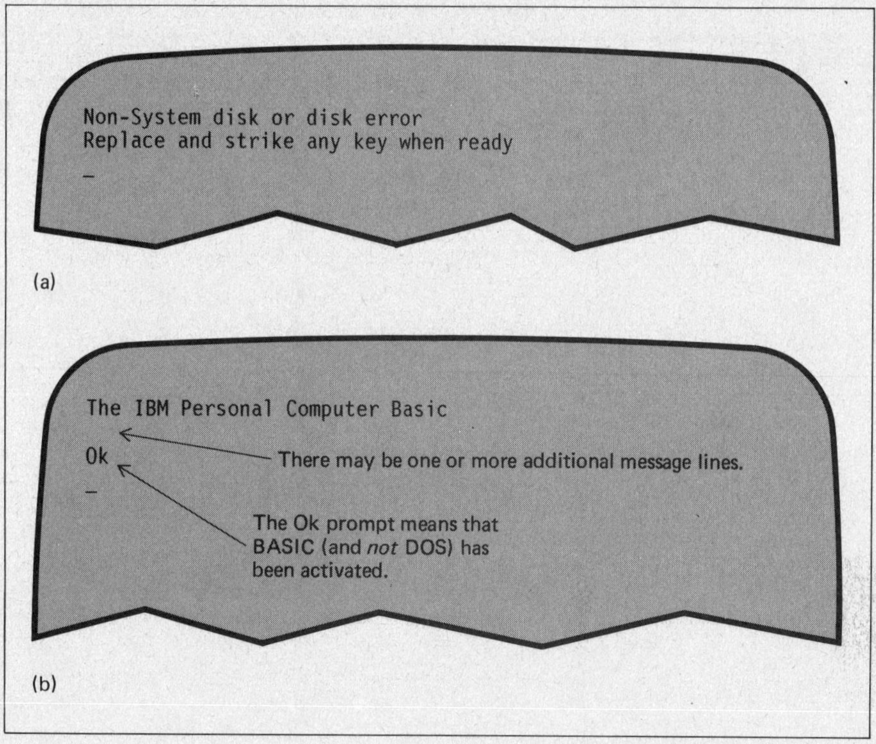

Figure 1-4
(a) The disk was read but not found to be a DOS system disk.
(b) The disk in the A drive could not be read.

Whenever DOS (as well as almost all software) completes an action and is awaiting a response, it gives you an indication. For instance, the messages of Figure 1-3 are called **prompts.** The prompt can be a message such as these or certain symbols that depend on the software in control of the computer. DOS uses the letter of the current drive followed by a right angle bracket >. Hence, the DOS prompt A> (or C>) tells us:

1. The computer is ready and waiting for something to be entered.
2. It is under the control of DOS.
3. The A drive (or C drive) is the current, or default, drive. The default drive is the one that DOS will automatically refer to if we do not specify otherwise (more about this later).

Boot Failure

If, instead of the date request (or DOS prompt), you receive either of the messages in Figure 1-4, then DOS has not booted properly. Causes and cures for these problems with a floppy disk computer are:

Case	Cause	Cure
(a)	The disk in the A drive is not a DOS system disk. For example, if you attempted to boot with the data disk included with this book, you would get such a message.	Replace the disk in the A drive with the proper DOS disk. When ready, strike Enter (or any other keyboard key).
(b)	There is no disk in the A drive; or the DOS disk is upside down or backward; or a new, initialized disk is in the A drive; or the disk drive is not latched.	Properly insert the DOS disk in the A drive. Then hold down the Ctrl and Alt keys, and while holding them down, strike the Del key.
Other	Something is wrong with your DOS disk.	Obtain another DOS disk, then follow the cure for Case (a).

If either the (a) or (b) error occurs with a hard disk computer, then you have inserted a disk in the A drive (you should not have done so). The recovery actions are the same as for a floppy system except that you must first remove the disk from the A drive. If you get some other error, then something is wrong with the DOS information on the hard disk; for this, refer to the DOS manual.

Cold Start and Warm Start

When the computer is first turned on, it runs through a hardware test cycle and then begins the boot process. This is called a *cold start*. Occasionally, the computer software gets things locked up so that it is not possible to progress further. Under these conditions, the computer must be rebooted. Rather than turn the computer off and then back on again, the rebooting process can be initiated by holding down both the Ctrl and Alt keys and then striking the Del key. This is the action taken to remedy the boot failure of Figure 1-4(a); it is called a *warm start*. Whenever instructions tell you to reboot the computer, use this method.

Assignment 1-1 may now be completed.

USING THE DISK OPERATING SYSTEM

About DOS Commands

One of the program files on the DOS system disk that is loaded into memory from the booting action is the command processor program named COMMAND.COM. One of the functions of this program is to communicate between you at the keyboard and the rest of the operating system. Although DOS keeps track of all files on a disk, it is up to you to take care of general "housekeeping" functions, such as preparing a new disk for use, deleting unneeded files from a disk, and making copies of needed files to ensure against loss. Actions such as these are done with DOS **commands,** instructions to DOS to take a given action. Whenever you request an action by entering a command, the command processor interprets that command and then takes appropriate action. Some of the commonly used commands are a part of the command processor and thus are always available whenever the computer has been booted up under DOS. As such they are called **internal commands.** DOS also includes **external commands;** these commands are not part of the command processor. Each is a separate program stored as a file on the DOS system disk. With a hard disk system, these are normally available from the hard disk so that the user sees little difference between them and internal commands. However, with a floppy disk computer, if an external command is used, then the DOS system disk must be available. Descriptions that follow will identify each command as being internal or external.

Entering a Command

A DOS command is entered from the DOS prompt merely by typing in the command name and striking Enter.

```
A> DIR
```

or

```
C> DIR
```

In this chapter, in order to distinguish between information entered from the keyboard and that displayed by the computer (the prompt), the keyed information will be shaded as in the preceding example; that is, in the first line, A> is displayed by the computer and DIR is entered by you from the keyboard. After each entry, the Enter key must be pressed to signal the computer that you have completed the entry.

Occasionally, it is convenient to change the default drive. This is easily done by typing the drive specification of the new default drive; for instance, the following would be the screen dialogue to change from the A drive to the B drive.

```
A> B:

B>
```

INSPECTING DISK CONTENTS

The DIR Command

Although it is standard practice to label each disk (using the gummed labels that accompany them), it is easy to forget the exact contents. Fortunately, DOS maintains a **directory** that includes the name of each file stored on the disk. You can view the directory on the screen with the DIR command. For instance, if you were to place the WordPerfect disk that accompanies this book in drive A, type the DIR command, and then strike Enter, the result would be similar to that in Figure 1-5. Here you have asked for a directory listing and have automatically been given that for drive A. The reason for this is that drive A is the default drive (as indicated by the A> prompt). Anytime you give DOS a command that does not refer to a specific disk drive, DOS automatically assumes that you are interested in the default drive (A in this case).

On the other hand, if you wanted a directory of the B drive, you would enter the DIR command in the following form.

```
A> DIR B:
```

Here you explicitly ask for the contents of drive B by including the drive specifier B: (B followed by a colon). (If the colon were omitted, DOS would think you were referring to a file named B.) If you were using a hard disk system operating from the C> prompt and you wanted to know the contents of the disk in the A drive, the form would be:

```
C> DIR A:
```

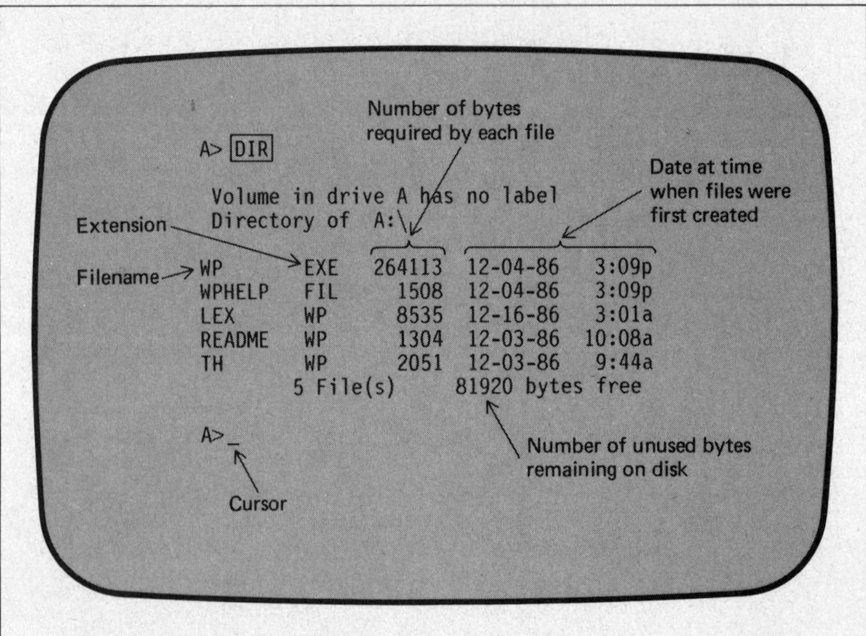

Figure 1-5
The DIR command and a disk directory.

Although all examples in the book show DOS commands entered in uppercase, it makes no difference whether you use upper- or lowercase. For instance, the earlier DIR command could just as well been entered as:

```
A> dir b:
```

The DIR command is convenient to determine if a particular file is stored on a disk. For instance, if you wanted to know if the disk in the B drive contained the Lotus 1-2-3 file BUDGET.WKS, you would use the following form of the DIR.

```
A> DIR B:BUDGET.WKS
```

If the file with that exact name exists on the disk in the B drive, DOS will display its name; if it does not, DOS displays the message, *File not found*.

Technically speaking, the DIR command consists of two components: the command name and an operand, a designation of the element to be involved in the operation. Some commands, such as DIR, have one operand; others that you shall learn about have two.

Other DIR Options

There are numerous options that can be used with the DIR command; the following examples illustrate most of them.

```
A> DIR B:/P
```

/P causes DOS to pause when the screen becomes full. This is useful if the directory to be displayed is too long to fit on the screen. At the pause, DOS displays the prompt:

```
Strike a key when ready...
```

Striking any keyboard key causes the next screenful of the directory to be displayed.

```
A> DIR B:/W
```

/W causes DOS to display the directory in wide-screen format. The filenames (including extensions) are displayed five across on the screen; file size, date, and time are omitted.

```
A> DIR B:>PRN
```

PRN is a special code for the printer; this option to the DIR command causes the directory to be printed on the printer. Note the use of the right angle bracket >; you can interpret this as indicating "send the directory listing to the device PRN."

```
A> DIR B:*.DBF
```

The asterisk (*) means "anything can go here." This form of the command causes the directory display to be limited to only those files with an extension of DBF. A typical directory display might include the files:

```
AUTO.DBF
CUSTOM.DBF
TEMP.DBF
```

`A> DIR B:CONTRACT.*` This is similar to the preceding example except that the directory listing is limited to files with a filename of CONTRACT and any extension. A typical directory display might include the files:

```
CONTRACT.AJC
CONTRACT.BW1
CONTRACT.BW2
CONTRACT.CW
```

`A> DIR B:CON_*.WP` Directory display is limited to only those files with CON_ as the first four letters of the filename, and with the extension WP. A typical directory display might include the files:

```
CON_PQ.WP
CON_5.WP
CON_GEN.WP
```

The first two examples use **command parameters** (also called **switches**) that allow the user to modify the action performed by the DIR command. Many of the DOS commands include switches for influencing the exact actions of the command.

In the third example, the directory display is redirected from the screen to the printer, thereby producing a directory listing. If you have many files on several disks, it is a good idea to include a directory listing in the envelope with the disk. This will help you locate needed files quickly.

The last three examples illustrate use of the **global filename character** * (often called the **wildcard** character), which indicates that any character can occupy that part of the name or the remaining positions (filename or extension). If you establish some consistent naming convention for files, it will make life much easier in attempting to find things later. For instance, assume that you have numerous contracts that you have drawn up. If you name each of them using CON_ as the first four letters of the filename, then you can isolate them in a directory display as shown in the last example.

If you feel somewhat overwhelmed with the variety of options available with the DIR, do not be concerned. The most important item is to become accustomed to using DOS commands and, in this case, to know how to get a directory. As you use the computer, you will come to recognize the value of this variety of options. Furthermore, do not be concerned about doing something wrong and causing trouble with the computer. As a rule, DOS will simply prompt you with an appropriate message and then allow you to go on. The few DOS commands that can cause you a loss of files are clearly identified in descriptions that follow.

Viewing a File: The TYPE Command

Every software package that you might purchase includes documentation—a manual for installing and using the software. No matter how careful the software manufacturer is, there will always be some errors in or omissions from the documentation that are not detected until after the manual has been printed. To accommodate this, manufacturers commonly include corrections and additions to the manual in the form of a file on the software disk. (If the software occupies more than one disk, it is usually on the first.) Most commonly, the name of the file includes the word *READ;* typical names used are README (no extension), READ.ME, and README.1ST. When you obtain a new software package or an upgraded version of a package you are currently using, you should first check the directory for such a file. If one is found, then you should do as the name suggests—read it. For instance, if you noticed the file README.1ST on a disk, you could view it on the screen with the following TYPE command (internal).

```
A> TYPE B:README.1ST
```

You should be aware that you will get garbage (an unintelligible display) on the screen when displaying most files created by any productivity software package because of special encoding used by the software. For instance, WordPerfect uses encoding techniques to achieve such things as centering a line and underscoring, and the DOS TYPE command will not decode these. (You can observe this by attempting to display the README.WP file on the Limited Use WordPerfect disk included with this book. It is a WordPerfect file and can only be read from WordPerfect.) Most read-me files can be displayed by the TYPE because they are specially prepared. Such files are called *text files* and do not include any special codes normally used by productivity software packages.

If you want a printed copy of a text file (for example, a read-me file), then you can use the >PRN form illustrated for the DIR command as follows:

```
A> TYPE B:README.1ST>PRN
```

However, be careful that the file you are sending to the printer is indeed a text file. You should first display it on the screen. If you find unintelligible characters (such as happy faces) interspersed in the display, then *do not send it to the printer.*

After the screen becomes full during the display of a file, room is made at the bottom of the screen for the next line to be displayed by moving each line up. Thus, the top line of the display is lost; this is called **scrolling.** To read each screenful before it scrolls into oblivion (unless you are an exceptionally fast reader) requires that you momentarily stop the scrolling action. This is accomplished by holding down the Ctrl key and striking the Num Lock key at the upper right of the keyboard. (If you are using a 101-key enhanced keyboard, simply strike the Pause key at the right of the top row of keys.) The continuous display of new text will be halted, and the screen contents will remain unchanged, giving you time to read the screen contents. To resume the display, simply strike any key on the keyboard (the Enter key is convenient).

GENERAL HOUSEKEEPING FUNCTIONS

The FORMAT Command

When a new disk leaves the factory, it is completely blank and not yet usable by DOS. Before any data can be stored on it, the disk must be **formatted** by DOS, an action that involves defining the track and sectors of the disk and writing special formatting information. Once completed, this information remains on the disk. Hence, formatting is not an operation that you constantly repeat with a given disk. (Note that if you have disks that were used by another operating system, you will need to reformat them for use by DOS.) It is very important to understand that formatting a disk wipes out everything that might be stored on the disk. Hence, the disk should be checked carefully before formatting; accidentally inserting the wrong disk in the drive for formatting can spell disaster. Do this check with the DIR command.

Unlike the DIR command, which is internal (part of COMMAND.COM in memory), the FORMAT command is external and so is a separate program stored on the DOS system disk. In order to execute it with a floppy disk computer, either a copy of the file (named FORMAT.COM) must be on the disk in drive A or a DOS system disk must be in drive A.

The standard way of formatting a new disk is to have the drives loaded as follows:

drive A	Contains the DOS system disk
drive B	Contains the new disk to be formatted

Then the formatting command may be entered as follows:

```
A> FORMAT B:
```

DOS will then display the following prompt (regardless of whether or not you already have the disk in the B drive).

```
Insert the new diskette for drive B:
and strike ENTER when ready
```

Striking the Enter key causes the formatting to begin. DOS will display a message when the formatting has been completed.

Actually, there are two ways to format a disk. When formatted as described in the preceding, the disk can be used as a data disk with a capacity of 360K bytes. It is also possible to format a disk as a bootable system disk—one from which it is possible to boot the computer. The command to format it as a system disk becomes

```
A> FORMAT B:/S
```

The /S (System) command parameter causes three files to be placed on the disk, requiring approximately 40K of disk space. One of them is the command processor COMMAND.COM, the presence of which you can see by issuing the DIR command. The other two are called **hidden files** because DOS defines them so that their names are not displayed with the DIR command. All three of these files are required on a system disk. If you prepare your own system disk in this way, you may wish to copy other DOS programs, for instance, FORMAT.COM and DISKCOPY.COM, using the COPY command. (DISKCOPY and COPY are described in sections that follow.)

The ERASE Command

As you continue to work with your computer, you will tend to accumulate more and more files. Eventually, you will find that a disk becomes full and cannot hold any more data. This can happen in either of two ways: the storage required by your files exceeds the 360K-byte disk capacity or the number of files exceeds the DOS directory limit of 112 files. There is nothing quite as frustrating as to be working on an application and to receive the DOS "Disk is full" message. When this happens, it is easy to end up losing work that you have done during the current work session, if not the entire file. To avoid this problem, you should pay careful attention to the amount of data you have stored on each disk and always delete files that you no longer need. For instance, assume that you have displayed a directory and found on the disk in drive B the files SAMPLE1.WKS, SAMPLE2.WKS, and SAMPLE3.WKS that you no longer need. You could erase them by using the ERASE command (an internal command) by entering:

```
A> ERASE B:SAMPLE1.WKS

A> ERASE B:SAMPLE2.WKS

A> ERASE B:SAMPLE3.WKS
```

Note that the DEL command (delete) can also be used; DEL and ERASE perform the same function.

If these were the only Lotus 1-2-3 SAMPLE files on the disk, then the global filename character * could be used.

```
A> ERASE B:SAMPLE*.WKS
```

However, be warned that this will delete all files with names that fit this global form. When using global characters in an ERASE command, it is best to always do a DIR with exactly the same form first. For example, assume that you asked for a directory and received the following:

```
A> DIR B:SAMPLE*.WKS

Directory of B:/

SAMPLE   WKS   980   1-08-89   8:48a
SAMPLETP WKS  3024   3-13-89   2:45p
SAMPLE1  WKS  2312   6-12-89  10:31a
SAMPLE2  WKS  1884   6-18-89  11:44a
SAMPLE3  WKS  1676   6-22-89   4:16p
```

If you used the preceding form of the ERASE command, then SAMPLE.WKS and SAMPLETP.WKS would also be deleted.

Use of the global filename character can be extended to both the filename and the extension with significant results. That is, the command

```
A> ERASE B:*.*
```

will cause all of the files to be erased from the B drive disk. Obviously, you should be careful when using this.

In general, be very careful when deleting a file. There are ways of getting a file back after it has been deleted, but special software is required (see the box).

Duplicating a Disk: The DISKCOPY Command

Eventually, we all lose a file on disk or even the entire disk contents. The best way to protect against this is to make a copy of each disk containing important data. This is called *backing up* the data, and a disk that duplicates the contents of another is called a *backup* disk. Back up is as important to the student who would not care to lose an entire semester's work as to the business person who would not care to lose accounting files. With the DISKCOPY command, it is possible to duplicate the contents of the disk in drive A onto the disk in drive B (or B to A, if desired). The recommended sequence is as follows.

1. Insert a DOS system disk into drive A.

2. Enter the DOS command:

   ```
   A> DISKCOPY A: B:
   ```

   This says to copy the contents of the disk in drive A to the disk in drive B. The first listed drive is said to be the **source drive** and the second is the **target drive.** The direction of transfer with commands that list two drives (or files) is from the source to the target. Note that the command and source drive designation, and the source and target drive designations are separated by spaces.

3. DOS will request that the two disks be inserted into the drives. Remove the DOS disk from the A drive and then insert the original (the disk to be copied). Insert the disk that will become the copy into the B drive. If the disk in B already has data on it, that data will be erased. If it is a new disk that has not yet been formatted, DOS will format it during the copy operation.

4. When the copy has been completed, DOS will display an appropriate message. After you respond, the disks may be removed.

Eventually, we all erase an important file from disk and then, after much teeth gnashing, set about to reenter it. This happened to a programmer named Peter Norton in 1982. However, Mr. Norton knew that deleting a file did not really delete the file. In fact, the action of DOS was the electronic equivalent of clipping a note to a file folder that said, "No longer needed." He knew that the file was still sitting on disk (even though DOS was ignoring it) and that it would remain there until something else was written over it. Actually, DOS marks a file as deleted by replacing the first character of the filename in the directory with an * character. So he wrote a program that allowed him to inspect the directory for names that started with an asterisk (those that DOS had deleted) and to change the asterisk to an "acceptable" character for files that he wanted back. Thus, in a blink of the eye, he had "unerased" his erased file. (In fact, he named his command to restore a file UNERASE.) Mr. Norton recognized the need for a general-purpose set of programs that would do things that cannot be done with DOS so he pulled together a collection of handy programs and called the package the Norton Utilities. These perform such actions as reorganizing the contents of the disk in order to make disk operations faster, rearranging the order of the directory entries (to alphabetic or date order), and actually erasing deleted information (convenient to get rid of confidential data). If you look around the desk of any devout PC user, you are likely to find a copy of the Norton Utilities or an equivalent program from another vendor. Consider such software essential to maintain your sanity in the transitory world of the computer.

If you are using a hard disk computer with only one floppy drive, then you must enter the command simply as DISKCOPY; no operands are required. The process will involve alternately inserting the original and new disks into the A drive as prompted by DOS.

Copying Files: The COPY Command

Individual files can be copied from one disk to another by the COPY command (internal). For instance, assume that you need to copy the file SAMPLE1.WP from the disk in drive A to the disk in drive B. The following command will do this.

```
A> COPY A:SAMPLE1.WP B:
```

As with the DISKCOPY, the first operand following the command name is the source and the second is the target. In this case, SAMPLE1.WP on drive A is to be copied to drive B; since no filename is specified in the target operand, the file is stored under the same name. Technically, the A: preceding the filename is not required because drive A is the default drive.

This command is especially convenient to use when you are experimenting with an application. For example, assume that yesterday you completed a spreadsheet named BUDGET3.WKS; today you want to try something new with it. However, you do not want to change the original copy. (It works; be careful of changing something that works.) Hence, you need a duplicate to work on. You can easily create the copy with the following form of the COPY command.

```
A> COPY B:BUDGET3.WKS B:BUDTEST.WKS
```

This causes DOS to find the file named BUDGET3.WKS on drive B and to make an exact copy of it named BUDTEST.WKS, also located on drive B. Now you can modify BUDTEST.WKS while the original BUDGET3.WKS remains unchanged.

The RENAME Command

Occasionally, you will need to change the name of a file on the disk. You do this with the RENAME command. For example, assume that you have the word processing document file that you had named TEST.WP. It has proved to be more than the simple test that you had begun so you want to change the name to COLUMNS.WP. You could do this with the following form of the RENAME command.

```
A> RENAME B:TEST.WP COLUMNS.WP
```

ABOUT SUBDIRECTORIES

One of the conveniences of the floppy disk drive is that you can keep applications separated on different disks. For instance, you may have a separate disk on which you store copies of all contracts, another for general correspondence, and so on. The removable nature of the medium simplifies the process of keeping organized. However, the situation with a hard disk is different: you may have several *thousand* files on a single 30-megabyte hard disk. Clearly, it would be a bookkeeping nightmare if all of the files of a hard disk were listed in a single directory. The way in which DOS handles this is to allow you to create **subdirectories,** which are separate directories within the main, or **root,** directory. For instance, consider how you might arrange a hard disk to use the software that accompanies this book. Since there are three distinct software packages (WordPerfect, a spreadsheet similar to Lotus 1-2-3, and dBASE III PLUS),

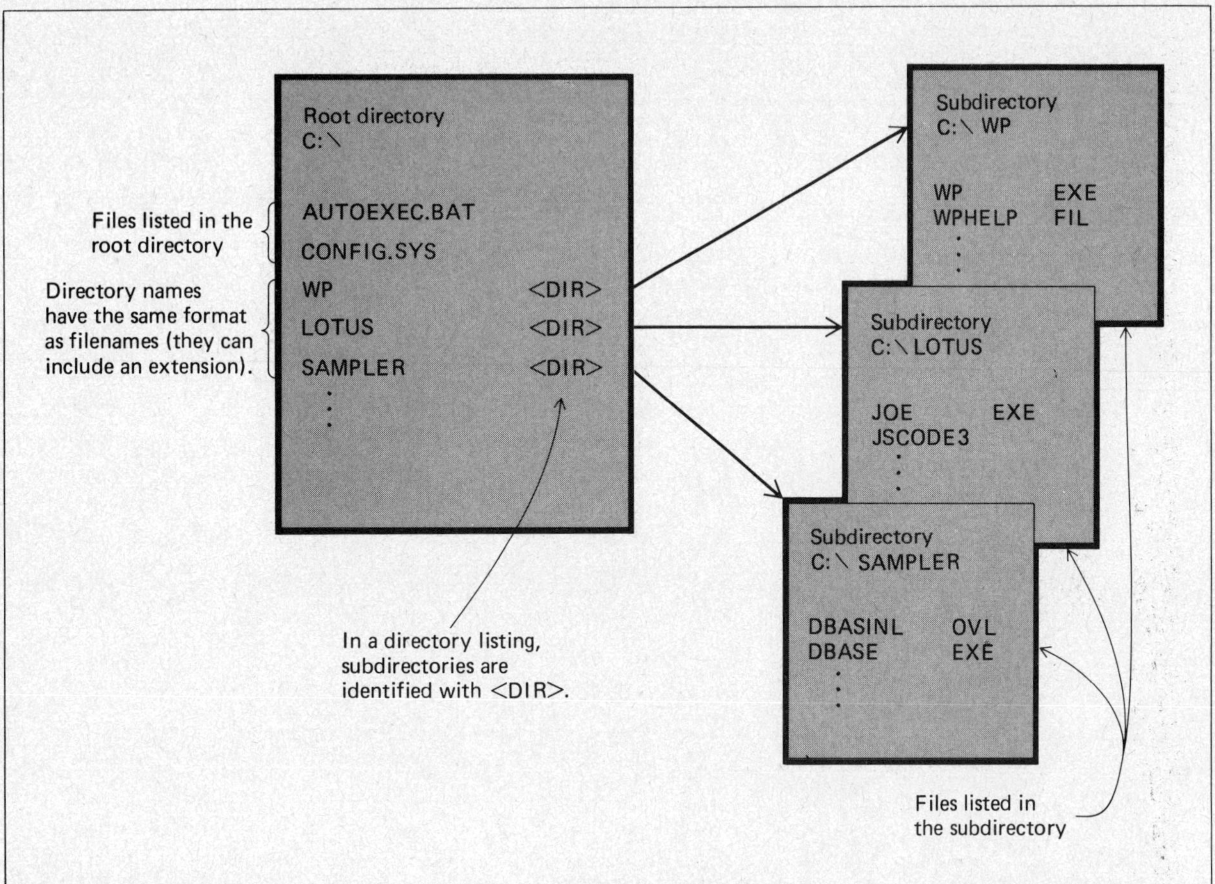

Figure 1-6
The concept of subdirectories.

three subdirectories, one for each package, would be sufficient. The relationship between these subdirectories and the root directory is illustrated in Figure 1-6. Then the filenames for each software package are neatly stored in its own subdirectory. This situation is somewhat analogous to working with two disk drives. If the A drive is the default, then the default directory is that of the disk in the A drive. You still have access to the directory of the disk in the B drive by explicitly referring to B:. As with subdirectories, the root directory or any of the subdirectories can be activated as the default at any time. Let us consider how to use subdirectories.

Assume that the three subdirectories of Figure 1-6 have been created (this is the activity of an exercise at the end of this chapter). With the normal DOS prompt of C>, you have no direct indication as to which subdirectory is the current default directory. It is easy to forget in which subdirectory you are working and to create a file that you cannot find later because you do not know where to look. (This is much the same problem that most of us encounter with many floppy disks. For instance, on which disk is the database you created last month?) The recommended way of resolving this is to modify the DOS prompt using the PROMPT command.

Without going into the details of this command, the following will cause the prompt to display both the default drive and the subdirectory.

```
C> PROMPT $P$G
```

With this change, the prompt will become:

C:>	When the default is the root directory
C:WP>	When the default is the WP subdirectory
C:LOTUS>	When the default is the LOTUS subdirectory

You should be aware that when the computer is rebooted, the prompt goes back to the C>. If you wish to use this subdirectory prompt form, then put the command in the AUTOEXEC.BAT file (refer to the DOS manual for instructions on this).

Notice that C:\ indicates the root directory—the backslash symbol is the element that denotes the root. The symbolism C:\WP indicates the WP subdirectory under the root directory. You can switch from one directory to another with the CD (change directory, an internal command) as illustrated by the following examples.

C:> CD\WP	Change from root directory to WP subdirectory.
C:WP> CD\LOTUS	Change from WP subdirectory to LOTUS subdirectory.
C:LOTUS> CD\	Change from LOTUS subdirectory back to root directory.

For instance, if you wish to work in WordPerfect, you should enter the first of the above CD commands. Then you could run WordPerfect from the C drive without using the floppy disk copy each time.

Note that subdirectories can be created on a floppy disk as well. This is sometimes convenient for storing a large number of small files, or simply for keeping different types of files separated. If you are using a hard disk computer, then you should become familiar with the concept of subdirectories—unless you have already done so. If you are using your own hard disk computer, then you should learn more about subdirectories from the DOS manual. This will allow you to use your computer more efficiently.

Assignment 1-2 may now be completed.

SUMMARY

This chapter has provided you with needed exposure to DOS. Summarizing, the important items from the chapter are:

- In DOS, every file must have a name consisting of a filename of up to 8 characters, and optionally a filename extension of up to 3 characters. The two parts must be separated by a period.

- Every new disk must be formatted before it can be used.
- A system disk is required to boot the computer under DOS; such a disk can be created with the FORMAT command using the /S command parameter.
- DOS commands can be considered in two categories: internal, which are included in the COMMAND.COM program, and external, which must be available from a disk to be executed.
- The global filename character * allows DOS operations to be performed on multiple files meeting the global definition.
- Following is a summary of the commands introduced in this chapter.

Command	Type	Action
CD	internal	Change to another directory; useful especially with a hard disk computer.
COPY	internal	Copy one or more files. Files may be copied to another disk, or to the same disk with a different name.
DIR	internal	Display or print a disk directory.
DISKCOPY	external	Make a duplicate of an existing disk.
ERASE	internal	Erase one or more files from a disk.
FORMAT	external	Format a disk so that it can be used by DOS.
PROMPT	internal	Change the DOS prompt.
RENAME		Change the name of a file.
TYPE	internal	Display or print a text file.

NEW TERMINOLOGY

The following are important new terms introduced in this chapter; you should be familiar with each of them.

Alt key
booting up
command
command parameter
Ctrl key
DOS
directory
drive specification
extension
external command
file specifiction
filename
format
global filename character
hidden file
internal command
prompt
root directory
scrolling
source drave
subdirectory
system disk
target drive
wildcard character

Name: ______________________________ Date: ______________

Assignment 1-1

1. How are the Ctrl and Alt keys on the PC keyboard used?

2. Identify which of the following names would not be valid for use as DOS filenames (according to the naming rules given in this chapter). For each, give the reason that it is not acceptable.
   (a) GOOD.LUCK

   (b) summary

   (c) LETTER-1.DOC

   (d) FORMLETTER.2

   (e) B:ACCT.WKS

Name: ______________________ Date: ______________

Assignment 1-1 (*continued*)

(f) HOLD/3.WP

(g) INV_SUM.DBF

(h) 6.6

3. Describe the distinction between the following two file references.
(a) ANALYSIS.DBF
(b) B:ANALYSIS.DBF

4. What types of files are stored on a DOS system disk? What is the role of this disk during the computer start-up operation?

5. What message would be displayed on the monitor if you did each of the following, then turned the computer on?
(a) Inserted the DOS disk in the B drive.

(b) Inserted the WordPerfect disk that accompanies this bock in the A drive.

(c) Inserted the DOS disk upside down in the A drive.

Name: ______________________ Date: ____________

Assignment 1-1 (*continued*)

6. During bootup, the computer displays a default date then asks you to enter the current date. If you simply strike the Enter key the default date is used. What is the disadvantage of using this default date?

7. What is the difference between a warm start and a cold start?

Name: ______________________ Date: ______________

Assignment 1-2

1. What is a DOS internal command? Contrast this with an external command.

2. Assuming that the A drive is the default, write a command to print a list of all files on the B drive with an extension of DBF.

3. A user becomes curious about the spreadsheet file SUMMARY.WKS so attempts to display it on the screen with the command:

```
TYPE SUMMARY.WKS
```

What would you expect to be displayed on the screen? Explain your answer.

4. How often must a floppy disk be formatted?

Name: ______________________ Date: ______________

Assignment 1-2 *(continued)*

5. What are the two conditions that can result in a floppy disk being full under DOS?

6. What do you think will be the difference in the directory displays of the following two forms of the DIR command?

```
A>DIR
A>DIR *.*
```

7. What is the maximum number of files that can be erased from a floppy disk with a single ERASE command?

8. What happens if the target disk of a DISKCOPY command has not been formatted?

Name: ______________________________ Date: ______________

Assignment 1-2 (*continued*)

9. What is wrong with the following command? How do you think DOS will respond to it?

```
A>COPY INVEN.WKS A:
```

10. What is the command needed to perform each of the following tasks, assuming that you are operating from the A> prompt?

(a) List the files in the B drive.

(b) List the files in the A drive with an extension of PRD.

(c) Print the names of the files in the B drive.

(d) Display on the screen the file READTHIS from the B drive.

(e) Format the disk in the B drive so that it can be used to boot the computer.

(f) Erase all files from the B drive with names starting with the letter C.

Name: ______________________ Date: ____________

Assignment 1-2 (*continued*)

(g) Copy the complete contents of the disk in drive B onto the disk in the A drive.

(h) Make a copy of the file HOLD.WKS (on the B drive) and call it HOLD2.WKS.

(i) Copy all of the files from the B drive to the A drive.

(j) Change from the current directory to the TEMP subdirectory.

Name: ______________________________ Date: ______________

OBJECTIVE QUESTIONS

MATCHING

Match each term in a to h with the most appropriate description or definition in 1 through 8.

a. Ctrl key	**e.** subdirectory
b. prompt	**f.** internal command
c. boot-up	**g.** drive specification
d. system disk	**h.** extension

____ **1.** Designates the location of a disk file.

____ **2.** Displayed to let the user know that a response is required.

____ **3.** Makes it easier to organize a hard disk and keep track of files stored on it.

____ **4.** The action that takes place when the computer is started.

____ **5.** Once the computer is operating under DOS, can be carried out without the DOS disk.

____ **6.** Part of the name of a file.

____ **7.** Needed to start the computer under DOS.

____ **8.** Used in conjunction with character keys on the keyboard.

True False

Circle either T or F to indicate whether the answer is True or False.

T F **1.** One of the characteristics of internal memory is that all data stored in it is lost when the computer is turned off.

T F **2.** An important feature of the floppy disk is that it is a removable storage medium so that one disk can be removed from a disk drive and another inserted.

T F **3.** Microcomputers with hard disks do not use floppy disks.

T F **4.** The F1 key on the keyboard is used to start the computer.

T F **5.** The Caps Lock key on the keyboard deactivates the Shift key.

T F **6.** It is possible to store data and programs on the same floppy disk.

T F **7.** The following are all valid names to use for files in DOS: A.A, heading.q, SAVE.DBF, 123.456, and HOLD.

T F **8.** Every file stored on a disk must be given a filename, but the extension is optional.

T F **9.** In referring to a file, the drive specification is not needed if the file is on the default drive.

Name: ______________________ Date: ______________

OBJECTIVE QUESTIONS (*continued*)

T F **10.** For a floppy disk computer the default drive is always the A drive and for a hard disk computer it is always the C drive. This is a permanent part of DOS and cannot be changed.

T F **11.** To boot up means to load and run a program such as WordPerfect or Lotus 1-2-3.

T F **12.** If the disk in the A drive during start-up is not a system disk, the computer will still boot up but the action will take longer because the programs in ROM will have more to do.

T F **13.** The DIR command always displays the contents of the disk in the default drive.

T F **14.** The file WORKER.B would not be listed in the directory display of the following command.

```
DIR WOR*.B*
```

T F **15.** The following command will cause the directory of the disk in the default drive to be sent to the printer.

```
DIR >PRN
```

T F **16.** A command parameter modifies the action of a command.

T F **17.** The TYPE command is not intended to be used with software packages such as WordPerfect because of the codes that are stored within the files.

T F **18.** The TYPE command can be used to print a copy of a text file.

T F **19.** Formatting a disk will destroy all of the data stored on the disk.

T F **20.** A disk needs to be formatted only when the type of application for which it is used is changed. For instance, a WordPerfect data disk must be reformatted if it is to be used for dBASE III.

T F **21.** A disk formatted as a data disk (without using the /S command parameter) can be converted to a bootable system disk merely by copying the file COMMAND.COM to it from a DOS system disk.

T F **22.** A single ERASE command can be used to erase more than one file from a disk.

T F **23.** The ERASE command itself does not remove the actual file from the disk.

T F **24.** Two floppy disk drives are required to use the DISKCOPY command.

T F **25.** When using the DISKCOPY command, if the target disk (the one to which the copy will be made) has not been formatted, the DISKCOPY command will automatically format it.

T F **26.** The copy of a file made on another disk with the COPY command can have either the same name as or a different name from the original.

OBJECTIVE QUESTIONS (*continued*)

T F **27.** The following command will copy all of the files from the disk in the A drive to the disk in the B drive.

```
COPY A:*.* B:
```

T F **28.** The RENAME command allows you to change the name of a file while you are making a copy.

T F **29.** Subdirectories cannot be used with a floppy disk.

T F **30.** The PROMPT command allows you to modify the DOS prompt to tell you which subdirectory you are working in.

Multiple Choice

In the space provided, record the letter of the choice that best completes or answers the statement.

____ **1.** The byte is capable of storing

A. one character.
B. one word.
C. one file.
D. the contents of a disk.

____ **2.** If the write enable notch on a floppy disk is covered, then it is impossible to

A. read the disk.
B. change the disk contents.
C. use the disk.
D. damage the disk.

____ **3.** The capacity of a hard disk is _____ that of a floppy disk.

A. less than
B. greater than
C. about the same as

____ **4.** Striking the F10 function key of the keyboard causes the computer to

A. boot up.
B. format a disk.
C. turn off.
D. perform an action that depends upon the software you are using.

____ **5.** The DOS disk includes

A. the word processing program.
B. files necessary to boot the computer.
C. the data files for this course.
D. all of the data files and programs for this course.

Name: ______________________ Date: ______________

OBJECTIVE QUESTIONS (*continued*)

____ **6.** Which of the following is NOT a valid file name?

A. WORK.OK
B. SUMMARY.THIRD
C. it
D. HOLD.4

____ **7.** For a computer with two floppy drives, which of the following would be an incorrect file specification?

A. C:ADDRESS.DBF
B. B:ADDRESS.DBF
C. A:ADDRESS.DBF
D. ADDRESS.DBF

____ **8.** The operation of the computer making itself ready for use when the power is first turned on is called

A. formatting.
B. spooling.
C. booting.
D. operational control.

____ **9.** Upon turning the computer on, the following message is displayed on the screen.

```
Non-system disk or disk error
```

The most likely reason for this is

A. the door on the disk drive is not latched.
B. you pressed the wrong key on the keyboard.
C. the disk drive has failed.
D. drive A does not contain a bootable disk.

____ **10.** Which of the following commands will cause a list of the contents of the B drive to be printed?

A. `DIR >PRN`
B. `DIR B:>PRN`
C. `PRINT DIR B:`
D. `DIR B: TO PRINTER`

____ **11.** Which of the following will list all of the files with an extension of DBF?

A. `LIST *.DBF`
B. `DIR *.DBF`
C. `DIR DBF`
D. `DIR ALL.DBF`

Name: ______________________ Date: ______________

OBJECTIVE QUESTIONS (*continued*)

____ **12.** Which of the following types of files will give a meaningful display when listed with the TYPE command?

A. database
B. formatted
C. word processing
D. text

____ **13.** The first thing to do with a new floppy disk is to

A. format it.
B. backup it up.
C. boot it up.
D. put a write protect tab on it.

____ **14.** What can you say about a disk that has just been formatted with the following command?

```
FORMAT B:/S
```

A. You can use it to boot the computer.
B. You cannot use it to boot the computer.
C. You cannot store data files on it.
D. You cannot store programs on it.

____ **15.** The ______ command can be used to get rid of one or more files from a disk.

A. ELIMINATE
B. FORMAT
C. ERASE
D. RENAME

____ **16.** You have a new disk and want to copy all of the files from another disk. The command to use would be

A. `COPY`
B. `DISKCOPY`
C. `FORMAT`
D. `COPY ALL`

____ **17.** When you use the ERASE command to delete a file from disk, the action of DOS is to

A. mark the file as deleted but leave it on the disk.
B. mark the file as deleted and erase it from the disk.
C. replace the file with all zeros.
D. simply erase the file from the disk.

Name: ______________________ Date: ____________

OBJECTIVE QUESTIONS (*continued*)

____ **18.** Which of the following would NOT change the number of files on a disk?

A. RENAME
B. COPY
C. FORMAT
D. DISKCOPY

____ **19.** One of the advantages of using subdirectories on a floppy disk is

A. it increases the capacity of the disk.
B. it makes it possible to store more than 112 files on a disk.
C. it gives the floppy all the advantages of a hard disk.
D. Subdirectories cannot be used on a floppy disk.

____ **20.** Your screen displays the following prompt.

```
C:\LOTUS>
```

This means that

A. the LOTUS program is currently running.
B. you are using an operating system other than MS DOS.
C. the LOTUS subdirectory is the current subdirectory.
D. It is not possible to get this prompt.

Fill In

In the space provided, fill in the correct answer. Note that the answer can be one or two words.

1. ______________________
Rebooting the computer by holding down the Ctrl and Alt key and striking the Del key (without turning the computer off then back on) is called a ____ start.

2. ______________________
DOS commands that are not part of the command processor and are carried out by a separate DOS program are called ____ commands.

3. ______________________
The ____ command allows you to display the names of the files that are stored on a disk.

4. ______________________
Both the FORMAT and ____ commands will destroy all the files stored on a disk.

5. ______________________
A ____ file can be viewed on the screen using the TYPE command.

Name: ______________________ Date: ______________

OBJECTIVE QUESTIONS (*continued*)

6. ______________________

If you format a disk as a system disk (using the /S), two of the three files that DOS places on the disk will not be listed with a DIR command. Files that do not show from the DIR are called ______ files.

7. ______________________

The operand to use with ERASE command to erase all of the files from the disk in the B drive is ______.

8. ______________________

The ______ command would be used to copy all files from one disk to another without destroying the existing files on the target disk.

9. ______________________

To change the name of the file SUMMARY.WK1 to SUMMARY.SAV, you would use the ______ command.

10. ______________________

By creating a ______ on a floppy disk, you can store more than the limit of 112 files on a floppy disk.

ASSIGNMENTS/PROJECTS

Before attempting these assignments, you will need a blank disk.

1. Obtain printed copies of the directories for each of the disks that accompanied this book.

2. This is an exercise to make a disk duplicate, and to delete and copy files.

1. Copy the contents of the data disk that accompanied this book onto a blank disk. When you are finished, remove the original and store it in a safe place.
2. Print a copy of the directory of the new disk.
3. Delete all files with extensions of DBF and NDX from the new disk (in the B drive) and print a directory again. Note the number of files now on the disk and the space remaining.
4. Copy all of the files from the Limited Use WordPerfect disk with an extension of WP from this disk to the new disk. Display a directory and note the number of files now on the disk and the space remaining.
5. Copy all of the files from Disk #1 of Limited Use dBASE III with names starting with the letter C.
6. Obtain a printed copy of the directory of this disk and check each entry against the disks from which you copied to ensure that files were deleted and copied properly.

3. For floppy disk computer users only. The objective of this exercise is to prepare a new disk to serve most of your needs for this book. For the sake of disk economy, you can use the disk you prepare as both the bootable DOS disk and as your data disk for completing assignments. To this end, you will need to reformat the new disk you used in the preceding assignment.

1. Insert a DOS disk in the A drive. Insert your disk from the preceding assignment in the B drive.
2. Format the disk in the B drive as a system disk with the command:

```
FORMAT B:/S
```

3. When the formatting operation is complete, display a directory. Notice that approximately 40K of the 360K capacity is used by the DOS files. (It may be more depending on the version of DOS you have.)
4. Copy the files FORMAT.COM and DISKCOPY.COM from the DOS system disk to your newly formatted system disk with the commands:

```
COPY FORMAT.COM B:
COPY DISKCOPY.COM B:
```

5. Remove the DOS disk from the A drive and insert the data disk that accompanied this book.
6. Copy all the files from this disk to your disk in the B drive with the command:

```
COPY A:*.* B:
```

Remove the data disk from the A drive and store it in a safe place. Do not use it except to copy its files to another disk.

7. If you have your own copy of Lotus 1-2-3 and are using it rather than the spreadsheet software included with this book, then rename the spreadsheet files with the following command.

```
RENAME B:*.WKQ *.WKS
```

8. Remove the disk from the B drive and label it as your boot/data disk.

4. For hard disk computer users only. The objective of this exercise is to prepare your hard disk to serve most of your needs for this book. For this you should create subdirectories for WordPerfect and JOE, the Lotus-like spreadsheet included with this book. (Setting up for dBASE III PLUS is described in the dBASE chapter.)

1. Insert the WordPerfect disk in the A drive.

2. From the C> prompt, create the subdirectory WP with the following DOS sequence.

```
CD\
MD WP
```

3. Change to the WP subdirectory and copy the WordPerfect files:

```
CD WP
COPY A:*.*
```

4. You can run with the data files on a floppy disk or on your hard disk.

   If you plan to work with your data files on a floppy disk, then do the preceding preparation for floppy disk users. However, you do not need the /S on the format nor do you need to copy the two files from the DOS disk.

   If you want your data on your hard disk, then replace the WordPerfect disk in the A drive with the data disk that accompanied this book. From the C> prompt, type the command:

```
COPY A:*.WP*
```

5. Replace the disk in the A drive with the JOE spreadsheet disk.

6. From the C> prompt, create the subdirectory JOE with the following DOS sequence.

```
CD\
MD JOE
```

7. Change to the JOE subdirectory and copy the JOE files:

```
CD JOE
COPY A:*.*
```

8. As with WordPerfect, if you intend to run with your data on a hard disk, you should replace the JOE disk in the A drive with the data disk that accompanied this book. From the C> prompt, type the command:

```
COPY A:*.WKQ
```

9. If you have your own copy of Lotus 1-2-3 and are using it rather than the spreadsheet software included with this book, then rename the spreadsheet files with the following command:

```
RENAME C:*.WKQ  *.WKS
```

PART TWO

Word Processing and Desktop Publishing

INTRODUCTION TO PART TWO

The first of the software tools that you will learn about is word processing: using the computer to prepare printed documents. This part of the book consists of two chapters with the focus on the popular word processor WordPerfect, which is included with this book. You will learn basic operations such as entering and editing a document, saving it to disk, and retrieving a previously saved document from disk (Chapter 2). You will also learn more advanced operations such as changing a document's appearance and rearranging text within the document (Chapter 3).

THE NEED FOR WORD PROCESSING CAPABILITIES

Preparing letters and other documents is not a task you might normally associate with the amazing processing speeds and number-crunching abilities of the computer. However, computer handling of the written word, or text, is another important application of the computer. The computer can streamline the tasks of text entry, storage, retrieval, modification, and printing in much the same way that it can streamline maintaining the financial records of a company. Word processing programs have placed the power of the microcomputer behind words, making it far easier for people to prepare and revise text than was possible with the typewriter. You as a student can prepare course papers and essays as well as a résumé. You as a businessperson can enter memos and letters directly into a word processor rather than writing them in longhand and then having them typed. Sales representatives who spend much time on the road can use portable microcomputers to prepare documents that are transmitted to the home office over telephone lines. The list of personal and business tasks made easier by word processors is endless.

The appearance of written communications prepared by a business or individual conveys an image (whether correct or not) of that business or individual. If your correspondence looks sloppy, the recipient is likely to feel that this reflects your expertise on the topic at hand. For instance, a student has to prepare essays and papers. No matter how good the content, if they are poorly presented, their appearance will produce a negative feeling on the part of the instructor who is doing the grading. A prospective employer will not be impressed with the person who does not take the effort to prepare a good-looking résumé. As a businessperson, your correspondence to people outside the company conveys a significant image of the company. Even the physical appearance of your memos within the company conveys an image of you to your employees (or employers). As the owner of a business, it is critical that your catalogs and price lists be accurate and easy to read. A potential customer who receives a poorly prepared catalog might well conclude that the quality of your product will be the same.

These are all word processing tasks involving text entry, storage, retrieval, modification, and printing. They can be done using a word processing program on a microcomputer equipped with one or more disk drives and a printer. There are also special-purpose computers dedicated solely to word processing that range in size from units not much larger than a typewriter to large systems with numerous workstations; these are commonly referred to as word processors. However, the focus in this book is on word processing as done on the general-purpose microcomputer. As used in this book, the term *word processor* refers to word processing programs such as WordPerfect described in the next two chapters. Word processing system refers to the combination of word processing software and microcomputer hardware.

PREPARING A LETTER USING A TYPEWRITER

Let us begin the consideration of word processing by looking at the preparation of a document on a typewriter, the predecessor of the word processing system. Note that descriptions in this chapter should not be interpreted to imply that the typewriter is obsolete. There are still some applications for which the typewriter is well suited, such as filling out forms or addressing envelopes.

Planning the Letter

Assume that you have been working with an attorney to prepare a sales representative contract for MCT Enterprises. After reviewing her draft for the contract and comparing it with some sample contracts, you decide that three items should be added. To that end, you write her the letter shown in Figure P2-1. Without the aid of a word processor, you might have written your draft of the letter in longhand, as shown in Figure P2-2. Note that the three contract items are to be inserted from another document.

Before beginning to type, the typist had to envision the general layout of the letter—its format—which depends on several factors. Many typewriters, such as the IBM Selectric and those that use daisy wheels, can type at either 10 characters per inch (commonly referred to as pica) or at 12 characters per inch (commonly referred to as elite). A short note that will occupy only a portion of a page may look better using pica; a long document for which you wish to minimize the number of pages would be best in elite.

The typist must also select the margins, which depend on the length of the document and the appearance that you desire. Typically, left and right

```
MCT Enterprises
124 Burnett Ave.


Jane Harlett, Attorney at Law
1551 A Street
San Francisco, CA

Dear Ms. Harlett:

We have received your draft of the sales representative contract.
If you would include the following items, the contract will be
satisfactory.

OPTION OF COMPANY TO APPROVE ORDERS - COMPANY shall have the
option to accept or reject any order taken by Sales
Representative, and no commission shall be payable to Sales
Representative except on goods actually shipped by COMPANY and
received, accepted, and paid for by the purchaser.

DISCOUNT POLICY - COMPANY shall set all discount rates.  The
following discounts are agreed upon and shall remain in effect
for a period of not less than 180 days from the date of this
agreement.

          Standard Line      19%
          Stylist Line       22%
          Classic Line       24%

TERMINATION - This contract may be terminated by either party at
any time upon 30 days written notice to the other, or as provided
in Paragraph 1.

We appreciate your concern in assisting us.


Sincerely yours,
```

Figure P2-1
A finished letter ready to be signed and mailed.

margins range from 1 to 1½ inches wide. There are numerous other considerations. Tab stops must be positioned for paragraph indents, and for alignment of columns if a table is to be printed. If the document is to be proofread and marked for modification, then double spacing should be used rather than single spacing. All of these are factors that must be taken into account when preparing a letter such as the one shown in Figure P2-1. Significantly, a word processor does not eliminate the need for this type of planning, but it makes changing much easier, as you will learn.

Typing the Letter

One of the nuisance factors of using a typewriter is the action required when the end of the line is near. As anyone knows who has ever used a typewriter, a bell tells the typist that a fixed number of spaces remain before reaching the right margin. A decision must be made regarding how

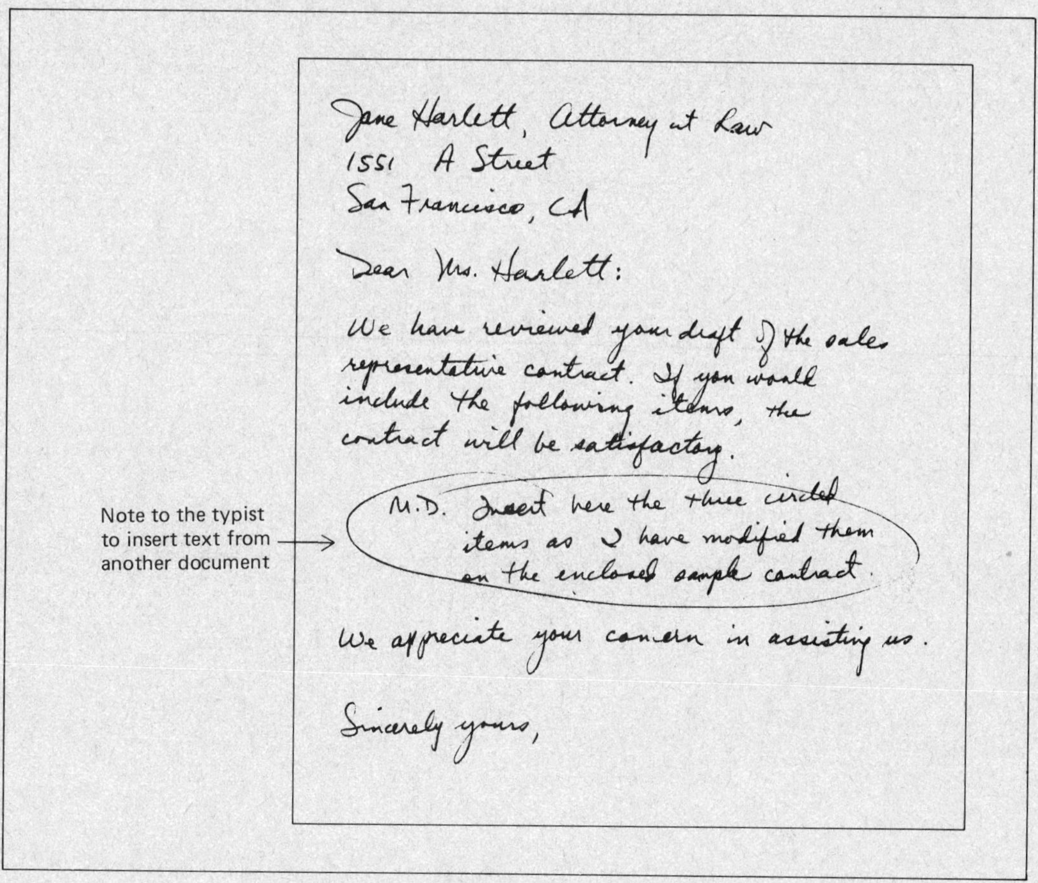
Jane Harlett, Attorney at Law
1551 A Street
San Francisco, CA

Dear Ms. Harlett:

We have reviewed your draft of the sales representative contract. If you would include the following items, the contract will be satisfactory.

N.D. Insert here the three circled items as I have modified them on the enclosed sample contract.

We appreciate your concern in assisting us.

Sincerely yours,

Figure P2-2
The handwritten original of the letter.

much more can be typed on the current line. Although this may appear to be a minor factor, it reduces both speed and accuracy by diverting the attention of the typist from the copy.

The letter shown in Figure P2-1 is the final error-free version that will be signed and mailed. However, it is quite unlikely that it was the original typed copy. You may have had a draft copy typed (double-spaced) so that you could read it over and make needed changes. In typing the final copy, if a minor error were made, such as omitting the letters *na* in *terminated* (producing *termited*), the typist would have to retype again. Because many businesses view their correspondence as an indication of their abilities, letters that must be "perfect" sometimes are typed two or three times.

ABOUT WORD PROCESSORS

What Can a Word Processor Do?

There are many similarities between typing a letter on a typewriter and preparing one with a word processing system. In both cases, the characters are produced from a keyboard, and the person at the keyboard must make

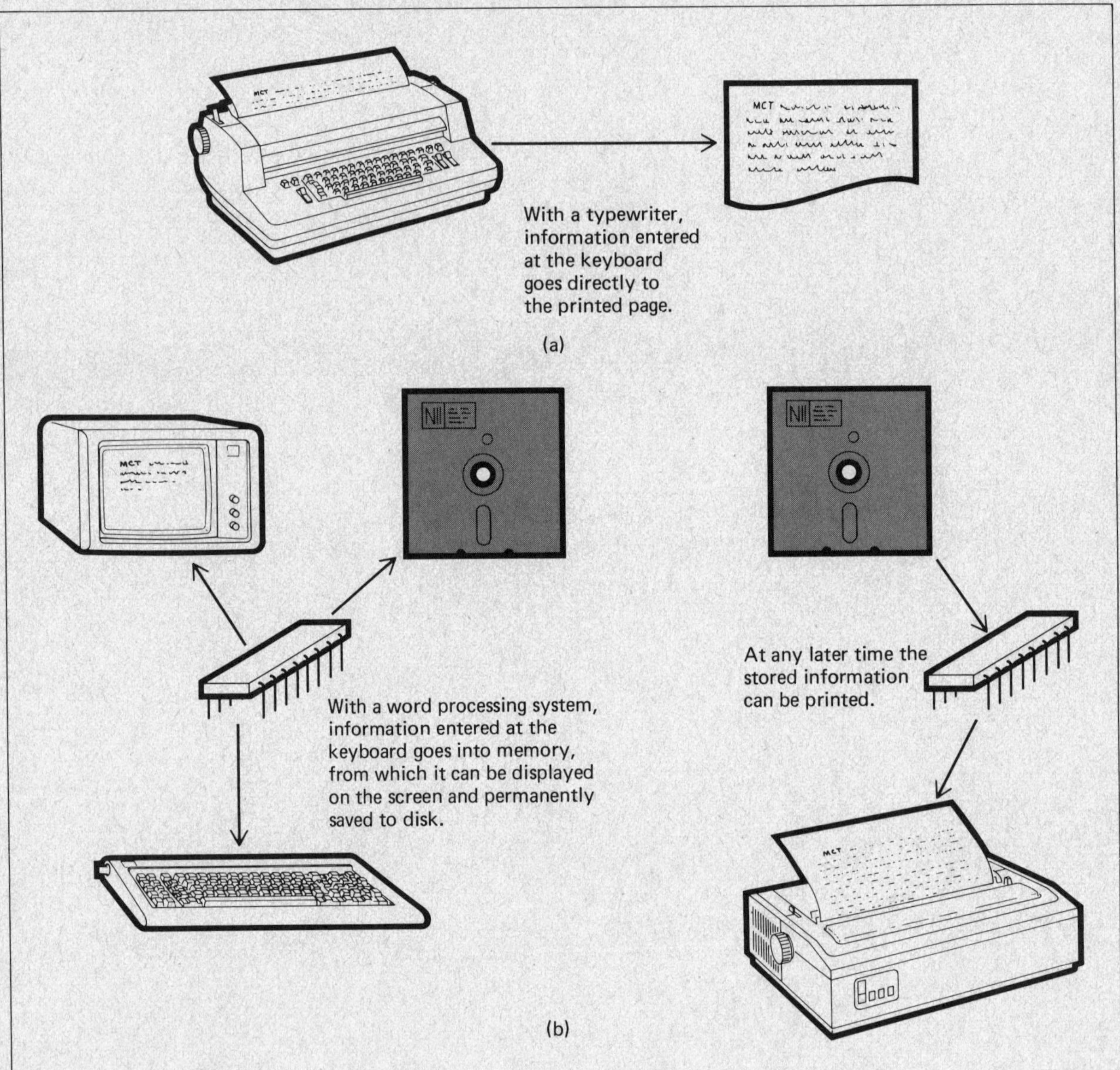

Figure P2-3
(a) Preparing a letter with a typewriter.
(b) Preparing a letter with a word processing system.

format decisions to control the final appearance of the document. However, the primary distinction between the two is that with a typewriter, keyboarded text goes directly to the printed page, but with a word processor, it goes into computer memory, where it can be manipulated. These concepts are illustrated in Figure P2-3. With a typewriter, the result is a typed page that, to be modified, must be retyped. With a word processor, the term **captured keystroke** is commonly used. This means that characters entered through the keyboard are stored in computer memory. Since entering and modifying are operations distinct from printing, a letter can be corrected and printed as many times as needed with little additional effort required to make it perfect. Without a doubt, the most significant characteristic of a word processor is that it allows changes to be made in a document without total retyping. These changes include the ability to perform the following actions with ease.

- Make editing changes.
- Reformat all or parts of the document.
- Move or copy sections of a document from one place to another.
- Insert a block of text into the current document from another stored on disk.
- Almost instantaneously find a word or phrase anywhere in a document.
- Automatically change all occurrences of a word or phrase in a document.
- Check the spelling of all words in the document on command.

You will learn how to do all of these in the two chapters that follow.

Chapter 2

Using WordPerfect

OBJECTIVES

The preceding introduction to word processing gave you a general idea of what it is all about. In this chapter, you will have the opportunity to work with the popular word processor WordPerfect. When you have completed this chapter, you should be able to:

- Activate the WordPerfect program.
- Enter and make corrections to a document.
- Save the document to disk.
- Print a document.
- Retrieve a document from disk that was previously saved.
- Terminate execution of the WordPerfect program and return to DOS.

PREVIEW

Getting Started

The WordPerfect program is run from DOS; once running, control of the computer is given by DOS to WordPerfect. The screen display awaiting your text entry is called the edit screen.

Entering Text and Correcting Text

As you enter text into the edit screen, word wrap occurs as each line becomes full. During the process of text entry, you may make corrections and changes to the text you have entered.

Commands and the Function Keys

The function keys are used to issue commands to WordPerfect. These allow you to request actions such as printing a document and searching for a phrase, and to insert formatting codes.

Rewriting a Document

At any time while entering text, you can insert or delete characters at any point in your document. If you change your mind about a portion of text you have deleted, then you may restore it with the Undelete command.

Saving Documents

Documents that you enter from the edit screen are stored in memory (RAM), the "temporary" working area of the computer. The Save command allows you to save your documents to disk storage.

The Exit Command

You can conclude your WordPerfect work session or stop work on one document and begin work on another with the Exit command.

Retrieving a Document from Disk

Any document that you have previously saved to disk can be retrieved and placed in memory so that you can work on it further.

More on Moving the Cursor

You can use the keyboard arrow keys to move the cursor character by character or line by line within your document. Other keys allow quicker movement, including scrolling from one screen to the next.

Summary of Cursor Moves

This section includes a table summarizing all of the cursor movements.

Printing a Document

You can produce a printed copy of your document at any time during your work session by following a simple command sequence.

GETTING STARTED

This chapter is slightly different from Chapter 1 in that you need to read *and* do—that is, read the chapter or a portion of it first, then do all of the described actions for yourself at the computer. The hands-on exercises are emphasized with a DO THIS NOW designation: for instance, DO THIS NOW 2-3 is the third one in this chapter. In discussions within the text, it would be referred to as DTN 2-3. If you wish to try some hands-on tasks before finishing the entire chapter, read up to the section on hidden codes and then go to the computer.

When reading, do not attempt to memorize exact keystrokes necessary to carry out the different actions; simply learn about the actions. When you try them on the computer, things will fall into place much more quickly.

Before you can begin to enter a document with WordPerfect, you must load the WordPerfect program into the computer's memory. Once it is loaded, control of the computer switches from DOS to WordPerfect. Let us consider this loading start-up process and the WordPerfect screen from which you will be working.

About the Limited-Use Software That Accompanies This Book

This book includes a Limited-Use version of WordPerfect 4.2 that is identical to the commercial version except for a relatively few restrictions on its capabilities. Those restrictions that you are likely to encounter are described in a screen display when the Limited-Use version program is run. If you try to execute a command not operational in the Limited-Use version, WordPerfect notifies you. The purpose of this version is to provide you with a means for learning basic principles of word processing without the expense of the commercial version of the software. All examples in this and the next chapter can be run on either the Limited-Use or commercial version.

Running WordPerfect

To work with WordPerfect, you will need the WordPerfect disk that accompanies this book, a DOS disk for booting the computer, and a formatted data disk (the data disk that accompanies this book can be used). Note that the DOS and data disks are those that you should have prepared in Chapter 1. To run WordPerfect, carry out the sequence of operations described in the boxes on the next page.

Floppy Disk Computer

1. Boot the computer with a DOS disk in the A drive.
2. Remove the DOS disk from the A drive and insert the WordPerfect disk.
3. Insert the data disk in the B drive.
4. From the A> prompt, change to the B drive as the default by typing

   `A> B:`

   and then striking the Enter key. The DOS prompt will then be:

   `B>`

5. The name of the WordPerfect program (located on the A drive) is WP; from the B prompt, type the following.

   `B> A:WP`

   Note that it is necessary to precede WP with A: in order to tell DOS to look on the A drive for the WordPerfect program.

Hard Disk Computer

Note: The following instructions assume that WordPerfect is stored in the subdirectory named WP as described in Chapter 1. If it is not, then you must modify these instructions accordingly.

1. Boot the computer from the hard disk (leave the door to the A drive open).
2. Change to the WP subdirectory by typing:

   `C> CD\WP`

3. From the C> prompt, change to the A drive as the default by typing

   `C> A:`

   and then striking the Enter key. The DOS prompt will then be:

   `A>`

4. The name of the WordPerfect program (located on the C drive) is WP; from the A> prompt, type the following.

   `A> C:WP`

   Note that it is necessary to precede WP with C: in order to tell DOS to look on the C drive for the WordPerfect program.

Whether you are using a floppy disk or hard disk computer, an announcement screen will be displayed describing restrictions of the Limited-Use version of WordPerfect. Striking the Enter key will cause this screen to be erased and the remainder of the WordPerfect program to be loaded into memory.

The WordPerfect Screen

Once you have loaded the WordPerfect program, your screen will be as shown in Figure 2-1. This is called the **edit screen** because it is the screen display from which you can enter and edit text. (As you will learn, there are other screen displays from which other functions can be performed.) Note that the cursor is initially located in the upper left of the screen; as with DOS, it is the position into which text will be entered. The line at the bottom of the screen is called the **status line;** from the descriptions in Figure 2-1, you can see that the information provided relates to the eventual printed page.

The position indicator also conveys other information. That is, if the keyboard is in uppercase shift, then the Pos indicator is displayed in caps

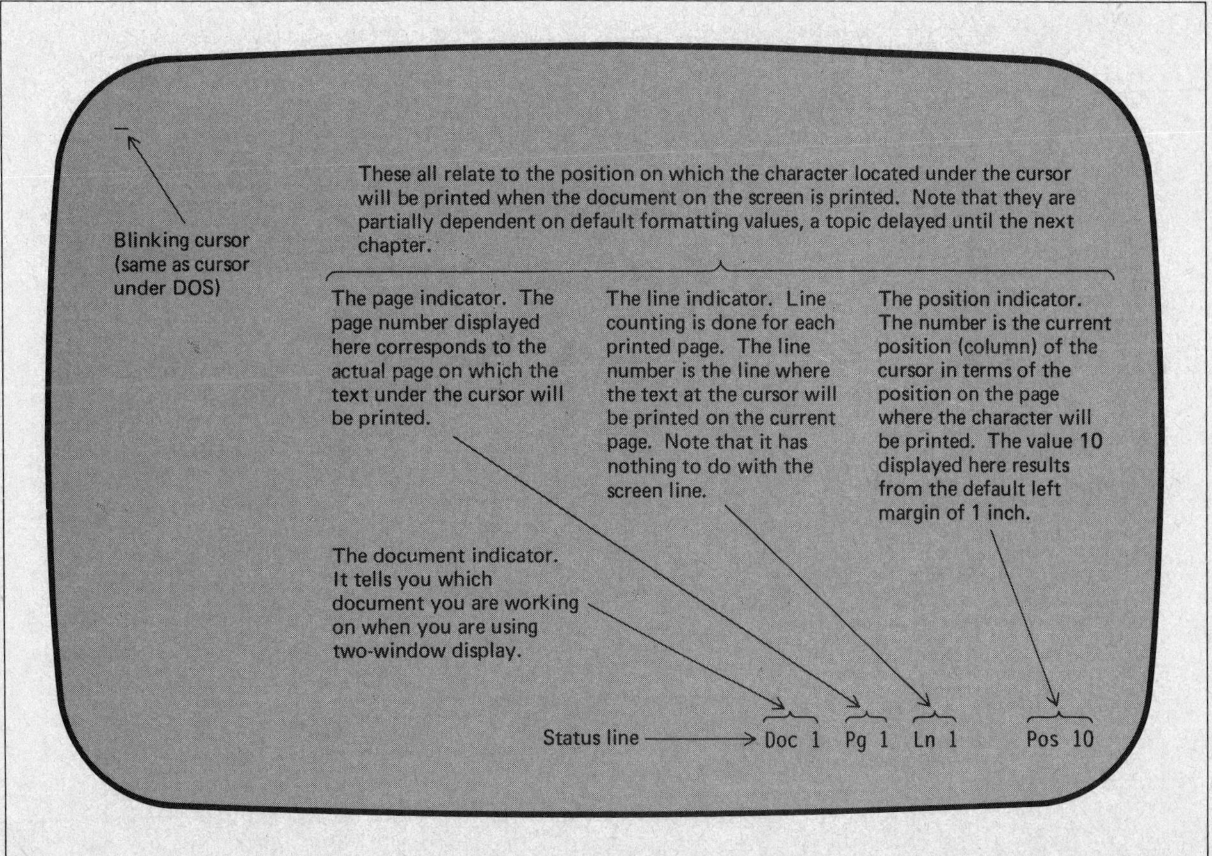

Figure 2-1
The empty WordPerfect screen.

as POS. If the NumLock key has been struck thereby switching the arrow keys to numeric data keys, the Pos (or POS) indicator will be blinking on and off. Try this by pressing the Caps Lock key; notice how the letters *os* in Pos alternate between lowercase and uppercase each time the key is pressed. Then do the same with the NumLock key and notice how the position indicator alternates between blinking and not blinking.

As you will learn later in this chapter, the status line serves as somewhat of a message center to you from WordPerfect. For instance, if you enter the command to save the document on which you are working to disk, WordPerfect will respond with a prompt asking you the name of the document. Once the document is named, the name will be displayed on the status line.

Getting Out of Trouble

Keystroke actions with a word processor are used both to enter text into the document (as with a typewriter) and to enter commands directing the word processor to take some action. For your first activity with WordPerfect, you will be entering text and hence will not be using commands. However, if you accidentally strike a key sequence that results in a command, you may cause WordPerfect to switch from accepting text to awaiting a response to a prompt. For instance, if you strike the F10 function key, the cursor will be moved to the bottom of the screen following the displayed prompt:

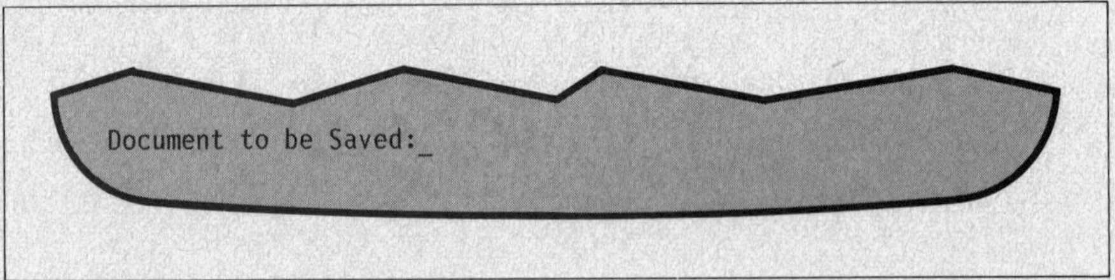

To get rid of this and return to text entry, simply strike the F1 function key. You should try this on your computer so that you recognize what takes place. Commands and their corresponding function keys are described later in this chapter.

ENTERING AND CORRECTING TEXT

Your First Document

Figure 2-2 is a memo that you will type into the computer as an exercise in learning about text entry and correction. As you type, do not be concerned about entering it perfectly. (In fact, be certain to type the word *otherer* as it is misspelled in the sixth line.) One of the strong points of word processors is the ease with which errors can be corrected.

Figure 2-2
The document to be entered.

```
To:      Readers of this book
From:    The Author
Subject: WordPerfect

This memo will be used to illustrate some of the many basic
features of WordPerfect.  With it as an example, you will learn
how to enter a simple document (such as this) into the computer.
If you are anything like I am, then you will need immediate
assistance on how to make corrections.  As you will learn, the
operation of correcting spelling and otherer errors is almost as
easy as making them in the first place.  You will learn how to
insert text, and delete text, and move text, and search for text,
and...

Although this chapter only scratches the surface of the things
that can be done with WordPerfect, there are some advanced topics
in the next chapter.  One of them involves breaking the screen
into two parts and viewing two different documents.  You will
even be able to move a portion of one of the documents into the
other with a few keystrokes.  Actually, the process is so simple
that it seems strange to classify it as an "advanced topic."  I
will leave that for you to decide.
```

DO THIS NOW 2-1 **Entering the memo of Figure 2-2.**

1. If you have not already done so, run WordPerfect to obtain the edit screen of Figure 2-1.
2. Using the keyboard in much the same way that you use a typewriter, type in the first few lines as shown in Figure 2-3. Note that each

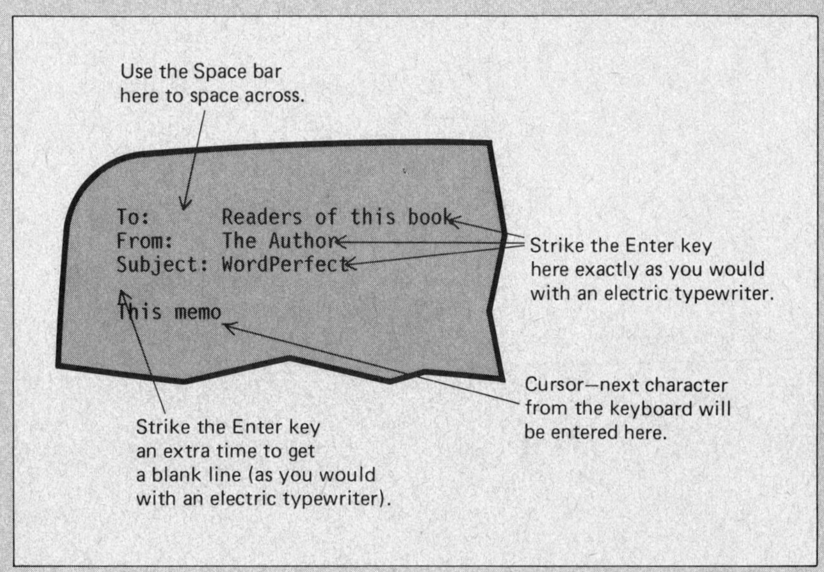

Figure 2-3
Entering text.

line is ended by striking Enter. Do not worry if you make mistakes while typing, because the next thing you will learn is how to correct them.

3. Continue typing the first sentence; remember not to strike the Enter key at the end of the line. As you near the end of the first line, observe how WordPerfect uses word wrap by automatically starting a new line. As shown in Figure 2-4(a), the first five letters of the word *features* will be at the right margin. Note that the cursor is to the immediate right of the last letter typed. What you do not see on the screen is that the line is full and that no characters can be entered beyond the "invisible" right margin.

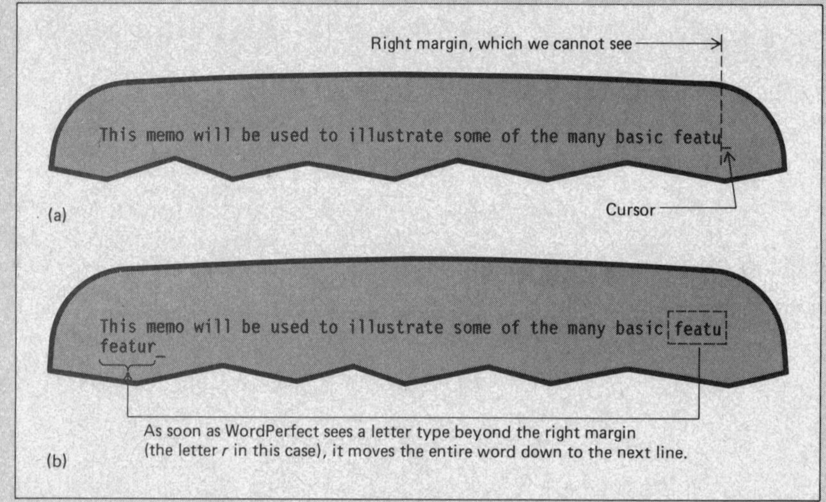

Figure 2-4
Entering text with word wrap.

4. Type the letter *r*. The moment you do this, WordPerfect moves this word to the next line, as shown in Figure 2-4(b), because no characters can be typed beyond the margin.
5. Type the rest of the first paragraph.
6. Tell WordPerfect that you want to start a new paragraph by striking Enter to force a new line (as was done in typing the first three lines in Figure 2-3).
7. Force a blank line between paragraphs by striking Enter a second time as shown in Figure 2-5.

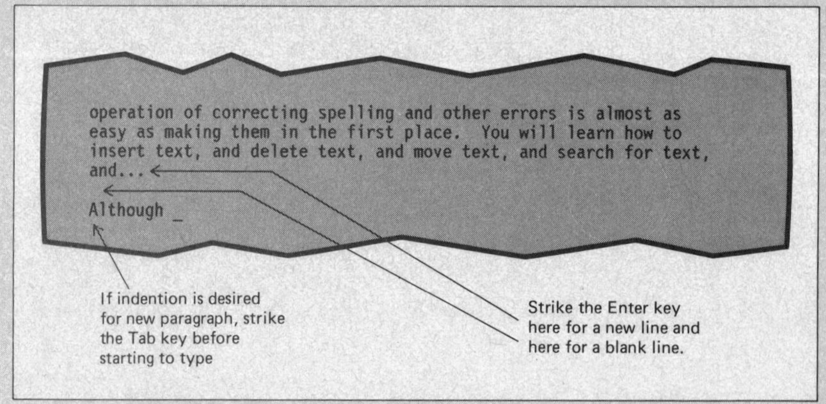

Figure 2-5
Beginning a new paragraph.

8. Type the second paragraph. If you wish to indent this paragraph, then strike the Tab key before beginning typing on the new line (preceding the word Although). If you do indent, your copy of the document will be slightly different from that of Figure 2-2.

In this exercise, you have used the default values for margins and tab settings (you will learn how to change margins in the next chapter). Each time you strike the Tab key, the cursor jumps to previously identified positions called tab stops. The default tab stop settings are positioned every five positions so that each time the Tab key is struck, the cursor moves right five positions.

Making Corrections While Typing

The backspace key.

Often when typing you will realize immediately when you have struck one or more incorrect keys. If so, you can use the Backspace key to delete the incorrect characters and then resume typing. Note that it is located in the upper right corner of the main part of the keyboard. On some keyboards, it is imprinted with the word Backspace.

To illustrate using the Backspace, assume that you misplaced your hand and hit the wrong keys while typing the word *example* as shown in Figure 2-6(a). With your completed document on the screen, begin a new

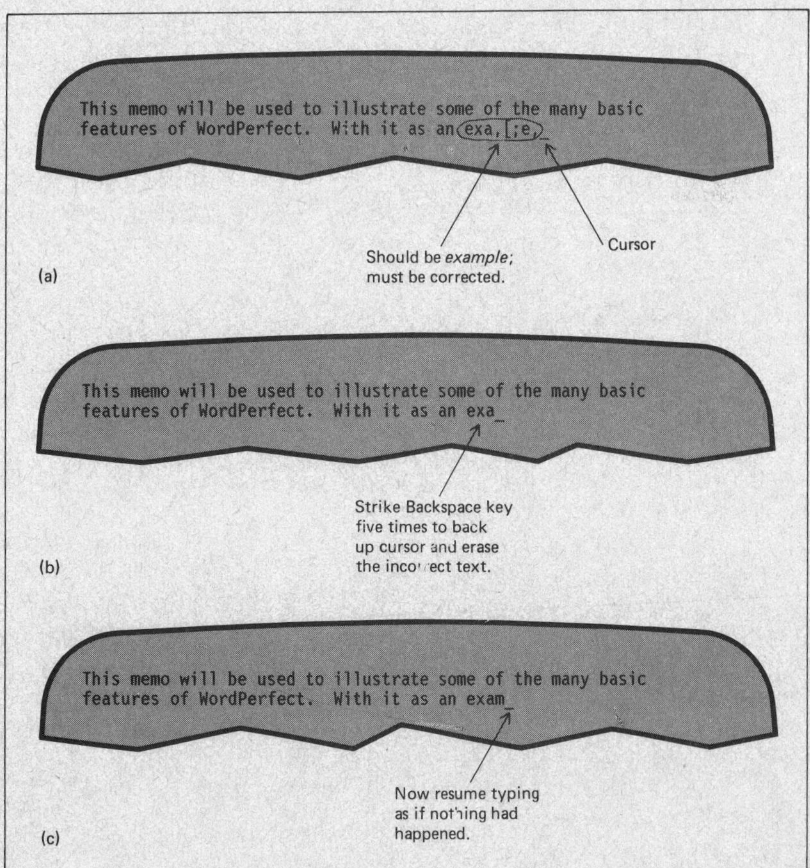

Figure 2-6
(a) Incorrect text that must be corrected.
(b) Deleting the incorrect entries.
(c) Resuming typing of the document.

paragraph and type two lines exactly as in Figure 2-6(a). Do not worry that they are a duplicate of the first two lines; you will delete them when finished.

DO THIS NOW 2-2 **Using the Backspace**

1. Strike the Backspace key five times; your screen will be as in Figure 2-6(b).
2. Resume typing as if you had made no error [Figure 2-6(c)].
3. You no longer need the two lines you entered from this exercise, so hold down the Backspace key and watch the characters to the left of it disappear. If you accidentally delete part of the preceding paragraph, then reenter it.

Positioning the Cursor and Correcting Typographical Errors

You will find that making corrections as in Figure 2-6 is convenient if you notice the error immediately. However, what happens if you notice the error upon proofreading after entering more text as shown in Figure 2-7(a)? Since the cursor defines the position at which characters are entered or deletions made, it must be repositioned to the portion of the text that requires correction. You can do this using combinations of the cursor movement keys. Each time you strike one of them, the cursor moves up or down one line or left or right one character, as indicated by the direction of the arrow. (Note: The enhanced keyboard includes a separate set of cursor movement keys.) If you hold an arrow key down, then you invoke the automatic repeat and the cursor moves continuously. In Figure 2-7(a), the letters *er* must be deleted from the word *otherer*.

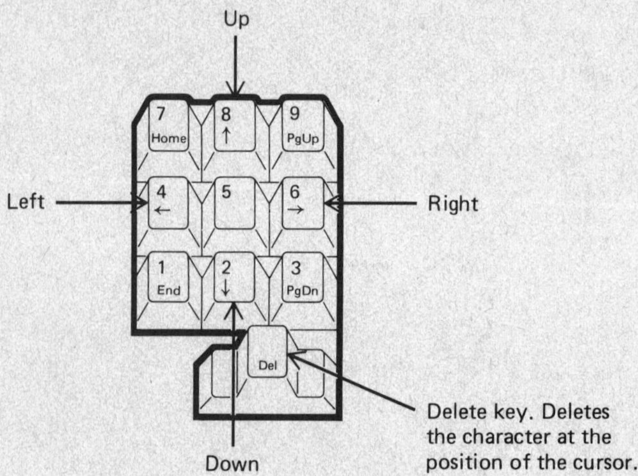

The cursor keys.

The cursor keys.

Figure 2-7
(a) An error to be corrected.
(b) Move the cursor to the incorrect entry.
(c) Strike the Del key to delete the character at the cursor.

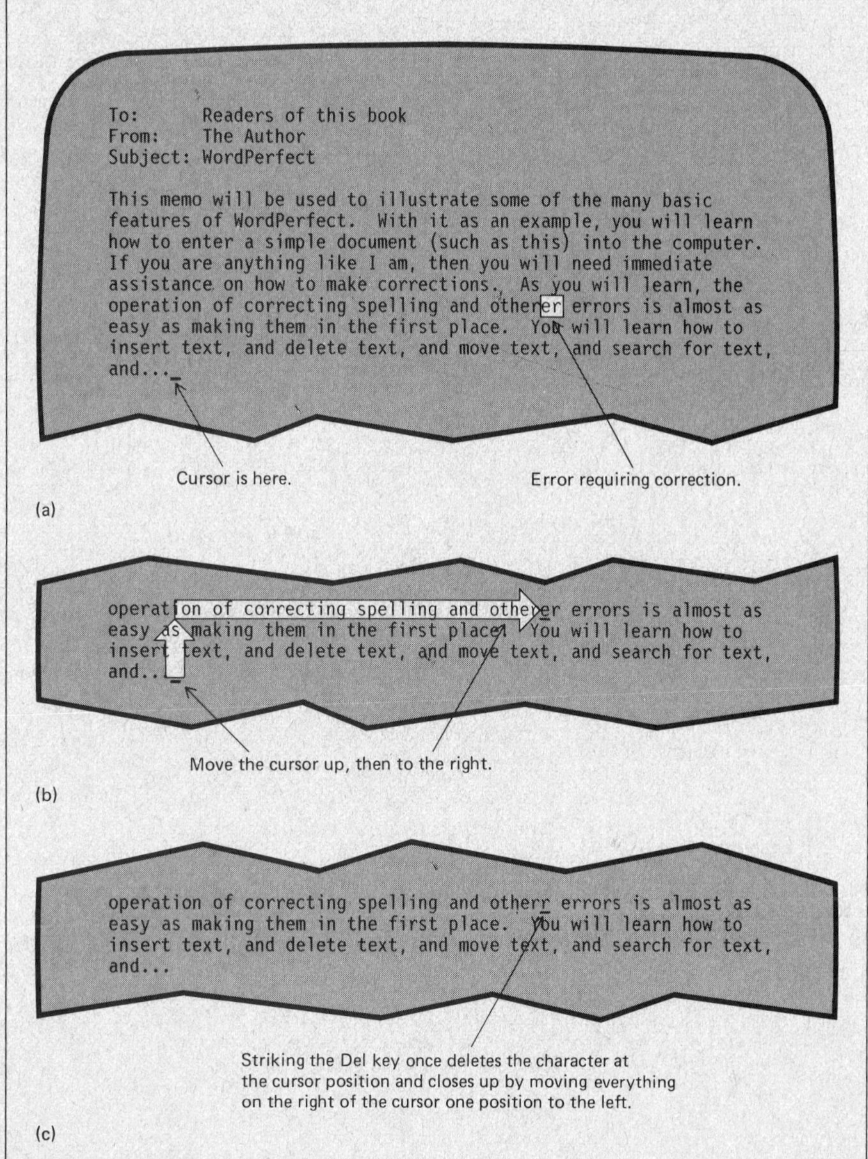

DO THIS NOW 2-3 **Cursor Repositioning for Correcting**

1. Move the cursor up (using the Up arrow key) to the desired line.
2. Move right (using the Right arrow key) to the first character to be deleted in Figure 2-7(b).
3. Delete the unwanted characters by striking the Del (Delete) key twice. Note that as each character is erased, everything that was to the right of it is moved left one position to fill the gap—see Figure 2-7(c).

At this point, you may move the cursor to some other point for additional corrections or back to the end of the document to resume text entry.

From the two examples of erasing characters, notice that you can use either the Backspace key or the Del key. Although the Backspace erases the character to the left of the cursor and the Del erases the character at the cursor position, they both produce the same result.

Assignment 2-1 may now be completed.

COMMANDS AND THE FUNCTION KEYS

Entering Commands

Now that you know how to enter text and make minor corrections, you need to learn about using commands,* the keystroke actions that allow you to control WordPerfect. Remember that there are two categories of commands: those that cause an action to take place, such as saving a document to disk, and those that cause the appearance of the document to change, such as changing the margin settings. In WordPerfect, these commands are entered using the function keys F1 through F10 in conjunction with the Shift, Ctrl, and Alt keys (see the keyboard layouts of Figure 2-1). With these, you can perform such actions as:

Command	Key Sequence
Save a document	F10
Center a line	Shift-F6
Replace a word	Alt-F2

You invoke the command to save a document by striking the F10 function key. In contrast, you invoke the command to center a line by striking the F6 function key while you are holding down the Shift key. This action is represented as:

Shift-F6

Some other keystroke actions require you to strike one key and release it, and then strike another. For instance, striking the Home key and then

*If you are using the commercial version of WordPerfect and have access to the WordPerfect reference manual, you should be aware of a difference in terminology in this book and in the manual regarding the word *command*. For instance, to initiate a search and replace action, this book will refer to the *replace command* whereas the manual will refer to the *replace key*. The latter can be confusing because it involves a key sequence rather than a single key. However, they both mean the same thing.

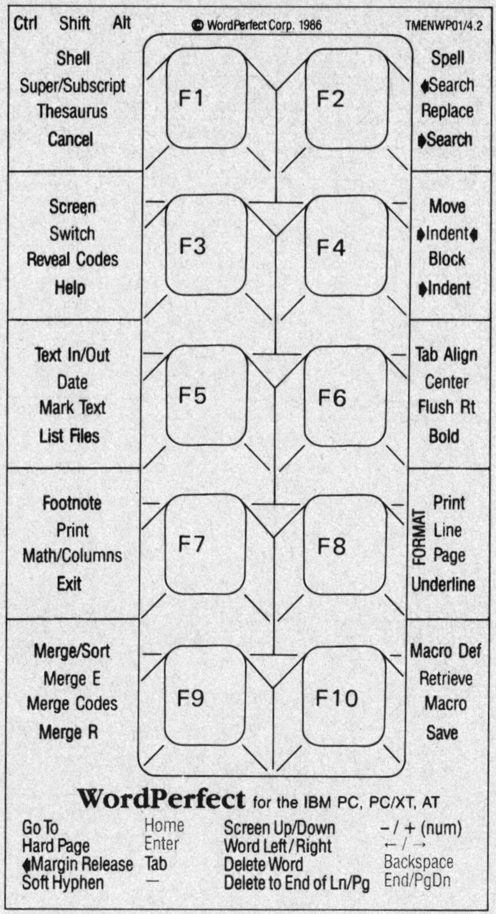

Figure 2-8
The function key template.

the left arrow key positions the cursor at the beginning of the current line. This action is represented as:

Home,Left

Remember, a keying action in which the keys are separated by a hyphen means to hold down the first key and strike the second. A keying action in which the keys are separated by a comma means to strike the first key and release it, and then strike the second. Do not type either the hyphen or the comma.

The Function Key Template

In combination with the Shift, Ctrl, and Alt keys, the ten function keys provide you with forty different commands. As it is difficult to remember all of these combinations (especially when beginning), you may find the function key template included with WordPerfect very useful. This template, which fits over the function keys as shown in Figure 2-8, uses color coding to designate whether to use the Shift, Ctrl, Alt, or no key in conjunction with the particular function key. For instance, commands invoked by the F2 key are:

Color	Key sequence	Command
Red	Ctrl-F2	Spell
Green	Shift-F2	<-Search
Blue	Alt-F2	Replace
Black	F2	->Search

If you misplace the template or find it inconvenient to use, you can use the Help command (F3), which displays the layout on the screen. You should invoke the Help command (by striking F3) and you will see that the screen display of your document is replaced by the Help screen of Figure 2-9. At first glance, this tends to be confusing but notice that the four entries for each of the function keys are identical to the template of Figure 2-8, that is:

Entry	Case	Keystrokes
First	Upper/lowercase	Ctrl + Function key
Second	Uppercase	Shift + Function key
Third	Upper/lowercase with underscore (highlighted with color monitors)	Alt + Function key
Fourth	Upper/lowercase	Function key alone

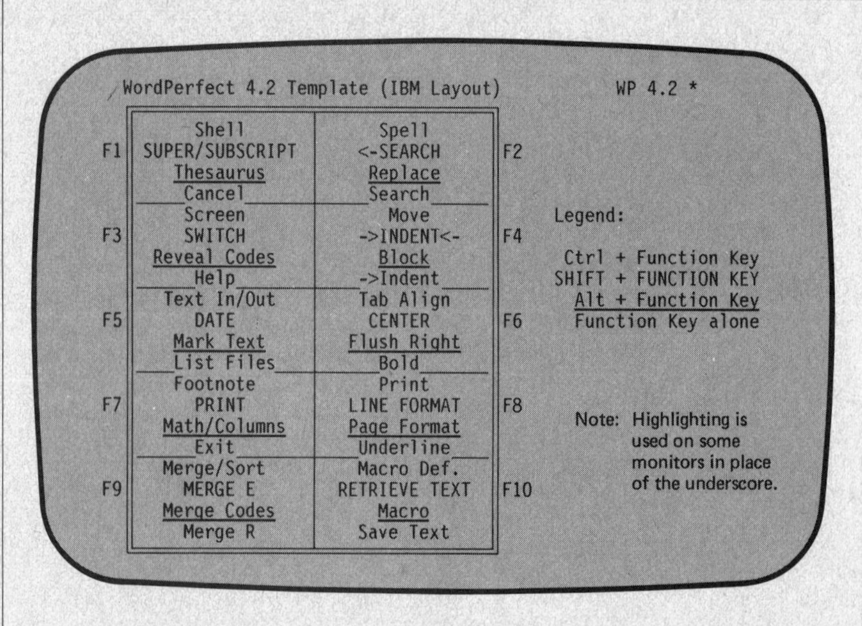

Figure 2-9
Screen display of the function key template; obtained by striking the F3 key.

When ready to return to the edit screen, simply strike any key on the keyboard and the Help screen will disappear. As you start using more of the features of WordPerfect, you will find the function key template very useful.

The Cancel Key

At the beginning of this chapter, you were told that if you accidentally pressed a command key sequence and were unable to continue typing text, you should strike the F1 key. This invokes the Cancel command, which causes the preceding action to be canceled. (WordPerfect refers to it as the Cancel key.) For instance, if you pressed the F2 function key, the following prompt would be displayed on the status line.

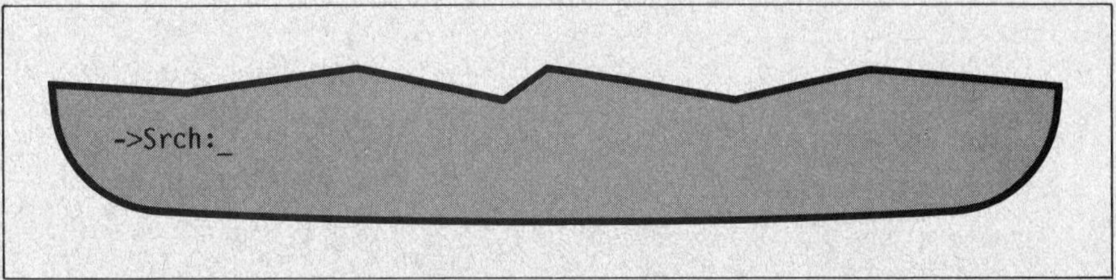

At this point, the cursor is positioned after the prompt and WordPerfect has stopped and is awaiting your entry. It will continue only when an appropriate response is entered to this prompt or else the command is canceled. Since this is not an action you wish to perform, you may cancel it by striking the F1 key. The prompt will disappear and control will be returned to the edit screen.

REWRITING A DOCUMENT

One of the features of word processors is the ease with which you can make changes, whether they are minor typographical corrections or major alterations to improve the message of the document. For instance, upon rereading the memo, assume that you decide to make the changes shown in Figure 2-10. Note that you must perform two tasks: insert a phrase and delete three words.

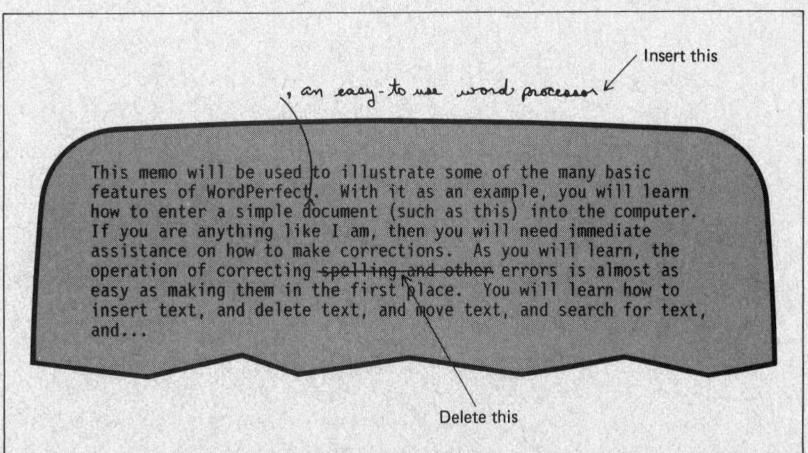

Figure 2-10
Portion of memo to be edited.

Inserting Text

First, let us consider inserting the desired phrase.

> DO THIS NOW 2-4 **Inserting Text**
>
> 1. Position the cursor (using the arrow keys) on the period following the word *WordPerfect* in the second line. This is the position at which you will begin typing.
> 2. Type the needed phrase in exactly the same way you would type any text. As you enter each character, WordPerfect inserts it at the position of the cursor and pushes the remaining text on that line to the right.

If you have done this correctly, your screen will look like that in Figure 2-11. As you typed, you probably noticed that the last portion of that line disappeared off the edge of the screen. The reason for this is that WordPerfect performs the word wrap operation only when the cursor reaches the right margin, or when the cursor is moved to another line if a situation such as that in Figure 2-11 occurs. Hence, you should move the cursor down to the next line (Down arrow key) and observe the screen being redisplayed conforming to the default right margin.

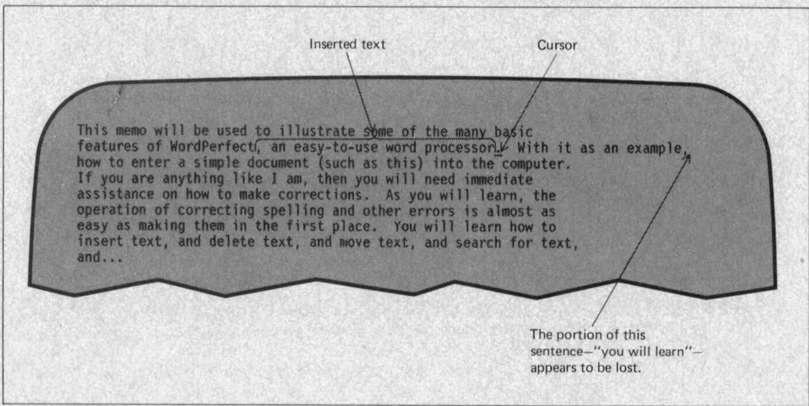

Figure 2-11
The document after insertion has been made.

In this example, you inserted text, thereby making the line longer. In some situations, you will want each new character to replace the character at the cursor. This is called **typeover.** You can switch from the insert mode to the typeover mode (and back again) by striking the Ins (Insert) key. As a simple illustration, assume you decide to change the word *memo* to *note*. To make this correction using typeover, you would:

> DO THIS NOW 2-5 **Using typeover**
>
> 1. Move the cursor to the letter *m* in *memo*.
> 2. Strike the Ins (Insert) key. The status line will tell you that WordPerfect is in the typeover mode by displaying Typeover at the lower left of the screen.

3. Type the word *note;* each letter will replace the corresponding letter of *memo*.
4. Strike the Ins key again to get out of the typeover mode.

Note that like the CapsLock key, the Insert key functions as a toggle. After making this change, change note back to memo.

Deleting More Than a Single Character

Referring to Figure 2-11, your next action is to delete the three words *spelling and other*. (You should have noticed that these were moved to the beginning of the sixth line when you performed the insertion operation.) Although you can delete these words one character at a time using either the Backspace or Delete key (automatic repeat works with them), WordPerfect provides other options for situations in which more than a few letters are to be deleted. For instance, whereas Backspace erases a single character, Ctrl-Backspace erases an entire word.

DO THIS NOW 2-6 **Deleting Words**

1. To delete the word *spelling* move the cursor so that it is positioned anywhere within the word or in the space following the word.
2. Enter the Ctrl-Backspace sequence to delete the entire word. You will see the word deleted and the remaining text in that line moved left so that the letter *a* in the word *and* is at the cursor position.
3. Enter the Ctrl-Backspace sequence twice more to delete the other two words. When you are finished, the screen will appear as shown in Figure 2-12.

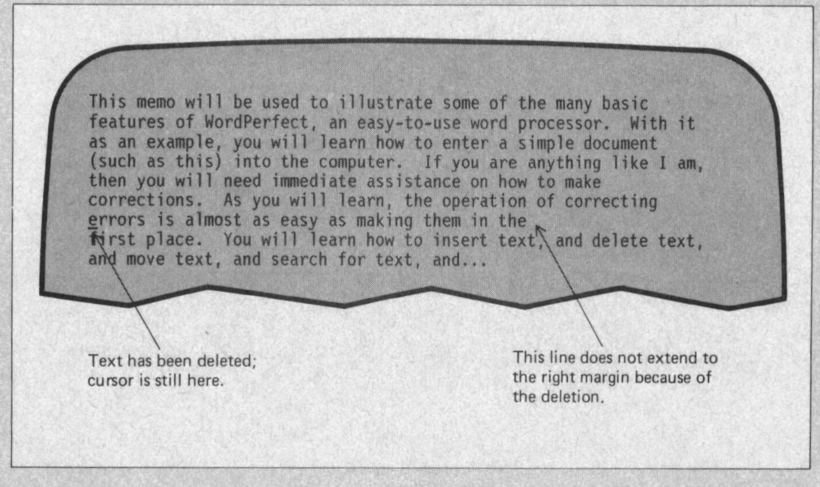

Figure 2-12
The document after deleting three words.

As with insertion, WordPerfect does not reformat paragraphs until the operation is completed (by moving the cursor to another line). Hence, the line from which the words were deleted is short. However, you need only move the cursor to another line to cause WordPerfect to reformat the display according to the default margin settings.

There are two other delete operations you can use to delete larger amounts of text. Ctrl-End deletes all text from the position of the cursor to the end of the current line. Ctrl-PgDn deletes all text from the cursor to the end of the current page. Note that this is the page as defined by the printer page size, not the screen display. Because this can be a large amount of text, WordPerfect prompts you for a confirmation before proceeding with the deletion. However, do not try it yet because the topic of the next section is how to restore text that has been deleted when you change your mind.

Undelete

Sometimes, when editing a document, you will delete a portion of text, and then change your mind and want it back. One feature of most word processors, including WordPerfect, is that deleted text is not discarded immediately and can be restored. To illustrate, assume that you have changed your mind about the previously deleted three words (*spelling and other*) and you want them back.

DO THIS NOW 2-7 **Undeleting**

1. If you moved the cursor, the first thing to do is to move it back to the point at which the deleted text is to be restored. In this example, it would be as shown in Figure 2-12.
2. Strike the F1 key and the text will be inserted and highlighted as shown in Figure 2-13.
3. Type the digit 1 to restore the deleted text to the document. The highlight will disappear and control will be returned to the edit screen.

When you use Undelete, WordPerfect displays a prompt on the status line with the following three options.

0 Striking the digit 0 causes a return to the edit screen without making any changes. In effect, this cancels the command.

1 Striking the digit 1 causes this deletion to be restored to the document as it is highlighted. The highlight is removed, control returns to the edit screen, and you can continue to work on your document.

2 Striking the digit 2 causes the highlighted (restored) text to be removed from the displayed document. The text being held from the previous deletion operation is then displayed.

To illustrate option 2, assume that after deleting these three words, you had moved the cursor and deleted the last sentence from the document. WordPerfect would now have two sets of deletions that it is saving as illustrated in Figure 2-14. After moving the cursor into position to

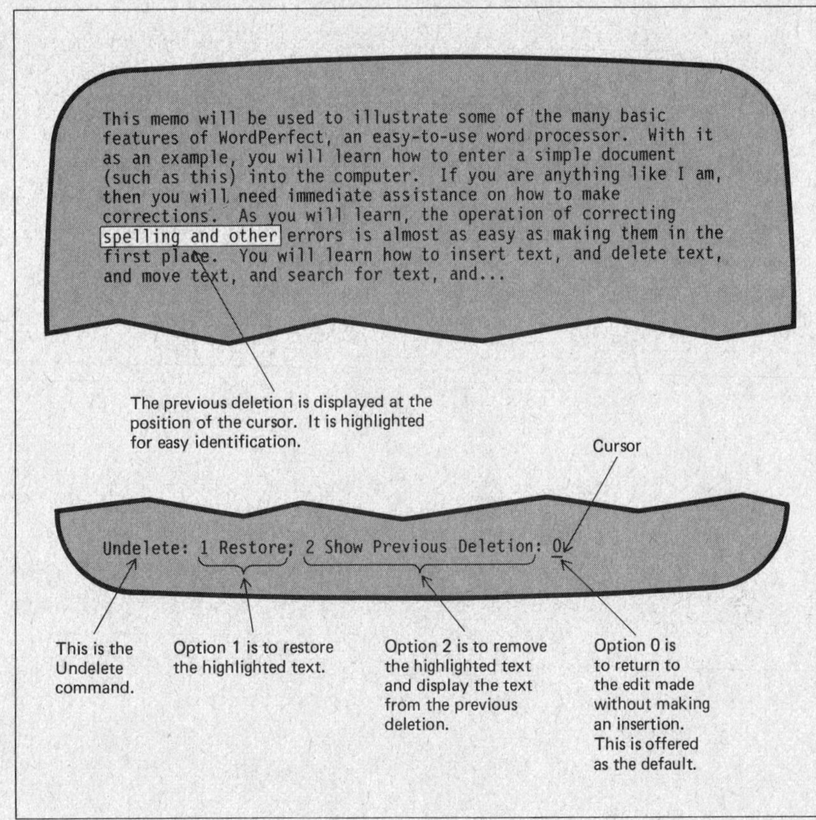

Figure 2-13
Restoring deleted text.

restore, when you strike the F1 key, WordPerfect displays text from the most recent deletion. In this case, it will be the sentence *I will leave that for you to decide.* However, since you want the text from the preceding deletion, you must select option 2 and the text from the preceding deletion (*spelling and other*) will be restored. WordPerfect keeps the three most recent deletions of text.

From the point of view of holding deleted text, what constitutes a delete action? For instance, you deleted the three words with three separate Ctrl-Backspaces. What if you had deleted them by striking the Del key

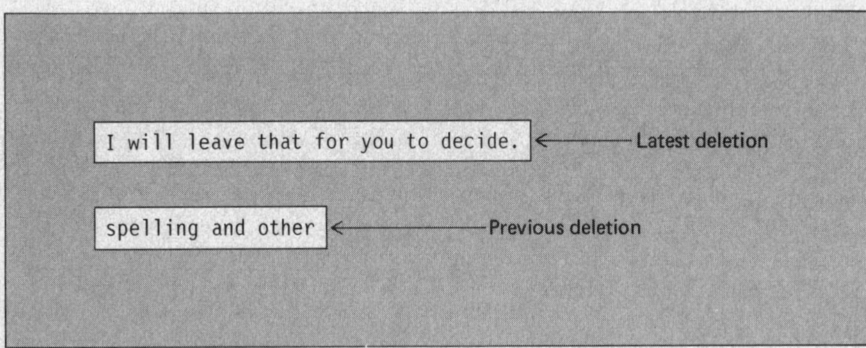

Figure 2-14
Deleted text.

nineteen successive times? The answer is that the results would have been the same. Any time you perform successive erasing actions without moving the cursor or entering another command, all of the deleted text is saved as a single deletion.

Regarding the F1 key, notice that it serves two different functions. If you press the F1 from the edit screen as illustrated by these examples, the Undelete command is executed and previously deleted text is restored. On the other hand, if a command has been executed that results in a prompt to which you must respond, then the Cancel command is executed. That is, the previous command is canceled and control returned to the edit screen.

Inserting and Deleting Return Codes

As you enter a document, both text and formatting codes are stored in memory. These codes control the way in which the text is displayed on the screen and printed on the page. Although a detailed discussion is reserved until the next chapter, a knowledge of the code caused by striking the Enter key during document entry will help you now when entering and editing a document. Figure 2-15 shows the screen display for the first three lines of the memo and the corresponding memory contents. The WordPerfect code resulting from striking the Enter key is called a hard return and is abbreviated HRt. When entering and editing a document, you can treat this code in exactly the same way you would treat any other characters entered from the keyboard. To illustrate, you should position the cursor on the letter *F* in the word *From* (beginning of the second line of your document) as shown in Figure 2-15. Then strike the Left key one time and the cursor will move left one position in memory to the code HRt; you will see this on the screen as the cursor jumping from the beginning of the second line to the end of the first.

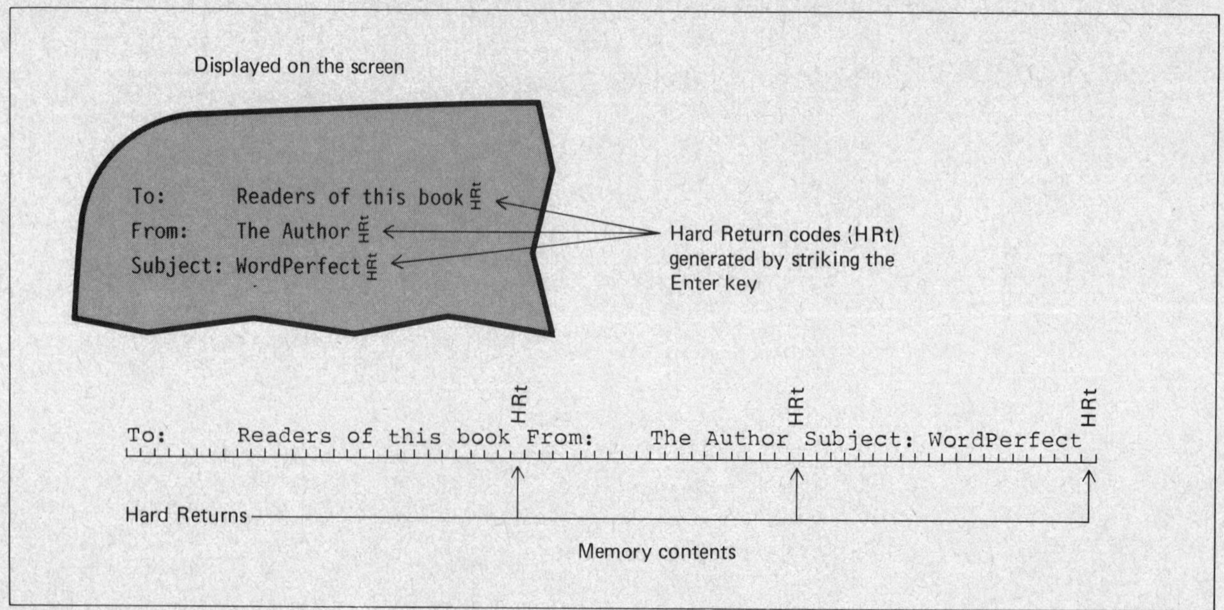

Figure 2-15
The Hard Return (HRt) code.

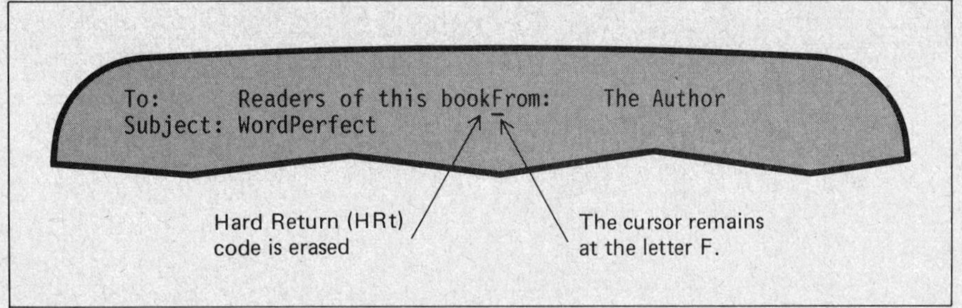

Figure 2-16
Deleting the HRt hidden code.

Using some logic, the answer to the next question should be apparent. What if you reposition the cursor to the letter *F* of the word *From* (in the second line) and strike the Backspace key? As you know, the Backspace erases the character to the left, which, in this case, is the HRt. Thus, your three lines become two, as shown in Figure 2-16. If this action were accidental, then all that would be necessary to restore it to the original form of Figure 2-15 would be to strike Enter. In other words, *even though you cannot see the HRt codes, they can be inserted and deleted the same as text characters that you see displayed on the screen.*

Assignment 2-2 may now be completed.

SAVING DOCUMENTS

About RAM and Disk Storage

If you have entered and corrected the memo, you may be ready to take a break or to terminate this work session. However, the first thing you should do is save a copy of your document to disk. The document you are working on is in RAM and will be lost when you terminate the WordPerfect program or turn the computer off, *or if there is any kind of power failure.* Once saved on disk, you can command WordPerfect to retrieve it from disk and place it in memory whenever you need it.

From your study of DOS in Chapter 1, you learned that anything saved to disk is saved as a file. This applies to documents created by WordPerfect, spreadsheets created by Lotus 1-2-3, and so on. Each file must be given a filename consisting of up to 8 characters and, optionally, an extension consisting of up to 3 characters. Let us save your memo to disk.

The Save Command

In WordPerfect, you transfer information from memory to disk with the Save command, which is invoked by striking the F10 key (refer to the function key template).

DO THIS NOW 2-8 **Saving a document**

1. Enter the Save command with F10; this will produce the following prompt.

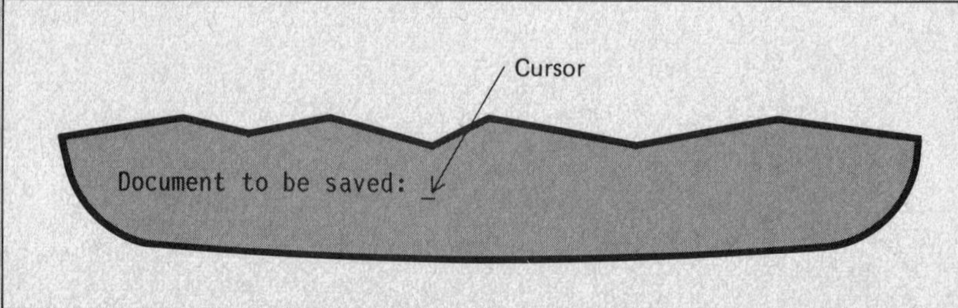

WordPerfect is asking you: "What is the name that you wish to use for the document you are about to save to disk?"

2. Type MEMO.WP1 and strike the Enter. While WordPerfect is copying your document to disk, it will display the message:

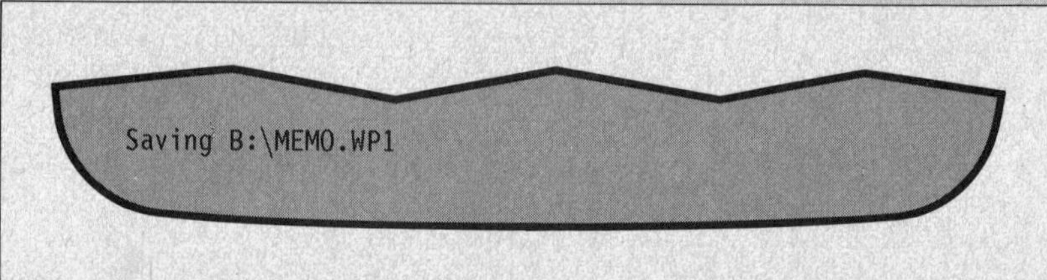

When WordPerfect completes the save operation, control is returned to the edit screen and text entry or editing can continue.

Although you can use any valid DOS filenames and extensions, to avoid confusing word processing files with spreadsheet or database files, use WP as the first two letters of the extension, as is done in this example.

Frequent Saving

If you have a long document to enter or a lot of editing to complete, do not wait until you have finished your work to save what you have done. You should save periodically while working. If you have a hardware or power failure, or you accidentally erase a large section of work without realizing it immediately, all your effort will be lost if you have not saved. For subsequent saves, the process is simplified because WordPerfect displays the document name as the default value:

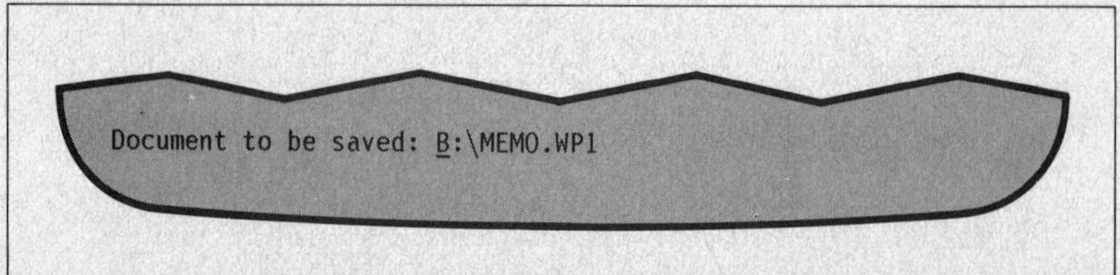

To save it again, simply strike Enter without typing anything and the displayed name will be used. However, whenever you save a document and there is an existing file on disk with the same name, WordPerfect warns you with the following message.

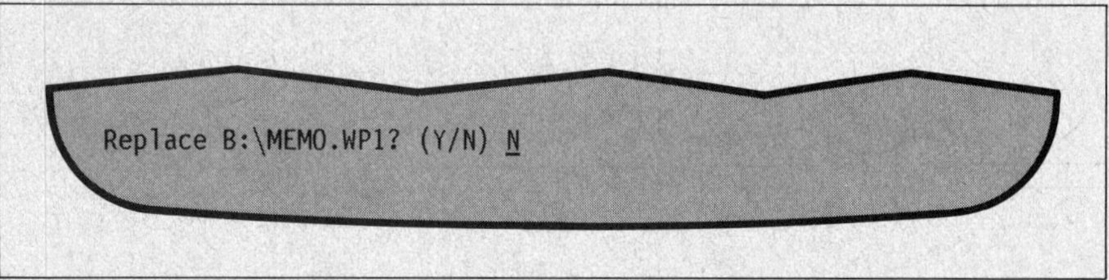

The reason for this is that the existing copy will be replaced with the copy from memory. Normally, each save will represent further work that you have done to the document, so you do want the version displayed on the screen to replace the old copy on disk. To effect the replacement, simply strike the letter *Y*.

When concentrating on your work, it is easy to become so involved that you forget to save frequently. Developing the habit of saving files regularly will save you a lot of grief.

THE EXIT COMMAND

Exiting WordPerfect

When you have finished working with WordPerfect and have saved your document, you may terminate WordPerfect with the Exit command (the F7 key). (This will cause control of the computer to be returned to DOS.) When you strike the F7 key, the first thing WordPerfect does is to ask if you wish to save to disk the document in memory.

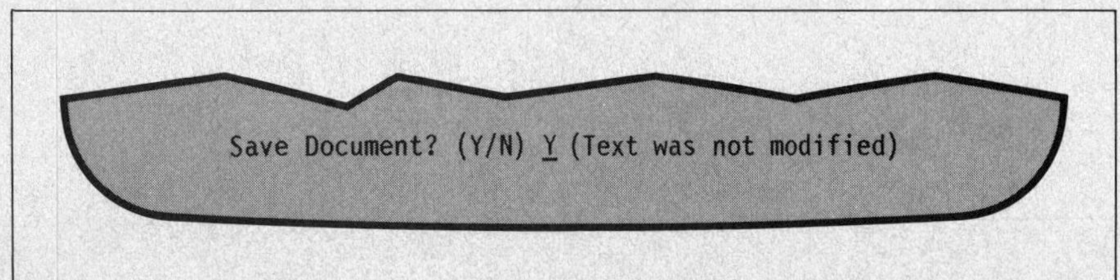

If there have been no changes since the last time you saved, the message *Text was not modified* is displayed to the right. Since you just saved the document using the Save command, there is no need to save it again. Whenever this *not modified* message is not displayed, be certain to respond with Y or else the most recent changes you made will not be saved. Requesting a save will result in exactly the same sequence of prompts as those resulting from the Save command.

Whether you save the document or not, you are then presented with the Exit prompt:

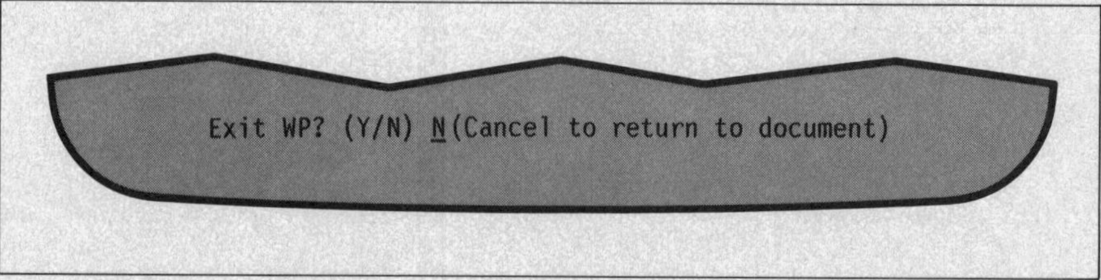

You can respond with one of the following three choices:

- Strike the letter *Y* to exit WordPerfect and return to DOS.
- Strike the Enter key, thereby accepting the default (No). This causes the current document to be erased from memory and control returned to the edit screen, which is blank.
- Strike the Cancel key (F1) if you have changed your mind and wish to return to the edit screen of the current document (the document currently in memory).

Clearing the Current Document from Memory

Assume that after completing the memo, you have another document that you must enter. However, after saving the memo, it is still in memory and on the screen. You need WordPerfect to clear the memory (and the screen) so that you can begin the next document. Responding with No to the Exit WP prompt does this.

To illustrate how this is useful, assume that you have another document to enter and save now that you have finished the memo. The overall sequence would be as follows:

DO THIS NOW 2-9 **Clearing Memory to Begin a New Document**

1. Enter the Exit command (F7); save if any changes have been made since the last save.
2. Enter N in response to the prompt asking if you wish to exit WordPerfect. This will clear the current document from memory and present you with the blank edit screen.
3. You may now proceed to enter your next document. After completing the second document, you would Exit again and respond with Y to the prompt regarding exiting WordPerfect.

About Starting WordPerfect

When you terminate a WordPerfect word session (and return to DOS) through the Exit command, WordPerfect erases some temporary files that it uses. If you terminate a work session by simply turning the computer off (a bad practice), then these files remain on your disk. The next time you attempt to run WordPerfect, it will detect these files and ask you if other copies of WordPerfect are currently running. Respond to the question by typing the letter *N* (for no) and WordPerfect will complete the start-up sequence.

RETRIEVING A DOCUMENT FROM DISK

If you have completed the first two steps of DTN 2-9, you have a blank edit screen. If you have not, then do so in order that you can step through the sequence of retrieving an existing document stored on disk.

The Retrieve Command

When you return to work on your document at some later time, reading it from disk back into memory is every bit as easy as saving it was.

DO THIS NOW 2-10 **Retrieving the Document MEMO.WP1**

1. Enter the Retrieve command with Shift-F10; this produces the following prompt.

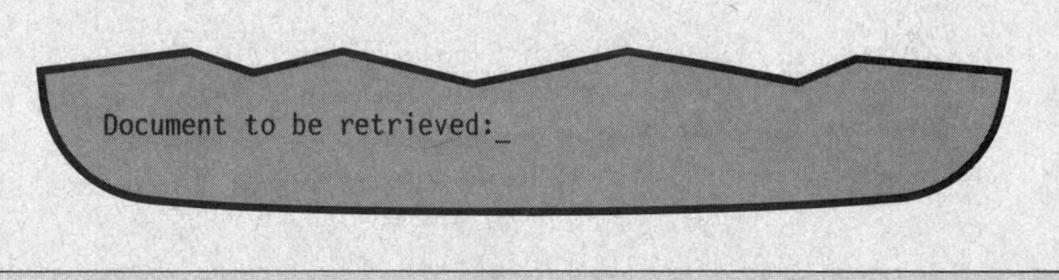

2. Type in MEMO.WP1 (the name of your document), then strike the Enter key. Do not forget to include the extension.

If WordPerfect cannot find the named file on the disk, it displays an error message for a few seconds and then returns to the preceding prompt asking for the document name.

During a word processing session, it is common to work on one document, save it, and then retrieve another and work on that one. If you attempt to retrieve one document while another is still on the screen, the new one will be inserted right at the position of the cursor. Note that *the previous document will not be erased from memory when a new one is retrieved.*

Starting WordPerfect with a Filename

You already know that when you load the WordPerfect program by typing A:WP from the DOS prompt, you are presented with a blank edit screen.

However, if you load WordPerfect by typing

```
B> A:WP MEMO.WP1

A> C:WP MEMO.WP1
```

(for hard disk computer)

the named document, MEMO.WP1 in this case, will be placed in memory by WordPerfect and will be ready for editing.

So that you know what to expect when using WordPerfect, you should experiment with the Retrieve command by trying each of the following:

- Load WordPerfect by designating a document name (use your MEMO.WP1).
- Load WordPerfect by designating a document name of a file that does not exist (use X.X as the document name).
- Load WordPerfect with a blank screen and then attempt to retrieve the nonexistent file X.X.
- Load WordPerfect with a blank screen and then retrieve MEMO.WP1 with the Retrieve command.
- With your MEMO.WP1 on the screen, position the cursor somewhere in the center of the document and retrieve the document name CONTRACT.WP1. (CONTRACT.WP1 is the name of a document on the data disk included with this book.)

Listing the Files Stored on Disk

Once you start working with a word processor, you will have many files stored on your disk. Unfortunately, it is easy to forget names that you have selected. For instance, assume that you remember your memo document name as MEMO.WP instead of MEMO.WP1. How do you locate a document that you need when you cannot remember the name? For this, WordPerfect allows you to inspect the contents of a disk without leaving WordPerfect by using the List Files command (F5). You should carry out the following actions with your data disk to get a feel for using the command. When you execute it by striking the F5 key, WordPerfect responds with the DOS DIR command on the status line as follows:

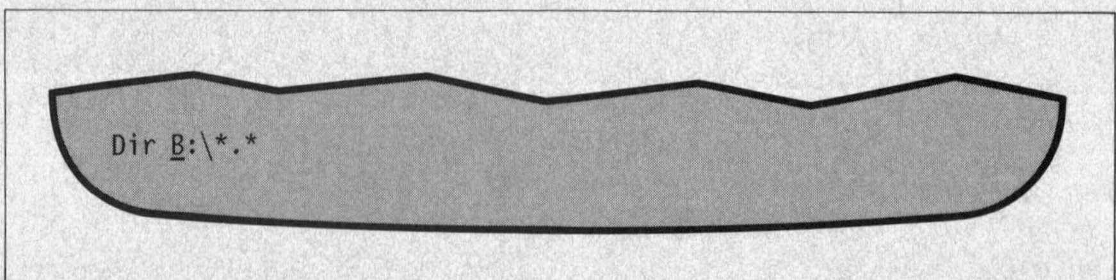

At this point, you may change the form of the directory command as you please, or simply strike the Enter key to accept the default. You will be presented with a directory screen such as that shown in Figure 2-17. (Note that the contents of your data disk will be different.) This disk contains six

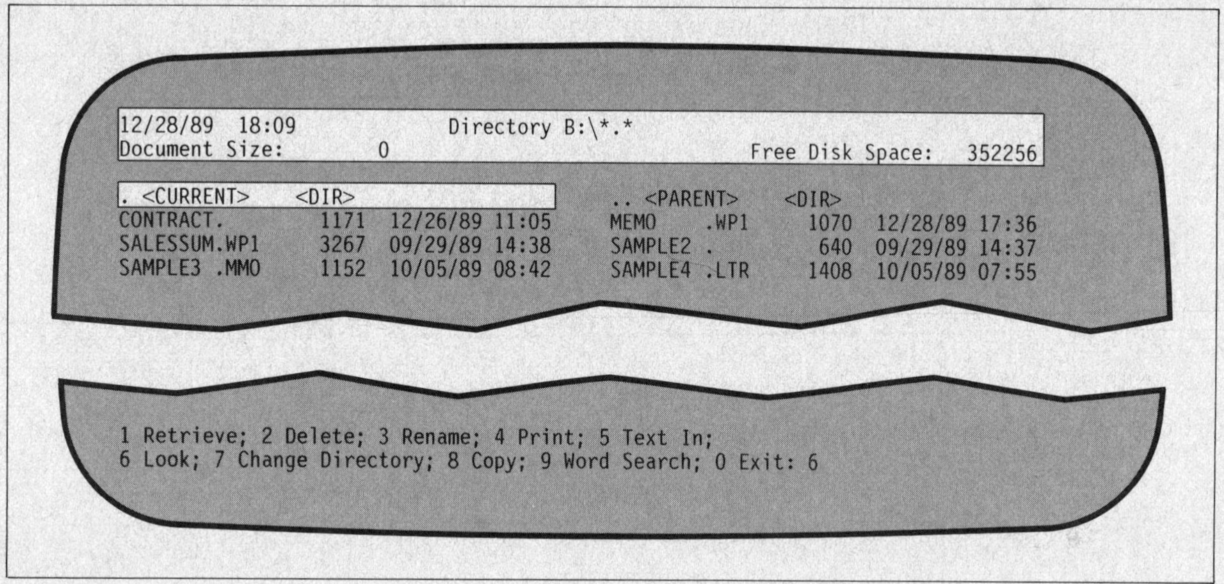

Figure 2-17
A directory listing.

data files listed in alphabetic order; note that they are *not necessarily* WordPerfect document files. On inspecting the list, it is evident that the name of the desired file is MEMO.WP1, not MEMO.WP. To retrieve it, simply move the highlight to that filename using the Right arrow key, then strike the digit 1 (for the Retrieve option). This document will be loaded into memory, and control will be returned to the edit screen, which will now display your memo.

Referring to the status line prompt in Figure 2-17, notice that there are nine options in addition to the Retrieve option you selected. The only other that we shall consider is the Look (6), which allows you to see any file in the listing without going through the routine of actually loading it into memory. For instance, if you want to check MEMO.WP1 to be certain that it is indeed the desired file, then highlight it and strike the 6 key. The first screen of the file will be displayed; you can inspect subsequent screens by striking the PgDn key.

Assignment 2-3 may now be completed.

MORE ON MOVING THE CURSOR

Now that you know how to save and retrieve documents, you are free to experiment without fear of losing the work you have done in entering and editing the document. Let us continue with some of the other basic features of WordPerfect.

About Positioning the Cursor on the Screen

If you have tried to move the cursor with a blank edit screen (after WordPerfect is loaded with no document), you noticed that the cursor would not move. (If you have not already done this, then try it.) The reason is that WordPerfect allows the cursor to be moved only within areas of the screen that display text from a document. To illustrate this, you should retrieve your completed memo and attempt to move the cursor throughout the screen. When you do so, you will find that movement is restricted to the highlighted portion shown in Figure 2-18.

If you position the cursor at the end of the first line (following the word *book*) and you strike the right arrow, the cursor will not be moved into the blank area to the right of the screen but to the beginning of the next line. (However, if you have entered spaces at the end of this line, the cursor will move over those spaces since WordPerfect treats the space as any other character.) Furthermore, if you position the cursor after the last character in the document, striking Right or Down keys to move it further will have no effect.

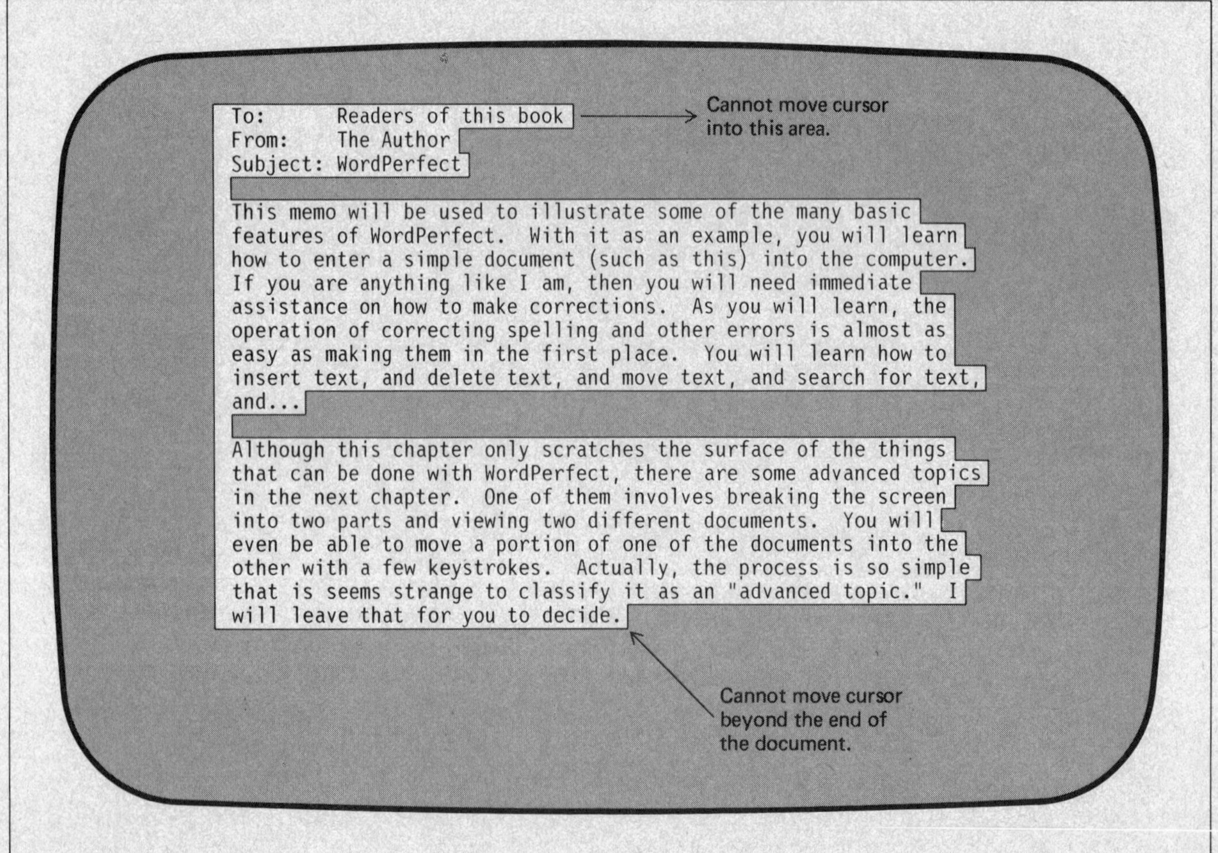

Figure 2-18
The document area on the screen.

Positioning the Cursor Within the Current Screen Display

Moving the cursor one character at a time (even with automatic repeat) is a simple approach but is not very fast when moving across an entire line once you begin to master WordPerfect. Fortunately, there are keystroke sequences that permit you to move the cursor by more than a single character or line. For instance, Ctrl-Right (the Right arrow key) causes the cursor to move to the right from one word to the next. If repeated movement is required, then simply hold down the Ctrl and arrow keys for automatic repeat. Ctrl-Left results in an equivalent cursor movement to the left. These are commonly referred to as Word Right and Word Left.

Frequently, when working in the middle of a line, you want to position the cursor at the beginning or at the end of the line for the next action. This is easily done by striking the Home key (do not hold it down) and then striking the Left key or the Right key. That is, Home,Left positions at the beginning of the line and Home,Right at the end. You should try each of these actions with your memo that is currently displayed on the screen.

Moving the Cursor Outside the Screen Display

Previous cursor movement actions have related to moving within the text displayed on the screen. However, what if you are editing a long document and the text you want to edit is not currently on the screen? Since the memo is short, you cannot experiment with it. However, you can retrieve the document CONTRACT.WP1 from the data disk that accompanies this book and try the following movement actions with it.

The Plus (+) key located in the numeric keypad at the right of the keyboard is defined by WordPerfect as the Screen Down key. If you strike it, you will see that the cursor moves to the bottom of the screen. If you strike it again, assuming that you have retrieved the document CONTRACT.WP1, the current screen display will be replaced by the rest of this document. In general, the Screen Down key causes the twenty-four lines of the document currently displayed to be replaced on the screen by the next twenty-four lines of the document.

Similarly, pressing the Screen Up, which is the minus (−) key on the numeric keypad, causes the cursor to move to the first line of the screen display. As with the Screen Down, striking the Screen Up again causes a twenty-four-line scroll toward the beginning of the document.

In addition to the screen-by-screen scrolling, you can move up or down in your document by page. Remember that WordPerfect keeps track of where each printed page ends and the next begins. Striking the PgDn key displays the first line of the next page of text. If the default page line count is in effect, then this is 54 lines. In a similar fashion, striking the PgUp key causes a full page to be scrolled toward the beginning of the document.

SUMMARY OF CURSOR MOVES

As you can see, you have many cursor positioning options to use when editing your document. It may seem as though it would be difficult to master all of the key sequences, but when you use a word processor regularly you quickly become familiar with them. The following summary of cursor movement options should help you learn them when working with WordPerfect.

Movement Command	Key or Keys	Action
Up Line	Up	Move cursor up one line.
Down Line	Down	Move cursor down one line.
Left Character	Left	Move cursor left one character.
Right Character	Right	Move cursor right one character.
Left Word	Ctrl-Left	Move cursor left one word.
Right Word	Ctrl-Right	Move cursor right one word.
Beginning of Line	Home,Left	Move cursor to beginning of current line.
End of Line	Home,Right	Move cursor to end of current line.
	End	Same as Home,Right.
Screen Up	– key (numeric keypad)	Move cursor to first line on current screen. Subsequently scrolls twenty-four lines toward beginning of the document.
Screen Down	+ key (numeric keypad)	Move cursor to last line on current screen. Subsequently scrolls twenty-four lines toward end of the document.
Page Up	PgUp	Move the cursor to the first line of the preceding page as defined by the printer.
Page Down	PgDn	Move the cursor to the first line of the following page as defined by the printer.

PRINTING A DOCUMENT

The Print Command

The final task we shall consider in this chapter is how to print your memo. Actually, at any point during the entry or editing of a document, you may print a copy. Usually, this is when you have completed typing and must proofread it. However, for a long document you may wish to enter a portion of it, print that part then read it to get a feel for the overall flow. In either case, you should always save the document before printing. Although the printing process does not change the document in memory, you want to be certain that the copy you have on disk is the same as the printed copy. It is simply a good habit.

Before printing, you should check that the printer is on and ready and that it contains paper.

DO THIS NOW 2-11 **Printing MEMO.WP1**

1. If you do not currently have MEMO.WP1 on the screen, clear your screen and then retrieve MEMO.WP1 from disk.
2. Enter the Print command with the Shift-F7. The following list of options is displayed on the status line.

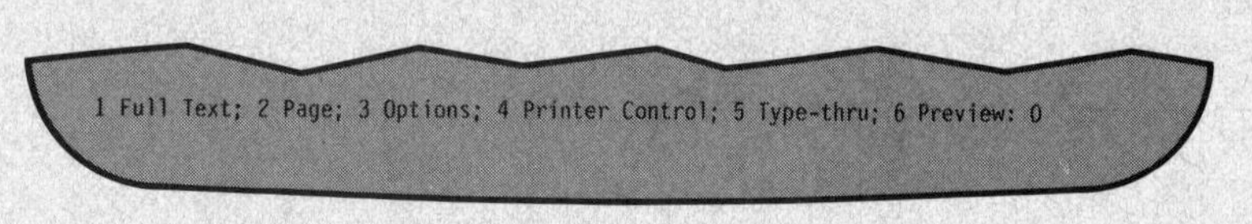

3. Type the digit 1 to cause the Full document to be printed. When printing is finished, WordPerfect returns to the edit screen.

Referring to the Print option menu, notice that the default option is 0, which, if selected, cancels the print request and returns to the edit screen.

If you examine the keyboard template, you will notice that Ctrl-F8 is also listed as Print. This provides for formatting of the printed output; it does not print so do not use it.

If you have entered and correctly edited your memo, your printed copy should be the same as that of Figure 2-19. Note the presence of *WPC at the

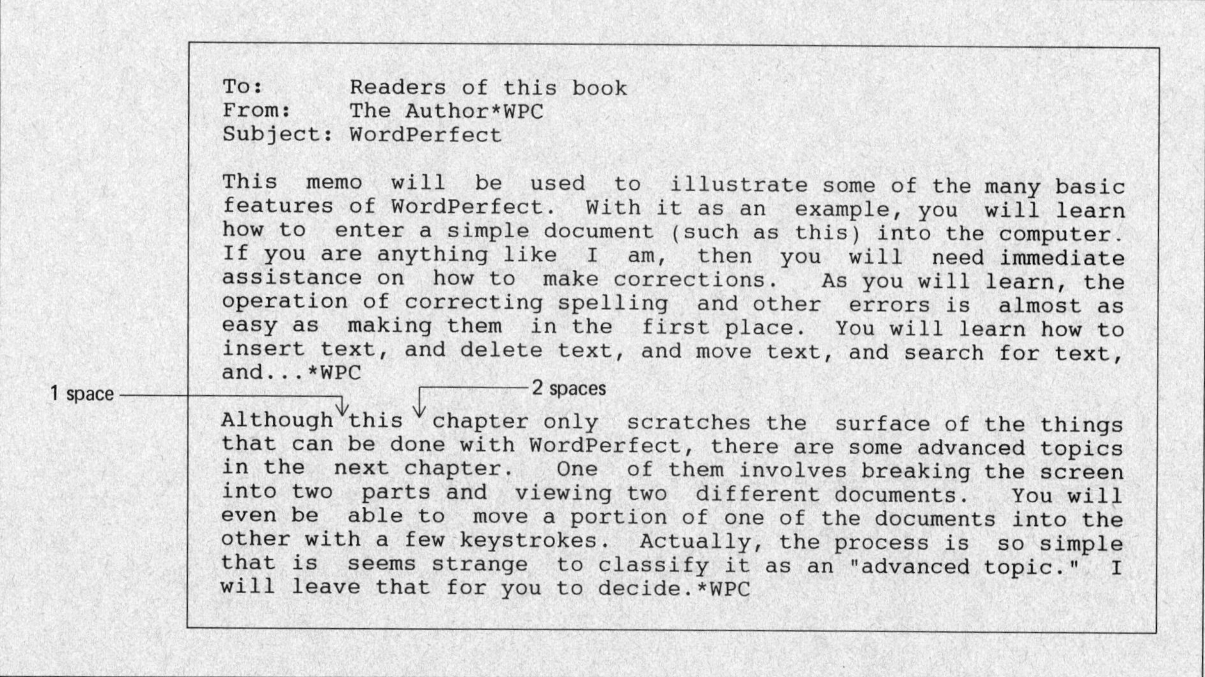


```
To:      Readers of this book
From:    The Author*WPC
Subject: WordPerfect

This  memo  will  be  used  to  illustrate some of the many basic
features of WordPerfect.  With it as an  example, you  will learn
how to  enter a simple document (such as this) into the computer.
If you are anything like  I  am,  then  you  will  need immediate
assistance on  how to  make corrections.   As you will learn, the
operation of correcting spelling  and other  errors is  almost as
easy as  making them  in the  first place.  You will learn how to
insert text, and delete text, and move text, and search for text,
and...*WPC

Although this  chapter only  scratches the  surface of the things
that can be done with WordPerfect, there are some advanced topics
in the  next chapter.   One  of them involves breaking the screen
into two  parts and  viewing two  different documents.   You will
even be  able to  move a portion of one of the documents into the
other with a few keystrokes.  Actually, the process is  so simple
that is  seems strange  to classify it as an "advanced topic."  I
will leave that for you to decide.*WPC
```

Figure 2-19
A printed copy of the memo.

end of some of the lines. These are included automatically at the position of some of the Hard Returns to identify this as a document printed by the Limited-Use version. They will not appear if you are using a commercial version of WordPerfect. In contrast to the copy of the memo in Figure 2-2, notice that the right margin is aligned: that is, the document is justified. The copy in Figure 2-2 was printed with justification disabled; you will learn how to do this in the next chapter.

Assignment 2-4 may now be completed.

SUMMARY

From this chapter you have learned the basic elements of using WordPerfect. You can now enter a document, edit it, save it to disk for later use, and print it. Yet to come in the next chapter are the many features of word processors described in Chapter 6, including formatting, cut and paste, and searching. Summarizing from this chapter, its important points are:

- After WordPerfect is loaded, you see the edit screen that contains the cursor and the status line. The status line serves as a general "message" area between WordPerfect and you, the user.
- Function keys are used to execute WordPerfect commands. Each function key causes four different actions depending on whether it is used with the Shift, Ctrl, or Alt key, or alone.
- When used from the edit screen, the F1 key performs an Undelete action; that is, F1 restores previously deleted text. When used after a command that displays a prompt to which the user must respond, it cancels that command.
- The Enter key should be struck only to force a new line or begin a new paragraph. Within a paragraph, WordPerfect automatically performs word wrap when a line reaches the right margin.
- Hard Returns (resulting from striking the Enter key) can be deleted and inserted in exactly the same way as other keyboard characters.
- You can modify a document with insertions and deletions. After such changes, WordPerfect realigns the text automatically.
- The Right, Left, Up, and Down arrow keys move the cursor to any position within the document. Other cursor movement actions allow the cursor to be positioned at the beginning or end of the current line, at the end or beginning of the current screen, or to the next or preceding page.

- Disk storage is for the long-term storage of documents. Documents are entered into and edited from main memory (RAM).
- The Save command copies the document in memory to disk.
- The Retrieve command copies a document from disk into memory. If a document is already in memory, the newly retrieved one will be inserted at the position of the cursor.
- The directory of a disk can be displayed from WordPerfect with the List Files command.
- The Exit command can be used either to end the WordPerfect session or to clear memory of the current document.

COMMAND AND FUNCTION SUMMARY

Following is a summary of the various commands other than those for cursor movement described in this chapter. Cursor movement commands are summarized in an earlier table of this chapter.

Command	Key or Keys	Action
Deletion of Text		
Delete Character	Backspace	Delete character to left of cursor.
Delete Character	Del	Delete character at position of cursor.
Delete Word	Ctrl-Backspace	Delete word in which cursor positioned.
Delete to Line End	Ctrl-End	Delete from cursor to end of line.
Delete to Page End	Ctrl-PgDn	Delete from cursor to end of page.
Other Commands		
Cancel	F1	Executed command, cancel the command.
Undelete	F1	Executed from edit screen, restore deleted text.
Help	F3	Display Help screen.
List Files	F5	Display a disk directory.
Exit	F7	Save document, clear memory, and/or exit WordPerfect.
Print	Shift-F7	Print the current document.
Save	F10	Save the current document to disk.
Retrieve	Shift-F10	Retrieve a document from disk.

NEW TERMINOLOGY

The new terminology introduced in the general word processing discussion of Chapter 1 carries over directly to WordPerfect. The following are important new terms introduced in this chapter; you should be familiar with each of them.

edit screen
hard return
status line
typeover

Name: ______________________ Date: ______________

Assignment 2-1

1. When starting WordPerfect with A:WP (or C:WP for the hard disk), why is the drive designator A: (or C:) used to precede WP?

2. What is the "status line" and what information does it contain?

3. While typing a letter, you typed the word *recieve* instead of *receive* and realized your error immediately. How can you correct this?

4. After completing a letter and proofreading, you notice that you typed the word *recieve* instead of *receive*. How would you make this correct?

5. What two keys delete a single character?

Name: ______________________________ Date: ______________

Assignment 2-2

1. What keystroke actions do each of the following tell you to take?
   (a) Home,End

   (b) Shift-F10

2. Referring to the function key template (or the screen Help), list the four actions and the key sequences that are initiated with the F4 key.

3. Which key in WordPerfect is called the Cancel key? What does it do?

4. How do you change from insert mode to typeover mode? Describe the difference between these two modes.

Name: ______________________ Date: ______________

Assignment 2-2 (*continued*)

5. What are the quickest ways to make the following deletions from your document?

   (a) Shorten the second sentence so that it ends with *simple document.*

   (b) Delete the word *different* in the fourth line of the second paragraph.

   (c) Delete the second paragraph.

6. Assume you have the following text on the screen

```
Sometimes when editing a document you will delete a portion
of text, then change your mind and want it back. One feature
of most good word processors is that deleted text is not
discarded immediately.
```

   and that you take the actions:

   1. Position the cursor on the word *most* in line 3.
   2. Delete this word with the Ctrl-Backspace.
   3. Position the cursor at the space following the word *document* in the first line.
   4. Strike the Backspace key 11 times.
   5. Move the cursor to the second line.

   (a) Describe the deletions the WordPerfect is holding for you at this moment.

   (b) Describe how you would undelete the word *most* (without simply retyping it).

Name: ______________________ Date: ____________

Assignment 2-3

1. Why should you save a document at intervals while working on it rather than waiting until it is all finished?

2. What key sequences for the Exit command cause the following actions to occur?
   (a) Save the document and continue editing it.

   (b) Save the document and begin a new one.

   (c) Clear the memory to begin a new document without saving the current one.

   (d) Retrieve another document without saving the current one.

3. What happens if you retrieve a document when another is already on the screen? If you do not know, try it to find out.

4. What happens if you attempt to retrieve a file that is not on disk? If you do not know, try it to find out.

Name: ______________________________ Date: ______________

Assignment 2-4

1. How do the Page Up and the Screen Up operations differ?

2. If you position the cursor on the letter *b* of the word *basic* (first line in your memo—refer to Figure 2-18), to where will it be moved by Ctrl-Right?

3. Position the cursor in the word *illustrate* (first line in your memo). What are three different key sequences that move it to the end of the line?

Name: ______________________ Date: ______________

OBJECTIVE QUESTIONS

Matching

The descriptions in 1 through 8 describe an activity requiring that one or more commands be invoked. Designate the first key sequence action to take by matching these actions with the key sequences in a through h.

a. F1
b. F10
c. F5
d. - key on numeric keypad
e. Shift-F10
f. Ctrl-Backspace
g. F7
h. F3

____ **1.** You have tried to retrieve a file and WordPerfect has told you that it cannot be found on the disk.

____ **2.** You must edit a line in your document that is about 30 lines above the current position of the cursor.

____ **3.** You accidentally deleted a line.

____ **4.** You have just completed a document, saved it, and are ready to begin another document.

____ **5.** You cannot remember the key sequence to print a document.

____ **6.** You have just completed a large number of editing changes and are ready to take a break.

____ **7.** When entering a document, you realize that you have typed the word *installation* twice in succession and you want to delete the second one. The cursor is still positioned immediately following the letter *n*.

____ **8.** You want to insert another document file into the current document at the position of the cursor.

TRUE/FALSE

Circle either T or F to indicate whether the answer is True or False.

T F **1.** The computer can be booted up from the WordPerfect disk that accompanies this book.

T F **2.** You can tell whether or not the keyboard is in uppercase shift by looking at the status line at the bottom of the screen.

T F **3.** If something goes wrong while you are entering a document and the computer freezes up, you can reboot by striking the F1 function key.

T F **4.** Corrections can be made to a document (at any place in the document) while the document is being entered.

T F **5.** Both the Backspace and the Del keys delete one character when you strike them.

Name: ______________________________ Date: ______________

OBJECTIVE QUESTIONS (*continued*)

T F **6.** Shift,F6 means to hold down the Shift key and (while holding it down) press the F6 function key.

T F **7.** The purpose of the Cancel key is to cancel any section of text that you do not wish to retain in a document.

T F **8.** Switching between the insert and typeover modes is done by striking the Insert key.

T F **9.** Typeover is the action of replacing a copy of a document stored on disk with the copy in memory.

T F **10.** Where striking the Backspace key deletes a single character, holding down the Ctrl key while striking the Backspace deletes an entire word.

T F **11.** If you delete a portion of text, then continue typing, then delete another portion of text, only the text from the latest deletion can be restored with the Restore command.

T F **12.** The action resulting from the F1 key depends on what you were doing prior to striking it.

T F **13.** If the cursor is positioned on the first character of a line (other than the first line of a document) and you strike the Backspace key, the last character of the preceding line will be deleted.

T F **14.** When you are editing a document, WordPerfect saves the latest three deletions. At any time, any of those deletions can be restored to any point in a document.

T F **15.** A hard return results from striking the Enter key. It ends a line regardless of the line length and causes a new line to be started.

T F **16.** All WordPerfect documents must be saved to disk with the file name extension of WP.

T F **17.** Every time you execute a Save command, a new copy of your document is added to existing copies on disk.

T F **18.** The save action resulting from invoking the Exit command is the same as the save action from the Save command.

T F **19.** The Exit command can be used to clear the current document from memory with or without saving it to disk.

T F **20.** The Insert command allows you to insert another document from disk at the point of the cursor in the document on the screen.

T F **21.** It is not possible to retrieve a document file from disk without first clearing the current document from memory.

T F **22.** It is possible to obtain a directory listing of the data disk with an appropriate WordPerfect command; it is not necessary to terminate WordPerfect then issue the DIR command from DOS.

T F **23.** If an attempt is made to retrieve a file not on disk, execution of the WordPerfect program is immediately terminated.

Name: ______________________ Date: ______________

OBJECTIVE QUESTIONS (*continued*)

T F **24.** Using the arrow cursor movement keys, the cursor can be positioned anywhere on the edit screen.

T F **25.** If you started WordPerfect with the following command from DOS

```
A:WP CONTRACT.WP5
```

and the file CONTRACT.WP5 did not exist then WordPerfect would not be loaded and control would be returned to DOS.

T F **26.** Where the Left and Right (arrow) keys cause the cursor to move one character at a time, the Ctrl-Left and Ctrl-Right cause the cursor to move one word at a time.

T F **27.** The PgDn key causes the screen to scroll 24 lines.

T F **28.** Striking the End key causes the cursor to be positioned at the end of the current line.

T F **29.** It is possible to print a document without first saving it.

T F **30.** The Ctrl-F8 key sequence is used to print the document currently displayed on the screen.

Multiple Choice

In the space provided, record the letter of the choice that best completes or answers the statement.

____ **1.** The line at the bottom of the screen when WordPerfect comes up is called the

A. status line.
B. edit screen.
C. edit line.
D. control line.

____ **2.** Which of the following keys will cause something to be deleted from the document?

A. Ctrl
B. Left
C. Backspace
D. Enter

____ **3.** Shift-F6 means

A. strike the Shift key then strike the F6 key.
B. hold down the Shift key and strike the F6 key.
C. shift over and begin using the F6 key.
D. strike the Caps Lock key then the F6 key.

Name: ______________________________ Date: ______________

OBJECTIVE QUESTIONS (*continued*)

____ **4.** Typeover is the action of

A. replacing one document with another.
B. replacing one disk with another.
C. inserting characters between existing characters.
D. replacing existing text with newly typed text.

____ **5.** The ______ key sequence deletes a full word.

A. Backspace
B. Ctrl-Backspace
C. Shift-Backspace
D. Alt-Backspace

____ **6.** You have just finished typing a sentence into a document and you strike the F1 key. Which of the following will happen?

A. The last command will be canceled.
B. Previously deleted text will be inserted at the cursor.
C. The Help screen will be displayed.
D. It depends on whether or not you have previously saved this document.

____ **7.** The maximum amount of text that can be held by WordPerfect from a deletion action is

A. one word.
B. one paragraph.
C. one screen.
D. the entire document.

____ **8.** Which of the following is NOT true about the hard return code.

A. It is entered by striking the Enter key.
B. It can be inserted in a document during editing the same as a text character.
C. It can be deleted from a document during editing the same as a text character.
D. Using the Right arrow key, you cannot move the cursor past a hard return.

____ **9.** If the cursor is positioned on the first character of a line (other than the first line of a document) and you strike the Backspace key, which character will be deleted?

A. The last character of the preceding line.
B. The hard return at the end of the preceding line.
C. The character at the position of the cursor.
D. Nothing will be deleted.

Name: ______________________________ Date: ______________

OBJECTIVE QUESTIONS (*continued*)

____ **10.** After WordPerfect completes the action of saving a document to disk (from the Save command), it

A. returns to the edit screen.
B. clears the screen so you can start on the next document.
C. asks you for the name of the next document.
D. returns control to DOS.

____ **11.** Which of the following actions cannot be carried out by the Exit command?

A. Save the current document.
B. Clear the screen.
C. Return control to DOS.
D. All of the above actions can be carried out by the Exit.

____ **12.** If you attempt to terminate WordPerfect (with the Exit command) and you have not saved the current document, what will happen?

A. WordPerfect will warn you.
B. WordPerfect will automatically save it.
C. The document will be lost.
D. The action WordPerfect takes will depend on whether or not you previously saved the document.

____ **13.** If you attempt to retrieve a document from disk without saving the document currently on disk, WordPerfect will

A. replace the current document with the one from disk.
B. warn you that the current document will be lost if you do not save it first.
C. insert the new document into the current document.
D. first save the current document then load the new one.

____ **14.** If you were in WordPerfect and wanted to retrieve a particular document but could not remember the spelling of its name, which key command would you use?

A. F3
B. F5
C. F7
D. Shift-F10

____ **15.** Printing a document is invoked by which of the following key sequences?

A. Ctrl-F8
B. Shift-F7
C. Ctrl,F8
D. Shift,F7

Name: ______________________ Date: ______________

OBJECTIVE QUESTIONS (*continued*)

Fill In

In the space provided, fill in the correct answer. Note that the answer can be one or two words.

1. ______________________
From the edit screen, the _____ provide(s) you information such as the cursor location and whether or not the Caps Lock key has been struck.

2. ______________________
The _____ key causes the character to the left of the cursor to be deleted.

3. ______________________
Striking the _____ key causes WordPerfect to display the function key template on the screen.

4. ______________________
When WordPerfect first comes up, it is in the _____ mode; striking the Insert key places it in the _____ mode.

5. ______________________
_____ occurs during text entry when the cursor reaches the end of the current line.

6. ______________________
With the _____ command, you can restore text that was previously deleted.

7. ______________________
The code entered into a document when the Enter key is struck is called a _____.

8. ______________________
If you wanted to insert a document stored on disk into the document currently on the screen, you would use the _____ command.

9. ______________________
The _____ command allows you to clear the currently displayed document so that you can begin entry of another.

10. ______________________
The Print command is invoked with the _____ key sequence.

ASSIGNMENTS/PROJECTS

1. The following document is to be entered into the computer using WordPerfect. (Your margins will not coincide with the margins of this copy; do not be concerned about this.) Entries enclosed within angle brackets are to be replaced with information as described within the brackets. For instance, <YOUR NAME> should be replaced with your name. In addition to the three problems described in the memo, add two of your own. Proofread carefully and make necessary corrections. Then save it to disk and print a copy on the printer.

```
To:  Chief of Security
From: <YOUR NAME>
Date: <TODAY'S DATE>

I recently had a problem with one of your officers (badge number 22)
in the parking lot regarding my car.  (It is a <MAKE OF YOUR CAR>,
license number <YOUR AUTO LICENSE NUMBER>.)  It is bad enough that the
officer would not allow me to park in our lot, but he was also rude.
Following are the problems that resulted because of him.

1.  I was late for my appointment with <PERSON OF YOUR CHOICE>.

2.  I twisted my ankle walking in from the outer parking lot.

3.  Someone backed into my car while it was parked in the outer lot
and put a dent in the <PART OF YOUR CHOICE>.

I want you to know that I am very unhappy about this entire incident
and I am thinking of seeing an attorney.  I would appreciate it if you
would investigate the entire matter and inform me of what will be
done.

None of this would have happened if the officer had taken the time to
listen to may explanation.  Our security force should be here to help
out, not to make life difficult for us.

May I hear from you soon?  Thank you.
```

2. Create and type a response from the Chief of Security to your memo of Assignment 1.

3. You are to prepare a personal résumé using the following format. Entries enclosed within angle brackets are to be replaced with information as described within the brackets. For instance, <YOUR NAME> should be replaced with your name. For your employment history (which is to include your last three jobs), include the dates you started and terminated, the name of your employer, and your job title. If you have not had three jobs, make them up. For your special interests or hobbies, describe the extent to which you participate or the nature of the activity; a single word such as "golf" is not sufficient.

If you are not comfortable including your address and vital statistics, then make them up (for instance, use a weight you would *like* to be). When you are finished, save your document to disk with the file name RESUME.WP; you will need it for an assignment in the next chapter.

```
PERSONAL SUMMARY
<DATE>

<YOUR NAME>
<STREET ADDRESS>
<CITY, STATE>

Vital Statistics

Birthdate:  <YOUR AGE>
Height:     <YOUR HEIGHT>
Weight:     <YOUR WEIGHT>

Employment

1. <FIRST JOB FROM DATE AND TO DATE>, <COMPANY NAME>, <JOB TITLE>

2. <SECOND JOB FROM DATE AND TO DATE>, <COMPANY NAME>, <JOB TITLE>

3. <THIRD JOB FROM DATE AND TO DATE>, <COMPANY NAME>, <JOB TITLE>

Special Interests or Hobbies

1. <FIRST INTEREST OR HOBBY>

2. <SECOND INTEREST OR HOBBY>

3. <THIRD INTEREST OR HOBBY>
```

4. The document at the top of the next page is to be entered into the computer using WordPerfect. (Your margins will not coincide with the margins of this copy; do not be concerned about this.) Entries enclosed within angle brackets are to be replaced with information as described within the brackets. For instance, <YOUR NAME> should be replaced with your name. You are to prepare detailed sequences of instructions for using the Exit command as described in this notice. The starting point of each of these two descriptions is that the user has completed entering a short document but has not yet saved or named it. The first sequence of steps is to describe each step in saving it, entering the filename to be used, and terminating execution of WordPerfect. Use your last name (or the first eight letters) for the filename and WP for the extension. (For instance, for the author, it would be PRICE.WP.) For the second sequence describe the steps necessary to clear the screen rather than terminate. As an example of the level of detail required, pattern your instructions after the following for printing a document.

1. Enter the Print command with the key sequence Shift-F7.
2. From the resulting selection menu, type the digit 1 to cause the Full document to be printed.
3. When printing is completed, WordPerfect returns to the edit screen.

```
Using the Exit Command
by
<YOUR NAME>
<CURRENT DATE>


The Exit command is used for more than simply terminating
execution of WordPerfect.  If your document has not already been
saved, Exit prompts you to save it.  Then you can terminate, or
you can direct WordPerfect to clear the current document so that
you can enter another.  Assume that you are working at the
computer and the document currently on the screen has not yet
been saved (or even given a file name).  Furthermore, assume that
you want to give your document the name <YOUR LAST NAME>.WP.  The
Exit sequence of steps you would take to terminate (and save the
document) would be as follows.

1.    <Detailed sequence of steps numbered 1, 2, 3,...>

The sequence of steps you would follow if you wished to save the
current document but wanted to clear the screen so that you could
enter another document would be:

1.    <Detailed sequence of steps numbered 1, 2, 3,...>
```

When you are finished, save your document to disk with the filename USEEXIT.WP; you will need it for an assignment in the next chapter.

5. The following document describing cut and paste is stored as MEMO-CP.WP on the data disk accompanying this book. Make the indicated corrections to it, then print a copy.

```
delete          and Future Experts                              Delete

To:   Students of WordPerfect
From: The Author

The cut and paste feature of WordPerfect is a powrful tool as you
shall soon learn.  One option of the Move command allows you to
deletete anything from a single word all the way up to the entire
document if you so desire.  For instance, this sentence should
not be here so it should be removed or at least moved somewhere
else.  The Retrieve Text command allows you to insert the most
recently cut text into your document--anyplace you desire, no
less.  In other words, this combination of commands allows you to
move text from one place in your document to another.

This is another paragraph but it does not say anything. In fact,
the "out of place" sentence in the preceding paragraph can be
inserted in front of this one. That operation will give this
paragraph some value.

Delete this
                                    This does seem to be a
                                    waste of time but the
```

6. In the Introduction to Part Two, word processing is introduced using a MCT letter to an attorney (see Figure P2-1). The data disk accompanying this book includes another version of that letter; it is named CONTRACT.WP1. You are to print a copy of this version and compare it to that in Figure P2-1. (In the output, ignore the justification of lines and the *WPC inserted by the Limited-Use version of WordPerfect.) You are to edit CONTRACT.WP1 as follows:

   (a) Make all corrections and changes so that it is identical to Figure P2-1.

   (b) Insert a date at the top of the letter.

   (c) Put your name at the bottom leaving ample space for your signature.

Chapter 3

More on WordPerfect

OBJECTIVES

From Chapter 2 you have learned how to enter, edit, save, retrieve, and print documents using WordPerfect. In this chapter, you will learn about using the other features of word processing described in the introduction. When you have completed this chapter, you should be able to:

- Format your document, including setting margins, centering lines, indenting paragraphs, and underlining text.
- Examine and change formatting codes that you have entered with formatting commands.
- Use the Search and the Search and Replace commands.
- Move a section of text from one place in a document to another (or into another document): cut and paste.
- Use the WordPerfect speller and thesaurus.

PREVIEW

Simple Formatting

WordPerfect formatting commands enable you to change margin settings, center lines, indent paragraphs, underline text, and set text in boldface.

Working with Hidden Codes

The Reveal Codes command causes WordPerfect to display the formatting codes in a document so that they can be deleted as you would delete text.

Formatting While Entering a Document

Formatting of a document can be done either after the document has been entered or while text entry is taking place.

Other Formatting Features

Other WordPerfect commands enable you to change line spacing, disable right justification of the printed document, and use specialized indenting.

Searching a Document

The Search command locates any word or combination of words in a document. The Search and Replace command finds designated text and replaces it.

Cutting and Pasting

Using the Move command, you can delete, cut, or copy a portion of text in a document and insert it at some other place in the document.

Working with Two Documents

WordPerfect maintains two memory areas so that you can have two independent documents in memory at the same time. You can split the screen and display both documents.

The WordPerfect Speller and Thesaurus

WordPerfect includes a built-in spelling checker that will check the spelling of all words in a document. The on-screen thesaurus helps you select synonyms for words in your document.

SIMPLE FORMATTING

A Notice to Be Formatted

In Chapter 2, you learned how to edit a document by inserting and deleting text. Now you will learn how to modify a document by changing its format; the text will be unchanged, but its appearance will be changed. For this activity, you will need the document NOTICE.WP1, which is stored on the data disk that accompanies this book. If you prepared your

Figure 3-1
The unformatted notice.

```
University Computer Center
Special Notice
11/26

Unfortunately, budget reductions are forcing us to curtail some
of our services this semester.  In an effort to minimize the
impact on your use of the facilities, we have attempted to reduce
in areas that will least affect you, the student.  During the
holiday period, the Center will not be open during the evening.
However, with the exception of both Tuesdays, we will maintain
the normal daytime hours.  We hope that this is not a major
inconvenience to any of you.

If you have any suggestions for improving our services, please
let us know.  Thank you for you cooperation.
```

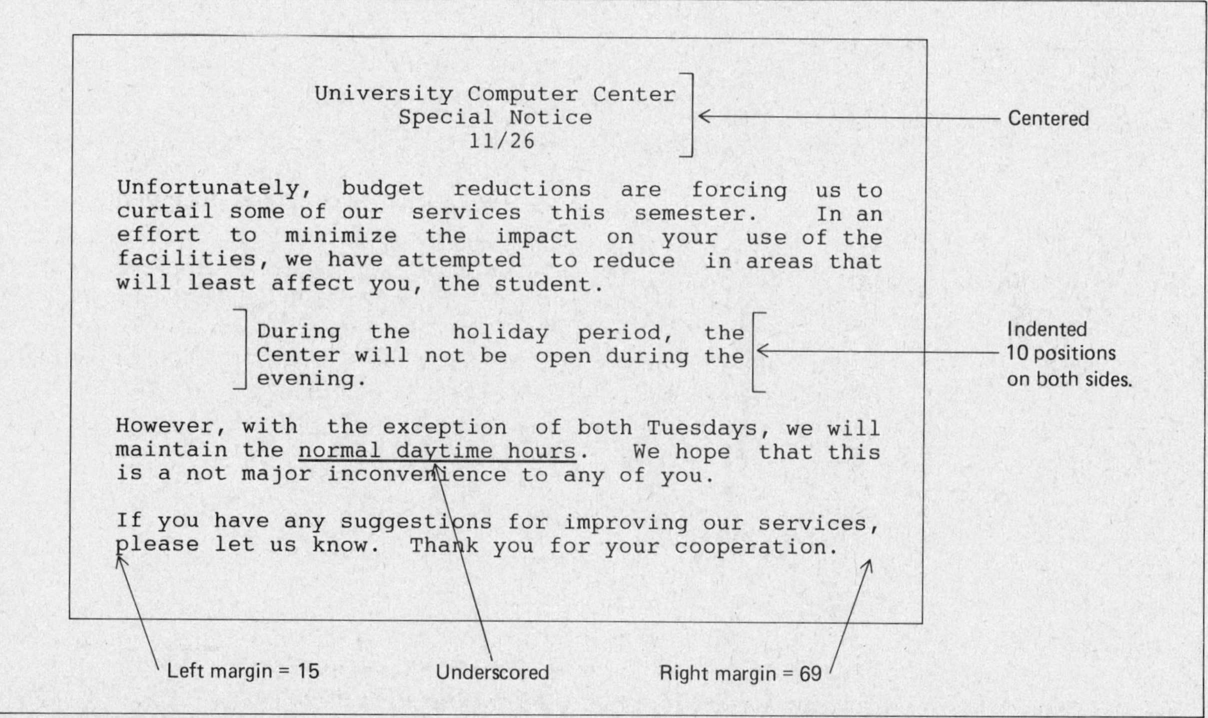

University Computer Center
Special Notice
11/26

Unfortunately, budget reductions are forcing us to curtail some of our services this semester. In an effort to minimize the impact on your use of the facilities, we have attempted to reduce in areas that will least affect you, the student.

During the holiday period, the Center will not be open during the evening.

However, with the exception of both Tuesdays, we will maintain the normal daytime hours. We hope that this is a not major inconvenience to any of you.

If you have any suggestions for improving our services, please let us know. Thank you for your cooperation.

Figure 3-2
The formatted notice.

data disk as described in Chapter 1, then you will have the document available. If you load WordPerfect with

```
B> A:WP NOTICE.WP1
```

you will be presented with the screen shown in Figure 3-1. Note that the message is adequate but the formatting is not very imaginative. Certain points need emphasis. Now compare this with the formatted version shown in Figure 3-2. Here, formatting has been used to produce a notice that is much more appealing to the eye. Note that the important message (that the Center is not open during the evening) is indented to make it more noticeable. The purpose of this portion of the chapter is to show you how simple it is to change the formatting of the document in Figure 3-1 so that it looks like that in Figure 3-2. At first, the variety of actions required in using the formatting commands might be confusing. As you use them and observe how they work and what they do, you will find most of the required actions quite logical. If you use WordPerfect often, using formatting commands will become as automatic as typing text. In reformatting the document of Figure 3-1, you will learn about the following formatting techniques:

- Changing margin settings—the notice in Figure 3-2 uses margin settings of 15 and 69.
- Centering lines—the first three lines of the notice are centered.
- Splitting a single paragraph into more than one paragraph—the third sentence of the first paragraph must be a separate paragraph. (Actually, you already know how to do this from Chapter 2.)
- Indenting a paragraph—referring to Figure 3-2, the second paragraph is indented 1 inch on both sides.
- Underlining—three words are underlined in this notice.

When performing the formatting actions described in the instructions that follow, be certain that you do exactly as described; that is, the cursor must be properly positioned and the key sequences must be entered correctly. If you do not do so, then your formatted version will not look like that in Figure 3-2. Furthermore, you may not be able to undo the action (you will learn how to undo an action after you learn to do the formatting). If you make a mistake that you cannot correct, then simply clear the screen (use F7) and retrieve the original copy of NOTICE.WP1 from disk.

Setting Margins

Before entering the new margin settings, make certain that the cursor is in the upper left corner of the screen. That will have been its position when you first retrieved the notice, so it will already be there unless you have moved it. Referring to the WordPerfect function key template, notice that the function key F8 is identified as the format key (however, it does not control all formatting operations). Setting margins is an option under the Format Line command and is done as follows.

DO THIS NOW 3-1 **Setting Margins**

1. Enter the Shift-F8 sequence that produces the following status line prompt.

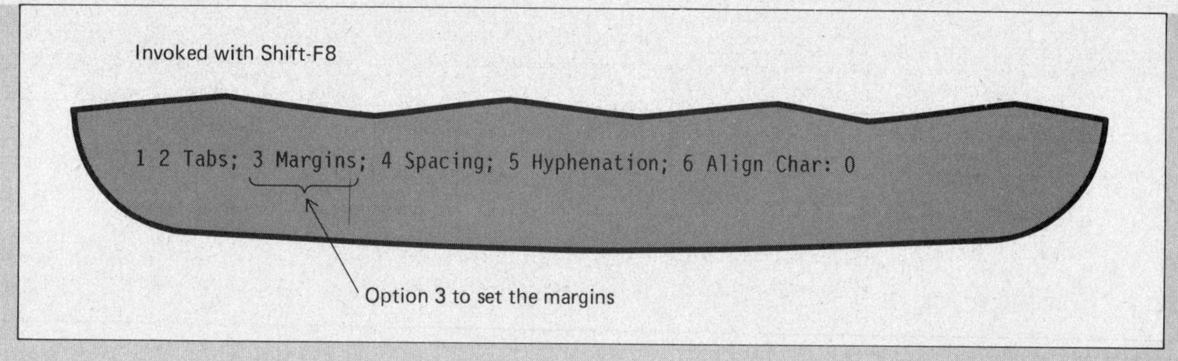

2. Strike the digit 3 key to select Margins. You will see the preceding prompt replaced by:

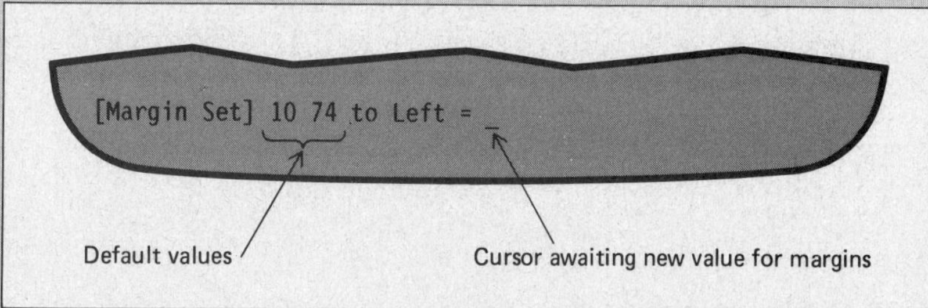

3. Type the new left margin, 15, and strike Enter.
4. You will then be prompted for the value of the right margin. Type the new right margin of 69 and strike Enter.

You will see the notice realigned immediately to conform to the new margin settings and control returned to the edit screen awaiting your next action.

Positioning a Line

Your next formatting action is to center each of the first three lines using the Center command (Shift-F6). Note that this command operates on a single line that is ended with a hard return. (The Enter key was pressed after the line was entered for each of these three lines.)

DO THIS NOW 3-2 **Centering a Line**

1. Before issuing the command, the cursor *must be at the extreme left of the line*. If it is not there, then reposition it with the Home,Left sequence.
2. Enter the Center command with the Shift-F6 sequence; the line will be shifted to the right. It may not be centered, but when you move the cursor to the next line, it will be positioned properly.

3. Repeat this action for each of the two lines that follow. Do not forget to position the cursor at the left of each line before centering it.

In addition to centering, the F6 key is also used to align lines on the right margin; this is called **flush right.** Although the notice of Figure 3-2 does not use flush right, you can experiment to see how it works. To do this, move the cursor beyond the last line of the document and do the following.

DO THIS NOW 3-3 **Setting a Line Flush Right**

1. Strike Enter to insert a blank line.
2. Type the following three lines (strike Enter after each line).

   First line
   Second line
   Last line

   Be certain to strike Enter after the last line.
3. Position the cursor on the first letter of the first line.
4. Enter the Flush Right command with Alt-F6.
5. Repeat this for each of the two remaining lines. Be certain to position the cursor at the beginning of the line before issuing the command.

When you finish, the lower portion of your screen will look like this:

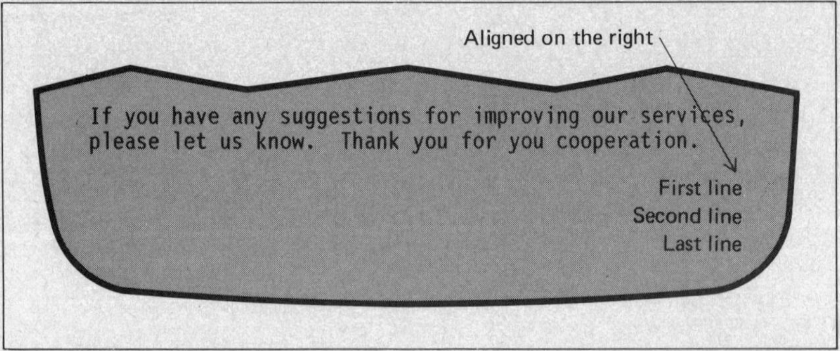

To delete these, simply position the cursor on the line to be deleted, strike the left arrow until the cursor is at the far left of the screen, and then use the Delete to End Of Line command (Ctrl-End).

Indention

Your next task is to break the first paragraph into three separate paragraphs and then indent the second one as shown in Figure 3-2. Remember from Chapter 2 that you create a paragraph by striking Enter, causing WordPerfect to insert a hard return. Thus, to create the new paragraphs you must do the following.

DO THIS NOW 3-4 **Creating a New Paragraph**

1. Position the cursor on the letter *D* of *During;* this is the first word of that which will become a new paragraph.
2. Strike the Enter twice—once to start the new paragraph and again to insert a blank line.
3. Move the cursor to the letter *H* in *However;* this is to begin the third paragraph.
4. Strike the Enter twice. Your document will now appear as in Figure 3-3.

Figure 3-3
Splitting one paragraph into two.

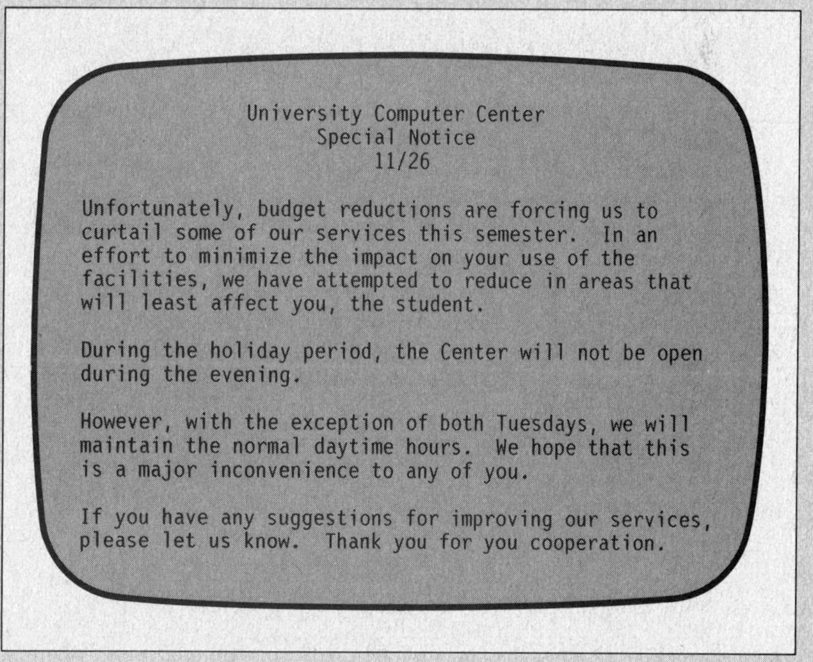

You are now ready to indent the newly created second paragraph.

In Chapter 2, you learned about tab settings whose default values are set every five positions. When the Tab key is struck, the cursor jumps to the next tab setting. Note that you cannot use the Tab key to achieve the desired indention of Figure 3-2 because you need the indention to act on all lines of the paragraph.

WordPerfect provides two ways to indent paragraphs. Look at the function key template (or display it on the screen with the F3 key) and you will notice that the F4 key lists indent in the following two forms:

```
->Indent<-      Shift-F4
```

and

```
->Indent        F4
```

The arrows indicate the direction of indention; for instance, Shift-F4 causes an entire paragraph to be indented from both the left and right margins an amount equal to one tab. You must use this command for the indention required in the second paragraph of Figure 3-2.

DO THIS NOW 3-5 **Indenting a Paragraph**

1. Position the cursor on the letter *D* of the word *During* (the first character in this paragraph).
2. Enter the Shift-F4 sequence; WordPerfect will indent this paragraph from both the left and right by five positions. Enter the Shift-F4 sequence a second time for the ten-position indents.

Blocks of Text

The various formatting commands are different with respect to the amount of text that they affect. For instance, the Center command acts on a single line; the Indent command acts on a paragraph. However, the Underline command is different in that it does *not* act on some predetermined amount of text. For instance, in the third paragraph of the notice, you must underline the words *normal daytime hours.* For this, you need the ability to operate on a portion of the text. WordPerfect provides that capability with the **Block** command, which allows you to mark a portion of text that can range in length from two characters to the entire document. WordPerfect indicates the blocked portion of text by highlighting it on the screen. It is possible to perform numerous operations on a block, such as underlining, deleting, and saving to a file. For now, our attention is focused on underlining.

Underlining and Boldface

In the following sequence, you must first block the text that you want to underline and then underline it.

DO THIS NOW 3-6 **Defining a Block and Underlining**

1. Move the cursor to the first position of the text to be marked as a block: that is, the letter *n* in *normal.*
2. Mark the beginning of the block with the Block command Alt-F4.

This turns on the block mode, causing a flashing message to be displayed on the status line as shown below.

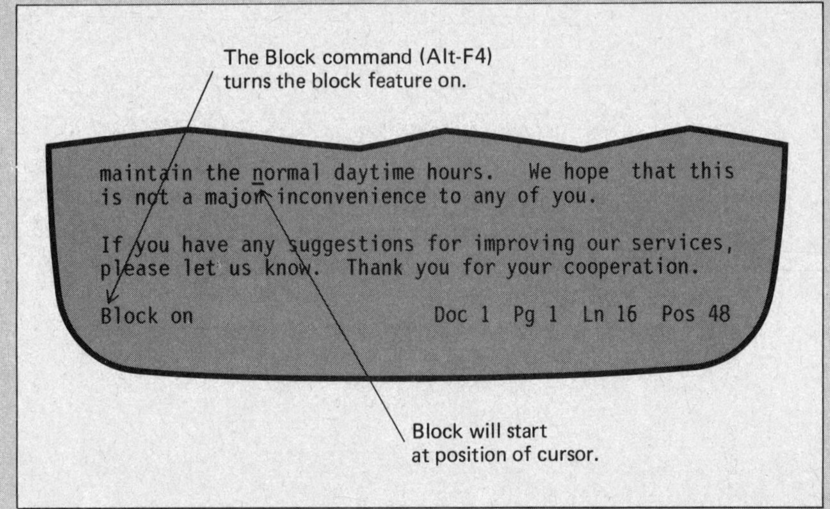

3. Move the cursor to the position of the last character in the block using the Right key. The entire blocked area will be highlighted.

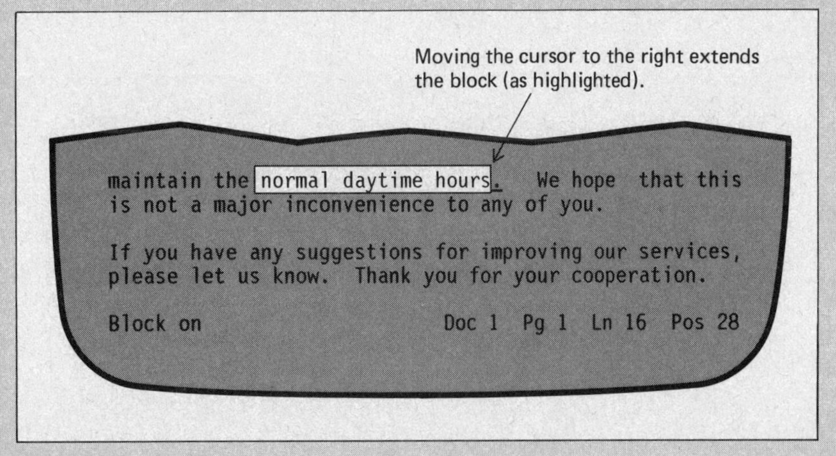

4. Enter the Underline command (F8) to cause the blocked text to be underlined. Note that this also turns off the block.

When defining a block of text, once you establish the starting point (with the Alt-F4), the cursor can be moved with any of the cursor movement keys in order to extend the block. For instance, in the preceding example, the Ctrl-Right key could have been used to move word by word. If two or more lines must be included in a block, you can use the Down (or

Up) keys. The best way to learn about blocking is to carry out some blocking actions; to cancel the block, use the Cancel command (F1).

Changing text to boldface (letters that are darker and stand out more) is done in the same way as underlining. The Boldface key is F6. You can further enhance the notice by using boldface on the entire second paragraph. To do this, block the paragraph and then strike the F6 key. Although you will see no difference on the screen display, when printed, the boldface portions will be printed twice, thereby making them slightly darker.

The formatting of your document is now complete. You should save it to disk (you will need it later) and then print a copy. When saving it, use a different filename, for instance, NOTICE.WP2. In this way, you will still have the original version as NOTICE.WP1 for other practice activities. Now that you have done the formatting, let us learn about the codes resulting from the formatting commands you used.

Assignment 3-1 may now be completed.

WORKING WITH HIDDEN CODES

From Chapter 2, you know that the formatting commands of WordPerfect cause formatting codes to be imbedded directly in the text within memory. One of the functions of the word processor program is to display the text according to the specifications of the codes and not display the codes themselves. Thus, for most activities, you need not be concerned about the actual codes. You have just seen this from the preceding example in which you formatted the notice. You simply issued the appropriate formatting commands and WordPerfect adjusted the document on the screen accordingly. Because you see the effect of these codes and not the codes themselves, in WordPerfect they are called **hidden codes.**

As a rule, it is best that they remain hidden so that you can focus on your document and its appearance. However, if you accidentally strike a wrong function key and enter a formatting command at the wrong place, the screen display of your document can be very confusing. It is sometimes quite difficult to diagnose the problem merely by looking at the edit screen display. For this, you need to have a basic understanding of these hidden codes.

If you formatted the notice exactly as described in the preceding sections, then your document will contain the hidden codes shown in Figure 3-4. Here, each code is enclosed in square brackets and positioned at the point where you issued the corresponding command during editing.

Hidden Code	Key Sequence	Description
[Margin Set:15,69]	Shift-F8,3	Defines the margins; resulted from the Format Line command.
[C] and [c]	Shift-F6	Line-centering code from the Center command. The code [C] marks the beginning of the text to be centered and is inserted at the position of the cursor when the command is issued. The code [c] marks the end of the text to be centered; it is automatically inserted by WordPerfect at the end of the line.
[HRt]	Enter	Hard Return inserted when the Enter key is pressed.
[SRt]		Soft Return inserted by WordPerfect when a word is wrapped to start a new line.
[->Indent<-]	Shift-F4	Specifies that this paragraph be indented from both left and right margins.
[U] and [u]	F8	Specifies that the text between [U] and [u] be underlined. The underlining in this notice involved first marking the text (Alt-F4) and then issuing the underline command.

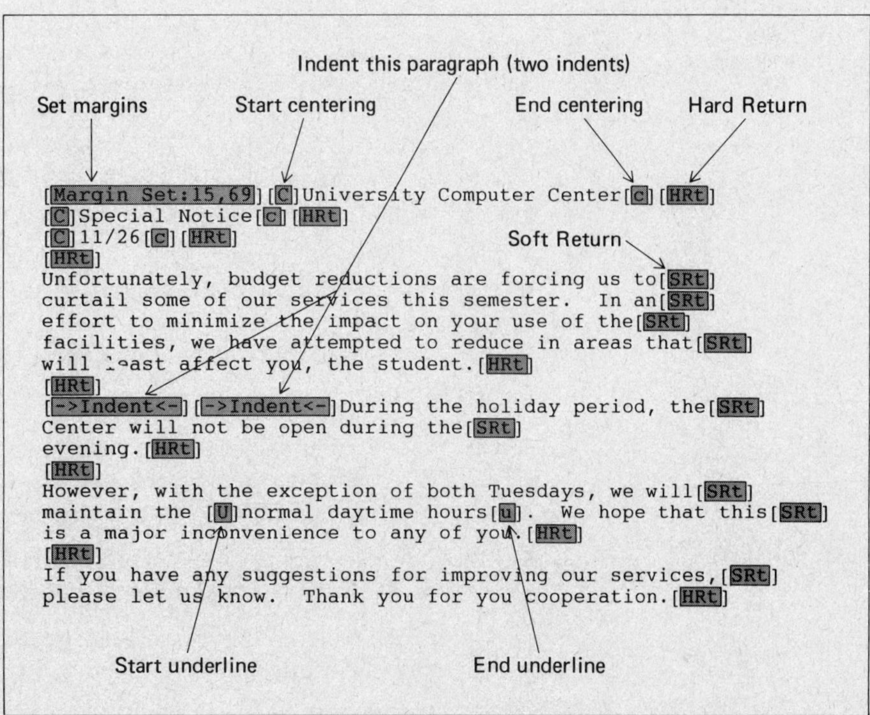

Figure 3-4
Hidden codes in the memo.

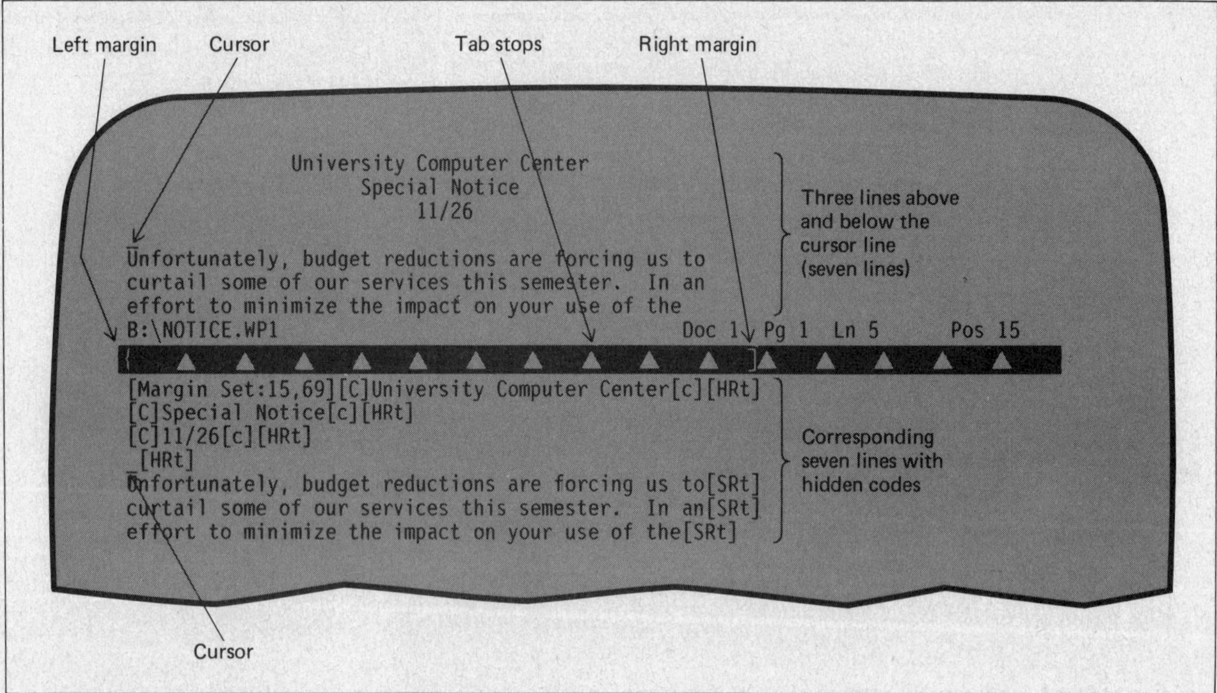

Figure 3-5
The Reveal Codes screen.

Displaying and Deleting Hidden Codes

Hidden codes are displayed with the Reveal Codes command (Alt-F3). To illustrate its use, you should have your formatted notice on the screen. Although you can issue this command with your cursor anywhere on the screen, position it for this example so that it is on the blank line that precedes the first paragraph. Then enter the Reveal Codes command with Alt-F3 and your screen display will be as shown in Figure 3-5. This Reveal Codes screen consists of the following parts (from the top of the screen down):

- An upper portion displaying up to seven lines of text as they appear from the edit screen. These include the line on which the cursor is located and three lines above and below it.
- The familiar status line.
- The tab ruler separates the two halves of the screen and indicates the locations of the margins and tab stops. (The brace is used if the margin falls on a tab stop; otherwise, the square bracket is used.)
- A lower portion of the screen displaying the seven lines of text (shown in the upper portion) together with the hidden codes.

As a simple illustration of deleting formatting codes, let us delete the margin and underline codes. With the Up arrow key, move the cursor to the first line and your screen should be as shown in Figure 3-6(a). In the upper portion of the screen note that the cursor is positioned beneath the

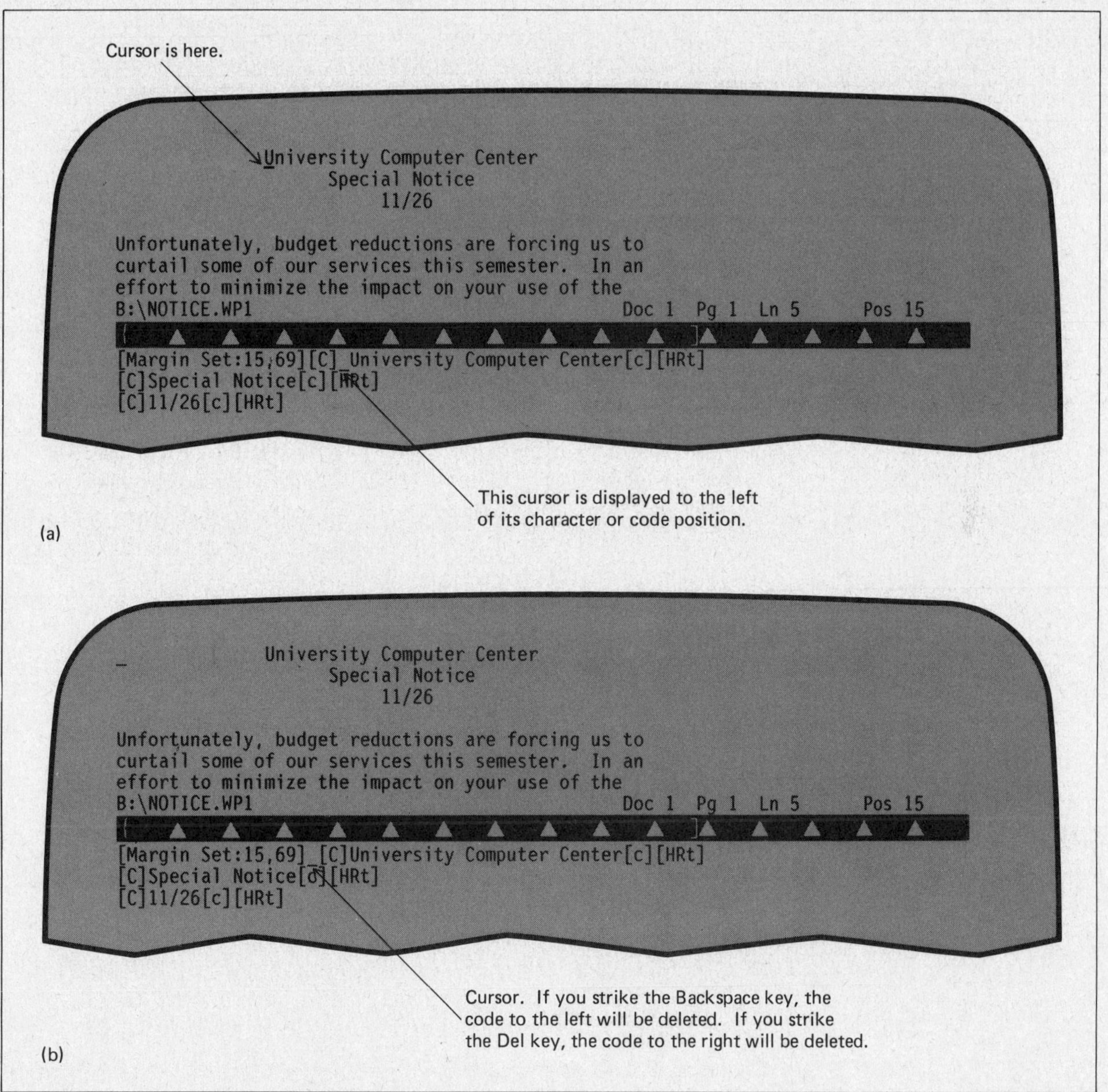

Figure 3-6
Positioning the cursor in the hidden codes.

letter *U* in *University*. In the lower portion of the screen, it is positioned between the center code [C] and the letter *U*. The cursor in the Reveal Codes screen is always positioned to the left of its character or code position.

DO THIS NOW 3-7 **Deleting Hidden Codes**

1. Position the cursor between the two codes as shown in Figure 3-6(b).

2. Strike the Backspace key to delete the margin code, and the displayed text will be rearranged conforming to the default values of 10 and 75.
3. Next, you must delete the underline, which is in a portion of the screen not displayed in Figure 3-6. With the Down key, move the cursor to the line containing the underlined text. Note that the screen scrolls when the cursor reaches the bottom line.
4. Position the Reveal Codes cursor to the right of the [U] underline code.
5. Strike the Backspace key.

When you do this, you will see that the ending code [u] is also deleted and that the underscore is removed from the text in the upper half of the screen. WordPerfect automatically deletes the matching code when you delete one of them. Since you are finished, you may return to the edit screen by striking the F1 key.

Deleting Hidden Codes from the Edit Screen

In Chapter 2, you learned that you can delete the Hard Return just as if it were another character. The same is true with other hidden codes. However, a problem is that you will be operating blindly if your document has two or more consecutive codes. To try this, you must clear the screen (Exit command) and then retrieve your copy of the formatted notice.

DO THIS NOW 3-8 **Deleting Hidden Codes**

1. Position the cursor under the letter *U* in *University* (the first line of the notice).
2. Strike the Backspace key. You will be prompted to confirm that you want the Center code deleted. If you respond with Y, the code will be deleted and the line moved to the left margin.
3. Leave the Center code unchanged by responding with N, the default.
4. Strike the Left arrow one time, thereby moving the cursor to a location between the left margin and the first title line.
5. Strike the Backspace and you will be prompted about deleting the margin code.
6. Respond with N and your document will be unchanged.

In both of these cases, WordPerfect asked you to confirm deleting the hidden code. For most (but not all) hidden codes, an attempt to delete from the edit screen results in a confirming prompt.

Correcting a Problem

To illustrate a situation in which the Reveal Codes screen can be invaluable, assume that you are making some minor changes in the notice. In this process, you are going to issue the Center command accidentally when the cursor is positioned in the middle of a paragraph. For your screen to correspond to the screen illustrations that follow, you must carry out the following sequence of steps exactly as described.

DO THIS NOW 3-9 **Creating a Problem**

1. Retrieve your formatted copy of the notice from disk. For this, use the Exit command without saving in order to clear the screen (remember the key sequence: F7,N,N). Then retrieve your formatted copy of the document.
2. Position the cursor under the letter *t* in *this* as shown in the following.

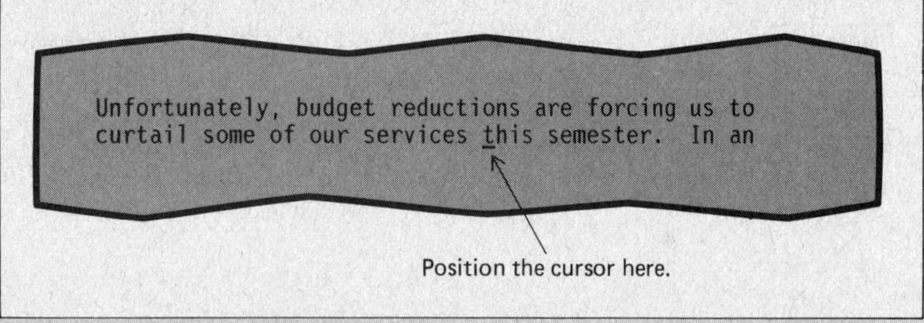

3. Enter the Center command with the Shift-F6.
4. Move the cursor down to the next line. Your display will now be as shown in Figure 3-7: the words *of our services* are missing.

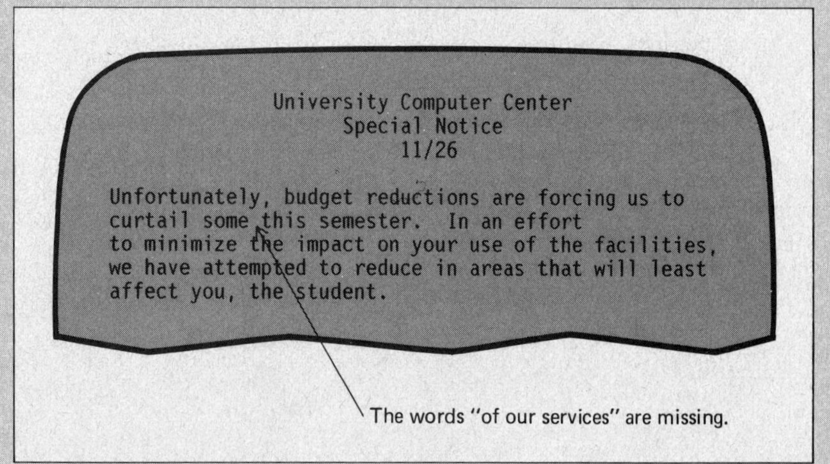

Figure 3-7
A puzzling screen display.

5. Move the cursor back up to the second line.
6. Using the Left and Right keys, move the cursor back and forth across the line (to the beginning of the line, then to the end, and then back again). Note how the cursor jumps when moved in the vicinity of the missing text and how that text is alternately redisplayed and then changed again. This is confusing indeed.

Whenever WordPerfect responds in a strange way such as this, you should use the Reveal Codes command (Alt-F3). The screen of Figure 3-8 tells the story. The errant Center command causes WordPerfect to center that portion of the line between the two codes, thus "overlaying" the earlier portion of the line. Once you know the problem, correcting it is easy.

DO THIS NOW 3-10 **Correcting a Problem**

1. Position the cursor to the immediate right of the Center code [C].
2. Strike the Backspace once.

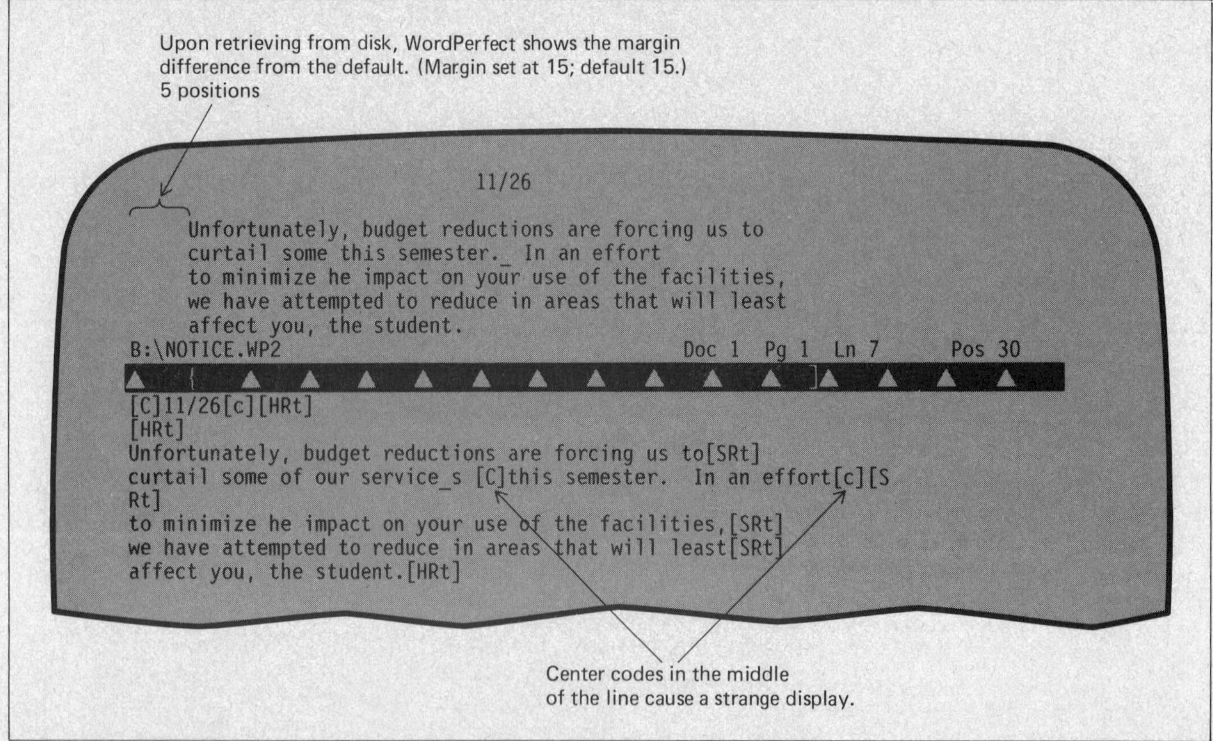

Figure 3-8
Misplaced hidden code that causes trouble.

Comparing Formatting Commands

From the earlier summary of commands used in this document and your knowledge of the actions required to format, you have probably noticed that the amount of text over which a command has an effect varies among commands. In this respect, the formatting commands can be grouped in three categories:

- First are those commands that act on all text that follows until another command is encountered. For instance, setting the margins results in a hidden code that applies to all text following the code until the next margin code is encountered (if there is another in the document).
- Second are those commands that act on a predetermined amount of text. For instance, the Indent command generates a code that indents that single paragraph.
- Third are those commands that operate on a user-defined amount of text. For example, the Underline command generates codes that define the beginning and ending of the affected text.

Keeping these distinctions in mind will help you understand the various formatting operations that are possible with WordPerfect.

Assignment 3-2 may now be completed.

FORMATTING WHILE ENTERING A DOCUMENT

For your first exposure to formatting a document, you worked with a document that had already been entered into the computer. Although you will frequently have occasion to change the formatting of a document, you will commonly enter formatting while you are entering the text. So that you become familiar with this, you should clear your screen (use the Exit statement) and then enter the document of Figure 3-2, together with formatting, as follows (you will find it convenient to have a printed copy of the notice in front of you).

DO THIS NOW 3-11 **Entering and Formatting**

1. Enter the margin settings with the following sequence:

Shift-F8	Enter the Format Line command
3	Selection 3 for margins
15,Enter	Enter value for left margin
69,Enter	Enter value for right margin

2. Enter the Center code with Shift-F6.
3. Type the first heading line; note that WordPerfect constantly maintains centering on the text as you enter it. When finished, strike the Enter key.
4. Repeat steps 2 and 3 for the second and third heading lines.
5. After leaving a blank line following the headings, type the first paragraph. When finished with this paragraph, strike the Enter key twice (you need a blank line before the second paragraph).
6. Enter two Indent commands by holding down the Shift and striking the F4 twice.
7. Type the second paragraph. When you strike the Enter to end this paragraph, note that the cursor returns to the left margin. Remember, the Indent code applies only to the single paragraph. Strike the Enter again to leave another blank line.
8. Type the third paragraph up to the words *normal daytime hours,* which require underlining.
9. Turn underlining on by striking the F8 key.
10. Type the words *normal daytime hours.*
11. Turn underlining off by striking the F8 key. Note that during text entry, the underline key F8 functions as a toggle: strike it once and underlining is on; strike it a second time and underlining is off.
12. Type the remainder of this paragraph and the next paragraph.

Entry of the notice is now complete. It should look exactly like the version that you formatted beginning with the unformatted NOTICE.WP1.

OTHER FORMATTING COMMANDS

Double Spacing

The documents you have prepared have been single spaced—the WordPerfect line spacing default. Sometimes it is convenient to double space a document, especially for a first draft that will require a lot of editing. You can change line spacing in the same way you change margin settings: by issuing a command that inserts hidden code in the document. Like the margin code, the line spacing code applies to all text that follows until another line spacing code is encountered. In fact, spacing is set from the same function key command as margins: Format Line (Shift-F8). To illustrate this, you should clear the screen and retrieve the original unformatted copy of the notice (NOTICE.WP1). Referring to Figure 3-1, note that it consists of the three heading lines followed by two paragraphs. You will double space the first paragraph only.

DO THIS NOW 3-12 **Double Spacing a Paragraph**

1. Move the cursor to the first position of the first paragraph (the letter *U* in *Unfortunately*).

2. Issue the Format Line command as follows:

Shift-F8	Format Line command
4	Selection 4 for spacing

3. From the resulting prompt

you can designate the line spacing. The default value is 1; values that can be entered are 1.5 for one and a half spacing, 2 for double spacing, and 3 for triple spacing. Type the digit 2 and then strike the Enter. Except for the first three lines, the entire document will be double spaced.

4. Move the cursor to the first position of the second paragraph (the letter *I* in *If you,* which should be the last displayed line on your screen).

5. Repeat the Format Line command but this time enter 1 for the line spacing. This will cause all text that follows (only two lines in this document) to be single spaced.

Disabling Right Justification

Although the edit screen displays documents with a ragged margin on the right, WordPerfect automatically inserts sufficient spaces to justify printing. However, in some situations, you might not want these extra spaces inserted. For instance, the additional spaces in the indented paragraph of the notice tend to be distracting.

```
During   the   holiday  period  the
Center will not be  open during the
```

You can insert hidden codes to turn justification on and off just as you insert margin and line spacing codes. For the notice that you have on the screen, you can turn justification off with the following sequence.

DO THIS NOW 3-13 **Disabling Right Justification**

1. Position the cursor at the beginning of the first paragraph (under the *U* in *Unfortunately*).
2. Enter the Print Format command with Ctrl-F8. WordPerfect then displays the Print Format list of eleven options, each of which can be used to change the way in which printing will be affected.
3. Since you want to turn justification off, strike the digit 3. Had you desired to turn it on (only necessary if you previously turned it off), then you would have entered the digit 4.

You should now print the document to confirm that its appearance is consistent with the formatting that you have performed.

Hanging Paragraphs

A **hanging paragraph** (also called a hanging indent) is one in which the entire paragraph, with the exception of the first line, is indented from the left. For example, the description of Figure 3-9 uses hanging paragraphs to set each of the three items apart. To try this, you might want to clear your screen first, although it is not necessary for this exercise.

Figure 3-9
Hanging paragraphs.

```
The amount of text over which a command has an effect varies from
one command to another.  In this respect, formatting commands can
be grouped in three categories.

1.    Those that act on all text that follows until another is
      encountered.  The margins code is such an example.

2.    Those that act upon a predetermined amount of text.  For
      instance, the Indent command used here generates a code that
      indents a single paragraph.

3.    Those that operate on a user defined amount of text.  For
      example, the underline command generates codes that define
      the beginning and ending of the affected text.
```

The first line of each paragraph
is positioned to the left.

DO THIS NOW 3-14 **Hanging Paragraph**

1. Enter the first paragraph and strike the Enter twice to produce the blank line.
2. Type the digit 1 and the period.
3. Enter a Left Indent command (F4). The cursor will jump to the first tab stop.
4. Enter the paragraph; each wrap begins the next line at the indent position.
5. Enter items 2 and 3 in exactly the same way as you entered item 1.

With this technique, you can use the left indent (F4) or the left-right indent (Shift-F4).

SEARCHING A DOCUMENT

The Search Command

Assume you prepared a long document and that somewhere within it you mentioned an *archive copier*. Later, you decide to check that passage to be certain your statement was accurate. If you did not remember where in the document you made the remark, you would have to scan the entire document looking for these words. For a long document, this could be time consuming. With a word processor, it is simple because the program will do the searching for you. For this, WordPerfect includes two versions of the Search command:

F2	Forward Search searches from the cursor position to the end of the document.
Shift-F2	Reverse Search searches from the cursor position to the beginning of the document.

Although the command is most useful with a long document, its use is easily illustrated with a short one. For this, use the document named CONTRACT.WP1; it is on the data disk that accompanies this book and was used for one of the Chapter 2 assignments. In it, the word *terminated* is misspelled as *terminted*. Let us find it with the Search command.

DO THIS NOW 3-15 **Searching**

1. Clear the screen and retrieve the file CONTRACT.WP1.
2. To issue a Search Forward command, strike the F2 key, which produces the following prompt on the status line.

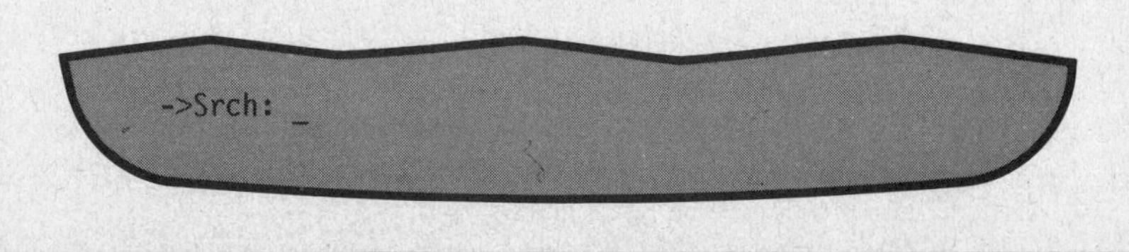

3. Type the characters for which you wish to search; this is called the **search string**. To illustrate the Search command more fully, type in the first four letters of the word *terminted*, or *term*.
4. Start the search by striking the F2 key again; the search will be successful and the cursor will be positioned as follows:

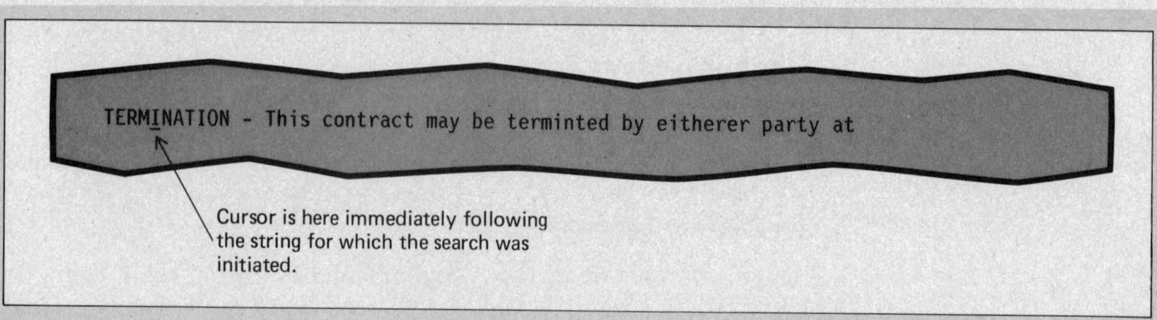

```
TERMINATION - This contract may be terminted by eitherer party at
```

Cursor is here immediately following the string for which the search was initiated.

When starting the search, be careful that you do not strike the Enter key. If you do, the code [HRt] will be entered as part of the search string. Then the search will be for the indicated text followed by a hard return.

5. Since this is not the portion of text that you want, you must execute the Search command again. However, the process is simplified by the fact that the last-used search string is offered as a default. Hence, to continue, strike the F2 key twice, and the cursor will be positioned on the word *terminted.*

This exercise illustrates three points. The first is how to repeat a search, as you have just done. The second is that the search action is looking for a sequence of characters that is exactly like the search string. In this example, WordPerfect found the four letters *term* as part of another word. A further point is that the search string can be one or more words or portions of two words—any combination of characters. The third point relates to the way in which WordPerfect handles lowercase and uppercase in the search action. If the search string is lowercase, then either uppercase or lowercase in the text will cause a match. For instance, with the search string *term,* WordPerfect found a match with both *TERM* and *term* (it would also have matched *Term*). However, had you used uppercase for the search string, that is, *TERM,* then only uppercase letters would have been matched.

In this example, the cursor was positioned at the beginning of the document so you used the Search Forward (search toward the end). Had the cursor been located somewhere within the document (or at the end), you could have used the reverse search by initiating the command with Shift-F2. This would have caused the search to progress from the cursor position back toward the beginning of the document.

If WordPerfect cannot find text that matches the search string, then the status line momentarily displays the message

```
*Not Found*
```

and you are returned to the edit screen. The cursor remains where it was before the search was started.

The Replace Command

In the letter CONTRACT.WP1 that you are working on, assume that you must change the word COMPANY to MCT wherever it occurs (see Figure P2-1 of the introduction to word processing). In this letter, the word appears only four times; in the complete contract, it would occur many times. In WordPerfect, the Replace command (which is an extension of the Search) automates your task of making this change. If you do not have the letter (CONTRACT.WP1) on the screen from the search example, then clear the screen and retrieve it for this example. After making certain that the cursor is at the beginning of the letter, you should do the following to change COMPANY to MCT.

DO THIS NOW 3-16 **Replacing Text**

1. Issue the Replace command with the key sequence Alt-F2; this produces the following prompt on the status line.

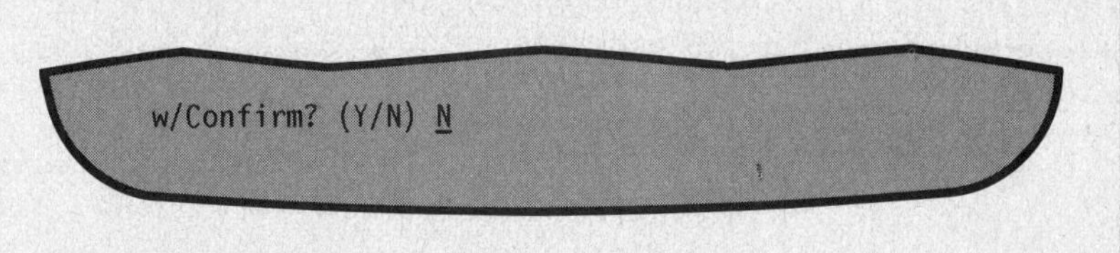

2. Strike the letter Y (this option is described later).
3. WordPerfect displays the following prompt on the status line requesting that the text to be replaced be entered.

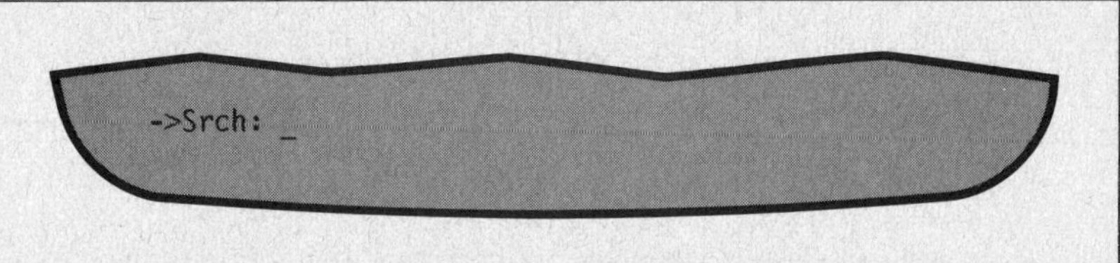

Notice that this is identical to the Search prompt.

4. Type the search string *COMPANY* and then strike F2 to indicate to WordPerfect that you have completed your entry. (As with the Search, you should not strike the Enter key.)
5. The prompt on the status line will be replaced with:

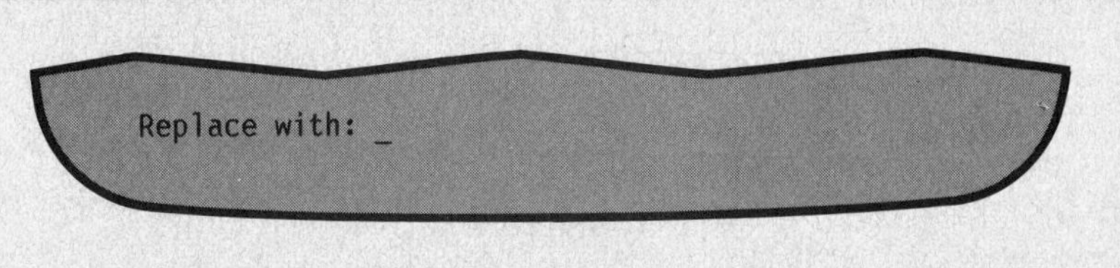

Type the replacement text *MCT* and then strike the F2 key.

6. The first match will be in the phrase *OPTION OF COMPANY TO APPROVE ORDERS*. The cursor will be positioned under the word *COMPANY*, and a prompt will appear on the status line asking for a confirmation. Strike the letter *Y* to replace and *N* (or Enter) to leave unchanged. You must repeat this for each occurrence of the word.

The Replace command offers you the option of confirming each replacement (as you did in this example) or allowing the program to make each one automatically. Usually, it is best to use the confirmation option. For instance, if you decided to change the word *which* to *that* everywhere it appeared, you could end up with such things as *thatever* (resulting from *whichever*). Before making an automatic replacement, it is a good idea to save your document to disk in the event of unforeseen problems.

CUTTING AND PASTING

Another feature of word processors is the ease of cutting and pasting—the moving of a section of text from one place in a document to another. As illustrated in Figure 3-10, this term is derived from the equivalent action of physically cutting a portion of text from one page and pasting it onto another. Because of the versatility of the computer, cutting and pasting with a word processor can involve moving a portion of text from one place to another in a document, or making a copy of a portion of text and inserting the copy at another place in the document. The general steps in performing a cut and paste are as follows:

1. Identify the text to be cut.
2. Cut (remove) the identified text from the document but retain it in a temporary memory area (called the *cut save area*).

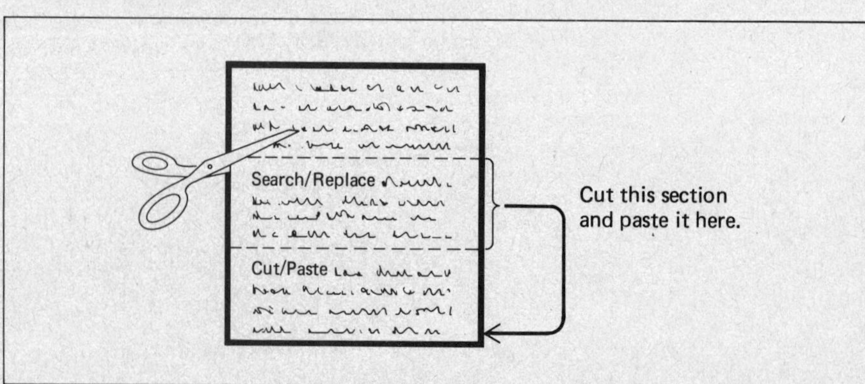

Figure 3-10
The concept of cut and paste.

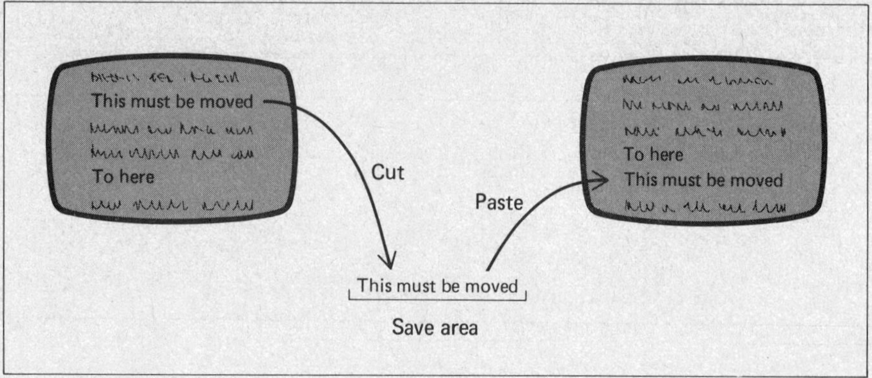

Figure 3-11
Using the save area to cut and paste.

3. Move the cursor to the location at which the cut text is to be inserted.
4. Insert the text currently held in the cut save area into the document at the position of the cursor.

The overall process is illustrated in Figure 3-11. In WordPerfect, this is done with various options of the Move command (Ctrl-F4). Let us try this.

Operating on a Block of Text

For an example of cutting and pasting, you may continue with the document CONTRACT.WP1 that you used in the preceding example for search and replace. Assume that you wish to move the DRESS CODE paragraph to precede the OPTION paragraph, as shown in Figure 3-12. The following steps perform the cut and paste by defining a block of text to be moved.

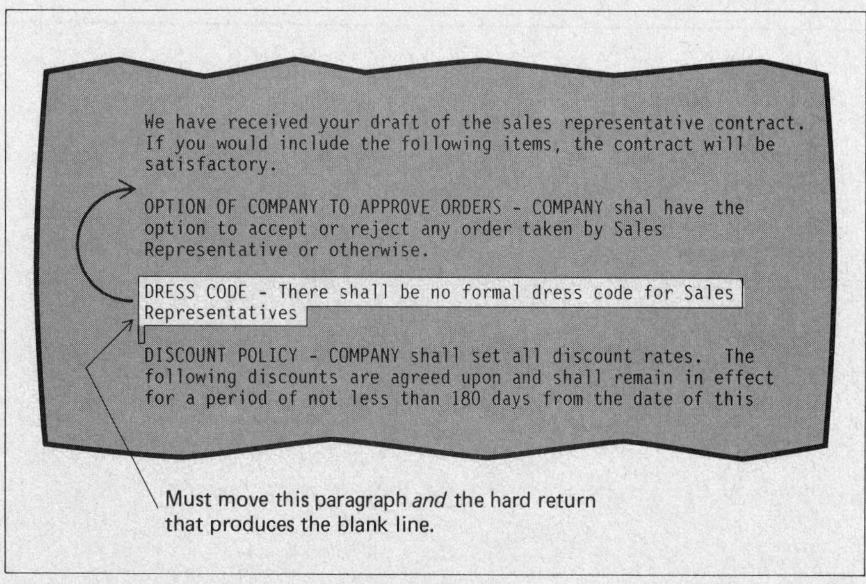

Figure 3-12
A section of text to be cut and pasted.

DO THIS NOW 3-17 **Using Cut and Paste**

1. Position the cursor at the first character of the text to be moved, in this case, under the letter *D* in *DRESS* (see Figure 3-12).
2. Begin blocking with the Alt-F4 key sequence.
3. Extend the block by moving the cursor down until the entire paragraph is highlighted. If you move the cursor to the letter *D* in *DISCOUNT* of the following paragraph, your block will include the hard return that produces the blank line following the desired paragraph.
4. Invoke the Move command with Ctrl-F4. This produces the status line selection menu shown in Figure 3-13.

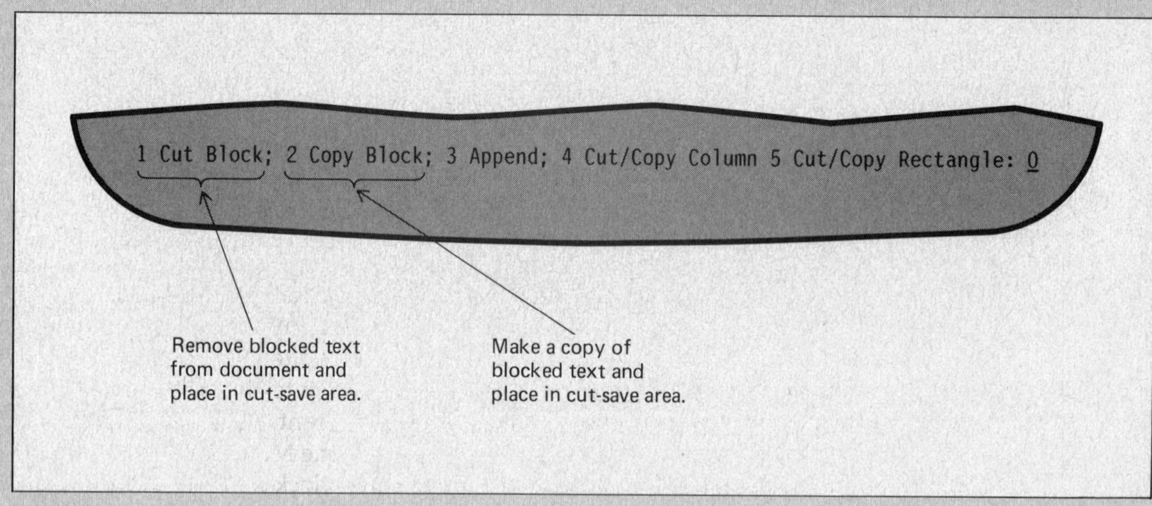

Figure 3-13

5. Options 1 and 2 both cause a copy of the blocked text to be placed in the cut save area of memory. Option 1 erases the block from the document, and option 2 leaves it unchanged. For this example, since you want to cut the block, strike the digit 1 key.
6. Move the cursor to the position to which the cut text is to be inserted; that is, its position is on the letter *O* in *OPTION* (see Figure 3-12).
7. Issue another Move command (Ctrl-F4); the status line prompt will be as shown in Figure 3-14.

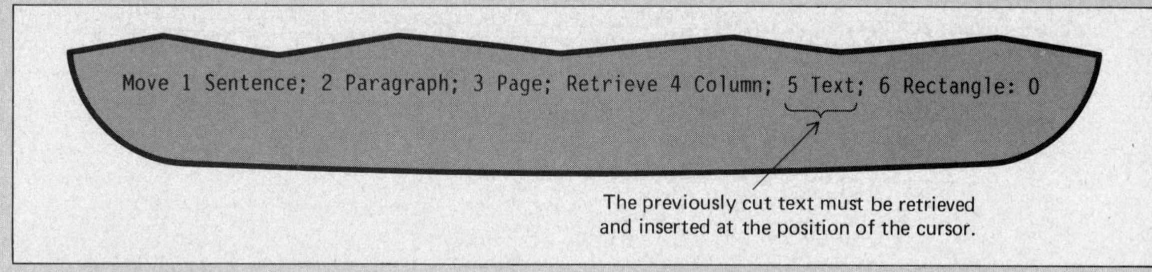

Figure 3-14
The two-window concept.

Notice that selections 1 through 3 pertain to the Move action and 4 through 6 pertain to the Retrieve action.

8. To insert the text at the point of the cursor, you need the Retrieve Text action; for this, type the digit 5. The text stored in the save area of memory is retrieved and inserted preceding the OPTIONS paragraph, thus completing the cut-and-paste action.

Operating on a Sentence, Paragraph, or Page

The cut-and-paste sequence for blocked text that you used in the preceding example allows you to operate on a block of any size, from a few words to many pages. However, if you need to operate on a full sentence, paragraph, or page, then you need not block the text. You have already seen that the Move command produces two different selection menus. That is, if you blocked an area of text before issuing the Move, the selection menu is as shown in Figure 3-13. If you did not block an area of text, then the selection menu is as shown in Figure 3-14. Thus, to perform the cut-and-paste operation of this example, you could have positioned the cursor anywhere in the paragraph that is to be moved. Then the Move command would have produced the menu of Figure 3-14. Striking the 2 key for Paragraph would produce a prompt asking if you want to Cut, Copy, or Delete. The Cut-and-Copy options are the same as previously described. The Delete option really is not a Move action at all. It simply deletes the text indicated from the document and permanently discards it (without placing a copy in the cut save area).

With regard to the cut save area of memory, whenever text is cut or copied, it is placed in this special area of memory. This area will always contain the text that was cut or copied with the last execution of the Move command. However, each cut or copy action causes the previous contents of the area to be replaced by the latest cut or copied text. Note that this save area is used only by the cut or copy action; text deleted with the Backspace and Del keys is not saved here.

The cut-and-paste sequence for blocked text that you used in the preceding example allows you to operate on a block of any size, from a few words to many pages. However, if you need to operate on a full sentence, paragraph, or page, then you need not block the text. You have already seen that the Move command produces two different selection menus. That is, if you blocked an area of text before issuing the Move, the selection menu is as shown in Figure 3-13. If you did not block an area of text, then the selection menu is as shown in Figure 3-14. Thus, to perform the cut-and-paste operation of this example, you could have positioned the cursor anywhere in the paragraph that is to be moved. Then the Move command would have produced the menu of Figure 3-14. Striking the 2 key for Paragraph would produce a prompt asking if you want to Cut, Copy, or Delete. The Cut-and-Copy options are the same as previously described. The Delete option really is not a Move action at all. It simply deletes the text indicated from the document and permanently discards it (without placing a copy in the cut save area).

With regard to the cut save area of memory, whenever text is cut or copied, it is placed in this special area of memory. This area will always contain the text that was cut or copied with the last execution of the Move command. However, each cut or copy action causes the previous contents of the area to be replaced by the latest cut or copied text. Note that this save area is used only by the cut or copy action; text deleted with the Backspace and Del keys is not saved here.

WORKING WITH TWO DOCUMENTS

Word processing was introduced to you via the letter to the attorney (see Figures P2-1 and P2-2) of the introduction to word processing. In fact, the handwritten original included directions to the typist to copy the three contractual items from another document: in word processing terminology, a cut-and-paste operation. However, this cut-and-paste operation is different from that of the preceding example in that it requires that text from one document be copied into another. Let us see how this can be done with WordPerfect.

Creating and Using Two Windows

To facilitate working with two documents, WordPerfect allows you to split the screen into two independent document screen areas or windows, as illustrated in Figure 3-15. Notice that WordPerfect splits the memory into two separate document areas so that each can function completely independently of the other. Before trying this, you should clear the screen with the Exit command and then carry out the sequence of DTN 3-18.

Figure 3-15
The two-window concept.

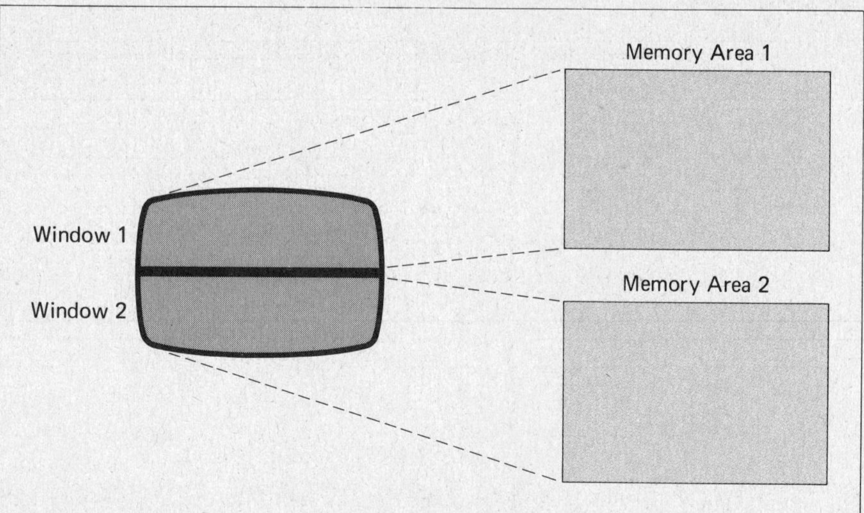

DO THIS NOW 3-18 **Creating Two Windows**

1. Enter the Screen command (Ctrl-F3), which produces the status line message:

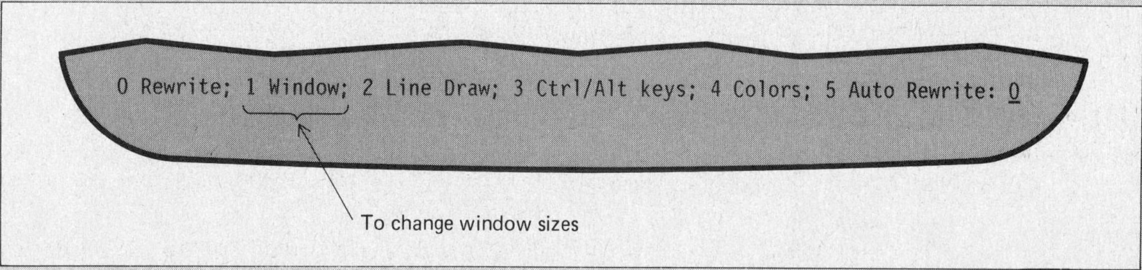

2. Select the Window option by typing the digit 1. WordPerfect then asks you how many screen lines you wish to devote to window 1 with the following prompt.

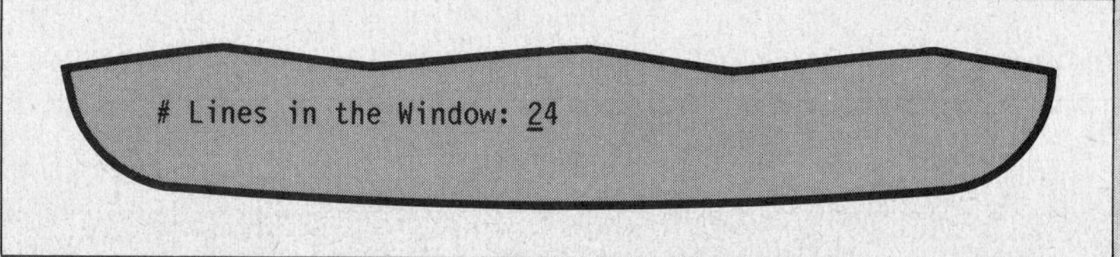

3. The smallest allowable window size is 2; the default of 24 results in a single window. For this exercise, enter 14 and strike the Enter. Your screen will then appear as in Figure 3-16.

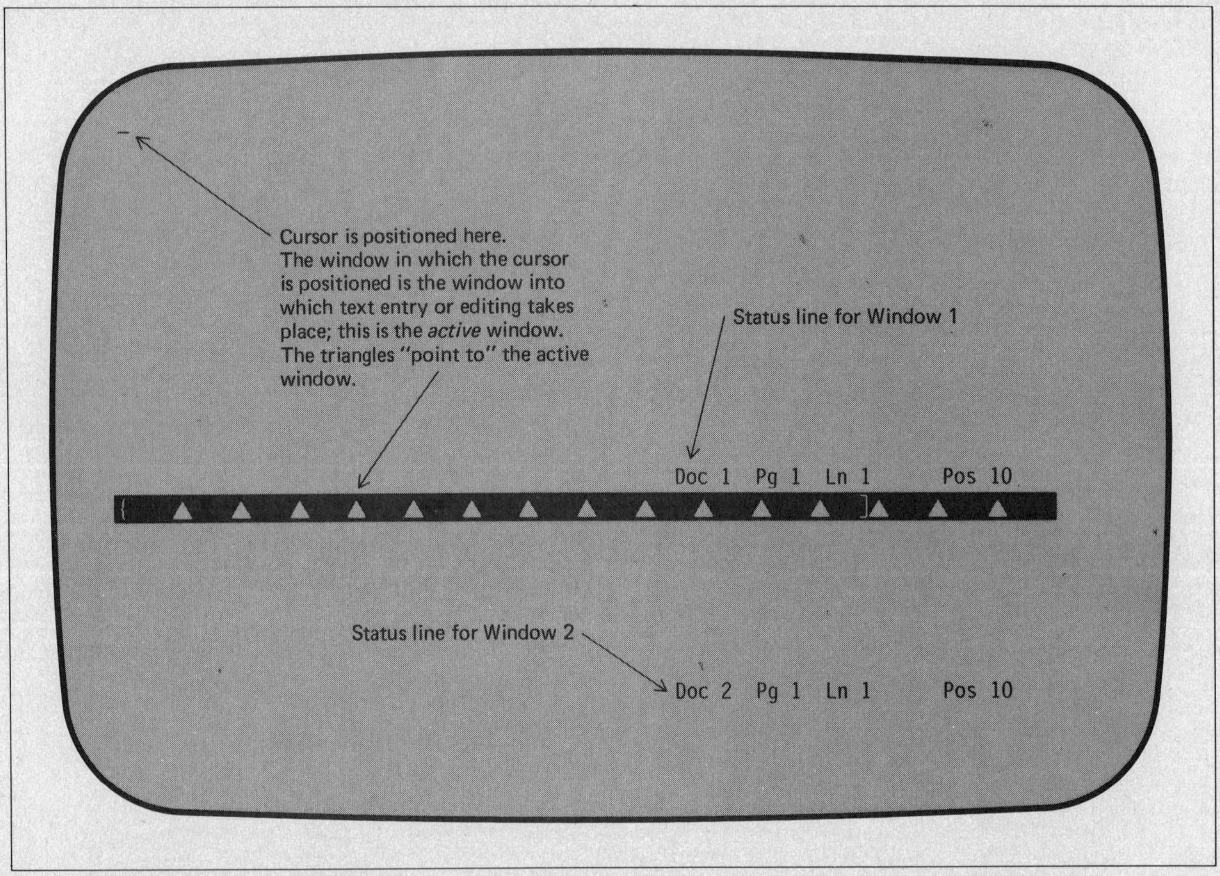

Cursor is positioned here.
The window in which the cursor is positioned is the window into which text entry or editing takes place; this is the *active* window.
The triangles "point to" the active window.

Status line for Window 1

Doc 1 Pg 1 Ln 1 Pos 10

Status line for Window 2

Doc 2 Pg 1 Ln 1 Pos 10

Figure 3-16
A two-window screen.

The two windows in Figure 3-16 are divided by the tab ruler. Note that each window includes its own status line. Initially, the upper window will be the active window and the cursor will be positioned in it. You can switch from one window to the next with the Switch command (Shift-F3). Try it. You will notice that you can tell at a glance which window is active by looking at the tab ruler. If the upper window (document 1) is active, the small triangles in the ruler point upward, as in Figure 3-16. If the lower window (document 2) is active, the small triangles point downward, as in Figure 3-16.

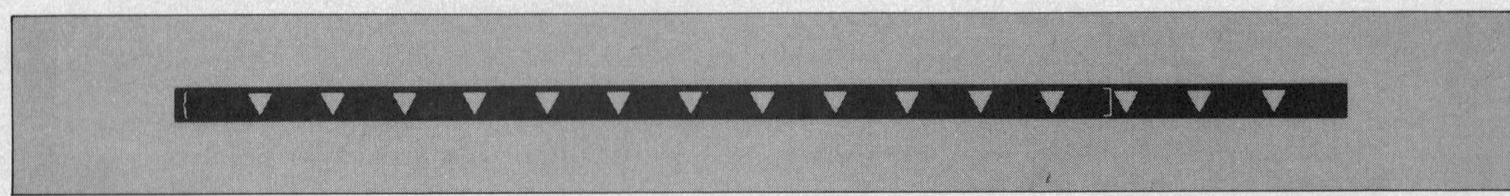

Figure 3-17
Tab ruler when window 2 is active.

Copying from One Document to Another

For this example, the data disk that accompanies this book contains two files: SKELETON.WP, which is the skeleton of the letter to the attorney (Figure P2-2) of the introduction to word processing; and LEGAL.WP1, which contains the legal items to be included in the letter. Before beginning, you should check to ensure that they are on the data disk currently in your computer. To retrieve these documents, carry out the following sequence (your screen should already display two windows, as shown in Figure 3-16).

DO THIS NOW 3-19 **Retrieving Two Documents**

1. If window 1 is not the active window, then change to it with the Switch command (Shift-F3).
2. Retrieve the document SKELETON.WP (Shift-F10). The skeleton of the letter will be displayed in the upper screen.
3. Switch to the lower window with the Switch command (Shift-F3).
4. Retrieve the document LEGAL.WP1. Your screen will now appear as shown in Figure 3-18. Notice that the status lines clearly identify each document.

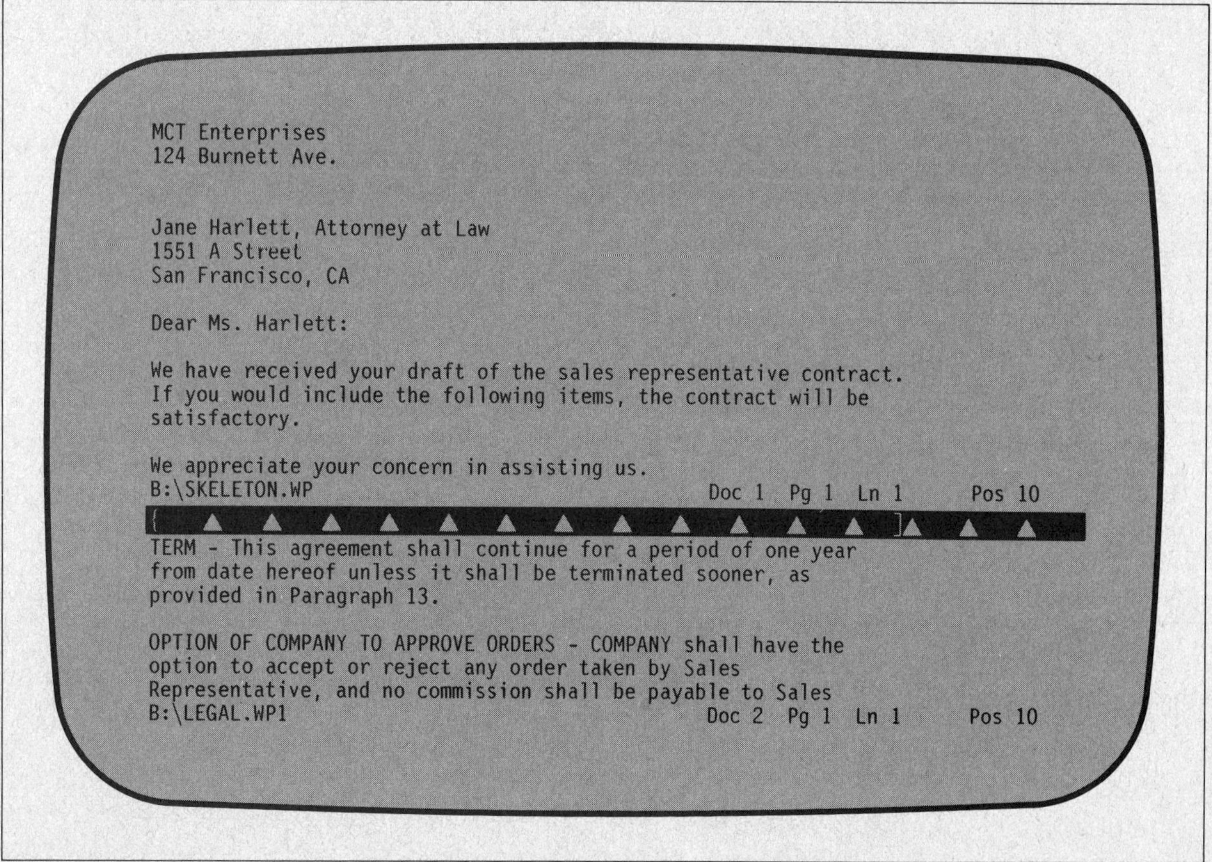

Figure 3-18
Two document display.

If you scroll the lower window, you will see that this document contains five items. You need to copy the second (OPTION OF COMPANY . . .), the fourth (DISCOUNT POLICY), and the fifth (TERMINATION) into the letter in the upper window with the following sequence of actions.

DO THIS NOW 3-20 **Copying from One Document to Another**

1. With the lower screen active, block the first item to be copied as follows:

   Position cursor under the letter *O* of *OPTION*.

   Enter the Block command (Shift-F3).

   Move the cursor to the letter *N* in *NOTICE* (of the next item).

2. Enter the Move command (Ctrl-F4); then select the Copy Block option (strike the digit 2). The highlight on the screen will disappear. The text will remain unchanged but a copy is now in the cut save area.
3. Switch to the upper window (Shift-F3) and move the cursor to the point at which the text in the cut save area is to be inserted (to the letter *W* in *We appreciate*).
4. Enter the Move command (Ctrl-F4); then select the Retrieve Text option (strike the digit 5). The text from the cut save area will be inserted into the letter. You may wish to scroll the screen to see that it is indeed in place.
5. To copy the other two items, switch to the lower screen and repeat the process. Since the last two items you need to copy are adjacent in document 2, you can begin the block with the letter *D* in *DISCOUNT*, and move it down to encompass the entire TERMINATION item. Then repeat steps 2 through 4.

Sometimes, when working with two windows, it becomes desirable to close one of the windows in order to devote the full screen to the document in the other window. For example, if after working with the two windows of Figure 3-18 you decided to devote the entire screen to the letter, you would carry out the following actions.

DO THIS NOW 3-21 **Closing a Window**

1. Switch to memory area 1 (the window that is to remain open).
2. Enter the Screen command (Ctrl-F3).
3. In response to the number of lines query, enter 24 and strike the Enter.

All twenty-four lines of the screen will then be devoted to document 1 and none to document 2. However, document 2 is still in memory and you can switch to it with the Switch command (Shift-F3), or reopen that window with the Screen command.

After you have finished working with two documents and decide to exit, you should be aware that WordPerfect will require that you issue the Exit twice, once for each document, before terminating processing.

THE WORDPERFECT SPELLER AND THESAURUS

There are two other useful tools found in most word processors: the spelling checker and the thesaurus. When invoked, a spelling checker checks spelling in all or part of your document against a dictionary stored on disk. With a thesaurus, you can request that a list of alternative words for a word in your document (these are called synonyms) be displayed from a thesaurus file on disk. However, these components of the Limited-Use version have access to a relatively few words. (The files for the full spelling checker and the thesaurus are very large.) Because of the restriction, the speller and thesaurus in the Limited-Use software are adequate only for you to learn how to use them.

Checking Spelling

The data disk accompanying this book includes a short document named SPELL.WPC that consists only of words in the abbreviated dictionary. This document, which is shown in Figure 3-19, is used here to illustrate principles of the WordPerfect Speller. In the illustration, spelling errors have been highlighted for convenient reference.

After clearing your screen, retrieve the document SPELL.WPC and then enter the Spell command Ctrl-F2. The first three options of the prompt on the status line allow you to check a single word, a page, or the entire document. Press the 2 key to select the document. WordPerfect will then begin checking word by word. Upon encountering the word *theese*

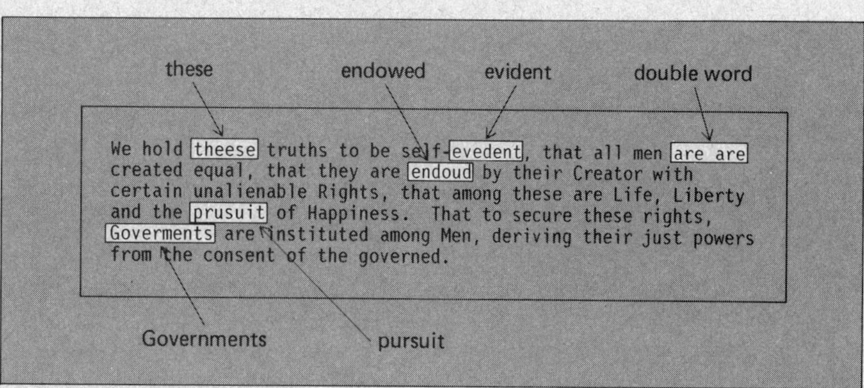

Figure 3-19
Document with spelling errors.

(see Figure 3-19), it will be highlighted and the message *Not Found!* displayed at the bottom of the screen, indicating that this word was not found in the dictionary. Just below the double line is a list of possible correct spellings for the word. Although only one word is offered in this example, there will commonly be several different possibilities, listed as alternative A, B, C, and so on. To select one of the alternatives, enter the letter that identifies it; in this case, type the letter *A*. The incorrectly spelled word will immediately be replaced with the selected alternative. The meanings of the menu selections 1 through 4 are as follows.

1 Skip only this occurrence of the word and leave it unchanged. However, if the same word is encountered again in the document, show it as misspelled.

2 Skip this word and all other occurrences of it, leaving it unchanged throughout the document.

3 Add this word to the Speller dictionary. Then it will become a regular part of the Speller dictionary on your disk and will not be marked as unrecognized in the future.

4 Type a replacement word from the keyboard.

As you respond to each misspelled word, WordPerfect searches for the next one; each should be handled in the same way. The third error that WordPerfect will detect is the double occurrence of *are* (see Figure 3-16). Entering the digit 3 causes the second occurrence to be deleted. After completing the spelling check, WordPerfect indicates how many words were checked. Strike the F1 key to return to the edit screen.

Using the Thesaurus

Assume that last week the manager of Slick Promotions presented a plan to your partner for advertising a new MCT product line. Your partner was impressed with some of the ideas but had reservations and so requested that you meet with Slick Promotions officials. After the meeting, you summed up your reactions in the memo of Figure 3-20 (it is stored as

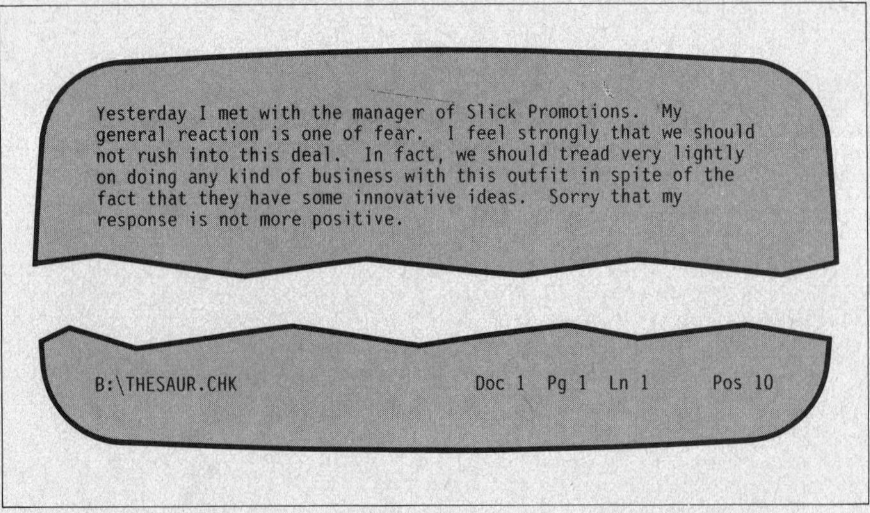

Figure 3-20
A memo expressing concern.

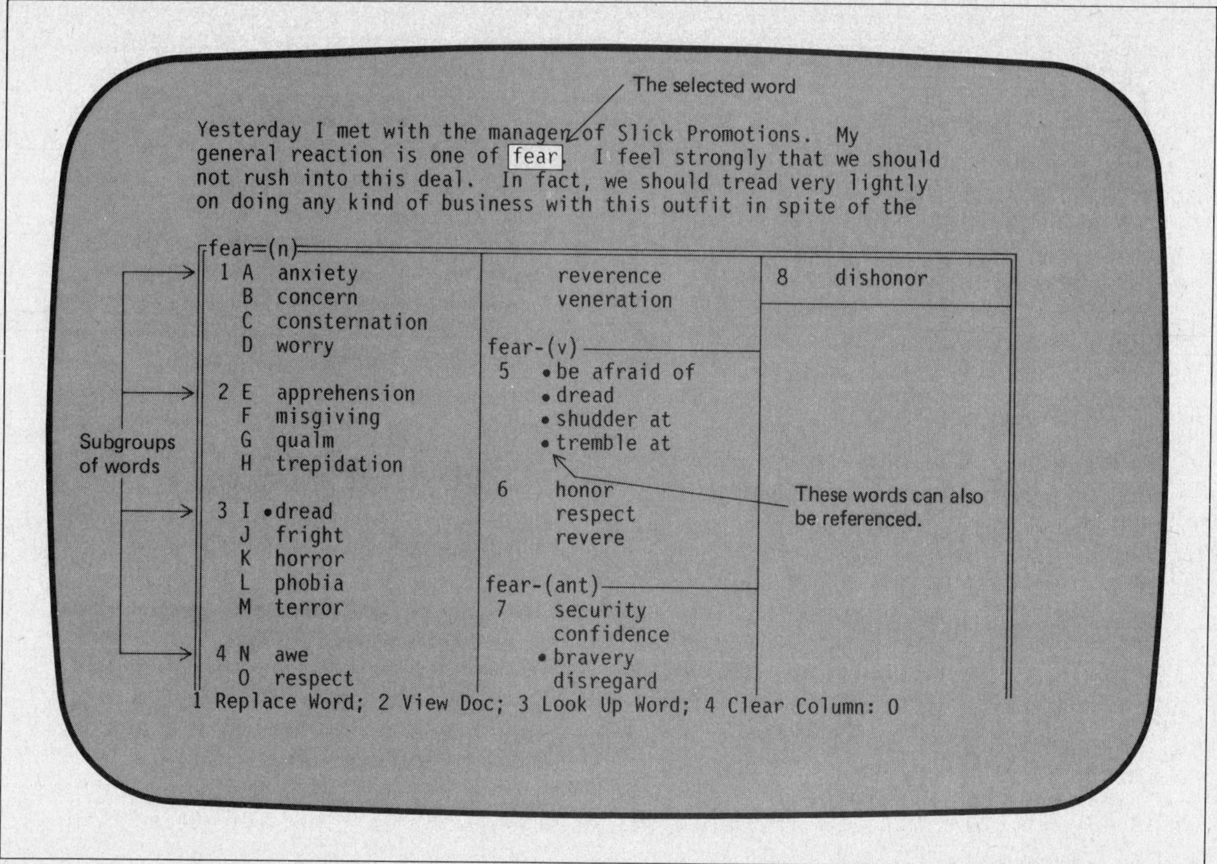

Figure 3-21
The Thesaurus display.

THESAUR.WPC on the data disk accompanying this book). Upon reading it over, you were not completely happy with the word *fear* so you decided to check the thesaurus.

To try this yourself, first clear the screen and then retrieve THESAUR.WPC. Next, position the cursor anywhere in the word *fear* and issue the thesaurus command Alt-F1. The resulting screen will be as shown in Figure 3-21. Here, four lines of the document remain at the top of the screen and groups of reference words occupy the rest of the screen. The selected word from the text, the one being referenced, is highlighted. Any word that can be found in the thesaurus is called a *headword*. The reference words in the lower portion of the screen are divided into four categories: nouns, adjectives (there are no adjectives for the word *fear* in this screen), verbs, and antonyms. (An antonym is a word that means the opposite of the selected word.) The numbered groups 1, 2, 3, . . . are groups of words with the same general connotation. Words that are preceded by a dot are also headwords, meaning that they can be found in the thesaurus.

For this example, assume that you decide to replace *fear* with *concern*. To do this, type the digit 1 (Replace Word selection), and the program will ask you which word is to be used as the replacement. Strike the letter B for *concern,* and the replacement will be made. WordPerfect will then return to the edit screen. If you are interested in reference words for one of the other headwords—for example, dread—type the digit 3 and respond to the prompt with the letter I.

Assignment 3-3 may now be completed.

SUMMARY

This chapter has built on the basic concepts you learned in Chapter 2. Summarizing, the important items from the chapter are:

- The general formatting actions described in this chapter include the following.

  Margin setting

  Line centering

  Paragraph indention

  Double spacing

  Disabling and enabling right justification

  Underscoring

  Boldfacing

- WordPerfect formatting commands produce hidden codes inserted into the document. The Reveal Codes command is used to display hidden codes within a document.
- Different formatting commands affect different amounts of text. For instance, if the margins are set at one point in a document, they remain at that setting until you insert another margin-setting code. On the other hand, centering affects only a single line.
- You can locate a portion of text with the Search command. The search operation is conducted from the location of the cursor and can be toward either the beginning of the document or the end.
- You can replace a word or phrase anywhere in the document with another word or phrase using the Search and Replace command. The replacement can be automatic for all occurrences or you can monitor each potential replacement.

- With the Move command, you can delete, cut, or copy a sentence, paragraph, or page. If you cut or copy, the text is saved in the cut-and-save area, from which it can be inserted at any point in the document.
- WordPerfect includes two memory areas, which allows for two independent documents to be in memory concurrently. You can switch from one document to the other with the Switch command. Documents in the two memory areas can be viewed at the same time by splitting the screen with the Screen command.
- Using the Block command, you can identify a portion of text ranging in size from one character to the entire document.
- The Speller can check the spelling of all words in a single paragraph or page, or in the entire document. If a word is determined to be misspelled, you have the option to select one of the words from a list of displayed alternatives, type in a correction, request WordPerfect to leave the word unchanged, or add the word to the dictionary.
- Invoking the thesaurus causes WordPerfect to display a list of synonyms for the word at the position of the cursor.

COMMAND AND FUNCTION SUMMARY

Following is a summary of the various commands and operations described in this chapter.

Command	Key or Keys	Action
Formatting		
Boldface	F6	Makes text boldface.
Center	Shift-F6	Centers a line between the margins.
Flush right	Alt-F6	Positions a line against the right margin.
Indent left	F4	Indents a paragraph one tab stop from the left margin.
Indent left/right	Shift-F4	Indents a paragraph one tab stop from both the left and right margins.
Justification	Ctrl-F8	Produces a selection menu. Allows right justification to be turned on or off.
Line spacing	Shift-F8	Produces a selection menu. Allows line spacing to be changed.
Margin set	Shift-F8	Produces a selection menu. Allows the left and right margins to be set.
Underline	F8	Underlines text.

Command	Key or Keys	Action
Other Commands		
Block	Alt-F4	Starts or ends the definition of a block.
Cut (Move)	Ctrl-F4	Produces a selection menu. Allows a sentence, paragraph, or page to be deleted, cut, or copied.
Replace	Alt-F2	Replaces occurrences of a user-designated search text with a user-designated replacement text.
Reveal codes	Alt-F3	Displays the text together with hidden codes.
Screen	Ctrl-F3	Produces a selection menu. Allows the screen to be split into two windows.
Search forward	F2	Searches from the location of the cursor to the end of the document for the occurrence of a specified search text.
Search reverse	Shift-F2	Same as Search forward except searches toward beginning of document.
Spell	Ctrl-F2	Invokes the Speller to check spelling.
Switch case	Shift-F3	Changes all letters in a block to uppercase or lowercase.
Switch documents	Shift-F3	Toggles between the documents in memory area 1 and memory area 2.
Thesaurus	Alt-F1	Invokes the thesaurus to find a synonym for a selected word.

NEW TERMINOLOGY

The following are important new terms introduced in this chapter; you should be familiar with each of them.

block
flush right
hanging paragraph
hidden code
indent
search string

Name: ____________________ Date: ____________

Assignment 3-1

1. What does each of the following key sequences cause?
   (a) Shift-F4

   (b) Shift-F6

   (c) Alt-F6

   (d) Shift-F8

   (e) F6

   (f) F8

2. What is the difference between the actions of the F4 and the Shift-F4?

Name: ______________________ Date: ______________

Assignment 3-1 (*continued*)

3. What is the minimum size of a block? What is the maximum size of a block?

4. The cursor is moved to the beginning of the first line of a paragraph and the Block command (Alt-F4) is entered. How much text is blocked by entering each of the following?
   (a) Ctrl-Right

   (b) Down,Down

   (c) Up

   (d) End

Name: ______________________ Date: __________

Assignment 3-1 *(continued)*

5. Over how much of the document do each of the following format commands operate?
   (a) Center

   (b) Indent left and right

   (c) Set margins

Name: ______________________ Date: ______________

Assignment 3-2

1. In the lower portion of the screen of Figure 3-6(b) the cursor is displayed to the left of the hidden code [C]. What do you think would happen if you struck the Del key?

2. In centering the first heading line of Figure 3-1, assume that the cursor was positioned on the letter *C* of *Center* when you entered the Center command. What do you think would happen?

3. Assume that you have just brought WordPerfect up with an empty screen so that you can enter a document. The first thing you do is to set the margins to 15 and 69, which you will use for the entire document. After entering part of your text, you decide that you want the margins at 10 and 74, so you position the cursor at the beginning of the document and enter these new settings. What margin codes will now exist in your document?

Name: ______________________________ Date: ______________

Assignment 3-3

1. Is it possible to set up a document so that the entire document prints unjustified except for one paragraph, which is to be printed justified? Explain your answer.

2. When performing a search, which is the better to use, a backward search or a forward search?

3. In doing replace operation you have entered the hyphen character (-) as the search string and entered nothing for replacement string. What do you think will happen?

Name: ______________________ Date: ______________

Assignment 3-3 *(continued)*

4. You have decided to compose a letter and at the same time to make some notes about the letter. For this, you use window 1 for the letter and window 2 for the notes. After completing your notes you decide to close the second window to have the full screen for the letter. However, you forget to save the notes as a file before closing the window. Have you lost the notes because of this action? Explain your answer.

5. In running a spelling check on a document, an abbreviation is displayed as not found. What action should you take?

Name: ______________________ Date: ______________

OBJECTIVE QUESTIONS

Matching

The descriptions in 1 through 8 describe an activity requiring that one or more commands be invoked. Designate the first key sequence action to take by matching these actions with the key sequences in a through h.

a. F2
b. Ctrl-F3
c. Alt-F3
d. F4
e. Alt-F4
f. Ctrl-F8
g. Shift-F8
h. Alt-F6

____ **1.** Set the margins to 20 and 60.

____ **2.** Indent a paragraph from the left margin only.

____ **3.** Figure out why the document is not displayed on the screen as it should be.

____ **4.** Find a misspelled word somewhere in a document.

____ **5.** Position a line so that it is against the right margin.

____ **6.** Identify a portion of text that is to be set to boldface.

____ **7.** Work with two documents.

____ **8.** Obtain printed output that is not justified.

True/False

Circle either T or F to indicate whether the answer is True or False.

T F **1.** Once margins are set they cannot be changed.

T F **2.** The Margin Set and Indent commands work the same in that they both affect all text that follows until another Margin Set or Indent command is entered.

T F **3.** The Center command cannot be used to center an entire paragraph.

T F **4.** The flush right command causes text to be aligned on the right.

T F **5.** Each successive indent command causes indention to the next tab stop.

T F **6.** A paragraph can be indented from the left only or from both the left and the right.

T F **7.** The Block command must be used to enter text into a document that is to be underlined.

T F **8.** Formatting codes cannot be stored with the document; that is, when a document is stored, all formatting codes are lost.

Name: ______________________________ Date: ______________

OBJECTIVE QUESTIONS (*continued*)

T F **9.** Hidden codes can be displayed by opening a second window with the Screen command.

T F **10.** Hidden codes can be deleted when working from the edit screen.

T F **11.** If you are formatting as you are entering text and you enter an Indent command, then all paragraphs that follow will be indented until you change the indent back to the default.

T F **12.** Some of the formatting codes cannot be entered after the document has been typed; they must be entered as the text is being entered.

T F **13.** Formatting commands must be entered as the text is being entered; it is not possible to go back and add them later.

T F **14.** To disable right justification, you must go through the document and erase all of the extra spaces inserted by WordPerfect in filling each line.

T F **15.** The appearance of the document on the screen is not changed if you disable justification.

T F **16.** Once a document has been converted to double spacing, it cannot be converted back to single spacing.

T F **17.** WordPerfect provides for triple spacing as well as double spacing.

T F **18.** Since the Indent command acts on a paragraph, you must be certain to position the cursor at the first position of the paragraph before entering the Indent command.

T F **19.** A hanging paragraph is one in which the entire paragraph, with the exception of the first line, is indented both from the left and the right.

T F **20.** In a Search command, if the search string is lowercase, then WordPerfect ignores case in performing the search. However, if the search string is uppercase, WordPerfect will search only for a corresponding uppercase occurrence.

T F **21.** A searching action always starts at the position of the cursor and either searches toward the beginning or the ending of the document depending on which of the two Search commands was selected.

T F **22.** You must not have any blank characters in the search string of the Search command.

T F **23.** When doing a search and replace, you can have WordPerfect perform all replacements automatically, or you can check and approve each replacement.

T F **24.** Before performing any cut-and-paste operation, the text to be moved must first be blocked.

T F **25.** The exact option menu from the Move command depends on the action that was taken before the Move command was executed.

T F **26.** The cut save area holds the text cut from the last three cuts that were performed. This is similar to the way in which deleted text is held in memory.

Name: ______________________________ Date: ______________

OBJECTIVE QUESTIONS (*continued*)

T F **27.** The primary purpose of using two windows is to be able to view two different portions of the same document at the same time.

T F **28.** When two windows are open, each will display its own status line.

T F **29.** A spelling checker will identify misspelled words such as using the word *there* instead of *their*.

T F **30.** You would use a thesaurus to find a synonym for a word you are not completely happy with.

Multiple Choice

In the space provided, record the letter of the choice that best completes or answers the statement.

____ **1.** If you enter a set margin command, that command applies to all text

A. in the entire document.
B. from the point of the command to the end of the document.
C. from the point of the command until another margin command is encountered.
D. in the current paragraph and no other text.

____ **2.** If you accidentally forget to position the cursor at the beginning of a line and you enter a flush right command,

A. WordPerfect will ignore the command.
B. the line will be positioned flush right correctly regardless of cursor position.
C. an error message will be displayed.
D. the line probably will not be positioned properly.

____ **3.** The amount of text over which an Indent command acts is

A. everything from the cursor to the next indent command.
B. the current paragraph.
C. the current line only.
D. the text that was blocked when the command was issued.

____ **4.** A left indent is performed with the ______ key sequence.

A. F4
B. Shift-F4
C. Ctrl-F4
D. Alt-F4

Name: ______________________________ Date: ______________

OBJECTIVE QUESTIONS (*continued*)

____ **5.** The key sequence

Alt-F4, {Right arrow 10 times}, F6

will cause

A. 10 characters to be made boldface.
B. 11 characters to be made boldface.
C. 10 characters to be underscored.
D. 11 characters to be underscored.

____ **6.** Hidden codes can be displayed on the screen

A. by using two windows.
B. with the Reveal Codes command.
C. by formatting the document.
D. Hidden codes cannot be displayed.

____ **7.** Some commands such as the Boldface cause a pair of codes to be entered, one at the start and the other at the end of the text to be displayed in boldface. If only one of these is deleted, then

A. WordPerfect will automatically delete the other.
B. the other will remain but WordPerfect will ignore it.
C. the other will pair up with another command, thus producing an error situation.
D. WordPerfect will flash an error message.

____ **8.** Of the following commands, which acts only on a single paragraph?

A. Boldface
B. Margin Set
C. Search
D. Indent

____ **9.** Text that is aligned only on the right is called

A. justified.
B. flush right.
C. indented.
D. unjustified.

____ **10.** With a hanging paragraph, the entire paragraph is indented

A. but the first line is not indented.
B. but the first line is indented one tab stop further.
C. only where the paragraph is split across two pages.
D. only where the paragraph is not split across two pages.

____ **11.** The search string of a Search command is Gold. Which of the following would NOT be found in a search?

A. Golden
B. GOLD
C. gold
D. All of the above would be found by this command.

Name: ______________________ Date: ______________

OBJECTIVE QUESTIONS (*continued*)

____ 12. Which of the following is NOT true regarding cutting and pasting with WordPerfect?

A. The cut-and-paste operation can be used to either move a section of text or copy it.
B. Text cannot be cut from one document and inserted into another.
C. The amount of text to be involved in a cut-and-paste sequence can be as much or as little as the user desires.
D. All of the above are true.

____ 13. If you are working with two documents (using two windows) and you close one of the windows without first saving the document in that window, which of the following will happen?

A. WordPerfect will automatically save the document.
B. The document will be lost.
C. WordPerfect will not allow you to close the window without first saving the document.
D. None of the above will occur.

Fill In

In the space provided, fill in the correct answer. Note that the answer can be one or two words.

1. ______________________
After entering a document, you decide to underscore a word. The first thing you would do is use the _____ command to designate the text to be underscored.

2. ______________________
Using the Indent command causes a _____ to be inserted into the text.

3. ______________________
A _____ paragraph is one in which the entire paragraph, with the exception of the first line, is indented.

4. ______________________
To find a misspelled word in a document, you could use the _____ command.

5. ______________________
If you needed to change the spelling of a misspelled word in several different places of a document, you could use the _____ command.

6. ______________________
The _____ and _____ feature of WordPerfect allows you to move text from one place in a document to another.

7. ______________________
If you were copying text from one document to another, you would probably be using two _____.

8. ______________________
A _____ allows you to display alternate words (synonyms) for a selected word.

ASSIGNMENTS/PROJECTS

1. The following document is to be entered into the computer using WordPerfect. Entries enclosed within angle brackets are to be replaced with information as described within the brackets. For instance, <YOUR STREET ADDRESS> should be replaced with your address. Use margins of 12 and 73. Note that the return address is flush right. Disable right justification. When finished, save it to disk and print a copy on the printer.

```
                                              <YOUR STREET ADDRESS>
                                                 <CITY, STATE, ZIP>
                                                             <DATE>

Jim Marconi
American Association for Improvement
5 Pacific Circle
Washington, DC  20036

Dear Jim:

Included is the consulting bill for the month of February; note
that I am including my time and telephone expenses.  Please have
these paid separately.  I am relieved that we were able to repair
the problems that resulted from what I sense as a system failure.
I suggest that you have the maintenance engineer do extended
checks on the disk drive.

Date     Activity                             Hours
----     --------                             -----
2/1-2/3  Modification to accounting system     7.0
         1. Modify edit to handle comps
         2. Modify the save record response
         3. Check for duplicate invoices
         4. Modify billing form
2/4      Modify nametag program                6.0
2/7      Diagnose apparent file corruption     2.0
2/11     Diagnose system failure               2.0
2/12     Repair corrupted files from failure   6.0
                                              ----
         TOTAL                                23.0

                         23.0 hours @ $50/hour              $1150.00


2/11,12  Telephone                             8.0


                AT&T weekend rate: $8.65/hour 8 hours        $69.20

Thank you for your assistance.

Sincerely yours,



<YOUR NAME>
```

2. You are to type two sections from this book (Disabling Right Justification and Hanging Paragraphs, pages 153 and 154). Format your copy so that its appearance is as much like that of the text as you can achieve. For text that is printed in italics, use the underscore. When finished, save it to disk and print a copy.

3. Copying text from one document to another is illustrated (DTN 3-20) by copying items from the document LEGAL.WP1 into the letter SKELETON.WP. For this assignment you will do the same thing except that you will be obtaining items from the document LEGAL.WP2 (stored on the data disk). The items that you must copy into the letter (and the order in which they must be inserted) are:

   INTENT

   EXCLUSIONS

   TERRITORY

   ARBITRATION

   PROCEDURE ON TERMINATION

   In addition, you must use boldface for each of these titles, and use hanging paragraphs for the separate elements defined as a, b, c, and d in the PROCEDURE item. When you are finished, save the letter to disk and print a copy.

4. In Chapter 2, you prepared a résumé and saved it as RESUME.WP. You are to retrieve that document and modify it so that it appears as follows. The changes that you are to make are:

   1. Center the title lines.
   2. Underscore as shown.
   3. Add the job description to each of the job entries.
   4. Indent from the left all items under the headings *Vital Statistics*, *Employment*, and *Special Interests or Hobbies*. After the indention, use a hanging paragraph for each of the numbered items. To do this, first enter a left indent command, type the item number, then do another left indent.

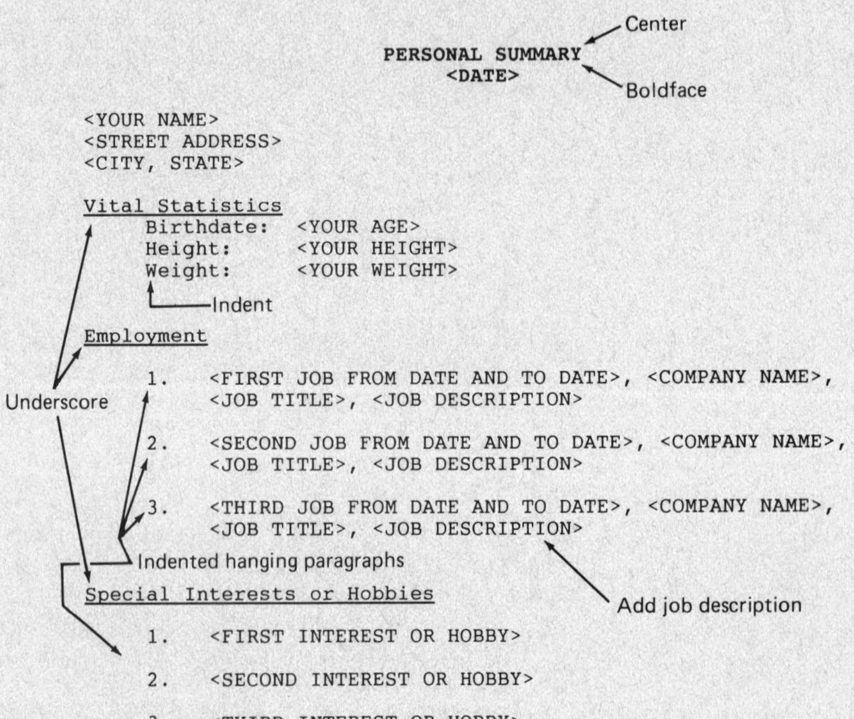

5. In Chapter 2, you created the document USEEXIT.WP. You are to retrieve that document and modify it so that it appears as follows. The changes that you are to make are:

1. Center the title lines.
2. Underscore the word Exit in the first line of the text.
3. Make the editing changes shown in the first paragraph and break the two conditions out as *a* and *b*. Use hanging paragraphs on them.
4. Disable right justification after the first paragraph.
5. Use boldface for the filename.
6. Break the Exit description into two parts as shown using hanging paragraphs for the Roman numerals I and II.
7. For the detailed sequences of steps, use hanging paragraphs which have first been indented from the left. To do this, first enter a left indent command, type the item number, then do another left indent.

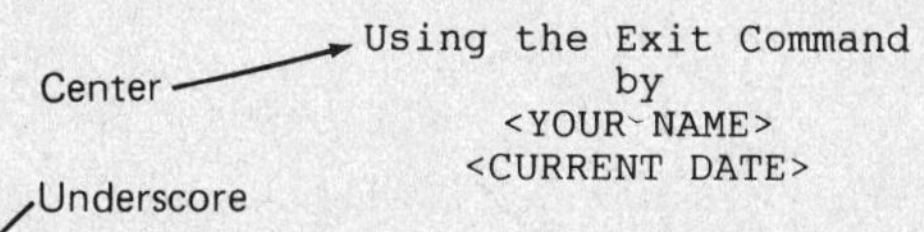

The <u>Exit</u> command is used for more than simply terminating execution of WordPerfect. If your document has not already been saved, Exit prompts you to save it. Then you can terminate, or you can direct WordPerfect to clear the current document so that you can enter another. For this example, assume that the conditions are as follows.

a. You are working at the computer and the document currently on the screen has not yet been saved (or even given a file name).

b. You want to give your document the name **<YOUR LAST NAME>.WP**.

Following are the detailed sequences of steps.

I. The Exit sequence of steps you would take to terminate (and save the document) would be as follows.

   1. <Detailed sequence of steps numbered 1, 2, 3,...>

II. The sequence of steps you would follow if you wished to save the current document but wanted to clear the screen so that you could enter another document would be:

   1. <Detailed sequence of steps numbered 1, 2, 3,...>

Boldface

PART THREE

Spreadsheets and Computer Graphics

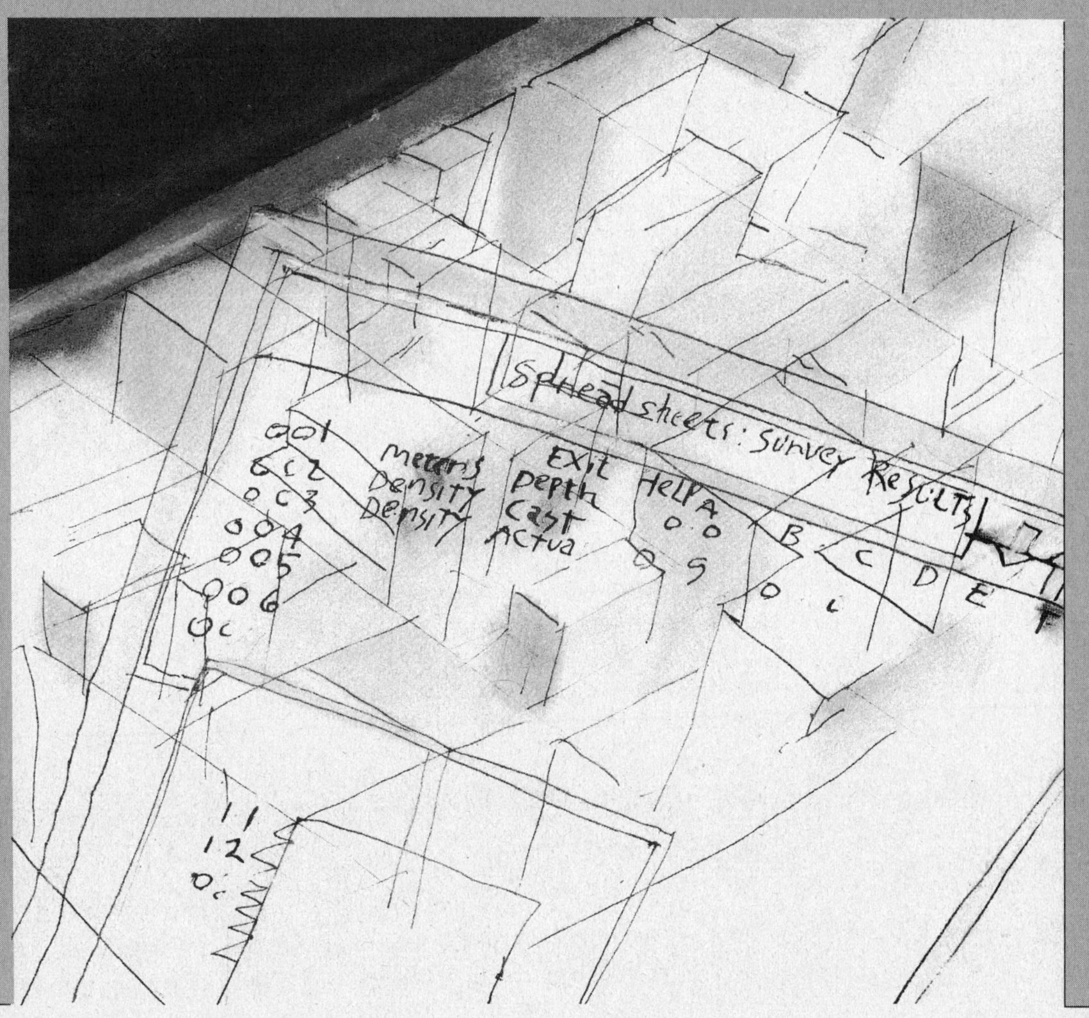

INTRODUCTION TO PART THREE

The next of the software tools described in this book is the electronic spreadsheet—using the computer to summarize data in a tabular form. Part Three consists of three chapters. In Chapters 3 and 4, you will learn how to use the popular program Lotus 1-2-3. If you have a copy of the commercially available Lotus 1-2-3 program, you can work with it. If not, you can use the JOE spreadsheet program that is included with this book. Its command structure is identical to that of Lotus 1-2-3. Whichever software you use, you will learn basic operations, such as entering and changing a spreadsheet, saving it to disk, and retrieving a previously saved spreadsheet from disk (Chapter 3). You will also learn more advanced operations, such as changing a spreadsheet's appearance and rearranging data in the spreadsheet (Chapter 4). In Chapter 5, you will learn about computer graphics with an emphasis on displaying spreadsheet information in graphics form.

A COST ANALYSIS PROBLEM

The electronic spreadsheet is patterned after the accountant's worksheet, in which numerical data is organized in rows and columns from which calculations are performed. As an introduction, let us consider a specific problem and how to solve it using a worksheet. This will give you a better understanding of how a worksheet is employed and will introduce you to the example that will be used in the next two chapters on Lotus 1-2-3.

The Problem

As a special promotion for first-time retail stores, you, as a partner in MCT Enterprises, decide to offer a "Special Collection Retail Module" consisting of the four basic styles shown in Table P3-1.

Table P3-1 SPECIAL COLLECTION SUMMARY

Garment Style	Your Cost	Quantity	Amount
Style A	13.97	12	167.64
Style B	15.83	12	189.96
Style C	13.42	18	241.56
Style D	14.59	8	116.72
		Total	715.88

You consider this a "foot-in-the-door" package and wish to keep the price below $675 in order to compete with promotions of other companies. However, this summary shows that you will not meet your price objective so you must consider the alternatives.

1. Go with the higher price.
2. Change the quantities offered in order to reduce the price.
3. Evaluate your costs to determine whether any reductions are possible.

As your promotion is to be oriented around the theme "less than $675," you wish to avoid the higher price. The quantities are based on your careful analysis of expected sales demand so you do not wish to change these numbers. The only alternative is to determine whether reductions in cost are possible. Because you wish to cover your costs in offering this deal, you must accurately assess the cost of the various components of the package. To do this, you break down the costs for each garment into three categories: Material, Labor, and Other. (In reality, the cost breakdown probably would be in greater detail; three broad categories are used here to illustrate worksheet principles.)

Using a Worksheet for a Cost Analysis

It is essential to see the overall effect of changing each of these factors for each garment. The best way to study something such as this is to create a worksheet model as shown in Figure P3-1. Notice that this is nothing more than a detailed expansion of Table P3-1 but it makes it possible to isolate the factors that contribute to the overall cost.

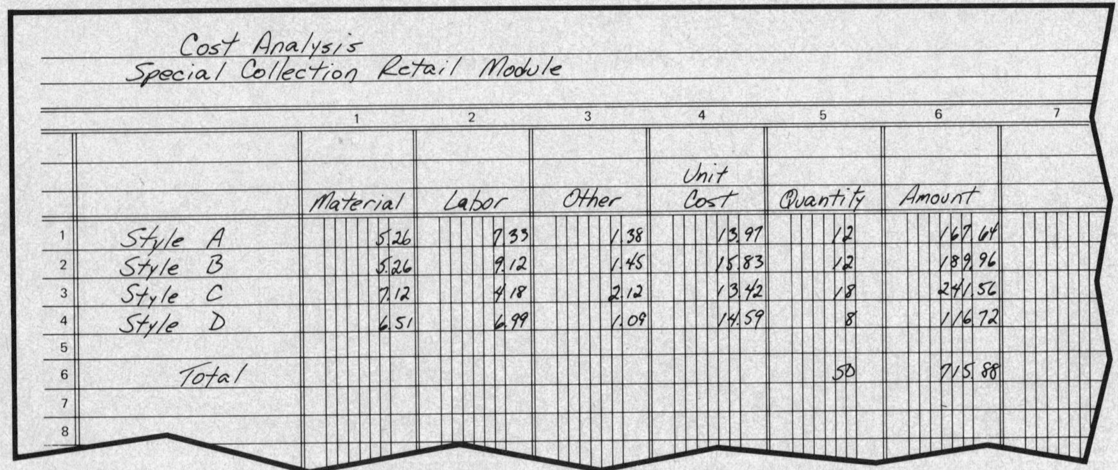

Cost Analysis
Special Collection Retail Module

	Material	Labor	Other	Unit Cost	Quantity	Amount
Style A	5.26	7.33	1.38	13.97	12	167.64
Style B	5.26	9.12	1.45	15.83	12	189.96
Style C	7.12	4.18	2.12	13.42	18	241.56
Style D	6.51	6.99	1.09	14.59	8	116.72
Total					50	715.88

Material + Labor + Other = Unit Cost

Unit cost X Quantity = Amount

Figure P3-1
A cost analysis worksheet.

Now the question is, "By how much is it necessary to change each of these amounts in order to achieve the $675 objective?" Here you must work within ground rules dictated by facts, that is:

1. The Material costs are fixed.
2. The Other costs can be reduced slightly.
3. You might be able to negotiate a reduction with the sewing contractor (Labor) because of the introductory nature of this offer.

After careful evaluation of your costs and a meeting with your contractor, you determine that you can make the following changes.

- Reduce the Labor cost for Styles A, B, and D by the amounts $0.55, 0.60, and 0.70, respectively.
- Reduce the Other cost for Styles A, B, C, and D by the amounts $0.41, 0.44, 0.31, and 0.21, respectively.

The question now is, "Does this meet the price objective?" You can make this assessment by entering new values for Labor and Other, and then recalculating, with the result shown in Figure P3-2. Although close to your $675 objective, it is obvious that further adjustments are needed. You could then examine the details of your costs even more closely to determine whether further reductions were possible. If they were not, you would be faced with the decision either to raise the price or to take a small loss on the promotion in order to maintain the target price. In the end, the worksheet will have proved a valuable tool in presenting information for making a decision.

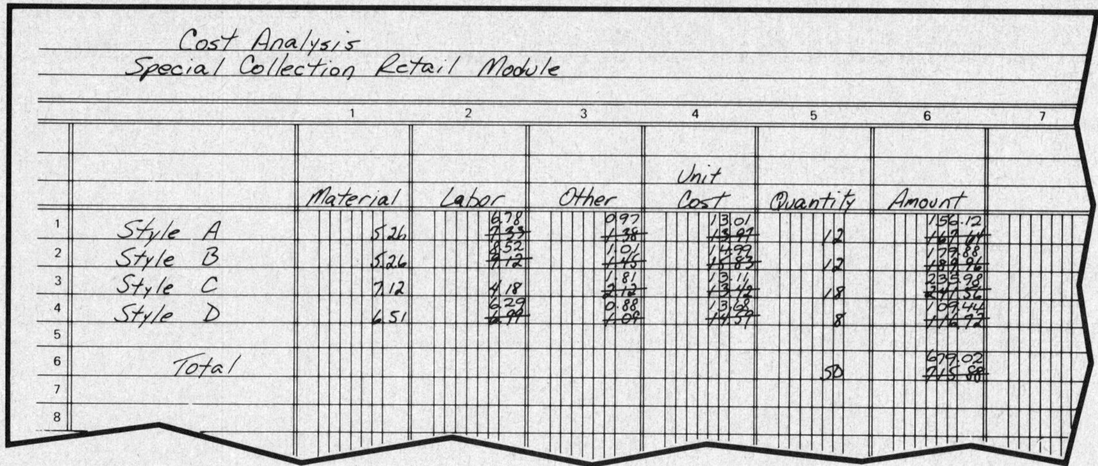

Figure P3-2
Changing the worksheet values.

About the Values Displayed in a Worksheet

From a casual glance at the worksheet of Figure P3-1, we see rows and columns of numbers. However, we know from the description of the example that some of these depend on others. In fact, we can represent the Unit Cost in a mathematical formula format as:

Unit Cost = Material + Labor + Other

When filling in this worksheet, we enter values for Material, Labor, and Other, and then calculate the Unit Cost by adding their values. Quantity is also a value that we enter. It is multiplied by the Unit Cost to obtain the amount for each style. These amounts are summed to give the total cost for this special retail module. Hence, in this worksheet, we are looking at two different entities: data, and results that are based on computation with that data. Data values are entered, and results calculated according to previously defined rules. If the results are not acceptable, then new values are entered into one or more of the data elements and the results are recalculated accordingly.

In making changes to the worksheet entries, notice that each change produces a "ripple" effect; that is, a change in one position requires calculated changes in other positions. This is a clumsy procedure, especially if repeated changes are made in attempting to determine an optimum configuration. In spite of this, manual worksheets were widely used tools of the businessperson before the invention of the computer because of their effectiveness in displaying data in a way that is easy to understand and manipulate.

Although performing calculations manually in a worksheet might be clumsy and error prone for most people, it is an activity in which the number-crunching capabilities of the computer shine. Let us see how these principles are implemented on electronic spreadsheets.

PRINCIPLES OF ELECTRONIC SPREADSHEETS

In the business world before the introduction of the microcomputer, the word *worksheet* was used to describe the tabular work form. In the microcomputer world, *spreadsheet* is used almost universally to describe this type of application program. That is, VisiCalc, Lotus 1-2-3, and JOE (the software included with this book) are called spreadsheet programs. However, in their reference manuals, many of the software companies, including Lotus, use the word *worksheet.* (In fact, Lotus 1-2-3 includes the Worksheet command to perform certain operations on the worksheet.) Hence, in your reading you will see the words used interchangeably. In this book, worksheet is used when referring to the electronic worksheet and spreadsheet is used in referring to the program (the spreadsheet program or software).

Cells and Their Contents

The electronic version of the cost summary worksheet in Figure P3-3 has the same form as the worksheet in Figure P3-1 in that it displays information in row-column form. Notice that rows are numbered 1, 2, 3, . . . and columns are identified by letters A, B, C, ... Each position into which an entry can be made is identified by its column letter and row number and is called a **cell.** For instance, the Labor cost for Style A is stored in the cell at the intersection of column C and row 2. This cell is identified by its **cell address** C2. Note that with this addressing scheme, the column letter is first and the row number is second. This is the standard way of addressing cells with spreadsheet systems that use the letter and number method. (Although most spreadsheet programs use letters and numbers, some use numbers to identify both rows and columns.)

We have already observed that the values displayed by the worksheet fall into two categories—those that we select (as data) and those that we calculate using previously defined relationships. With the electronic

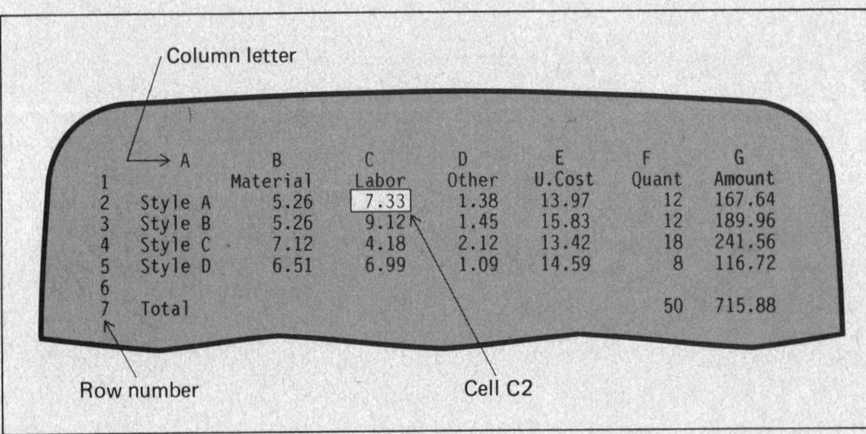

Figure P3-3
The cost summary worksheet.

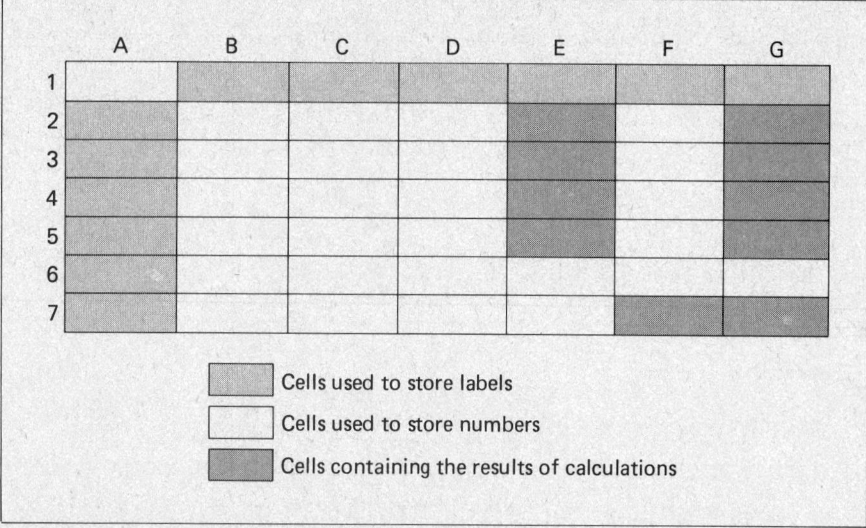

Figure P3-4
General layout of the cost summary worksheet.

spreadsheet, cell entries can be either of three general types; for the spreadsheet of Figure P3-3, these are identified in Figure P3-4. The first type of entry, shown in the first row and column, contains the English descriptions that identify parts of the spreadsheet for us. These entries are commonly called **labels,** although in some spreadsheet programs they are called *alpha* data (alphabetic) and in others they are called *titles.*

The second type of cell entry is numeric data, values that we select and enter in performing the analysis. In Figure P3-4, these cells are shown in blue. In some spreadsheets, these are called numbers, and in others, they are called values. The word *numbers* is used in this book to be consistent with the Lotus 1-2-3 usage.

The third type of cell entry is the value resulting from calculations with quantities stored in other cells, the green cells in Figure P3-4. When making both label and number entries into a spreadsheet, you type the actual value to be entered. However, for any cell that is to display results of calculations, you must enter the exact instructions for making those calculations. This is called a **formula,** and it is the topic of the next section.

Formulas

For each cell that is to display a calculated value, you must define the data to be used and the operations to take place. For instance, the Unit Cost for Style A would be calculated as follows:

1. Add the values in cells B2, C2, and D2.
2. Display the result in cell E2.

The use of cell addressing as defined in the preceding section allows the language of mathematics to be used, resulting in the following very concise formula.

```
E2 = +B2+C2+D2
```

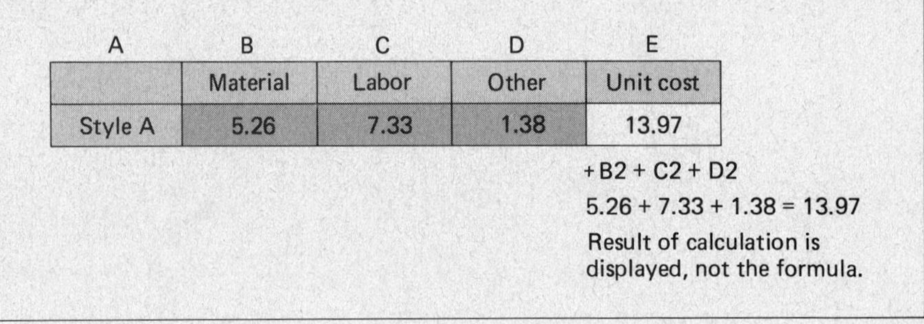

Figure P3-5
The concept of formulas associated with cells.

The portion on the right-hand side of the equals sign is commonly called an **expression.** This expression is then assigned to the cell named to the left of the equals sign, as illustrated in Figure P3-5. When we look at cells of a worksheet containing data, we expect to see that data. When looking at cells with formulas, we do *not* expect to see the formulas; we expect to see the numbers resulting from the calculations performed by the formulas. As you see, the underlying concept of formulas is that they determine the value in one cell based on values in other cells. Once you understand this, you have a basic understanding of how a worksheet is used. After you have a worksheet set up, whenever you enter a new number into a cell, the spreadsheet program automatically recalculates the values for every cell that depends on the one with the new entry. Thus, with the cost analysis worksheet, you can focus your attention on weighing all of the possibilities represented by your model. You need not be concerned with the details of calculating each time you make a change as the computer recalculates and displays the results. In a matter of minutes, you can try many variations of the cost figures in an attempt to find the optimum cost structure.

A Spreadsheet Template

A spreadsheet program such as Lotus 1-2-3 is a tool that you can use to assist you in solving problems. Using it for performing the cost analysis of the preceding sections involves a two-step approach: (1) defining and entering relationships between cells, and (2) entering and changing data values. The first, setting up the worksheet, requires entering all of the labels and formulas. This is sometimes called programming the worksheet. The end result of this phase is called a worksheet **template**: a complete worksheet except that no data has yet been entered into it. As often as not, a given template will be used and reused. For instance, many instructors maintain their student grade records with spreadsheet programs that automatically compute totals and averages. With a template stored on disk, beginning the new semester process involves making a copy for each class and then entering the student names. Templates, many of which include highly complex calculations, can be purchased for different applications. Application systems are available that consist of many interrelated templates for performing a particular set of operations. Once a worksheet template has been created, it can be used as an aid to solving the problem for which it was designed.

FUNDAMENTAL STEPS IN COMPUTER PROBLEM SOLVING

Word processing programs such as WordPerfect provide a powerful tool for managing documents. The other two productivity tools described in this book, Lotus 1-2-3 and dBASE III, are significantly different in that they are tools of analysis. They both include such provisions for performing operations as:

- Manipulating both numeric and nonnumeric data.
- Performing mathematical computations based on forms that are similar to those of algebra.
- Carrying out actions on a conditional basis depending on the relationship between two quantities.

To utilize these capabilities, the user must prepare appropriate instructions describing the exact actions to be taken under the conditions to be considered. This is called *programming*. Although the term is most commonly associated with preparing sequences of statements to solve a problem using a conventional programming language, it is equally applicable to problem solving using spreadsheet and database programs.

Without a doubt, the single biggest difficulty the beginning student encounters is to sit down at the computer to solve a problem without thoroughly understanding what is to be done or how to do it. The "instant gratification" generated by the computer responding is usually short-lived and superficial. The computer can only do what we tell it to do; it cannot define a problem or tell us what formulas to use. In preparing an application (such as the cost analysis) for computer solution, an organized approach is essential. Following is a straightforward set of steps to use in preparing computer solutions.

1. *Define the desired results.* Analyze the problem to see what useful results (or output) are required. Decide exactly what information you wish to come out of the computer. In the case of the cost analysis worksheet, you wanted the ability to vary the data values and observe how the total cost changed.

2. *Analyze the input data.* Does the data contain everything that is needed to produce the desired results? If the needed data is not there in exactly the desired form, is it possible to combine some of the data quantities to produce the desired output? If the answer to one of these questions is Yes, you can go ahead. However, if the answer to both is No, you do not have the necessary input data to produce the desired output. For the cost analysis, the input data was the individual cost items and the quantity. Had you, for example, been unable to determine the Other cost element accurately, the analysis would have been of little value.

3. *Devise an overall plan for the solution.* The objective of a computer solution is to obtain the desired results from the input. The operations necessary to do this must be clearly defined. They commonly include such things as specifying calculations to be carried out and

conditions under which various actions are taken. The calculations for the cost analysis were relatively simple. However, what if your evaluation had shown that some of the cost items would decrease with increased sales? Then it would have been necessary to devise a relationship between these cost items and the sales.

4. *Express the solution in a form that can be communicated to the computer.* For a spreadsheet program, it includes defining formulas describing calculations to be performed.

5. *Test the solution.* Once the solution has been entered into the computer, it should be tested thoroughly. One of the lessons that the programmer learns very early in her or his training cycle is the importance of thoroughly testing a program. Frequently, output generated by a computer is accepted as correct simply because it is produced by a computer. This is unfortunate. For instance, consider a formula to apply a discount to a customer purchase, in which the discount is added rather than subtracted. The computer, knowing nothing of the context of this task, will calculate as directed and customers will be overcharged. Errors such as these are detected and corrected by preparing and entering test data.

Because of the interactive nature of productivity software and the microcomputer, it is easy to fall into the bad habit of skipping over the problem planning and solution and immediately to sit down at the computer. Although this might be adequate for your first, relatively simple tasks, the results are usually poor for tasks that are more complex. Do not slip into that habit.

NEW TERMINOLOGY

The following are important new terms introduced in this introduction; you should be familiar with each of them now because you will be using them in chapters that follow.

cell
cell address
column
expression
formula
label
row
spreadsheet
template
worksheet

Chapter 4

Using Lotus 1-2-3 and JOE Spreadsheet

OBJECTIVES

From the introduction to Part Three, you learned how spreadsheet programs can be used to assist you in solving problems. In this chapter you will have the opportunity to use some of these features by learning to work with the popular spreadsheet program Lotus 1-2-3. The vehicle that you will use in learning these basic spreadsheet principles is the MCT cost analysis spreadsheet that you studied in the introduction. When you have completed this chapter, you will be able to:

- Identify the parts of the 1-2-3 screen: the worksheet area, cell address border, control panel, information line.
- Save a worksheet that you have created to disk as a file.
- Retrieve a worksheet from disk.
- Terminate running of the 1-2-3 program, thus ending a work session.
- Move around on the worksheet to select the desired cell for action, such as entering data.
- Enter labels, numbers, and formulas into cells.
- Use the worksheet as a tool in attempting to adjust individual costs to achieve the cost goal set for the Special Collection Group described in the introduction.
- Edit the contents of individual cells.
- Print a worksheet.

This chapter is like Chapters 2 and 3 (WordPerfect) in that you need to read *and* do. That is, read the chapter first, and then do all of the described actions for yourself at the computer. When reading, do not attempt to memorize exact keystrokes necessary to carry out the different actions; simply learn about the actions. When you try them on the computer, things will fall into place much more quickly. If you wish to try some hands-on activity before finishing the entire chapter, read at least to the section entitled "Moving the Cell Pointer" before going to the computer.

PREVIEW

Getting Started

To follow the examples of this chapter, you need spreadsheet software. This section describes running the software on either a floppy disk or hard disk computer.

The Display Screen

The 1-2-3 spreadsheet screen display includes rows and columns of cells and the control panel from which activities are monitored.

Saving and Retrieving Worksheets Using Commands

As with a word processing document, a worksheet is created and manipulated in memory. For permanent retention, it must be stored to disk using a conventional DOS filename. At any time, it can be retrieved from disk and loaded into memory.

Moving the Cell Pointer

One of your first needs in working with a spreadsheet program is to be able to move the cursor from one cell to another. The currently selected cell is the cell into which data is always entered from the keyboard.

Entering Labels and Numbers into the Worksheet

Labels and numbers are entered into a cell by moving to the cell and then typing the desired entry. The entry of labels and numbers is illustrated by entering those for the cost analysis spreadsheet of the introduction.

Formulas

Formulas define the calculations to be carried out. They are assigned to cells of the worksheet in much the same way that labels and numbers are entered. The formulas for the cost analysis spreadsheet are entered.

Rules for Building Formulas

The arithmetic operations that can be performed with formulas are addition, subtraction, multiplication, division, and raising to a power. These are used in accordance with the precedence rules of mathematics.

About Worksheet Errors and Correcting Them

A worksheet should be carefully checked to ensure that all formulas are correct before using it. Erroneous formulas can be corrected through the Edit command.

More About Commands

Most of the spreadsheet operations are carried out by commands. Descriptions of commands and other operations are available from the program in the form of Help screens.

Printing a Worksheet

The Print command allows all or a portion of a spreadsheet to be sent directly to a printer or to a file for later printing.

GETTING STARTED

About the Software

Since this chapter involves learning by doing, you will need spreadsheet software. If you have access to a copy of Lotus 1-2-3, then you can use it. If you do not, then you can use the JOE spreadsheet that is included with this book. The appearance on the screen as well as the command sequences are similar. In descriptions in this book, reference will almost always be to Lotus 1-2-3, but the remarks apply equally to JOE. In cases where the screen displays are significantly different, displays from both Lotus 1-2-3 and JOE are included.

Before you can begin to enter a spreadsheet, you must load the Lotus 1-2-3 or the JOE program into the computer's memory. Once loaded, control of the computer switches from DOS to Lotus 1-2-3 or to JOE. Let us consider this loading start-up process.

Running 1-2-3

To work with 1-2-3, you will need the Lotus 1-2-3 system disk or the JOE disk that accompanies this book, a DOS disk for booting the computer, and a formatted data disk (the data disk that accompanies this book can be used). Note that the DOS and data disks are those that you should have prepared in Chapter 1. If you have not already prepared the data disk, then you should refer to Chapter 1 and prepare it before proceeding. To run 1-2-3, carry out the following sequence of operations.

Floppy Disk Computer.

1. Boot the computer with a DOS disk in the A drive.
2. Remove the DOS disk from the A drive and insert the Lotus 1-2-3 or JOE disk.
3. Insert the data disk in the B drive.
4. To load and run the spreadsheet program, type the following and then strike Enter.

   A> `JOE` (for JOE)

   A> `123` (for Lotus 1-2-3)

Hard Disk Computer. *Note*: The following instructions assume that JOE or Lotus 1-2-3 is stored in the subdirectory named JOE or 123 as described in Chapter 1. If it is not, then you must modify these instructions accordingly.

1. Boot the computer from the hard disk (leave the door to the A drive open).
2. Change to the spreadsheet program subdirectory by typing:

   C> `C\JOE` (for JOE)

   C> `C\123` (for Lotus 1-2-3)
3. To load and run the spreadsheet program, type the following and then strike Enter.

   C> `JOE` (for JOE)

   C> `123` (for Lotus 1-2-3)

Whether you are using a floppy disk or hard disk computer, an announcement screen will be displayed. Striking the Enter key will cause this screen to be erased and the main worksheet screen to be displayed. For users of JOE, the first time that you run the program, you will be prompted to identify the type of monitor connected to your computer. When you do so, this information will be stored on the JOE disk and you will not be asked again.

THE DISPLAY SCREEN

Once the spreadsheet program is running, your screen display will appear as shown in Figure 4-1(a) for JOE and as shown in Figure 4-1(b) for Lotus 1-2-3—see page 214. (Note: The highlighting for cell E14 will not be dis-

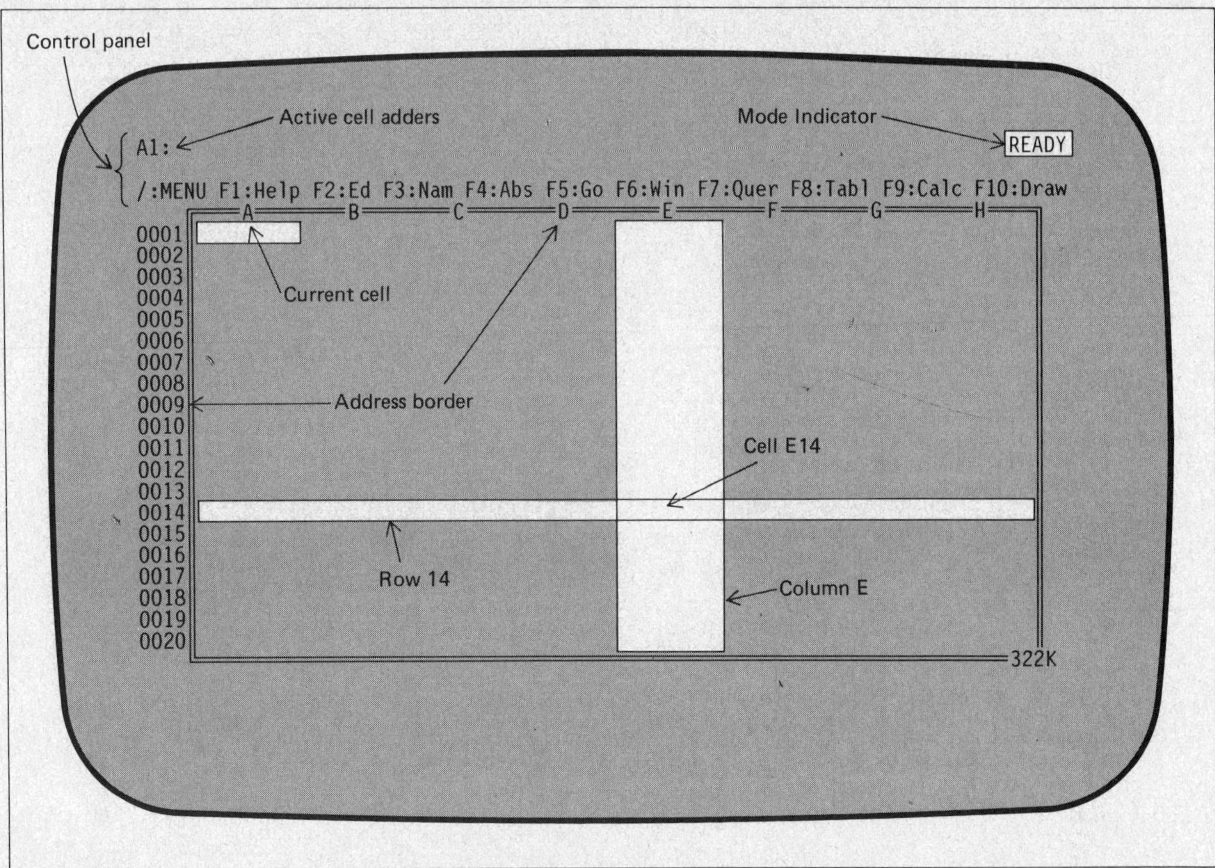

Figure 4-1
(a) The JOE Spreadsheet screen.

played on your screen.) Although some details are different, the general layouts of the two are identical. The screen can be considered as consisting of the following four components:

- The worksheet area
- The cell address border
- The control panel
- The information line

The Worksheet and Border

As you know from the introduction, the worksheet is made up of columns and rows, with the columns identified by letters and the rows by numbers. In Figure 4-1, the main portion of the screen is taken up by the worksheet itself. The cell address border clearly identifies each screen row (1 through 20) and each screen column (A through H). The intersection of each row and column represents a 1-2-3 cell. For instance, Figure 4-1 shows cell E14,

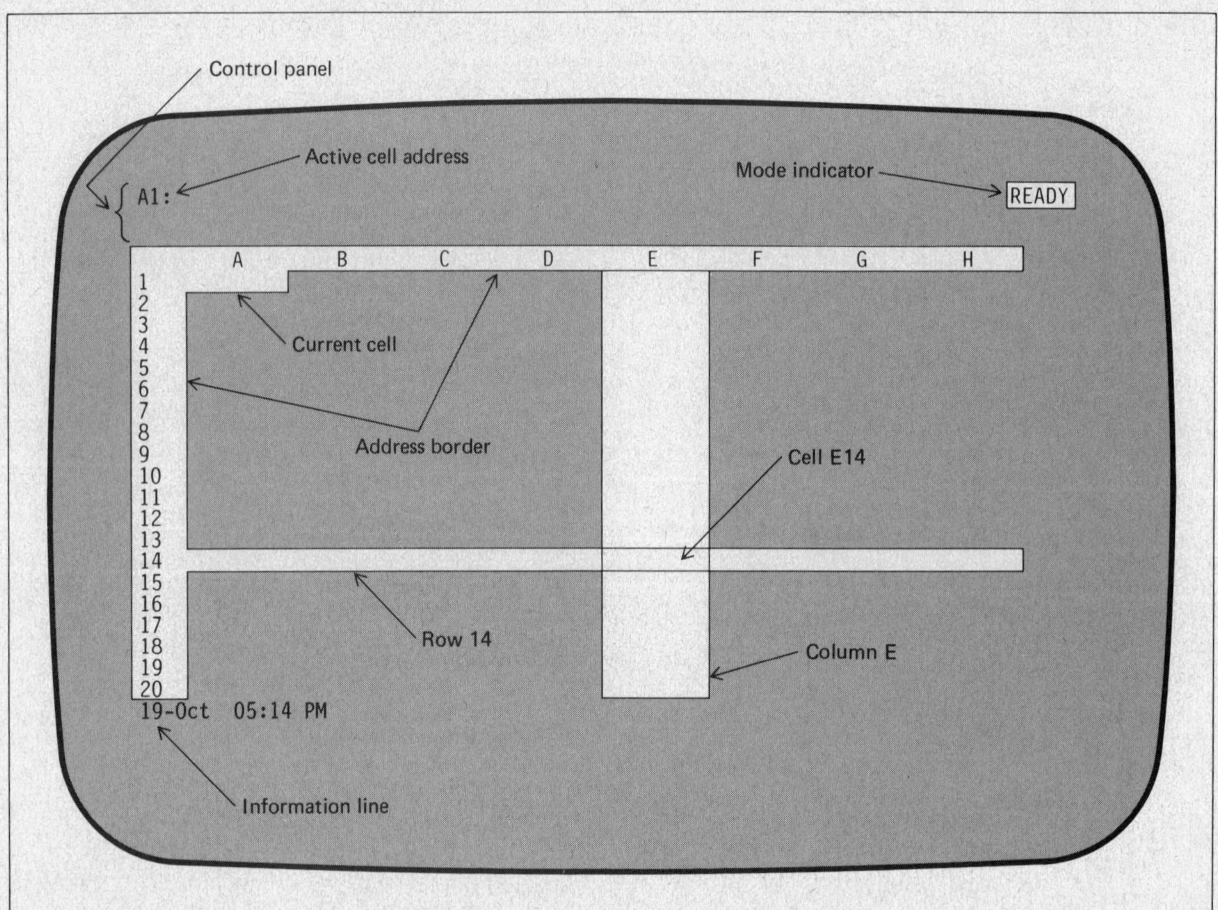

Figure 4-1
(b) The Lotus 1-2-3 Spreadsheet screen.

the intersection of column E and row 14. Although only 20 rows and 8 columns are displayed here, the full worksheet consists of 256 columns named A through IV. The first 26 are A through Z, the next 26 are AA through AZ, then BA through BZ, and so on up to IA through IV. The number of rows depends on the particular version of the software. In Lotus 1-2-3, Release 1A has 2048 rows and Release 2 has 8192 rows; later releases have more. JOE has 8192 rows.

The **cell pointer** is the highlighted area on the worksheet (in this case, cell A1) that indicates the **current cell,** the cell that is the current focus of 1-2-3's attention. For instance, to enter data into a cell from the keyboard, that cell must be the current cell. One of your first activities will be learning how to move the cell pointer.

If you look at your screen display carefully, you will see that the screen width of each cell is 9 positions. This is the default display cell size set by the program. You will learn how to change this value in the next chapter.

Terminology

The word *worksheet* is commonly used ambiguously. That is, it is used to describe both the entire collection of cells in computer memory (for instance, 256 columns by 8192 rows) and the portion of cells into which entries have been made (for instance, the cost analysis spreadsheet of Figure P3-3 in the introduction would occupy columns A through G and rows 1 through 7). Usually, you will know which is meant by the context. In some cases with examples that follow, the latter is identified as "your" worksheet, meaning the rectangular block of cells into which you have made your entries.

The Control Panel

The **control panel** consists of the top three lines on the screen and describes most of the 1-2-3 activities. Information displayed by the control panel includes the following.

- The cell address of the current cell. In the example of Figure 4-1, we see that the cell pointer is at cell A1.
- To the immediate right of the cell address, 1-2-3 displays the contents of the current cell. In this case, nothing is displayed because the current cell is empty; however, you will see how this works when you enter values into the worksheet.
- To the extreme right is the mode indicator, which indicates the current mode of operation of 1-2-3. For instance, when 1-2-3 is first loaded, READY is displayed, indicating that 1-2-3 is ready to respond to a request. When you enter a label into the spreadsheet, LABEL is displayed, indicating that 1-2-3 is ready to accept a label.
- Lines 2 and 3 of the control panel display information that depends on the particular operation you are performing. Notice that JOE uses line 3 to tell you the actions produced by each function key. You will learn about some of these in later sections of this chapter.

The Information Line

The bottom line of the screen provides three items of information. In Release 2 (and higher) of Lotus 1-2-3, the date and time are displayed. In place of the date and time, JOE displays the name of the worksheet file that is currently loaded. The second item of information displayed on this line is the status of the toggle keys of the keyboard. For example, if the keyboard has been shifted to uppercase by striking the CapsLock key, the word CAPS is displayed. Similar displays appear for the Numlock and Scroll Lock keys. The third information item displayed on this line is error messages. If an error occurs during a worksheet operation, the mode indicator is changed to ERROR and a short description of the error is displayed.

SAVING AND RETRIEVING WORKSHEETS USING COMMANDS

Before you start learning how to enter values into the cells of a worksheet, you should know how to save a worksheet to disk as a file and to retrieve the file from disk. Then you will be able to stop your activity at any point, save your work to disk, and return later to resume where you left off. Saving and retrieving are done with 1-2-3 commands. Although there is much to say about commands, for the moment we will be concerned only with the bare essentials needed to save and retrieve files and to terminate the program.

To get to the command menu from the READY mode, you must strike the slash key (/). When you do this, your screen will appear as shown in Figure 4-2; note that the READY indicator in the upper right has now

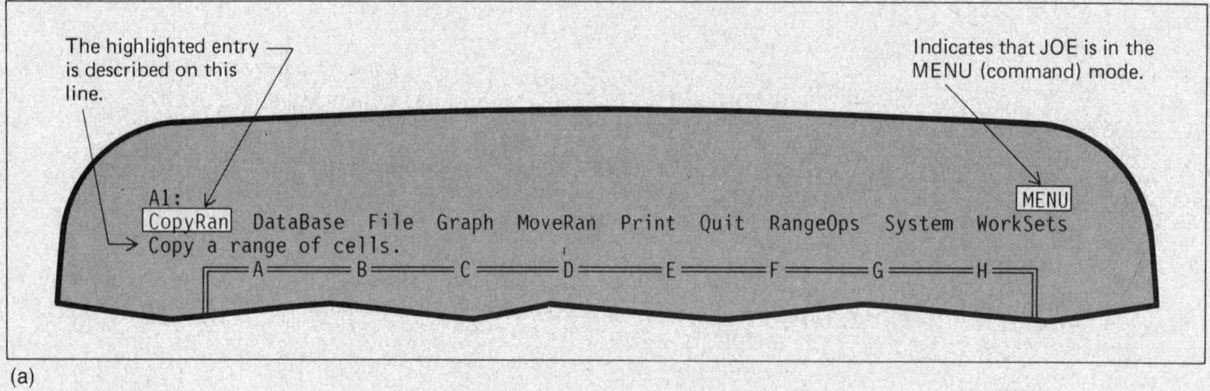

(a)

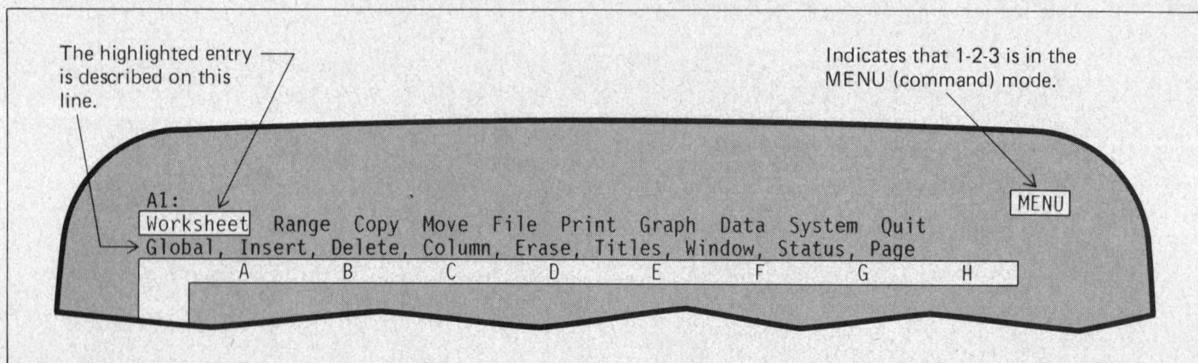

Figure 4-2
(a) Command menu for JOE.
(b) Command menu for Lotus 1-2-3.

changed to MENU. In both control panels, the second line contains a list of commands. (Although the command names and the order in which they are listed are slightly different for Lotus 1-2-3 and JOE, the first letters of corresponding commands are the same. This is a key point.)

About the Escape Key

As you will learn in working with 1-2-3, you control actions of the program through keystrokes. Some keystrokes move the cell pointer, others enter different types of data, and still others bring up commands. When you are first learning, it is easy to strike the wrong key, with totally unexpected results. Often the program is awaiting a response from you and will not continue until you respond properly. If that happens, then you should strike the Escape (Esc) key one or more times. This key is somewhat of a "back up one step" key and will usually get you out of trouble.

Initial Setup for the Data Drive

Your first action is to define for your software (Lotus 1-2-3 or JOE) to which disk drive files are to be written. If you are using a floppy-based computer, this is the B drive. If you are using a hard disk computer, it can be the C drive and the same subdirectory as your software (Lotus 1-2-3 or JOE).

Without being concerned about the details of what happens as a result of the following command sequence, carrying out the sequence will change the default data drive to B. Be certain that the disk you plan to use as a data disk is formatted and in drive B.

DO THIS NOW 4-1 **Setting the Default Data Drive**

For this, you must carry out the keystroke sequence exactly as listed in the following steps. For instance, strike the W, then the G, and so on. The descriptions to the right tell you which JOE/Lotus 1-2-3 command is being executed or the action being taken. If you make a wrong entry, strike the Escape key to return to the READY mode. Depending on the action you have taken, you may have to strike it two or more times. When you are back to READY, you may start over. If you are using a hard disk computer, the entry at step 6 must be different from the one shown here; see the description that follows. Remember, in the following sequence, type the letter W (either upper- or lowercase), then type the letter G, and so on.

1. Type a W	Worksheet/WorkSet command
2. Type a G	Globals/Global command
3. Type a D	Defaults/Default command
4. Type a D	Directory/Directory command
5. Press the Esc key	Erase the current default

6. Type B:\	Enter the new default drive
7. Press the Enter	Accept the entry
8. Type a U	Update/Update command
9. Type a Q	Quit menu/Quit command

If you are using a hard disk as described in Chapter 1 (software and data in a single subdirectory), then at step 6 you must enter:

`C:\JOE` (For JOE)
`C:\123` (For Lotus 1-2-3)

After entering the letter *Q* (the last step), you will be returned to the READY mode. The default data disk is now permanently stored on your program disk; you need not run this sequence again unless you want to change the value.

Saving a Worksheet to Disk

After entering a worksheet, you might be a bit unhappy if, upon turning the computer off, the worksheet were to disappear. In fact, this is exactly what will happen if you do not save it to disk. Both saving a worksheet to disk and retrieving one from disk are done through the File command. Even though the worksheet currently on the screen is empty, it can still be saved to disk. Although an empty worksheet on disk is of little value, the exercise will show you how to carry out the operation.

DO THIS NOW 4-2 **Saving a Worksheet to Disk**

1. Switch to command mode by striking the / key; the mode indicator will be MENU and the menu of Figure 4-2 will be displayed.
2. Strike the letter F for File. This will produce the File submenu of Figure 4-3.
3. Strike the letter S for Save. This will produce the prompt of Figure 4-4. Note that the system shows the drive B (or your hard disk subdirectory) as the default disk drive for saving the file (assuming that you carried out the procedure to set the default in DTN 4-1).
4. You must now type the name by which you want the worksheet stored on disk. Remember, the worksheet name is a DOS filename and therefore is limited to 8 characters. To be consistent with example procedures that follow, type COST for the filename and strike the Enter key.

Figure 4-3
(a) The JOE File submenu.
(b) The Lotus 1-2-3 File submenu.

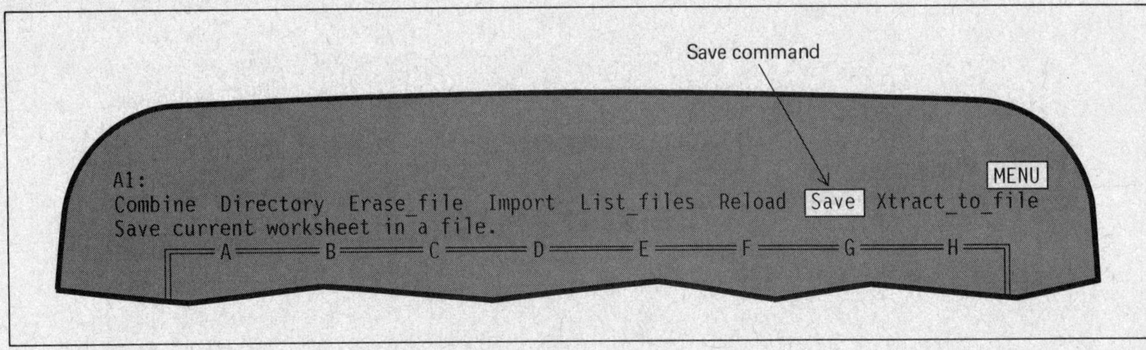

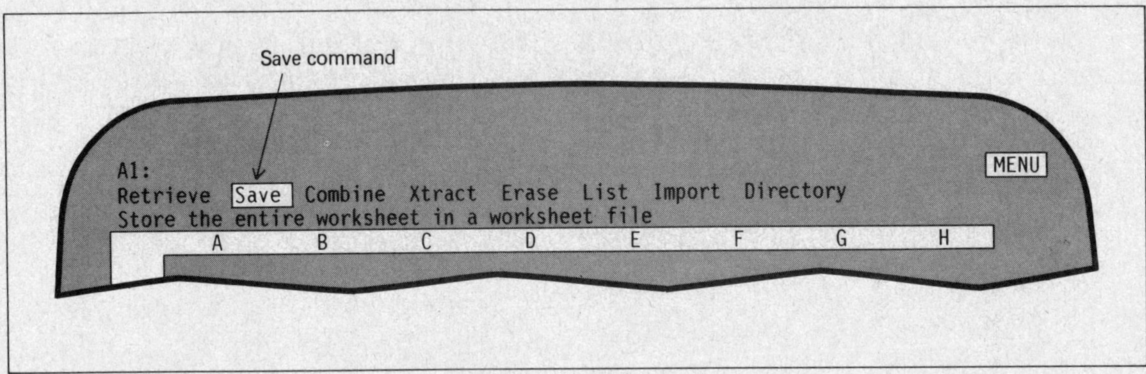

Figure 4-4
Saving a worksheet as a file.

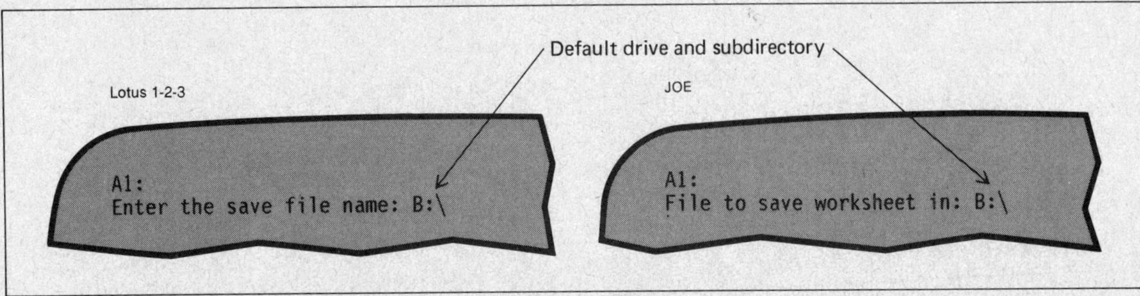

When the file is saved, a predetermined extension is automatically attached. If you are using JOE, the extension will be WKQ. If you are using Lotus 1-2-3 Release 1A, the extension will be WKS; if you are using Release 2, it will be WK1. Hence, this worksheet will be saved as COST.WKQ, COST.WKS, or COST.WK1, depending on the software you are using.

As you know, everything in memory is lost when the computer is turned off or if there is any kind of electric power failure even though momentary. Think of how unhappy you would be if the electricity were to go off after you had just completed entering a complex worksheet. The solution to the loss of a large amount of work is to save the worksheet frequently (this is no different from working on a document with a word processor). If you have saved a worksheet while working on it, the next time you execute the File Save command sequence, the filename will be listed as a default in the prompt of Figure 4-4. Then you need only strike the Enter key and the worksheet will be saved again.

Ending a Work Session

Whenever you complete a work session with any piece of software, you should terminate the program with the appropriate command (for most software, it is QUIT or EXIT). This terminates execution in an orderly fashion and returns control to DOS. Then, if you are all finished, you can turn the computer off. Turning the computer off while your software program still controls the computer is poor practice. Some software performs cleanup activities when you terminate; they will not be performed if the computer is simply turned off. Also, if you have not saved your latest changes, most software warns that work will be lost if you terminate, a warning you would not get by simply turning the computer off.

DO THIS NOW 4-3 **Terminating Execution of the Program**

1. Switch to command mode by striking the / key; the mode indicator will be MENU and the menu of Figure 4-2 will be displayed.
2. Strike the letter Q for Quit.
3. The prompt on the control panel asks you to confirm that you indeed wish to quit. Striking the Y key (for Yes) returns control of the computer to DOS.

With JOE, whenever you terminate processing, if any changes have been made to the worksheet since the last save, you will be warned. If you override the warning, the most recent changes will not be on the disk copy.

Retrieving a Worksheet from Disk

Upon returning to work on the worksheet at some later time, reading it from disk back into memory is every bit as easy as saving it. For instance, assume that you have entered a portion of a worksheet and have realized that you cannot finish it now. You would then save as much as you have entered with the intention of completing it later. At some later time, when bringing the spreadsheet program (Lotus 1-2-3 or JOE) up on the computer, you would be confronted with an empty worksheet screen. The first thing to do would be to load the worksheet so that you could continue your entry or editing tasks. This process is almost identical to that of saving. If you performed the sequence of DTN 4-3 properly, you will be at the DOS prompt; start your spreadsheet program.

DO THIS NOW 4-4 **Retrieving a Worksheet File**

1. Switch to command mode by striking the / key; the mode indicator will be MENU and the menu of Figure 4-2 will be displayed.
2. Strike the letter *F* for File, then strike the letter *R*. In the submenu of Figure 4-3, note that it means Reload for JOE and Retrieve for Lotus 1-2-3. These are different names for the same thing.
3. In the resulting screen of Figure 4-5, you have two options for selecting the worksheet to be retrieved from disk. Since you know that you want to retrieve the worksheet file COST, simply type in the name (the extension is not required) and strike the Enter key. Your worksheet will be retrieved from disk. If there is no worksheet file with the name you enter, an error message will be displayed.

Referring to Figure 4-5, notice that the third line of the control panel includes a list of the worksheet files stored on the data disk. (They are listed alphabetically.) The file to be retrieved can be identified either by typing the name as in step 3 or by selecting from this list. To select from the list, you must move the highlight with the right arrow key to the desired worksheet name, and then strike Enter. If you have more than five files on the disk, the one you desire may not appear on the screen. If you continue to strike the right arrow, the list of names will scroll. When the desired name is highlighted, strike Enter.

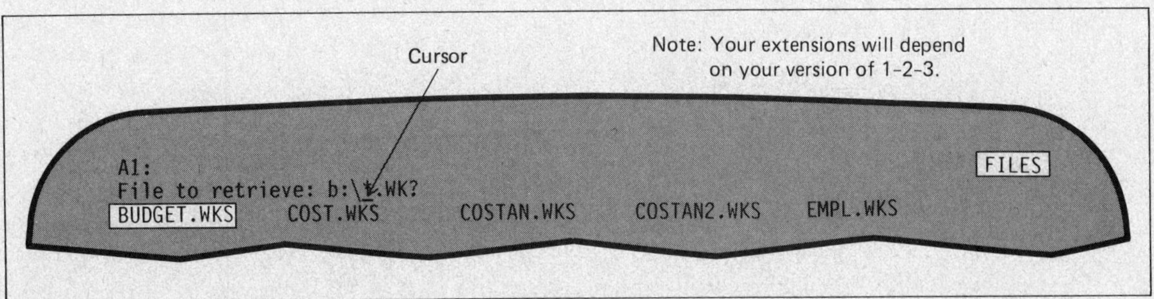

Figure 4-5
Retrieving a worksheet file from disk.

Options for Starting JOE

As you know, you start JOE simply by typing JOE and striking the Enter key. You can also specify a worksheet file to be loaded when starting, thus causing JOE to be loaded and run *and* a worksheet to be retrieved from disk. The following examples illustrate this.

`JOE /L`	Retrieves the last worksheet that was saved from the previous JOE session.
`JOE /FCOST`	Retrieves the worksheet COST.WKQ (WKQ is the JOE default extension).
`JOE /FCOSTAN.WKS`	Retrieves the worksheet COSTAN.WKS (created with Lotus 1-2-3, Version 1A).

The /L is a code representing "Last" and /F is a code representing "File."

Assignment 4-1 may now be completed.

MOVING THE CELL POINTER

From the earlier discussion of the screen, recall that cell A1 is highlighted when the spreadsheet program is first run (see Figure 4-1). Remember, the highlighting is called the cell pointer (the cell address is displayed in the upper-left corner of the screen); the cell pointer identifies the current cell. Since all keyboard entries are placed in the current cell, the action of entering labels, numbers, and formulas involves first moving the cell pointer to the cell into which the entry is to be made, and then making the entry.

Using the Arrow Keys

Moving the cell pointer is done with the group of four arrow keys on the numeric keypad portion of the keyboard shown in Figure 4-6. (Note: The

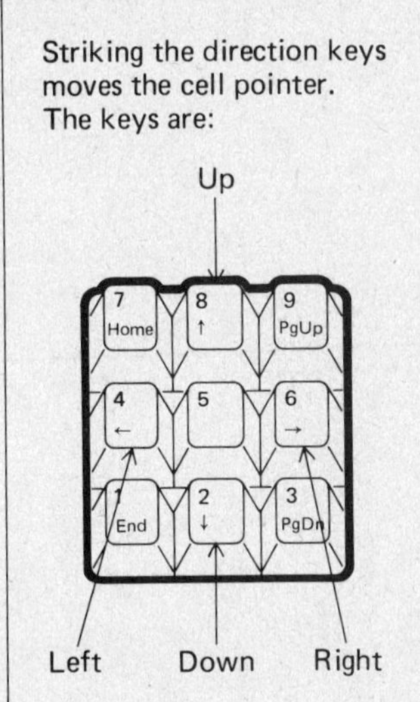

Figure 4-6
The numeric keypad.

enhanced keyboard described earlier includes a separate set of arrow keys.) In this book, these keys are referred to as the Left, Right, Up, and Down keys. To move the cell pointer to, for instance, cell B6, you would strike the:

Right key one time
Down key five times

This is illustrated in Figure 4-7, where the cell pointer was originally in column A, row 1 (A1). There is nothing magic about this particular sequence. That is, the cell pointer could have been moved from A1 to B6 by the following actions:

Down key five times
Right key one time

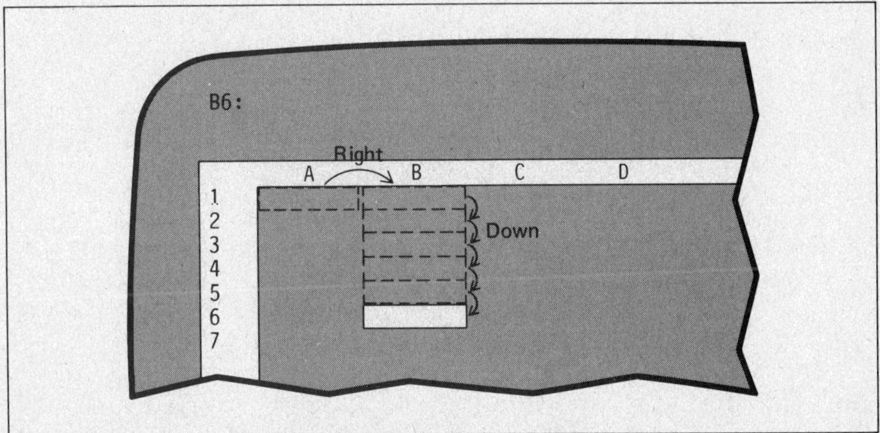

Figure 4-7
Moving the cursor.

In moving the cell pointer, the arrow keys will automatically repeat if you hold them down. This is convenient for moving up or down several rows. When moving to the left or the right, be careful because the movement is very quick.

When you have a worksheet on your screen, you see only 8 columns and 20 rows of the total 256 columns and 8192 rows in memory. If you try to move beyond the rightmost column (or the bottom row) displayed on the screen, it causes your "view" into the worksheet to move to the right (or down). What you see on the screen is that the cell pointer stays at its current position on the screen but the worksheet columns move to the left (or up). For instance, starting from cell B6 (Figure 4-7), the result of successively pressing the Right key after reaching the right border is as illustrated in Figure 4-8. This action of moving your view of the worksheet is called **scrolling.** You should try these actions.

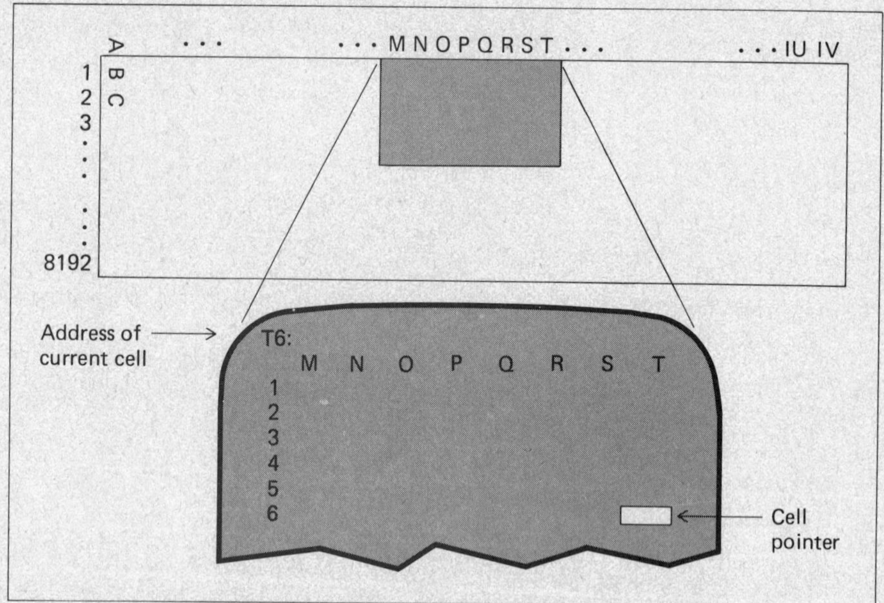

Figure 4-8
Scrolling the spreadsheet.

DO THIS NOW 4-5 **Moving the Cell Pointer**

1. Make certain the cell pointer is at cell A1.
2. Strike the Right key one time and the Down key five times; this moves the cell pointer to cell B6.
3. Hold the Right key down and observe the empty worksheet scroll. Release the Right key when the active cell is T6. If you go beyond it, use the Left key to move left.
4. Move to cell T50 by holding the Down key down. If you go beyond cell T50, use the Up key to back up.
5. To move the cell pointer back to cell A1, you could hold down the Up key until reaching row 1. (You will hear a beep if you continue to hold the Up key after reaching row 1.) Then hold down the Left key until reaching column A. However, a quicker way is to strike the Home key; it is on the 7 key of the numeric keypad (see Figure 4-6). This immediately moves the cell pointer to cell A1 regardless of current location.

Other Cell Pointer Movement Actions

Assume that you have just retrieved from disk one of your worksheets consisting of 40 rows and 20 columns and that you need to make some changes in row 30. One way to get there is simply to hold down the Down key until that portion of the worksheet scrolls into view. A simpler method is to use the PgDn key (see the numeric keypad of Figure 4-6), which moves the next 20 rows into view. Thus, if rows 1–20 are displayed, striking the PgDn key will cause rows 21–40 to be displayed. Striking the PgUp key causes the view to be moved up 20 rows.

To move a full screen (8 columns) to the right or left requires use of the Control key. That is, holding down the Ctrl key and striking the Right key will progress from columns A–H to columns I–P. Correspondingly, holding down the Ctrl key and striking the Left key moves to the 8 columns at the left. Keystroke actions in which one key is held down while another is struck are represented in this book by separating them with a hyphen. For instance, Ctrl-Right means hold down the Ctrl key and strike the Right key. (This is the same as with WordPerfect.)

In DTN 4-5, you moved the cell pointer to cell T50 using the arrow keys. If you must move the cell pointer to a specific cell that is not currently on the screen, you can use the GOTO command, which is invoked by striking the F5 function key. In response to the program prompt asking you the desired cell address, you would type it and then strike the Enter key. (For instance, type T50 and then strike Enter.) The view will be moved to the portion of the worksheet surrounding the requested cell and that cell will be made the current cell.

One other positioning key that is sometimes convenient is the End (see Figure 4-6). Striking this key causes the lowest, rightmost cell used by your worksheet to be made the current cell.

SUMMARY OF CELL POINTER MOVEMENT KEYSTROKES

Keystroke	Action
Right	Move current cell right 1 column.
Left	Move current cell left 1 column.
Up	Move current cell up 1 row.
Down	Move current cell down 1 row.
Ctrl-Right	Scroll 8 columns to the right.
Ctrl-Left	Scroll 8 columns to the left.
PgUp	Scroll 20 rows up.
PgDn	Scroll 20 rows down.
Home	Make cell A1 the current cell.
End	Make the cell at the last row and column used by your worksheet the current cell.

ENTERING LABELS AND NUMBERS INTO THE WORKSHEET

Now that you know how to position the cell pointer at any cell in the worksheet, you need to know how to make entries into the cells. You will learn how to do this by entering the cost analysis example of the introduction to Part Three. From this introduction, you know that there are three types of information that you will enter:

- *Labels* (descriptive titles)
- *Numbers* (numeric data)
- *Formulas* (for calculating values from numbers that have been entered)

When you make an entry into a cell, 1-2-3 determines the type of entry by inspecting the first keystroke. This principle of 1-2-3 reacting to a keystroke is not new; for example, you have already experienced the following.

Keystroke	Action
Arrow key	Moves the cell pointer.
/	Changes from READY mode to MENU mode and awaits a command.
F5	Changes from READY mode to POINT mode and awaits the cell address of the cell to be made the current cell.

Other keys on the typewriter portion of the keyboard are interpreted by 1-2-3 to indicate whether a label, number, or formula is being entered. For instance, if the first keystroke from the READY mode is a letter, 1-2-3 assumes that a label is being entered. If the first keystroke is a digit, it assumes that a number is being entered. A partial summary of the first keystroke actions and the keys that trigger them are shown in Figure 4-9.

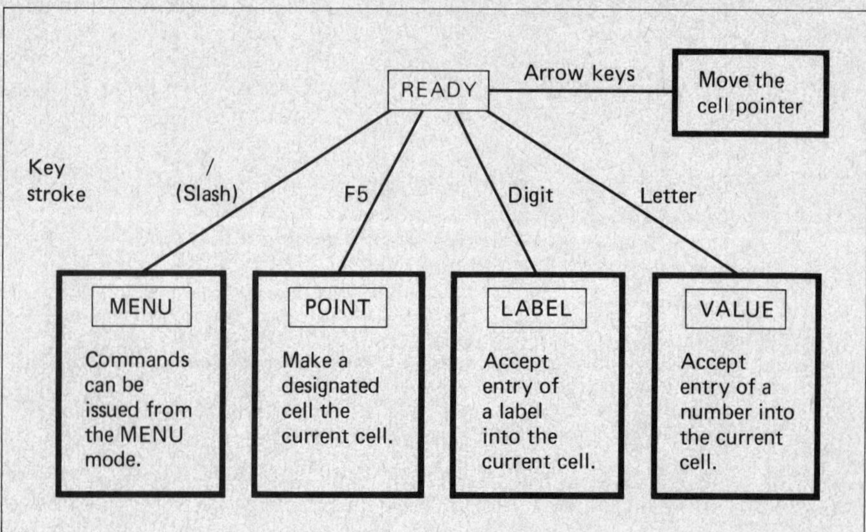

Figure 4-9
The effect of keystroke actions from the READY mode.

Figure 4-10
The cost analysis worksheet.

	A	B	C	D	E	F	G
1		Material	Labor	Other	Unit Cost	Quantity	Amount
2	Style A	5.26	7.33	1.38	13.97	12	167.64
3	Style B	5.26	9.12	1.45	15.83	12	189.96
4	Style C	7.12	4.18	2.12	13.42	18	241.56
5	Style D	6.51	6.99	1.09	14.59	8	116.72
6							
7	Total					50	715.88

Simple Label Entry

For your convenience, the cost analysis worksheet that you will be entering is repeated here as Figure 4-10.

DO THIS NOW 4-6 **Entering a Label Into Cell A2**

1. Move the cell pointer to A2 by striking the Down key.
2. Strike the letter S (in *Style A*) to begin the entry; this will produce the following screen display.

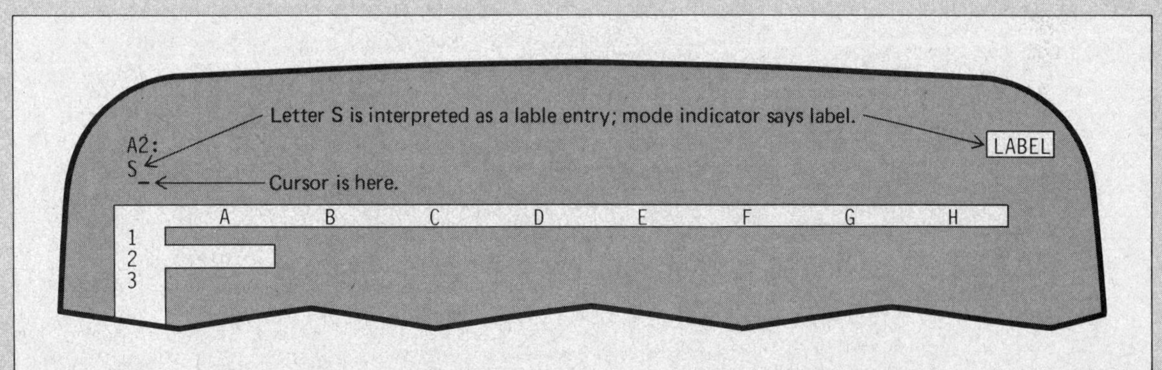

Notice that this keystroke has caused two things to happen. First, 1-2-3 switched to the label mode, as indicated by the word LABEL in the mode indicator. This tells you that 1-2-3 is in the LABEL mode, accepting the entry of a label from the keyboard. Second is that 1-2-3 accepted this first keystroke as the first character of the label; in doing so, 1-2-3 placed it on the second line of the control panel.

3. Type in the remainder of the label. As the label is being keyed in, notice that it is entered into the second line of the control panel as follows:

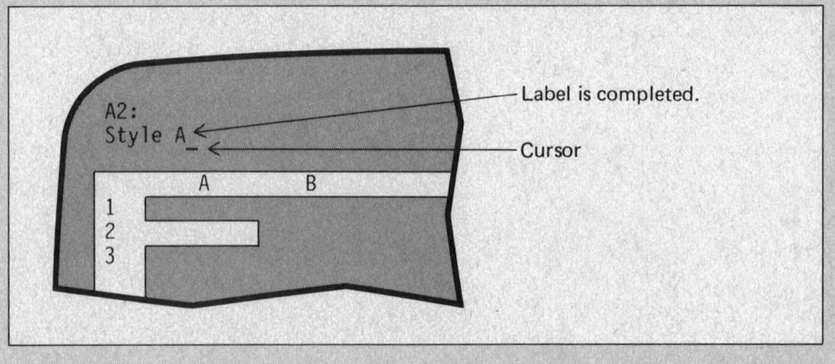

4. As with most computer programs, you must "tell" the computer that you have finished an entry. Do this by striking Enter and your final result will be as follows (for the moment, ignore the single quote that is displayed following the cell address):

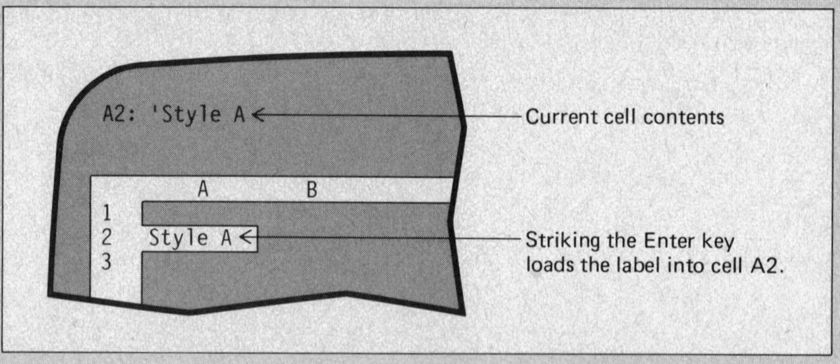

In the preceding example, you caused 1-2-3 to place your entry in the current cell by striking Enter. However, there is another way that is usually more convenient. That is, if you strike *any* of the direction keys, the entry is completed *and* the cell pointer is moved. In the preceding example, had you pressed the Down key, the entry in cell A2 would have been completed and the cell pointer moved to cell A3, ready and waiting for the next entry.

You should now proceed to enter the rest of the labels in column A. Then move the cell pointer to cell B1 and begin entry of the top row of titles. When you are finished, your screen should appear as shown in Figure 4-11. Check your worksheet on the screen to ensure that all entries are correct. If you have made any errors, you can correct them simply by moving the cell pointer to the cell containing the incorrect value and reentering it. The new entry will replace the current one. In other words, it makes no difference whether a cell is empty or contains something else (another label, number, or formula) when an entry is made. The previous contents are always replaced by the newly typed quantity.

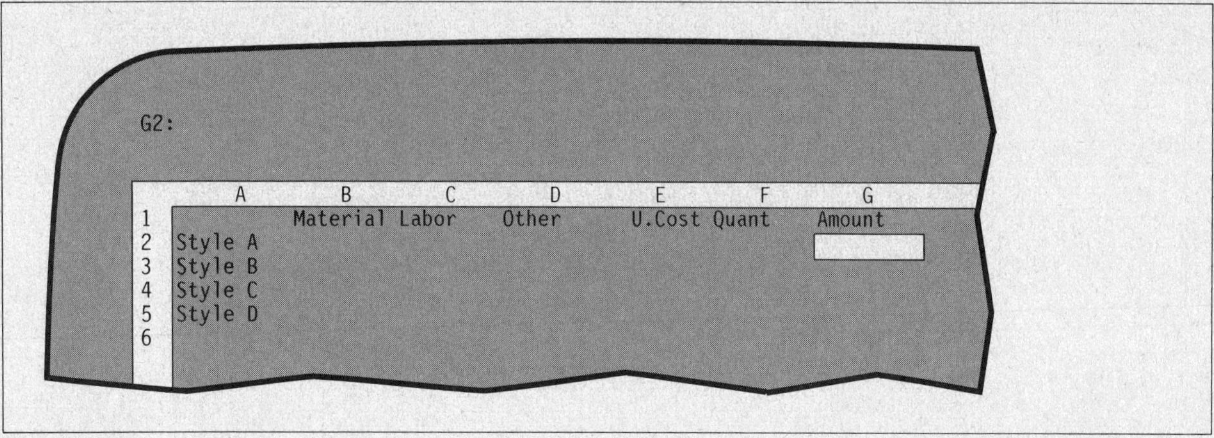

Figure 4-11
The worksheet labels.

Positioning of Labels in the Cell Display

Perhaps you noticed when entering the labels that they are positioned to the left in the cell. Left alignment is the default. In contrast, numbers are positioned to the right, or right-aligned. For this worksheet, the default position will give you a result in which the labels are positioned poorly over the numbers they describe. Fortunately, you can override the default left alignment of labels.

Move the cell pointer to any label cell on the screen and you will see the label displayed on the second line of the control panel preceded by a single quote ('). This is one of three characters that indicate a label to 1-2-3; the other two are the double quote (") and the caret (^). The single quote is the default value and is automatically used when you strike a letter key from the READY mode. In addition to identifying an entry as being a label, the label indicators also designate the positioning of the label within the display cell as follows:

' (single quote)	Label left-aligned
" (double quote)	Label right-aligned
^ (caret)	Label centered

DO THIS NOW 4-7 **Entering a Label Left-Aligned**

1. Move the cell pointer to cell C1 (it contains the label *Labor*).
2. Type a double quote. This switches 1-2-3 to the LABEL mode, enters the double quote, and causes 1-2-3 to await the entry of the label (see next page).

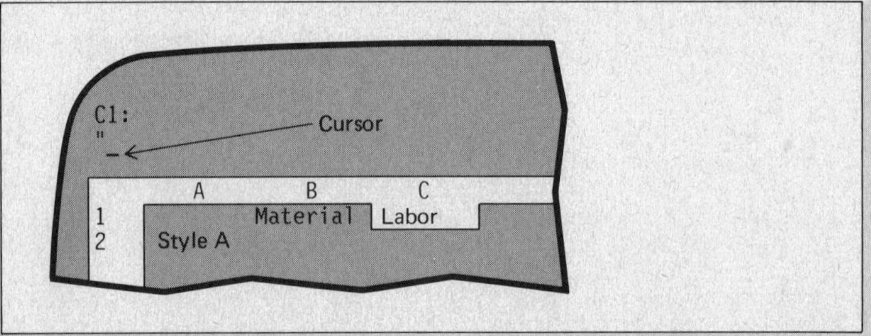

3. Type the label (Labor) and strike Enter. The label will be entered into cell C1 and the screen display will be as shown in the following. Notice that the double quote is not displayed in the screen cell but is included in the corresponding memory cell.

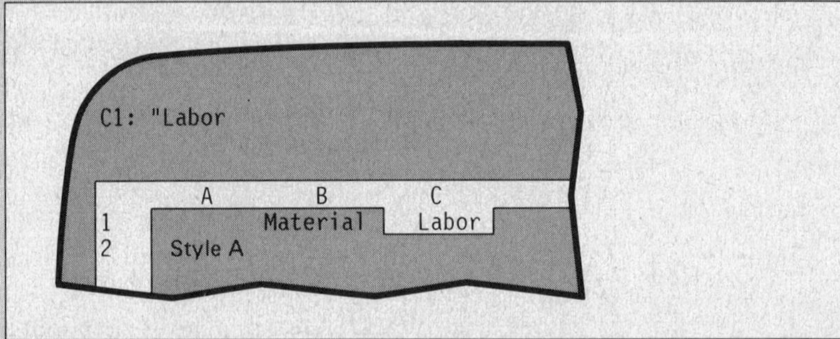

4. Reenter the rest of the labels in Row 1 so that they are all right-aligned.

Entering Numbers

If you were creating a template for the cost analysis, you would enter the formulas next and save a copy without data. Then, for your cost studies, you would enter data values and observe the effect on total cost. However, for this learning sequence, you will learn how to enter numeric quantities next. Remember that this data will be used by formulas in performing the calculations. Hence, each cell entry must be identified as a number when it is entered.

Numbers take a variety of forms; for instance, the number 125 might appear in a worksheet in any of the following ways.

125	–125
12.5	+125
.125	$125.00
0.0125	

Consistent with these needs, any of the following characters causes 1-2-3 to switch from the READY mode to the VALUE mode and accept the entry as a number. (As you will learn in the next section, the VALUE mode is used to enter both numbers and formulas.)

Any digit 0–9

Decimal point (.)

Minus sign (–)

Plus sign (+)

Dollar sign ($)

You can now proceed to enter the data into your worksheet.

DO THIS NOW 4-8 **Entering Data into the Worksheet**

1. Move the cell pointer to cell B2, the cell into which the material cost for Style A is to be entered.
2. Type in the number 5.26. Notice that when you strike the digit 5, the mode indicator displays VALUE. Your screen should appear as shown below.

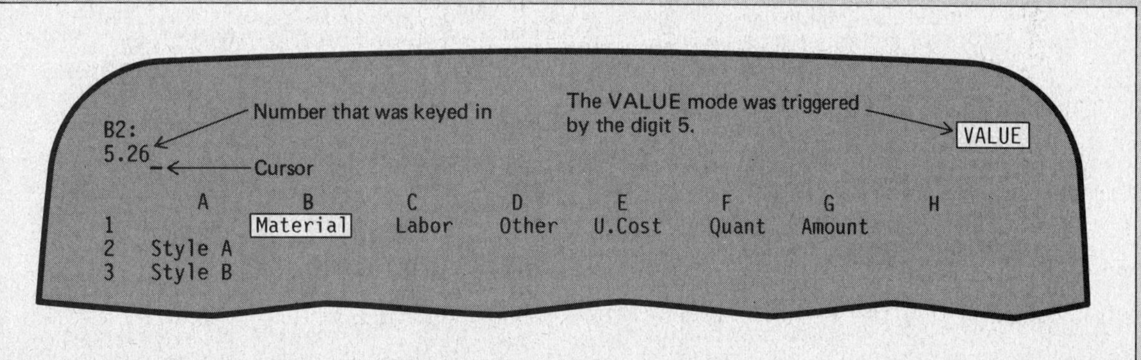

3. As with labels, you can enter this value into the current cell either by striking the Enter or one of the direction keys. In this case, strike the Down key in order to be ready for data entry into cell B3.
4. Enter the data for the rest of the worksheet.
5. When data entry is complete, check your values to make certain they are correct. For any that are incorrect, reenter the correct value in the same way that you corrected label entries.

Perhaps, as you entered your numbers for this worksheet, you accidentally entered an amount ending with a digit 0. If you did, you noticed that it was displayed as, for instance, 5.2 rather than 5.20. The default display for 1-2-3 is not to display digits to the right of the decimal point that are not significant. You will learn how to control this in the next chapter.

More About Entering Labels

Since 1-2-3 inspects the first character to determine whether a label or number is about to be entered, perhaps you have wondered about entering labels with default left alignment such as the following.

```
97 Print
--Tax--
```

Here, the first character you enter will cause 1-2-3 to change to the VALUE mode, not the LABEL mode as desired. In cases such as this, you must first type a single quote, thereby switching to LABEL mode, and then proceed to type the label. If you use centering or right alignment, you will have no problem.

Assignment 4-2 may now be completed.

FORMULAS

The Introduction to Part Three describes how formulas in spreadsheets automatically calculate and display values in cells based on the contents of other cells. For example, the formula

```
+B2+C2+D2
```

directs 1-2-3 to add the values stored in cells B2, C2, and D2. If this formula is assigned to cell E2 (the Unit Cost cell in the cost analysis), the sum will be displayed in that screen cell. Completing the cost analysis worksheet requires that you enter formulas into the cells of columns E and G.

About the VALUE Mode

In the preceding descriptions, you used the VALUE mode for entering numbers into the worksheet. Actually, the word *value* has a much broader implication in 1-2-3: it means that the cell contents will be a numeric quantity. The quantity can be a number that has been entered into the cell, *or it can be the calculated result of a formula assigned to the cell*. Hence, when a keystroke changes the mode to VALUE, 1-2-3 is ready to accept either a number or a formula.

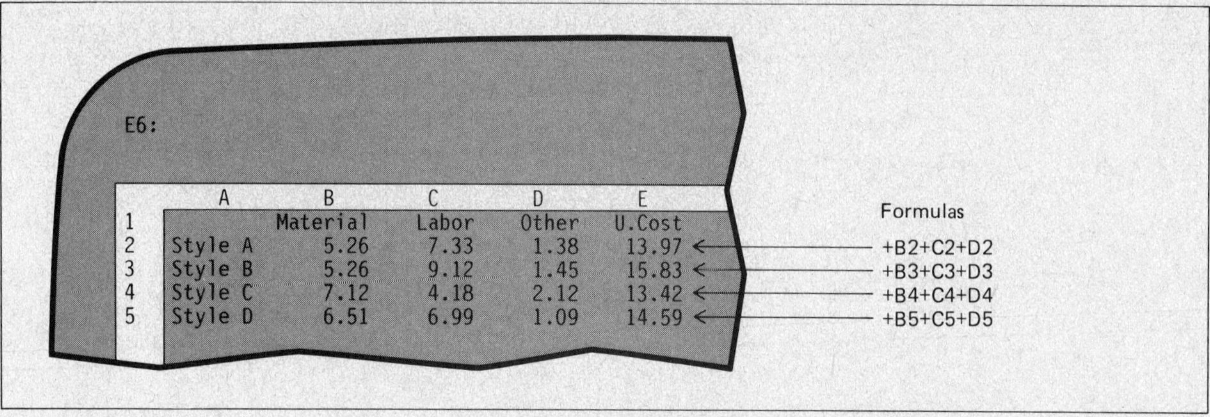

Figure 4-12
Formulas for column E.

Entering Formulas to Calculate Unit Costs

The first group of formulas that will be entered are those for calculating the Unit Cost (column E) shown in Figure 4-12. As the first character in the formula

```
B2+C2+D2
```

is a letter, 1-2-3 will automatically switch to LABEL mode rather than VALUE mode. To avoid this, you must enter the formula as:

```
+B2+C2+D2
```

In the following example, you will enter the formulas into the Unit Cost. If the basic format of the formula is wrong (for instance, you enter +B2#C2 instead of +B2+C2), the computer will beep and switch to the EDIT mode. Working from the EDIT mode is described in a later section of this chapter. For now, if that occurs, simply strike the Escape key twice to return to the READY mode. Then you can reenter the formula.

DO THIS NOW 4-10 **Entering the Formula into Cell E3 by Pointing**

1. Move the cell pointer to E2.
2. Type a + sign to switch to VALUE mode. The upper portion of your screen will appear as shown below.

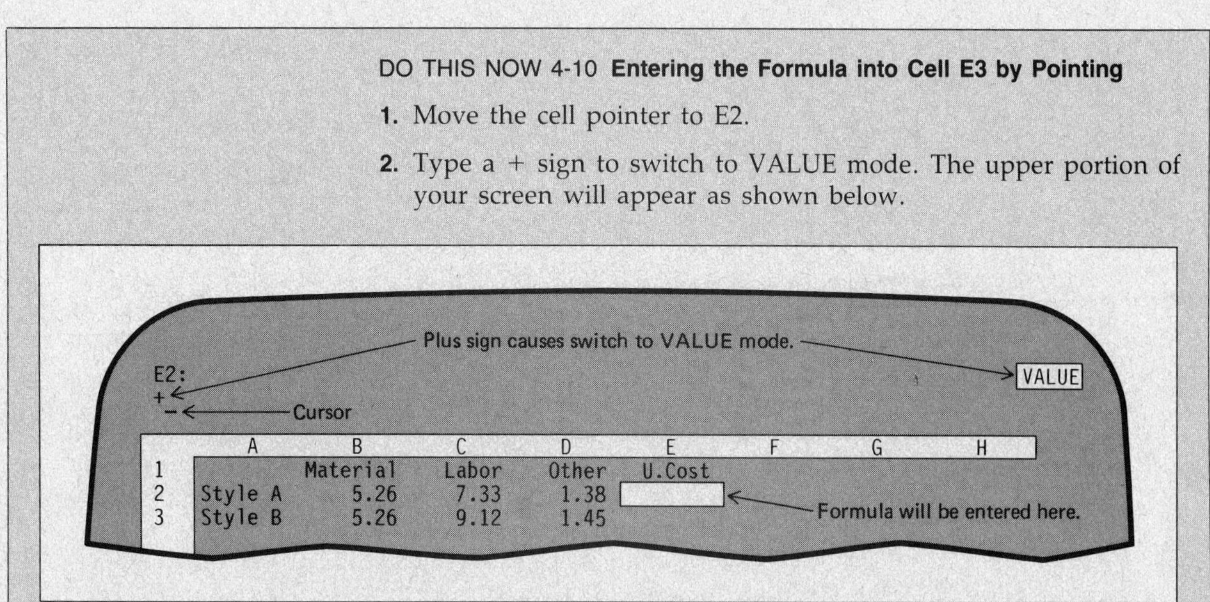

3. Type in the formula. Check it before striking Enter. If it is not the same as the following display, correct it.

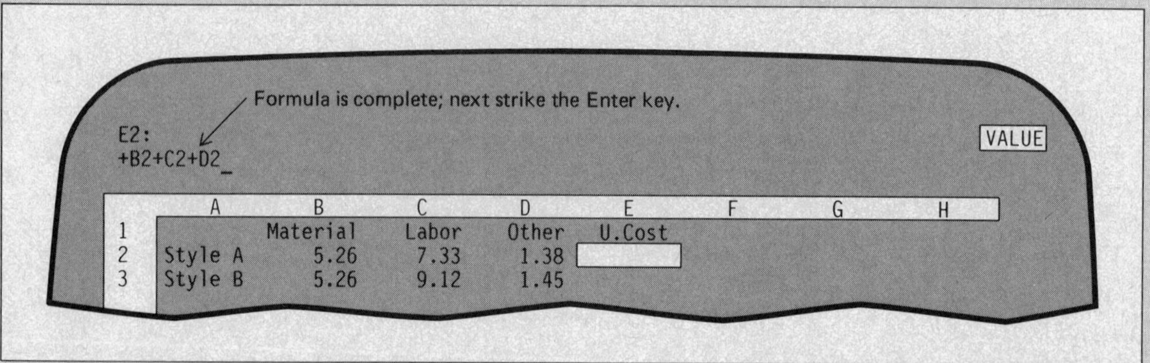

Make needed corrections by striking the Backspace key, which backs up the cursor and deletes as it goes. For instance, if you observed that you had entered

```
+B2+C1+D2
```

you would use the Backspace key and erase until you had

```
+B2+C
```

Then you would complete the entry.

4. Although you can complete the entry of this formula with either an arrow key or the Enter, strike the Enter key so that your screen will be as exactly as follows:

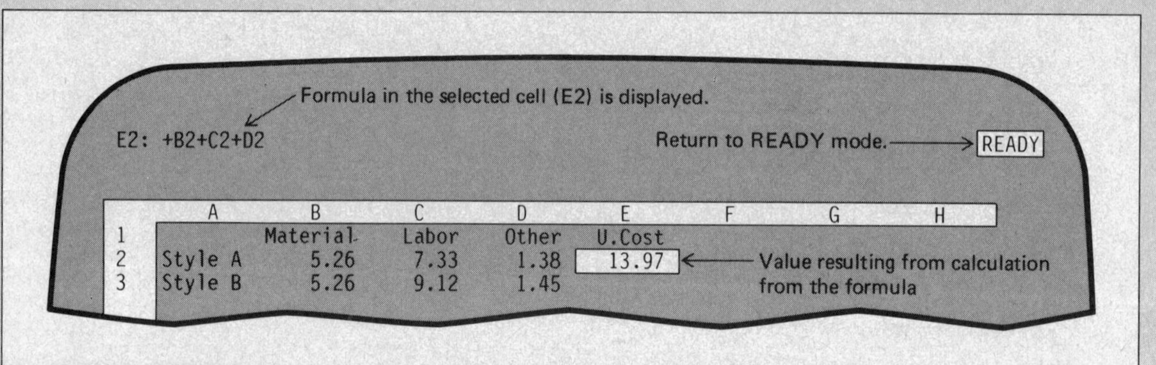

5. If the displayed result in cell E2 is different from the preceding display, something is wrong with your entries. First, check the numbers in cells B2, C2, and D2. Reenter any that are different. If the value in cell E2 is still incorrect, then check your formula. Notice that the formula of the current cell is displayed on the first line of the control panel. If the formula is incorrect, then reenter it just as you would a label or number.

If you forget to begin a formula with a +, you can see it because the mode indicator will say LABEL. If you do not notice this while typing the formula, it will be quite evident when you strike the Enter because the formula rather than the calculated result will be displayed in the cell. If this happens, simply reenter the formula properly.

Creating Formulas by Pointing

There is another way of entering formulas that many users prefer. The method is called *pointing* and involves moving the cursor to the cell to be included in the formula. To illustrate, let us create the formula for the cost of Style B (B3+C3+D3). In the following sequence of steps, the appearance of the appropriate portion of the screen is shown below the description.

DO THIS NOW 4-10 **Entering the Formula into Cell E3 by Pointing**

1. Position the cell pointer to cell E3, the cell into which the formula is to be entered.

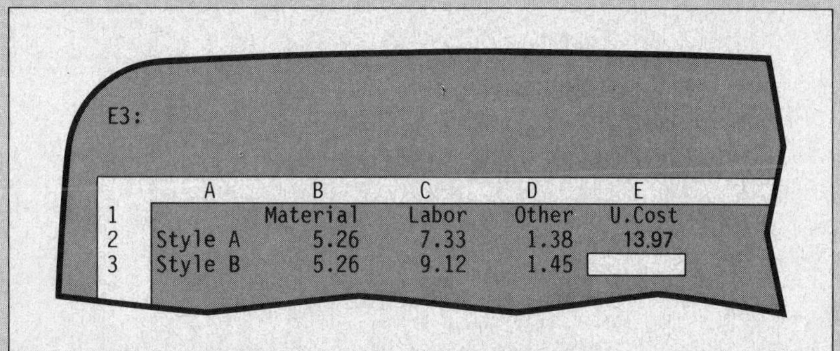

2. Enter the plus sign (+) to indicate that a value entry is to be made.

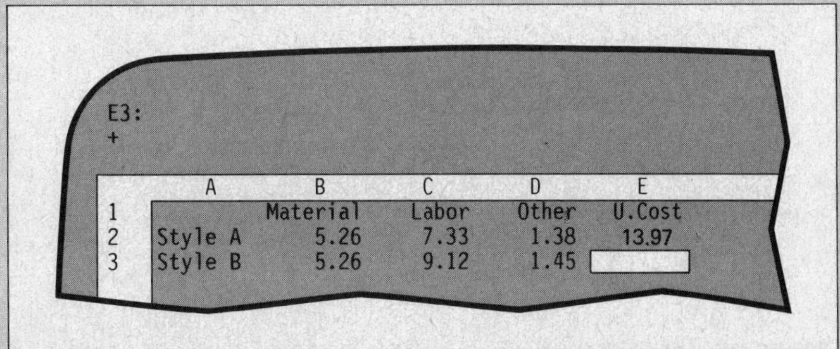

3. Strike the Left arrow key three times, thus moving the cell pointer to cell B3. This is the first cell address required in the formula. Note that the corresponding address has been entered into the formula that is being constructed on the second line of the control panel.

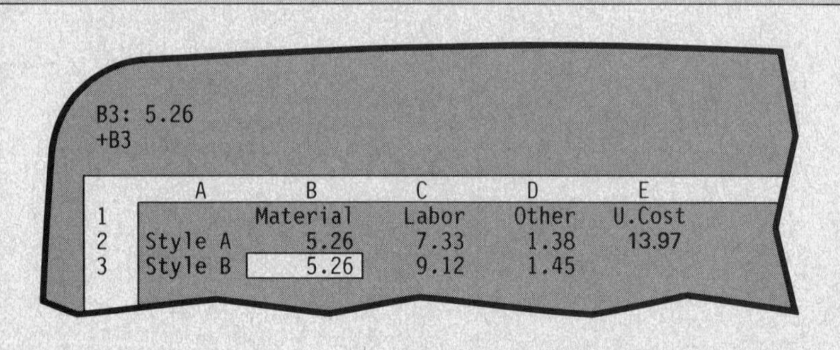

4. Enter a + sign, the next part of the formula. Notice that it has been added to the emerging formula in the control panel.

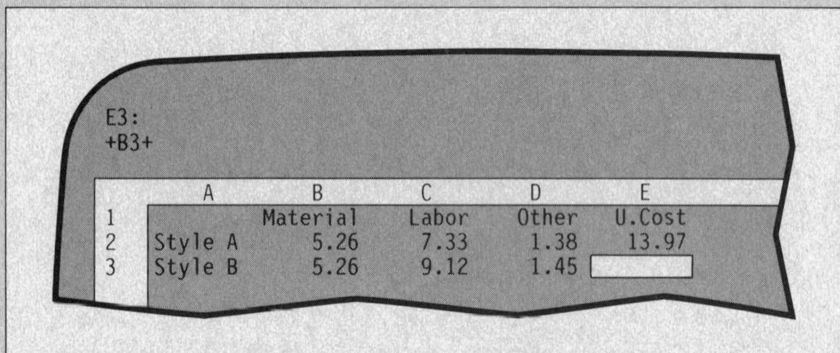

5. Move the cell pointer to cell C3, causing the next element of the formula to be displayed.

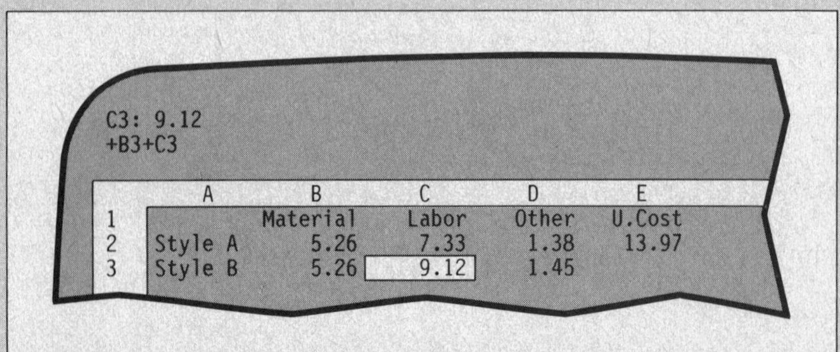

6. Enter a + sign, the next part of the formula.

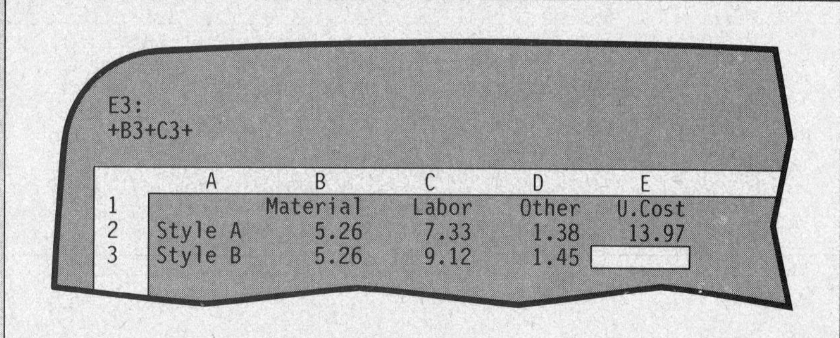

7. Move the cell pointer to cell D3, causing the final element of the formula to be displayed.

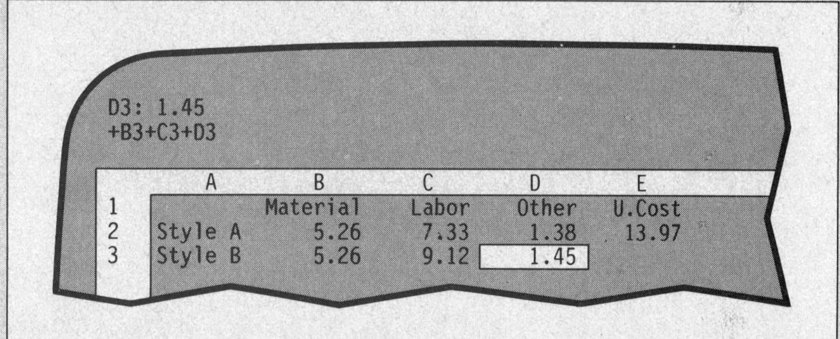

8. As the formula is now complete, strike the Enter key to enter it into cell E3.

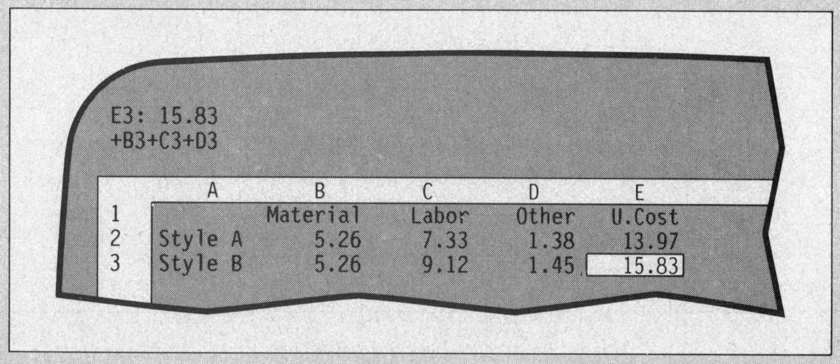

At first, this method for entering formulas may appear to be slower and clumsier than simply keying them in. However, once you get the knack of it, the process is reasonably quick. Most important, it reduces the chance for error. That is, it is much easier to overlook the address D3 keyed in as D2 than to make the corresponding mistake with the visual operation of positioning the highlight to the desired cell.

To complete this portion of your worksheet, you must enter each of the formulas for cells E4 and E5. You may either type the formula or use pointing.

Entering the Remaining Formulas

To complete the cost analysis worksheet, you must enter the remaining formulas summarized in Figure 4-13. Using cell G2 as an example, notice that the Amount value for this line is calculated as the contents of cell E2 times the contents of cell F2. Using the asterisk for multiplication, this formula must be entered as:

```
+E2*F2
```

You should proceed to enter the formulas into your worksheet, thus completing all entries. Do not forget the plus sign to indicate that a value entry is being made. The formulas for cells G3, G4, and G5 are identical except that the row designations differ as appropriate. The final formulas (in cells F7 and G7) are the totals of the values above them in the worksheet.

There is a subtle point about formulas that is illustrated by this worksheet. The formula of cell F7, for example, uses the contents of cells F2 through F5, all of which contain numbers. However, the formula of cell G7 uses the contents of cells G2 through G5, all of which have formulas associated with them. In other words, the calculated value displayed by cell G7 is the result of the contents of cells G2 through G5, themselves calculated values. This is quite valid and, in fact, is very common in worksheets.

Using the Completed Worksheet

When you have completed your worksheet, you should carefully check each cell display to ensure that it is correct. Then save it to disk; you will need this worksheet for later examples. Note that a copy of it is also

Figure 4-13
The remaining formulas.

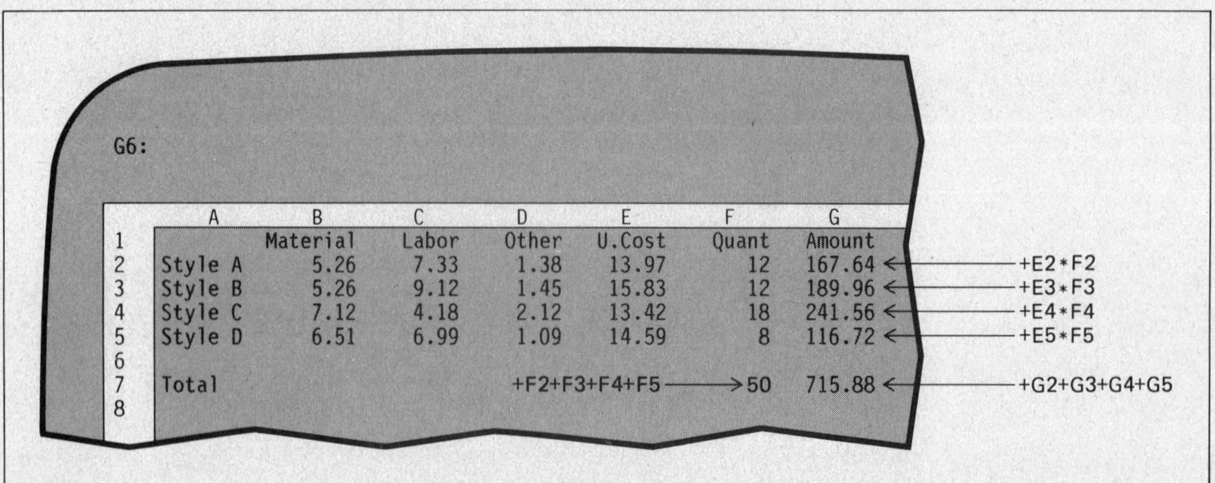

available to you on the data disk that accompanies this book under the name COSTAN.WKS.

You can now proceed to experiment by changing the data in the worksheet in order to achieve the desired $675 cost total.

DO THIS NOW 4-11 **Changing Data Entries in the Cost Analysis Worksheet**

1. Change the values of items identified for cost reduction in the introduction to Part Three; that is, incorporate the following reductions into your worksheet.

Labor Reduction		Other Reduction	
Style A	.55	Style A	.41
Style B	.60	Style B	.44
Style D	.70	Style C	.31
		Style D	.21

   For instance, the Material cost for Style A is to be reduced from 7.33 (refer to your worksheet on the screen or to Figure 4-13) to 6.78, which is a reduction of .55. As you type in each new data value, notice the "ripple" effect it has on the Unit Cost, Amount, and Total. When you have completed these changes, the new total should be 679.02. If it is not, check all of your values.

2. Make additional small changes to these data values and bring the total as close to 675 as you can. In deciding how small (or large) to make your changes, notice that a change in Unit Cost of 1 cent reduces the amount for Styles A and B by 12 cents, for Style C by 18 cents, and for Style D by 8 cents.

RULES FOR BUILDING FORMULAS

The formulas you entered for the cost analysis worksheet are relatively simple, consisting of adding the contents of several cells or multiplying the contents of two cells. For examples yet to come, the calculations are more complex. In order to construct them, you must know the rules used by 1-2-3 when performing the calculations.

Operators and Their Precedence

Consider the simple arithmetic expression:

```
24+7x3
```

24 + 7 X 3	24 + 7 X 3
31 X 3	24 + 21
93	45

Which of the following two sets of calculations to the left is correct and how do we know which form to use?

The answer is that the multiplication must be performed first (as on the right) because the rules of mathematics say that multiplication takes precedence over addition.

This example involves two of the basic arithmetic operations of mathematics; in all, there are five:

Raise to a power

Multiplication and division

Addition and subtraction

They are listed here in their order of **precedence,** that is, the order in which the operations will be carried out in a calculation sequence. Notice that multiplication and division have the same precedence level as do addition and subtraction. These precedence rules are illustrated by the following examples.

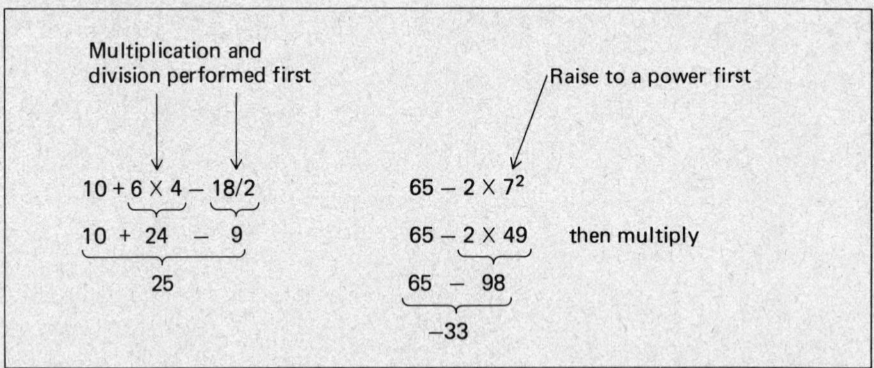

As in algebra, parentheses can be used to group items and change the precedence. That is, when parentheses are used, calculations are performed first on those elements within the parentheses, as illustrated by the following set of examples. In the right-most example of those that follow (representing a compound interest calculation for $100 at 8 percent for 3 years), the addition within the parentheses is performed first. Then the resulting quantity is raised to a power.

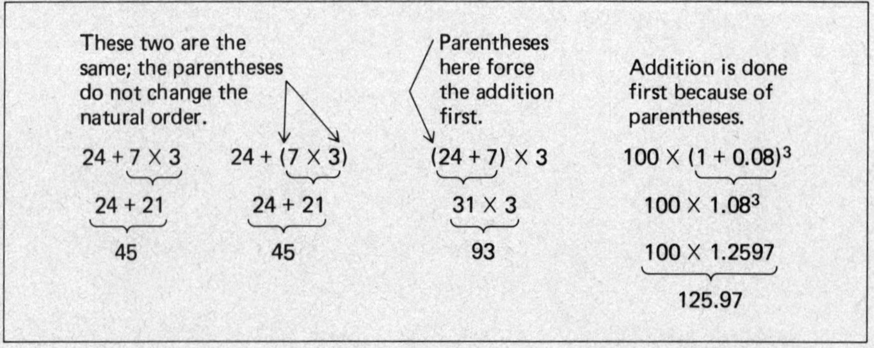

Formulas in 1-2-3

These precedence rules illustrated here with numbers also apply to 1-2-3 formulas. (In fact, they are used almost universally in computing.) In 1-2-3, formulas are constructed by relating variable quantities (for instance, B2, C2, and D2) and numbers with the following **arithmetic operators.**

^ Raise to a power

* Multiplication

/ Division

+ Addition

– Subtraction

The following examples illustrate the major points of constructing 1-2-3 formulas.

Formula	Explanation
+C3+D3-E3	Add the contents of cells C3 and D3 and then subtract the contents of E3.
+F4*F5+23	Multiply the contents of cells F4 and F5 and then add 23 to that result. Note that numbers can be used in forming formulas.
+23+F4*F5 +23+(F4*F5)	Both of these perform exactly the same operation as the preceding example. Note that the rules of precedence are applied: multiplications and divisions are done first and then additions and subtractions. In the second form, parentheses are included. This has no effect on the operation carried out in this case. However, you can use parentheses to make the sequence clear to you.
+C5+C6/4	Divide the contents of cell C6 by 4 and add the result to the contents of cell C5.
(D3+D4+D5)/3	Add the contents of D3, D4, and D5 then divide the result by 3. Parentheses are necessary in this case in order to force the desired sequence of operations.
+D10*(1+D12)^C3	This is the 1-2-3 version of the interest calculation in the last precedence example. Here the value 1 is added to the contents of cell D12 before raising to the power (the number in cell C3).

Notice that none of the preceding examples include any spaces within the formulas. If you have studied a programming language such as BASIC, you know that spaces in formulas are ignored and hence can be inserted to make the forms more readable. This is not true with 1-2-3, which *does not allow spaces anywhere within formulas.*

The earlier examples of entering numbers illustrate most of the initial characters that cause 1-2-3 to switch to the VALUE mode (for entry of a number or formula). Following is the complete set of characters that can be used to start a value entry.

```
1 2 3 4 5 6 7 8 9 0 . + - ( @ # $
```

Note that the open parenthesis, used for grouping in a formula, is also valid as the first character.

Assignment 4-3 may now be completed.

ABOUT WORKSHEET ERRORS AND CORRECTING THEM

In the preceding exercises, you were instructed to make entries and then to check to ensure that they were correct. For your check, you compared your worksheet with the sample in this book. When preparing your own worksheets, you must do the checking. In this section, we will consider a version of the cost analysis worksheet that includes an error, and will show how to detect errors and how to correct them. For this example, you will be using a worksheet from the data disk that accompanies this book. Hence, if your cost analysis worksheet is still on the screen and you wish to save the current version, you should do so before continuing.

Errors in Worksheets

For this example, you must retrieve the worksheet named COSTAN2.WKS from the data disk. In your resulting screen display, which should match Figure 4-14, you can see that this is a cost analysis worksheet with an

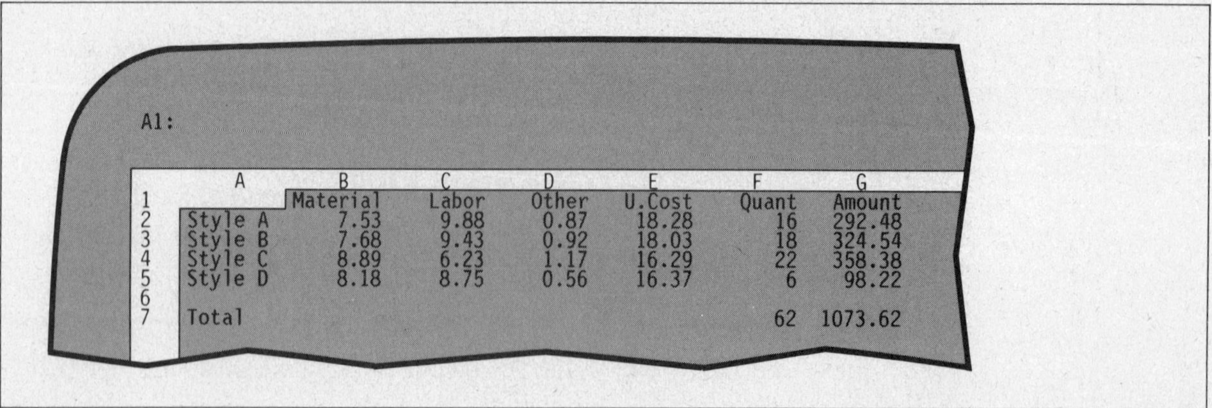

A1:

	A	B	C	D	E	F	G
1		Material	Labor	Other	U.Cost	Quant	Amount
2	Style A	7.53	9.88	0.87	18.28	16	292.48
3	Style B	7.68	9.43	0.92	18.03	18	324.54
4	Style C	8.89	6.23	1.17	16.29	22	358.38
5	Style D	8.18	8.75	0.56	16.37	6	98.22
6							
7	Total					62	1073.62

Figure 4-14
The worksheet COSTAN2.WKS.

entirely different set of data values. At a glance, it appears to be all right. However, let us experiment with it.

DO THIS NOW 4-12 **Finding an Error**

1. Increase each of the Other cost values by 10 cents (for example, change the Style A Other cost in cell D2 to 0.97).
2. As you make each entry, observe the change in each of the computed cells. Pay particular attention to Style D. Notice that when you increase the Other amount, the Unit Cost *decreases*. This is a distressing fact.
3. Manually add the three component values for Style D and you will see the discrepancy of Figure 4-15. It would appear that something is wrong with the way in which 1-2-3 is calculating this sum.

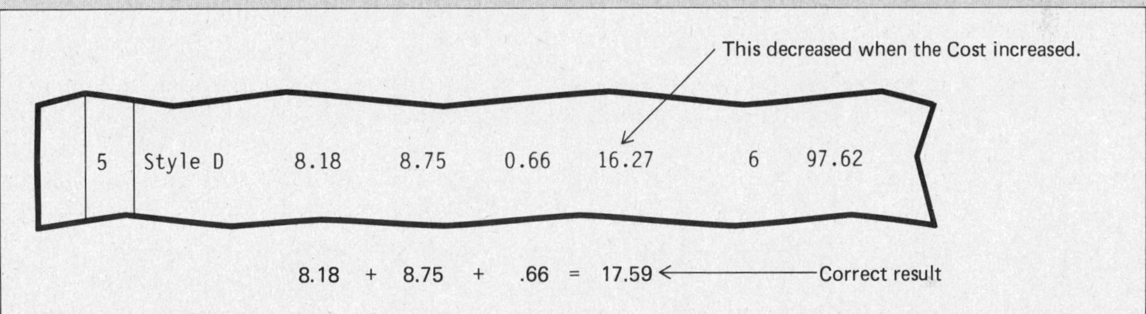

Figure 4-15
Suspicious results from the worksheet.

4. Move the cell pointer to cell E5 so that you can inspect the formula. Your screen display should correspond to that in Figure 4-16 in which the formula has been incorrectly entered with a minus sign. This is easily corrected by reentering. However, do not change it as this formula is used in the next section to illustrate editing.

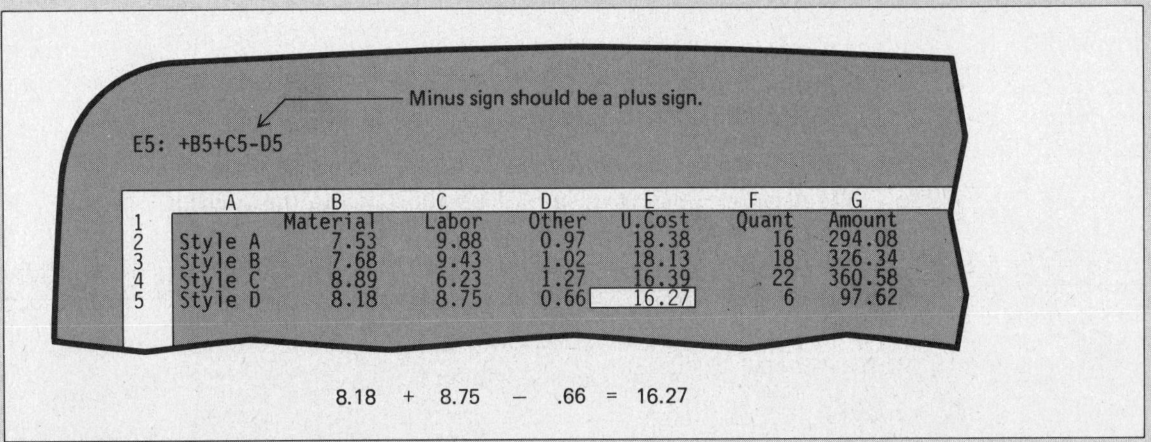

Figure 4-16
An erroneous formula.

This example illustrates an extremely important factor when working with the computer. That is, never assume that the output from any type of program (and your template represents a program) is correct without double checking. Whenever you create a worksheet, check the value displayed from each formula by performing the calculations manually and comparing them to the displayed results. Once each formula has been checked in this way, it is safe to proceed with manipulating data values in the optimization process. Any businessperson who bases decisions on worksheets that have not been properly checked might find it difficult to stay in business.

The EDIT Mode

As you know, you can change the contents of any cell simply by reentering; this applies to formulas as well as numbers and labels. However, reentering an entire formula (or a long label) is a nuisance if only one character is incorrect. To simplify this process, 1-2-3 allows you to perform editing operations on any cell entry by switching to the EDIT mode. Switching from the READY mode to the EDIT mode is done by striking the F2 key. (If you are using JOE, the third line of the control panel displays F2:Ed as a reminder. If you are using Lotus 1-2-3, then you should have a template that fits around the function keys that tells you the action of each.) To illustrate editing, let us correct the error in the formula of Figure 4-16.

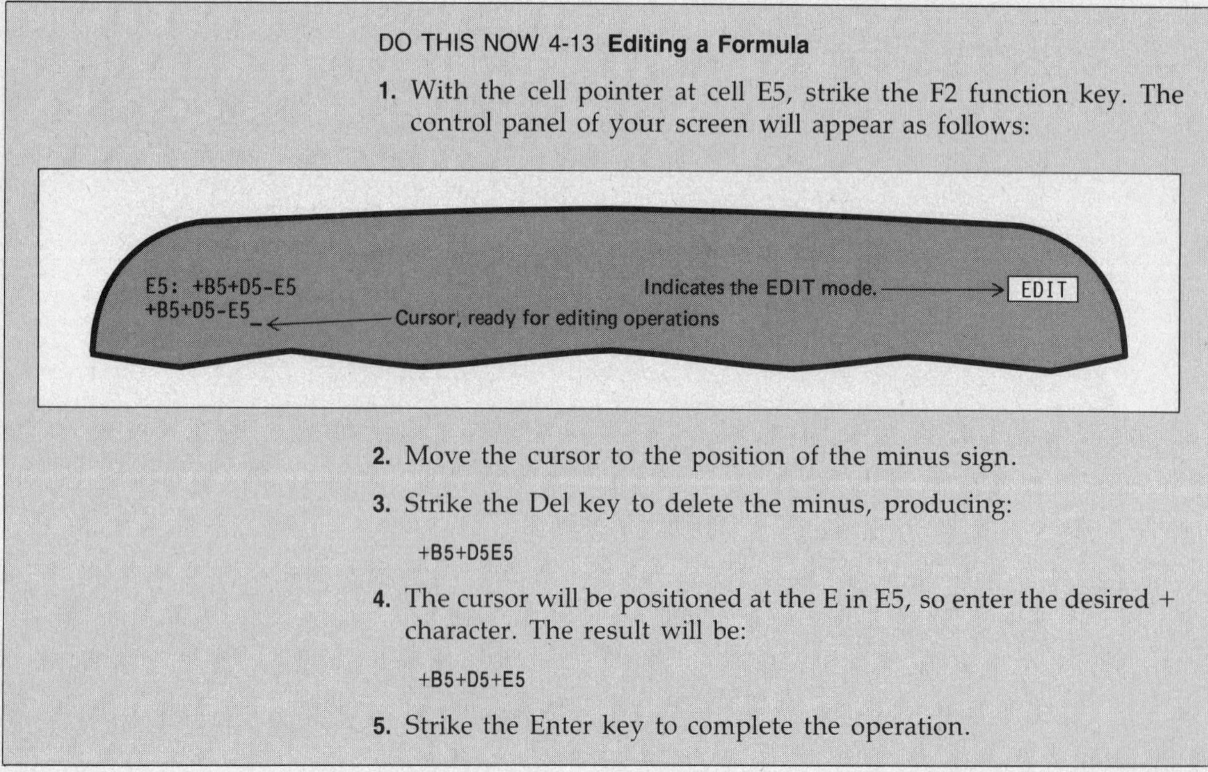

DO THIS NOW 4-13 **Editing a Formula**

1. With the cell pointer at cell E5, strike the F2 function key. The control panel of your screen will appear as follows:

2. Move the cursor to the position of the minus sign.
3. Strike the Del key to delete the minus, producing:

   +B5+D5E5

4. The cursor will be positioned at the E in E5, so enter the desired + character. The result will be:

   +B5+D5+E5

5. Strike the Enter key to complete the operation.

The keys to be used during editing operate in exactly the same way as they do with word processing. Summarizing, you can use them as follows:

- *Left and Right arrows.* Move the cursor to the left or the right.
- *Backspace.* Delete the character to the left of the cursor.
- *Del.* Delete the character at the position of the cursor.
- *Ins.* Toggle between Insert mode and Overtype mode (the newly entered character replaces the character at the position of the cursor). The edit begins in the Insert mode. If the Ins key is used to switch to Overtype, the bottom line of the screen displays the letters OVR.

If you attempt to enter an invalid form into a cell, 1-2-3 beeps and then automatically switches to the EDIT mode without placing anything in the cell. For example, assume that you accidentally keyed in the formula for cell E2 as follows:

```
B2+C2#D2
```

When you strike the Enter or an arrow key, the computer will beep, the mode indicator will change to EDIT, and the cursor will be positioned for editing the formula. When you have corrected it, you can strike the Enter and continue.

MORE ABOUT COMMANDS

You received your introduction to worksheet commands at the beginning of this chapter so that you could save and retrieve worksheets and terminate a work session. The approach at that point was, "Do it because it works." Let us consider some more details of 1-2-3 commands.

Basic Principle of Commands

From the READY mode, striking the slash key (/) causes 1-2-3 to switch to the MENU mode, thus producing the control panel of Figure 4-17. (This is repeated from earlier in the chapter.) Although the command names and their order are slightly different for JOE and Lotus 1-2-3, the first letter of corresponding commands are the same. This is important because, as you recall, you can execute a command by typing the first letter of the command name. When the MENU mode is first entered, the first command is highlighted, as we see in Figure 4-17. The third line of the control panel contains a brief description of the highlighted command. If information regarding any of the other commands is desired, the highlight can be moved from one command to the next by striking the Left or Right keys. The description changes with the changing highlight. Try this and you will see how the third line display changes.

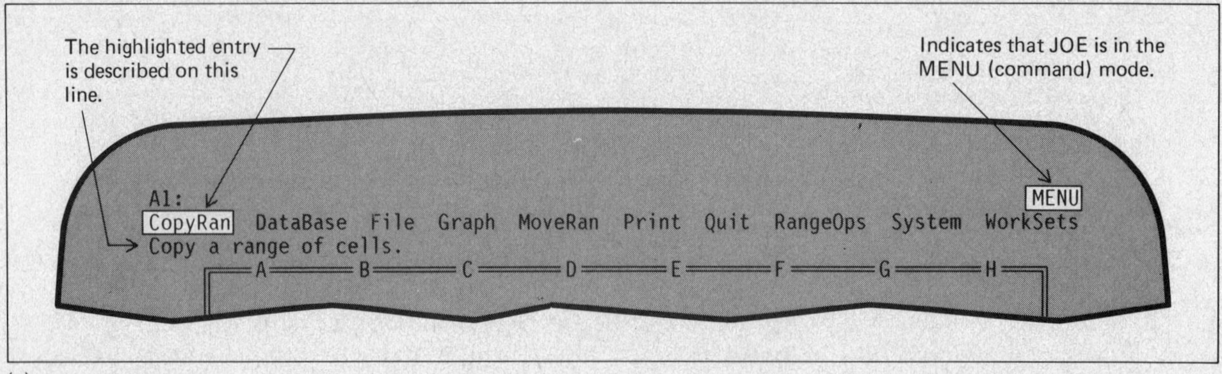

(a)

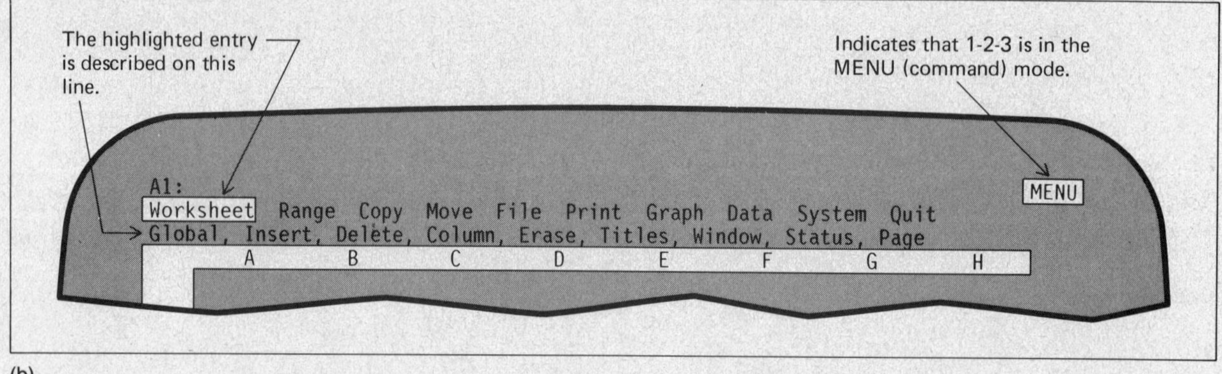

(b)

Figure 4-17
(a) Command menu for JOE.
(b) Command menu for Lotus 1-2-3.

To issue the Save, Retrieve, and Quit commands, you have been typing the first letter of the command name. There is another way of issuing a command—by moving the highlight to the desired command and striking the Enter key. This is identical to the method for selecting the name of a worksheet file to be retrieved. In general, issuing a command by striking the first letter is quicker than moving the highlight.

The execution of some commands produces a submenu of commands from which an option must be selected. You are familiar with that from the File command that produces the submenu shown in Figure 4-3. If you set your default data drive as described earlier in this chapter, you probably noticed that you had to work through several levels of menus.

Getting Help

It is difficult to remember everything about the commands, especially if you do not use 1-2-3 on a regular basis. If you need more information about a command (or many other possible 1-2-3 actions) while working with 1-2-3, you can get assistance from the program. The F1 function key is called the Help key; striking it from the READY mode switches to the HELP mode. To illustrate its use, let us see what descriptive information is available for the File command, one that you have already used in saving and retrieving worksheets. To get a feel for using the Help, you should carry out these actions.

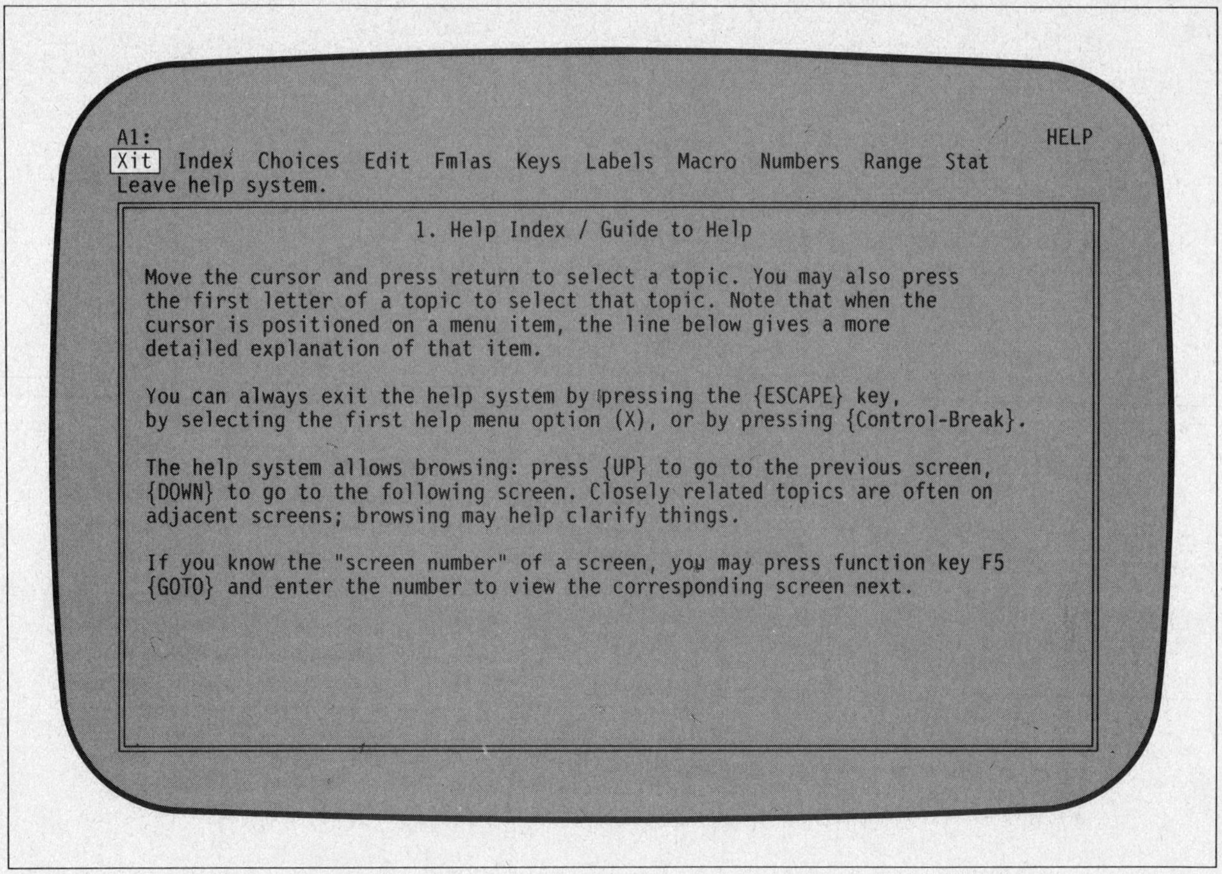

A1:
HELP
Xit Index Choices Edit Fmlas Keys Labels Macro Numbers Range Stat
Leave help system.
1. Help Index / Guide to Help
Move the cursor and press return to select a topic. You may also press
the first letter of a topic to select that topic. Note that when the
cursor is positioned on a menu item, the line below gives a more
detailed explanation of that item.
You can always exit the help system by pressing the {ESCAPE} key,
by selecting the first help menu option (X), or by pressing {Control-Break}.
The help system allows browsing: press {UP} to go to the previous screen,
{DOWN} to go to the following screen. Closely related topics are often on
adjacent screens; browsing may help clarify things.
If you know the "screen number" of a screen, you may press function key F5
{GOTO} and enter the number to view the corresponding screen next.

Figure 4-18
The general Help screen for JOE.

Help with JOE. Striking the F1 key from the READY mode will cause your worksheet to be replaced with the general Help screen shown in Figure 4-18. This gives you a capsule description of how to use Help. The selection menu at the top lists the various categories. Selecting the Choices option (striking the letter C or moving the highlight to Choices and striking Enter) produces the following menu in the control panel.

A1:
HELP
Xit Index Data Entering_Ranges File Graph Print OpRange Worksheet
Leave help system.

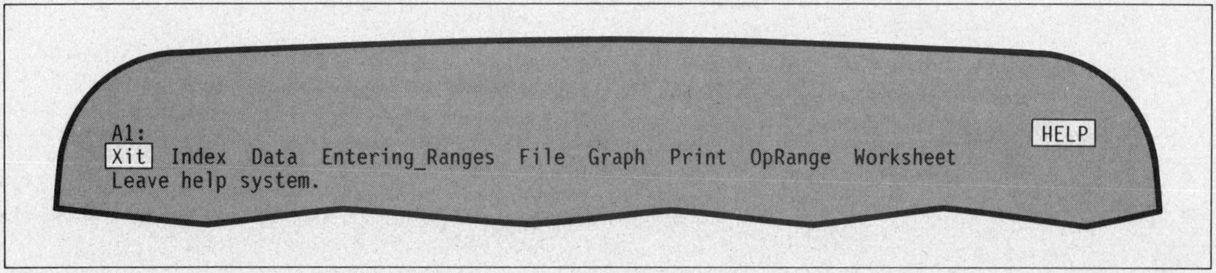

Since we are interested in the File command, type the letter F (for File) or move the highlight to File and strike Enter. Your initial Help screen will be replaced with the File help screen shown in Figure 4-19. Here we see a

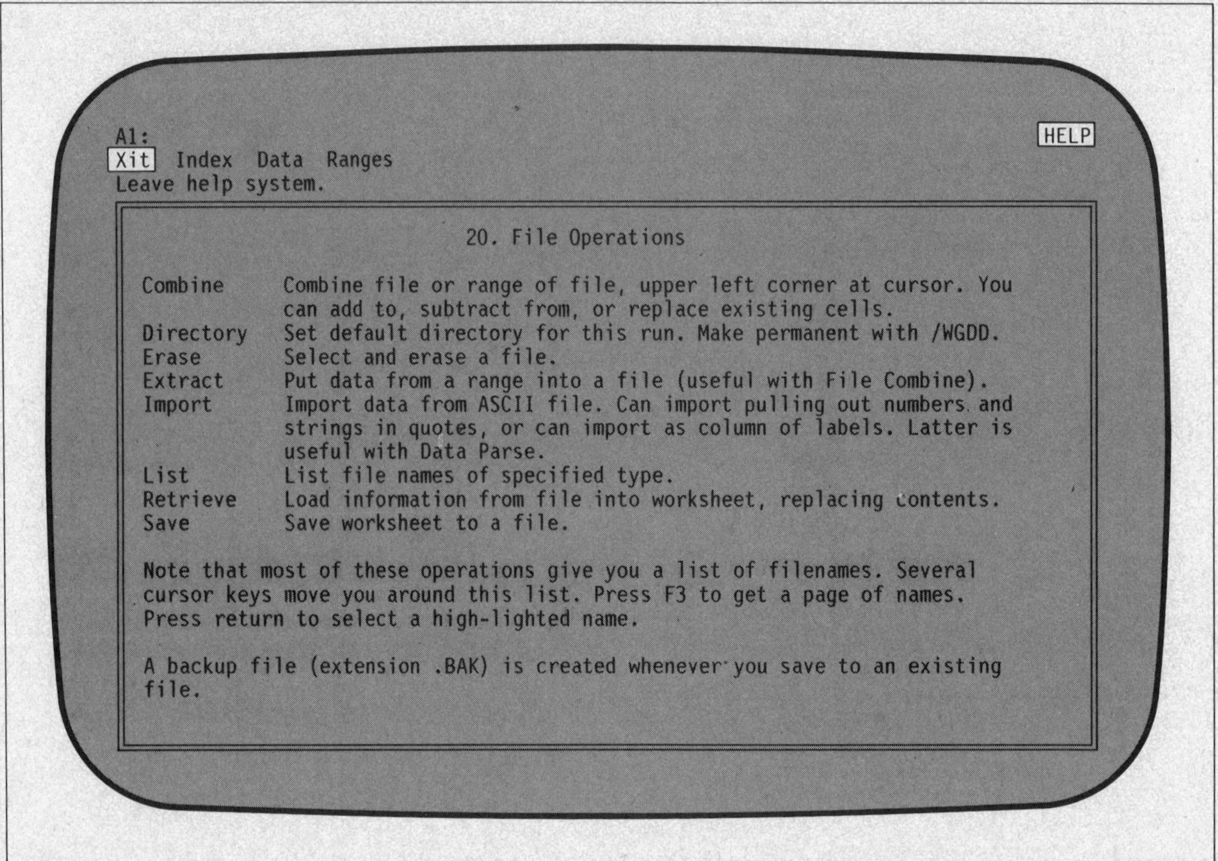
A1: HELP
Xit Index Data Ranges
Leave help system.

20. File Operations

Combine — Combine file or range of file, upper left corner at cursor. You can add to, subtract from, or replace existing cells.
Directory — Set default directory for this run. Make permanent with /WGDD.
Erase — Select and erase a file.
Extract — Put data from a range into a file (useful with File Combine).
Import — Import data from ASCII file. Can import pulling out numbers and strings in quotes, or can import as column of labels. Latter is useful with Data Parse.
List — List file names of specified type.
Retrieve — Load information from file into worksheet, replacing contents.
Save — Save worksheet to a file.

Note that most of these operations give you a list of filenames. Several cursor keys move you around this list. Press F3 to get a page of names. Press return to select a high-lighted name.

A backup file (extension .BAK) is created whenever you save to an existing file.

Figure 4-19
The File Help screen for JOE.

brief description of each of the eight File commands. Although the descriptions may seem too short to be of much value, remember that they are designed as an aid to users in recalling how JOE features work. They are not designed specifically as learning tools. To get a feel for using the Help feature, you should experiment. You cannot get into trouble while in the MENU or HELP modes; striking the Escape key one or more times will always get you back to the READY mode.

Help With Lotus 1-2-3. Striking the F1 key from the READY mode will give you an abbreviated summary of actions you can take from READY. Since we are interested in the File command, first switch to MENU mode (strike the / key), and then strike F1. This will cause your worksheet to be replaced with the general Help screen shown in Figure

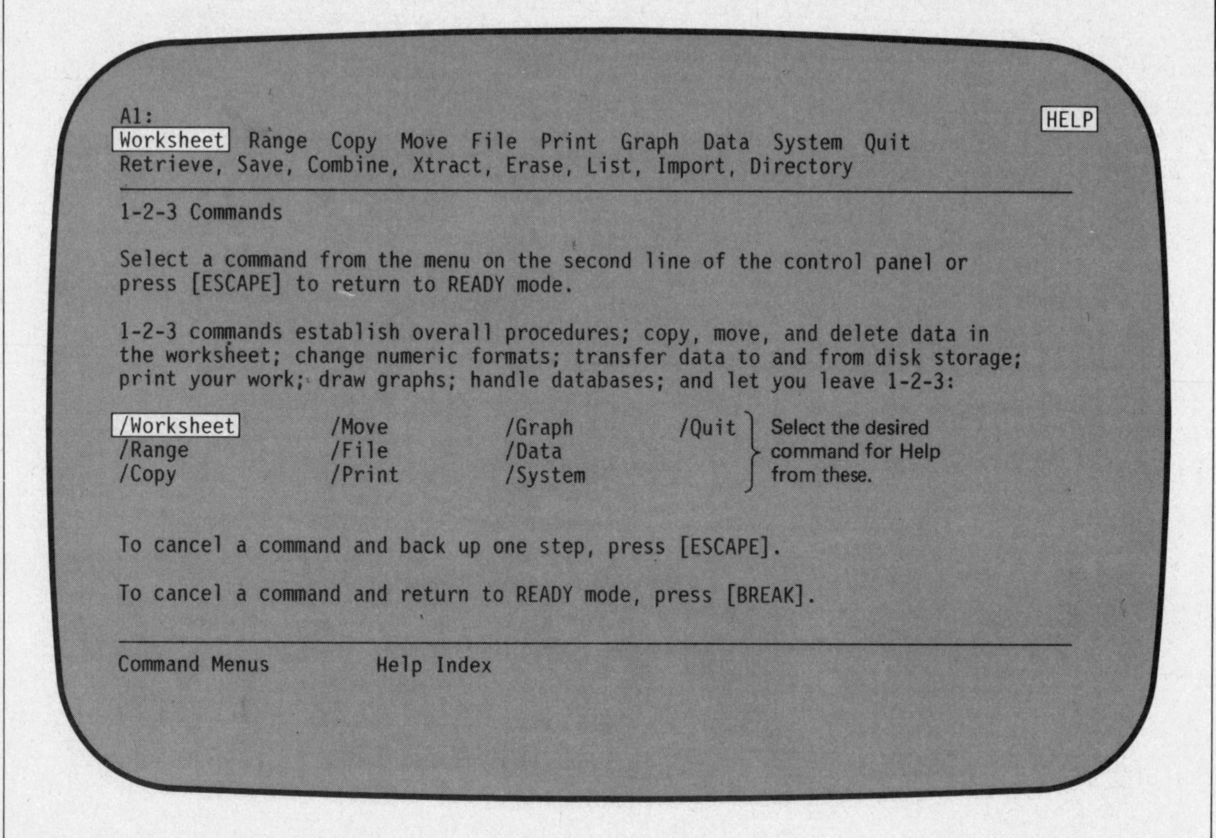

Figure 4-20
Command Help screen for Lotus 1-2-3.

4-20, which gives you a brief description of commands in general. (The Help screens of this section were obtained using Lotus 1-2-3, Version 2; the screens for Version 1A are similar.) To obtain help for any of the commands listed in the center of the screen (/Worksheet is highlighted), move the highlight to that command with the arrow keys and then strike the F1 key again. Moving it to /File and striking the F1 key again produces the File help screen shown in Figure 4-21. If you wanted information on the Save command, you would move the highlight to /Save and strike the F1 once more. Although these descriptions are useful in helping you to recall features of Lotus 1-2-3, remember that they are designed for reference rather than as learning tools. To get a feel for using the Help feature, you should experiment. You cannot get into trouble while in the MENU or HELP modes; striking the Escape key one or more times will always get you back to the READY mode.

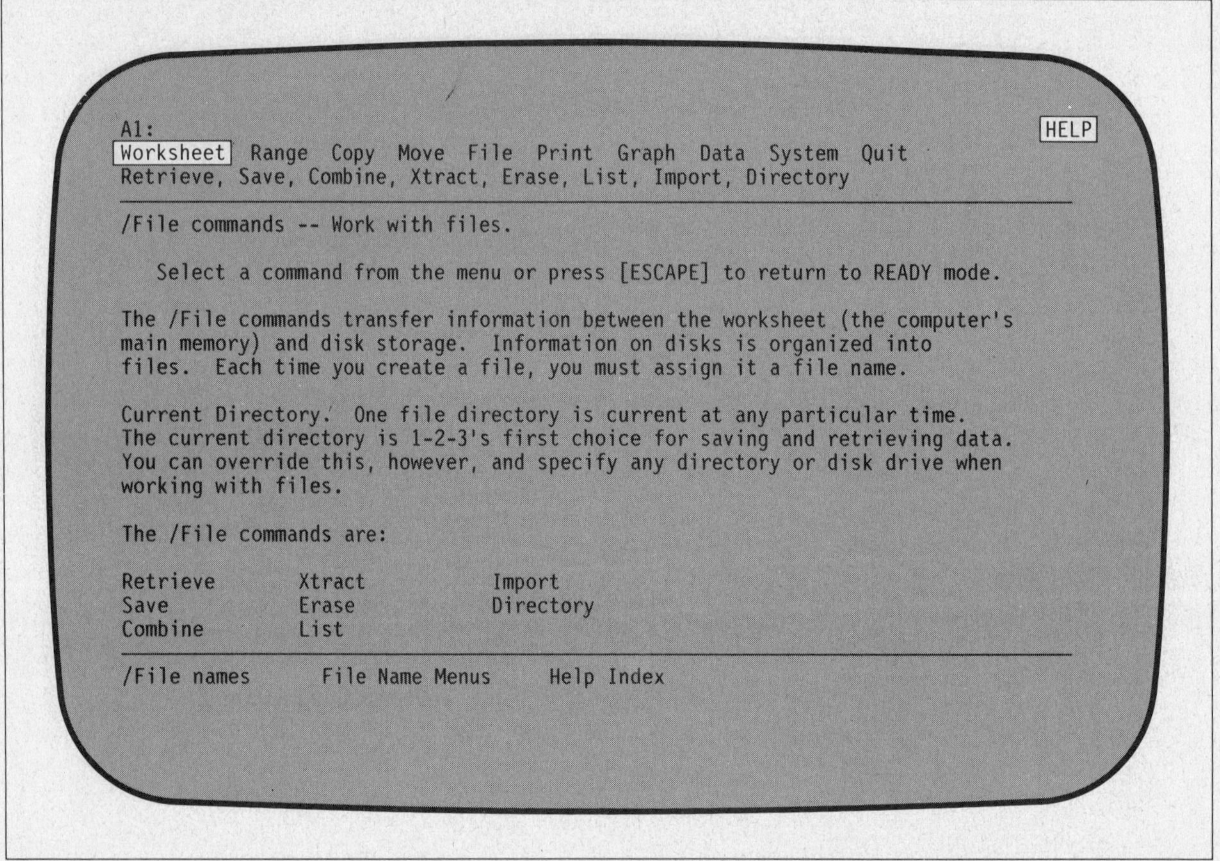

Figure 4-21
The File Help screen for Lotus 1-2-3.

PRINTING A WORKSHEET

About Printed Output

The final action that we will consider in this chapter is printing your worksheet. When printed from 1-2-3, the printed page is the same as the worksheet portion of the screen display (row numbers and column letters are not printed). Your first thought about the Print command is probably that the output goes directly to the printer. Actually, 1-2-3 allows you to send the output either to the printer or to a file on disk in a standard text file (ASCII) format. At first thought, sending the "printed" output to disk might seem a little strange. However, there are several reasons for doing this. One is that the worksheet file in this form can be incorporated into a word processing document. For instance, a worksheet summary of projected sales might be included as part of a letter to sales representatives intended to spark their enthusiasm for emphasizing the products of MCT Enterprises.

As you will see, 1-2-3 allows you to print the entire worksheet or a portion of it. You also have other options, such as inserting special information just for the printout and defining word processing types of options. However, for this example, you will simply print the entire worksheet. In doing so, you must deal with the concept of cell range, a topic discussed in great detail in the next chapter.

Using the Print Command

If you do not have the cost analysis worksheet on your screen, you should retrieve it so you can carry out the following steps.

DO THIS NOW 4-14 **Printing the Worksheet**

1. Strike the / key to switch to MENU mode.
2. Strike the letter *P* for Print. This causes a submenu to appear, which gives you the option of sending the output to the printer or to a file.
3. Strike the letter *P* for Printer output. This produces a menu of several options for controlling the printing.
4. Strike the letter *R* for the Range to print (that is, the portion of the displayed worksheet that you want printed).
5. Move the cell pointer to cell A1 if it is not already there; the second line of the control panel should say:

   ```
   Enter print range: A1
   ```

6. Strike the period key (.) to set the beginning of the range of cells to be printed; the second line of the control panel will now say:

   ```
   Enter print range: A1..A1
   ```

7. Successively strike the Down arrow key and then the Right arrow key until the entire worksheet is highlighted (rows 1 through 7 and columns A through G), as shown in Figure 4-22. (This is the

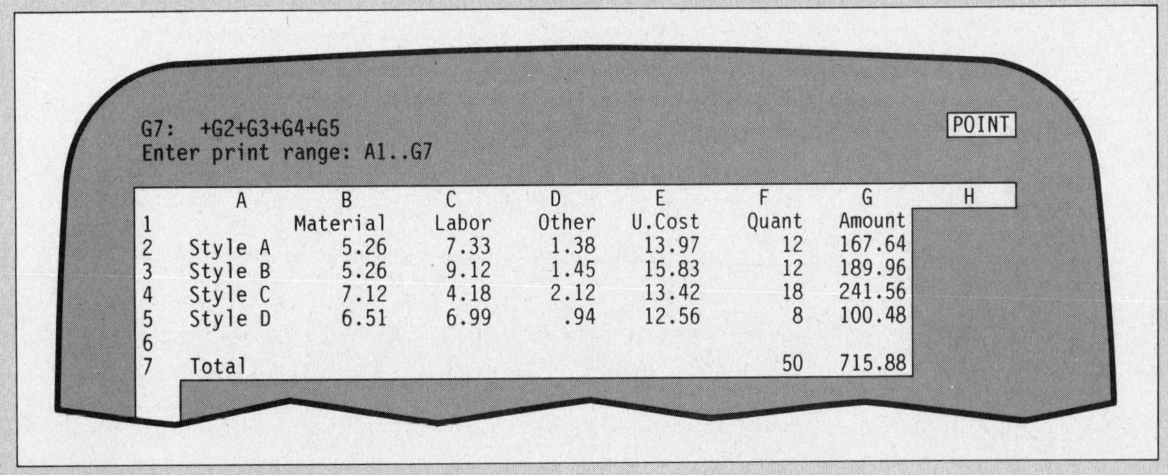

Figure 4-22
The selected print range.

display for 1-2-3; the display for JOE is identical except that the borders are different.) Notice that as you move the cell pointer, the size of the highlighted area is increased. If this does not happen, you have done something wrong and you must try again. Strike the Escape key; the sequence will back up one step for each time the Escape key is struck.

8. To record this range, strike the Enter key and control will be returned to the printer submenu.
9. Check your printer to make certain that it is turned on and ready. Strike the letter *G* (for Go to printing) and your worksheet will be printed.
10. When the printing is completed, strike the letter *Q* for Quit and control is returned to the READY mode.

Your printed output will look exactly like the worksheet area of your screen. You can now proceed with other worksheet activities or terminate your session.

Assignment 4-4 may now be completed.

SUMMARY

This chapter has provided you the basic tools for using 1-2-3. Through the cost analysis worksheet, you have learned how to create a worksheet consisting of labels, numbers, and formulas; to change the data values in using the worksheet as a tool to achieve an objective; to save the worksheet to disk; and to print a copy of the worksheet on the printer. Summarizing, the important items from the chapter are:

- The 1-2-3 display screen comprises four components: worksheet area, cell address border, control panel, and information line.
- The cell pointer identifies the current cell; this is the cell into which keyboard entries are made.
- The control panel is the center of many of the 1-2-3 activities. Information displayed by the control panel includes the cell address of the current cell, the contents of the current cell, the mode indicator, and command menus.
- The mode indicator tells you the current operating mode of 1-2-3. The principal modes under which you have operated in this chapter are:

- READY Default mode
- MENU For execution of commands
- LABEL Allows entry of labels into cells
- VALUE Allows entry of numbers and formulas into cells

- The MENU mode (for entry of commands) is activated by striking the / key.
- Saving a worksheet to disk and retrieving one from disk are done with the File command.
- A 1-2-3 work session should be terminated with the Quit command. This returns control of the computer to DOS.
- The cell pointer can point to a cell at a time, or to a screen at a time, or to the beginning or ending of your worksheet.
- Entry of information into a cell is done from the READY mode. The first keystroke signals to 1-2-3 the type of entry (label or value).
- Formulas are constructed by relating cell contents and numbers by the arithmetic operations:

  Raising to a power

  Multiplication and division

  Addition and subtraction
- The preceding arithmetic operations are listed in the order that calculations are carried out when evaluating a formula. This is called the precedence of operations.
- The Edit command, invoked with the F2 function key, allows you to edit the contents of the current cell.
- By striking the F1 key from any point in 1-2-3, you can display a Help screen, which is a written description of a command or concept.
- The Print command, which is executed from the MENU mode (strike / key), allows you to print all or part of the worksheet on the screen. The worksheet can be directed to either a printer or a disk for later printing or inclusion in a word processing document.

NEW TERMINOLOGY

Many of the spreadsheet terms introduced in the introduction to Part Three are used in this chapter. The following are additional new terms; you should be familiar with each of them.

arithmetic operator
cell address border
cell pointer
control panel
current cell
help screen
mode indicator
operator
precedence
scroll

Name: ______________________ Date: ______________

Assignment 4-1

1. What is the control panel and what information does it contain?

2. How many rows and columns are visible on the screen?

3. How would you refer to the cell in the third row and sixth column?

4. What is the purpose of setting the default data drive to B?

5. You have just turned on the computer and brought 1-2-3 up. You enter the sequence /FR. What will you see on the screen?

Name: ______________________ Date: ______________

Assignment 4-1 (*continued*)

6. Why is it important to save a worksheet at intervals as you are working on it rather than waiting until it is all finished?

7. Describe the keystroke sequence to save a worksheet to disk.

Name: ______________________ Date: ______________

Assignment 4-2

1. What is meant by scrolling a worksheet?

2. Describe what will happen (from the READY mode) with each of the following keystrokes.
   (a) Right key

   (b) Ctrl-Right

   (c) PgDn

   (d) End

3. What are the three types of entries that you can make into a cell?

Name: ______________________ Date: ____________

Assignment 4-2 *(continued)*

4. The following labels are to be entered into a worksheet with positioning as indicated. In each case, which key should be struck first?

   (a) March (centered)

   (b) Points (right-aligned)

   (c) Summer (left-aligned)

   (d) -TITLE- (left-aligned)

5. As you type the first few digits of a number, you realize that the cell pointer is at the wrong cell. How do you cancel this action?

6. After entering a number into a cell, you realize that it is the wrong value. How can you correct the contents of the cell?

7. The text states that if the first keystroke from the READY mode is a single quote that 1-2-3 switches to LABEL mode and awaits the entry of a label which will be left-aligned. Since the default positioning of labels is left-aligned, what is the value of the single quote?

Name: ______________________ Date: ____________

Assignment 4-3

1. The quantity displayed in cell G12 (which contains a formula) does not appear to be correct. How can you inspect the formula in that cell?

2. To enter the formula into cell E2 of Figure 4-12, a user carries out the following sequence of steps.

   Move the cell pointer to cell E2.
   Key in the formula: B2+C2+D2
   Press the Up key to enter the formula.

   What is wrong with this sequence and what would happen?

3. A user gets carried away and enters the following formula into cell E2 of Figure 4-12. What is wrong and what do you think will happen?

   +A2+B2+C2+D2

Name: ______________________ Date: ______________

Assignment 4-3 (*continued*)

4. Assume that the contents of cells are as follows:

A1 = 6, A2 = 14, A3 = –5, A4 = 20

What will be the value stored in A6 as a result of each of the following formulas?

(a) A2–A3+A4

(b) A4–A1*A2

(c) A4+A1–A2/2

(d) (A4+A1–A2)/2

Name: ______________________________ Date: ______________

Assignment 4-4

1. What action is necessary to get to the EDIT mode in order to edit a formula?

2. Of the three types of cell entries (labels, numbers, and formulas) which can be edited using the edit function?

3. What action is required to place 1-2-3 in the MENU mode?

4. What happens when the F1 function key is struck?

5. The text describes printing a worksheet to a file so that it can be included in a word processing document. Why go to that trouble? Why not simply insert the worksheet file into the document and edit it as needed?

Name: ______________________________ Date: ______________

OBJECTIVE QUESTIONS

Matching

Match each term in a to h with the most appropriate description in 1 through 8.

a. READY mode
b. precedence of operations
c. Help
d. control panel
e. VALUE mode
f. LABEL mode
g. cell pointer
h. MENU mode

____ **1.** Striking the letter E while 1-2-3 is in the READY mode causes this.

____ **2.** Results from striking the F1 function key.

____ **3.** Allows you to enter commands.

____ **4.** Important when constructing formulas.

____ **5.** Necessary in order to move the cell pointer with the arrow keys.

____ **6.** Identifies the current cell.

____ **7.** From this, it is possible to enter a number or a formula into a cell.

____ **8.** Includes the mode indicator.

TRUE/FALSE

Determine whether each of the following is true or false.

T F **1.** The control panel is located at the bottom of the screen and provides you general information such as the status of toggle keys on the keyboard and error messages.

T F **2.** Assume that you have loaded a worksheet into memory and made corrections. If you issue a Quit command to terminate processing without first saving the worksheet, all changes will be lost because the Quit does not save automatically.

T F **3.** The cell address of the cell at the fourth row and third column is D3.

T F **4.** The cell pointer must first be positioned at the cell into which a keyboard entry is to be made before the entry is typed in.

T F **5.** If 1-2-3 is in VALUE mode, striking the / key causes it to switch to MENU mode.

T F **6.** Saving a worksheet to disk is done through the File command.

T F **7.** The Ctrl-Right key sequence entered from any of the operating modes will cause the display to scroll right eight columns.

T F **8.** Scrolling a worksheet is much the same as scrolling a document using a word processing program.

OBJECTIVE QUESTIONS (*continued*)

T F **9.** The positioning of a label within the screen cell is determined by the first key struck when entering the label.

T F **10.** Both numbers and formulas are entered from the VALUE mode.

T F **11.** To enter

```
++++
```

into a cell as a label would require more than four keystrokes.

T F **12.** A formula in cell D9 includes the cell address C4. The only allowable entry for cell C4 is a number.

T F **13.** When entering data into a worksheet, care should be taken to avoid errors because once a data value has been entered into a worksheet, it is difficult to change.

T F **14.** There are three types of cell entries: labels, numeric data, and alphabetic data.

T F **15.** A formula uses values from other cells to determine the value displayed in the cell to which it is assigned. The values from the other cells can either be data or numbers resulting from another calculation.

T F **16.** When a data value in a cell is changed, the worksheet automatically recalculates and redisplays the new value for all cells depending on the value in that cell.

T F **17.** The precedence rule defines the order in which the user enters labels, numbers and formulas into the worksheet.

T F **18.** If you were in the LABEL mode and struck the Escape (Esc) more than one time, execution of the spreadsheet program would be terminated and control returned to DOS.

T F **19.** The digit 6, the decimal point, and the dollar sign are typical first keystroke characters that indicate to 1-2-3 that a value entry is about to be made.

T F **20.** In the following formula, the first arithmetic operation that would be performed would be the addition.

```
C2/(D5+D6-D7)
```

T F **21.** In the following formula, the first arithmetic operation that would be performed would be the subtraction.

```
G4-G5*C3
```

T F **22.** If a formula is entered incorrectly, for instance, you wanted to add the interest amount in cell D6 to the principal amount in cell B8 but you subtracted instead, 1-2-3 would indicate an error and switch to the Edit mode.

Name: ______________________ Date: ______________

OBJECTIVE QUESTIONS (*continued*)

T F **23.** If the contents of cells B3, B4, and B5 were 24, 16, and 8, respectively, then the following formula would give a value of 19.

```
B4+B3/B5
```

T F **24.** Both parentheses and spaces can be used within 1-2-3 formulas in order to make them more easily understandable.

T F **25.** To put the formula

```
C5+D5
```

into cell C5 would probably represent an error condition.

T F **26.** Although spreadsheet programs are useful for experimenting, their computational capabilities are severely limited because they are capable of only the simplest arithmetic operations.

T F **27.** From the EDIT mode, which is invoked with the F2 key, it is possible to edit the contents of the current cell whether they are a label, number, or formula.

T F **28.** From the MENU mode, a command can be invoked either by typing the first letter of the command name or by moving the highlight to that command and striking Enter.

T F **29.** One shortcoming of the Print command is that it is not possible to print only a part of the worksheet displayed on the screen.

T F **30.** The Print command can be used to send the printer output to either a printer or to a disk file.

Multiple Choice

In the space provided, record the letter of the choice that best completes or answers the statement.

____ **1.** The ______ identifies the current cell.

A. cell pointer
B. information line
C. mode indicator
D. default drive

____ **2.** One of the items of information displayed on the control panel is the

A. toggle settings.
B. default drive.
C. current mode.
D. worksheet name.

Name: ______________________ Date: ______________

OBJECTIVE QUESTIONS (*continued*)

____ **3.** The ______ command is used to save a worksheet to disk.

A. Save
B. File
C. Quit
D. Hold

____ **4.** Striking which of the following keys will NOT terminate entry of data into a cell?

A. Backspace
B. Left arrow
C. Down arrow
D. PgDn

____ **5.** You are about to make an entry into a cell. Which of the following keys will NOT result in a label's being entered?

A. Single quote
B. Double quote
C. Period
D. Caret

____ **6.** You want to check the formula that you have entered into cell F7. To do this, you would

A. obtain a printout of the worksheet.
B. execute the Display Formula command.
C. move the cell pointer to cell F7.
D. refer to the information line of the worksheet.

____ **7.** If 1-2-3 is in the READY mode and you strike the minus key (–), 1-2-3 immediately switches to the ______ mode.

A. LABEL
B. NUMBER
C. FORMULA
D. VALUE

____ **8.** In building your cost analysis worksheet, you make an error and divide unit cost by quantity rather than multiply. When you enter this incorrect formula, 1-2-3 will

A. store it in the cell.
B. correct it automatically.
C. warn you about the error.
D. warn you about the error and switch to edit mode.

Name: ______________________ Date: ______________

OBJECTIVE QUESTIONS (*continued*)

____ **9.** In the following formula, which arithmetic operation will be performed first?

4*B3+(B4-25)/7.5

A. multiplication
B. addition
C. subtraction
D. division

____ **10.** Which of the following is an invalid formula?

A. B7+5
B. 2(B4-B5)
C. C5^3
D. C5^2*B4

____ **11.** Which of the following actions cannot be done from the EDIT mode?

A. Move the cell pointer.
B. Change a formula.
C. Enter a new number in the current cell.
D. Correct the spelling in a word of a label.

____ **12.** To get help in 1-2-3, you must strike the ______ key.

A. Ready
B. Escape
C. F3
D. F1

____ **13.** To switch from READY mode to MENU mode, you must strike the ______ key.

A. Menu
B. slash (/)
C. F1
D. Enter

____ **14.** After 1-2-3 completes printing a document, it

A. returns to the MENU mode.
B. terminates and returns to DOS.
C. destroys the copy of the worksheet in memory.
D. destroys the copy of the worksheet in memory but reloads it back into memory from disk.

Name: ______________________________ Date: ______________

OBJECTIVE QUESTIONS (*continued*)

____ **15.** If you wanted to include a worksheet in a WordPerfect document, you would probably

A. insert the worksheet in the document then edit it as needed.
B. print a copy, then bring up WordPerfect and type it in.
C. print a copy of the worksheet to a file.
D. bring up WordPerfect, open a second window in WordPerfect, then bring up 1-2-3.

Fill In

In the space provided, fill in the correct answer. Note that the answer can be one or two words.

1. ______________________________
The three top lines on the screen are called the ______ ______.

2. ______________________________
You must be in the ______ mode to move the cell pointer.

3. ______________________________
To make cell A1 the current cell, you would strike the ______ key.

4. ______________________________
If you strike the double quote to start the entry of a label, that label will be positioned to the ______ within the cell.

5. ______________________________
The action of ______ enables you to designate the cell addresses of formulas by moving the cell pointer to each cell to be included in the formula.

6. ______________________________
If cell B4 contains 5 and cell C7 contains 8, then the value displayed by the following formula will be ______.

```
B4+3*C7
```

7. ______________________________
The ______ rules determine which arithmetic operation is performed first in a 1-2-3 formula.

8. ______________________________
When entering a formula into a cell, you must not include any ______ within the formula.

9. ______________________________
If you switch to the ______ mode, you can make a correction to a formula without reentering it entirely.

10. ______________________________
If you have accidentally switched to the MENU mode while entering data into cells, you can return to the READY mode by striking the ______ key.

ASSIGNMENTS/PROJECTS

1. This assignment involves making changes to the cost analysis worksheet, so you should make a copy, then work on the copy. You must add Style E to row 6. Data for this style must be:

   Labor cost: 5.88

   Other cost: 1.04

   Quantity: 10

   Material cost for Styles B, C, D, and E are to be based on the Material cost for Style A as follows:

   Style B Equal to that of Style A

   Style C Equal to 1.22 times that of Style A

   Style D Equal to 1.09 times that of Style A

   Style E Equal to 0.94 times that of Style A

2. In planning for a school year, a student creates the quarterly budget worksheet shown in Figure 4-23. Based on the descriptions of the labels and the values displayed, the formulas should be evident. For this assignment, you are to enter this as a 1-2-3 worksheet with appropriate formulas for the two Total lines and the Balance line. When you have completed it, print a copy. Notice that because of the auto insurance in the Fall quarter, the expenses exceed the income. The insurance company will allow this to be paid in two $435 installments (Fall and Spring), or four quarterly installments of $237. Make these changes to determine the effect on the Balance line.

	Fall	Winter	Spring	Summer
Income				
Job	400	400	400	2000
Grant	400	400	400	0
Parents	150	0	200	0
Total	950	800	1000	2000
Expenses				
Auto ins.	800	0	0	0
Auto exp.	200	200	200	300
Tuition	300	300	300	0
Books	100	120	120	0
Misc.	150	300	200	400
Total	1550	920	820	700
Balance	-600	-720	-540	760

Fall Income Total – Fall Expenses Total

Fall Balance + (Winter Income Total – Winter Expenses Total)

Figure 4-23
Budget worksheet for Assignment 2.

3. You decide to create a payroll worksheet for the employees of MCT Enterprises. Entries in the respective columns are to be as follows:

Column	Information
A	Employee last name (assume names no more than 9 characters)
B	Hours worked
C	Pay rate
D	Total deductions
E	Formula: Pay = Hours times Rate minus Deductions

The data to be entered is the following.

Name	Hours	Rate	Deductions
Finch	40	9.60	26.15
Baker	36	8.50	31.07
Zener	44	8.00	33.28
Sparks	40	11.35	44.57
Olson	48	9.60	43.98
Peters	20	9.60	13.84
Ito	40	8.50	27.77
Mier	37	9.60	21.89

Rows 1 and 2 should be used for descriptive headings; leave row 3 blank and enter data beginning row 4. Directly under the Hours column (column B), enter a formula to calculate the total hours worked by all employees so that this number will be displayed directly under the hours worked by the last employee.

4. In running your business, you must pay particular attention to your inventory of goods. On the one hand, you do not want to be out of stock frequently, thus delaying shipments to customers. On the other hand, your inventory represents money that is committed and cannot be used for other purposes. Hence, you must keep your inventory as low as possible without the danger of running out frequently. You decide on the rule of thumb that your stock in inventory should turn over three times per year. Another way of viewing this is by comparing your sales to your inventory value. For example, if you have an inventory value of $50,000, then your gross sales should be three times that or $150,000. To make a comparison of your major product lines, you must create a spreadsheet that includes the following for each item in the inventory.

Column	Information
A	Product line description
B	Gross sales for Quarter 1
C	Gross sales for Quarter 2
D	Gross sales for Quarter 3
E	Gross sales for Quarter 4
F	Formula: Total gross sales
G	Average inventory value
H	Formula: Total gross sales divided by Inventory value

Rows 1 and 2 should be used for descriptive headings; leave row 3 blank and enter data beginning row 4. Following is the data to be entered; note that all money values are in thousands of dollars. For instance, the entry for men's casual wear for the first quarter of 2.3 means $2300.

Product		Quarter			Inventory
Line	1	2	3	4	Average
Men's					
Casual Wear	2.3	5.2	4.8	5.9	5.9
Summer Sports	1.5	6.1	5.6	1.6	5.0
Winter Sports	5.9	1.2	3.1	6.4	7.3
Work Uniforms	2.7	3.1	2.9	2.8	3.0
Women's					
Casual Wear	3.5	7.3	6.9	9.3	9.0
Summer Sports	1.6	8.8	7.5	3.1	7.1
Winter Sports	7.3	2.1	4.9	9.1	7.0
Work Uniforms	1.1	1.6	1.2	1.1	2.1

Do not be concerned that the entire product line description will not display in the cell when you begin entering data. You will learn how to make screen cells wider in the next chapter.

Chapter 5

More on Lotus 1-2-3 and JOE Spreadsheet

OBJECTIVES

From Chapter 4, you learned how to perform some of the basic spreadsheet operations. In this chapter, you will learn how to use the other features of spreadsheet software. When you have completed this chapter, you should be able to:

- Insert new rows or columns into a worksheet with the Worksheet Insert command sequence.
- Change the default column width from 9 to any needed value. Also, change the width of selected columns.
- Copy the contents of one or more cells from one place in the worksheet to another, and recognize the effect on formulas of the copy operation.
- Format the display of cells displaying numeric quantities defining the number of decimal places to be displayed, and include punctuation such as commas and dollar signs.
- Erase the contents of a group of cells.
- Move the contents of a group of cells from one place in the worksheet to another.
- Use functions to compute the sum and average and to determine the largest and smallest values from a group of cells.
- Use relational operators that allow you to compare the values in different cells and display results based on such comparisons.
- Prepare a worksheet so that it can be incorporated into a word processing document.

These concepts will be introduced with an expansion of the cost analysis worksheet, an employee-retraining progress worksheet, and a sales summary worksheet.

PREVIEW

A Task and the Needed Tools

The expansion of the cost analysis worksheet will include adding more information. This includes adding 2 columns so that the cost breakdown can be expanded from three cost components to five. Column widths are also changed and formatting of displayed cell contents added.

Changing the Size of Your Worksheet

The worksheet size can be increased by inserting blank rows or columns at any place in the worksheet using the Worksheet Insert command. The size also can be decreased by deleting rows or columns.

Changing Column Widths

The default cell display width is 9 columns. You can reset the default width as needed with the Worksheet command. You can also set the widths of individual columns. This gives you the capability to set column widths to display your worksheet entries better.

Correcting a Formula and Copying It

With the addition of two new cost components, the Unit Cost formula must be edited. The Copy command allows you to duplicate it into other cells without retyping it for each one.

Formatting Displayed Values

Formatting allows you to control the appearance of numeric values in the display. Using the Format command, it is possible to include such punctuation as decimal points, commas, and dollar signs.

Other Commands

There are two commands not illustrated by the cost analysis worksheet: Erase and Move. With the Erase command, you can erase the contents of cells. With the Move command, you can move the contents of a group of cells from one place in the worksheet to another.

Basic Principles of Functions

A function is a predefined procedure for performing a particular operation. Some of the functions used in this section perform the following actions on a group of cells: summing the values, counting the number of nonempty entries, calculating the average, and finding the smallest and largest values.

Conditional Operations Using Functions

Relational operators in 1-2-3 allow you to compare quantities and define actions to be taken depending on the results of the comparison.

Absolute Cell Addresses in Formulas

When copying a formula from one cell to another, 1-2-3 automatically adjusts the cell address references of the formula to conform to the new location. In some instances, this is not desirable. Absolute cell addressing allows you to specify certain cell addresses as being fixed.

Combining a Worksheet with a Word Processing Document

You can send the printed output of a worksheet (or portion of a worksheet) either to the printer or to a disk file. Once it is stored on disk, you can insert the worksheet into a word processing document.

A TASK AND THE NEEDED TOOLS

Problem Definition

In the preceding chapter, you used the File command to save and retrieve worksheet files. In addition to these basic operations, commands give you the capability to change a worksheet to adjust to your changing needs. This ability is essential because, when you use a worksheet to analyze a problem, the process of setting it up and experimenting with values provides more insight into the nature of the problem. As you perform your "what if" studies with a worksheet, you will find that often subtle (and sometimes major) modifications will make it more effective. Such changes can include expanding the worksheet to include additional data or more calculations, and deleting unneeded portions.

Assume that this has happened to you with the cost analysis worksheet. In order to pinpoint costs more precisely, you have broken labor costs down into two components: labor costs and contracted services. Furthermore, you have separated overhead costs from the other costs. Also, you have decided to improve the appearance of your worksheet. Its final form is shown in Figure 5-1.

To convert your original COST worksheet to this form will require that you know how to do the following.

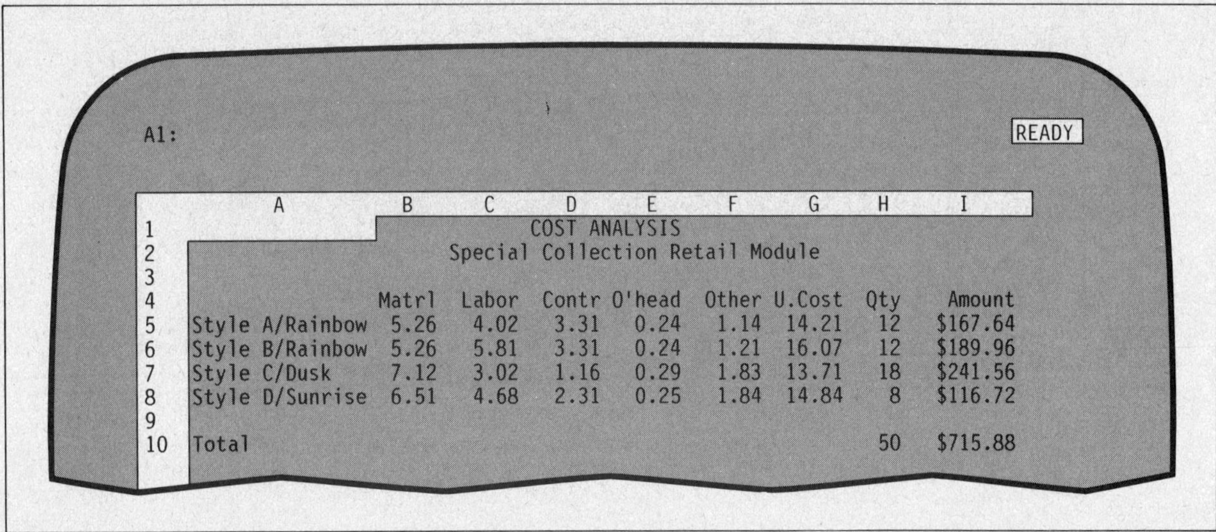

A1: READY

	A	B	C	D	E	F	G	H	I
1				COST ANALYSIS					
2			Special Collection Retail Module						
3									
4		Matrl	Labor	Contr	O'head	Other	U.Cost	Qty	Amount
5	Style A/Rainbow	5.26	4.02	3.31	0.24	1.14	14.21	12	$167.64
6	Style B/Rainbow	5.26	5.81	3.31	0.24	1.21	16.07	12	$189.96
7	Style C/Dusk	7.12	3.02	1.16	0.29	1.83	13.71	18	$241.56
8	Style D/Sunrise	6.51	4.68	2.31	0.25	1.84	14.84	8	$116.72
9									
10	Total							50	$715.88

Figure 5-1
The expanded cost analysis worksheet.

- Insert empty rows and columns into a worksheet. Three blank rows must be inserted at the top of the worksheet for the headings, and 2 blank columns must be inserted for the additional cost components.
- Change column width. Column A must be made wider to accommodate the wider headings. Also, the width of other columns is reduced in order to conveniently display the entire worksheet on the screen without scrolling. Notice that Figure 5-1 displays 9 columns.
- Include format descriptions for the display of values. The amount column includes the $ symbol. Also, all dollar and cent amounts are printed with two digits to the right of the decimal point even if the digits are 0.
- Copy the contents of a cell into other cells. A new formula entered into cell G5 will be copied into cells G6, G7, and G8.

Command Nomenclature

To save your worksheet file in Chapter 4, your sequence of keystrokes was:

/ To switch to MENU mode.

F To invoke the File command from the main command menu.

S To invoke the Save command from the File submenu.

Example descriptions in this chapter detail your step-by-step actions in performing the necessary steps. However, all key sequence actions will be summarized in a concise form. For instance, the preceding sequence of command invoking keystrokes will be represented as:

/FS

As each command is first introduced, the following form will also be used.

```
/ File Save
```

Note that only the first letter of each command is printed in boldface; these are the only letters to be keyed in to select the command. Since striking the first command letter (F in this case) leads to a submenu in which another option is to be selected, you may wish to inspect each level of the menu as you enter the sequence.

Your sequence of keystrokes in saving also included typing the filename and striking the Enter key. The complete sequence will be indicated as:

```
/FS filename {Enter}
```

where *filename* means that you must type the name to be used for the file and {Enter} means to strike the Enter key.

Ranges of Cells

When you printed your worksheet in Chapter 4, you had to designate the group of cells, or **range,** to be printed. Many 1-2-3 commands operate on a range of cells (this includes commands for column width change, format, and copy that are required to achieve Figure 5-1). A range is any rectangular portion of a worksheet, as illustrated by Figure 5-2. Not only can a range comprise many columns or rows, but it can also consist of a portion of a single column or row. Technically, even the current cell is a range. You may think that a single cell does not fit the definition of a *range of cells.* However, we must be able to designate a cell as a range because many

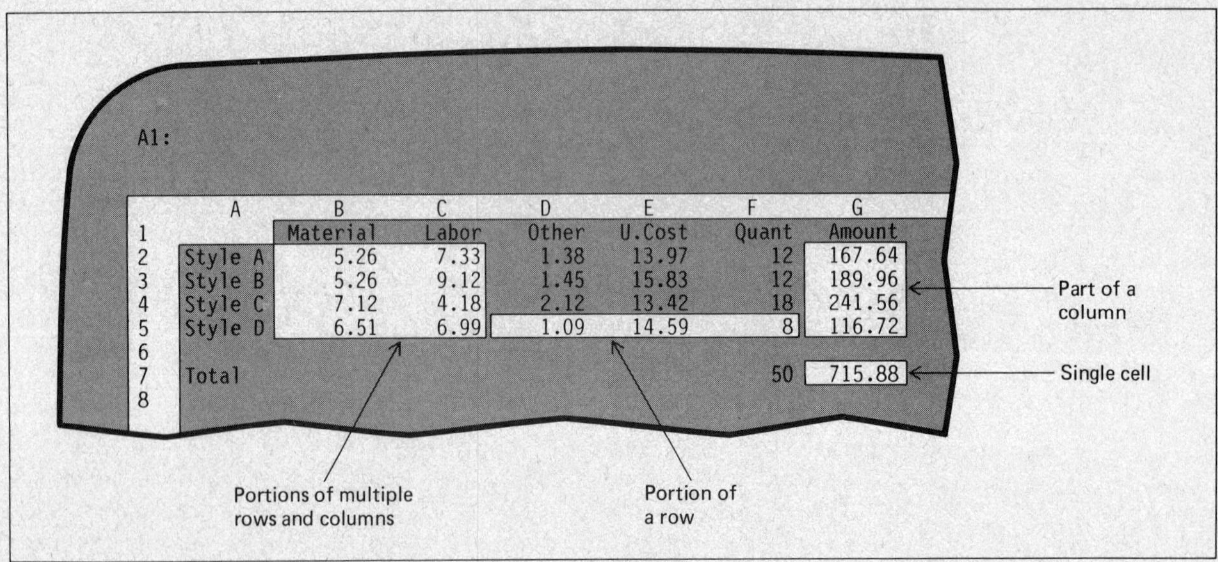

Figure 5-2
Worksheet ranges.

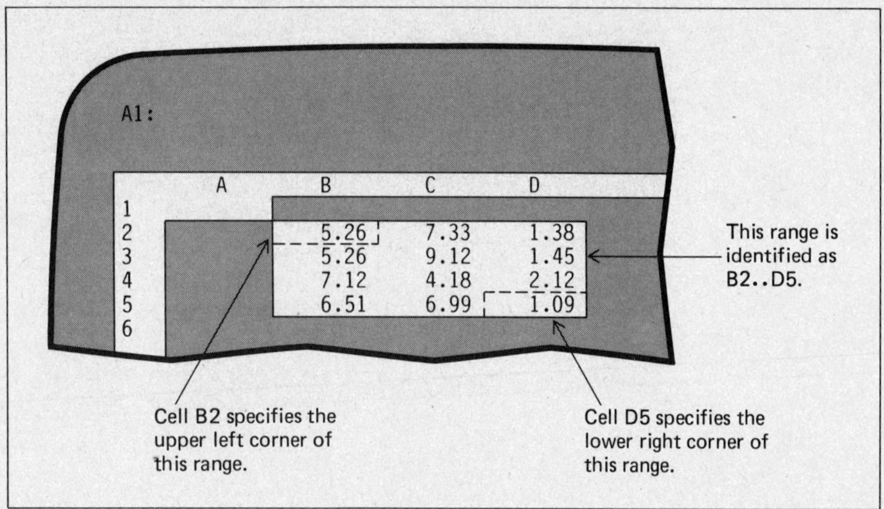

Figure 5-3
Specifying a range by cell addresses.

range commands operate on single cells. The key notion is that a range can only be a *rectangular* collection of cells.

To that end, a range can be pinpointed exactly by two cells located at the corners (at opposite ends of the diagonal), as illustrated in Figure 5-3. In this case, the range is specified by the upper-left cell, B2, and the lower-right cell, D5. The standard method for identifying a range is by the upper-left cell address, followed by two periods, followed by the lower-right cell address, as in Figure 5-3. The sample ranges of Figure 5-2 are:

B2..C5 Rectangular area consisting of columns B and C and rows 2 through 5.

D5..F5 A portion of row 5.

G2..G5 A portion of column G.

G7..G7 The single cell, G7.

CHANGING THE SIZE OF YOUR WORKSHEET

The Insert Command: Inserting Rows

All spreadsheet programs allow the user to open up new (blank) rows or columns anywhere in the worksheet. Existing cell entries are not disturbed other than being moved either down or to the right. To modify your worksheet to the form in Figure 5-1, you must insert 3 new rows and 2 new columns. Let us first insert the 3 blank rows. Since you will be working with the original cost analysis worksheet, you should retrieve either your copy that you saved as COST or the copy COSTAN.WKS included on the data disk. Then proceed with the following.

DO THIS NOW 5-1 **Inserting 3 Blank Rows**

1. Position the cell pointer at cell A1 (for row insertion, it can be anywhere in the first row).
2. Switch to the command mode by striking the / key.
3. Strike the W key for the Worksheet command; this will produce the following Worksheet submenu.

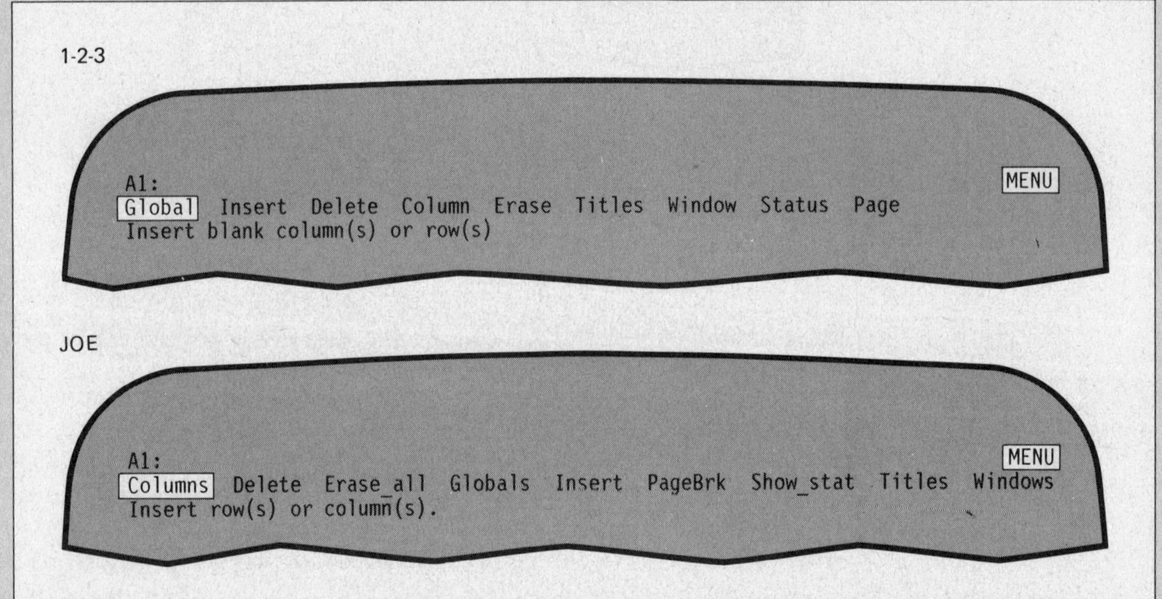

4. You want the Insert command so strike the letter *I* (or move the highlight to Insert and strike Enter); you will be given your choice of inserting columns or rows.

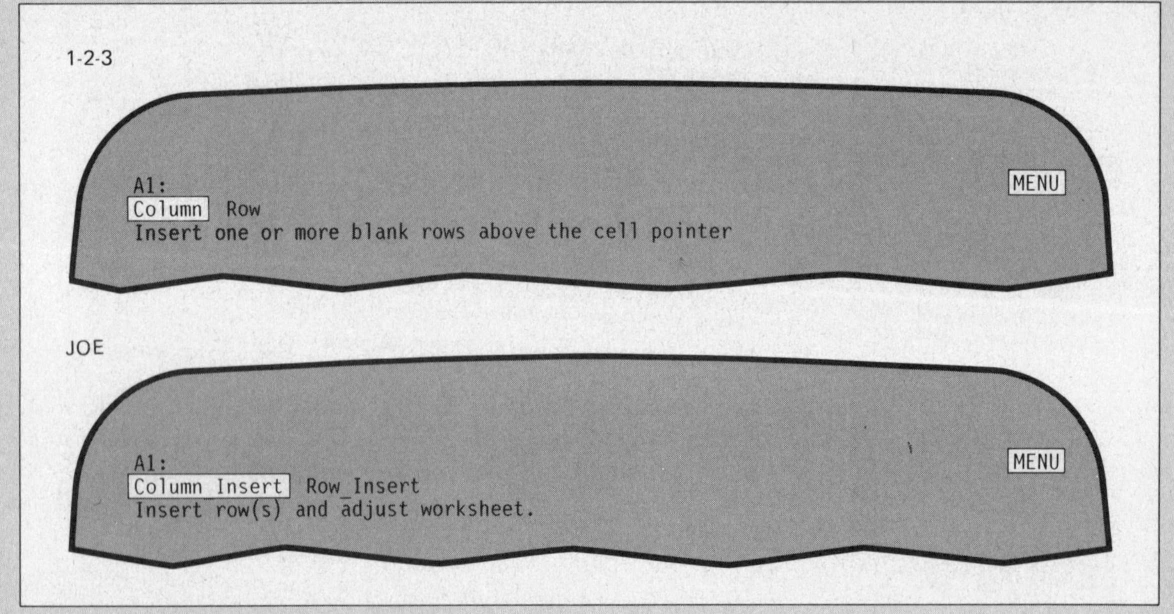

5. Strike the letter *R* for Row; your control panel will change to:

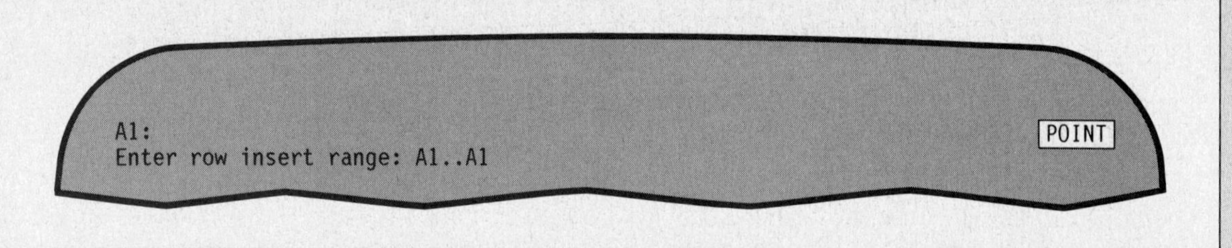

The current range of rows into which blank rows will be inserted is the current cell, or A1..A1.

6. Strike the Down key twice to define the range A1..A3, as shown in the following.

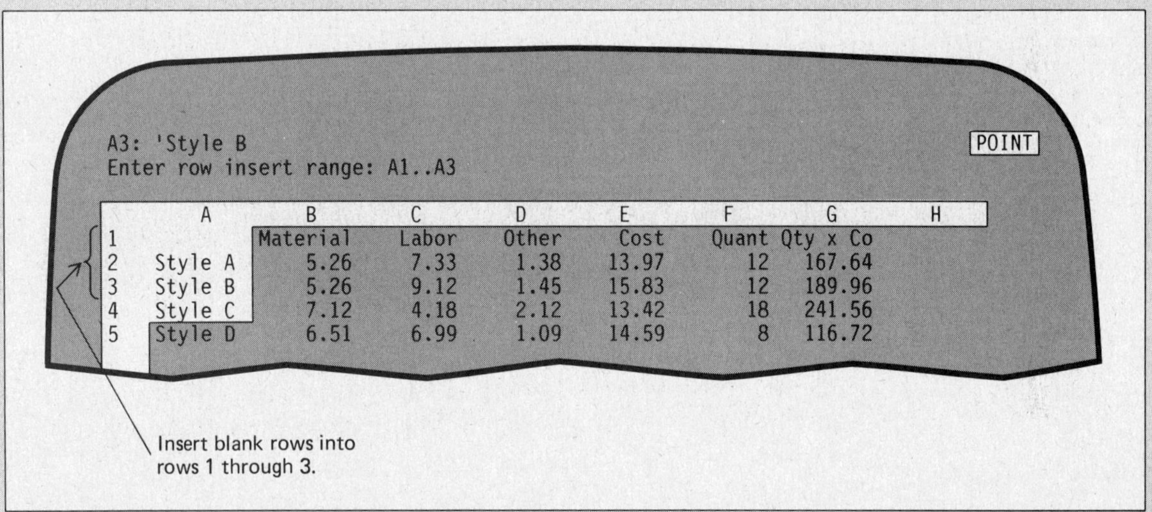

This range specifies that new rows are to be inserted from row 1 through row 3. Note that it is possible to move the cell pointer to the right; for instance, the selected range could be A1..D3. Additional columns in the range have no effect on the insert operation.

7. Strike Enter to carry out the insertion operation. The resulting worksheet is shown in Figure 5-4.

Summarizing, the keystroke sequence necessary to insert these three blank rows is as follows:

```
/WIR {Down} {Down} {Enter}
```

The command sequence is:

```
/ Worksheet Insert Row          (Lotus 1-2-3)
/ WorkSet Insert Row Insert     (JOE)
```

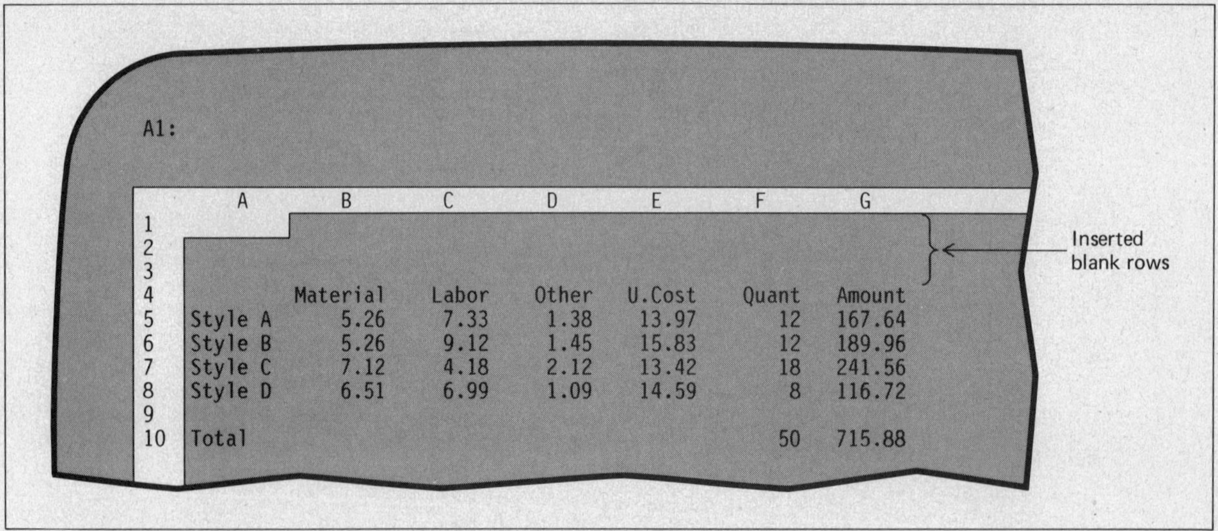

A1:

	A	B	C	D	E	F	G
1							
2							
3							
4		Material	Labor	Other	U.Cost	Quant	Amount
5	Style A	5.26	7.33	1.38	13.97	12	167.64
6	Style B	5.26	9.12	1.45	15.83	12	189.96
7	Style C	7.12	4.18	2.12	13.42	18	241.56
8	Style D	6.51	6.99	1.09	14.59	8	116.72
9							
10	Total					50	715.88

Figure 5-4
The inserted blank rows.

Although this example involves inserting rows at the top of the worksheet, row insertion is not so restricted. That is, rows can be inserted anywhere in the worksheet.

The Insert Command: Inserting Columns

The next step in modifying this worksheet is to insert 2 additional columns for the further breakdown of cost components. The column insertion procedure is almost identical to that for inserting rows.

DO THIS NOW 5-2 **Inserting 2 Blank Columns Into Columns D and E**

1. Position the cell pointer at cell D1 (actually, any cell in column D will be adequate).
2. Enter the following keystroke sequence.

   /WIC {Right} {Enter}

   The control panel sequence will be similar to that of DTN 5-1. If you wish to observe the changing control panel, pause after each keystroke. The cell range in the last step will be D1..E1.

At this point, the previous contents of column D (the Other cost) and everything to the right have been moved 2 columns to the right, leaving columns D and E blank as shown in Figure 5-5. Notice that the Amount column is now scrolled off the right edge of the screen.

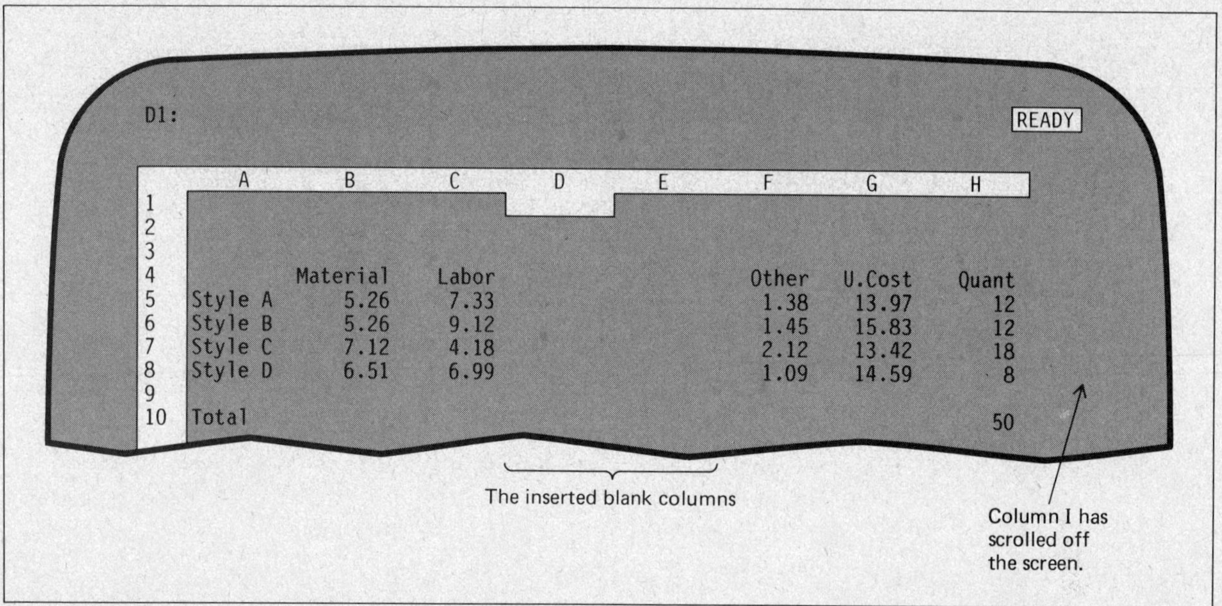

Figure 5-5
The inserted blank rows and columns.

The Effect of Row Insertion on Formulas

Before continuing with the modification of your worksheet, let us consider the effect of row and column insertions on the formulas. For example, remember that the Unit Cost for Style A previously stored in cell E2 was computed with the formula:

```
+B2+C2+D2
```

Since this item is now in cell G5, move your cell pointer to that cell and you will see the following formula displayed in the first line of the control panel.

```
+B5+C5+F2
```

Notice that 1-2-3 has adjusted the cell addresses of this formula consistent with the repositioning of the data cells resulting from the insertions. Also note that the cell addresses D5 and E5 (which will be required in the new form) are not inserted automatically into this formula.

Entering Data Into the New Rows and Columns

You can now proceed to make the necessary changes and entries to the labels and numbers so that your worksheet will have the same values as those in Figure 5-1.

DO THIS NOW 5-3 **Entering New Labels and Numbers**

1. For the descriptions in column A, use the EDIT mode and it will not be necessary to retype. For instance, position the cursor on cell A5, strike the F2 key, type "/Rainbow", and then strike Enter.
2. Position the cell pointer at cell D1 and enter the label COST ANALYSIS. Then enter the label Special Collection Retail Module into cell C2.
3. Change the column headings in row 5 so that they are the same as those in Figure 5-1. Shorter headings will be necessary when the column width is decreased.
4. Enter the new data values and change others that need changing. When you make the entries into columns D and E, you will notice that the Unit Cost does *not* change. Remember that these cells are not yet included in the Unit Cost formulas. You will change these later.

When you entered the titles in the first 2 rows, you may have been surprised that the entire labels (which are longer than the cell width of 9) were displayed on the screen. Although each screen cell has a default size of 9 positions, each memory cell can hold up to 240 characters. Just as the screen provides us with a view of a portion of the worksheet in memory, so does the screen cell provide us with a view of the contents of a memory cell. On your screen (as in Figure 5-1), you see that 1-2-3 uses additional cells to the right for displaying long labels (if those cells are not used for something else). Even though the label in row 2 is stored in memory cell C2, its screen display spills over into cells D2, E2, and F2.

Before proceeding further, you should save this version of the worksheet; use the name COST3.

Deleting Rows or Columns

Sometimes, in reorganizing a worksheet, you will need to eliminate rows or columns. You do this with the Delete command, which is the opposite of the Insert. Note that this command does *not* simply erase the contents of cells; it eliminates rows or columns and moves those that follow up (or to the left). In other words, it is the opposite of the Insert command. Although the modification necessary to expand your cost analysis worksheet to that of Figure 5-1 does not require deletion, you should try the command so that you will be familiar with it. For the deletion exercise, you will be using the worksheet that you have been modifying, *so be certain that you have saved it to disk.*

DO THIS NOW 5-4 **Deleting Rows 6 and 7 of the Figure 5-5 Worksheet**

1. Position the cell pointer in cell A6 (actually, anywhere in row 6 is acceptable).
2. Enter the following command sequence:

   ```
   /WDR
   ```

   That is:

   ```
   / Worksheet Delete Row              (Lotus 1-2-3)
   / WorkSet Delete Row_Delete         (JOE)
   ```

3. Strike the Down key one time to define the range A6..A7. These are the rows to be deleted.
4. Strike Enter to carry out the delete operation. The selected range will be deleted and the previous contents of rows 8 and 10 will be moved up.

When the action has been completed, notice that cell H8 (the total of the cells above it) now displays the letters ERR. If you move the cell pointer to this cell, the formula displayed in the control panel will be:

```
+H5+ERR+ERR+H6
```

Since elements from the 2 deleted rows were used in this formula, 1-2-3 did not know what to do. Hence, it replaced them with the error code ERR. You can proceed to correct this formula through the EDIT mode. That is, strike the F2, and then delete them as you would any other unwanted entries in a formula. You will see that the display of cell H8 changes from ERR to the computed value.

This completes the exercise on deletion. You should now retrieve the copy of COST3 from disk. When you do so, JOE will warn you that changes have been made to the worksheet on the screen and that they will be lost. Do not save the screen version of the worksheet.

CHANGING COLUMN WIDTHS

The 9-position default column width is a good compromise for both labels and numbers. However, in many instances, it is convenient to make one or more columns wider to display longer labels or larger numbers. Also, if a worksheet is to contain numbers consisting of only a few digits, using narrower columns allows more of them to be displayed on the screen or printed on a single page. There are two ways you can change column width. One is to change the default value, which will change the screen cell width of every column in the worksheet. Any change to parameters (such as column width) that affects all elements in the worksheet is said to be

global. The other way of changing column widths is to change individual columns one at a time. If you make a global width change after changing one or more columns, the columns that were changed will *not* be affected by the global change. If, when you change the width of a column, a displayed number is replaced with a row of asterisk(*) characters, then the cell width is not adequate to display the number and the width must be increased.

To better fit the data of the revised cost analysis worksheet in Figure 5-1, the column widths have been adjusted. These widths, which you will use in your copy of the worksheet, are:

Columns	Width
A	15
B..G	7
H	5
I	10

Since most of the columns will have a width of 7, let us first make the global change to 7, and then proceed with the column changes.

DO THIS NOW 5-5 **Changing Column Widths**

1. Enter the following command sequence.

```
/WGC
```

That is:

```
/ Worksheet Global Column-Width            (Lotus 1-2-3)
/ WorkSet Globals Column-Width             (JOE)
```

2. You will then see one of the following prompts.

```
Enter global column width (1..240): 9      (Lotus 1-2-3)
Default column width (1..240): 9           (JOE)
```

Enter the new value of 7 to replace the default value of 9 and strike Enter. The cell width of all cells on the screen will change to 7.

3. To change the width of column A to 15, position the cell pointer at cell A1.

4. Enter the following command sequence.

```
/WCS
```

That is:

```
/ Worksheet Column Set-Width               (Lotus 1-2-3)
/ WorkSet Columns Set_column_width         (JOE)
```

5. You will then see one of the following prompts; note that the newly defined default is now displayed.

```
Enter column width (1..240): 7
New column width (1..240): 7
```

(Lotus 1-2-3)
(JOE)

Enter the new value of 15 and strike Enter. Note that the first line of the control panel now displays [15]; this indicates that the cell width for this column has been set to 15. Move the cell pointer to A5 and you will see that the contents are displayed after this width code.

6. Repeat steps 3, 4, and 5 for column H using a cell width of 5.
7. Repeat steps 3, 4, and 5 for column I using a cell width of 10.

This completes the task of changing column width; check to ensure that all width values are set properly and that your screen display is the same as that in Figure 5-1. Correct any differences. To ensure that you do not lose this latest round of work, save your worksheet to disk.

CORRECTING A FORMULA AND COPYING IT

Editing the Formula to Sum the Cost Components

The next step in modifying this worksheet is to correct the formulas for calculating the Unit Cost. Remember, when you inserted 3 new rows and 2 new columns, 1-2-3 adjusted these formulas; for instance, that for Style A was changed to:

```
+B5+C5+F5
```

With the addition of two new cost components, the formula should be:

```
+B5+C5+D5+E5+F5
```

You can easily correct this with the Edit command.

DO THIS NOW 5-6 **Correcting the Formula in Cell G5**

1. Move the cell pointer to cell G5.
2. Strike the Edit key (F2).
3. Insert +D5+E5 into the formula and strike Enter.

The next step is to make the corresponding correction to cells G6, G7, and G8. However, rather than edit each of them, let us use the Copy command, which is specifically designed to simplify the task of entering repetitive information.

Copying the Contents of a Single Cell Into a Range of Cells

Spreadsheet programs allow you to copy the contents from cells into other cells. This includes formulas as well as labels and numbers. However, when a formula is copied, the program automatically adjusts cell addresses. (In some spreadsheet software, this action is called replication.) For instance, when the formula

```
+B5+C5+D5+E5+F5
```

in cell G5 is copied to cell G6, the row numbers must be changed, producing:

```
+B6+C6+D6+E6+F6
```

In 1-2-3, this is done with the Copy command.

DO THIS NOW 5-7 **Copying the Formula in Cell G5 Into Cells G6, G7, and G8**

1. Position the cell pointer at cell G5.
2. Execute the Copy (Lotus 1-2-3) or CopyRan (JOE) command with the sequence:

   ```
   /C
   ```

   In the following control panel display, note that the prompt requests that you specify the range of cells to be copied (the FROM range). The range consisting of the single current cell appears as the default.

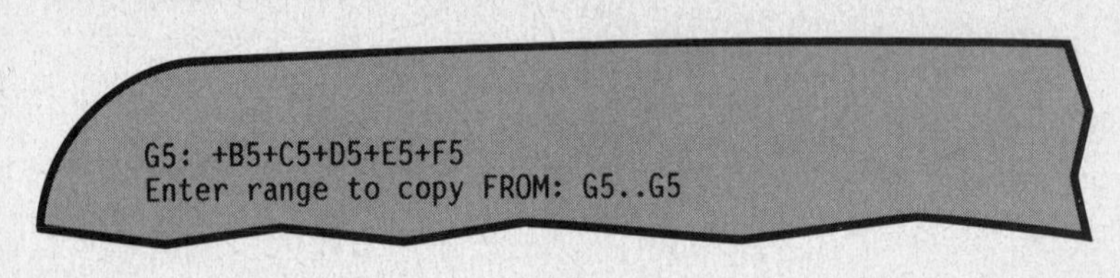

3. Because you want to copy only one cell, strike Enter. The prompt now requests the range of cells into which the FROM range (single cell, in this case) is to be duplicated.

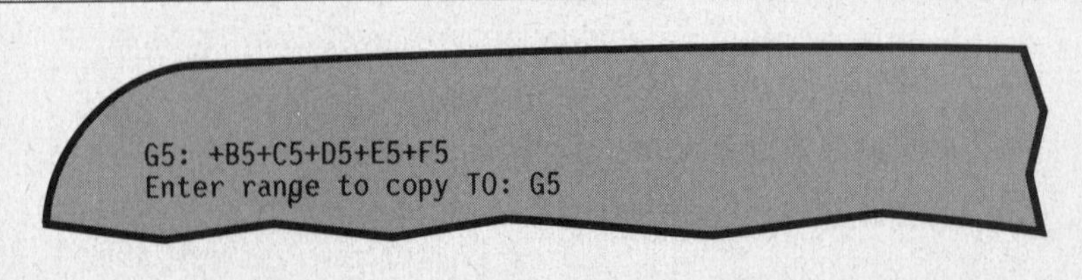

4. Move the cell pointer to the beginning of the range to which the duplication is to occur, This is called the **anchor cell** because it is the "anchor" point from which the range is to be defined. In this case, move the cell pointer to cell G6.

5. Strike the period key (.) to anchor the range.

6. Move the cell pointer to the end of the range; in this case, move it to cell G8.

7. Strike Enter to complete the command. The contents of the FROM cell (the formula in this case) will be duplicated into each cell of the TO range. These new formulas will change the values displayed for these cells. You should compare the values displayed with those of Figure 5-1 to ensure that they are correct. You might also move the cell pointer to each of these cells and inspect the new formulas.

The preceding detailed sequence of steps makes copying seem more tedious than it really is. However, when you master the steps, you will find that the actual process is quick and relatively simple.

The Copy command is not limited to copying the contents of a single cell into other cells. For instance, if for your studies, you decided to copy the range of cells B5..F8 to another portion of the worksheet, the sequence of steps would have been almost the same as the steps of DTN 12-7. The only difference would be in specifying the FROM range as B5. .F8 and the TO range appropriately.

FORMATTING DISPLAYED VALUES

Displaying Numbers

In Chapter 11 (DTN 11-11), you adjusted the cost entries in attempting to bring the total price to $675. In the process, you probably noticed that the dollar and cent amounts were not always displayed with two digits to the right of the decimal point. For instance, you might have seen 4.8 instead of 4.80, or even 5 instead of 5.00. The reason for this is that the 1-2-3 default number display format prints a decimal point only if there are digits to the right of the decimal. You probably found that the displayed column of numbers in which the decimal points are not aligned is very difficult to read.

Fortunately, just as you can override the default column width, you can also override the number display format of one or more cells. To better illustrate the effect of this formatting, make the following changes to the Contractor costs of your spreadsheet

Current Value	Adjustment	New Value	Displayed
3.31	–0.31	3.00	3
3.31	–0.07	3.24	3.24
1.16	–0.26	0.90	0.9
2.31	–0.24	2.07	2.07

You should notice in your worksheet that some of the entries in the Unit Cost and Amount columns also reflect this column alignment problem now.

You can avoid this problem and control the way in which numeric data is displayed on the screen with the Format command. Following are some of the formatting options of this command.

Format	Description
General	No trailing zeros after the decimal point are displayed; very large and small numbers are displayed in scientific notation. This is the default format.
	Examples: 5.2 7.55 165
Fixed	A fixed number of places (0 to 15) to the right of the decimal point are displayed.
	Examples for three decimal places: 165.000 165.230 165.238
(comma)	Same as fixed except commas are added between thousands and negative values are enclosed in parentheses. Fixed number of decimal places (0 to 15) must be specified.
	Examples for one decimal place: 3,526.1 48.0 (356.5)
Currency	Same as comma except that dollar sign is included.
	Examples for two places: $2,561.00 $1.28 ($55.06)

The Format is a subcommand of the Range command. Entering the command sequence

```
/RF
```

That is:

```
/ Range Format     (Lotus 1-2-3)
/ RangeOps Fmt     (JOE)
```

produces the formatting submenu shown in Figure 5-6. Let us use these formatting capabilities to improve the appearance of your worksheet to that of Figure 5-1.

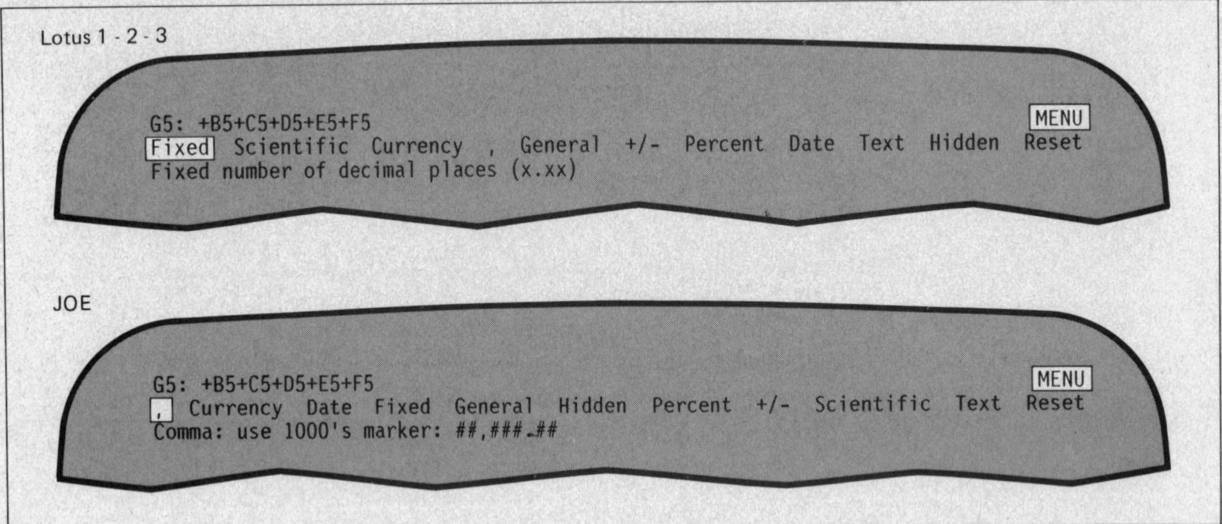

Figure 5-6
Format submenu options.

Formatting the Numeric Data of the Worksheet

Following is the formatting that you need to do for your cost analysis worksheet to complete this modification.

Cell Range	Formatting
B5..G8	Fixed with two places to the right of the decimal.
H5..H10	No formatting required; default is acceptable.
I5..I10	Currency with two places to the right of the decimal.

You should carry out the following sequence of steps to format your worksheet display.

DO THIS NOW 5-8 **Formatting the Cells Containing Value Entries**

1. Position the cell pointer at cell B5.
2. Enter the following command sequence:

   ```
   /RFF
   ```

   That is:

   `/ Range Format Fixed` (Lotus 1-2-3)
   `/ RangeOps Fmt Fixed` (JOE)

3. You will see the prompt:

```
Enter number of decimal places (0..15) 2
```

Note that the default value is 2. Accept this value by striking Enter.

4. You are then prompted for the range with:

```
Enter range to format: B5..B5
```

Move the cell pointer to cell G8; the range B5..G8 will be highlighted.

5. Strike Enter to complete the command. Notice that the numbers previously displayed with fewer digits to the right of the decimal point now include zeros. Also, the first line of the control panel now displays:

```
G5: (F2) 5.26
```

The code preceding the data means that this cell has been formatted to Fixed with two places to the right of the decimal. Moving the cell pointer to any cell within the range that has just been formatted will yield the same code. On the other hand, no such code will be displayed if the cell pointer is moved to column H (Qty) because it still retains the default format.

6. The next task is to format column I to currency. First, position the cell pointer at cell I5.

7. Enter the following command sequence:

```
/RFC
```

That is:

```
/ Range Format Currency      (Lotus 1-2-3)
/ RangeOps Fmt Currency      (JOE)
```

8. Repeat the sequence of steps 3, 4, and 5 using the range I5 to I10.

Your revised worksheet is now completed. If you changed the Contractor entries earlier, you should change them back to their original values. Your worksheet should appear exactly as that in Figure 5-1. If it does not, make the necessary corrections. When you are finished, save this latest version to disk.

The careful formatting of a worksheet is not a matter to be taken lightly. Obviously, unaligned columns make it difficult for even the creator of the worksheet to use it as a tool. We often set up worksheets that others will read. For instance, a summary of needs for a departmental budget will be presented to a manager; projected sales for a new product line will be prepared by an employee for presentation to the management. Each of these is to convey a message—often as part of gaining approval for pursuing a particular course of action. The more professional appearing the information presented, the more successful it will be in conveying your message.

OTHER COMMANDS

In addition to the preceding commands illustrated with the cost analysis example, there are a few other commands that are convenient when modifying a worksheet. These include the ability to erase part or all of the cell contents of a worksheet, and to move a range of cell contents from one place to another.

The Range Erase

The Delete command gives you the ability to delete rows and columns from a worksheet, an action that repositions remaining rows or columns. There is also the need to erase the contents of a range of cells without disturbing the general layout. This is done with the Range Erase. To try this command, first *make certain that you have saved the final version of your revised cost analysis worksheet.* Then with the screen copy, you can use the Range Erase as follows:

DO THIS NOW 5-9 **Erasing the Contents of the Cell Range B5..F8**

1. Position the cell pointer at cell B5.
2. Enter the command sequence

   ```
   /RE
   ```

   That is:

   ```
   / Range Erase        (Lotus 1-2-3)
   / RangeOps Erase     (JOE)
   ```

3. The following prompt and default will be displayed.

   ```
   Enter erase range: B5..B5
   ```

4. Extend the range to cell F8. The prompt will be:

   ```
   Enter erase range: B5..F8
   ```

5. Strike Enter and the contents of the highlighted cells will be erased.

The Worksheet Erase

After completing a worksheet and saving it to disk, you will often wish to begin a new one starting with an empty screen. For this, you need to erase the entire worksheet from the screen. This is done from the Worksheet (Lotus 1-2-3) or WorkSet (JOE) command; the action is one that will affect the entire worksheet as opposed to a selected range.

DO THIS NOW 5-10 **Erasing the Contents of All Cells in the Worksheet**

1. Enter the following command sequence (the position of the cell pointer does not make any difference).

```
/WE
```

That is:

```
/ Worksheet Erase
/ WorkSet Erase_all
```

2. In response to the request for confirmation, enter the letter *Y* for Yes. All cells will be erased.

Note that upon selecting the Erase command, 1-2-3 asks for a confirmation. If your key sequence was the result of striking a wrong key, you could easily abort the operation by striking the letter *N* for No.

The Move Command

Sometimes, in revising a worksheet, it is necessary to move the contents of a range from one place in the worksheet to another. The Move command allows you to move the contents of any range of cells up, down, left, or right, as needed. Figure 5-7 illustrates the action of moving the contents of the cell range B3..D6 to corresponding positions anchored at cell F8. The sequence of steps to carry out this operation is almost identical to that for copying. If you wish to try it, retrieve one of your worksheets and try moving the contents of some of the cells. Remember first to position the cell pointer to the anchor point of the range to be moved. Then invoke the Move command with the sequence /M. The prompts will be almost identical to those of the Copy.

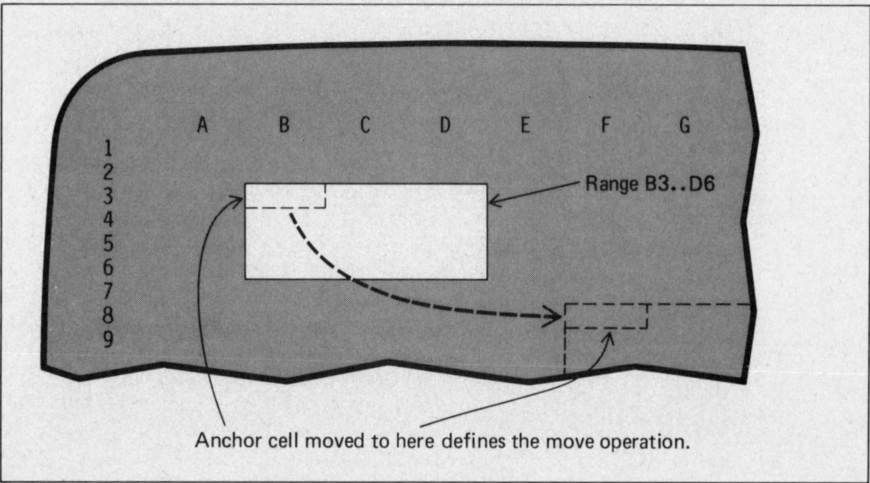

Figure 5-7
Moving the contents of a range of cells.

Assignment 5-1 may now be completed.

BASIC PRINCIPLES OF FUNCTIONS

The five arithmetic operators of 1-2-3 provide you with the basic calculating tools. Like most computer software systems, 1-2-3 includes an extensive set of *functions*, which can be thought of as "predefined" formulas. For instance, there are functions to do the following.

- Calculate the square root of a number.
- Sum the values in a range of cells.
- Calculate the average of a range.
- Determine the payment required for a loan given the amount, interest, and time period.
- Compare two quantities in determining an action to take.

The next two examples are designed to give you an understanding of how functions are used in spreadsheet design.

Example Definition

Assume that the management of the company for which you work is in the process of completely modernizing the work facility. An integral part of the modernization is the upgrading of the work force through specialized training units. For training purposes, the employees have been assigned to groups (such as the office group, warehouse group, and so on). For each group, the training consists of a series of units specifically designed to upgrade the skills in the occupational area. One of your colleagues has been assigned to monitor the progress of the different training groups. After a short period of time, your friend is transferred and you are given the task. Figure 5-8 is an example of one of the record sheets that your friend was using to maintain a record of progress manually. As each training unit is completed, the rating for that employee is entered in the appropriate position. After all employees complete a unit, you must calculate the average for that unit. Furthermore, as each unit is completed, you must maintain a total for each employee. After looking this over, you decide that you could maintain these records much more easily on the computer. Furthermore, you feel that you could provide more information that would be useful in evaluating the performance of employees as well as the success of the training program. To this end, you decide that you will design a spreadsheet that will provide the following.

For each employee:

Total rating for all units completed.

Average rating for all units completed.

Figure 5-8
Maintaining a record of employee progress manually.

Employee Name	Unit 1	Unit 2	Unit 3	Total
Anderson, John	68			
Balcer, Anna	79			
Dexter, Howard	69			
Franklin, Benjamin				
Harrison, Albert	48			
Irvin, Shirley				
Knowland, Jeanette	89			
McDaniel, Nancy	89			
Pierce, William	85			
Sutherland, Carol	75			
Thomas, John	81			
Wilson, Raleigh				
Average rating	76			

For each unit:

Average rating for employees completing the unit.

Number of employees completing the unit.

Highest rating achieved for the unit.

Lowest rating for the unit.

Your expansion of your friend's manual worksheet, as you hope it to appear when all the data entries have been made, is shown in Figure 5-9. Now you need to know how to define the formulas to compute the values in which you are interested. This cannot be done with only the arithmetic operators that you have used in preceding examples. You will need to use 1-2-3 functions. Specifically, typical cell needs for this example are as follows:

Cell	Operation
E3	Sum the values in the cell range B3..D3.
F3	Average the values in the cell range B3..D3.
B17	Average the values in the cell range B3..B14.
B18	Count the number of nonblank entries in the cell range B3. .B14.
B19	Find the maximum (largest) value from the cell range B3. .B14.
B19	Find the minimum (smallest) value from the cell range B3. .B14.

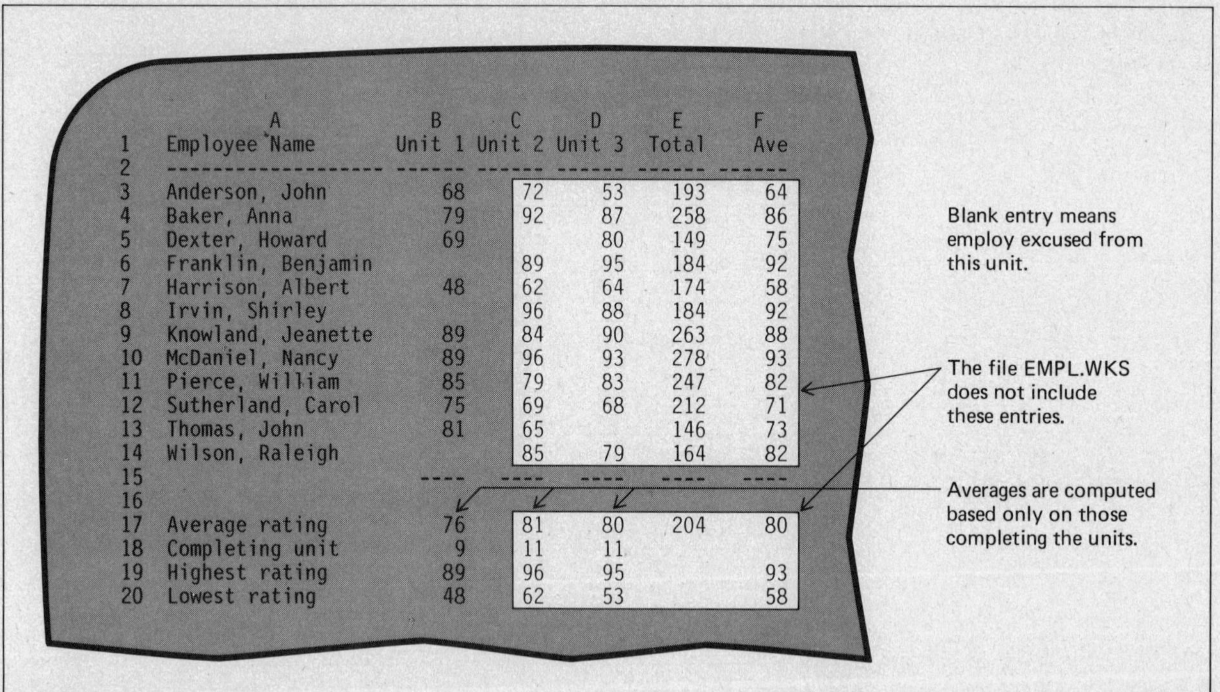

	A	B	C	D	E	F
1	Employee Name	Unit 1	Unit 2	Unit 3	Total	Ave
2	------------------	------	------	------	------	------
3	Anderson, John	68	72	53	193	64
4	Baker, Anna	79	92	87	258	86
5	Dexter, Howard	69		80	149	75
6	Franklin, Benjamin		89	95	184	92
7	Harrison, Albert	48	62	64	174	58
8	Irvin, Shirley		96	88	184	92
9	Knowland, Jeanette	89	84	90	263	88
10	McDaniel, Nancy	89	96	93	278	93
11	Pierce, William	85	79	83	247	82
12	Sutherland, Carol	75	69	68	212	71
13	Thomas, John	81	65		146	73
14	Wilson, Raleigh		85	79	164	82
15		----	----	----	----	----
16						
17	Average rating	76	81	80	204	80
18	Completing unit	9	11	11		
19	Highest rating	89	96	95		93
20	Lowest rating	48	62	53		58

Figure 5-9
Employee progress worksheet.

For the examples of this portion of the chapter, the data disk includes the worksheet file EMPL.WKS, which is an incomplete version of that shown in Figure 5-9. That is, it includes only the data for the first unit, and none of the needed formulas. You can use it to serve as the beginning point for examples that follow. Thus, you should retrieve that worksheet from the disk so that you can follow the example instructions.

Using a Function

Let us begin this study of functions with the function to sum the values in a range of cells. In the cost analysis example, you added up, or summed, the values in a range of cells to obtain the Unit Cost using such formulas as:

```
B5+C5+D5+E5+F5
```

@SUM. The @SUM function provides the following alternative (which is especially convenient if the sum includes many cells).

```
@SUM(B5..F5)
```

Here the name of the function is @SUM and it operates on the range of cells B5 through F5. As you shall learn, all function names begin with the @ character. This signals a function to 1-2-3. Let us enter this into your worksheet.

DO THIS NOW 5-11 **Entering the @SUM Function Into Cell E3**

1. Move the cell pointer to cell E3, the cell into which the function is to be entered.
2. Type the @ character and 1-2-3 will switch to the VALUE mode and the @ will be entered to the second line of the control panel. Continue to type SUM(and the control panel display will be:

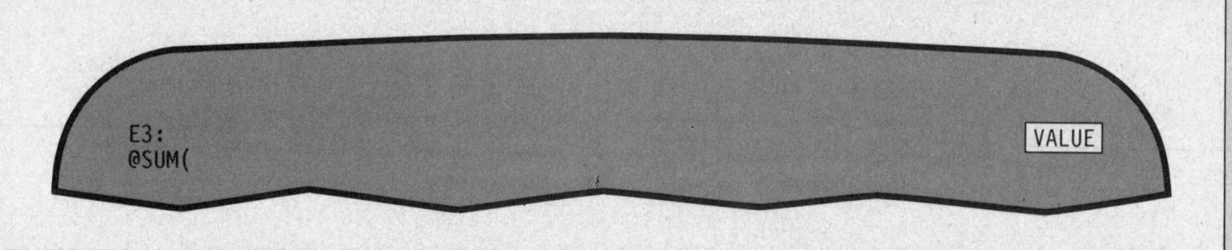

3. Move the cell pointer to cell B3. This identifies the anchor of the range for this function. The control panel display will be:

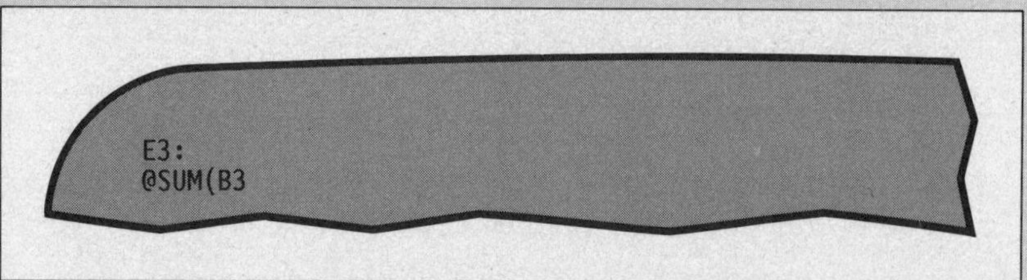

4. Strike the period (.) key to set the anchor for the beginning of the range, giving:

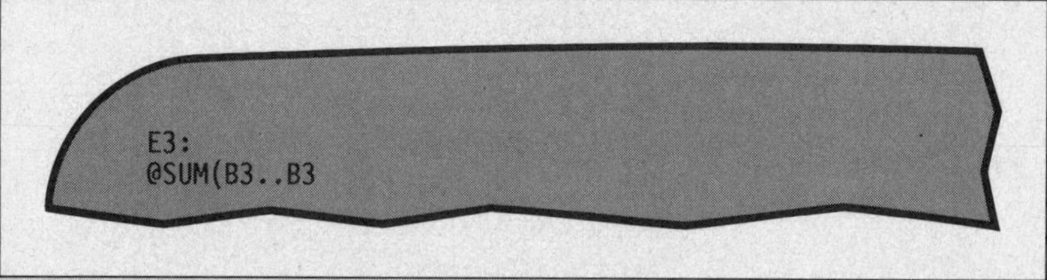

5. Move the highlight to cell D3; this extends the range to cover all cells that you need in the sum, giving:

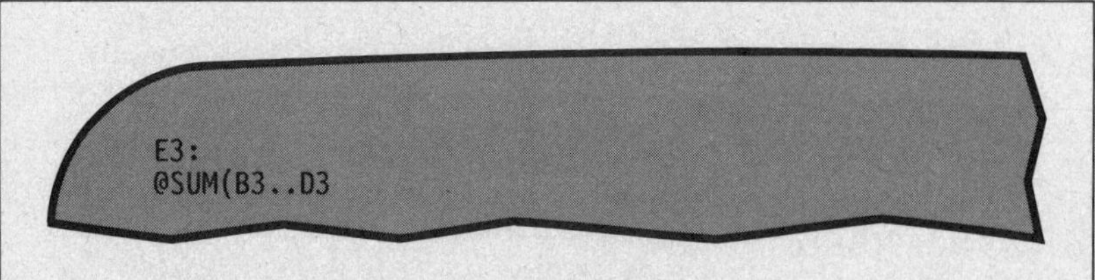

6. Strike the) key to close the parentheses, giving:

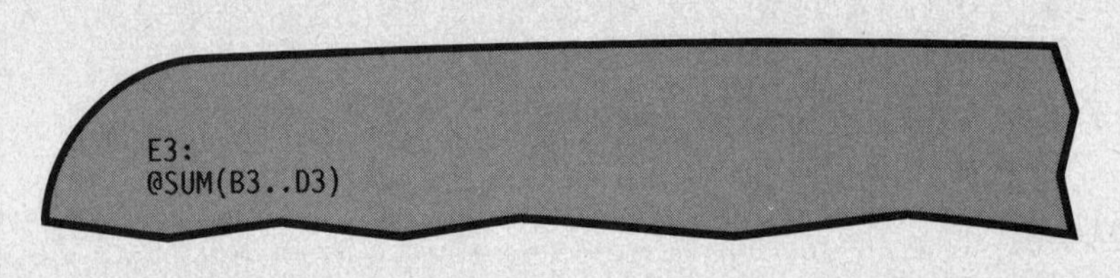

7. Strike Enter, thus completing the operation and entering the function into the cell. The value displayed in this cell should be 68, the only unit completed by this employee.
8. Copy this function entry from cell E3 into the cell range E4..E14 using the /C (Copy) command. Remember to position the cell pointer at cell E3 if you have moved it. Then invoke the command. Your FROM range is E3..E3 and your TO range is E4..E14.

In general, since the function yields a single number, it can be used in building formulas as if it were an ordinary cell address or number. For example, the following formula obtains the sum of cells B8 through D8, multiplies it by 4, and then adds 50.

```
4*@SUM(B8..D8)+50
```

Other Statistical Functions

Following is a brief description of each of the functions you need to complete the worksheet of Figure 5-9.

@AVG. This function calculates the average value of a range. The average is calculated as the sum of the numbers in the range divided by the count of entries, with blank entries being ignored. For instance, in Figure 5-9, the average for column B is the sum of all the ratings divided by 9, the number of employees completing the unit. Sample functions for cells B17 and F3 are:

```
@AVG(B3..B14)
@AVG(B3..D3)
```

@COUNT. This function counts the number of entries in the specified cells. For example, in Figure 5-9, rows 3 through 14 contain information for twelve employees. Referring to column B, we see that three of the employees were exempted from Unit 1 (there are no entries for three of the cells). Thus, the entry count for this range is 9. This count could be determined and displayed in cell B18 by the following function.

```
@COUNT(B3..B14)
```

@MAX and @MIN. These functions search the specified range and return the maximum and minimum values from those cells. They are required to obtain the highest and lowest ratings for individual units, as well as for the average. For cells B19 and B20, the functions take the following form.

```
@MAX(B3..B14)
@MIN(B3..B14)
```

Completing the Employee Progress Worksheet

You should now proceed to enter these functions into your copy of the worksheet.

DO THIS NOW 5-12 **Completing the Employee Progress Worksheet**

1. For the average of cells B3..D3, enter the @AVE function into cell F3, and then duplicate it into the range F3..F14. The sequence of steps is the same as that of DTN 5-11 for the @SUM.
2. Enter the @AVE function into B17 for the range B3..B14. Then duplicate it into C17..F17.
3. Enter the @COUNT function into B18 for the range B3..B14. Then duplicate it into C18..D18.
4. Enter the @MAX function into B19 for the range B3..B14. Then duplicate it into C19..D19, and then to F19.
5. Enter the @MIN function into B20 for the range B3..B14. Then duplicate it into C20..D20, and then to F20.

When you are finished, save your worksheet to disk. Then enter the data for Unit 2 (column C) and observe how all of the calculated values change as you are entering. Then enter the data for Unit 3. Check all values to ensure that your calculations are correct.

CONDITIONAL OPERATIONS USING FUNCTIONS

Problem Definition

Owning a sales-oriented company, you and your partner have considered all types of techniques to promote sales. Your latest thought is to promote sales by your part-time sales representatives with a bonus plan. This plan is to be based on the following monthly bonus quotas for your "high season" sales period (the months April through August).

Month	Bonus Quota
April	$4500
May	$5000
June	$7500
July	$8000
August	$6000

Part-time representatives are currently paid 10 percent of their total sales. You propose to change this as follows:

- Each month for which a sales representative equals or exceeds the bonus quota, you will award a bonus point.
- At the end of the high season, the bonus points are totaled. If the total is four or more, a bonus of $1000 is paid.

In deciding whether or not to proceed with this plan, you decide to evaluate its effect using the data you have stored in a worksheet for the sales for the last high season. (A copy of this worksheet, shown in Figure 5-10, is stored on the data disk as SALES.WKS.) Your plans are to expand this worksheet as follows:

- Column I to contain the total bonus points earned.
- Column H to contain the earnings, which is the 10 percent commission amount plus $1000 if the bonus points are four or more.

Figure 5-10
High season sales representative summary.

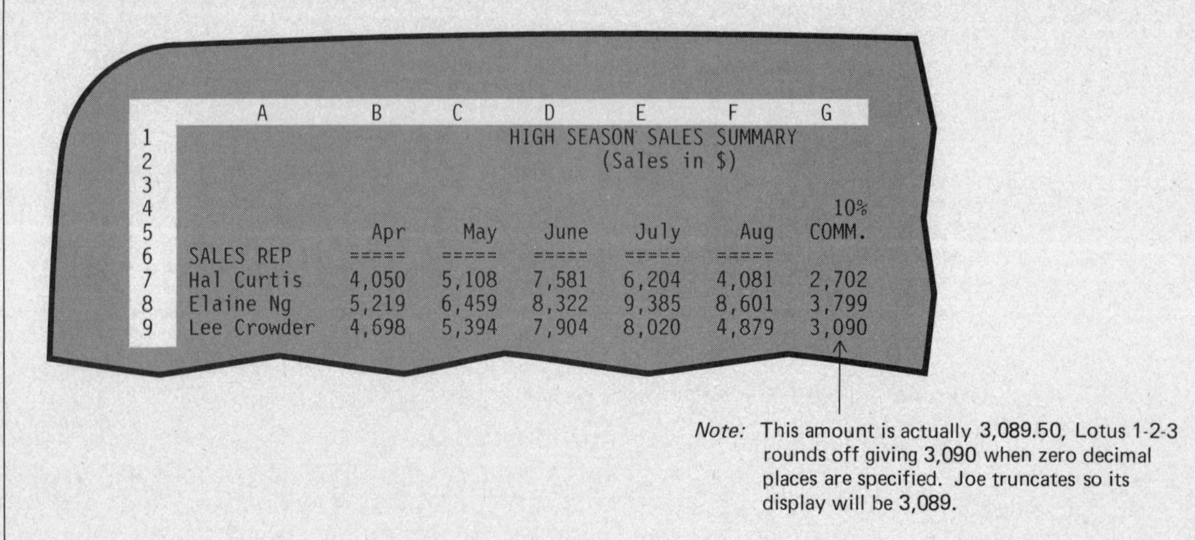

	A	B	C	D	E	F	G
1				HIGH SEASON SALES SUMMARY			
2				(Sales in $)			
3							
4							10%
5		Apr	May	June	July	Aug	COMM.
6	SALES REP	=====	=====	=====	=====	=====	
7	Hal Curtis	4,050	5,108	7,581	6,204	4,081	2,702
8	Elaine Ng	5,219	6,459	8,322	9,385	8,601	3,799
9	Lee Crowder	4,698	5,394	7,904	8,020	4,879	3,090

Note: This amount is actually 3,089.50, Lotus 1-2-3 rounds off giving 3,090 when zero decimal places are specified. Joe truncates so its display will be 3,089.

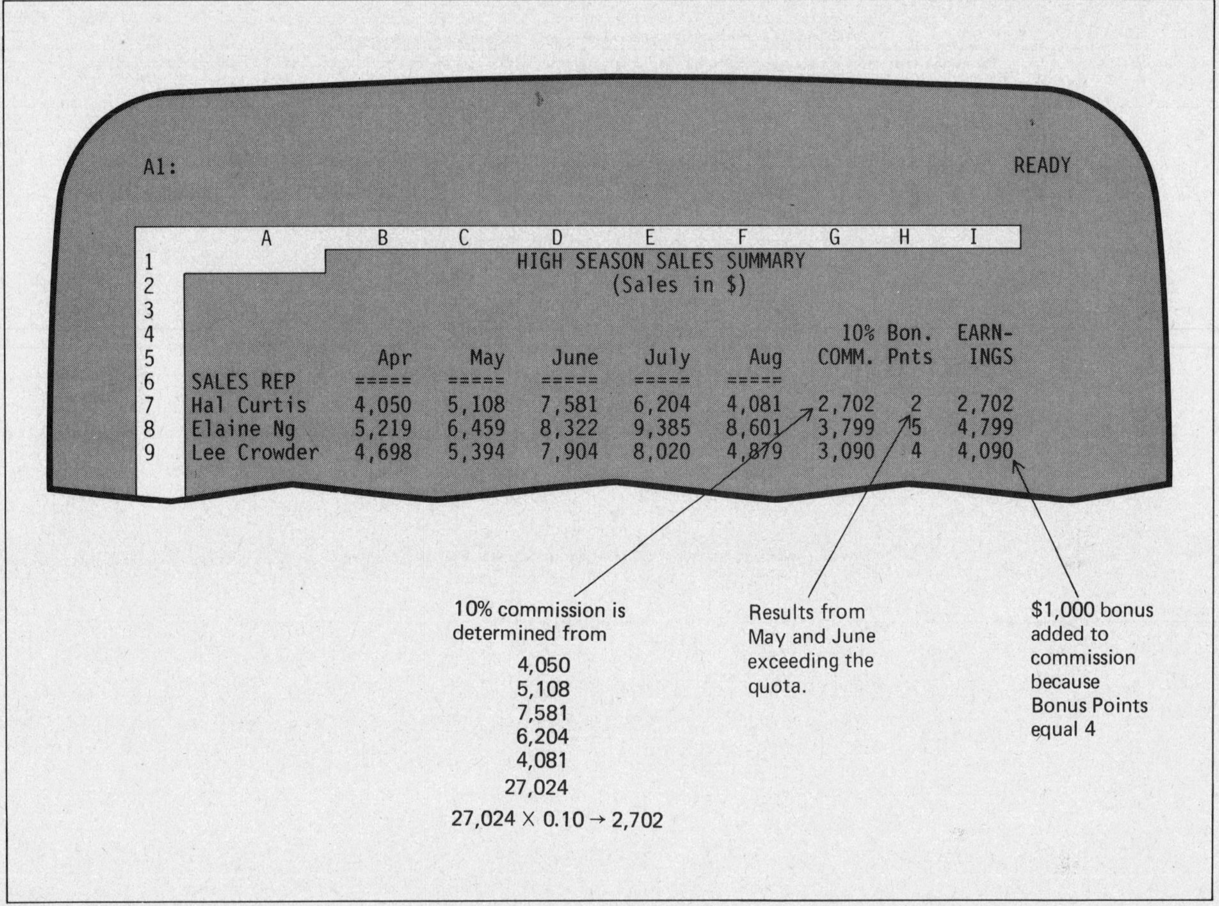

A1: READY

	A	B	C	D	E	F	G	H	I
1				HIGH SEASON SALES SUMMARY					
2				(Sales in $)					
3									
4							10%	Bon.	EARN-
5		Apr	May	June	July	Aug	COMM.	Pnts	INGS
6	SALES REP	=====	=====	=====	=====	=====			
7	Hal Curtis	4,050	5,108	7,581	6,204	4,081	2,702	2	2,702
8	Elaine Ng	5,219	6,459	8,322	9,385	8,601	3,799	5	4,799
9	Lee Crowder	4,698	5,394	7,904	8,020	4,879	3,090	4	4,090

Figure 5-11
The expanded worksheet with bonus calculations.

When you are finished, the worksheet will be as shown in Figure 5-11.

To do this, you need the ability to instruct 1-2-3 to perform an operation on a conditional basis. That is, the amount to be paid to a sales representative must be increased by $1000 if the employee accumulates four or more bonus points. For this, 1-2-3 includes, in addition to arithmetic operators, special operators that allow you to compare quantities.

Relational Operators

We have already learned about formulas built with arithmetic operators (+, –, and so on) that define the arithmetic actions. Similarly, we can create formulas by using the set of **relational operators*** shown on the next page; these define actions in which quantities are compared.

*In the Lotus 1-2-3 manual, these operators are called *logical* operators. Since, in general computer use, there is a distinction between relational and logical operators, the term *relational operator* is used in this book.

Operator	Meaning
=	Equal to
<>	Not equal to
<	Less than
<=	Less than or equal to
>	Greater than
>=	Greater than or equal to

In 1-2-3, you use these operators to build **relational expressions,** which allow you to compare two quantities, as illustrated by the following two examples.

Relational Expression	Explanation
D3>8000	If the value in cell D3 is greater than 8000, then this expression is true and has a value of 1 else this expression is false and has a value of 0.
F5=F10+500	If the value in F5 is equal to the value in F10 plus 500, then this expression is true and has a value of 1 else this expression is false and has a value of 0.

Using Relational Operators in Building Formulas

Let us first consider how to use relational expressions in constructing the formula for the bonus points (column H), and then how to use them for comparing two quantities in determining the earnings (column I). Since relational expressions produce numerical values of 0 or 1, they can be used in building formulas. For example, consider the sales of Curtis (row 7 in Figure 5-11).

Month	Cell	Sales	Bonus Quota	Relational Expression	→	Points
April	B7	4050	4500	B7>=4500		0
May	C7	5108	5000	C7>=5000		1
June	D7	7581	7500	D7>=7500		1
July	E7	6204	8000	E7>=8000		0
August	F7	4081	6000	F7>=6000		0

Figure 5-12
Using relational expressions in a formula.

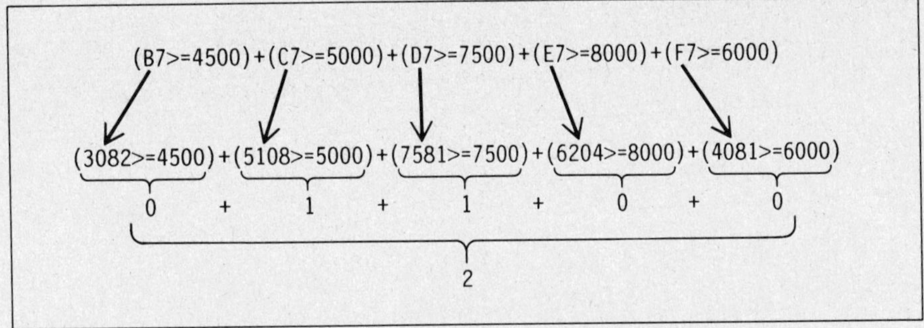

From this table, we see that each of the relational expressions yields a value of 0 or 1. In this specific case, we get the total points by summing the points for each month. Exactly the same approach is used in 1-2-3, except that we use the relational expressions to build the needed formulas, as shown in Figure 5-12.

The second expansion to the worksheet is to calculate the earnings for each sales representative. Stated in a form that is consistent with computer representations, the contents of the cells of column I are to be determined as follows:

> If total bonus points value is equal to or greater than four,
> then the amount of earnings is 10 percent of sales plus $1000,
> else the amount of earnings is 10 percent of sales.

To see how this statement corresponds to the features of 1-2-3, consider the illustration in Figure 5-13. In 1-2-3, the conditional form is handled by the @IF function. Notice that it has three components inside the parentheses: the condition, the value to use if the condition is true, and the value to use if the condition is false. The English statement of this function is, "If the value in cell H7 is greater than or equal to four, then return a value that is

Figure 5-13
The @IF function in cell I7.

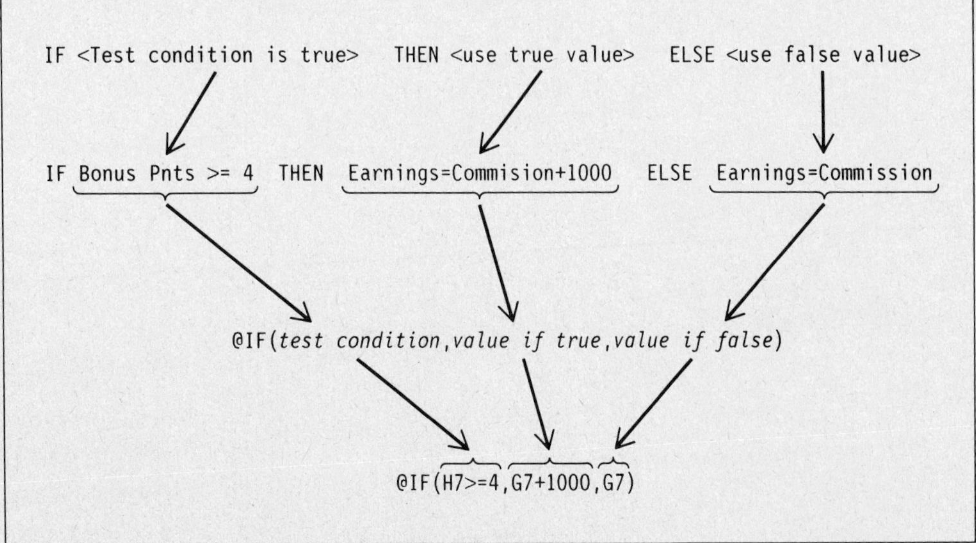

the sum of the contents of cell G7 and the number 1000; else, return a value equal to the value in cell G7.′ In other words, add 1000 to the commission if the condition is true.

Completing the Worksheet

You now have the tools to expand the SALES.WKS worksheet to include calculations for bonus points and total earnings.

DO THIS NOW 5-13 **Expanding the Worksheet to Include Bonus Payments**

1. Retrieve the SALES.WKS worksheet.
2. Set the column width of column H to 4 with the command sequence /WGC.
3. Enter the new column headings for columns H and I (see Figure 5-11).
4. Move the cell pointer to cell H7, the cell into which the bonus points formula is to be entered.
5. You must now enter the formula of Figure 5-12. Notice that when you strike the (key, 1-2-3 switches to VALUE mode. When you have finished, line 2 of the control panel should display:

   ```
   (B7>=4500)+(C7>=5000)+(D7>=7500)+(E7>=8000)+(F7>=6000)
   ```

6. Strike Enter to assign this formula to cell H7. Notice that the value displayed in cell H7 is 2.
7. Move the cell pointer to cell F7. Change the sales from 4081 to 6000, the minimum to qualify for a bonus point. Notice that the value now displayed in cell H7 increases from 2 to 3. You just entered a qualifying sales amount for August. Change the contents of cell F7 back to 4081.
8. With the Copy command (/C), copy the formula in cell H7 into the range H8..H9.
9. Next, you must enter the @IF function for cell I7. Move the cell pointer to cell I7.
10. Enter the formula of Figure 5-13. Notice that when you strike the @ key, 1-2-3 switches to the VALUE mode. When you have finished, line 2 of the control panel should display:

    ```
    @IF(H7>=4,G7+1000,G7)
    ```

11. Strike Enter to assign this formula to cell I7. Notice that the value displayed in cell H7 is 2702. This salesperson did not qualify so the earnings are the same as the commission.
12. With the Copy command (/C), copy the formula in cell I7 into the range I8..I9.

As this version of the worksheet is complete, save it to disk as SALES2 (you will need it for the next example).

Testing Your Worksheet

The fact that your worksheet displays values that are identical to those of Figure 5-11 does not necessarily mean that your formulas are correct. For instance, the first relational expression of your formula could be

`(B7>=4600)` instead of `(B7>=4500)`

and your display would still be the same. Errors of this type are usually detected by inspecting the formulas, although such errors are easily overlooked. Similar errors in larger, more complex worksheets are often much more difficult to locate. Hence, before using a worksheet, you should always check all elements with sample data. Each cell that contributes to the results in columns H and I should be checked. A good test would be to change the values in row 8 as summarized in the following.

Test Values					Expected Results		
April	May	June	July	August	Commission	Points	Earnings
4500	5000	7500	8000	6000	3100	5	4100
4499	4999	7499	7999	5999	3099.50	0	3099.50

Concerning this set of values, notice that the first test set consists of amounts that are the exact value at which bonus points are awarded. The second set is a dollar less. The expected results were calculated with a pocket calculator. These values should be entered into row 8, thereby testing a version of the formula resulting from the Copy operation.

DO THIS NOW 5-14 **Testing Formulas in a Spreadsheet**

1. Enter the first set of test values into row 8 and check your results.
2. Enter the second set of test values into row 8 and check your results.

ABSOLUTE CELL ADDRESSES IN FORMULAS

Expanding the Capabilities of the Sales Summary Worksheet

After completing the worksheet of Figure 5-11, you decide to experiment with different bonus quota amounts to see whether some other set of

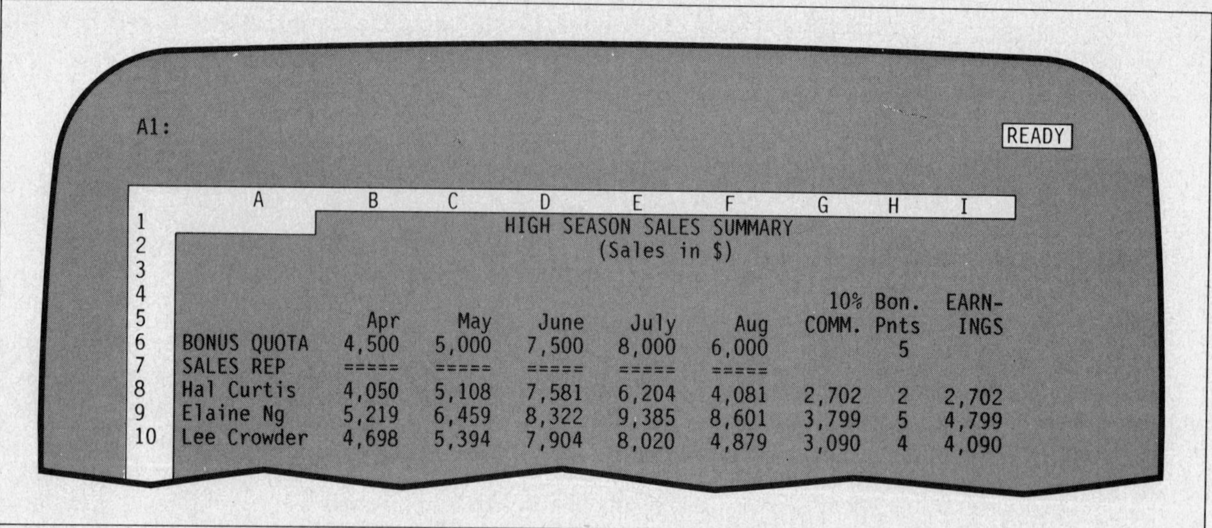

A1: READY

	A	B	C	D	E	F	G	H	I
1				HIGH SEASON SALES SUMMARY					
2				(Sales in $)					
3									
4							10%	Bon.	EARN-
5		Apr	May	June	July	Aug	COMM.	Pnts	INGS
6	BONUS QUOTA	4,500	5,000	7,500	8,000	6,000		5	
7	SALES REP	=====	=====	=====	=====	=====			
8	Hal Curtis	4,050	5,108	7,581	6,204	4,081	2,702	2	2,702
9	Elaine Ng	5,219	6,459	8,322	9,385	8,601	3,799	5	4,799
10	Lee Crowder	4,698	5,394	7,904	8,020	4,879	3,090	4	4,090

Figure 5-14
Including the bonus quota in the worksheet.

values might better meet your objectives. The form that you wish the worksheet to take is shown in Figure 5-14, where a row containing the monthly bonus quotas has been inserted at row 6. To take advantage of these entries, the formula for Curtis that we considered in Figure 5-12 becomes:

```
(B8>=B6)+(C8>=C6)+(D8>=D6)+(E8>=E6)+(F8>=F6)
```

This form of the worksheet serves a double duty for you. Not only are the bonus quotas displayed, but you can easily change them and observe the effect on the earnings.

Unfortunately, there is a subtle problem with this example when you attempt to copy the formula of cell I8 into cells I9 and I10. Remember that whenever a formula is copied from one row to the next, each row addressed is changed to account for this repositioning. Thus, when you copy, the formula in cell I9 will be

```
(B9>=B7)+(C9>=C7)+(D9>=D7)+(E9>=E7)+(F9>=F7)
```

instead of

```
(B9>=B6)+(C9>=C6)+(D9>=D6)+(E9>=E6)+(F9>=F6)
```

To copy this formula, we must be able to designate to 1-2-3 that some of the cell addresses must not be changed when the formula is moved.

Absolute Addressing

In all of the examples that we have considered to this point, 1-2-3 changes cell addresses in formulas when the formula is moved or copied to another cell. This is an automatic consequence of the fact that 1-2-3 determines the location of the addressed cells that make up the formula relative to the location of the cell containing the formula. For instance, in Figure 5-15, the

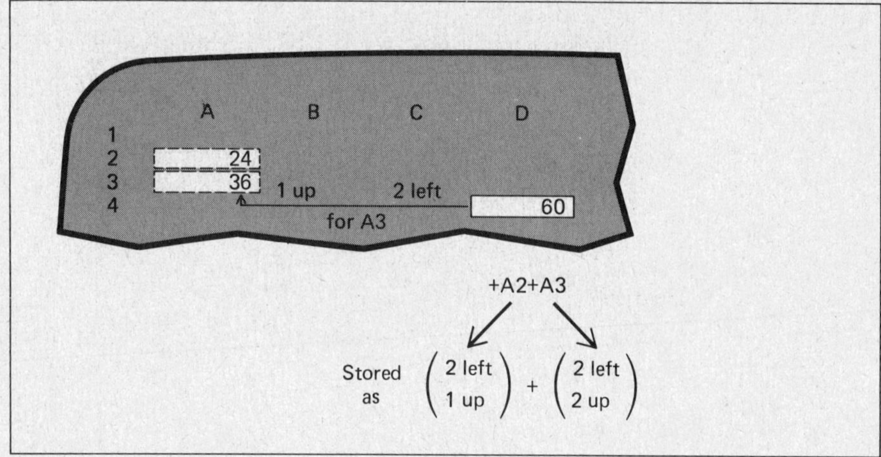

Figure 5-15
Relative addressing.

formula in cell D4 that we see as +A2+A3 is actually stored in memory as "the cell two left and one up plus the cell two left and two up." Consequently, this formula can be moved anywhere and we see it displayed with cell addresses that change according to where we have positioned it. This cell addressing is called **relative addressing** because the addresses are determined relative to the location of the formula cell.

For this formula, you need to be able to designate that the 6's in B6, C6, D6, E6, and F6 remain unchanged when the formula is copied. In 1-2-3, cell addressing in which a row or column reference remains unchanged when the formula is moved is called **absolute addressing.** A row or column reference in a cell is designated as absolute by preceding the row or column with the $ character. Hence, the formula must be entered into the worksheet as:

```
(B8>=B$6)+(C8>=C$6)+(D8>=D$6)+(E8>=E$6)+(F8>=F$6)
```

DO THIS NOW 5-15 **Modifying the Sales Summary Worksheet to Include the Bonus Quota as in Figure 5-14**

1. Either reenter the correct data values for row 7 (those that you changed in DTN 5-14) or retrieve the copy of SALES2 from disk.
2. Use the Insert command to insert a blank row at row 6 (/WIR).
3. Enter the label and data values shown in Figure 5-14.
4. Enter the preceding formula (with the absolute row address for row 6) into cell I8.
5. Copy the formula assigned to cell I8 to I9..I10.

Check your display to ensure that it is identical to that of Figure 5-14; if you find any differences, investigate the causes and make needed corrections. When your version of the worksheet is the same as Figure 5-14, save it to disk as SALES3. You will use this version of the sales summary worksheet for creating graphs in the next chapter.

When you use absolute addresses in a worksheet, be careful regarding the operations of moving, inserting, and deleting. Remember, if you perform an operation such as inserting one or more rows, 1-2-3 automatically adjusts the relative address references. However, if you were to insert a blank row at row 1 of Figure 5-14, the bonus quota values would be moved to row 7, but the references in the formula, being absolute, would remain at row 6. On the other hand, this entire worksheet could be moved one or more columns to the right with no ill effects since all column references are relative.

Technically, an address such as B$6 is called a **mixed address** because one part is relative and the other part is absolute. It is equally valid to use an absolute column address if the circumstances require it. For example, in the cell address $K13, the column address K is absolute but the row address 13 is relative. Only if both the column and row designations are fixed—for instance, $B$22, which refers to column B and row 22—is the address called absolute.

Assignment 5-2 may now be completed.

COMBINING A WORKSHEET WITH A WORD PROCESSING DOCUMENT

Assume that you decide to send a memo to each sales representative describing the activities of the past season. You wish to include the portion of the worksheet output that lists the monthly sales for each sales representative (columns A through F of Figure 5-10). There are three ways in which you can do this. First (and the least desirable), as the memo is being created on the word processor, simply type in the worksheet table by using a printed copy from 1-2-3. Second, type the letter and leave space for the worksheet table. Then paste in the desired portion of the worksheet as printed by 1-2-3 and make the required copies on a copying machine. Actually, the third approach is essentially the same as the second. The difference is that the pasting is done electronically rather than with scissors and paper.

Your first task is to send the printed output of the worksheet to a file so that it can be inserted into the memo. Referring to Figure 5-10, you will need the range A1..F9.

DO THIS NOW 5-16 **Inserting a Worksheet into a Document**

1. Retrieve the worksheet file SALES.WKS.
2. In order to give the resulting printout a more balanced appearance, move row 1 and 2 headings 2 columns to the left.
3. Position the cell pointer at cell A1, the anchor for the print range.
4. Enter the following command sequence.

   `/PF`

   That is:

   `/ Print File` (Lotus 1-2-3)
   `/ Print File_output` (JOE)

5. You will see the prompt:

   `Enter print file name: B:\_.PRN`

   Notice that the displayed default extension is PRN.

6. Type the filename SALES. When your entry has been completed, this line will be:

   `Enter print file name: B:\SALES`

   Strike the Enter key to complete this action. Even though you do not include an extension, PRN will be used as it is the default. Hence, the file will be stored on drive B as SALES.PRN and the original worksheet file will remain.

7. The following submenu will be displayed. From this, select the Range option (to define the range of cells to be printed) by striking the letter *R*.

`Range Line Page Options Clear Align Go Quit` (Lotus 1-2-3)
`Align_top Clear Go_print Line Page Option_menu Quit Range_to_print` (JOE)

8. You will see the prompt:

   `Enter Print range: A1`

   Strike the period to accept A1 as the range anchor.

9. Move the cell pointer to cell F9, and then strike Enter to complete the range.
10. The submenu of step 7 is redisplayed. Select the Go_print (JOE) or Go (Lotus 1-2-3) option by striking the letter G. This causes the print file to be created.
11. After a few moments, the submenu of step 7 is redisplayed. To complete the operation, it is essential to execute the Quit command by striking the letter *Q*. If this is not done, the print file stored on the disk will be empty.

Upon completing this sequence, the output will be stored as the file SALES.PRN. At this point, you can terminate the 1-2-3 session and use DOS commands to send it to a printer or display it on the screen. In fact, it is always a good idea to check to ensure that it is correct. Displaying it is done with the following DOS command.

```
A>TYPE SALES.PRN
```

The file SALES.PRN could then be treated as if it were a document created by WordPerfect. It could be retrieved with WordPerfect and edited as required. To insert it into the memo to your salespeople:

1. Create the memo with WordPerfect.
2. Position the cursor at the point in the document at which you wish to insert the text version of your worksheet SALES.PRN.
3. Retrieve SALES.PRN. Remember, if WordPerfect is displaying a document on the screen and another is retrieved, the newly retrieved document is inserted into the one on the screen at the position of the cursor.
4. Insert spacing or otherwise edit the inserted text as desired.

SUMMARY

This chapter has built on the basic concepts you learned in Chapter 4. Summarizing, the important items from the chapter are:

- A range is any rectangular collection of cells; this includes a single cell, a portion of a row, or a portion of a column.
- If you change the size of a worksheet by inserting or deleting rows or columns, 1-2-3 automatically adjusts formulas. However, sometimes deletions produce results that 1-2-3 cannot resolve.
- The default display cell width is 9 positions. This default can be overridden with the WGC (global) command sequence. Individual column widths can be changed with the /WCS command sequence.
- The Copy command allows you to copy the contents of one or more cells to another portion of the worksheet. If a single cell is being copied into a range, it will be duplicated in each cell of that range. Cell addresses in formulas are adjusted by 1-2-3 automatically.
- The four formatting options described in this chapter are: General, the default; Fixed, in which the user specifies the number of decimal places; Comma, which inserts commas for large numbers; Currency, the same as Comma except it includes a $ character.
- The Format is a subcommand under the Range command; it operates on a user-designated range of cells.

- The Erase command erases the contents of a range of cells. Do not confuse this with the Delete command, which removes rows or columns.
- Functions perform mathematical operations on designated cells. A function is indicated to 1-2-3 by preceding its name with the @ character. (The command summary following this section lists the functions covered in this chapter.)
- Relational operators allow you to construct relational formulas in which two quantities are compared. If the comparison is true, a value of 1 is assigned; if false, a value of 0 is assigned.
- The @IF function gives you a conditional capability. It allows you to assign a formula to a cell that display the result of one expression if a stated condition is true and another if it is false.
- Addresses in building a formula can be relative, absolute, or mixed. A relative address is one that is adjusted when the formula is moved. An absolute address is one that remains unchanged if the formula is moved. A reference in which one element (row or column) is relative and the other is fixed is called a mixed address.
- To prepare a worksheet for inclusion in a word processing document, use the Print command and send the "printed" output to a disk file.

COMMAND AND FUNCTION SUMMARY

Following is a summary of the various commands and operations described in this chapter.

Command	Key Sequence	Action
Column width	/WGC	Change the default column width.
	/WCS	Change the width of the current column.
Copy	/C	Copy the contents of a range of cells to another portion of the worksheet.
Delete	/WDR or /WDC	Delete rows or columns.
Erase	/RE	Erase the contents of a range of cells.
	/WE	Erase the contents of all cells in the worksheet.
Format	/RF	Format the display of numeric quantities in a range of cells.
Insert	/WIR or /WIC	Insert rows or columns.
Move	/M	Move the contents of a range of cells to another portion of the worksheet.

Function Name	Action
@AVG	Average the values of a range of cells.
@COUNT	Count the number of nonblank entries in a range of cells.
@MAX	Determine the largest value from a range of cells.
@MIN	Determine the smallest value from a range of cells.
@SUM	Sum the values of a range of cells.

NEW TERMINOLOGY

The following are important new terms introduced in this chapter; you should be familiar with each of them.

absolute address
anchor cell
function
global
mixed address
range
relational expression
relational operator
relative address

Name: ______________________________ Date: ______________

Assignment 5-1

1. How many cells are in each of the following ranges?
   (a) B5..B9

   (b) C6..C6

   (c) M23..Q42

   (d) F12..E11

2. What is the sequence of operations to insert 3 blank rows in rows 7–9 of the current worksheet?

3. What is the sequence of operations to delete columns F–J of the current worksheet?

Name: ______________________ Date: ______________

Assignment 5-1 (*continued*)

4. The following column width changes have been made using the **/WCS** command sequence: column A to 15, columns E–G to 6, and column M to 10. Then the default width is changed to 7 using the command sequence **/WGC.** What will be the widths of the columns in the worksheet?

5. Five asterisk characters (*) are to be entered into all of the cells of the first column, rows 5 through 20. What are the steps to do this?

6. How will the values 25, 3669.1234, and –65.1 be displayed with each of the following format definitions?
   (a) General.

   (b) Fixed with three decimal places.

   (c) Comma with one decimal place.

   (d) Currency with two decimal places.

Name: ______________________ Date: ____________

Assignment 5-2 (*continued*)

7. Is it possible to format part of the cells in a column one way and others in the same column another way? For instance, could cells B3..B6 be formatted as fixed with 4 decimal places and cells B7..B10 be formatted as currency? Explain your answer.

8. What will happen if the following sequence of operations is carried out?

   Move the cell pointer to cell C6.
   Enter the command sequence **/RE.**
   Strike the Down key three times and the Right key twice.
   Strike the Enter key.

9. Referring to the cost analysis worksheet, tell what would happen to the formulas originally in column E if column A were erased? What would happen if column A were deleted?

Name: ______________________________ Date: ______________

Assignment 5-2

1. What changes would be required to the formulas in the worksheet of Figure 5-9 if a blank row were inserted at row 8 to insert the employee Anthony Hobbs?

2. Cell D14 contains the formula @SUM(D3..D12). Four rows are inserted beginning row 5. In which cell will the formula now reside, and what will its form be?

3. Answer the preceding question if three rows are deleted beginning row 7.

4. What is the difference between an arithmetic formula and a relational formula?

Name: ______________________ Date: ____________

Assignment 5-2 (*continued*)

5. Assume that the following cells contain the indicated values.

   D1 –2 F6 110 D6 135 F9 137

   What will be displayed by a cell containing each of the following logical formulas?

   (a) D6>500 **(b)** D6<=F6+25

   (c) D6<>D1+F9 **(d)** D1*D6<0

6. Using the cell contents of the preceding exercise, what will be displayed by a cell containing each of the following @IF functions?

   (a) @IF(D6>0,F9,F6+F9)

   (b) @IF(F6+F9<=D6,F9,F6+F9)

   (c) @IF(D1<D6,0,D1)

7. What is the difference between a relative address and an absolute address?

8. The following formula in cell H10 is copied to cell H11. What will be the appearance of this formula in H11?

   +C10-D10*A$10+$K$4

Name: ______________________ Date: ______________

OBJECTIVE QUESTIONS

Matching

Match each command key sequence in a to h with the corresponding action in 1 through 8.

a. /PF	**e.** /FS
b. /WDR	**f.** /WIC
c. /RF	**g.** /RFC
d. /RE	**h.** /C

____ **1.** Provide for the display of very large numbers in the worksheet.

____ **2.** Eliminate the second row from a worksheet.

____ **3.** Make room for three additional columns to be inserted after column D.

____ **4.** Save a worksheet to disk.

____ **5.** Erase the contents of the current cell.

____ **6.** Prepare a worksheet to be included in a word processing document.

____ **7.** Duplicate the formula currently in cell D5 into the range D5..G12.

____ **8.** Display a dollar sign preceding a numeric quantity.

True/False

Determine whether each of the following is true or false.

T F **1.** Technically, B4..B4 is not a range because it includes only one cell.

T F **2.** The cell range C5..F9 includes 20 cells.

T F **3.** The two rows of cells B3..B9 and D3..D9 represent a cell range.

T F **4.** When new rows are inserted or deleted, the formulas are always adjusted by 1-2-3 to give the proper result.

T F **5.** To insert a row in a worksheet, the cell pointer must first be positioned in the row into which the blank row will be inserted. The existing row (and all following it) will be moved down with the insertion.

T F **6.** Cell C9 contains the formula C5+C6+C7. If a new row is inserted at row 8, this formula will not be changed.

T F **7.** If a column width is too narrow to display a numeric value, asterisks are displayed in that cell.

T F **8.** The Delete command erases information stored in a row or a column without affecting other rows or columns.

Name: ______________________ Date: ______________

OBJECTIVE QUESTIONS (*continued*)

T F **9.** If cell F9 contains the formula +F3+F4+F5+F6 and you delete row 4, an error condition will occur.

T F **10.** If the width of column D is set to 22, then the default column width is changed to 15, the width of column D will not be changed.

T F **11.** In using the Copy command, the size of the range into which the copy is being made must be identical to the size of the range being copied.

T F **12.** If a formula is copied to other cells, all addresses in the formula will be changed automatically to account for the location of the copy of the formula.

T F **13.** The Erase allows you to erase the contents of the entire worksheet or of only a selected range.

T F **14.** With default formatting, the dollar and cent amount 5.20 will be displayed as 5.2.

T F **15.** If the quantity stored in a cell is 1547.6312, it could be displayed by the Currency format at $1,547.63.

T F **16.** Currency formatting can be applied to a cell whether it contains numbers or a formula.

T F **17.** The first line of the control panel displays:

```
G7: [F2] 7.28
```

This means that the formatting of cell G7 is Fixed with two decimal places.

T F **18.** The actions of the Move and Copy commands are the same.

T F **19.** To erase a range of cells, you must first use the Range command to select the desired range, then use the Range Erase command.

T F **20.** The Worksheet Erase command will destroy the worksheet copy that is stored on disk.

T F **21.** All function names begin with the & character.

T F **22.** The following two formulas would produce the same result.

```
B7+B8+C7+C8     @SUM(B7..C8)
```

T F **23.** The following two formulas will always produce the same result.

```
(F7+F8+F9)/3     @AVE(F7..F9)
```

T F **24.** If row 5 is deleted from a worksheet, the following formula would still display the correct result.

```
@SUM(C3..C20)
```

Name: ______________________________ Date: ______________

OBJECTIVE QUESTIONS (*continued*)

T F **25.** The contents of selected cells are:

```
B3   25      C7   125
B4   30      C8   211
```

The following formula will display a value of 2.

```
(C7>5*B3)+(B3<B4)+(4*B4=C7)
```

T F **26.** The @MAX function finds the largest entry in the entire worksheet.

T F **27.** A relational expression used in a formula returns a value of either 0 or 1.

T F **28.** The contents of selected cells are:

```
B3   25      C7   125
B4   30      C8   211
```

The following function will cause 125 to be displayed.

```
@IF(B4>=B3+5,C7,C8+100)
```

T F **29.** Cell F5 contains the following formula.

```
2*$A$5+C5-D5
```

If this were copied to cell F6, its form would be:

```
2*$A$5+C6-D6
```

T F **30.** If an entire worksheet is to be included in a word processing document, then the worksheet file itself could be inserted. It is only necessary to print to a file when a portion of the worksheet is needed.

Multiple Choice

In the space provided, record the letter of the choice that best completes or answers the statement.

____ **1.** The cell range B3..G10 includes ______ cells.

A. 6
B. 42
C. 48
D. 35

____ **2.** Which of the following is NOT true about the Insert command?

A. It can cause the contents of one or more rows or columns to be erased.
B. It can be used to insert blank rows into a worksheet.
C. It can be used to insert blank columns into a worksheet.
D. It can cause one or more formulas in other cells to be changed.

Name: ______________________________ Date: ______________

OBJECTIVE QUESTIONS (*continued*)

____ **3.** Cell D12 of a spreadsheet contains the formula:

```
+D5+D6-D8/D9
```

The Delete command is used to delete row 7. What can be said about this formula?

A. It will not be changed.
B. All of the cell addresses will be changed.
C. Some of the cell addresses will be changed.
D. It is not possible to say for certain what will be changed without knowing what is stored in the cells.

____ **4.** Cell D12 of a spreadsheet contains the formula:

```
+D6-D8/D9
```

The Erase command is used on row 7. What can be said about this formula?

A. It will not be changed.
B. All of the cell addresses will be changed.
C. Some of the cell addresses will be changed.
D. It is not possible to say for certain without knowing what is stored in the cells.

____ **5.** A label consisting of 20 characters has been entered into a cell with the default width value. Which of the following is a true statement regarding this entry?

A. Everything in excess of the cell width will be lost.
B. The entire label will be stored but only part of it will be displayed.
C. The cell width will be increased automatically.
D. It is not possible to say whether or not the entire label will be displayed without more information.

____ **6.** The width of columns A, B, and C has been increased from 9 to 12. A global width change is then made changing the column width to 7. What can be said of this action?

A. It is illegal because A, B, and C cannot be changed again.
B. The widths of columns A, B, and C will not be changed.
C. The width of every column in the spreadsheet is changed whenever "global" is used.
D. It is not possible to say without knowing the contents of the cells in columns A, B, and C.

Name: ______________________________ Date: ______________

OBJECTIVE QUESTIONS (*continued*)

____ **7.** The contents of several screen cells containing numbers is displayed as: 6.30, 7391.25, and 24.00. The format for these cells is probably

A. general (the default).
B. currency.
C. comma.
D. fixed.

____ **8.** Which of the following commands would you use if you wished to clear all cells of the current worksheet so that you could start a new one?

A. Range Erase
B. Worksheet Erase
C. Range Delete
D. Worksheet Delete

____ **9.** Which of the following commands would not change the cell addresses of any formulas in a worksheet?

A. Format
B. Move
C. Copy
D. Delete

____ **10.** Which of the choices is true regarding the following function?

```
@SUM(B7..D13)
```

A. This function can operate only on the elements of a single row or column so it will sum only the elements B7..B13 and ignore the rest.
B. This function can operate only on the elements of a single row or column so it will sum only the elements B7..D7 and ignore the rest.
C. This function can operate only on the elements of a single row or column so this form is invalid.
D. It will sum all the cells in the range B7..D13.

____ **11.** Which of the following could NOT be used to find the average value of the contents of cells C4, C5, C6, and C7 (assume that they all contain data)?

A. `(C4+C5+C6+C7)/4`
B. `@SUM(C4..C7)/4`
C. `@AVE(C4..C7)`
D. All of the above could be used.

Name: ______________________________ Date: ______________

OBJECTIVE QUESTIONS (*continued*)

____ **12.** Which of the following formulas will cause a value of 1 to be displayed in the cell to which it is assigned? Assume that the values in selected cells are:

```
C7  22       C8  9       C9  22
```

A. (C9>=23)
B. (C7<C9)
C. (3*C8>24)
D. +C9–C8

____ **13.** Based on your knowledge of the @IF function, what would you say about the following?

```
@IF(B9>=23,"Good","Bad")
```

A. If B9 contains 23, the label *Good* will be displayed.
B. If B9 contains 23, the label *Bad* will be displayed.
C. If B9 contains 22, the label *Good* will be displayed.
D. This is an invalid form because the alternatives to be displayed must be the contents of other cells.

____ **14.** If a particular cell address in a formula is said to be "absolute," which of the following is true?

A. That cell contains a number that cannot be changed.
B. The cell address will not be changed if the formula is moved.
C. The cell contents will not be recalculated if the formula is moved.
D. The formula cannot be moved.

____ **15.** Some of the cell addresses of the formula in a particular cell are relative. This means that

A. the value in the cell is related to values in nearby cells.
B. the cell can be moved anywhere on the spreadsheet.
C. the formula can be used only in its relative position and nowhere else in any form.
D. some cell address changes will be made if the formula is copied to another cell.

Fill In

In the space provided, fill in the correct answer. Note that the answer can be one or two words.

1. ______________________________
A group of cells treated as a unit is called a ______.

2. ______________________________
You would like to include another descriptive line in the second row of your worksheet. To provide the space for this, you would use the ______ command.

Name: ______________________ Date: ____________

OBJECTIVE QUESTIONS (*continued*)

3. ______________________
A ______ change is one that affects all elements of a worksheet.

4. ______________________
The quantity 3,526.1 is displayed in a cell; the Format command has been used to give this cell the ______ format.

5. ______________________
The ______ command can be used to blank out the contents of a group of cells.

6. ______________________
You have a worksheet in which you would like to switch the contents of columns E and F. To do this you would use the ______ command.

7. ______________________
The first character of a function name is the ______ character; this serves to identify the form to 1-2-3 as being a function.

8. ______________________
The entry of cell F12 is to be the number of cells in the range F2..F10 that contain data (are not empty). For this, you would use the ______ function.

9. ______________________
______ operators (also called logical operators) are used to construct forms that give conditional results.

10. ______________________
A cell address that is to remain unchanged if a formula is copied to other cells is called a(n) ______ address.

ASSIGNMENTS/PROJECTS

	A	B	C	D	E
1		Fall	Winter	Spring	Summer
2	INCOME				
3	Job	400	400	400	2000
4	Grant	400	400	400	0
5	Parents	150	0	200	0
6	Total	950	800	1000	2000
7					
8	EXPENSES				
9	Auto Ins	800	0	0	0
10	Auto Exp	200	200	200	300
11	Tuition	300	300	300	0
12	Books	100	120	120	0
13	Misc	150	300	200	400
14	Total	1550	920	820	700
15					
16	BALANCE	-600	-720	-540	760

Fall Income Total – Fall Expenses Total

Fall Balance + (Winter Income Total – Winter Expenses Total)

Figure 5-16
Budget worksheet
BUDGET.WKS.

1. In Project Assignment 2 of Chapter 4 you entered a quarterly budget (repeated here as Figure 5-16). For this assignment, you are to expand the worksheet to include a two-year summary as follows:

   a. Add a second year to the worksheet using columns F through I.
   b. The year-end balance in the lower right corner of the Chapter 4 worksheet must be placed in cell F2 and must be added to the Fall income in arriving at the total in cell F6. Thus the formula in cell F6 will be different from those in the other cells of row 6.
   c. Reduce the widths of the columns containing numbers so that the spreadsheet will fit entirely on the screen (and will be printed on one page).
   d. Insert a description line in Row 1 that tells the reader that there are two separate years.
   e. For the sample data of the second year, increase the first year values by 10 percent. There are two ways of doing this. One approach is to type the new values as a complete new data set. The other is to enter formulas relating them to corresponding first-year entries.

Column	Information
A	Employee last name (assume names no more than 9 characters)
B	Hours worked
C	Regular hours worked If Hours worked <= 40 then equals Hours worked else equals 40
D	Overtime hours worked If Hours worked <= 40 then equals 0 else equals Hours worked minus 40
E	Pay rate
F	Regular pay = Regular hours worked times Pay rate
G	Overtime pay = Overtime hours worked times Pay rate times 1.5
H	Gross pay = Regular pay plus Overtime pay
I	Total deductions
J	Net pay = Gross pay minus Deductions

2. In Project Assignment 3 of Chapter 4 you entered a payroll worksheet. For this assignment, you are to expand the worksheet to include overtime calculations for all hours worked over 40, with the display according to the following table. Include totals for all columns F through J.

3. In Project Assignment 4 of Chapter 4 you entered a worksheet to study inventory turnover. For this assignment, you are to expand the worksheet as follows.

a. Average each of the columns B through H for the men (this summary should follow the men's group).

b. Average each of the columns B through H for the women (this summary should follow the women's group).

c. In column I, display an asterisk character if the value in column H is less than 3. Note: The @IF can be used to display a label value by including the label within double quotes.

d. Adjust the column widths so that the entire worksheet fits on your screen.

4. A stock summary worksheet is to be created with the general form shown at the bottom of this page. Note that this form represents all label and data entries. The positions into which formulas are to be entered have been left blank. The assignment is to enter this spreadsheet and create the formulas. The Profit and Percent columns are to be computed as follows:

Profit = (Sales Price minus Purchase Price) times Num of Shares

Percent Profit = (Profit divided by (Pur. Price times Num of shares)) times 100

Display the result correct to two decimal places.

Totals are to be computed for the columns as indicated by the single asterisks in the Totals row. Special calculations are to be performed as indicated in the analysis portion of the spreadsheet. The computed values are to be displayed in the positions indicated by the double asterisks. Set column widths so that it is possible to get the entire spreadsheet on the screen. Change the column heading descriptions if you feel that is needed.

```
                          Pur.   Sale  Num of Broker         Percent
Stock                     Price  Price Shares Comm.   Profit Profit

Dickerson Computer        25.25  25.80   100  35.45
Peach Software             8.75  11.30   100  20.55
HAL Limited               12.85  10.20   100  19.75
Hardly Peripherals        45.65  75.20    20  34.38
Slippery Diskettes        32.85  33.05    40  29.87
Microhard, Inc.            6.25   2.68   200   7.80
Vaporware Development     11.85  18.65   100  27.65
Vaporware Development     13.97  18.65    50  15.87
Tardy Products            14.01  15.63    75  19.56

Totals                                     *      *      *
--------------------------------------------------------------------

Analysis:     Average Purchase Price              **
              Average Sale Price                  **
              Average Profit                      **
              Maximum Profit                      **
              Maximum Percent value               **
```

Name	Reg Hours	OT Hours	Pay Rate	Reg Pay	OT Pay	Deduct	Net Pay
Arnold Finch	40.0		9.60				
Alice Baker	40.0	6.5	8.50				
John Zener	36.0		8.00				
Howard Sparks	30.0		11.35				
Frank Olson	40.0	13.5	9.60				
Jane Peters	40.0	3.3	11.35				
George Ito	40.0	5.5	8.50				
Ann Miller	37.5		9.60				
Fran Wong	0.0		9.60				
June Frank	40.0	7.5	8.50				
Ed Brister	40.0	4.5	9.60				
Fred Grant	40.0		8.50				
Sue Miller	40.0		8.00				
Charles Inns	40.0	3.0	8.50				
Totals	*	*		*	*		

Average overtime hours: ** Total pay: ***

5. A payroll summary worksheet is to be created with the general form of the above worksheet. Note that this form shows all label and data entries. The positions into which formulas are to be entered have been left blank. The assignment is to enter this spreadsheet and create the formulas. The following calculations are required.

   Regular pay = Regular hours times Pay rate

   Overtime pay = Overtime hours times Pay rate times 1.5

   Deductions = 10% of the Regular plus Overtime Pay

   Net Pay = Regular Pay plus Overtime Pay minus Deductions

   Totals are to be computed for the columns as indicated by the single asterisks in the Totals row. The Average overtime hours worked is to be computed and displayed in the position indicated by the double asterisks. The Total pay (Regular plus Overtime) for all employees is to be computed and displayed in the position indicated by the triple asterisks. Use appropriate column widths to get the entire spreadsheet on the screen. If necessary, modify column headings.

6. In the worksheet of Assignment 5, insert another column between the current columns 1 and 2 into which you can enter total hours worked. Then the regular hours and overtime hours entries are to be calculated using an @IF function.

Chapter 6

Computer Graphics

OBJECTIVES

One of the most dramatic applications of computers is in the area of graphics. With appropriate software, you can do such things as include drawings in printed documents (desktop publishing), use the computer as an art medium, create engineering drawings, transform spreadsheet data into multiple-color graphs, and simulate events with animation. The objectives of this chapter are twofold: (1) to provide you with a broad survey of computer graphics and its many application areas; (2) to give you hands-on experience using 1-2-3 to create business graphs that summarize the data stored in worksheets. When you have completed this chapter, you should be able to:

- Distinguish between business graphics and design graphics.
- Describe the uses of pie charts, bar graphs, and line graphs for displaying data.
- Create the following types of graphs with 1-2-3: pie chart, bar graph, stacked-bar graph, and line graph.
- Save graphs as part of a worksheet.
- Print graphs on a graphics printer.

PREVIEW

About Computer Graphics

Computer graphics is the use of the computer to prepare visual materials. This includes everything from displaying graphs of spreadsheet data to engineering design.

Presentation Graphics

Design graphics programs are used by such professionals as engineers, architects, and interior designers to automate much of their work. For instance, the engineer can enter specifications for a machine into a computer. From this, the computer can display the image on the screen and print detailed drawings.

Business Graphics

Graphs and charts plotted from tabular data are called business graphics. Using spreadsheet data, we can create line and bar graphs and pie charts.

Using 1-2-3 to Create Business Graphs

Data stored in worksheets can be used by 1-2-3 to prepare graphs.

Preparing Pie Charts with 1-2-3

The pie chart illustrates the proportion that each value of a data set represents with regard to the whole. With the Graph command of 1-2-3, you will create a pie chart from the sales summary spreadsheet of Chapter 5.

Saving Your Work

After the specifications for a 1-2-3 graph have been entered, they become a part of the worksheet. Each graph associated with a worksheet must be given a name.

Creating Other Types of Graphs

You will use the sales summary worksheet of Chapter 5 to create line and bar graphs that plot and compare the sales of each sales representative.

Recalling a Graph

Each graph created for a worksheet is given a name and stored with the worksheet. A simple command sequence makes any of these graphs available during a 1-2-3 work session.

Printing a Graph

If a graphics printer is attached to your computer, any worksheet graph can be printed.

ABOUT COMPUTER GRAPHICS

Assume that you work for a manufacturing company and that management has made the decision to install a new software package in your department. Three software companies have made bids to sell you their software: Whizzer, Flash, and Wow. Management is leaning toward Whizzer because it is the most widely used. You and your group have studied each package in detail and have determined that any of the three would do the job. However, on the basis of your evaluations, you feel that Wow is clearly superior. Your manager has given you 5 minutes to present your case at the weekly management meeting. As part of your argument, you have compiled results of studies and testing. Two of the tables to be included in your report showing the superiority of Wow are indicated in Figure 6-1. In the first, you have summarized the time required for each software package to complete a run for each of your four main applications. Inspecting this table shows that Wow is clearly faster for three of the four applications. The second table summarizes how the better speed of

Time Test Summary
(Time in Minutes)

Application	Whizzer	Flash	Wow
Doodle	8.25	8.07	5.44
Abbreviate	15.15	13.28	7.50
Consolidate	12.30	13.44	13.50
Terminate	5.55	6.45	1.38

(a)

Technical Staff Time Allocation

Activity	Whizzer	Flash	Wow
Programming	40%	45%	35%
Testing	35%	25%	20%
Development	25%	30%	45%

Development = 100% - Programming - Testing

(b)

Figure 6-1
Tables of data.

Wow and its ease of use would allow your technical people to spend less time programming and testing and more time in creative development activities. These tables will indeed convey your point to management, *if* you can get your managers to study them; they do not make much of an impression unless they are studied.

On the other hand, think of the extent to which your presentation would be enhanced if you were to flash the graphic summaries shown in Figure 6-2 on a projection screen. With these, the managers need not study tables of data; the superiority of Wow is clear at a glance.

Figure 6-2
Graphic display of data.

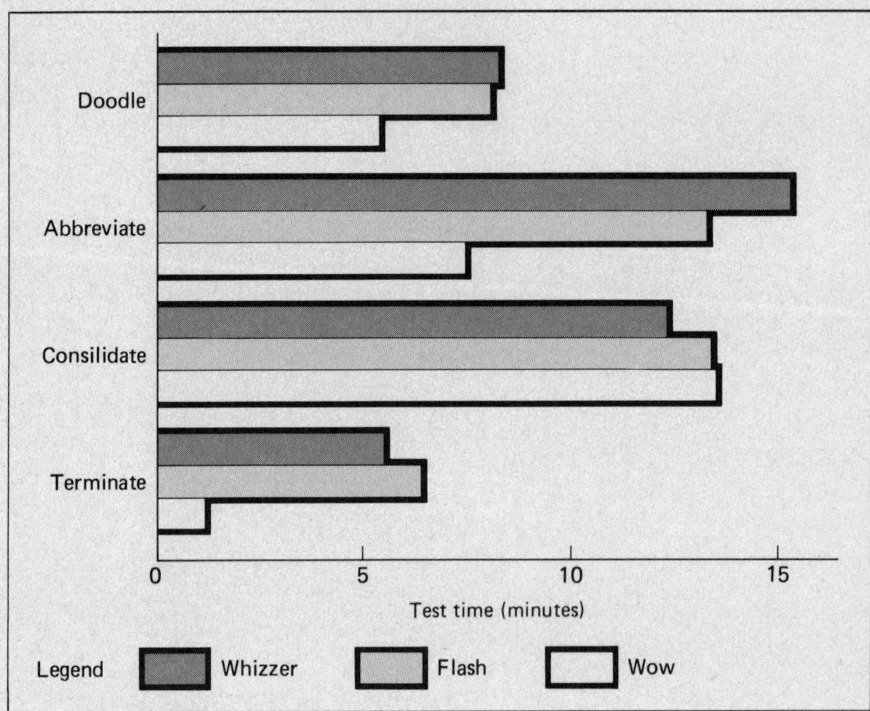

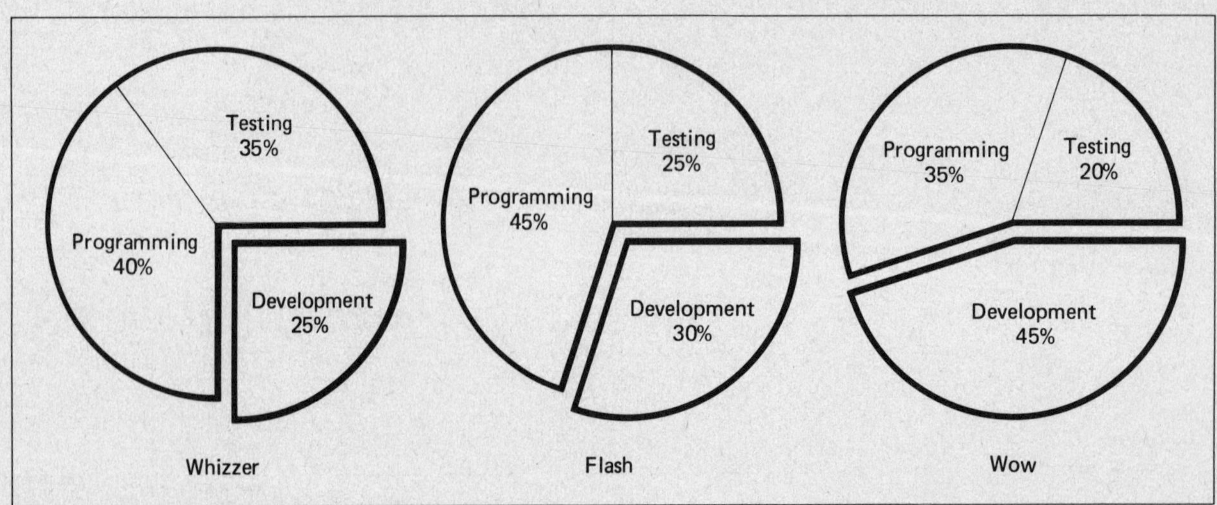

Graphics such as that in Figure 6-2 can be produced easily using a microcomputer and appropriate software. However, this represents only one small segment of computer graphics. We see examples of computer graphics when we observe special effects in movies and on television. Almost everyone is familiar with video games. In fact, some of the auto racing games are so realistic that one almost has a tendency to lean into the turn when a sharp curve in the roadway appears. We also see art shows devoted entirely to art generated using the computer as a medium. In industry, engineers use computers to produce drawings for mechanical parts from which specifications can be furnished for automatic machine tools to produce the parts. It is apparent that **computer graphics,** which is the use of the computer to prepare visual presentations, embraces a wide range of activities.

Some applications software has built-in graphics as part of the package. For instance, in this chapter you will learn how to use the graphics capabilities of 1-2-3 to prepare graphic displays from data in a worksheet. Other graphics software is available that allows you to create your own graphic output, much as a draftsperson makes drawings. Some drawing software that allows you to use the computer as an electronic pencil and paper is used both for design and art applications.

The many different types of computer graphics software and applications fall in several categories. For the purpose of description in this chapter, the following classifications are used: presentation or business graphics, design graphics, and graphics for entertainment. The entertainment category is a general one encompassing a variety of applications in animation, education, art, and games.

To use graphics on a computer, both software and hardware are required. When purchasing a computer system, you must evaluate your objectives and applications, select the software that will do the job, and then select the hardware required by the software. If you intend to use a computer for graphics, you must make sure that the hardware you obtain is compatible with the software. The two basic elements are the monitor and the printer. If you intend to use color, then a color monitor and printer (or plotter) are needed. Other specialized peripheral devices are required for different graphics software.

DESIGN GRAPHICS

Engineers and other professionals make wide use of design graphics software in design work. Many design software packages are available, with capabilities ranging from highly specialized to general purpose. For instance, developers using specialized software can do the layout planning for housing developments on the computer and print copies on plotters to present at meetings with appropriate agencies and citizen groups. Changing and adjusting the plan to meet the needs and concerns of all involved can be done on the screen using a mouse or light pen and a new plan can be printed immediately for consideration. Just as spreadsheet software makes it easy to perform "what if" analyses with data, design software allows the user to perform "what if" studies with graphic layouts. Similarly, architects can prepare plan views and detailed floor plans of homes to be built for clients. A client's request to rearrange fixtures or appliances in the bathroom or kitchen can be met almost immediately and the new version displayed or printed. Even the office manager can work with the interior designer in performing space studies. A careful analysis to make the most efficient use of a facility is critical considering the high cost of office space. In the past, many office layout studies were carried out by making paper cutouts of desktops, file cabinets, and other furniture, and then manually arranging them on a drawing of the room floor plan. With interior layout software, corresponding images can be moved and rotated with ease.

Computer-aided design (CAD) programs are sophisticated software systems that have revolutionized the design of mechanical devices ranging from automobile parts to electrical appliances for the kitchen. For instance, with CAD software, automotive engineers can design a new transmission with all specifications stored in the computer. They can display the transmission housing on the screen in three-dimensional perspective, rotate it to view it from different angles, and explode it to show the parts it comprises. Changes in specifications are easily incorporated into the display. At any time, detailed three-view drawings of all components can be printed.

We constantly read about the extent of automation and use of robot devices in the workplace. All types of factory operations are automated, including electronic circuit board assembly of parts for your computer, welding on the automobile assembly line, and machining operations such as those performed by lathes and grinders. Each automatic device needs a set of specifications defining the exact motions and actions required to do its task; in other words, these tools must be programmed. The logical extension of CAD is to prepare these specifications or programs on the basis of the design information stored in the computer. This is called computer-aided manufacturing (**CAM**); the use of **CAD/CAM** software is revolutionizing the manufacturing industry.

PRESENTATION GRAPHICS

The purpose of presentation graphics software is to turn numbers into pictures of graphs, charts, and diagrams so that they can be understood easily. The tables of data in Figure 6-1 are illustrated graphically in Figure 6-2. These are two of the three commonly used methods for the graphic representation of numeric data: bar chart, pie chart, and line graph. Later in this chapter, you will generate graphs such as these using the graphics capabilities of 1-2-3 operating on data stored in worksheets. This type of graphics is also referred to as business graphics, because it is so widely used to display business data. However, it is not confined to business applications; indeed, the scientist commonly uses these graphic techniques to display scientific data.

Basic Graphics Terminology

Assume that your department manager has assigned you the task of evaluating the expenditures of several projects that have been completed by the department. One of your tasks is to compare actual and budgeted expenditures. Typical of the data you must present is the following table, which summarizes expenditures for the Harcourt project.

	Expenditures	
Year	Budgeted	Actual
1	34,000	39,400
2	34,000	41,100
3	44,000	46,100
4	51,000	57,300
5	48,000	55,500

Here, the expenditures are tabulated by the year. To find the expenditure for a given year, we run down the column on the left to the desired year, and then read across to the columns to the right. Basically, we can say that the expenditures depend on the year, or in mathematical terminology, the expenditures are a *function* of the year. Business data is commonly represented in terms of time such as this. For instance, sales quotas are designated by the month, company earnings by the quarter, departmental budgets by the year, and so on.

The Line Graph

One way of illustrating this table is with a **line graph,** as shown in Figure 6-3. This uses the conventional coordinate system of mathematics in which two axes at right angles to each other are used to plot data. In this example, the **X axis** (horizontal) displays time in units of a year. That is, each increment of time shown on this graph is 1 year. The **Y axis** (vertical) displays expenditures in units of 1000: each expenditure increment represents $1000. The relationship between the physical entity and the unit of length on the graph is called the **scale.** If the time period were 15 years instead of 5, then a different scale would be used to keep the graph from running off the edge of the paper. Computer graphics programs automatically select the scale on the basis of the range of the data values to be graphed. In the graph of Figure 6-3, the expenditures scale ranges from 0 to

Figure 6-3
Line graphs.

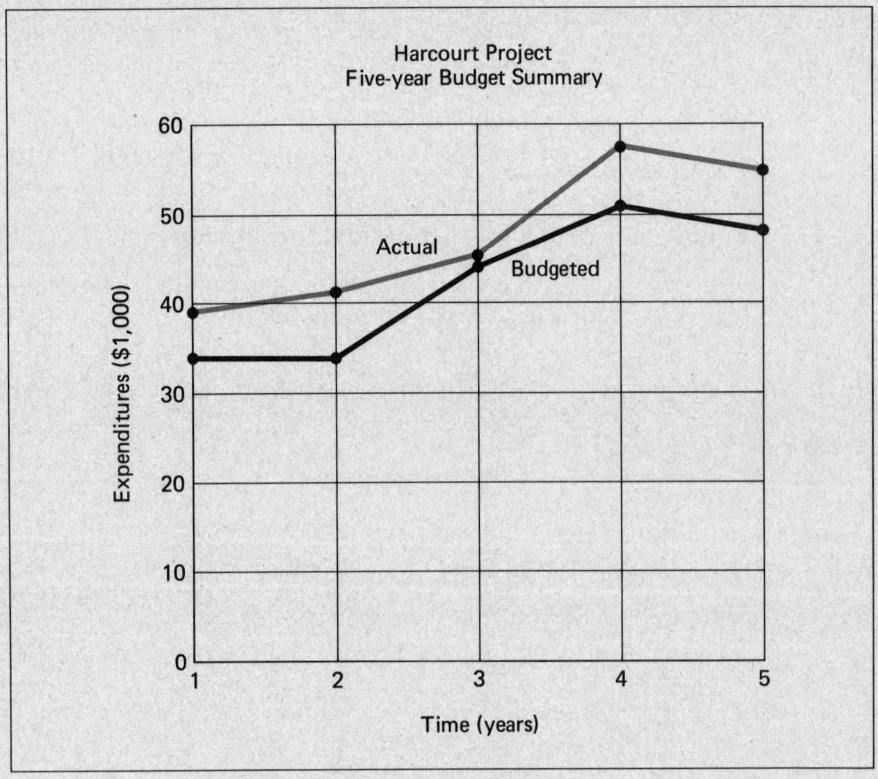

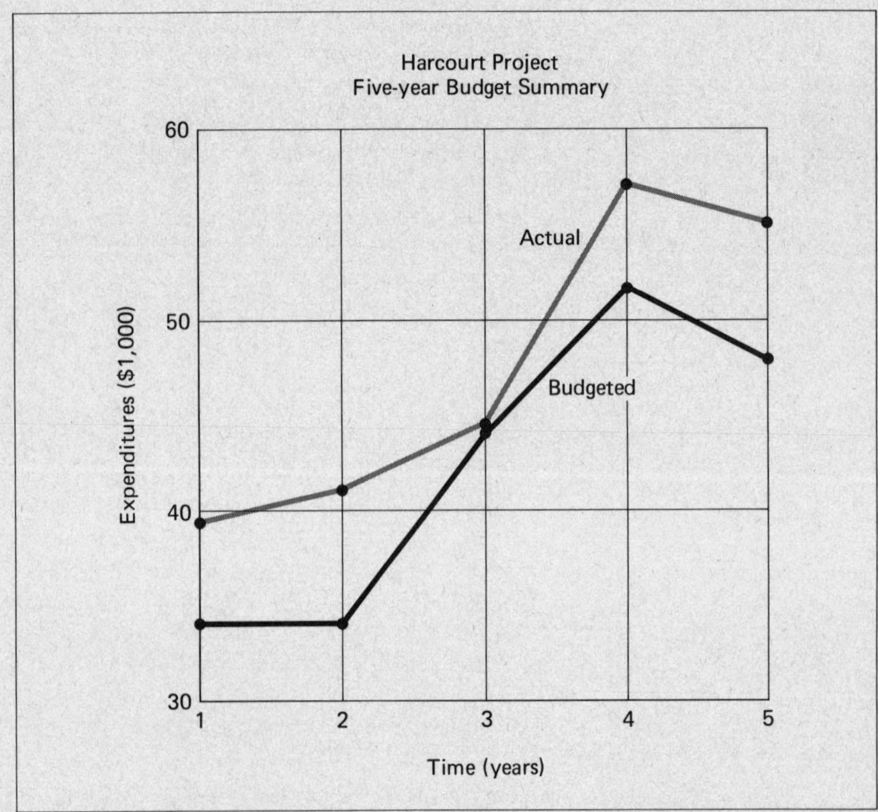

Figure 6-4
Using a different scale for a graph.

60 (60,000). Since there are no values below 30, the scale can be changed by using a lower limit of 30 and an upper limit of 60, with the result shown in Figure 6-4. Note that this has the effect of accentuating the difference between the two graphs. Scaling such as this is often used to emphasize differences and changes. It is sometimes used to mislead the reader; at a glance, the first-year actual expenditure appears to be twice the budgeted amount.

Using Graphs for Analysis

Anticipating the future is an important part of running a business. For instance, the manufacturer must estimate the sales for a new product in determining the price and the quantity to manufacture. Department managers must estimate their budget needs for the coming year. The programming consultant must predict how much time will be required to complete a job. More often than not, such estimates are "educated guesses" based on a feeling derived from past experience. In many cases it is possible to organize past data and to use statistical analysis to extrapolate into the future and predict what will occur. For instance, consider a sales company that has accurate monthly sales data for the past 2 years and wishes to use it to predict the sales growth for the coming year. In Figure 6-5, each of the monthly sales figures has been plotted. Then a "best fit" curve has been drawn that demonstrates the sales growth trend. Extending the curve gives an estimate of the future. Statistical analysis programs are available for analyzing data and producing trends such as this.

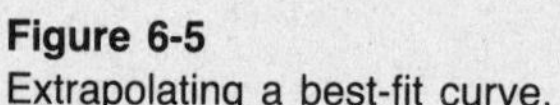

Figure 6-5
Extrapolating a best-fit curve.

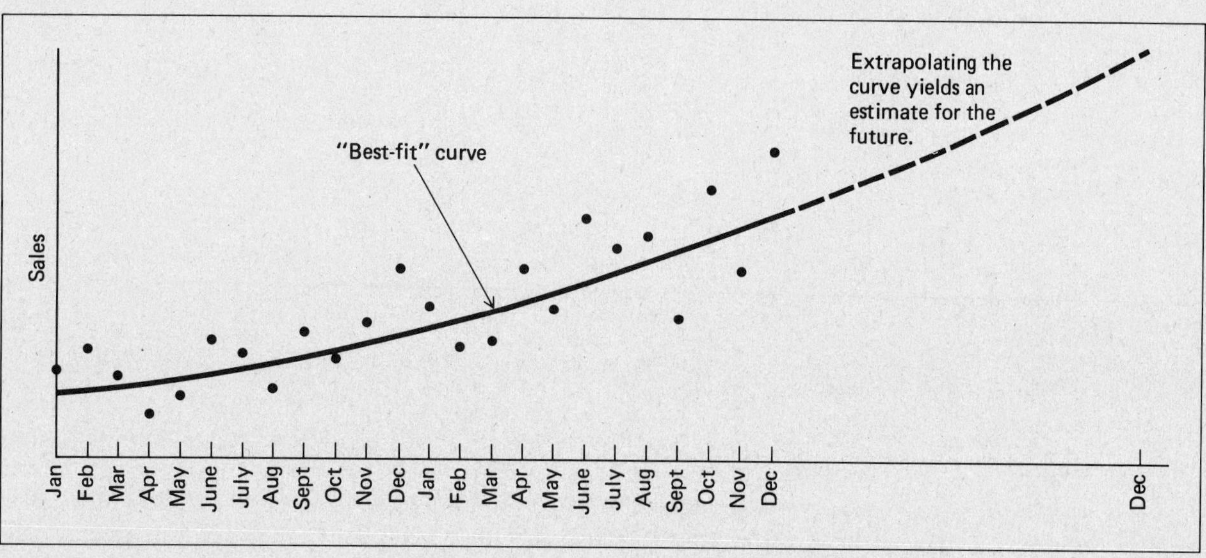

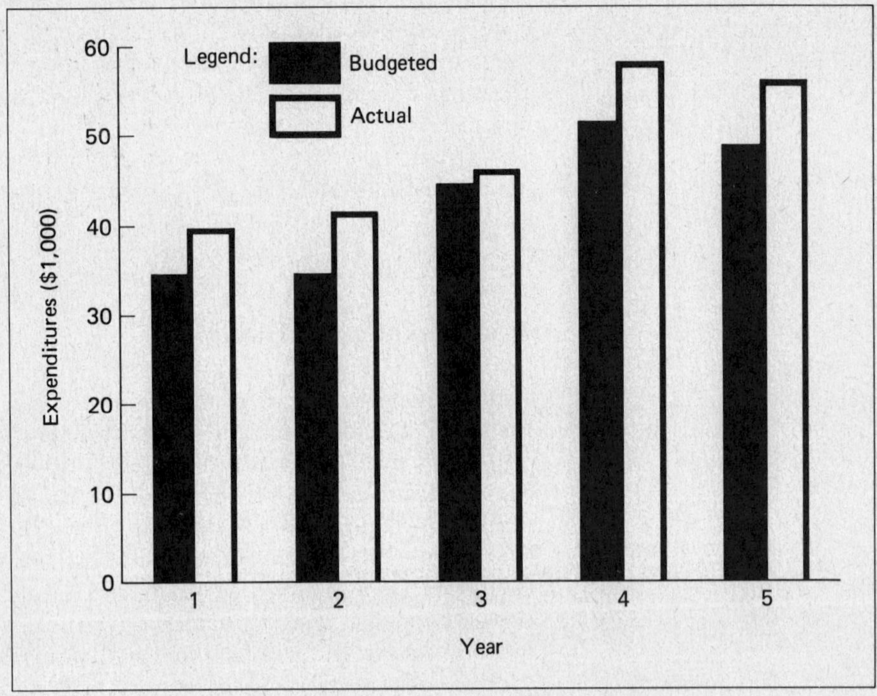

Figure 6-6
A bar graph comparing budgeted and actual expenditures.

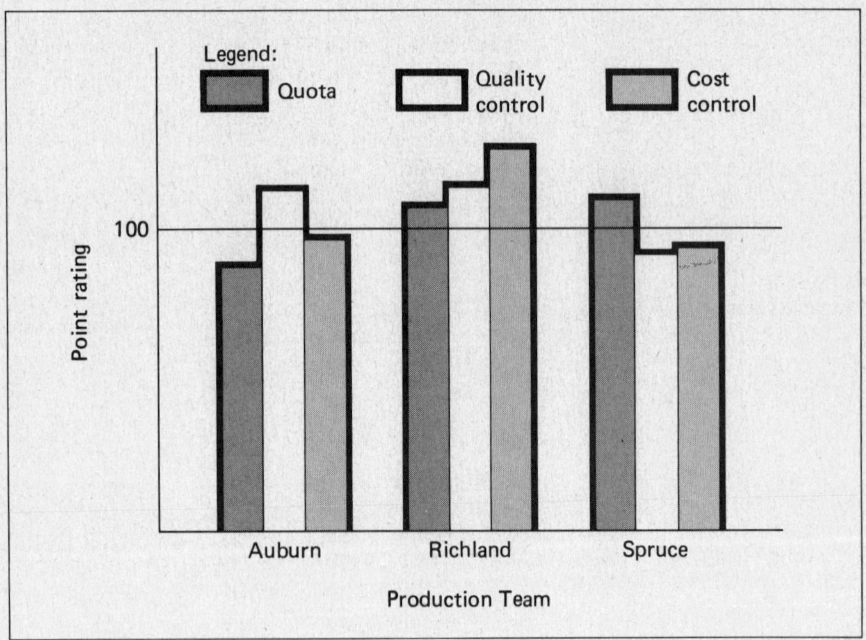

Figure 6-7
A bar graph illustrating the performance of production teams.

The Bar Graph

The **bar graph** is another method of displaying the budget summary data of the preceding table. Bar graphs use rectangles to represent each of the data values, as illustrated in Figure 6-6. Bar graphs, which are also called histograms, are especially useful when there is a need to compare and

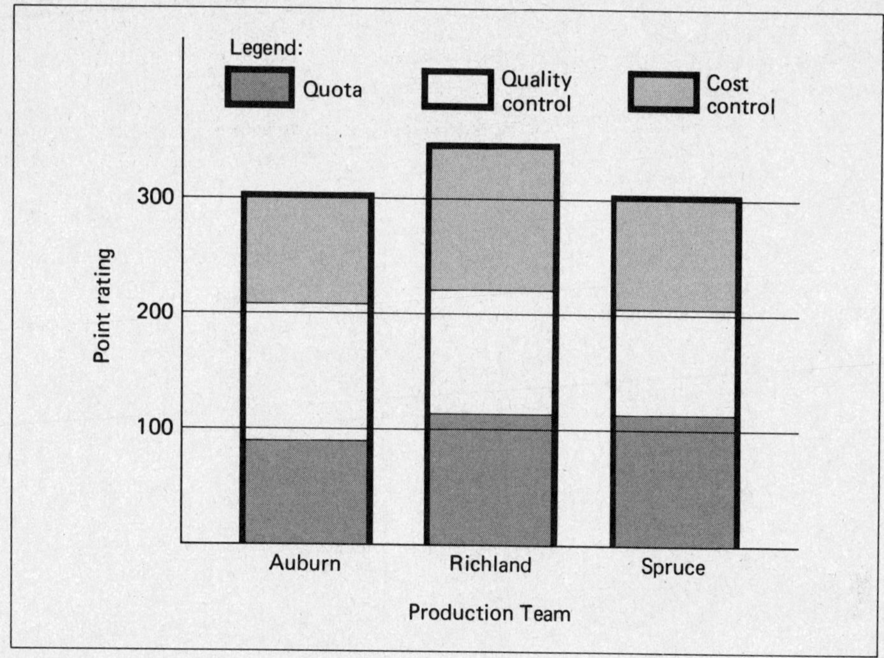

Figure 6-8
A stacked bar graph showing the effect of components on the total.

contrast quantities. They are also commonly used when the X axis does not represent a continuous range. For example, Figure 6-7 compares the performance of three production teams where each team is rated on the basis of an assigned quota, quality control, and cost control. Whether the Auburn team or the Richland team is listed first is of little consequence. However, in the bar graph of Figure 6-6, the X axis represents consecutive years; to list them in any but their numerical order would be confusing.

A different perspective of the data can be obtained by stacking the rectangles to illustrate both the total and the individual components making up that total, as shown in Figure 6-8. In this stacked-bar graph, we can clearly see the contribution to the total of each element. The expenditures of Figure 6-6 might also be plotted as a stacked-bar graph by breaking them down into individual categories, such as equipment purchase, repair, staff training, and so on.

Sometimes turning the bar graph on its side makes it easier to understand. This technique is used in Figure 6-2(a), which compares the time required for software packages to complete designated operations.

The Pie Chart

One characteristic of the line and bar graphs is that they display actual data values. The stacked bar chart takes this one step further in that it also illustrates the contribution of the various elements in terms of the whole. The purpose of the **pie chart** is solely to illustrate the percentage that each component contributes to the whole. For example, consider the computer software company that markets the software product Widget. As part of an effort to obtain venture capital for a major expansion, the company prepares a detailed report of all aspects of the product, including market penetration. One set of data that is to be included is the following regional sales summary.

Region	Units	Percentage
Northeast	3,221	29.7
South	2,120	19.5
Midwest	2,703	24.9
Rocky Mountains	1,133	10.4
Pacific Coast	1,684	15.5
Total	10,861	

This data could be represented in the form of a bar graph as shown in Figure 6-9(a) or as a pie chart as in Figure 6-9(b). The pie chart is produced by dividing the units sold for each region by the total units sold, producing the percentage of the total for each region. These percentages are used to determine the "slice" size in the pie. Even though the pie chart does not include an X axis and a Y axis, it still uses two items: a set of descriptions of the data and the data in forming the chart. This will have implications when you create a pie chart with 1-2-3.

Sometimes it is desirable to emphasize one or more segments of a pie chart. This is done by setting that segment or segments apart from the others, as shown in Figure 6-10. The segment that is removed in this way is said to be an exploded slice. As you will learn, with the facilities of 1-2-3 you can easily explode one or more slices of a pie chart.

Figure 6-9
(a) Sales information by region.
(b) A pie chart showing proportions.

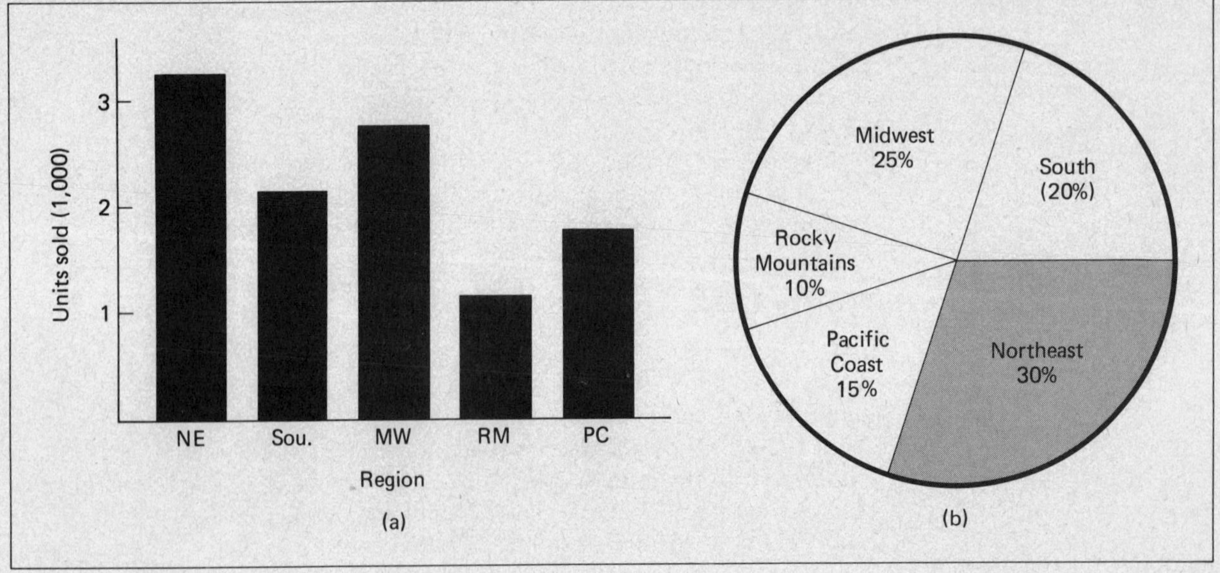

Figure 6-10
An exploded segment from a pie chart.

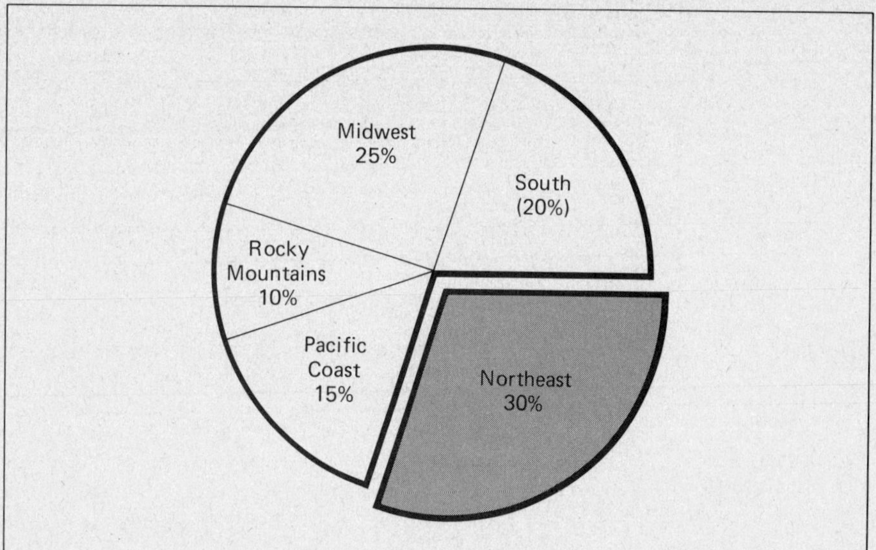

Assignment 6-1 may now be completed.

USING 1-2-3 TO CREATE BUSINESS GRAPHS

The remainder of this chapter is devoted to preparing business graphs from worksheets using the graphics capabilities of 1-2-3. With 1-2-3, you can prepare each of the types that you studied earlier in this chapter: line, bar, stacked-bar, and pie charts. The first type that you will learn to prepare is the pie chart because it involves the fewest parameter specifications and is the simplest to set up. All of the examples are based on the worksheet SALES3 that you completed in the preceding chapter. It is repeated here as Figure 6-11 for convenient reference.

Figure 6-11
The SALES3 worksheet.

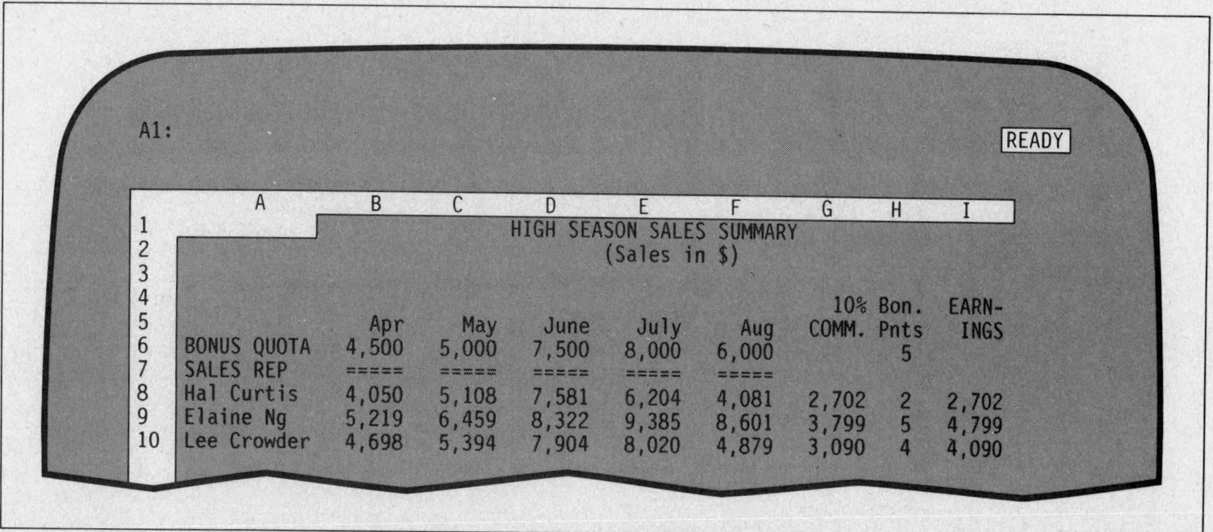

A1: READY

	A	B	C	D	E	F	G	H	I
1				HIGH SEASON SALES SUMMARY					
2				(Sales in $)					
3									
4							10%	Bon.	EARN-
5		Apr	May	June	July	Aug	COMM.	Pnts	INGS
6	BONUS QUOTA	4,500	5,000	7,500	8,000	6,000		5	
7	SALES REP	=====	=====	=====	=====	=====			
8	Hal Curtis	4,050	5,108	7,581	6,204	4,081	2,702	2	2,702
9	Elaine Ng	5,219	6,459	8,322	9,385	8,601	3,799	5	4,799
10	Lee Crowder	4,698	5,394	7,904	8,020	4,879	3,090	4	4,090

PREPARING PIE CHARTS WITH 1-2-3

Creating the Chart

As part of your year-end sales summary reports, you decide to include a pie chart that displays the bonus quotas for each of the 5 months of the high season (see row 6 of Figure 6-11). This will present a clear picture of the relative proportion that each monthly amount contributes to the whole. In creating this pie chart, you must:

- Specify the range of data that is to be used in the chart (B6..F6).
- Specify the range of labels that is to be used in identifying each segment of the pie (B5..F5).

You know from the preceding that, unlike the line and bar graphs, the pie chart does not use the conventional X axis and Y axis. As you will see in the following example, the 1-2-3 nomenclature of the pie chart identifies labels as the x-entry; do not be confused as this has nothing to do with an X axis.

DO THIS NOW 6-1 **Creating a Pie Chart**

1. If you have not already started 1-2-3 and retrieved SAVE3, then do so now.
2. From the READY mode, position the cell pointer at cell B5. Although this is not necessary, it will minimize cell pointer movement when you select the ranges.
3. Execute the Graph command with the key sequence /G. This produces the submenu of Figure 6-12.

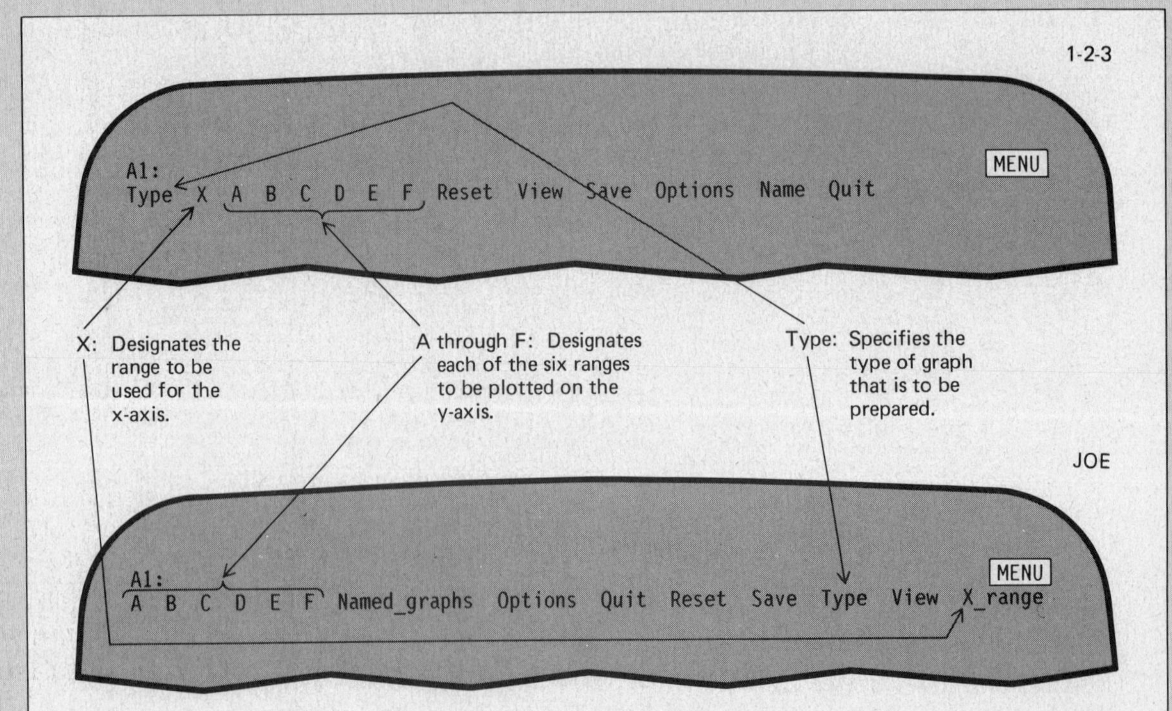

Figure 6-12
The Graph submenu.

4. Execute the Type command (to designate the type of graph) by striking the letter *T*; this will cause the following submenu to be displayed.

```
Line Bar  XY  Stacked-bar  Pie                                   (Lotus 1-2-3)
Bar_graph  Line_graph  Pie_graph  Stacked_bar_plot  XY_graph     (JOE)
```

5. Strike the letter *P* for Pie. The Pie option will be selected and the submenu of Figure 6-12 will reappear.

6. The next step is to specify the labels to be used. For pie charts, this is identified as the X range. Strike the letter X; the following prompt and anchor cell default will appear.

```
Enter X axis range: B5    (Lotus 1-2-3)
Enter X data range: B5    (JOE)
```

7. If you did not position the cell pointer at cell B5 prior to the Type command, your default cell address will not be B5. If it is not, then move the cell pointer to B5.

8. Strike the period key to anchor the cell range.

9. Move the cell pointer to cell F5 to complete the range.

10. Strike Enter to identify the range. The Graph submenu of Figure 6-12 will be redisplayed.

11. The next step is to identify the range of the data to be used in determining the number of sections and their sizes. Strike the letter *A* to enter the first range (the A range). The following prompt and default will appear.

```
Enter first data range: B5    (Lotus 1-2-3)
Enter A data range: B5        (JOE)
```

12. Enter the range B6..F6 (anchor at B6, move highlight to F6, and strike Enter).

13. Upon returning to the submenu of Figure 6-12, display the chart on the screen by striking the letter *V* for the View command. Your pie chart should look like Figure 6-13. (If you are using Lotus

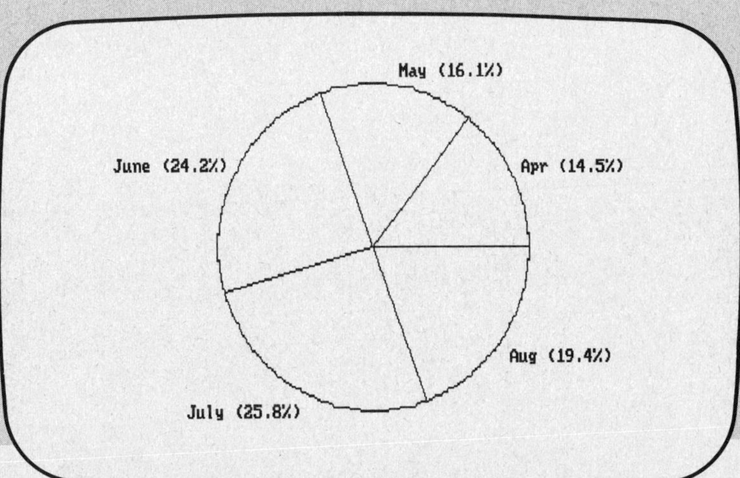

Figure 6-13
A basic pie chart.

1-2-3, the pie slices may be oriented differently. However, the proportions are the same.)

14. Strike the Escape key and your spreadsheet, together with the menu of Figure 6-12, will reappear.

Further Enhancements to the Pie Chart

One of the purposes of creating charts and graphs is to present information so that it is clear and easy to interpret. To this end, they must be complete and self-contained; it should not be necessary to refer to the spreadsheet to interpret the graph or chart. One way to improve the ability of charts and graphs to convey information is to give them titles; 1-2-3 allows you to include two title lines.

DO THIS NOW 6-2 **Entering Title Lines to the Pie Chart**

1. Your screen should still display the menu of Figure 6-12. If it does not, then take whatever action is necessary to display it.
2. For the first title line, enter the command sequence /OTF. That is:

```
Options  Titles  First          (Lotus 1-2-3)
Options  Titles  First_Title    (JOE)
```

3. The following prompt will appear:

```
Enter graph title, top line:   (Lotus 1-2-3)
Top title (above graph):       (JOE)
```

4. Type the following title and strike Enter.

```
MCT Enterprises
```

   You will be returned to the MENU mode and the Options submenu will be redisplayed.

5. For the second title line, select Title again by striking the letter *T*. Then strike the letter *S* for Second title line.
6. In response to the prompt, type the following and strike Enter.

```
High Season Monthly Sales Quotas
```

   You will be returned to the MENU mode and the Options submenu will be redisplayed.

7. To get back to the Graph submenu of Figure 6-12, strike the letter *Q* (for Quit) twice. You must back out of two menu levels. You can display your pie chart with the View command.

In the earlier descriptions of graphics, all the examples of graphs and pie charts were shown in color. For instance, different colors were used to distinguish one data set from the other in a bar graph and clearly to mark the slices of the pie chart. This same effect can be achieved with the cross-hatching features found in both JOE and Release 2 of Lotus 1-2-3. In order to use cross-hatching with a pie chart, each data value (cell) in the data range requires a corresponding cross-hatching code. There are seven different cross-hatch patterns that can be coded into the display by using the digits 1 through 7; 0 causes no cross-hatching and is the default.

The pie chart of Figure 6-13 is constructed from the data in B6..F6 of the Figure 6-11 worksheet. To cross-hatch each of these five cells, you must specify a corresponding set of five cross-hatching codes. This is done by entering the cross-hatching codes into a cell range that corresponds to the data cell range. For this example, we will enter the codes for the data in B6..F6 in the cell range B12..F12.

DO THIS NOW 6-3 **Designating Cross-Hatching for the Pie Chart**

1. If your screen is not already at the READY mode, then strike the Escape key until it is.
2. Enter the numbers 1 through 5 into the cell range B12..F12. The display for this range of cells will be as shown in Figure 6-14.

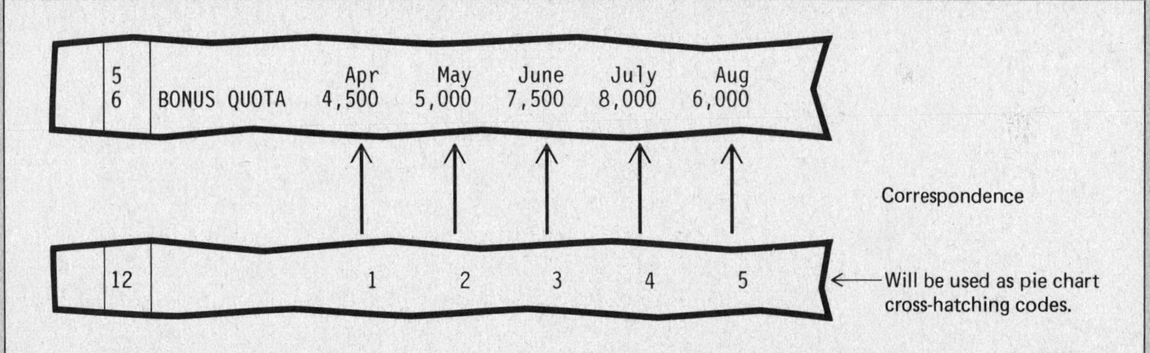

Figure 6-14
Cross-hatch codes to be used with the pie chart.

3. Execute the Graph command with the sequence /G. This causes the submenu of Figure 6-12 to be displayed.
4. When you created the pie chart, you used the A range (refer to the menu) to specify the worksheet data range. You assign cross-hatching codes by selecting the *B* range. Strike the letter B to select the B range.
5. Designate the cell range by anchoring the cell pointer at B12 and then extending the range to cell F12. When you have the range specified, strike the Enter key.
6. The submenu of Figure 6-12 will be displayed again. Strike the letter *V* (for View) to display the pie chart shown in Figure 6-15.

Figure 6-15
The pie chart with cross-hatching.

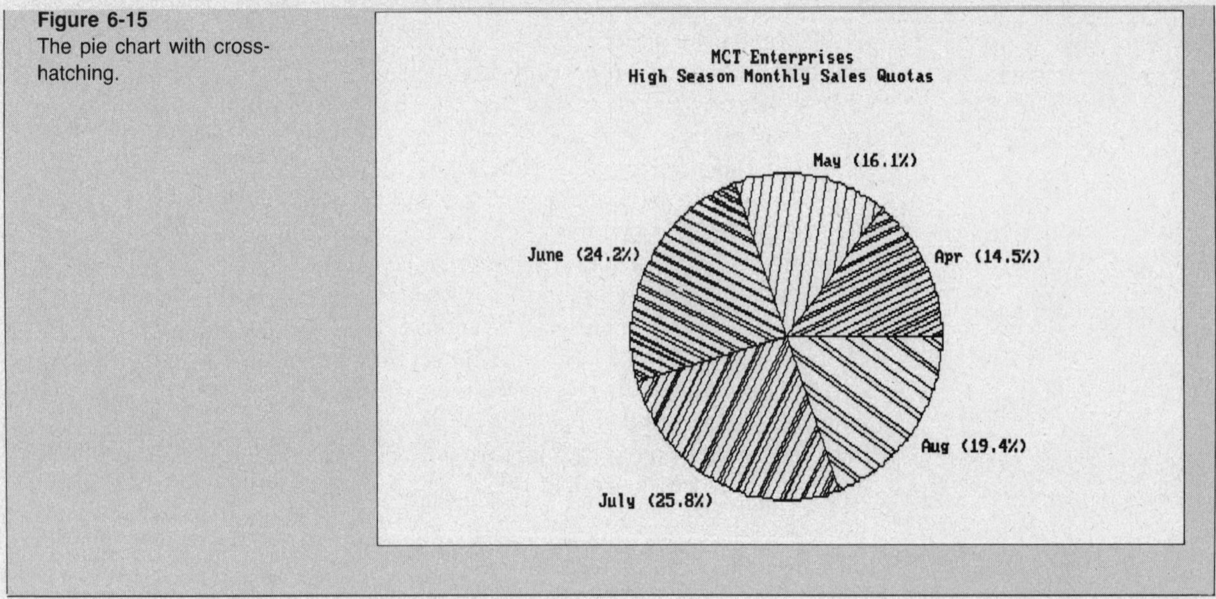

If you want to change the cross-hatching, you need only return to the READY mode and change the codes in the cell range B12..F12. Although the codes in Figure 6-14 are consecutive integers (1, 2, ...), they need not be in sequence as in this example. For instance, your entries in these five cells could have been 6, 0, 4, 0, and 3. The 0 entries would cause the May and July slices to be displayed without cross-hatching. In this example, the cell range B12..F12 was used for the cross-hatching codes because it corresponds conveniently to the data range. However, this range could have been positioned anywhere (for instance, A11..A15), but it must be included somewhere. The software simply matches the codes defined by the B range to the data defined by the A range.

You can explode any of the slices of your pie chart by adding 100 to the cross-hatching code that corresponds to the data cell for that slice. For example, return to the READY mode and change the entry in cell E12 from 4 to 104, as shown in Figure 6-16. Then invoke the Graph menu (with /G) and display the graph with the View command. The result will be as shown in Figure 6-17.

Figure 6-16
Cross-hatch codes to explode the July segment.

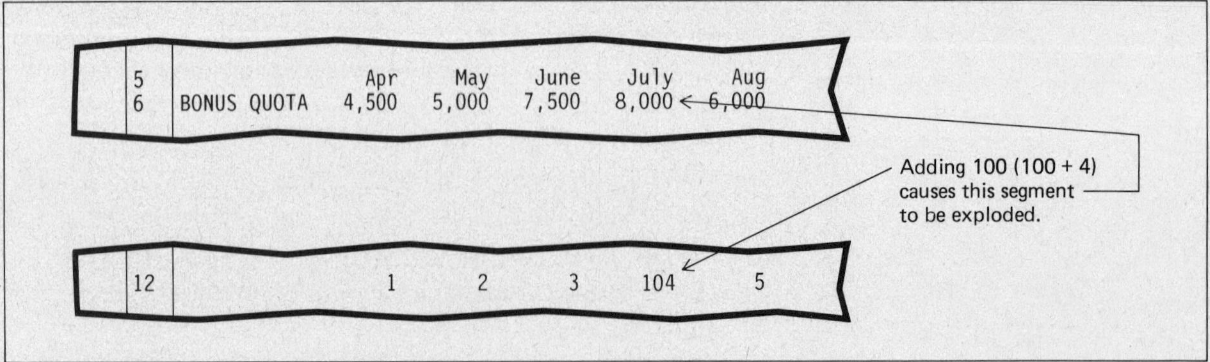

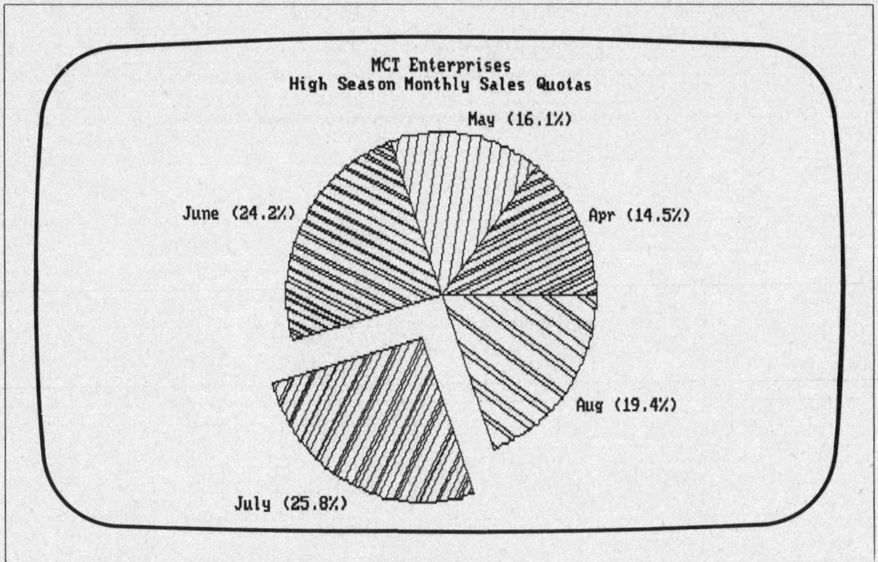

Figure 6-17
Exploding a section of a pie chart.

SAVING YOUR WORK

The Action of the File Save Command

Preparing the pie chart has required numerous, detailed steps. Fortunately, the specifications for this graph are now a part of this worksheet, just as are the formulas. Defining one or more graph specifications for a worksheet involves a change to the worksheet just as does adding a new column or row. Hence, after one or more graph settings have been defined, you must save the worksheet back to disk. In fact, you should issue the File Save command (/FS from the READY mode) to save your worksheet *including the pie chart specifications that you have just entered*. At any later time that you use this worksheet, the graph will be available as if you had never terminated the work session at all. Be aware that the saving operation *is not done with the Save from the Graph submenu* (Figure 6-12). The Graph Save sequence writes a printer image of the graph to the disk for later printing.

Naming a Graph

In preparing graphics presentations from data in a worksheet, you will commonly create more than one graph or chart. For instance, in addition to this pie chart, you will also create line and bar graphs for the monthly sales of the sales representatives. Once they are completed, you will be able to retain all of them as part of your worksheet file (as illustrated in Figure 6-18) and switch from one graph to another. However, in order to create and retain more than one graph with a worksheet, each must be given a name. The graph that you have access to at any time is called the **current graph.** With a simple sequence of 1-2-3 commands, you can make any of the defined graphs in the worksheet the current graph. Before proceeding further, let us use the sequence of DTN 6-4 to give this graph the name QUOTA_PIE so that we might create another.

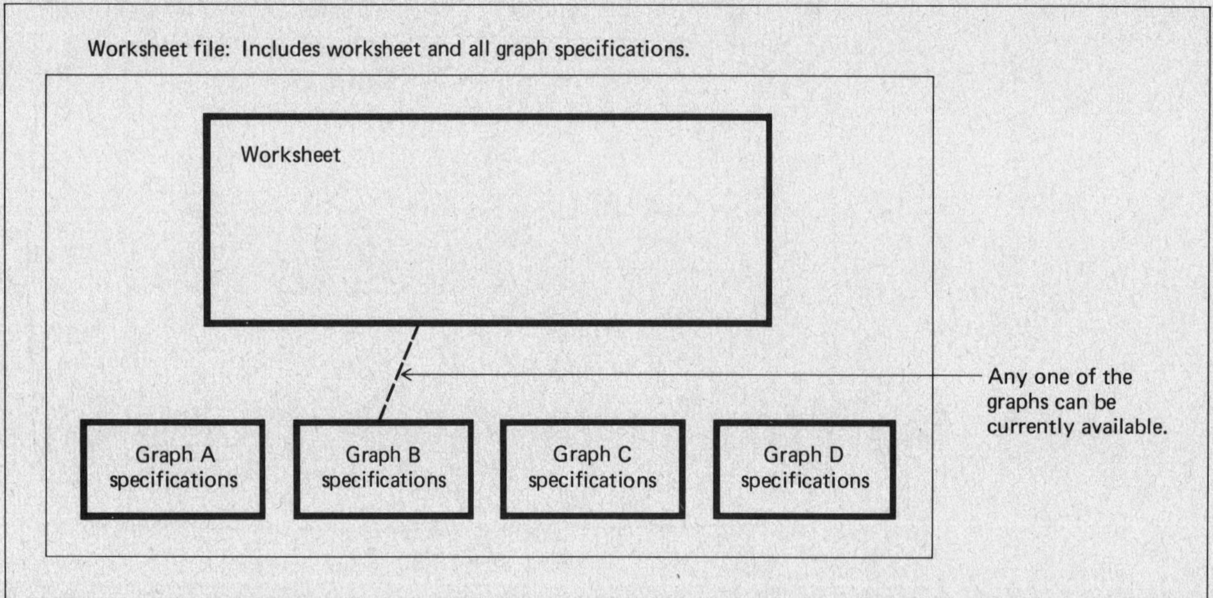

Figure 6-18
Graph specifications in a worksheet file.

DO THIS NOW 6-4 **Naming the Graph**

1. If you are at the READY mode, use the Graph command (/G) to get the graph submenu of Figure 6-12.

2. From the Graph submenu, execute the Named_graph (JOE) or Name (Lotus 1-2-3) command by striking the letter *N*. This produces the following submenu.

`Use  Create  Delete  Reset` (Lotus 1-2-3)
`Create_named_graph Delete_one_named_graph Reset_all Use_named_graph` (JOE)

3. Execute the Create command by striking the letter *C*. *This does not mean create a graph; it means to create a name for the current graph.* You will be prompted to enter a name. Type the name QUOTA_PIE (use an underscore to separate the two words), and then strike Enter. This gives a name to the set of specifications for this graph so that you can make it current at any time. The name can be up to 15 characters in length (it is *not* a DOS filename).

You must be aware that the action of naming the graph *does not save the worksheet or the graph specifications to disk.* It only makes the appropriate additions to the version of the worksheet currently in memory. To update the copy on disk, you must use the Save command from the main menu.

Resetting Before Creating a New Graph

Now that you have named the current graph, you can proceed to define another. The first thing you must do is to "clear the slate" so that you can enter the specifications for the new graph; remember, QUOTA_PIE is not only safely named and stored, but it is also the current graph. This overall sequence of steps is much like creating a worksheet, saving it to disk, and then erasing all cells to enter another. The following example resets the current graph specifications so that you can begin anew.

DO THIS NOW 6-5 **Resetting the Graph Specifications**

1. From the Graph submenu (Figure 6-12), execute the Reset command by striking the letter *R*. Note that there is the Reset command in the Name submenu. Do not execute the Name Reset command or *all* of the named graph definitions will be deleted. The Graph Reset command produces the following submenu.

```
Graph X A B C D E F Quit          (Lotus 1-2-3)
A B C D E F Graph Quit X_range    (JOE)
```

2. Execute the Graph subcommand by striking the letter *G*. The graph settings will be initialized, and you may proceed to define the next graph settings.

CREATING OTHER TYPES OF GRAPHS

The pie graph that you created involves most of the basic principles of graph creation. The following overall actions of creating a graph or chart are the same for all types. The details differ from one graph to the next according to the nature of the graph or chart.

- Designate the type.
- Designate the cell range for the x range. For a pie chart, these cell contents are the descriptions that are placed next to each slice. For bar and line graphs, they are the entries to be placed on the X axis (the horizontal axis of the graph).
- Designate the cell range for the X range. For a pie chart, these cell contents are the descriptions that are placed next to each slice. For bar and line graphs, they are the entries to be placed on the X axis (the horizontal axis of the graph).

Bar Graphs

For this example, assume that you are preparing a postseason report analyzing the results of the past selling season to go to all the sales representatives. In it you wish to include a bar graph comparing each representative's monthly sales with the bonus quota. In this way, the representatives will be able to assess their performances relative to the bonus quota and to the performances of others.

DO THIS NOW 6-6 **Creating a Bar Graph**

1. You must first designate the graph type (bar). From the Graph submenu of Figure 6-12, set the graph type as Bar by striking the letters *TB*. The Graph submenu will remain on the screen.
2. Now specify the range of cells that form the X axis by striking the letter *X*.
3. Enter the X axis range as B5..F5. To do this, move the cell pointer to B5, anchor it, move it to cell F5, and strike Enter. When the action has been completed, the Graph submenu will be redisplayed.
4. The A value range will be used for the bonus quota, so strike the letter *A*. In response to the prompt to enter the A value range, the first data range is B6..F6. To do this, move the cell pointer to B6, anchor it, move to cell F6, and strike Enter.
5. At this point, if you are curious about the graph, execute the View command by striking the letter *V*. The bar graph shown in Figure 6-19 will be displayed. Strike the Escape to get back to the Graph submenu.

Figure 6-19
The beginning of the desired bar graph.

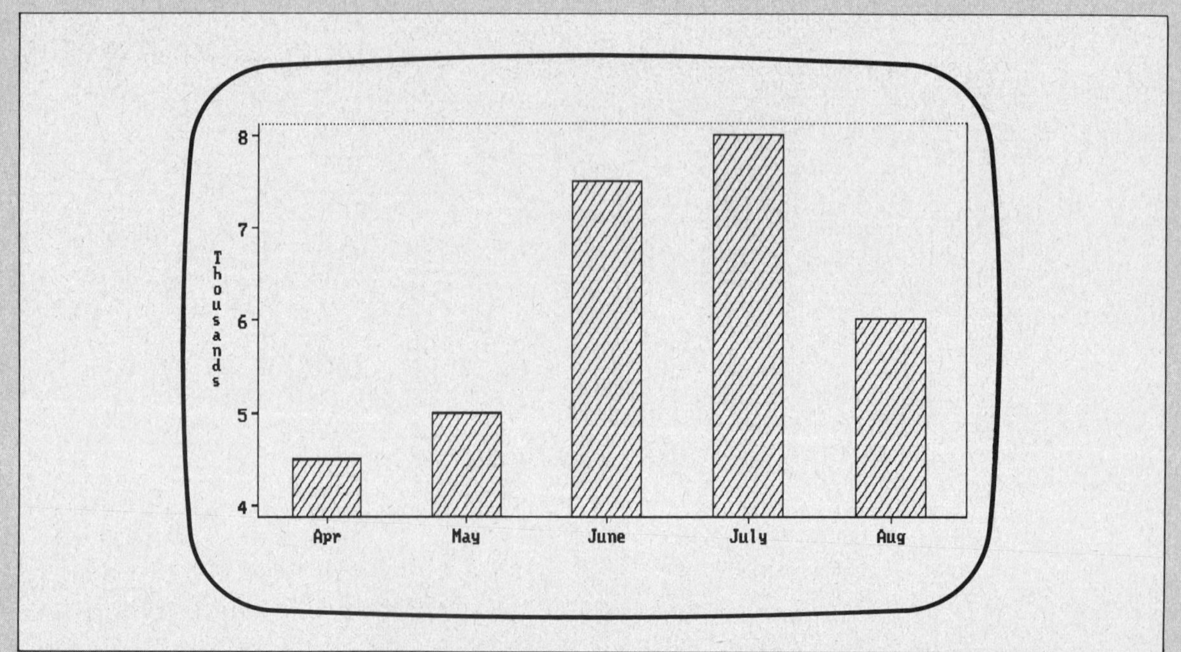

6. Continuing, the B value range will be used for salesperson Hal Curtis. Strike the letter *B* and enter the second data range as B8..F8, using the same procedure as you did for the A range.

7. Repeat the range definitions with the C value range as the data range B9..F9 and the D value range as the data range B10..F10.

8. Viewing the graph once again, you should have the form of Figure 6-20. This bar graph is rapidly taking form.

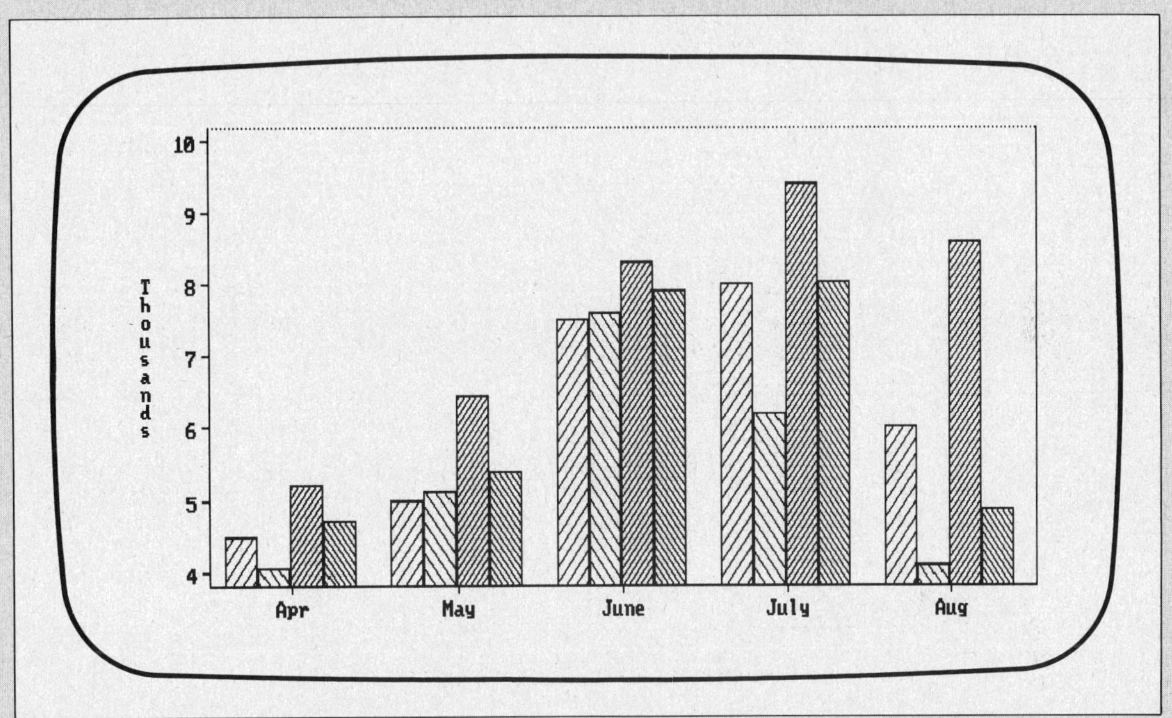

Figure 6-20
The bar graph with four ranges.

Although this bar graph has a nice appearance, it does not tell us the entire story; that is, we do not know the association between bars and data ranges. Refer to any of the bar graphs from earlier descriptions (for instance, Figure 6-7 or 6-8) and you will see that each color bar is identified by a **legend.** Let us enter a legend into your bar graph.

DO THIS NOW 6-7 **Entering a Legend into a Bar Graph**

1. From the Graph menu (Figure 6-12), execute the Options and Legends commands by striking O and then L. The displayed submenu will consist of a list of ranges (A through F).

2. To define the legend for the A range (bonus quota), strike the letter *A* and you will be prompted to enter the A range legend.

3. You can type in whatever description you desire. Since this is the bonus quota, type QUOTA and strike Enter.

4. For ranges B, C, and D, execute the Legends command and repeat steps 2 and 3 using the legends Curtis, Ng, and Crowder, respectively.

5. As this completes legend definition, strike the letter *Q* to Quit the Options submenu, and control is returned to the Graph menu of Figure 6-12. To view your graph, strike the *V* and your display should be as in Figure 6-21.

Figure 6-21
The bar graph with legends.

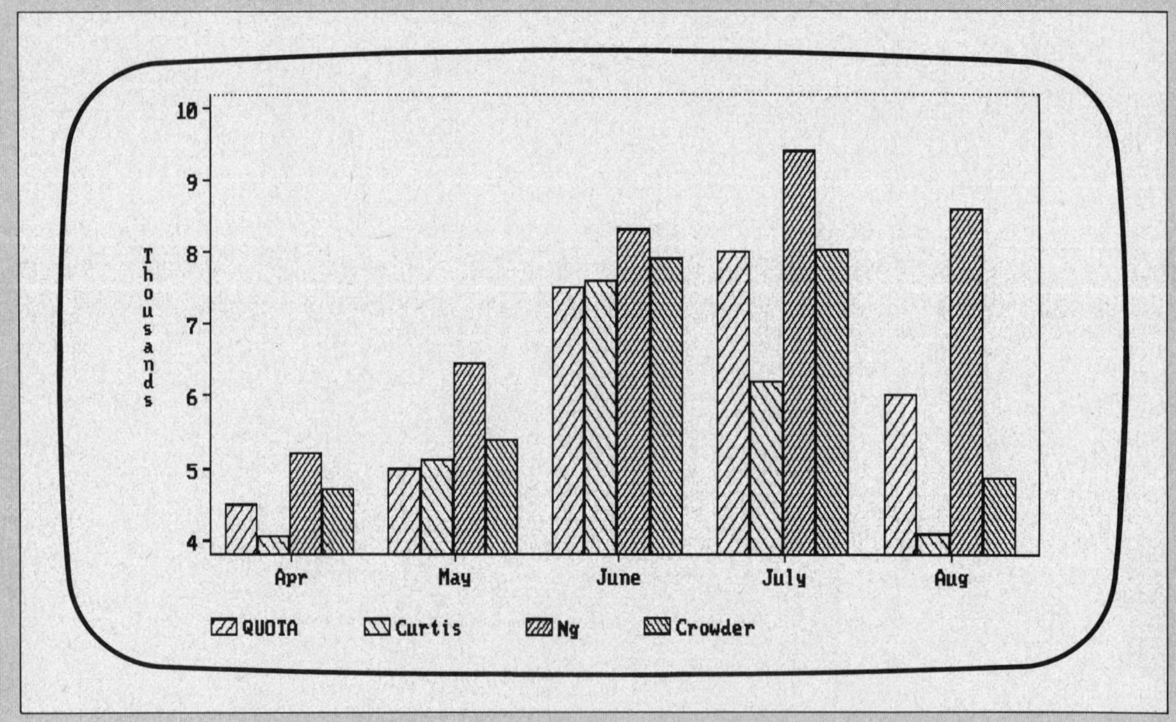

If you wish to include a label, the procedure is identical to that for the pie chart. To retain these graph settings, use the Name Create sequence.

Changing the Y Axis

Earlier in this chapter, you saw the effect of changing the Y axis scaling on the appearance of a graph. In Figure 6-3, the range of values displayed on the Y axis was 0 to 60. By contrast, in Figure 6-4 the scale was changed to be consistent with displaying a range of 30 to 60. To simplify creating graphs, 1-2-3 automatically scales to fit the data range. Hence, in your bar graph

(Figure 6-21), the Y axis starts at slightly less than 4 (4000), consistent with the smallest data value. In some instances, the form of Figure 6-21 is desirable. However, by starting at $4000 rather than 0, the differences are exaggerated. For instance, at a glance, the August sales of Curtis appear to be only a fraction of the quota. Let us consider how to override the automatic scaling of the program and change the Y axis display so that it starts at 0.

DO THIS NOW 6-8 **Changing the Y-Axis Range to 0–10,000**

1. From the Graph submenu, execute the following command sequence

```
Options  Scale  Y_scale
```

by typing the letters *O*, *S*, and *Y*. You may wish to inspect each resulting submenu as you go. When finished, the following submenu will be displayed on your screen.

`Automatic Manual Lower Upper Format Indicator Quit` (Lotus 1-2-3)
`Automatic_scale Format_# Indicator Lower_bound Manual_Quit Upper_bound` (JOE)

2. You must first designate that you want to use manual specification of the scale. To do this, strike the letter *M* for Manual. Do not be concerned that nothing appears to happen and the menu does not change; 1-2-3 has "logged" this change.
3. You can now specify the lower and upper limits of values that you want used for the Y axis. Select the Lower option by striking the letter *L*.
4. Enter a value of 0 and strike Enter.
5. Select the Upper option by striking the letter *U*.
6. Enter a value of 10,000 and strike Enter.
7. To return to the Graph menu, strike the letter *Q* twice (there are two submenus requiring the Quit action).

If you view your graph now, it will appear as shown in Figure 6-22. This graph is now complete and so you should give it a name before going on to the next one; you should then save the worksheet to disk. Using the sequence of DTN 6-4, name the graph QUOTA_BAR. Then return to the main 1-2-3 menu and execute the File Save command sequence to ensure that your latest work is not lost.

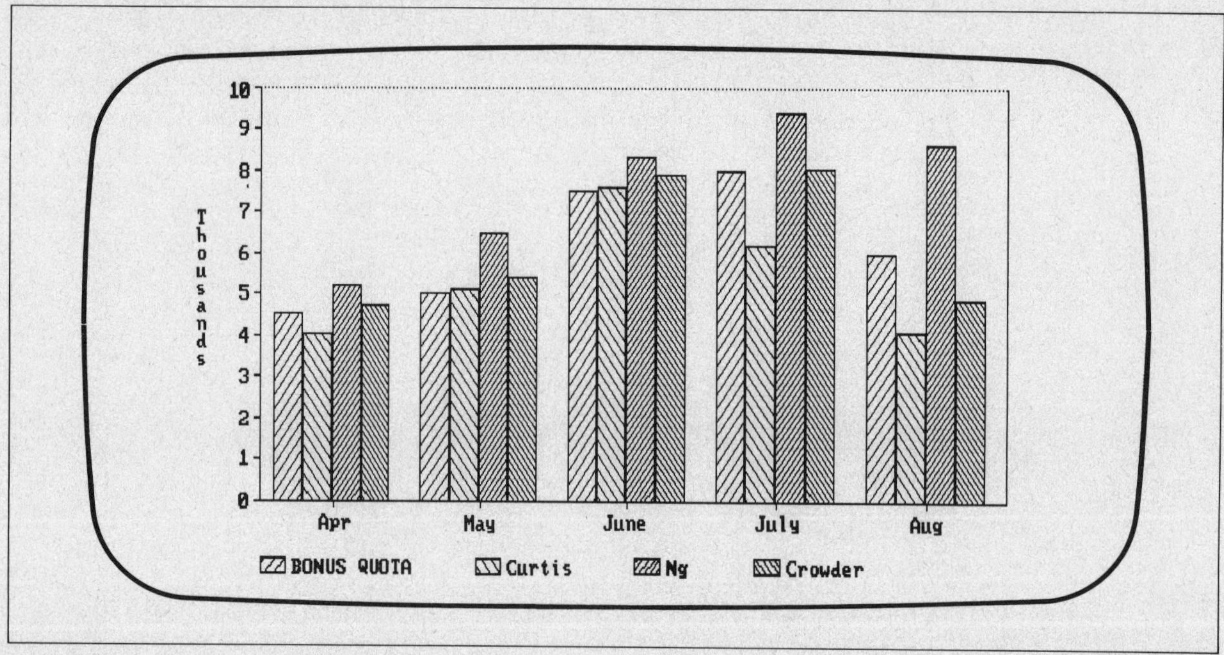

Figure 6-22
Bar graph with a manually scaled Y-axis.

A Line Graph

Your next step is to create the line graph equivalent of the bar graph for the sales data. Actually, the data requirements and graph specifications for a line graph are almost identical to those for a bar graph. In this case, you can change your bar graph to a line graph merely by changing the type. Do this from the Graph submenu (Figure 6-12) by striking the letter *T* for Type. From the resulting Type submenu, select the Line graph option by typing an *L*. If you view the graph, it should look like Figure 6-23. In doing this, you have changed the current set of graph specifications; you have not changed QUOTA_BAR as stored in your worksheet. If you wish to save this line graph as a separate named graph, then return to the Graph submenu and use the sequence of DTN 6-4 to name it. The name QUOTA_LINE would be descriptive.

If you had no bar graph from which to work (the normal situation) and you wanted to create a line graph, then you would need to reset and enter all the specifications. Other than specifying the Type as Line instead of Bar in the first step of DTN 6-6, the sequence of steps is identical to that of DTNs 6-6 and 6-7. However, there is one other specification that determines the appearance of the line graph. Referring to Figure 6-23, notice that each data point is marked by a symbol, and that the points for each data range are connected by line segments. With line graphs, you can specify lines only, symbols only, or both; the default is lines with no symbols. You can change this with the Graph Format command. To see how this works, let us change your line graph so that you have only lines.

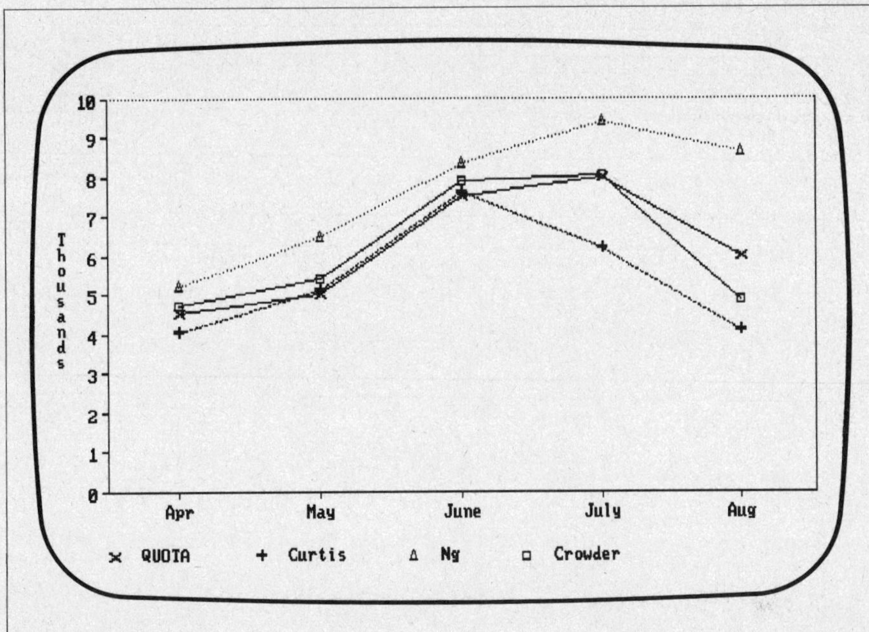

Figure 6-23
A line graph.

DO THIS NOW 6-9 **Changing the Line/Symbol Display of a Line Graph**

1. From the Graph submenu, enter the Options Format Graph command sequence, that is, OFG.
2. The resulting submenu will be:

```
                        Lines  Symbols  Both  Neither        (Lotus 1-2-3)
Both_lines_and_symbols  Lines_only  Symbols_only  Neither;label_only  (JOE)
```

   Select Lines by typing the letter *L*.
3. To return to the Graph submenu, strike the letter *Q* twice (there are two submenus requiring the Quit action). Then view the graph and you will see that it consists only of the lines.

A Stacked-Bar Graph

The bar graph of Figure 6-22 is a good vehicle for comparing the sales quotas and monthly sales for each sales representative. However, it does not show us total monthly sales. As you recall from the earlier descriptions, a stacked-bar graph displays totals and the contribution of each element to the totals. To create a stacked-bar graph, you must first reset (DTN 6-5), and then enter the graph specifications. The steps are identical to those of DTNs 6-6 and 6-7, with the following exceptions.

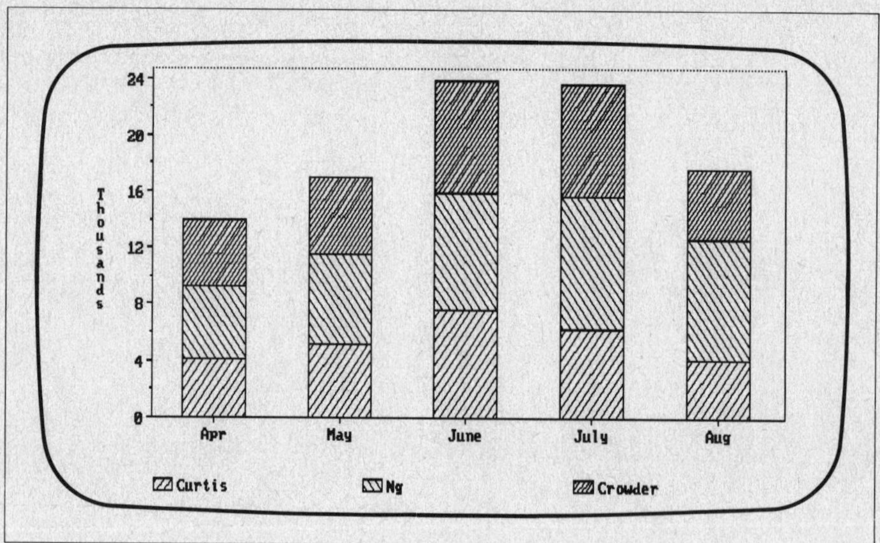

Figure 6-24
A stacked bar graph.

- The graph type must be designated by typing *S* for Stacked_bar.
- The bonus quota has no meaning in the total. Thus, the A, B, and C ranges should be the monthly sales for the three sales representatives.

When you are finished, executing the View command from the Graph submenu will produce the graph shown in Figure 6-24. Note that it is not necessary to designate the scaling, as 1-2-3 defaults to 0 for the lower value of the Y axis. You should now name this graph; use QUOTA_SBAR. Then return to the main menu and save your worksheet using the File Save command.

RECALLING A GRAPH

You now have four graph specifications defined for this worksheet (three if you did not name the line graph). Whenever you begin a 1-2-3 work session and retrieve this worksheet, the current graph will always be the one that was current when you last used the worksheet. You can switch from one graph to another at any time; for instance, the following example makes the pie chart (QUOTA_PIE) the current graph.

DO THIS NOW 6-10 **Switching Graphs**

1. From the Graph submenu (Figure 6-12), execute the Name command by striking the letter *N;* the following Name submenu will be displayed.

```
Use  Create  Delete  Reset      (Lotus 1-2-3)
Create_named_graph Delete_one_named_graph Reset_all Use_named_graph (JOE)
```

2. Execute the Use command by striking the letter *U*. A prompt will be displayed requesting the name of the graph to be made current. Also, a list of named graphs will be displayed on the third line of the control panel. If you have named all four graphs, it will be:

```
QUOTA_BAR  QUOTA_LINE  QUOTA_PIE  QUOTA_SBAR
```

3. Select the graph QUOTA_PIE either by typing the name or by moving the highlight to that name and striking Enter. The Graph submenu of Figure 6-12 will reappear.

You can then display or modify your pie chart as desired. Remember, if you make any changes, you must save your worksheet.

PRINTING A GRAPH

The procedures for printing a graph are different for Lotus 1-2-3 and JOE. Hence, you should read the first of the following sections if you are using JOE and the second if you are using Lotus 1-2-3.

Printer Initialization and Printing a JOE Graph

The first time you ran JOE, the program asked you to enter the type of monitor; this information is required by JOE to produce the correct screen images. In order to print graphics, JOE must be told the brand of graphics printer you are using. You specify this information in much the same way that you specified the default data drive (DTN 4-1).

DO THIS NOW 6-11 **Setting the Printer Type**

1. To avoid possible confusion, return to the READY mode by striking the Escape key as many times as is necessary.
2. Enter the command sequence

```
/ WorkSets Globals Defaults Install Printer
```

   by typing /WGDPI.
3. A list of printers will be displayed. Select your printer from this list by moving the highlight to it and striking the Enter.
4. Exit this menu by typing Q (Quit_menu). You will be returned to the READY mode.
5. If your printer is connected to printer port 1 (the standard printer port), then you can skip to step 6. Otherwise, you must specify the port with the command sequence

```
/ WorkSets Globals Defaults Printer_sets Interface_port
```

   by typing /WGDPI. You will be presented with a list of selections 1–8. Select the one that corresponds to your computer configuration by moving the highlight and then striking the Enter. Repeatedly strike the Escape key to return to the READY mode.

6. To save your printer information, enter the command sequence

```
/ WorkSets Globals Defaults Update
```

by typing /WGDU. Then return to the READY mode.

This action saves the printer information to the JOE disk so that it will be available whenever you want to print a graph. The only reason to perform this action again would be to designate another printer.

For printing, you have two options: print the current graph or print a graph that you designate. First, check the printer to be certain that it is turned on. Then, from the READY mode, use either of the following key combinations:

`Alt-F10`	Print the current graph.
`Shift-F10`	Print a named graph; JOE will ask for the name of the graph to be printed.

As printing takes place, the graph will be displayed on the screen. When finished, the worksheet will be redisplayed in the READY mode. To cancel a graph printing operation, enter the Ctrl-Break key sequence.

Printing With Lotus 1-2-3

Lotus 1-2-3 consists of several programs; you have been using the worksheet program 123.EXE. To print a graph, 123.EXE creates a separate graphics image file. This file is then printed by the Lotus program PGRAPH.EXE. However, before you can print a graph, you must have specified to Lotus the type of graphics printer connected to your computer. If you are using Lotus 1-2-3, then you should already have run the INSTALL program (from DOS) to specify your computer configuration. If you have not, then do so and specify the graphics printer that you have on your computer.

When this is done, run Lotus 1-2-3 and retrieve the worksheet SALES3, which includes specifications for four graphs. As an illustration, let us print the pie chart.

DO THIS NOW 6-12 **Printing the Pie Chart QUOTA_PIE with Lotus 1-2-3**

1. Make QUOTA_PIE the current graph with the sequence of DTN 6-10.

2. Execute the command sequence

```
/ Graph Save
```

by typing /GS. Lotus 1-2-3 is ready to save an image of this graph to disk. The resulting prompt will be as follows (the default drive will be different if you are using a hard disk):

```
Enter you graph file name B:\*.PIC
```

3. You must enter a DOS filename; the default extension for graph files is PIC. Type Q_PIE and strike Enter. The graph file image will then be written to disk with the filename Q_PIE.PIC. Note that you cannot use QUOTA_PIE because it is too long for use as a DOS filename.
4. When control is returned to the Graph submenu, terminate execution of Lotus 1-2-3 and return to DOS.
5. Run the graph program from DOS by typing PGRAPH and striking the Enter. (If you have been operating from the Lotus Access System, select the PrintGraph option.)
6. The graph program will display the menu:

   ```
   Image-Select Settings Go Align Page Exit
   ```

   You will also see the full definition of the current print specifications. The Hardware Setup section is a result of the INSTALL program.
7. You must select the graph image file to be printed; do this by typing the letter *I* (Image-Select). A list of graph image files will be displayed.
8. Select the desired graph image file by highlighting the name and striking the Enter. (Your disk has only one file, so it is already highlighted.)
9. Select the Go command by typing the letter *G*.

As printing takes place, Lotus 1-2-3 will flash WAIT in the upper right of the screen. When printing is finished, strike the letter *E* (for Exit) and control of the computer will be returned to DOS.

Assignment 6-2 may now be completed.

SUMMARY

The purpose of this chapter has been both to provide you with a general understanding of computer graphics, and to give you specific experience using the graphics features of 1-2-3. By using 1-2-3, you have been able to create, save, and print line and bar graphs and pie charts. Summarizing, the important items from the chapter are:

- Computer graphics is the use of the computer to prepare visual presentations.
- Business graphics is the representation of tabular data in graph form. The three common graphic forms are line graph, bar graph, and pie chart.
- A pie chart is used to illustrate the percentage contribution that each data item makes to the whole.
- Design graphics programs are used by professionals such as engineers, architects, and interior designers to automate much of their work.
- Computer-aided design (CAD) software allows the designer to enter design data into the computer and from that data to display the item on the screen and to print detailed drawings. CAD/CAM software extends this to creating detailed instructions to machines for manufacturing the item.
- All graphics activity in 1-2-3 takes place through the Graph command.
- With 1-2-3, five graph types can be created; the four described in this chapter are line, bar, stacked-bar, and pie chart.
- The overall 1-2-3 steps in creating a graph are:
  1. Designate the type (line, bar, stacked bar, or pie).
  2. Designate the cell range for the x range. For a pie chart, these cell contents are the descriptions that are placed next to each slice. For bar and line graphs, they are the entries to be placed on the X axis (the horizontal axis of the graph).
  3. Designate the cell range(s) for the Y axis. For a pie chart, these cell contents contain the data to be used in determining the relative sizes of the slices. For bar and line graphs, they are the values to be plotted on the Y axis (the vertical axis of the graph). With 1-2-3, it is possible to include up to six ranges.
- Graphs can include descriptions, legends, and cross-hatching to better convey their meaning.
- When a graph is created for a worksheet, it becomes part of that worksheet until it is erased (in much the same way as adding a new row to a worksheet). After creating a graph, the worksheet must be saved using the /File Save command if the graph is to be retained.
- If more than one graph is specified for a worksheet, then each must be given a graph name using the /Graph Name command. This command is also used to make any graph the current graph.
- The current graph is the set of graph specifications to which 1-2-3 has access at any give time. It is the graph that is displayed with the View command and is available for modification or for printing.
- Bar and line graphs are automatically scaled by 1-2-3. Manual scaling can be used, which allows you to specify the smallest and largest values to be utilized in setting the X axis and Y axis.

- Graphs can be printed if you have a graphics printer.
- Before a graph can be printed, the printer characteristics must be defined for the program. This is done differently with JOE and with Lotus 1-2-3.
- From the READY mode with JOE, use either of the following key combinations to print a graph.

Alt-F10	Print the current graph
Shift-F10	Print a named graph

- To print a graph from Lotus 1-2-3, a graph image file of the current graph must be created with the /Graph Save command. Then from DOS run the program PGRAPH to print the image file.

NEW TERMINOLOGY

The following are important new terms introduced in this chapter; you should be familiar with each of them.

bar graph
CAD (computer-aided design)
CAD/CAM
computer graphics
current graph
legend
line graph
pie chart
presentation graphics
scale
X axis
Y axis

Name: ______________________ Date: ______________

Assignment 6-1

1. What is computer graphics?

2. What is meant by X axis and Y axis?

3. What is the difference between a bar graph and a stacked-bar graph?

4. Referring to the pie charts of Figure 6-2, do they tell you how much time each employee can devote to various activities? What information is conveyed?

5. What does it mean that a pie chart is exploded?

Name: ______________________ Date: ______________

Assignment 6-2

1. What do you think would happen to the pie chart display of QUOTA_PIE (see Figure 6-15) if the entries of row 12 were changed to each of the following sets?
   (a) 1 0 2 0 3

   (b) 3 0 1 0 2

   (c) 100 100 100 100 100

   (d) 1 100 2 0 100

2. What is the purpose of naming a graph specification?

Name: ______________________ Date: ______________

Assignment 6-2 (*continued*)

3. When a graph definition is named and saved, what is the extension used by DOS?

4. What happens to a newly specified graph if 1-2-3 is exited without executing the File Save command sequence from the main menu?

5. How many data ranges can be included in a line or a bar graph?

6. What is the purpose of changing the range of the Y axis in the line graph of Figure 6-21 to 0–10000?

Name: ______________________ Date: ______________

OBJECTIVE QUESTIONS

Matching

Match each key sequence in a to h with the corresponding action in 1 through 8.

a. /GNC
b. /GT
c. /GOL
d. /GRG
e. /GNU
f. /GOSY
g. /GX
h. /FS

___ **1.** Designate the type of graph.

___ **2.** Specify the descriptions to be used for each slice of a pie chart.

___ **3.** Enter a name for the current graph.

___ **4.** Save the recently created graph to disk.

___ **5.** Clear the current graph settings so that a new set of specifications can be entered.

___ **6.** Create legends for a bar graph.

___ **7.** Change the lower limit of the Y axis from 1000 to 500.

___ **8.** Make the graph QUOTA_LINE the current graph.

TRUE/FALSE

Determine whether each of the following is true or false.

T F **1.** The primary use of CAD software is to generate computer artwork.

T F **2.** The distinguishing feature of a line graph is that it is shaped like a pie.

T F **3.** The X axis of a line graph always displays time.

T F **4.** The purpose of a pie chart is to display the relative sizes of quantities that make up a whole.

T F **5.** From a CAD/CAM program an engineer might get a detailed drawing for a part to be manufactured and a set of instructions to machine tools for making the part.

T F **6.** One distinction between a bar graph and a stacked-bar graph is that one displays data values but the other does not.

T F **7.** In 1-2-3, an exploded stacked-bar chart is one in which some of the elements have been separated from others for emphasis.

T F **8.** Even though the pie chart does not have X and Y axes as do bar and line graphs, the X range is used to describe the data range being used.

Name: ______________________________ Date: ______________

OBJECTIVE QUESTIONS (*continued*)

T F **9.** Once the cross-hatching codes have been set up for a pie chart, they can be deleted from the worksheet and 1-2-3 will still retain the information.

T F **10.** Any slice of a pie chart can be exploded by adding 100 to the cross-hatching code for that segment.

T F **11.** You can create more than one graph from a single worksheet.

T F **12.** It is not necessary to name a graph if it is the only one to be created for a worksheet.

T F **13.** When you name a graph, that set of graph specifications is automatically saved to disk as part of the worksheet.

T F **14.** A reason that you might use the Graph Reset command would be so that you can create a new graph for your worksheet.

T F **15.** A completely different procedure is used for creating a bar graph than for creating a pie chart.

T F **16.** The purpose of a legend on a graph is to identify different sets of data displayed by the graph.

T F **17.** The Graph Reset command is used to clear all the graphs that are stored for a particular worksheet.

T F **18.** Legends are commonly used with graphs to identify the different sets of data that comprise the graph.

T F **19.** Graphs created by 1-2-3 are automatically scaled (by default).

T F **20.** The action of making another graph the current graph (using /GNU) requires that an entirely new file be read from disk.

T F **21.** The only shortcoming of graphics capabilities of 1-2-3 is that it is not possible to print a graph.

Multiple Choice

In the space provided, record the letter of the choice that best completes or answers the statement.

____ **1.** The floor plan layout for an office might be done with ______ software.

A. CAD
B. bar graph
C. business graphics
D. graphical analysis

____ **2.** Presentation graphics might be used to

A. design a mechanical part.
B. prepare a pie chart.
C. display business data.
D. scale the Y axis of a line graph.

Name: ______________________________ Date: ______________

OBJECTIVE QUESTIONS (*continued*)

____ **3.** On a graph, the scale is the

A. direction of the X axis.
B. direction of the Y axis.
C. the relationship between the different segments of a bar graph.
D. the relationship between a physical entity and the graph unit of measure.

____ **4.** If you wanted to show the relative contributions of different elements to the whole, you would use a

A. line graph.
B. pie chart.
C. bar graph.
D. stacked-bar graph.

____ **5.** Which of the following does not have X and Y axes?

A. line graph
B. pie chart
C. bar graph
D. stacked-bar graph

____ **6.** An exploded pie chart is one in which one or more segments of the pie are

A. moved out from the others.
B. cross-hatched.
C. colored.
D. pie charts cannot be exploded.

____ **7.** To add cross-hatching to a pie chart, you must

A. add 100 to pie codes.
B. first save the chart.
C. revert to the default values.
D. enter a sequence of codes in the worksheet.

____ **8.** A graph created for a worksheet is saved to disk

A. automatically when the graph is created.
B. automatically when you exit 1-2-3.
C. only when you save the worksheet to disk.
D. when you begin the next graph.

____ **9.** The purpose of naming a graph is so that

A. DOS will be able to retrieve it for you.
B. you can create more than one graph for a worksheet.
C. you know what type of graph it is.
D. DOS knows what type of graph it is.

Name: ______________________ Date: ______________

OBJECTIVE QUESTIONS (*continued*)

____ **10.** In a bar graph, the purpose of the legend is to

A. indicate the relationship between the data entity and the physical unit of measure on the graph.
B. make predictions based on displayed data.
C. identify the different sets of data in the graph.
D. give the graph a name so that it can be retrieved later.

Fill In

In the space provided, fill in the correct answer. Note that the answer can be one or two words.

1. ______________________

______ programs are used in mechanical design and allow the engineer to create designs with the computer.

2. ______________________

In a graph, the relationship between the physical entity (for instance, dollars spent) and the unit of length on the graph is called the ______.

3. ______________________

If you needed to represent the temperature as a function of the hour of the day, you would probably use a ______ graph.

4. ______________________

You have current and last year's reading scores for a small group of children and you want to show a comparison of the two for each child. For this, you would probably use a ______ graph.

5. ______________________

The stacked-bar graph and the ______ graph display the same information in a slightly different form.

6. ______________________

The ______ does not use a conventional X and Y axis as does a line graph.

7. ______________________

One way of emphasizing a particular segment in pie chart is to move it out from the others, or to ______ it.

8. ______________________

If you intend to create more than one graph for a worksheet, then you must ______ each graph.

ASSIGNMENTS/PROJECTS

1. Using the sales analysis worksheet of Chapter 5 (COST3), create a pie chart that shows the portion of the total cost contributed by each of the four styles. Use cross-hatching and include appropriate titles.

2. From COST3, create a stacked-bar graph that shows the unit cost and the five cost components of which it is comprised. Include appropriate graph titles and titles for the X axis and Y axis.

3. Using the version of the EMPL worksheet of Chapter 5 that you completed, create a stacked-bar chart showing the total score for each employee as consisting of scores on each of the three training units. Include appropriate graph titles and titles for the X axis and Y axis.

4. Using the version of the EMPL worksheet of Chapter 5 that you completed, create a line graph with scores plotted against the three training units. This graph is to include three data ranges: the average rating, the highest rating, and the lowest rating. Include appropriate graph titles and titles for the X axis and Y axis.

5. Using the worksheet BUDGET.WKS stored on your data disk, make a bar graph displaying the quarterly expenses and income against the quarter. Include appropriate graph titles and titles for the X axis and Y axis.

6. In Project Assignment 1 of Chapter 5 you extended a budget worksheet to 2 years. For this assignment, you are to create two pie charts, one for income and the other for expenses (first year). There must be four pie segments, one for each of the four quarters.

7. For the budget worksheet, create a line graph of the quarterly balance for the entire 2-year period.

8. In Project Assignment 4 of Chapter 4 you included quarterly sales for various product lines. For this assignment, you are to create a stacked-bar graph displaying gross sales. Along the X axis, you should have each of the four quarters. Stack Casual Wear, Summer Sports, Winter Sports, and Work Uniforms; prepare separate graphs for the men and the women.

9. From the worksheet of Project Assignment 4 of Chapter 4, create a bar graph displaying the total sales for each of the four product line categories comparing the data for men and women. (Each of the four product line categories must be along the X axis.)

PART FOUR

Database Management

INTRODUCTION TO PART FOUR

You have already seen how word processing streamlines the entry, editing, and storage of documents, and how spreadsheet programs make "what-if" analyses of data quick and efficient. You have also learned that one characteristic of spreadsheet programs is that they provide you the ability to organize data and to relate data elements (by formulas) to produce useful information. The third of the software tools that you will use is the database management system (DBMS); it will give you the ability to manage and manipulate data in files to produce useful information. This is the topic of the final two chapters.

In Chapters 7 and 8, you will use the popular database management program dBASE III PLUS which is included with this book. You will learn basic operations such as creating a database file, inspecting data in the file, rearranging the order of data in the file, and operating on data on a conditional basis. The vehicle for learning will be three data files, two of them taken from the MCT Enterprises example.

- MCT Enterprises customer file.
  Each customer of MCT has a record in this file. Data stored in it includes the customer number, name, and account balance.
- MCT Enterprises accounts receivable file.
  There is a record for each MCT sale that has an outstanding balance in this file. Data stored in it includes the invoice number (this identifies the sale), the customer number, and the amount of the sale.
- Assembly bill file.
  This is a new application involving information about legislative bills in a state assembly. This example is described in detail in this introduction in order to give you your first insight to the nature of database concepts.

Although the treatments in these chapters are necessarily limited in scope (with only two chapters), they will provide you a firm foundation in the principles of database management.

Typical Information Needs

In all aspects of our lives, both personal and business, we see the need for information. Let us consider a variety of examples that illustrate a broad range of applications to provide us information based on data stored in computer files.

To find out the current balance in your bank account, you call your bank and give your name and account number. The clerk types this information into a computer terminal and the computer finds your record among the many thousands in the file and displays it on the monitor. Speed is essential; the information must be located in seconds, *not* minutes. The bank management does not want employees standing around waiting for information, nor does it want you to change banks because of slow service.

As the owner of MCT Enterprises, say you receive a call from a customer requesting the immediate shipment of 200 of your light-blue, Sunset-style jackets. Do you have them in stock? With a computer inventory system, you can enter the stock number and receive an immediate display from the inventory file telling you the exact status of this item. With the computer at your fingertips, the customer need wait only a few moments for you to say (with confidence), "Yes, they will be shipped late this afternoon."

Another of your needs as a business owner is mass mailing, an important part of your business. Periodically, you send sale information and announcements to everyone in a special mailing file. In order to use the bulk mailing rate, the Post Office requires that the pieces be in order by postal ZIP code. One of the functions of data management software is to sort data stored in the file. With this, you can have the computer print address labels in ZIP code order regardless of the order in which the names and addresses were entered into the file.

Where each of the preceding examples involves actions with data in a single file, the monthly preparation of customer bills requires data from three files. The customer's name, address, and current balance come from a customer file. Data regarding purchases comes from the accounts receivable file, which contains data on all sales. Data regarding payments comes from the payments file. All of this must be brought together for each customer in preparing the bill.

For a completely different example, consider the task of keeping records for the issuance of keys to offices and buildings at the institution where you are studying. One or more keys are issued to faculty and staff according to their needs. Some keys open only a single door. Others open doors to several rooms. Still others open the doors to all rooms in an area or building. Now consider the plight of the facilities manager who is faced with the loss of equipment from one of the rooms and wants the names of all key holders with access to that room. First, she would need to determine which keys open the room; then she would have to find out to whom each of these keys has been issued. This may sound simple, but with a large institution, it is a huge and painstaking manual task. Data management software provides the means for getting such information almost instantly.

These are typical data management applications: data in files must be managed to provide needed information. Let us focus on these concepts by considering a typical data management application. In this example, you will consider a problem to be solved and the "common-sense" steps in solving it. From it, you will learn about the storage of data in files and about data management software that make it easy to convert the stored data to useful information.

A MANUAL DATA PROCESSING APPLICATION

Assume that you have taken a job with an organization dedicated to protecting the environment. You have been given the task of monitoring all bills in your state assembly that in any way relate to the environment. This is to be an expansion of a small project begun by your predecessor in which he tracked a few important bills.

The Assembly Bill File

For monitoring the bills, your predecessor had written information about each assembly bill of interest on a 3 × 5 card as shown in Figure P4-1. There are some things about this collection of cards that have direct significance to computer processing of data files. Each card, or record, contains data

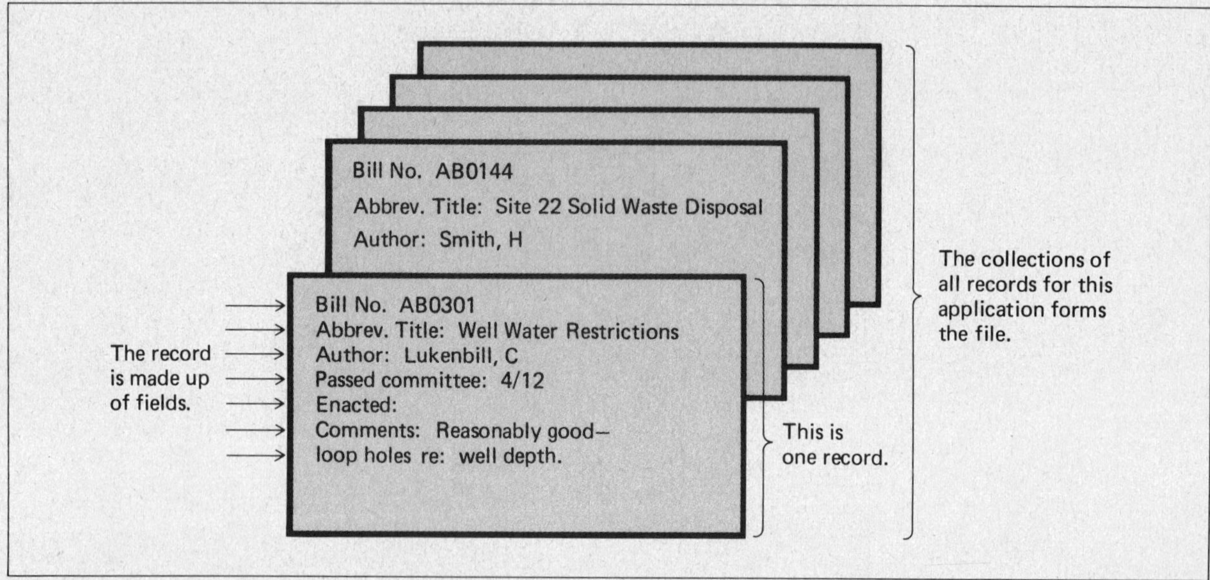

Figure P4-1
A card file containing assembly bill data.

about one bill. That is, this record comprises the following data items, or fields:

Bill number

Abbreviated title

Author (member of the assembly who is sponsoring the bill)

Date the bill was passed in committee

Date the bill was approved

Comments

The collection of all of these cards form the assembly bill file. Hence, we have a hierarchy of data.

Field A basic unit of data (such as bill number, author, and date approved).

Record A group of related facts or fields of information treated as a unit.

File The organized collection of all records of a given type.

Each field of a record contains information about a given entity, in this case, an assembly bill. The bill number identifies a given bill. The title, author, and other data pertain to that bill. These facts are related and they are relevant to a particular application or group of applications. Notice that the author's name is included because he or she is the author of this proposed legislation. However, data about the author is not included in this record; the record is for data about the bill, not the author. In setting up files, it is important to maintain this type of distinction.

Your predecessor had certain procedures for working with this file. He had to add a new record for each bill introduced. As each bill left its working committee, he entered the date; as each bill was enacted he entered that date. In using the file, he prepared reports listing, for example, bills that had been enacted, and those that were still being worked on by committee. He also prepared summaries of the bills introduced by each member of the assembly. We can consider these activities in two broad categories: file maintenance and file use. Together they make up a **file management system,** a set of procedures for managing the data in a data file. These manual procedures illustrated in this example are found in file management programs for automating the maintenance and use of data files on the computer.

Interrelating the Data in Two Files

In addition to the assembly bill card file, your predecessor maintained a separate assembly member file, which is illustrated in Figure P4-2. Each card record of this file contains the needed data about a member of the assembly. Together, the Bill and Member files provided the necessary data for your predecessor to do his job. For instance, if he was working on bill AB0301 and needed to address a letter to the author, he would:

Figure P4-2
A card file containing assembly member data.

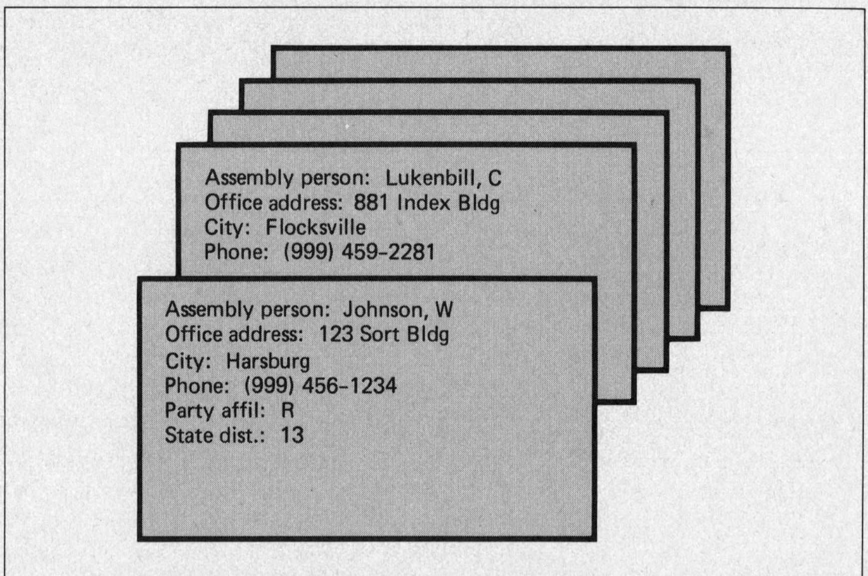

1. Find the record for AB0301 in the Bill file and get the name of the assembly member who wrote the bill.
2. Find the record for that assembly member in the Member file to get the address.

In other words, these two files are used together, as illustrated in Figure P4-3. Note that they are interrelated by a common field: the author of the bill. This has important implications in database processing.

These data files provide information because they are structured and organized. For instance, in the Bill file each record contains the data in the same layout or format: the records are *structured*. Furthermore, the cards

Figure P4-3
Relationship between the Bill file and Member file.

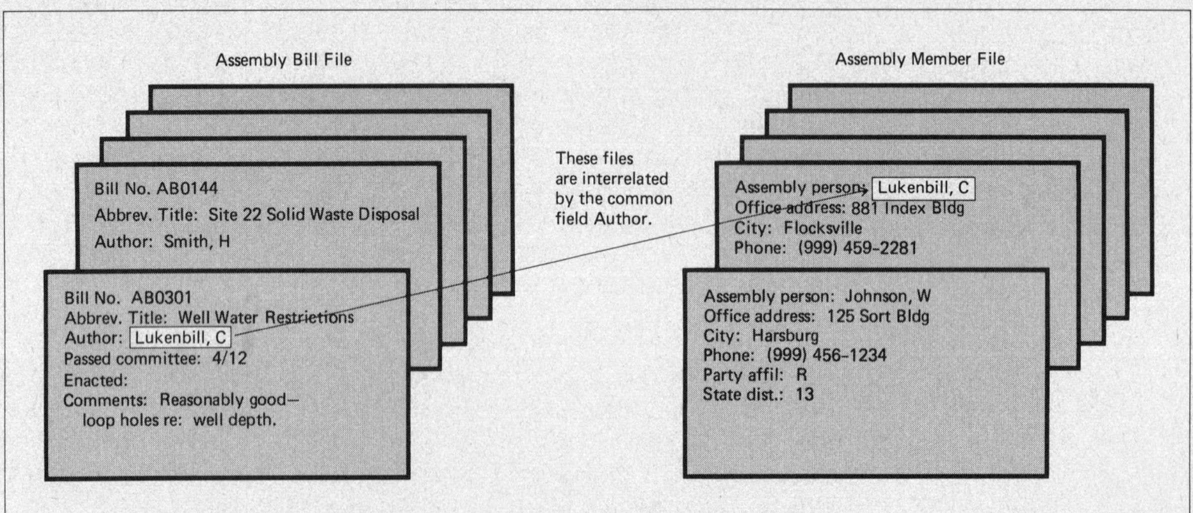

are probably arranged in the file in sequence by bill number: the file is *organized*. (The Member file is probably sequenced by assembly member name.) Structure and organization are keys to the usefulness of these two sets of data.

Key Field

One of the cornerstones of database theory is that any record in a database can be accessed without ambiguity by specifying a data file, and a record in that file. This has an important implication. That is, for every file, there must be a field (or combination of fields) in the record that uniquely identifies each record. For example, the Bill file record includes the bill number field; no two bills ever have the same bill number—it is **unique**. If, in doing a particular operation, you request the record for AB0212, the DBMS program will locate that specific record for you. This field is called the **key field**. Contrast requesting a record using the key field with requesting the Bill record of bills written by Smith; there is more than one such record so it is not possible to access a particular one in this way.

In the representation of the Member file, the member name is used as the key field. In an actual application, a name would not be used as a key field because two people might have the same name, for example, there might be two people in the file named Helen Smith. For the Member file, the number of the district represented by the assembly member would be a good choice as a key field. For many applications, the person's Social Security number is used.

Database Management

In this application, your predecessor kept information about each bill in the Bill file, and information about each assembly member in the Member file. You are looking at the essence of a **database,** a collection of interrelated files. A DMBS is a program (or collection of programs) that allows you to manage and use data stored in multiple, interrelated files: the database.

In reading computer literature, you will encounter the terms **file management system** and **database management system.** A file management system is considerably less powerful than a DBMS. One of the distinctions between the two is that a file management system cannot interrelate multiple files, whereas a DBMS can.

If you have worked with a programming language such as BASIC or COBOL, you know that writing programs to enter data into a file and edit data already in the file is not a simple task. Furthermore, you know that each file requires its own set of programs. For instance, a program to edit data in a customer file could not be used to perform the same editing operations on data in an inventory file. It would be necessary to write another program. On the other hand, DBMS is designed specifically for managing and manipulating data stored in files. In fact, most of the following actions can be done on a database data file with a few simple database commands.

- Create a new file.
- Enter a new record into a file.
- Change the contents of a record in the file.
- Delete a record from a file.
- Find a record in the file according to some selection criterion.
- Rearrange the records of a file in a specific order.
- Define relationships between two or more files.
- Generate reports consisting of data from the file.

PLANNING FOR A DATABASE APPLICATION

After careful consideration, you decide to put this application on the computer using a DBMS. You feel that the use of a computer will be essential to accomplishing your goals of maintaining data on all bills that have any effect on the environment, and of storing more data for each bill. Furthermore, you feel that a computer is necessary to get the utmost information from available data. You are faced with devising a computer solution.

Computer problem solving was the topic of the last section in the Part Three Introduction to spreadsheets. Similar techniques are used to prepare a computer solution for a problem whether the software tool used is a spreadsheet, a DBMS, or a conventional programming language. That is, (1) define the results you want from your solution, (2) analyze the available data and determine if the necessary data is available, (3) devise an overall plan for the solution, (4) express the solution in a form that can be conveyed to the computer, and (5) test the solution. Let us first consider the results you are seeking.

Capabilities of the Assembly Bill Information System

After careful consideration, you have decided that your assembly bill information system should provide you with the ability to:

- Assign a quality rating (0–100) to each bill and get statistical information based on ratings.
- Classify the bills as having their principal impact on the air, the water, or the ground.
- Designate each bill as regional (you have divided the state into five regions) or statewide, so that you can categorize the bills.
- Assess the performance of members of the legislature with regard to the number and ratings of the bills they write.
- Arrange the records in order based on any of the fields in the file.
- List information for all bills or for those meeting some criterion such as water-related bills with a rating of 90 or greater.

- Display on the screen the entire record for any selected bill plus the author's office address and telephone number.
- List each assembly member and the bills written by the member.

Your next step is to designate the data that you will require to obtain this information, that is, the fields that will make up your record in this file. Your data needs for the Bill file are an expansion of those from the manual system in Figure P4-1.

Bill number

Abbreviated title

Author (member of the assembly who is sponsoring the bill)

Bill type (relates to air, water, or land)

Region to which this bill applies

Rating (0–100)

Recommendation for support (Yes or No)

Date the bill was passed in committee

Date the bill was approved

Comments

You would then detail your needs for the Member file in exactly the same way. For this illustration, assume that you have decided that the data contained in the card file of Figure P4-2 will be adequate for your application. You must now assess each data field and determine the type of data it will contain and its size.

Data Types

Four data classifications are common to virtually all DBMSs: character, numeric, date, and logical. Let us consider each of these relative to the fields of this application.

Character Data. The bill title and author's name are typical examples of character data. Such can consist of letters, digits, and special characters, for instance:

Bill: Restrictions on Insecticide 99-X

Author: Pamella O'Hara

Thus, fields of a data file designated as character fields (often called alphanumeric fields) can contain any character that can be entered from the keyboard.

Numeric Data. The legislation file includes only one numeric data field: the rating, which can have a value of from 0 to 100. Notice that although the first field is identified as the bill *number,* this field is not truly numeric. For instance, one of the sample bill numbers is AB0224. There are many examples of data fields, that we refer to as numbers (which contain only digits), that are not treated as numeric data. For instance, your Social Security number (without the hyphens) consists of nine digits. Your account number with VISA, the loan number for your home or automobile, and many other "numbers" consist only of digits. However, almost always these are designated in data files as character fields. On the other hand, fields such as amount owed on an account, number of items in inventory, and score achieved on an examination are designated as numeric fields. These are fields on which arithmetic operations might be performed.

Date Data. Your legislation file will contain two dates (date passed by committee and date signed into law). You could define these fields as being character and use the standard form month/day/year; for example, 11/18/90. However, your ability to manipulate date fields would be very limited. For instance, arranging records in sequence by date would be very clumsy with normal sorting methods. Simple date arithmetic such as adding 45 days to a date would be difficult. The date-type data found in most DBMSs allows comparing and simple arithmetic operations to be performed on date data almost as if it were numeric.

Logical Data. Most database applications include fields that will contain a yes or no value. For instance, the legislation file includes the recommendation field: the value stored in this field will be either yes or no, depending on whether or not you recommend passage of the bill. This is commonly called logical data because it can have either of two values: yes or no (or true or false). Although you could use a character field (into which you store Y or N), database management systems include the logical data type specifically for yes/no data.

Field Width

In addition to the data type, the width of character and numeric fields must be designated. This is necessary because a DBMS reserves a specified amount of space in memory (and on disk) for each field of a record. For some fields, the width is predetermined by the field itself. For instance, the bill number consists of two letters and four digits; hence, its width is six characters. On the other hand, the title and author field widths must be selected based on your knowledge of the data. The abbreviated title width should be sufficiently long that each entry is clearly meaningful. Fields containing people's names should be long enough to avoid chopping off the last few letters of the name. Numeric fields must be long enough to hold the largest possible number that will be stored in them. This includes a decimal point if the number can have a fractional part and a sign if it can be negative, as illustrated by the two examples at the left.

One approach to selecting a field width is: "A width of twenty should be good enough, so I will double it to forty to be certain." This is a poor approach because it results in wasted disk space; for large files, the percentage of wasted space on a disk can be significant. Table P4-1 summarizes the data type and reasonable field widths for the Bill record.

Once all of these characteristics of the fields that make up the file have been determined, the needed data files can be created and data records

Table P4-1 RECORD DEFINITION FOR BILL FILE

Field	Type	Width	Comments
Bill number	Character	6	
Title	Character	30	
Author	Character	20	
Bill type	Character	1	A—Air W—Water G—Ground
Region	Character	1	1–5—Regions 1–5 9—Statewide
Rating	Numeric	3	0–100
Recommendation	Logical	1	
Date passed in committee	Date	8	
Date approved	Date	8	
Comments	Character	80	

entered and edited. These are basic file maintenance operations of a DBMS; they allow us to manage the data stored in the data files.

ACCESSING RECORDS IN A FILE

File maintenance operations are essential to any database application, but it is the file processing operations that allow us to make that data available in a useful form—as information. Let us first consider the ways in which records read from disk into memory (accessed) are made available for processing.

Sequential Processing

The records of the Bill file are shown in Figure P4-4 in the physical order in which they were entered into the file (physical record numbers are included to the left of the first field for convenient reference). This is called a *file listing* because it is a printout of each field and record of the file. It was generated by a command to access records and print them one after the other from the file in their physical order; the listing task was completed when the end of the file was reached. Reading and processing records in this way are called *sequential processing*, or **sequential access** of the records in the file; sequential access is illustrated by the diagram of Figure P4-5. In sequential accessing, the DBMS program always accesses the next record after the current one.

Two of the examples at the beginning of this introduction involve sequential processing of all the records in a file. For example, in preparing mailing labels from the data in the mailing file of MCT Enterprises, the

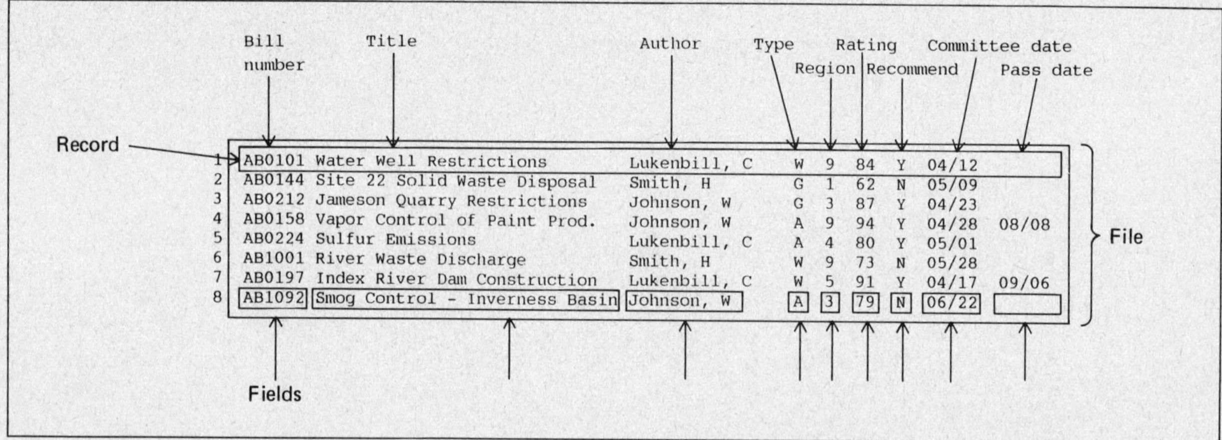

Figure P4-4
Listing of the Bill file.

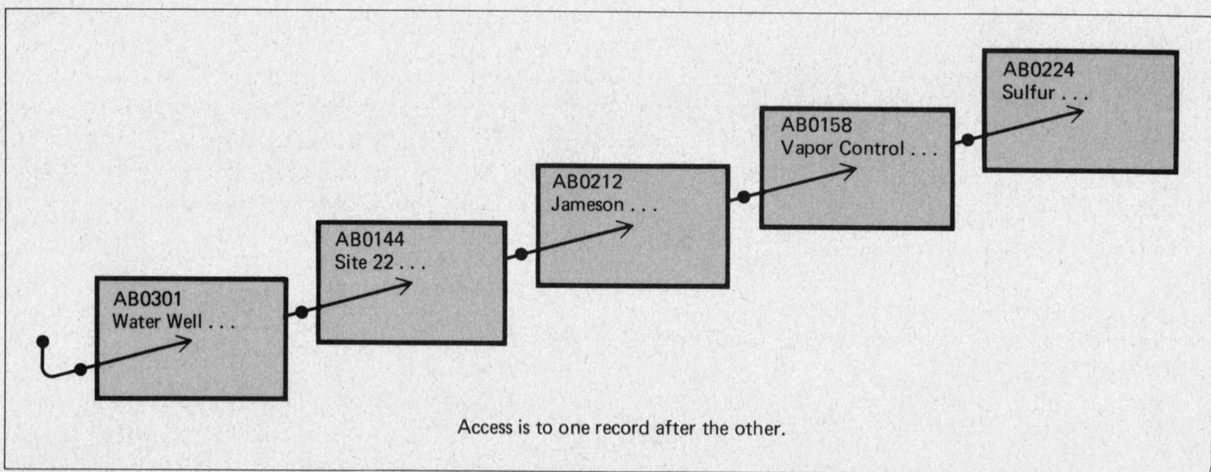

Figure P4-5
Sequential file access.

DBMS program must access records and print labels one after the other. One of the features of DBMS programs is that records can be processed in the order in which they were entered into the file (the physical sequence), or in sequence according to almost any field of the record. The processing action of printing the labels involves reading the record with the next higher ZIP code from disk into memory and then printing the address label.

Direct Processing

Sequential processing is one way of working with data in files. On the other hand, three of the examples at the beginning of this chapter involved obtaining information from a file for a particular record. For instance, in checking the inventory file to determine if you had 200 light-blue, Sunset-style jackets, you needed information from one record in the file. At that time, you had no interest in any other record in the file. Similarly, with the legislation file, if someone asked you for information on bill AB0224, you

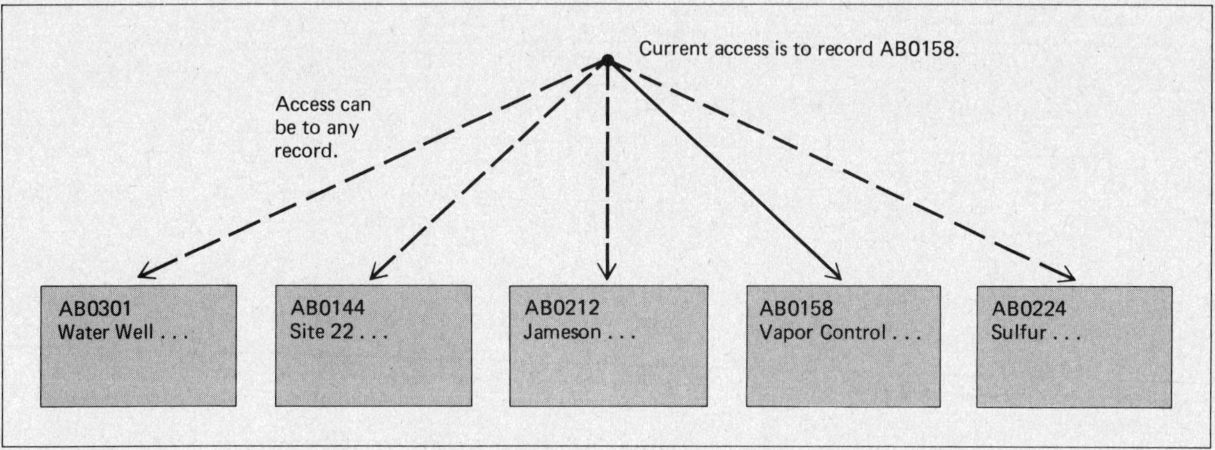

Figure P4-6
Direct file access.

would want to display the record for that bill. To obtain this, you would enter an appropriate command that would say, "Find the record with the bill number AB0224 and display it on the screen." This is called *direct processing* or **direct access** of the records in the file because it involves directly locating the single record in which you are interested. (It is also called **random** processing or access.) Direct access is illustrated by the diagram of Figure P4-6. In direct processing, the program accesses whichever record you request.

INDEXING

The sequence of records in a file can be changed by sorting them, but a better way is by indexing. Sorting changes the physical order of the records in a file. Using an index changes the **logical order** of the records in the file. That is, the physical order is unchanged but the order in which records are accessed by the DBMS program is changed as dictated by the index. Indexes serve two useful functions for file processing. First, they are vital to direct processing, the random accessing of records; and second, they make it possible to process records in the file in an order other than their physical order.

Using an index in everyday life is nothing new. For example, the directory in a large building is an index. It displays a list of the building's occupants in alphabetic order, not in room number order, and makes "direct access" of a particular occupant's room possible. To find the office of Dr. Hargrove, we would look up the name in the directory (index) and read the corresponding office number. Then we would go directly to that room. It is much faster to search the index than to search the building door by door looking for her name. Similarly, the index makes it possible to access a selected record from the file without searching the entire file in the same way that we use the directory in a building.

The indexing principle is illustrated in Figure P4-7, where we see a representation of two files: the data file and a corresponding index file that is based on the bill number. (In this example, a five-record file is used to

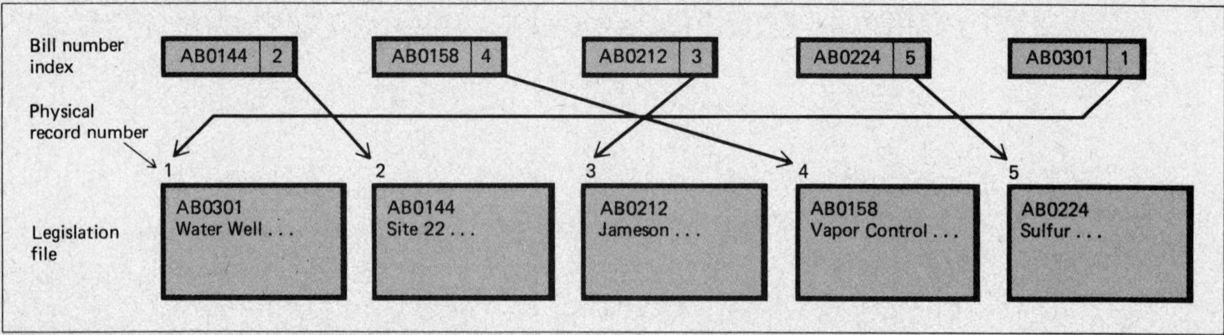

Figure P4-7
The relationship between a data file and an index file.

simplify the illustration.) Notice that each entry of the index file includes only two fields: the data value from the indexing field (bill number in this case) and the physical record number of the data record corresponding to that bill number. Each index entry is said to *point* to a record in the legislation file because it contains the physical record number of that record.

In using this index to access a selected record—for instance, the record for bill AB0224—the DBMS program would:

1. Find the entry in the index for AB0224.
2. Read the physical record number for AB0224, which is 5.
3. Obtain the fifth record from the Bill file.

This process is much faster and more efficient than searching the data file itself for two reasons. First, the index file entries are in sequence based on the index field. This sequence is maintained automatically by the DBMS program, even when records are added or changed, making it possible to use special search techniques that locate a desired record very quickly. Second, the index is much smaller than the data file so considerably less data must be handled during the search. Sometimes the index is sufficiently small that most or all of it can be kept in memory by the DBMS program during processing.

As you shall learn, indexing is central to most of the activities in Chapter 8.

NEW TERMINOLOGY

The following are important new terms introduced in this Introduction; you should be familiar with each of them now because you will be using them in chapters that follow.

character data type
database
database management system
date data type
direct access
field width
index
key field
logical data type
logical record order
numeric data type
random access
sequential access
unique

Chapter 7

Creating and Using dBASE III PLUS Data Files

OBJECTIVES

The introduction to Part Four has given you your first insight into how a DBMS can be used to assist you in managing data. In this chapter, you will use dBASE III PLUS to create the MCT customer file and add records to it. You will also use the Bills file that served as the basis for descriptions of the introduction. When you have completed this chapter, you should be able to:

- Create a new database data file by defining the record format.
- Make changes to the record format of your data file.
- Add records to a data file.
- Display on the screen or print the contents of a data file.
- Display on the screen or print the record format of a data file.
- Terminate a dBASE work session.
- Use the dBASE Assistant, a simplified menu form for carrying out dBASE operations.
- Make a copy of a data file from within dBASE.
- Sequentially access records in a data file.
- Directly access records in a data file.
- Edit records in a data file.
- Delete records from a data file.
- Permanently erase deleted records from a data file.

PREVIEW

Getting Started

The procedures to install and run dBASE and the initial screen display are described.

Creating a New dBASE File

Generating a new database data file is a two-step process in which the first step is defining the record format using the CREATE command. Following the examples of this section, you will define the record format for the Customer file.

Adding Records to a File

The second step in generating a new database data file is adding records to the file using the APPEND command. You will enter ten records to the Customer file.

Using the Assistant

dBASE includes a feature called the Assistant, which provides access to the many actions of dBASE commands through a menu system. You will use the Assistant to inspect the records of the file you have created.

Accessing and Changing Records in a File

The primary focus of this section is using the EDIT command to edit records in a file. You will edit all records in a file using sequential file access and edit selected records using direct access.

Deleting Records From a File

Records are deleted from a file with the DELETE command. Each deleted record is "marked" for deletion but not physically removed, and can be ignored during processing. Deleted records are physically removed with the PACK command.

The Browse Command

The BROWSE command provides the ability to display on the screen records of a file (inspect the data), to edit records, and to delete records.

GETTING STARTED

Since this chapter involves learning by doing, you will need DBMS software. If you have access to a copy of dBASE III, dBASE III PLUS, or dBASE IV, you can use it. If you do not, you can use the special Limited-Use

Educational version of dBASE III PLUS included with this book. The primary difference between the commercial and Limited-Use versions of dBASE III PLUS is that you can have no more than thirty records in a file with the Limited-Use version. If you will be using this version, then read the following section for setting up.

Setting Up for Using dBASE III PLUS (Limited-Use Version)

The Limited-Use version of dBASE III PLUS is stored on two disks that accompany this book:

dBASE III PLUS Sampler Demo Disk #1.

dBASE III PLUS Sampler Demo Disk #2.

Once installed, it can run on a computer with any of the following four computer configurations:

256K of memory and two floppy drives.

More than 256K of memory and two floppy drives.

256K of memory, one floppy drive, and one hard disk.

More than 256K of memory, one floppy drive, and one hard disk.

To run this version of dBASE III PLUS from a floppy-based computer, the system disk that you use to boot the computer must contain a special start-up file. Fortunately, the dBASE disk contains a program to write this file to a system disk that you use to boot the computer. (If you need to format a disk as a system disk, Chapter 1 describes how to create a DOS system disk.) Whether dBASE III PLUS is to run from a floppy or a hard disk, it is necessary to carry out the following installation procedure.

1. Boot the computer up with a normal DOS system disk.
2. Insert the dBASE III PLUS Demo Disk #1 into the A drive.
3. If you are using a floppy-based computer, insert the system disk that will normally be used into the B drive. This is not necessary if you are using a hard-disk-based system.
4. From the DOS A> prompt, type in the following command

   ```
   INSTALL
   ```

   and strike Enter.

The INSTALL program will give you instructions. When the process is completed, dBASE III PLUS will be ready for use. If you are using a hard disk computer, the install procedure will create a subdirectory named SAMPLER on the C drive. All the components of the dBASE software from the Demo Disks #1 and #2 will be copied to that subdirectory. You can use your data disk as is, or you can copy all of the data files to your hard disk. Note that these setup procedures need be carried out only once; it is not necessary to do so each time you use dBASE III PLUS.

Throughout the book, continual reference is made to dBASE III PLUS by name. In the interest of brevity, the word dBASE is used. In all cases, you should interpret dBASE to mean dBASE III PLUS, the software made available with this book. (Note that most of the descriptions and commands are equally applicable to the predecessor, dBASE III, as well as the successor dBASE IV.)

Running dBASE

Activating dBASE (or bringing the program up) involves a slightly different sequence for a floppy disk system than for a hard disk system.

Floppy Disk System

1. Insert the system disk in the A drive. Reboot the computer by holding down the Ctrl and Alt keys and pressing the Del key.
2. After the booting operation is complete and the A> prompt displayed, remove the system disk from the A drive and insert dBASE III PLUS Sampler Demo Disk #1.
3. Insert your data disk in the B drive.
4. From the DOS A> prompt, type the following command.

   ```
   DBASE
   ```

5. Press the Enter key.
6. After about 30 seconds, you will be prompted to remove Demo Disk #1 from the A drive, insert Demo Disk #2, and press the Enter key. Do so.

Hard Disk System

1. Change to the appropriate subdirectory by typing the following command sequence from the C> prompt.

   ```
   C:
   CD\SAMPLER
   ```

2. From the C:> DOS prompt, type the following command.

   ```
   DBASE
   ```

3. Press the Enter key.

When dBASE first loads, it will be in the ASSIST mode; to exit ASSIST, strike the Escape (Esc) key (you will learn about ASSIST later). The bottom of your screen will be as shown in Figure 7-1. The first of the last three lines on the screen is called the **status bar**; descriptions in this chapter will refer to it frequently. Note that the cursor is positioned following a period. The period is used as the dBASE prompt (much like the DOS prompt A>), and is commonly called the **dot prompt**. When using the Limited-Use version, the dot prompt will be preceded by (DEMO), as shown in Figure 7-1. At this point, dBASE is ready to accept a command.

If the entry on the status bar following the words Command Line is <B:>, then the system is ready to go. If it is not, then you must indicate to

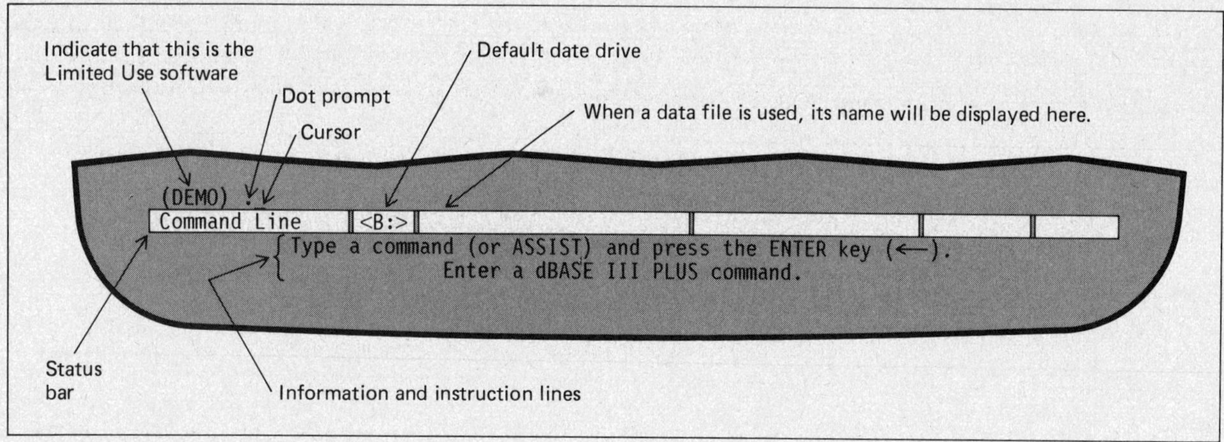

Figure 7-1
The dBASE III PLUS announcement screen.

dBASE the default location of the data disk. To this end, enter the following and strike the Enter key.

```
SET DEFAULT TO B
```

If you are using a hard disk computer, then use the letter of the drive where your data files are located (A if in the A drive and C if together with dBASE in the SAMPLER subdirectory).

dBASE Commands

dBASE is a DBMS: a programming system that allows us to manipulate files that make up a database. To that end, dBASE includes commands to perform a wide variety of operations on files. For instance, you will use dBASE commands to create a new data file (CREATE), add a new record to a file (APPEND), create an index (INDEX), and change the contents of a selected field in every record of a file (REPLACE). These commands (of which there are over 100) can be executed through a menu from the dBASE Assist mode (described later in this chapter), or from the dot prompt mode (Figure 7-1) by typing the command name and striking Enter.

Getting Help

Most quality software includes *on-line help* that provides the program user with instructions or explanations. For instance, assume that you cannot remember the form of the various options of the LIST command. You can obtain the description from information stored in a special file on the disk with the command HELP followed by the keyword for which you need help. (*Keywords* are words with special meaning to dBASE.) For instance, type the following from the dot prompt and strike Enter.

```
HELP LIST
```

The result will be the screen display of Figure 7-2. Here, you see a syntax description (the structure of a command is called its **syntax**) and a brief

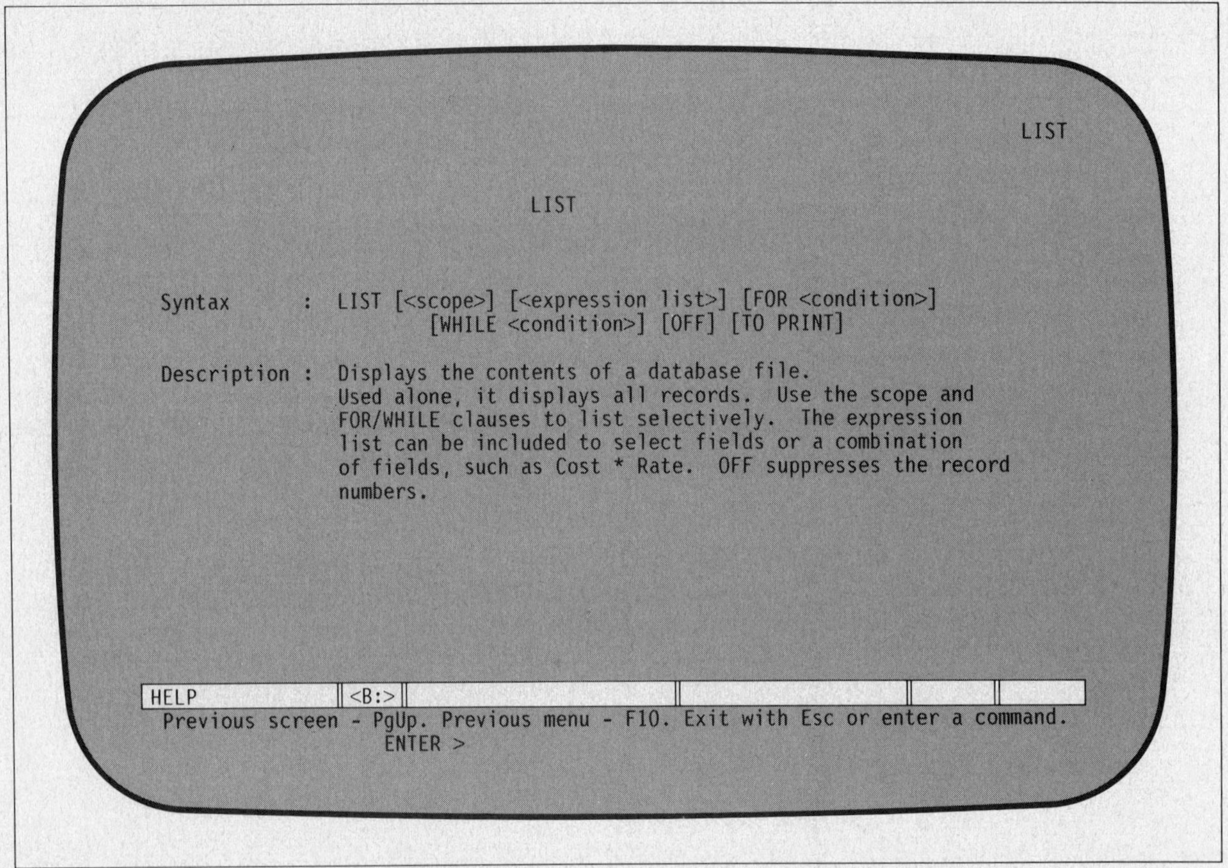

Figure 7-2
Description of the LIST command from Help.

description. Many of the dBASE commands have a variety of optional parameters that can be used. Each command is designated by an action word followed by its permissible options. The syntax convention uses both angle <> and square [] brackets. The angle brackets indicate that you must insert something (as described by the words enclosed in the brackets). The square brackets indicate an optional item. Words shown in uppercase must be typed exactly as shown if that portion of the command is used. Based on this syntax definition, the following examples of this command are valid.

```
LIST
LIST TO PRINT
LIST FOR BALANCE>LIMIT TO PRINT
```

Note that you must not type the angle or square brackets when entering a command. To return to the dot prompt from the Help, strike the Escape (Esc) key.

CREATING A NEW dBASE DATA FILE

To learn how to create and work with a new file, we will focus our attention on the Customer file of MCT Enterprises. We will assume that all of the planning and design has been completed and that you are ready to create the data file. The process of entering a new file requires two steps: (1) Create the data file, which involves defining each field of the record, and (2) Enter data records into the file.

Record Requirements

During the planning phase of creating a database application, details of each data file are spelled out. Assume that this task has been completed and that the exact record format of the Customer file is as summarized in Table 7-1.

Table 7-1 CUSTOMER File

Field Description	Field Name	Type	Length	Decimal Positions
Customer number	CUSTNUM	Character	5	
Sales region	REGION	Character	2	
Customer company name	COMPANY	Character	27	
Year-to-date sales	YTDSALES	Numeric	8	2
Current unpaid balance	BALANCE	Numeric	7	2
Date account opened (anniversary date)	ANNIV	Date	8	

As you can see, the record is relatively small, consisting of six fields requiring a total of 47 bytes. This is well within dBASE limits of 128 fields and 4000 bytes per record for a database file.

Field Names

As you know, each file stored on a disk is given a unique filename by which we can retrieve the file at any time. Similarly, within a database data file, each field must be given a name by which we can refer to that field. Each field name should be selected so that it describes the field that it represents, as illustrated by the names that have been selected in Table 7-1. As with DOS filenames, you must follow dBASE rules for field names.

- Names are limited to 10 characters. Note that this size restriction applies to the field *name*. It has nothing to do with the length of the data value that will be stored in that field.
- The first character must be a letter.
- Succeeding characters may be letters, digits, or the underscore character. You *cannot* use the hyphen.
- No two fields in a data file can have the same name. (The same name *can* be used in two different data files of a database.)

The underscore is commonly used to separate words as the space is not allowed. In that respect, an alternate to CUSTNUM would be CUST_NUM. (The underscore is used sparingly in this book *only* because it can easily disappear from view in various printed illustrations.)

Using the CREATE Command to Define the Record Format of a Data File

Your first exercise in this chapter is to create the CUSTOMER data file. If you do not have dBASE running on your computer, you should bring it up now. Do not forget to set the default data drive. If your screen shows the ASSIST mode, then switch to the dot prompt by striking the Esc key.

DO THIS NOW 7-1 **Creating a New Data File Named CUSTOMER**

1. From the dot prompt, type the following command and strike Enter.

```
CREATE CUSTOMER
```

This places dBASE in the field entry mode with the screen shown in Figure 7-3. Ignore the boxed area at the top of the screen for

Figure 7-3
The data file creation screen.

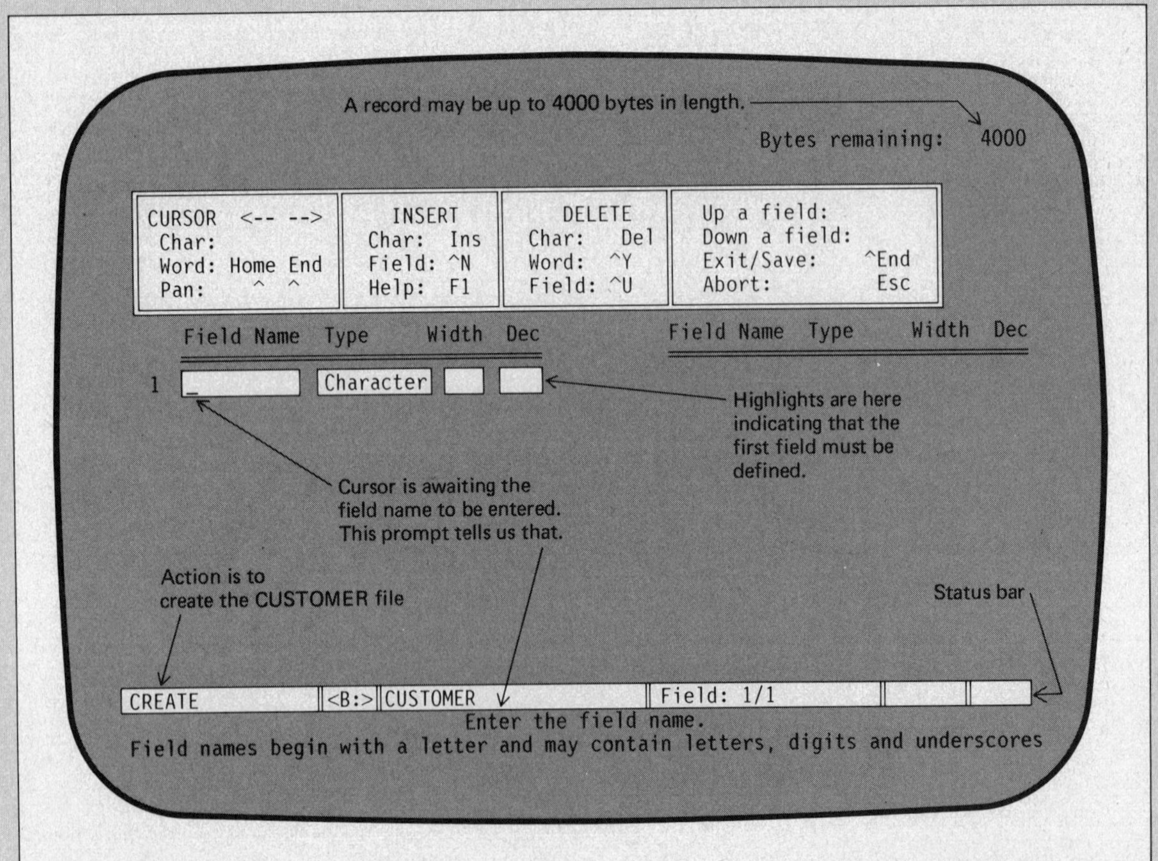

now; you will learn about it after you have entered the field definitions. The highlighted line is numbered 1. This line will define the first data field of the record, in this case, the customer number.

2. In entering the field definitions, you must use the record layout of Table 7-1. Type the name of the first field in the record, CUSTNUM, and then strike Enter; this portion of the screen will appear as shown below. (When typing a field name, it makes no difference whether uppercase or lowercase is used; the name is displayed in uppercase.)

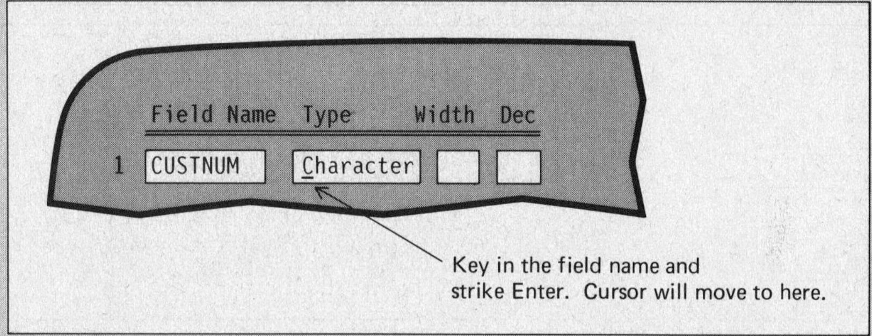

If, after completing an entry, you notice that you entered it incorrectly, do not worry, as you will learn how to make corrections when you have finished.

3. dBASE is waiting for you to enter the type of field that this will be. (Remember from the introduction to Part Four that fields can be character, numeric, date, or logical.) Since Character is offered as the default, strike Enter to accept it and the cursor will move to the Width highlight.

4. The width of the CUSTNUM field is 5 (see Table 7-1), so type the digit 5 as shown below.

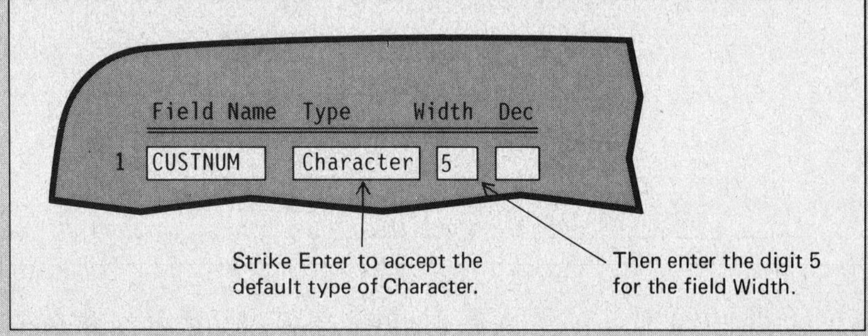

Notice that no attempt is made to position the number within the highlighted area. Knowing that this is a number, dBASE automatically positions it after you strike Enter.

5. Strike the Enter and this portion of your screen will appear as follows.

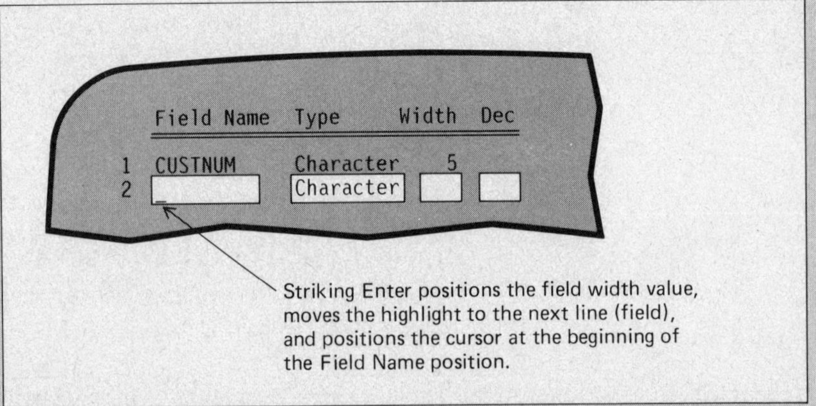

6. Enter the REGION and COMPANY fields in the same way as the CUSTNUM field.

7. The fourth field YTDSALES is numeric. For the Type entry, strike the letter *N*, which will cause Character to be replaced with Numeric. Then enter a width of 8 and strike Enter. Your screen will now appear as:

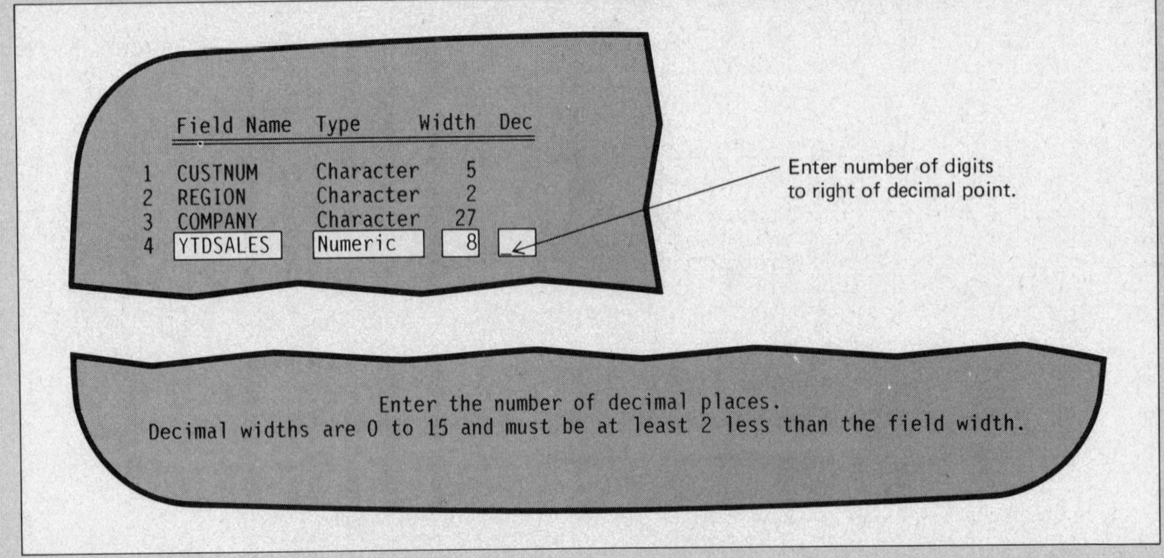

The cursor is awaiting your entry of the Dec (Decimals) value. Since this is to be a dollar and cent amount (two places to the right of the decimal), type 2 and strike Enter.

8. For field 5 of this record, enter the BALANCE field definition in the same way as YTDSALES.

9. The last field definition is the date the account was opened (ANNIV). Type the name, strike Enter, and then strike the letter *D* (for Date) for the Type. A value of 8 will be entered automatically for the Width and the highlight will progress to line 7.

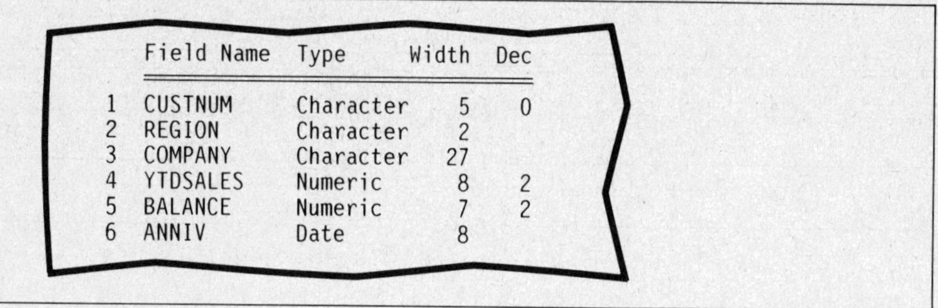

	Field Name	Type	Width	Dec
1	CUSTNUM	Character	5	0
2	REGION	Character	2	
3	COMPANY	Character	27	
4	YTDSALES	Numeric	8	2
5	BALANCE	Numeric	7	2
6	ANNIV	Date	8	

Figure 7-4
The completed record definition.

The completed record definition is shown in Figure 7-4. You should check your screen contents to be certain that your entries are correct. If you made an error while entering information, you can correct it easily as described next.

Making Changes to the Record Structure

The boxed areas in the upper portion of your screen (refer to Figure 7-3) is called a **Help** window and summarizes all of the key sequences to be used for editing record definitions. (If your screen does not display the boxed areas, then strike the F1 key; the display is toggled on and off with this key.) Most of the key actions for editing a file structure are described in Figure 7-5. To illustrate making corrections, assume the following.

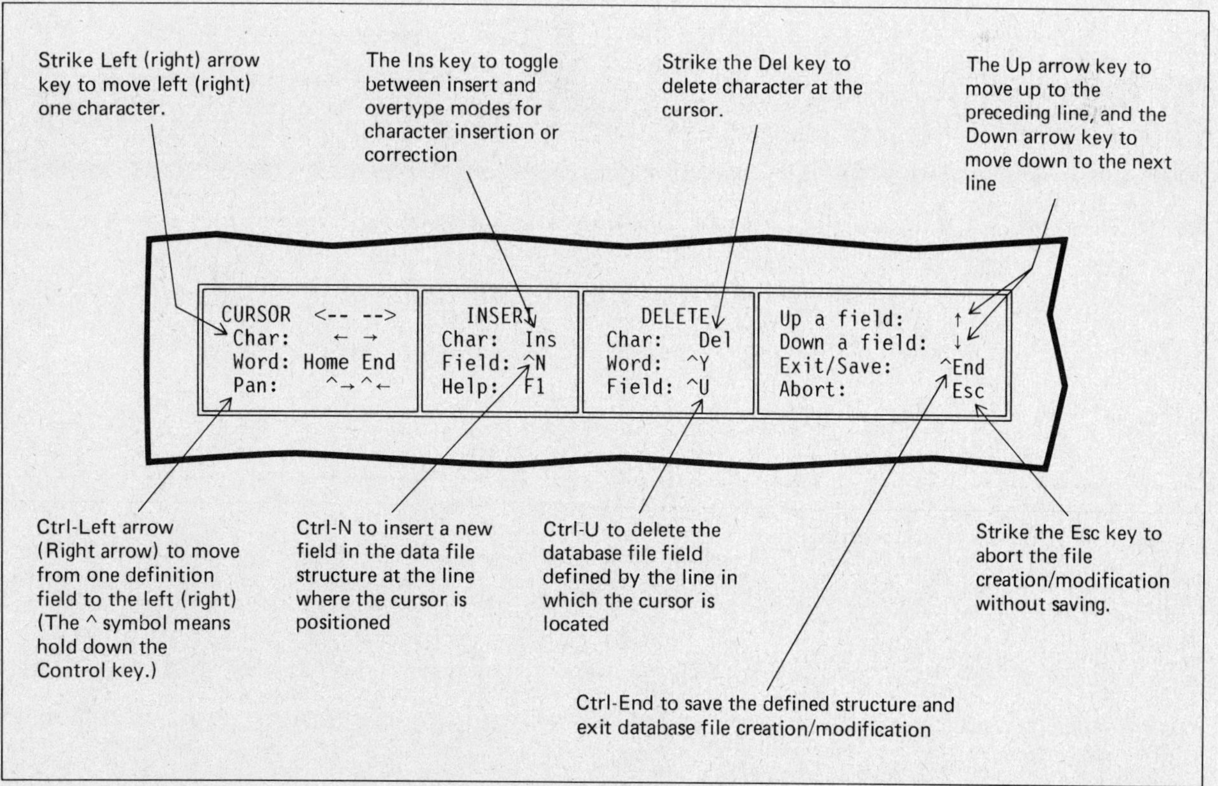

Figure 7-5
Editing actions of CREATE.

- The Field Name of the first field must be CUSTOMER rather than CUSTNUM.
- You entered the field REGION as numeric rather than character.
- You entered the length of the field COMPANY as 37 rather than 27.
- You forgot the BALANCE field.

Even if your record definition is correct, carry out the steps of the following example so that you will be familiar with the actions.

DO THIS NOW 7-2 **Changing a Record Definition**

1. Using the arrow keys, move the cursor to the Field Name entry of the first field (this will be CUSTNUM, if you entered it correctly). Position the cursor on the letter *N* in CUSTNUM.
2. Strike the Del key three times, leaving CUST.
3. Type OMER to make the name CUSTOMER, and then strike Enter. You have changed the name of this field. Now repeat the process and change it back to CUSTNUM.
4. Move the cursor to the Type definition of the REGION field using the arrow keys. The current definition is Character.
5. Change the field to Numeric (you will change it back after this) by striking the letter *N*. dBASE will make the change.
6. Change it back to Character by repositioning the cursor and striking the letter *C*.
7. Move the cursor to the Width entry for the third field COMPANY. Type 37 and strike Enter. Reposition the cursor and change it back to 27.
8. Move the cursor to line 5 (the BALANCE entry).
9. Delete this field definition with a Ctrl-U (hold down the Ctrl key and strike the letter *U*). The entries of line 5 (BALANCE) will be deleted and the ANNIV field will be moved into its place.

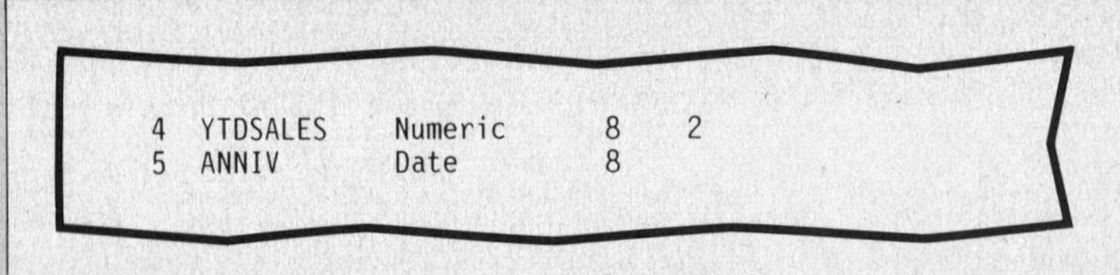

```
4  YTDSALES    Numeric     8   2
5  ANNIV       Date        8
```

10. You must now insert the BALANCE field to restore your record definition to its complete form. Enter the Ctrl-N sequence to

insert a new field. The ANNIV field will be moved down one line and line 5 will blank as shown below.

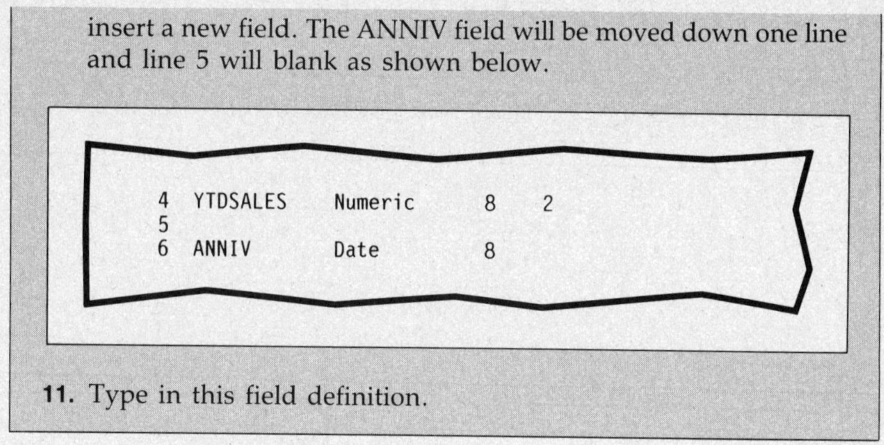

```
4  YTDSALES    Numeric    8   2
5
6  ANNIV       Date       8
```

11. Type in this field definition.

This completes the definition of our CUSTOMER data record structure.

Terminating a CREATE Session

There are two ways that you can end a CREATE session. If you decide at any time during the session that you do not wish to proceed and do not want any of your work saved, then strike the Esc key. dBASE will ask for a confirmation that you wish to abort. However, you will usually want to save your work and have dBASE complete the action by creating the empty data file you have defined.

DO THIS NOW 7-3 **Saving the File Definition and Exiting CREATE**

1. Enter the Ctrl-End sequence (hold down the Control key and strike the End key). In response, dBASE displays the following message.

   ```
   Strike ENTER to confirm.  Any other key to resume.
   ```

2. If, upon reflecting, you realize that you are not finished, strike any key (for instance, the space bar) and the exit will be aborted. You can then continue entering or editing field definitions.
3. Since you are finished, strike Enter. This will cause dBASE to write a new, empty file to disk. When the action is complete, the following prompt is displayed.

   ```
   Input data records now? (Y/N)
   ```

4. At this point, you could proceed to enter data into the file (respond with Y) or return to the dot prompt (respond with N or any other key). Return to the dot prompt by striking the letter *N*.

When this action is complete, your data disk will contain the data file CUSTOMER.DBF. Notice that dBASE automatically adds the extension DBF (meaning database file).

ADDING RECORDS TO A FILE

The Contents of a Data File

The contents of your newly created file CUSTOMER.DBF are illustrated in Figure 7-6(a). In addition to the defining information about this data file, it includes a special "marker" called an EOF, meaning end of file. As records are entered, dBASE moves the EOF so that it is always positioned after the last record; Figure 7-6(b) illustrates a file containing two records. The EOF is always positioned to indicate to dBASE the physical end of the file. The process of adding records is called *appending* and is done with the dBASE APPEND command.

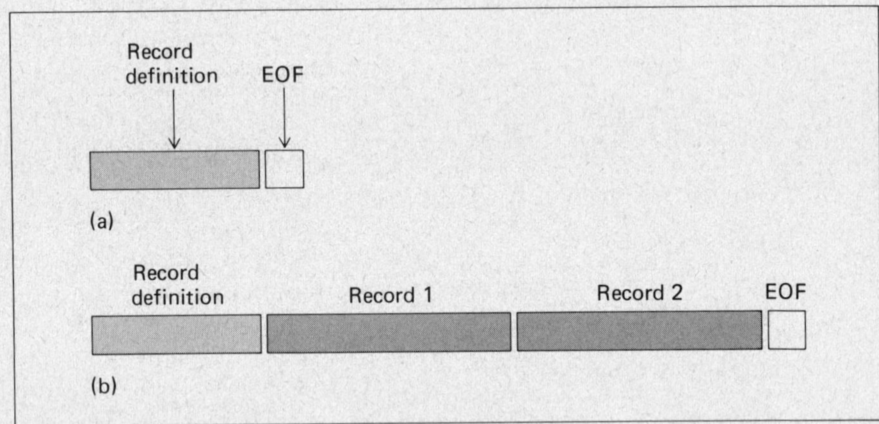

Figure 7-6
(a) An empty data file.
(b) Two records in a data file.

The USE Command

In using WordPerfect and 1-2-3 in the earlier chapters, you accumulated word processing and spreadsheet files on your data disk. To work with one of them, you first had to retrieve it from disk. Somewhat the same is true of working with a dBASE data file. You must first designate to dBASE the name of the file that you want. This is called *opening* the file; it causes dBASE to find the file on the disk and set aside memory for making records available to you. The dBASE command to open a file is USE followed by the filename:

```
USE CUSTOMER
```

Notice that the extension DBF need not be included because dBASE assumes DBF as a default in the same way that Lotus 1-2-3 uses a default of WKS (or WK1). Once opened, the file remains open until it is closed by opening another file, by entering a USE command without a data filename (USE by itself), or by terminating processing with the QUIT. The QUIT is described later in this chapter.

The APPEND Command

You can enter records using the APPEND command at any time whether the file is empty or already contains records. For this data file, you are to enter the ten records shown in Figure 7-7. (This is a listing of the CUSTOMER file that was entered during the writing of this book.) First, you will enter the first two records and terminate the append. Then you will issue the APPEND command again and enter the rest of the records.

Figure 7-7
Input data for CUSTOMER file.

Record#	CUSTNUM	REGION	COMPANY	YTDSALES	BALANCE	ANNIV
1	13069	12	ABC Retail Outlet	12633.70	248.88	06/13/86
2	12573	23	Boardwalk Sportswear Sales	8003.46	1280.22	06/24/86
3	12626	12	Mr. Casual, Limited	8933.48	0.00	08/19/87
4	11882	37	Harlicorn Operations	1012.66	1012.66	06/06/89
5	12292	23	Coast Concepts	5990.86	0.00	06/12/87
6	13312	37	Paradise Leisure Clothing	14889.83	2701.73	04/22/86
7	12272	12	Grand Times	7932.82	876.33	02/28/88
8	13189	37	Crow Canyon Casual Wear	19833.22	2912.29	03/28/86
9	13117	23	Blue Ridge Sport & Casual	1788.29	448.98	09/22/87
10	12217	12	Falcon Ridges Enterprises	5880.10	0.00	04/02/86

Indicates the order in which the records are to be entered

DO THIS NOW 7-4 **Appending the First Two Data Records to the CUSTOMER File**

1. Open the CUSTOMER file with the command:

```
USE CUSTOMER
```

The file CUSTOMER is now available for use. Note that, in this instance, the USE was not necessary because, when the CREATE was completed, dBASE had left this file open. However, this is the general sequence that you will use; you will create a given file once but you will use it many times.

2. From the dot prompt, you must issue the APPEND command by typing

```
APPEND
```

and striking Enter. You will be presented with the entry screen of Figure 7-8. At the top of the screen is a record number counter

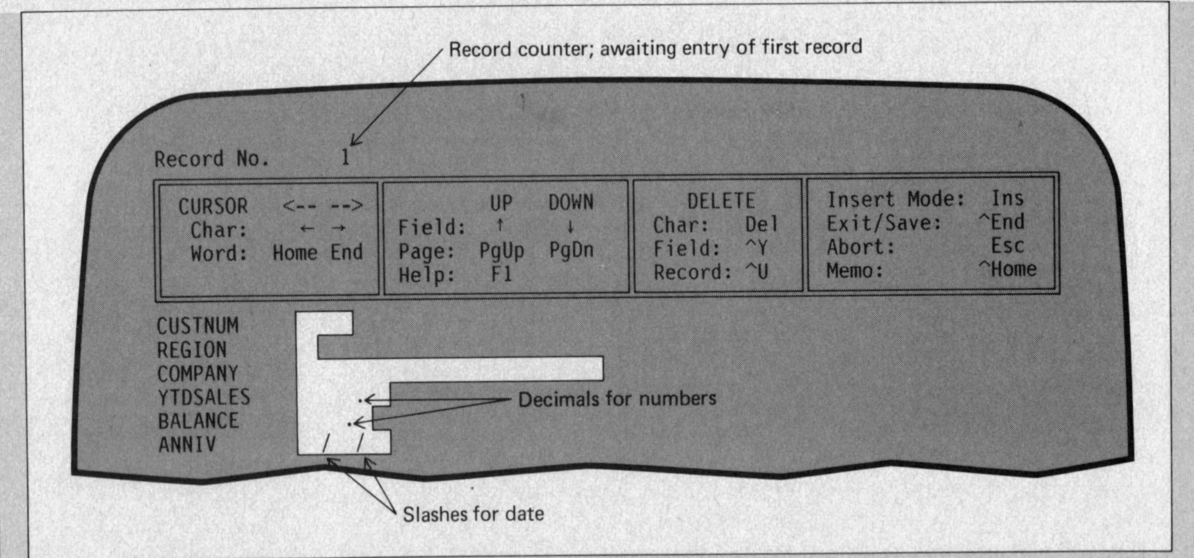

Figure 7-8
Data entry screen.

indicating that dBASE is awaiting entry of record number 1. Notice that the fields are listed in the same order as they are defined in the record. Furthermore, the highlighted area designates the space allocated for each field. The boxed display describing keystroke actions is similar to that of the CREATE screen (Figure 7-3). If you want to get rid of it, strike the F1 key.

3. Type the customer number for the first record (13069). dBASE will cause your computer to beep, indicating that the field is full. Strike Enter to progress to the next field.

4. Enter the values for REGION and COMPANY in the same way.

5. For the YTDSALES field, attempt to enter a letter and notice what happens. Then enter the correct values for both YTDSALES and BALANCE (from Figure 7-7).

6. Make an incorrect entry of 16/13/86 for the year. As you enter the digits, notice that the cursor jumps over the slashes. When you strike Enter, an error message will be displayed. Strike any key to continue. Type the correct entry over the incorrect one; do not strike the Enter key when you finish. Your screen should appear as shown below.

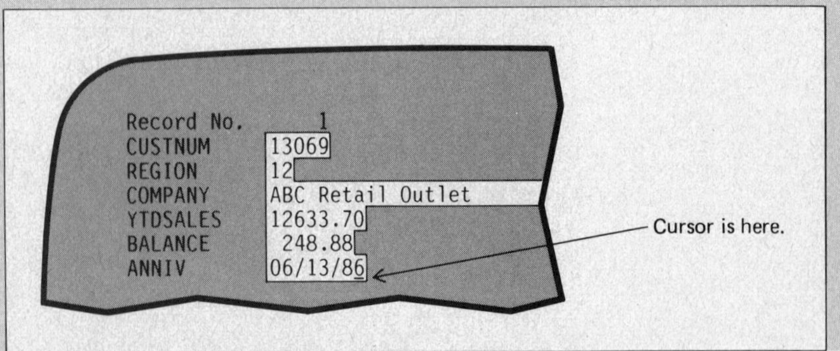

7. If you have any errors, correct them by using the arrow keys to move the cursor (the same methods you used in correcting the record definition in DTN 7-2).

8. If you have moved the cursor to another field entry, move it back to the ANNIV field (the last one) and strike Enter. The highlighted data entry portion of the screen will be cleared and the record number will be increased to 2.

9. Type the values for the fields of the second record in the same way you typed the first. However, since you wish to terminate after this record, *do not strike Enter after typing the date.*

10. With record number 2 still on the screen, use the Ctrl-End key sequence (hold down the Ctrl key and strike the End key). This saves the newly entered record *and* terminates the APPEND mode, returning control to the dot prompt.

When entering a number of records, striking Enter after each field is almost automatic. If you strike Enter after the last field of the last record, then a blank screen appears. *Do not use Ctrl-End at this point.* If you do, a blank record will be written to the file. You can avoid having a blank record added to your file by striking the Escape key to abort the append. Then the append operation will be terminated without the blank screen being saved to disk as a blank record.

Changing the Environment and Continuing Data Entry

As you entered data, dBASE beeped when any field became full. Some people find this distracting; it is especially annoying if a number of people are working with APPEND. There are various working environment parameters that dBASE allows you to change. This is done with the SET command. You have already used this command to set the default data drive to B (if you are using a floppy disk computer). You can also use it to turn the beep (called the bell in dBASE) off by typing the following command from the dot prompt.

```
SET BELL OFF
```

To turn it back on, use the word ON instead of OFF. You may turn it off or leave it on, whichever you desire; it has no effect on the entry of the data. You must now enter the rest of the data records.

DO THIS NOW 7-5 **Entering the Rest of the Data Records From Figure 7-7**

1. Return to the APPEND mode by typing the command:

```
APPEND
```

You should be presented with the data entry screen of Figure 7-8; the record number should be 3. If it is 4, you have entered a blank record into the file. To fix that, strike the PgUp key and the record counter will be reduced to 3.

2. Enter the data for each of the remaining records listed in Figure 7-7. Remember to use Ctrl-End, *not* Enter, after the last field of the last record.

FINISHING UP

Listing the Contents of a File

Before terminating this session, you might want to display or print a copy of your work; this is done with the LIST command. To get a complete display of your data file, you must type

```
LIST
```

from the dot prompt and strike Enter. dBASE will display the records of your file as shown in Figure 7-7. Notice that the field names are used for column headings and the physical record number is printed. If you do not want the record number, use the OFF option with list; that is:

```
LIST OFF
```

If your record is so large that not all of the fields will fit on a single line, you might want to list selected fields. For instance, LIST followed by the word FIELDS and a list of fields (called the *expression list* in the general form of Figure 7-2) could take the following form.

```
LIST FIELDS CUSTNUM, COMPANY, BALANCE
```

This will produce a display consisting only of the listed fields from the records of the file. (Note: You can omit the word FIELDS.)

If you have a printer attached to your computer and would like a printed copy, then use the TO PRINT option of the command and enter it as:

```
LIST TO PRINT
```

Your file contents will be printed to the printer and also displayed on the screen.

Listing the Structure of a Data File

When working with a data file, you will occasionally need to check the record format. You can get this with the following variation of the LIST:

```
LIST STRUCTURE
```

or

```
LIST STRUCTURE TO PRINT
```

The display (or printout) will be as shown in Figure 7-9. One thing to notice about this display is that the sum of the field widths is 57 but the total given is 58. This number will always be one higher than the sum of the field widths because dBASE adds an extra position for its own use.

You probably noticed that your listings caused the contents of the screen to scroll upward, leaving the previous display on the upper half of

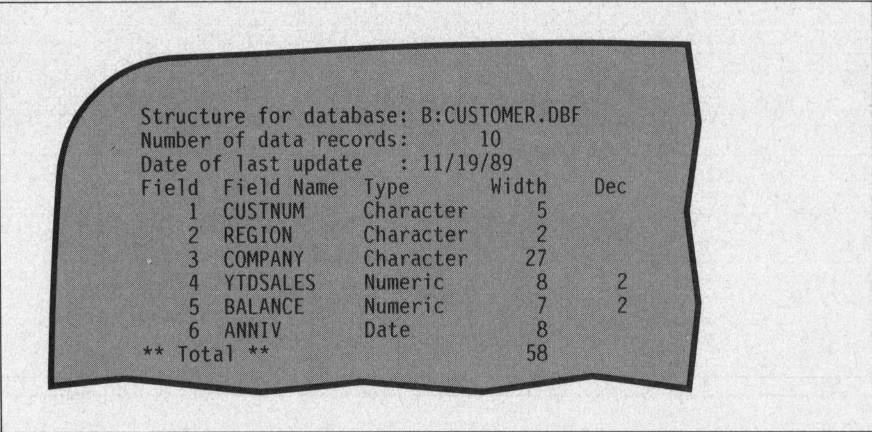

```
Structure for database: B:CUSTOMER.DBF
Number of data records:       10
Date of last update   : 11/19/89
Field  Field Name  Type       Width    Dec
    1  CUSTNUM     Character      5
    2  REGION      Character      2
    3  COMPANY     Character     27
    4  YTDSALES    Numeric        8      2
    5  BALANCE     Numeric        7      2
    6  ANNIV       Date           8
** Total **                      58
```

Figure 7-9
Structure of CUSTOMER.

the screen and yours on the lower half. The CLEAR command will remedy this; just type CLEAR and strike Enter to clear the screen and position the cursor at the upper left screen position. Then enter the LIST or LIST STRUCTURE command.

Terminating a dBASE Work Session

As with WordPerfect and 1-2-3, a work session must be ended by terminating execution of the dBASE program. This will ensure that everything needed for your data file is properly stored on disk.

DO THIS NOW 7-6 **Terminating the Work Session**

1. Terminate by typing, from the dot prompt, the command

```
QUIT
```

and striking Enter. You will be returned to the DOS prompt.

You will recall from WordPerfect and 1-2-3 that before terminating the program you saved your latest work because all additions or changes during the session are in memory, not on disk. With dBASE, as each record is entered during the APPEND (or during editing, which you will do later), it is written to disk. When you terminate execution of the dBASE program, dBASE saves to the file a count of the number of records in the file and then closes it.

Assignment 7-1 may now be completed.

USING ASSIST

When you first bring dBASE up, you are presented with the ASSIST screen shown in Figure 7-10. (You got out of this by striking the Esc key.) The purpose of ASSIST is to provide the occasional user with easy access to all commands and their forms through a menu system; the dot prompt mode

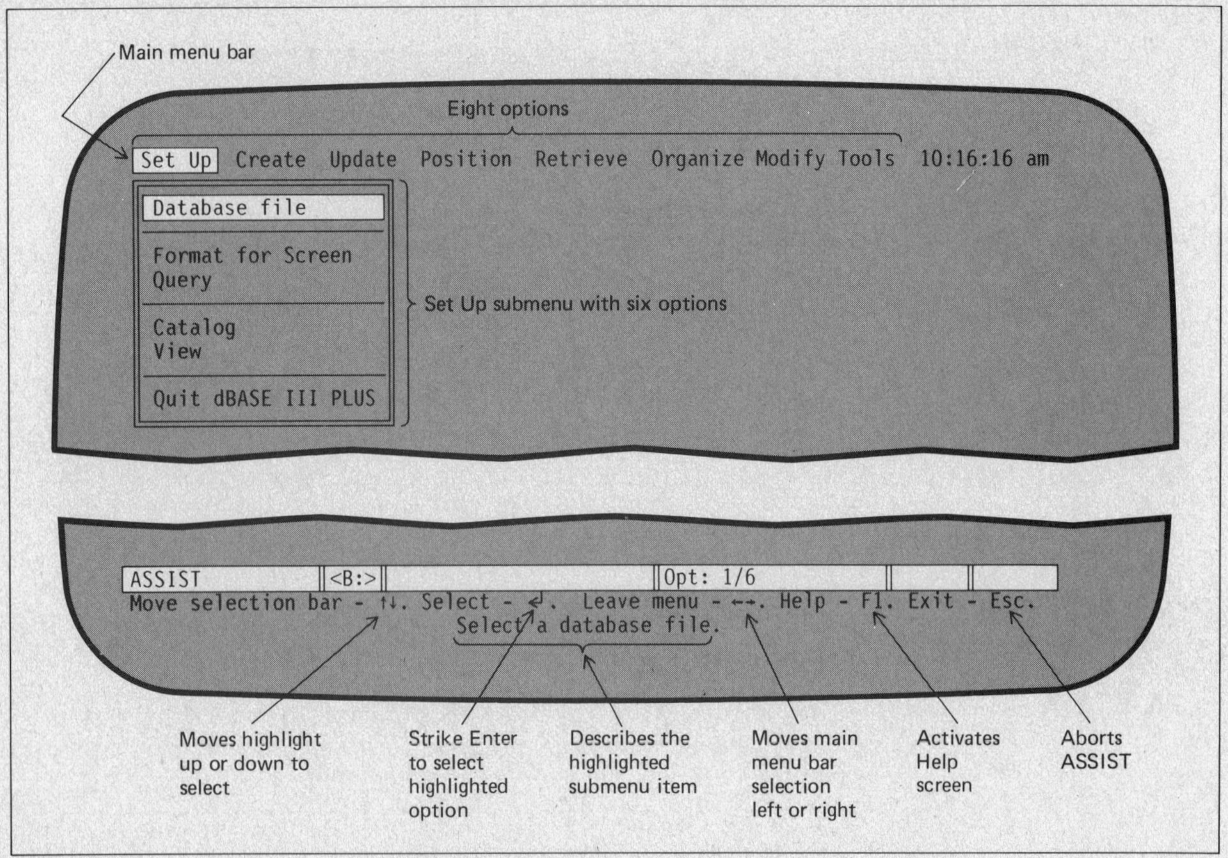

Figure 7-10
The ASSIST screen.

is not used. Some people prefer ASSIST; others consider it clumsy and prefer working from the dot prompt. In this section, you will learn how to open a file (USE) and to list selected fields using ASSIST. To activate ASSIST, it is only necessary to type in the ASSIST command and then press Enter.

Menus

Across the top of the screen is a *bar menu,* which represents the first-level options. The highlighted entry (*Set Up,* in this case) is the currently selected menu item. Directly beneath is the *Set Up* submenu; it includes six options. At the bottom of the screen are three lines. The first is a general information line; you will see how its contents change as you use ASSIST. The second describes the actions you can take regarding selecting a menu item or switching to another menu. The third line is a brief description of the nature of the highlighted menu option.

In general, the four arrow keys are used to "navigate" the menu structure. At the main bar menu level, the left and right arrows move the highlight to the adjacent menu option. The up and down arrows move the highlight up or down in a submenu. For instance, if you were to press the down arrow key one time, the highlight would move from *Database File* to *Format for Screen* (Figure 7-10).

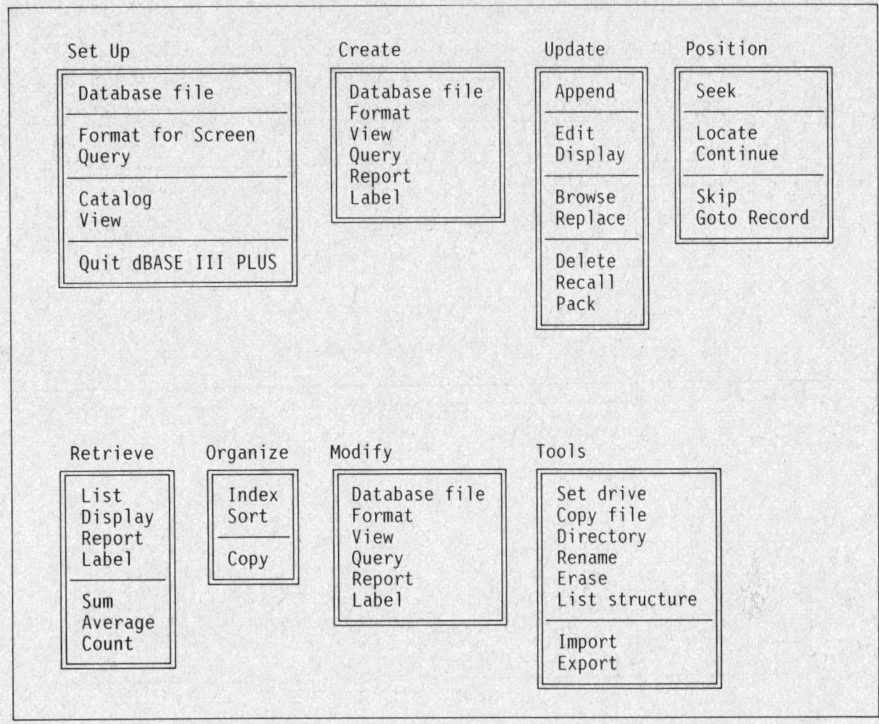

Figure 7-11
The ASSIST submenus.

As the highlight is moved across the main menu bar with the right (or left) arrow key, dBASE displays successive submenus on the screen. Their appearance is similar to that of the *Set Up* submenu shown in Figure 7-10. Figure 7-11 shows each of these. These are the dBASE commands that you can execute from ASSIST. For instance, under *Create* you can create a *Database* file. If you were to select this, you would be placed in the create mode exactly as if you typed the CREATE command from the dot prompt. Similarly, the *List* option of the *Retrieve* submenu represents the LIST command.

Opening the Data File and Listing Records with ASSIST

To illustrate using ASSIST, let us perform the equivalent of the dot prompt command sequence of opening the CUSTOMER file and listing part of its contents.

DO THIS NOW 7-7 **Using ASSIST**

Execute the following command sequence from ASSIST:

```
USE CUSTOMER
LIST CUSTNUM, COMPANY, BALANCE
```

1. Your first action, opening the database data file, is done from the *Set Up* option of the main menu (Figure 7-10). Here, you see that the currently highlighted items allow you to select a database (the bottom line of the screen). To make this selection, strike Enter, which produces the following display. Notice the next to the last

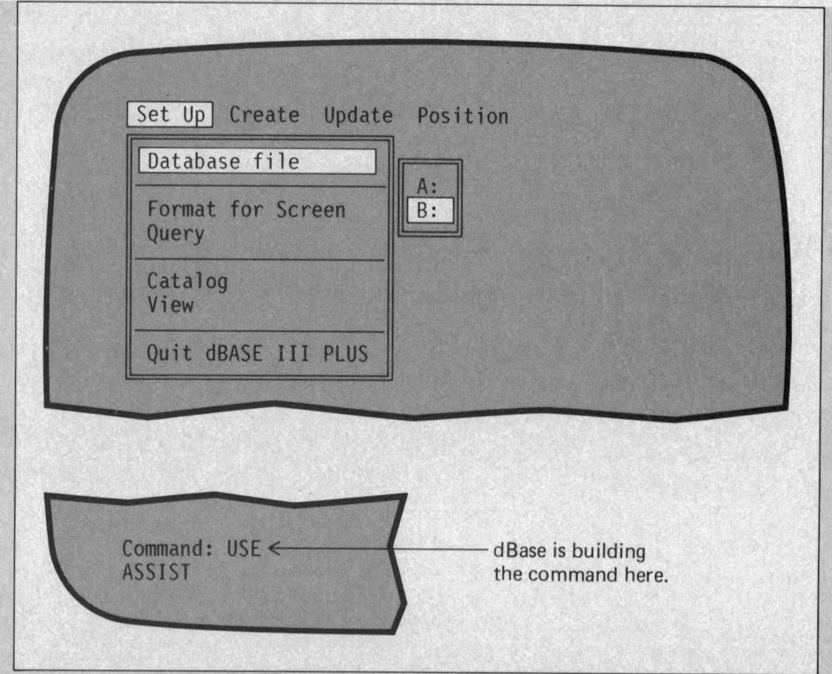

line of the display entitled *Command;* ASSIST is "building" the USE command (necessary to open the file).

2. Select the disk drive that contains the desired file by moving the highlight to it and striking Enter. (The drive highlighted by ASSIST is always the default drive.) dBASE will then display a list of data files on your disk as follows (notice in your display that the *Command* line now shows the partial command as USE B:)

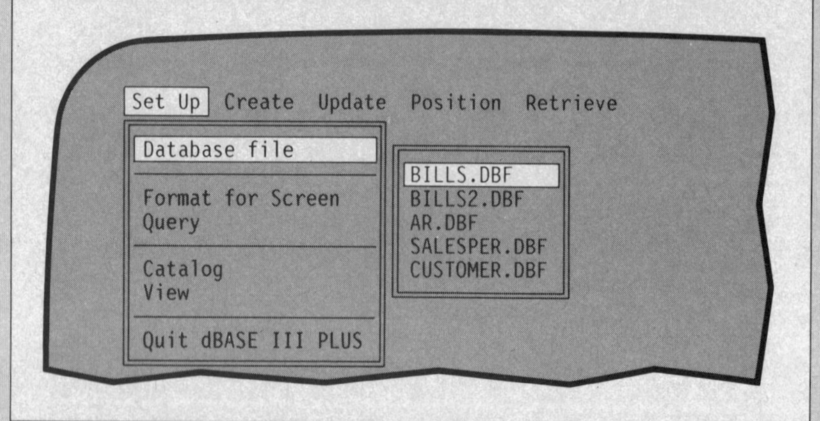

3. To select the CUSTOMER file, use the down arrow key and move the highlight with CUSTOMER.DBF, and then strike Enter. The command at the bottom of the screen will now be

```
USE B:CUSTOMER
```

The query

```
Is the file indexed? [Y/N]
```

is also displayed.

4. If you wanted to use an index with this file (indexing is described in the next chapter), then you would respond with Y and be presented with a list of index files. Since you do not intend to use an index with this file, type the letter *N*. ASSIST will execute the USE command as if you had entered it from the keyboard and the screen display will return to that of Figure 7-10. You can now proceed to build the LIST command.

When "building" a command from ASSIST, be careful to make the proper selections because *it is not possible to undo a mistake*. Had the wrong file been selected in the preceding step, its name would have been appended to the USE command. The only way to correct such an error is to press the Escape and start over again.

5. Referring to Figure 7-11, we see that the List is a subcommand under Retrieve. Move the main menu bar selection to *Retrieve* with the right arrow key. This produces the following submenu.

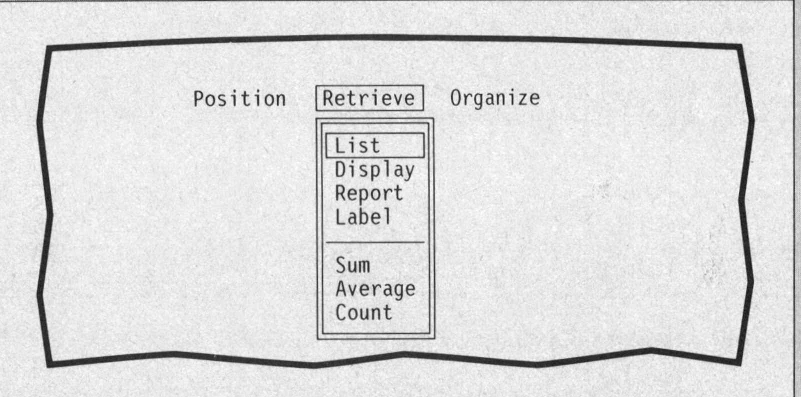

6. Since *List* is already highlighted, select it by striking Enter. This produces the following set of actions that can be taken under the List.

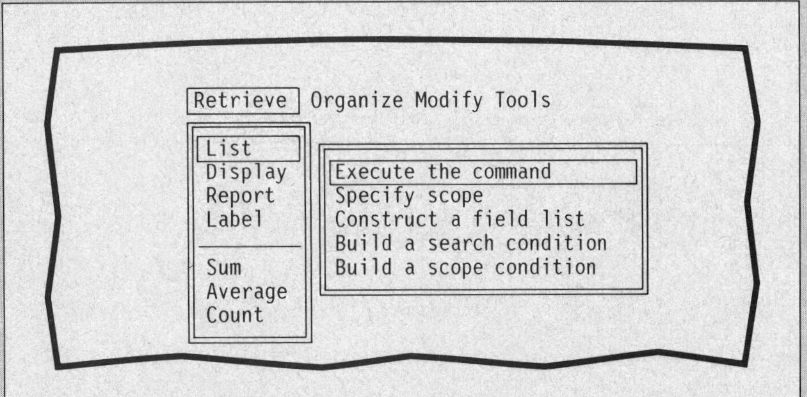

7. You must now designate the fields that you want listed. Do this by moving the highlight to the *Construct a field list* option and striking Enter. One of the convenient aspects of ASSIST is that it displays the fields that make up the database file, as you can see here (and on your screen). Furthermore, details of the highlighted field are also displayed.

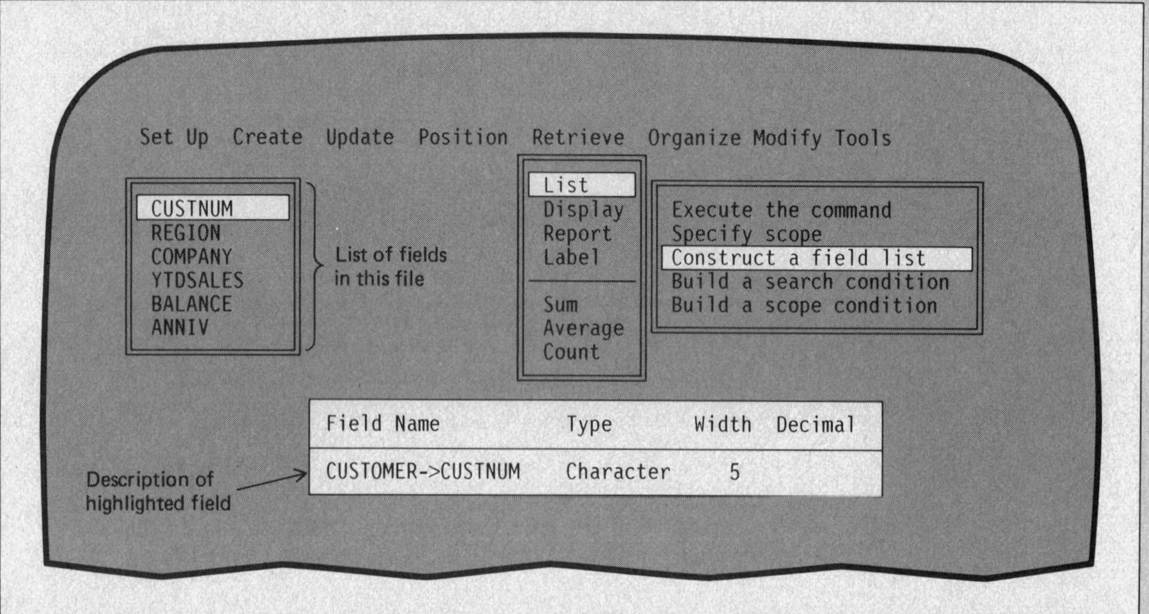

8. Since the CUSTNUM field is highlighted, select it for listing by striking Enter. This will cause the highlight to move to the next field (REGION), the display of the name CUSTNUM in the field list to be changed so that you can tell it has been selected, and CUSTNUM to be added to the command. The *Command* line will now be:

```
LIST CUSTNUM
```

9. Move the cursor to COMPANY with the Down key. Be careful not to strike Enter for fields you do not want. Once one is selected, it cannot be removed. Select COMPANY, and then BALANCE. Your *Command* line will now be:

```
LIST CUSTNUM, COMPANY, BALANCE
```

10. To exit this field selection mode, strike the Right key (see the prompt on the message line at the bottom of the screen). This returns control to the List submenu of Step 7.

11. The command is now complete and you may execute it. Move the selection to the *Execute the command* option and strike Enter. You will be asked if you want your output printed. Respond with Y if you do and with N if you do not.

12. When the listing is complete, strike any key and the ASSIST menu is redisplayed.

13. Terminate ASSIST by striking the Escape key.

For someone using dBASE on a regular basis, ASSIST is slow and somewhat clumsy. However, for the infrequent user, it does offer some advantages. If you find it helpful, then use it. If you are comfortable with the dot prompt, then continue typing your commands.

ACCESSING AND CHANGING RECORDS IN A FILE

In the introduction to Part Four, you learned about the principles of DBMSs using a legislative bill application as an example database. One of the example files, BILLS.DBF, is included on the data disk that accompanies this book and will be used to illustrate the remainder of the topics in this chapter. If you followed the instructions of Chapter 1 for preparing your data disk, then you should have a copy of it on your data disk. For convenient reference, a listing of the records in this file is shown in Figure 7-12. (The printed listing has been edited so that it would fit on a page.) This is identical to the listing of Figure P4-4 except that the logical field RECOMMEND values are displayed as .T. (meaning true or yes) and .F. (meaning false or no); dBASE displays logical data in this way.

Making a Copy of a Data File

Three of the next dBASE commands that you will be learning in this chapter change the contents of data in the files. You will be making these changes to the BILLS file. (You may also wish to experiment with CUSTOMER or with other files that you create.) So that you do not destroy

```
Record#                                                  REGION RECOMMEND
    BILL   TITLE                          AUTHOR       TYPE   RATING  COMMITTEE APPROVED

  1  AB0301 Water Well Restrictions        Lukenbill, C  W  9   84 .T. 04/12/90   /  /
  2  AB0144 Site 22 Solid Waste Disposal   Smith, H      G  1   62 .F. 05/09/90   /  /
  3  AB0212 Jameson Quarry Restrictions    Johnson, W    G  3   87 .T. 04/23/90   /  /
  4  AB0158 Vapor Control of Paint Prod.   Johnson, W    A  9   94 .T. 04/28/90 08/08/90
  5  AB0224 Sulphur Emissions              Lukenbill, C  A  4   80 .T. 05/01/90   /  /
  6  AB1001 River Waste Discharge          Smith, H      W  9   73 .F. 05/28/90   /  /
  7  AB0197 Index River Dam Construction   Lukenbill, C  W  5   91 .T. 04/17/90 09/06/90
  8  AB1092 Smog Control - Inverness Basin Johnson, W    A  3   79 .F. 06/22/90   /  /
```

Figure 7-12
The BILLS file listing.

data that you want to keep, you should make a copy and use the copy. You can do this with the DOS COPY command or from dBASE using the dBASE COPY TO command.

DO THIS NOW 7-8 **Making a Copy of the Data File BILLS.DBF**

1. From the dBASE dot prompt, enter the following command.

```
USE BILLS
```

2. With the dBASE COPY TO command, make a copy of BILLS (the open file) and call it BILLS9:

```
COPY TO BILLS9
```

If there is already a copy of BILLS9 on your disk (the result of a previous COPY command), you will get a warning message. Tell dBASE to replace it with the new copy.

3. Open the new file BILLS9:

```
USE BILLS9
```

The action of the COPY TO command is to create a new file on disk from records in the currently open file. As you will learn in the next chapter, you can copy all or part of the fields of the file and all or part of the records in the file. Notice that, in this example, the file duplicate has been named BILLS9.DBF; you should adopt some type of naming convention so that you can easily recognize such copies when you want to delete unwanted files from your disk. Whenever you create the copy for experimenting, do not forget to open it with a USE command; remember, opening a new file also closes the one previously open (BILLS in this case).

Accessing Records

When you open a data file with a USE command, dBASE does the following.

1. Reserves an area of memory into which records from disk can be placed during processing; this is called a **record buffer.**
2. Reads the first record from the file, places it in the buffer, and makes it available to you. The record available to you at any time is called the **current record.**
3. Displays on the status bar (as shown in Figure 7-13) the name of the file, which record is the current record, and the number of the records in the file.

At any given time, dBASE gives you access to one record from the file. In the introduction to Part Four, you learned about the two methods of accessing data from a file: sequential access and direct access. With sequential access, records are read one after the other in the order in which they

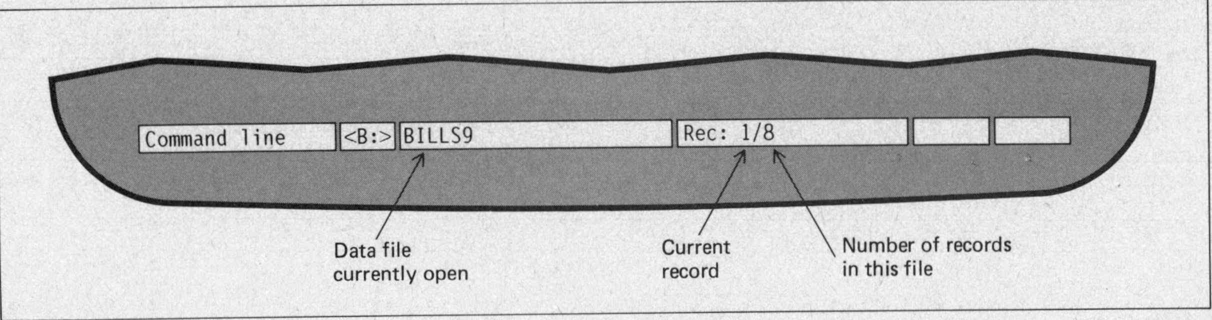

Figure 7-13
The status bar.

are stored in the file (or as indicated by an index). With direct access, a single record is accessed without regard to which record was accessed previously or where in the file it is located. The LIST command is a sequential access command because it begins with the first record in the file, and then reads and displays the records one after the other. You may have noticed on your status bar after you listed CUSTOMER that the record number indicator displayed EOF/10. dBASE was telling you that it had reached the end of the file and that the current "record" was the EOF.

One way to change the current record is with the GOTO command. With it, you can make any record in the file the current record. For instance, if you wanted to make physical record 5 the current record, you could do it with the command:

```
GOTO 5
```

Try this and you will see the current record number on the status bar change. In addition to positioning the pointer by designating a record number, it is possible to position it to the first or the last data record available. (As you will learn in the next chapter, these will not necessarily be the first and last physical records of the file when an index is used.) These GOTO forms are:

```
GOTO TOP
GOTO BOTTOM
```

The TOP causes dBASE to position to the first record of the file, and the BOTTOM to the last.

Let us now consider the EDIT command to make changes to records in a data file. With this command, you can access records for editing either sequentially or directly.

The EDIT Command

Changing the contents of a record is done via a screen that is identical to the data entry screen (see Figure 7-8 for the CUSTOMER data entry screen). To illustrate, assume that the values for RATING in BILLS9 must be increased by three for all records except records 6 and 8 (bills AB1001 and AB1092). For this, you will need to process records of the file sequentially.

DO THIS NOW 7-9 **Editing BILL9 to Increase the RATING Field Values by 3**

1. If record 1 is not the current record (check the status bar), then go to the top of the file with the command:

```
GOTO TOP
```

2. Issue the EDIT command:

```
EDIT
```

The resulting screen display will be as shown in Figure 7-14.

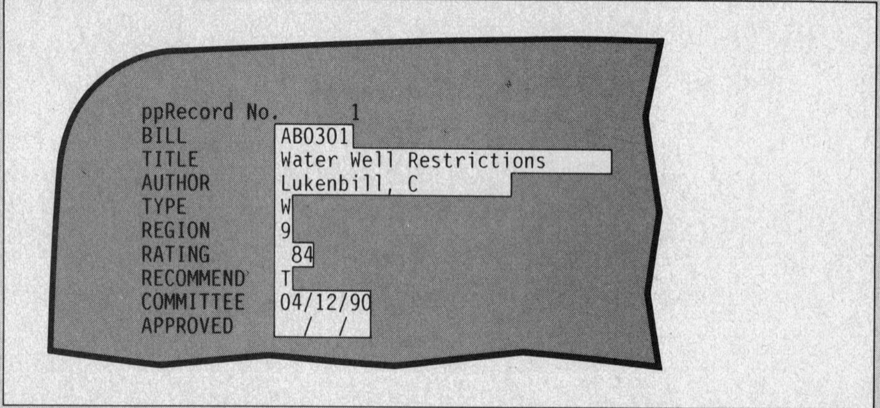

Figure 7-14
The edit screen for BILLS9.

3. Move the cursor to the RATING field, and type the corrected value of 87, and strike Enter.
4. The first record is corrected, so progress to the next by striking the Page Down (PgDn) key; the second record in the file will be displayed. If, during the editing process, you must back up to the preceding record (for instance, you accidentally strike the Page Down twice), use the Page Up (PgUp) key. In other words, it is possible to move from record to record with these two keys. If you strike the Page Down key when the last record in the file is on the screen, an end-of-file condition occurs and you are returned to the dot prompt. If you strike the Page Up key when the first record is displayed, you are returned to the dot prompt.
5. Correct the RATING field in the same way as with the first record.
6. Repeat this process for records 3, 4, and 5.
7. After editing record 5, strike the Page Down key to progress to record 6; since this is not to be changed, strike the Page Down again.
8. Correct the RATING field for record 7.

9. You have completed the editing task. Terminate editing with the Ctrl-End key sequence.

10. To check your work, you should list this file. However, because of the length of the record, the lines wrap on the screen, making reading it difficult. To avoid that problem, use the following form of the LIST.

```
LIST FIELDS BILL, TITLE, AUTHOR, RATING
```

11. Compare your display with Figure 7-12.

If your values of RATING are not three greater than those in Figure 7-12 for all records except 6 and 8, you will need to make appropriate corrections.

The preceding example illustrates a situation in which most or all of the records in a file must be edited. However, what about the situation in which you must edit only one or two records in a file consisting of several hundred records? Clearly, progressing from one record to the next until you find the desired ones would be impractical. Let us consider the direct access capability of the EDIT command by changing RATING of record 6 from 73 to 79.

DO THIS NOW 7-10 **Editing Record 6**

1. Make record 6 the current record with the command:

```
GOTO 6
```

The status bar will tell you that record 6 is the current record.

2. Issue the EDIT command:

```
EDIT
```

The edit screen will appear and record 6 will be displayed. Note that the EDIT command with no options always edits the current record.

3. Change RATING from 73 to 79.

4. Return to the dot prompt with Ctrl-End.

Actually, the GOTO and EDIT can be combined to gain access for a single record for editing. For example,

```
EDIT RECORD 6
```

makes record 6 the current record and switches to the edit mode. Using this form, either Page Down or Ctrl-End will return you to the dot prompt. Note that Page Down does not progress to the next record because you have asked to edit the single record 6.

If you made any errors in DTN 7-9, use this method to edit those records now.

DELETING RECORDS FROM A FILE

The DELETE Command

You can delete records from a file with the DELETE command. Like EDIT, DELETE alone deletes the current record; DELETE RECORD deletes the designated record.

DO THIS NOW 7-11 **Deleting Records 2 and 6–8 from BILLS9**

1. To delete record 2, enter the command:

```
DELETE RECORD 2
```

dBASE will delete this record and respond with the message:

```
1 record deleted
```

2. To delete records 6–8 (the last three records in the file), enter the command sequence:

```
GOTO 6
DELETE REST
```

dBASE will delete all records from record 6 to the end of the file (the REST of the records) and display the message:

```
3 records deleted
```

3. List your file with the command:

```
LIST BILL, TITLE, AUTHOR
```

If you performed the delete actions properly, your display will be identical to that shown below. Note that each of the deleted records is flagged with an asterisk.

```
Record#  BILL   TITLE                            AUTHOR
      1  AB0301 Water Well Restrictions          Lukenbill, C
      2 *AB0144 Site 22 Solid Waste Disposal     Smith, H
      3  AB0212 Jameson Quarry Restrictions      Johnson, W
      4  AB0158 Vapor Control of Paint Prod.     Johnson, W
      5  AB0224 Sulphur Emissions                Lukenbill, C
      6 *AB1001 River Waste Discharge            Smith, H
      7 *AB0197 Index River Dam Construction     Lukenbill, C
      8 *AB1092 Smog Control - Inverness Basin Johnson, W
```

4. Enter the following command.

```
SET DELETED ON
```

5. Repeat the preceding LIST command and note that your display does not include the deleted records.

One of the things about the DELETE command is that deleting a record does not physically remove it from the file, but only marks it for removal. There are two factors that the dBASE designers took into account with the DELETE. The first is that there is commonly a need to "remove" a record from a file but to have it accessible in the event that circumstances change and it must be made available again. For instance, you might decide to remove from current processing the record of any customer who has not made a purchase for the past 12 months, and yet have the record available if that customer orders again. Second, actually erasing a record from a file is fatal for that record; once it is gone...

In DTN 7-11, you used two forms of the DELETE. The following examples illustrate each of the forms that you can use.

Command	Action
`DELETE`	Delete the current record.
`DELETE RECORD 12`	Delete record 12.
`DELETE NEXT 3`	Delete current record and the next two (a total of three).
`DELETE REST`	Delete all records from the current one to the end of the file.
`DELETE ALL`	Delete all of the records in the file.

Recalling Deleted Records

This method of deleting records is of limited value if you cannot get them back again. For this purpose, dBASE includes the RECALL command. It has the same forms as the DELETE: one or more records can be restored with execution of the command. For instance, the following will recall deleted records as indicated.

Command	Action
`RECALL`	Recall the current record.
`RECALL RECORD 12`	Recall record 12.
`RECALL NEXT 3`	Recall current record and the next two.
`RECALL REST`	Recall all deleted records from the current one to the end of the file.
`RECALL ALL`	Recall all of the deleted records in the file.

DO THIS NOW 7-12 **Recalling Records 6 and 7**

1. Make record 6 the current record with the command:

```
GOTO 6
```

Check your status bar to be certain that record 6 is the current record.

2. Recall the next two records with:

```
RECALL NEXT 2
```

dBASE will recall (remove the delete flag) records 6 and 7 and then display the message:

```
2 records recalled
```

3. List your file with the command

```
LIST BILL, TITLE, AUTHOR
```

and you will see that these records are now displayed.

Permanently Erasing Records

Since deleted records remain in the file, they continue to occupy disk space, which can be a problem if you have limited storage. Also, as a file becomes larger, file processing activities take longer. There commonly comes a time when you must remove deleted records from a file. This is done with the PACK command as shown in the following.

DO THIS NOW 7-13 **Packing the File**

1. To pack the file, type the command:

```
PACK
```

If you have performed the delete and recall actions of the preceding examples, after the packing operation, dBASE will display the message:

```
6 records copied
```

The record counter on the status bar will display 1/6; your file now has only six records.

2. List your file with the command:

```
LIST BILL, TITLE, AUTHOR
```

Notice that the records for bills AB0144 and AB1092 are gone and the records have been renumbered; for instance, AB0212 was record 3 but it is now record 2.

THE BROWSE COMMAND

The last command that we consider in this chapter allows us to inspect records in a file and make changes: it is BROWSE. To illustrate its use, let us inspect BILL9, delete the bill AB0224 record, and change RATING for bill AB1001.

DO THIS NOW 7-14 **Using the BROWSE Command to Inspect and Change BILL9**

1. Type the command:

```
BROWSE
```

Your screen display (Figure 7-15) includes all the records in the file. If you do not have the Help window, strike the F1 key. In the display, the first record is highlighted; it is the current record. Since the screen is not wide enough to display the entire record, only those fields that will fit on the screen are displayed (six fields, in this case).

Figure 7-15
The BROWSE screen.

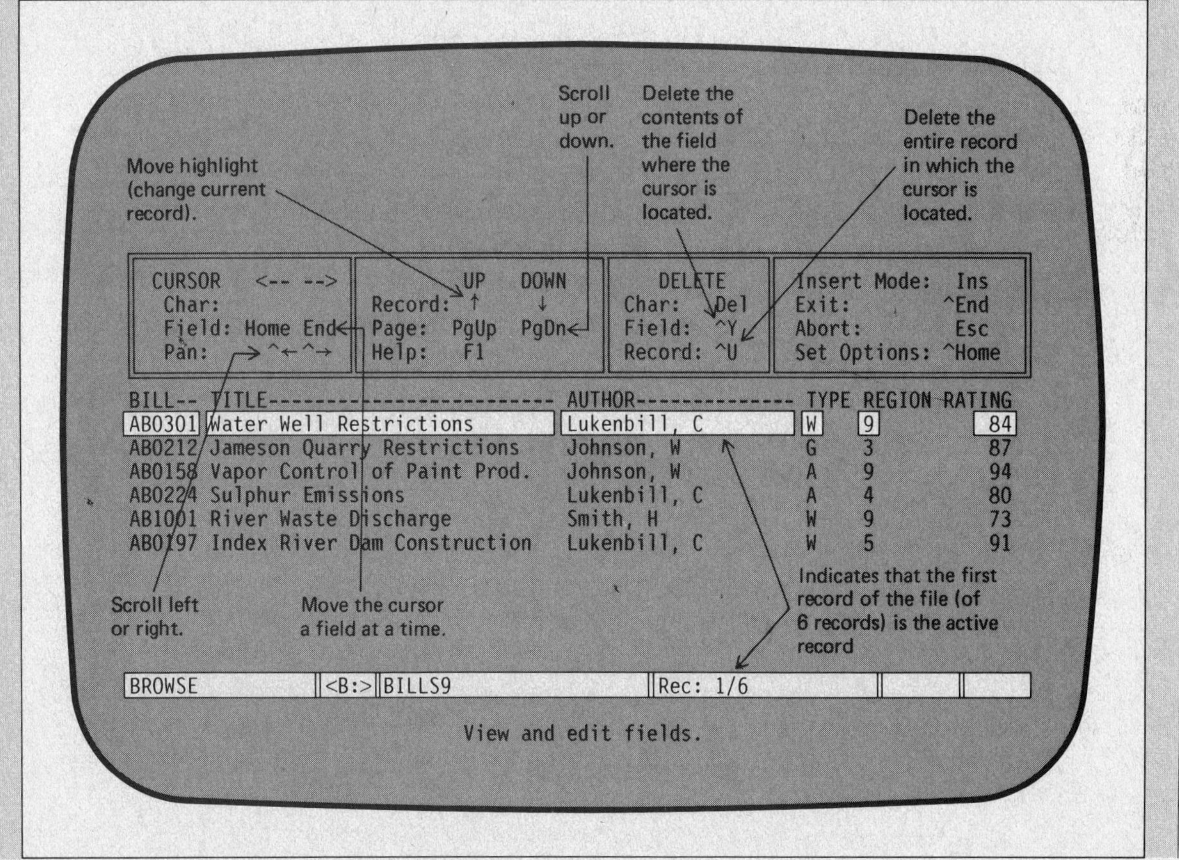

2. To scroll right (bring other fields into view), use the Ctrl-Right key sequence. Enter Ctrl-Right twice to produce the following display of your data.

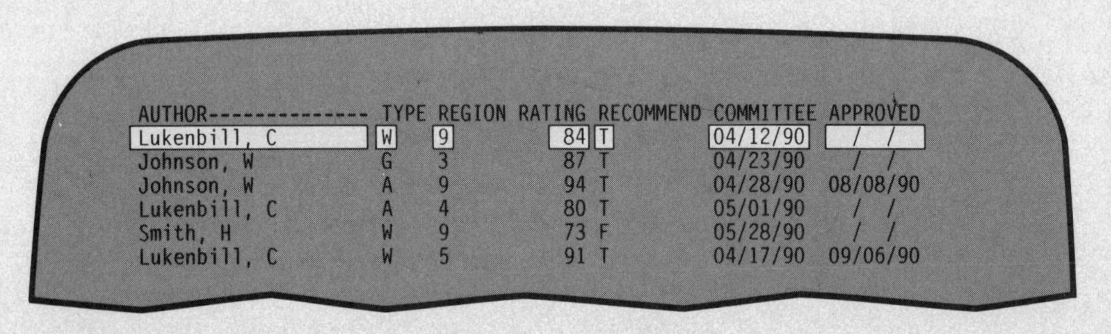

AUTHOR--------------	TYPE	REGION	RATING	RECOMMEND	COMMITTEE	APPROVED
Lukenbill, C	W	9	84	T	04/12/90	/ /
Johnson, W	G	3	87	T	04/23/90	/ /
Johnson, W	A	9	94	T	04/28/90	08/08/90
Lukenbill, C	A	4	80	T	05/01/90	/ /
Smith, H	W	9	73	F	05/28/90	/ /
Lukenbill, C	W	5	91	T	04/17/90	09/06/90

3. Use the Ctrl-Left to scroll back to Figure 7-15.
4. Move the highlight to the fourth record (AB0224) with the Down key.
5. Delete this record with a Ctrl-U. Notice that the word Del now appears on the status bar.
6. Move the highlight to the AB1001 record.
7. Successively strike the End key to move the cursor field by field to RATING.
8. Type 74 and strike Enter.
9. Terminate this BROWSE command with Ctrl-End.

Whenever you enter a BROWSE command, the current record is displayed at the top of the screen. To scroll upward (toward the beginning of the file), strike the Page Up key.

Like the LIST command, you can display selected fields with BROWSE. For example, assume that you wished to scan the date fields for records in the file. For this, you might use the following form of BROWSE.

```
BROWSE FIELDS BILL, TITLE, COMMITTEE, APPROVED
```

From the resulting screen, you can proceed to inspect the records, making corrections to the displayed fields or deleting records. The BROWSE is a convenient and versatile command.

Assignments 7-2 and **7-3** may now be completed.

SUMMARY

This chapter has provided you with the basic tools for generating and changing data files using dBASE. Through the Customer file, which you created and entered, and the Bill file that you edited you have learned how to define a record structure, enter records into a file, edit records in the file, delete records from the file, and display and print the contents of a file. Summarizing, the important items from the chapter are:

- Creating a new database file is a two-step process: first the structure must be defined, and then records may be added.
- The CREATE command is used to define the structure of a new database file.
- Field names for a database file may be selected at the discretion of the user but within the following limitations.
  - The name length is limited to 10 characters.
  - The first character must be a letter.
  - Succeeding characters may be letters, digits, or the underscore character.
- Once a file structure is created, records can be added immediately or at any later time.
- The APPEND command adds a blank record to the end of a file and then allows for data entry.
- After entering the last field of the last record when appending, do not strike Enter; use Ctrl-End or else a blank record will be added to your file on disk. If you must terminate appending from a blank entry screen, then use the Escape key.
- The USE command opens a specified data file. If another file is already open, it will be closed.
- If a file is open when you issue the QUIT command to terminate a dBASE session, that file will be closed without loss of data before dBASE is terminated.
- The LIST command allows you to display on the screen or print to the printer records from a file; you can print all or part of the fields of the record.
- ASSIST allows you to perform dBASE operations from a sequence of menus. This is helpful for occasional users of dBASE. To activate ASSIST, type the ASSIST command from the dot prompt.
- With the EDIT command, it is possible to make changes to the current record or to any selected record.

- The GOTO command has the ability to position the record pointer to any desired record or to the first or last record in the file (make it the current record).
- The DELETE command marks records for deletion but does not actually eliminate them from the file.
- The command

```
SET DELETED OFF
```

- will cause dBASE to act as if deleted records do not exist.
- The delete status can be removed from deleted records with the RECALL command. Records that have been recalled are unchanged from what they were prior to their deletion.
- The PACK command is used to physically remove deleted records from a file. The physical records numbers are changed corresponding to the records deleted.
- With the BROWSE command, it is possible to view, edit, and add records to a data file.

COMMAND SUMMARY

The following commands have been used in this chapter. Each is shown in its general form. Remember that <> enclose a description of something you must enter and [] enclose an optional item. Words in lowercase describe the entry you must make and words in uppercase must be entered as shown if that portion of the command is used. Some of the forms included in this summary are incomplete. Examples of this chapter have not illustrated all of the forms summarized here.

APPEND
Adds records to the end of a database file.

ASSIST
Switches to the ASSIST mode.

BROWSE [FIELDS <field list>]
Allows full-screen display and editing of records.

CREATE <filename>
Allows for the definition of a new file structure.

DELETE [<scope>]
Marks the specified records for deletion.

EDIT [<scope>] [FIELDS <field list>]
Permits changes to database file contents.

GOTO <record number> or GOTO TOP/BOTTOM
Positions the record pointer to the specified record.

HELP <keyword>
Displays dBASE command and function Help screens.

LIST [[FIELDS] <field list>] [TO PRINT]
Displays the records from the active database file.

LIST STRUCTURE [TO PRINT]
Displays the active database file structure.

PACK
Permanently removes records marked for deletion from a data file.

RECALL [<scope>]
Reinstates records marked for deletion.

SET BELL ON/OFF
Turns the bell on/off during data entry.

SET DELETED ON/OFF
Hides/Does not hide records marked for deletion.

USE [<filename>]
Opens the designated file (if no filename is included, then closes the current file).

NEW TERMINOLOGY

Many of the database terms used in the introduction to Part Four are also used in this chapter. The following are additional important new terms introduced in this chapter; you should be familiar with each of them.

current record
dot prompt
eof
help
record buffer
status bar
syntax

Name: ______________________ Date: ______________

Assignment 7-1

1. What is the purpose of executing the command:

```
SET DEFAULT TO B
```

2. Each of the following is to be used as a field name in a data file definition. Identify those that are not valid as field names and give the reason.

(a) DISCOUNT

(b) CREDIT_LIMIT

(c) LIMIT4

(d) X

(e) 25_QUANT

(f) MAX AMNT

Name: ______________________ Date: ____________

Assignment 7-1 (*continued*)

(g) STUDENT#

(h) DISC-RATE

3. After creating a data file, you enter exactly 10 data records and then terminate. The next day when you execute APPEND to add more records, the record number at the top of the screen is 12 rather than 11. What is the most likely reason for this? What would you do to correct this problem?

4. Consider this scenario. Yesterday you created a new data file, entered twenty records, and terminated. Today you appended ten more, then immediately opened another file to work on without telling dBASE to close your first file. What will happen to the newly entered ten records of this file?

Name: ______________________________ Date: ______________

Assignment 7-1 (*continued*)

5. If you set the bell off during entry of records in a data file, how will this affect the entry of data?

6. The text describes several variations of the LIST command. List and describe each of them.

7. From the APPEND command you have just entered five records into a file and have returned to the dot prompt. Without saving the file, you issue the QUIT command. Will any records that you entered be lost? Explain your answer.

Name: ______________________________ Date: ______________

Assignment 7-2

1. Do you prefer using ASSIST or working from the dot prompt? Give your reasons. (Note that there is no "correct" answer to this question.)

2. You have just entered the following commands.

```
USE PERSONS
COPY TO PERSONSX
```

Which file is now open? Explain your answer.

3. What is the purpose of the record buffer?

4. What is the difference between the following?

```
GOTO 7      and      EDIT RECORD 7
EDIT
```

Name: ______________________________ Date: ____________

Assignment 7-2 (*continued*)

5. When editing, you may progress from one record to the next by striking the PgDn key. There is another key stroke action that will cause the next record to be brought up on the screen. What is it?

6. A file contains twenty-two records and the current record is 14. How many records will be deleted by each of the following?

(a) DELETE

(b) DELETE NEXT 3

(c) DELETE NEXT 12

(d) DELETE REST

(e) DELETE ALL

7. What is the difference between LIST and BROWSE?

Name: ______________________________ Date: ______________

Assignment 7-3

For these questions, you will need to use dBASE.

1. Create a data file that includes at least one record with each of the four data types. While you are making your entries, determine the answers to each of the following questions.
   a. What is the maximum allowable length for a character field (look at the screen when the cursor is in the Width definition field)?

   b. What are the restrictions on a numeric field regarding both the maximum field width and the decimal definition?

   c. What happens if you attempt to change the length of a date field to something other than 8?

   d. What happens if you strike the Escape key while defining the file? What do you expect will happen if you complete the Escape operation?

   e. Do the following after completing definition of this file: Move the cursor to the second field that you have defined. Strike the Ctrl-N sequence. Strike the Ctrl-U sequence. What do these two Ctrl sequences do?

Name: ______________________ Date: ______________

Assignment 7-3 (*continued*)

2. The BILLS file includes eight records plus the EOF. Open this file and describe what happens when you attempt to GOTO each of the following record numbers?
   a. 9

   b. –10

   c. 100

Name: ______________________________ Date: ______________

OBJECTIVE QUESTIONS

Matching

Match each of the commands in a to h with the most appropriate action in 1 through 8.

a. LIST STRUCTURE
b. GOTO
c. CREATE
d. HELP
e. SET DELETED OFF
f. ASSIST
g. PACK
h. USE

____ **1.** Permanently get rid of unwanted records in a file.

____ **2.** Check the general form of the DELETE command.

____ **3.** Find out the width of each field of a data file.

____ **4.** Enter field names.

____ **5.** Temporarily make certain records unavailable for processing.

____ **6.** Open a data file.

____ **7.** Make record 20 of a thirty-record file the current record.

____ **8.** Enter commands through menu selection.

True/False

Determine whether each of the following is true or false.

T F **1.** Each time you run dBASE, you must first run the INSTALL program.

T F **2.** To get Help about a command from dBASE, you would type in HELP followed by the name of the command.

T F **3.** In a description of a command, if something is enclosed in square brackets, that item may be omitted when using the command.

T F **4.** The syntax of the LIST command is the number of fields that can be printed when the command is executed.

T F **5.** CUSTOMER, PRES_NAME, Q5, and MAX_AMOUNT are all valid for use as field names in a dBASE file.

T F **6.** The CREATE command can be used to either create a new database file or add records to an existing one.

T F **7.** Both dBASE database file names and field names can be 10 (or fewer) characters in length.

T F **8.** If you terminate the CREATE command after defining the last field, your newly created data file will contain no data records.

Name: ______________________ Date: ______________

OBJECTIVE QUESTIONS (*continued*)

T F **9.** If you have just completed working with the file CHECKS and wish to work with the file ACCOUNTS, you must first close CHECKS before USEing ACCOUNTS or data that you have entered into CHECKS could be lost.

T F **10.** Once the record structure of a data file has been defined, it cannot be changed.

T F **11.** Pertaining to the eventual contents of a data file, it makes no difference whether you enter records immediately upon terminating file creation or at a later time using the APPEND command.

T F **12.** In adding a record to a file, you have just typed the last field and not yet pressed Enter. If you strike the Escape key, that record will not be saved to disk.

T F **13.** The LIST command displays the contents of a data file on the screen; the PRINT command prints the contents of a data file on a printer.

T F **14.** ASSIST can be used to enter dBASE commands through a menu system. However, new files must be created through the dot prompt as it is not possible to perform the CREATE function through ASSIST.

T F **15.** If you have a file open and issue a USE command designating another file, dBASE first closes the currently open file, then opens the new one.

T F **16.** A file must first be opened with a USE command (unless you are already using it) before records can be appended to it.

T F **17.** The record buffer is a memory area set up to hold the values being typed in for a new record during the APPEND operation.

T F **18.** Since the APPEND command uses the bell to indicate an error condition during data entry, issuing the command SET BELL OFF is a bad idea because it will stop dBASE from warning you when you enter incorrect data.

T F **19.** With the LIST command, you can get a printed copy of a data file as well as a display on the screen.

T F **20.** The advantage of ASSIST is that you have access to many commands that are not available from the dot prompt.

T F **21.** It is possible to delete records from the BROWSE command.

T F **22.** If you issued the command EDIT from the dot prompt, the current record would be displayed on the edit screen.

T F **23.** The COPY TO command allows you to copy entries from one or more fields of a record into corresponding fields of other records.

T F **24.** The GOTO is a direct access command.

T F **25.** If a record is deleted with the DELETE command, that record is not actually removed from the file.

Name: ______________________ Date: ______________

OBJECTIVE QUESTIONS (*continued*)

T F **26.** The command DELETE REST could delete one record or it could delete many.

T F **27.** The command SET DELETED OFF permanently erases deleted records from the file.

T F **28.** The PACK command is normally used after records of a file have been edited; it gets rid of blanks within fields resulting from the edit operation.

T F **29.** The RECALL command cannot recall records that have been physically removed from a file.

T F **30.** One disadvantage of the BROWSE command is that the number of fields that can be displayed from a record is limited to the width of the screen.

Name: ______________________ Date: ____________

OBJECTIVE QUESTIONS (*continued*)

Multiple Choice

In the space provided, record the letter of the choice that best completes or answers the statement.

____ **1.** In a description of a command, angle brackets < > mean that the enclosed part

A. is optional and can be omitted.
B. is a description of the item to be entered.
C. must be typed exactly as shown if you use that part of the command.
D. is simply a description for you and is not actually a part of the command.

____ **2.** Names that you select for fields in a data file

A. must not exceed eight characters.
B. can include a three-character extension.
C. must not exceed ten characters.
D. The user does not select field names: dBASE determines them automatically.

____ **3.** During a CREATE session, you can abort at any time without saving the work you have done by

A. striking the Escape key.
B. entering the ABORT command.
C. entering the QUIT command.
D. You cannot abort without saving because dBASE automatically saves your work as you enter it.

____ **4.** With the APPEND command, you can

A. add fields to a previously created data file.
B. add fields to or delete fields from a previously created data file.
C. add records to a previously created data file.
D. add records to or delete records from a previously created data file.

____ **5.** Which of the following dBASE commands would you use to open a data file?

A. OPEN
B. CREATE
C. APPEND
D. USE

____ **6.** The command LIST OFF causes

A. the list option to be turned off.
B. the file contents to be displayed without record numbers.
C. output to the printer to be suppressed.
D. output to the screen to be suppressed.

Name: ______________________________ Date: ______________

OBJECTIVE QUESTIONS (*continued*)

____ **7.** If you wanted to see the record format of your file, you would use the ______ command.

A. LIST STRUCTURE
B. LIST FORMAT
C. STRUCTURE
D. FORMAT

____ **8.** ASSIST operates on the basis of

A. the dot prompt.
B. automatic execution of commands.
C. the Escape key.
D. a set of menus.

____ **9.** One of the shortcomings of ASSIST is

A. if you make an error in building a command, it is not possible to correct the error without starting over.
B. many useful dBASE commands are not available through ASSIST.
C. the user must memorize all of the command forms in order to use it.
D. indexed files cannot be used with ASSIST.

____ **10.** Which of the following dBASE commands would you use if you wanted to make a copy of the current file?

A. CREATE
B. COPY
C. COPY TO
D. APPEND

____ **11.** Which of the following actions does NOT occur when you open a file with the USE command?

A. The previously opened file is closed.
B. A record buffer is created.
C. The first record is read from the file and made the current record.
D. The first record in the file is displayed.

____ **12.** You want to make the seventh record in a data file the current record. Which of the following commands would you use?

A. GOTO 7
B. FIND 7
C. LOCATE 7
D. POSITION AT 7

____ **13.** Which of the following is NOT true of the EDIT command?

A. You can progress from one record to the next by striking the PgDn key.
B. You can access records sequentially for editing.
C. You can access records directly for editing.
D. You can use it to change the width of any field in the record.

Name: ____________________ Date: ____________

OBJECTIVE QUESTIONS (*continued*)

____ **14.** The command that you would use to get rid of records in a file permanently is

A. DELETE.
B. PACK.
C. KILL.
D. DELETE ALL.

____ **15.** The purpose of the RECALL command is to

A. display record format information.
B. restore the record format to its original form after editing changes have been made.
C. make records available that have previously been deleted.
D. restore the data file to its previous form after a PACK command has been issued.

Fill In

In the space provided, fill in the correct answer. Note that the answer can be one or two words.

1. ____________________
From the dot prompt, you use ______ to tell dBASE which action to take.

2. ____________________
The general structure of a command is called its ______.

3. ____________________
The first character of a field name must be a ______.

4. ____________________
The ______ command is used to define a new data file.

5. ____________________
The last record in a data file is followed by a(n) ______ to indicate to dBASE that there are no more records in the file.

6. ____________________
The ______ command opens a file and makes it ready for use.

7. ____________________
You would use the ______ command to add more records to a data file.

8. ____________________
If you wanted to display the record format of your data file, you would use the ______ command.

Name: ______________________ Date: ____________

OBJECTIVE QUESTIONS (*continued*)

9. ______________________

_____ allows you to use the functions of dBASE through a series of menus.

10. ______________________

The GOTO command gives you _____ access to records in a data file.

11. ______________________

If you want to make a record available for processing that was previously deleted, you would use the _____ command.

12. ______________________

The _____ command permanently gets rid of records in a file that are marked for deletion.

ASSIGNMENTS/PROJECTS

1. The BILLS2 file is identical to BILLS except that it includes several blank records. You are to do the following to this file. When completed, print a listing that includes the fields BILL, AUTHOR, TYPE, REGION, RATING, RECOMMEND, and APPROVED.
   a. Permanently eliminate all blank records.
   b. Enter today's date for APPROVED for bills AB0212 and AB1092.
   c. For bill AB0212, change RATING from 87 to 79 and RECOMMEND from True to False.
   d. Change REGION for bill AB0224 from 4 to 9.

2. A group of bike racers maintains a database file of their progress. You are to create a data file to store the following racing data.

Field	Type	Width
Last name	Character	10
First name	Character	10
Birthdate	Date	8
Club name	Character	12
Bike make	Character	10
Best placement	Numeric	2
Earned points	Numeric	3

Following are the first five records that you must enter into this file.

Name Last	First	Birthdate	Club	Bike	Best Finish	Points
Pratt	Janet	03/22/66	Quicksilver	Cicco	10	20
Nickazy	Eva	05/20/67	Quicksilver	Schwinn	1	55
Sovin	Dorothy	04/19/64	Quicksilver	Lotus	8	25
Damir	Monica	10/07/68	Felines	Cicco	6	38
Lee	Amy	01/04/65	Quicksilver	Cicco	1	101

In addition to these, there are nineteen other records for this file. To simplify your task, these nineteen records are included on the data disk that accompanies this book in the file BIKERS.ASC. They are recorded in a special ASCII format to be compatible with your database data file. After you have typed in the preceding five records, you can append the remaining nineteen by typing the following command from the dot prompt.

```
APPEND FROM BIKERS.ASC DELIMITED
```

For this to work properly, you must have defined your record format as described in the preceding table. After the APPEND, list your file and check to ensure that the values loaded are reasonable.

3. Create a database data file for an automobile leasing agency; the record format must be as follows:

Field	Type	Length	Remark
License number	Character	6	
Make	Character	10	
Year	Character	2	
Size code	Character	2	CO (compact) MI (midsize) LU (luxury)
Lessee acct. number	Character	4	
Lessee name	Character	18	
Lease expiration date	Date	8	
Lease type	Character	1	Q (quarter) Y (year)
Monthly lease rate	Numeric	7	2 decimal places

Following are the first five records that you must enter into this file. Note that no value is listed for the Lease expiration date. You must fill in these entries with current values.

				Lessee		Lease	
License	Make	Year	Size	Number	Name	Type	Rate
ABX108	Ford	90	MI	2199	E Z Insurance	Q	194.66
DIJ155	Ford	90	MI	2701	Hart Construction	Y	183.82
EEF908	Chevrolet	90	MI	2001	JP Designs	Y	180.72
EEF921	Chevrolet	90	CO	2001	JP Designs	Y	164.97
BQJ063	Chevrolet	90	CO	2001	JP Designs	Y	164.98

In addition to these, there are twenty other records for this file. To simplify your task, these twenty records are included on the data disk that accompanies this book in the file VEHICLE.ASC. They are recorded in a special ASCII format to be compatible with your database data file. After you have typed in the preceding five records, you can append the remaining twenty by typing the following command from the dot prompt.

```
APPEND FROM VEHICLE.ASC DELIMITED
```

For this to work properly, you must have defined your record format as described in the preceding table. After the APPEND, use EDIT to fill in the Lease expiration dates. Then list your file and check to ensure that the values loaded are reasonable.

4. A software evaluator decides to computerize records of productivity software evaluations by creating a database. The software is grouped in four major categories: Word processing (WP), spreadsheet (SS), file management (FM), and graphics (GR). The following fields are to be included in the database. Study this list and decide on appropriate field widths and types. Then create the data file and enter 21 records evenly divided between the three software types.

Field	Sample Value
Software product	Beginners Word Processor
Company name	Supersoft, Incorporated
Category of software	WP, SS, FM, GR
Price	999.99 (maximum)
Typical discounted price	999.99 (maximum)
Date of evaluation	
Software rating	1 through 9
Recommended	Y or N

5. A member of a quarter horse owners association decides to create a database file of horses owned by members of the association. The following fields are to be included in the database.

Field	Sample Value
Horse's name	Giant Stride
Gender	M for mare S for stallion
Date of birth	
Best race finish	1 through 9
Association rating	1 through 100
Owner	Erica Price
Owner in good standing	Y or N

Study this list and decide on appropriate field widths and types. Then create the data file and enter 20 records that satisfy the following.

Field	Data Distribution
Gender	11 mares and 9 stallions
Best race finish	5 first
	4 second
	4 third
	2 fourth
	2 sixth
	1 seventh
	1 eighth
	1 ninth
Association rating	6 rated 90–100
	5 rated 80–89
	you select the rest
Owner in good standing	3 No; the rest Yes

Chapter 8

More on dBASE III PLUS

OBJECTIVES

Chapter 7 provided you with the ability to perform basic maintenance on database data files: creating a file, adding records, deleting records, and editing. The focus in this chapter is on using the data to provide information by creating indexes to give record access in a desired sequence, selecting records based on conditions you specify, and generating reports. When you have completed this chapter, you should be able to:

- Generate an index based on any field in the record of a file.
- Limit access to records of a file to those with data values satisfying a condition that you specify.
- Directly access a desired record in a file based on the value in any field of the record.
- Interactively obtain the sum or average of any field in a data file.
- Use the dBASE report generator to specify the format of a report using data from a data file.
- Prepare reports in which common records are grouped and subtotals are calculated for designated fields.

PREVIEW

Principles of Indexing

An index provides access to records of a file based on a sequence determined by a designated field in the file. Index files are not created automatically when a data file is created; each needed index must be created using the INDEX command. dBASE can maintain index files automatically when the corresponding data files are changed.

Conditional Operations

Relational expressions allow you to compare quantities and to control actions taken by dBASE depending on the results of the comparison. Used with the FOR command option, you can limit your access to records in a file to those meeting a designated condition.

Obtaining Information From a File

Indexes provide the means for fast direct access to any record in a file based on a data value (as opposed to a record number as in Chapter 7). Statistical commands allow you to obtain the count of the number of records meeting a specified condition and to compute the sum and average of specified fields of a file that satisfy a stated condition.

Report Generation

The LIST command allows you to generate a list of the records in a file. The CREATE REPORT command allows you to specify the exact format that printed output is to take. You can designate that totals for selected numeric fields be computed for all records of the file and subtotals on groups of records with a common field entry.

Using Two or More Files

With dBASE, you can interrelate two or more files to generate reports consisting of data from both files.

PRINCIPLES OF INDEXING

Records of a data file are commonly processed in order based on the contents of one or more fields of the file. For instance, a printout of customers and their purchases might be in sequence based on either the customer number or the customer name. Printed labels for mailing advertising information would be in sequence based on the customer ZIP code to take advantage of bulk postal rates. There are two methods to accomplish this: sorting the records of the file thus putting them in the desired sequence; or creating an index that gives access to the records in the desired sequence. In most database processing applications, indexing is used because a separate index file can be created for each field on which sequencing is required. Furthermore, the index provides direct access to records in a data file.

Creating an Index File

In order to use an index with a file, you must first create it; indexes are *not* created automatically when a data file is created. In creating one, you must:

1. Open the data file that is to be indexed.
2. Designate the field on which the index is to be built.
3. Provide a name that dBASE will use for the index filename. Remember: dBASE builds the index as a separate file and uses the extension NDX.

To illustrate this process, let us use CUSTOMER; the following fields make up its record.

CUSTNUM	Customer number
REGION	Sales region
COMPANY	Company name
YTDSALES	Year-to-date sales
BALANCE	Current account balance
ANNIV	Anniversary date

Assume that your processing actions require indexes on the four fields CUSTNUM, COMPANY, YTDSALES, and ANNIV. From the introduction to Part Four, you know that the customer number is the key field—the unique field for which no two records have the same value. Almost all data files in a database application have an index file based on the key field.

In contrast, there can be two or more records with the same value for the year-to-date sales and anniversary date fields. In such a case, the index will cause records with the same values to be grouped together.

Although dBASE does not include a naming convention for index files, it is recommended that one be used. In this book, the following guidelines are employed.

- The index file associated with the key field of the data file is always given the same name as the data file.
- Names are selected for other index files so that they indicate both the data file to which they correspond and the field to which they are related. For instance, an index file for CUSTOMER based on the COMPANY field might be named CUS-COMP. Here, the first three letters represent the data file and the last four the field on which it is based.

DO THIS NOW 8-1 **Creating Index Files for CUSTOMER**

The following files are to be created.

CUSTOMER.NDX	Based on the customer number (CUSTNUM)
CUS-COMP.NDX	Based on the company name (COMPANY)
CUS-YTD.NDX	Based on the year-to-date sales (YTDSALES)
CUS-ANNV.NDX	Based on the anniversary date (ANNIV)

1. Open CUSTOMER with the command:

```
USE CUSTOMER
```

2. Create the index CUSTOMER.NDX with the command in Figure 8-1.

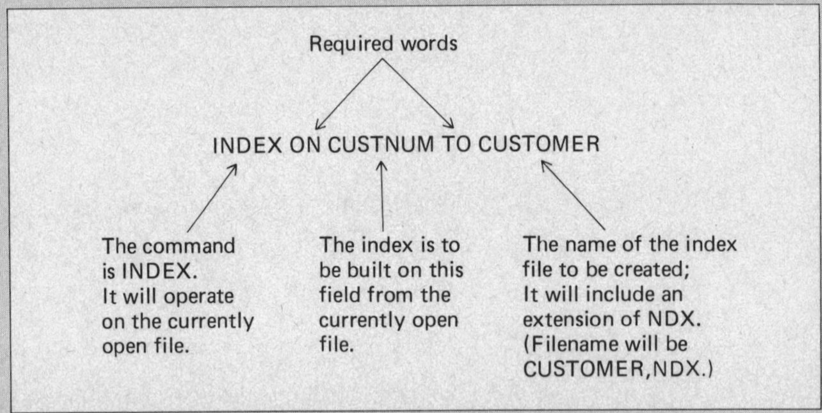

Figure 8-1
Creating an index file.

When the indexing action is complete, dBASE will display a message indicating the number of records indexed.

3. The index just created is stored on disk and is now active; confirm this by listing the file with the command:

```
LIST
```

If your index was created correctly, the records of your file will be listed in sequence based on the customer number.

4. Create the index CUS-COMP.NDX with the following command.

```
INDEX ON COMPANY TO CUS-COMP
```

5. You now have two index files for this data file: CUSTOMER.NDX and CUS-COMP.NDX. The one just created is the active one; confirm this by listing the file. Note that the records are now displayed in sequence based on the company name.

6. Create the index CUS-YTD with the command:

```
INDEX ON YTDSALES TO CUS-YTD
```

One index, CUS-ANNV, is yet to be created. That one will be created using ASSIST in the next section.

Before dBASE creates an index, it checks to see if there is already an index with that name. For instance, in creating CUS-YTD, had your disk contained a file name CUS-YTD.NDX, dBASE would have given you the option of aborting the index command or proceeding, thus replacing the existing file with a new one.

Creating an Index File Using ASSIST

You can also create an index file from ASSIST. This is helpful in that ASSIST will display a list of the fields making up the record, from which you simply select the field for indexing from the list.

DO THIS NOW 8-2 **Creating the Index File CUS-ANNV Using ASSIST**

1. Get into the ASSIST mode by typing the command ASSIST.
2. Open the CUSTOMER file from Setup by striking Enter, with *Database File* highlighted on the Setup menu.
3. Select the data drive, and then the file CUSTOMER.DBF.
4. Respond with N to the question of whether or not the file is indexed; you do not want to use an existing index.
5. With the Right key, move the bar menu highlight to *Organize.*
6. Select the *Index* option. dBASE will respond with the query:

   ```
   Enter an index key expression:
   ```

7. You may type the name of the field or strike F10 for a display of the fields in this record. Strike F10. The fields composing the CUSTOMER record will be displayed.
8. With the Down arrow, position the highlight on the field ANNIV and strike Enter. The field name will be entered in response to the dBASE query for the field name.
9. Strike Enter to signal dBASE that you are ready to continue. dBASE will query you regarding the disk on which to write the index file. As the default data drive is highlighted, select it by striking Enter.
10. You are then requested to enter the name of the file (the index filename). Type CUS-ANNV and strike Enter. The index will be created.
11. You may return to the dot prompt by striking Escape.

As with other actions, you should use whichever you find the simplest: command entry from the dot prompt or from ASSIST.

Opening a Data File That Has Indexes

Your data disk now includes four indexes for the CUSTOMER file. Whenever you wish to use the file, you can open without an index (USE CUSTOMER, as you have already done), or open it with any of the indexes. Obviously, only one of these can be activated at any given time. That is, you can see the data based on the sequence of CUS-COMP or of CUS-YTD, but not both at the same time. Although a variety of methods can be used in switching between indexes, descriptions in this book will be

Figure 8-2
Opening a data file with an index.

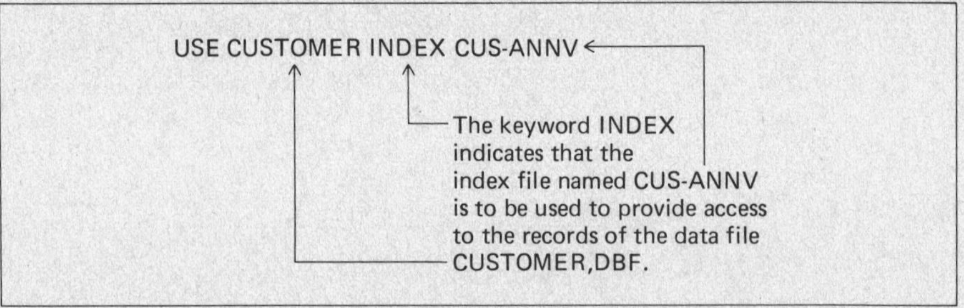

limited to specifying the needed index in the USE statement. For example, to open CUSTOMER with the CUS-ANNV index, you would enter the USE command in the form in Figure 8-2. This causes dBASE to open both the data file CUSTOMER and the associated index file CUS-ANNV. At any time in your work session, you could open CUSTOMER again with another index. Remember, the USE statement always closes any open data

Figure 8-3
Using different indexes.

```
USE CUSTOMER INDEX CUS-COMP
LIST CUSTNUM, COMPANY
```

Record#	CUSTNUM	COMPANY
1	13069	ABC Retail Outlet
9	13117	Blue Ridge Sport & Casual
2	12573	Boardwalk Sportswear Sales
5	12292	Coast Concepts
8	13189	Crow Canyon Casual Wear
10	12217	Falcon Ridges Enterprises
7	12272	Grand Times
4	11882	Harlicorn Operations
3	12626	Mr. Casual, Limited
6	13312	Paradise Leisure Clothing

```
USE CUSTOMER INDEX CUS-YTD
LIST CUSTNUM, YTDSALES
```

Record#	CUSTNUM	YTDSALES
4	11882	1012.66
9	13117	1788.29
10	12217	5880.10
5	12292	5990.86
7	12272	7932.82
2	12573	8003.46
3	12626	8933.48
1	13069	12633.70
6	13312	14889.83
8	13189	19833.22

```
USE CUSTOMER INDEX CUS-ANNV
LIST CUSTNUM, ANNIV
```

Record#	CUSTNUM	ANNIV
8	13189	03/28/86
10	12217	04/02/86
6	13312	04/22/86
1	13069	06/13/86
2	12573	06/24/86
5	12292	06/12/87
3	12626	08/19/87
9	13117	09/22/87
7	12272	02/28/88
4	11882	06/06/89

and index files first. (This is true only to the extent that we will use dBASE in this book; dBASE does include procedures for having more than one data file open.) The USE and LIST sequences of Figure 8-3 produce the corresponding record listings.

The Effect of Data Changes on Indexes

Any command that will change the contents of a data file can potentially affect indexes created for the file. For instance, assume that you must make the following changes to CUSTOMER.

1. Change the customer number of record 7 from 12272 to 32272.
2. Append a record using a customer number of 11133.

To avoid changing your copy of customer, you can make a copy (call it CUSTOM9), and then perform the operations on the copy. Since CUSTOM9 will be identical to CUSTOMER, you can use any of the index files that you created for customer.

DO THIS NOW 8-3 **Editing Record 7 and Appending a Record to CUSTOM9**

1. Begin by closing CUSTOMER with the command:

```
USE
```

2. Make the CUSTOM9 copy with the dBASE command:

```
COPY FILE  B:CUSTOMER.DBF  TO  B:CUSTOM9.DBF
```

   Be certain to type this command exactly as shown; do not omit the extension DBF from either filename.

3. Open CUSTOM9 with the command:

```
USE CUSTOM9
```

4. Bring record 7 up in the edit screen by entering the command:

```
EDIT 7
```

5. Change the value of the customer number field from 12272 to 32272. Return to the dot prompt with a Ctrl-End.
6. Use the APPEND command to add the new record; the customer number must be 11133 and the company name *Direct Sales*. Make up your own values for the other fields. Be certain to avoid striking Enter after typing the last field; use the Ctrl-End sequence so that the append operation will be terminated without adding a blank record.

Figure 8-4
The modified CUSTOM9 file in physical order (no index).

7. From the dot prompt, list the file (LIST command). Your screen display will be as shown in Figure 8-4. Notice that record 7 has been changed and that the new record is displayed as record 11.

8. Open CUSTOM9 with the index file CUSTOMER.NDX as follows:

```
USE CUSTOM9 INDEX CUSTOMER
```

9. List the file once again and you will see the display of Figure 8-5. Notice that record 7 is out of sequence and the newly added record 11 is missing.

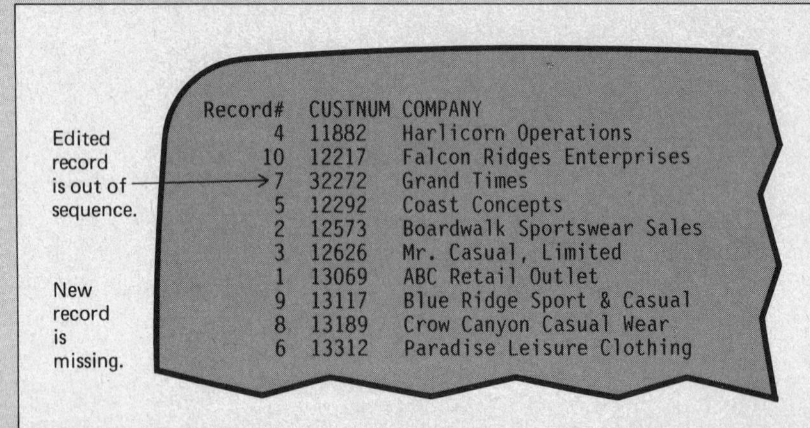

Figure 8-5
The modified CUSTOM9 file as displayed with an obsolete index.

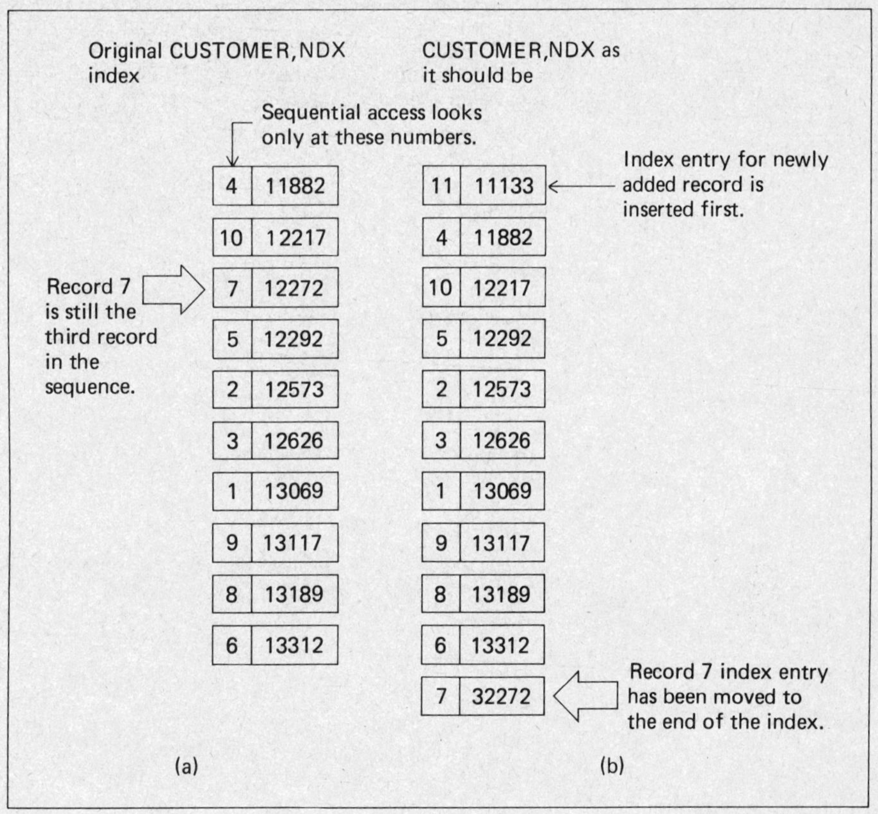

Figure 8-6
(a) Entries of the original CUSTOMER.NDX file.
(b) Entries of an updated CUSTOMER.NDX file.

The problem here is due to the fact that the index file is independent of the data file. Since the index file was not open with the data file when the preceding changes were made to the data file, *the index file was left unchanged.* Even though the file was changed, the index file contents remain as shown in Figure 8-6(a), and the file is thus inconsistent with the data file. When subsequently used with CUSTOM9, dBASE used as the record entries records 4, 10, 7, and so on, to access the records sequentially from the data file. When using indexes in conjunction with data files, it is important to remember that *only the indexes designated with the data file when the file is opened will be modified when the data file is modified.* This means that had the file been opened with the command

```
USE CUSTOM9 INDEX CUSTOMER
```

before making the changes, then the index file CUSTOMER.NDX would have been adjusted automatically, as shown in Figure 8-6(b).

If several indexes have been created for a file, only those designated in the USE will be updated automatically. For instance, DTN 8-1 involves four indexes for the CUSTOMER file. It is possible to designate all of them in a USE command as follows:

```
USE CUSTOMER INDEX CUSTOMER, CUS-COMP, CUS-YTD, CUS-ANNV
```

Here, although the CUSTOMER.NDX index is the only one that is active (effects access to the file), the others will be modified as appropriate when changes are made to the file. There are numerous methods for working with multiple indexes that you would learn about in a course devoted solely to dBASE.

Assignment 8-1 may now be completed.

Indexing a file allows you to change the order in which records of the file are presented to you. This is only one of the many database processing needs; another is the ability to be selective about available records. For this, you need conditional capabilities.

The FOR Command Option

To display all of the records in a file, you have used the LIST command. Furthermore, you have used it together with some of the available command options. For instance, in Chapter 7, you used the FIELDS option to select the fields that you wanted displayed. There are also cases in which you want to see only those records that meet a certain criterion—you want to be selective of the records. For instance, you might want to generate a list of all customers in the CUSTOMER file who have made more than $10,000 in purchases so that you can offer them a special discount on quantity purchases. Selecting records according to some condition is done with the FOR command option. For instance, the following form of the LIST will display all customers for whom the value of the year-to-date sales field is greater than $10,000.

```
LIST FOR YTDSALES > 10000
```

This is a *conditional action;* a record will be selected only on the condition that the value stored in the YTDSALES field is greater than 10,000. The ability to select records or, more generally, to perform actions conditionally is fundamental to data processing. This is an essential element of DBMSs, as well as all programming languages, or even the machine language of the computer itself.

In this example, the condition is specified with the FOR option. As we will learn, the FOR can be used with many commands. Its general form is

FOR <*condition*>

where *condition* is a comparison form that can be either true or false. Let us learn how to set up these forms.

Relational Operators and Expressions

In programming languages, comparisons are made using **relational operators.** They are so called because they indicate the relationship between two quantities. For example: "Is the amount owed larger than the credit limit?" "Is the sales region equal to 12?"

As do most programming languages, dBASE includes the following six relational operators for operating on numeric as well as character data.

Comparison	Symbol	Examples
Less than	<	CHARGE < LIMIT
Greater than	>	YTDSALES > 10000
Equal to	=	AGE = 21
Less than or equal to	<=	QUANT <= BREAK
Greater than or equal to	>=	PRICE >= 17.95
Not equal to	<>	GRADE <> "A"

The examples shown are called **relational expressions;** they are essentially comparisons between two quantities. For instance,

```
YTDSALES > 10000
```

compares the value stored in YTDSALES with 10,000. If YTDSALES contains a value of 15,000, this relationship will be true, that is,

```
15000 > 10000
```

(15,000 is greater than 10,000) is indeed true. However, if YTDSALES contains 5000, the relationship will be false, that is,

```
5000 > 10000
```

is false. In general, the result of evaluating a relational expression will be either true or false.

When used in conjunction with a command that processes a file sequentially, each record is evaluated to determine whether it meets the condition. For instance, in executing the LIST command

```
LIST FOR YTDSALES > 10000
```

dBASE reads each record from disk and compares the value in YTDSALES with 10,000. If the comparison is true, the record is displayed; otherwise, it is ignored.

Arithmetic Expressions

Assume that you have decided to pay a special bonus to all sales representatives who have sold at least twice the sales quota amount. Your relational expression would then take the form:

```
SALES >= 2*QUOTA
```

The form 2*QUOTA is called an **arithmetic expression** and is virtually identical to expressions of 1-2-3. It says, "Multiply the value in QUOTA by 2." Although large, complex expressions can be formed in dBASE, examples and assignments in this book will require only relatively simple forms, such as adding two quantities or dividing one by another. These will be constructed using the four **arithmetic operators** illustrated in the following examples.

Operator	Example	Description
*	`2*QUOTA`	Multiply 2 by QUOTA.
/	`TCOST/QUANT`	Divide TCOST by QUANT.
+	`MATERIAL + LABOR + OTHER`	Add MATERIAL, LABOR, and OTHER.
–	`AMOUNT - DISCOUNT + SHIP`	Subtract DISCOUNT from AMOUNT, then add SHIP.

Unlike 1-2-3, spaces can be inserted in an expression to make it more readable. In the preceding examples, spaces are included around the + and – signs but not around the * and /; dBASE ignores all such spaces when performing the calculations.

In setting up comparisons, the quantities on each side of the relational operator can be constant values, field names, or arithmetic expressions such as those illustrated in the preceding set of examples.

Using Relational Operators with Character Data

In addition to comparing numeric data, you can use relational operators with character and date data types to form relational expressions. For instance, Assignment 3 in Chapter 7 requires creating a data file for an automobile leasing agency. One of the fields is a two-position size code in which CO means compact, MI means midsize, and LU means luxury. If you wanted a display of all compact vehicles (those with a CO for the SIZE field), you would use the form:

```
LIST FOR SIZE = "CO"
```

Notice that the CO is enclosed in quotes. If the quotes were omitted, then dBASE would interpret CO as the name of a field in the data file and would give an error message that no such field (or variable) exists. Quoted quantities such as this are called **literals.**

If the character field to be compared contains numbers, do not forget the quotes. For example, if you wanted to display all customers (from the CUSTOMER file) in region 12, you would use the LIST in the following form.

```
LIST FOR REGION = "12"
```

In this case, if the quotes were omitted, dBASE would interpret the quantity 12 as type numeric and would indicate an error because REGION is a type character. The data types on each side of the relational operator must be the same.

Although examples in this book use the double quotation marks, you can use either single or the double quotation marks to specify a literal. Note that the single and double quotes are on the same key of the keyboard.

Testing Logical Variables

Remember that the BILLS data file of Chapter 7 includes the logical field RECOMMEND; it can have a value of true or false (yes or no). If you wanted to display the bills and their titles that have been recommended, then you would want all of the records for which this field is true. To test these, you must not use a relational operator; for instance, the following LIST produces the desired display.

```
LIST FIELDS BILL, TITLE FOR RECOMMEND
```

If you use the form FOR RECOMMEND = .T., dBASE III PLUS will indicate an error.

Logical Operators

Frequently, situations arise in which your selection criterion is based on the values of two or more fields. For instance, you might want to initiate a special promotional effort with customers in region 12 with year-to-date sales of $8000 or more. The English form of the condition is:

REGION value equals 12 *and*
YTDSALES value equals or exceeds 8000

With this form, the overall expression will be true only if both parts are true (because of the *and*). The dBASE form is almost identical to this English form, as we see when it is used with the LIST.

```
LIST FOR REGION = "12" .AND. YTD SALES >= 8000
```

Notice that the .AND. operator, which is called a **logical operator,** includes a period before and after the word AND.

The companion logical operator is .OR., which allows either of two conditions to be true. For instance, assume that you are working with the BILLS data file of Chapter 7 and a special study must be made of bills that are water oriented or pertain to region 3. The English form of the condition is:

TYPE value equals W *or* REGION value equals 3

In this form, the overall expression will be true if either part is true (or if both parts are true). Used in the LIST command, the condition takes the form:

```
LIST FOR TYPE = "W" .OR. REGION = "3"
```

Hands-on Examples

The preceding sections describe numerous examples of using conditions. Let us try each of these on the computer to confirm the results.

DO THIS NOW 8-4 Using Conditionals

1. Open the CUSTOMER file with the command:

```
USE CUSTOMER INDEX CUSTOMER
```

   Notice that the file is opened with the index CUSTOMER.NDX; conditional forms are completely independent of whether or not the data file is opened with an index file.

2. List the records with YTDSALES greater than 10,000 with the command:

```
LIST FOR YTDSALES > 10000
```

   Your screen display should consist of records 1, 8, and 6.

3. List the REGION 12 records with the command:

```
LIST FOR REGION = "12"
```

   Your screen display should consist of records 10, 7, 3, and 1.

4. Attempt to list the REGION 12 records with the command:

```
LIST FOR REGION = 12
```

   If you are using dBASE III PLUS you will get:

```
Data type mismatch
```

5. List the REGION 12 records with YTDSALES equal to or exceeding 8000 using the command:

```
LIST FOR REGION = "12" .AND. YTDSALES >= 8000
```

   Your screen display should consist of records 3 and 1.

6. The next two examples use the BILLS file. Open it with the command:

```
USE BILLS
```

7. List the bills that have been recommended, that is, have a value of true in the RECOMMEND field. Use the command:

```
LIST FIELDS BILL, TITLE FOR RECOMMEND
```

   Your screen display should consist of records 1, 3, 4, 5, and 7.

8. Attempt to list the recommended bills with:

```
LIST FIELDS BILL, TITLE FOR RECOMMEND = .T.
```

   With dBASE III PLUS, you will get the error message:

```
Invalid operator
```

9. List the bills that are water oriented or pertain to region 3 using the command:

```
LIST FIELDS BILL, TITLE FOR TYPE = "W" .OR. REGION = "3"
```

Your screen display should consist of records 1, 3, 6, 7, and 8.

For the purpose of illustration, all of these examples have used the FOR in conjunction with the LIST. However, you should not conclude that the FOR option can be applied only to LIST; indeed, it can be used with a number of dBASE commands, as will be seen with some of the examples that follow.

Using ASSIST to Build a Condition

In step 9 of the preceding set of exercises, you used the .OR. operator in the LIST command. Let us see how this is done using ASSIST.

DO THIS NOW 8-5 **Using ASSIST to Execute the Command:**

```
LIST FIELDS BILL, TITLE FOR TYPE = "W" .OR. REGION = "3"
```

1. Enter ASSIST by typing the command:

```
ASSIST
```

2. The BILLS file should still be open from the preceding exercise. If you closed it, then reopen it from the *Set Up* option of the ASSIST bar menu.

3. With the Right key, move the highlight to the *Retrieve* option of the bar menu. The submenu *List* option is highlighted; select it by striking Enter. The resulting List submenu shown in Figure 8-7 will be displayed.

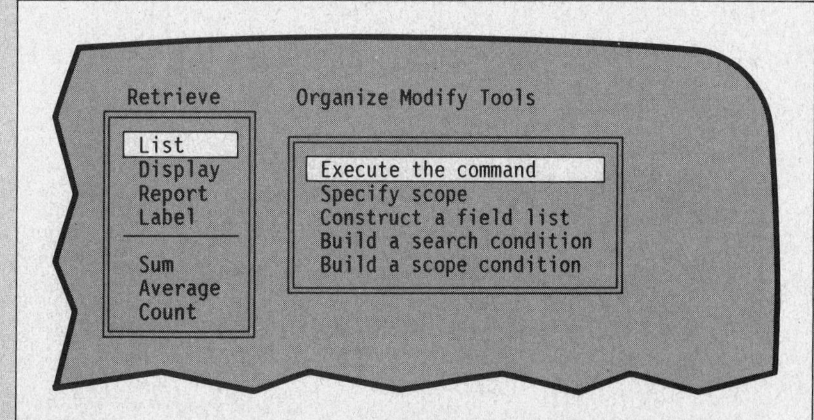

Figure 8-7

4. The first action is to specify the fields to be listed. Move the highlight to the *Construct a search condition* option and strike Enter. The list of fields composing this record will be displayed (Figure 8-8).

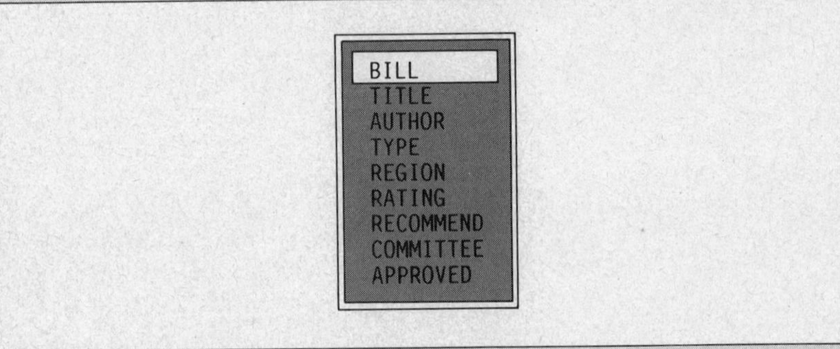

Figure 8-8

5. You want to display the fields BILL and TITLE. Since BILL is highlighted, strike Enter. Notice that the command is being assembled at the bottom of the screen. It is now:

   ```
   LIST BILL
   ```

   ASSIST does not include the optional word FIELDS in assembling this command.

6. The highlight is at the TITLE field; select it by striking Enter.

7. As you have completed the field selection, strike the Right key to get out of this portion of the menu.

8. You must now define the first of your conditions:

   ```
   TYPE = "W"
   ```

   Do this by selecting the *Build a search condition* option of the menu in Figure 8-7. You will again be presented with the field list of Figure 8-8.

9. Select the field TYPE by moving the highlight to it and striking Enter. This produces the following set of relational operators.

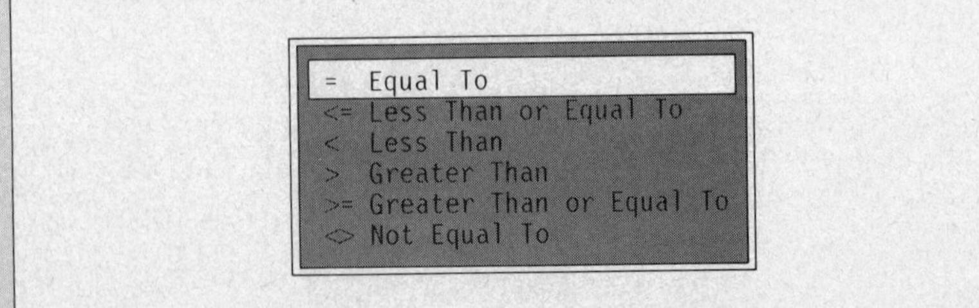

10. You want the *Equal to* operator; since it is highlighted, strike Enter. The following prompt is displayed.

```
Enter a character string (without quotes):
```

11. As the field to be compared (TYPE) is only one position in width, ASSIST only allows a one-position field to be entered. Enter the letter W (do not forget to use uppercase), and then strike Enter. Notice that the command being built at the bottom of your screen now includes this FOR condition. You also have the following options.

```
No more conditions
Combine with .AND.
Combine with .OR.
```

12. Since you must use .OR. with another condition, select the *Combine with .OR.* option.

13. You must then repeat steps 9, 10, and 11 for the

    ```
    REGION = "3"
    ```

    portion of the command.

14. Select the *No more conditions* to return to the submenu of Figure 8-7.

15. As the command is complete, select the *Execute the command* option and the list will be displayed.

This sequence of steps in using ASSIST might appear to be tedious but it goes quickly once you are familiar with it. The principal advantage is that dBASE is continually prompting you, especially in listing the fields from which you must select.

OBTAINING INFORMATION FROM A DATA FILE

Direct Access Using an Index

Indexing allows us to access records of a file in a desired sequence (sequential access); it also allows us to locate a desired record quickly (direct access). For instance, assume that you must edit the record of customer number 13189 of the CUSTOMER file. Using the record number to edit a record as you did in Chapter 7 is clumsy because the record number is not a meaningful number to the end user. You need to be able to say to dBASE, "Find the record with a customer number of 13189." You can do exactly this if you have opened the file with the index on the customer number field (CUSTOMER.NDX). Let us try this form of direct access.

DO THIS NOW 8-6 **Using an Index for Direct Access of Customer 13189**

1. Open CUSTOMER with the command:

```
USE CUSTOMER INDEX CUSTOMER
```

2. Enter the FIND command in the following form:

```
FIND "13189"
```

   dBASE will indicate on the status bar that record 8 is the current record.

3. To confirm that this is indeed the desired record, enter the EDIT command. Record 8 (Crow Canyon Casual Wear) will be displayed on the screen.
4. Strike the Escape key to return to the dot prompt.
5. To illustrate what happens if there is no such record in the file, enter the command:

```
FIND "13198"
```

   dBASE displays the message

```
No find
```

   and returns to the dot prompt. Note that the current record is listed as EOF.

In using the FIND command, follow the keyword FIND with the value of the index field that you want dBASE to locate. Because the index is arranged in sequence on this field, dBASE can use special techniques to locate the desired record very quickly.

You could also use the FIND if you needed to locate the record based on the customer name. For instance, assume that you are working on some customer records and you do not have the customer numbers readily available. However, you do know the company names of the records you need to access. For this, you can use the index built on the COMPANY field.

DO THIS NOW 8-7 **Using an Index for Direct Access of Crow Canyon Casual Wear**

1. Open the file with the index CUS-COMP as follows:

```
OPEN CUSTOMER INDEX CUS-COMP
```

   Remember that this closes both the data file and the index file previously opened before opening.

2. Enter the FIND command in the following form.

```
FIND "Crow Canyon"
```

   dBASE will indicate on the status bar that record 8 is the current record. In this example, notice that the entire company name is not required (the name is Crow Canyon Casual Wear). For a search such as this, dBASE uses only as many characters as you specify in the FIND statement when doing the comparing.

3. Enter the FIND command in the following form:

```
FIND "CROW CANYON"
```

   You will receive the *No find* message because the characters must match exactly; uppercase and lowercase are *not* the same.

Accessing a Selected Record Without Using an Index

Relational expressions and the FOR command option allow us to select records from a file (sequential access); they also give us the means for searching the file for a record satisfying a particular condition. There are frequently situations in which you want to find a particular record based on the value of a field for which there is no index. For this, dBASE includes the LOCATE command, which searches the data file beginning with the first record. For example, assume that you would like to check the bill (in the BILLS file) that pertains to sulfur. You remember that the first word of the name is Sulfur but you do not remember the bill number. You could find the desired record with the LOCATE command.

DO THIS NOW 8-8 **Using the LOCATE Command to Find the Sulfur Bill**

1. Open the BILLS file with:

```
USE BILLS
```

2. The name of the field on which you must do the search is TITLE (see Figure 7-12). Enter the LOCATE command as follows.

```
LOCATE FOR TITLE = "Sulfur"
```

The message

```
Record =     5
```

is displayed and the current record will be indicated on the status bar as record 5.

3. You may inspect the record with the EDIT command. When finished, strike the Escape key.

   Note that this form of the LOCATE command includes the FOR command option in exactly the same form in which you used it when listing records in a previous section.

In general, the LOCATE is much slower than the FIND because it must search the data file record by record until it finds the desired one. In doing these exercises, you probably did not notice any difference in speed between the FIND and LOCATE. This was so because of the small size of the files. Had the files consisted of several thousand records, the LOCATE would have taken a considerable amount of time.

Tabulating Data in a File

Data processing is commonly defined as the converting of data to useful information. Thus far, in using dBASE we have inspected selected fields and records from a file but have done no processing. To get an idea of how easy it is to process data with dBASE, let us consider three commands that perform statistical operations on all or part of the records in a file.

COUNT	Counts the number of records in a file that satisfy a stated FOR condition.
SUM	Totals the values of a selected numeric field for all or part of the records of a file.
AVERAGE	Computes the average of the values of a selected numeric field for all or part of the records of a file.

To illustrate, assume that you, as the person responsible for the BILLS file, receive a telephone call from your supervisor, who urgently needs to know the average rating of all bills in the file and how many bills in the file have a rating value of 85 or greater. For a large file, a manual count would be time consuming. With dBASE, it can be done in a matter of seconds.

DO THIS NOW 8-9 **Computing the Average Rating Value and Counting the Number of Bills with a Rating of 85 or Greater**

1. Open the BILLS file with:

```
USE BILLS
```

2. Count the number of bills with a value of the field RATING that is 85 or greater with the following command.

```
COUNT FOR RATING >= 85
```

dBASE will check each record in the file, counting those that meet the specified FOR condition. Upon completing this action, it will display the message:

```
3 records
```

3. Determine the average of the field RATING for all records with the following command.

```
AVERAGE RATING
```

4. dBASE will total the values from the field RATING of each record in the file and then divide by the number of records. Upon completing this action, it will display:

```
8 records averaged
RATING
81
```

5. When you give these figures to your supervisor, she tells you that she wanted the average rating of only the water-related bills. For this, you only need add the FOR option to the AVERAGE command as follows:

```
AVERAGE RATING FOR TYPE = "W"
```

6. dBASE will select only those records meeting the FOR condition. The result will be:

```
3 records averaged
RATING
83
```

Assignment 8-2 may now be completed.

REPORT GENERATION

A file listing (many of which you have generated) is a file printout consisting of one line per selected record from the file. Although this has been adequate for learning about dBASE, businesses require much more information—they require reports. Reports commonly include more extensive headings, the numbering of pages and column headings on each page

Figure 8-9
The structure of the AR file.

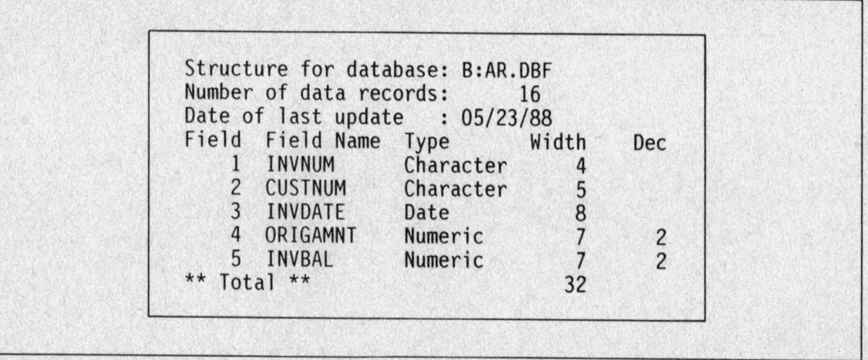

```
Structure for database: B:AR.DBF
Number of data records:       16
Date of last update   : 05/23/88
Field  Field Name  Type       Width    Dec
    1  INVNUM      Character      4
    2  CUSTNUM     Character      5
    3  INVDATE     Date           8
    4  ORIGAMNT    Numeric        7      2
    5  INVBAL      Numeric        7      2
** Total **                      32
```

for reports longer than a single page, summary lines that display totals of portions of the output, and often data from more than one file. In dBASE, the process of preparing reports is simplified with a special component of the dBASE program called the report generator. To illustrate how the report generator works, we will use the MCT Enterprises Accounts Receivable file (named AR). The record format of this file is shown in Figure 8-9. Characteristics of this file are:

1. It contains one record for each customer sale.
2. The key field is the invoice number; there will never be two records with the same invoice number.
3. A customer will have one record for each purchase. For instance, referring to the file listing of Figure 8-10, notice that most customers have more than one record. However, the invoice number is different for each.
4. As payments are received, the payment is credited against the invoice.
5. As part of the month-end processing, reports are prepared using data from this file. These include a summary report of all customers and their balances due, and a statement of account for each customer. Records with 0 balances are deleted from this file at this time.

A Simple Report

For our first exposure to the report generator, we will use it to print the report shown in Figure 8-11. Notice that it includes a *page heading* and *column headings* that are much more descriptive than the data file field names. It also includes a page number. The dBASE report generator allows us to specify the number of lines to be printed per page. When the page becomes full, dBASE causes the printer to position the continuous-form printer paper to the top of the next page, where the column headings are printed again, together with the page number. The main part of the report is made up of *detail lines,* with each line representing a record from the input file. The last line of the report is a *total line,* which includes the total for the original amount and current balance fields.

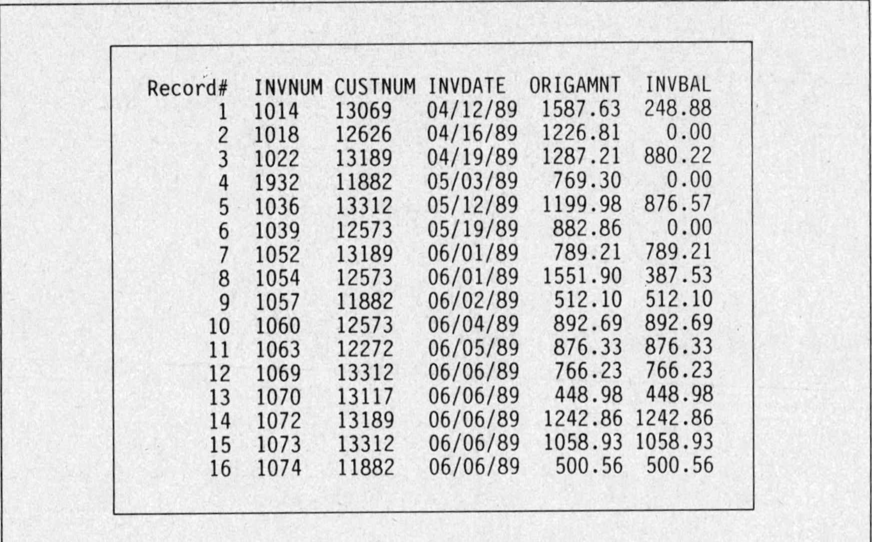

Record#	INVNUM	CUSTNUM	INVDATE	ORIGAMNT	INVBAL
1	1014	13069	04/12/89	1587.63	248.88
2	1018	12626	04/16/89	1226.81	0.00
3	1022	13189	04/19/89	1287.21	880.22
4	1932	11882	05/03/89	769.30	0.00
5	1036	13312	05/12/89	1199.98	876.57
6	1039	12573	05/19/89	882.86	0.00
7	1052	13189	06/01/89	789.21	789.21
8	1054	12573	06/01/89	1551.90	387.53
9	1057	11882	06/02/89	512.10	512.10
10	1060	12573	06/04/89	892.69	892.69
11	1063	12272	06/05/89	876.33	876.33
12	1069	13312	06/06/89	766.23	766.23
13	1070	13117	06/06/89	448.98	448.98
14	1072	13189	06/06/89	1242.86	1242.86
15	1073	13312	06/06/89	1058.93	1058.93
16	1074	11882	06/06/89	500.56	500.56

Figure 8-10
The AR file.

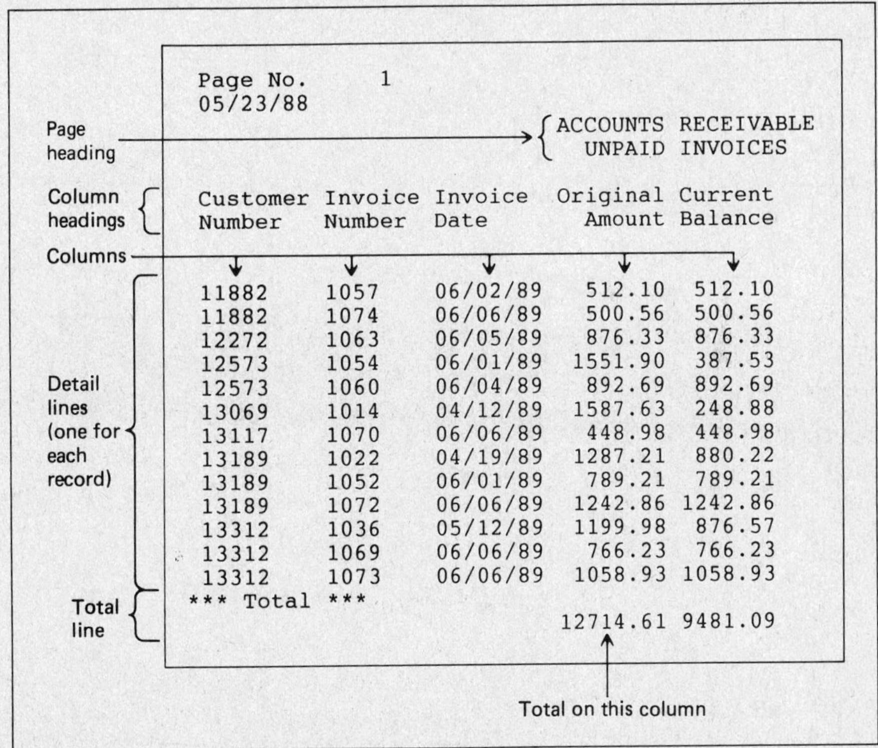

Page No. 1
05/23/88

ACCOUNTS RECEIVABLE
UNPAID INVOICES

Customer Number	Invoice Number	Invoice Date	Original Amount	Current Balance
11882	1057	06/02/89	512.10	512.10
11882	1074	06/06/89	500.56	500.56
12272	1063	06/05/89	876.33	876.33
12573	1054	06/01/89	1551.90	387.53
12573	1060	06/04/89	892.69	892.69
13069	1014	04/12/89	1587.63	248.88
13117	1070	06/06/89	448.98	448.98
13189	1022	04/19/89	1287.21	880.22
13189	1052	06/01/89	789.21	789.21
13189	1072	06/06/89	1242.86	1242.86
13312	1036	05/12/89	1199.98	876.57
13312	1069	06/06/89	766.23	766.23
13312	1073	06/06/89	1058.93	1058.93
*** Total ***				
			12714.61	9481.09

Figure 8-11
A simple report.

The report of Figure 8-11 was generated from a report specification generated with the dBASE report generator and stored on disk as a separate report specification file. That file is not included on your data disk; in fact, you will learn how to use the report generator by creating this specification file. In doing so, you will need to designate:

1. Information about the printed page (for instance, number of printed lines per page) and the report heading.
2. Each field to be printed (each column of the report) and the column heading.
3. The format of each numeric field (number of decimal positions to be printed).
4. The numeric fields to be totaled for the total line.

The report specification is created using the CREATE REPORT command and, once created and stored to disk, it can be used whenever needed for preparing the report. Let us now create this specification.

DO THIS NOW 8-10 **Creating a Report Specification to Generate the Report of Figure 8-11 from Data in the AR File**

1. Since this report specification is to use data from the AR file, that file must first be opened with the command:

```
USE AR
```

2. To create the report specification, enter the command:

```
CREATE REPORT AR1
```

   AR1 will be used as the name of this report specification file: AR to signify the AR data file and 1 to indicate that this is the first of two that you will create. Your screen display will be as shown in Figure 8-12. The *Options* submenu allows you to specify page characteristics. The default values are for standard 8 1/2 × 11 paper but you easily can change them to suit the needs of the particular report.

3. The *Page title* option is highlighted; select it by striking Enter. The window of Figure 8-13 will be displayed on your screen with the cursor awaiting entry of the report title. The small triangle (arrowhead) on the *Page title* line indicates that this menu option has been selected.
4. Type the following two report title lines:

```
ACCOUNTS RECEIVABLE
UNPAID INVOICES
```

   The page title can consist of up to four lines.

5. Terminate report title entry with the Ctrl-End sequence. Your screen display will be the same as that of Figure 8-13 except that the first part of the title will be on the *Page title* line.

   Next you must specify the data fields to be printed. For each column of the output report (refer to Figure 8-11), you will need to designate the field to be printed (the column contents), the column heading, the number of positions to allocate on the printed page, and the number of decimal places for numeric data.

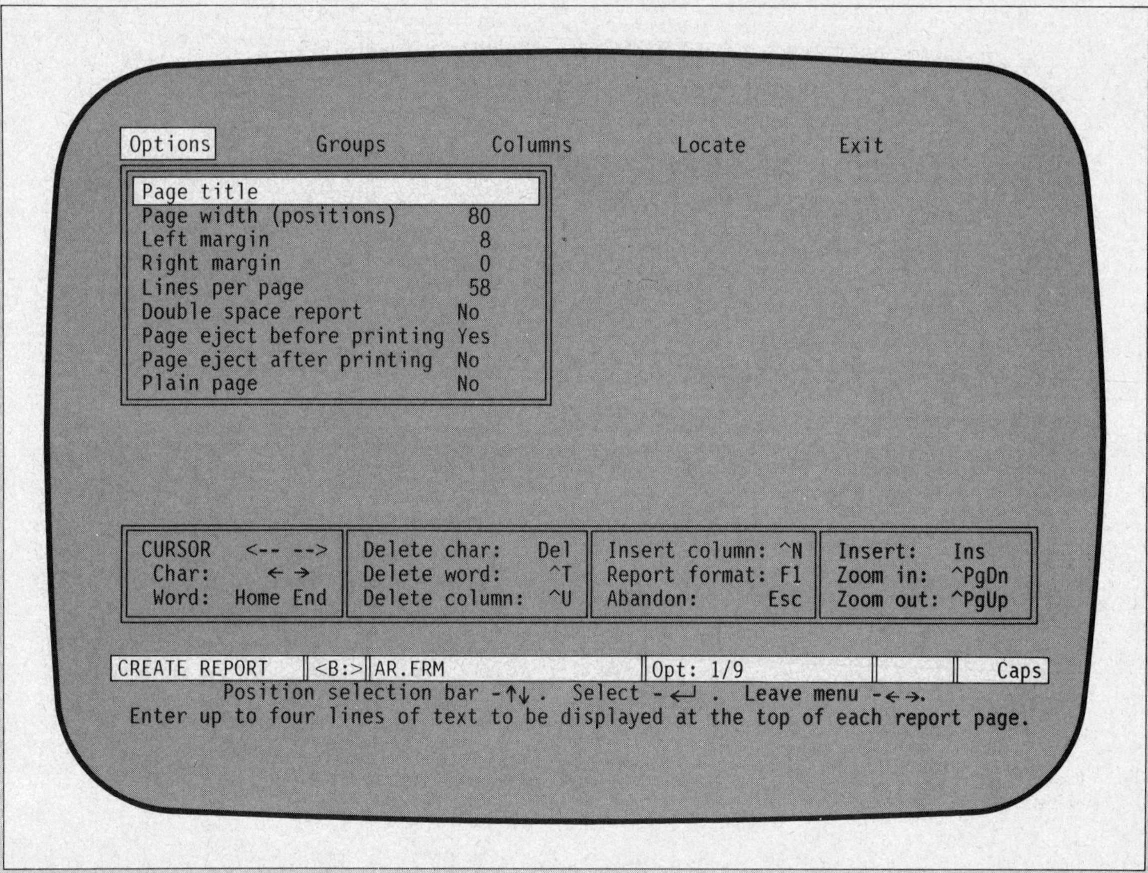

Options
Groups
Columns
Locate
Exit
Page title
Page width (positions) 80
Left margin 8
Right margin 0
Lines per page 58
Double space report No
Page eject before printing Yes
Page eject after printing No
Plain page No
CURSOR <-- -->
Char: ← →
Word: Home End
Delete char: Del
Delete word: ^T
Delete column: ^U
Insert column: ^N
Report format: F1
Abandon: Esc
Insert: Ins
Zoom in: ^PgDn
Zoom out: ^PgUp
CREATE REPORT
<B:>
AR.FRM
Opt: 1/9
Caps
Position selection bar - ↑↓. Select - ↵. Leave menu - ←→.
Enter up to four lines of text to be displayed at the top of each report page.

Figure 8-12
The CREATE REPORT Option submenu.

Options
Groups
Columns
Locate
Exit
Page title
Page width (positions) 80
Left margin 8
Right margin 0
Lines per page 58
Double space report No
Page eject before printing Yes
Cursor is positioned here awaiting entry of report title.

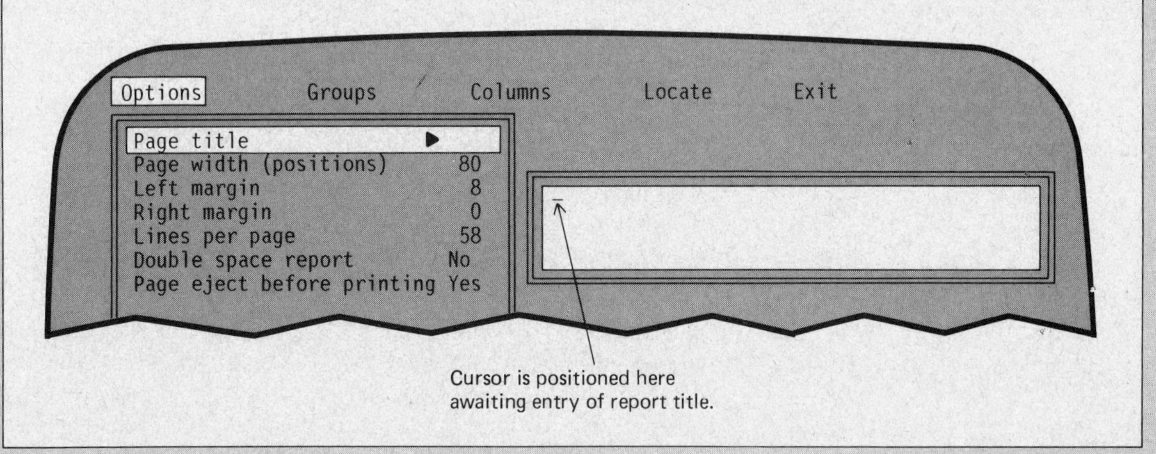

Figure 8-13
Entering the main heading.

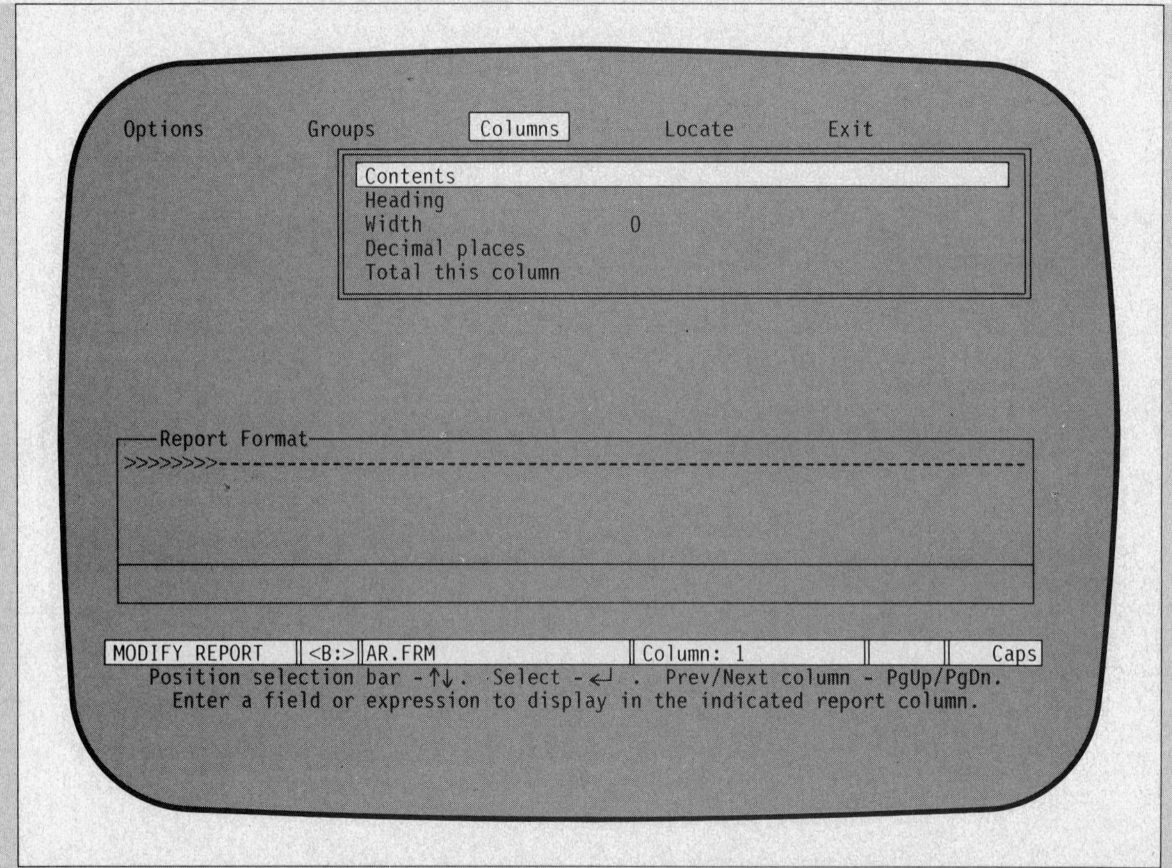

Figure 8-14
The Columns submenu.

6. With the Right key, move the menu bar selection to *Columns;* this will produce the screen shown in Figure 8-14.

7. Select the *Contents* option by striking Enter. A small arrowhead will be displayed in the highlighted area, indicating that you must enter the name of the field whose values are to be printed in this column.

8. You can type the field name (or an expression), or you can obtain a field list of the data file by pressing the F10 key. Strike F10 to obtain the display of Figure 8-15.

9. Since the customer number is to be in the first column of the report, move the highlight to CUSTNUM and strike Enter to select it. CUSTNUM will be displayed in the *Contents* line; strike Enter to tell dBASE to accept it.

10. Strike the Down key to highlight the *Heading* option, and then strike Enter to select it. Your display will be as shown in Figure 8-16; dBASE is awaiting entry of the heading for this column.

11. Type the two-line heading:

```
Customer
Number
```

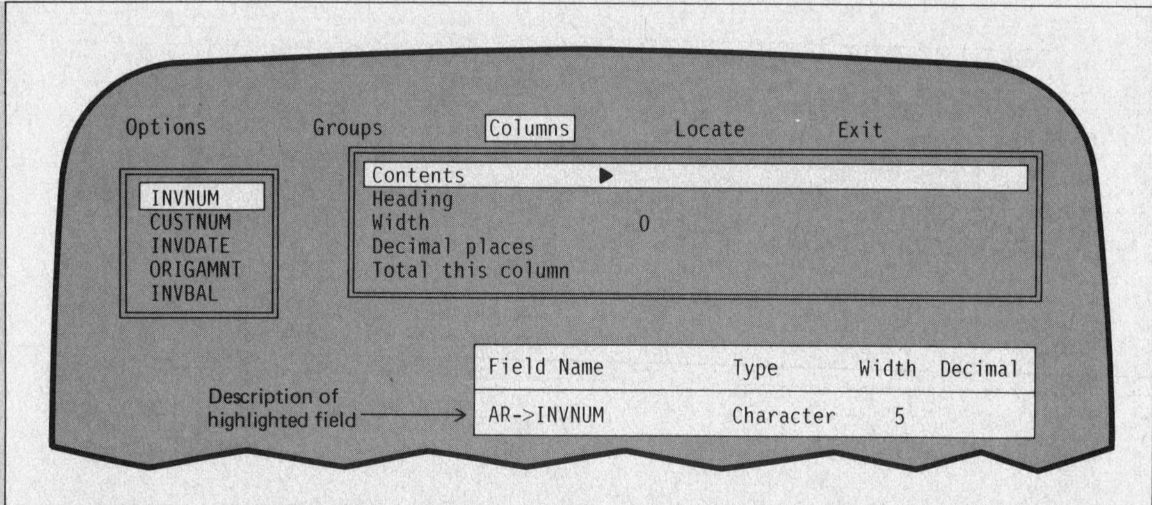

Figure 8-15
Data file field display.

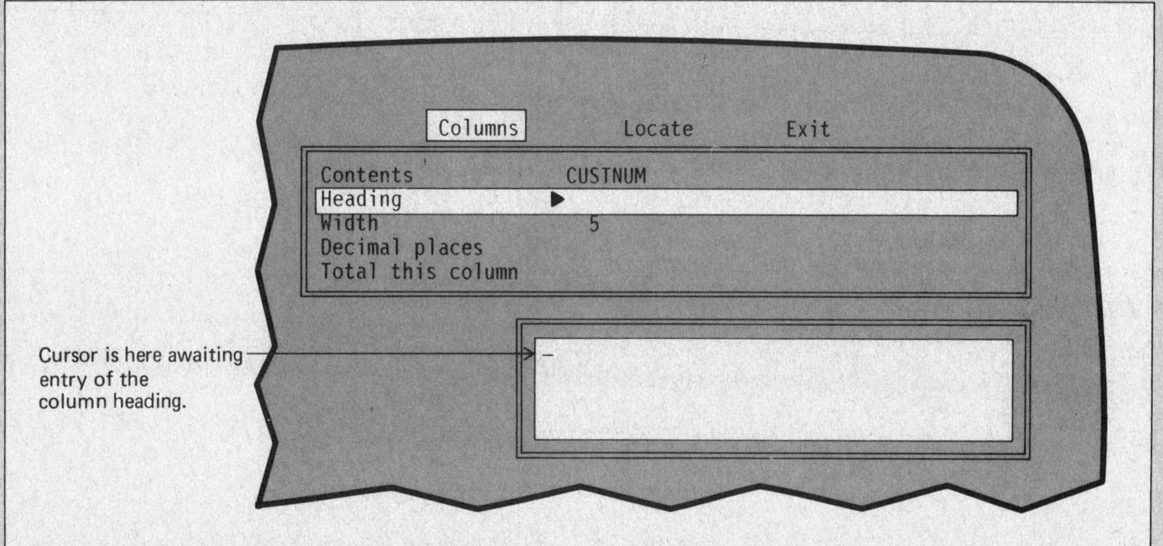

Figure 8-16
Entering column headings.

Complete this action with the Ctrl-End key sequence. Your screen display will be as shown in Figure 8-17. The box entitled *Report Format* displays the current form of the output line. Notice that the margin, heading, and number of remaining positions on the output line are indicated in the upper portion of the box. In the lower portion of the box, the location of the field (CUSTNUM) is indicated by XXXXX. The uppercase letter X indicates a character field.

12. Strike the PgDn key to complete the first column; the blank *Columns* submenu of Figure 8-14 will be displayed again.

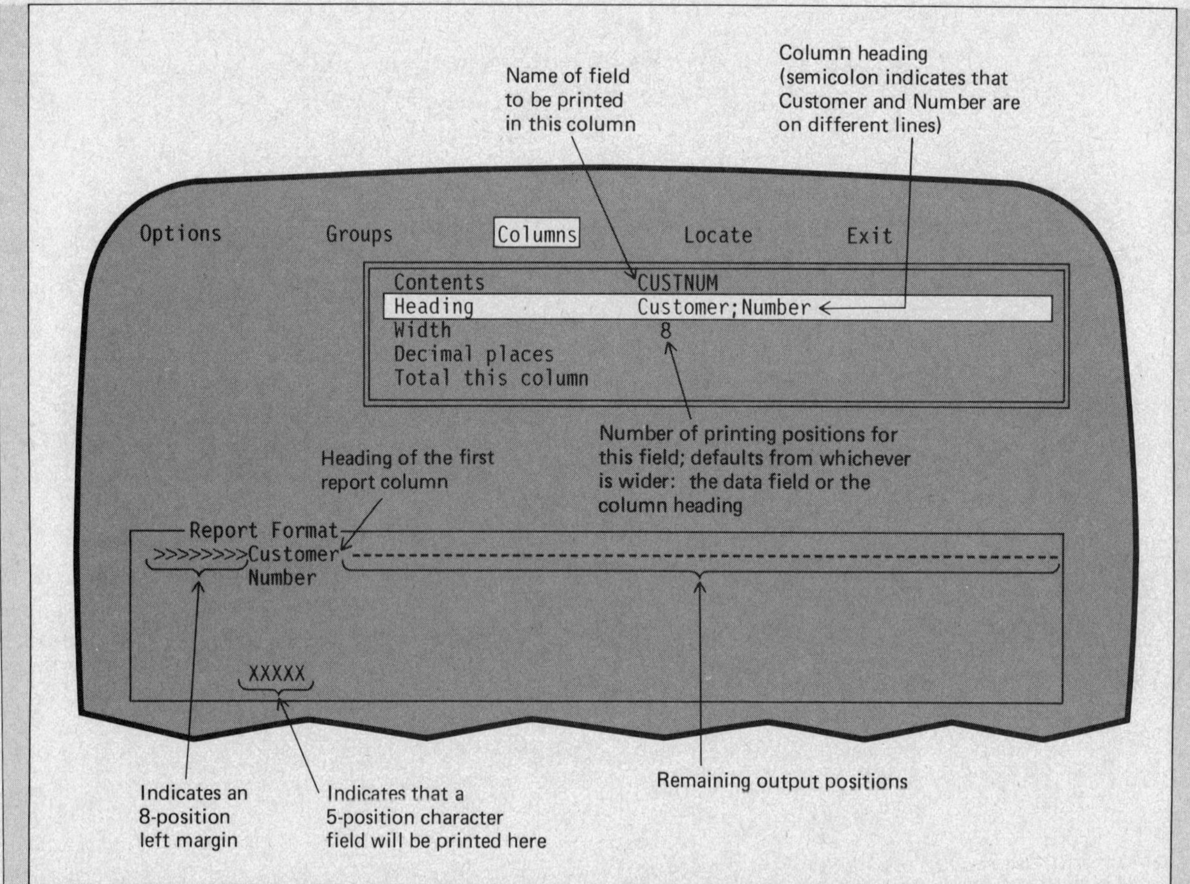

Figure 8-17
The Columns screen.

13. Repeat steps 8 through 12 for the second column, using the field INVNUM, then for the third column, using the field INVDATE. The column headings are to be:

```
Invoice   Invoice
Number    Date
```

14. Repeat steps 8 through 11 (do not strike PgDn when finished) for the fourth column using the field ORIGAMNT. Use the column headings:

```
Original
Amount
```

Your screen should appear as shown in Figure 8-18.

In your line format, you can see that the numeric output is indicated by ####.## where the # character indicates a digit position. The largest number that could be displayed is 9999.99. In this case, the report generator uses as a default the field width and decimal places from the structure of the data file.

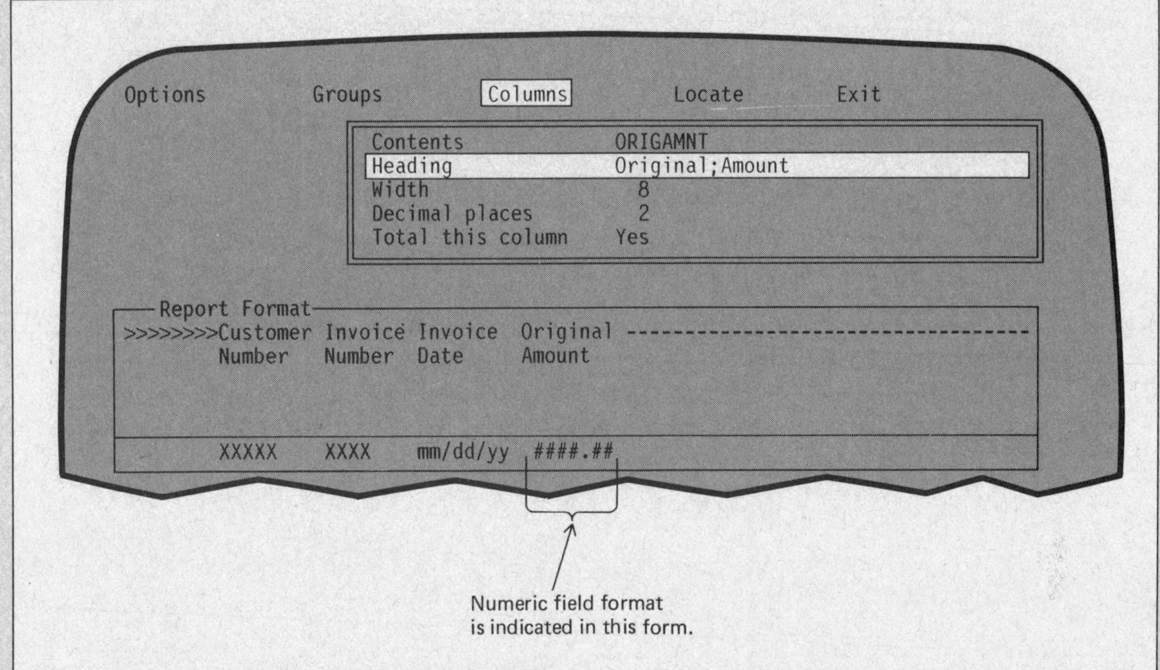

Figure 8-18
Defining a numeric field in a report.

The last menu option, *Total this column*, defaults to Yes for each numeric field. This will cause dBASE to calculate and print a total for this column (refer to the report of Figure 8-11). When a column is to be totaled, you should keep in mind that the total will require more digits than any component value. Hence, you must designate a field width for that column large enough to display the largest possible total. In this example, the report generator set the width as 8 to accommodate the heading. If the total of this column were to exceed 99999.99, then you would need to set the width at 9. If you did not want a total on this column, then you would change the Yes to No.

15. Complete the specification for the ORIGAMNT field by striking the PgDn key.

16. Enter the specification for the INVBAL field as you did with ORIGAMNT. Use the following column heading.

```
Current
Balance
```

17. Check each of your column specifications by moving from one field to the next with the PgUp or PgDn key. Correct any error by selecting the same way that you did when entering.

18. When you have checked everything, move the bar menu highlight to the *Exit* option; highlight the *Save* suboption and strike Enter.

Your report specification will be saved to disk using the name AR1 (that you designated at the beginning) and a default extension of FRM; the full name will be AR1.FRM. When the saving action has been completed, you will be returned to the dot prompt.

Printing the Report

Now that the report specification has been stored as a file, you could immediately generate a report, or you could terminate the dBASE work session and generate a report at any later time. As with a listing from the LIST command, you can have the records accessed in their physical file order or in order based on an index. In Figure 8-11, the records are in order by customer number. Notice that this causes all records for a given customer to be grouped together. The data disk contains the index file AR-CUST, which is based on the customer number field. You will use this in the following sequence.

DO THIS NOW 8-11 **Generating an Accounts Receivable Report Using AR1.FRM**

1. Open the AR file with the index AR-CUST as follows:

```
USE AR INDEX AR-CUST
```

2. Generate the report by entering the following command.

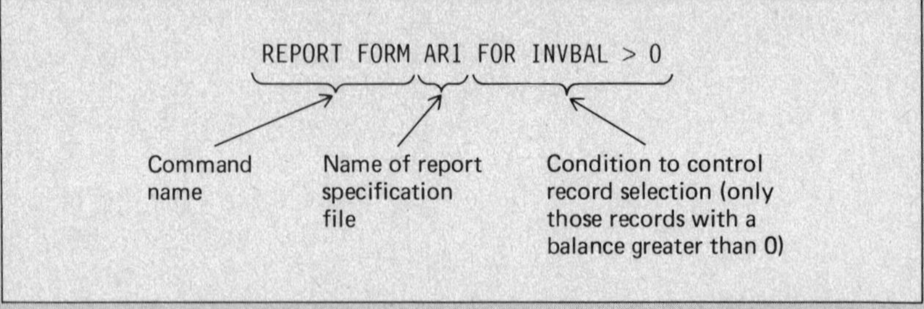

The report displayed on your screen should be identical to that of Figure 8-11.

In the REPORT FORM command, you may select records using the FOR option exactly as you did with the LIST command in the preceding section. Also, if you want a printed copy of the report, you need only include the TO PRINT option, that is:

```
REPORT FORM AR1 FOR INVBAL > 0 TO PRINT
```

For a report in which the records are in invoice number sequence, you would create an index on that field and open the AR file with it.

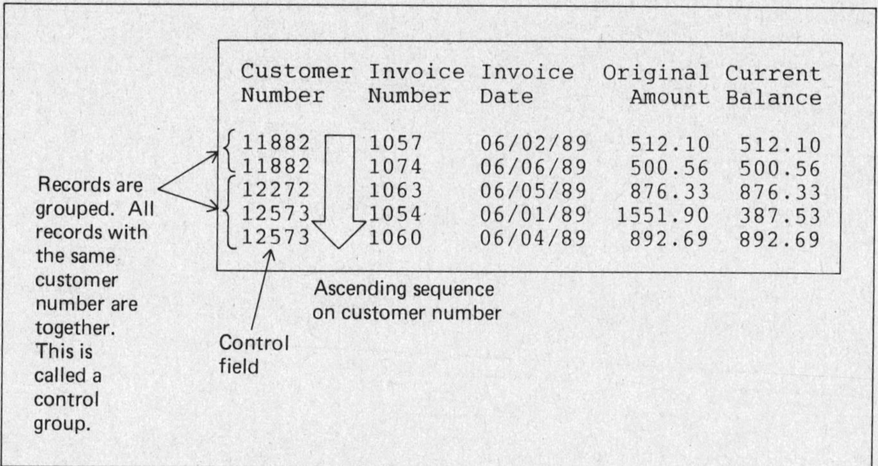

Customer Number	Invoice Number	Invoice Date	Original Amount	Current Balance
11882	1057	06/02/89	512.10	512.10
11882	1074	06/06/89	500.56	500.56
12272	1063	06/05/89	876.33	876.33
12573	1054	06/01/89	1551.90	387.53
12573	1060	06/04/89	892.69	892.69

Figure 8-19
Groups of records.

Control Groups

Figure 8-19 is a portion of the report produced by AR1. Since the records are in order by the customer number field, all records with identical customer numbers are grouped together. Each group of records with the same customer number is called a **control group;** the field on which they are grouped (customer number in this case) is called the **control field.** Each control group represents a semi-independent element of the report. As such, the report becomes more useful if it includes a summary for each control group.

With only some minor additions to AR1.FRM, we would be able to generate the report of Figure 8-20 (see the next page). Here, we see that the customer number is not repeated for each record of a control group; it serves as a heading for that group. Furthermore, the total for each control group is included following the last record of the group. These are commonly called **group totals.**

Generating a Report Specification with Group Totals

The creating of a report specification that gives group totals requires one additional step beyond that of creating AR1.FRM: you must identify the group. The easiest way to do this is to use the MODIFY REPORT command that will bring up the screen of Figure 8-12. Then you can continue working on this specification as if you had never terminated the CREATE REPORT work session. To preserve the original, you will make a copy, and then modify the copy. The changes that you will make will be both to improve the appearance of that which you already have and to add subtotals. The modifications will be:

- Change the left margin and page width to center the heading better.
- Specify the group field (CUSTNUM).
- Remove the customer number from the column output because the group heading will include it (see Figure 8-20).

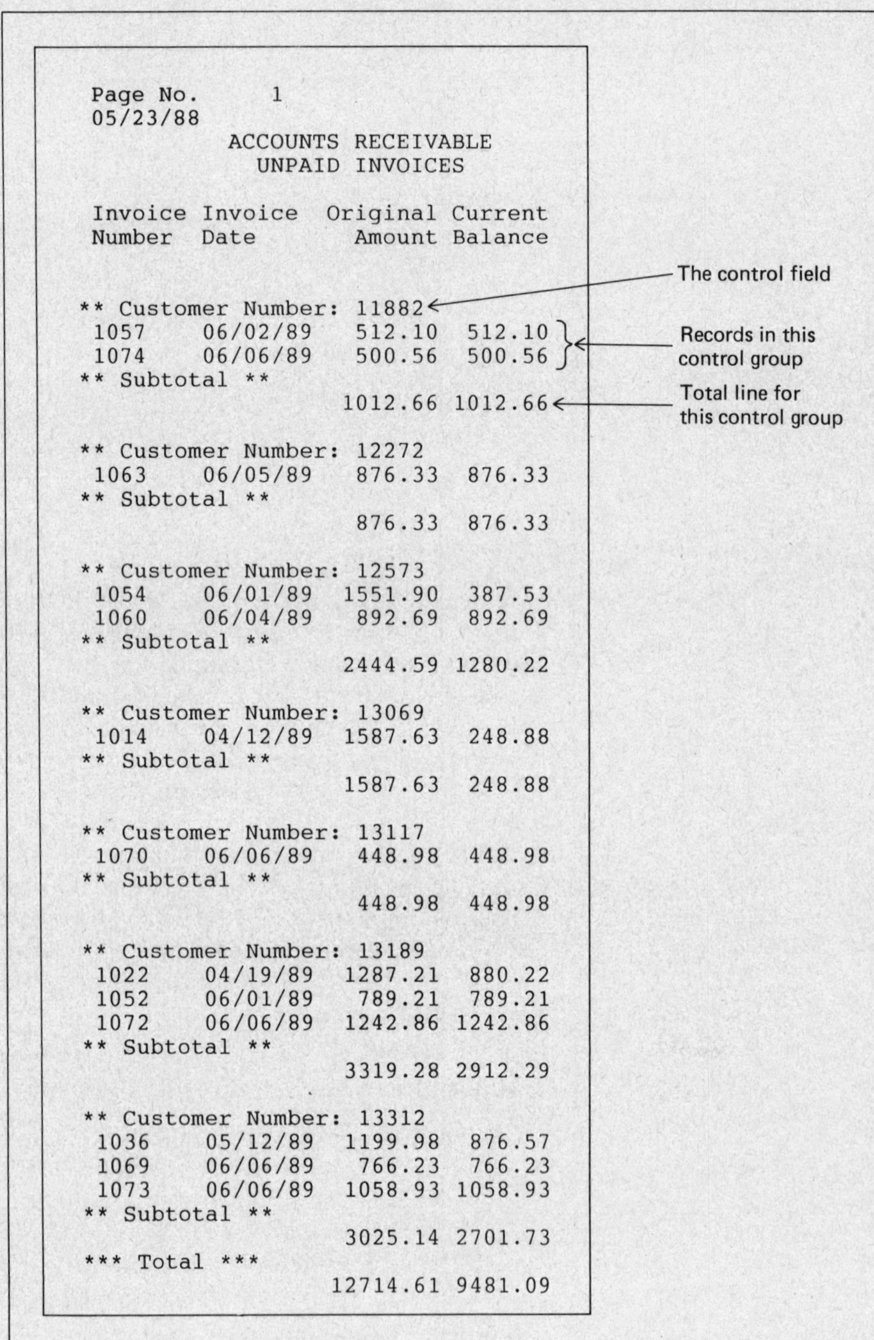

```
Page No.      1
05/23/88
         ACCOUNTS RECEIVABLE
           UNPAID INVOICES

Invoice Invoice  Original Current
Number  Date       Amount Balance

** Customer Number: 11882
 1057    06/02/89   512.10  512.10
 1074    06/06/89   500.56  500.56
** Subtotal **
                   1012.66 1012.66

** Customer Number: 12272
 1063    06/05/89   876.33  876.33
** Subtotal **
                    876.33  876.33

** Customer Number: 12573
 1054    06/01/89  1551.90  387.53
 1060    06/04/89   892.69  892.69
** Subtotal **
                   2444.59 1280.22

** Customer Number: 13069
 1014    04/12/89  1587.63  248.88
** Subtotal **
                   1587.63  248.88

** Customer Number: 13117
 1070    06/06/89   448.98  448.98
** Subtotal **
                    448.98  448.98

** Customer Number: 13189
 1022    04/19/89  1287.21  880.22
 1052    06/01/89   789.21  789.21
 1072    06/06/89  1242.86 1242.86
** Subtotal **
                   3319.28 2912.29

** Customer Number: 13312
 1036    05/12/89  1199.98  876.57
 1069    06/06/89   766.23  766.23
 1073    06/06/89  1058.93 1058.93
** Subtotal **
                   3025.14 2701.73
*** Total ***
                  12714.61 9481.09
```


Figure 8-20
Group totals.

DO THIS NOW 8-12 Making a Copy of AR1.FRM and Modifying It to Include Group Totals

1. From the dBASE dot prompt, make a copy of AR1.FRM using the dBASE COPY FILE command as follows:

```
COPY FILE B:AR1.FRM TO B:AR2.FRM
```

2. If the AR file is not still open from DTN 8-11, then open it with a USE command.
3. Enter the command:

```
MODIFY REPORT AR2
```

   The resulting screen will be that shown in Figure 8-12.

4. The first step is to change the page width and margins to center the report better. For this, select the *Page width* option (move the highlight to it and strike Enter). Type in the value 60, and then strike Enter to register the new value.
5. Select the *Left margin* option and enter a value of 20. This completes the page setup changes.
6. With the Right key, move the highlight to the *Groups* menu bar selection. Your screen will display the submenu shown in Figure 8-21.

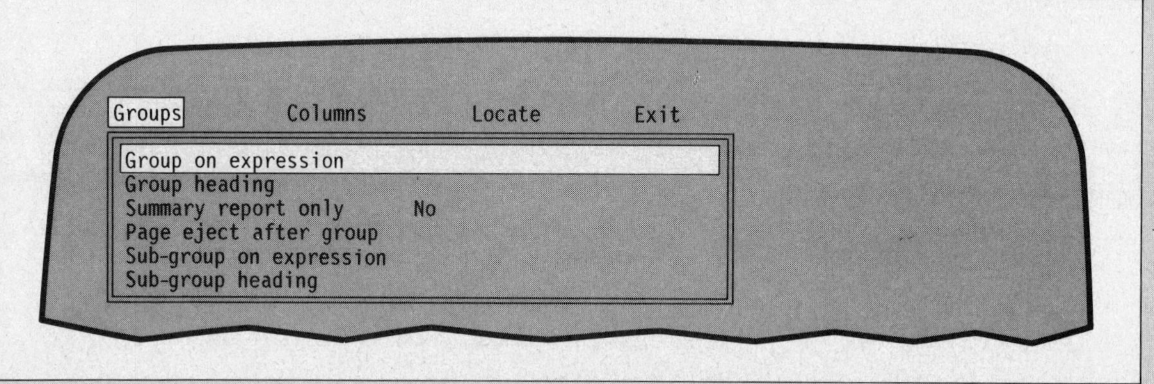

Figure 8-21
The Groups submenu.

7. The first option, *Group on expression,* is used to specify the control field; select this option by striking Enter.
8. The cursor will be positioned following the arrowhead on the *Group on expression* line. Type CUSTNUM, the name of the control field, and then strike Enter. (Note that you could display the field list by striking the F10 key.)
9. You must now describe the heading that is to precede each group. Strike the Down key to move the highlight to the Group heading option then strike Enter.
10. Type the group heading

```
Customer number:
```

and then strike Enter. Your screen will be as shown in Figure 8-22. This completes the group designation. The remaining items are left at their default values.

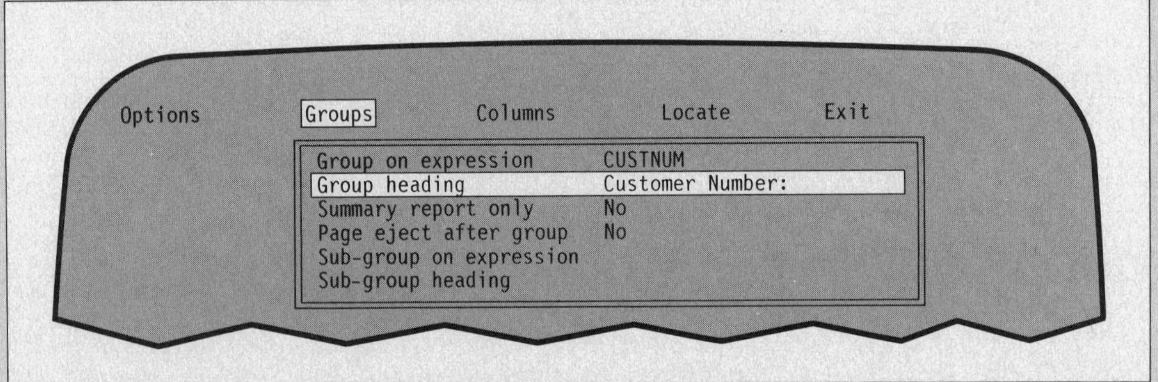

Figure 8-22
Entering the group heading.

11. To remove the CUSTNUM field from the column specifications, move the highlight to the *Columns bar* menu option. The description of the CUSTNUM column will be displayed.

12. Strike the F1 key to display the Help frame shown in Figure 8-23. Upon inspecting this, you will see that a column can be deleted with the Ctrl-U sequence. Hold down the Control key and strike the letter U. This causes the currently displayed column (CUSTNUM) to be deleted from the report.

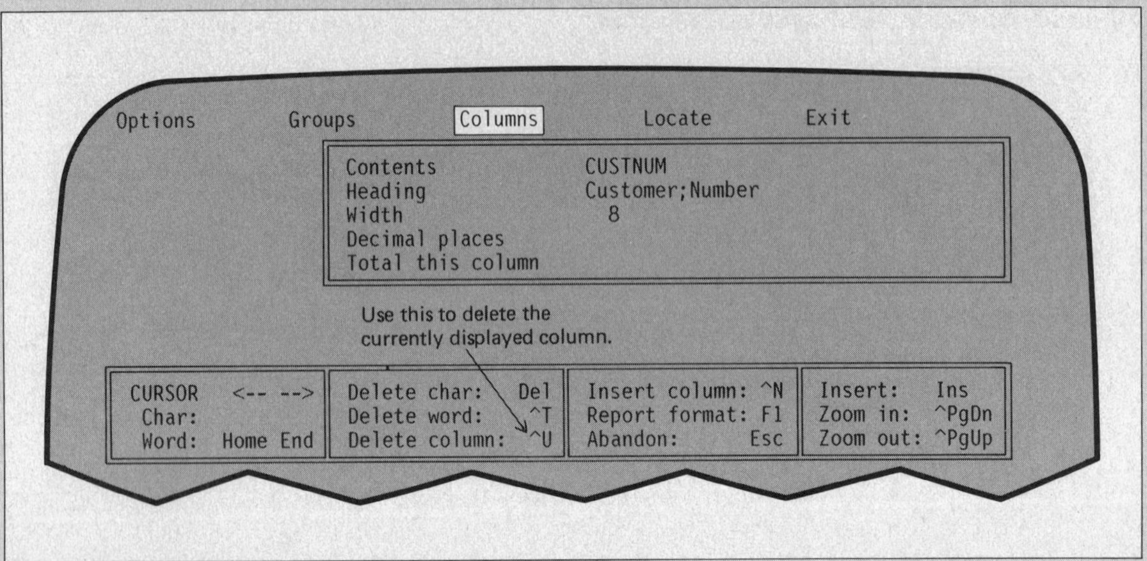

Figure 8-23
Deleting a report column.

13. The task is complete. The final step is to highlight the *Exit* option and select the *Save*. You will be returned to the dot prompt.

You now have two report specification files on your disk: AR1.FRM and AR2.FRM. To generate a report with AR1, you must first open the AR data file. If you do not specify an index when opening, the records will be listed in their physical file order. Designation of an index upon opening will cause the records to be listed according to the index. On the other hand, AR2.FRM does group totaling using the customer number as the group control field. Hence, if AR is not opened with the customer number index, the printed group totals will be meaningless.

DO THIS NOW 8-13 **Generating the Group Total Report Using AR2.FRM**

1. Open the AR file with the command:

```
USE AR INDEX AR-CUST
```

2. Generate the report with the command:

```
REPORT FORM AR2 FOR INVBAL > 0
```

Your output should be identical to that of Figure 8-20.

Assignment 8-3 may now be completed.

SUMMARY

From this chapter, you have learned some of the basic methods for turning data into useful information. The three broad areas covered in this chapter were indexing, which allows you to change the sequence in which you access records; selecting records by using conditional forms; and report generation. Summarizing, the important items from this chapter are:

- An index can be created on any character, numeric, or date field of a data file record.
- Access to data in a file is controlled by an index file only when the file is opened together with that index file.
- If records are to be added to a file for which indexes have been created, the indexes will be updated with the addition of records only if they were opened when the file was opened.
- When a file is opened with an index, the FIND command allows direct access to any record in the file based on the value of the field on which the index was built.

- If a data field of a file on which an index is built is changed, then that index must be open when the change is made or else the index file will not be updated.
- Relational operators are used to build relational expressions that compare two quantities. The relational operators are:

<	Less than
>	Greater than
=	Equal to
<=	Less than or equal to
>=	Greater than or equal to
<> or #	Not equal to

- A relational expression can be either true or false.
- The FOR command option uses a relation expression to select records according to the condition designated by the relational expression.
- Compound conditions can be formed using the .AND. and .OR. logical operators.
- Calculations are performed in dBASE using arithmetic operators to form arithmetic expressions.
- With the LOCATE command, you can search a file based on a desired value for any field of a record.
- The COUNT command will count the number of records meeting a specified condition.
- The SUM and AVERAGE commands will sum and average the contents of a designated field for all records or selected records of a file.
- With the CREATE REPORT command, you can specify the exact form that a report will take. This includes page layout, headings, data to be printed, and totals and subtotals of numeric fields. This specification information is stored in a file with an extension of FRM.
- Before a report can be generated from an FRM file, the data file must first be opened. If the FRM computes group totals, then the data file must be opened with the index file created from the group control field.

COMMAND SUMMARY

Following are general forms for commands introduced in this chapter.

AVERAGE <field name> [FOR condition>]
Computes the arithmetic mean of numeric expressions.

COPY FILE <filename1.ext> TO <filename2.ext>
Makes an exact duplicate of the file *filename1.ext* and names it *filename2.ext*.

COUNT [FOR <condition>]
Tallies the number of records specified by the FOR condition.

INDEX ON <key expression> TO <index filename>
Create an index file on the specified fields.

LOCATE [FOR <condition>]
Positions the record pointer to the first record that satisfies the specified conditions.

MODIFY REPORT <.frm filename>
Allows for the creation and editing of a report form file.

REPORT FORM <.frm filename> [FOR <condition>] [TO PRINT]
Displays a tabular report of data.

SUM <field name> [FOR <condition>]
Computes and displays the sum of an expression for database records specified in the scope.

NEW TERMINOLOGY

Many of the database terms used in the introduction to Part Four are also used in this chapter. The following are additional new terms introduced in this chapter; you should be familiar with each of them.

arithmetic expression
arithmetic operator
control field
control group
group total
literal
logical operator
relational expression
relational operator

Name: ______________________ Date: __________

Assignment 8-1

1. In addition to the command COPY FILE, dBASE includes the COPY TO command which will copy the currently open file to a new file record by record. For instance, consider the command sequence:

```
USE CUSTOMER INDEX CUS-YTD
COPY TO CUSTOM8
```

This COPY command will cause the records of CUSTOMER to be copied to another file on disk with the name CUSTOM8. Do you think that CUSTOM8 will be identical to CUSTOMER? Explain your answer. You may want to inspect the newly created file. To do so, you must first open it.

2. The customer file is opened with the following USE command.

```
USE CUSTOMER INDEX CUS-YTD, CUSTOMER, CUS-COMP CUS-ANNV
```

If the LIST command is executed, what will be the sequencing of the records?

3. Only one index can affect the sequence of the records in a file at any given time. What is the value of listing all of the index files in a USE as is done in the preceding question?

4. What is the maximum number of index files that you think could be created for the CUSTOMER file? Explain your answer.

Name: ______________________ Date: ____________

Assignment 8-2

1. Consider the relational expression:

```
3.2*AMNT>=16
```

What will be the result of evaluating for each of the following values of the field AMNT?

a. –10

b. 5

c. 20

2. Prepare a LIST command to list records from the CUSTOMER file according to the following conditions.

a. Account balances greater than 1000.

b. In region 12 with zero balances.

c. Year-to-date sales between 5000 and 8000.

d. The first two digits of the customer number 12.

Name: ______________________ Date: ______________

Assignment 8-2 (*continued*)

3. Assume that you opened the CUSTOMER file with the index on the customer name field (CUS-COMP) intending to open it on the customer number field. Then you attempted to find the record with a customer number of 11882 (this is record 4) with the command:

```
FIND "11882"
```

What do you think would happen?

4. Both the FIND and LOCATE commands can be used for accessing a selected record. What are the advantages of each?

5. What would happen if you entered the following sequence of commands?

```
USE CUSTOMER INDEX CUS-COMP
FIND "C"
```

6. Give the command sequence to obtain the average customer balance from the CUSTOMER file both with and without including the zero balance values. Execute the commands and check the results against the data.

Name: ______________________ Date: ______________

Assignment 8-3

1. Why do you think dBASE requires that the data file be opened before you issue the CREATE REPORT command to prepare a report specification?

2. The BILL file includes three fields on which a group total report might be run. (This excludes the logical field RECOMMEND because dBASE does not allow an index to be built on a logical field.) Identify these fields and the significance of each group.

3. What would be the nature of a report generated with the following sequence of commands? Notice that no index file is designated.

```
USE AR
REPORT FORM AR2
```

Name: ______________________ Date: ____________

OBJECTIVE QUESTIONS

Matching

Match each of the commands in a to h with the most appropriate action in 1 through 8.

a. logical operators
b. detail line
c. control group
d. index
e. relational expression
f. LOCATE
g. FIND
h. arithmetic operators

____ **1.** Allows you to process the records of a file in other than their physical order in the file.

____ **2.** Results in a value of either true or false.

____ **3.** Provide the ability to perform calculations in dBASE.

____ **4.** Gives you the ability to include two or more comparisons in a single FOR option.

____ **5.** Requires that a file be opened with an index.

____ **6.** Searches a file (without the use of an index) for a record meeting a stated condition.

____ **7.** A set of consecutive records with the same value for a particular identifying field.

____ **8.** A portion of a report made up of data from a single record.

True/False

Determine whether each of the following is true or false.

T F **1.** Whenever a file is created (with the CREATE command), dBASE automatically creates one index file for it. This index is based on the key field.

T F **2.** A data file must first be opened before an index can be created on that data file.

T F **3.** As each index is created, dBASE automatically changes the physical sequencing of the records in the data file.

T F **4.** You cannot create an index for a data file from ASSIST; you must use the INDEX command from the dot prompt.

T F **5.** Although dBASE does not include a convention for index file names, the default file extension is NDX.

T F **6.** When opening a file for which several indexes have been created, the USE statement can include no index files, any one of the index files, or even all of them.

Name: ______________________ Date: __________

OBJECTIVE QUESTIONS (*continued*)

T F **7.** Whenever a data file is edited, all indexes associated with that data file must be recreated using the INDEX command.

T F **8.** When listing the contents of a data file using the FOR option, it is possible to get no records at all displayed.

T F **9.** If a file is opened with an index, it is not possible to use the FOR option in a LIST command.

T F **10.** The FOR option is designed solely for use with the LIST command.

T F **11.** Relational operators can be used to compare character data as well as numeric data.

T F **12.** If the following LIST were executed, only records with values in the SALES field that are twice the value in the QUOTA field will be listed.

```
LIST FOR 2*SALES >= QUOTA
```

T F **13.** If the following LIST were executed, only records for which the logical field CREDIT is True will be listed.

```
LIST FOR CREDIT
```

T F **14.** Like Lotus 1-2-3, dBASE does not allow spaces to be included within an expression.

T F **15.** According to the rules for using relational operators in dBASE, the following would list all records with a value in the field CHARGES between 400 and 800 (inclusive).

```
LIST FOR CHARGES >= 400 .AND. <= 800
```

T F **16.** If ACCTNUM is a five-position character field, the following would NOT be a valid form.

```
FOR ACCTNUM=12596
```

T F **17.** If APPROVED is a logical field, the following would be a valid command.

```
LIST FOR APPROVED
```

T F **18.** A logical operator is one that can be Yes or No.

T F **19.** ASSIST can be used to build simple conditions but it cannot be used to build compound conditions that use logical operators.

T F **20.** The advantage of the FIND over the LOCATE for direct access is that the FIND is much faster, especially for large files.

T F **21.** It is not necessary to use the entire field contents when searching for a record based on the value of one of the character fields of the record.

T F **22.** The FIND command can be used only in conjunction with the index that is built on the key field of a data file.

Name: ______________________ Date: ______________

OBJECTIVE QUESTIONS (*continued*)

T F **23.** Using the AVERAGE command to average the values in a particular field of a file does not change the values stored in the records for that field.

T F **24.** Both the SUM and the AVERAGE commands can be used with the FOR option to restrict records included in the calculation.

T F **25.** The commands COUNT, SUM, and AVERAGE will give different results if the file is opened with an index than if it is opened without an index.

T F **26.** The FOR option can be used with the REPORT FORM command to limit the records that are used in generating the report. This has nothing to do with the report specification created with the CREATE REPORT command.

T F **27.** In generating a report, totals can be calculated for numeric fields only if the data file is opened with an index.

T F **28.** Before issuing the REPORT FORM command to print a report, the file from which the report is generated must first be opened with a USE. However, creating the report specification does not require data from the file so it is not necessary to open the data file prior to issuing the CREATE REPORT command.

T F **29.** Using the REPORT FORM command to generate a report does not change either the report specification file or the data file.

T F **30.** It would be meaningless to speak of control groups in respect to a file that is opened on its key field.

Multiple Choice

In the space provided, record the letter of the choice that best completes or answers the statement.

____ **1.** Which of the following is NOT true about indexes?

A. An index can be created based on any numeric or character field in the record.
B. An index must be created for the key field.
C. Each index for a data file is stored as a separate index file.
D. An index can be created using ASSIST.

____ **2.** Which of the following is true regarding editing a data file that has indexes?

A. All index files must be opened with the data file.
B. The index built on the key field must be opened with the data file.
C. In some circumstances, it is not necessary to include all of the indexes in the data file open.
D. A file with indexes cannot be edited.

Name: ______________________ Date: ____________

OBJECTIVE QUESTIONS (*continued*)

____ **3.** The following is called a ______.

```
AMOUNT>=100
```

A. relational expression
B. relational operator
C. logical expression
D. logical operator

____ **4.** The element <> in the following form is called a ______.

```
CODE<>"ACF"
```

A. relational expression
B. relational operator
C. logical expression
D. logical operator

____ **5.** To designate calculations to be carried out, you use

A. relational expressions.
B. relational operators.
C. logical operators.
D. arithmetic operators.

____ **6.** If TEST is a logical variable, which of the following statements is true regarding the command:

```
LIST FOR TEST = .T.
```

A. Only records for which the value in the variable TEST is true will be displayed.
B. The periods should not be included around the letter T.
C. A logical operator should be used.
D. It is an invalid form.

____ **7.** In the following form, the .AND. is called a ______.

```
LIST FOR LOC="CENTRAL" .AND. AMNT<100
```

A. logical operator
B. relational operator
C. arithmetic operator
D. connective

Name: ______________________ Date: ______________

OBJECTIVE QUESTIONS (*continued*)

____ **8.** You have opened a file with an index on the Social Security number of the people in the file. The quickest way to access a record with a particular Social Security number would be to use the ______ command.

A. LIST
B. LOCATE
C. FIND
D. BROWSE

____ **9.** You need to access a particular record of a file based on the last name of a person. There is no index for this file. Which command would you use?

A. LIST
B. LOCATE
C. FIND
D. BROWSE

____ **10.** Assuming that BALANCE and LIMIT are both numeric fields in the currently open file, which of the choices is NOT true of the following command?

```
COUNT FOR BALANCE<500 .AND. BALANCE>600
```

A. A value of 0 will be displayed.
B. The value displayed will not depend on LIMIT.
C. Only values between 500 and 600 will be counted.
D. It will not matter what the values are in the BALANCE field of the records.

____ **11.** In a report, which of the following consists of data taken from a single record?

A. Column heading
B. Page heading
C. Detail line
D. Summary line

____ **12.** To print a report according to a previously generated report specification, you would use the ______ command and include the name of the report specification.

A. LIST
B. CREATE REPORT
C. RUN REPORT
D. REPORT FORM

____ **13.** A group total is a total

A. printed at the end of the report.
B. of all lines printed on a given page.
C. for a field of a particular set of consecutive records.
D. count of the records in a given group.

Name: ______________________ Date: ______________

OBJECTIVE QUESTIONS (*continued*)

Fill In

In the space provided, fill in the correct answer. Note that the answer can be one or two words.

1. ______________________
A(n) ______ gives access to the records in a file in other than their physical order in the file.

2. ______________________
The ______ command option allows you to be selective about the records to be accessed by a command.

3. ______________________
Comparisons are made using ______ operators.

4. ______________________
If you want to select records based on either of two conditions, you would need to use a(n) ______ operator to connect the conditions.

5. ______________________
An index provides ______ access to records of a data file.

6. ______________________
To find a record based on a particular condition, you would use the ______ command.

7. ______________________
If you wanted to add up the values for a given field of a file, you would use the ______ command.

8. ______________________
The ______ command is used to define a report specification.

9. ______________________
The ______ command is used to run a report using a previously defined report specification.

ASSIGNMENTS/PROJECTS

1. Print a listing in sequence based on the Points field of all bikers (Assignment 2, Chapter 7) belonging to the Quicksilver club with best finishes of 1, 2, or 3.
2. Print a listing in sequence based on the License Number field of all vehicles (Assignment 3, Chapter 7) that are Type MI and are on yearly leases.
3. Print a listing in sequence based on the Date of Evaluation field of all software evaluation records (Assignment 4, Chapter 7) that are type WP or SS.
4. Prepare a report specification file that will print a report from the BILLS file with records grouped on author and subtotals on the RATING field. Run the report.
5. Create a report specification for the bikers of Assignment 2, Chapter 7. Total only the Points field. Run two copies of the report: one consisting of all records in sequence based on the bikers' last name, and the other consisting of bikers with a Best Finish of 4 or better in sequence based on Points.
6. Expand the report specification of Assignment 5 to group by the Club field. Include a subtotal and total on the Points field.
7. Create a report specification for the vehicles of Assignment 3, Chapter 7. Total the Monthly Lease Rate field. Run two copies of the report: one consisting of all records in sequence based on the License Number field, and the other consisting only of vehicles with a Size field of CO or MI with all CO entries preceding MI entries.
8. Expand the report specification of Assignment 5 to group by the Customer Name field. Include a subtotal and total on the Monthly Lease Rate field.
9. Create a report specification for the software of Assignment 4, Chapter 7. Total both price fields. Run two copies of the report: one consisting of all records in sequence based on the Software product name field, and the other consisting only of vehicles with a Category field of FM or SS with all FM entries preceding SS entries.
10. Expand the report specification of Assignment 9 to group by the Category field. Include subtotals and totals on price fields.
11. Create a report specification for the horse owners association of Assignment 5, Chapter 7. Group by gender; thus there will be two groups, mares and stallions. Include subtotals and totals on the Rating field. Run two copies of the report; the first must include all of the horses and the second must include only those horses with best race finishes of third or better.

Index

Microcomputer Applications

Microcomputer Applications

Featuring:
WordPerfect®
Lotus® 1-2-3® and Joe Spreadsheet™ (a 1-2-3® Workalike)
dBASE III PLUS®

WILSON T. PRICE

The Dryden Press
Chicago Fort Worth San Francisco Philadelphia
Montreal Toronto London Sydney Tokyo

Acquisitions Editor: David Chodoff
Production Manager: Roger Kasunic
Production Coordinator: Donna Conte, Spectrum Publisher Services, Inc.
Interior Design: Rita Naughton
Cover Design: Marsha Cohen/Parallelogram
Part opening illustrations: Robert Andrew Parker
Photo Research: Teri Stratford
Illustrations: J & R Services
Composition: Kachina Typesetting
Printing and Binding: Arcata

Address editorial correspondence:
One Salt Creek Lane
Hinsdale, IL 60521

Printed in the United States of America

Library of Congress Cataloging-in-Publication Data

Price, Wilson T.
Microcomputer applications.

Includes Index.
1. Microcomputers. I. Title.
QA76.5.P7215 1989 004.16 88–31077
ISBN 0–03–026403–0
ISBN 0–03–026394–8

ISBN 0–03–026403–0 without software

9 0 1 2 069 9 8 7 6 5 4 3 2

The Dryden Press
Holt, Rinehart and Winston, Inc.
Saunders College Publishing

Picture credits appear on page 669.

Important: Please read this page before using the dBASE III PLUS program, a copy of which is being made available to you for use in conjunction with this Textbook pursuant to the terms of this Agreement for educational, training and/or demonstration purposes. By using the dBASE III PLUS program, you show your agreement to the terms of this license.

EXCLUSIONS OF WARRANTIES AND LIMITATIONS OF LIABILITY

THE COPY OF THE dBASE III PLUS PROGRAM MADE AVAILABLE FOR USE WITH THIS TEXTBOOK IS A LIMITED FUNCTIONALITY VERSION OF dBASE III PLUS, AND IS INTENDED SOLELY FOR EDUCATIONAL, TRAINING AND DEMONSTRATION PURPOSES. ACCORDINGLY, THIS COPY OF dBASE III PLUS IS PROVIDED "AS IS," WITHOUT WARRANTY OF ANY KIND FROM ASHTON-TATE OR HOLT RINEHART & WINSTON. ASHTON-TATE AND HOLT RINEHART & WINSTON HEREBY DISCLAIM ALL WARRANTIES OF ANY KIND WITH RESPECT TO THIS LIMITED FUNCTIONALITY COPY OF dBASE III PLUS, INCLUDING WITHOUT LIMITATION THE IMPLIED WARRANTIES OF MERCHANTABILITY AND FITNESS FOR A PARTICULAR PURPOSE. NEITHER ASHTON-TATE NOR HOLT RINEHART & WINSTON SHALL BE LIABLE UNDER ANY CIRCUMSTANCES FOR CONSEQUENTIAL, INCIDENTAL, SPECIAL OR EXEMPLARY DAMAGES ARISING OUT OF THE USE OF THIS LIMITED FUNCTIONALITY COPY OF dBASE III PLUS, EVEN IF ASHTON-TATE OR HOLT RINEHART & WINSTON HAS BEEN APPRISED OF THE LIKELIHOOD OF SUCH DAMAGES OCCURRING. IN NO EVENT WILL ASHTON-TATE'S OR HOLT RINEHART & WINSTON'S LIABILITY (WHETHER BASED ON AN ACTION OR CLAIM IN CONTRACT, TORT OR OTHERWISE) ARISING OUT OF THE USE OF THIS LIMITED FUNCTIONALITY COPY OF dBASE III PLUS EXCEED THE AMOUNT PAID FOR THIS TEXTBOOK.

LIMITED USE SOFTWARE LICENSE AGREEMENT

Definitions

The term "Software" as used in this agreement means the Limited Use version of dBASE III PLUS which is made available for use in conjunction with this Textbook solely for educational, training and/or demonstration purposes. The term "Software Copies" means the actual copies of all or any portion of the Software, including back-ups, updates, merged or partial copies permitted hereunder.

Permitted Uses

You may:

- Load into RAM and use the Software on a single terminal or a single workstation of a computer (or its replacement).
- Install the Software onto a permanent storage device (a hard disk drive).
- Make and maintain up to three back up copies provided they are used only for back-up purposes, and you keep possession of the back-ups. In addition, all the information appearing on the original disk labels (including copyright notice) must be copied onto the back-up labels.

This license gives you certain limited rights to use the Software and Software Copies for educational, training and/or demonstration purposes. You do not become the owner of and Ashton-Tate retains title to, all the Software and Software Copies. In addition, you agree to use reasonable efforts to protect the Software from unauthorized use, reproduction, distribution or publication.

All rights not specifically granted in this license are reserved by Ashton-Tate.

Uses Not Permitted

You may not:

- Make copies of the Software, except as permitted above.
- Rent, lease, sublicense, time-share, lend or transfer the Software, Software Copies or your rights under this license except that transfers may be made with Ashton-Tate's prior written authorization.
- Alter, decompile, disassemble, or reverse-engineer the Software.
- Remove or obscure the Ashton-Tate copyright and trademark notices.

Duration

This agreement is effective from the day you first use the Software. Your license continues for fifty years or until you return to Ashton-Tate the original disks and any back-up copies, whichever comes first.

If you breach this agreement, Ashton-Tate can terminate this license upon notifying you in writing. You will be required to return all Software Copies. Ashton-Tate can also enforce our other legal rights.

General

This agreement represents the entire understanding and agreement regarding the Software and Software Copies and supersedes any prior purchase order, communication, advertising or representation.

This license may only be modified in a written amendment signed by an authorized Ashton-Tate officer. If any provision of this agreement shall be unlawful, void, or for any reason unenforceable, it shall be deemed severable from, and shall in no way affect the validity or enforceability of the remaining provisions of this agreement. This agreement will be governed by California law.

The Limited Use Educational Version of WordPerfect 4.2 included with this textbook is licensed to the person who purchased the book. The purchaser is free to make backup copies for his or her own archival purposes only. He or she can use the software on different computers provided the software is never used on more than one computer at a time. Under no circumstances can this software be resold.

The Limited Use Educational Version of WordPerfect 4.2 contains certain limitations:

No file larger than 50K (roughly 25 to 30 single spaced pages) can be saved to disk. Documents of any size, however, can be edited on screen.

A data file created with the Limited Use Educational Version cannot be imported into regular WordPerfect, nor can a file created in regular WordPerfect be imported into the Limited Use Educational Version.

The message "WPC" will be printed after every paragraph.

Data files of any size can be printed through parallel printer port 1 without defining a printer, but font changes and extended ASCII characters are not allowed.

One cannot use the Limited Use Educational Version's speller and thesaurus with any of one's own documents because there are only a limited number of words in the Limited Use Educational Version's speller and thesaurus. To use the thesaurus and speller in the Limited Use Educational Version, follow the instructions in the file called "readme.wp".

The help file of the Limited Use Educational Version allows the user to retrieve the function key template, but space will not allow the full help files on the Limited Use Educational Version disk.

The Limited Use Educational Version of WordPerfect 4.2 is designed for introductory word processing courses. It is not, however, meant to substitute for the regular full-featured version of WordPerfect 4.2. The full-featured version may be obtained directly from WordPerfect Corporation at a 75 percent discount by means of the enclosed order form.

To my wife
Jean
with love
and
to our next adventure

Brief Contents

Contents

Preface

The premise of this book is simple: The best way to learn is to do, so the best way to learn about computers is to "do" computers.

A computer textbook that claims to teach you to learn by doing has to meet certain criteria:

- It must provide clear instructions on the use of specific applications on specific computers. And if those instructions are to be of any value to students, both the programs and the computers must be widely used in the business world.
- It must provide abundant opportunities for hands-on practice in the form of examples, exercises, and assignments.
- It must do all this in the context of a business environment—the environment for which students want to learn computer skills in the first place.

Microcomputer Applications meets all these criteria. It provides hands-on instruction—for the IBM PC—on WordPerfect®; Lotus® 1–2–3® and Joe Spreadsheet™, a keystroke compatible 1–2–3 workalike; and dBASE III PLUS®. It provides frequent hands-on examples keyed to an accompanying data disk. It provides abundant end-of-chapter exercises and assignments. Furthermore, it puts it all in a business context.

Microcomputer Applications, however, isn't just a software manual. It is, rather, a general introduction to computers in business, with a special emphasis on microcomputers and applications software.

ORGANIZATION OF THE TEXT

Microcomputer Applications is organized into five parts. Part One, "Computers and Microcomputers: An Overview," provides general background information on basic computer concepts and on the role of computers in business. It concludes with a chapter on DOS.

Part Two, "Word Processing and Desktop Publishing," Part Three, "Spreadsheets and Computer Graphics," and Part Four, "Database Management," are the hands-on core of the text. These parts can, of course, be covered in any order.

Part 5, "Advanced Topics," includes chapters on other types of software, on programming using dBASE III PLUS's programming language, and on communications.

SPECIAL FEATURES

Microcomputer Applications has several special features that distinguish it from other texts: It is available with and without software; the hands-on chapters contain "DO THIS NOW" exercises, as well as assignments; all versions of the text include a data disk keyed to the exercises and assignments; and the dBASE III PLUS programming language is used to illustrate programming principles.

Available with or Without Software

Microcomputer Applications is available with limited use educational versions of WordPerfect 4.2 and dBASE III PLUS, and a full-featured version of Joe Spreadsheet, a keystroke compatible Lotus 1–2–3 workalike. The software comes packaged with the book.

For those of you who already have the appropriate software available in your computer labs, the text is also available without software.

Three Chapters on Each Type of Software

Each of the three parts that make up the hands-on core of the text has a similar organization. The first chapter in each of these parts is a generic introduction to the type of software covered in the part. The next two chapters in each part is software specific—covering WordPerfect in Part Two, Lotus 1–2–3 and Joe Spreadsheet in Part Three, and dBASE III PLUS in Part Four. The first in each pair of software-specific chapters covers basics; the second, advanced topics. Part Two ends with a chapter on desktop publishing, and Part Three ends with a chapter on computer graphics.

"Do This Now" Sections

Throughout the hands-on, software-specific chapters are student exercises called "DO THIS NOW," each of which defines an activity (for example, editing a document with WordPerfect) and then describes, step by step, the procedures that the student should follow to carry out the activity.

There are over 100 "DO THIS NOW" exercises in the book. Each consists of activities ranging from simple, such as typing text into a word processor, to complex, such as preparing a bar graph from data in a spreadsheet.

Abundant Hands-on Assignments

Each of the hands-on chapters ends with a set of "Assignments" for students to do on their own that allows them to review the procedures presented in the chapter.

Data Disk

Both versions of the text—with and without software—come with a data disk with files keyed to the examples, exercises, and assignments in the text.

dBASE Programming

Although most computer users will never have to write a program in BASIC or other traditional high-level programming languages, they may well need to take advantage of the advanced features of a spreadsheet or a database program. To do so effectively, they need to understand the principles of good programming. For this reason, *Microcomputer Applications* teaches the principles of programming (in Chapters 18 and 19) using dBASE III PLUS's programming language.

OTHER FEATURES

Each chapter employs a number of learning aids to help students master the material. These include, for each chapter:

- A list of learning Objectives.
- A chapter Preview containing brief descriptions of each major section of the chapter.
- Boldfaced Key Terms throughout the text, which are also repeated in the New Terminology section and in the Glossary at the end of the book.
- A New Terminology section that lists the key terms in the chapter.
- A bulleted Summary
- A set of Review Questions, including discussion, matching, and true/false. Answers to the matching and true/false questions are found at the end of each chapter. Answers to the discussion questions are in the *Instructor's Manual.*

INSTRUCTIONAL PACKAGE

Microcomputer Applications comes with a full set of instructional support materials. These include, in addition to the software available with the book, an *Instructor's Manual, Transparency Acetates,* a *Test Bank* (in both printed and computerized form), and a student *Study Guide.*

Instructor's Manual

The *Instructor's Manual* includes an introduction with detailed suggestions for using the text for a variety of course schedules. For each chapter of the text, the *Instructor's Manual* contains:

- An expanded set of objectives.
- An overview of the chapter.
- A detailed lecture outline.
- Teaching tips and suggestions.
- Answers to review questions.
- Additional homework assigments.

Transparency Acetates

Microcomputer Applications comes with a set of over 100 Transparency Acetates. These include important figures from the text, as well as new figures.

Test Bank

The *Test Bank* contains over 2000 questions in a variety of formats, including true/false, multiple choice, matching, and fill-in. It comes in printed form and on disk for the Apple II family and the IBM PC. The computerized test bank system allows you to create tests using the existing questions and to create your own questions.

ACKNOWLEDGMENTS

Although only one name appears on the cover of this book, many people, including students and colleagues, have contributed to the finished product. I would like to mention first of all the people who reviewed the book in its many drafts. Your comments kept me in touch with the needs of those teaching and taking courses in microcomputer applications:

Wesley E. Nance	Cerritos College, California
Peter L. Irwin	Richland College, Texas
Travis D. Walker	Mineral Area College, Missouri
Kevin Halvorson	Willmar Community College, Minnesota
Stephen J. Brown	Gannon University, Pennsylvania
Pat Fenton	West Valley College, California
Lister Wayne Horn	Pensacola Junior College, Florida
Richard Bernardin	Cape Cod Community College, Massachusetts
Stanley Niemczycki	El Camino College, California
Leah Rose Pietron	University of Nebraska, Omaha

My colleagues Richard Bidleman of Vista College, Steve Brown of Computerland, Fred Cisin and Jack Olson of Merritt College, and Jim Mahoney of the American Association of Community Colleges all provided valuable insight and assistance.

One person, Marjorie Anderson, who served as developmental editor on the book, I cannot thank enough. Although I often felt bruised after reading her chapter reviews, I found that her comments were always on target. She improved the book immeasurably.

Donna Conte of Spectrum Publisher Services, Inc., coordinated the many pieces of the project through production under an incredibly tight schedule. Rita Naughton provided the attractive design. And Teri Stratford provided photo research.

I must express a special thanks to David Chodoff (also a special friend) and Ted Buchholz for their strong support of this project. Thanks are also due to many others at Holt and Dryden: DeVilla Williams, Butch Gemin, Roger Kasunic, Doug Chilcott, and Elaine Pascal.

To all of the people who helped make this a better book, I offer a very special "Thank you."

Wilson T. Price

PART ONE

Computers and Microcomputers: An Overview

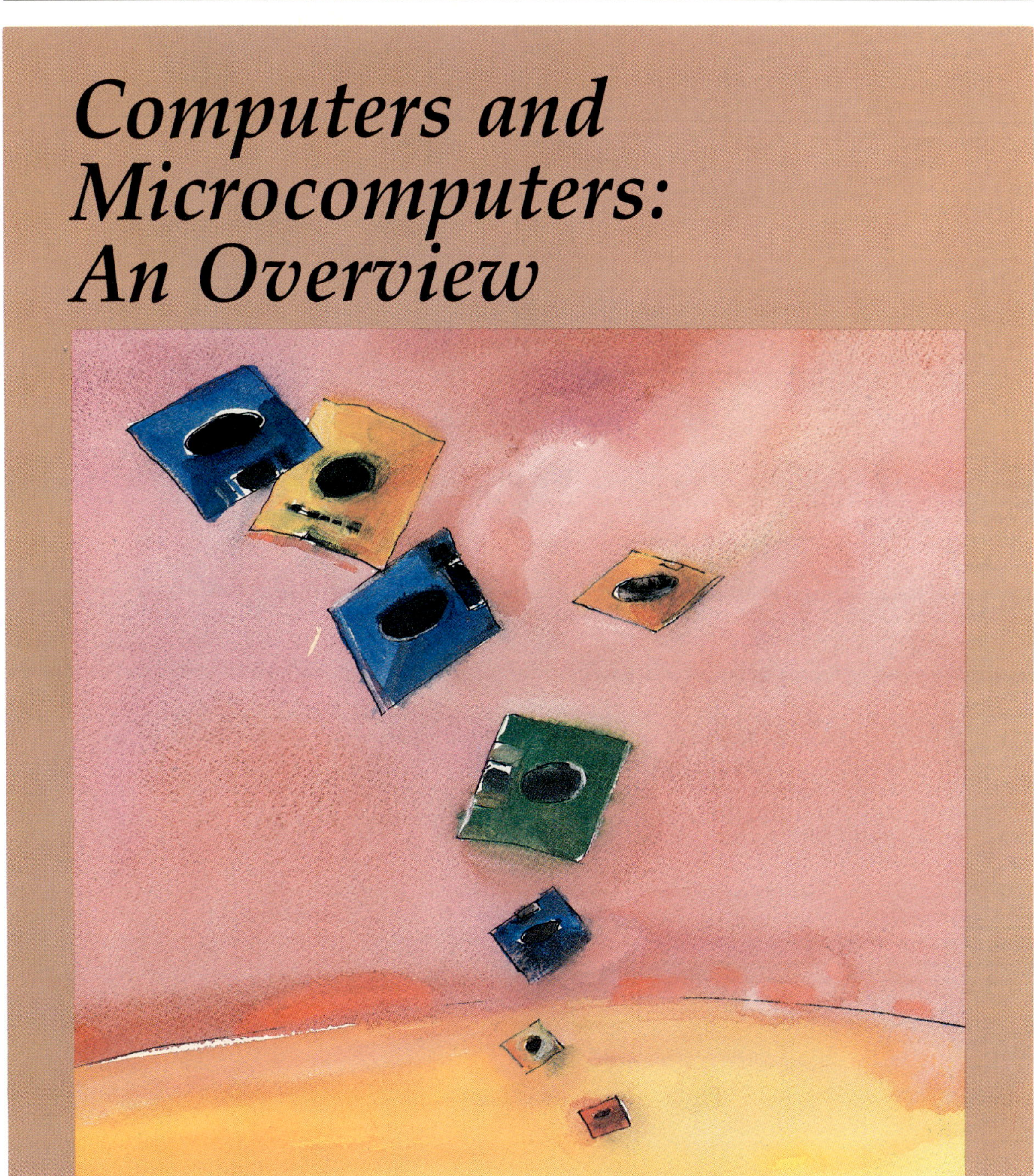

PROLOGUE TO PART ONE

The principle focus of this book is learning about computers by using one. However, before you begin, there are some basic things that you should know about computers and the programs that make them work. The purpose of Part One is to give you that basic knowledge. Since the orientation of this book is on the computer in business, Chapter 1 describes ways in which the computer is used in the business world. In Chapter 2 you will have an introduction to computer software: programs that make the computer work for you. Most of these topics will be expanded in later chapters. Chapters 3 and 4 describe computer hardware. In Chapter 5 you will begin working with the computer.

Chapter 1

Data Processing: What Is It?

OBJECTIVES

This chapter sets the broad framework for data processing by describing the needs of a newly formed small business. When you have completed this chapter, you should be able to describe:

- A variety of ways in which the computer is used in business.
- The hierarchy structure of data—file, record, and field—and how these concepts are related to a customer's accounting application.
- A typical sequence of steps in performing a distinct data processing operation.

PREVIEW

The Computer and Its Influence

The computer is a tool. It extends our ability to do things. It influences our lives in many powerful ways, ranging from entertainment to changing the nature of our jobs. It is an essential tool in all areas of business.

Starting a Business

The person who starts a business is faced with many problems. They include problems engendered by the specific activity as well as by data processing actions that are essential to every business.

Processing an Order

In addition to making and selling garments, the small business of this chapter must manage data. Filling an order and processing all of the associated data (such as customer data and inventory data) is an essential and complex task. The example in this section provides a basis for understanding some of the basic concepts of data processing.

THE COMPUTER AND ITS INFLUENCE

Better Ways to Do Things

Most of us have been to the beach and have dug holes in the sand with our hands. For a large hole, the digging is slow and a lot of work. However, the task is much simpler if we have a shovel; this tool allows us to do a better and faster job of something that we can already do in another way. If we had been digging holes for the foundation of a building, however, then the shovel would leave much to be desired; a tractor equipped with a backhoe would be more practical. Notice something about the nature of these tools: they improve our ability to do things that we are capable of doing without them, though perhaps less efficiently. Computers are much like the shovel and backhoe in this respect. For instance, assume that you must write a detailed set of lab procedures for the computer lab in which you will be working. You could certainly perform the task using a pencil and paper, although hand-printing the final document would be slow and cumbersome. A typewriter would be much faster. And the entire process could be made much more efficient if you used a computer word processor. (Word processing is the subject of Chapters 6 through 8.) Similarly, if you performed a survey of all students using the lab, you could tabulate the results by hand. If totals and averages were to be computed, a calculator would improve your speed and accuracy. However, if the survey consisted of many components requiring complex summaries, a computer spreadsheet program or a computer database management system would make the task much easier. (Spreadsheet programs are described in Chapters 10 through 12. Database management is the subject of Chapters 14 through 16.) As the shovel and backhoe expand the ability of our hands to do things, the computer expands the ability of our minds to do things.

There are few aspects of modern life that are not touched by computers. We read about spectacular events such as controlling the landing of astronauts on the moon. As each election day rolls around, we are bombarded by computer-generated election predictions. Each day on the news we are given computer-prepared predictions of the weather. Many of us use microcomputers for computer-aided learning or simply for playing games for entertainment. In the grocery store, we see items passed over the check-out scanner and the price automatically registered (from information stored in a computer). Most of us have observed lines (or stood in them) at automatic teller machines that allow us to make immediate cash withdrawals from our bank accounts. Little do we realize that through the push buttons of the machine and the telephone lines connecting them to

There are few aspects of modern life that are not touched by computers. Here a cowboy uses a portable computer and database software to keep accurate records of his herd.

large computers, we have direct access to our small portion of the bank's huge customer account data base.

One way of viewing the computer and computer access is by considering the cost of computing. For instance, the cost to perform a particular set of operations with a computer can be calculated as including a portion of the cost of the computer, the operating staff, and the programs to perform the task. Since the beginning of the computer age, the cost of computing has been decreasing at a rapid pace. For instance, today's microcomputers that cost but a few thousand dollars have computing power equivalent to full-sized computers that cost 50 to 100 times as much just 2 decades ago. However, as the cost of computing power has decreased, the cost of labor in general has increased. Under these circumstances, it becomes cost-effective to put computing power behind more and more tasks in all aspects of our lives. Replacing people with computers to improve productivity is commonplace in business and industry in order to compete in the global marketplace. In the factory, workers who worked with mechanical systems in the past must work with computer-controlled equipment. The accountant who kept records manually in the past must become familiar with computerized record keeping. The office person who in the past would use a typewriter to type a memo to another person in the organization must learn to use an electronic message system in which the memo is handled through interconnected computers. The need for computer-related skill is not confined only to computer professionals; the computer touches an increasingly wide circle of job and professional areas. However, using the computer (like using the backhoe to dig a hole) extracts a price: it requires more skill to operate than a typewriter or calculator.

The purpose of this book is to provide a basic insight into the many aspects of the computer and how to use it. Computing is commonly considered in two broad categories: business and scientific. The latter generally relates to extensive mathematics and engineering. Few of us come into direct contact with the scientific use of computers. However, most of us do have direct contact with the many business uses of the computer, both in our personal lives and on the job. The focus of this book is on the use of the computer as a tool for processing information in a business environment.

The Computer in the Business Environment

It is difficult to imagine a medium- or large-size business of today functioning without a computer. Computers in the business environment are used to organize and sort information and to provide the wide variety of reports needed by workers throughout the company. To get an idea of the types of computer-generated information, examine the partial organization chart of a typical manufacturing company as illustrated in Figure 1-1. The person performing the function of each of these boxes needs current information from the computer pertaining to his or her area of the company. Typical needs are:

President—General profit and loss summaries and projections of future profit and loss figures.

Vice President, Sales and Marketing—Sales figures for the current year and sales projections for future years.

Regional Sales Manager—Sales and projected sales of assigned region; performances of individual salespeople.

Sales Representative—Detailed customer information.

Vice President, Engineering—Information on performance of products currently on the market; market research to define new products for the marketplace.

Manager, Research—Status of all research projects currently under way.

Scientist—Theoretical evaluation of new processes and techniques.

Vice President, Business/Finance—Accurate data on current expenditures in all areas to maintain proper control over the corporation budget and to evaluate investment in new projects.

Manager, Accounting—Financial summaries of money owed by the corporation and money owed to the corporation.

Accountant—Details of transactions with each customer to ensure that money owed is properly collected.

Secretary (at all levels)—Prepare and maintain records about letters and documents.

In a large corporation, these needs are usually handled by numerous computers, ranging from very small to very large. For instance, overall central control of the corporation information is commonly handled by one or more large-scale computers costing hundreds of thousands, or even

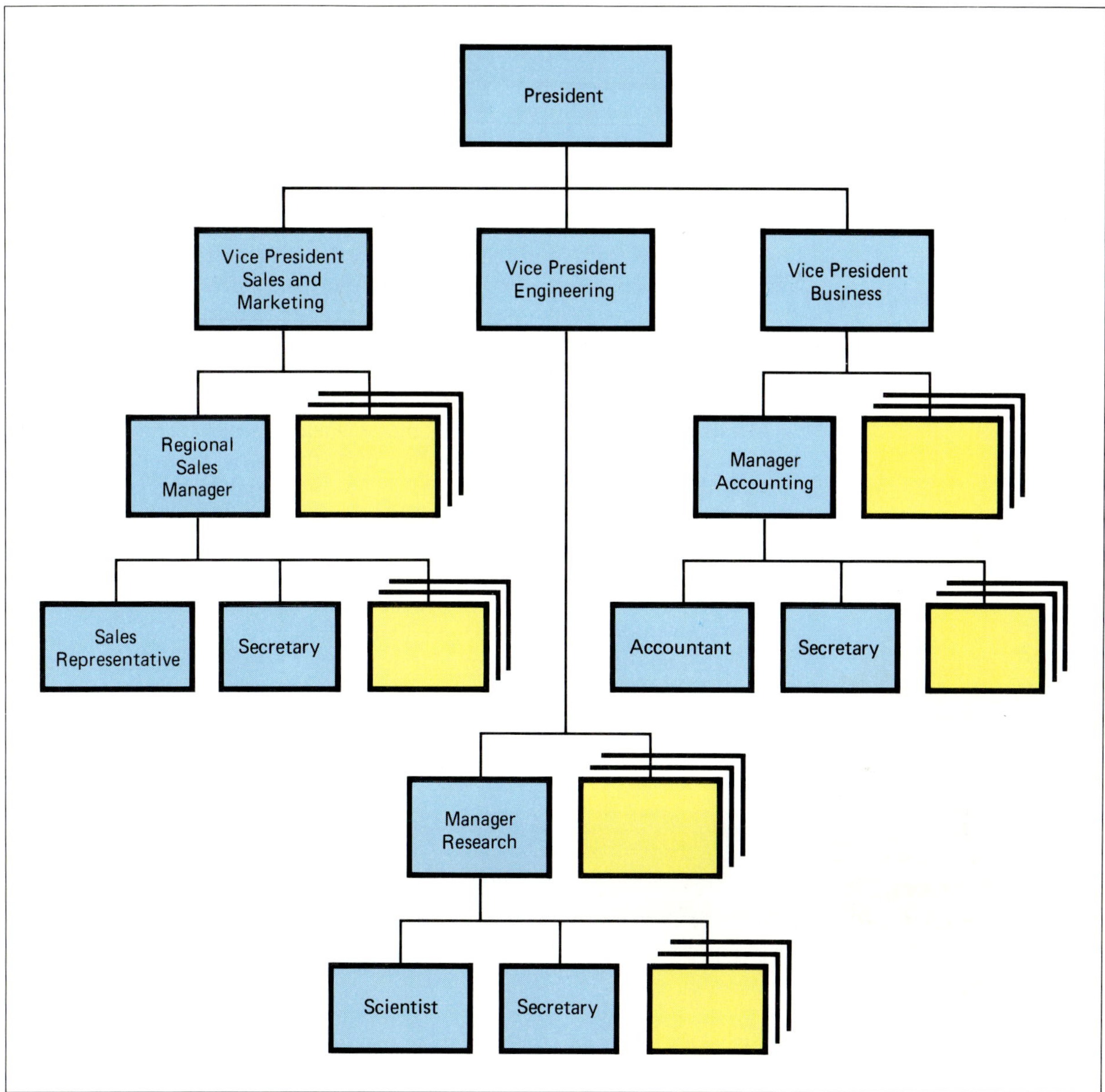

Figure 1-1
Abbreviated organizational chart.

millions, of dollars. They are characterized by their ability to process huge quantities of data very quickly and to handle the needs of many different users concurrently. For instance, such a computer might be performing an investment analysis for the president, calculating sales performance of the sales staff for a vice president, and checking the credit rating of a customer for a salesperson, all at the same time. At the other end of the cost spectrum, small desktop microcomputers costing as little as several hundred dollars are also used to perform a wide variety of tasks. For instance, the sales manager might use a microcomputer to maintain a special set of records containing data about sales performance that is not maintained in the main computer. Through electronic interconnection to the main computer, she might also use the microcomputer to work in conjunction with the main computer in performing special sales analyses that she needs.

Regardless of the size of the computer, every application for which it is used requires a set of detailed instructions (known as a program) describing the exact sequence of steps to perform the desired operation. These include special accounting programs to keep track of the company's financial status, statistical programs to analyze sales trends, computer-aided design programs to assist the engineer, and word processing programs used by the secretary (and many others in the organization). Interestingly, very different operations within the company may involve virtually identical data-handling techniques. For instance, the scientist in performing experiments will require special data management programs to catalog and analyze experimental data. The sales representative might use those same programs to keep track of customers and their purchasing habits.

Learning about computers is made easier if the various ideas are introduced through examples. To that end, this book relies heavily upon placing the new concepts in the framework of a small business. The small business environment is used for two reasons. First, many of the processing needs of the small business mirror those of large companies. For instance, both must keep track of money that is owed, both must file tax returns, and both must pay employees. Second, it is easier for most of us to visualize and relate to the needs of a small business, which are on a more personal level than the needs of a large, abstract corporation. Furthermore, by using a new business venture, we can examine the planning necessary to maintain efficient record keeping and to fulfill these needs with a computer. Figure 1-2 shows some typical applications.

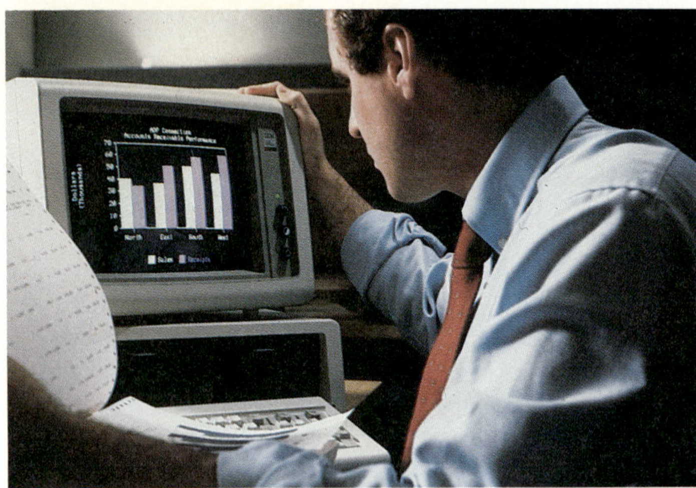

Figure 1-2
(a) A sales manager studies data on projected sales.

(b) A scientist perfects a design.

STARTING A BUSINESS

The Idea for a Business

Let us consider this small business venture as one that you and an acquaintance have decided to start. Your proposed partner might be a colleague at work who was laid off when the company retrenched, a brother or sister with an idea, or a fellow graduate who simply is not interested in starting a career by working for someone else. During your summer vacations from college, you had worked at the beach selling general casual wear such as sweatshirts, T-shirts, and shorts. Being observant, you learned from the experience. You saw what people buy, you understand the needs of the specialty shops, *and* you have a bold idea for marketing a new line that should appeal to impulse buying. You decide to approach your school acquaintance regarding a partnership because he studied business in college and spent his summers assisting in managing the office of his mother's small business. In that capacity, he used a computer extensively. (In addition, he has some savings that might be available for the right situation.) Here we have the right ingredients for a business venture: knowledge about the business activity, knowledge about running a business, and capital. All too often, a person with a good knowledge of a product or service will start a business and fail because he or she does not know how to run the business. Planning of expenditures, keeping accurate records of money owed, and maintaining records for tax purposes are only a few of the many information processing activities that are essential to running a business. You recognized this in selecting a partner with the necessary

(c) Anyone in an organization can use a computer to send a message electronically to another computer.

(d) Management decisions can be made with the help of a computer.

Computers are used in all areas of business; for instance, in the garment industry they are used in such diverse areas as designing textile patterns and controlling cutting machines.

skills and abilities that you lack. A handshake between you and your friend is followed by a trip to the local governmental agency where the partnership papers are filed and the new company, MCT Enterprises, becomes a reality.

Defining a Business Plan

In starting your business, you must give careful consideration to the way in which you commit your resources, both money and time. Since you do not have lavish financing, you must define precisely your particular niche in the marketplace. You already know the exact products with which you wish to make your entry. After considerable discussion and weighing of various alternatives, you decide to position your company as a wholesaler selling to retail stores. One of your high-priority actions is to contract with independent sales representatives to handle your product line. With the exception of a mail order operation that you decide to pursue, you have no intention of getting into retail sales.

The careful management of your money requires many basic decisions regarding the exact way in which you plan to organize your company. For instance, some activities are best done by you and your partner and others by outside contractors. To these ends, you decide to lease a small space in an industrial park that you can use as a combination office, work area, and warehouse. From this facility, you, your partner, and a person working as a part-time pattern maker will:

- Handle all record keeping.
- Maintain your inventory of finished garments.

- Fill and ship all orders.
- Design and make all patterns for new garments to be manufactured.

All cutting and sewing will be done by an outside sewing contractor. You will place orders to your suppliers for needed fabrics and accessories, which will be shipped to and inventoried at the contractor's facility. As each sewing run is completed, the finished product will be delivered to your office/warehouse.

Data Processing Needs

Carefully analyzing your market, designing your product line, and planning your mode of operation are essential aspects of your business plan. Another critical aspect is managing data that you collect. For instance, as the result of a series of telephone calls, you may have a variety of notes relating to fabric qualities and prices from different suppliers. In this raw form, the data is of limited value. However, by arranging it into an organized form, such as tabulations by vendor, fabric type, quantity, and price, the data provides information that can be used in making decisions. The unorganized collection of facts is **data***; data that has been organized into a useful form is information. The objective of data processing is to convert data into information. Following are some of the data processing needs that you and your partner discuss.

General Ledger. In operating a business, it is essential to be able to identify precisely and summarize the wide variety of your income and expenses. This is done with a general ledger system that represents the financial lifeblood of the company. It provides the information needed for you and potential lenders to evaluate the performance of your company and the tax information required by the Internal Revenue Service. It can be accomplished manually using common accounting forms or it can be done on a computer. The computer makes it possible to maintain and manage a broader range of data that provides the information necessary to make good management decisions.

Inventory Control. Keeping accurate records of your inventory is essential. On the one hand, you must have enough stock in the warehouse to avoid constantly running out of product items and delaying orders. On the other hand, the amount of money available for inventory is limited. Keeping accurate, up-to-date records of how many of each item is in stock

---

*Technically speaking, the word *data* is plural. For instance, in speaking of sales figures for several different items in the product line, it could be said that "the sales data *are* encouraging." However, in the data processing industry data used in this sense is generally treated as the singular, that is, "The sales data *is* encouraging." Here data is used synonymously with the term *data set*, which is consistent with "the sales data set *is* encouraging." In this book, the word is used in the singular, thus implying a set of data that may consist of one or more individual data values.

One area in which large amounts of data must be processed is the stock market. Here stock brokers literally are surrounded with computer display devices that give them the latest status of stocks.

is critical to achieving the optimum balance. This task is greater than it might first appear. For instance, assume that your marketing plans include:

Fifteen different items,

each with five sizes,

each in six colors,

each for both men and women.

The total number of inventory items is 15 x 5 x 6 x 2, or 900, which is not a small number. Each time a sale is made, the quantities sold must be deducted from the appropriate inventory balance. Maintaining these records manually is a tedious and time-consuming task. A good computer inventory control program can do much of the processing automatically when coupled with an order-processing system.

Order Processing. No matter how high the quality of your product, you will have difficulty with your customers if orders are not filled accurately and shipped promptly. Errors such as shipping an order to the wrong customer, sending the wrong item, charging the wrong price for an item, or accepting a rush order for an item that is not in stock does not lead to customer satisfaction. Up-to-date customer and inventory information from a computer system significantly reduces the probability of such problems and speeds up the necessary paperwork.

Customer Billing. Your billing must be accurate and timely if you are to avoid cash shortages. As a rule, customers like to delay payment as long as possible—and you must collect as soon as possible. A good computer accounts receivable system (a system of processing information regarding money owed) can be linked to the order-processing system so that customer accounts are kept up to date automatically.

Product Sales Analysis. With a wide variety of items in your product line, some will have appeal during particular seasons, others will have appeal the year around, and still others will have little appeal at any time. Sales analysis is essential to evaluate the sales performance of the current product line and to project future needs. Such analyses can take days to perform if all processing is done manually. With a computerized system and the proper programs, this type of information can be an immediately available by-product of other components of the system.

Product Cost Analysis. To remain competitive and profitable, each new item will require a detailed cost analysis. Such analyses will take into account both the direct and indirect costs of producing the item, as well as the projected income for various levels of target sales. Most people who have been in business for 20 years or so are familiar with laying out a sheet of paper with rows and columns of cost details, summaries, and totals, and then changing values in order to achieve an optimum. (These are called spreadsheets.) Today's computerized spreadsheet systems provide results in minutes that would take days to calculate manually.

Management of Documents. Routine correspondence with suppliers, contractors, customers, and creditors requires letter and memo writing. Streamlining this operation with a word processing program will simplify the task of preparing a rough draft and making the needed corrections and changes to convert it into a perfect original. The preparation of personalized form letters, an impractical task without the aid of a computer word processing system, will become routine.

Direct Mailing. Since you have decided to put a significant percentage of your advertising budget into direct mailing, accurate address information regarding current and potential customers is critical. A database program will enable you to maintain timely information.

All businesses, both large and small, have similar record-keeping needs and computers with appropriate programs help to satisfy them. If you and your partner are going to make the most of your creative and business talents, you cannot afford to devote time to exhaustive record keeping and reporting. It will be far more profitable to learn something about the computer and let it convert the data into the information necessary to market your product and operate the business efficiently. With that goal in mind, let us examine a typical, yet crucial, task for which you will use the computer—order processing. This is a good task to analyze because it requires the manipulation of many pieces of information, it must interact with a number of other components of the overall record-keeping system, and it will help you see what computers can do.

PROCESSING AN ORDER

Files, Records, and Fields

When you receive an order from a customer, a number of actions take place; the process includes much more than simply shipping the requested items. The paperwork portion of the action includes bringing together data about the customer from the customer component of the system with data about the items ordered from the inventory component of the system. This will generate an invoice, which is basically a bill consisting of a listing of all items purchased and their prices, and a packing slip to be used in assembling all of the items purchased. Inventory records will have to be brought up to date, called **updating,** and the transaction will need to be recorded in the accounts receivable for collection.

Central to these activities will be computer *files* containing the data needed to do your processing. Order processing requires the following files (or sets of files), with information flow as illustrated in Figure 1-3.

- Customer file containing needed information for each customer such as mailing address, credit limit and terms, and current amount owed.
- Inventory file containing information about each item in your product line, including quantity on hand and unit price.
- Accounts receivable file containing a detailed record for each unpaid order that has been shipped.

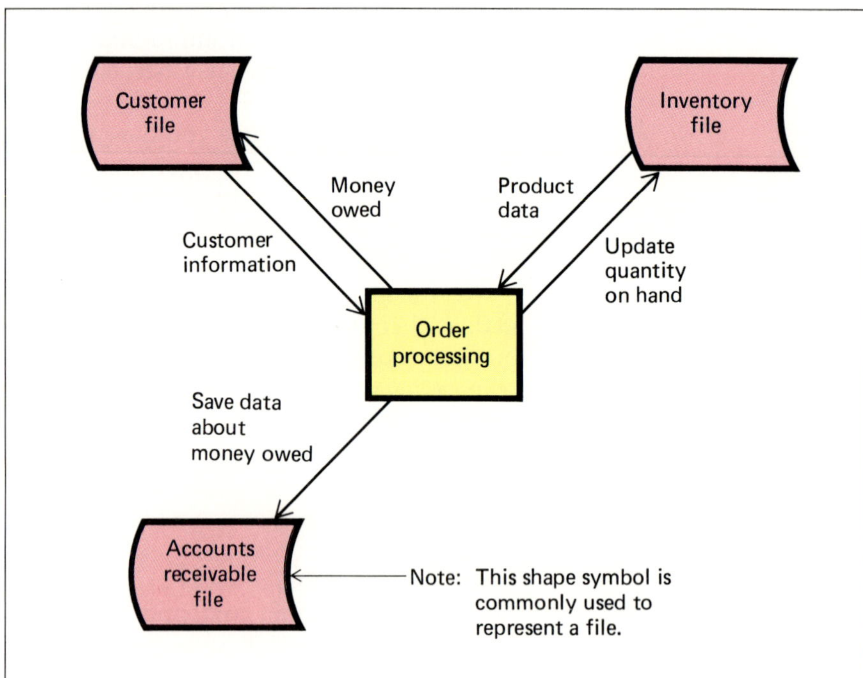

Figure 1-3
Using files in processing an order.

The word *file* is familiar; it is easy to surmise its general meaning in the context above. However, in computer terminology, it has a much more precisely defined meaning. Actually, a good way to understand the computer definition is to examine how information is stored in a manual processing system where customer information is hand-written or typed on ledger cards and stored in a file cabinet as illustrated in Figure 1-4. For each customer, *a customer record* is maintained which includes the company name, address, credit information, and current balance. Note that the customer record is standard and that each record contains the same type of information as the other records. All of these cards are stored alphabetically in a file cabinet; collectively they are the *customer file.* Notice that file is simply the collection of all records of a given type arranged in a useful order. The file does not contribute any information above and beyond that in the individual records.

As we see in Figure 1-4, each record in the file contains a number of pieces of data: the company name, address, credit rating, and so on. When such a record is part of a computer system, these basic units of information are called *fields.* Considering the manual representation of Figure 1-4, we see that data can be considered in a hierarchy form.

File The organized collection of all records of a given type. For instance, Figure 1-3 illustrates, in addition to the customer file, the inventory file consisting of a record for each item in the product line. It also shows the accounts receivable file, which includes one record for each recorded sale.

Record A group of related fields of information treated as a unit. Each inventory record will include the inventory item code

Figure 1-4
The customer master record and file.

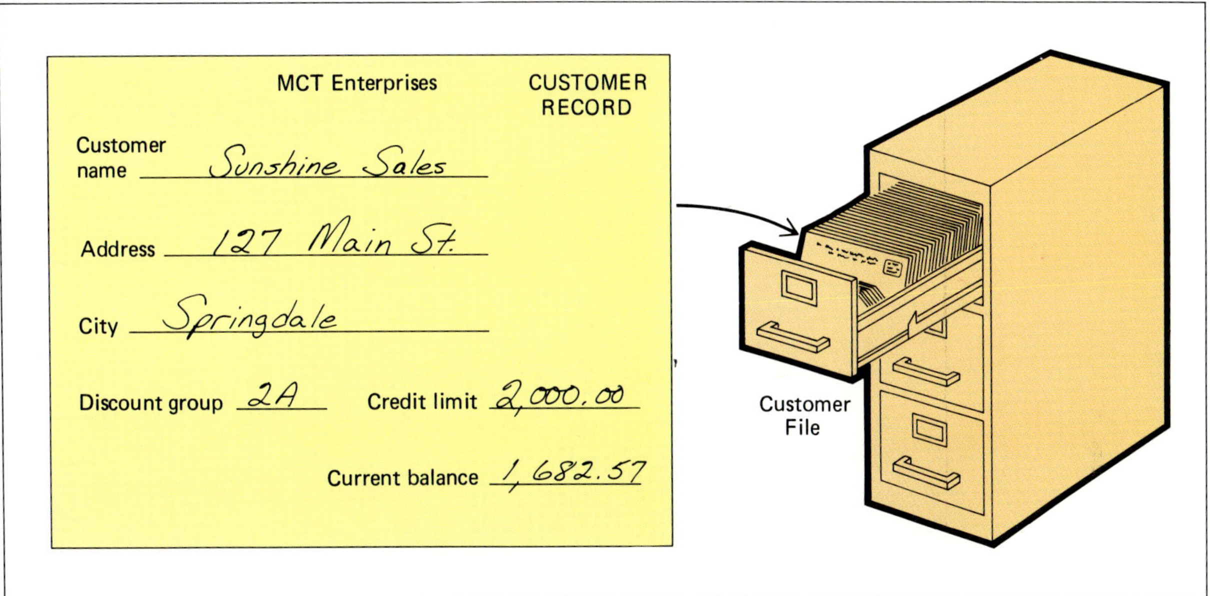

and description, its price, and the quantity on hand. Each accounts receivable record will include the customer number, the invoice number, and the amount due.

Field A basic unit of information such as customer name or address.

Thus we see that a collection of related fields forms a record, and all the records of a given type form a file. Organizing data in this way provides broad versatility for manipulating and accessing data stored in the files. With this background, let us consider some details of the customer and inventory files if you were to implement them on a computer.

For even a medium-size company files can require large amounts of computer storage. This photograph shows banks of computer disk drives and tapes for storing information. You will learn about these in Chapter 4.

The Customer and Inventory Files

The primary focus of your entire company is your customers and your product line. To this end, you will need to maintain an accurate and comprehensive customer file and inventory file. A typical customer record is illustrated (as the information might be stored in a computer storage unit) in Figure 1-5, where the customer is identified by a customer number assigned by you. In addition to other information, this record will include the current balance owed by the customer and the customer's credit limit. This file is commonly referred to as the customer **master file** because it contains the master reference information, most of which does not change, about this customer. Because of the way in which this data is stored within the computer, you can inquire into this file at any time. For instance, if you want to know the current balance of a particular customer, by using an appropriate program, you can simply key in the customer number and the computer will show the contents of that customer record on its display screen (which is similar to an ordinary television screen). You can also do such things as request a list of all customers who have been allowed to exceed their credit limits. Whereas such a task might take 15 to 20 minutes thumbing through the file cabinet of Figure 1-4 (and be prone to error), the computer could compile and display an accurate list almost instantly.

Central to maintaining close control over the stock in the warehouse is the inventory file, which consists of one record for each item in your product line. A typical record is illustrated in Figure 1-6. Note that it includes information describing the product, the price, and the number of

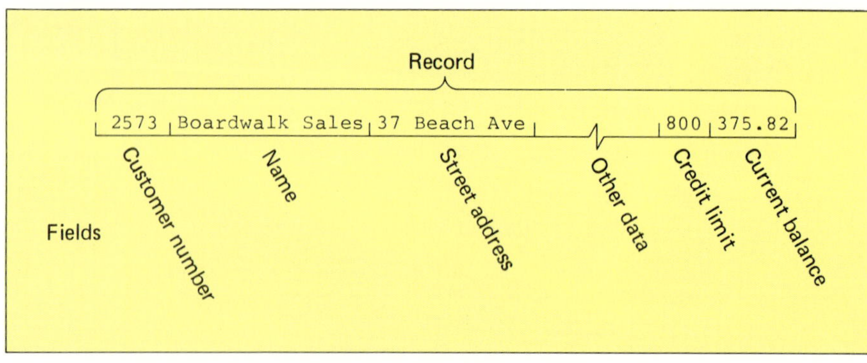

Figure 1-5
A typical customer record.

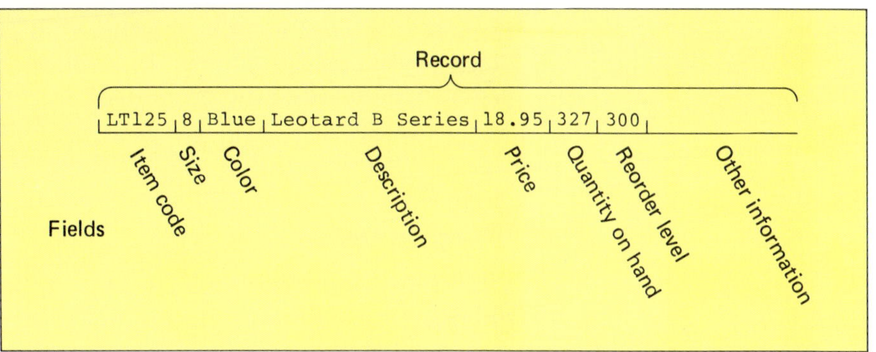

Figure 1-6
A typical inventory record.

units in inventory. The most obvious function of the inventory file is to keep track of how much of each item is in stock. To that end, as new garments are manufactured and placed in stock, the value in the quantity-on-hand field of the corresponding record is increased; as each order is filled (and stock taken from the inventory), the value is decreased. Hence, the inventory file will always include a current count of everything in your inventory. The input of data is illustrated in Figure 1-7. Notice that reports generated from this file include a list of items that have fallen below the

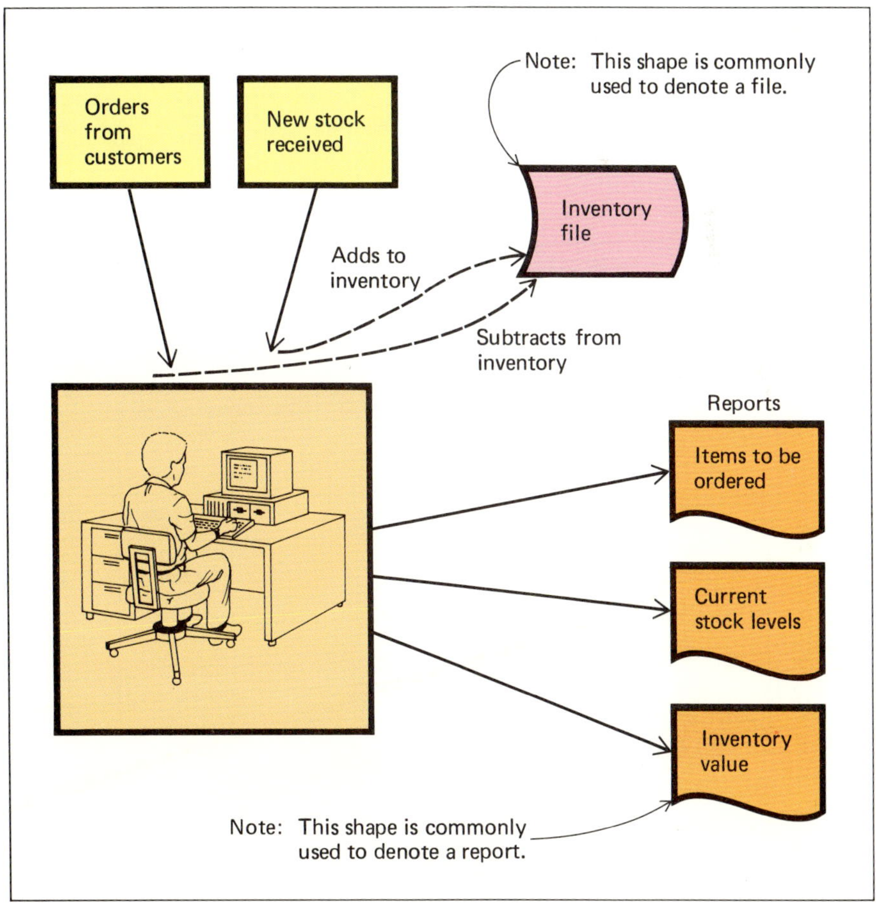

Figure 1-7
Inventory processing.

reorder level (and must be reordered), a general summary of the current stock levels, and the value of the inventory. As with the customer file, you can also inquire into the inventory file. For instance, if you want to know whether a particular item is in stock, you can request the computer to show the contents of that item record on the screen.

Filling an Order

What will take place when an order is received from a customer? Customer information must be obtained from the customer file and product information from the inventory file in preparing the paperwork. If the processing is done with a computer using the files illustrated in Figures 1-5 and 1-6, then, using an appropriate program, most of the required paperwork actions would be done automatically by the computer. To illustrate, assume that you have received an order from a customer for three different items in your product line.

1. The customer number first is entered into the computer. The customer name, address, and credit information are accessed by the computer from the customer file and displayed on the screen.

Figure 1-8
A sample invoice.

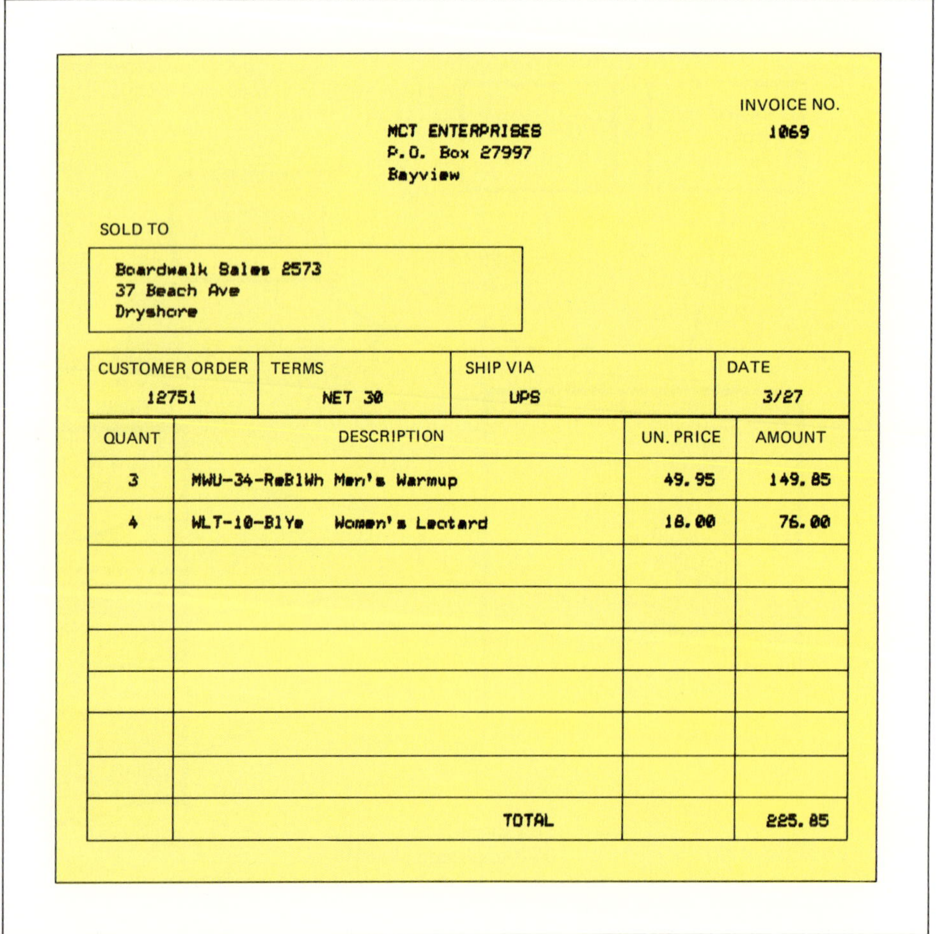

MCT ENTERPRISES
P.O. Box 27997
Bayview

INVOICE NO.
1069

SOLD TO

Boardwalk Sales 2573
37 Beach Ave
Dryshore

CUSTOMER ORDER	TERMS	SHIP VIA	DATE
12751	NET 30	UPS	3/27

QUANT	DESCRIPTION	UN. PRICE	AMOUNT
3	MWU-34-ReBlWh Men's Warmup	49.95	149.85
4	WLT-10-BlYe Women's Leotard	18.00	76.00
	TOTAL		225.85

2. The first item ordered is entered (identified by the item code, size, and color), and the information for that item is accessed by the computer from the inventory file and displayed on the screen.
3. The quantity ordered is entered and compared against the current quantity in stock. If there is sufficient inventory to fill this portion of the order, the total for this item is calculated and displayed. This step is repeated for each of the other two items ordered.
4. After the last item has been entered (the order completed), the total amount of this order is calculated by the computer.
5. Several copies of the invoice are printed; one will be used as the packing slip, another as a bill, and a third retained in your files. As we can see by referring to Figure 1-8, this invoice contains detailed information concerning the order. Handling it as quickly as possible is important: the sooner you get it into the mail, the sooner you will receive your money.
6. The inventory file is updated (automatically by the computer) by subtracting the ordered quantity for each item from the quantity-on-hand field of the corresponding inventory record.
7. The amount owed by the customer is updated (automatically by the computer) in the customer record by adding the total for this order to the customer's current balance field.
8. In addition, a new record for this transaction is placed in the accounts receivable file (the topic of the next section).

The overall action of processing an order is diagrammed in Figure 1-9.

Figure 1-9
Order processing.

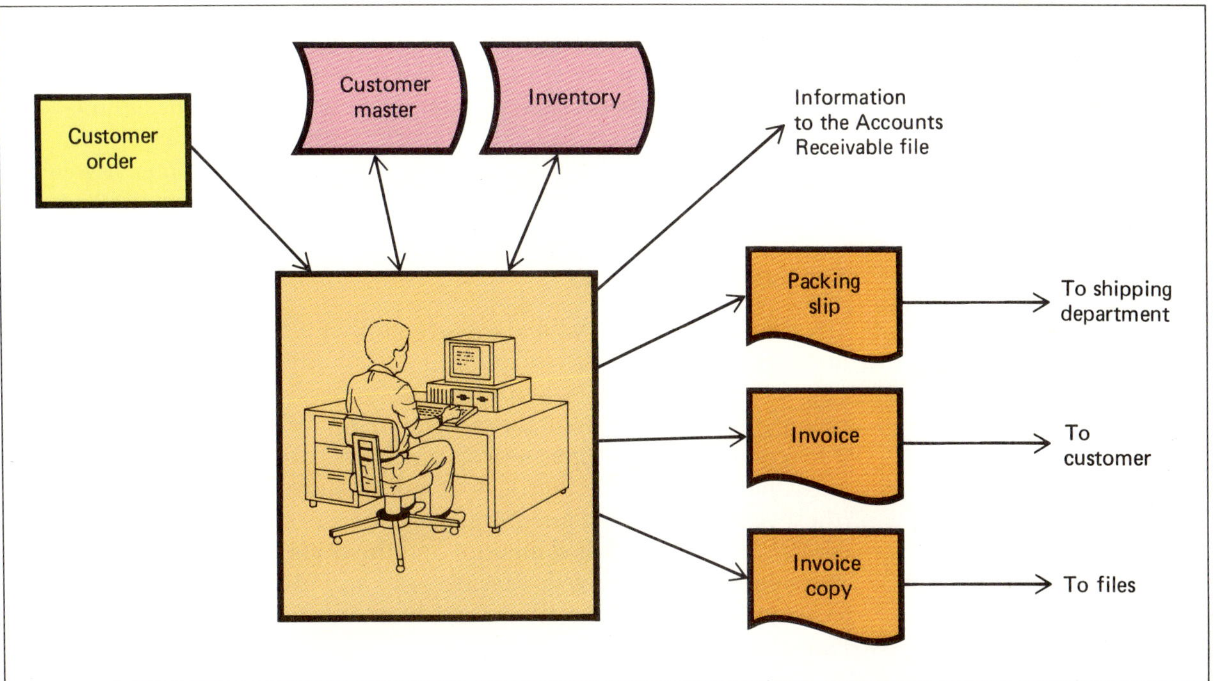

A large company may have thousands of items in a warehouse. The warehouse shown in this photograph is completely automated.

You should keep in mind that the actions performed by the computer in this process can be carried out in less time than it took you to read the preceding description of the process. Furthermore, all calculations will be accurate and the invoice will be correctly printed. The slowest part of the entire operation will be your action of entering the customer number and items and quantities ordered.

Accounts Receivable

The third of the files we have considered that plays a role in order processing is the accounts receivable file; a record from this file is illustrated in Figure 1-10. This file will contain one record for each order processed (invoice generated). It will include the customer number, which will relate it to a particular customer, and an invoice number, which will relate it to a particular sale. Notice that it does not include the details of the invoice (these are stored in yet another file, not described here). However, it does contain the original billed amount and the unpaid balance for this invoice. As payments are received, the customer and invoice numbers are entered to locate this record, and then the amount paid is entered (illustrated in Figure 1-11).

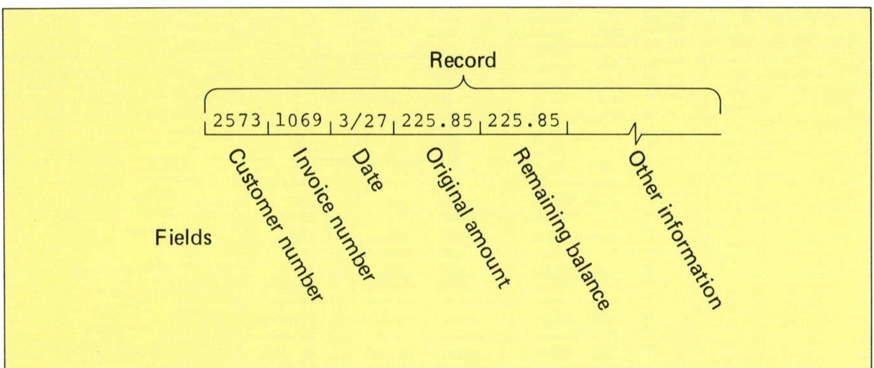

Figure 1-10
Accounts receivable record.

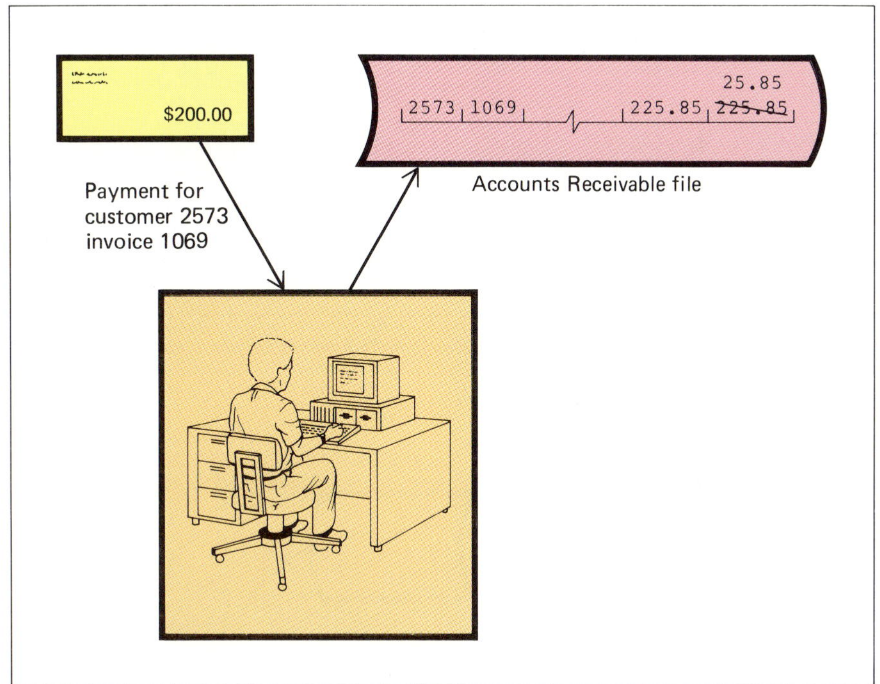

Figure 1-11
Entering a customer payment.

At the end of each month, you will rely on the computer to prepare a statement of account for each customer. As illustrated in Figure 1-12, this operation will require information from the customer and accounts receivable files (as well as the payment file, which we have not discussed). A sample customer statement is shown in Figure 1-13.

It should be apparent from the preceding descriptions that the overall actions relating to processing an order involve numerous details and access to many different sets of data. Although the entire operation can be handled manually, the process is time consuming and error-prone. By using a computerized system, the process takes much less time, is much less susceptible to error, and allows for record keeping that would be impractical without the computer.

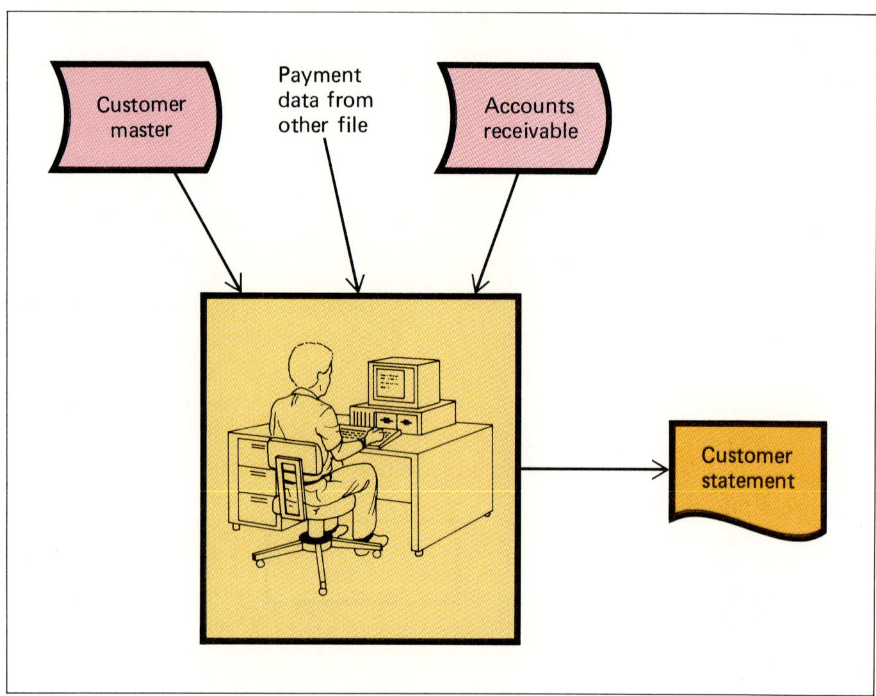

Figure 1-12
Customer statement preparation.

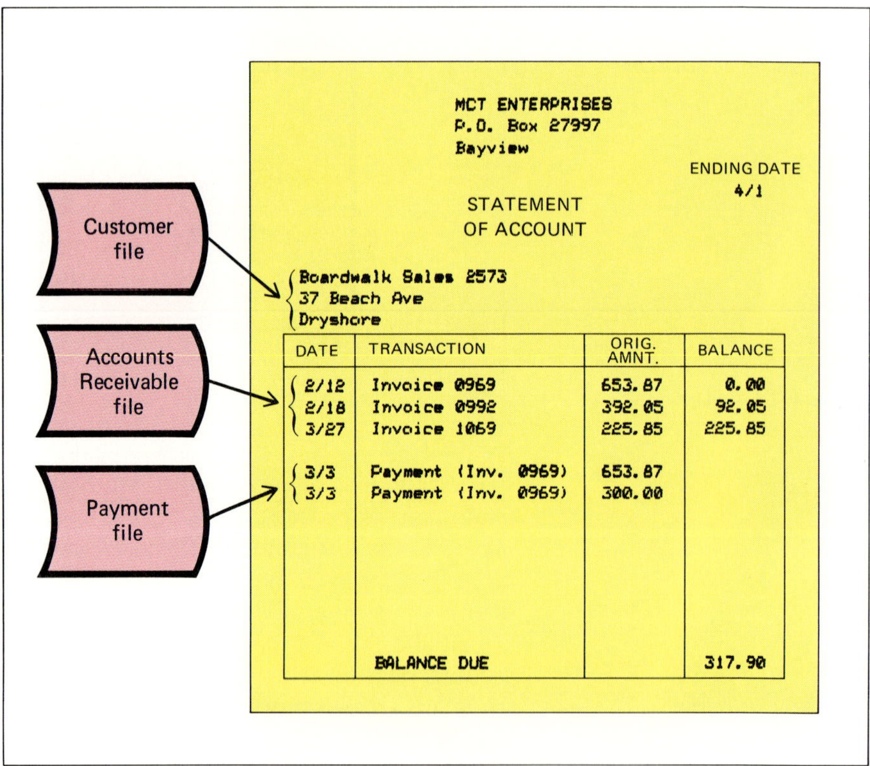

MCT ENTERPRISES
P.O. Box 27997
Bayview

ENDING DATE
4/1

STATEMENT OF ACCOUNT

Boardwalk Sales 2573
37 Beach Ave
Dryshore

DATE	TRANSACTION	ORIG. AMNT.	BALANCE
2/12	Invoice 0969	653.87	0.00
2/18	Invoice 0992	392.05	92.05
3/27	Invoice 1069	225.85	225.85
3/3	Payment (Inv. 0969)	653.87	
3/3	Payment (Inv. 0969)	300.00	
	BALANCE DUE		317.90

Figure 1-13
A sample customer statement.

Assume that you are in New York and your colleague is in San Francisco making a presentation. She needs some descriptive charts from you immediately. One solution might be to send them over the telephone system using Fax machines: The one at your end would scan the page and send the images; the one at her end would receive the signals, convert them to their original form, and then print them.

SUMMARY

The purpose of this chapter has been to give you a broad overview of the field of data processing and to set the stage for the chapters that follow. Through this chapter, you have gained a brief insight into some of the data processing problems and considerations involved in beginning and operating a business. Many of the computer concepts and principles to come are related to the framework established for MCT Enterprises. The study of microcomputer hardware and software will expand upon many of the questions arising in this chapter. Summarizing, the important points from this chapter are:

- As the cost of computing continues to decrease, more and more applications become cost-effective to computerize. In the workplace, this results in the loss of many jobs and in significantly changing the nature of many others.
- Employees at all levels in businesses and industry utilize the computer as a tool. Applications range from generating profit and loss summaries for the president, to doing engineering analyses for the engineer, to maintaining letters and correspondence for the secretary.
- The objective of data processing is to convert raw data (unorganized) into information that is useful for making decisions.
- Data is stored in the computer in a hierarchical form. The basic unit of information is the field. A group of related fields form a record; the organized collection of all records of a given type is a file.
- Most computer applications in business involve operating on data stored in one or more files. For instance, order processing involves a customer file, an inventory file, and an accounts receivable file. The customer file described in this chapter serves as the basis for the descriptions of dBASE III in Chapters 14, 15, and 16.

NEW TERMINOLOGY

The following are important new terms introduced in this chapter; you should be familiar with each of them.

data
field
file
master file
record
update

REVIEW QUESTIONS

1. What is meant by "cost of computing"? How does the cost of computing influence the use of the computer in the business environment?
2. What are the three necessary ingredients of starting a business?
3. What is the difference between data and information?
4. What is the difference between a file and a record?
5. In talking with a friend about your plan to use the computer for inventory control, the friend makes the following point: "I do not see why you go to the trouble of computerizing your inventory. It will take a huge amount of time to enter all of that information into the computer, and then with each order you must change the inventory value. It would be much easier to just go out to the warehouse and count the number of each item whenever you need to know." Comment on this attitude.
6. What are some of the operations performed by the computer that make order processing faster and more accurate than if the task were to be done manually?
7. What is the nature of the information stored in the accounts receivable file?

TRUE/FALSE

Determine whether each of the following is true or false.

______ 1. Even though inflation in recent years has driven the cost of computing up, computer applications continue to proliferate because of the high speeds of modern computers.

______ 2. Microcomputers might be adequate for small businesses, but they have no place in large corporations that have heavy data processing demands.

______ 3. All computers, large and small, require programs that define the steps to be carried out for each application.

______ 4. It is impossible to run a small business in today's competitive environment without a computer to handle bookkeeping chores.

_______ **5.** A general ledger system contains information that describes the overall financial status of the company.

_______ **6.** One of the advantages of using a computer for order processing is that the order-processing action can be related to inventory control and an accurate record of stock on hand can be maintained by the computer.

_______ **7.** The accounts receivable file contains one record for each customer in the customer file.

_______ **8.** A general ledger system is a system for maintaining records of income and expenditures; such a system can be maintained manually or with a computer.

_______ **9.** A field is a group of related records.

_______ **10.** The action of subtracting the count of sweatshirts sold to a customer from the inventory count of that record in the inventory file is called updating the record.

_______ **11.** Details of every purchase ever made by a customer would be stored in the customer master file.

_______ **12.** An invoice is a billing to a customer for goods purchased.

ANSWERS TO OBJECTIVE QUESTIONS

True/False

1. F 2. F 3. T 4. F 5. T 6. T 7. F 8. T 9. F
10. T 11. F 12. T

Chapter 2

Focusing on Software

OBJECTIVES

Chapter 1 provided you with an insight into the nature of a business's data processing needs. To use a computer, you need programs to tell it what to do—software. This chapter is about software. When you have completed the chapter, you should be able to describe:

- The relationship between software and hardware.
- The basic operations of which a computer is capable: data input, data storage, arithmetic/logic, and output.
- The following categories of computer software:
  - Operating systems that provide for overall control of the computer.
  - Programming languages with which the trained programmer can prepare computer solutions to problems.
  - Productivity software systems that provide the user with powerful access to computer capabilities without extensive, detailed computer training.
  - Applications systems that are "ready-to-go" software systems for handling specific applications such as order processing.
- Factors to consider in selecting software.

PREVIEW

The Essentials of a Computer

A computer system consists of hardware, the physical components, and software, the programs that tell the hardware what to do. The combination of hardware and software provides us with the ability to manage data: to enter it into the computer, to store it, to manipulate it, and to retrieve it.

Looking at Software

Software can be grouped into four categories: operating and control programs, programming languages, productivity software, and applications software.

Basic Concepts of an Operating System

The operating system is the component that provides the underlying control functions that make the computer work. Without an operating system, a present-day computer is of little value.

Programming Languages

Programming languages allow the trained programmer to write instructions that describe in detail the actions for the computer to carry out in performing a particular task.

Productivity Software

Productivity software is software that allows an individual with a relatively small amount of training to prepare applications on the computer. The five basic components of productivity software are commonly considered to be word processing, spreadsheet, database management, graphics, and communications.

Applications Software

There are certain data processing tasks that are common to almost every business. Typical is general accounting. A wide variety of software companies sell off-the-shelf accounting software with a "load it up and it runs" sales pitch.

Software Requirements

Assessing software requirements by defining the needs of a small business is the first step in selecting a computer system. The software decisions for the small business illustrated in this chapter are described.

THE ESSENTIALS OF A COMPUTER

Analyzing the order-processing procedure in Chapter 1 has shown you what a computer can do in a particular application. However, to achieve the portion of your business plan devoted to electronic data processing and to expand it to all tasks you hope to computerize, you must learn about the components of a computer and the types of programs that make it work. This chapter focuses on the programs, or software; Chapters 3 and 4 describe the computer, or hardware. However, in order to have some basis for the software discussions of this chapter, you need a brief introduction to some hardware concepts.

About Automobiles and Computers

Virtually all of us have had some experience with automobiles. We all view our automobiles differently. For instance, a car can be seen as a status symbol or an embarrassment, a hobby or a necessary evil, a smoothly functioning machine or an unreliable piece of junk. Let us be more abstract and view the automobile from an entirely different point of view; that is, it is a machine (a piece of *hardware*) that is designed to perform a particular function—to get us from one place to another. Note that it does not allow

Modern microcomputers and associated software give us capabilities far beyond those of noncomputer methods.

us to do anything basic that we cannot already do ourselves. We do not need an automobile (or any other modern means of transportation) to get from New York to Boston; we can always walk. Of course, the automobile allows us to make the trip much faster (except perhaps on Labor Day weekend). As a matter of fact, we can walk to places that are impossible to drive to. For example, when is the last time you heard of someone driving to the top of Mount Everest? Overall, it is probably safe to say that the automobile certainly *extends* our ability to move from one place to another.

Now let us view the automobile as a transportation system that can be used to perform a certain function. What are the basic components of that system? One way of looking at it is to say that this system consists of two broad components: the automobile itself and the fuel that makes it run. Both are essential. Without fuel, the automobile is not much of a transportation device except for coasting from the top of a hill to the bottom. This is not to suggest that it would be *totally* useless without fuel. Indeed, with the top removed, it might make an interesting large planter box, or it could be deposited at the bottom of the ocean as an artificial reef, or it could serve any number of other creative functions. But if someone asks you which is most important, the machine or the fuel, you can answer, "One is not much good without the other."

In the event that you skipped the first section and started reading here, do not think that you accidently picked up a book on auto mechanics. Let us consider what all of this has to do with data processing. The answer is that if, in the foregoing descriptions, *automobile* were changed to *computer hardware* and *fuel* to *software,* and a few other changes made, the statements would be completely valid (especially those about one's feelings toward one's auto).* A usable computer system consists of two basic components: the machine itself, commonly called **hardware,** and the sets of instructions that make it work, called **software.** One without the other has little value. Like the auto without fuel, the computer without software might make a good planter box or part of an artificial reef.

What Can a Computer Do?

Much of what we read about computers or see about them on television tends to show them as modern marvels or technological instruments of doom. In reality, the computer itself is capable of only very elementary operations, which include:

1. *Input operations,* such as accepting information from a human-operated keyboard for entry of a customer order.
2. *Storage of data* that has been read by an input device (such as the customer order information from the keyboard) or created as a result of calculations within the computer.

---

*An analogy is useful to get an idea across by relating something new to something that is familiar. The intent of this analogy is to emphasize the fact that hardware and software are equally necessary. However, if taken too literally, an analogy can be misleading. For instance, an automobile consumes gasoline; the computer does not consume software (it does consume electricity). Obviously, this analogy is not intended in that way.

3. *Basic arithmetic operations* of addition, subtraction, multiplication, and division. They are the simple functions that we can all perform ourselves such as calculating the cost of a purchased product by multiplying the unit cost of the item by the number ordered.

4. *Logical operations,* such as comparing the current inventory level of an item with a predetermined allowable minimum to determine if it is time to reorder.

5. *Output operations,* such as displaying on a screen the status of a particular customer's account based on information stored within the computer.

The computer is like the automobile. We can get from New York to Boston on foot, but the automobile is much faster (and more comfortable). The strength of the computer is that it can process information with phenomenal speed and accuracy. The computer can perform the order-processing actions of looking up a customer in the customer file, finding records for the items ordered in the inventory file, updating both files, creating a new record in the accounts receivable file, and performing all needed calculations in less time than it would take you to position a manual invoice form in a typewriter. The many amazing feats of which the computer is capable are the result of carefully planned (and often very clever) programs of instructions (software) written by people.

Components of the Computer

The automobile (which started this discussion) can be broken down into functional parts: the engine, the drive train, the fuel system, and so on. In a similar fashion, the computer can be broken down into the basic functional components—*input, output, processor, memory,* and *auxiliary storage*—shown in Figure 2-1 for microcomputers, such as the IBM Personal Com-

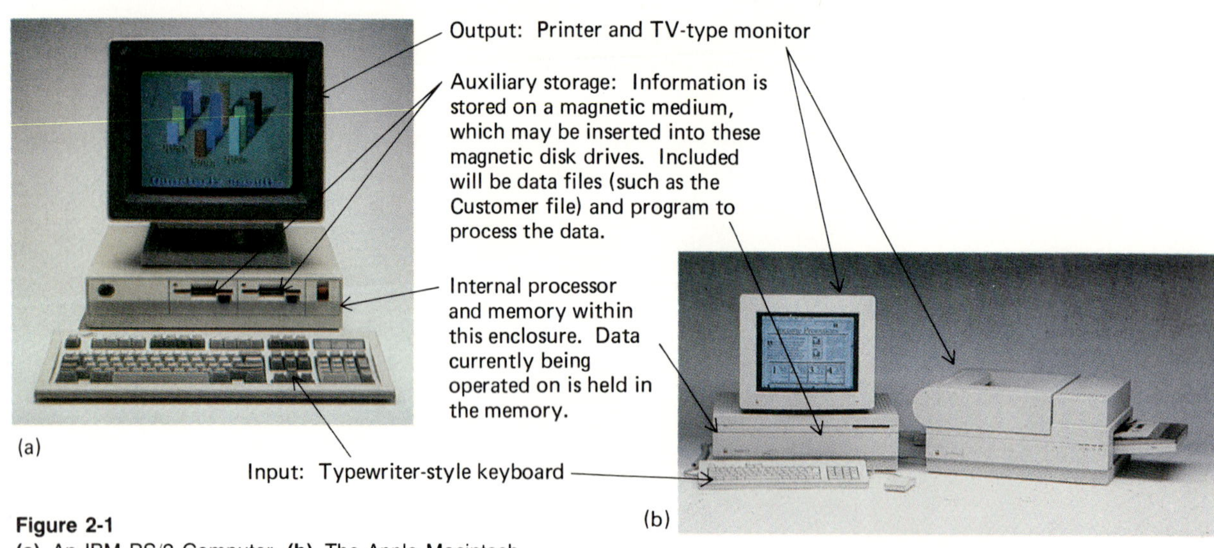

Figure 2-1
(a) An IBM PS/2 Computer. **(b)** The Apple Macintosh.

puter (PC) and the Apple Macintosh. The standard input device for microcomputers is the keyboard. For the basic output device, all microcomputers include a video monitor, also called the CRT or screen. In addition to a monitor for output, most microcomputers are also equipped with a printer. We shall learn much more about the details of computer hardware in Chapters 3 and 4. This limited description will allow us to place some of the topics that follow in their proper perspective.

You should not get the impression that the identified components of Figure 2-1 relate solely to microcomputers. Indeed, these basic components are as representative of large-scale computers used by big corporations and government agencies as they are of microcomputers. As might be expected, the differences relate to size, speed, and capacity, as well as numerous features that are beyond the scope of this chapter.

About the Word *System*

Because both hardware and software are required for a computer to do useful work, the two together are referred to as a unit and are commonly called a computer system. Like many terms in our English language, the word *system* is used in many different contexts with different meanings. For instance, in almost any company, when the accountant refers to a general accounting system, the accountant is probably talking about an overall set of procedures and standards (and everything else required) for maintaining financial records. Mention accounting system to the supervisor who is responsible for the computer in the installation, and the supervisor will probably think of the general accounting software for storing and managing the accounting data. Note that the supervisor's notion of the system is actually one part of that which the accountant considers the system. At the other extreme, if you talk to the technician who repairs the computers, the technician is interested in the computer hardware itself: the boxes of gadgets that techies appreciate. To the technician, the computer together with all of its hardware components, such as magnetic disk units and printers, make up the computer system—all strictly hardware. Between the extremes might be a person who has a small computer on a desk used solely for preparing publications, a word processing function. This person does not care about the technical details of either the hardware or software; the only concern is whether the *word processing system* (combination of hardware and software) is adequate to do the job. Here we see the word **system** applied to: (1) a combination of people, procedures, and machines; (2) computer software; (3) computer hardware; and (4) the combination of computer hardware and software. When everyone uses the word system differently, how is a beginner in the field to know what it means? The answer is, "by context." We are quite accustomed to that because there are many words in the English language that have different meanings and we interpret them in the context in which they are used. Throughout this book, system will be used in the preceding four different ways. If you are aware of this, you should not find it confusing because the context will make the meaning clear.

LOOKING AT SOFTWARE

On Evaluating Computer Needs

Convinced of the value of a computer system for MCT Enterprises, your next step is to determine which hardware and software will best satisfy your needs. There are two general approaches that might be used to select the needed computer system.

Look at this

Before this

> Survey the computer market carefully and evaluate the relative merits of different computers that are available. Armed with this information, buy the hardware configuration that seems most appropriate, making certain to get a good printer and other equipment. Once the computer is installed, then integrate it into your business by obtaining suitable software.

To "survey the market carefully and evaluate" has a very good ring to it; it sounds like the way to do things. Before getting too excited about this approach, remember that the reason you are getting a computer is to use it in your business to assist with many of the tasks necessary in running the business. The focus must first be on the problem-solving aspect of the computer—the software available to do the job. The greatest computer in the world is of little value if the software you need to run your business is not available for it. Unfortunately, in many situations, potential computer users get carried away by the attractions of particular hardware. They acquire it and then go looking for software to serve their needs. It should be emphasized that this mistake is not unique to first-time microcomputer purchasers. Many people at various levels of management of large companies make the same mistake.

Computers are used at all educational levels for such tasks as teaching typing, testing, generating art, and developing analytical skills.

Although the preceding approach is common, it leaves much to be desired. The second, and much more realistic, of the two approaches is as follows:

> Survey and evaluate the general processing needs of the company. Find the appropriate software that appears to fit these needs. Then determine what computer hardware is necessary to run the software.

Except for the relatively few people who make their livings as computer experts, in general, we should treat the computer as a means to an end (the way of getting things done), not the end itself. A computer system must provide *solutions*. The latest, the best, the fastest, the most elegant, the most powerful, and so on, do not necessarily represent the best for your company. Before making any decisions, let us look at an overall picture of what software is all about.

Categories of Software

Most computer neophytes who have ever talked to computer enthusiasts have come away completely confused by the need for things such as DOS, Pascal, Lotus, data managers, and compilers. It is easy to become intimidated by such dazzling displays of "profound knowledge." However, there are only a few general concepts about software that the beginner need know in order to avoid being the victim of a complete "snow job." The first thing to understand is that there are various levels of software. For purposes of discussion in this book, software is grouped into the following four general categories.

1. Operating and control programs. These make the computer work. For general applications use, present-day computers are virtually useless without them. They usually are furnished by the computer manufacturer.

2. Programming languages. These are used by programmers to prepare programs of instructions for the computer to perform a particular task.

3. Productivity software systems. These are specialized software tools that give the user a powerful means for solving problems of special types. They might be classified as the "next step beyond" conventional programming languages. Chapters 6 through 16 focus on this type of software.

4. Applications programs, which are designed and written to handle particular applications. For instance, your order-processing operation will be computerized with a series of programs written by a software company and purchased by MCT Enterprises.

Figure 2-2 illustrates some of the characteristics of these components and their relationships to one another. Let us consider each of these and its place in the overall scheme of the computer.

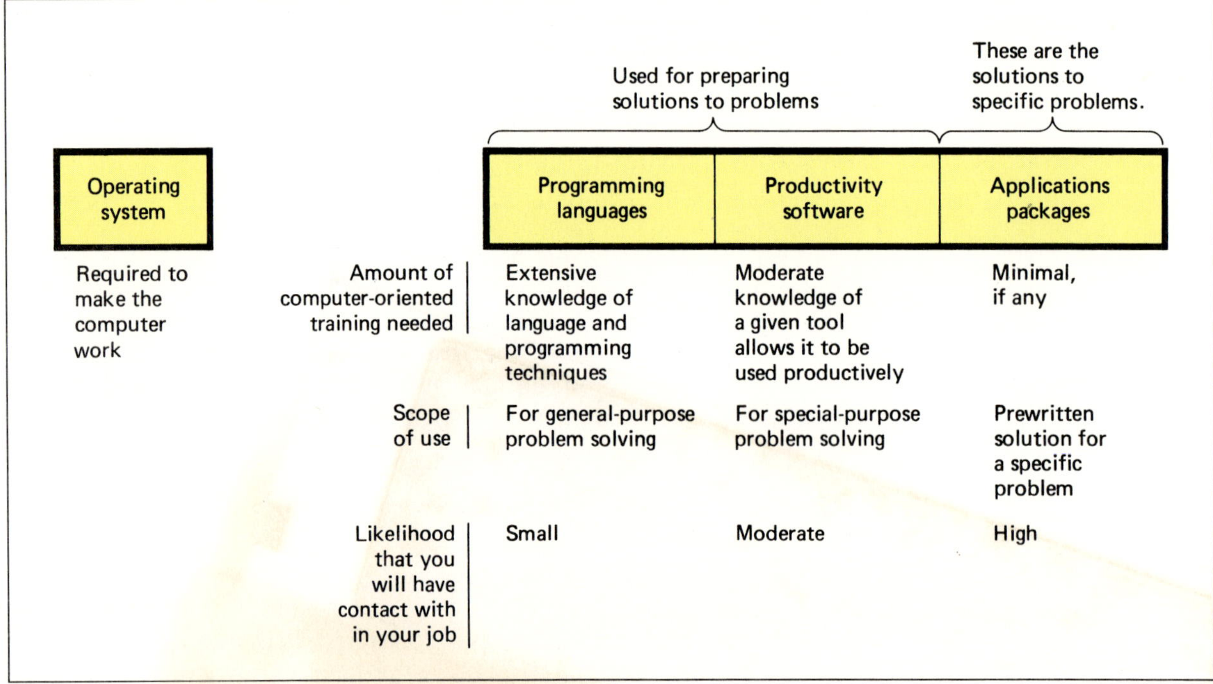

Figure 2-2
Categories of software.

THE OPERATING SYSTEM

As we learned in an earlier section, the computer is capable of only the simplest types of operations. There are numerous tasks that must be performed on a regular basis that are elementary to almost everything we might do on a computer. For instance, consider some of the actions we learned about earlier when entering a customer order. As the customer number is keyed in, each keystroke must be accepted by the computer, placed in an appropriate position of the computer memory, and displayed on the screen. To locate the customer record, the computer must search the customer file until the record with the matching customer number is found. Although the operations sound simple, the programs to perform them are highly complex. The collection of these basic programs is called the operating system. The **operating system** of a computer is a set of programs designed to manage the hardware resources of the computer. Some of the operations performed by various programs of the operating system are as follows:

- Keeping track of files of data and user programs that are stored in the computer's auxiliary storage units.
- Controlling the efficient operation of input and output devices and providing access to the data stored in the auxiliary storage units.

- In some cases, controlling the environment such that two or more programs can be in the computer memory and operating at the same time.

For some simple types of operations, such as making a duplicate copy of a data file or deleting a file that we no longer need, we can command the operating system directly. However, the overall actions of the operating system are accomplished automatically as the result of directives from programs or productivity software actions. In this sense, the many and intense activities of the operating system components are carried out in the background with little or no "visibility."

As the capacity and sophistication of microcomputer hardware have mushroomed in recent years, so has the technology of operating systems. Indeed, microcomputer operating systems are available today with many features superior to those of full-scale computers of 2 decades ago. In Chapter 5 we will learn about the Disk Operating System (DOS), which is widely used with the IBM Personal Computer.

PROGRAMMING LANGUAGES

The next category of computer software is that encompassing programming languages. Many high school (and even some elementary school) students are familiar with the BASIC programming language, which is almost universally available on microcomputers. (The word *BASIC* is an acronym meaning Beginners' All-purpose Symbolic Instruction Code.) Using BASIC, a person can describe a sequence of steps instructing the computer to perform any desired action. For instance, the sequence of BASIC statements in Figure 2-3 calculates the sum of two numbers entered from the keyboard. We need not be a computer expert to appreciate the action of each of these statements. One feature of BASIC is that the instructions to the computer (called statements) use English words and common math notation. This contrasts with the form of the internal computer instructions. That is, within the computer, all instructions must be in a numerically coded form (actually consisting only of the digits 0 and 1) called **machine language.** BASIC, used for the program in Figure 2-3, is called a **high-level language;** such languages are people oriented and allow

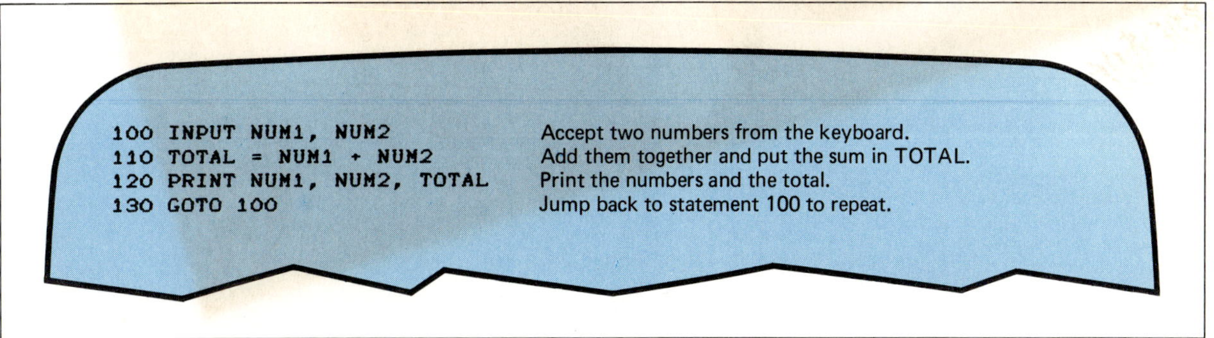

Figure 2-3
A simple BASIC program.

the programmer to avoid the intricate detail required by the computer. The statements of a high-level language must be converted to machine language (by a special translating program) before they can be understood by the computer.

A wide variety of programming languages is available to the programmer, each designed for a different type of applications. In a sense, the distinction between languages is similar to that between mechanical tools. For instance, the auto mechanic will require a different type of wrench to remove the carburetor of your automobile than the plumber will require to remove the faucet in your kitchen.

COBOL is the predominant language in business data processing (COBOL is an acronym for COmmon Business Oriented Language). It is well suited to business programming needs in which data in a variety of files must be manipulated, selected, and rearranged. Remember that the order-processing application involves working with several files, including the customer and inventory files. Because of the way in which the language is designed, it is not well suited to complex mathematical calculations such as those needed for solving an engineering type of problem. Although COBOL has been used mostly on full-scale computers, in recent years, powerful COBOL systems have become available for microcomputers and have gained considerable acceptance.

In contrast to COBOL, FORTRAN (from which BASIC was derived) is widely used in engineering and mathematics (FORTRAN is an acronym for FORmula TRANslating language). Its design includes special provisions

Wind farms such as the one shown generate electricity for input to our electrical distribution system. Here, information about the performance of each windmill is maintained by microcomputers.

for performing complex mathematical operations and the extended repetition that is characteristic of engineering/mathematical problem solutions. Although FORTRAN was developed for full-sized computers, it is also available for microcomputers. However, BASIC is much more widely used in the microcomputer environment than FORTRAN.

BASIC, FORTRAN, and COBOL, as well as a variety of other languages available to the programmer, are called **procedural languages** because they require the definition of procedures (programs) describing the steps for the computer to take to solve a given problem. As a rule, using a procedural language to program an application of any substance requires a significant level of training and experience. To an extent, these languages are most commonly used by professional programmers.

PRODUCTIVITY SOFTWARE

Some programming languages, such as BASIC, are deceptively easy for a new computer user to learn. However, mastering them sufficiently to produce the programs commonly used in business is not nearly as simple. For instance, writing a set of programs to perform all the needed processing operations on the inventory file would require considerable programming skill and training. Furthermore, the task would require an enormous number of programming hours.

For special needs, there are software tools available that offer the casual computer user very powerful capabilities. These are collectively referred to as **productivity software,** the third category of software represented in Figure 2-2. The term *productivity software* is derived from the notion that it enhances the productivity of a person in his or her area of work (without the need to become a computer expert). Many different types of software fall in the productivity category. The five commonly encountered productivity tools (which are described in this book) are word processing, spreadsheet, data management, graphics, and communications. The following sections give a preview of these tools; Chapters 6 though 16 are devoted to learning about them.

Word Processing

All businesses generate written communications. For example, for MCT Enterprises, you will need to write letters to vendors inquiring about raw material prices and availability, and you will have written contracts with sales representatives defining the working arrangements. Anyone who has ever had a letter typed that needed to be "perfect" is quite familiar with the sequence of steps illustrated in Figure 2-4 using a conventional typewriter. After the letter is composed, a typist types a rough copy to which appropriate changes and corrections can be made. After these are completed, the entire letter must be retyped to produce the final copy. Frequently, the "final" copy will not be exactly as desired and the entire letter must be retyped once again. The retyping of an entire letter because of errors in only one part of it is an inefficient process.

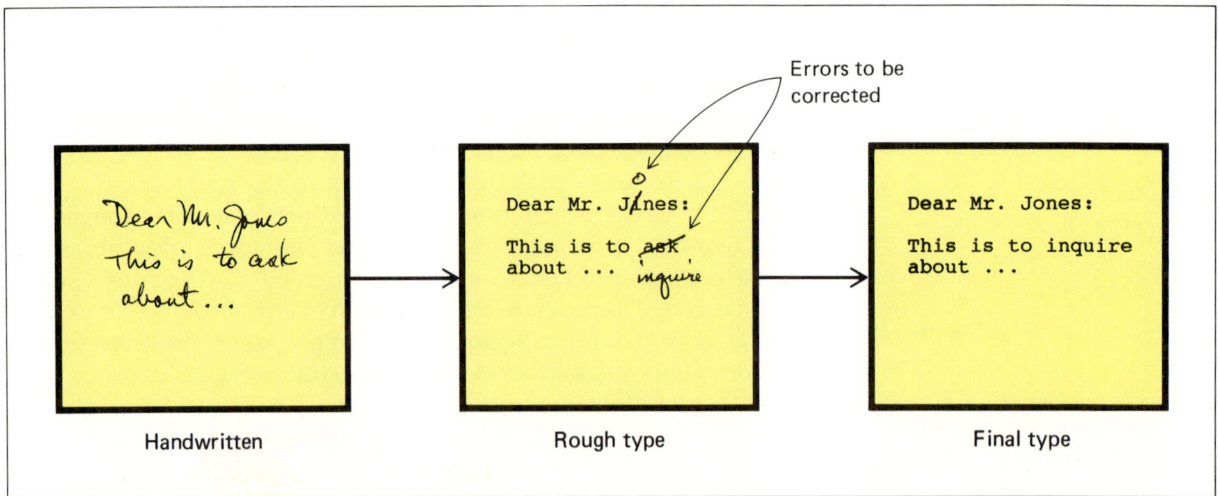

Figure 2-4
Preparing a letter.

Figure 2-5
A comparison of a typewriter and a word processor.

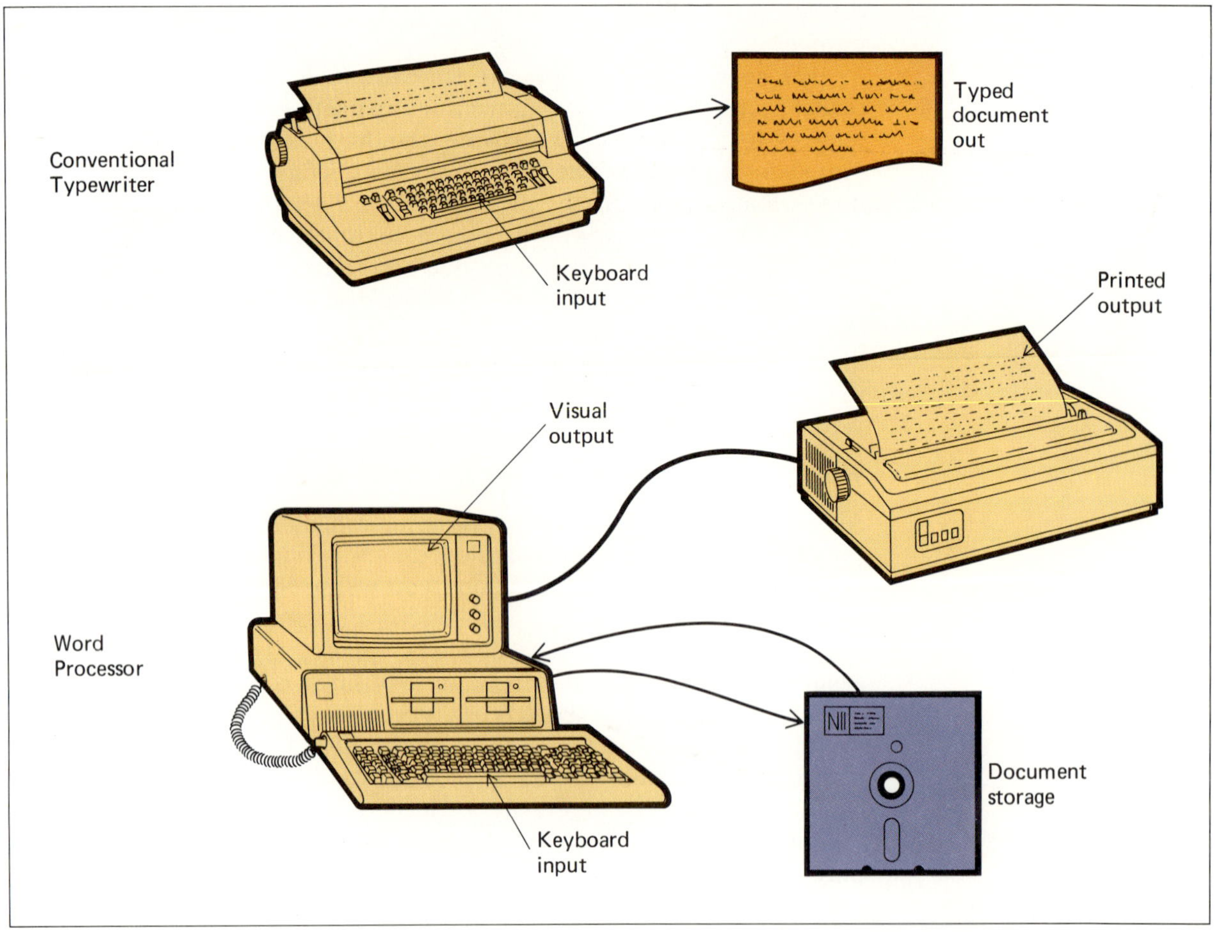

A word processor eliminates much of this duplication of effort. What is a word processor? It is a software system that allows for the entry, storage, retrieval, modification, and printing of documents. This concept is illustrated in Figure 2-5, which shows the difference between a conventional typewriter and a word processor. The objective of both is the same: the production of printed documents. As we can see, the concept of word processing relies on a computer. With the wide availability of microcomputers and good word processing software, it is very likely that the letter of Figure 2-4 would have been created by the originator by keying it directly into the computer (via a word processor). Once stored on disk, it is no longer necessary to retype the entire letter to make changes. To change, for instance, the wording of a phrase, only those portions to be changed need be retyped. Changing the overall appearance, such as making the margins wider, is easily done with a few keystrokes.

As we have already learned, a word processing system consists of both hardware and software. Many companies market computers that are specifically designed for word processing alone. As we might expect, these single-purpose machines are very versatile and powerful with respect to their word processing capabilities. On the other hand, within recent years many outstanding word processing software packages have become available for microcomputers. One of these is WordPerfect, the topic of Chapters 7 and 8.

Spreadsheets

A tool that you will encounter in almost any accountant's office is the *worksheet*, a technique for laying out data in the form of rows and columns for tabulation and analysis. Worksheet applications are so common that, in 1978, Daniel Bricklin and Robert Frankston, who were graduate students at the time, devised a technique for computerizing the worksheet concept. Their software, called *VisiCalc*, was first introduced for the Apple II microcomputer and was an instant success, finding use in a wide variety of applications. (Some computer industry observers argue that more Apple computers were sold for business use as a result of VisiCalc than for any other reason.)

One of the most common business uses is to study costs and expenditures. For instance, assume that you are trying to decide how to allocate your advertising money. You have four different product lines and you have categorized your spending into three categories. You can enter this information into the computer with a spreadsheet program and study it from the display of Figure 2-6. Notice that this display includes data (expenditure for each category) and calculated results (total and average). The calculated results are determined by the computer based on instructions for performing the calculations. If you change one of the data values, the computer will automatically recalculate all values that depend upon it. Thus, with a spreadsheet such as this, you can experiment with individual values to achieve your objectives—which might be a particular distribution of expenses as restricted by a maximum total amount. This process is commonly called a "what-if" analysis because you approach it from the viewpoint of "What happens if I make this change?"

You will learn more about spreadsheets in general in Chapter 10. In Chapters 11 through 13, you will learn about Lotus 1-2-3, a very powerful spreadsheet software tool and one of the most spectacular software successes in the microcomputer software field.

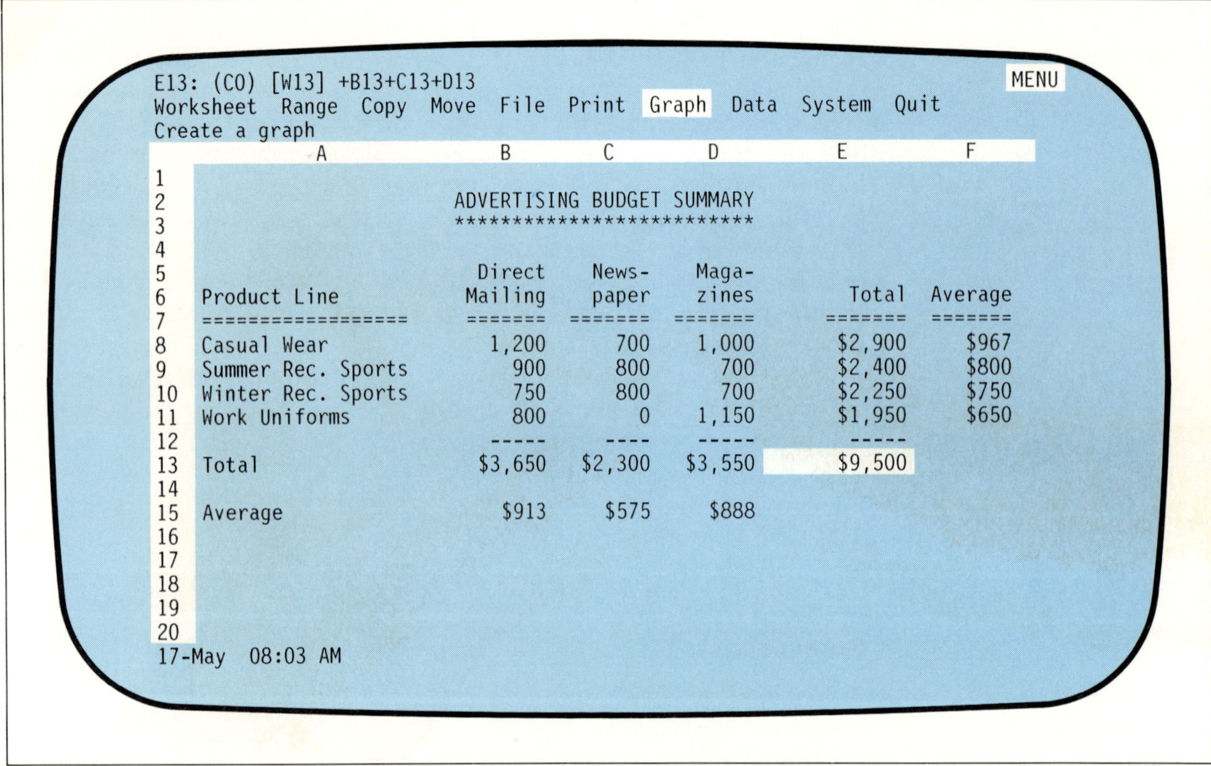

Figure 2-6
A spreadsheet.

Database Management Systems

From the descriptions of order processing, we learned that this system consists of two components: the data files and the programs (software) to process them as illustrated in Figure 2-7. Remember that the system includes several files that are used together to carry out the desired processing. This is commonplace for applications in the business environment. In

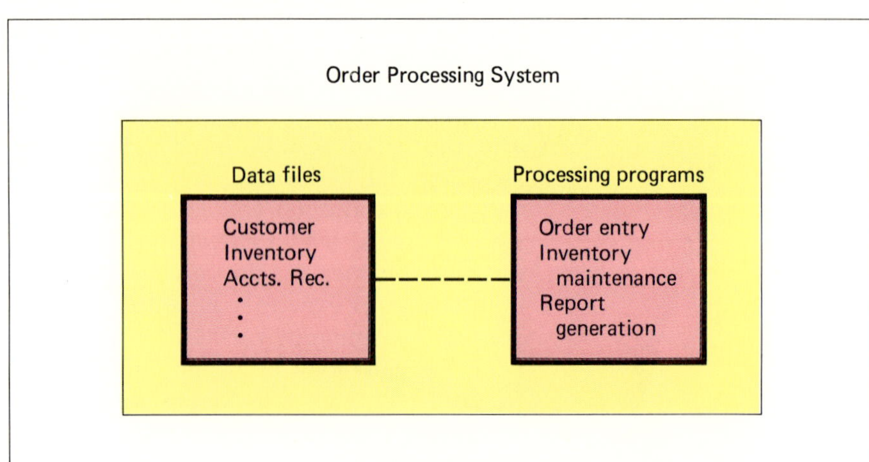

Figure 2-7
Data files and their processing programs.

any application such as this, some of the files are closely related to others. For instance, the accounts receivable file contains one record for each invoice that has been prepared. Each accounts receivable record contains the invoice number for that sale, the number of the customer to whom the sale was made, and other data pertaining to the sale. However, it does not include such customer data as the customer's name and address. Hence, the accounts receivable file by itself has limited value. In order to prepare, for instance, a customer statement, the customer file and accounts receivable file must be used together. Figure 2-8 illustrates how information from the customer file would be linked to that in the accounts receivable file to generate a customer statement.

In using such a system, there are many types of operations that must be performed in managing the collection of files; these are independent of

Figure 2-8
Linking records of two files to create an invoice.

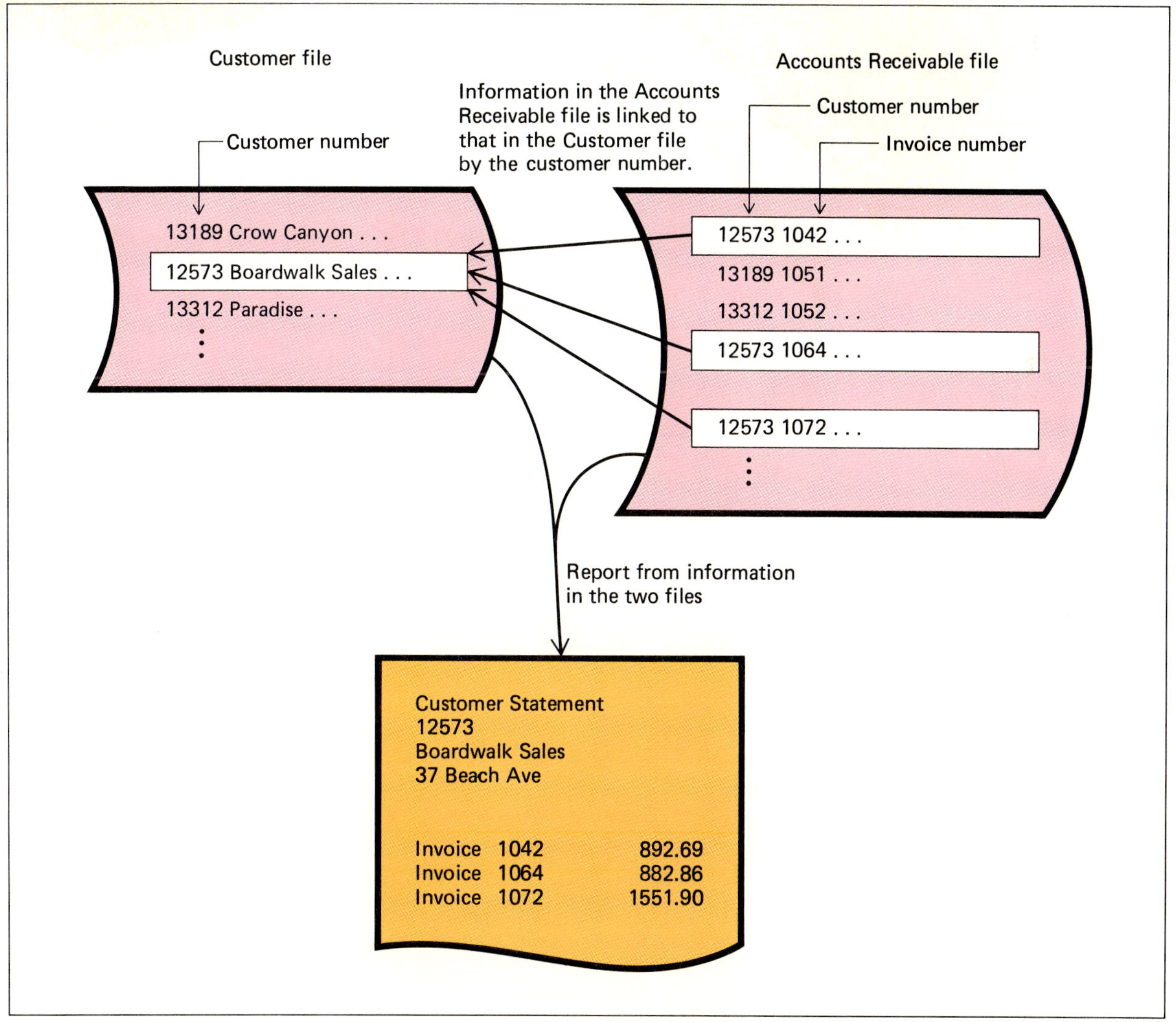

Software comes in many "shapes and sizes." This photograph shows some of the software products available from Ashton-Tate, the company that produces dBASE III PLUS, about which you will learn in later chapters.

the particular application. They include such actions as creating a new file, interrelating two files as illustrated by the example of Figure 2-8, and arranging the records of a file into a desired order. For each such application written in a programming language (such as COBOL), the programmer must write programs for these "utility" actions as well as programs to perform the desired processing (such as processing an order).

A database management system (DBMS) is a software system designed specifically to address the varied needs of file processing. With a DBMS, the composite of all the files for a given application are said to form the **database** of the system. In addition to the data files, a DBMS includes a variety of other files that define such things as characteristics of each file in the system, relationships between files, and limitations on the data in the files. Many of the functions that would require considerable programming effort by the programmer in setting up a business application with a programming language are built-in components of database management software. For instance, a DBMS user can combine the data in two different database files by issuing one simple command. With the tools of a DBMS and a limited amount of training, a computer user can set up database files and do many different processing operations. These are operations that would require considerable time and effort by a trained programmer to duplicate with a conventional programming language. However, this is not to suggest that the powers of a DBMS can be fully exploited by a casual user. It requires considerable training similar to that required by a programmer of a conventional programming language.

One such DBMS is dBASE III; it is the most widely used microcomputer DBMS. Although dBASE IV with a number of important new features became available in 1988, dBASE III is completely adequate to illustrate basic principles of the DBMS concept. You learn how to use dBASE III beginning in Chapter 15.

As you will learn in later chapters, both spreadsheets and DBMS's require a degree of programming, although the word *programming* has a slightly different meaning in each of the cases. At this stage of our learning, it is difficult to recognize the distinctions between programming as it applies to a programming language and as it applies to a spreadsheet or a DBMS. These distinctions will become more apparent in later chapters. For now, it is sufficient to recognize that:

1. Spreadsheets and database DBMS's are relatively specialized tools; programming languages are more generalized tools (although there is a distinction between business and scientific programming languages).
2. Spreadsheets and DBMS's can be used to program useful (although simple) applications with far less training than is possible using a programming language.

Computer Graphics

Computers are sometimes called number crunchers because of the speed with which they can perform calculations. Although the spreadsheet form of Figure 2-6 clearly displays all of the data, graphs are much more effective in communicating information to others. For instance, in the Total column of Figure 2-6 we can see the amount allocated to each product line. Upon inspecting it carefully, we see that Casual Wear is allocated the most and Work Uniforms the least. With a pocket calculator, we could determine the percentage of the whole for each product line. On the other hand, we see this relationship at a glance in the pie chart of Figure 2-9, which was prepared from this data. Displayed as a bar graph in Figure 2-10, the same data takes on a different form and conveys more information. These are examples of business graphics, a common method for illustrating all types of data, not simply that from spreadsheets.

Figure 2-9
Business graphics—a pie chart.

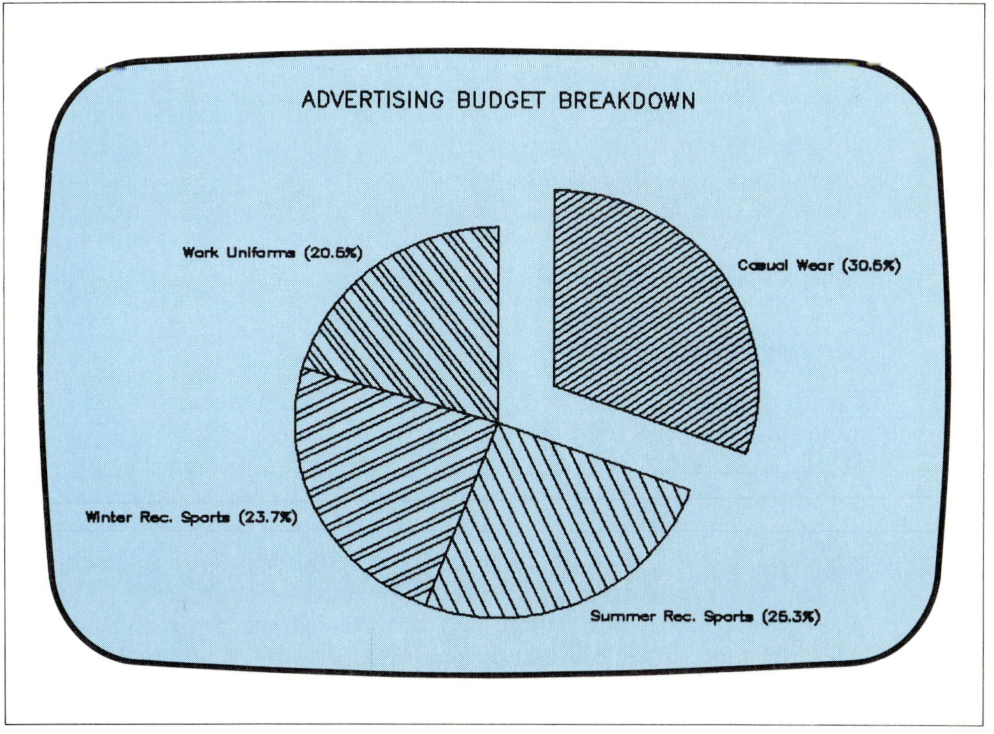

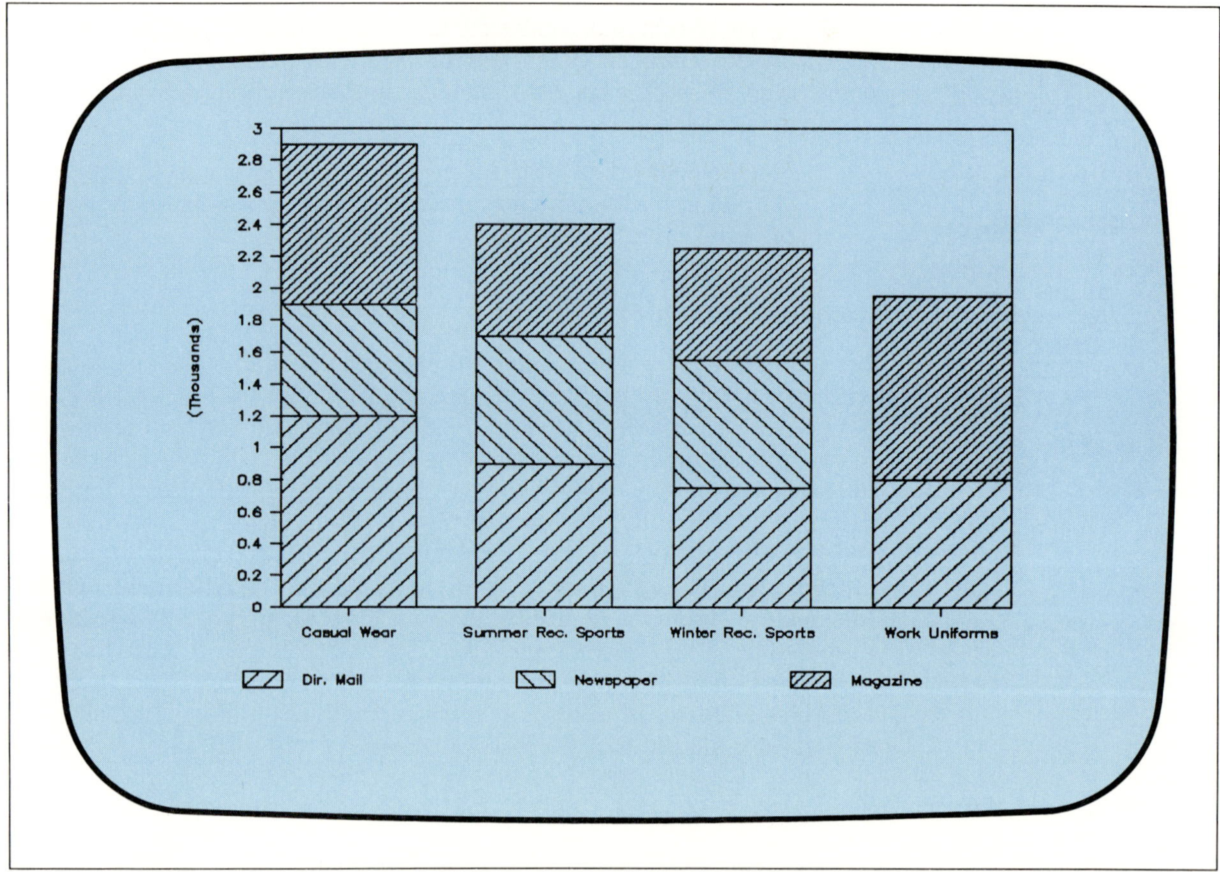

Figure 2-10
Business graphics—a bar graph.

Computer graphics is not limited to preparing business graphs. Indeed, paint and draw programs allow you to prepare drawings and pictures directly on the computer screen. Design programs allow professionals such as engineers and architects to produce engineering drawings and specifications on the computer. You will learn more about computer graphics in Chapter 13.

Data Communication

Communication between computers over the telephone network is vital to the information sharing that is such an essential element of many aspects of our lives. At a personal level, there is communication between an automatic teller machine from which you might make a withdrawal and the computer that contains the data for your bank account. On a much larger scale, there is communication between the computers of different banks for processing large fund transfers electronically. For the microcomputer owner, there is communication from his or her microcomputer to an information service or to another microcomputer. As you will learn in Chapter 20, a hardware device called a modem is necessary to connect a personal computer to the telephone line. Special software is also needed to allow two computers to "talk" to each other. For example,

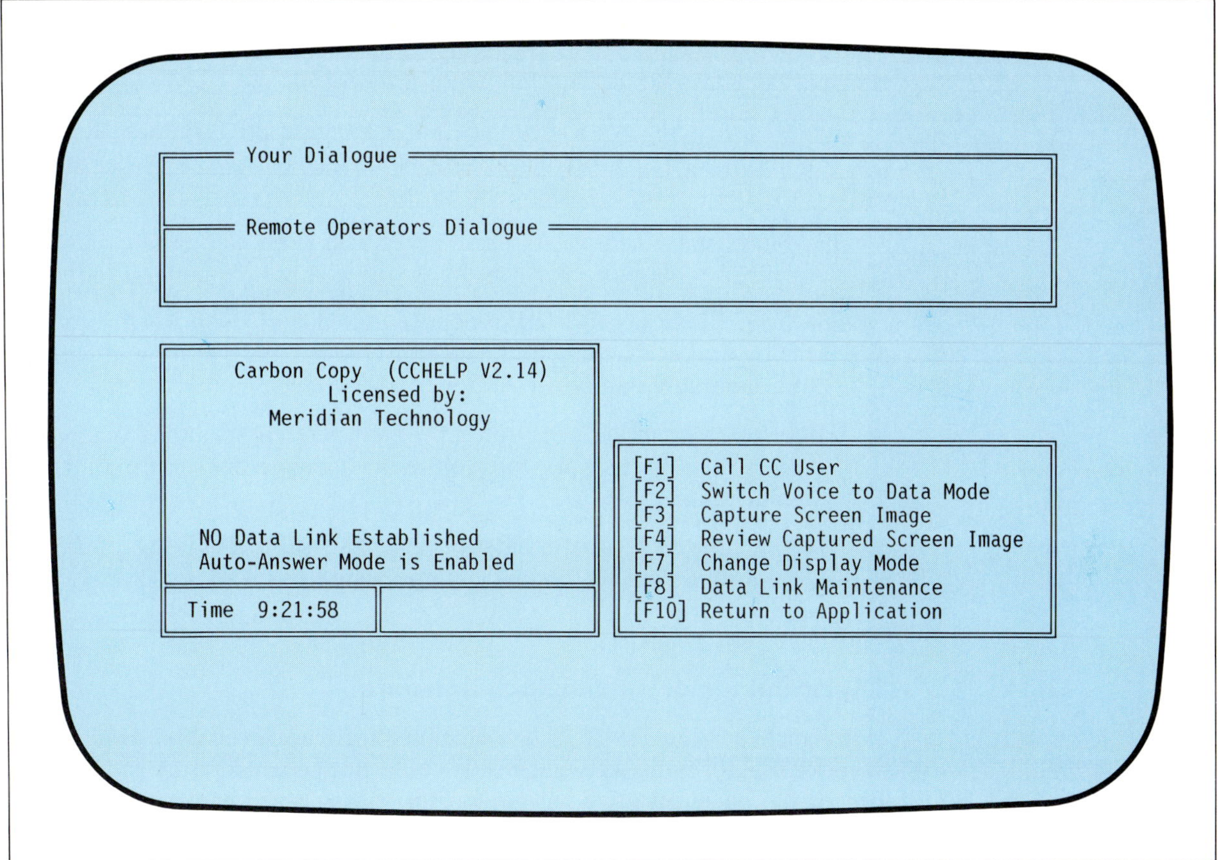

Figure 2-11
A data communications display.

a program named Carbon Copy allows a user to dial into a remote computer and operate the remote computer from his or her keyboard even though it may be 3000 miles away. Notice in the Carbon Copy main menu of Figure 2-11 that the upper part of the screen is dedicated to sending messages back and forth. The lower right summarizes the commands, including calling a computer and switching between using the telephone for computer communication and for voice communication between you and the other person.

APPLICATIONS SOFTWARE

The fourth broad software category is applications software. Whereas both programming languages and productivity software provide tools for developing (programming) solutions to specific problems, applications software represents those solutions. A particular software package might be prepared using a programming language or one of the productivity tools. Applications software is developed to meet the needs of many people or companies with the same processing needs. For instance, the general accounting system that you will require is much like the general accounting need of any manufacturing/sales-oriented company. There are literally hundreds of categories of applications software and thousands of application packages available. The following are typical.

QUIKEY Key Management System. For managing the issuance of room/building keys to employees. Tells who has what key, who has access to various rooms, and much more.

BPI Budget and Analysis. Assesses and tracks your company's financial health by following the activity in the company's general ledger.

MedEase. Medical office administrative package. Includes insurance, billing and accounting and also analyzes patient history and clinical and laboratory data.

Property Management. Accounting program for owners and managers of residential, industrial, and commercial properties of up to 1,000 rental units.

The Tax Advantage. Tax-assistance and year-round planning program. Supports Forms 1040 and 4562, and Schedules A, B, C, D, E, G, SE, and W.

Shortcomings of Applications Software

With such a wide range of applications software available, you might wonder if all of your software needs could not be satisfied by purchasing prewritten packages. The answer is that packages are necessarily general in nature and may not conform to the exact way you like to do things. To illustrate, let us consider some of your data needs for the inventory file. After careful consideration of your product line, you have decided upon an item code that will uniquely identify each item in the line. It is to consist of three components that will identify the style, the size, and colors. For instance, a particular style of your men's warm-up suit, size 34, red, black, and white, has the following item code (this is typical of your needs).

Style	MWU7
Size	34
Colors	ReBlWh

With this as a general form, your item code will consist of twelve positions broken down as follows:

Style	Four positions
Size	Two positions
Colors	Six positions (up to three colors, two positions per color)

Another of your needs for any order-processing package relates to product pricing; that is, for each item in your line you will have a:

Unit wholesale price for quantity 1–11

Unit wholesale price for quantity 12 or more

Retail price (mail order sales)

In other words, for wholesale sales, you have a price break at quantity 12. For example, if a local store were to purchase eleven sweatshirts (or any fewer), the unit price might be $15.95; if the store were to purchase twelve or more, the unit price would be $15.25. The retail price to a person purchasing by mail order would be $29.95. It is important that this information be stored in the inventory file to make it possible for all prices to be looked up and calculations made automatically when you are entering an order.

Now, let us consider how your particular needs might relate to a typical order-processing package on the market. Studying the specifications of their system, you see that the inventory record includes the following fields.

Field	Length
Item code	8
Description	30
Quantity on hand	6
Base price	7
Second price	7
Second price break quantity	5
Third price	7
Third price break quantity	5

You have problems with this package. First, the item code field provides for only an 8-position value; you need 12 positions. The solution to this dilemma is to reduce the length of your item code to 8 positions, or else look for another order-processing package. In general, making necessary changes to the applications package is not practical. Second, the package is not capable of handling two different pricing scales; you need retail as well as wholesale. Notice that it can handle your wholesale structure in which you have a price break at quantity 12. In fact, it includes a second price break point—a feature that you do not currently require. Entering retail orders with this system would require that the unit price for each item be typed from the keyboard, a slow and error-prone process. All factors considered, the best solution is to look at other order-processing packages.

The preceding problems are typical of those that are encountered when evaluating applications packages. That is, a user has specialized needs (or desires) that cannot be handled by a general-purpose package. With such potential problems, the beginner in business might consider hiring a programmer to do the necessary programming in order to produce a system to fill the exact needs of the company. The problem with this approach is cost. An application system to do the common order-processing, invoicing, and inventory control operations might cost anywhere between $100 and $500. An equivalent system would cost many thousands of dollars to write. The

Applications packages are available to do almost anything. These drawings of a new aircraft were prepared using special design software.

bottom line with most applications packages is that if the company can adjust to the standards of the package, then using such a package is quite realistic.

SOFTWARE REQUIREMENTS

By now we are well aware that acquiring a computer system for a business involves much more than simply purchasing and installing a computer. Indeed, we have learned that the correct process requires:

1. Assessing processing needs of the business.
2. Selecting software to satisfy those needs.
3. Selecting hardware that will handle the chosen software.

Although the preceding descriptions do not involve the detailed assessment necessary to make sound software decisions, they are sufficient to give you an idea of the many factors involved. However, there is one common pitfall that we have not considered: the tendency to overestimate what the computer can do in a cost-effective way.

About Assessing Needs

There are numerous bad reasons why people acquire a particular piece of software, such as:

- Everyone is using it and we must stay in step. The current rage is not necessarily the best for your applications. On the other hand, if, in your business area, a particular software product is widely used *and* it fits your needs, then staying in step can be desirable.

- It has all the bells and whistles. Your acquisition should not be based simply on the number of features of a product but, rather, on the features needed for your applications.
- It is cheaper than competing software. Saving a few hundred dollars might seem to be a good idea at the time of purchase. However, if the software is mediocre or is poorly suited to your needs, the long-term cost in time wasted and working with inadequate results will far outweigh the initial saving.
- It is the most expensive, the Cadillac. The "best" does not mean that it is the best for your needs. There are many high-quality, low-priced software products on the market.

The bottom line should be, "Will use of the software be cost effective on an overall basis and will it do the job that we need done?" Some tasks are less costly and time consuming to do manually; others are best done by using outside services. For instance, consider one of your many needs—care labels. The federal government requires that every garment include a label with care instructions, such as that shown in Figure 2-12. Assume that a young salesperson has been knocking on your door to sell database software that will store all of your care label information and print care labels. She explains that you would be able to print your own care labels if you were to purchase her care label software. The alternative is to use a local label service. Let us consider the costs.

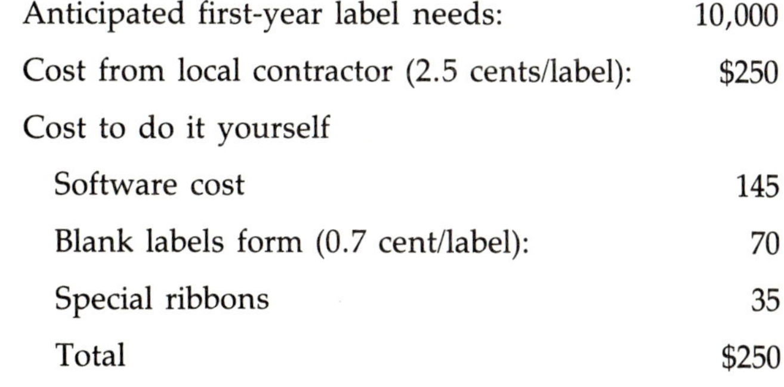

Anticipated first-year label needs:	10,000
Cost from local contractor (2.5 cents/label):	$250
Cost to do it yourself	
Software cost	145
Blank labels form (0.7 cent/label):	70
Special ribbons	35
Total	$250

Figure 2-12
A care label. Courtesy of Max-Tech, Oceanside, CA.

We see in this brief cost summary that the savings in printing your own labels will pay for the software the first year. This appears to be a good investment and one worth pursuing. However, there are other factors. Let us consider advantages and disadvantages of both possibilities.

Print them yourself:

Save money after the first year.

Needed labels can be run immediately.

Convenient for low-quantity runs.

Occupies your time and computer.

Use outside service:

No initial outlay.

Two-day service.

Extra charge for low-quantity runs.

Someone else does it for you.

The final point is an extremely important one. Let us consider some of the inconveniences of running your own labels.

1. Someone will have to learn how to use the software. Although this is not a major task, it will require valuable time. It is important to recognize that each software product (as well as each piece of hardware) takes time to learn how to use. This is commonly called a learning curve. The learning process for some software products is long and tedious, and details are easily forgotten if the software is not used frequently.
2. When labels must be run, the computer will not be available for other use.
3. Running labels requires changing the printer setup and carefully monitoring the printing operation.

After assessing the situation, you decide that the convenience and long-term cost savings simply do not justify the inconvenience of preparing your own labels. The convincing argument is that your area of expertise is the garment business, not the label business. You decide to focus on what you do best and to hire someone who specializes in preparing labels to handle that task.

Software Decisions

At the beginning of this chapter when looking at your business plan, the following typical data processing needs were considered:

- General ledger
- Inventory control
- Order processing
- Customer billing
- Product sales analysis
- Product cost analysis
- Management of documents
- Direct mailing

The final choice of activities to implement on the computer requires a careful assessment of your needs, capabilities, and resources. After a thorough evaluation, you decide to begin operations using the following software.

Software Product	Source	Functions
WordPerfect	WordPerfect Corp.	Word processor for general document management. Also used in conjunction with database system for direct mailing.
Lotus 1-2-3	Lotus Development Corp.	Spreadsheet for product sales analysis and product cost analysis.
dBASE III PLUS	Ashton-Tate	DBMS required for use of selected general ledger system.
General ledger	Business software vendor	Applications package programmed using dBASE III.
Order processing	Business software vendor	Applications package that includes order processing, accounts receivable, and inventory control components. Compatible with selected general ledger system.

Overall, this software list will provide a solid foundation for handling the business aspects of the company.

SUMMARY

Many of the computer concepts and principles to come are related to the framework established for MCT Enterprises. The study of microcomputer hardware and software will expand upon many of the questions arising in this chapter.

- A computer system consists of hardware and software. Hardware comprises the physical elements; software comprises the programs of instructions that direct the hardware operations. The microcomputer user need not be a hardware expert to make use of the computer, but the basic understanding provided by Chapter 2 allows for more intelligent use of the system.
- The computer is capable of only very elementary operations with data: input, storage, arithmetic, comparing, and output. These are described in detail in Chapters 3 and 4.
- In the computer field, the word *system* is used in a variety of ways. It can refer to: (1) a combination of people, procedures, and machines; (2) computer software; (3) computer hardware; and, (4) the combination of computer hardware and software. As with many English words, its meaning in a specific instance will be evident by the context in which it is used.

- The computer system must provide solutions. To that end, when obtaining a computer, the problems to be solved (the needs) must be clearly defined. Then software that will satisfy these needs must be found. Finally, hardware required by the software must be obtained.

- The operating system is an essential set of programs designed to manage the resources of the computer. A basic knowledge of how to use an operating system is essential to the intelligent use of a microcomputer. The disk operating system for the IBM PC (MS DOS) is described in Chapter 5. More advanced operating system concepts are described in Chapter 17.

- Programming languages provide the trained programmer with the tools necessary to prepare sets of instructions to solve wide classes of problems. Principles of various types of languages are described in Chapter 18. Simple programming using the programming language of dBASE III is included in Chapter 19.

- Software tools, collectively referred to as productivity software, are available that allow a user with a minimum of training to prepare solutions to problems. The five productivity tools are word processing, spreadsheet, database management, graphics, and communications. These topics are described in more detail in later chapters as follows:

    - General principles of word processing in Chapter 6; using WordPerfect in Chapters 7 and 8.
    - General principles of spreadsheet software in Chapter 10; using Lotus 1-2-3 in Chapters 11 and 12.
    - General principles of DBMS's in Chapter 14; using dBASE III in Chapters 15 and 16.
    - Graphics in conjunction with Lotus 1-2-3 in Chapter 13.
    - Communications in Chapter 20.

- Applications software is off-the-shelf software ready to be used. It is developed to meet the needs of many people or businesses with the same processing needs. An applications package to, for instance, handle order processing might cost hundreds of dollars whereas to prepare the necessary programs in a programming language might cost many thousands. Applications packages usually require that the user adjust his or her way of doing things to conform to the way in which the package is designed.

- In obtaining software to implement solutions on a computer, the first criterion must be, "Is it cost effective?" Software (and hardware) should not be obtained for "emotional" reasons in the business environment.

Chapter 3

Hardware: The Processor and Memory

OBJECTIVES

Chapter 2 has provided you with your first look at computer software. This chapter is the first of two chapters about hardware. When you have completed the chapter, you should be able to describe:

- The basic components of the computer—input, output, processor, memory, and auxiliary storage—and their interactions when running a program.
- The components and functions of the microprocessor, the processing and control center of the microcomputer.
- The characteristics of computer memory, including the concepts of the byte, memory size, memory speed, and random accessing capability.
- The basic means by which information is encoded in memory, including the ASCII code and error checking concepts.
- The data bus, the "lifeline" through which data flows between components of the computer.

PREVIEW

Introduction to Hardware

The basic components of any computer are input, output, processor, memory, and auxiliary storage. This is as true of microcomputers (the focus of this book) designed to serve individual users as it is of larger computers designed to handle much greater work loads.

Inside the Computer

The main circuitry of the computer is mounted on an electronic circuit board called the motherboard. Included is the microprocessor, which provides both the overall control of the computer and the ability to perform arithmetic operations.

Internal Memory

Before anything can take place in a computer, the program of instructions must be placed in memory. While the program is being run, it moves data in and out of memory. The basic memory element is the byte.

Technical Aspects of the Computer Interior

Within memory, the byte is used in a variety of ways to store different types of data (for instance, numbers as opposed to letters). Data is moved from one place in the computer to another through an "electronic freeway" called a data bus.

INTRODUCTION TO HARDWARE

Chapter 2 has provided you with enough knowledge of the computer needs of your business to formulate a basic plan for the tasks you wish to automate and to select the software packages to perform these jobs. Using the "software first, then hardware" method of system selection, you are now ready to investigate the available hardware to get your business moving. Making the best decision for hardware acquisition is not an easy task for a person new to the computer field. Purchasing a computer is somewhat like purchasing an automobile: not only must you select the make and model, but you must also decide upon accessories. Furthermore, computer "accessories" (like automobile accessories) can add significantly to the cost of the system. How much must you know about hardware in order to make a wise decision concerning your computer acquisition? One solution is to work with a reputable computer dealer in selecting both your software and hardware and rely upon the expertise of the dealer. With this approach, you need to have very little knowledge of hardware. However, in this situation, you can end up with serious problems if the dealer lacks in qualifications and/or honesty. Assuming that you were successful in acquiring a system in this way, would you be able to use it without a knowledge of the hardware? The answer to this question is Yes.

With this alternative, you might wonder why you need any knowledge of hardware. To answer this, let us return to the automobile. You hardly need to be a mechanic to drive and own one. However, a basic knowledge of how the automobile works is very helpful in being a good owner. It can be especially helpful in recognizing particular symptoms and knowing what *not* to do when trouble develops, thereby saving yourself expensive repairs. It can also be helpful in recognizing the limitations of the vehicle. For instance, if you are constantly carrying heavy loads, then you might want to install overload springs and heavy-duty tires. A computer is much the same. The more you know about it and how it works, the better able you are to use it and to make wise decisions.

Computers: Micro, Mini, and Mainframe

The focus of this book is on using microcomputers. However, in learning about them, we should not lose sight of the fact that there is a huge world of much larger computers. The popular classifications, listed in order by computer size, are microcomputer, minicomputer, and mainframe. Without using the terms and concepts that you have yet to learn about, it is difficult to define characteristics that distinguish one from the other. In fact, changes in technology come at such a rapid pace that a particular feature that distinguishes a minicomputer from a microcomputer today might be an important characteristic of a microcomputer tomorrow. Much the same is true of the relationship between the minicomputer and the mainframe. In fact, the comparisons that distinguished the minicomputer from the mainframe when the minicomputer was first introduced during the 1960s are really no longer meaningful. Indeed, some of the so-called minicomputers manufactured by the Digital Equipment Corporation (DEC), the dominant minicomputer company, are larger and more powerful than some of the mainframes manufactured by IBM, the dominant mainframe company. Rather than there being a distinct line of division between the two categories, computers are available in almost a continuous range of sizes, from small to very large. (This is not unlike the automobile industry in which we see automobiles ranging from the smallest two-seaters to huge limousines.) At the low end of the computer spectrum (excluding microcomputers), there are minicomputers that are able to handle several users at once. Such a computer might serve as the next major step upward in data processing capability for MCT Enterprises as the business expands. At the high end of the spectrum are supercomputers with enormous power used by some government agencies and the largest corporations. As a general rule, larger size means increased speed, more memory, and higher cost with a resulting ability to handle larger and more complex tasks that might be impossible to accomplish on a smaller machine.

It is generally true that microcomputers are intended for one-to-one use: one person sitting at the computer and directly interacting with it. The minicomputer and mainframe usually serve many individuals or departments, however, and most can be working on many different programs concurrently. Others are designed with many workstations (keyboard and display monitor) to allow tens, or even hundreds, of people to use the computer at the same time. Another feature that is typical of the larger minicomputer and the mainframe installation is the need for a comprehensive staff. As a rule, this includes people to manage the computer and data processing center, to program at different levels, and to coordinate the day-to-day operations.

As you study the materials that follow, you should keep in mind that the microcomputer represents one important component of the overall capability for processing data. Microcomputers can be used alone or they can be used in conjunction with minicomputers and mainframes. That is,

Minicomputers allow many people to have access to the computer at the same time. The minicomputers of today have capabilities that large-scale computers had 10 years ago.

The Cray-2 supercomputer. Where microcomputers operate with speeds of millions of operations per second, supercomputers operate at speeds of many hundreds of millions of operations per second.

by connecting a microcomputer to a larger computer to serve as a **workstation,** it is possible to have the advantages of both the microcomputer and the host computer at the disposal of the user. Much emphasis has been placed by computer companies on this aspect of the market. The IBM PS/2 is especially designed to accommodate this need. The Apple Corporation and DEC reached an agreement in 1988 to include provisions for the Macintosh to function as a workstation for the DEC computers.

Descriptions that follow of hardware (and many of the topics in later chapters) are related specifically to microcomputers. However, keep in mind that, on a broad basis, they apply to mainframes as well. For instance, the concepts of input and output, of memory, and of auxiliary storage are as applicable to mainframes as they are to microcomputers.

Computer Logical Structure

From Chapter 2, we know that the computer is capable of the basic operations of data input, output, storage, arithmetic, and comparing. These actions correspond to the components of the computer illustrated in Figure 3-1.

- *Input.* Input devices bring input data into the computer system; the keyboard is the standard input device for the microcomputer.
- *Output.* Output devices deliver processed results for "people" use; the monitor and printer are standard output devices for the microcomputer.
- *Processor.* The processor is the heart of the computer. It contains the electronic circuitry to perform arithmetic operations, make comparisons, and provide overall control of the computer's actions.
- *Memory.* The computer memory, also called *internal memory,* is the electronic component of the computer into which information is temporarily stored when processing takes place. For instance, to process an order, the order-processing program must be in memory. During processing activities, data will be moved into and out of

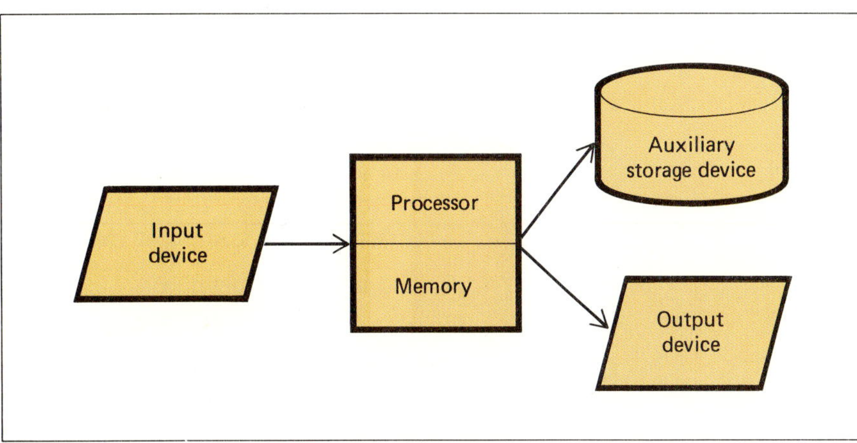

Figure 3-1
The logical structure of a computer.

memory. Information in memory is lost when another application is loaded into memory or when the computer is turned off.

- *Auxiliary storage.* Auxiliary storage is the component of the computer in which software and data are permanently stored. The floppy disk is the auxiliary storage medium for microcomputers. Because most auxiliary storage units use rotating disks, the term *disk storage* is commonly used. During operation of the computer, software is copied from auxiliary storage to memory; data is also transferred back and forth between auxiliary storage and memory.

Running a Program

To get an idea of how these components work together, let us consider the actions that would take place if an order were entered into the computer and an invoice printed. This is an operation that we learned about in Chapter 1.

1. From the keyboard, you issue an appropriate command to cause the order-processing program to be loaded (copied) from auxiliary storage into memory. This command also causes the computer to *execute* or *run* the program, that is, to perform the actions described by the instructions of the program. The processor controls the execution of each instruction in the program, one after the other.
2. Through the monitor, you are asked for the customer number of the customer for whom you wish to process an order.
3. Through the keyboard, you type the desired customer number.
4. The processor directs the auxiliary storage device to copy the record for that customer into memory so that it will be available for processing.
5. Through the monitor, you are asked to enter information regarding the item to be ordered.
6. Through the keyboard, you type the item number of the item desired.
7. The processor directs the auxiliary storage device to copy the inventory record for that item into memory.
8. Changes in the quantity on hand for each item ordered are copied from memory back into auxiliary storage.
9. The actions of steps 5 through 8 are repeated for each product item in the order. Note that in this sequence, you are *interacting* with the computer: the computer makes a request and you respond.
10. The invoice is printed.
11. If you are finished with order processing, you might go on to some other application such as printing mailing labels for mass mailing. This will involve loading and running another program, thereby replacing the previous contents of memory.

In this sequence, notice the movement of data between memory and auxiliary storage. Data is permanently stored in auxiliary storage (however, it can be erased) but must be copied into memory in order to be operated upon. Actually, we can think of memory and auxiliary storage as corresponding to a desktop (where the "action" takes place) and a file cabinet. This concept is illustrated in Figure 3-2.

Personal Computer Models

This book is written to be used in conjunction with software that accompanies it—software for use on IBM personal computers and compat-

Figure 3-2
Relationship between internal memory and auxiliary storage.

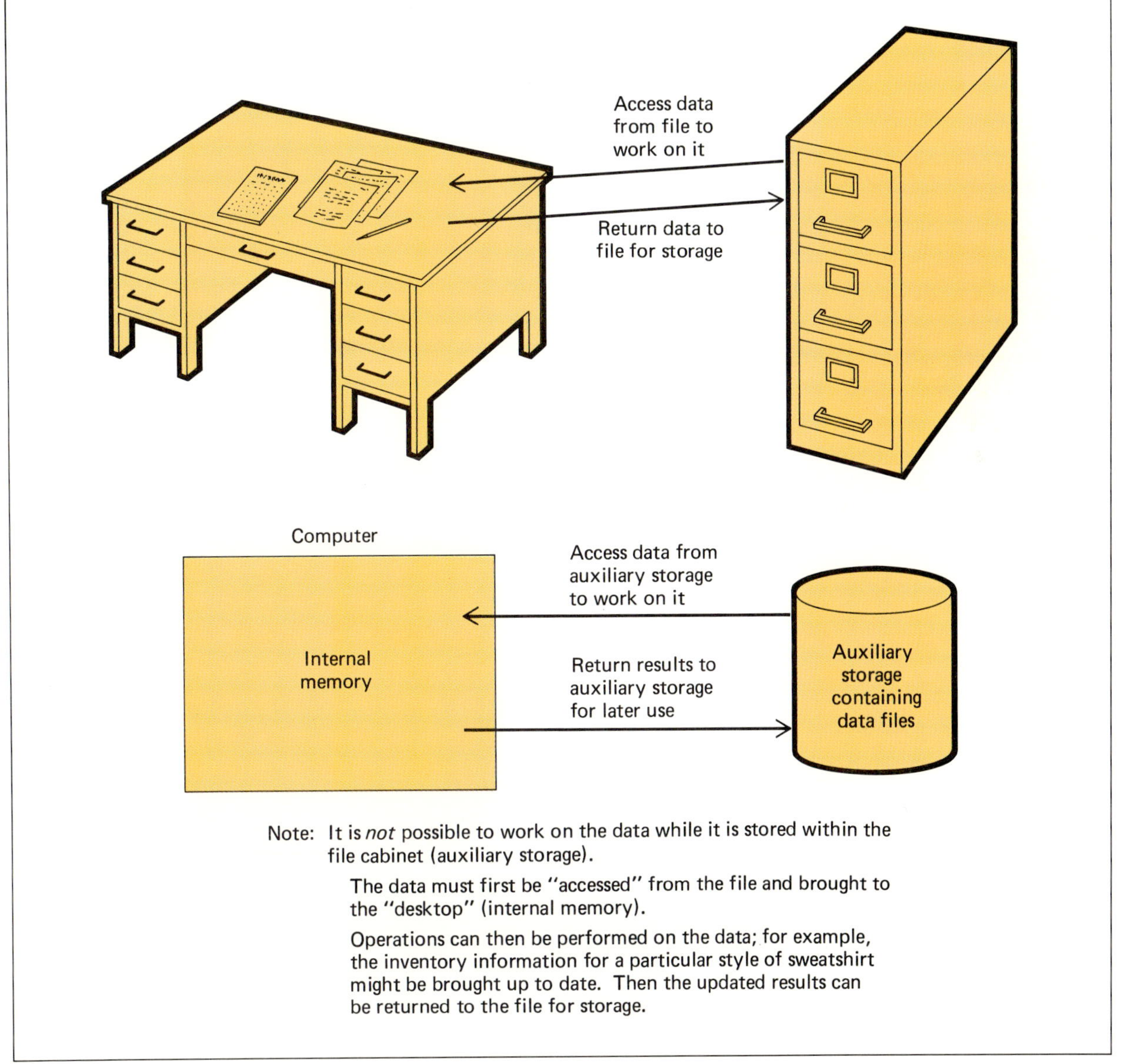

ible machines made by other companies. Consequently, most descriptions in the book relate to the IBM computers. With this heavy emphasis, it is important that you avoid concluding that IBM is "the only" computer. (Many users, for example, prefer the Apple Macintosh series of computers.) It is simply a case in which you will be using a particular type of computer so the emphasis is on equipment that will be familiar to you.

The oldest of the IBM personal computer line is the PC, the computer most commonly encountered in college computer laboratories and offices. This computer was introduced by IBM in 1981 and quickly became an industry standard, primarily because of the dominance of IBM in the computer field. Later came the IBM XT, which was practically identical to the PC except that it included a high-capacity disk storage unit. After the XT, IBM followed up with the AT, which was considerably different from its predecessors. However, for most owners and users, the AT functions essentially as a faster, higher-capacity XT. In 1987, IBM introduced its Personal System/2 (PS/2) line, which featured a number of concepts new to microcomputers.

This IBM equipment has set significant standards for both software and hardware, so much so that the model designations (for instance, XT) are commonly used in a generic sense; that is, a wide variety of companies market "clones" of these computers, which are, in most instances, less expensive and faster than the IBM product. (*Note*: IBM ceased manufacturing the PC, XT, and AT with the introduction of the PS/2. However, clones are still available from a large number of companies.) Almost all descriptions in this book (unless otherwise indicated) apply to all models in a generic sense; that is, reference to a PC means an IBM PC, XT, AT, PS/2, or the *equivalent*.

INSIDE THE COMPUTER

Figure 3-3 shows what you would see if you removed the cover from a microcomputer. Both the older IBM PC and the newer IBM PS/2 include the same basic components. Clearly visible are the power supply, disk

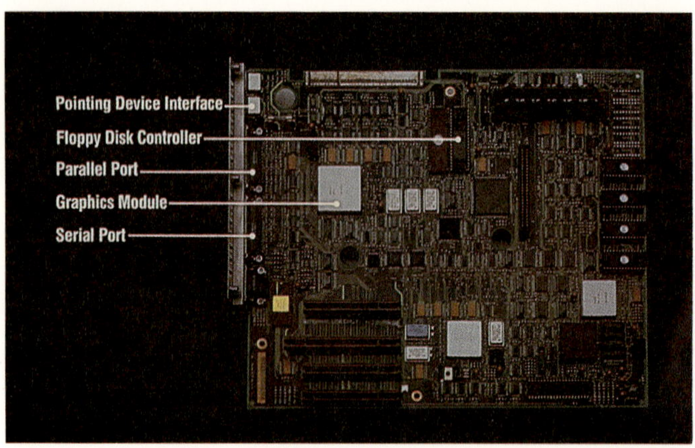

Figure 3-3
The IBM PS/2 motherboard.

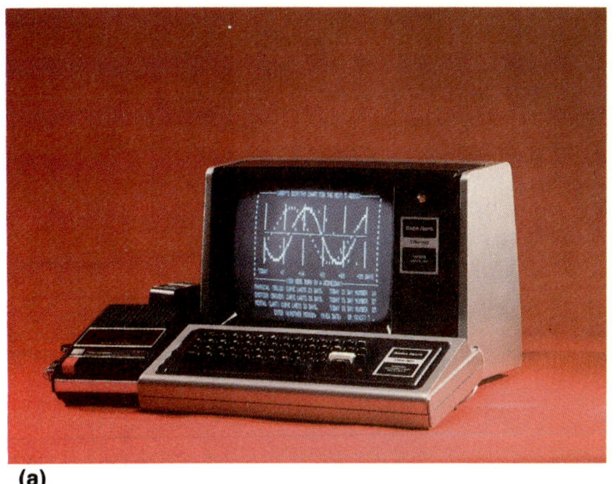
(a)

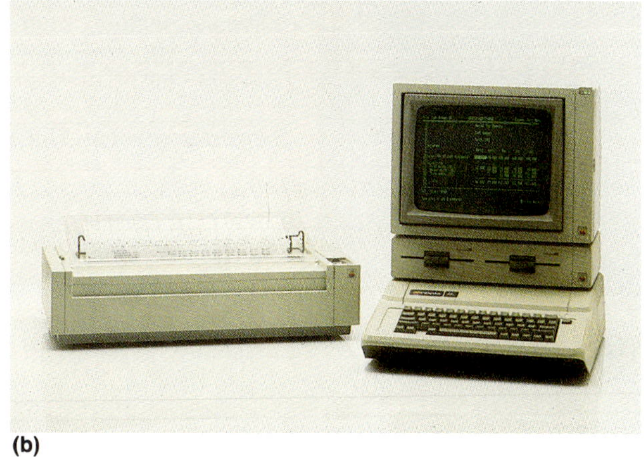
(b)

(c)

(d)

(e)

This brief pictorial history of the microcomputer shows some of the highlights: **(a)** the Radio Shack TRS80 Model 1; **(b)** the venerable Apple II; **(c)** The trend-setting IBM Personal Computer; **(d)** the Apple Macintosh; and **(e)** an IBM PS/2 computer.

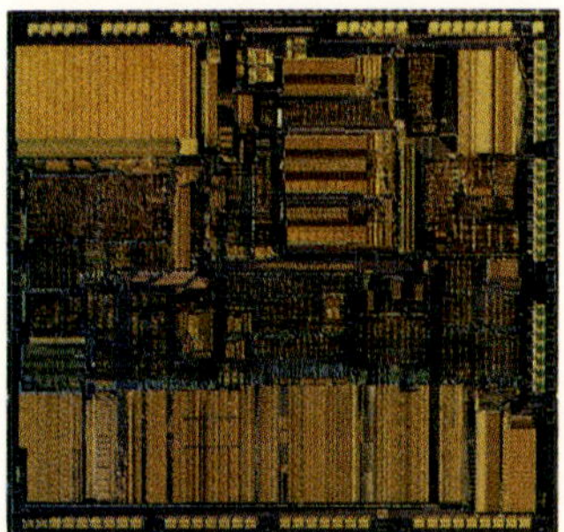

Figure 3-4
Microprocessor chip.

drives, speaker, main system board, and expansion slots. Let us first consider the system board and some of its elements.

Semiconductor Chips and the System Board

Modern electronics is based on microtechnology that uses special semiconductor materials placed on miniature silicon chips to form complex electronic circuitry. Commonly called **integrated circuits,** the sample shown in Figure 3-4 contains thousands of individual circuits. Over the years, improvements in chip technology have seen huge increases in the number of circuits on a chip, the speed of operation, and reliability. The result is continually increasing power and reliability of computers. The basic components of the microcomputer are mounted on a special circuit board called a **system board,** or a **motherboard.** A variety of chips are mounted on the system board. The processor chip controls the computer. Others function as memory chips, and still others to control communication between various components of the computer. Astonishingly, thousands of electronic circuits in each chip are interconnected to those of other chips through electrical tracings on the surface of the board. A computer of the 1960s with the amount of circuitry on this single small board would have required a cabinet the size of several full-size office file cabinets.

The Processor

The "nerve center" of any computer is the processor, the component that performs all calculations and comparisons and controls overall operation of the computer and its components. In the microcomputer, these actions are carried out by the **microprocessor** (see Figure 3-4). Introduced by Intel Corporation in 1971, microprocessors have had a huge impact not only on the computer industry, but on many other industries as well. The low cost and small size of microprocessors have made it possible to put "intelligence" in all sorts of machines. We can even buy a sewing machine controlled by a microprocessor. Automobiles with microprocessors to optimize the control of the engine and provide better pollution control are commonplace.

The task of directing operations within the computer is the function of the **control unit,** one of the basic components of the microprocessor. This unit can be considered analogous to a combination of traffic officer and automatic telephone switchboard. It obtains instructions from **memory,** interprets them, and makes certain that they are carried out as required. These functions require the opening and closing of appropriate circuits, starting and stopping of input/output (I/O) devices, and, in general, directing the flow of information within the computer.

The **arithmetic/logic unit,** another component of the microprocessor, performs all arithmetic and logical (comparing) operations. Herein lies the key to the versatility of the modern computer, because logical operations provide decision-making capability. For example, in Chapter 1, we studied the process of entering an order. An item from the inventory can be entered into the order only if the stock balance is greater than 0. The program to perform this action will need instructions to *compare* the requested quantity with the quantity on hand. Similarly, if the application happened to be payroll, the hours worked for each employee would likely be *compared* with 40 in order to determine overtime. In other words, a **logical operation** is simply a comparison of two quantities that produces a "yes" or "no" type of result. For instance:

"Is the value of total hours > 40?"

"Is the employee code = E?"

"Is employee number > previous employee number?"

Once the comparison is made within the arithmetic/logic unit, other instructions can decide what to do on the basis of the result of the comparing operation. Interestingly, this simple comparing ability represents the extent of the computer's ability to make decisions. It is the well-conceived and often sophisticated programs written by people using this simple feature that make the computer appear almost human in its decision-making abilities.

The vast array of activities taking place within the microprocessor are synchronized by the **system clock,** an element that oscillates millions of times per second. The clock speed is of significance to the typical user because it is a determinant of how fast the computer runs. For instance, if you were to go into a computer store to purchase a computer, the salesperson might show you an XT that operates at either 4.77 or 8 megahertz. If you needed something faster, a step upward could be an AT operating at 8 megahertz or another operating at 12. (The price increases as the speed increases.) What does all of this mean? First, the word **hertz** means cycles per second. For instance, your household electric power is 60 cycles per second, or 60 hertz. Hence, 4.77 megahertz is 4.77 million cycles per second (**mega** is an abbreviation for million). Within the computer, the clock speed is important because it represents the pace at which internal activities take place. The fastest single operation can take place in one clock cycle; other operations take two or more clock cycles. The original IBM PC operated at a speed of 4.77 megahertz. Most PC clones available now operate at a speed of 8 megahertz. This is important to you as a user because it determines how fast a given program will run. Although 4.77 million action cycles per second sounds unbelievably fast, it is not when considered in light of the heavy processing demands of some current software systems. A particular program that is agonizingly slow when run on a 4.77-megahertz computer might be acceptable on an 8-megahertz machine.

Just as automobile engines are different in their design, so are microprocessors, as it is within their electronic circuitry that primary characteristics of the computer are defined. Regarding automobile engines, we find gasoline, diesel, and rotary. The manner in which each of these operates is completely different from the others. However, the purpose of each is the same: to propel the auto. Much the same can be said of microprocessors used in microcomputers. There are many different designs, but they are all designed to "propel" the computer. Following are some of the most widely known microprocessors and the computers with which they are commonly associated.

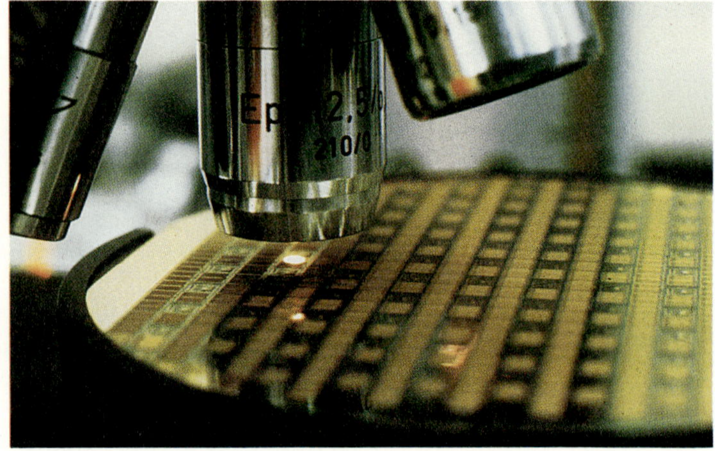

The microscopic size and fragility of the microprocessor require that they be manufactured in ultraclean conditions. Here, manufactured chips are being inspected under a microscope.

Microprocessor	Computer
Motorola 6502	Apple II
Zytel Z80	TRS80 Model III
Intel 8088	IBM PC/XT
Intel 80286	IBM AT, IBM PS/2 Model 50
Intel 80386	IBM PS/2, Model 80
Motorola 68000	Apple Macintosh

The above computers are not the *only* ones that use the indicated microprocessors. In fact, the Z80 was widely used by a variety of computer companies, as are others on this list. From the point of view of software, the microprocessor used is very significant as it is this component that includes the machine language used in the computer. Thus, the machine language would be the same for two Z80-based computers even though they might be manufactured by different companies.

Expansion Slots

Purchasing a microcomputer is much like purchasing an automobile—you must decide upon the model and also upon the accessories. In fact, some of the "accessories" of the PC/XT/AT are to the computer as tires are to an automobile: you would not get very far without them. For instance, the motherboard of these computers does not include circuitry for such basic elements as controlling devices for the monitor or disk drives. This capability is provided through **expansion circuit boards** that plug into the expansion slots of the motherboard (see Figure 3-3). Almost any PC/XT/AT that you might purchase already includes the disk controller board in one of the slots. However, you must make a decision regarding the type of monitor you intend to use and purchase the monitor board accordingly (monitors are discussed in a later section of this chapter). In addition, expansion cards can be inserted to provide for such needs as additional memory or a modem for communicating with other computers over telephone lines (described in Chapter 20). If you purchase a PS/2, then you need not be concerned about separate boards to serve the basic needs (such as disk and monitor controller) as the needed circuitry is included in the motherboard.

INTERNAL MEMORY

Computer Memory

Programs to be run and data to be processed must be placed in memory before anything can take place. To understand how memory is used, we can think of it as analogous to a large housing tract situated on one very long street, as illustrated in Figure 3-5(a). The houses are all identical (having been built on a large scale by a single contractor). It is possible to distinguish one from the other only by the address. In Figure 3-5, the first house that we see has the address 132, the next 133, and so on. Note that the address identifies the house and has nothing to do with the people living in it. The family living in the house represents its "contents." The address is permanent, but the contents are not; they come and go. Computer memory as illustrated in Figure 3-5(b) is much the same. It consists of a series of memory cells, each identical to the other and each with its own memory address. Furthermore, each memory cell can hold one piece of information at any one time. As do families in a house, information items in memory cells come and go.

Two important characteristics of memory are that any given position of memory can be accessed just as easily and quickly as any other, and that

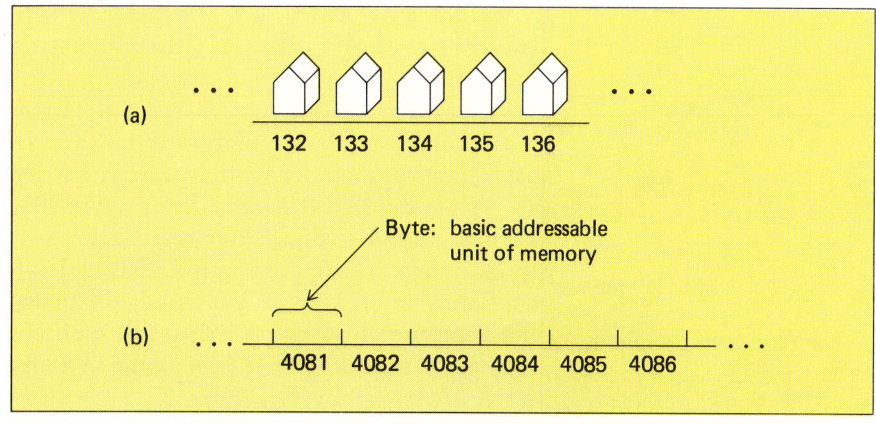

Figure 3-5
The concept of computer memory.

the contents of a given location can be changed easily. The accessibility characteristic is significant because, for example, customer data and inventory data that have been brought into memory might be held in widely separated portions of memory. Speed of operations will be jeopardized if it takes longer to get data from "the other end" of memory. By comparison, consider "accessing" a particular piece of music on a tape cassette. Its accessibility will depend upon its placement on the tape: if it is at the opposite end of the tape, the fast-forward action will take some time to complete. Because of the fact that any location can be accessed just as quickly as any other, internal memory is commonly referred to as random access memory, or simply **RAM.** The second characteristic of memory (the easily changed feature) is significant because new data is constantly being read into memory and modified by the program.

Another of the characteristics of semiconductor RAM is that all stored information is lost if the power is turned off. Hence, it is referred to as **volatile memory.** By contrast, auxiliary storage units retain the stored information when the power is turned off; these are called **nonvolatile memory** units.

When the power to a microcomputer is turned on, the computer performs a start-up sequence of operations. This includes checking to see if all of its components are in place and functioning, and reading the needed portions of the operating system into memory. However, if everything in RAM was lost when the computer was last turned off (remember, RAM is volatile), then where do the instructions to perform these initial operations come from? The answer is, "from **read-only memory (ROM)**." In addition to RAM, all computers include ROM, which is manufactured with fixed information encoded within. Unlike RAM, ROM is nonvolatile in that it retains the encoded information even when the power to the computer is turned off.

In the PC (and virtually all microcomputers), the basic addressable unit of memory is the **byte.** A byte consists of 8 binary digits, or bits (you will learn some of the technical details of memory in a later section of this chapter). For the moment, to give you an idea of the significance of this unit, a byte has the capacity to store one character (letter, digit, or special character such as the hyphen). Thus, for example, the Social Security number 123-45-6789 would require 11 bytes to be stored in memory (each of the hyphens requires a byte).

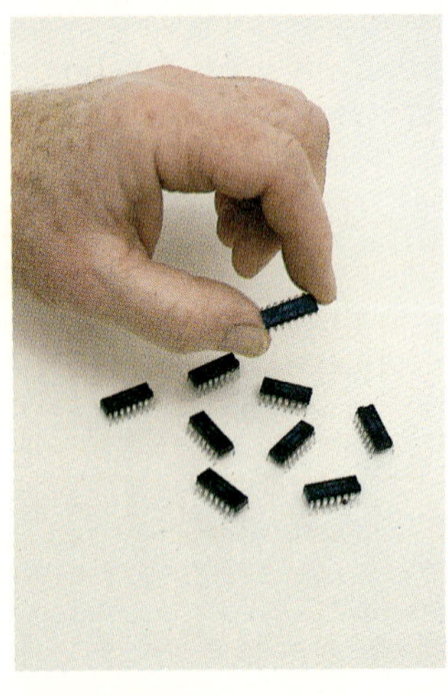

Figure 3-6
Memory chips.

Whereas prices have *decreased,* the storage capacity and speed of digital computers have *increased* remarkably in the past 20 years. Early computers had memory capacities from the equivalent of a few hundred to a few thousand bytes. Microcomputers are now commonly available with storage capacities of 640K bytes at a cost of less than $1000. (The letter K is used in the computer field to represent the amount 1024. Thus, a computer with 640K bytes of memory would have a capacity slightly larger than 640,000.)

When the IBM PC was introduced in 1981, it used memory chips, such as those shown in Figure 3-6, with a storage capacity of 16K *bits* (equivalent to 2K bytes). These are commonly called 16K chips because a set of them consisting of eight chips provided 16K bytes of memory. Two years later, the computer was upgraded to use a chip of the same size but with an equivalent capacity of 64K bits. Some models of the IBM PS/2 use 1-megabit

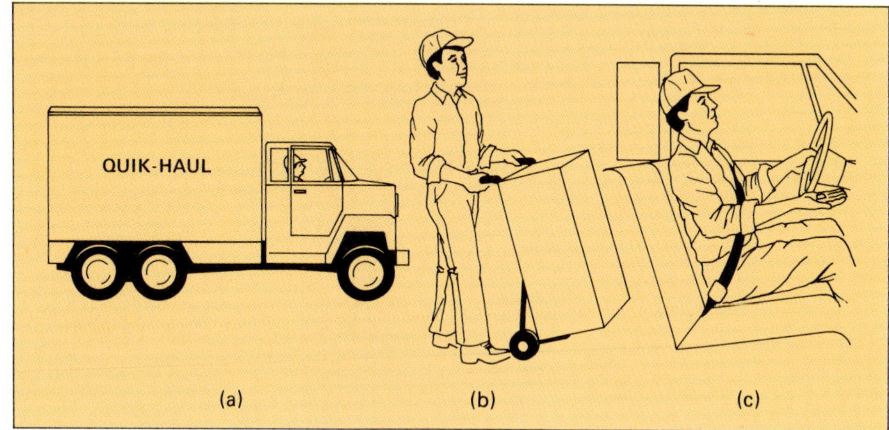

Space required for 1 megabyte (1 million bytes) of internal memory.
(a) 1953. 1 megabyte of memory would fully occupy the space in a medium-sized moving truck.
(b) 1971. 1 megabyte of memory would fit into a large-sized box commonly available from the moving company.
(c) 1987. 1 megabyte of memory and its packaging would now easily fit in the palm of the truck driver's hand.

chips; that is, each chip has the capacity of 1 million bits. In spite of their increased capacity, they are still the same size as those shown in Figure 3-6. An interesting thing about the chip of Figure 3-6 is that most of the bulk of the unit is taken up by the pin connectors; the actual electronics of the memory occupies but a fraction of the overall chip.

Memory Speed

Another characteristic of a memory chip is its speed, which is a measurement of the time required to access data from the chip. As you might expect, this speed of the memory used in a computer and the speed of the processor must be coordinated; that is, if you have an AT with a fast microprocessor, you will need faster memory chips than you would for a slower XT microprocessor. This is important to keep in mind when purchasing a memory expansion board: the memory speed must be consistent with that of the microprocessor. The PC/XT models commonly use memory chips with an **access time** (time to access a single byte) of 150 nanoseconds, where a nanosecond is a millionth of a second. Commonly

Technology has decreased the size and increased the speed of computer memory. The chip in the eye of the needle has ten times the capacity and hundreds of times the speed of the magnetic core assembly (to the left) of an earlier generation of computers.

encountered AT models require 100- to 120-nanosecond memory. When the IBM PS/2 Model 80 was first introduced, it included 80-nanosecond, 1-megabit memory chips.

TECHNICAL ASPECTS OF THE COMPUTER INTERIOR

Internal Coding

Computer memory, being electronic, operates on the on-off principle; that is, a circuit is either on or off, an electrical storage element is either charged or not charged. It is through this simple principle that the computer is capable of storing information ranging from customer data to month-by-month company earnings to images of charts showing monthly sales increases. As mentioned in the preceding section, each memory byte consists of eight component elements called binary digits, abbreviated to **bits.** They are called bits because they are based on the binary number system in which only two digits (0 and 1) are used. Through a variety of coding methods, it is possible to store in one or more bytes numeric (for instance, the cost of an inventory item) as well as nonnumeric data (for instance, a customer's name or address).

Nonnumeric data is commonly called **alphanumeric** because it can consist of letters, digits, or even special characters such as the hyphen or the space. It is also called **character data** and **string data.** All three of these terms refer to the same thing. For this type of data, each byte is used to store one character. Thus, for example, the following telephone number would require 14 bytes in memory (assuming that there is a space following the area code).

(415) 555-1212

There are two commonly used methods for encoding character data. One of them, the Extended Binary Coded Decimal Interchange Code (EBCDIC), was introduced by IBM with its System/360 computer in 1964. It is currently used by IBM in all of its computers except the microcomputers. The EBCDIC coding method is based on the 8 bits of the storage byte. Each letter, digit, and special character has its combination of digits 0 and 1. For instance, the code for the letter A is 11000001 and for the comma is 01101011. Fortunately for the computer user, all handling of codes is done internally by the computer. As it uses the full 8 bits, the EBCDIC character set includes coding for 256 characters.

The other data coding method, the American Standard Code for Information Interchange (ASCII), is virtually universal in the microcomputer area (including IBM microcomputers). The standard ASCII coding method is based on a 7-bit code and hence includes provisions for 128 characters. (There are 128 different combinations of 0 and 1 in a 7-bit code.) In the IBM PC world, the ASCII code set has been expanded to utilize the full 8 bits, thereby yielding an array of special graphics characters (such as double lines to draw borders around the screen and Greek letters). The binary coding for the letter A in IBM 8-bit ASCII is 0100001, and for the comma, it is 00101100. As with computers using EBCDIC, all handling of the encoding is done automatically by the computer and the user need not be concerned about these details.

Error Checking

With the millions of operations per second that take place within the computer, malfunctions are bound to happen. When driving an automobile, if a sparkplug fails to fire during one cycle, we do not even notice it. However, the situation is different with the computer. For instance, let us assume that you are entering a customer order and that the program has completed the total due calculation and is copying this amount into a memory area from which the invoice is to be printed. During this operation, the electronic failure of losing a single 1-bit could change the amount due from $743.25 to $343.25. A computer prone to such undetected errors would be of little value to anyone. To detect such errors, a technique called **parity checking** is used. Each memory byte includes, in addition to the 8 bits for storage of data, a ninth bit called the **parity bit** for error checking. Whenever a character is placed in memory, the number of 1-bits is counted. If the count is even, the parity bit is set to 1 to make the total count odd; if the count is already odd, the parity bit is set to 0. This is illustrated in Figure 3-7 for the letters *s* and *t*. Then whenever the contents of a byte are moved, the number of 1-bits is counted. If the count is not odd, a 1-bit has been lost (changed to 0) and an error is indicated. The computer will automatically retry the operation. If the error is repeated a set number of times, the computer will stop and display on the monitor screen that a parity error has occurred. If this happens repeatedly, then the computer probably has a bad chip and requires servicing.

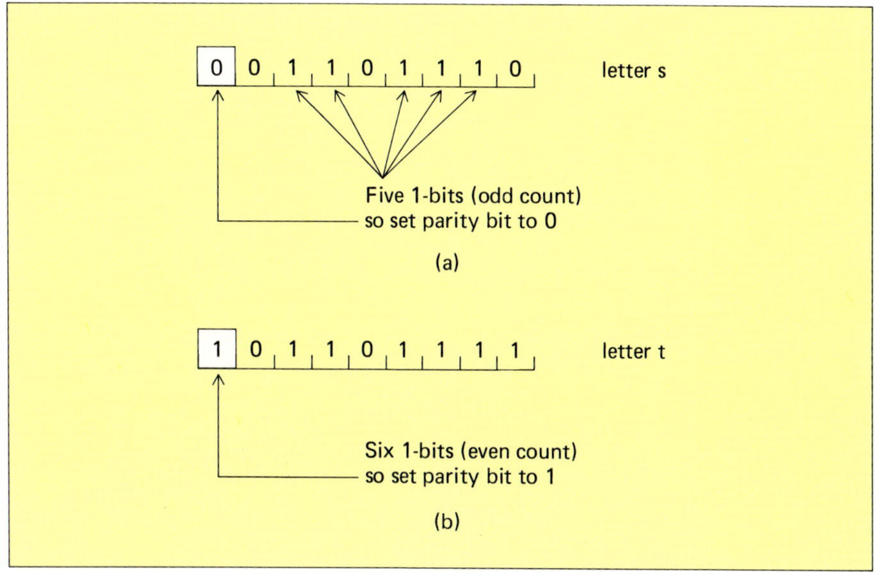

Figure 3-7
The concept of the parity bit.

The Data Bus

Within the computer, bytes of data are continuously being moved from one computer element to another. For instance, a data record must be copied from disk storage to memory; a numeric value must be copied from memory into the arithmetic/logic unit to perform calculations. Rather than using a single wire to connect parts of the computer, groups of wires are used in order to speed up the movement of data. Figure 3-8 illustrates a situation in which the contents of a memory location are copied into a register (a small working memory unit) of the microprocessor. Using this method, data can be transmitted eight times faster than if only a single wire were used. The multiple-wire connection is commonly referred to as a data bus or data path; as it consists of eight conductors it is called an 8-bit **bus.** The size of the data path is an important feature of a microprocessor. The Motorola 6502 used by the Apple II has an 8-bit data path; hence, this microprocessor in commonly referred to as an 8-bit microprocessor.

At first thought, the use of an 8-bit data path might seem quite logical because the basic memory unit, the byte, is 8 bits in size. However, this does not necessarily follow. In general, the byte is used in a variety of ways. For instance, 2 bytes together are used to store a whole-number quantity and either 4 or 8 bytes may be used to store a number with a fractional part. Thus, multiple operations are required to access such a numeric quantity from memory and perform desired operations. One way of making internal operations faster and more efficient is to design the microprocessor with a wider data path. This, in fact, was one of the features of the IBM PC when it was introduced. It uses the Intel 8088 microprocessor, which features a 16-bit data path for operations within the microprocessor. The Apple Macintosh and the IBM PS/2 (Models 40 and above) use 32-bit microprocessor.

As we might expect, the larger the data path of a microprocessor, the more expensive it is to make. What then are the advantages of a larger data path? One advantage is increased speed. A record can be moved from one place in memory to another much faster if data is being moved in blocks of

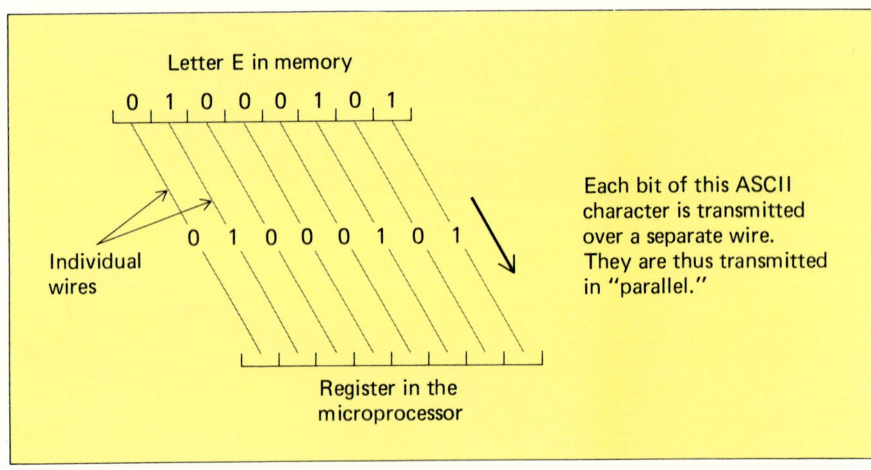

Figure 3-8
Parallel data transmission.

4 bytes rather than 1 byte. Another advantage relates to technical considerations that make it practical to design the computer with the capability of having greater memory sizes. For instance, the Apple II cannot have more than 64K of memory; the PC/XT cannot have more than 1 megabyte (1 million bytes), of which 640K is available to the user. Although 640K might appear to be a large amount, as programming systems become more complex and powerful, the 640K becomes more and more of a problem. (Note that there are special memory boards available to overcome this limitation but their use has a number of limitations.) In contrast, when first introduced, the PS/2 Models 50 and 80 had the capability to accommodate 7 and 16 megabytes of memory, respectively. However, full use of this memory capability is a function of the operating system. Although the operating system DOS (described in Chapter 5), can be used with these PS/2 models, it does not provide full use of many of the broad features of the computer (including increased memory capacity).

This rush to increased speed and memory capacity is not simply a matter of "putting more horsepower in an automobile for marketing appeal." As computer users become more sophisticated, they demand software that is more powerful and easier to use. Powerful software, in turn, requires more powerful hardware.

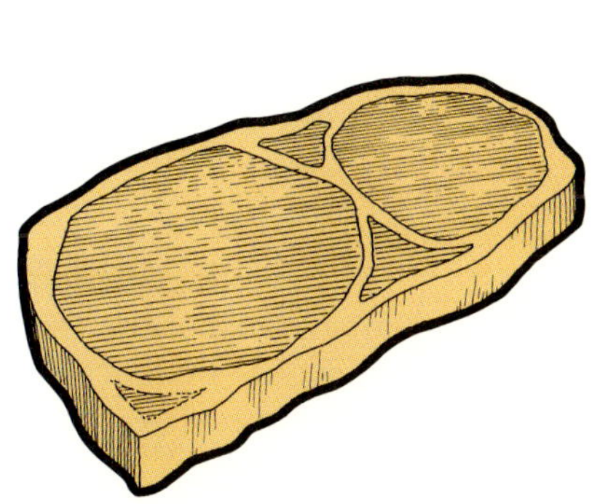

Thirty years ago it cost $1.26 to do 100,000 multiplications by computer. Today it costs less than a penny. If other costs had gone down the same, you would be able to buy a sirloin steak for less than a penny per pound and an around-the-world airline trip for modest pocket change.

Built in 1946, the first fully electronic computer contained 18,000 vacuum tubes. The technology of today can pack much more than that much computing power in a space the size of one of these tubes.

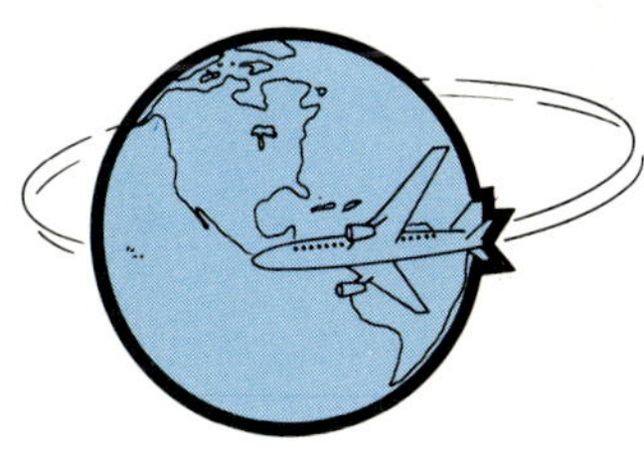

If technology and productivity in other industries had progressed at the same rate as computer technology, an around-the-world airline flight would take a few minutes, and a standard-size car would get over a million miles per gallon.

SUMMARY

This chapter has provided your first exposure to computer hardware by focusing on the processor and memory. The important items from the chapter are:

- Computers are commonly classified as microcomputers, minicomputers, and mainframe computers. With the changes in technology, the distinction between minicomputers and mainframes is unclear. Microcomputers are generally categorized as "one person, one computer" in nature.
- The focus of this book is the microcomputer or, more specifically, the PC, XT, and AT originally marketed by IBM. The concepts and descriptions also relate to the later IBM PS/2.
- The system board, also called the motherboard, is the main circuit board of the computer. It includes expansion slots into which other circuit boards can be inserted in order in increase the capabilities of the computer.
- The microprocessor is the controlling nerve center of the computer. It includes a control unit for controlling overall operation of the computer, an arithmetic/logic unit for performing arithmetic and comparing operations, and a system clock for timing coordination.
- Internal memory is the "work area" of the computer. Whenever a program is to be run, it must first be copied into memory, from which its instructions can be carried out. Memory also serves to store data temporarily as it is being processed.
- Memory is commonly referred to as RAM (meaning random access memory). This describes a significant characteristic of the computer's internal memory: data in any part of memory can be accessed just as quickly as data in any other part of memory.
- ROM (meaning read-only memory) is memory manufactured with encoded information that cannot be changed and is not lost when power to the computer is turned off.
- The basic unit of storage in the computer is the byte, which consists of 8 binary digits (bits). A single byte of memory can store one letter, digit, or special character using the ASCII coding method. Two or more bytes can be combined to store numeric data.
- The parity bit is a device used for automatic error detection within the computer.

NEW TERMINOLOGY

The following are important new terms introduced in this chapter; you should be familiar with each of them.

access time
alphanumeric
arithmetic/logic unit
ASCII
bit
bus
byte
character data
control unit
expansion board
hertz
integrated circuit
logical operation
mainframe
mega
memory
microprocessor
minicomputer
motherboard
nonvolatile memory
parity bit
parity checking
processor
RAM
ROM
string data
system board
system clock
volatile memory
workstation

REVIEW QUESTIONS

1. The microcomputer can be distinguished from a minicomputer or mainframe based on the way that it is used. Describe this distinction.
2. Why is it difficult to distinguish a minicomputer from a mainframe (or in some cases, a microcomputer from a minicomputer) solely on the basis of hardware or software features?
3. What is meant by computer "logical structure"?
4. Distinguish between a motherboard and an expansion board.
5. Describe the three components of the microprocessor (referred to in this chapter) and the function of each.
6. What is a "logical operation"?
7. Distinguish between a byte and a bit.
8. What is the difference between RAM and ROM?
9. What is ASCII?
10. Explain how the parity bit is used to prevent errors within the computer.
11. The text states that the Intel 8088 microprocessor (that used in the PC and XT) has a 16-bit bus. What does this mean?
12. What is the advantage of a 16-bit bus over an 8-bit bus?

MATCHING

Match each term in a to h with the most appropriate description in 1 through 8.

a. system board
b. microprocessor
c. RAM
d. parity bit
e. system clock
f. access time
g. ROM
h. byte

1. The basic storage unit of memory.

2. Memory that is easily changed and provides quick access to stored data.

3. The amount of time required to obtain data from memory.

4. Provides the timing control for all actions within the computer.

5. Contents of this type of memory are not lost when the power is turned off.

6. Includes expansion slots.

7. The arithmetic/logic unit is contained in this component of the computer.

8. Provides for the detection of errors.

TRUE/FALSE

Determine whether each of the following is true or false.

______ **1.** The primary distinction between a mainframe and a minicomputer is that a mainframe can run many programs at once whereas a minicomputer cannot.

______ **2.** A characteristic of the microcomputer is that it is designed for a one-to-one relationship between the user and the computer.

______ **3.** The primary components of the computer are input, output, processor, and auxiliary storage.

______ **4.** In general, if a microcomputer has sufficient memory, then it does not need auxiliary storage.

______ **5.** The action of running a program involves the computer loading the program from auxiliary storage into memory, then carrying out the actions described by the instructions of the program.

______ **6.** Since PC, XT, and AT are IBM computers, they are available only from IBM.

______ **7.** The words *microprocessor* and *control unit* are two terms for exactly the same thing: the component of the computer that controls all actions of the computer.

______ **8.** The speed of the system clock of a microprocessor is an indication of how fast the computer will run programs.

______ **9.** An expansion slot is an electrical receptacle in the motherboard into which other circuit boards can be plugged in order to increase the capabilities of the computer.

______ **10.** One characteristic of RAM is that stored information is lost when the electric power is turned off.

______ **11.** ROM is nonvolatile.

______ **12.** The bit is the basic unit of memory in the computer; each bit consists of 8 bytes.

______ **13.** If a computer is described as a 640K machine, then it has exactly 640,000 bytes of memory.

______ **14.** The ASCII code is a coding method used to store numeric values within the computer.

______ **15.** The data bus is the "channel" through which information is moved from one component of the computer to another.

ANSWERS TO OBJECTIVE QUESTIONS

Matching

1. h 2. c 3. f 4. e 5. g 6. a 7. b 8. d

True/False

1. F 2. T 3. F 4. F 5. T 6. F 7. F 8. T
9. T 10. T 11. T 12. F 13. F 14. F 15. T

Chapter 4

Hardware: Peripheral Devices

OBJECTIVES

Chapter 3 has provided you with an insight into the inner workings of the computer. This chapter focuses on devices that get data into and out of the computer. When you have completed the chapter, you should be able to describe:

- The nature of the computer monitor, the display device used with the microcomputer, how information is displayed, and how color and noncolor monitors work.
- The computer keyboard together with its similarities to and differences from the typewriter keyboard.
- The variety of printers available and the general types of applications for which each is commonly used.
- The distinction between serial and parallel interconnection between the computer and printer.
- Factors to consider in selecting a printer: compatibility with software, the need for multiple-copy printing, cost, speed, and print quality.
- The nature and uses of other input devices: optical page reader, bar code reader, graphics tablet, light pen, and voice recognition.
- Principles of information storage and retrieval on disk storage, an auxiliary storage device.
- Characteristics of the floppy disk, the "standard" auxiliary storage device used with microcomputers.

- The nature of hard disks, which provide high-speed, high-capacity auxiliary storage.
- The use of magnetic tape units for making copies of stored data in order to ensure against loss.

PREVIEW

Basic Input/output for Microcomputers

The two essential I/O elements of the microcomputer are the televisionlike monitor and the typewriterlike keyboard. As with television sets, both color and black-and-white computer monitors are available. In addition to the keys found on a typewriter, the computer keyboard includes a variety of keys for different computer-related control operations.

Printers

The selection of a printer is the area in which the user probably has the widest choice of options. Some printers print in much the same way as typewriters; others form characters with dots as is done with an athletic scoreboard. Some use the impact of a printing element striking a ribbon; others use copying machine principles. Some yield high-quality printing; others yield the low-quality printouts that we stereotypically identify with computer output.

Other Features of Printers

In selecting a printer, there are numerous factors that you must consider. How much can you afford? What speed do you need? What print quality do you need? Do you need to print multiple copies? Is the printer compatible with your software? What type of interconnection to the computer do you need?

Other Peripherals

Although the keyboard is the primary input device for microcomputers, other special-purpose devices are commonly encountered—devices that can read a printed page or special bar codes, devices that allow graphics to be entered in much the same way as drawing a picture, and voice sensitive units. The mouse is a widely used pointing and selection device. For output, plotters are common that provide the capability for drawing multicolored graphs.

Auxiliary Storage

Auxiliary storage devices are used for long-term storage of programs and data. They include the means by which the stored information can be read into computer memory quickly and replaced by new data. The magnetic surfaced floppy disk is the standard auxiliary storage device for microcomputers. Hard disks provide greater storage capacities and higher speeds.

Deciding Upon Hardware

In purchasing a computer, the needs of both today and tomorrow must be considered. Will the computer you are purchasing handle future needs or be capable of being expanded as needs grow? These are critical considerations when investing time and money in a computer system.

BASIC INPUT/OUTPUT FOR MICROCOMPUTERS

From Chapter 3 you learned about a number of components inside the computer that provide the capability for processing data. Obviously, you need ways to get data into the computer and to retrieve the results of processing. This is done with I/O or **peripheral devices** (or simply peripherals); in general, a peripheral device is any device that performs an I/O function. There are many different types of peripheral devices (some used for very specialized purposes) but the keyboard and monitor are standard devices found on all microcomputers. In fact, because the keyboard and monitor are such integral parts of the microcomputer, they are not commonly thought of as peripherals.

The Monitor

The basic output device used with the microcomputer is the televisionlike video monitor. (It is frequently referred to as a CRT, for cathode ray tube.) Since the motherboard circuitry of the PC, XT, and AT do not include provisions for a monitor, it is necessary to install a **video display adapter** in one of the expansion slots. The video board includes the necessary circuitry for communicating between the microprocessor and monitor and defining the desired images to be displayed on the screen.

For a basic idea of how a monitor works in conjunction with the rest of the computer, let us consider how information is displayed on the screen. In addition to the main memory of the computer, other devices include memory. For instance, video adapters include sufficient memory to store information that is being displayed on the screen. This is commonly called **video memory.** For the display of character information only, the conventional screen (consisting of 25 rows and 80 columns) requires 2000 bytes (25 times 80) to hold the entire screen display. However, the character itself is not the only information that must be retained. A character can be shown in normal display, or it can be displayed highlighted, extra bright, or blinking. For these purposes, video memory also includes 1 byte for each screen position to hold the video attributes of that position. This overall concept is illustrated in Figure 4-1. Internally, the task of changing the screen display involves changing the contents of video memory. Thus,

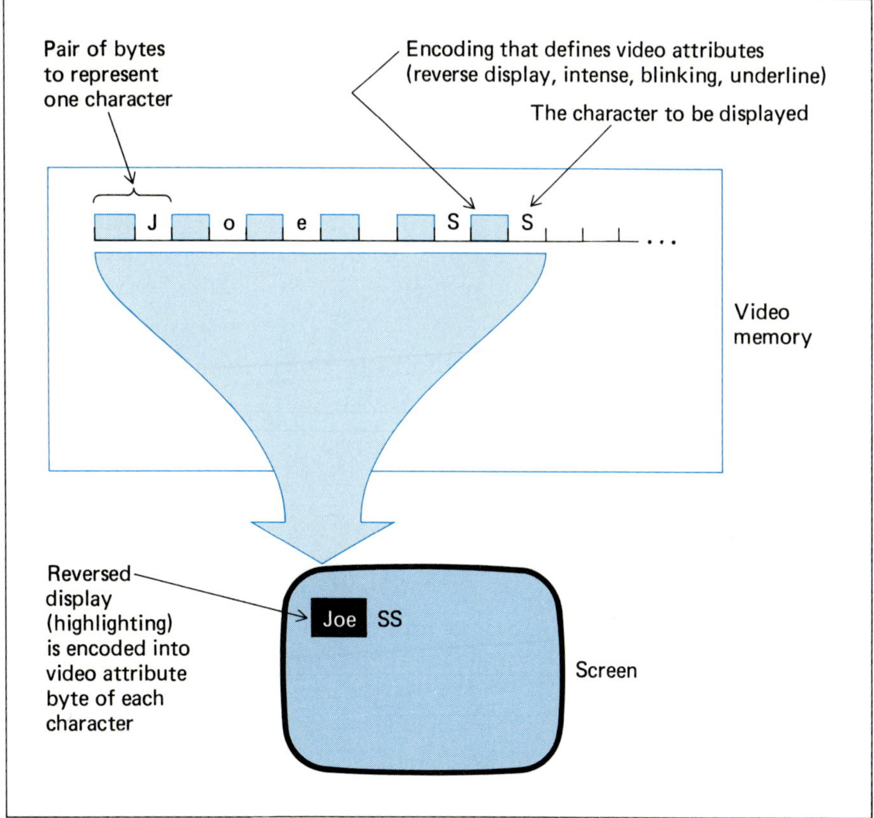

Figure 4-1
Relationship between information in video memory and on the screen.

the simple task of moving the displayed information up by one line on the screen involves moving the entire contents of video memory. We observe this while watching the screen scroll as the operation requires a perceivable amount of time.

Characters that are displayed on the screen are formed by a series of pinpoints of light—the more points, the clearer is the image. This is evident by referring to the formation of the letter P in Figure 4-2 where the area has been broken down into successively smaller elements. The measure of the number of elements is called the **resolution**: the more elements used to form a character, the higher is the resolution of the monitor. The basic element of screen illumination (resolution) is called the **pixel,** meaning picture element. A pixel is a single point on the screen that can be illuminated.

When the IBM PC was first introduced, it included the choice of two video display adapters (and corresponding monitors): the monochrome adapter and the color graphics adapter (CGA). The monochrome adapter featured a resolution of 720 pixels horizontally and 348 pixels vertically, resulting in a sharp, clear character display. However, its display was limited to characters only; it could not display graphics. On the other hand, the CGA provided for the display of both text and graphics in color. Unfortunately, the screen resolution was a relatively low 640 by 200 pixels, resulting in a character display significantly inferior to that of the monochrome adapter. At that time, the choice was simple: obtain the

Figure 4-2
Forming the letter P with a series of points.

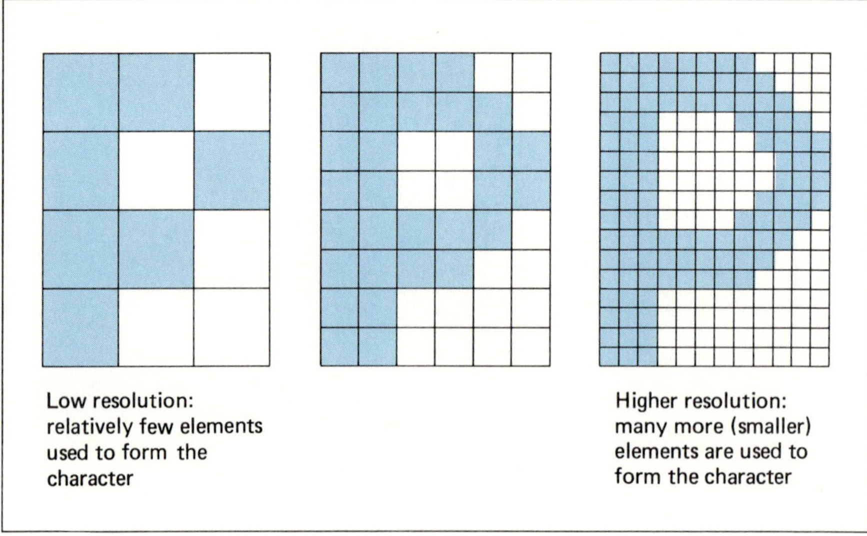

monochrome (because of its high-quality text display) unless graphics capabilities were required.

Because of the inability of the monochrome adapter to display graphics, a small company (Hercules Computer Technology) introduced a monochrome graphics adapter in 1982. (It was one of the first add-on boards for the IBM PC.) The board provided the same high-quality character display but also included graphics capability based on the individual pixel. Characters are displayed using the technique of the monochrome adapter (see Figure 4-2). However, displaying graphics information involves setting the value of each of the 250,000 pixels (resulting from the 720-by-348 resolution) to produce the desired result. This technique of displaying graphics information (which is used by the CGA) is commonly called **bit-mapped graphics** as each screen pixel is represented in video memory by 1 (or more) bits. Because of the larger amount of memory to manipulate, the display of graphics information is slower than that of straight text. Software developers quickly recognized the value of this monochrome graphics adapter and immediately extended their software to take advantage of its features. The Hercules card has become a de facto standard for the PC/XT/AT. Most clones feature Hercules-compatible video adapters.

The CGA, introduced with the PC by IBM, uses the bit-mapping concept but extends it by including appropriate color codes for each pixel. Because the quality of the CGA system was relatively poor (low-quality color and poor resolution), better adapters became available from a wide variety of vendors. The next standard from IBM was the IBM Enhanced Graphics Adapter (EGA), which featured a resolution of 640 by 350 pixels. It is still widely used.

With the introduction of System/2, IBM fully acknowledged the importance of graphics, because this system includes provision for the new IBM VGA (Video Graphics Array) standard with a resolution of 640 by 480 pixels. More significantly, the graphics hardware capabilities are built

The Apple Macintosh is designed to intermix graphics and text while displaying information on the screen.

directly into the computer (by being included on the motherboard). The extent to which IBM has integrated graphics hardware, graphics software in the operating system OS/2, and other peripheral hardware and software makes IBM's view of the importance of graphics in the business market quite apparent.

The Computer Keyboard

Whereas the monitor is the basic microcomputer output device, the typewriterlike keyboard is the primary data input device. The combination of the keyboard and monitor is somewhat analogous to the typewriter. As each key of a typewriter is struck, the corresponding character is printed on the paper. As each key of the computer keyboard is struck, the corresponding character is displayed on the monitor screen. (Actually, the computer detects which key was struck, stores the character into memory, and then sends an image to the monitor.) The position at which each character from the keyboard is displayed on the screen is marked by an element called the **cursor.**

Figure 4-3(a) shows the keyboard included with the IBM PC when the PC was first introduced. Unfortunately, there were some relatively minor decisions regarding key layout that resulted in a significant nuisance in using the keyboard. One relates to the positioning of the left Shift key (too far to the left) and another to the small sizes of the Shift and Enter keys. As a result, other keyboards (with different layouts) became available from a variety of manufacturers. (IBM eventually followed suit and changed the layout of its keyboard.)

If you purchase a PC, XT, or AT clone, then you will probably have the option of designating the particular style of keyboard best adapted to your needs. For instance, one style has a key layout that is almost the same as

Figure 4-3
(a) The IBM PC keyboard.
(b) The 101-key enhanced keyboard.

that of Figure 4-3(a), except that a few of the keys have been repositioned and others made larger. Still another keyboard, the 101-key enhanced keyboard, is commonly encountered; it includes additional keys as seen in Figure 4-3(b). This key layout is standard with the IBM PS/2.

PRINTERS

Assume that you are working at your desk and a customer telephones questioning a charge that appeared on last month's bill. With the appropriate software, it is a simple matter to display on the monitor screen information about the customer and each invoice for that customer. If the customer requests a copy of the invoice in question, then you need to print one on the printer attached to your computer. Notice here that you are dealing with two forms of output: the printed copy and the screen displayed copy. The printed output is commonly called **hard copy** as it has a permanent form. The screen display is called **soft copy** because it does not give a permanent copy; it "disappears" the moment something else is displayed. Although a microcomputer can operate without a printer (it cannot operate without a monitor), a printer is really a necessity for almost all applications. Except for the rare situation in which only soft copy is needed, the question is not "Do I need a printer?" but rather "What type of printer do I need to best fit my needs and budget?"

Categories of Printers

There are a number of ways to classify printers. One is by the way in which the characters are placed on the page. For instance, a typewriter is called an **impact** device because it places the characters on the page through the impact of a printing element with the paper. Many computer printers use the impact principle. On the other hand, a copying machine places an image on the page with a special fusing process (Xerox technology) that does not involve the impact of an element. Hence, they are called **nonim-**

pact devices. Numerous computer printers use nonimpact methods for printing.

Another way of classifying printers is by the way in which the characters are formed. For instance, a typewriter incorporates a printing element for each character with the exact shape of that character. The character is said to be fully formed. In contrast, **dot-matrix printers** have long been available that form characters with a series of dots in much the same way that an athletic scoreboard forms characters.

Let us consider the features of this variety of types by grouping them as follows:

- Impact/fully formed character.
- Impact/dot matrix.
- Nonimpact.

Fully Formed Character Printers

One of the factors of which every business owner is aware is the importance of maintaining a quality image to customers. Numerous things can detract from the image, including correspondence that looks less than professional. For instance, the image projected by the sharp, clear type of the letter opening in Figure 4-4(a) is obviously better than that projected by the opening in Figure 4-4(b). The former was typed on an IBM Selectric typewriter, which has been considered the standard of comparison for quality typing. Since the typewriter has been replaced in the office to a large extent by a computer, printer, and word processor, this same standard has carried over to computer printers. In fact, printers that print with or near the quality shown in Figure 4-4(a) are called **letter-quality printers.** The unit shown in Figure 4-5(a) is called a **daisy-wheel printer** because the

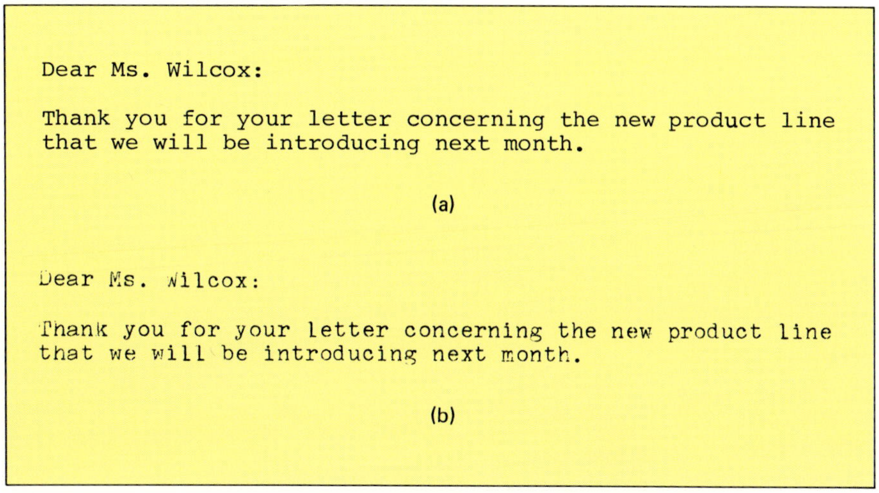

Dear Ms. Wilcox:

Thank you for your letter concerning the new product line that we will be introducing next month.

(a)

Dear Ms. Wilcox:

Thank you for your letter concerning the new product line that we will be introducing next month.

(b)

Figure 4-4
(a) High-quality type.
(b) Type quality that leaves something to be desired.

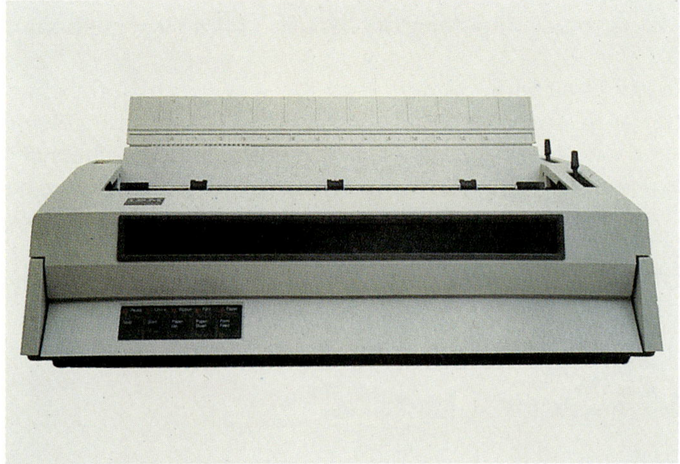

Figure 4-5
(a) A letter-quality daisy-wheel printer.
(b) A daisy-wheel print element.

print characters are molded into the ends of radial arms of a print element that has the appearance of a daisy [see Figure 4-5(b)].

The principal feature of impact letter-quality printers is the high quality of print they produce. However, one objection to them is that they are noisy enough to be very distracting in an otherwise quiet office work area. Another problem for some office applications is that they are relatively slow with typical speeds ranging from 30 to 60 characters per second (cps). At this rate, approximately 1 minute would be required to print a full page. Although this might be adequate for most word processing needs, it is lacking for many other data processing requirements. For instance, a detailed inventory summary report might consist of 100 or more pages and require time measured in hours to print. Similarly, month-end billing where the bills for several hundred customers must be printed could require time also measured in hours. There are two considerations for printing applications such as this. First, letter-quality printing is not needed; second, high printing speed is needed. The solution to these needs is the dot-matrix printer.

Dot-Matrix Printers

The most commonly encountered printer is the dot-matrix printer, which prints a dot pattern that forms the shape of the desired character. An illustration of the dot array and some printed characters is shown in Figure 4-6. The **print heads** of a matrix printer consist of a column of pins, each of which is pressed forward by a magnetic device. This causes impacting against the ribbon, and in turn the paper, thus forming the printed characters as the unit progresses across the page.

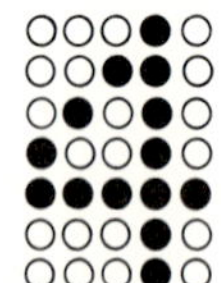

MATRIX
PRINTING
1234567890

Figure 4-6
Sample print from a dot-matrix printer.

Most commonly, matrix printers print 10 characters per inch (cpi). However, with the versatility of the matrix technique, printing is not so limited. For instance, in Figure 4-7 you can see that characters can be printed compressed (17 cpi), enlarged, double high, and in other forms. Condensed printing is convenient for printing a report in which the line will not fit on a normal 8.5-inch page width at 10 cpi. It is also useful for

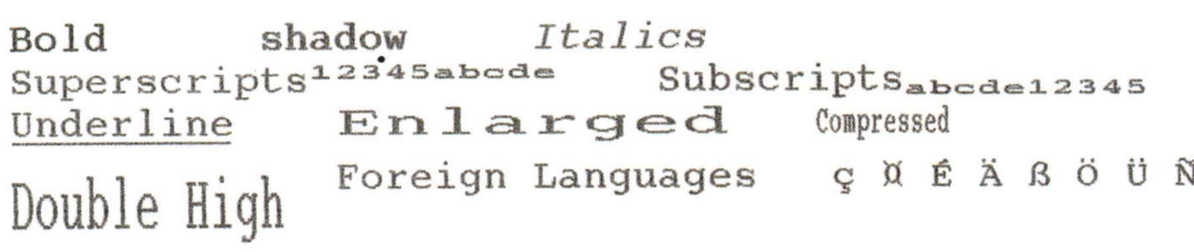

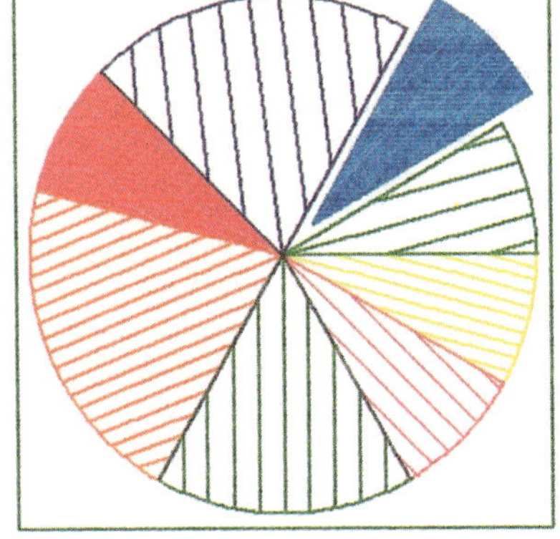

Figure 4-7
Some of the printing capabilities of the Fujitsu DL3000 dot-matrix printer.

printing a large spreadsheet, the subject of Chapters 11 and 12. Enlarged printing can be used effectively for report and paragraph headings whenever emphasis is needed. Switching the printing mode from one of these forms to another is achieved by the computer software sending appropriate codes to the printer.

The dot-matrix output of Figure 4-7 is acceptable for data processing needs such as printing the 100-page inventory summary. However, there are many applications in which a better quality is desired but that of a daisy-wheel printer is not necessary. For the diversity of needs of both the business and home user, present-day dot-matrix printers represent a versatile solution. For example, the sample output lines of Figure 4-8 were all printed by the same printer. Note that the print speed for the high-speed draft is 288 cps whereas that for the near-letter quality is 72 cps. (These output qualities and speed ranges are typical.) The high-quality print in Figure 4-8 is commonly referred to as near-letter quality (NLQ) or correspondence quality.

There are a number of technical factors that designers utilize in achieving the higher quality. One method is by using a larger number of pins in the print head; typically this count ranges from 9 to 24. Another method is to print a line, shift the position of the paper ever so slightly, then reprint

```
The DL3000 Series prints at a rapid 288 cps
```

```
Courier at 10 characters per inch
Prestige Elite at 12 characters per inch
```

Figure 4-8
Different print qualities of the Fujitsu DL3000 printer.

the line. Printers that make two passes to print a line of higher quality are common. Selecting a printer can be confusing because, in addition to the number of pins and print passes, the buyer is also presented with such details as the matrix size and the graphics resolution. In general, the best way to make a selection is to ignore the technicalities. Look for the printer that best matches your speed requirements, pocketbook restrictions, and print quality needs. One other consideration, software compatibility, is described later in this section.

The Laser Printer: A Nonimpact Device

The introduction of the $3500 Laserjet **laser printer** by Hewlett-Packard Corporation in 1984 marked an important shift in the direction of "high-end" letter quality printers. (Figure 4-9 shows the Laserjet II, the successor to the Laserjet.) This product brought together features of speed significantly faster than those of dot-matrix printers, high print quality approaching that of a top-line daisy-wheel printer, and broad flexibility for graphics. The Laserjet uses the copying machine components of the low-priced

Figure 4-9
The Laserjet II printer.

O W

(a)

O W

(b)

Figure 4-10
(a) Output from a laser printer. **(b)** Laser printer output magnified three times.

Canon office copier (as do numerous other laser printers now available) and works on the basic principle of ordinary copying machines. This printer prints at the rate of eight pages per minute—at the time, an astonishing speed for a printer used in conjunction with a microcomputer.

Technically, the laser printer is a dot-matrix device since it forms characters using the dot technique of monitor screens and impact matrix printers. However, the laser printer quality is high because it uses a dot resolution of 300 by 300 per inch. That is, to fully darken a 1-inch square would require 300 rows of dots where each row consists of 300 dots; this is 90,000 dots per square inch. Although the quality of print is excellent, for some letters, such as the O and W, the jagged edges are noticeable, as we can see by inspecting Figure 4-10(a). This effect is clearly visible in the copy of these letters in Figure 4-10(b), where they have been enlarged to three times their original size.

In addition to speed, the laser printer offers versatility in the type styles that are available to the user. For instance, the printed output shown in Figure 4-11 was generated by an AST Turbo Laser using a word processor. All of the types and type sizes were simultaneously available as the text was being entered.

Other Nonimpact Printers

Historically, the first nonimpact printers used with computers formed dot-matrix images on specially treated paper using heat (thermal printers) or electrical techniques (electrostatic printers). Their principal feature was the relatively low cost but this was partially offset by the need for treated

Figure 4-11
Laser printer output.

This is small, but the next line is larger.
This is **bold** and this is *italic.*

Perhaps you like this **typeface** better,
or in an *easier* to read size,
or still larger,
or now BIG.

Standard typewriter type style is also available including **bold** and *italic*.

This is a commonly used type style.
but this is the more commonly used size (**bold** and *italic*).

For size, this is SIZE.

A little of everything *on the* **same** line.

paper. They do not find wide general use because they no longer offer a huge price advantage over impact dot-matrix printers, and the treated paper is a nuisance to deal with. However, they do find use in special applications in which portability is important.

The **ink-jet printer** produces printed copy by spraying a fine jet of ink onto the printing surface, which may be ordinary paper or even have a textured surface. Individual characters to be printed are formed using electrostatic charges to deflect the tiny droplets of ink in much the same way that electrons are deflected in a television tube. As the ink jet is not a continuous stream, images are formed with discrete dots as with dot-matrix printers. In general, ink-jet printers have found slow acceptance because they offer little advantage over impact matrix printers at one extreme and daisy-wheel printers at the other. Furthermore, they experienced numerous technical problems, including clogging of the spray nozzles by the ink. However, many of these problems have been solved and ink-jet printers are gaining wider acceptance. In addition, some ink-jet printers have the capability to print in full color, a useful feature for many graphics applications. Another factor relating to their growing acceptance is that in 1988 Hewlett-Packard announced an ink-jet printer (for under $1000) featuring a dot resolution of 300 by 300, equivalent to the laser. This printer combines low cost, letter-quality printing and impact matrix printer speed.

OTHER FEATURES OF PRINTERS

Using Buffers to Improve Efficiency

During the printing operation, the computer processor sends characters to the printer one after the other. Because the computer speed is many times greater than the printer speed, the computer must spend most of its time waiting for the printing action to be completed. This results in a very inefficient use of the computer and waste of the user's time. For instance, with a 120-cps matrix printer, you would sit and wait approximately 1 minute for two pages to be printed. One way of getting around this inefficiency is to include a limited amount of memory in the printer into which the printed output can be transferred at computer speed. Then the computer is available for the user to continue while the printer independently prints the information stored in its memory area. Memory areas intended to hold data temporarily during input or output operations are called **buffers;** printers are commonly available with buffers ranging from 2K to 64K bytes. To place this in perspective, a single-spaced page requires approximately 3K bytes.

In addition to a buffer in the printer, special programs are commonly used to handle printed output. These programs, called **print spoolers,** are programs that remain in memory and control output operations. That is, when printing takes place, the computer operates at electronic speeds in sending the to-be-printed information out. However, the spooler intercepts the output and stores it in a reserved area of memory. Then, in between other operations of the processor, the spooler program sends it out to the printer at the slower printer speed. Thus, the computer is doing two things at once: sending output to the printer via the spooler and performing whatever task the user is requesting.

Connecting the Printer to the Computer

To connect a printer to a computer requires special interface circuitry (an **interface** is a device for connecting two dissimilar components). There are two commonly encountered interfaces used with printers. With the serial interface (more commonly used for communications as described in Chapter 20), data is transmitted from the computer to the printer over a single data wire. The parallel interface uses eight wires for transmitting data, thus providing a separate wire for each bit of the byte to be transmitted (as illustrated in Figure 3-8). It is called the Centronics interface and is available with almost all printers currently manufactured for microcomputers. Many printers include both the serial and Centronics capabilities. A few are available only with serial. The disadvantage of the serial interface is that communications needs require a complex communications standard that is simply not needed (or used) by printers. Because of its relative complexity, it is often difficult to get different varieties of printers and microcomputers to "talk" to each other. In general, it is simpler to use the Centronics interface. Most PC, XT, and AT computers include at least one serial and one Centronics interface (or port) on the variety of expansion cards normally installed. The IBM PS/2 includes both serial and Centronics interfaces on the motherboard.

Factors to Consider in Selecting a Printer

There are five major factors to consider in selecting a printer:

- Software compatibility.
- Need for multiple copy printing.
- Cost.
- Speed.
- Print quality.

Software/printer compatibility is a factor that many beginners overlook when purchasing a computer system. For instance, if you are preparing a report and you want to use double-width printing for your headings (refer to Figure 4-7), then your word processor must "know" the required codes for the printer that you are using. Unfortunately, each printer company uses it own coding methods to change the printing characteristics; there is no standard. The way in which software companies handle this is to supply printer drivers for commonly encountered printers. Each driver is a table of codes and/or a program for a particular printer. If your software does not support your printer (does not include a driver for it), then you will not be able to take full advantage of the features of your printer or your software. Because the Epson matrix printer is so widely used, many matrix printers provide Epson emulation, a feature that allows a non-Epson printer to function as if it were an Epson. Most software supports the Epson.

For some applications, the distinction between impact and nonimpact is an important consideration. For instance, when preparing an order and printing the invoice, a **multiple-part form** is used (multiple part means that the form consists of two or more "layers" of paper in order to produce one or more copies of the document). Since the second (and beyond) copies require an impacting action, an impact printer is essential.

For the business person, a printer decision requires compromising among cost, speed, and print quality to best meet the needs of a business. If a large volume of high-quality printed output is to be generated, then a laser printer is a good solution. If only a moderate volume of business reports (for instance, inventory summaries) is to be generated, then a low-cost impact matrix printer is usually a good solution. An office computer used for generating business reports and outside correspondence might be equipped with both matrix and daisy-wheel printers.

OTHER PERIPHERALS

Input Devices

Where the keyboard is the standard input device for the microcomputer, there are many other devices that serve specialized input functions. Some of the following are more often used with mainframe and minicomputer systems but have also found their way into the microcomputer world.

An **optical page reader** can read pages of printed text, convert the text to internal computer codes, and store the information as if it had been entered from the keyboard. This is useful in a situation in which preprinted documents must be entered into the computer.

The bar codes on groceries and the reading device at the grocery store checkout counter is a familiar sight (see the following box). Through a **bar code reader** embedded in the counter, encoded data on each product item is read into a computer. Use of bar code systems is not confined to the grocery industry; they are also used for such applications as automatic car identification by the railroads (the first use of bar codes), book identification and checkout in the library, and inventory control in warehouses. Bar code readers range from stationary units such as those in the grocery store to hand-held devices that can be attached to a microcomputer, or even a small portable device that uses a standard tape cassette for storing information.

A **graphics tablet** is a pressure-sensitive surface that is used much like a drawing board. For instance, a line drawn on the surface is "read" by the computer, converted to a coded image in memory, and displayed on the screen. At any time, the created image can be stored for later use.

A **light pen** used in conjunction with a special monitor screen functions somewhat like a graphics tablet. Through a light-sensitive element at the end of the pen and interconnection to the computer, movement of the light pen across the screen can be tracked and stored within the computer as a graphics image.

The Universal Product Code

During the late 1960s, the grocery industry began investigating methods to control escalating costs through automation. Finally, in 1970, the manufacturing and distribution sides of the food industry, in a rare burst of cooperation, agreed to a study that led to many of the automation concepts we see today. Management consultants, graphics arts experts, computer specialists, and even the Massachusetts Institute of Technology were enlisted to ensure that planning and implementation of the system would leave no stone unturned. In 1973, the means for encoding computer-readable information on items in the store was introduced; it is called the Universal Product Code, or just UPC. (A sample UPC is shown below.) The basic elements of the system are:

- Encoded product-identifying information on each item in the supermarket.
- Light-beam scanning devices at each checkout counter for reading the encoded information.
- Linking of the scanners and cash registers to a central computer.

Integration of the checkout procedure with a central computer system, which provides a host of advantages over manual systems. These include speedier checkout, the virtual elimination of errors in prices charged, and better inventory control. The grocery industry had taken a sophisticated step forward, receiving praise from many other industries for this cooperative effort.

If you cannot take the data to the computer, you can take a computer input device to the data. Here, a portable bar-code scanner is used to record inventory data in the warehouse.

Voice recognition devices are programmed with vocabularies and can recognize and interpret voice commands spoken into a microphone connected to the computer. Current applications of this technology require that a person have an initial session with the computer in which each word command is spoken into the computer, defined as to its meaning (that is, the vocabulary is built). Then as a command is spoken during a work session, the recognition device compares it with words in its vocabulary. Although finding limited use in certain areas, the widespread use of voice recognition still appears to be in the future. The ability to recognize different voices with a variety of accents and speech patterns is a formidable technical problem.

The Mouse

Much software currently available provides for the use of a pointing device called a **mouse** that can streamline editing and input operations. A mouse is a hand-sized unit connected to the computer that, as it is dragged across a flat surface, relays positioning information to the computer (see Figure 4-12). This information can be used to position the cursor quickly at any desired point. The mouse has one or more buttons that can be pressed to control positioning of the cursor and selection operations. It is especially convenient for designating one or more characters or words to be deleted, moved, or changed in appearance. Although the same actions can be performed with the keys of the keyboard, many of them are done much more quickly with a mouse.

One of the important features of the Apple Macintosh is that the mouse is standard; consequently, its use is widely incorporated into all Macintosh software. It is used for actions that include cursor positioning, making freehand drawings on the screen, and selecting actions to be taken from a *menu* of actions. In Macintosh software, the selection procedure is based on **icons,** symbols that represent the action to be performed. A

Figure 4-12
A mouse used to position the cursor on the screen.

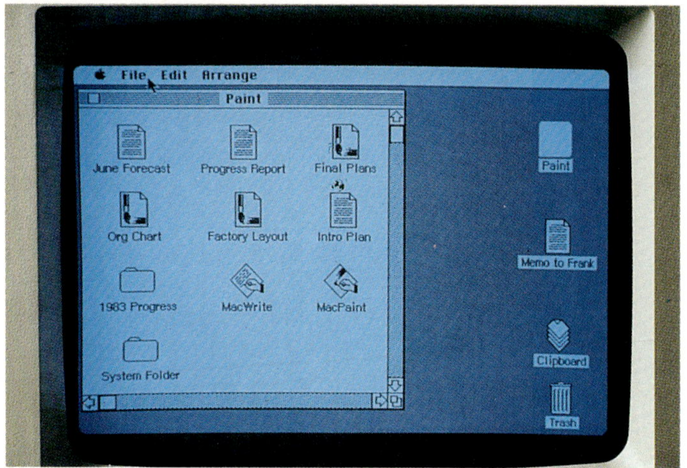

Figure 4-13
An Apple Macintosh icon-based menu.

typical icon-selection screen of the Macintosh is shown in Figure 4-13. To select a particular option, it is only necessary to move the mouse pointer to the appropriate icon and click the mouse button. The popularity of the mouse for many Macintosh applications has spurred the demand for IBM-compatible software that use it. Numerous programs are available that allow the user to interact with the PC in much the same way as with the Macintosh.

The Plotter

The plotter is an output device designed specifically to generate graphics output. Mechanisms of the plotter allow a pen holder to move anywhere on a sheet of paper, up and down or left to right, to form the desired images. They are used, for instance, by engineers for engineering drawings, by electronic engineers for electronic circuit layouts, by architects for floor plan layouts, and by surveyors to print contour maps. Many have provisions for printing in color.

You name it, and plotters can plot it. Here, two large plotters are preparing engineering drawings.

AUXILIARY STORAGE

The Need for Auxiliary Storage

The components of the computer that we have discussed up to this point provide for the entry of information into the computer, processing of that information, and output of the results. A computer system consisting of only these elements would not be very useful. The reason is that it includes no provisions for the long-term storage of data and programs. (Remember, storage of information in memory is temporary; when the computer is turned off or another program is placed into memory, the current contents are lost.) Long-term storage is provided by auxiliary storage devices that work hand in hand with memory. For instance, all of the data files and processing programs for the MCT Enterprises' order-processing system, sales analysis summaries, word processing activities, and other activities would be permanently stored in auxiliary storage. To perform a sales analysis, the sales analysis program would be read into memory and would then read appropriate data into memory for processing. Remember that the relationship between internal memory and auxiliary storage is somewhat analogous to the relationship between a desktop and a file cabinet, as illustrated in Chapter 3 (see Figure 3-2).

Two types of auxiliary storage devices are commonly encountered today. One uses magnetic tape (much like that of the home tape recorder) for storage of information. The other uses rotating magnetic disks that utilize the same magnetic recording methods as tape. Both of these methods for storing information involve two basic elements: the magnetic storage medium and the hardware unit for reading information from or writing it to the storage medium. The basic principle of magnetic encoding of information is illustrated in Figure 4-14. As the magnetic material is moved beneath the reading element (read/write head), the element senses the magnetically encoded information on the surface and transmits it in the form of electrical pulses to the computer. This element is called the *read/write* head because it is capable of encoding new information on the magnetic surface, as well as reading that which is already encoded. For

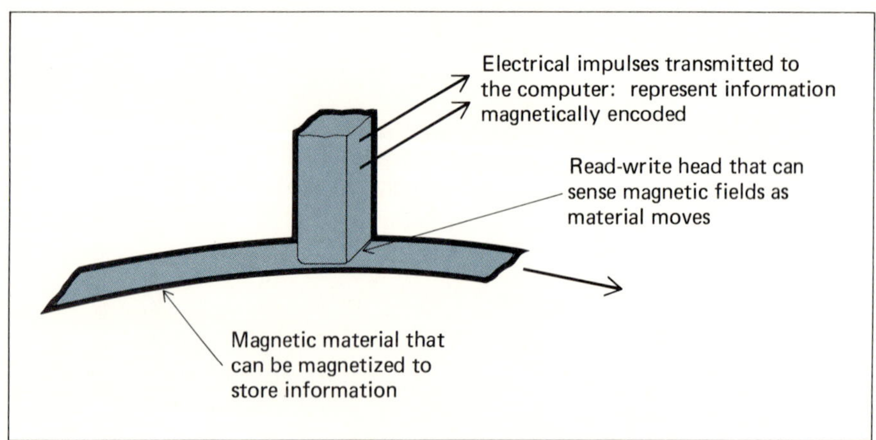

Figure 4-14
Reading magnetically encoded information.

disk storage, the hardware unit is called a **disk drive;** for tape storage, it is called a **tape drive.** The combination storage medium and drive hardware is analogous to the home tape recorder in which music is stored on a tape cassette that must be inserted into a tape deck in order to play (or record) it.

The Magnetic Disk Concept

Magnetic disk storage units are of two broad types: those in which the storage medium is removable (such as the tape cassette used with a cassette recorder), and those in which the storage medium is fixed and cannot be removed. Both are used with microcomputers and both are based on the same principles for storing and accessing information from the disk.

To illustrate the disk storage concept, consider a circular piece of paper (a disk) that is attached to a smooth surface with a pin in the center so that it can rotate. If you rotate the disk while holding a felt marking pen to the surface, a circle will result. If you repeat the process but move the marking pen toward the center as illustrated in Figure 4-15, another circle will result that is concentric with the first. If you are careful when positioning the pen, you can repeat this process, thus producing a series of distinct circles, none of them overlapping the adjacent circles.

This is the principle of the magnetic disk storage device in which the rotating disk has a magnetic material coating and the marking pen is a mechanism containing a magnetic read/write head. Although the disk surface is a continuous sheet of magnetic material, the design of the drive is such that the read/write head may be positioned through **access arms** at any of a number of predetermined positions. The resulting "circles," called **tracks,** represent circular "strips" for recording information, as illustrated in Figure 4-14.

From Chapter 3, Figure 3-5, we know that memory is designed so that individual positions of memory are addressable. Hence, a program can

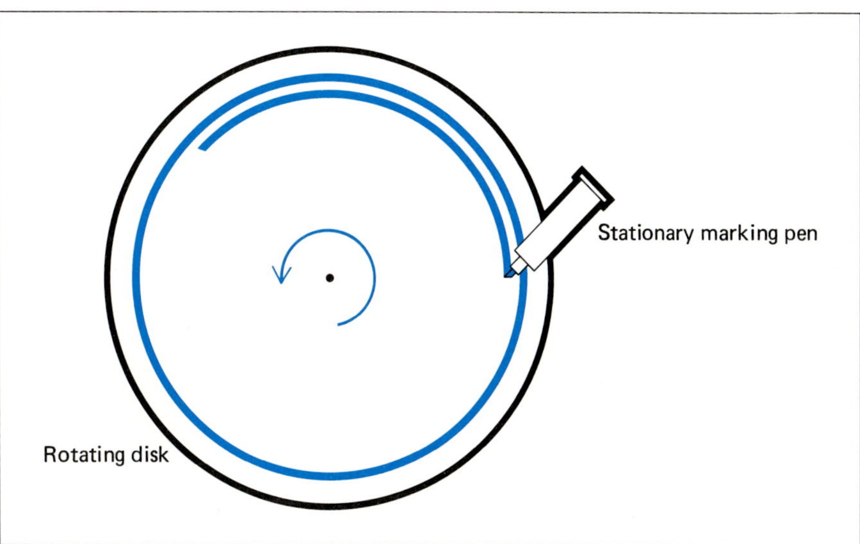

Figure 4-15
Marking concentric circles on a rotating disk.

easily refer to a single character, a field, or an entire record stored in memory. Because of the nature of the disk medium, this capability is not possible with disk storage. Instead, information is stored as large blocks that conform to the design of the operating system and features of the disk drive. This means, for example, that if you were entering an order and the program required the price from the disk of a particular item, the entire data block containing the price would be read into memory. Then the program would find the single field that was needed for the calculation. Fortunately, this is handled automatically by the operating system software and the user or programmer need not be concerned with what actually takes place.

For the purpose of storing data, each track is divided into **sectors** as illustrated in Figure 4-16. In this illustration, there are nine sectors per track; this number depends upon the operating system and hardware design. It is the combination of the number of bytes per sector, the number of sectors per track, and the number of tracks per surface that determine the storage capacity of the disk surface. For the PC floppy disk (described next), the number is:

512 bytes/sector × 9 sectors/track × 40 tracks/surface = 184,320 bytes

Referring again to the paper/pen illustration of Figure 4-15, for a given diameter of disk, the number of circles you could draw (without one touching another) would depend upon the width of the pen point and the accuracy with which you could position it. Similarly, with a disk drive, the more precise the access mechanism and the magnetic elements of the read/write head, the greater is the number of tracks that can be used. Increasing the number of tracks and packing the data more tightly on a track increases the amount of data that can be stored on the disk. The **density** of a disk is a measure of how much data can be stored on the disk.

One of the features of a magnetic disk is that it provides quick access to stored data. For instance, to read a particular sector from the disk of Figure

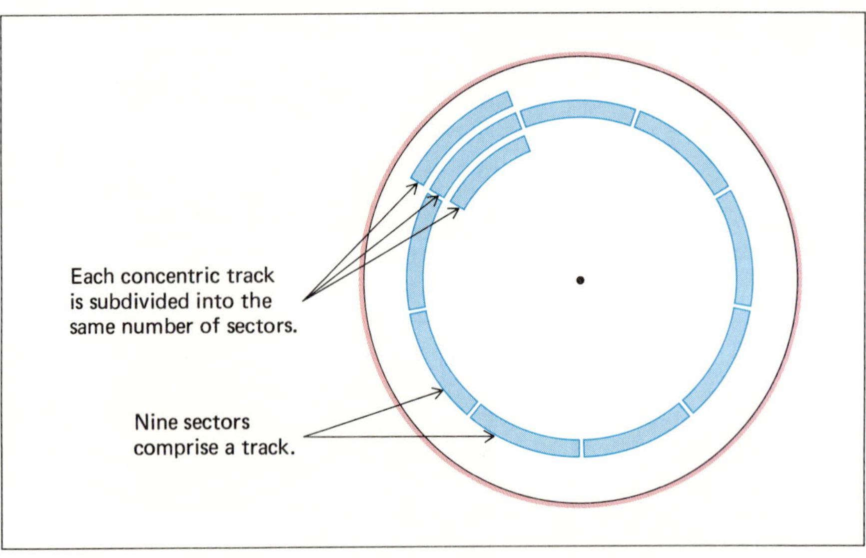

Figure 4-16
A track subdivided into sectors.

4-16, the program must move the read/write head in or out to the desired track, and then wait for the needed sector to rotate beneath the head. The time required for each of these operations is measured in milliseconds (there are 1000 milliseconds in a second), with actual times dependent upon the type of drive. Because of this ability to obtain information from anywhere on the surface, disk storage is referred to as a random-access device. It is well suited to both processing in which records are accessed one after the other in some predetermined sequence (sequential processing), and in random order (random or direct processing).

The Floppy Disk

For several years, virtually the only disk medium used with personal computers was the 5¼-inch flexible diskette, more commonly known as the **floppy disk.** Floppy disk drives are called removable media devices because a disk (see Figure 4-17) can easily be removed from the unit and replaced with another. This provides the user with the ability to store information limited in amount only by the number of relatively low-cost disks that she or he is willing to buy. When inserted into a disk drive unit in the computer, the plastic disk surface, which is coated with a magnetic material, rotates inside the protective jacket at a rate of 300 to 400 revolutions per minute (the exact speed depends upon the drive design). Under program control, data in memory can be written to disk and information previously written can be copied into memory. Writing to a disk containing files that must not be changed or deleted can be prevented by covering the write protect notch (see Figure 4-17) with a small piece of tape.

Early disk drives had only one read/write head and were thus capable of recording only on one side of the disk. With the density allowed by the technology of that time, the capacity of a disk was approximately 80,000 or

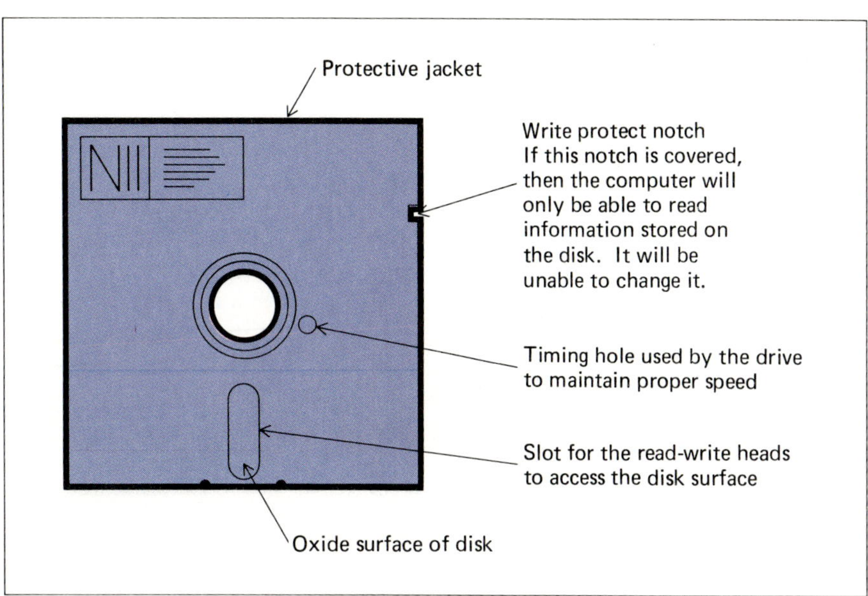

Figure 4-17
A 5¼-inch floppy disk.

80K bytes. With improved technology, the recording density was doubled and a pair of read/write heads (one for each side of the disk) was designed into the disk drive. These units, which were labeled "double-sided, double-density," are standard with the PC. (The calculation in the preceding section corresponds to the current capacity of each side of the disk as used on the PC. The total capacity of disk is 368,640 bytes; the disk is commonly referred to as the 360K disk.)

Disks are rated according to the capacity that the manufacturer guarantees. The most common (and those to use with the PC) are designated as DSDD, meaning double-sided, double-density. You may also encounter SSDD (single-sided, double-density) disks, which are used on disk drives with a read head only for one side of the disk. Both disks are the same. The only difference is that DSDD disks have been tested and certified for writing on both sides; SSDD disks have been tested and certified for writing on only one side and not the other. SSDD-certified disks are commonly used in DSDD drives, but there is an increased risk of losing data.

When the IBM AT was introduced, one of its features was a 5¼-inch floppy disk drive with a capacity of 1.2 megabytes. Although the disk is identical to its 360K cousin, it is especially manufactured for the higher density needed to achieve this capacity. The disk drive can read information from standard 360K disks (written by a PC) as well as its own high-density disks.

One of the disadvantages of the common floppy disk is its relatively fragile packaging. That is, the jacket and direct openings exposing the recording surface offer only minimal protection. More than one student has seen a major project lost because a disk was left in the direct heat of sunlight in an automobile. The international warnings shown in Figure 4-18 are found on the storage envelopes of many disks; they tell the story.

One of the features of the Apple Macintosh when it was introduced was the use of the 3½-inch disk that is enclosed in a rigid plastic container with self-closing cover over the access opening. This unit, shown in Figure 4-19, was adopted as the standard removable disk medium by IBM for the PS/2. The low-end Model 30 disk drive provides a disk capacity of 720K bytes. Other models use a high-density unit providing a capacity of 1.44 megabytes. The 3½-inch drive is also commonly used in portable microcomputers.

Floppy disks have two significant limitations, both relating to their overall characteristics. One is the relatively slow speed of accessing data. For instance, it takes approximately 1/50 second to read a sector from a 360K disk. Although this may not sound like a long time, remember that the processor operates in nanoseconds. Rotating the disk faster to speed up this process is not practical because of the fragile nature of the medium. The other limitation is the small capacity relative to the needs of today's software. For instance, all the components for the word processor Microsoft Word occupy six 360K disks.

Hard Disk Drives

Both the speed and the capacity shortcomings of the floppy disk are resolved through the use of hard disks. (Figure 4-20 shows a hard disk

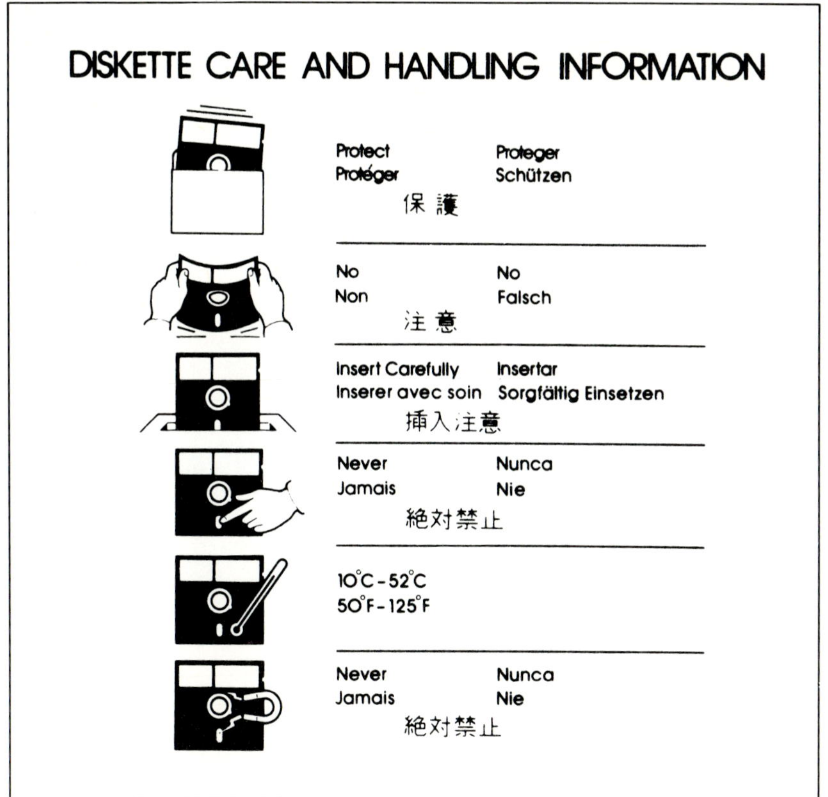

Figure 4-18
Floppy disks require special care.

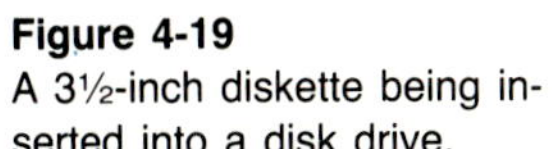

Figure 4-19
A 3½-inch diskette being inserted into a disk drive.

Figure 4-20
A hard disk.

unit.) Whereas the recording medium for a floppy disk drive is a flexible plastic, that for a hard disk is a rigid metal surface; hence, **hard disk.** Because of the rigidity of the metal disk, the rotating speeds can be much higher (ten times that of a floppy) with the result that data is read and transferred at a much higher rate.

Furthermore, the disk platters, of which there might be several in a disk drive, are sealed, thus providing an environment free of contamina-

Row upon row of magnetic tapes can be accessed by automatic tape library equipment. The tapes in this photograph store billions of characters of data.

tion. With this contaminant-free environment, a number of technological features are incorporated to provide significantly greater storage capacity. Where the storage capacity of the first hard disk drives for microcomputers were 5 megabytes, the 20-megabyte drive is commonly thought of as the minimum to purchase. Capacities of 40 and 70 megabytes and beyond are now common. Although these capacities seem huge when compared with the floppy, there is a very important difference between these two auxiliary storage devices; that is, a floppy drive uses a removable medium. Many microcomputer owners have 100 or more floppy disks to store their programs and data. (The capacity of 100 360K floppies is in excess of 30 megabytes.) On the other hand, the hard disk is not a removable medium so the total storage available is limited to the capacity of the disk. With the planned computer applications for MCT Enterprises (discussed in Chapter 1), the capacity of a 20-megabyte hard disk could be exceeded very quickly.

The Need For Magnetic Tape

In preceding descriptions, care has been taken to refer to magnetic disk storage as *long-term* storage and not as *permanent* storage. The reason is that information stored on disk is easily lost, either by purposely replacing outdated data with new data or accidentally writing over data, or by physical failure of the drive. Needless to say, the accidental loss of data is quite undesirable. To protect against this, it is a simple matter to make **backup** copies of an entire disk, as most floppy-based microcomputers include two disk drives. With the appropriate command (which we learn about in the next chapter), the computer can be directed to make an exact copy of the disk in one of the drives to the disk in the other drive.

On the other hand, with a hard disk system, backup of the set of files stored on the disk becomes a problem. It does not take much arithmetic to

Figure 4-21
A microcomputer tape cartridge and drive unit for backup.

determine that the complete backup of a 20-megabyte disk to floppy disk (removable medium) would require about sixty 360K disks. As always seems to be the case, a problem is soon followed by solutions; this is indeed the case for backup of hard disks. In the mainframe world, magnetic tape units have long been used both as auxiliary storage devices for processing involving moving data into and out of memory, and for backup purposes. Certain of the tape technology has been scaled down, producing tape drives for backup of microcomputer hard disks. Figure 4-21 shows a special ¼-inch tape cassette designed especially for computer use. Units such as these have capacities in the 20- to 60-megabyte range (and more). A tape drive for backup of a hard disk is an important element in a business environment. It provides a convenient means for guarding against the possible loss of part or all the computer records that could result from a hardware failure or a catastrophic blunder that the computer operator could conceivably make.

DECIDING UPON HARDWARE

About Obsolescence

The rapid advance of computer technology leaves the average person (and even the computer professional) with many more questions than answers. Should we buy now or wait a few months for the arrival of something that is more powerful and less expensive? In general, there is little use in waiting because the field is constantly evolving at an unbelievable pace. The important consideration in acquiring a microcomputer is to purchase hardware and software that will best do the needed job. In other words, buy solutions—not hardware labels. Furthermore, the purchaser should distinguish between the technology and the functionality of computing hardware and software; that is, both hardware and software become obsolete in a technological sense very quickly. For instance, a piece of equipment purchased today might well be obsolete in a year (or even less) because newly invented equipment does the job faster and better and is less expensive. However, as long as a piece of equipment can be used to perform its intended function in an efficient way, it will not be functionally obsolete. Computer hardware and software become technologically obsolete long before they become functionally obsolete.

Upgrading a Computer System

In purchasing a computer for business or personal use, you want to be certain that the investment you make today is also a good one for your needs of tomorrow. For instance, as the owner of a new business, you anticipate that your data processing needs will be significantly greater in 2 years than they are now. You know that as more powerful software becomes available to do things that are not practical for you now, you will need more computer power. Over a period of time, you will become more and more dependent on the computer and associated software, some of which you may have had tailored or written for your specific needs. You certainly do not wish to reach a point at which your entire system, software and hardware, must be replaced. Because technology changes so rapidly, it seems as though the owner of a computer will soon possess obsolete equipment. In some cases, this has occurred, but generally, computer hardware manufacturers have provided the owner with good alternatives for upgrading. To illustrate, let us assume that you started your business in 1984 and purchased an IBM PC with two disk drives and 256K of memory on the motherboard. As time progressed, you saw your hardware needs increase as you continually installed new software and upgraded old. (Periodically, software companies make available new releases of their software products; these upgrades usually include new features and sometimes require additional hardware.) Following is a typical sequence of hardware upgrades that you might have made.

- Add a memory card to increase the memory capacity to 640K.
- Expand auxiliary storage with a hard disk to increase the capacity to 20 megabytes.
- Add accelerator expansion card with a faster microprocessor to speed up (by 3-6 times) some of the operations of applications that had become cumbersome with the latest software.
- Replace the PC with an AT, thus providing increased internal and disk storage speed and increased disk storage capacity.

In the first three upgrades, the capacity of the PC is expanded; in the last upgrade, the computer is replaced. This is all possible because manufacturers are careful to ensure that new equipment is compatible with software used on previous equipment.

With the PS/2 in 1987, IBM introduced a significantly different computer system, including models with capacities far beyond those of the AT. Even though the more powerful models are designed for use with a new operating system, provisions were made to accommodate without change programs used on the PC/XT/AT computers.

Optical storage technology is a fast emerging area in the microcomputer field. The 5-inch optical disk shown here can store over a half-billion characters. An entire multivolume encyclopedia can be stored on one of these with plenty of room to spare.

Hardware Selection for MCT Enterprises

As the owner of a small business, your goal must be to select hardware that will run your selected software to satisfy your processing needs. You must be careful to avoid the desire to have the "fastest and most powerful computer on the block." Since you have selected software that requires an IBM PC-compatible computer, you must make a choice between the PC, XT, AT, and PS/2. A careful evaluation of your needs and the features of the various computers would indicate that a good cost-effective solution would be an AT-clone (an AT compatible computer manufactured by a company other than IBM). As with any computer purchase, whether for personal or business use, there must be compromises between cost and features. Some features are desirable but their cost is simply not justifiable. The following hardware represents a realistic compromise for the needs of a small business such as MCT Enterprises.

IBM AT clone with 640K memory: selected over the XT because of its faster processor speed. The entering of data and processing using the general ledger and order-processing software were found to be too slow (and aggravating) with the slower speed of the XT.

A 1.2-megabyte floppy drive: standard equipment with the AT.

A 40-megabyte hard disk: selected over the 20-megabyte drive because the cost difference was relatively small for 100 percent more capacity (which will likely be needed in 12 to 18 months).

Tape drive for backup: considered to be essential in order to simplify the backup procedure and ensure that all stored information is safe from loss.

Monochrome graphics display: less costly than color and adequate for the needs of MCT Enterprises.

Dot-matrix printer: to be used for all output. The model selected has good near-letter quality printing for correspondence. At a later date, a daisy-wheel printer may be added to the system but other expenditures have a higher priority.

As is the case with any computer acquisition, this is the first step for handling initial needs. As data processing activities grow, the system can be expanded. When your needs have outgrown the system, then you can assess the market, which certainly most offer more powerful equipment at lower prices than available today.

SUMMARY

This chapter completes the basic information you should have about computer hardware. Summarizing, the important items from the chapter are:

- A peripheral device is any device that performs an input or output function. Although, technically speaking, the keyboard and monitor are peripherals, they are such an integral part of the microcomputer that they are not commonly referred to as peripherals.
- Monitors are generally classified as color or monochrome (black and white). The PC/XT/AT require a special monitor adapter card corresponding in type (color or monochrome) to the monitor. This circuitry is built into the motherboard of the PS/2.
- The elementary screen display unit is called a pixel, meaning picture element. The quality of the display (its resolution) is commonly measured in pixels.
- The keyboard is similar in design to that of a typewriter. In addition, it includes a Control key and an Alternate key, which, when used together with other keys, alter the codes entered. Function keys provide the ability to enter commands and directives that depend upon the software being used.
- One way of categorizing printers is as impact and nonimpact. Impact printers create the letter images by a printing element striking the paper through an inked ribbon. Nonimpact printers use copying machine techniques (laser printers).
- The daisy-wheel printer is an impact printer in which the print characters are molded into the ends of radial arms of a print element. The print quality of the daisy-wheel printer is commonly referred to as letter quality.
- A dot-matrix printer forms characters with dot patterns in a manner similar to that of an athletic scoreboard. Most dot-matrix printers can be controlled to produce different sizes of print; for instance, printing

can be at 10 characters per inch (cpi) or 17 cpi. Most also have the capability to print at high speeds, producing a relatively low quality print, or at lower speeds to produce near-letter quality print.

- The laser printer represents the high end of printer cost and overall versatility. Lasers commonly used with microcomputers form images (both printing and graphics) by using a dot resolution of 300 dots by 300 dots per inch. The fact that images are formed by dots is barely perceptible.
- A buffer is a memory device used with a printer to account for the fact that the computer can send the printer information to print far faster than the printer can print. Output is stored in the buffer memory, to await the printer while the computer proceeds with other tasks.
- A printer can be connected to the computer through either a parallel or a serial interface. The Centronics parallel interface is specifically designed for printers.
- In selecting a printer, you should consider the following factors: compatibility with your software, your need for multiple-copy printing, what you can realistically afford (cost), printer speed as compared with your needs, and your needed print quality.
- Other specialized input devices include: optical page reader for reading printed text; bar code reader for reading printed bar codes; graphics tablet that is used much like a drawing board; light pen used in conjunction with a special monitor for pointing and drawing; and voice recognition systems that recognize verbal commands.
- The mouse is a pointing device used in conjunction with the monitor that streamlines editing and input operations.
- The magnetic disk auxiliary storage device consists of two fundamental components: the magnetic disk on which information is recorded and the disk drive mechanism that performs the reading and writing operations. They are analogous to the home tape cassette and the tape recorder.
- The 5¼-inch floppy disk is the standard auxiliary storage medium used with the PC/XT/AT. Drives used with the PC/XT can record up to 360K bytes on a single disk. Those used with the AT have a capacity of 1.2 megabytes.
- The 3½-inch disk is used with the IBM PS/2 and the Apple Macintosh.
- Hard disks provide the user with far greater storage capacity and much faster access than floppy disks. However, the medium is not removable as it is with floppy disks.
- Magnetic tape units are commonly used to make backup copies of data stored on hard disks to protect against accidental loss of data.

NEW TERMINOLOGY

The following are important new terms introduced in this chapter; you should be familiar with each of them.

access arm
auxiliary storage
backup
bar code reader
bit-mapped graphics
buffer
cursor
daisy-wheel printer
density
disk drive
dot-matrix printer
floppy disk
function key
graphics tablet
hard copy
hard disk
icon
impact printer
ink-jet printer
interface
laser printer
letter-quality printer
light pen
mouse
multiple-part form
nonimpact printer
optical page reader
peripheral device
pixel
print head
print spooler
printer driver
resolution
sector
soft copy
tape drive
track
video display adapter
video memory
voice recognition
write protect notch

REVIEW QUESTIONS

1. Is the disk drive a peripheral device? Explain your answer.
2. In a computer store, you are comparing two monitors. One has been described to you as "640 by 200 pixels" and the other as "640 by 480 pixels." What would be the difference in the display between these two monitors?
3. What are the purposes of the Control and Alternate keys on the PC keyboard?
4. What is the difference between hard copy and soft copy?
5. List the "strengths" and "shortcomings" of each of the following categories of printers: daisy wheel, impact dot matrix, ink jet, and laser.
6. How does a print spooler improve the overall efficiency of the computer?
7. How would your need to print multiple copies of invoices affect your choice of a printer?
8. Which is generally more preferable for connecting a printer to a computer, a parallel interface or a serial interface? Explain your answer.
9. What is a read/write head?
10. You have made a request through the keyboard of your computer to display the current balance of one of your customers stored on disk. Describe in as much detail as you can the actions that occur in finding and isolating that data for you. What part do the access arms play in this operation?
11. What is meant by a DSDD disk?

12. Describe two advantages of a hard disk drive over a floppy disk drive. Describe the advantage(s) of the floppy drive over the hard disk drive (if there are any).
13. What purpose does a microcomputer tape drive serve?

MATCHING

Match each term in a to h with the most appropriate description in 1 through 8.

a. Centronics
b. buffer
c. daisy wheel
d. laser
e. sector
f. peripheral
g. impact dot matrix
h. mouse

1. Basic unit of storage of a disk drive.
2. A type of interface for connecting a printer to a microcomputer.
3. A printer type that is associated with high-quality print and high printing speed.
4. Allows the processor to proceed without waiting for the printer to complete a printing operation.
5. A highly versatile, low-cost type of printer.
6. Any device used to get information into or out of computer memory.
7. A hand-held device that can be used to reposition the cursor on the screen.
8. An impact printer type that produces letter-quality printing.

TRUE/FALSE

Determine whether each of the following is true or false.

______ 1. A pixel is a unit of measure that specifies the resolution of a dot-matrix printer.

______ 2. The complete image displayed on the monitor screen at any given time is stored in video memory.

______ 3. The display quality of a VGA (video graphics array) monitor is superior to that of the CGA (color graphics adapter).

______ 4. The Caps Lock key on the keyboard is identical to the shift lock key on a typewriter.

______ 5. The action caused by striking one of the keyboard function keys depends upon the particular software being used.

______ 6. Dot-matrix printers that form characters by printing many dots slightly overlapped to produce good-quality printing are called fully formed character printers.

______ 7. Near-letter quality usually refers to print quality produced by a dot-matrix printer whereas correspondence quality refers to print quality produced by a daisy-wheel printer.

______ 8. It is not possible to print multiple-part forms with a laser printer.

______ 9. Because of the high-quality print of the laser printer, they are commonly referred to as fully formed character printers.

______ 10. Ink-jet printers print by spraying a fine stream of ink on the paper; some can even print in full color.

______ **11.** A print spooler is a memory unit built directly into the printer so that the processor does not need to wait for the completion of each printing operation.

______ **12.** Bar code readers are used only on minicomputers and mainframes for such applications as inventory control and marking products in the grocery store. Their use on microcomputers is not practical.

______ **13.** The number of tracks on a disk is determined by the disk-accessing mechanism in the drive.

______ **14.** The floppy disk drive offers no advantages over the hard disk drive as the hard disk has more capacity and is faster.

______ **15.** A tape drive would be of little value on a PC equipped only with two floppy disk drives.

ANSWERS TO OBJECTIVE QUESTIONS

Matching

1. e 2. a 3. d 4. b 5. g 6. f 7. h 8. c

True/False

1. F 2. T 3. T 4. F 5. T 6. F 7. F 8. T
9. F 10. T 11. F 12. F 13. T 14. F 15. T

Chapter 5

Using MS DOS

OBJECTIVES

Chapters 2, 3, and 4 have provided you with the basic concepts of software and hardware. This chapter is designed to give you the background needed to work with the PC and to run the software systems described in the chapters that follow. When you have completed this chapter, you should be able to describe:

- Characteristics of the keyboard and its features that are unique to computer usage.
- The nature of the Disk Operating System (DOS) used with the PC.
- Controlling the computer system with DOS commands.
- Subdirectories that allow a hard disk to be "divided" into smaller working areas.

Skills in this chapter involve using DOS commands. With them you will be able to do the following:

- Inspect the contents of a disk (DIR command).
- Display the contents of a file (TYPE command).
- Initialize a new disk so that information can be stored on it (FORMAT command).
- Make a copy of a file or an entire disk (COPY and DISKCOPY commands).
- Create and use a subdirectory on a hard disk (MD and CD commands).

PREVIEW

Some Additional Details on PC Hardware

The computer keyboard has, in addition to the normal keys associated with a typewriter, a number of keys that take advantage of the capabilities of a computer. Under the PC operating system, floppy disk drives are identified by letters A and B (C for a hard disk).

Introduction to DOS

The operating system most commonly used with the PC is the MS DOS. DOS manages the files stored on disk; through DOS you have access to files by name stored on either disk drive of the computer.

Computer Start-up

Although read-only memory contains basic instructions to start the computer, a special DOS system disk is required to make the computer operational under DOS.

Using the Disk Operating System

You direct DOS with commands to perform such operations as deleting files and making a duplicate of a disk.

Inspecting Disk Contents

DOS maintains a directory of all files stored on a disk; you can view the contents of the directory using a variety of forms of the DIR command. The TYPE command allows you to display the contents of certain types of files directly from DOS.

General Housekeeping Functions

To use the computer intelligently, you need relatively few DOS commands. New disks are made ready with the FORMAT command; the ERASE command allows you to get rid of unwanted files; the COPY and DISKCOPY commands give you the means to make duplicates of files or an entire disk.

About Subdirectories

The large storage capacity of a hard disk requires some way of organizing stored data; subdirectories provide this capability.

HANDS-ON NATURE OF THIS CHAPTER

The first four chapters of this book contain descriptions of numerous topics that you need to know about. Your involvement has been one of reading and assimilating. This chapter is distinctly different in that it involves topics about which you read and activities that you must perform: it is *hands-on*. For example, you will read about the need for preparing a floppy disk for use (formatting) and how to do it, and you will do it. In fact, a primary focus of this book is learning by doing. You will learn about the PC operating system by using it; you will learn about each of the productivity software packages WordPerfect, Lotus 1-2-3, and dBASE III by using them. In all of these software-specific chapters, you should first read the chapter or a portion of it, making notes and asking questions as you go, and then sit down at a computer and perform each of the actions described. In working with the computer, do not be timid; you cannot damage it by making a mistake. Although there are a few ways in which you can destroy information stored on a disk, you need not be concerned that your disk will go up in smoke with the slightest wrong move. Those actions that can cause problems are called to your attention in the text, so do not allow your fear of doing something wrong interfere with your learning about the software by using it.

At the end of this chapter, you will prepare a data disk for use in the chapter that follows. All hands-on activity for this chapter is deferred until the end. In the chapters that follow, hands-on activities are an integral part of the chapter.

SOME ADDITIONAL DETAILS ON PC HARDWARE

The Computer Keyboard

In order to use the computer and the software described in this book, there are some things that you need to know about the keyboard. Even though it is much like that of an ordinary typewriter, it has special keys specifically for controlling the actions of the software that you are using. These are identified in Figure 5-1 for both the original PC keyboard and the enhanced keyboard. Following are descriptions of some of the special keys; others are described in later chapters.

- Letters (uppercase and lowercase), digits, and special characters are entered as with a typewriter. After each line is entered, it is necessary to strike the **Enter key** to notify the computer to accept the line. This is identical to the return key on an electric typewriter.

- The **Caps Lock** key is similar but not identical to the shift lock on a typewriter. Striking the Caps Lock shifts to uppercase for the letter keys but not for the other keys. For instance, after you press the Caps Lock key, striking the letter G key gives you an uppercase letter, but striking the 5 key would give a 5, not the % character. Striking the Caps Lock a second time shifts back to lowercase. This

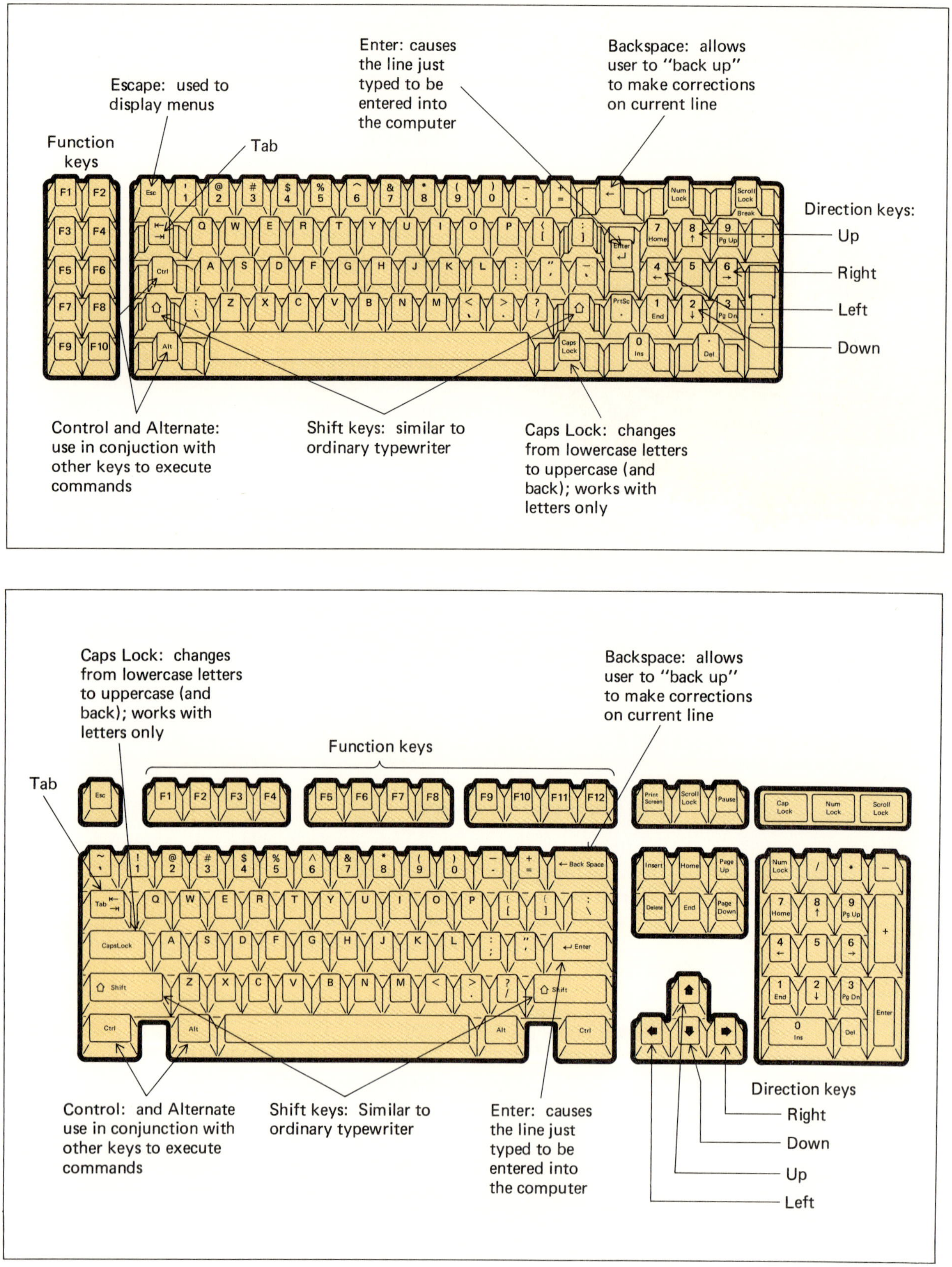

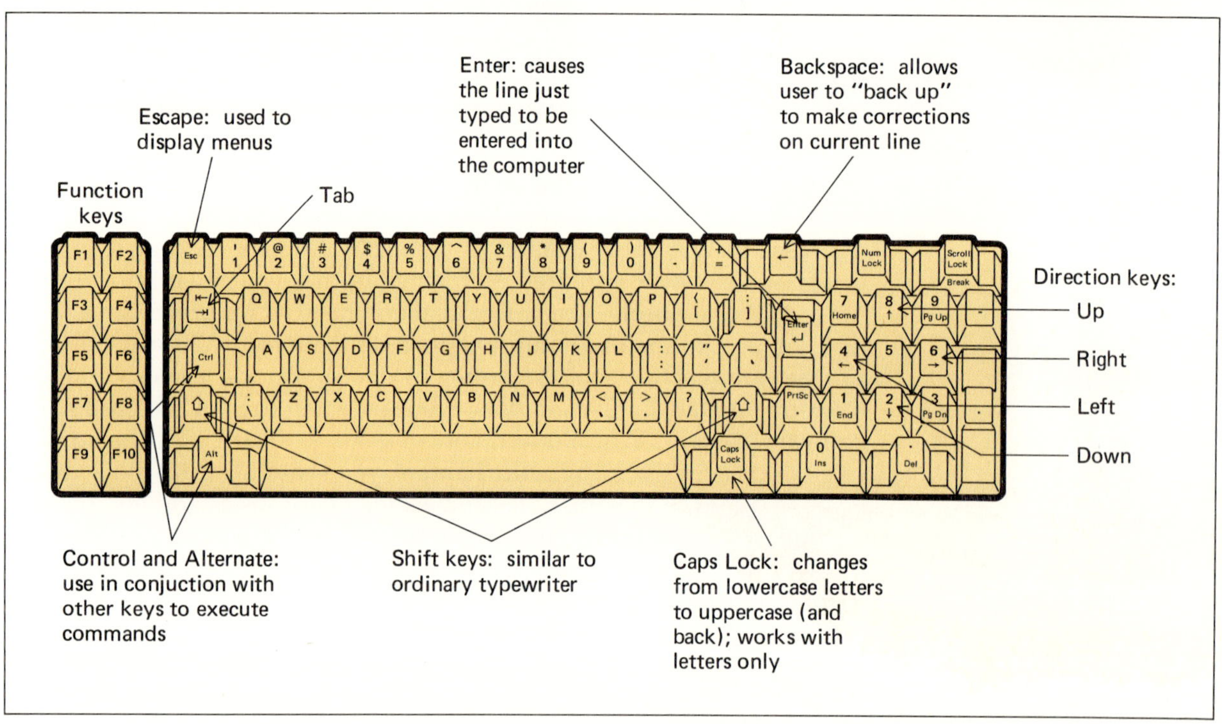

Caps Lock: changes from lowercase letters to uppercase (and back); works with letters only

Backspace: allows user to "back up" to make corrections on current line

Function keys

Tab

Control: and Alternate use in conjunction with other keys to execute commands

Shift keys: Similar to ordinary typewriter

Enter: causes the line just typed to be entered into the computer

Direction keys

Right

Down

Up

Left

Figure 5-1
(a) The IBM PC keyboard. **(b)** The 101-key enhanced keyboard.

key "toggles" back and forth between uppercase and lowercase; hence, it is commonly called a toggle.

- The **Shift key** works much like its counterpart on a typewriter. That is, it is activated only as long as it is held down. Depressing it gives you access to the characters on the upper part of the keys (for instance, % instead of 5). However, for letters it gives uppercase if the Caps Lock has not been activated and lowercase if it has.

- If you strike the Backspace key, the cursor will move one position to the left, erasing the character in that position in the process.

- The Control key (**Ctrl**) and the Alternate key (**Alt**), like the Shift key, do not do anything by themselves. They are always used in conjunction with another key to change the action caused by that key. The functions performed by these keys are defined within the software being used.

- Both keyboards have function keys. The original PC keyboard has ten, labeled F1 through F10, and the enhanced keyboard has twelve, labeled F1 through F12. The specific action of each is defined by the software being used.

- In using the software in this book, many actions require that you move the cursor. This is done with the group of keys with arrows pointing up, down, left, and right.

You should note that all of the character keys have automatic repeat. If you hold one of them down, the character will be entered continuously.

IBM PC Disk Drives

You know from Chapter 4 that programs and data are stored on floppy diskettes or on hard disks, and that in order to use them, they must be copied into memory. Because a PC can have two or more drives, some way is needed to distinguish one from the other. The operating system that you will be using assigns each an identifying letter. The standard IBM PC includes two floppy disk drives; the one on the left is identified as the A drive and the one on the right is the B drive (refer to Figure 2-1). With the exception of start-up operations described later in this chapter, the drives are identical in every respect and each can be made to perform the same operations as the other. The XT, AT, and PS/2 include at least one floppy drive and a hard disk drive. The floppy is designated as drive A and the hard disk as drive C.

Recall from Chapter 4 (Figure 4-17) that floppy drives include a special feature used in conjunction with the disk to protect information stored on disks from being accidentally destroyed. That is, if the write-protect notch in the disk is covered, then it is impossible to change the contents of the disk.

INTRODUCTION TO DOS

For most of us, acquiring something new is immediately followed by the urge to try it out. Taking the time to learn how to use it properly or how it functions is often thought of as an unnecessary impediment to action. Learning something about the PC operating system falls into this same category. The urge is to get on with WordPerfect. However, without some knowledge of the operating system, situations will continually arise in which you do not know what to do next.

MS DOS

By far the most commonly used operating system for the PC is the Disk Operating System written by Microsoft Corporation. The name is abbreviated DOS and pronounced as if it rhymed with the word boss; because it was written by Microsoft, it is commonly identified as MS DOS. The first version of DOS was identified as Version 1.0. Most software packages are written to be used with Version 2.0 or higher. The computer on which the manuscript for this book was prepared used Version 3.2 (successive releases of this version were Versions 3.0, 3.1, 3.2, 3.3, and 4.0). Each version or release provides capabilities not available with the previous version or release. When the computer is first started (described in the next section), a message appears on the screen that identifies the version of DOS. Descriptions in this chapter are relatively basic and apply to all versions of DOS.

DOS is not a item that automatically comes with the computer but is a software package that is purchased separately. The package includes a large number of programs (there are more than forty-two in DOS 3.2) that are stored on a disk called the DOS System Disk. This disk includes programs that are necessary to start the computer and use it under DOS, as well as programs that you will need for doing things such as preparing a new disk for use.

Naming Disk Files

In order for DOS to keep track of files stored on disk, you must give a name to each file when it is first created. For instance, a letter to Boardwalk Sales might have the name BWSALES.LTR or a customer database file might have the name CUSTOMER.DBF. The three parts of the name are described in Figure 5-2. Restrictions imposed by DOS are as follows:

1. The filename can consist of up to 8 characters.
2. The filename extension, which is optional, can consist of up to 3 characters.

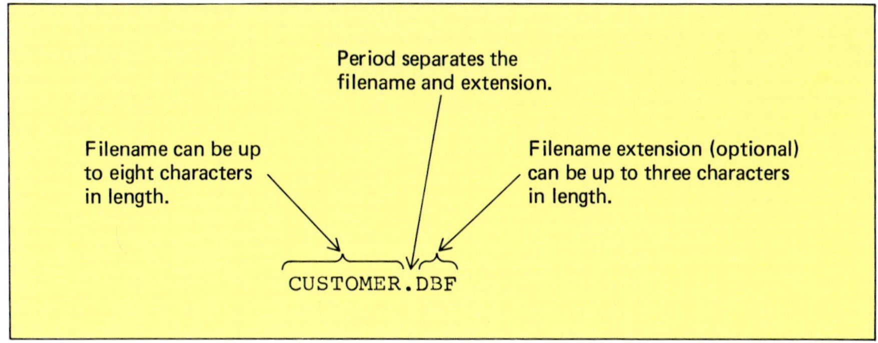

Figure 5-2
File name structure.

3. Any of the letters and digits can be used; there is no distinction between lowercase and uppercase. Thus, for example, the following are valid filenames.

   ```
   X.X   x.x   LETTER.WP   MANAGER.DOC   7.SAV
   ```

4. Many of the special characters can also be used in forming filenames and extensions, but a number of them are not valid because they have special meaning to DOS. Some software packages restrict the use of special characters even further. However, almost all allow the use of the underscore character and the hyphen. This is convenient to separate two parts of a name (the space is not allowed). For instance, a WordPerfect-prepared contract with AR Stevens Corporation might be named:

   ```
   CON_ARS.WP     or     CON-ARS.WP
   ```

   To avoid any problems, avoid using special characters other than the underscore or the hyphen in creating names.

DOS manuals clearly define the single word **filename** to mean the portion of the name preceding the period. However, in common usage (including within the IBM DOS manual itself), the word *filename* is often used to indicate the entire name, including the extension. It will usually be evident from the context what is meant; remember that DOS can only find a file for you if you give it the complete name.

Although DOS allows you to select both the name and extension as needed, software packages commonly use the extension to indicate the type of file. For instance, Lotus 1-2-3 Version 2 uses the extension WK1 to indicate a worksheet file and dBASE III uses the extension DBF to represent a database file. As you will learn, when working with these software packages, you need not specify the extension if you allow the default to be used.

Drive Specification

Whenever you refer to a file, DOS requires that you specify the complete name and the drive on which it is located if the file is not on the default drive (you will learn about the default drive next). This is done by preceding the name by a **drive specification.** For instance, if the file

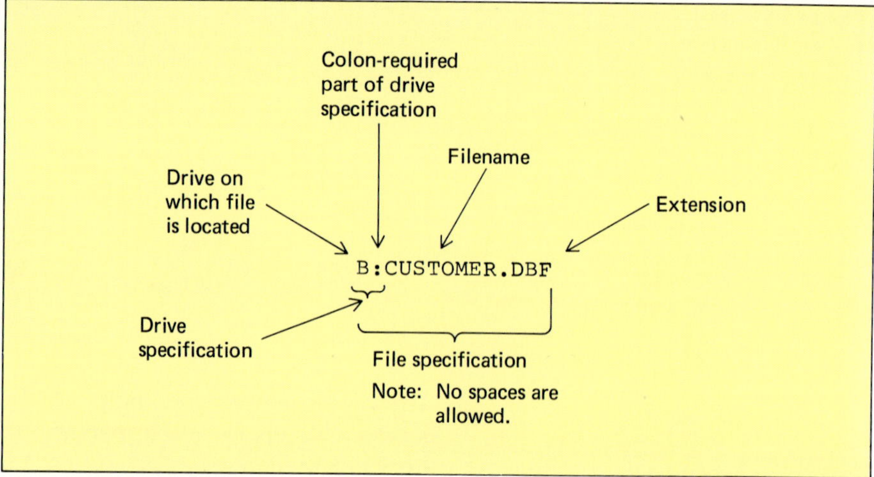

Figure 5-3
File specification structure.

CUSTOMER.DBF is on the B drive, the drive specification is B: (the letter B followed by a colon with no space between them). The complete **file specification** is B:CUSTOMER.DBF, as illustrated in Figure 5-3. Notice that no spaces are allowed within the file specification.

COMPUTER START-UP

Booting up Under DOS

In Chapter 3 you learned that microcomputers include two types of memory: RAM for general use and ROM with permanent contents. These permanent contents include special bootstrap start-up and hardware-test programs that allow the computer to start itself when the power is turned on. This start-up operation is called **booting up** the system; the term comes from the nature of the start-up operation in which the action is somewhat akin to "lifting yourself by the bootstraps." It includes reading needed DOS components from disk and placing them in RAM. If you are using a floppy disk computer (one with two floppy drives and no hard disk), you must have a DOS system disk. (*This is not one of the disks that came with the book;* it is one that came with DOS.) If you are using a hard disk computer, the needed DOS programs will be on the hard disk. To start the computer, follow these steps:

1. With a *floppy disk computer,* insert the DOS disk into the A drive; the read/write slot must be inserted first (see Figure 4-17) and the side with printing should face upward. Close the latch on the drive. With a *hard disk computer,* make certain the latch on the floppy drive is opened in order to force the computer to boot up from the C drive.

2. Make certain that the monitor power switch is on. In some configurations, the monitor power cord is plugged into the computer and controlled by the computer power.

3. Turn the power to the computer on.

If the start-up tests find no hardware malfunctions, the A drive (or the C for a hard disk) will be activated and the needed DOS programs will be read into memory. When the operation is complete, the message shown in Figure 5-4(a) will be flashed on the screen and the system will be waiting for you to enter the date. It is important to enter the correct date because DOS attaches the date to every file that you create. In response to the date request, enter the current date in month/day/year form then strike Enter. Note that you can use either slashes or hyphens, for example, both 12/3/89 and 12-3-89 are acceptable. Next, DOS displays the message of Figure 5-4(b), then waits for you to enter the time (based on a 24-hour clock). For instance, if it is 2:35 p.m., then enter 14:35; you need not be concerned with seconds and fractions of seconds as shown in Figure 5-4. (Many computers have a battery-powered clock/calendar and the DOS disk is set up to read it automatically when booting. In this case, you will not be asked the date and time.) When the booting operation is complete, control is given to DOS. It is easy to tell that a successful booting operation has occurred by checking the screen for the following DOS display.

A> (for a floppy disk system)
C> (for a hard disk system)

Whenever DOS (as well as almost all software) completes an action and is awaiting a response, it gives you an indication. For instance, the messages of Figure 5-4 are called **prompts.** The prompt can be a a message such as these or certain symbols that depend upon the software in control of the

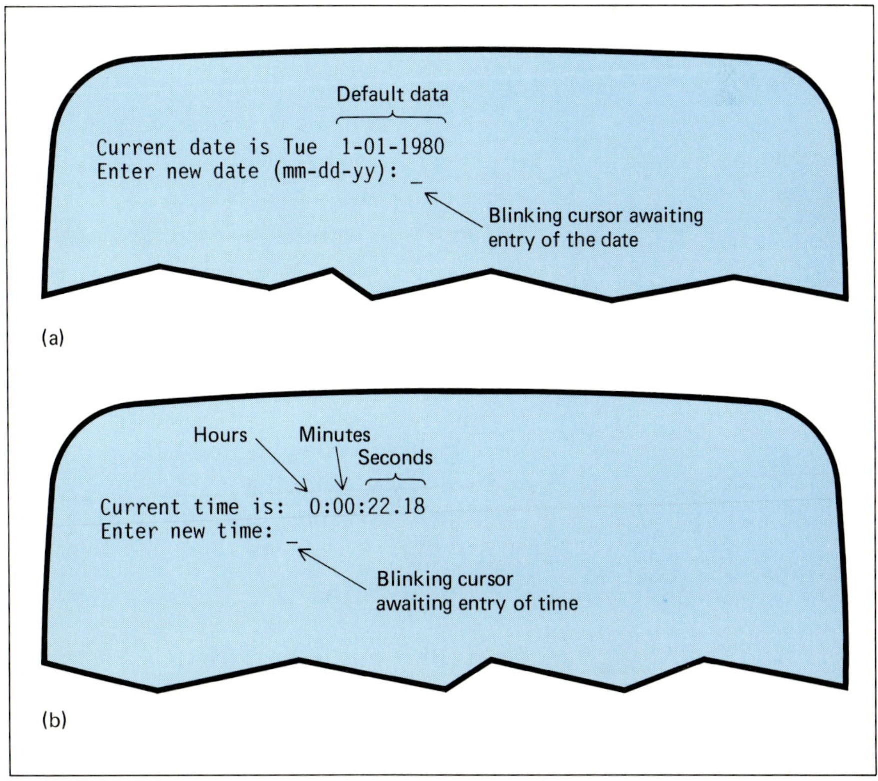

Figure 5-4
(a) Date prompt.
(b) Time prompt.

computer. DOS uses the letter of the current drive followed by a right angle bracket >. Hence, the DOS prompt A> (or C>) tells us:

1. The computer is ready and waiting for something to be entered.
2. It is under the control of DOS.
3. The A drive (or C drive) is the current, or default, drive. The default drive is the one that DOS will automatically refer to if we do not specify otherwise (more about this later).

Boot Failure

If, instead of the date request (or DOS prompt), you receive either of the messages in Figure 5-5, then DOS has not booted properly. Causes and cures for these problems with a floppy disk computer are:

Case	Cause	Cure
(a)	The disk in the A drive is not a DOS system disk. For example, if you attempted to boot with the data disk included with this book, you would get such a message.	Replace the disk in the A drive with the proper DOS disk. When ready, strike Enter (or any other keyboard key).
(b)	There is no disk in the A drive; or the DOS disk is upside down or backward; or a new, unitialized disk is in the A drive; or the disk drive is not latched.	Properly insert the DOS disk in the A drive. Then hold down the Ctrl and Alt keys, and while holding them down, strike the Del key.
Other	Something is wrong with your DOS disk.	Obtain another DOS disk, then follow the action for Case (a).

If either the (a) or (b) error occurs with a hard disk computer, then you have inserted a disk in the A drive (you should not have done so). The recovery actions are the same as for a floppy system except that you must first remove the disk from the A drive. If you get some other error, then something is wrong with the DOS information on the hard disk; for this, refer to the DOS manual.

Cold Start and Warm Start

When the computer is first turned on, it runs through a hardware test cycle and then begins the boot process. This is called a *cold start*. Occasionally,

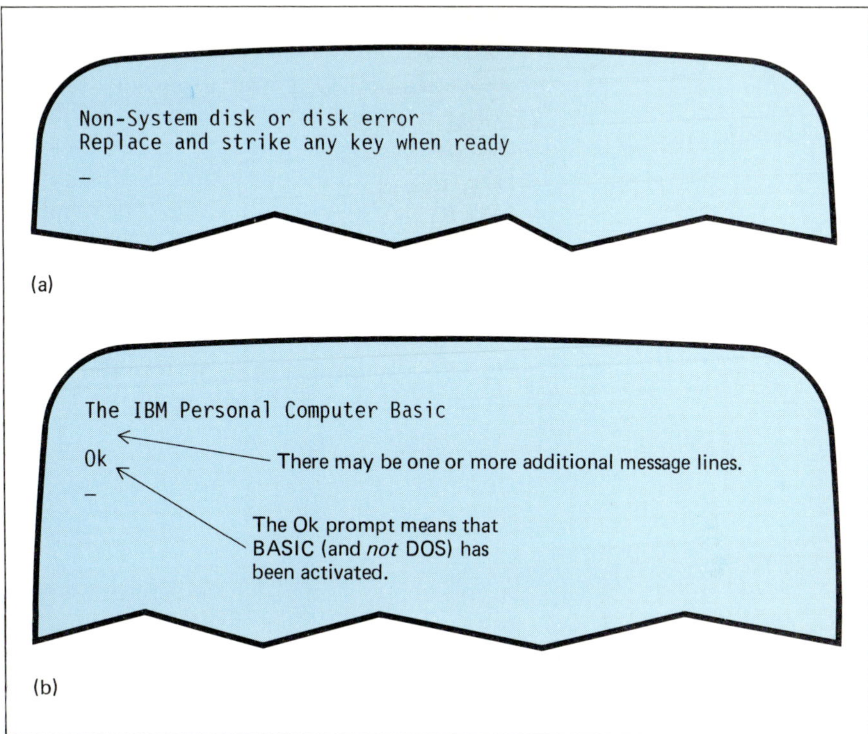

Figure 5-5
(a) The disk was read but not found to be a DOS system disk.
(b) The disk in the A drive could not be read.

the computer software gets things locked up so that it is not possible to progress further. Under these conditions, the computer must be rebooted. Rather than turn the computer off and then back on again, the rebooting process can be initiated by holding down both the Ctrl and Alt keys and then striking the Del key. This is the action taken to remedy the boot failure of Figure 5-5(a); it is called a *warm start*. Whenever instructions tell you to reboot the computer, use this method.

USING THE DISK OPERATING SYSTEM

About DOS Commands

One of the program files on the DOS system disk that is loaded into memory from the booting action is the command processor program named COMMAND.COM. One of the functions of this program is to communicate between you at the keyboard and the rest of the operating system. Although DOS keeps track of all files on a disk, it is up to you to take care of general "housekeeping" functions, such as preparing a new disk for use, deleting unneeded files from a disk, and making copies of needed files to ensure against loss. Actions such as these are done with DOS **commands,** instructions to DOS to take a given action. Whenever you request an action by entering a command, the command processor interprets that command and then takes appropriate action. Some of the commonly used commands are a part of the command processor and thus are always available whenever the computer has been booted up under

DOS. As such they are called **internal commands.** DOS also includes **external commands;** these commands are not part of the command processor. Each is a separate program stored as a file on the DOS system disk. With a hard disk system, these are normally available from the hard disk so that the user sees little difference between them and internal commands. However, with a floppy disk computer, if an external command is used, then the DOS system disk must be available. Descriptions that follow will identify each command as being internal or external.

Entering a Command

A DOS command is entered from the DOS prompt merely by typing in the command name and striking Enter.

```
A> DIR
```

or

```
C> DIR
```

In this chapter, in order to distinguish between information entered from the keyboard and that displayed by the computer (the prompt), the keyed information will be shaded as in the preceding example; that is, in the first line, A> is displayed by the computer and DIR is entered by you from the keyboard. After each entry, the Enter key must be pressed to signal the computer that you have completed the entry.

Occasionally, it is convenient to change the default drive. This is easily done by typing the drive specification of the new default drive; for instance, the following would be the screen dialogue to change from the A drive to the B drive.

```
A> B:

B>
```

INSPECTING DISK CONTENTS

The DIR Command

Although it is standard practice to label each disk (using the gummed labels that accompany them), it is easy to forget the exact contents. Fortunately, DOS maintains a **directory** that includes the name of each file stored on the disk. You can view the directory on the screen with the DIR command. For instance, if you were to place the WordPerfect disk that accompanies this book in drive A, type the DIR command, and then strike Enter, the result would be similar to that in Figure 5-6. Here you have asked for a directory listing and have automatically been given that for drive A. The reason for this is that drive A is the default drive (as indicated by the A> prompt). Anytime you give DOS a command that does not refer to a specific disk drive, DOS automatically assumes that you are interested in the default drive (A in this case).

Figure 5-6
The DIR command and a disk directory.

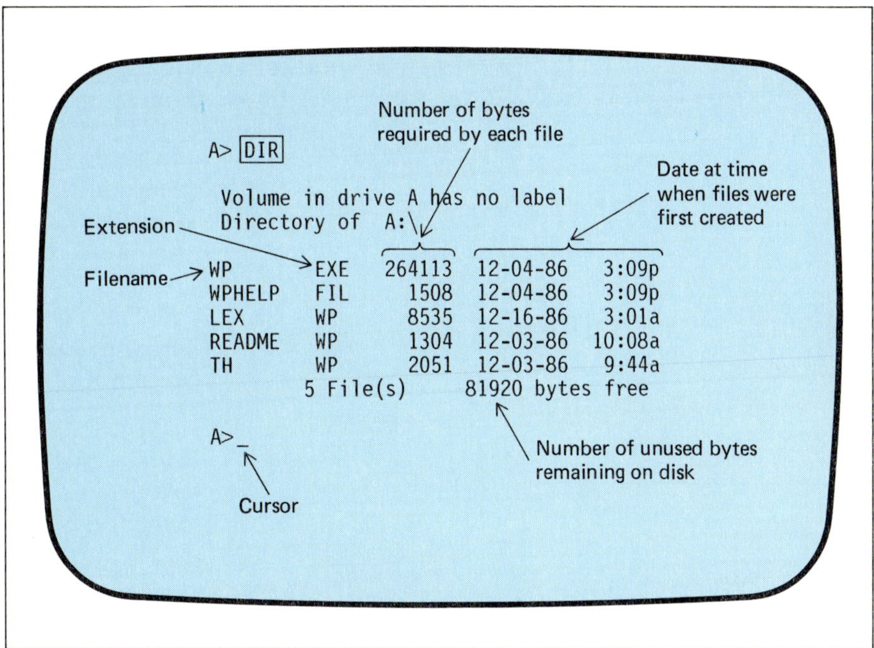

On the other hand, if you wanted a directory of the B drive, you would enter the DIR command in the following form.

A> DIR B:

Here you explicitly ask for the contents of drive B by including the drive specifier B: (B followed by a colon). (If the colon were omitted, DOS would think you were referring to a file named B.) If you were using a hard disk system operating from the C> prompt and you wanted to know the contents of the disk in the A drive, the form would be:

C> DIR A:

Although all examples in the book show DOS commands entered in uppercase, it makes no difference whether you use upper- or lowercase. For instance, the earlier DIR command could just as well been entered as:

A> dir b:

The DIR command is convenient to determine if a particular file is stored on a disk. For instance, if you wanted to know if the disk in the B drive contained the Lotus 1-2-3 file BUDGET.WKS, you would use the following form of the DIR.

A> DIR B:BUDGET.WKS

If the file with that exact name exists on the disk in the B drive, DOS will display its name; if it does not, DOS displays the message, *File not found.*

Technically speaking, the DIR command consists of two components: the command name and an operand, a designation of the element to be involved in the operation. Some commands, such as DIR, have one operand; others that you shall learn about have two.

Other DIR Options

There are numerous options that can be used with the DIR command; the following examples illustrate most of them.

A> `DIR B:/P`

/P causes DOS to pause when the screen becomes full. This is useful if the directory to be displayed is too long to fit on the screen. At the pause, DOS displays the prompt:

```
Strike a key when ready...
```

Striking any keyboard key causes the next screenful of the directory to be displayed.

A> `DIR B:/W`

/W causes DOS to display the directory in wide-screen format. The filenames (including extensions) are displayed five across on the screen; file size, date, and time are omitted.

A> `DIR B:>PRN`

PRN is a special code for the printer; this option to the DIR command causes the directory to be printed on the printer. Note the use of the right angle bracket >; you can interpret this as indicating "send the directory listing to the device PRN."

A> `DIR B:*.DBF`

The asterisk (*) means "anything can go here." This form of the command causes the directory display to be limited to only those files with an extension of DBF. A typical directory display might include the files:

```
AUTO.DBF
CUSTOM.DBF
TEMP.DBF
```

A> `DIR B:CONTRACT.*`

This is similar to the preceding example except that the directory listing is limited to files with a filename of CONTRACT and any extension. A typical directory display might include the files:

```
CONTRACT.AJC
CONTRACT.BW1
CONTRACT.BW2
CONTRACT.CW
```

A> `DIR B:CON_*.WP`

Directory display is limited to only those files with CON_ as the first four letters of the filename, and with the extension WP. A typical directory display might include the files:

```
CON_PQ.WP
CON_5.WP
CON_GEN.WP
```

The first two examples use **command parameters** (also called **switches**) that allow the user to modify the action performed by the DIR command. Many of the DOS commands include switches for influencing the exact actions of the command.

In the third example, the directory display is redirected from the screen to the printer, thereby producing a directory listing. If you have many files on several disks, it is a good idea to include a directory listing in the envelope with the disk. This will help you locate needed files quickly.

The last three examples illustrate use of the **global filename character** * (often called the **wildcard** character), which indicates that any character can occupy that part of the name or the remaining positions (filename or extension). If you establish some consistent naming convention for files, it will make life much easier in attempting to find things later. For instance, assume that you have numerous contracts that you have drawn up. If you name each of them using CON_ as the first four letters of the filename, then you can isolate them in a directory display as shown in the last example.

If you feel somewhat overwhelmed with the variety of options available with the DIR, do not be concerned. The most important item is to become accustomed to using DOS commands and, in this case, to know how to get a directory. As you use the computer, you will come to recognize the value of this variety of options. Furthermore, do not be concerned about doing something wrong and causing trouble with the computer. As a rule, DOS will simply prompt you with an appropriate message and then allow you to go on. The few DOS commands that can cause you a loss of files are clearly identified in descriptions that follow.

Viewing a File: The TYPE Command

Every software package that you might purchase includes documentation—a manual for installing and using the software. No matter how careful the software manufacturer is, there will always be some errors in or omissions from the documentation that are not detected until after the manual has been printed. To accommodate this, manufacturers commonly include corrections and additions to the manual in the form of a file on the software disk. (If the software occupies more than one disk, it is usually on the first.) Most commonly, the name of the file includes the word *READ;* typical names used are README (no extension), READ.ME, and README.1ST. When you obtain a new software package or an upgraded version of a package you are currently using, you should first check the directory for such a file. If one is found, then you should do as the name suggests—read it. For instance, if you noticed the file README.1ST on a disk, you could view it on the screen with the following TYPE command (internal).

```
A> TYPE B:README.1ST
```

You should be aware that you will get garbage (an unintelligible display) on the screen when displaying most files created by any productivity software package because of special encoding used by the software. For instance, WordPerfect uses encoding techniques to achieve such things as centering a line and underscoring, and the DOS TYPE command will not decode these. (You can observe this by attempting to display the README.WP file on the Limited Use WordPerfect disk included with this book. It is a WordPerfect file and can only be read from WordPerfect.) Most read-me files can be displayed by the TYPE because they are specially prepared. Such files are called *text files* and do not include any special codes normally used by productivity software packages.

If you want a printed copy of a text file (for example, a read-me file), then you can use the >PRN form illustrated for the DIR command as follows:

```
A> TYPE B:README.1ST>PRN
```

However, be careful that the file you are sending to the printer is indeed a text file. You should first display it on the screen. If you find unintelligible characters (such as happy faces) interspersed in the display, then *do not send it to the printer.*

After the screen becomes full during the display of a file, room is made at the bottom of the screen for the next line to be displayed by moving each line up. Thus, the top line of the display is lost; this is called **scrolling.** To read each screenful before it scrolls into oblivion (unless you are an exceptionally fast reader) requires that you momentarily stop the scrolling action. This is accomplished by holding down the Ctrl key and striking the Num Lock key at the upper right of the keyboard. (If you are using a 101-key enhanced keyboard, simply strike the Pause key at the right of the top row of keys.) The continuous display of new text will be halted, and the screen contents will remain unchanged, giving you time to read the screen contents. To resume the display, simply strike any key on the keyboard (the Enter key is convenient).

GENERAL HOUSEKEEPING FUNCTIONS

The FORMAT Command

When a new disk leaves the factory, it is completely blank and not yet usable by DOS. Before any data can be stored on it, the disk must be **formatted** by DOS, an action that involves defining the track and sectors of the disk and writing special formatting information. Once completed, this information remains on the disk. Hence, formatting is not an operation that you constantly repeat with a given disk. (Note that if you have disks that were used by another operating system, you will need to reformat them for use by DOS.) It is very important to understand that formatting a disk wipes out everything that might be stored on the disk. Hence, the disk should be checked carefully before formatting; accidentally inserting the wrong disk in the drive for formatting can spell disaster. Do this check with the DIR command.

Unlike the DIR command, which is internal (part of COMMAND.COM in memory), the FORMAT command is external and so is a separate program stored on the DOS system disk. In order to execute it with a floppy disk computer, either a copy of the file (named FORMAT.COM) must be on the disk in drive A or a DOS system disk must be in drive A.

The standard way of formatting a new disk is to have the drives loaded as follows:

drive A Contains the DOS system disk

drive B Contains the new disk to be formatted

Then the formatting command may be entered as follows:

```
A> FORMAT B:
```

DOS will then display the following prompt (regardless of whether or not you already have the disk in the B drive).

```
Insert the new diskette for drive B:
and strike ENTER when ready
```

Striking the Enter key causes the formatting to begin. DOS will display a message when the formatting has been completed.

Actually, there are two ways to format a disk. When formatted as described in the preceding, the disk can be used as a data disk with a capacity of 360K bytes. It is also possible to format a disk as a bootable system disk—one from which it is possible to boot the computer. The command to format it as a system disk becomes:

```
A> FORMAT B:/S
```

The /S (System) command parameter causes three files to be placed on the disk, requiring approximately 40K of disk space. One of them is the command processor COMMAND.COM, the presence of which you can see by issuing the DIR command. The other two are called **hidden files** because DOS defines them so that their names are not displayed with the DIR command. All three of these files are required on a system disk. If you prepare your own system disk in this way, you may wish to copy other DOS programs, for instance, FORMAT.COM and DISKCOPY.COM, using the COPY command. (DISKCOPY and COPY are described in sections that follow.)

The ERASE Command

As you continue to work with your computer, you will tend to accumulate more and more files. Eventually, you will find that a disk becomes full and cannot hold any more data. This can happen in either of two ways: the storage required by your files exceeds the 360K-byte disk capacity or the number of files exceeds the DOS directory limit of 112 files. There is nothing quite as frustrating as to be working on an application and to receive the DOS "Disk is full" message. When this happens, it is easy to end up losing work that you have done during the current work session, if not the entire file. To avoid this problem, you should pay careful attention to the amount of data you have stored on each disk and always delete files that you no longer need. For instance, assume that you have displayed a directory and found on the disk in drive B the files SAMPLE1.WKS,

SAMPLE2.WKS, and SAMPLE3.WKS that you no longer need. You could erase them by using the ERASE command (an internal command) by entering:

```
A> ERASE B:SAMPLE1.WKS
A> ERASE B:SAMPLE2.WKS
A> ERASE B:SAMPLE3.WKS
```

Note that the DEL command (delete) can also be used; DEL and ERASE perform the same function.

If these were the only Lotus 1-2-3 SAMPLE files on the disk, then the global filename character * could be used.

```
A> ERASE B:SAMPLE*.WKS
```

However, be warned that this will delete all files with names that fit this global form. When using global characters in an ERASE command, it is best to always do a DIR with exactly the same form first. For example, assume that you asked for a directory and received the following:

```
A> DIR B:SAMPLE*.WKS

Directory of B:\

SAMPLE   WKS   980   1-08-89   8:48a
SAMPLETP WKS  3024   3-13-89   2:45p
SAMPLE1  WKS  2312   6-12-89  10:31a
SAMPLE2  WKS  1884   6-18-89  11:44a
SAMPLE3  WKS  1676   6-22-89   4:16p
```

If you used the preceding form of the ERASE command, then SAMPLE.WKS and SAMPLETP.WKS would also be deleted.

Use of the global filename character can be extended to both the filename and the extension with significant results. That is, the command

```
A> ERASE B:*.*
```

will cause all of the files to be erased from the B drive disk. Obviously, you should be careful when using this.

In general, be very careful when deleting a file. There are ways of getting a file back after it has been deleted, but special software is required (see the box).

Duplicating a Disk: The DISKCOPY Command

Chapter 4 describes the need for backup of information stored on disk to ensure against loss. This is as important to the student who would not care to lose an entire semester's work as to the business person who would not care to lose accounting files. With the DISKCOPY command, it is possible to duplicate the contents of the disk in drive A onto the disk in drive B (or B to A, if desired). The recommended sequence is as follows.

1. Insert a DOS system disk into drive A.

2. Enter the DOS command:

Eventually, we all erase an important file from disk and then, after much teeth gnashing, set about to reenter it. This happened to a programmer named Peter Norton in 1982. However, Mr. Norton knew that deleting a file did not really delete the file. In fact, the action of DOS was the electronic equivalent of clipping a note to a file folder that said, "No longer needed." He knew that the file was still sitting on disk (even though DOS was ignoring it) and that it would remain there until something else was written over it. Actually, DOS marks a file as deleted by replacing the first character of the filename in the directory with an * character. So he wrote a program that allowed him to inspect the directory for names that started with an asterisk (those that DOS had deleted) and to change the asterisk to an "acceptable" character for files that he wanted back. Thus, in a blink of the eye, he had "unerased" his erased file. (In fact, he named his command to restore a file UNERASE.) Mr. Norton recognized the need for a general-purpose set of programs that would do things that cannot be done with DOS so he pulled together a collection of handy programs and called the package the Norton Utilities. These perform such actions as reorganizing the contents of the disk in order to make disk operations faster, rearranging the order of the directory entries (to alphabetic or date order), and actually erasing deleted information (convenient to get rid of confidential data). If you look around the desk of any devout PC user, you are likely to find a copy of the Norton Utilities or an equivalent program from another vendor. Consider such software essential to maintain your sanity in the transitory world of the computer.

```
A> DISKCOPY A: B:
```

This says to copy the contents of the disk in drive A to the disk in drive B. The first listed drive is said to be the **source drive** and the second is the **target drive.** The direction of transfer with commands that list two drives (or files) is from the source to the target. Note that the command and source drive designation, and the source and target drive designations are separated by spaces.

3. DOS will request that the two disks be inserted into the drives. Remove the DOS disk from the A drive and then insert the original (the disk to be copied). Insert the disk that will become the copy into the B drive. If the disk in B already has data on it, that data will be erased. If it is a new disk that has not yet been formatted, DOS will format it during the copy operation.

4. When the copy has been completed, DOS will display an appropriate message. After you respond, the disks may be removed.

If you are using a hard disk computer with only one floppy drive, then you must enter the command simply as DISKCOPY; no operands are required. The process will involve alternately inserting the original and new disks into the A drive as prompted by DOS.

The DISKCOPY command allows you to make backup copies to avoid losing all of your data in the event of a power failure. If, however, you have a power failure while a file is being saved to disk, the disk can be unusable. An uninterruptable power supply like the one shown here will allow the computer to keep operating (from batteries) long enough for you to save all of your work.

Copying Files: The COPY Command

Individual files can be copied from one disk to another by the COPY command (internal). For instance, assume that you need to copy the file SAMPLE1.WP from the disk in drive A to the disk in drive B. The following command will do this.

```
A> COPY A:SAMPLE1.WP B:
```

As with the DISKCOPY, the first operand following the command name is the source and the second is the target. In this case, SAMPLE1.WP on drive A is to be copied to drive B; since no filename is specified in the target operand, the file is stored under the same name. Technically, the A: preceding the filename is not required because drive A is the default drive.

This command is especially convenient to use when you are experimenting with an application. For example, assume that yesterday you completed a spreadsheet named BUDGET3.WKS; today you want to try something new with it. However, you do not want to change the original copy. (It works; be careful of changing something that works.) Hence, you need a duplicate to work on. You can easily create the copy with the following form of the COPY command.

```
A> COPY B:BUDGET3.WKS B:BUDTEST.WKS
```

This causes DOS to find the file named BUDGET3.WKS on drive B and to make an exact copy of it named BUDTEST.WKS, also located on drive B. Now you can modify BUDTEST.WKS while the original BUDGET3.WKS remains unchanged.

The RENAME Command

Occasionally, you will need to change the name of a file on the disk. You do this with the RENAME command. For example, assume that you have the word processing document file that you had named TEST.WP. It has proved to be more than the simple test that you had begun so you want to change the name to COLUMNS.WP. You could do this with the following form of the RENAME command.

```
A> RENAME B:TEST.WP COLUMNS.WP
```

ABOUT SUBDIRECTORIES

One of the conveniences of the floppy disk drive is that you can keep applications separated on different disks. For instance, you may have a separate disk on which you store copies of all contracts, another for general correspondence, and so on. The removable nature of the medium simplifies the process of keeping organized. However, the situation with a hard disk is different: you may have several *thousand* files on a single 30-megabyte hard disk. Clearly, it would be a bookkeeping nightmare if all of the files of a hard disk were listed in a single directory. The way in which DOS handles this is to allow you to create **subdirectories,** which are separate directories within the main, or **root,** directory. For instance, consider how you might arrange a hard disk to use the software that accompanies this book. Since there are three distinct software packages (WordPerfect, a spreadsheet similar to Lotus 1-2-3, and dBASE III PLUS), three subdirectories, one for each package, would be sufficient. The relationship between these subdirectories and the root directory is illustrated in Figure 5-7. Then the filenames for each software package are neatly stored in its own subdirectory. This situation is somewhat analogous to working with two disk drives. If the A drive is the default, then the default directory is that of the disk in the A drive. You still have access to the directory of the disk in the B drive by explicitly referring to B:. As with subdirectories, the root directory or any of the subdirectories can be activated as the default at any time. Let us consider how to use subdirectories.

Assume that the three subdirectories of Figure 5-7 have been created (this is the activity of an exercise at the end of this chapter). With the normal DOS prompt of C>, you have no direct indication as to which subdirectory is the current default directory. It is easy to forget in which subdirectory you are working and to create a file that you cannot find later because you do not know where to look. (This is much the same problem that most of us encounter with many floppy disks. For instance, on which disk is the database you created last month?) The recommended way of resolving this is to modify the DOS prompt using the PROMPT command. Without going into the details of this command, the following will cause the prompt to display both the default drive and the subdirectory.

```
C> PROMPT $P$G
```

With this change, the prompt will become:

C:\>	When the default is the root directory
C:\WP>	When the default is the WP subdirectory
C:\LOTUS>	When the default is the LOTUS subdirectory

You should be aware that when the computer is rebooted, the prompt goes back to the C>. If you wish to use this subdirectory prompt form, then put

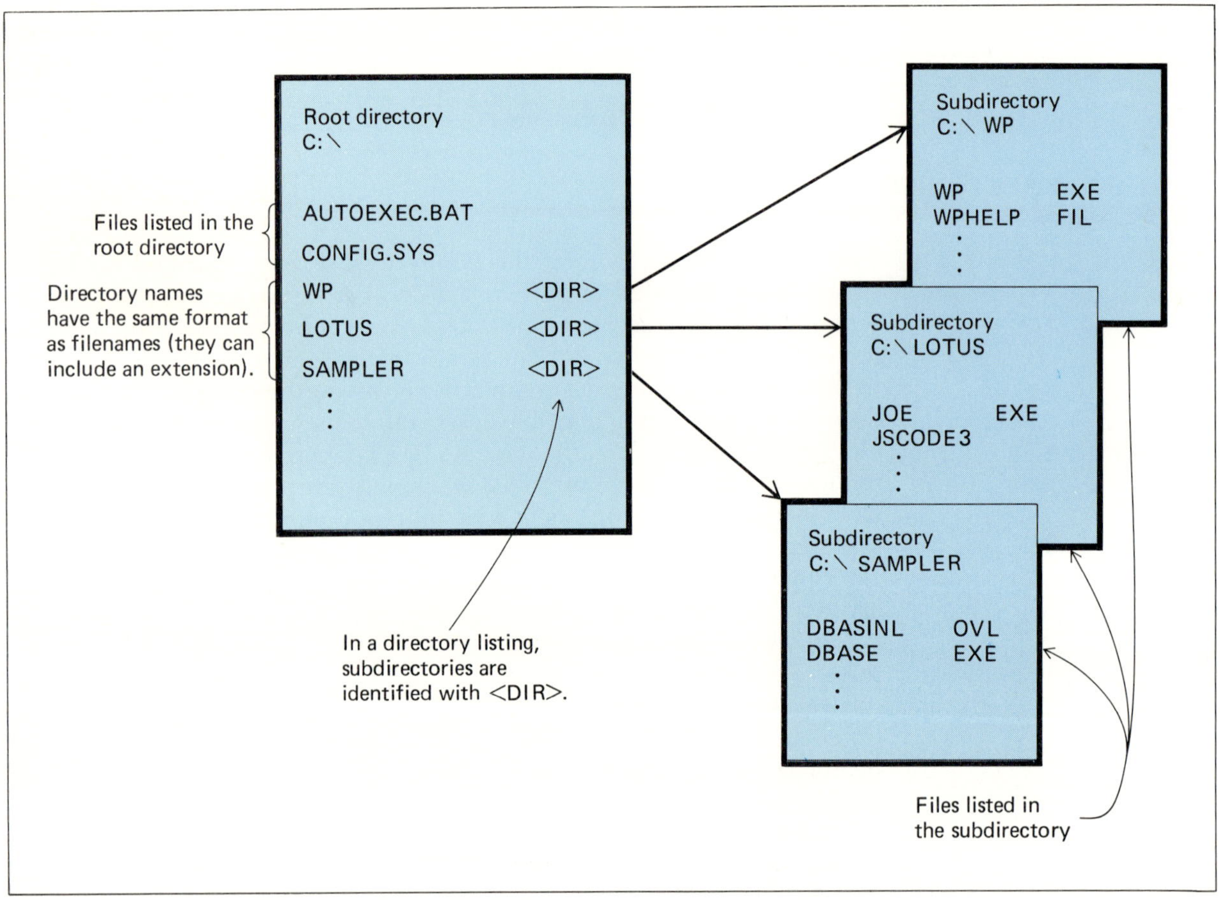

Root directory
C:\

Files listed in the root directory
AUTOEXEC.BAT
CONFIG.SYS

Directory names have the same format as filenames (they can include an extension).
WP <DIR>
LOTUS <DIR>
SAMPLER <DIR>
⋮

In a directory listing, subdirectories are identified with <DIR>.

Subdirectory
C:\ WP
WP EXE
WPHELP FIL
⋮

Subdirectory
C:\ LOTUS
JOE EXE
JSCODE3
⋮

Subdirectory
C:\ SAMPLER
DBASINL OVL
DBASE EXE
⋮

Files listed in the subdirectory

Figure 5-7
The concept of subdirectories.

the command in the AUTOEXEC.BAT file (refer to the DOS manual for instructions on this).

Notice that C:\ indicates the root directory—the backslash symbol is the element that denotes the root. The symbolism C:\WP indicates the WP subdirectory under the root directory. You can switch from one directory to another with the CD (change directory, an internal command) as illustrated by the following examples.

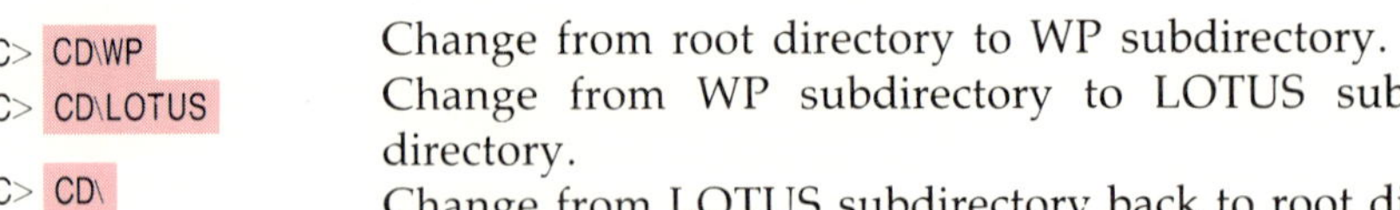

C> CD\WP	Change from root directory to WP subdirectory.
C> CD\LOTUS	Change from WP subdirectory to LOTUS subdirectory.
C> CD\	Change from LOTUS subdirectory back to root directory.

For instance, if you wish to work in WordPerfect, you should enter the first of the above CD commands. Then you could run WordPerfect from the C drive without using the floppy disk copy each time.

Note that subdirectories can be created on a floppy disk as well. This is sometimes convenient for storing a large number of small files, or simply for keeping different types of files separated. If you are using a hard disk computer, then you should become familiar with the concept of subdirectories—unless you have already done so. If you are using your own hard disk computer, then you should learn more about subdirectories from the DOS manual. This will allow you to use your computer more efficiently.

DOS 4.0

In mid-1988, IBM introduced DOS Version 4.0 to the computing community. The most widely acclaimed aspect of this release is its menu-driven feature, graphical "shell." (You will learn about menu-driven software when you study dBASE III in Chapter 15 and other software in Chapter 17.) With the menu-driven feature of 4.0, the user can execute commands either by typing them from the command line prompt (which you have studied in this chapter) or by selecting them from a graphical screen display. With the latter, the user can select a command from a list displayed on the screen either through the keyboard, with a mouse, or by using a combination of the two. The system presents users with two major screens. One is the "Start Program" screen, which displays a list of DOS programs available. The other is the "File System" screen, which shows the organization of the disk directories and directory contents.

One of the disadvantages of this new version is its memory requirements; that is, 4.0 requires nearly twice the memory of its predecessor. Furthermore, to install the full 70 files of the complete system requires over one megabyte of disk storage.

There are numerous features of 4.0 that are beyond the basic needs of those described in this chapter. However, all of the commands of earlier versions of DOS, including those that you have learned about in this chapter, work exactly the same with 4.0 as they do with earlier DOS versions.

SUMMARY

This chapter has provided you with needed exposure to DOS. Summarizing, the important items from the chapter are:

- The PC keyboard, in addition to typewriter keys, includes special keys to be used in conjunction with the computer. The Ctrl and Alt keys are used in conjunction with other keys (as is the Shift key) to change the meaning of the other keys. The specific meanings of these key combinations, as well as those of the function keys, depend upon the software package.

- Most floppy disk computers have two disk drives, identified as drives A and B. Hard disk computers commonly have one floppy drive identified as A and a hard disk identified as C.
- In DOS, every file must have a name consisting of a filename of up to 8 characters, and optionally a filename extension of up to 3 characters. The two parts must be separated by a period.
- Every new disk must be formatted before it can be used.
- A system disk is required to boot the computer under DOS; such a disk can be created with the FORMAT command using the /S command parameter.
- DOS commands can be considered in two categories: internal, which are included in the COMMAND.COM program, and external, which must be available from a disk to be executed.
- The global filename character * allows DOS operations to be performed on multiple files meeting the global definition.
- Following is a summary of the commands introduced in this chapter.

Command	**Type**	**Action**
CD	internal	Change to another directory; useful especially with a hard disk computer.
COPY	internal	Copy one or more files. Files may be copied to another disk, or to the same disk with a different name.
DIR	internal	Display or print a disk directory.
DISKCOPY	external	Make a duplicate of an existing disk.
ERASE	internal	Erase one or more files from a disk.
FORMAT	external	Format a disk so that it can be used by DOS.
PROMPT	internal	Change the DOS prompt.
RENAME	internal	Change the name of a file.
TYPE	internal	Display or print a text file.

NEW TERMINOLOGY

The following are important new terms introduced in this chapter; you should be familiar with each of them.

Alt key
booting up
command
command parameter
command processor
Ctrl key
DOS
directory
drive specification
extension
external command
file specification
filename
format
function key
global filename character
hidden file
internal command
prompt
root directory
scrolling
source drive
subdirectory
switch
system disk
target drive
wildcard character

REVIEW QUESTIONS

1. How are the Ctrl and Alt keys on the PC keyboard used?
2. What are the restrictions on choosing names for disk files in DOS?
3. What types of files are stored on a DOS system disk? What is the role of this disk during the computer start-up operation?
4. During boot-up, the computer displays a default date and then asks you to enter the current date. If you simply strike the Enter key, the default date is used. What is the disadvantage of using this default date?
5. What is the difference between a warm start and a cold start?
6. What is a DOS internal command? Contrast this with an external command.
7. Assuming that the A drive is the default, write a command to print a list of all files on the B drive with an extension of DBF.
8. A user becomes curious about the spreadsheet file SUMMARY.WKS and attempts to display it on the screen with the command:

   ```
   TYPE SUMMARY.WKS
   ```

   What would you expect to be displayed on the screen? Explain your answer.
9. How often must a floppy disk be formatted?
10. What are the two conditions that can result in a floppy disk being full under DOS?
11. What do you think will be the difference in the directory displays of the following two forms of the DIR command?

    ```
    A> DIR
    A> DIR *.*
    ```

12. What is the maximum number of files that can be erased from a floppy disk with a single ERASE command?

13. What happens if the target disk of a DISKCOPY command has not been formatted?

14. What is wrong with the following command? How do you think DOS will respond to it?

```
A> COPY INVEN.WKS A:
```

15. What command is needed to perform each of the following tasks, assuming that you are operating from the A> prompt?

    a. List the files in the B drive.
    b. List the files in the A drive with an extension of PRD.
    c. Print the names of the files in the B drive.
    d. Display on the screen the file READTHIS from the B drive.
    e. Format the disk in the B drive so that it can be used to boot the computer.
    f. Erase all files from the B drive that contain names starting with the letter C.
    g. Copy the complete contents of the disk in drive B onto the disk in the A drive.
    h. Make a copy of the file HOLD.WKS (on the B drive) and call it HOLD2.WKS.
    i. Copy all of the files from the B drive to the A drive.
    j. Change from the current directory to the TEMP subdirectory.

MATCHING

Match each term in a to h with the most appropriate description in 1 through 8.

a. Ctrl key
b. prompt
c. boot-up
d. system disk
e. subdirectory
f. internal command
g. drive specification
h. extension

1. Designates the location of a disk file.
2. Displayed to let the user know that a response is required.
3. Makes it easier to organize a hard disk and keep track of files stored on it.
4. The action that takes place when the computer is started.
5. Once the computer is operating under DOS, can be carried out without the DOS disk.
6. Part of the name of a file.
7. Needed to start the computer under DOS.
8. Used in conjunction with character keys on the keyboard.

TRUE/FALSE

Determine whether each of the following is true or false.

______ 1. The F1 key on the keyboard is used to start the computer.

_______ **2.** The following are all valid names to use for files in DOS: A.A, heading.q, SAVE.DBF, 123.456, and HOLD.

_______ **3.** Every file must be given a filename, but the extension is optional.

_______ **4.** In referring to a file, the drive specification is not needed if the file is on the default drive.

_______ **5.** For a floppy disk computer, the default drive is always the A drive, and for a hard disk computer, it is always the C drive. This is a permanent part of DOS and cannot be changed.

_______ **6.** If the disk in the A drive during start-up is not a system disk, the computer will still boot up but the action will take longer because the programs in ROM will have more to do.

_______ **7.** The file WORKER.B would not be listed in the directory display of the following command.

```
DIR WOR*.B*
```

_______ **8.** A command parameter modifies the action of a command.

_______ **9.** The TYPE command is not intended to be used with productivity software packages because of the codes that are stored within the files.

_______ **10.** The TYPE command can be used to print a copy of a text file.

_______ **11.** A disk needs to be formatted only when the type of application for which it is used is changed. For instance, a WordPerfect data disk must be reformatted if it is to be used for dBASE III.

_______ **12.** A disk formatted as a data disk (without using the /S command parameter) can be converted into a bootable system disk merely by copying the file COMMAND.COM to it from a DOS system disk.

_______ **13.** Two floppy disk drives are required to use the DISKCOPY command.

_______ **14.** The copy of a file made on another disk with the COPY command can have either the same name as or a different name from the original.

_______ **15.** Subdirectories cannot be used with a floppy disk.

ANSWERS TO OBJECTIVE QUESTIONS

Matching

1. g 2. b 3. e 4. c 5. f 6. h 7. d 8. a

True/False

1. F 2. T 3. T 4. T 5. F 6. F 7. F 8. T
9. T 10. T 11. F 12. F 13. F 14. T 15. F

ASSIGNMENTS/PROJECTS

Before attempting these assignments, you will need a blank disk.

DO THIS NOW 5-1 **Obtain a directory of a disk as follows:**

1. Boot up the computer as described in the section entitled "Computer Start-up."
2. Insert the data disk that accompanied this book into the B drive.
3. Obtain a printed directory of the disk in the B drive (refer to the section entitled "Inspecting Disk Contents"). Note the number of files on the disk and the amount of space remaining.
4. Remove the data disk from the B drive.

DO THIS NOW 5-2 **Make a copy of the data disk.**

1. From the previous exercise, the A drive contains the DOS disk and the B drive is empty. From the A> prompt, type the command

```
DISKCOPY A: B:
```

and strike the Enter key.

2. In response to the message on the screen, remove the DOS disk from the A drive and insert the data disk; insert the blank disk in the B drive. When ready, strike Enter. DOS will proceed to copy the data disk in the A drive to the blank disk in the B drive, formatting the disk as it is copying.
3. When DOS asks if you want to duplicate another, respond by typing the letter N (for No).

DO THIS NOW 5-3 **Add and delete files using the new disk.**

1. Remove the data disk that accompanied this book from the A drive. Set it aside; do not use it for the following operations.
2. Delete all files with extensions of DBF and NDX from the new disk (in the B drive) with the commands:

```
DELETE B:*.DBF
DELETE B:*.NDX
```

3. Display a directory and note the number of files now on the disk and the space remaining.

4. Insert the Limited Use WordPerfect disk in the A drive. Copy all of the files with an extension of WP from this disk to the new disk with the command:

```
COPY *.WP B:
```

Display a directory and note the number of files now on the disk and the space remaining.

5. Remove the WordPerfect disk from the A drive and insert Disk 1 of the Limited Use dBASE III software. Copy all of the files with names starting with the letter C from the dBASE III disk with the command:

```
COPY C*.* B:
```

Display a directory and note the number of files now on the disk and the space remaining.

6. Obtain a printed copy of the directory of this disk and check each entry against the disks from which you copied to ensure that files were deleted and copied properly.

DO THIS NOW 5-4 **Preparing a disk for assignments; floppy disk computer.**

The purpose of DTN 5-3 was to familiarize you with interacting with DOS. The objective of this exercise is to prepare a new disk to serve most of your needs for this book. For the sake of disk economy, you can use the disk you prepare as both the bootable DOS disk and your data disk for completing assignments. To this end, you will need to reformat the new disk you used in DTN 5-2 and 5-3.

1. Insert a DOS disk in the A drive. Insert your disk from DTN 5-3 into the B drive.

2. Format the disk in the B drive as a system disk with the command:

```
FORMAT B:/S
```

3. When the formatting operation is complete, display a directory. Notice that approximately 40K of the 360K capacity is used by the DOS files. (It may be more, depending upon the version of DOS you have.)

4. Copy the files FORMAT.COM and DISKCOPY.COM from the DOS system disk to your newly formatted system disk with the commands:

```
COPY FORMAT.COM B:
COPY DISKCOPY.COM B:
```

5. Remove the DOS disk from the A drive and insert the data disk that accompanied this book.

6. Copy all the files from this disk to your disk in the B drive with the command:

```
COPY A:*.* B:
```

Remove the data disk from the A drive and store it in a safe place. Do not use it except to copy its files to another disk.

7. If you have your own copy of Lotus 1-2-3 and are using it rather than the spreadsheet software included with this book, then rename the spreadsheet files with the following command:

```
RENAME B:*.WKQ *.WKS
```

8. Remove the disk from the B drive and label it as your boot/data disk.

DO THIS NOW 5-5 **Preparing a hard disk for assignments.**

If you have your own hard disk computer, you should create subdirectories for WordPerfect and Joe, the Lotus-like spreadsheet included with this book. (Setting up for dBASE III PLUS is described in the dBASE chapter.)

1. Insert the WordPerfect disk in the A drive.

2. From the C> prompt, create the subdirectory WP with the following DOS sequence.

```
CD\
MD WP
```

3. Change to the WP subdirectory and copy the WordPerfect files:

```
CD WP
COPY A:*.*
```

4. You can run with the data files on a floppy disk or on your hard disk. If you plan to work with your data files on a floppy disk, then do the preparation of DTN 5-4. However, you do not need the /S on the format nor do you need to copy the two files from the DOS disk. If you want your data on your hard disk, then replace the WordPerfect disk in the A drive with the data disk that accompanied this book. From the C> prompt, type the command:

```
COPY A:*.WP*
```

5. Replace the disk in the A drive with the Joe spreadsheet disk.

6. From the C> prompt, create the subdirectory JOE with the following DOS sequence.

```
CD\
MD JOE
```

7. Change to the JOE subdirectory and copy the JOE files:

```
CD JOE
COPY A:*.*
```

8. As with WordPerfect, if you intend to run with your data on a floppy disk, you should replace the JOE disk in the A drive with the data disk that accompanied this book. From the C> prompt, type the command:

```
COPY A:*.WKQ
```

When these operations are completed, you will have the word processing and spreadsheet software loaded onto your hard disk ready to begin.

PART TWO

Word Processing and Desktop Publishing

PROLOGUE TO PART TWO

The first of the productivity tools that you will learn about is word processing: using the computer to prepare printed documents. This part consists of four chapters. Chapter 6 provides a generic description of word processing and discusses the features found in most word processing programs. In Chapters 7 and 8 you will use the popular word processor WordPerfect. You will learn basic operations such as entering and editing a document, saving it to disk, and retrieving a previously saved document from disk (Chapter 7). You will also learn more advanced operations such as changing a document's appearance and rearranging text within the document (Chapter 8). In Chapter 9 you will learn about desktop publishing, a natural extension of word processing.

Chapter 6

Word Processing Concepts

OBJECTIVES

In Chapter 2, you learned that a word processor is a computer-based system that provides for the entry, storage, retrieval, modification, and printing of documents. This chapter describes some of the distinct features of word processing and provides the basis for detailed descriptions of using WordPerfect in the two chapters that follow. When you have completed this chapter, you should be able to describe:

- Entering, saving, and editing text.
- Controlling the appearance of a document through formatting commands.
- Moving text from one place to another in a document.
- Working with two documents at the same time.
- Automatically finding and changing text within a document.
- The concept of the codes inserted into the document to control the appearance of the document.

PREVIEW

The Need for Word Processing Capabilities

The microcomputer when combined with word processing software automates the tedious typing necessary to prepare accurate, neat, and attractive documents.

Preparing a Letter Using a Typewriter

The significant characteristic of a typewriter is that as each key is struck, the corresponding character is transferred directly to the page. Changes to the document (other than minor corrections) require that the entire document be retyped.

About Word Processors

In contrast to a typewriter, each keystroke results in something stored in the computer's memory. Through the keyboard and the screen display of the document in memory, you can make changes (without total retyping) and print hard copy.

Word Processor Capabilities

Word processing programs enable users to enter, save, and recall documents; make editing changes without reentering the entire document; move sections of a document from one place to another; search a document for a word or phrase; automatically change all occurrences of a word or phrase in a document; merge text from one document into another; and alter the appearance of a document without retyping.

Printing Capabilities of Word Processors

Word processing programs include a number of features to give a professional appearance to the document as it is printed.

Controlling the Word Processor

Actions of the word processor are controlled from the keyboard by commands entered by the user. These give the user the ability to perform operations ranging from saving the document to disk to changing the appearance of the document.

THE NEED FOR WORD PROCESSING CAPABILITIES

Preparing letters and other documents is not a task you might normally associate with the amazing processing speeds and number-crunching abilities of the computer. However, as you learned in Chapter 2, computer handling of the written word, or text, is another important application of the computer. The computer can streamline the tasks of text entry, storage, retrieval, modification, and printing in much the same way that it can streamline maintaining the financial records of a company. Word processing programs have placed the power of the microcomputer behind words, making it far easier for people to prepare and revise text than was possible with the typewriter. You as a student can prepare course papers and essays as well as a resumé. You as a business person can enter memos and letters directly into a word processor rather than writing them in longhand and then having them typed. Sales representatives who spend much time on the road can use portable microcomputers to prepare documents that are transmitted to the home office over telephone lines. The list of personal and business tasks made easier by word processors is endless.

The appearance of written communications prepared by a business or individual conveys an image (whether correct or not) of that business or individual. If your correspondence looks sloppy, the recipient is likely to feel that this reflects your expertise on the topic at hand. For instance, a student has to prepare essays and papers. No matter how good the content, if they are poorly presented, their appearance will produce a negative feeling on the part of the instructor who is doing the grading. A prospective employer will not be impressed with the person who does not take the effort to prepare a good-looking resumé. As a business person, your correspondence to people outside the company conveys a significant image of the company. Even the physical appearance of your memos within the company convey an image of you to your employees (or employers). As the owner of a business, it is critical that your catalogs and price lists be accurate and easy to read. A potential customer who receives a poorly prepared catalog might well conclude that the quality of your product will be the same.

These are all word processing tasks involving text entry, storage, retrieval, modification, and printing. They can be done using a word processing program on a microcomputer equipped with one or more disk drives and a printer. There are also special-purpose computers dedicated solely to word processing that range in size from units not much larger than a typewriter to large systems with numerous workstations; these are commonly referred to as word processors. However, the focus in this book is on word processing as done on the general-purpose microcomputer. As used in this book, the term *word processor* refers to word processing programs such as WordPerfect described in the next two chapters. Word processing system refers to the combination of word processing software and microcomputer hardware.

PREPARING A LETTER USING A TYPEWRITER

Let us begin the consideration of word processing by looking at the preparation of a document on a typewriter, the predecessor of the word processing system. Note that descriptions in this chapter should not be interpreted to imply that the typewriter is obsolete. There are still some applications for which the typewriter is well suited, such as filling out forms or addressing envelopes.

Planning the Letter

Assume that you have been working with an attorney to prepare a sales representative contract for MCT Enterprises. After reviewing her draft for the contract and comparing it with some sample contracts, you decide that three items should be added. To that end, you write her the letter shown in

```
MCT Enterprises
124 Burnett Ave.


Jane Harlett, Attorney at Law
1551 A Street
San Francisco, CA

Dear Ms. Harlett:

We have received your draft of the sales representative contract.
If you would include the following items, the contract will be
satisfactory.

OPTION OF COMPANY TO APPROVE ORDERS - COMPANY shall have the
option to accept or reject any order taken by Sales
Representative, and no commission shall be payable to Sales
Representative except on goods actually shipped by COMPANY and
received, accepted, and paid for by the purchaser.

DISCOUNT POLICY - COMPANY shall set all discount rates.  The
following discounts are agreed upon and shall remain in effect
for a period of not less than 180 days from the date of this
agreement.

        Standard Line     19%
        Stylist Line      22%
        Classic Line      24%

TERMINATION - This contract may be terminated by either party at
any time upon 30 days written notice to the other, or as provided
in Paragraph 1.

We appreciate your concern in assisting us.


Sincerely yours,
```

Figure 6-1
A finished letter ready to be signed and mailed.

Figure 6-1. Without the aid of a word processor, you might have written your draft of the letter in longhand, as shown in Figure 6-2. Note that the three contract items are to be inserted from another document.

Before beginning to type, the typist had to envision the general layout of the letter—its format—which depends upon several factors. Many typewriters, such as the IBM Selectric and those that use daisy wheels, can type at either 10 characters per inch (commonly referred to as pica) or at 12 characters per inch (commonly referred to as elite). A short note that will occupy only a portion of a page may look better using pica; a long document for which you wish to minimize the number of pages would be best in elite.

The typist must also select the margins, which depend upon the length of the document and the appearance that you desire. Typically, left and right margins range from 1 to 1½ inches wide. There are numerous other

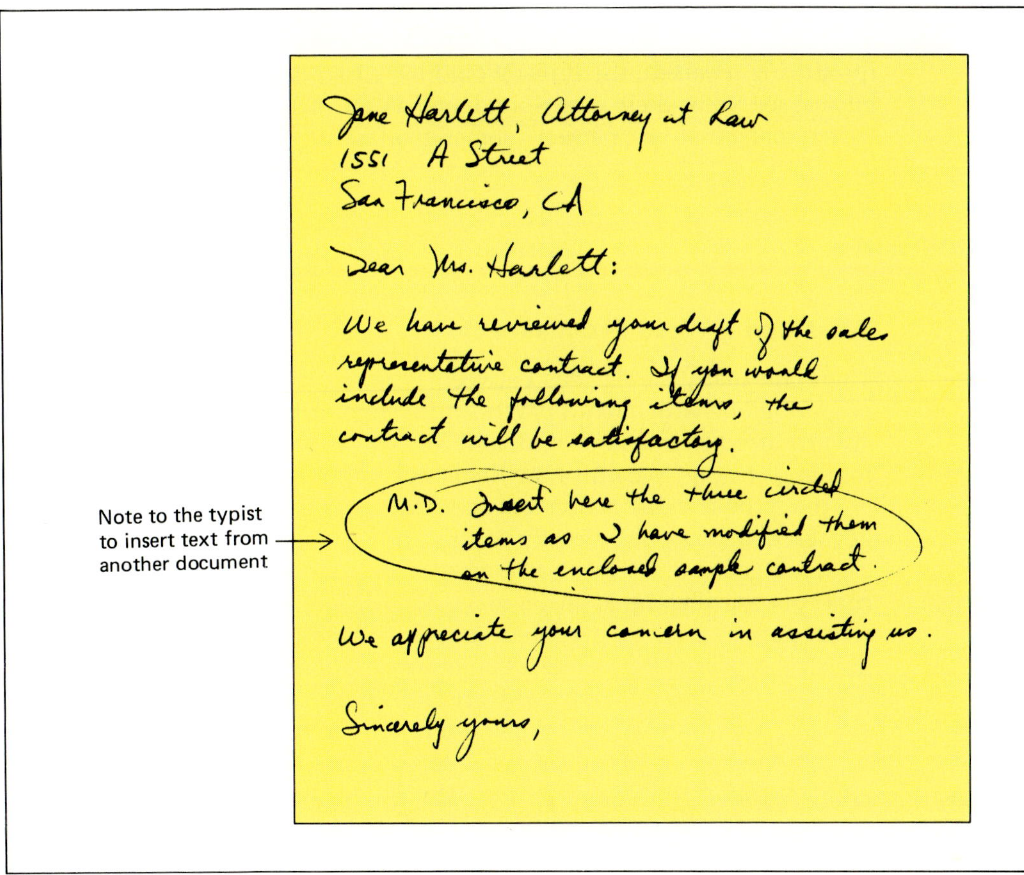

Jane Harlett, Attorney at Law
1551 A Street
San Francisco, CA

Dear Ms. Harlett:

We have reviewed your draft of the sales representative contract. If you would include the following items, the contract will be satisfactory.

N.B. Insert here the three circled items as I have modified them on the enclosed sample contract.

We appreciate your concern in assisting us.

Sincerely yours,

Figure 6-2
The handwritten original of the letter.

considerations. Tab stops must be positioned for paragraph indents, and for alignment of columns if a table is to be printed. If the document is to be proofread and marked for modification, then double spacing should be used rather than single spacing. All of these are factors that must be taken into account when preparing a letter such as that shown in Figure 6-1. Significantly, a word processor does not eliminate the need for this type of planning, but it makes changing much easier, as you will learn.

Typing the Letter

One of the nuisance factors when using a typewriter is the action required when the end of the line is near. As anyone knows who has ever used a typewriter, a bell tells the typist that a fixed number of spaces remain before reaching the right margin. A decision must be made regarding how much more can be typed on the current line. Although this may appear to be a minor factor, it reduces both speed and accuracy by diverting the attention of the typist from the copy.

The letter shown in Figure 6-1 is the final error-free version that will be signed and mailed. However, it is quite unlikely that it was the original typed copy. You may have had a draft copy typed (double-spaced) so that you could read it over and make needed changes. In typing the final copy, if a minor error were made, such as omitting the letters *na* in *terminated* (producing *termited*), the typist would have to retype again. Because many businesses view their correspondence as an indication of their abilities, letters that must be "perfect" sometimes are typed two or three times.

ABOUT WORD PROCESSORS

What Can a Word Processor Do?

There are many similarities between typing a letter on a typewriter and preparing one with a word processing system. In both cases, the characters are produced from a keyboard, and the person at the keyboard must make format decisions to control the final appearance of the document. However, the primary distinction between the two is that with a typewriter, keyboarded text goes directly to the printed page, but with a word processor, it goes into computer memory, where it can be manipulated. These concepts are illustrated in Figure 6-3. With a typewriter, the result is a typed page that, to be modified, must be retyped. With a word processor, the term **captured keystroke** is commonly used. This means that characters entered through the keyboard are stored in computer memory. Since entering and modifying are operations distinct from printing, a letter can be corrected and printed as many times as needed with little additional effort required to make it perfect. Without a doubt, the most significant characteristic of a word processor is that it allows changes to be made in a document without total retyping. These changes include the ability to perform the following actions with ease.

- Make editing changes.
- Reformat all or parts of the document.
- Move or copy sections of a document from one place to another.
- Insert a block of text into the current document from another stored on disk.
- Almost instantaneously find a word or phrase anywhere in a document.
- Automatically change all occurrences of a word or phrase in a document.
- Check the spelling of all words in the document upon command.

Viewing the Document on the Screen

The screens of microcomputers typically display twenty-four (or twenty-five) lines, 80 positions in width. Hence, whenever you are entering or editing (making changes to) a document of any length, you see only part of it. The standard way that this is handled by the computer is to retain the entire document in memory (or at least a large part of it for a very long one) and display that portion in which you are working. In this respect, the

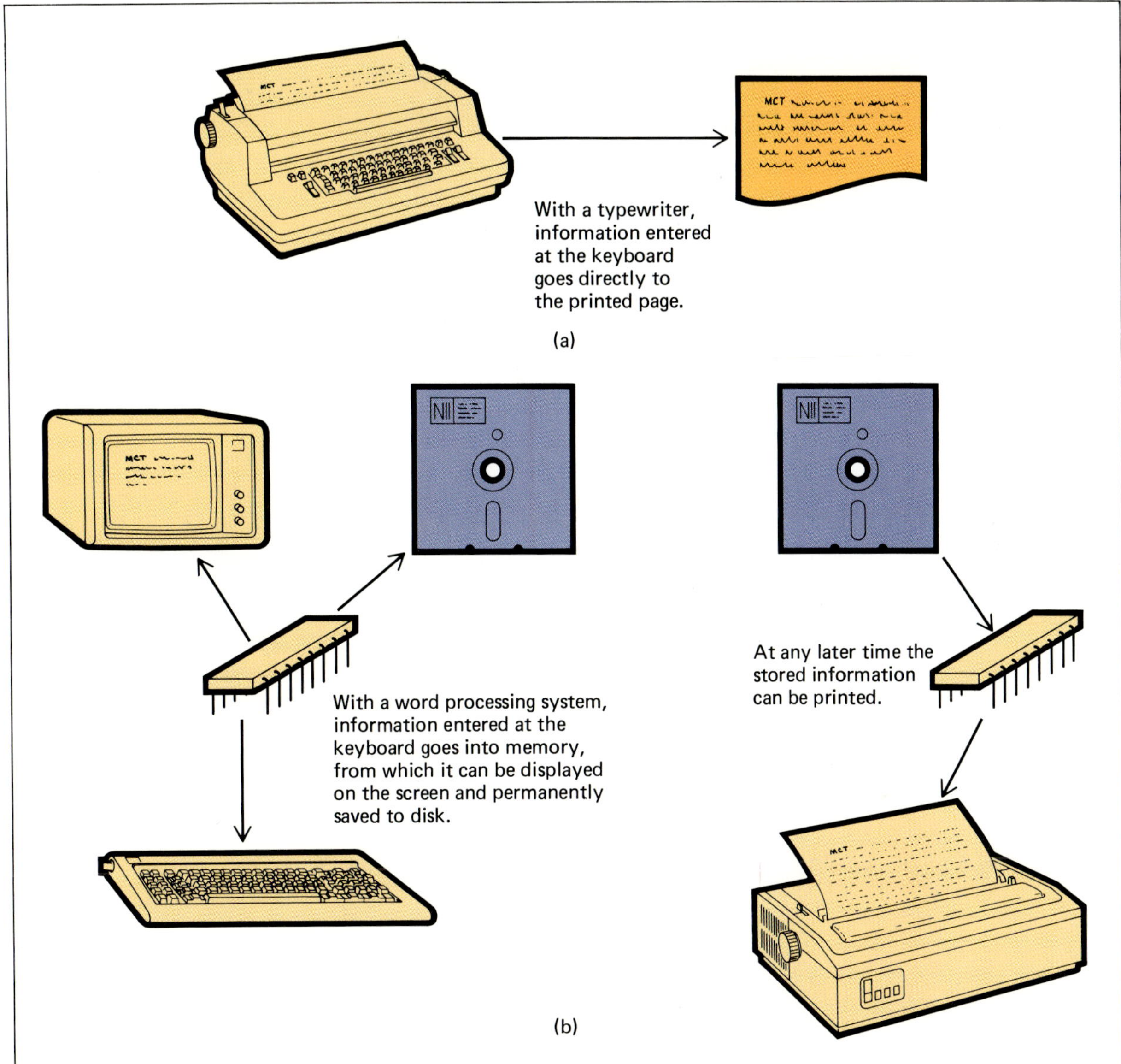

Figure 6-3
(a) Preparing a letter with a typewriter.
(b) Preparing a letter with a word processing system.

screen represents a view into the document as illustrated in Figure 6-4. Using appropriate keys on the keyboard, you can cause the text to scroll upward or downward to display a desired portion of the document.

As each change is made to a document, the screen display reflects it. For instance, if you change the margins, the document is immediately reformatted on the screen so that you see it in its latest form. One of the objectives of word processing software designers is to make the displayed form of a document as close in appearance to the final printed form as the monitor allows. This feature is commonly referred to as *what you see is what you get,* or **WYSIWYG** (pronounced "whizzy wig"). It is highly desirable because it makes it possible to do a maximum amount of work interactively by viewing the document on the screen.

Figure 6-4
Viewing a portion of the document in memory through the monitor screen.

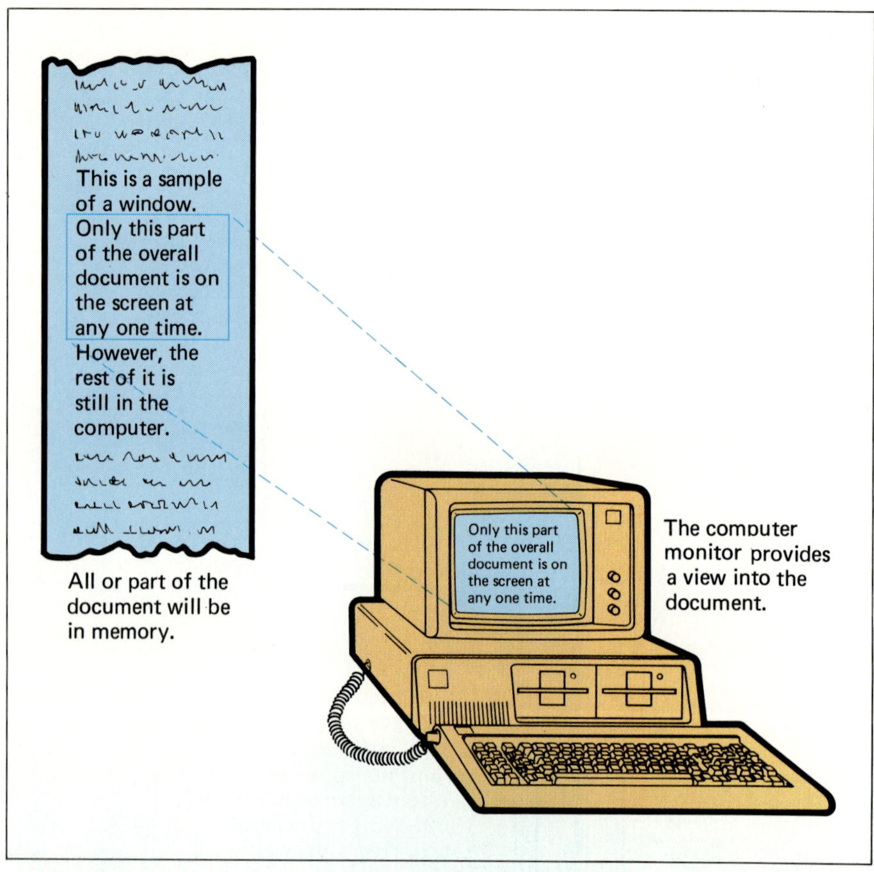

WORD PROCESSOR CAPABILITIES

Text Entry and Editing

One of the advantages of a word processor over a typewriter is that during text entry you can almost ignore the Enter (Return) key. As you type, the entered text is displayed on the current line. When the right margin is reached, the word processor program automatically takes the first word

People from all walks of life, including former President Jimmy Carter, find the computer and a word processor invaluable.

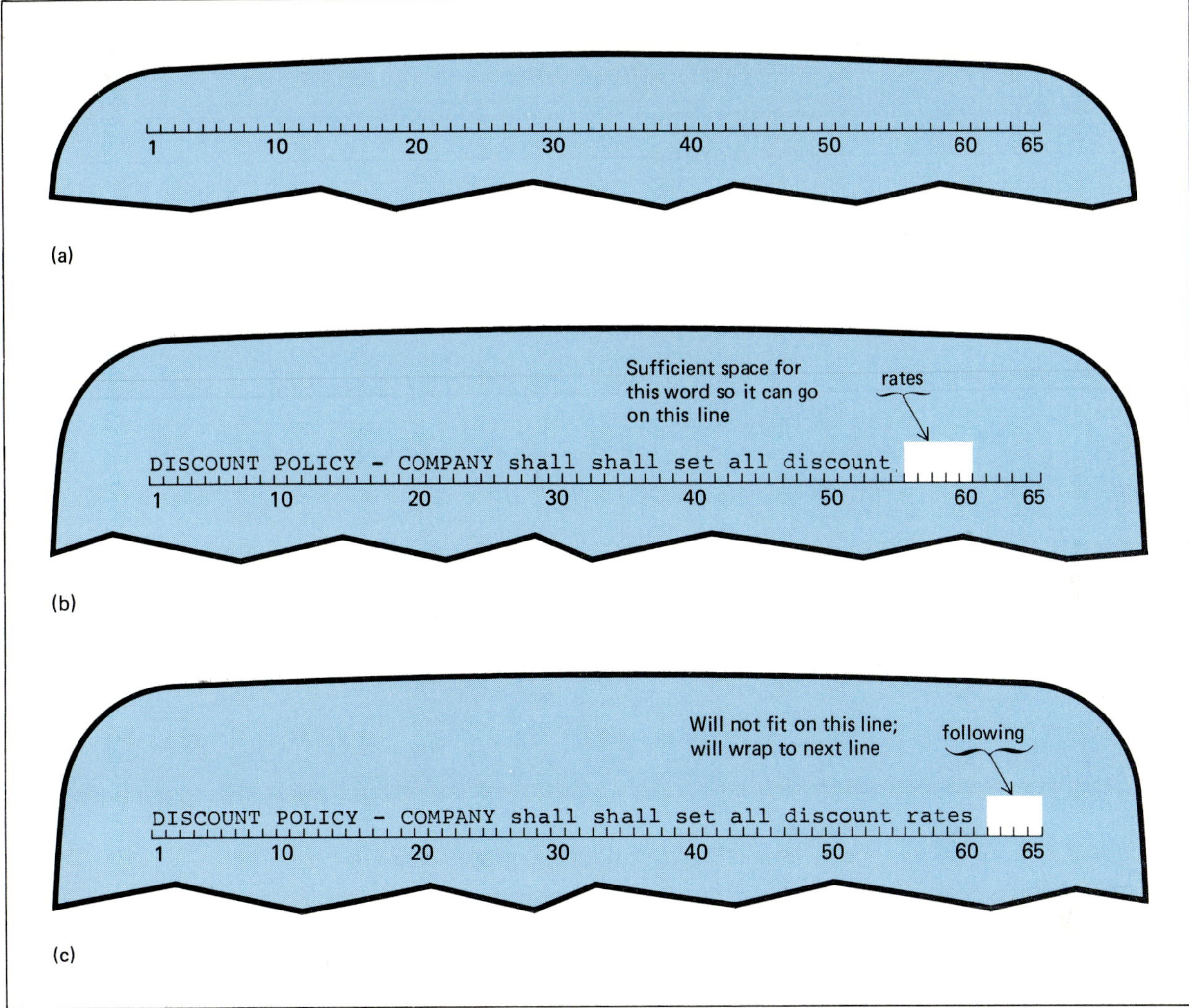

Figure 6-5
Automatic word wrap.

that overflows the line and moves it to the next line, as illustrated in Figure 6-5. This is called **word wrap;** it allows you to focus all of your attention on entering the document without the annoyance of noting the end of each line.

At any time, you may print the portion of the document you have entered or store it to disk. As you are entering, or at a later time, you can move the cursor to any point on the screen (or reposition the screen view into the document) and make insertions or deletions. The inserted (or deleted) text can be a single character, a word, a sentence, a paragraph, or any block of text that you specify. It is even possible to insert all or a portion of another document stored on disk.

Saving to and Retrieving from a Disk

Work on a word processing document is done with the document in main memory. At any time during the entry or editing process, the document can be saved to disk. If it is not saved before terminating the word processing program, the document will be lost. Once stored on disk, it can be retrieved for further entry or editing as necessary.

Format Control

Word processors give you broad control over document formatting. In fact, at any point during the entry of a document (or after entry has been completed), the format of any portion of the document can be changed with a few keystrokes, causing that portion of the document to be reformatted before your eyes. This includes such actions as changing the margins, changing tab settings, centering headings, and underscoring words.

For instance, you can specify that one or more lines be centered and the word processor automatically centers as the text is entered. To illustrate, the following heading might be keyed in as:

The Ocean Currents
Southern Hemisphere Study
by
James T. Kirk

However, the word processor would arrange it as follows:

The Ocean Currents
Southern Hemisphere Study
by
James T. Kirk

Cut and Paste and Boilerplate Insertion

How often have you written an essay or other document and decided to move a paragraph from one place to another? This is commonly referred to as **cut and paste,** taken from the manual operation of physically cutting a portion of a page and pasting it elsewhere (Figure 6-6). With a word processor, it is a simple matter to select a portion of a document by pinpointing the beginning and the ending of it and then to move it to some other place in the document.

In fact, the action of the typist in typing the handwritten letter of Figure 6-2 essentially involves a cut-and-paste type of operation: the three

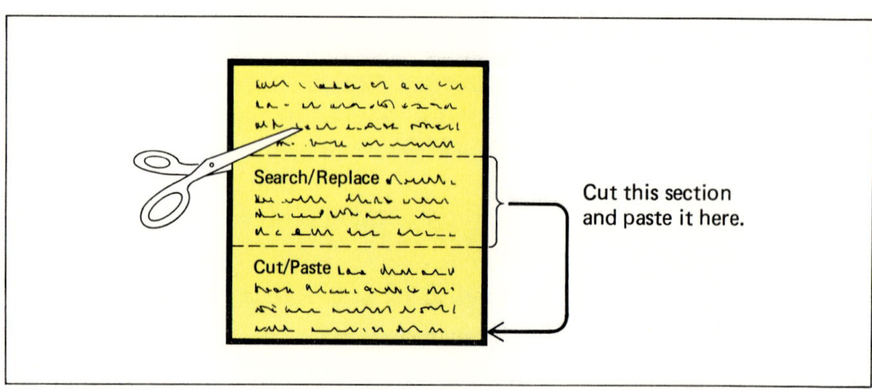

Figure 6-6
The concept of cut and paste.

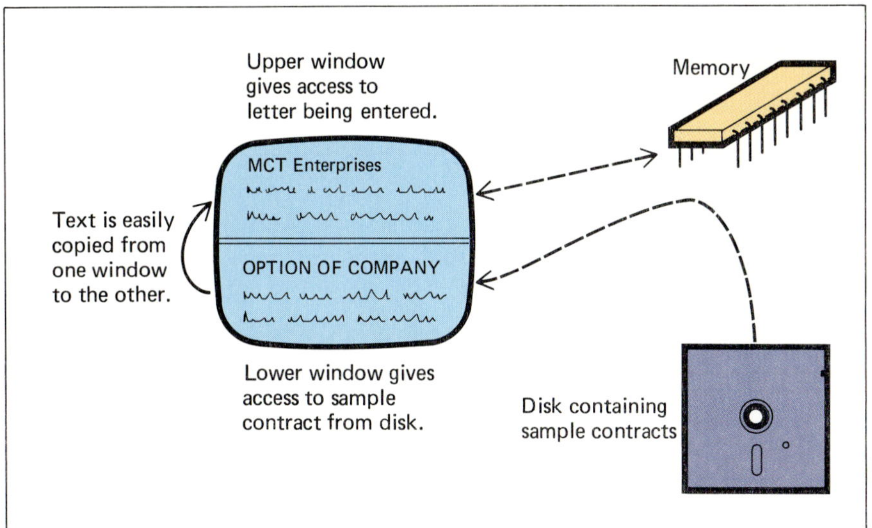

Figure 6-7
Using two windows.

legal items from another document must be "pasted" where indicated. A word processor offers considerable versatility in this respect. For instance, assume that you have copies of the sample contracts stored on disk. If you can copy the needed items from the sample contracts into your letter, then you need not retype them.

Most word processors allow you to split the screen into two parts, called **windows,** and to have access to two different documents at the same time. In Figure 6-7, the upper window is used for entering the letter and the lower window is used for displaying the desired sample contract. Moving or copying text from one window to another is as simple as the same action within a single document. Actually, the attorney probably prepared your contract draft by copying standard items, commonly called **boilerplate,** from her word processing files set up specifically for this type of use.

Search and Search/Replace

Assume that you have entered a very long report and have spelled an author's name Allyn. After working on the report for awhile, you realize that the correct spelling is Allen. However, you do not remember exactly where it was misspelled, so you must search from the beginning until you find it. For a large document, this could take a long time. With a word processor, the computer can do it in a matter of seconds, even for a very large document. This capability is appropriately called *searching* and leaves the cursor positioned at the point where the computer finds the name Allyn. Once the name is located, you can make the correction.

The **search and replace** action is a logical extension of the search in that it not only finds the designated characters, but also replaces them with a correction. For instance, assume that in the contract of Figure 6-1 you decide to change the word COMPANY everywhere it occurs to MCT. Using the search and replace, you could command the word processor to replace COMPANY with MCT for each occurrence. Replacement is not limited to a single word; a portion of a word or several words can be replaced with one or more characters as needed—for instance, the replacement could have been MCT Enterprises. Some word processors have a limit on the number of characters in a search operation but it usually is not very restrictive. Most include the ability to verify each replacement. That is, as each occurrence of the specified text is encountered, the operation temporarily stops. At that point, that portion of the document is displayed and the user is given the option to have the replacement take place or to leave that occurrence unchanged.

Spelling Checking and Other Aids

Most word processors include dictionary files and the capability to check the spelling of every word in a document. When a word is detected that does not match any word in the dictionary, the word processor can either flag it for later correction or allow the operator to make an immediate decision as to what to do. Some will display one or more words that might represent the correct spelling. For instance, if you typed the word *beleive*, the checker would offer *believe* as its "best guess" for the correct word. Needless to say, not all words are in the dictionary, especially abbreviations, proper names, and many technical words. To accommodate this, checkers allow you to add words of your own choosing.

How many times have you overworked a word in a document and searched for another word with the same meaning—a synonym? Not everyone has a thesaurus (a book of synonyms) on their desks that would solve the problem. However, many word processing programs include an electronic thesaurus that is activated by selecting the desired word in the text and entering the appropriate command. The computer displays a list of synonyms almost instantly, any of which can be selected to replace your offending word automatically.

The step beyond the relatively mechanical speller and thesaurus is the style checking program. Such programs check for improper syntax, poor usage, and other related items. However, since the English language does not adhere to hard, fast rules regarding style, this aid has limited value.

Here is a screen display of synonyms for a selected word. The user can even request the computer for synonyms of many of the words in this list.

```
honest=(a)                  honorable=(a)
 1    •ethical               1 A •ethical            •illustrious
      •honorable               B •honest             •venerable
      •moral                   C •scrupulous
      •trustworthy             D •upstanding      6  •estimable
      •upright                                       •respectable
      •virtuous              2 E •decent             •worthy
                               F •fair
 2    •candid                  G •right
      •forthright
      •frank                 3 H •dependable
      •sincere                 I •reliable
                               J •responsible
honest-(ant)
 3    •corrupt               4 K •constant
      •devious                 L •faithful
                               M •loyal

                             5 N •distinguished
1 Replace Word; 2 View Doc; 3 Look Up Word; 4 Clear Column: 0
```

PRINTING CAPABILITIES OF WORD PROCESSORS

Early microcomputer word processing programs were a far cry from being WYSIWYG. That is, much of the needed formatting was done as text was being sent to the printer. Even though, with each generation of software, the screen display becomes more and more like the actual printed copy, there are some variations between the screen display and the final printed form. There is even a variation from one word processor to another regarding the degree to which the screen display is like the printed page.

For example, in the letter of Figure 6-1 notice that the each line ends at a different position (depending upon the length of the last word); the right edge of a typed document is said to be ragged. Because of the ability of the computer to manipulate data, it is a relatively simple task to cause the computer to insert sufficient extra spaces between words so that each line ends on the right margin. This is called left and **right justification,** or simply **justification,** and is illustrated by the following samples.

```
This is a                          This    is    a
very simple                        very    simple
example of no                      example     of
justification                      justification
```

Most word processors, including WordPerfect, insert appropriate spaces to justify each line before sending it to the printer.

Other, more sophisticated features allow a standard heading to be included automatically at the top of each page; these are called **running heads.** For instance, at the top of each right-hand page of this book is the chapter title. If desired, the pages will also be numbered by the word processor. If a footnote is needed at the bottom of the page, the word processor, given the footnote, will leave sufficient space at the bottom of the page to insert the footnote where it belongs. These are all actions carried out by the word processor as text is sent to the printer for printing.

CONTROLLING THE WORD PROCESSOR

The Notion of Commands

In using an electric typewriter, almost all of the keystrokes result in text being printed on the paper. However, there are a few that cause some action to take place other than printing a character. For instance, striking the return key causes a new line to be begun; striking the tab key causes the printing element to skip to the next tab stop. We can think of these as keystrokes that cause a control action.

Word processors are the same except that there are many keystrokes and keystroke sequences that produce control functions. These are commonly called **commands** and must be entered to perform the variety of word processing operations described in the preceding sections. Some of the commands cause actions to take place, such as saving the document in memory to disk, printing the current document, searching for a text entry, or moving a section of text from one place to another. Others cause formatting actions to occur that change the appearance of the document on the screen.

Formatting Codes

One of the methods used by word processing designers for achieving desired format control is to include formatting commands directly in the text as they are entered. To illustrate, assume that you are writing a sales manual for your sales representatives, and to emphasize your point, you use the following (in which the second line is centered):

> . . . Always remember:
>
> Your Commissions Can Be Increased!
>
> The best approach . . .

Your actions when entering this line text would include:

- Upon completing the first line, strike the Enter key to force a new line, then strike it again for a blank line.
- Enter the command to center the line to be typed.
- Type the words *Your Commissions.*
- Enter the command to begin underscoring.
- Type the word *Can.*
- Enter the command to end underscoring.
- Type the rest of the line.
- Strike the Enter key twice for a new and a blank line.
- Resume typing.

Both the coded form of the commands and the text will be entered into memory, as illustrated in Figure 6-8. As each command key sequence is struck, the appropriate formatting code is entered into the string of text in memory. To display the text on the screen, the word processing program shows the effect of the codes rather than the codes themselves. When you make a format change in a document, the word processor changes the appropriate codes automatically. Hence, you are "insulated" from the actual memory codes themselves. In the characterization of Figure 6-8, the formatting codes are shown as letter codes enclosed in brackets. In reality, they would be special binary codes not used for normal character display.

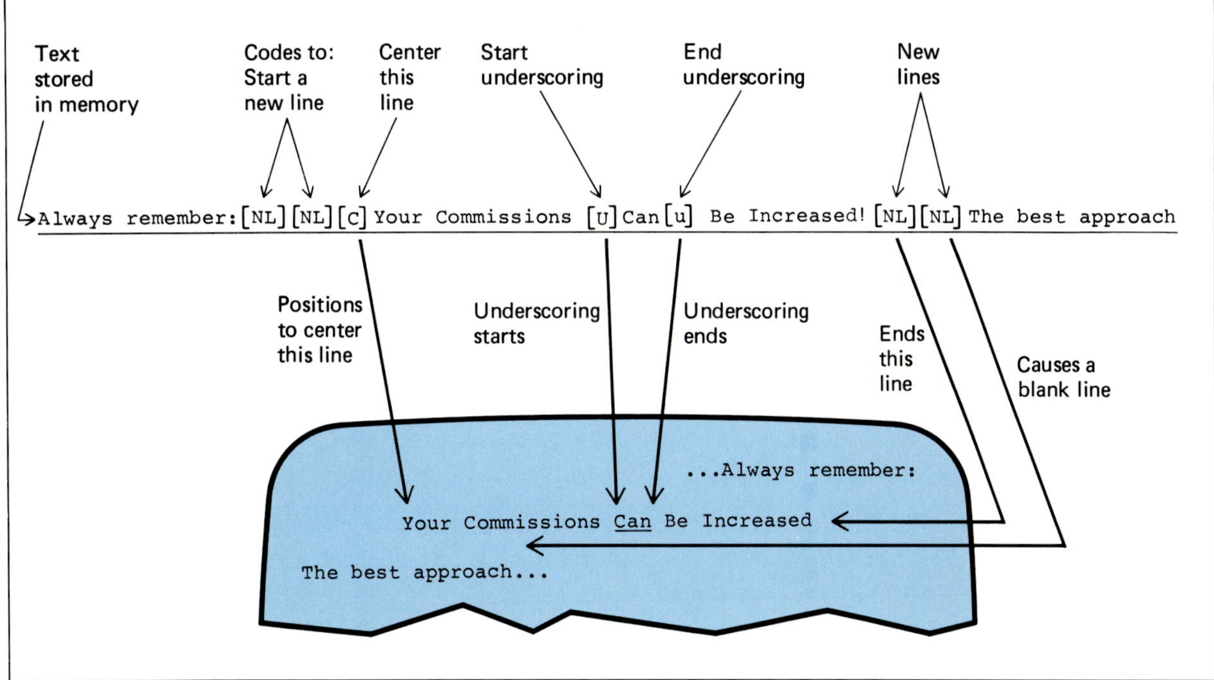

Figure 6-8
Formatting codes embedded in the text.

As described in Chapter 5, you can observe these codes by displaying the README.WP from the WordPerfect disk using the TYPE command.

SUMMARY

This chapter has provided you with a limited understanding of what a word processor is and how it works. The topics of this chapter will serve as the basis for a detailed description of using the word processing package WordPerfect. Summarizing, the important items from the chapter that will be explored in the next two chapters are:

- Document entry: Each keystroke is captured (retained in memory), thus allowing changes to be made without total retyping. As the right margin is reached when entering text, the word processor automatically begins a new line (word wrap).
- Screen editing: The cursor can be positioned anywhere in the document to make changes. These may involve the deletion of existing material or the insertion of new material.
- Format control: The appearance of the document is controlled by formatting commands that give the user the ability to do such things as change margins or tab settings. The results of these changes are immediately displayed on the screen.

- Cut and paste: Sections of text can easily be moved from one place to another in a document without retyping.
- Windows: The screen can be split into two parts, each of which may display a separate document.
- Searching: A particular word, phrase, or any combination of characters can be found within a text very quickly by the word processor.
- Search and replace: A designated combination of characters (for instance, a misspelled word) can be found and replaced with something else.
- Document storage: Documents can be saved to disk and retrieved at any later time as needed for printing or revising.

NEW TERMINOLOGY

The following are important new terms introduced in this chapter; you should be familiar with each of them.

boilerplate
captured keystroke
cut and paste
justification
right justification
search and replace
spelling checker
thesaurus
window
word wrap
WYSIWYG

REVIEW QUESTIONS

1. What are the variables that affect the appearance of a document?
2. What is meant by the term "captured keystrokes"?
3. What is the value of a word processor being "WYSIWYG"?
4. How does word wrap improve the efficiency of text entry with word processors over that of the typewriter?
5. Describe an example of cut and paste.
6. How can a word processor user examine a document that consists of many pages using only the twenty-four (or twenty-five) lines of display common to most monitors?
7. What is the value of using two windows when entering a document?
8. Distinguish between a spelling checker and a syntax checker.
9. After entering an essay on the ocean and tides, much to your embarrassment you notice that you have used the word *see* instead of *sea* throughout the

document. What word processing feature would you use to correct this? What precautions would you have to take in making the correction?

10. Regarding formatting codes, the text says that the user is "insulated" from the codes. What does this mean?

MATCHING

Match each term in a to h with the most appropriate description in 1 through 8.

a. cut and paste
b. format code
c. thesaurus
d. captured keystroke
e. window
f. justified
g. word wrap
h. pica

1. Makes it possible to have access to two separate documents at the same time.

2. Useful if you have overworked a particular word in a document.

3. Would be used to move a paragraph from one place in a document to another.

4. Automatically invoked in a word processor when the end of a line is reached.

5. A measure of the size of the characters printed on the page.

6. Controls the appearance of a document on the screen.

7. The alternative is a ragged margin.

8. Characteristic of a word processor because information is entered into the memory of a computer.

TRUE/FALSE

Determine whether each of the following is true or false.

_____ **1.** Captured keystroke relates to the notion that as each word is entered with a word processor, it is stored in the computer's memory.

_____ **2.** The characteristic that a word processor displays the text on the screen as it will look when printed on paper is called WYSIWYG.

_____ **3.** It is not possible to perform a cut-and-paste operation unless the word processor can divide the screen into two windows.

_____ **4.** A spelling checker would be unable to recognize as a spelling error the fact that you misspelled *their* as *there*.

_____ **5.** To justify a document means to insert sufficient spaces between words so that both the right and left margins are even.

_____ **6.** The purpose of a thesaurus is to check for poor usage within a document.

_____ **7.** If you had a document in which a phrase used several times had to be changed, you would use boilerplate.

______ **8.** Once a document is printed with a word processor, it must be entirely reentered from the keyboard.

______ **9.** One of the actions of word processor commands is to change the format of a document.

______ **10.** The codes entered into a document from a command are normally displayed on the screen.

ANSWERS TO OBJECTIVE QUESTIONS

Matching

1. e 2. c 3. a 4. g 5. h 6. b 7. f 8. d

True/False

1. T 2. T 3. F 4. T 5. T 6. F 7. F 8. F 9. T 10. F

Chapter 7

Using WordPerfect

OBJECTIVES

From Chapter 6, you learned how using the combination of word processing software and a computer makes document preparation more efficient than using a typewriter. That chapter provided you with a general knowledge of the nature of word processors and the basic operations of which they are capable. In this chapter, you will have the opportunity to use some of these features by learning to work with the popular word processor WordPerfect. When you have completed this chapter, you should be able to:

- Activate the WordPerfect program.
- Enter and make corrections to a document.
- Save the document to disk.
- Print a document.
- Retrieve a document from disk that was previously saved.
- Terminate execution of the WordPerfect program and return to DOS.

PREVIEW

Getting Started

The WordPerfect program is run from DOS; once running, control of the computer is given by DOS to WordPerfect. The screen display awaiting your text entry is called the edit screen.

Entering Text and Correcting Text

As you enter text into the edit screen, word wrap occurs as each line becomes full. During the process of text entry, you may make corrections and changes to the text you have entered.

Commands and the Function Keys

The function keys are used to issue commands to WordPerfect. These allow you to request actions such as printing a document and searching for a phrase, and to insert formatting codes.

Rewriting a Document

At any time while entering text, you can insert or delete characters at any point in your document. If you change your mind about a portion of text you have deleted, then you may restore it with the Undelete command.

Saving Documents

Documents that you enter from the edit screen are stored in memory (RAM), the "temporary" working area of the computer. The Save command allows you to save your documents to disk storage.

The Exit Command

You can conclude your WordPerfect work session or stop work on one document and begin work on another with the Exit command.

Retrieving a Document from Disk

Any document that you have previously saved to disk can be retrieved and placed in memory so that you can work on it further.

More on Moving the Cursor

You can use the keyboard arrow keys to move the cursor character by character or line by line within your document. Other keys allow quicker movement, including scrolling from one screen to the next.

Summary of Cursor Moves

This section includes a table summarizing all of the cursor movements.

Printing a Document

You can produce a printed copy of your document at any time during your work session by following a simple command sequence.

GETTING STARTED

This chapter is like Chapter 5 in that you need to read *and* do—that is, read the chapter or a portion of it first, then do all of the described actions for yourself at the computer. The hands-on exercises are emphasized with a DO THIS NOW designation: for instance, DO THIS NOW 7-3 is the third one in this chapter. In discussions within the text, it would be referred to as DTN 7-3. If you wish to try some hands-on tasks before finishing the entire chapter, read up to the section on hidden codes and then go to the computer.

When reading, do not attempt to memorize exact keystrokes necessary to carry out the different actions; simply learn about the actions. When you try them on the computer, things will fall into place much more quickly.

Before you can begin to enter a document with WordPerfect, you must load the WordPerfect program into the computer's memory. Once it is loaded, control of the computer switches from DOS to WordPerfect. Let us consider this loading start-up process and the WordPerfect screen from which you will be working.

About the Limited-Use Software That Accompanies This Book

This book includes a Limited-Use version of WordPerfect 4.2 that is identical to the commercial version except for a relatively few restrictions on its capabilities. Those restrictions that you are likely to encounter are described in a screen display when the Limited-Use version program is run. If you try to execute a command not operational in the Limited-Use version, WordPerfect notifies you. The purpose of this version is to provide you with a means for learning basic principles of word processing without the expense of the commercial version of the software. All examples in this and the next chapter can be run on either the Limited-Use or commercial version.

Running WordPerfect

To work with WordPerfect, you will need the WordPerfect disk that accompanies this book, a DOS disk for booting the computer, and a formatted data disk (the data disk that accompanies this book can be used). Note that the DOS and data disks are those that you should have prepared in Chapter 5.) To run WordPerfect, carry out the sequence of operations described in the boxes on the next page.

Floppy Disk Computer

1. Boot the computer with a DOS disk in the A drive.
2. Remove the DOS disk from the A drive and insert the WordPerfect disk.
3. Insert the data disk in the B drive.
4. From the A> prompt, change to the B drive as the default by typing

   A> B:

   and then striking the Enter key. The DOS prompt will then be:

   B>

5. The name of the WordPerfect program (located on the A drive) is WP; from the B prompt, type the following.

   B> A:WP

   Note that it is necessary to precede WP with A: in order to tell DOS to look on the A drive for the WordPerfect program.

Hard Disk Computer

Note: The following instructions assume that WordPerfect is stored in the subdirectory named WP as described in Chapter 5. If it is not, then you must modify these instructions accordingly.

1. Boot the computer from the hard disk (leave the door to the A drive open).
2. Change to the WP subdirectory by typing:

   C> CD\WP

3. From the C> prompt, change to the A drive as the default by typing

   C> A:

   and then striking the Enter key. The DOS prompt will then be:

   A>

4. The name of the WordPerfect program (located on the C drive) is WP; from the A: prompt, type the following.

   A> C:WP

   Note that it is necessary to precede WP with C: in order to tell DOS to look on the C drive for the WordPerfect program.

Whether you are using a floppy disk or hard disk computer, an announcement screen will be displayed describing restrictions of the Limited-Use version of WordPerfect. Striking the Enter key will cause this screen to be erased and the remainder of the WordPerfect program to be loaded into memory.

The WordPerfect Screen

Once you have loaded the WordPerfect program, your screen will be as shown in Figure 7-1. This is called the **edit screen** because it is the screen display from which you can enter and edit text. (As you shall learn, there are other screen displays from which other functions can be performed.) Note that the cursor is initially located in the upper left of the screen; as with DOS, it is the position into which text will be entered. The line at the bottom of the screen is called the **status line;** from the descriptions in

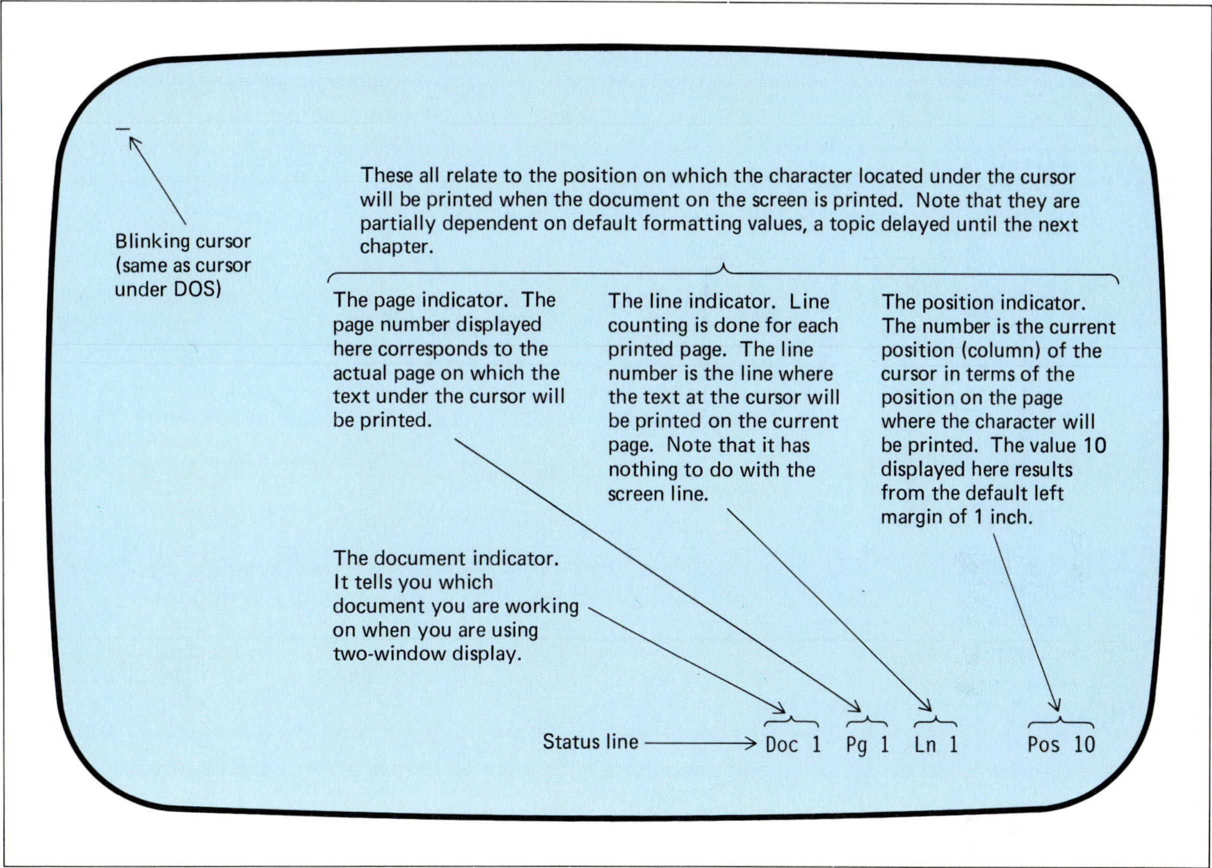

Figure 7-1
The empty WordPerfect screen.

Figure 7-1, you can see that the information provided relates to the eventual printed page.

The position indicator also conveys other information. That is, if the keyboard is in uppercase shift, then the Pos indicator is displayed in caps as POS. If the NumLock key has been struck thereby switching the arrow keys to numeric data keys, the Pos (or POS) indicator will be blinking on and off. Try this by pressing the Caps Lock key; notice how the letters *os* in Pos alternate between lowercase and uppercase each time the key is pressed. Then do the same with the NumLock key and notice how the position indicator alternates between blinking and not blinking.

As you will learn later in this chapter, the status line serves as somewhat of a message center to you from WordPerfect. For instance, if you enter the command to save the document on which you are working to disk, WordPerfect will respond with a prompt asking you the name of the document. Once the document is named, the name will be displayed on the status line.

Getting Out of Trouble

In Chapter 6, you learned that keystroke actions with a word processor are used both to enter text into the document (as with a typewriter) and to enter commands directing the word processor to take some action. For your first activity with WordPerfect, you will be entering text and hence will not be using commands. However, if you accidentally strike a key sequence that results in a command, you may cause WordPerfect to switch from accepting text to awaiting a response to a prompt. For instance, if you strike the F10 function key, the cursor will be moved to the bottom of the screen following the displayed prompt:

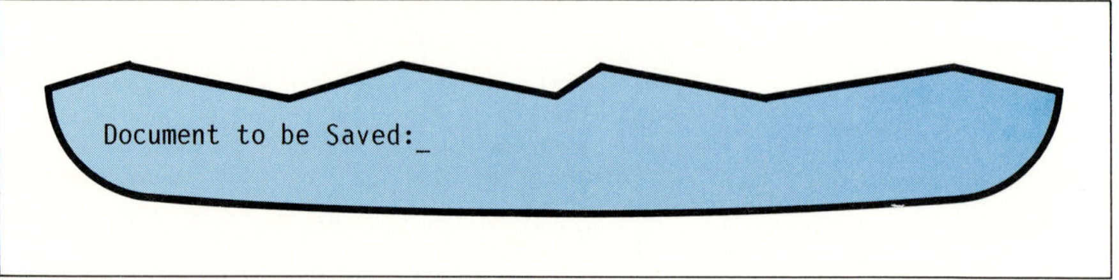

To get rid of this and return to text entry, simply strike the F1 function key. You should try this on your computer so that you recognize what takes place. Commands and their corresponding function keys are described later in this chapter.

ENTERING AND CORRECTING TEXT

Your First Document

Figure 7-2 is a memo that you will type into the computer as an exercise in learning about text entry and correction. As you type, do not be concerned

```
To:      Readers of this book
From:    The Author
Subject: WordPerfect

This memo will be used to illustrate some of the many basic
features of WordPerfect.  With it as an example, you will learn
how to enter a simple document (such as this) into the computer.
If you are anything like I am, then you will need immediate
assistance on how to make corrections.  As you will learn, the
operation of correcting spelling and otherer errors is almost as
easy as making them in the first place.  You will learn how to
insert text, and delete text, and move text, and search for text,
and...

Although this chapter only scratches the surface of the things
that can be done with WordPerfect, there are some advanced topics
in the next chapter.  One of them involves breaking the screen
into two parts and viewing two different documents.  You will
even be able to move a portion of one of the documents into the
other with a few keystrokes.  Actually, the process is so simple
that it seems strange to classify it as an "advanced topic."  I
will leave that for you to decide.
```

Figure 7-2
The document to be entered.

about entering it perfectly. (In fact, be certain to type the word *otherer* as it is misspelled in the sixth line.) One of the strong points of word processors is the ease with which errors can be corrected.

DO THIS NOW 7-1 **Enter the memo of Figure 7-2.**

1. If you have not already done so, run WordPerfect to obtain the edit screen of Figure 7-1.
2. Using the keyboard in much the same way that you use a typewriter, type in the first few lines as shown in Figure 7-3. Note that each line is ended by striking Enter. Do not worry if you make mistakes while typing, because the next thing you will learn is how to correct them.

Figure 7-3
Entering text.

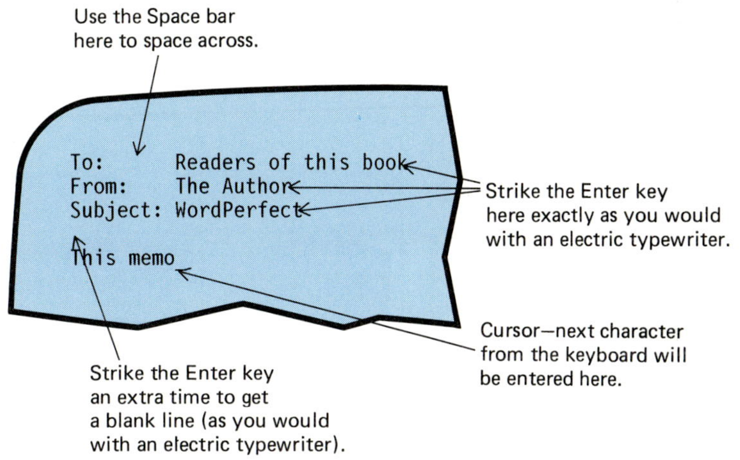

3. Continue typing the first sentence; remember not to strike the Enter key at the end of the line. As you near the end of the first line, observe how WordPerfect uses word wrap by automatically starting a new line. As shown in Figure 7-4(a), the first five letters of the word *features* will be at the right margin. Note that the cursor is to the immediate right of the last letter typed. What you do not see on the screen is that the line is full and that no characters can be entered beyond the "invisible" right margin.
4. Type the letter *r*. The moment you do this, WordPerfect moves this word to the next line, as shown in Figure 7-4(b), because no characters can be typed beyond the margin.
5. Type the rest of the first paragraph.
6. Tell WordPerfect that you want to start a new paragraph by striking Enter to force a new line (as was done in typing the first three lines in Figure 7-3).

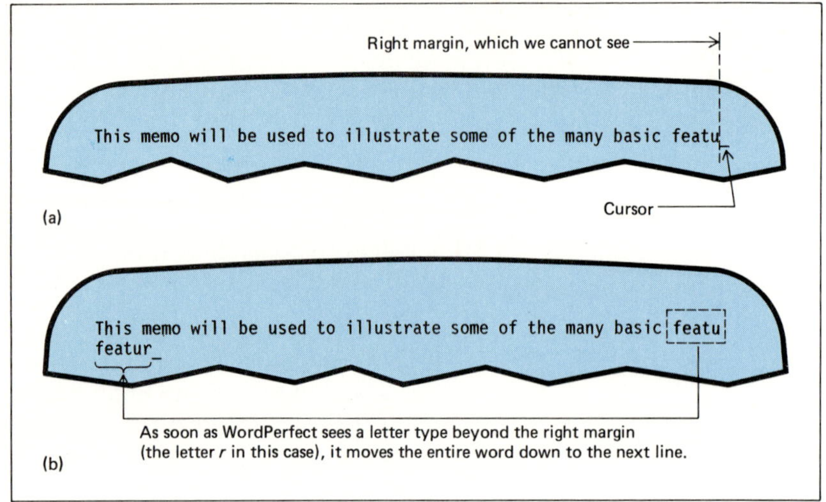

Figure 7-4
Entering text with word wrap.

7. Force a blank line between paragraphs by striking Enter a second time as shown in Figure 7-5.

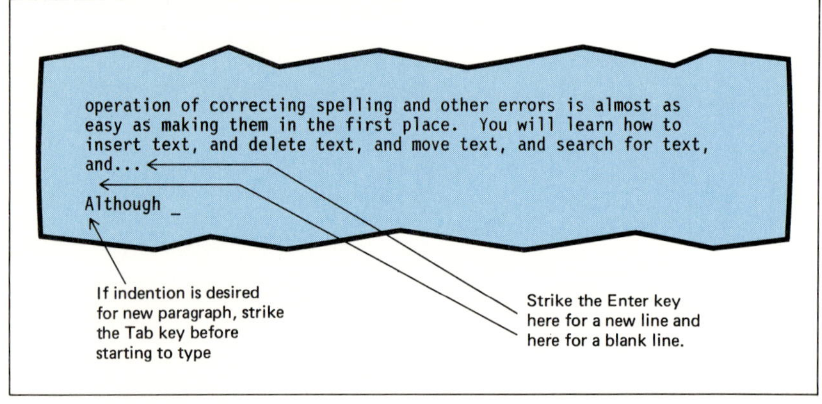

Figure 7-5
Beginning a new paragraph.

8. Type the second paragraph. If you wish to indent this paragraph, then strike the Tab key before beginning typing on the new line (preceding the word Although). If you do indent, your copy of the document will be slightly different from that of Figure 7-2.

In this exercise, you have used the default values for margins and tab settings (you will learn how to change margins in the next chapter). Each time you strike the Tab key, the cursor jumps to previously identified positions called tab stops. The default tab stop settings are positioned every five positions so that each time the Tab key is struck, the cursor moves right five positions.

Making Corrections While Typing

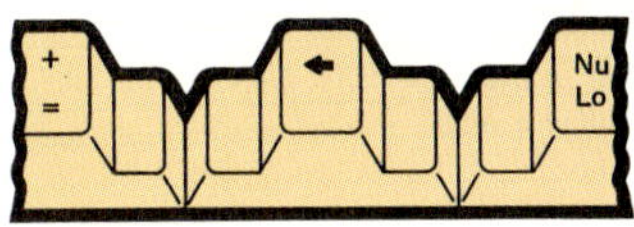

The backspace key.

Often when typing you will realize immediately when you have struck one or more incorrect keys. If so, you can use the Backspace key to delete the incorrect characters and then resume typing. Note that it is located in the upper right corner of the main part of the keyboard. On some keyboards, it is imprinted with the word Backspace.

To illustrate using the Backspace, assume that you misplaced your hand and hit the wrong keys while typing the word *example* as shown in Figure 7-6(a). With your completed document on the screen, begin a new paragraph and type two lines exactly as in Figure 7-6(a). Do not worry about them being a duplicate of the first two lines; you will delete them when finished.

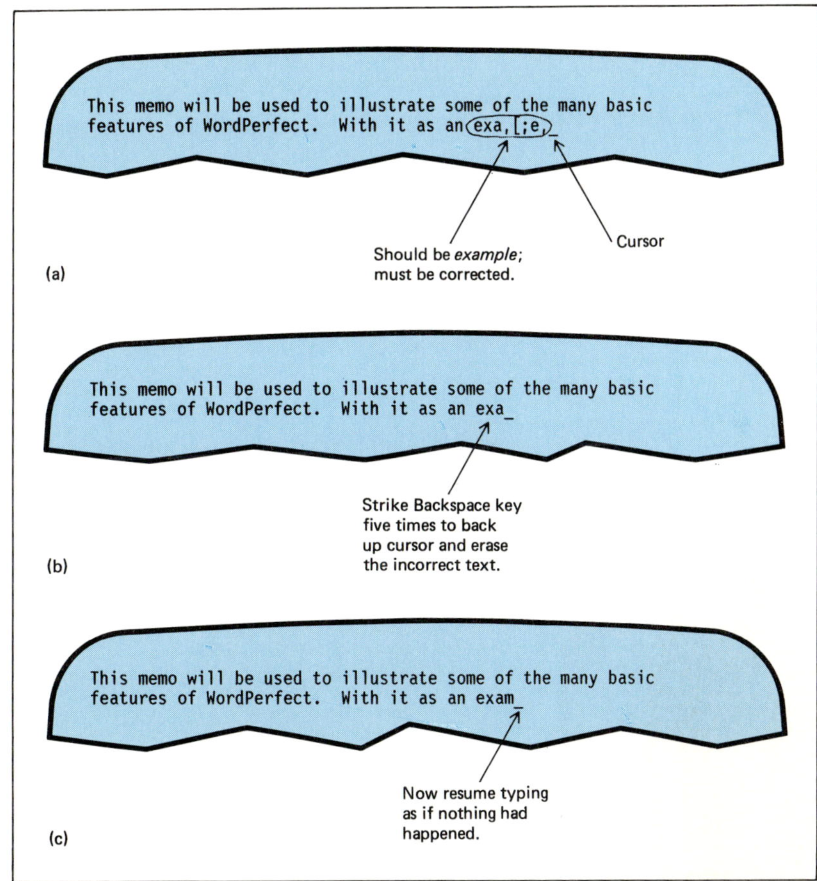

Figure 7-6
(a) Incorrect text that must be corrected.
(b) Deleting the incorrect entries.
(c) Resuming typing of the document.

DO THIS NOW 7-2 **Using the Backspace**

1. Strike the Backspace key five times; your screen will be as in Figure 7-6(b).
2. Resume typing as if you had made no error [Figure 7-6(c)].

3. You no longer need the two lines you entered from this exercise, so hold down the Backspace key and watch the characters to the left of it disappear. If you accidentally delete part of the preceding paragraph, then reenter it.

Positioning the Cursor and Correcting Typographical Errors

You will find that making corrections as in Figure 7-6 is convenient if you notice the error immediately. However, what happens if you notice the error upon proofreading after entering more text as shown in Figure 7-7(a)? Since the cursor defines the position at which characters are entered or deletions made, it must be repositioned to the portion of the text that requires correction. You can do this using combinations of the cursor movement•keys. Each time you strike one of them, the cursor moves up or down one line or left or right one character, as indicated by the direction of the arrow. (Note: The enhanced keyboard includes a separate set of cursor movement keys.) If you hold an arrow key down, then you invoke the automatic repeat and the cursor moves continuously. In Figure 7-7(a), the letters *er* must be deleted from the word *otherer.*

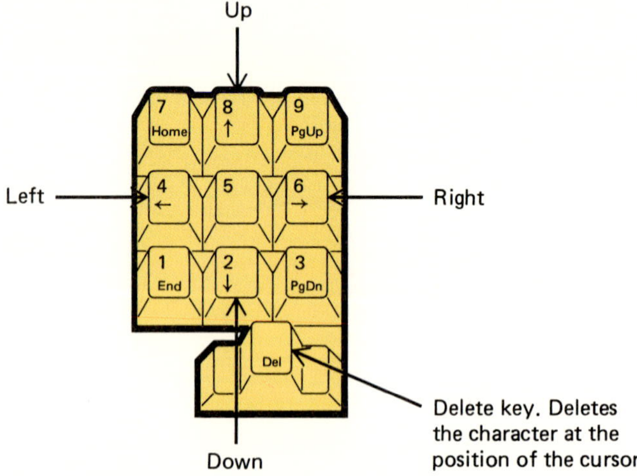

The cursor keys.

Figure 7-7
(a) An error to be corrected.
(b) Move the cursor to the incorrect entry.
(c) Strike the Del key to delete the character at the cursor.

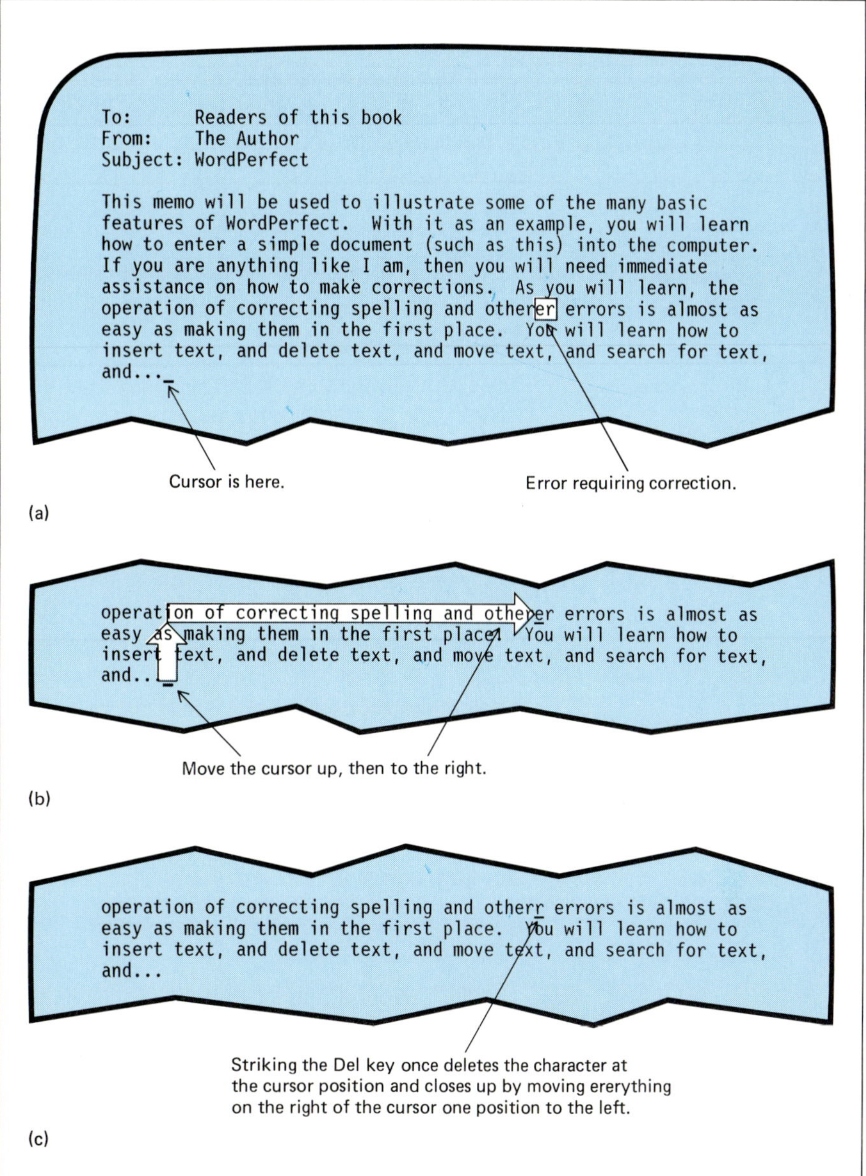

DO THIS NOW 7-3 **Cursor Repositioning for Correcting**

1. Move the cursor up (using the Up arrow key) to the desired line.
2. Move right (using the Right arrow key) to the first character to be deleted [see Figure 7-7(b)].
3. Delete the unwanted characters by striking the Del (Delete) key twice. Note that as each character is erased, everything that was to the right of it is moved left one position to fill the gap—see Figure 7-7(c).

At this point, you may move the cursor to some other point for additional corrections or back to the end of the document to resume text entry.

From the two examples of erasing characters, notice that you can use either the Backspace key or the Del key. Although the Backspace erases the character to the left of the cursor and the Del erases the character at the cursor position, they both produce the same result.

COMMANDS AND THE FUNCTION KEYS

Entering Commands

Now that you know how to enter text and make minor corrections, you need to learn about using commands,* the keystroke actions that allow you to control WordPerfect. Remember from Chapter 6 that there are two categories of commands: those that cause an action to take place, such as saving a document to disk, and those that cause the appearance of the document to change, such as changing the margin settings. In WordPerfect, these commands are entered using the function keys F1 through F10 in conjunction with the Shift, Ctrl, and Alt keys (see the keyboard layouts of Figure 5-1). With these, you can perform such actions as:

Command	Key Sequence
Save a document	F10
Center a line	Shift-F6
Replace a word	Alt-F2

You invoke the command to save a document by striking the F10 function key. In contrast, you invoke the command to center a line by striking the F6 function key while you are holding down the Shift key. This action is represented as:

Shift-F6

Some other keystroke actions require you to strike one key and release it, and then strike another. For instance, striking the Home key and then the left arrow key positions the cursor at the beginning of the current line. This action is represented as:

Home,Left

*If you are using the commercial version of WordPerfect and have access to the WordPerfect reference manual, you should be aware of a difference in terminology in this book and in the manual regarding the word *command*. For instance, to initiate a search and replace action, this book will refer to the *replace command* whereas the manual will refer to the *replace key*. The latter can be confusing because it involves a key sequence rather than a single key. However, they both mean the same thing.

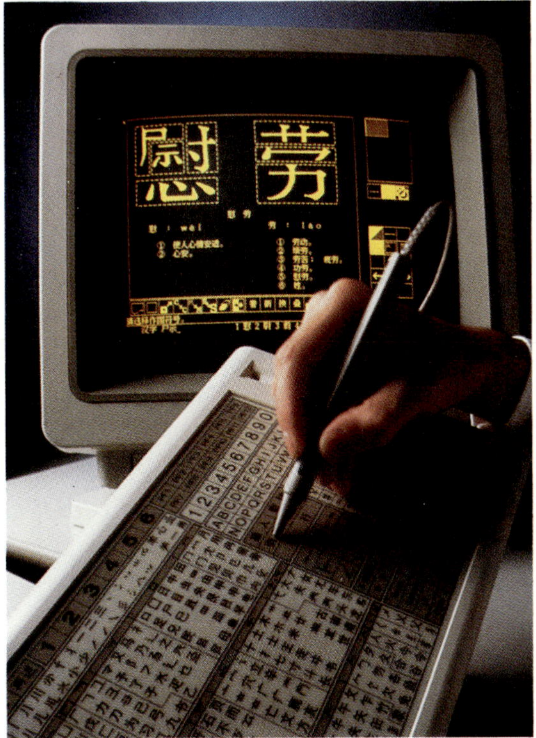

Word processing systems have been developed for languages such as Chinese, which have many more symbols than the twenty-six letters of our alphabet.

Remember, a keying action in which the keys are separated by a hyphen means to hold down the first key and strike the second. A keying action in which the keys are separated by a comma means to strike the first key and release it, and then strike the second. Do not type either the hyphen or the comma.

The Function Key Template

In combination with the Shift, Ctrl, and Alt keys, the ten function keys provide you with forty different commands. As it is difficult to remember all of these combinations (especially when beginning), you may find the function key template included with WordPerfect very useful. This template, which fits over the function keys as shown in Figure 7-8, uses color coding to designate whether to use the Shift, Ctrl, Alt, or no key in conjunction with the particular function key. For instance, commands invoked by the F2 key are:

Color	Key sequence	Command
Red	Ctrl-F2	Spell
Green	Shift-F2	<-Search
Blue	Alt-F2	Replace
Black	F2	->Search

Figure 7-8
The function key template.

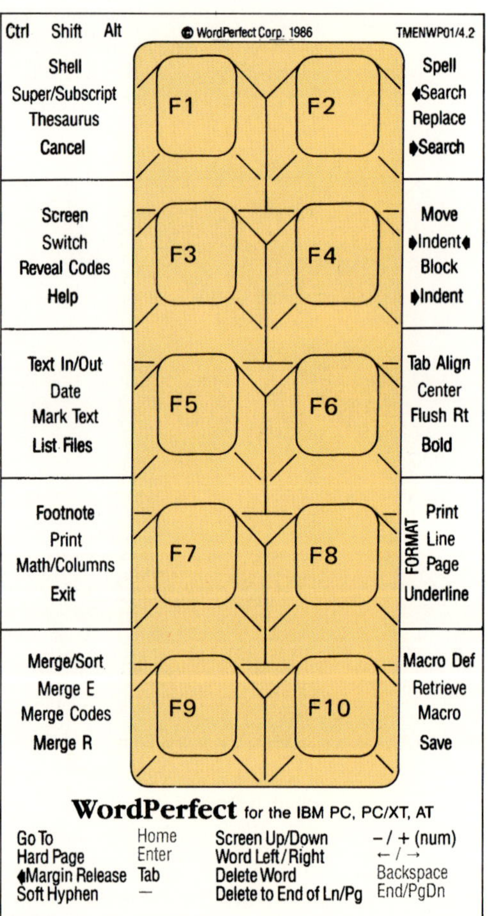

If you misplace the template or find it inconvenient to use, you can use the Help command (F3), which displays the layout on the screen. You should invoke the Help command (by striking F3) and you will see that the screen display of your document is replaced by the Help screen of Figure 7-9. At first glance, this tends to be confusing but notice that the four entries for each of the function keys are identical to the template of Figure 7-8, that is:

Entry	Case	Keystrokes
First	Upper/lowercase	Ctrl + Function key
Second	Uppercase	Shift + Function key
Third	Upper/lowercase with underscore (highlighted with color monitors)	Alt + Function key
Fourth	Upper/lowercase	Function key alone

Figure 7-9
Screen display of the function key template; obtained by striking the F3 key.

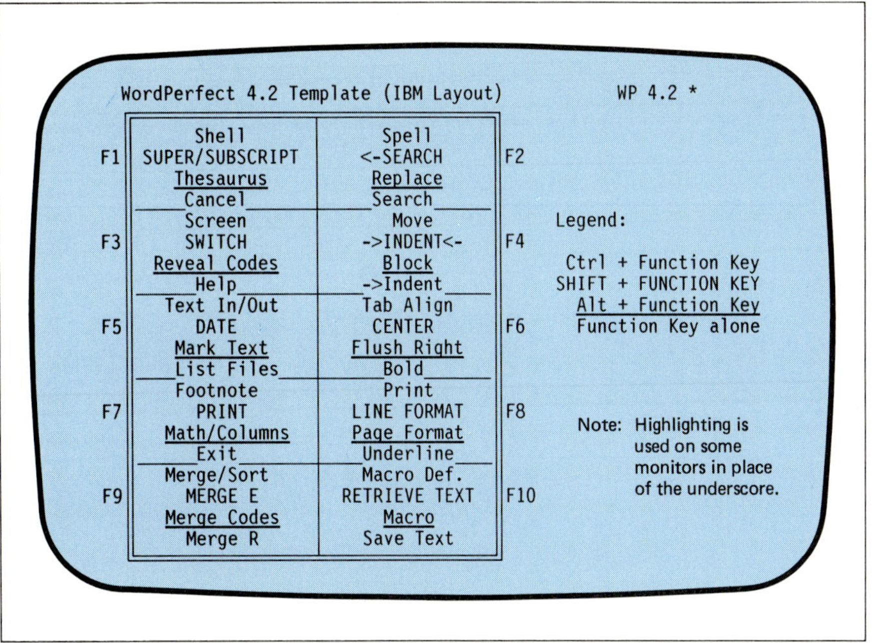

When ready to return to the edit screen, simply strike any key on the keyboard and the Help screen will disappear. As you start using more of the features of WordPerfect, you will find the function key template very useful.

The Cancel Key

At the beginning of this chapter, you were told that if you accidentally pressed a command key sequence and were unable to continue typing text, you should strike the F1 key. This invokes the Cancel command, which causes the preceding action to be canceled. (WordPerfect refers to it as the Cancel key.) For instance, if you pressed the F2 function key, the following prompt would be displayed on the status line.

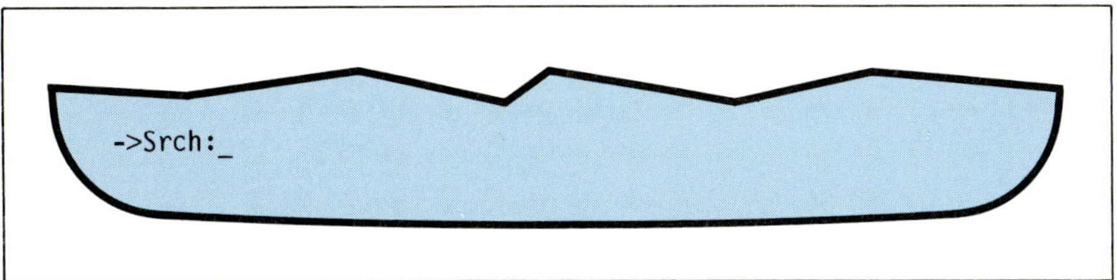

At this point, the cursor is positioned after the prompt and WordPerfect has stopped and is awaiting your entry. It will continue only when an appropriate response is entered to this prompt or else the command is canceled. Since this is not an action you wish to perform, you may cancel it by striking the F1 key. The prompt will disappear and control will be returned to the edit screen.

REWRITING A DOCUMENT

One of the features of word processors is the ease with which you can make changes, whether they are correcting minor typographical errors or are making major changes to improve the message of the document. For instance, upon rereading the memo, assume that you decide to make the changes shown in Figure 7-10. Note that you must perform two tasks: insert a phrase and delete three words.

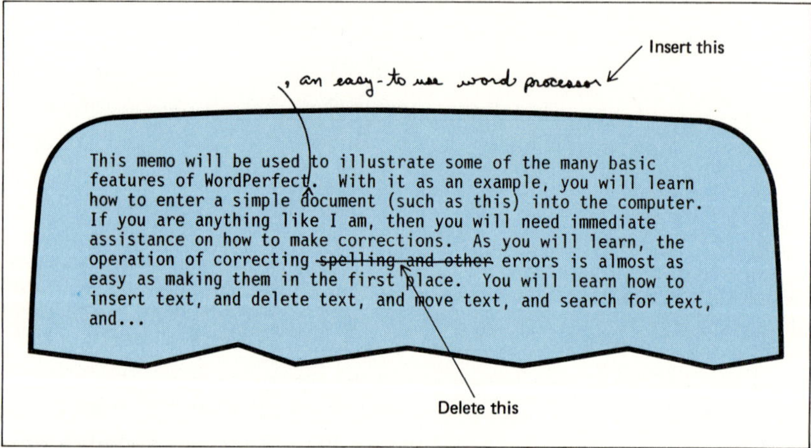

Figure 7-10
Portion of memo to be edited.

Inserting Text

First, let us consider inserting the desired phrase.

DO THIS NOW 7-4 **Insertion**

1. Position the cursor (using the arrow keys) on the period following the word *WordPerfect* in the second line. This is the position at which you will begin typing.
2. Type the needed phrase in exactly the same way you would type any text. As you enter each character, WordPerfect inserts it at the position of the cursor and pushes the remaining text on that line to the right.

If you have done this correctly, your screen will look like that in Figure 7-11. As you typed, you probably noticed that the last portion of that line disappeared off the edge of the screen. The reason for this is that WordPerfect performs the word wrap operation only when the cursor reaches the right margin, or when the cursor is moved to another line if a situation such as that in Figure 7-11 occurs. Hence, you should move the cursor down to the next line (Down arrow key) and observe the screen being redisplayed conforming to the default right margin.

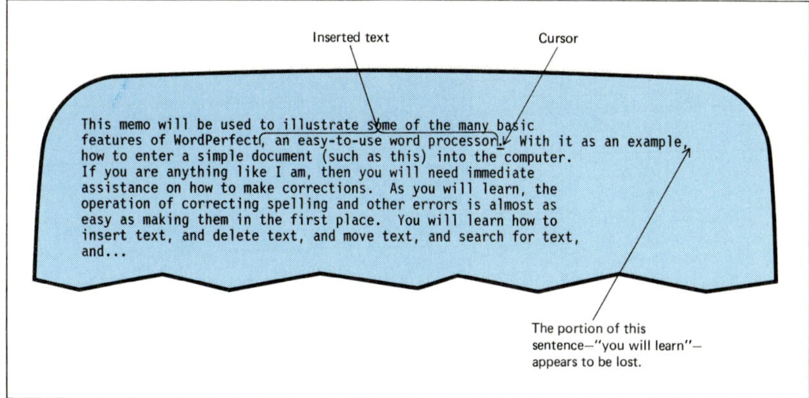

Figure 7-11
The document after insertion has been made.

In this example, you inserted text, thereby making the line longer. In some situations, you will want each new character to replace the character at the cursor. This is called **typeover.** You can switch from the insert mode to the typeover mode (and back again) by striking the Ins (Insert) key. As a simple illustration, assume you decide to change the word *memo* to *note.* To make this correction using typeover, you would:

DO THIS NOW 7-5 **Typeover**

1. Move the cursor to the letter *m* in *memo.*
2. Strike the Ins (Insert) key. The status line will tell you that WordPerfect is in the typeover mode by displaying Typeover at the lower left of the screen.
3. Type the word *note;* each letter will replace the corresponding letter of *memo.*
4. Strike the Ins key again to get out of the typeover mode.

Note that like the CapsLock key, the Insert key functions as a toggle. After making this change, change note back to memo.

Deleting More Than a Single Character

Referring to Figure 7-11, your next action is to delete the three words *spelling and other.* (You should have noticed that these were moved to the beginning of the sixth line when you performed the insertion operation.) Although you can delete these words one character at a time using either the Backspace or Delete key (automatic repeat works with them), WordPerfect provides other options for situations in which more than a few letters are to be deleted. For instance, whereas Backspace erases a single character, Ctrl-Backspace erases an entire word.

DO THIS NOW 7-6 **Deleting Words**

1. To delete the word *spelling* move the cursor so that it is positioned anywhere within the word or in the space following the word.
2. Enter the Ctrl–Backspace to delete the entire word. You will see the word deleted and the remaining text in that line moved left so that the letter *a* in the word *and* is at the cursor position.
3. Enter the Ctrl–Backspace sequence twice more to delete the other two words. When you are finished, the screen will appear as shown in Figure 7-12.

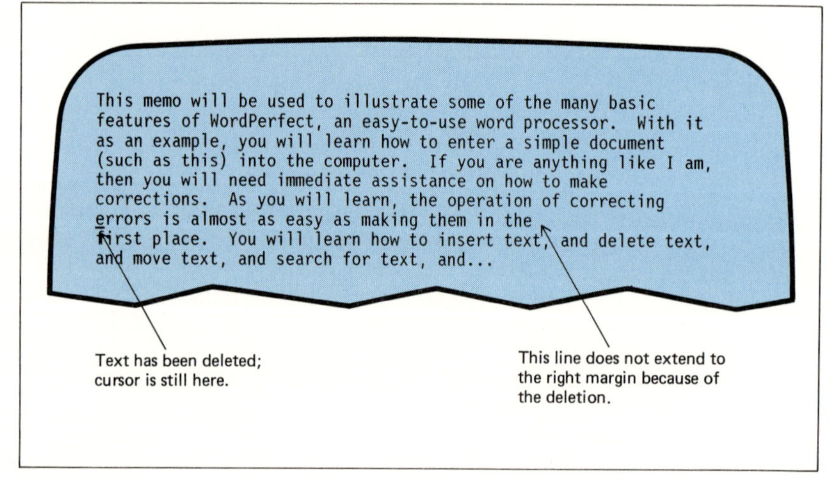

Figure 7-12
The document after deleting three words.

As with insertion, WordPerfect does not reformat paragraphs until the operation is completed (by moving the cursor to another line). Hence, the line from which the words were deleted is short. However, you need only move the cursor to another line to cause WordPerfect to reformat the display according to the default margin settings.

There are two other delete operations you can use to delete larger amounts of text. Ctrl-End deletes all text from the position of the cursor to the end of the current line. Ctrl-PgDn deletes all text from the cursor to the end of the current page. Note that this is the page as defined by the printer page size, not the screen display. Because this can be a large amount of text, WordPerfect prompts you for a confirmation before proceeding with the deletion. However, do not try it yet because the topic of the next section is how to restore text that has been deleted when you change your mind.

Undelete

Sometimes, when editing a document, you will delete a portion of text, and then change your mind and want it back. One feature of most word processors, including WordPerfect, is that deleted text is not discarded immediately and can be restored. To illustrate, assume that you have changed your mind about the previously deleted three words *(spelling and other)* and you want them back.

DO THIS NOW 7-7 **Undeleting**

1. If you moved the cursor, the first thing to do is to move it back to the point at which the deleted text is to be restored. In this example, it would be as shown in Figure 17-12.
2. Strike the F1 key and the text will be inserted and highlighted as shown in Figure 7-13.

Figure 7-13
Restoring deleted text.

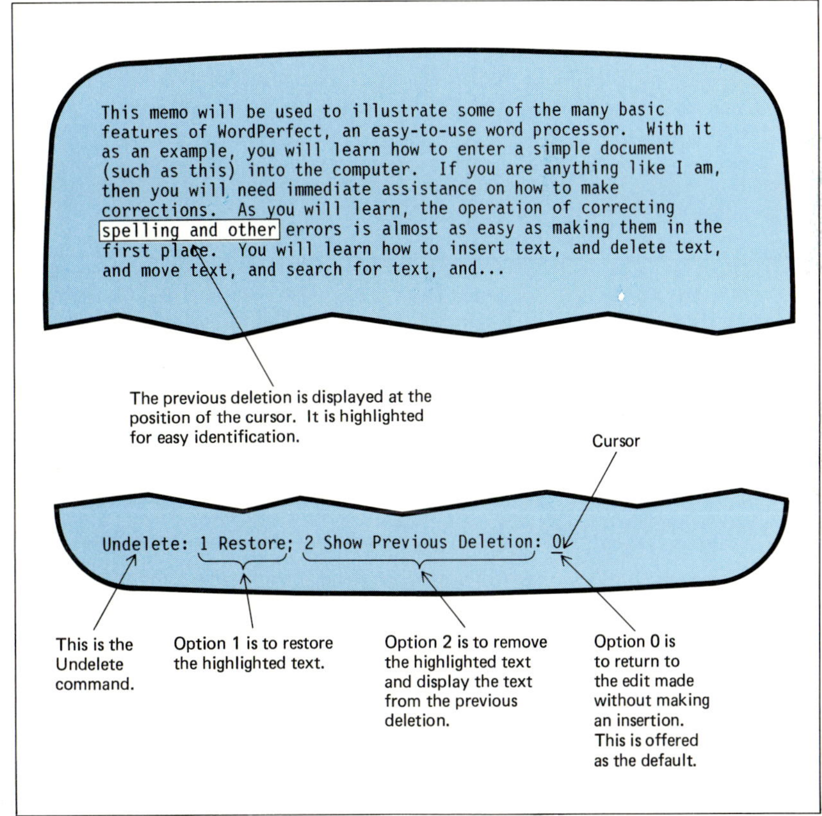

3. Type the digit 1 to restore the deleted text to the document. The highlight will disappear and control is returned to the edit screen.

When you use Undelete, WordPerfect displays a prompt on the status line with the following three options.

0 Striking the digit 0 causes a return to the edit screen without making any changes. In effect, this cancels the command.

1 Striking the digit 1 causes this deletion to be restored to the

document as it is highlighted. The highlight is removed, control returns to the edit screen, and you can continue to work on your document.

2 Striking the digit 2 causes the highlighted (restored) text to be removed from the displayed document. The text being held from the previous deletion operation is then displayed.

To illustrate option 2, assume that after deleting these three words, you had moved the cursor and deleted the last sentence from the document. WordPerfect would now have two sets of deletions that it is saving as illustrated in Figure 7-14. After moving the cursor into position to restore , when you strike the F1 key, WordPerfect displays text from the most recent deletion. In this case, it will be the sentence *I will leave that for you to decide.* However, since you want the text from the preceding deletion, you must select option 2 and the text from the preceding deletion *(spelling and other)* will be restored. WordPerfect keeps the three most recent deletions of text.

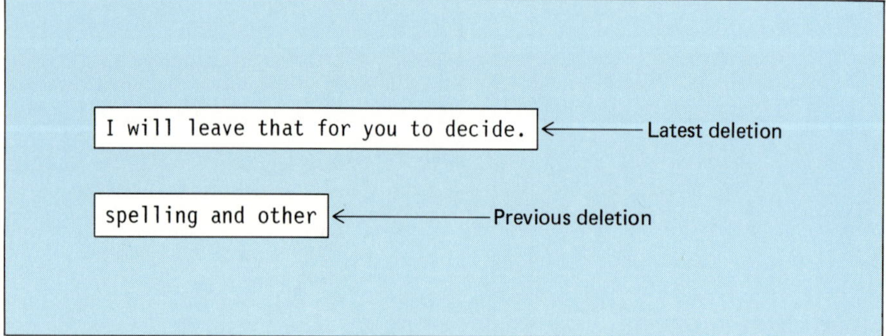

Figure 7-14
Deleted text.

From the point of view of holding deleted text, what constitutes a delete action? For instance, you deleted the three words with three separate Ctrl-Backspaces. What if you had deleted them by striking the Del key nineteen successive times? The answer is that the results would have been the same. Anytime you perform successive erasing actions without moving the cursor or entering another command, all of the deleted text is saved as a single deletion.

Regarding the F1 key, notice that it serves two different functions. If you press the F1 from the edit screen as illustrated by these examples, the Undelete command is executed and previously deleted text is restored. On the other hand, if a command has been executed that results in a prompt to which you must respond, then the Cancel command is executed. That is, the previous command is canceled and control returned to the edit screen.

Inserting and Deleting Return Codes

In Chapter 6, you learned that as you enter a document, both text and formatting codes are stored in memory (see Figure 6-8). These codes control the way in which the text is displayed on the screen and printed on the page. Although a detailed discussion is reserved until the next chapter, a knowledge of the code caused by striking the Enter key during document entry will help you now when entering and editing a document. Figure 7-15 shows the screen display for the first three lines of the memo and the corresponding memory contents. The WordPerfect code resulting from striking the Enter key is called a hard return and is abbreviated HRt (this corresponds to the new line code described in the general word processing discussion illustrated by Figure 6-8). When entering and editing a document, you can treat this code in exactly the same way you would treat any other characters entered from the keyboard. To illustrate, you should position the cursor on the letter F in the word *From* (beginning of the second line of your document) as shown in Figure 7-15. Then strike the Left key one time and the cursor will move left one position in memory to the code HRt; you will see this on the screen as the cursor jumping from the beginning of the second line to the end of the first.

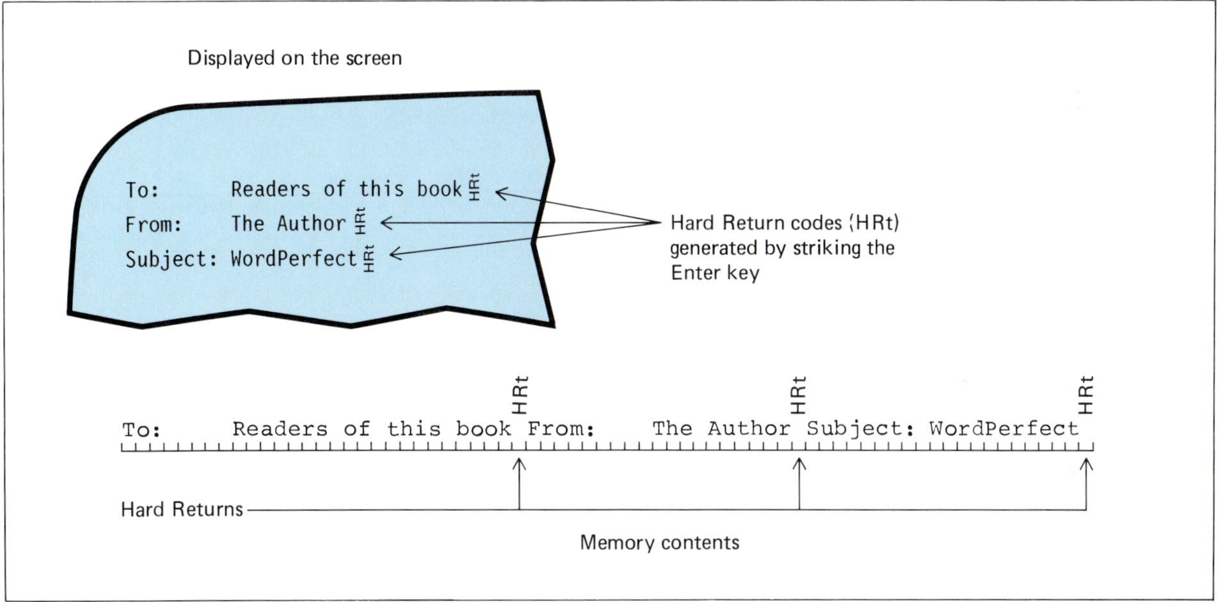

Figure 7-15
The Hard Return (HRt) code.

Using some logic, the answer to the next question should be apparent. What if you reposition the cursor to the letter *F* of the word *From* (in the second line) and strike the Backspace key? As you know, the Backspace erases the character to the left, which, in this case, is the HRt. Thus, your three lines become two, as shown in Figure 7-16. If this action were

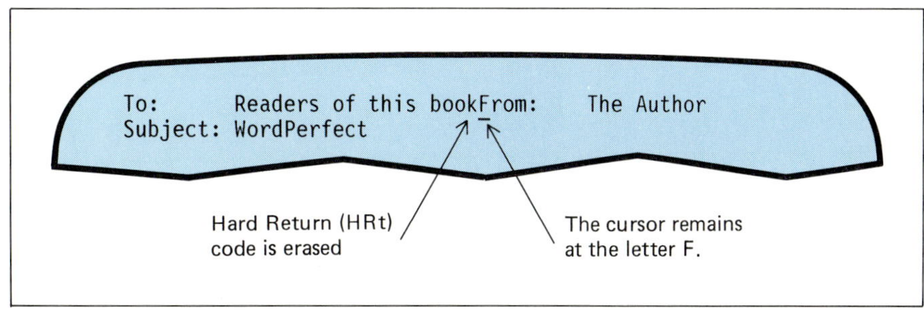

Figure 7-16
Deleting the HRt hidden code.

accidental, then all that would be necessary to restore it to the original form of Figure 7-15 would be to strike Enter. In other words, *even though you cannot see the HRt codes, they can be inserted and deleted the same as text characters that you see displayed on the screen.*

SAVING DOCUMENTS

About RAM and Disk Storage

If you have entered and corrected the memo, you may be ready to take a break or to terminate this work session. However, the first thing you should do is save a copy of your document to disk. Remember from Chapter 6 that the document you are working on is in RAM and will be lost when you terminate the WordPerfect program or turn the computer off, *or if there is any kind of power failure.* Once saved on disk, you can command WordPerfect to retrieve it from disk and place it in memory whenever you need it.

From your study of DOS in Chapter 5, you learned that anything saved to disk is saved as a file. This applies to documents created by WordPerfect, spreadsheets created by Lotus 1-2-3, and so on. Each file must be given a filename consisting of up to 8 characters and, optionally, an extension consisting of up to 3 characters. Let us save your memo to disk.

The Save Command

In WordPerfect, you transfer information from memory to disk with the Save command, which is invoked by striking the F10 key (refer to the function key template).

DO THIS NOW 7-8 **Saving**

1. Enter the Save command with F10; this will produce the following prompt.

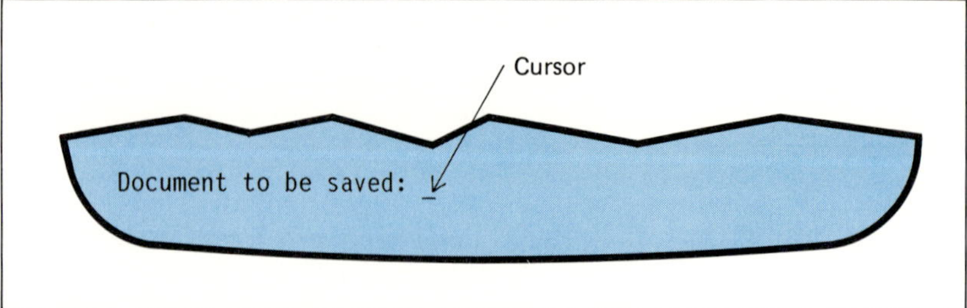

   WordPerfect is asking you: "What is the name that you wish to use for the document you are about to save to disk?"

2. Type MEMO.WP1 and strike the Enter. While WordPerfect is copying your document to disk, it will display the message:

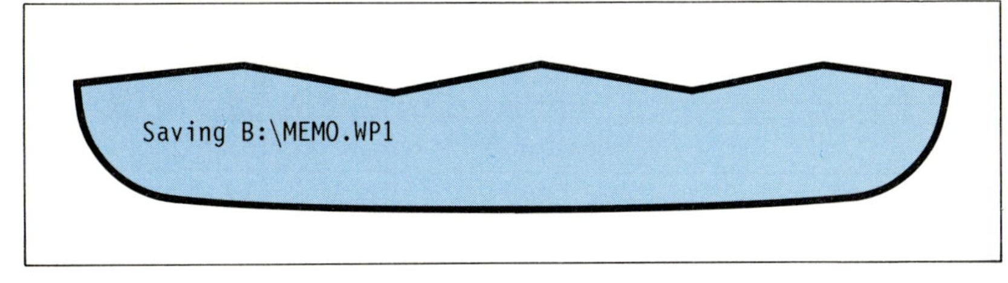

When WordPerfect completes the save operation, control is returned to the edit screen and text entry or editing can continue.

Although you can use any valid DOS filenames and extensions, to avoid confusing word processing files with spreadsheet or database files, use WP as the first two letters of the extension, as is done in this example.

Frequent Saving

If you have a long document to enter or a lot of editing to complete, do not wait until you have finished your work to save what you have done. You should save periodically while working. If you have a hardware or power failure, or you accidentally erase a large section of work without realizing it immediately, all your effort will be lost if you have not saved. For subsequent saves, the process is simplified because WordPerfect displays the document name as the default value:

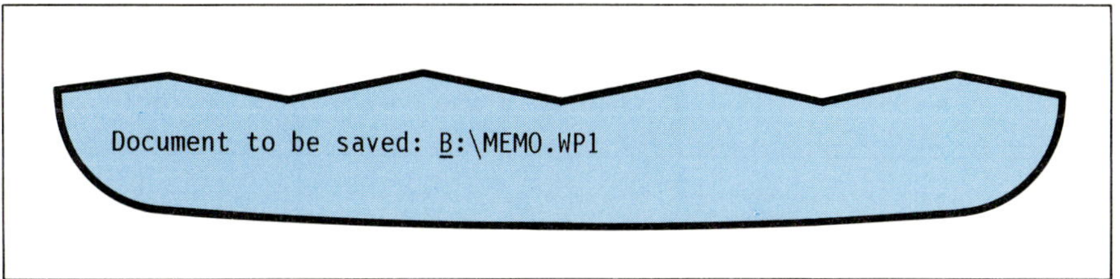

To save it again, simply strike Enter without typing anything and the displayed name will be used. However, whenever you save a document and there is an existing file on disk with the same name, WordPerfect warns you with the following message.

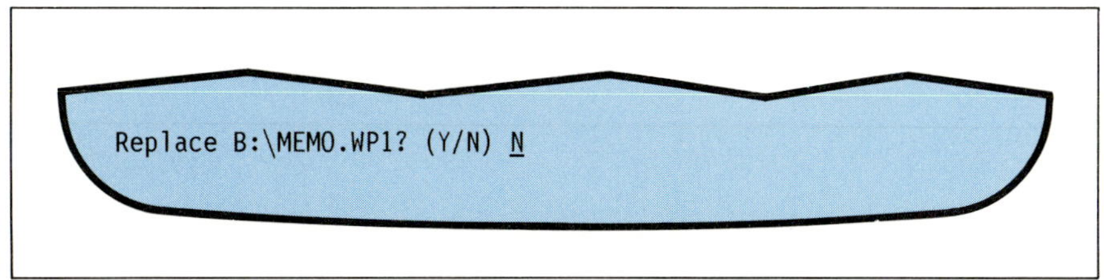

The reason for this is that the existing copy will be replaced with the copy from memory. Normally, each save will represent further work that you have done to the document, so you do want the version displayed on the screen to replace the old copy on disk. To effect the replacement, simply strike the letter *Y*.

When concentrating on your work, it is easy to become so involved that you forget to save frequently. Developing the habit of saving files regularly will save you a lot of grief.

THE EXIT COMMAND

Exiting WordPerfect

When you have finished working with WordPerfect and have saved your document, you may terminate WordPerfect with the Exit command (the F7 key). (This will cause control of the computer to be returned to DOS.) When you strike the F7 key, the first thing WordPerfect does is to ask if you wish to save to disk the document in memory.

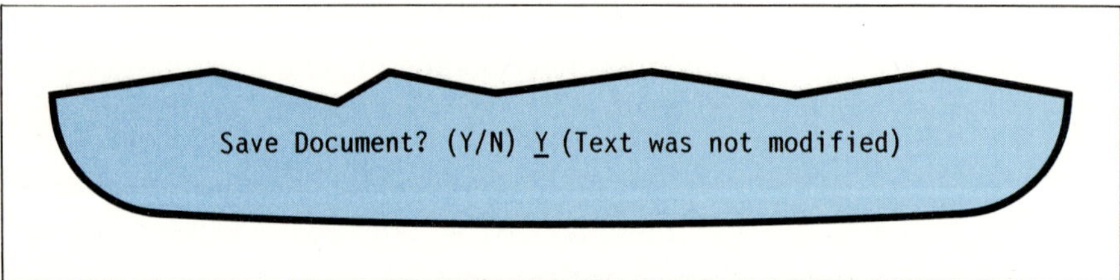

If there have been no changes since the last time you saved, the message *Text was not modified* is displayed to the right. Since you just saved the document using the Save command, there is no need to save it again. Whenever this *not modified* message is not displayed, be certain to respond with Y or else the most recent changes you made will not be saved. Requesting a save will result in exactly the same sequence of prompts as those resulting from the Save command.

Whether you save the document or not, you are then presented with the Exit prompt:

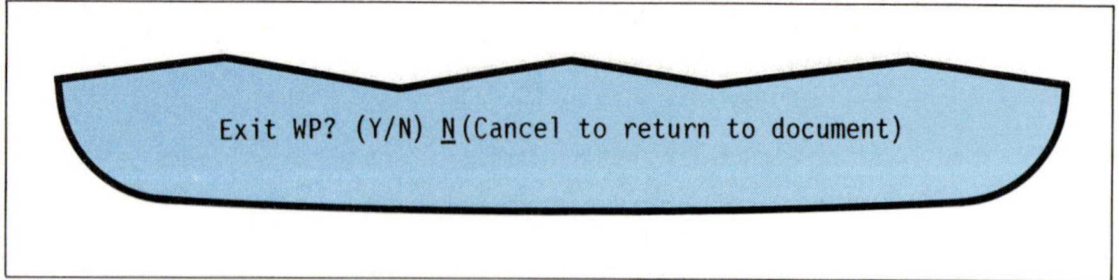

You can respond with one of the following three choices:

- Strike the letter *Y* to exit WordPerfect and return to DOS.
- Strike the Enter key, thereby accepting the default (No). This causes the current document to be erased from memory and control returned to the edit screen, which is blank.

- Strike the Cancel key (F1) if you have changed your mind and wish to return to the edit screen of the current document (the document currently in memory).

Clearing the Current Document from Memory

Assume that after completing the memo, you have another document that you must enter. However, after saving the memo, it is still in memory and on the screen. You need WordPerfect to clear the memory (and the screen) so that you can begin the next document. Responding with No to the Exit WP prompt does this.

To illustrate how this is useful, assume that you have another document to enter and save now that you have finished the memo. The overall sequence would be as follows:

DO THIS NOW 7-9 **Clearing Memory to Begin a New Document**

1. Enter the Exit command (F7); save if any changes have been made since the last save.
2. Enter N in response to the prompt asking if you wish to exit WordPerfect. This will clear the current document from memory and present you with the blank edit screen.
3. You may now proceed to enter your next document. After completing the second document, you would Exit again and respond with Y to the prompt regarding exiting WordPerfect.

You need not be confined to a desk to use a word processor. Here, one person is taking notes in a library and another is working in an airplane using portable computers equipped with word processing programs.

About Starting WordPerfect

When you terminate a WordPerfect word session (and return to DOS) through the Exit command, WordPerfect erases some temporary files that it uses. If you terminate a work session by simply turning the computer off (a bad practice), then these files remain on your disk. The next time you attempt to run WordPerfect, it will detect these files and ask you if other copies of WordPerfect are currently running. Respond to the question by typing the letter *N* (for no) and WordPerfect will complete the start-up sequence.

RETRIEVING A DOCUMENT FROM DISK

If you have completed the first two steps of DTN 7-9, you have a blank edit screen. If you have not, then do so in order that you can step through the sequence of retrieving an existing document stored on disk.

The Retrieve Command

When you return to work on your document at some later time, reading it from disk back into memory is every bit as easy as saving it was.

DO THIS NOW 7-10 **Retrieve the Document MEMO.WP1**

1. Enter the Retrieve command with Shift-F10; this produces the following prompt.

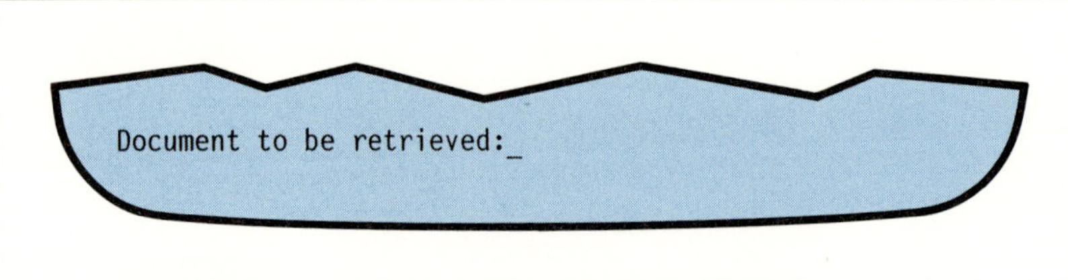

2. Type in MEMO.WP1 (the name of your document), then strike the Enter key. Do not forget to include the extension.

If WordPerfect cannot find the named file on the disk, it displays an error message for a few seconds and then returns to the preceding prompt asking for the document name.

During a word processing session, it is common to work on one document, save it, and then retrieve another and work on that one. If you attempt to retrieve one document while another is still on the screen, the new one will be inserted right at the position of the cursor. Note that *the previous document will not be erased from memory when a new one is retrieved.*

Starting WordPerfect with a Filename

You already know that when you load the WordPerfect program by typing A:WP from the DOS prompt, you are presented with a blank edit screen. However, if you load WordPerfect by typing

B> A:WP MEMO.WP1

A> C:WP MEMO.WP1   (for hard disk computer)

the named document, MEMO.WP1 in this case, will be placed in memory by WordPerfect and will be ready for editing.

So that you know what to expect when using WordPerfect, you should experiment with the Retrieve command by trying each of the following:

- Load WordPerfect by designating a document name (use your MEMO.WP1).
- Load WordPerfect by designating a document name of a file that does not exist (use X.X as the document name).
- Load WordPerfect with a blank screen and then attempt to retrieve the nonexistent file X.X.
- Load WordPerfect with a blank screen and then retrieve MEMO.WP1 with the Retrieve command.
- With your MEMO.WP1 on the screen, position the cursor somewhere in the center of the document and retrieve the document name CONTRACT.WP1. (CONTRACT.WP1 is the name of a document on the data disk included with this book.)

Listing the Files Stored on Disk

Once you start working with a word processor, you will have many files stored on your disk. Unfortunately, it is easy to forget names that you have selected. For instance, assume that you remember your memo document name as MEMO.WP instead of MEMO.WP1. How do you locate a document that you need when you cannot remember the name? For this, WordPerfect allows you to inspect the contents of a disk without leaving WordPerfect by using the List Files command (F5). You should carry out the following actions with your data disk to get a feel for using the command. When you execute it by striking the F5 key, WordPerfect responds with the DOS DIR command on the status line as follows:

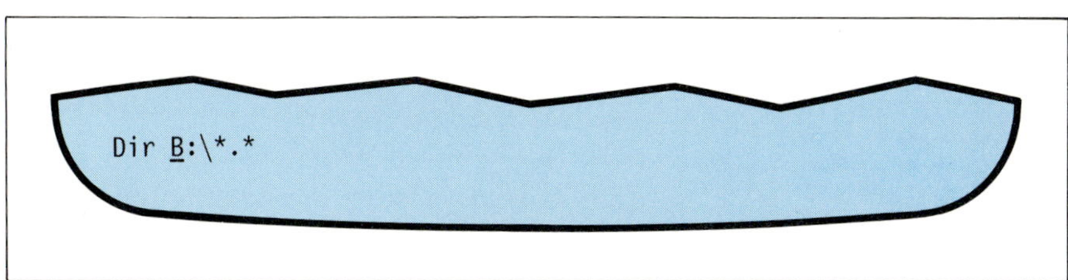

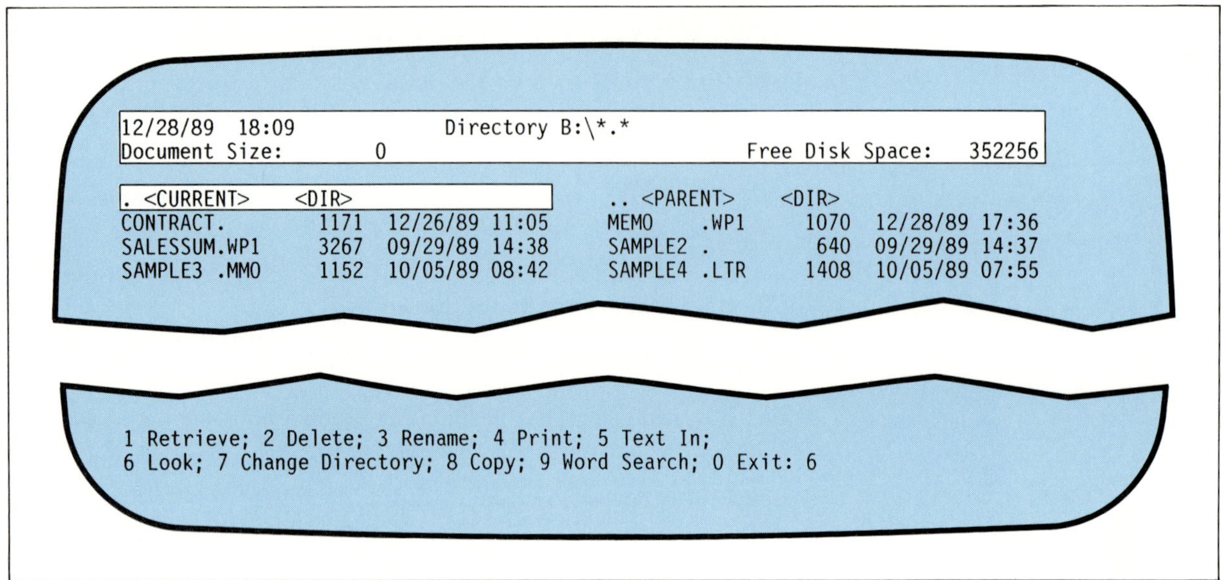

Figure 7-17
A directory listing.

At this point, you may change the form of the directory command as you please, or simply strike the Enter key to accept the default. You will be presented with a directory screen such as that shown in Figure 7-17. (Note that the contents of your data disk will be different.) This disk contains six data files listed in alphabetic order; note that they are *not necessarily* WordPerfect document files. Upon inspecting the list, it is evident that the name of the desired file is MEMO.WP1, not MEMO.WP. To retrieve it, simply move the highlight to that filename using the Right arrow key, then strike the digit 1 (for the Retrieve option). This document will be loaded into memory, and control will be returned to the edit screen, which will now display your memo.

Referring to the status line prompt in Figure 7-17, notice that there are nine options in addition to the Retrieve option you selected. The only other that we shall consider is the Look (6), which allows you to see any file in the listing without going through the routine of actually loading it into memory. For instance, if you want to check MEMO.WP1 to be certain that it is indeed the desired file, then highlight it and strike the 6 key. The first screen of the file will be displayed; you can inspect subsequent screens by striking the PgDn key.

MORE ON MOVING THE CURSOR

Now that you know how to save and retrieve documents, you are free to experiment without fear of losing the work you have done in entering and editing the document. Let us continue with some of the other basic features of WordPerfect.

About Positioning the Cursor on the Screen

If you have tried to move the cursor with a blank edit screen (after WordPerfect is loaded with no document), you noticed that the cursor would not move. (If you have not already done this, then try it.) The reason is that WordPerfect allows the cursor to be moved only within areas of the screen that display text from a document. To illustrate this, you should retrieve your completed memo and attempt to move the cursor throughout the screen. When you do so, you will find that movement is restricted to the highlighted portion shown in Figure 7-18.

If you position the cursor at the end of the first line (following the word *book*) and you strike the right arrow, the cursor will not be moved into the blank area to the right of the screen but to the beginning of the next line. (However, if you have entered spaces at the end of this line, the cursor will move over those spaces since WordPerfect treats the space as any other character.) Furthermore, if you position the cursor after the last character in the document, striking Right or Down keys to move it further will have no effect.

Figure 7-18
The document area on the screen.

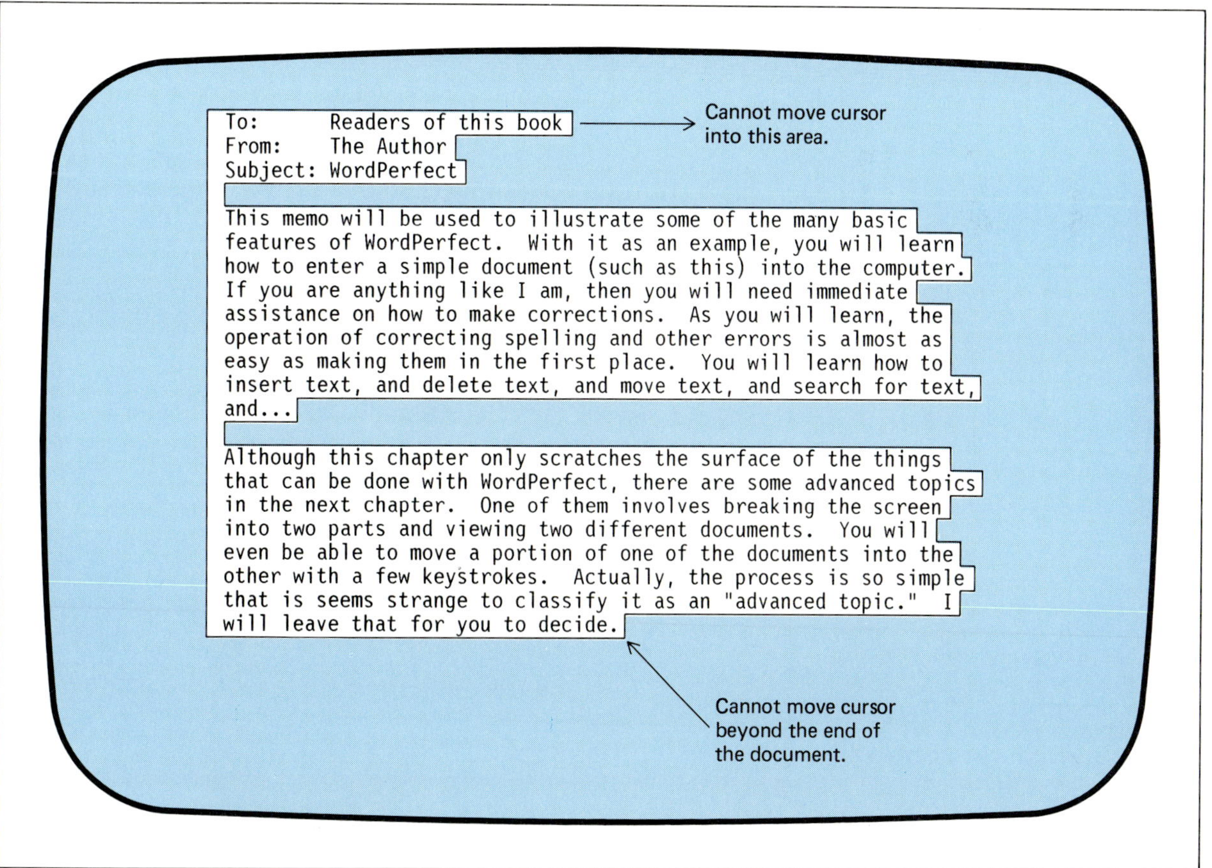

Positioning the Cursor Within the Current Screen Display

Moving the cursor one character at a time (even with automatic repeat) is a simple approach but is not very fast when moving across an entire line once you begin to master WordPerfect. Fortunately, there are keystroke sequences that permit you to move the cursor by more than a single character or line. For instance, Ctrl-Right (the Right arrow key) causes the cursor to move to the right from one word to the next. If repeated movement is required, then simply hold down the Ctrl and arrow keys for automatic repeat. Ctrl-Left results in an equivalent cursor movement to the left. These are commonly referred to as Word Right and Word Left.

Frequently, when working in the middle of a line, you want to position the cursor at the beginning or at the end of the line for the next action. This is easily done by striking the Home key (do not hold it down) and then striking the Left key or the Right key. That is, Home,Left positions at the beginning of the line and Home,Right at the end. You should try each of these actions with your memo that is currently displayed on the screen.

Moving the Cursor Outside the Screen Display

Previous cursor movement actions have related to moving within the text displayed on the screen. However, what if you are editing a long document and the text you want to edit is not currently on the screen? Since memo is short, you cannot experiment with it. However, you can retrieve the document CONTRACT.WP1 from the data disk that accompanies this book and try the following movement actions with it.

The Plus (+) key located in the numeric keypad at the right of the keyboard is defined by WordPerfect as the Screen Down key. If you strike it, you will see that the cursor moves to the bottom of the screen. If you strike it again, assuming that you have retrieved the document CONTRACT.WP1, the current screen display will be replaced by the rest of this document. In general, the Screen Down key causes the twenty-four lines of the document currently displayed to be replaced on the screen by the next twenty-four lines of the document.

Similarly, pressing the Screen Up, which is the minus (-) key on the numeric keypad, causes the cursor to move to the first line of the screen display. As with the Screen Down, striking the Screen Up again causes a twenty-four-line scroll toward the beginning of the document.

In addition to the screen-by-screen scrolling, you can move up or down in your document by page. Remember that WordPerfect keeps track of where each printed page ends and the next begins. Striking the PgDn key displays the first line of the next page of text. If the default page line count is in effect, then this is 54 lines. In a similar fashion, striking the PgUp key causes a full page to be scrolled toward the beginning of the document.

SUMMARY OF CURSOR MOVES

As you can see, you have many cursor positioning options to use when editing your document. It may seem as though it would be difficult to master each of the key sequences, but when you use a word processor regularly you quickly become familiar with them. The following summary of cursor movement options should help you learn them when working with WordPerfect.

Movement Command	Key or Keys	Action
Up Line	Up	Move cursor up one line
Down Line	Down	Move cursor down one line.
Left Character	Left	Move cursor left one character.
Right Character	Right	Move cursor right one character.
Left Word	Ctrl-Left	Move cursor left one word.
Right Word	Ctrl-Right	Move cursor right one word.
Beginning of Line	Home,Left	Move cursor to beginning of current line.
End of Line	Home,Right	Move cursor to end of current line.
	End	Same as Home,Right.
Screen Up	− key (numeric keypad)	Move cursor to first line on current screen. Subsequently scrolls twenty-four lines toward beginning of the document.
Screen Down	+ key (numeric keypad)	Move cursor to last line on current screen. Subsequently scrolls twenty-four lines toward end of the document.
Page Up	PgUp	Move the cursor to the first line of the preceding page as defined by the printer.
Page Down	PgDn	Move the cursor to the first line of the following page as defined by the printer.

PRINTING A DOCUMENT

The Print Command

The final task we shall consider in this chapter is how to print your memo. Actually, at any point during the entry or editing of a document, you may print a copy. Usually, this is when you have completed typing and must proofread it. However, for a long document you may wish to enter a portion of it and print that part and read it to get a feel for the overall flow. In either case, you should always save the document before printing. Although the printing process does not change the document in memory, you want to be certain that the copy you have on disk is the same as the printed copy. It is simply a good habit.

Before printing, you should check that the printer is on and ready and that it contains paper.

DO THIS NOW 7-11 Printing MEMO.WP1

1. If you do not currently have MEMO.WP1 on the screen, clear your screen and then retrieve MEMO.WP1 from disk.
2. Enter the Print command with the Shift-F7. The following list of options is displayed on the status line.

3. Type the digit 1 to cause the Full document to be printed. When printing is finished, WordPerfect returns to the edit screen.

Referring to the Print option menu, notice that the default option is 0, which, if selected, cancels the print request and returns to the edit screen.

If you examine the keyboard template, you will notice that Ctrl-F8 is also listed as Print. This provides for formatting of the printed output; it does not print so do not use it.

If you have entered and correctly edited your memo, your printed copy should be the same as that of Figure 7-19. Note the presence of *WPC at the

Figure 7-19
A printed copy of the memo.

```
To:      Readers of this book
From:    The Author*WPC
Subject: WordPerfect

This  memo  will  be  used  to  illustrate some of the many basic
features of WordPerfect.  With it as an  example, you  will learn
how to  enter a simple document (such as this) into the computer.
If you are anything like  I  am,  then  you  will  need immediate
assistance  on  how to  make corrections.   As you will learn, the
operation of correcting spelling  and other  errors is  almost as
easy as  making them  in the  first place.  You will learn how to
insert text, and delete text, and move text, and search for text,
and...*WPC

Although this  chapter only  scratches the  surface of the things
that can be done with WordPerfect, there are some advanced topics
in the  next chapter.   One  of them involves breaking the screen
into two  parts and  viewing two  different documents.   You will
even be  able to  move a portion of one of the documents into the
other with a few keystrokes.  Actually, the process is  so simple
that is  seems strange  to classify it as an "advanced topic."  I
will leave that for you to decide.*WPC
```

1 space

2 spaces

end of some of the lines. These are included automatically at the position of some of the Hard Returns to identify this as a document printed by the Limited-Use version. They will not appear if you are using a commercial version of WordPerfect. In contrast to the copy of the memo in Figure 7-2, notice that the right margin is aligned: that is, the document is justified. The copy in Figure 7-2 was printed with justification disabled; you will learn how to do this in the next chapter.

SUMMARY

From this chapter you have learned the basic elements of using WordPerfect. You can now enter a document, edit it, save it to disk for later use, and print it. Yet to come in the next chapter are the many features of word processors described in Chapter 6, including formatting, cut and paste, and searching. Summarizing from this chapter, its important points are:

- After WordPerfect is loaded, you see the edit screen that contains the cursor and the status line. The status line serves as a general "message" area between WordPerfect and you, the user.
- Function keys are used to execute WordPerfect commands. Each function key causes four different actions depending upon whether it is used with the Shift, Ctrl, or Alt key, or alone.
- When used from the edit screen, the F1 key performs an Undelete action; that is, F1 restores previously deleted text. When used after a command that displays a prompt to which the user must respond, it cancels that command.
- The Enter key should be struck only to force a new line or begin a new paragraph. Within a paragraph, WordPerfect automatically performs word wrap when a line reaches the right margin.
- Hard Returns (resulting from striking the Enter key) can be deleted and inserted in exactly the same way as other keyboard characters.
- You can modify a document with insertions and deletions. After such changes, WordPerfect realigns the text automatically.
- The Right, Left, Up, and Down arrow keys move the cursor to any position within the document. Other cursor movement actions allow the cursor to be positioned at the beginning or end of the current line, at the end or beginning of the current screen, or to the next or preceding page.
- Disk storage is for the long-term storage of documents. Documents are entered into and edited from main memory (RAM).
- The Save command copies the document in memory to disk.
- The Retrieve command copies a document from disk into memory. If a

document is already in memory, the newly retrieved one will be inserted at the position of the cursor.

- The directory of a disk can be displayed from WordPerfect with the List Files command.
- The Exit command can be used either to end the WordPerfect session or to clear memory of the current document.

COMMAND AND FUNCTION SUMMARY

Following is a summary of the various commands other than those for cursor movement described in this chapter. Cursor movement commands are summarized in an earlier table of this chapter.

Command	Key or Keys	Action
Deletion of Text		
Delete Character	Backspace	Delete character to left of cursor.
Delete Character	Del	Delete character at position of cursor.
Delete Word	Ctrl-Backspace	Delete word in which cursor positioned.
Delete to Line End	Ctrl-End	Delete from cursor to end of line.
Delete to Page End	Ctrl-PgDn	Delete from cursor to end of page.
Other Commands		
Cancel	F1	Executed command, cancel the command.
Undelete	F1	Executed from edit screen, restore deleted text.
Help	F3	Display Help screen.
List Files	F5	Display a disk directory.
Exit	F7	Save document, clear memory, and/or exit WordPerfect.
Print	Shift-F7	Print the current document.
Save	F10	Save the current document to disk.
Retrieve	Shift-F10	Retrieve a document from disk.

NEW TERMINOLOGY

The new terminology introduced in the general word processing discussion of Chapter 5 carries over directly to WordPerfect. The following are important new terms introduced in this chapter; you should be familiar with each of them.

edit screen
hard return
status line
typeover

REVIEW QUESTIONS

1. When starting WordPerfect with A:WP (or C:WP for the hard disk), why is the drive designator A: (or C:) used to precede WP?
2. What is the "status line" and what information does it contain?
3 While typing a letter, you typed the word *recieve* instead of *receive* and realized your error immediately. How can you correct this?
4. After completing a letter and proofreading, you notice that you typed the word *recieve* instead of *receive.* How would you make this correct?
5. What two keys delete a single character?
6. What keystroke actions do each of the following tell you to take?
   a. Home,End
   b. Shift-F10
7. Which key in WordPerfect is called the Cancel key? What does it do?
8. What are the quickest ways to make the following deletions from your document?
   a. Shorten the second sentence so that it ends with *simple document.*
   b. Delete the word *different* in the fourth line of the second paragraph.
   c. Delete the second paragraph.
9. Why should you save a document at intervals while working on it rather than waiting until it is finished?
10. What key sequences for the Exit command cause the following actions to occur?
    a. Save the document and continue editing it.
    b. Save the document and begin a new one.
    c. Clear the memory to begin a new document without saving the current one.
    d. Retrieve another document without saving the current one.
11. What happens if you retrieve a document when another is already on the screen? If you do not know, try it to find out.

12. What happens if you attempt to retrieve a file that is not on disk? If you do not know, try it to find out.
13. How do the Page Up and the Screen Up operations differ?
14. If you position the cursor on the letter *b* of the word *basic* (first line in your memo), to where will it be moved by Ctrl-Right?
15. Position the cursor on the word *illustrate* (first line in your memo). What are three different key sequences to move it to the end of the line?

MATCHING

Items in 1 through 8 describe activities requiring that one or more commands be invoked. Designate the first key sequence action to take by matching these actions with the key sequences in a through h.

a. F1
b. F10
c. F5
d. - key on numeric keypad
e. Shift-F10
f. Ctrl-Backspace
g. F7
h. F3

1. You have tried to retrieve a file and WordPerfect has told you that it cannot be found on the disk.
2. You must edit a line in your document that is about thirty lines above the current position of the cursor.
3. You accidentally deleted a line.
4. You have just completed a document, saved it, and are ready to begin another document.
5. You cannot remember the key sequence to print a document.
6. You have just completed a large number of editing changes and are ready to take a break.
7. When entering a document, you realize that you have typed the word *installation* twice in succession and you want to delete the second one. The cursor is still positioned immediately following the letter n.
8. You want to insert another document file into the current document at the position of the cursor.

TRUE/FALSE

Determine whether each of the following is true or false.

_____ 1. Corrections can be made to a document (at any place in the document) while the document is being entered.

_____ 2. A hard return results from striking the Enter key. It ends a line regardless of its length and causes a new line to be started.

_____ 3. Typeover is the action of replacing a copy of a document stored on disk with the copy in memory.

_______ **4.** If you delete a portion of text, then continue typing, then delete another portion of text, only the text from the latest deletion can be restored with the Restore command.

_______ **5.** Every time you execute a Save command, a new copy of your document is added to existing copies on disk.

_______ **6.** The save action resulting from invoking the Exit command is the same as the save action from the Save command.

_______ **7.** The Exit command can be used to clear the current document from memory with or without saving it to disk.

_______ **8.** The action resulting from the F1 key depends upon what you were doing before striking it.

_______ **9.** It is not possible to retrieve a document file from disk without first clearing the current document from memory.

_______ **10.** It is possible to obtain a directory listing of the data disk with an appropriate WordPerfect command; it is not necessary to terminate WordPerfect and then issue the DIR command from DOS.

_______ **11.** If an attempt is made to retrieve a file not on disk, execution of the WordPerfect program is immediately terminated.

_______ **12.** Using the arrow cursor movement keys, the cursor can be positioned anywhere on the edit screen.

_______ **13.** Whereas the Left and Right (arrow) keys cause the cursor to move one character at a time, the Ctrl-Left and Ctrl-Right cause the cursor to move one word at a time.

_______ **14.** The PgDn key causes the screen to scroll twenty-four lines.

_______ **15.** It is possible to print a document without first saving it.

ANSWERS TO OBJECTIVE QUESTIONS

Matching

1. c 2. d 3. a 4. g 5. h 6. b 7. f 8. e

True/False

1. T 2. T 3. F 4. F 5. F 6. T 7. T 8. T 9. F
10. T 11. F 12. F 13. T 14. F 15. T

ASSIGNMENTS/PROJECTS

1. The following document is to be entered into the computer using WordPerfect. (Your margins will not coincide with the margins of this copy; do not be concerned about this.) Entries enclosed within angle brackets are to be replaced with information as described within the brackets. For instance,

<YOUR NAME> should be replaced with your name. In addition to the three problems described in the memo, add two of your own. Proofread carefully and make necessary corrections. Then save it to disk and print a copy on the printer.

```
To:  Chief of Security
From: <YOUR NAME>
Date: <TODAY'S DATE>

I recently had a problem with one of your officers (badge number 22)
in the parking lot regarding my car.  (It is a <MAKE OF YOUR CAR>,
license number <YOUR AUTO LICENSE NUMBER>.)  It is bad enough that the
officer would not allow me to park in our lot, but he was also rude.
Following are the problems that resulted because of him.

1.  I was late for my appointment with <PERSON OF YOUR CHOICE>.

2.  I twisted my ankle walking in from the outer parking lot.

3.  Someone backed into my car while it was parked in the outer lot
and put a dent in the <PART OF YOUR CHOICE>.

I want you to know that I am very unhappy about this entire incident
and I am thinking of seeing an attorney.  I would appreciate it if you
would investigate the entire matter and inform me of what will be
done.

None of this would have happened if the officer had taken the time to
listen to may explanation.  Our security force should be here to help
out, not to make life difficult for us.

May I hear from you soon?  Thank you.
```

2. Create and type a response from the chief of security to your memo of Assignment 1.

3. The following document describing cut and paste is stored as MEMO-CP.WP on the data disk accompanying this book. Make the indicated corrections to it and then print a copy.

delete   and Future Experts   Delete

```
To: Students of WordPerfect
From: The Author

The cut and paste feature of WordPerfect is a powrful tool as you
shall soon learn.  One option of the Move command allows you to
deletete anything from a single word all the way up to the entire
document if you so desire.  For instance, this sentence should
not be here so it should be removed or at least moved somewhere
else.  The Retrieve Text command allows you to insert the most
recently cut text into your document--anyplace you desire, no
less.  In other words, this combination of commands allows you to
move text from one place in your document to another.

This is another paragraph but it does not say anything. In fact,
the "out of place" sentence in the preceding paragraph can be
inserted in front of this one. That operation will give this
paragraph some value.
```

Delete this

This does seem to be a waste of time but the

4. In Chapter 6, word processing was introduced using an MCT letter to an attorney (see Figure 6-1). The data disk accompanying this book includes another version of that letter; it is named CONTRACT.WP1. You are to print a copy of this version and compare it with that in Figure 6-1. (In the output, ignore the justification of lines and the *WPC inserted by the Limited-Use version of WordPerfect.) You are to edit CONTRACT.WP1 as follows:

- **a.** Make all corrections and changes so that it is identical to Figure 6-1.
- **b.** Insert a date at the top of the letter.
- **c.** Put your name at the bottom, leaving ample space for your signature.

Chapter 8

More on WordPerfect

OBJECTIVES

From Chapter 7 you have learned how to enter, edit, save, retrieve, and print documents using WordPerfect. In this chapter, you will learn about using the other features of word processing described in Chapter 6. When you have completed this chapter, you should be able to:

- Format your document, including setting margins, centering lines, indenting paragraphs, and underlining text.
- Examine and change formatting codes that you have entered with formatting commands.
- Use the Search and the Search and Replace commands.
- Move a section of text from one place in a document to another (or into another document): cut and paste.
- Use the WordPerfect speller and thesaurus.

PREVIEW

Simple Formatting

WordPerfect formatting commands enable you to change margin settings, center lines, indent paragraphs, underline text, and set text in boldface.

Working with Hidden Codes

The Reveal Codes command causes WordPerfect to display the formatting codes in a document so that they can be deleted as you would delete text.

Formatting While Entering a Document

Formatting of a document can be done either after the document has been entered or while text entry is taking place.

Other Formatting Features

Other WordPerfect commands enable you to change line spacing, disable right justification of the printed document, and use specialized indenting.

Searching a Document

The Search command locates any word or combination of words in a document. The Search and Replace command finds designated text and replaces it.

Cutting and Pasting

Using the Move command, you can delete, cut, or copy a portion of text in a document and insert it at some other place in the document.

Working with Two Documents

WordPerfect maintains two memory areas so that you can have two independent documents in memory at the same time. You can split the screen and display both documents.

The WordPerfect Speller and Thesaurus

WordPerfect includes a built-in spelling checker that will check the spelling of all words in a document. The on-screen thesaurus helps you select synonyms for words in your document.

SIMPLE FORMATTING

A Notice to Be Formatted

In Chapter 7, you learned how to edit a document by inserting and deleting text. Now you will learn how to modify a document by changing its format; the text will be unchanged, but its appearance will be changed. For this activity, you will need the document NOTICE.WP1, which is stored on the data disk that accompanies this book. If you prepared your data disk as described in Chapter 5, then you will have the document available. If you load WordPerfect with

```
B> A:WP NOTICE.WP1
```

you will be presented with the screen shown in Figure 8-1. Note that the message is adequate but the formatting is not very imaginative. Certain

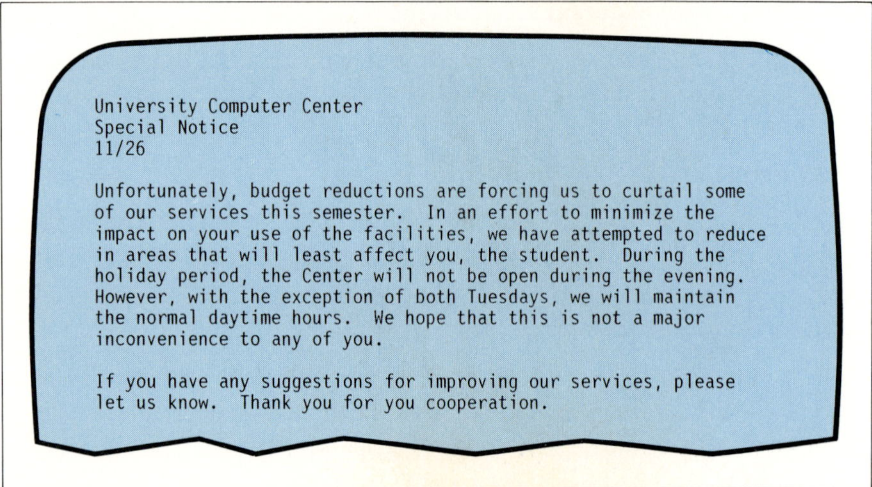

Figure 8-1
The unformatted notice.

points need emphasis. Now compare this with the formatted version shown in Figure 8-2. Here, formatting has been used to produce a notice that is much more appealing to the eye. Note that the important message (that the Center is not open during the evening) is indented to make it more noticeable. The purpose of this portion of the chapter is to show you how simple it is to change the formatting of the document in Figure 8-1 so that it looks like that in Figure 8-2. At first, the variety of actions required in using the formatting commands might be confusing. As you use them and observe how they work and what they do, you will find most of the required actions quite logical. If you use WordPerfect often, using format-

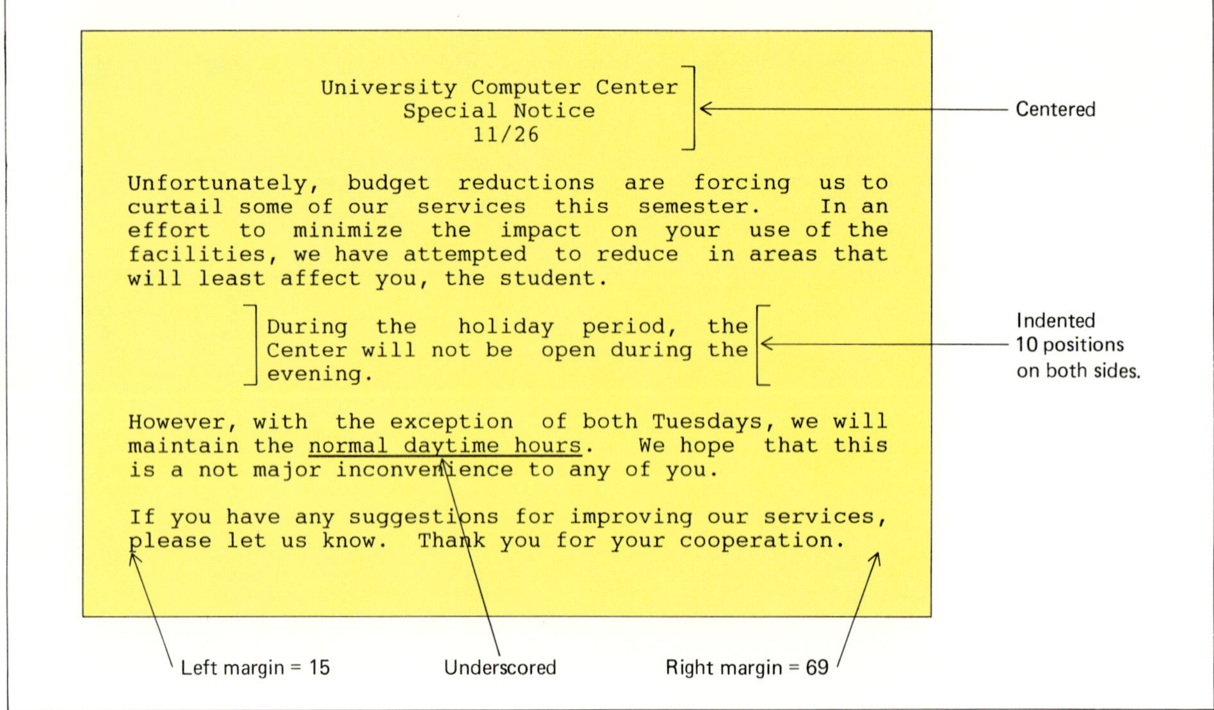

Figure 8-2
The formatted notice.

ting commands will become as automatic as typing text. In reformatting the document of Figure 8-1, you will learn about the following formatting techniques:

- Changing margin settings—the notice in Figure 8-2 uses margin settings of 15 and 69.
- Centering lines—the first three lines of the notice are centered.
- Splitting a single paragraph into more than one paragraph—the third sentence of the first paragraph must be a separate paragraph. (Actually, you already know how to do this from Chapter 7.)
- Indenting a paragraph—referring to Figure 8-2, the second paragraph is indented 1 inch on both sides.
- Underlining—three words are underlined in this notice.

When performing the formatting actions described in the instructions that follow, be certain that you do exactly as described; that is, the cursor must be properly positioned and the key sequences must be entered correctly. If you do not do so, then your formatted version will not look like that in Figure 8-2. Furthermore, you may not be able to undo the action (you will learn how to undo an action after you learn to do the formatting). If you make a mistake that you cannot correct, then simply clear the screen (use F7) and retrieve the original copy of NOTICE.WP1 from disk.

Setting Margins

Before entering the new margin settings, make certain that the cursor is in the upper left corner of the screen. That will have been its position when you first retrieved the notice, so it will already be there unless you have moved it. Referring to the WordPerfect function key template, notice that the function key F8 is identified as the format key (however, it does not control all formatting operations). Setting margins is an option under the Format Line command and is done as follows.

DO THIS NOW 8-1 **Setting Margins**

1. Enter the Shift-F8 sequence that produces the following status line prompt.

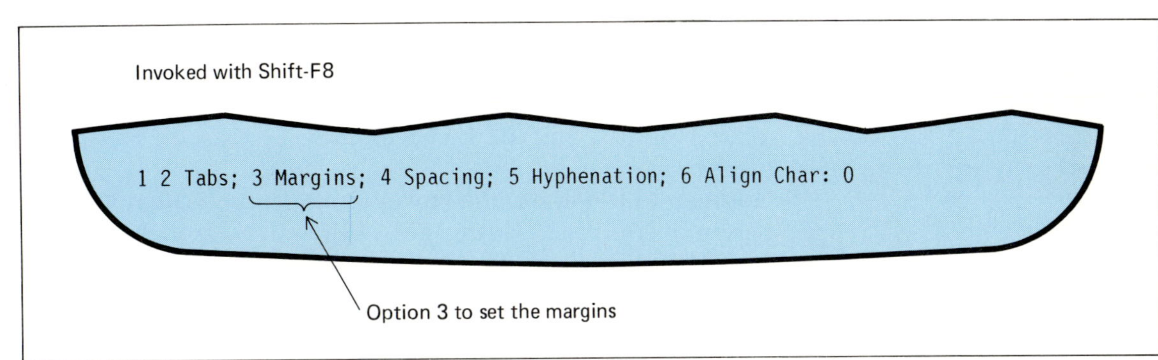

2. Strike the digit 3 key to select Margins. You will see the preceding prompt replaced by:

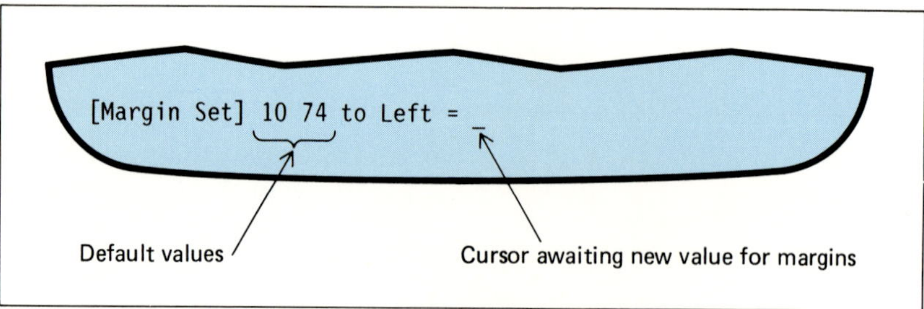

3. Type the new left margin, 15, and strike Enter.
4. You will then be prompted for the value of the right margin. Type the new right margin of 69 and strike Enter.

You will see the notice realigned immediately to conform to the new margin settings and control returned to the edit screen awaiting your next action.

Positioning a Line

Your next formatting action is to center each of the first three lines using the Center command (Shift-F6). Note that this command operates on a single line that is ended with a hard return. (The Enter key was pressed after the line was entered for each of these three lines.)

DO THIS NOW 8-2 **Centering a Line**

1. Before issuing the command, the cursor *must be at the extreme left of the line.* If it is not there, then reposition it with the Home,Left sequence.
2. Enter the Center command with the Shift-F6 sequence; the line will be shifted to the right. It may not be centered, but when you move the cursor to the next line, it will be positioned properly.
3. Repeat this action for each of the two lines that follow. Do not forget to position the cursor at the left of each line before centering it.

In addition to centering, the F6 key is also used to align lines on the right margin; this is called **flush right.** Although the notice of Figure 8-2 does not use flush right, you can experiment to see how it works. To do this, move the cursor beyond the last line of the document and do the following.

DO THIS NOW 8-3 **Setting a Line Flush Right**

1. Strike Enter to insert a blank line.
2. Type the following three lines (strike Enter after each line).

    First line
    Second line
    Last line

    Be certain to strike Enter after the last line.
3. Position the cursor on the first letter of the First line.
4. Enter the Flush Right command with Alt-F6.
5. Repeat this for each of the two remaining lines. Be certain to position the cursor at the beginning of the line before issuing the command.

When you finish, the lower portion of your screen will look like this:

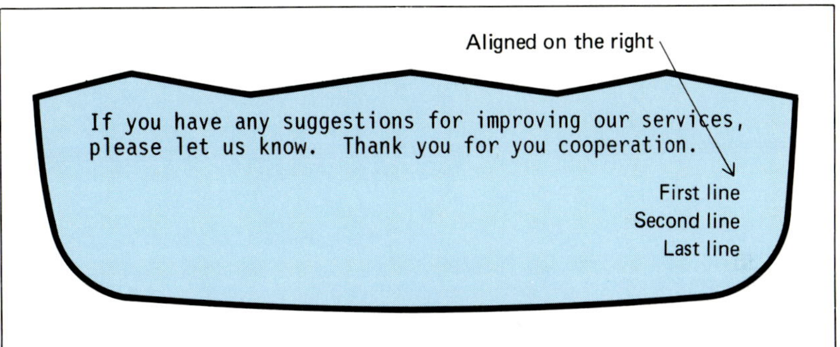

To delete these, simply position the cursor on the line to be deleted, strike the left arrow until the cursor is at the far left of the screen, and then use the Delete to End Of Line command (Ctrl-End).

Indention

Your next task is to break the first paragraph into three separate paragraphs and then indent the second one as shown in Figure 8-2. Remember from Chapter 7 that you create a paragraph by striking Enter, causing WordPerfect to insert a hard return. Thus, to create the new paragraphs you must do the following.

DO THIS NOW 8-4 **Creating a New Paragraph**

1. Position the cursor on the letter *D* of *During;* this is the first word of that which will become a new paragraph.

2. Strike the Enter twice—once to start the new paragraph and again to insert a blank line.
3. Move the cursor to the letter *H* in *However;* this is to begin the third paragraph.
4. Strike the Enter twice. Your document will now appear as in Figure 8-3.

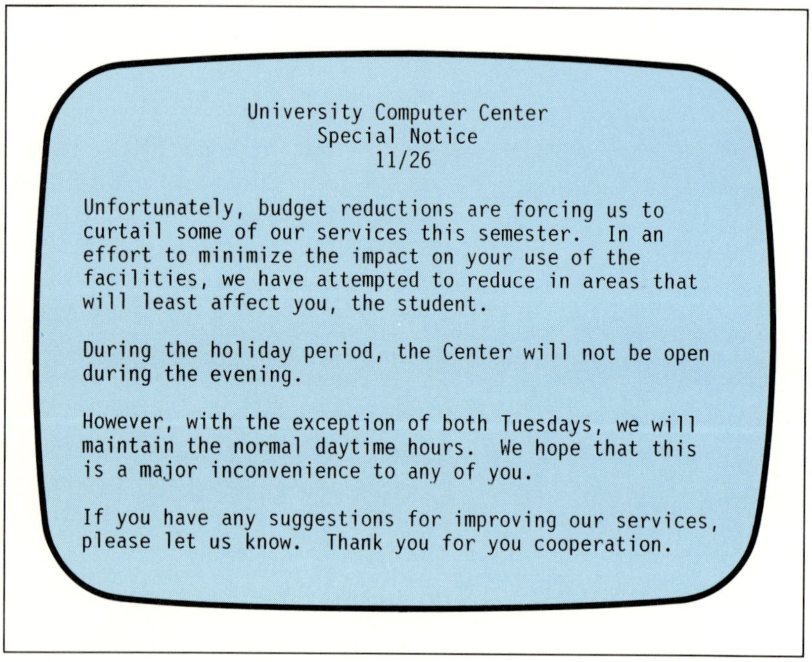

Figure 8-3
Splitting one paragraph into two.

```
                University Computer Center
                      Special Notice
                          11/26

Unfortunately, budget reductions are forcing us to
curtail some of our services this semester.  In an
effort to minimize the impact on your use of the
facilities, we have attempted to reduce in areas that
will least affect you, the student.

During the holiday period, the Center will not be open
during the evening.

However, with the exception of both Tuesdays, we will
maintain the normal daytime hours.  We hope that this
is a major inconvenience to any of you.

If you have any suggestions for improving our services,
please let us know.  Thank you for you cooperation.
```

You are now ready to indent the newly created second paragraph.

In Chapter 7, you learned about tab settings whose default values are set every five positions. When the Tab key is struck, the cursor jumps to the next tab setting. Note that you cannot use the Tab key to achieve the desired indention of Figure 8-2 because you need the indention to act on all lines of the paragraph.

WordPerfect provides two ways to indent paragraphs. Look at the function key template (or display it on the screen with the F3 key) and you will notice that the F4 key lists indent in the following two forms:

```
->Indent<-     Shift-F4
```

and

```
->Indent       F4
```

The arrows indicate the direction of indention; for instance, Shift-F4 causes an entire paragraph to be indented from both the left and right margins an amount equal to one tab. You must use this command for the indention required in the second paragraph of Figure 8-2.

DO THIS NOW 8-5 **Indenting a Paragraph**

1. Position the cursor on the letter *D* of the word *During* (the first character in this paragraph).
2. Enter the Shift-F4 sequence; WordPerfect will indent this paragraph from both the left and right by five positions. Enter the Shift-F4 sequence a second time for the ten-position indents.

Blocks of Text

The various formatting commands are different with respect to the amount of text that they affect. For instance, the Center command acts on a single line; the Indent command acts on a paragraph. However, the Underline command is different in that it does *not* act upon some predetermined amount of text. For instance, in the third paragraph of the notice, you must underline the words *normal daytime hours.* For this, you need the ability to operate on a portion of the text. WordPerfect provides that capability with the **Block** command, which allows you to mark a portion of text that can range in length from two characters to the entire document. WordPerfect indicates the blocked portion of text by highlighting it on the screen. It is possible to perform numerous operations on a block, such as underlining, deleting, and saving to a file. For now, our attention is focused on underlining.

Underlining and Boldface

In the following sequence, you must first block the text that you want to underline and then underline it.

DO THIS NOW 8-6 **Defining a Block and Underlining**

1. Move the cursor to the first position of the text to be marked as a block: that is, the letter *n* in *normal.*
2. Mark the beginning of the block with the Block command Alt-F4. This turns on the block mode, causing a flashing message to be displayed on the status line as shown below.

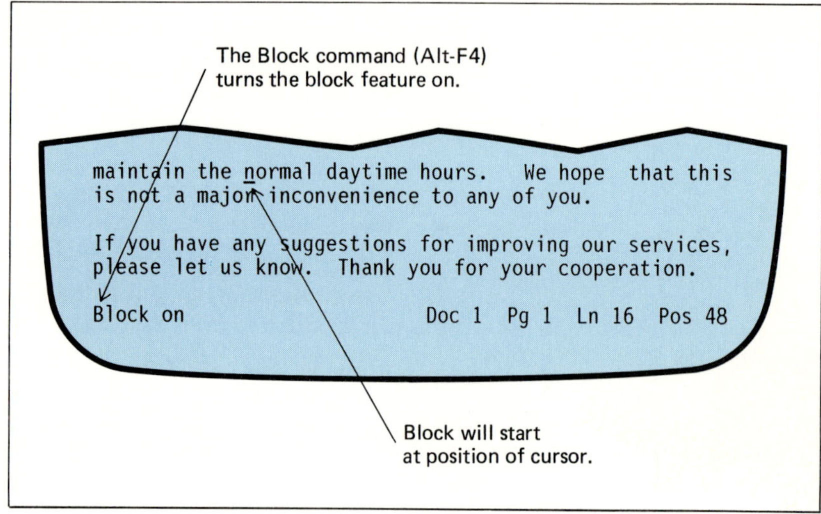

3. Move the cursor to the position of the last character in the block using the Right key. The entire blocked area will be highlighted.

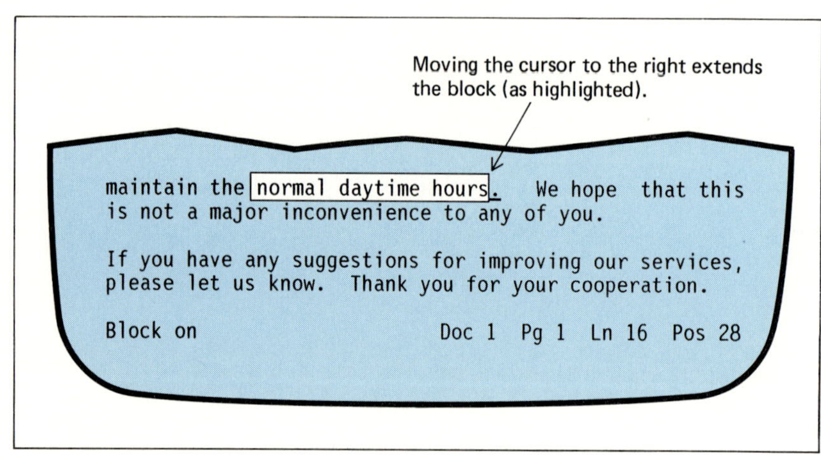

4. Enter the Underline command (F8) to cause the blocked text to be underlined. Note that this also turns off the block.

When defining a block of text, once you establish the starting point (with the Alt-F4), the cursor can be moved with any of the cursor movement keys in order to extend the block. For instance, in the preceding example, the Ctrl-Right key could have been used to move word by word. If two or more lines must be included in a block, you can use the Down (or Up) keys. The best way to learn about blocking is to carry out some blocking actions; to cancel the block, use the Cancel command (F1).

Changing text to boldface (letters that are darker and stand out more) is done in the same way as underlining. The Boldface key is F6. You can further enhance the notice by using boldface on the entire second paragraph. To do this, block the paragraph and then strike the F6 key. Although you will see no difference on the screen display, when printed, the boldface portions will be printed twice, thereby making them slightly darker.

The formatting of your document is now complete. You should save it to disk (you will need it later) and then print a copy. When saving it, use a different file name, for instance, NOTICE.WP2. In this way, you will still have the original version as NOTICE.WP1 for other practice activities. Now that you have done the formatting, let us learn about the codes resulting from the formatting commands you used.

WORKING WITH HIDDEN CODES

From Chapter 6, you know that the formatting commands of many word processors cause formatting codes to be imbedded directly in the text within memory (refer to Figure 6-8). One of the functions of the word processor program is to display the text according to the specifications of the codes and not display the codes themselves. Thus, for most activities, you need not be concerned about the actual codes. You have just seen this from the preceding example in which you formatted the notice. You simply issued the appropriate formatting commands and WordPerfect adjusted the document on the screen accordingly. Because you see the effect of these codes and not the codes themselves, in WordPerfect they are called **hidden codes.**

As a rule, it is best that they remain hidden so that you can focus on your document and its appearance. However, if you accidentally strike a wrong function key and enter a formatting command at the wrong place, the screen display of your document can be very confusing. It is sometimes quite difficult to diagnose the problem merely by looking at the edit screen display. For this, you need to have a basic understanding of these hidden codes.

If you formatted the notice exactly as described in the preceding sections, then your document will contain the hidden codes shown in Figure 8-4. Here, each code is enclosed in square brackets and positioned at the point where you issued the corresponding command during editing.

Hidden Code	Key Sequence	Description
[Margin Set:15,69]	Shift-F8,3	Defines the margins; resulted from the Format Line command.
[C] and [c]	Shift-F6	Line centering code from the Center command. The code [C] marks the beginning of the text to be centered and is inserted at the position of the cursor when the command is issued. The code [c] marks the end of the text to be centered; it is automatically inserted by WordPerfect at the end of the line.
[HRt]	Enter	Hard Return inserted when the Enter key is pressed.
[SRt]		Soft Return inserted by WordPerfect when a word is wrapped to start a new line.
[->Indent<-]	Shift-F4	Specifies that this paragraph be indented from both left and right margins.
[U] and [u]	F8	Specifies that the text between [U] and [u] be underlined. The underlining in this notice involved first marking the text (Alt-F4) and then issuing the underline command.

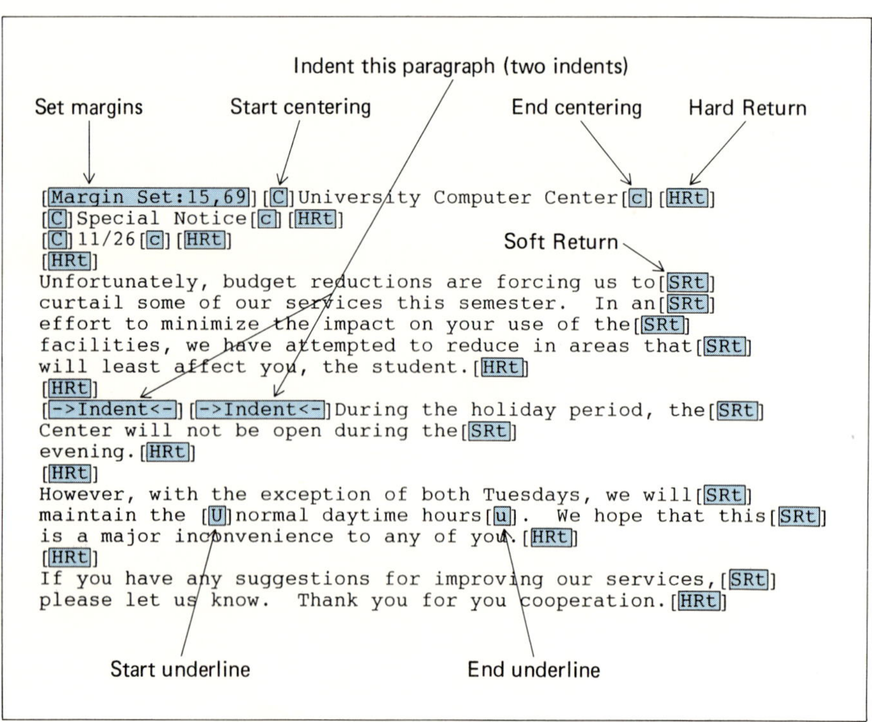

Figure 8-4
Hidden codes in the memo.

Displaying and Deleting Hidden Codes

Hidden codes are displayed with the Reveal Codes command (Alt-F3). To illustrate its use, you should have your formatted notice on the screen. Although you can issue this command with your cursor anywhere on the screen, position it for this example so that it is on the blank line that precedes the first paragraph. Then enter the Reveal Codes command with Alt-F3 and your screen display will be as shown in Figure 8-5. This Reveal Codes screen consists of the following parts (from the top of the screen down):

- An upper portion displaying up to seven lines of text as they appear from the edit screen. These include the line on which the cursor is located and three lines above and below it.
- The familiar status line.
- The tab ruler separating the two halves of the screen and indicating the locations of the margins and tab stops. (The brace is used if the margin falls on a tab stop; otherwise, the square bracket is used.)
- A lower portion of the screen displaying the seven lines of text (shown in the upper portion) together with the hidden codes.

As a simple illustration of deleting formatting codes, let us delete the margin and underline codes. With the Up arrow key, move the cursor to the first line and your screen should be as shown in Figure 8-6(a). In the upper portion of the screen note that the cursor is positioned beneath the

Figure 8-5
The Reveal Codes screen.

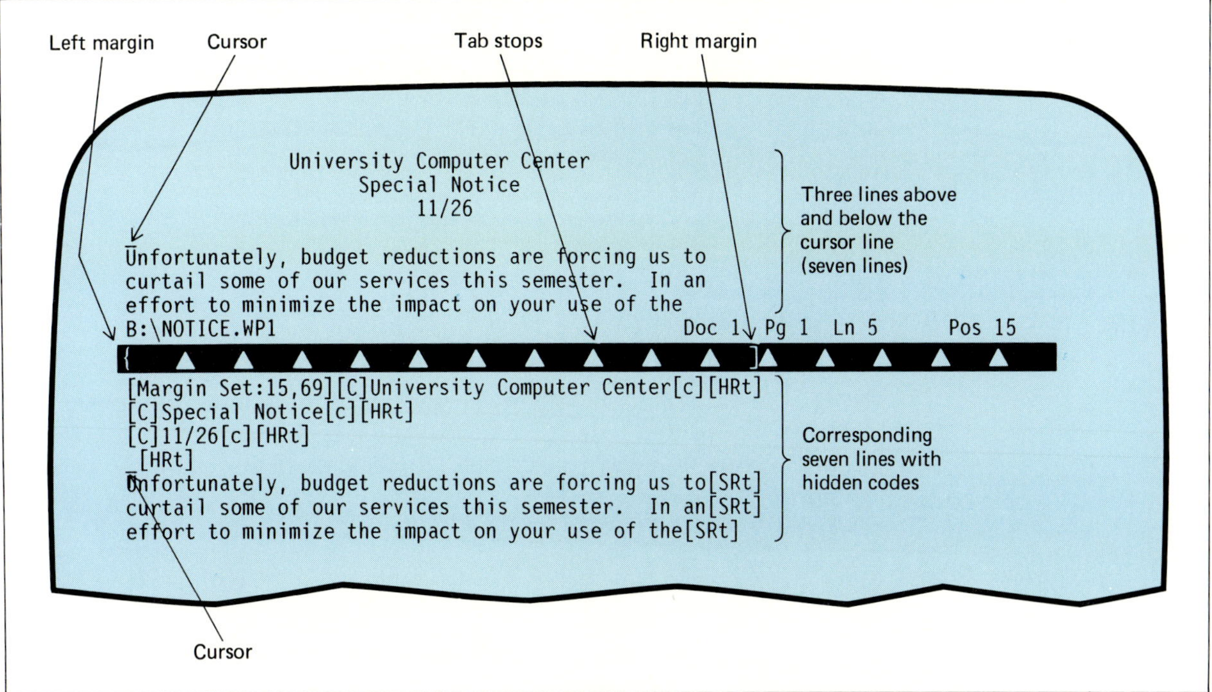

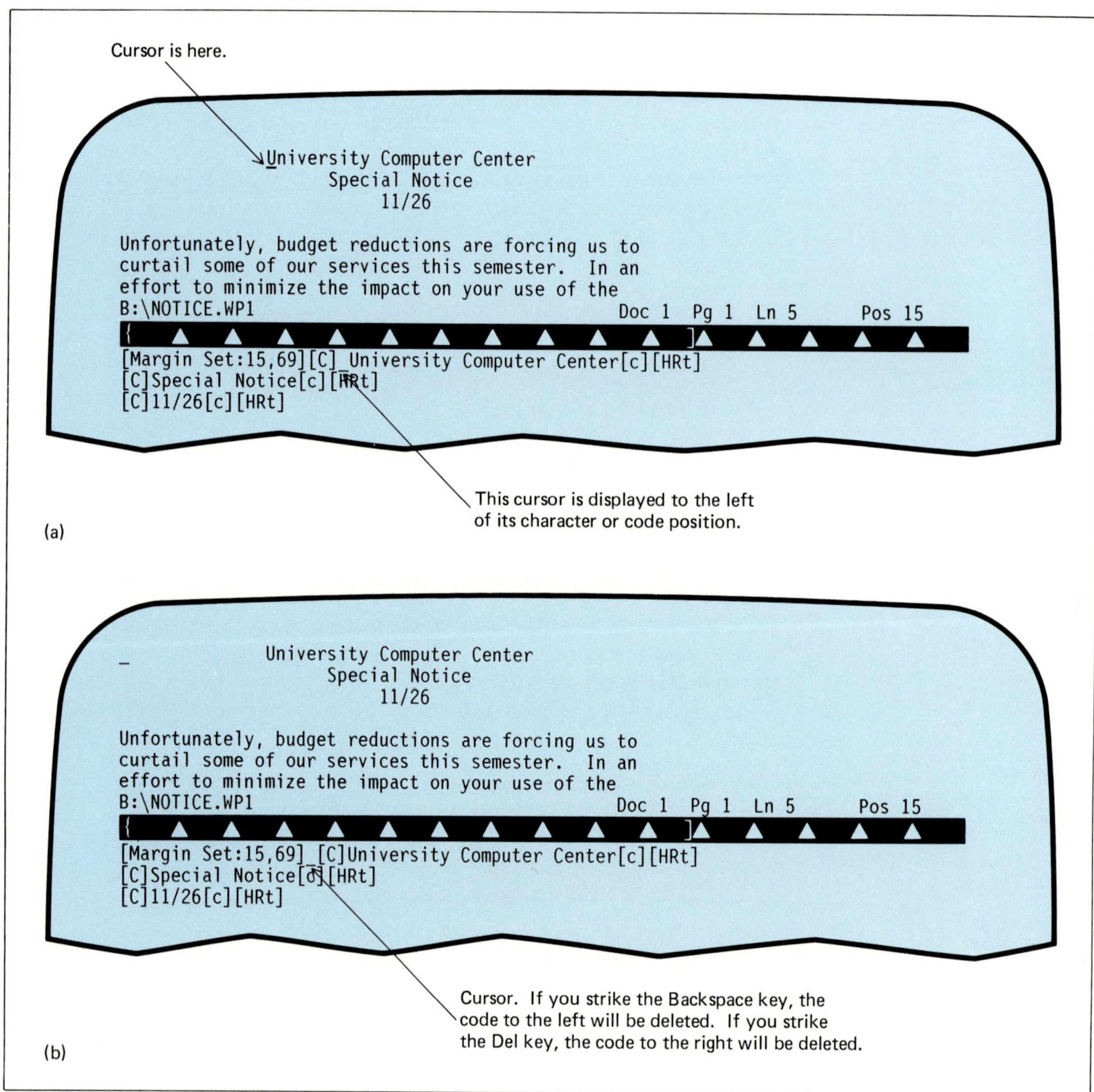

Figure 8-6
Positioning the cursor in the hidden codes.

letter *U* in *University*. In the lower portion of the screen, it is positioned between the center code [C] and the letter *U*. The cursor in the Reveal Codes screen is always positioned to the left of its character or code position.

DO THIS NOW 8-7 **Deleting Hidden Codes**

1. Position the cursor between the two codes as shown in Figure 8-6(b).

2. Strike the Backspace key to delete the margin code, and the displayed text will be rearranged conforming to the default values of 10 and 75.
3. Next, you must delete the underline, which is in a portion of the screen not displayed in Figure 8-6. With the Down key, move the cursor to the line containing the underlined text. Note that the screen scrolls when the cursor reaches the bottom line.
4. Position the Reveal Codes cursor to the right of the [U] underline code.
5. Strike the Backspace key.

When you do this, you will see that the ending code [u] is also deleted and that the underscore is removed from the text in the upper half of the screen. WordPerfect automatically deletes the matching code when you delete one of them. Since you are finished, you may return to the edit screen by striking the F1 key.

Deleting Hidden Codes from the Edit Screen

In Chapter 7, you learned that you can delete the Hard Return just as if it were another character. The same is true with other hidden codes. However, a problem is that you will be operating blindly if your document has two or more consecutive codes. To try this, you must clear the screen (Exit command) and then retrieve your copy of the formatted notice.

DO THIS NOW 8-8 **Deleting Hidden Codes**

1. Position the cursor under the letter *U* in *University* (the first line of the notice).
2. Strike the Backspace key. You will be prompted to confirm that you want the Center code deleted. If you respond with Y, the code will be deleted and the line moved to the left margin.
3. Leave the Center code unchanged by responding with N, the default.
4. Strike the Left arrow one time, thereby moving the cursor to a location between the left margin and the first title line.
5. Strike the Backspace and you will be prompted about deleting the margin code.
6. Respond with N and your document will be unchanged.

In both of these cases, WordPerfect asked you to confirm deleting the hidden code. For most (but not all) hidden codes, an attempt to delete from the edit screen results in a confirming prompt.

Correcting a Problem

To illustrate a situation in which the Reveal Codes screen can be invaluable, assume that you are making some minor changes in the notice. In this process, you are going to issue the Center command accidentally when the cursor is positioned in the middle of a paragraph. For your screen to correspond to the screen illustrations that follow, you must carry out the following sequence of steps exactly as described.

DO THIS NOW 8-9 **Creating a Problem**

1. Retrieve your formatted copy of the notice from disk. For this, use the Exit command without saving in order to clear the screen (remember the key sequence: F7,N,N). Then retrieve your formatted copy of the document.
2. Position the cursor under the letter *t* in *this* as shown in the following.

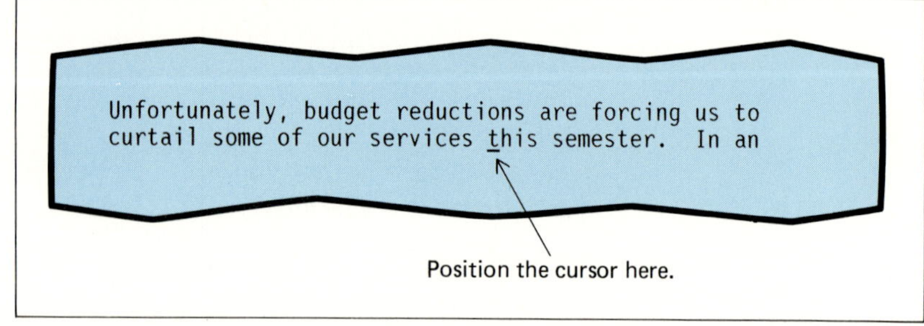

3. Enter the Center command with the Shift-F6.
4. Move the cursor down to the next line. Your display will now be as shown in Figure 8-7: the words *of our services* is missing.

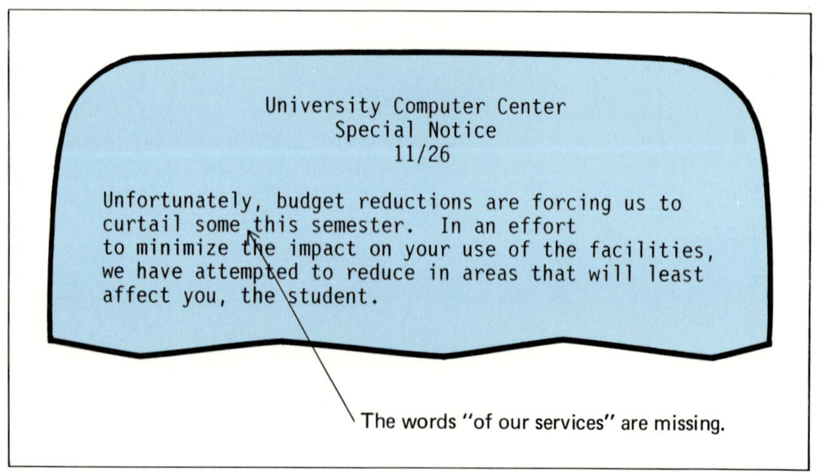

Figure 8-7
A puzzling screen display.

5. Move the cursor back up to the second line.
6. Using the Left and Right keys, move the cursor back and forth across the line (to the beginning of the line, then to the end, and then back again). Note how the cursor jumps when moved in the vicinity of the missing text and how that text is alternately redisplayed and then changed again. This is confusing indeed.

Whenever WordPerfect responds in a strange way such as this, you should use the Reveal Codes command (Alt-F3). The screen of Figure 8-8 tells the story. The errant Center command causes WordPerfect to center that portion of the line between the two codes, thus "overlaying" the earlier portion of the line. Once you know the problem, correcting it is easy.

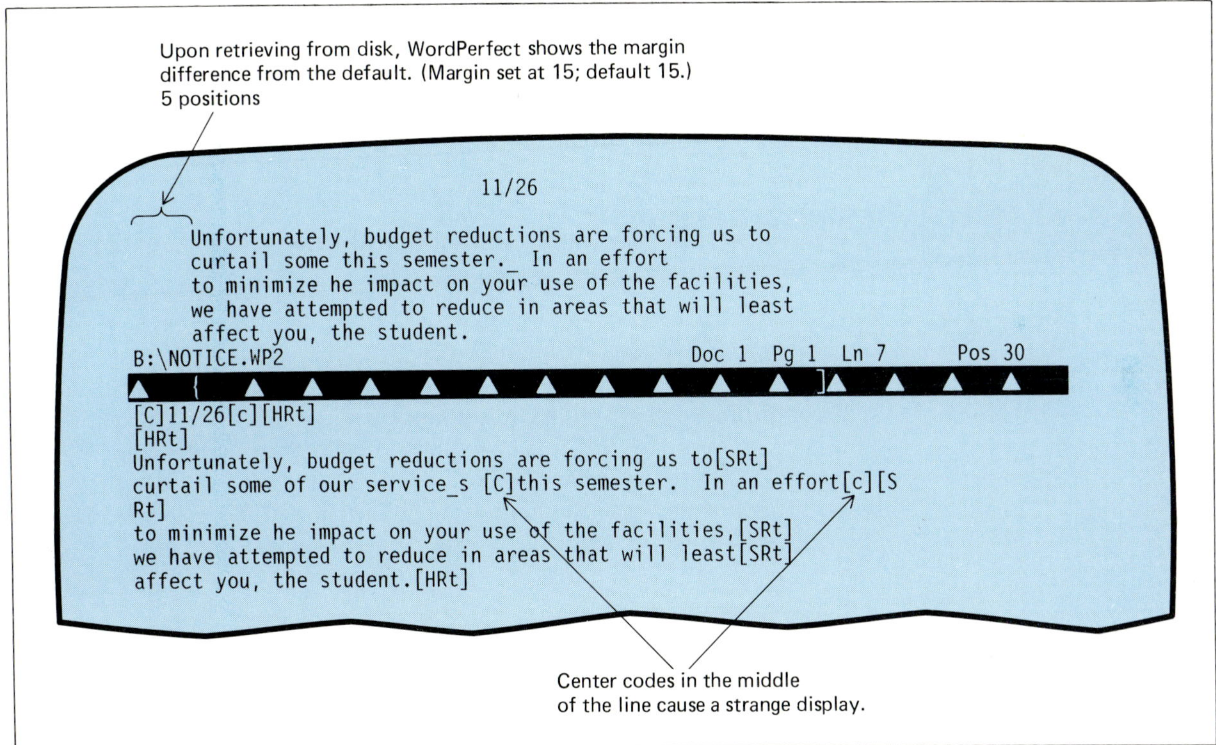

Figure 8-8
Misplaced hidden code that causes trouble.

DO THIS NOW 8-10 **Correcting a Problem**

1. Position the cursor to the immediate right of the Center code [C].
2. Strike the Backspace once.

Comparing Formatting Commands

From the earlier summary of commands used in this document and your knowledge of the actions required to format, you have probably noticed that the amount of text over which a command has an effect varies among commands. In this respect, the formatting commands can be grouped in three categories:

- First are those commands that act on all text that follows until another command is encountered. For instance, setting the margins results in a hidden code that applies to all text following the code until the next margin code is encountered (if there is another in the document).
- Second are those commands that act upon a predetermined amount of text. For instance, the Indent command generates a code that indents that single paragraph.
- Third are those commands that operate on a user-defined amount of text. For example, the Underline command generates codes that define the beginning and ending of the affected text.

Keeping these distinctions in mind will help you to understand the various formatting operations that are possible with WordPerfect.

FORMATTING WHILE ENTERING A DOCUMENT

For your first exposure to formatting a document, you worked with a document that had already been entered into the computer. Although you will frequently have occasion to change the formatting of a document, you will commonly enter formatting while you are entering the text. So that you become familiar with this, you should clear your screen (use the Exit command) and then enter the document of Figure 8-2, together with formatting, as follows (you will find it convenient to have a printed copy of the notice in front of you):

DO THIS NOW 8-11 **Entering and Formatting**

1. Enter the margin settings with the following sequence:

Shift-F8	Enter the Format Line command
3	Selection 3 for margins
15,Enter	Enter value for left margin
69,Enter	Enter value for right margin

2. Enter the Center code with Shift-F6.
3. Type the first heading line; note that WordPerfect constantly maintains centering on the text as you enter it. When finished, strike the Enter key.
4. Repeat steps 2 and 3 for the second and third heading lines.

5. After leaving a blank line following the headings, type the first paragraph. When finished with this paragraph, strike the Enter key twice (you need a blank line before the second paragraph).
6. Enter two Indent commands by holding down the Shift and striking the F4 twice.
7. Type the second paragraph. When you strike the Enter to end this paragraph, note that the cursor returns to the left margin. Remember, the Indent code applies only to the single paragraph. Strike the Enter again to leave another blank line.
8. Type the third paragraph up to the words *normal daytime hours,* which require underlining.
9. Turn underlining on by striking the F8 key.
10. Type the words *normal daytime hours.*
11. Turn underlining off by striking the F8 key. Note that during text entry, the underline key F8 functions as a toggle: strike it once and underlining is on; strike it a second time and underlining is off.
12. Type the remainder of this paragraph and the next paragraph.

Entry of the notice is now complete. It should look exactly like the version that you formatted beginning with the unformatted NOTICE.WP1.

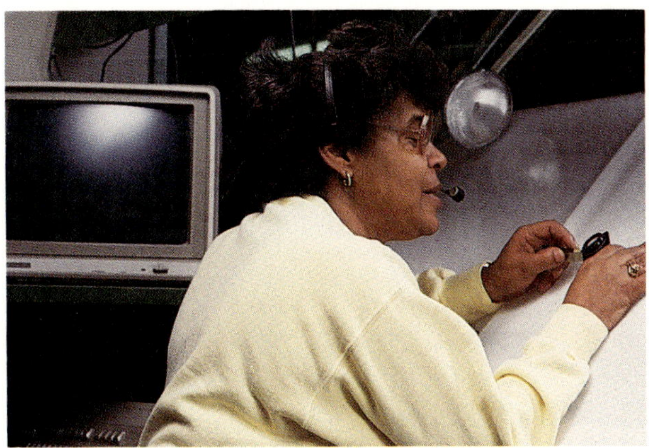

Voice input to a computer is a field that has evolved slowly because of significant technical problems. However, it is used in many different applications. It has great potential as a means of simplifying the use of word processing by the handicapped.

OTHER FORMATTING COMMANDS

Double Spacing

The documents you have prepared have been single spaced—the WordPerfect line spacing default. Sometimes it is convenient to double space a document, especially for a first draft that will require a lot of editing. You can change line spacing in the same way you change margin settings: by issuing a command that inserts hidden code in the document. Like the margin code, the line spacing code applies to all text that follows until another line spacing code is encountered. In fact, spacing is set from the same function key command as margins: Format Line (Shift-F8). To illustrate this, you should clear the screen and retrieve the original unformatted copy of the notice (NOTICE.WP1). Referring to Figure 8-1, note that it consists of the three heading lines followed by two paragraphs. You will double space the first paragraph only.

DO THIS NOW 8-12 **Double Spacing a Paragraph**

1. Move the cursor to the first position of the first paragraph (the letter *U* in *Unfortunately*).
2. Issue the Format Line command as follows:

Shift-F8	Format Line command
4	Selection 4 for spacing

3. From the resulting prompt

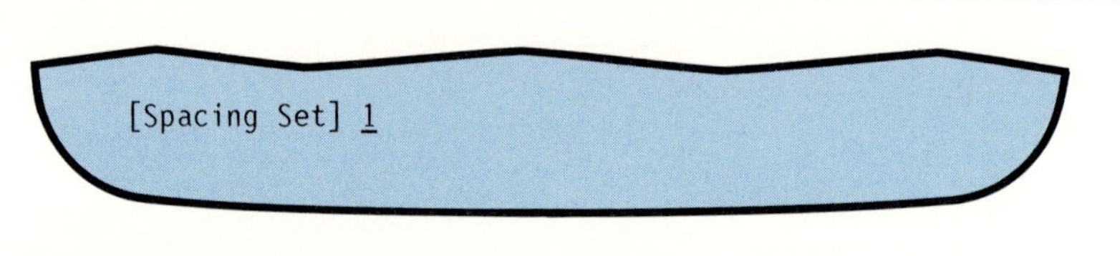

   you can designate the line spacing. The default value is 1; values that can be entered are 1.5 for one and a half spacing, 2 for double spacing, and 3 for triple spacing. Type the digit 2 and then strike the Enter. Except for the first three lines, the entire document will be double spaced.
4. Move the cursor to the first position of the second paragraph (the letter *I* in *If you,* which should be the last displayed line on your screen).
5. Repeat the Format Line command but this time enter 1 for the line spacing. This will cause all text that follows (only two lines in this document) to be single spaced.

Disabling Right Justification

Although the edit screen displays documents with a ragged margin on the right, WordPerfect automatically inserts sufficient spaces to justify printing. However, in some situations, you might not want these extra spaces inserted. For instance, the additional spaces in the indented paragraph of the notice tend to be distracting.

```
During   the   holiday  period  the
Center will not be  open during the
```

You can insert hidden codes to turn justification on and off just as you insert margin and line spacing codes. For the notice that you have on the screen, you can turn justification off with the following sequence.

DO THIS NOW 8-13 **Disabling Right Justification**

1. Position the cursor at the beginning of the first paragraph (under the *U* in *Unfortunately*).
2. Enter the Print Format command with Ctrl-F8. WordPerfect then displays the Print Format list of eleven options, each of which can be used to change the way in which printing will be affected.
3. Since you want to turn justification off, strike the digit 3. Had you desired to turn it on (only necessary if you previously turned it off), then you would have entered the digit 4.

You should now print the document to confirm that its appearance is consistent with the formatting that you have performed.

Hanging Paragraphs

A **hanging paragraph** (also called a hanging indent) is one in which the entire paragraph, with the exception of the first line, is indented from the left. For example, the description of Figure 8-9 uses hanging paragraphs to set each of the three items apart. To try this, you might want to clear your screen first, although it is not necessary for this exercise.

DO THIS NOW 8-14 **Hanging Paragraph**

1. Enter the first paragraph and strike the Enter twice to produce the blank line.
2. Type the digit 1 and the period.
3. Enter a Left Indent command (F4). The cursor will jump to the first tab stop.

4. Enter the paragraph; each wrap begins the next line at the indent position.
5. Enter items 2 and 3 in exactly the same way as you entered item 1.

With this technique, you can use the left indent (F4) or the left-right indent (Shift-F4).

Figure 8-9
Hanging paragraphs.

```
The amount of text over which a command has an effect varies from
one command to another.  In this respect, formatting commands can
be grouped in three categories.

1.    Those that act on all text that follows until another is
      encountered.  The margins code is such an example.

2.    Those that act upon a predetermined amount of text.  For
      instance, the Indent command used here generates a code that
      indents a single paragraph.

3.    Those that operate on a user defined amount of text.  For
      example, the underline command generates codes that define
      the beginning and ending of the affected text.
```

The first line of each paragraph is positioned to the left.

SEARCHING A DOCUMENT

The Search Command

Assume you prepared a long document and that somewhere within it you mentioned an *archive copier.* Later, you decide to check that passage to be certain your statement was accurate. If you did not remember where in the document you made the remark, you would have to scan the entire document looking for these words. For a long document, this could be time consuming. With a word processor, it is simple because the program will do the searching for you. For this, WordPerfect includes two versions of the Search command:

F2	Forward Search searches from the cursor position to the end of the document.
Shift-F2	Reverse Search searches from the cursor position to the beginning of the document.

Although the command is most useful with a long document, its use is easily illustrated with a short one. For this, use the document named CONTRACT.WP1; it is on the data disk that accompanies this book and was used for one of the Chapter 7 assignments. In it, the word *terminated* is misspelled as *termінted.* Let us find it with the Search command.

DO THIS NOW 8-15 **Searching**

1. Clear the screen and retrieve the file CONTRACT.WP1.
2. To issue a Search Forward command, strike the F2 key, which produces the following prompt on the status line.

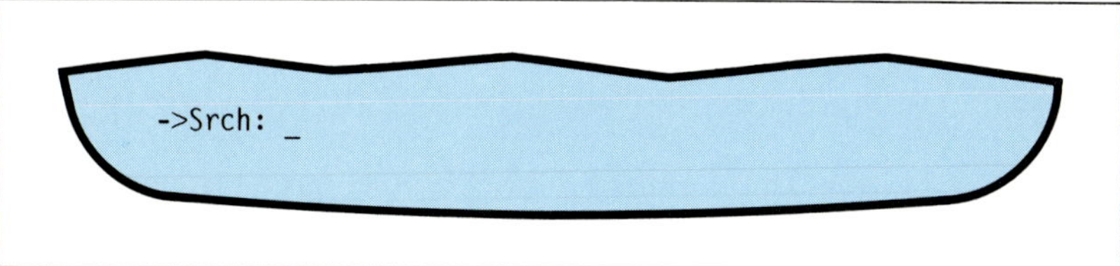

3. Type the characters for which you wish to search; this is called the **search string**. To illustrate the Search command more fully, type in the first four letters of the word *terminted,* or *term.*
4. Start the search by striking the F2 key again; the search will be successful and the cursor will be positioned as follows:

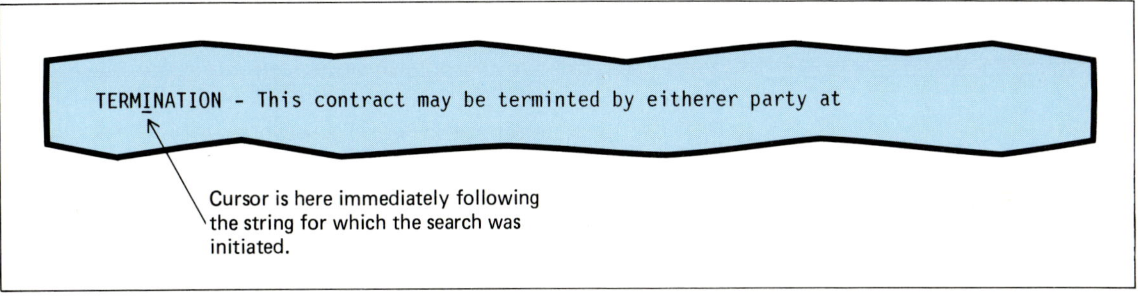

When starting the search, be careful that you do not strike the Enter key. If you do, the code [HRt] will be entered as part of the search string. Then the search will be for the indicated text followed by a hard return.

5. Since this is not the portion of text that you want, you must execute the Search command again. However, the process is simplified by the fact that the last-used search string is offered as a default. Hence, to continue, strike the F2 key twice, and the cursor will be positioned on the word *terminted.*

This exercise illustrates three points. The first is how to repeat a search, as you have just done. The second is that the search action is looking for a sequence of characters that is exactly like the search string. In this example, WordPerfect found the four letters *term* as part of another word. A further point is that the search string can be one or more words or portions of two words—any combination of characters. The third point relates to the way in which WordPerfect handles lowercase and uppercase in the search action. If the search string is lowercase, then either uppercase or lowercase in the text will cause a match. For instance, with the search string *term*, WordPerfect found a match with both *TERM* and *term* (it would also have matched *Term*). However, had you used uppercase for the search string, that is, *TERM*, then only uppercase letters would have been matched.

In this example, the cursor was positioned at the beginning of the document so you used the Search Forward (search toward the end). Had the cursor been located somewhere within the document (or at the end), you could have used the reverse search by initiating the command with Shift-F2. This would have caused the search to progress from the cursor position back toward the beginning of the document.

If WordPerfect cannot find text that matches the search string, then the status line momentarily displays the message

```
*Not Found*
```

and you are returned to the edit screen. The cursor remains where it was before the search was started.

The Replace Command

In the letter CONTRACT.WP1 that you are working on, assume that you must change the word COMPANY to MCT wherever it occurrs (see Figure 6-1). In this letter, the word appears only four times; in the complete contract, it would occur many times. In WordPerfect, the Replace command (which is an extension of the Search) automates your task of making this change. If you do not have the letter (CONTRACT.WP1) on the screen from the search example, then clear the screen and retrieve it for this example. After making certain that the cursor is at the beginning of the letter, you should do the following to change COMPANY to MCT.

DO THIS NOW 8-16 **Replacing Text**

1. Issue the Replace command with the key sequence Alt-F2; this produces the following prompt on the status line.

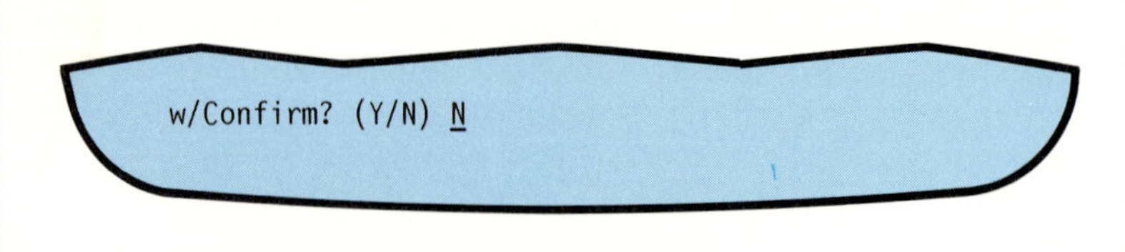

2. Strike the letter Y (this option is described later).
3. WordPerfect displays the following prompt on the status line requesting that the text to be replaced be entered.

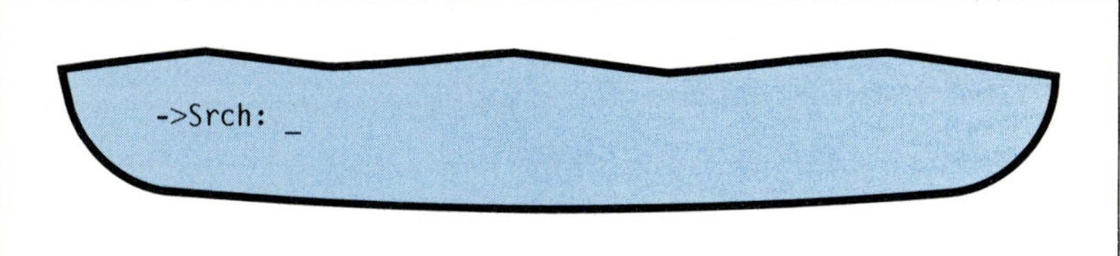

Notice that this is identical to the Search prompt.

4. Type the search string *COMPANY* and then strike F2 to indicate to WordPerfect that you have completed your entry. (As with the Search, you should not strike the Enter key.)
5. The prompt on the status line will be replaced with:

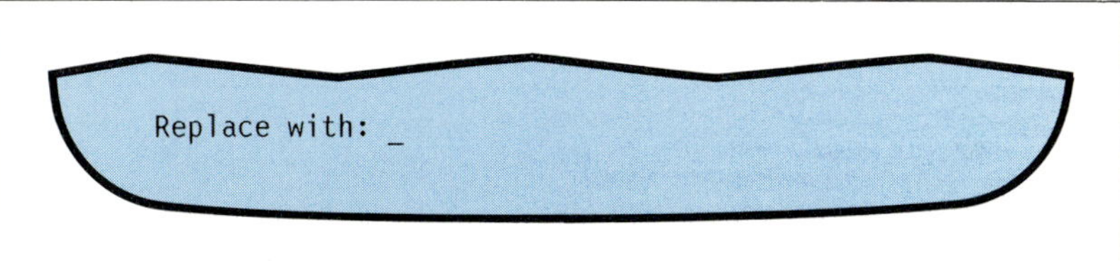

Type the replacement text *MCT* and then strike the F2 key.

6. The first match will be in the phrase *OPTION OF COMPANY TO APPROVE ORDERS.* The cursor will be positioned under the word *COMPANY,* and a prompt will appear on the status line asking for a confirmation. Strike the letter Y to replace and N (or Enter) to leave unchanged. You must repeat this for each occurrence of the word.

The Replace command offers you the option of confirming each replacement (as you did in this example) or allowing the program to make each one automatically. Usually, it is best to use the confirmation option. For instance, if you decided to change the word *which* to *that* everywhere it appeared, you could end up with such things as *thatever* (resulting from *whichever*). Before making an automatic replacement, it is a good idea to save your document to disk in the event of unforeseen problems.

CUTTING AND PASTING

In Chapter 6, you learned that another of the features of word processors is the ease of cutting and pasting. As illustrated in Figure 6-6, this term is derived from the equivalent action of physically cutting a portion of text from one page and pasting it onto another. Because of the versatility of the computer, cutting and pasting with a word processor can involve moving a portion of text from one place to another in a document, or making a copy of a portion of text and inserting the copy at another place in the document. The general steps in performing a cut and paste are as follows:

1. Identify the text to be cut.
2. Cut (remove) the identified text from the document but retain it in a temporary memory area (called the *cut save area*).
3. Move the cursor to the location at which the cut text is to be inserted.
4. Insert the text currently held in the cut save area into the document at the position of the cursor.

The overall process is illustrated in Figure 8-10. In WordPerfect, this is done with various options of the Move command (Ctrl-F4). Let us try this.

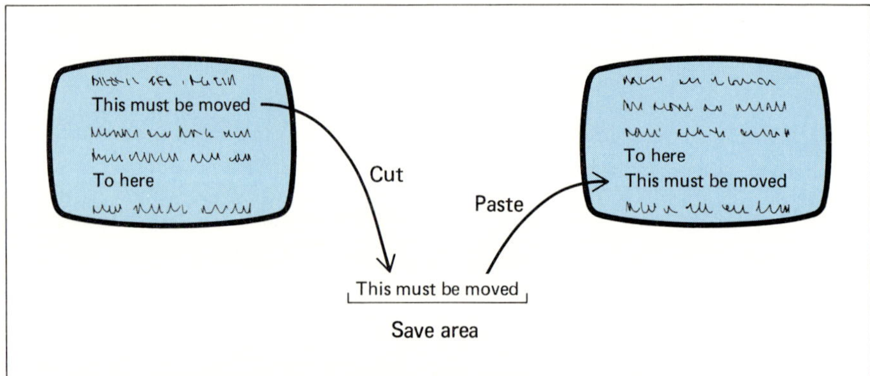

Figure 8-10
Using the save area to cut and paste.

Operating on a Block of Text

For an example of cutting and pasting, you may continue with the document CONTRACT.WP1 that you used in the preceding example for search and replace. Assume that you wish to move the DRESS CODE paragraph to precede the OPTION paragraph, as shown in Figure 8-11. The following steps perform the cut and paste by defining a block of text to be moved.

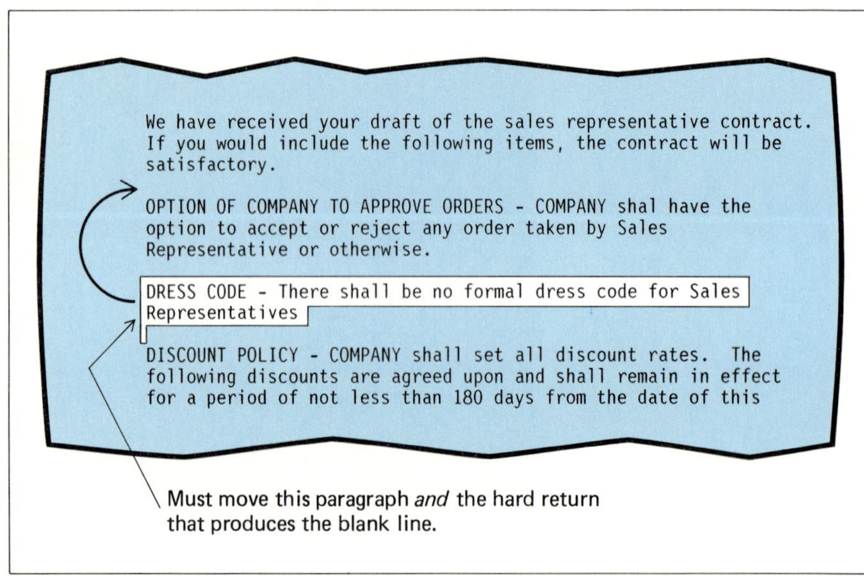

Figure 8-11
A section of text to be cut and pasted.

DO THIS NOW 8-17 **Cut and Paste**

1. Position the cursor at the first character of the text to be moved, in this case, under the letter *D* in *DRESS* (see Figure 8-11).

2. Begin blocking with the Alt-F4 key sequence.

3. Extend the block by moving the cursor down until the entire paragraph is highlighted. If you move the cursor to the letter *D* in *DISCOUNT* of the following paragraph, your block will include the hard return that produces the blank line following the desired paragraph.

4. Invoke the Move command with Ctrl-F4. This produces the status line selection menu shown in Figure 8-12.

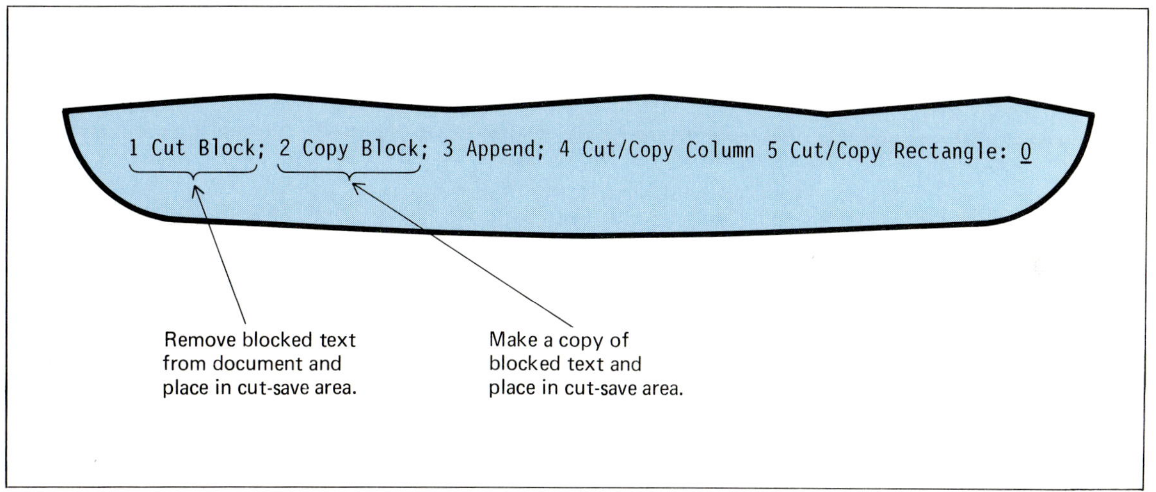

Figure 8-12

5. Options 1 and 2 both cause a copy of the blocked text to be placed in the cut save area of memory. Option 1 erases the block from the document, and option 2 leaves it unchanged. For this example, since you want to cut the block, strike the digit 1 key.

6. Move the cursor to the position to which the cut text is to be inserted; that is, its position is on the letter *O* in *OPTION* (see Figure 8-11).

7. Issue another Move command (Ctrl-F4); the status line prompt will be as shown in Figure 8-13.

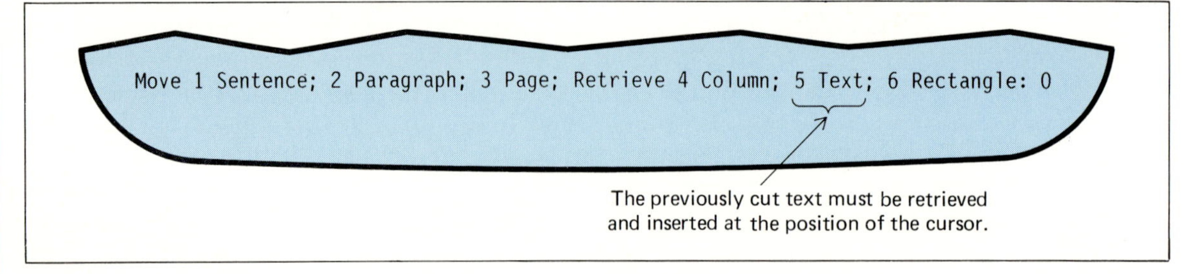

Figure 8-13

Notice that selections 1 through 3 pertain to the Move action and 4 through 6 pertain to the Retrieve action.

8. To insert the text at the point of the cursor, you need the Retrieve Text action; for this, type the digit 5. The text stored in the save area of memory is retrieved and inserted preceding the OPTIONS paragraph, thus completing the cut-and-paste action.

Operating on a Sentence, Paragraph, or Page

The cut-and-paste sequence for blocked text that you used in the preceding example allows you to operate on a block of any size, from a few words to many pages. However, if you need to operate on a full sentence, paragraph, or page, then you need not block the text. You have already seen that the Move command produces two different selection menus. That is, if you blocked an area of text before issuing the Move, the selection menu is as shown in Figure 8-12. If you did not block an area of text, then the selection menu is as shown in Figure 8-13. Thus, to perform the cut-and-paste operation of this example, you could have positioned the cursor anywhere in the paragraph that is to be moved. Then the Move command would have produced the menu of Figure 8-13. Striking the 2 key for Paragraph would produce a prompt asking if you want to Cut, Copy, or Delete. The Cut-and-Copy options are the same as previously described. The Delete option really is not a Move action at all. It simply deletes the text indicated from the document and permanently discards it (without placing a copy in the cut save area).

With regard to the cut save area of memory, whenever text is cut or copied, it is placed in this special area of memory. This area will always contain the text that was cut or copied with the last execution of the Move command. However, each cut or copy action causes the previous contents of the area to be replaced by the latest cut or copied text. Note that this save area is used only by the cut or copy action; text deleted with the Backspace and Del keys is not saved here.

WORKING WITH TWO DOCUMENTS

Word processing was introduced to you in Chapter 6 via the letter to the attorney (see Figures 6-1 and 6-2). In fact, the handwritten original included directions to the typist to copy the three contractual items from another document: in word processing terminology, a cut-and-paste operation. However, this cut-and-paste operation is different from that of the preceding example in that it requires that text from one document be copied into another. Let us see how this can be done with WordPerfect.

Creating and Using Two Windows

To facilitate working with two documents, WordPerfect allows you to split the screen into two independent document screen areas or windows, as illustrated in Figure 8-14. Notice that WordPerfect splits the memory into two separate document areas so that each can function completely independently of the other. Before trying this, you should clear the screen with the Exit command and then carry out the sequence of DTN 8-18.

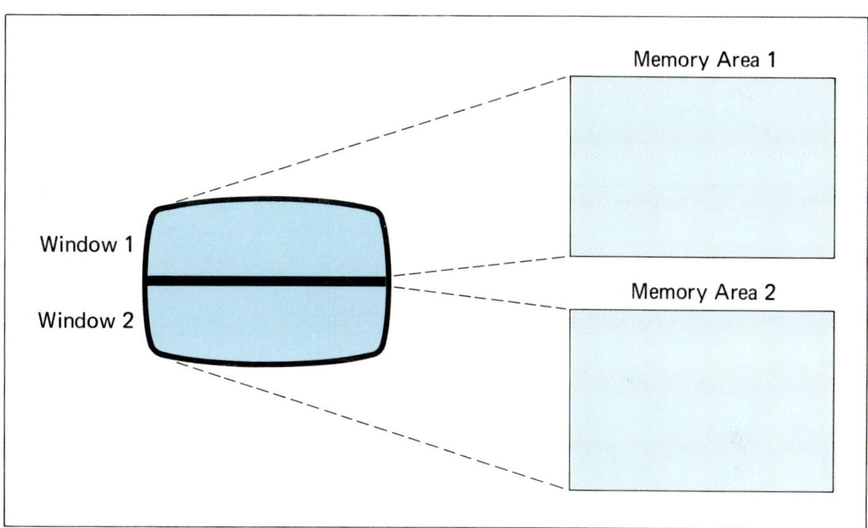

Figure 8-14
The two-window concept.

DO THIS NOW 8-18 **Creating Two Windows**

1. Enter the Screen command (Ctrl-F3), which produces the status line message:

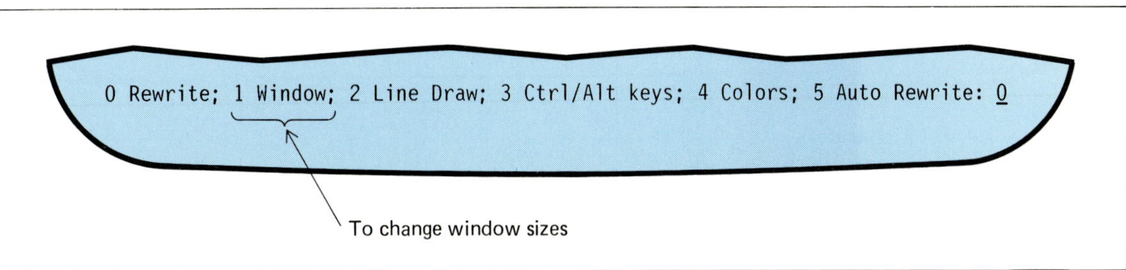

2. Select the Window option by typing the digit 1. WordPerfect then asks you how many screen lines you wish to devote to window 1 with the following prompt.

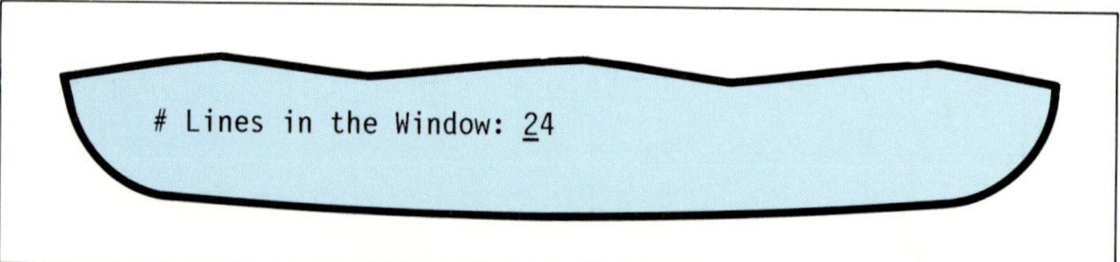

3. The smallest allowable window size is 2; the default of 24 results in a single window. For this exercise, enter 14 and strike the Enter. Your screen will then appear as in Figure 8-15.

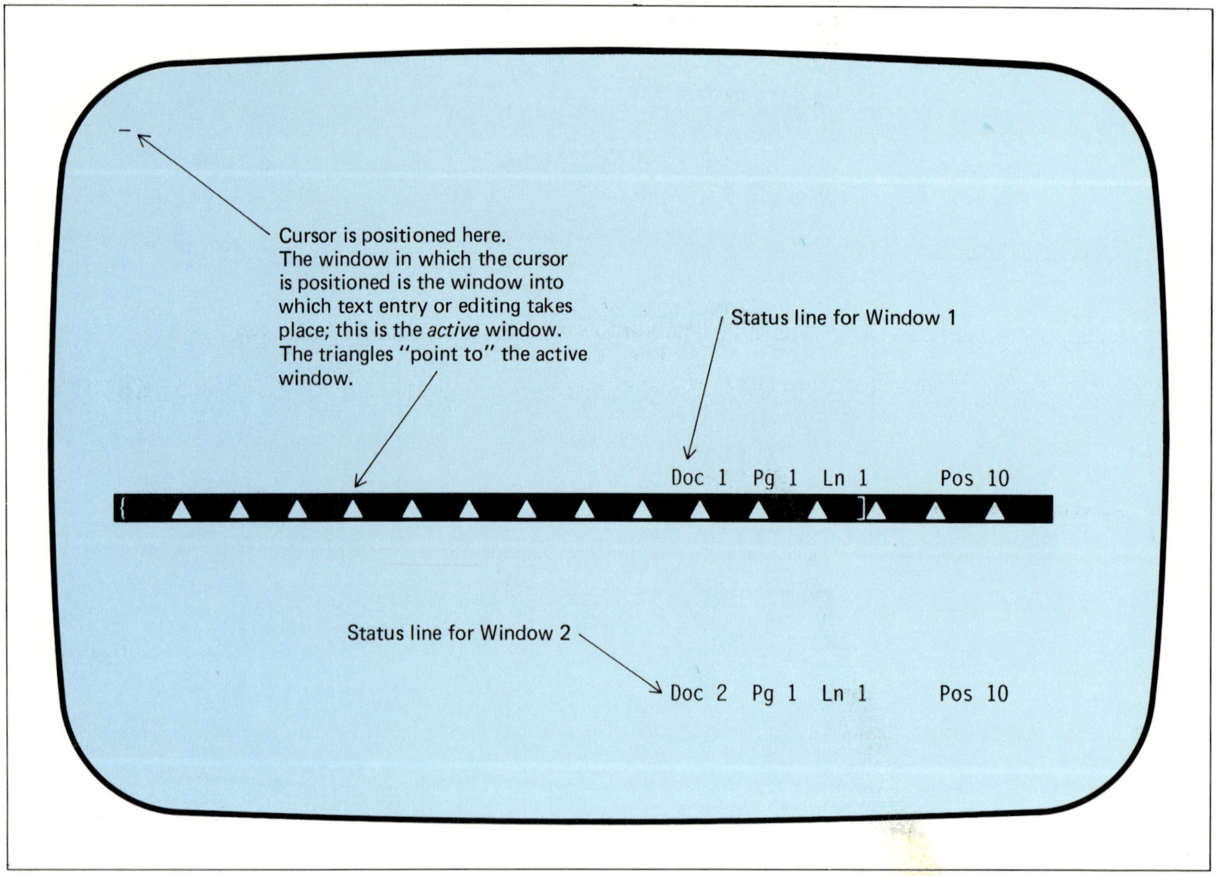

Cursor is positioned here.
The window in which the cursor is positioned is the window into which text entry or editing takes place; this is the *active* window. The triangles "point to" the active window.

Status line for Window 1

Doc 1 Pg 1 Ln 1 Pos 10

Status line for Window 2

Doc 2 Pg 1 Ln 1 Pos 10

Figure 8-15
A two-window screen.

The two windows in Figure 8-15 are divided by the tab ruler. Note that each window includes its own status line. Initially, the upper window will be the active window and the cursor will be positioned in it. You can switch from one window to the next with the Switch command (Shift-F3). Try it. You will notice that you can tell at a glance which window is active by looking at the tab ruler. If the upper window (document 1) is active, the small triangles in the ruler point upward, as in Figure 8-15. If the lower window (document 2) is active, the small triangles point downward, as in Figure 8-16.

Figure 8-16
Tab ruler when window 2 is active.

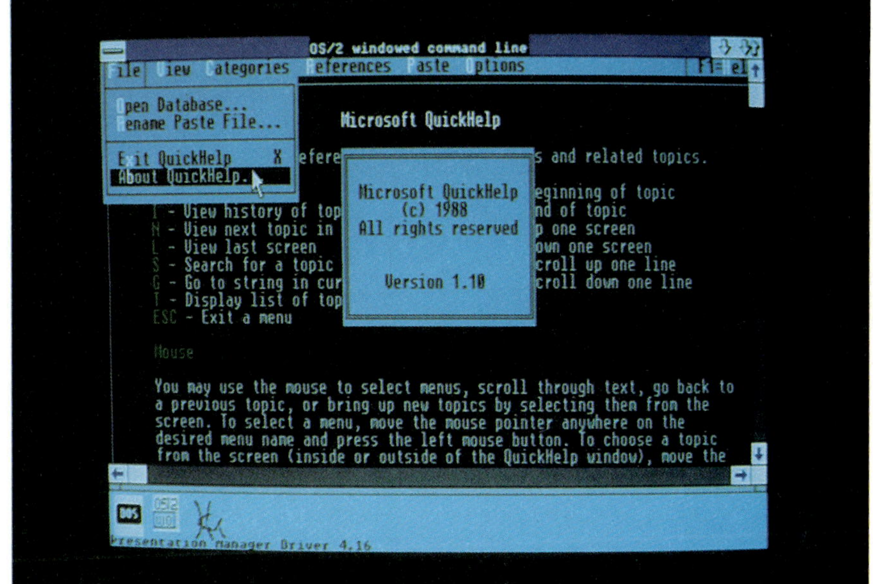

In later chapters you will learn about spreadsheets. The computer screen here shows the combination of data from a spreadsheet program with that from a word processing document.

Copying from One Document to Another

For this example, the data disk that accompanies this book contains two files: SKELETON.WP, which is the skeleton of the letter to the attorney (Figure 6-2); and LEGAL.WP1, which contains the legal items to be included in the letter. Before beginning, you should check to ensure that they are on the data disk currently in your computer. To retrieve these documents, carry out the following sequence (your screen should already display two windows, as shown in Figure 8-15).

DO THIS NOW 8-19 **Retrieving Two Documents**

1. If window 1 is not the active window, then change to it with the Switch command (Shift-F3).
2. Retrieve the document SKELETON.WP (Shift-F10). The skeleton of the letter will be displayed in the upper screen.

3. Switch to the lower window with the Switch command (Shift-F3).
4. Retrieve the document LEGAL.WP1. Your screen will now appear as shown in Figure 8-17. Notice that the status lines clearly identify each document.

Figure 8-17
Two document display.

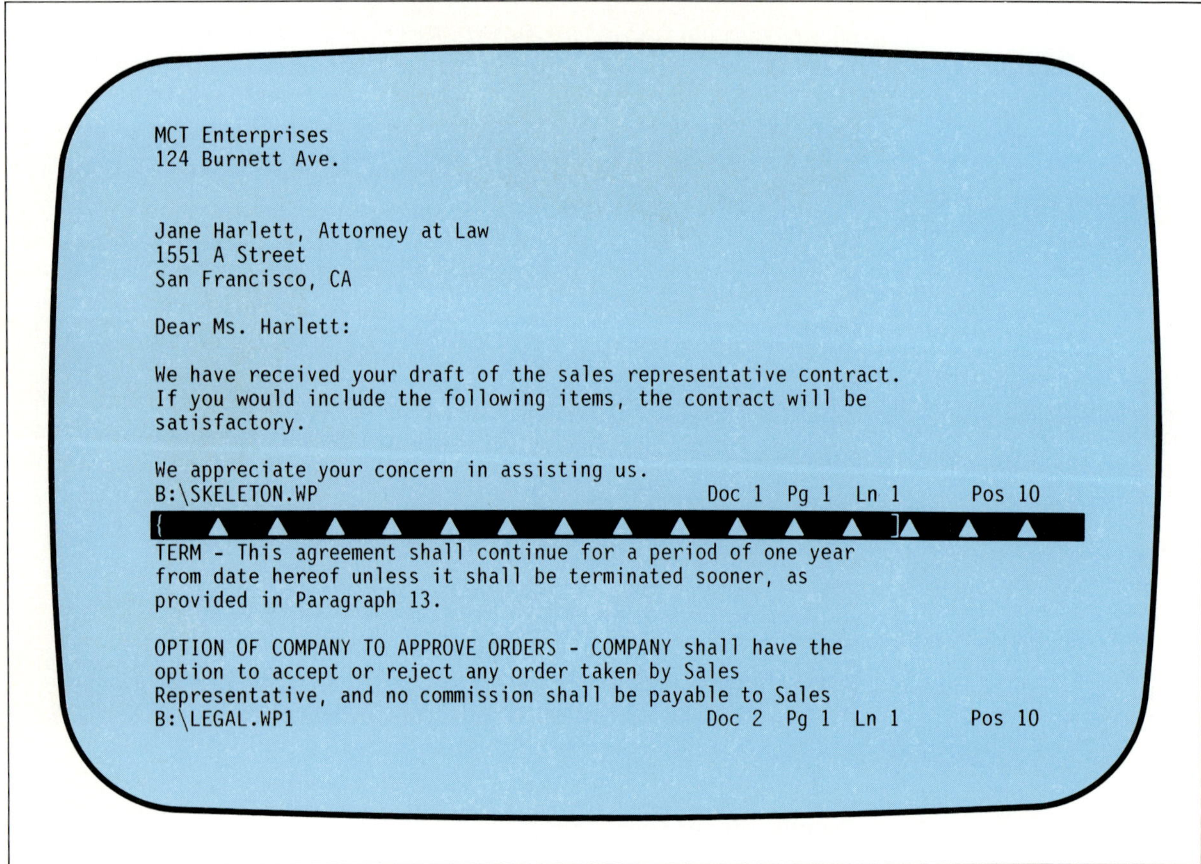

If you scroll the lower window, you will see that this document contains five items. You need to copy the second (OPTION OF COMPANY . . .), the fourth (DISCOUNT POLICY), and the fifth (TERMINATION) into the letter in the upper window with the following sequence of actions.

DO THIS NOW 8-20 **Copying From One Document to Another**

1. With the lower screen active, block the first item to be copied with:

   Position cursor under the letter *O* of *OPTION*.

   Enter the Block command (Shift-F3).

   Move the cursor to the letter *N* in *NOTICE* (of the next item).

2. Enter the Move command (Ctrl-F4); then select the Copy Block option (strike the digit 2). The highlight on the screen will disappear. The text will remain unchanged but a copy is now in the cut save area.
3. Switch to the upper window (Shift-F3) and move the cursor to the point at which the text in the cut save area is to be inserted (to the letter *W* in *We appreciate*).
4. Enter the Move command (Ctrl-F4); then select the Retrieve Text option (strike the digit 5). The text from the cut save area will be inserted into the letter. You may wish to scroll the screen to see that it is indeed in place.
5. To copy the other two items, switch to the lower screen and repeat the process. Since the last two items you need to copy are adjacent in document 2, you can begin the block with the letter *D* in *DISCOUNT*, and move it down to encompass the entire TERMINATION item. Then repeat steps 2 through 4.

Sometimes, when working with two windows, it becomes desirable to close one of the windows in order to devote the full screen to the document in the other window. For example, if after working with the two windows of Figure 8-17 you decided to devote the entire screen to the letter, you would carry out the following actions.

DO THIS NOW 8-21 **Closing a Window**

1. Switch to memory area 1 (the window that is to remain open).
2. Enter the Screen command (Ctrl-F3).
3. In response to the number of lines query, enter 24 and strike the Enter.

All twenty-four lines of the screen will then be devoted to document 1 and none to document 2. However, document 2 is still in memory and you can switch to it with the Switch command (Shift-F3), or reopen that window with the Screen command.

After you have finished working with two documents and decide to exit, you should be aware that WordPerfect will require that you issue the Exit twice, once for each document, before terminating processing.

THE WORDPERFECT SPELLER AND THESAURUS

In Chapter 6, you learned about two special word processing tools: the spelling checker and the thesaurus. When invoked, a spelling checker checks spelling in all or part of your document against a dictionary stored on disk. With a thesaurus, you can request that a list of alternative words for a word in your document (these are called synonyms) be displayed from a thesaurus file on disk. However, these components of the Limited-Use version have access to a relatively few words. (The files for the full spelling checker and the thesaurus are very large.) Because of the restriction, the speller and thesaurus in the Limited-Use software are adequate only for you to learn how to use them.

Checking Spelling

The data disk accompanying this book includes a short document named SPELL.WPC that consists only of words in the abbreviated dictionary. This document, which is shown in Figure 8-18, is used here to illustrate principles of the WordPerfect Speller. In the illustration, spelling errors have been highlighted for convenient reference.

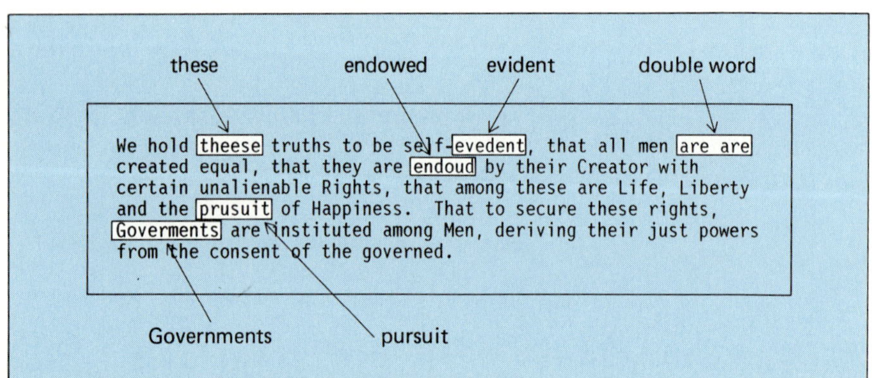

Figure 8-18
Document with spelling errors.

After clearing your screen, retrieve the document SPELL.WPC and then enter the Spell command Ctrl-F2. The first three options of the prompt on the status line allow you to check a single word, a page, or the entire document. Press the 2 key to select the document. WordPerfect will then begin checking word by word. Upon encountering the word *theese* (see Figure 8-18), it will be highlighted and the message *Not Found!* displayed at the bottom of the screen, indicating that this word was not found in the dictionary. Just below the double line is a list of possible correct spellings for the word. Although only one word is offered in this example, there will commonly be several different possibilities, listed as alternative A, B, C, and so on. To select one of the alternatives, enter the letter that identifies it; in this case, type the letter *A*. The incorrectly spelled word will immediately be replaced with the selected alternative. The meanings of the menu selections 1 through 4 are as follows.

1 Skip only this occurrence of the word and leave it unchanged. However, if the same word is encountered again in the document, show it as misspelled.

2 Skip this word and all other occurrences of it, leaving it unchanged throughout the document.

3 Add this word to the Speller dictionary. Then it will become a regular part of the Speller dictionary on your disk and will not be marked as unrecognized in the future.

4 Type a replacement word from the keyboard.

As you respond to each misspelled word, WordPerfect searches for the next one; each should be handled in the same way. The third error that WordPerfect will detect is the double occurrence of *are* (see Figure 8-18). Entering the digit 3 causes the second occurrence to be deleted. After completing the spelling check, WordPerfect indicates how many words were checked. Strike the F1 key to return to the edit screen.

Using the Thesaurus

Assume that last week the manager of Slick Promotions presented a plan to your partner for advertising a new MCT product line. Your partner was impressed with some of the ideas but had reservations and so requested that you meet with Slick Promotions officials. After the meeting, you summed up your reactions in the memo of Figure 8-19 (it is stored as THESAUR.WPC on the data disk accompanying this book). Upon reading it over, you were not completely happy with the word *fear* so you decided to check the Thesaurus.

To try this yourself, first clear the screen and then retrieve THESAUR.WPC. Next, position the cursor anywhere in the word *fear* and issue the Thesaurus command Alt-F1. The resulting screen will be as shown in Figure 8-20. Here, four lines of the document remain at the top of the screen and groups of reference words occupy the rest of the screen. The selected word from the text, the one being referenced, is highlighted. Any word that can be found in the Thesaurus is called a *headword*. The reference words in the lower portion of the screen are divided into four categories: nouns, adjectives (there are no adjectives for the word *fear* in this screen), verbs, and antonyms. (An antonym is a word that means the

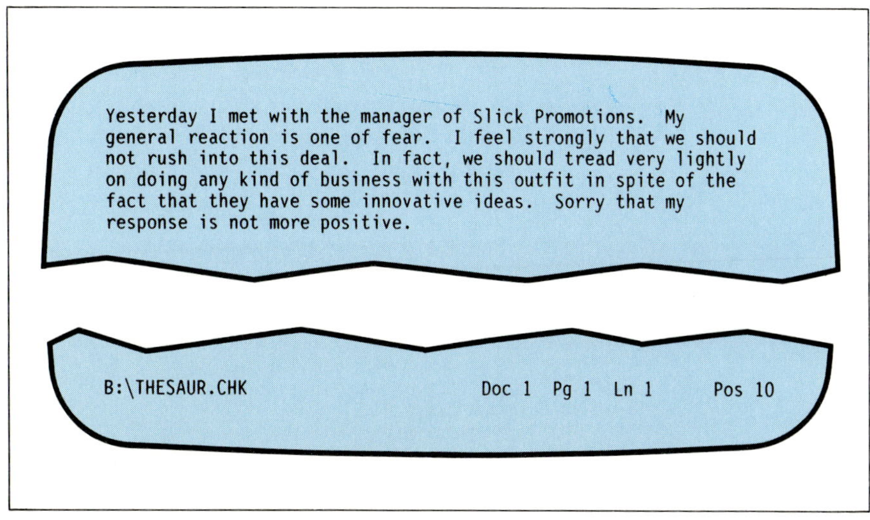

Figure 8-19
A memo expressing concern.

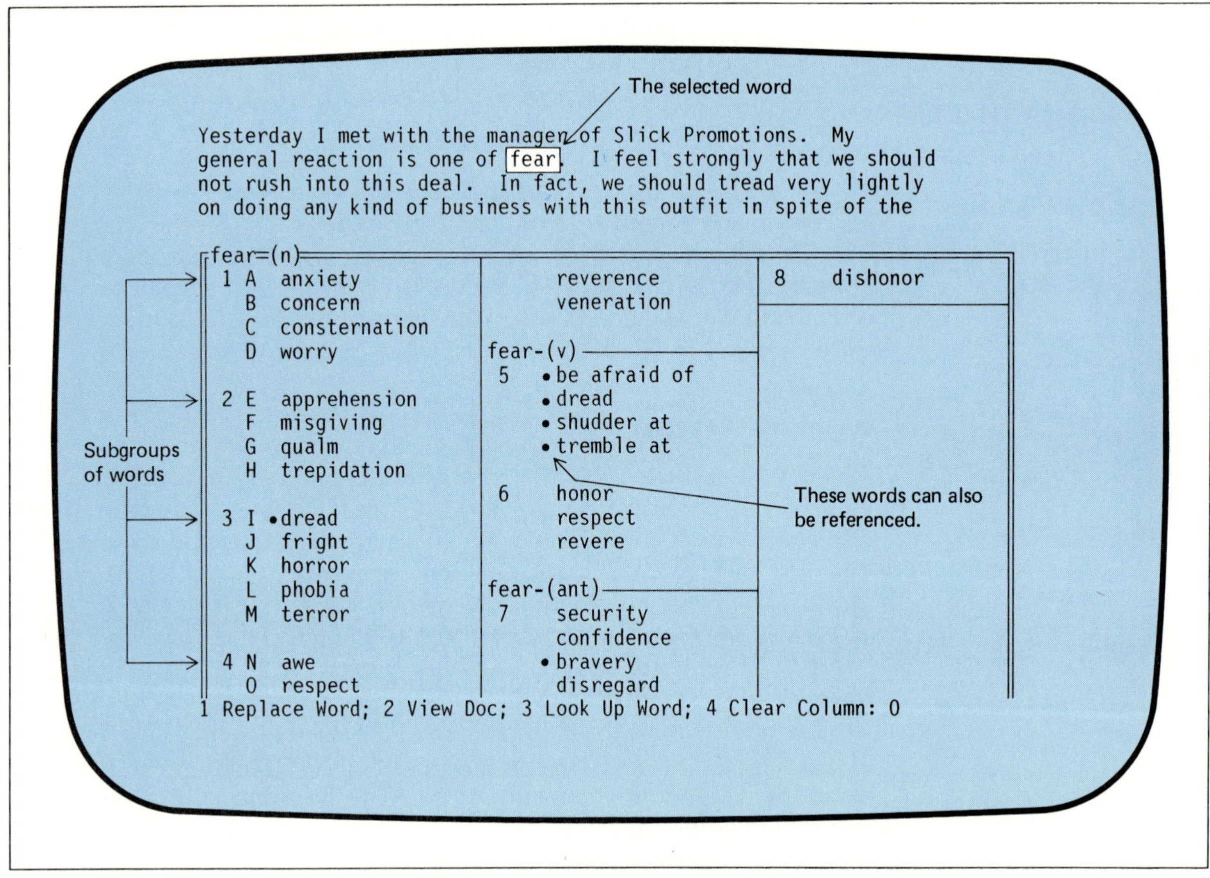

Figure 8-20
The Thesaurus display.

opposite of the selected word.) The numbered groups 1, 2, 3,. . . are groups of words with the same general connotation. Words that are preceded by a dot are also headwords, meaning that they can be found in the Thesaurus.

For this example, assume that you decide to replace *fear* with *concern.* To do this, type the digit 1 (Replace Word selection), and the program will ask you which word is to be used as the replacement. Strike the letter B for *concern,* and the replacement will be made. WordPerfect will then return to the edit screen. If you are interested in reference words for one of the other headwords—for example, dread—type the digit 3 and respond to the prompt with the letter I.

SUMMARY

This chapter has built upon the basic concepts you learned in Chapter 7. Summarizing, the important items from the chapter are:

- The general formatting actions described in this chapter include the following.

Margin setting

Line centering

Paragraph indention

Double spacing

Disabling and enabling right justification

Underscoring

Boldfacing

- WordPerfect formatting commands produce hidden codes inserted into the document. The Reveal Codes command is used to display hidden codes within a document.
- Different formatting commands affect different amounts of text. For instance, if the margins are set at one point in a document, they remain at that setting until you insert another margin-setting code. On the other hand, centering affects only a single line.
- You can locate a portion of text with the Search command. The search operation is conducted from the location of the cursor and can be toward either the beginning of the document or the end.
- You can replace a word or phrase anywhere in the document with another word or phrase using the Search and Replace command. The replacement can be automatic for all occurrences or you can monitor each potential replacement.
- With the Move command, you can delete, cut, or copy a sentence, paragraph, or page. If you cut or copy, the text is saved in the cut-and-save area, from which it can be inserted at any point in the document.
- WordPerfect includes two memory areas, which allows for two independent documents to be in memory concurrently. You can switch from one document to the other with the Switch command. Documents in the two memory areas can be viewed at the same time by splitting the screen with the Screen command.
- Using the Block command, you can identify a portion of text ranging in size from one character to the entire document.
- The Speller can check the spelling of all words in a single paragraph or page, or in the entire document. If a word is determined to be misspelled, you have the option to select one of the words from a list of displayed alternatives, type in a correction, request WordPerfect to leave the word unchanged, or add the word to the dictionary.
- Invoking the Thesaurus causes WordPerfect to display a list of synonyms for the word at the position of the cursor.

COMMAND AND FUNCTION SUMMARY

Following is a summary of the various commands and operations described in this chapter.

Command	Key or Keys	Action
Formatting		
Boldface	F6	Makes text boldface.
Center	Shift-F6	Centers a line between the margins.
Flush right	Alt-F6	Positions a line against the right margin.
Indent left	F4	Indents a paragraph one tab stop from the left margin.
Indent left/right	Shift-F4	Indents a paragraph one tab stop from both the left and right margins.
Justification	Ctrl-F8	Produces a selection menu. Allows right justification to be turned on or off.
Line spacing	Shift-F8	Produces a selection menu. Allows line spacing to be changed.
Margin set	Shift-F8	Produces a selection menu. Allows the left and right margins to be set.
Underline	F8	Underlines text.
Other Commands		
Block	Alt-F4	Starts or ends the definition of a block.
Cut (Move)	Ctrl-F4	Produces a selection menu. Allows a sentence, paragraph, or page to be deleted, cut, or copied.
Replace	Alt-F2	Replaces occurrences of a user-designated search text with a user-designated replacement text.
Reveal codes	Alt-F3	Displays the text together with hidden codes.
Screen	Ctrl-F3	Produces a selection menu. Allows the screen to be split into two windows.
Search forward	F2	Searches from the location of the cursor to the end of the document for the occurrence of a specified search text.
Search reverse	Shift-F2	Same as Search forward except searches toward beginning of document.
Spell	Ctrl-F2	Invokes the Speller to check spelling.
Switch case	Shift-F3	Changes all letters in a block to uppercase or lowercase.
Switch documents	Shift-F3	Toggles between the documents in memory area 1 and memory area 2.
Thesaurus	Alt-F1	Invokes the Thesaurus to find a synonym for a selected word.

NEW TERMINOLOGY

The following are important new terms introduced in this chapter; you should be familiar with each of them.

block
flush right
hanging paragraph
hidden code
indent
search string

REVIEW QUESTIONS

1. What does each of the following key sequences cause?

   a. Shift-F4
   b. Shift-F6
   c. Alt-F6
   d. Shift-F8
   e. F6
   f. F8

2. In the lower portion of the screen of Figure 8-6(b), the cursor is displayed to the left of the hidden code [C]. What do you think would happen if you struck the Del key?

3. What is the difference between the actions of the F4 and the Shift-F4?

4. What is the minimum size of a block? What is the maximum size of a block?

5. The cursor is moved to the beginning of the first line of a paragraph and the Block command (Alt-F4) is entered. How much text is blocked by entering each of the following?

   a. Ctrl-Right
   b. Down,Down
   c. Up
   d. End

6. In centering the first heading line of Figure 8-1, assume that the cursor was positioned on the letter C of *Center* when you entered the Center command. What do you think will happen?

7. Over how much of the document do each of the following format commands operate?

   a. Center.
   b. Indent left and right.
   c. Set margins.

8. Is it possible to set up a document so that the entire document prints unjustified except for one paragraph, which is to be printed justified? Explain your answer.

9. When performing a search, is it better to use a backward search or a forward search?
10. In doing replace operation, you have entered the hyphen character (-) as the search string and entered nothing for replacement string. What do you think will happen?
11. You have decided to compose a letter and at the same time to make some notes about the letter. For this, you use window 1 for the letter and window 2 for the notes. After completing your notes, you decide to close the second window to have the full screen for the letter. However, you forget to save the notes as a file before closing the window. Have you lost the notes because of this action? Explain your answer.
12. In running a spelling check on a document, an abbreviation is displayed as "not found." What action should you take?

MATCHING

The descriptions in 1 through 8 describe an activity requiring that one or more commands be invoked. Designate the first key sequence action to take by matching these actions with the key sequences in a to h.

a. F2
b. Ctrl-F3
c. Alt-F3
d. F4
e. Alt-F4
f. Ctrl-F8
g. Shift-F8
h. Alt-F6

1. Set the margins to 20 and 60.
2. Indent a paragraph from the left margin only.
3. Figure out why the document is not displayed on the screen as it should be.
4. Find a misspelled word somewhere in a document.
5. Position a line so that it is against the right margin.
6. Identify a portion of text that is to be set to boldface.
7. Work with two documents.
8. Obtain printed output that is not justified.

TRUE/FALSE

Determine whether each of the following is true or false.

______ 1. The Margin Set and Indent commands work the same in that they both affect all text that follows until another Margin Set or Indent command is entered.

______ 2. Each successive Indent command causes indention to the next tab stop.

______ 3. Hidden codes can be displayed by opening a second window with the Screen command.

______ 4. Hidden codes can be deleted when working from the edit screen.

______ **5.** If you are formatting as you are entering text and you enter an Indent command, then all paragraphs that follow will be indented until you change the indent back to the default.

______ **6.** Some of the formatting codes cannot be entered after the document has been typed; they must be entered as the text is being entered.

______ **7.** The appearance of the document on the screen is not changed if you disable justification.

______ **8.** WordPerfect provides for triple spacing as well as double spacing.

______ **9.** You must be certain to position the cursor at the first position of the paragraph before entering the Indent command.

______ **10.** You must not have any blank characters in the search string of the Search command.

______ **11.** When doing a search and replace, you can have WordPerfect perform all replacements automatically, or you can check and approve each replacement.

______ **12.** The exact option menu from the Move command depends upon the action that was taken before the Move command was executed.

______ **13.** The cut-and-save area holds the text cut from the last three cuts that were performed. This is similar to the way in which deleted text is held in memory.

______ **14.** The primary purpose of using two windows is to be able to view two different portions of the same document at the same time.

______ **15.** You would use a thesaurus to find a synonym for a word with which you are not completely happy.

ANSWERS TO OBJECTIVE QUESTIONS

Matching

1. g 2. d 3. c 4. a 5. h 6. e 7. b 8. f

True/False

1. F 2. T 3. F 4. T 5. F 6. F 7. T 8. T 9. T
10. F 11. T 12. T 13. F 14. F 15. T

ASSIGNMENTS/PROJECTS

1. The following document is to be entered into the computer using WordPerfect. Entries enclosed within angle brackets are to be replaced with information as described within the brackets. For instance, <YOUR STREET ADDRESS> should be replaced with your address. Use margins of 12 and 73. Note that the return address is flush right. Disable right justification. When finished, save it to disk and print a copy on the printer.

```
                                        <YOUR STREET ADDRESS>
                                           <CITY, STATE, ZIP>
                                                       <DATE>


Jim Marconi
American Association for Improvement
5 Pacific Circle
Washington, DC  20036

Dear Jim:

Included is the consulting bill for the month of February; note
that I am including my time and telephone expenses.  Please have
these paid separately.  I am relieved that we were able to repair
the problems that resulted from what I sense as a system failure.
I suggest that you have the maintenance engineer do extended
checks on the disk drive.

Date     Activity                              Hours
----     --------                              -----
2/1-2/3  Modification to accounting system      7.0
         1. Modify edit to handle comps
         2. Modify the save record response
         3. Check for duplicate invoices
         4. Modify billing form
2/4      Modify nametag program                 6.0
2/7      Diagnose apparent file corruption      2.0
2/11     Diagnose system failure                2.0
2/12     Repair corrupted files from failure    6.0
                                               ----
         TOTAL                                 23.0

                  23.0 hours @ $50/hour                   $1150.00


2/11,12  Telephone                              8.0


          AT&T weekend rate: $8.65/hour 8 hours             $69.20

Thank you for your assistance.

Sincerely yours,



<YOUR NAME>
```

2. You are to type two sections from this book (Disabling Right Justification and Hanging Paragraphs, pages 220 and 221). Format your copy so that its appearance is as much like that of the text as you can achieve. For text that is printed in italics, use the underscore. When finished, save it to disk and print a copy.

3. Copying text from one document to another is illustrated (DTN 8-20) by copying items from the document LEGAL.WP1 into the letter SKELETON.WP. For this assignment, you will do the same thing except that you will be obtaining items from the document LEGAL.WP2 (stored on the data disk). The items that you must copy into the letter (and the order in which they must be inserted) are:

   INTENT

   EXCLUSIONS

   TERRITORY

ARBITRATION

PROCEDURE ON TERMINATION

In addition, you must use boldface for each of these titles and use hanging paragraphs for the separate elements defined as a, b, c, and d in the PROCEDURE item. When you are finished, save the letter to disk and print a copy.

Chapter 9

Desktop Publishing

OBJECTIVES

Desktop publishing is the use of a microcomputer to create printed materials (publications) involving both text and graphics with a quality nearly equal to that of professional typesetting systems. From Chapters 7 and 8 you have learned how to use WordPerfect for preparing documents. WordPerfect Version 4.2 (the version of the Limited Use software) has many features beyond those described in this book, including a multitude of formatting capabilities essential to desktop publishing. In a sense, desktop publishing is a next step beyond basic word processing. When you have completed this chapter, you will have an understanding of desktop publishing and will be able to describe:

- The hardware and software components that make up a desktop publishing system.
- The eight steps of the publishing process: writing, designing, editing, typesetting, artwork preparation, paste-up, printing, and binding.
- Characteristics of type styles (typefaces) such as those you are reading.
- Factors to consider when designing a page layout: page size, margins, typeface and size selection, headings and subheadings, headers and footers, and artwork.
- Features of the laser printer that provide the user with the ability to use different typefaces and sizes on a single page and to combine text and graphics.

PREVIEW

Basic Concepts of Desktop Publishing

Central to desktop publishing is page layout software, which allows the integration of text and graphics in constructing pages, and the laser printer, which can perform the printing.

The Publishing Process

Conventional publishing (such as that used in publishing this book) involves eight basic steps: authoring, design, editing, typesetting, artwork preparation, paste-up, printing, and binding. These steps still exist for the desktop publisher, but software tools available for the microcomputer change their nature somewhat.

About Typefaces

In designing a publication, the desktop publisher must make many decisions. One of them relates to the selection of the style of the type (typeface) and its size (the measurement of its height). Typeface, size, and spacing must be selected so as to convey best the type of message of the document.

Page Design

In preparing a document for publication, care must be taken with the page layout. Standards must be defined to maintain a consistent appearance throughout the document. Word processing, as well as desktop publishing, includes features that assist in providing a high-quality page.

The Laser Printer

The dot-matrix printer forms images by imprinting patterns of dots on a page. Laser printers use the same principle except that the resolution of the dot patterns is finer and printing is done on equipment similar to a copying machine. The laser printer is driven by its own built-in computer designed specifically to handle the processing needs of the printer.

BASIC CONCEPTS OF DESKTOP PUBLISHING

What Is Desktop Publishing?

Figure 9-1 includes four pieces of printed communication: an invoice printed by a dot-matrix printer, a letter prepared with a word processor, an advertising piece prepared on a desktop publishing microcomputer, and part of a brochure prepared by a professional publication service. We can see at a glance that they differ significantly in their quality. There is another important distinction that is not so obvious. The first two (invoice and

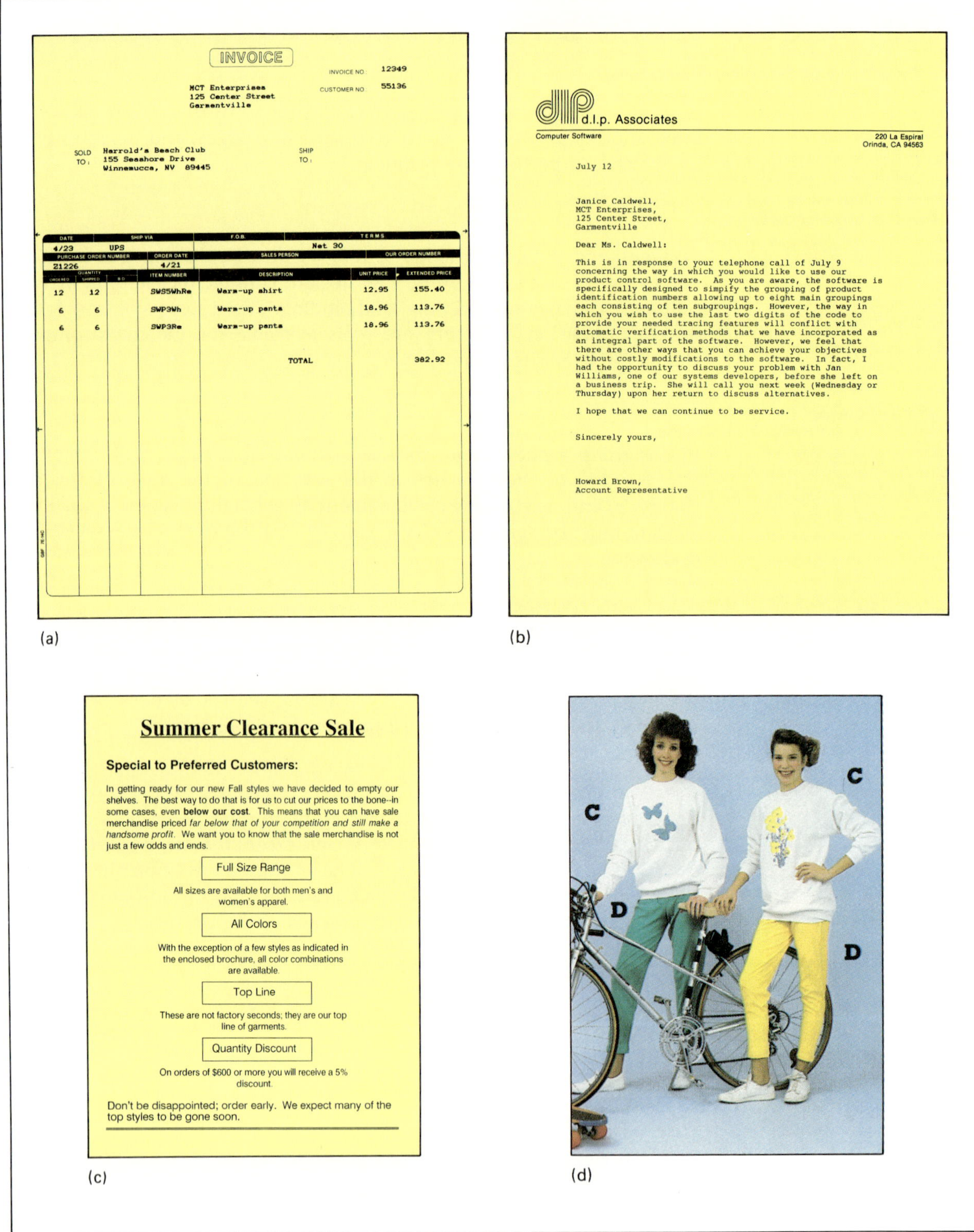

INVOICE

INVOICE NO: 12349
CUSTOMER NO: 55136

MCT Enterprises
125 Center Street
Garmentville

SOLD TO: Harrold's Beach Club
155 Seashore Drive
Winnemucca, NV 89445

SHIP TO:

DATE	SHIP VIA	F.O.B.	TERMS
4/23	UPS		Net 30

PURCHASE ORDER NUMBER	ORDER DATE	SALES PERSON	OUR ORDER NUMBER
21226	4/21		

QUANTITY ORDERED	QUANTITY SHIPPED	B.O.	ITEM NUMBER	DESCRIPTION	UNIT PRICE	EXTENDED PRICE
12	12		SWS5WhRe	Warm-up shirt	12.95	155.40
6	6		SWP3Wh	Warm-up pants	18.96	113.76
6	6		SWP3Re	Warm-up pants	18.96	113.76
				TOTAL		382.92

(a)

d.l.p. Associates
Computer Software
220 La Espiral
Orinda, CA 94563

July 12

Janice Caldwell,
MCT Enterprises,
125 Center Street,
Garmentville

Dear Ms. Caldwell:

This is in response to your telephone call of July 9 concerning the way in which you would like to use our product control software. As you are aware, the software is specifically designed to simpify the grouping of product identification numbers allowing up to eight main groupings each consisting of ten subgroupings. However, the way in which you wish to use the last two digits of the code to provide your needed tracing features will conflict with automatic verification methods that we have incorporated as an integral part of the software. However, we feel that there are other ways that you can achieve your objectives without costly modifications to the software. In fact, I had the opportunity to discuss your problem with Jan Williams, one of our systems developers, before she left on a business trip. She will call you next week (Wednesday or Thursday) upon her return to discuss alternatives.

I hope that we can continue to be service.

Sincerely yours,

Howard Brown,
Account Representative

(b)

Summer Clearance Sale

Special to Preferred Customers:

In getting ready for our new Fall styles we have decided to empty our shelves. The best way to do that is for us to cut our prices to the bone--in some cases, even **below our cost**. This means that you can have sale merchandise priced *far below that of your competition and still make a handsome profit*. We want you to know that the sale merchandise is not just a few odds and ends.

Full Size Range

All sizes are available for both men's and women's apparel.

All Colors

With the exception of a few styles as indicated in the enclosed brochure, all color combinations are available.

Top Line

These are not factory seconds; they are our top line of garments.

Quantity Discount

On orders of $600 or more you will receive a 5% discount.

Don't be disappointed; order early. We expect many of the top styles to be gone soon.

(c)

(d)

Figure 9-1
(a) Invoice printed with a dot-matrix printer. **(b)** A letter prepared with a word processor. **(c)** An advertising piece prepared on a microcomputer. **(d)** Professionally prepared material from a brochure.

letter) are destined for a single person (or organization); one copy will be mailed. Hence, we shall refer to these categorically as *documents.* Copies of the other two (advertising piece and brochure) are to be printed and sent to many people. As one of the definitions of the word *publish* is "to print and put into circulation," we shall call them *publications.* We are all familiar with publications. At one extreme are books such as this; it required the efforts of many people and the use of specialized machines. At the other extreme are simple, one-page newsletters that are prepared on a typewriter and duplicated on a copying machine. The process of creating and preparing all of these is called *publishing.*

In Chapter 6, you learned that the quality of an organization's documents conveys an image of the organization. The same is true of its publications. For instance, an advertising piece promoting a sale, such as that in Figure 9-1, is much more likely to capture the reader's attention and interest than would one typed on a typewriter. The nature of competition also dictates the "par" level of publications. For instance, in the garment business in which MCT Enterprises is engaged, full color in a product line brochure is essential because color selection is as important as styling.

The current level of technology is another factor that establishes a distinction between that which is acceptable and that which leaves something to be desired. For instance, 40 years ago organizations commonly typed their newsletters on special master sheets from which copies could be printed with a mimeograph machine. The quality was somewhat lower than that produced by the typewriter itself. With a word processor, microcomputer, and laser printer sitting on a desktop, a person can prepare the same newsletter with a quality approaching that of a professional printer of 40 years ago.

Perhaps it has occurred to you from these descriptions that publishing can be divided into two categories. First is that done by a professional publishing service using equipment especially designed for publishing. Second is that done using equipment available in the average office. Forty years ago, this equipment was the typewriter, now, it is the microcomputer and software. With today's microcomputer hardware and software, you can prepare publications from your desktop with a quality that several years ago would have required the services of a professional publisher. This has come to be known as **desktop publishing;** as a businessperson it allows you to bring many of your publishing activities "in-house." Through desktop publishing, you can publish professional-appearing material that would have been prohibitively expensive if prepared by an outside service. Even some of the work previously done by a publishing service can be brought in-house and done more conveniently and cheaply with desktop publishing. Typical users and their applications include:

- The office manager who must circulate internal documents such as company performance reports and meeting agendas.
- The real estate salesperson who must prepare mailings to prospective home buyers.
- The sales manager who must send out advertisement mailing.
- The health club owner who sends out a monthly newsletter.

- The church secretary who prepares and mails the church activity agenda.
- The student who can prepare reports that include graphs and charts having a finished, professional appearance.

Even though most of these can be prepared with a simple word processor, use of desktop publishing capabilities provide the professional appearance that can make the difference. The success of a publication depends not only on its contents but also on its appearance.

What Comprises a Desktop Publishing System

It could be argued that a typewriter represents a desktop publishing system since it provides the means to prepare publications. However, the term *desktop publishing* was coined to describe systems that allow professional-appearing materials to be prepared on a microcomputer. The term actually evolved with the introduction of the Apple Macintosh in 1984. Let us consider a simple example of what can be achieved with this computer; it will give you your first insight into the meaning of desktop publishing. The partial page shown in Figure 9-2 was prepared on an Apple Macintosh equipped with a mouse and printed on an Apple Imagewriter dot-matrix printer. Here you see both text and graphics. The sequence of steps in preparing this page was as follows.

1. The illustration was created using MacPaint, a program that allows you to utilize your artistic skills in creating drawings on the screen using the mouse as pencil. Figure 9-3 shows the MacPaint work screen. Along the left edge of the screen are icons (symbols) representing the action you may take. For instance, by selecting the rectangle, you can move the mouse pointer anywhere on the screen and, with a few clicks of the mouse button, create a rectangle of any size. The rows of squares at the bottom edge of the screen are the various designs that you can use to fill in portions of the drawing. These features were used to created the illustration shown. When it was completed, it was saved to disk.
2. The text was entered using MacWrite, the word processor included with the Macintosh. As the text was being entered, it was formatted much as you formatted text with WordPerfect. Notice that both the size and style of the printed characters are varied to provide emphasis where needed. During entry of the text, space was made for the illustration. When the document was completed, it was saved to disk.
3. The illustration was retrieved from disk and inserted into the allocated space within the text. Note that this action is similar to an action you carried out with WordPerfect in Chapter 8. That is, using two windows in DTNs 8-19 and 8-20, you retrieved two documents from disk and inserted a portion of one into the other. However, the action of inserting graphics into text is much more complex because it involves the merging of two completely different types of information, created by two different programs.

Figure 9-2
Output from an Apple Macintosh.

MCT Enterprises
Annual Report Page 7

State-by-State Summary

Nevada

Market penetration in the State of Nevada has been almost non-existent in the past. However, our sales manager Janelle Bowker recently completed a detailed survey and analysis that shows great promise for the newly designed Banner and Desert Air product lines.

In order to best focus our resources on what we consider to be a very lucrative market, we have divided the State into three sales regions (numbered 1, 2 and 3) as shown at the right. As indicated, the focus of activities will be:

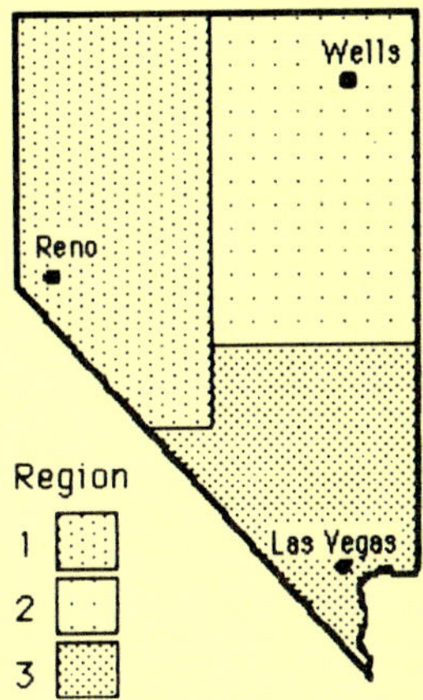

Region	City
1	Reno
2	Wells
3	Las Vegas

The overall state activity will be coordinated out of the Reno office under the direction of Howard Hongisto, one of our top promotions people.

The current projections for next season's sales activity is summarized on the next page in Tables 4 and 5.

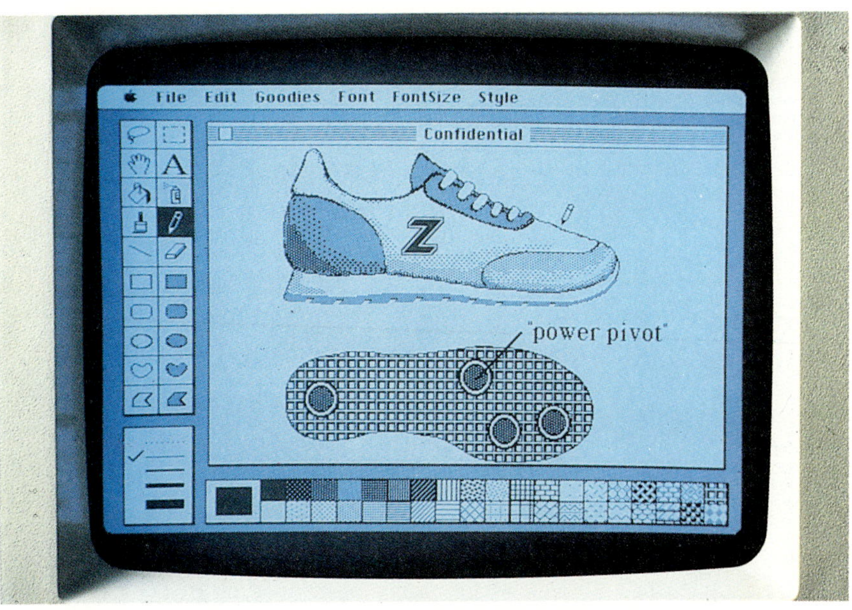

Figure 9-3
The MacPaint work screen.

One of the characteristics of the Macintosh as the basis for desktop publishing is the ease with which both text and graphics can be manipulated. With the mouse, you can build a page on the screen in much the same way you would use scissors and transparent tape to cut and lay out the equivalent page on paper. By doing it electronically, you can easily rearrange the layout of a page and see your result on the screen instantly. You can even reduce or expand an illustration or trim portions of it (called cropping) as you would with a printed illustration and a pair of scissors.

One of the significant features of the Macintosh is its software interface. That is, in order for a program to function in the Macintosh environment, the software designer must adhere to the strict standards set by Apple. Thus, computer files saved to disk by one application are intelligible to another application. Note that this is not limited to the drawings created by a program such as MacPaint, but to all software. For instance, we learned about spreadsheet programs in Chapter 2. The output from a spreadsheet program can be a table of numbers, a graph, or a chart. All of these can be stored to disk as files and incorporated into a document.

Hardware Components of a Desktop Publishing System

The preceding example introduces you to the nature of the software and hardware needed for a desktop publishing system. Let us consider first the hardware components and then the software components in more detail.

Hard-Disk-Equipped Microcomputer. Although a low level of desktop publishing is possible with a floppy disk computer, software commonly used in desktop publishing requires a hard disk. Furthermore, the text and graphics manipulation software place a heavy load on the processor. Without a large amount of memory, operations of preparing a page layout can be agonizingly slow. In the PC world (the focus of this book), 640K bytes of memory for an XT and 1 megabyte for an AT are common.

Graphics Printer. Although almost all dot-matrix printers can print graphics as well as text, the dot-matrix printer has two shortcomings for desktop publishing. One of them is obvious by inspecting Figure 9-2. The quality of the output is not suitable for most publications: it has the dot-matrix look. The other disadvantage is that dot matrix printers are exceedingly slow when printing in the graphics mode. For instance, printing the portion of the page in Figure 9-2 took approximately two minutes. In general, when speaking of desktop publishing, to most people "printer" means "laser printer."

Mouse. General editing and formatting functions with text are greatly simplified with the mouse. For instance, the tasks of blocking a portion of text for underlining and cutting and pasting are done much more quickly with a mouse than with command key sequences. Software that allows you to manipulate graphics in building your page layout (doing such things as moving an illustration from one place to another or cropping it to fit better) is generally built around the use of a mouse.

With this hand-held scanner the user can store an image in a computer and then incorporate it into a document.

Whereas the preceding three hardware elements are essential to a desktop publishing system, the following item is useful if existing drawings or photographs are commonly used in preparing documents.

Scanner/Digitizer. Software such as MacPaint allows the desktop publisher to create illustrations much as does an artist or draftsperson. A scanner/digitizer is a hardware peripheral that is capable of scanning any printed image (such as a photograph or a drawing) and converting it to a bit-mapped image in the computer's memory. (The concept of bit mapping was described in Chapter 4 in relation to monitors.) Once in memory, it can be stored to disk as a file and inserted into a document as if it were text.

Software Components of a Desktop Publishing System

In studying WordPerfect, you learned that an important part of preparing a document is to lay it out in a neat and easy-to-read form. For this, you learned about relatively simple operations such as setting margins and indenting in order to achieve the appearance you desire. When preparing publications, there are numerous other factors to consider, including the incorporation of graphics into the text. The following software components are necessary for these tasks.

Word Processor. Text must be entered and edited as you did in Chapters 7 and 8. Indeed, WordPerfect is commonly used for this.

Page Layout. The key software element of a desktop publishing system is the component that allows you to lay out on the screen the pages as they will appear in the final document. This page layout software must provide the ability to work with text created with a word processor. It must have the ability to perform not only those relatively simple formatting operations that you learned in the preceding two chapters, but also many of the formatting operations found in professional typesetting systems.

(These are described in a later section.) The software must also be capable of inserting into the text the output of other programs in order to assemble the publication. For instance, you might be preparing an annual sales report that will incorporate a narrative you entered and edited with a word processor, charts and graphs you created from Lotus 1-2-3, and summary tables that you obtained from dBASE III database files.

Two of the commonly encountered page makeup software systems available for both the Macintosh and the IBM PC are Ventura Publishing Edition from Xerox Corporation and PageMaker from Aldus Corporation. (Ventura requires an IBM AT.) Until recently, specialized page layout programs such as these were necessary elements in desktop publishing. However, WordPerfect Version 5.0 includes sufficient page layout features to make it adequate for handling desktop publishing needs for all but the most sophisticated users. This version of WordPerfect includes the capabilities for using various typefaces and sizes and including graphics, topics of later sections of this chapter.

Graphics Software. For many desktop publications, specialized graphics software is used to create illustrations, charts, and diagrams.

Page Layout Software and Word Processing Software

From your studies of word processing, you know that WYSIWYG is a feature of most word processors. The ability to see on the screen the form of the printed page saves time and effort in preparing an attractive document. How, then, does a word processor differ from page layout software? Let us consider the answer to this from a historical perspective.

With all software, including word processors, software companies continually upgrade their products by adding features to meet market demand. At one point, microcomputer users were happy with word processing software that included little more than the basic features you learned about in Chapters 7 and 8. Now, however, word processing users have grown in sophistication and require features on their word processors that parallel features available to the professional typesetter. This has evolved largely as a result of the laser printer with its capability of placing images of any shape at any position on the page. Each new round of upgrades to the various page layout software packages sees additional features that were previously the province of professional typesetting systems. Similarly, each new round of upgrades to the various word processors sees additional features that were previously the province of page layout systems. Hence, the distinction between word processors and page layout software is continually changing. Without becoming too technical, the following are three common distinctions between page layout software and midrange word processors.

- More precise control over positioning of text. This is essential to optimizing the overall appearance and setting such items as mathematical formulas and tables.
- True WYSIWYG whereby the page is displayed on the screen ex-

actly as it will be printed, including graphics, lines at the tops and bottoms of the pages (headers and footers, described later), and page numbers.

- The manipulation and insertion of graphics into the text. This includes the ability to size, trim, and rotate the graphic.

However, as indicated earlier, the latest version of WordPerfect includes these capabilities.

Some Costs of Desktop Publishing

A first reaction of a businessperson after seeing someone demonstrate the capabilities of a desktop publishing system might be, "Let's go this route and reduce our publishing costs." If the prospective purchaser already owns a hard disk microcomputer and can justify the cost of a laser printer, then the additional cost is limited to software. (Page layout software typically sells in the $500 to $1000 range.) However, this cost is only part of the overall picture. Although the tools are compact and relatively inexpensive, the publishing process is complex and involves numerous steps.

If you use a professional publishing service to prepare your publication, your role is limited to authoring and editing (the word processor simplifies the editing task). However, if you decide to use a desktop publishing system and prepare your own publications, then you must learn a plethora of new skills. In addition to being the author and editor, you will also be the designer, typographer, and artist. For simple publishing tasks using a little or no graphics, much can be done with a limited investment of time in training. But to use the full capabilities of a desktop publishing system requires a large investment of time and effort. A basic knowledge of the many facets of desktop publishing will provide you with a useful understanding of this important office phenomenon. Let us consider the essentials of the publishing process.

THE PUBLISHING PROCESS

Eight Steps in Preparing a Publication

Publications range in size from a one-page flier, to a multipage pamphlet, to a full-scale book such as this. The flier might be prepared entirely at one sitting with a word processor. However, the pamphlet would likely involve a number of production steps. Certainly, the publication of this book involved numerous detailed steps. Since these represent the formal steps of publishing, let us consider them, and then use them as a basis for assessing the necessary activities for various levels of desktop publishing.

Authoring. The obvious first step in preparing any publication is writing it. When this book was completed, a typed manuscript was submitted to the publisher.

Designing. The physical appearance of the publication is determined by its design—the way that text and illustrations appear on the page. For instance, examine the pages of this book. The page size, margin size, typefaces (the different styles of print), heading positioning, and color use are all design decisions. Although in reading books, magazines, or advertisements, you barely notice the design, they are important to the effectiveness of the publication and its ability to get its message across. You are less reluctant to tackle a twenty-page reading assignment that uses color and contains illustrations and tables to break up solid text than a ten-page reading assignment that is solid text. No matter how significant the message of a document, poor design will hinder getting it across.

Editing. The purpose of a publication is to communicate information. One in which ideas are poorly expressed and basic English fundamentals are lacking will not be effective in getting the message across and often in justifying the existence of the publication. The editor attends to the relatively mechanical tasks of checking spelling, usage, and sentence structure, as well as the more creative task of ensuring that concepts and ideas are conveyed concisely and clearly. In addition, the editor must indicate design instructions for the typesetter on the manuscript.

Typesetting. The typesetter enters the manuscript into a typesetting computer. Keyboarding the text is only a small portion of the typesetter's work; he or she must format the text as well. This is similar to the formatting that you did with WordPerfect except that it is much more extensive. For instance, the keystrokes to format a complex mathematical formula can far outnumber the keystrokes to enter the formula text.

Artwork Preparation. There is a saying, "A picture is worth a thousand words." For some publications (such as a mail-order catalog), artwork—also called graphics—consisting of photographs and drawings is essential. For others, it assists the printed materials in communicating the message. If you inspect the artwork in this book, you will see two types. Photographs are called **halftones** because they consist of various shades of gray (or color). In contrast, **line art** is artwork that consists of a solid color on white. For instance, a bar graph might be printed in black with no gray shades. Laser printers used with desktop publishing systems have limited capabilities for printing halftones.

Paste-up. Once the text is typeset and the artwork is complete, they can be assembled as pages. This is done by a person who physically pastes the text and artwork onto a piece of heavy paper or cardboard to form a separate mechanical for each page of the document. The mechanicals are photographed, thereby creating a photographic negative from which the page is eventually printed. Although electronic paste-up (one of the features of desktop publishing systems) is finding wider use with book publishers, many books are still prepared by mechanical paste-up methods.

Printing. From the negatives, the printer must prepare master plates from which the printing is done. Depending upon the size of the publication, each master can consist of up to thirty-two pages from the publication. The plates are mounted on a printing press on which the publication is printed.

Binding. The final step in the process is binding the individual pages together. For a textbook such as this, pages are folded in groups of thirty-two (conforming to the way in which they were printed) and glued. A workbook designed to lie flat when opened might use a plastic tubular device with fingers that fit through rectangular holes punched along the edge of the page. Magazines commonly use saddle stitching in which the pages are folded in the center and stapled together.

Moving Publishing to the Desktop

Now, let us assess each of these steps from the point of view of desktop publishing. This consideration will range from how the conventional publication process can be streamlined with the aid of a microcomputer to how most of these operations can be performed with a desktop publishing system.

Authoring. Obviously, new inventions will not affect authoring; the formulating and writing down of ideas and their conversion to written communication remain a human endeavor. However, many writers rely on the microcomputer with word processing software to simplify the mechanics of writing. (In response to the question, "Do you find writing difficult?" a well-known author replied: "No. I write whatever occurs to me. The writing is easy, it is the occurring that is difficult.")

Designing. Similarly, design results from the creativity of the human mind. In fact, in much advertising the design is far more creative than the message being conveyed.

Editing. Using a word processor simplifies the task of the author in making editing corrections during the entry and checking phase. In fact, spelling and thesaurus components of word processors, as well as sophisticated programs to check for grammatical errors such as verb-noun disagreements, help to automate the process. However, only a human editor can ensure that ideas are expressed clearly and accurately.

Typesetting. Although needed typesetting skills are not altered by microcomputer, word processing software has changed the way that typesetting is done. Since the page layout software can read from disk the text created with a word processor, a separate keying operation is not necessary. In fact, many publishers accept word processor prepared manuscripts on disk for publications ranging from magazine articles to entire books. However, a person still must insert formatting codes to match the design specifications.

Artwork Preparation. For the desktop publisher, artwork can come from several sources. Drawing programs make it possible to create your own illustrations. Many software programs such as Lotus 1-2-3 allow you to create graphs and charts from spreadsheet data. Scanner/digitizer hardware provides the means for converting pictures and images into digitized files stored on disk.

Paste-up. With a desktop publishing system, both the text and graphics are stored within the computer. Hence, by using page layout software, you can accomplish the electronic equivalent of paste-up quickly and easily on the screen. With the mouse, you can position the graphic on the page as easily as you can insert text. You can also move it, resize or crop it, or add a border.

Printing and Binding. These needs are the same for both desktop publishing and conventional publishing. However, as a rule, the finished product from a desktop publishing system is a copy of the publication from which needed copies can be printed and bound using methods of the professional publisher.

With this desktop publishing system, users can view the page exactly as it will be printed.

The Place of the Microcomputer in Publishing

As you can see, the organization that brings its publishing in-house using desktop publishing will require specialized training for one or more people. Design and typographical skills normally found in typesetting services will be required in the office. However, there are different levels at which the microcomputer can be used to streamline the publishing process. For instance, at the "low end," many organizations prepare their publications on their word-processing-equipped microcomputers. Once the material has been carefully edited, the electronic version is sent to a publishing service, either by sending a disk through the mail or by transmitting the information through the telephone system. Graphics can be handled in the same way. Then the remaining steps of the process are carried out by the publishing service.

At the other extreme is the organization that uses a desktop publishing system to do all but the most complex of its publications. Individuals within the organization are responsible for the design, formatting, and electronic paste-up, which is done with page layout software.

Except for some small, low-volume publications, the laser printer is not suitable for handling the volume printing task. Its per-page cost is relatively high, the fusing process used by laser printers to transfer the image to the paper produces printing that is not as durable as conventional printing, and desktop laser printers are not designed for heavy printing loads. A single copy to serve as a master is commonly sent to a printing company for printing and binding.

ABOUT TYPEFACES

The laser printer provides the microcomputer user with printing versatility previously available only to the professional typesetter. To take advantage of these capabilities, the user needs a knowledge of some of the basic principles affecting design. Even the person who uses only a word processor such as WordPerfect can produce, for instance, a professional appearing document using 10-point Times Roman with 11-point leading for the text and 14-point Helvetica for the headings. These descriptions use common terms from publishing. Let us consider some of the technical factors that are important to the desktop publisher.

Type Size

One of the first considerations that you will be confronted with if you wish to use the versatility of a laser printer is the type size. Where we commonly measure in terms of inches, halves, quarters, eighths, and so on, the typographer measures in terms of picas and points. A **pica** is approximately 1/6 inch.* The **point** is 1/12 pica, or approximately 1/72 inch.

---

*Although commonly treated as 1/6 inch, this is not correct. The pica is 0.16604 inch, whereas 1/6 is 0.16667.

With a dot-matrix or daisy-wheel printer, printing is commonly at 10 or 12 characters per inch, which represents some measure of size of the type. However, the typographer measures type size differently: it is based on a the sum of two values, as illustrated in Figure 9-4. Basically, it is the distance from the top of the highest letter to the bottom of the lowest. Figure 9-5 gives you an idea of various sizes. Note that any or all of these can be used on a single page of a document when using the commercial version of WordPerfect. In fact, Figure 9-5 was printed using WordPerfect.

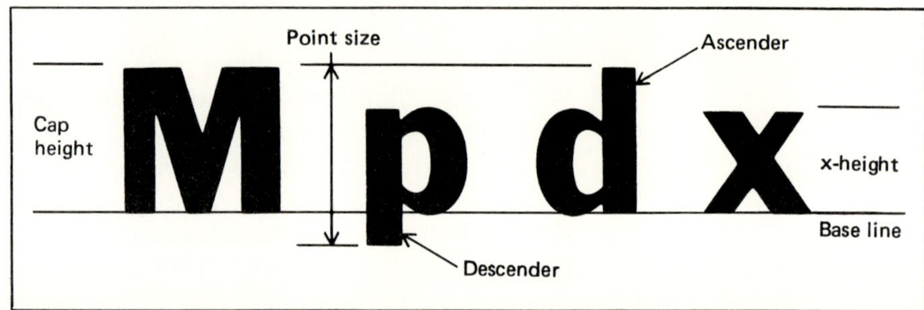

Figure 9-4
Major characteristics of a typical typeface.

abcdefghABCDEFGH 8 pt.

abcdefghABCDEFGH 10 pt.

abcdefghABCDEFGH 14 pt.

abcdefghABCDEFGH 24 pt.

abcdefghABC 36 pt.

Figure 9-5
Type sizes.

Typeface

Another of the features of laser printers is that different typefaces can be used for the text. Within this book, you can see that the letters of the words you are reading now are a different style (typeface) from those that form the headings. A **typeface** is a set of characters, numerals, punctuation marks, and related symbols that have been designed to have a consistent appearance.

The sample in Figure 9-5 includes five different sizes of the Times Roman typeface. The typeface of the material you are reading now is Palatino; that of the headings is Helvetica. In electronic publishing, the word **font** is used almost interchangeably with the word *typeface.** Howev-

*Technically speaking, the words *face* and *font* are different. The distinction is historical in nature and has no relevance to this overview of desktop publishing.

er, as used in conjunction with laser printers, each typeface *and* size is designated as a different font. In other words, in Figure 9-5 you see five different fonts, all being the Times Roman typeface. In reading the advertisements for printers, it is easy to be misled if you are unaware of this distinction. Do not conclude that you will get a printer with ten completely different typefaces if the printer is advertised with "ten built-in fonts."

Classification of Typefaces

Few people other than those engaged in publishing give much conscious thought to the typefaces of books or magazines they read. However, most are affected by these details without even realizing it. For instance, some faces are designed to be bold and austere and to give a decidedly mechanical appearance; many of these require special mental effort to read a line and comprehend the message. Such a face would hardly be appropriate for a novel intended to evoke emotions of sympathy. Others are designed to provide a smooth, flowing feeling so that the eye can drift easily across the line.

There are several ways to categorize typefaces. The basic divisions are *serif* and *sans serif,* and *roman* and *italic.* Understanding the association between the forms and functions of these will help you to make good decisions when selecting typefaces for your applications.

The distinction between **serif** and **sans serif** is explained and illustrated in the following two examples.

This is an example of a serif typeface. It has small counterstrokes at the end of the character's main stroke. This gives the feeling of a smooth transition from the top of one character to the top of the next.

By contrast, this is an example of a sans serif typeface (meaning without serif). Note that the appearance is somewhat bolder and that without the serifs the eye does not move across the line quite as smoothly.

Several commonly used typefaces are shown in Figure 9-6. The commercial typesetter has hundreds of typefaces from which to choose. The desktop

This is a sample of the typeface Univers in medium and *this is a sample of Univers italic.*

This is a sample of the typeface Press Roman in medium and *this is a sample of Press Roman italic.*

This is a sample of the typeface Baskerville in medium and *this is a sample of Baskerville italic.*

This is a sample of the typeface Optima in medium and *this is a sample of Optima italic.*

Figure 9-6
A variety of typefaces.

publisher is limited by a combination of the software (word processor or page layout software) and by the fonts that are available for the specific laser printer. For instance, even though a Bodini font might be available for your laser printer, you would not be able to use it with your word processor if the word processor did not include provisions for that font. The Times Roman serif and. Helvetica sans serif typefaces are commonly used with laser printers.

Another basic division among typefaces is based on the slant of the characters. That is, a typeface in which the letters are vertical such as these is called a roman typeface (you are reading Palatino roman). *One in which the letters are slanted such as this is called an* ***italic*** *typeface (you are now reading Palatino italics).* These are commonly used for emphasis or to set a particular passage apart for whatever reason. As a rule, every roman typeface has a corresponding italic typeface.

Character Spacing and Line Spacing

Printing in which each character of the line is allocated the same amount of space (from a typewriter or a typical computer printer) is said to be **monospaced.** With wide letters such as W and narrow letters such as i occupying the same amount of space, the overall effect is one of unevenness. To compensate for the differences in widths of letters, laser printers (and many other computer printers, as well) are capable of **microspacing** or proportional spacing, where the space provided for each letter depends upon the width of the letter. By examining the following two lines, you can see the difference between these two forms.

```
This is monospaced
```

This is microspaced (proportional spaced)

Whereas most word processors provide for microspacing, page layout software takes this even further. For instance, if a word must be positioned on a line but there is not quite enough room for it, the letters in the entire line can be moved imperceptibly closer in order to make the necessary room. This action of varying the spacing between letters is called **tracking.**

For character positioning, professional typesetting systems and some desktop publishing systems also include a feature called **kerning.** This is the controlling of the space between certain pairs of letters in order to give a more pleasing appearance. Kerning pairs of characters are defined for each typeface in the form of a table and are invoked automatically by the controlling software.

Another way of controlling the appearance of the text is by adjusting line spacing. In Chapter 8, you changed a portion of a document from single spacing to double spacing. When used in conjunction with a laser printer, page layout software and most word processors provide much more precise control over line spacing. For instance, 14 point type printed at six lines per inch (remember, 1/6 of an inch is 12 points) would not be very readable. Hence, for typesetting it is necessary to specify the size of the typeface and the distance from one baseline (refer to Figure 9-4) to the next, which is commonly referred to as the **leading.** The effect of two different leading values is illustrated in Figure 9-7 (the narrative describes the origin of the word *leading*). The first line of a new paragraph is often set with extra leading to make it easier for readers to separate the paragraphs. For instance, in Figure 9-8, the leading is 11 points but 15 points are used to separate the paragraphs.

Figure 9-7
Basic principles of leading.

Solid leading (10 point type on 10 point lead)

Leading relates to the amount of space between lines. The word is derived from the days in which type was prepared from metal elements and strips of lead were inserted between lines of type to increase spacing.

2 points leading (10 point type on 12 point lead)

Leading relates to the amount of space between lines. The word is derived from the days in which type was prepared from metal elements and strips of lead were inserted between lines of type to increase spacing.

Figure 9-8
Additional leading for the first line of a paragraph.

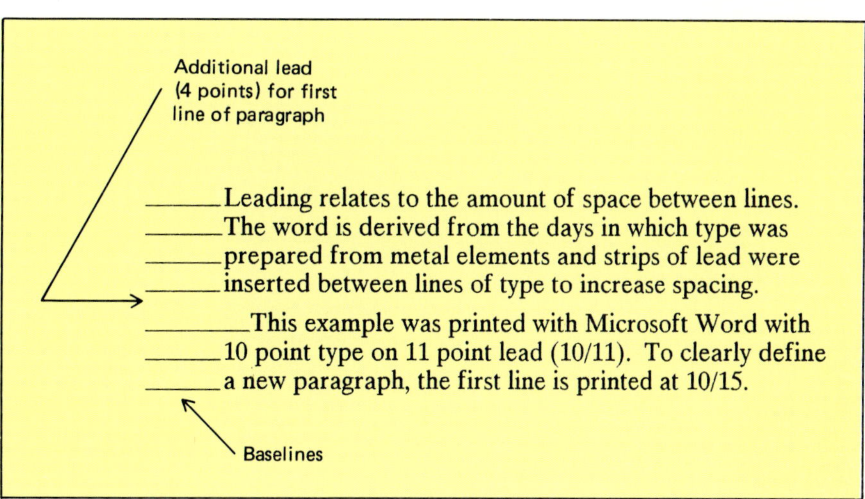

PAGE DESIGN

About Page Design

In designing your publication, an early decision must be the selection of typefaces, type sizes, and line spacing. In addition, you must make decisions concerning the overall page appearance that you want to achieve. This is called page design. Page layout programs streamline the paste-up process for the desktop publisher by eliminating most of the manual work in laying out each page. They also are useful for experimenting with page design because page samples can be displayed on the screen and easily changed in searching for the most appealing form. Pages are not designed one at a time; the design is a characteristic of the overall publication. For an office procedure manual with few illustrations, the document must be designed to avoid the boring appearance of the massive gray area that can result from pages of solid text. For a sales summary, the basic layout must be able to accommodate charts, tables, and illustrations. A more formal type of publication might require chapter or section headings and footnotes, as well as illustrations.

A portion of the section you are reading now is shown (reduced in size) in Figure 9-9. This copy, which was prepared with the commercial version of WordPerfect, illustrates the following page design factors.

DESKTOP PUBLISHING

PAGE DESIGN

About Page Design

In designing your publication, selection of typefaces, sizes, and line spacing are early decisions that you must make. In addition, you must make decisions concerning the overall page appearance that you want to achieve. This is called page design. Page layout programs streamline the paste-up process for the desktop publisher by eliminating most of the manual work in laying out each page. They also are useful for experimenting with page design because page samples can be displayed on the screen and and easily changed in searching for the most appealing form. Pages are not designed one at a time; the design is a characteristic of the overall publication itself. For an office procedure manual with few illustrations the document must be designed to avoid the boring appearance of a massive gray area resulting from pages of solid text. For a sales summary, the basic layout must be able to accomodate charts, tables, and illustrations. A more formal type of publication might require chapter or section headings, footnotes, as well as illustrations.

Selecting Page Size and Margins

The example in Figure 9-9 uses standard typing paper size of 8 1/2 x 11 with margins on the left, right, top, and bottom of one inch. For most desktop publishing the standard typewriter page size tends to prevail because it is the paper size used by the laser printer. The half-page, 5 1/2 x 8 1/2, is also commonly encountered; it is used for most microcomputer hardware and software manuals. However, the desktop publisher can specify to the word processor or page layout software almost any size smaller than 8 1/2 x 11. Changing page size is much like changing margins or indents: the software rearranges the text immediately. Then the person doing the printing can make appropriate adjustments to obtain the desired finished page size in the publication. There is a disadvantage to using a size that is different than the full or half typewriter page: cost. That is, most small print shops have an additional charge for publications that are not full or half-page in size.

One disadvantage of using 8 1/2 x 11 and a typeface such as 10-point Times Roman with one inch margins, is that it produces a line so long that it is uncomfortable to read. One way of resolving this problem is to use wider margins. Although this results in a shorter text line that is easier to follow, it suffers from two potential problems. First, the appearance of the wide margins might be objectionable for the particular publication. Second, the number of pages required for the document will be increased significantly.

Headers and Footers

Another design item that the desktop publisher can consider is the use of headers or footers. At the top of the sample page is a single line that identifies the current chapter. This is called a header; a **header** is one or more lines of standard text that appears at the top of each page. (If you look at the top of the pages of this book you see a header on both the left and the right pages.) Although less commonly used, a **footer** is one or more lines that appear at the bottom of each page. When used, the footer is often the page number, although one or more footer lines can be used in the same way as headers.

Figure 9-9
A very wide line.

Special large-screen monitors allow the user to view the entire page exactly as it will appear when it is printed.

- Page size.
- Margins.
- Typeface and type size selection.
- Headings and subheadings.
- Headers and footers.

Selecting Page Size and Margins

The example in Figure 9-9 uses standard typing paper size of 8½ × 11 inch with margins on the left, right, top, and bottom of 1 inch each. For most desktop publishing, the standard typewriter page size tends to prevail because it is the paper size used by the laser printer. The half-page, 5½ × 8½, is also commonly encountered; it is used for most microcomputer hardware and software manuals. However, the desktop publisher can specify to the word processor or page layout software almost any size smaller than 8½ × 11. Changing page size is much like changing margins or indents: the software rearranges the text immediately. Then the person doing the printing can make appropriate adjustments to obtain the desired finished page size. There is a disadvantage in using a size that is different from the full or half typewriter page, and that is cost. Most small print shops have an additional charge for publications that are not a full or half-page in size.

One disadvantage of using 8½ × 11 and a typeface such as 10-point Times Roman with 1-inch margins is that it produces a line so long that it is uncomfortable to read. One way to resolve this problem is to use wider margins. Although this results in a shorter text line that is easier to follow, it suffers from two potential problems. First, the appearance of the wide margins might be objectionable for the particular publication. Second, the number of pages required for the document will be increased significantly.

Another way to deal with this problem is to use double columns as shown in Figure 9-10. This produces a form that economizes on space and is relatively easy to read. Notice that justification is not used with the double-column version of the page whereas it is with the single-column sample of Figure 9-9. Because justifying short lines tends to produce exaggerated unevenness in the spacing between words, multiple-column text is commonly set unjustified. (*Note:* WordPerfect, as well as many other word processors, includes provisions for printing double columns.)

Figure 9-10
Double columns.

DESKTOP PUBLISHING

PAGE DESIGN

About Page Design

In designing your publication, selection of typefaces, sizes, and line spacing are early decisions that you must make. In addition, you must make decisions concerning the overall page appearance that you want to achieve. This is called page design. Page layout programs streamline the paste-up process for the desktop publisher by eliminating most of the manual work in laying out each page. They also are useful for experimenting with page design because page samples can be displayed on the screen and and easily changed in searching for the most appealing form. Pages are not designed one at a time; the design is a characteristic of the overall publication itself. For an office procedure manual with few illustrations the document must be designed to avoid the boring appearance of a massive gray area resulting from pages of solid text. For a sales summary, the basic layout must be able to accomodate charts, tables, and illustrations. A more formal type of publication might require chapter or section headings, footnotes, as well as illustrations.

Selecting Page Size and Margins

The example in Figure 9-9 uses standard typing paper size of 8 1/2 x 11 with margins on the left, right, top, and bottom of one inch. For most desktop publishing the standard typewriter page size tends to prevail because it is the paper size used by the laser printer. The half-page, 5 1/2 x 8 1/2, is also commonly encountered; it is used for most microcomputer hardware and software manuals. However, the desktop publisher can specify to the word processor or page layout software almost any size smaller than 8 1/2 x 11. Changing page size is much like changing margins or indents: the software rearranges the text immediately. Then the person doing the printing can make appropriate adjustments to obtain the desired finished page size in the publication. There is a disadvantage to using a size that is different than the full or half typewriter page: cost. That is, most small print shops have an additional charge for publications that are not full or half-page in size.

One disadvantage of using 8 1/2 x 11 and a typeface such as 10-point Times Roman with one inch margins, is that it produces a line so long that it is uncomfortable to read. One way of resolving this problem is to use wider margins. Although this results in a shorter text line that is easier to follow, it suffers from two potential problems. First, the appearance of the wide margins might be objectionable for the particular publication. Second, the number of pages required for the document will be increased significantly.

Headers and Footers

Another design item that the desktop publisher can consider is the use of headers or footers. At the top of the sample page is a single line that identifies the current chapter. This is called a header; a **header** is one or more lines of standard text that appears at the top of each page. (If you look at the top of the pages of this book you see a header on both the left and the right pages.) Although less commonly used, a **footer** is one or more lines that appear at the bottom of each page. When used, the footer is often the page number, although one or more footer lines can be used in the same way as headers.

Type Size, Headings, and Subheadings

Notice that the page of Figure 9-9 is broken up through the use of headings. This introduces white space, or areas between elements of the page that are empty, thus relieving the monotonous appearance resulting from line after line of text. (Positioning of artwork within text also contributes to white space.) In this example, two levels of headings are used: main headings and subheadings. Both are set in the Helvetica typeface; the main heading is 14 point and the subheading is 12 point. Notice that these sans serif typefaces give a stark appearance that sets them aside from the smoother, more flowing appearance of the text, which is set in the 10-point Times Roman serif typeface.

Headers and Footers

Another design item that the desktop publisher can consider is the use of headers or footers. At the top of the sample page is a single line that identifies the current chapter; it is set in 8-point Helvetica. This is called a header. A **header** is one or more lines of standard text that appears at the top of each page. (If you look at the tops of the pages of this book, you see headers on both the left- and right-hand pages.) Although less commonly used, a **footer** is one or more lines that appear at the bottom of each page. When used, the footer is often the page number, although one or more footer lines can be used in the same way as headers.

About Planning with Artwork

Although the example of Figure 9-9 does not include artwork, the type of artwork and the way in which it is incorporated into the design are essential elements of design. Artwork not only adds another avenue of communication, but can also make the page layout much more interesting. If a publication is to include many illustrations, especially large ones, a smaller page size can be clumsy because there is less room for maneuvering in positioning illustrations and text on each page.

As a rule, simplicity produces the best results, with illustrations placed at either the top or bottom of the page. However, page layout software affords the desktop publisher considerable versatility. You can even position a small illustration in the center of a page and direct the software to fill in text on each side of it as well as above and below.

In general, page design as it relates to artwork and all aspects of the document is an activity that must be well thought out and adhered to throughout the publication. Good page design results in a high-quality, professional-looking product.

THE LASER PRINTER

With the laser printer such an integral part of the desktop publishing system, a description of desktop publishing would not be complete without a discussion of some basic characteristics of this printer.

Resolution

From Chapter 4, you learned that dot-matrix printers and laser printers both form images with a series of dots. Indeed, even the letters of the words of this book you are reading were formed from a series of dots. The difference in quality between the printers is attributable to the **resolution**—

the number of dots per inch used by the device to generate images. Laser printers commonly used with personal computers generate 300 dots per inch in both directions; their resolution is said to be 300 dots per inch. Equipment used to generate the text on this page uses a resolution of 960 dots per inch. Although it might seem that dots 1/300 inch across would be small enough that the eye would see a series of them as a smooth line, that is not the case. In Figure 9-11, the jagged edges are visible in the sample printed by the laser printer. In the sample printed from photo typesetting at 960 dots per inch, the edges are sharp and clear. For contrast, a sample using the graphics capability of a dot-matrix printer generated using special software is shown at left. The clarity is amazingly good, considering that it was printed with a low-cost dot-matrix printer.

Figure 9-11
Print resolution.

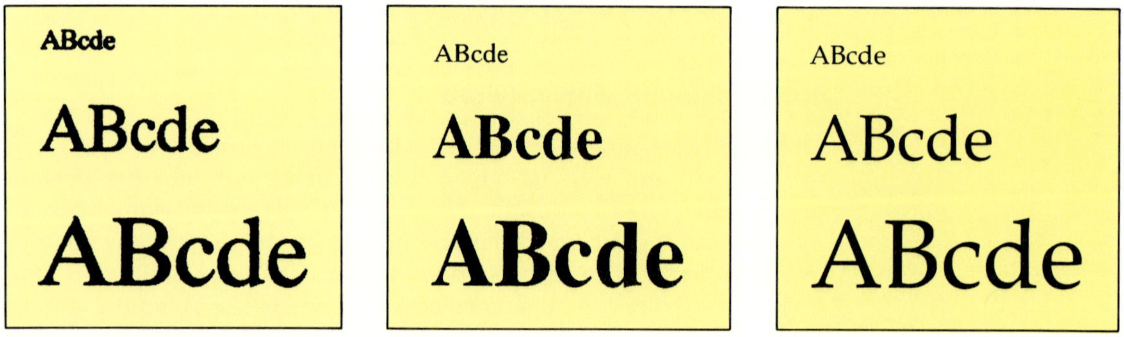

ABcde
ABcde
ABcde

Printed by a dot-matrix printer with Fancy Font® software from Softcraft, Inc.

ABcde
ABcde
ABcde

Printed by a laser printer; 300 dots per inch

ABcde
ABcde
ABcde

Printed by a phototypesetting machine; 960 dots per inch

Laser-Printer Memory Requirements

When observing a computer printer while it is printing, you see it as a line-by-line printing device. This is not the case with a laser printer in which the 8½ × 11 inch page, rather than the character position or line, is the major unit. This means that the electronic component of the laser printer (called the controller) must convert codes from word processing or page layout software to the binary images required by the computer, as illustrated in Figure 9-12. (The laser printer controller that does this is itself a microcomputer. It includes a processor, ROM, RAM, and I/O components.) Each page to be printed is assembled (as a bit map) in the memory of the printer. When the page is completely assembled, it is printed.

The fact that the page is treated as a single, huge array of positions at which a dot can be printed (or omitted) is a significant feature of the laser printer. That is what gives the laser printer its flexibility and allows for easy mixing of text and graphics. However, in order to have full 300 by 300 graphics capability for the entire page, the printer memory requirements are substantial. That is, with a resolution of 300 dots per inch, there is a total of 90,000 dot positions in a 1-inch square. With an 8½ × 11 page, this

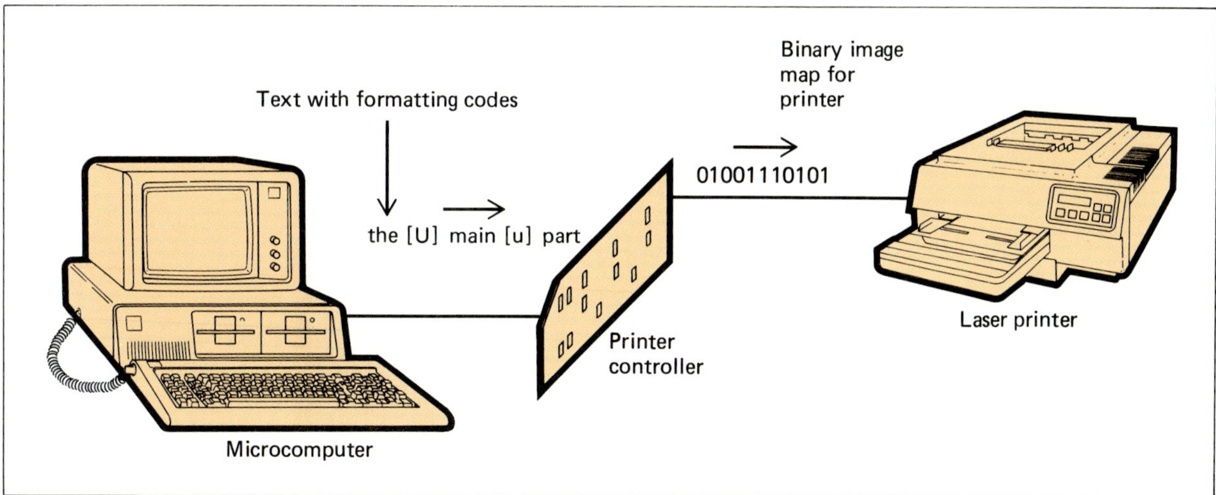

Figure 9-12
The action of the laser printer controller.

is over 8 million dots, requiring approximately 8 million memory bits to store, or about 1 megabyte of memory. If text only is to be printed, the memory requirements are significantly less because of the way in which character images are stored. For instance, the original Hewlett-Packard (HP) Laserjet included only 64K bytes of memory.

Printer Fonts

For each font to be used with a laser printer, the printer controller requires an exact definition of the dot placement for each character of the font.

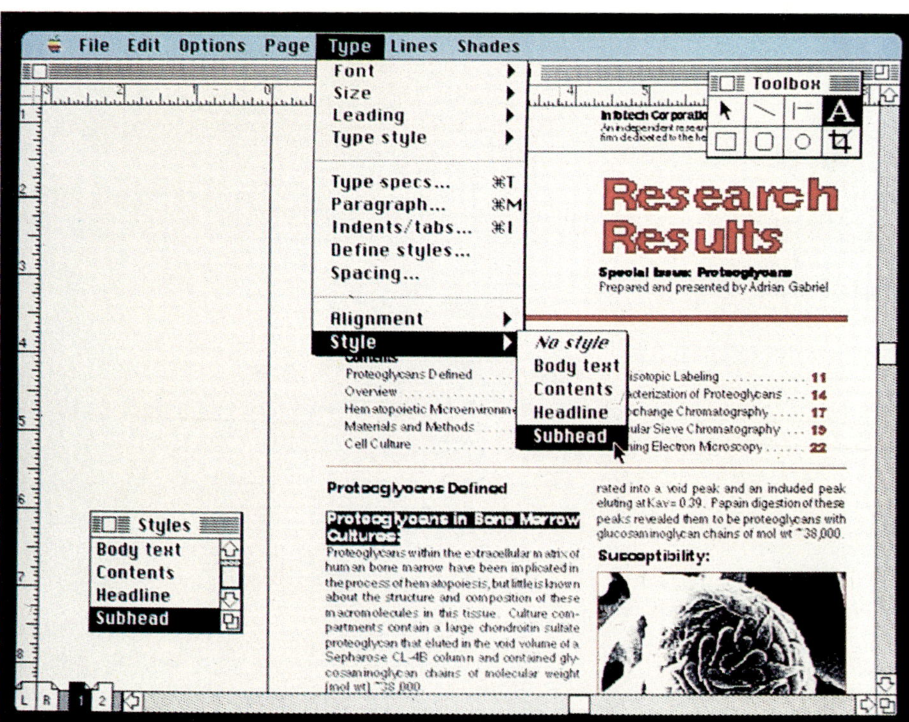

All aspects of formatting and page layout are controlled by means of "pop-up" menus in this page layout program.

These definitions come from three sources. The first is the ROM of the printer controller. With the original HP Laserjet, as well as most other laser printers, a default character set definition is stored in ROM. This is commonly the

```
10 character per inch Courier typeface
which is used to print these two lines.
```

Beyond the default Courier typeface, most laser printers use font cartridges for additional fonts. A **font cartridge,** which is about the size of a pocket calculator, is a ROM device into which the manufacturer has stored the complete dot patterns (font definitions) for several fonts. These are made available to the printer by inserting the cartridge into a receptacle in the printer. When the HP Laserjet was first introduced it was accompanied by the B cartridge, which contains definitions for 8- and 10-point Times Roman and 8- and 14-point Helvetica. Numerous font cartridges are now available for the Laserjet. However, the cost is not insignificant, ranging upward from approximately $200 for a single cartridge containing one or two typefaces in a variety of sizes.

The third method of providing the printer font definitions is with **downloaded fonts.** They are called downloaded because they are loaded into the printer's RAM from the disk drive of the microcomputer. Since printer RAM is used, it is a simple matter to load one set of fonts and then change the characteristics of the printer entirely by loading a different set. The printer needs substantial memory to store a complete font definition. For instance, the AST TurboLaser memory requirements of 10-point Times Roman is approximately 10K bytes; that for the 36-point face is approximately 93K bytes. The entire set in Figure 9-5 requires approximately 175K bytes. Most laser printers can use both cartridges and downloading.

SUMMARY

This chapter extends the principles of word processing to desktop publishing. Summarizing, the important items from the chapter are:

- Desktop publishing is the activity of preparing professional-appearing publications with a microcomputer. A desktop publishing system is commonly made up of a hard-disk-equipped microcomputer with a mouse and a laser printer (hardware) and a word processor and page layout program (software).
- The publishing process can be broken down into eight steps: authoring, designing, editing, typesetting, artwork preparation, pasteup, printing, and binding. Each of these requires specialized skills.

- The activities and associated skills of publishing are not eliminated by the microcomputer with desktop publishing capabilities. However, the desktop publishing software simplifies some of the procedures.
- Page layout programs provide the ability to lay out pages on the screen exactly as they will appear when printed. They have the capabilities to use text that has been prepared with a word processor and to insert graphics created by other programs.
- One of the activities facing the desktop publisher is design. Designing the publication requires that decisions be made on such items as typefaces and type sizes, page size, margins, number of columns of text, headings, and general placement of illustrations.
- Because of the versatility of the laser printer, the desktop publisher can choose from a variety of typefaces and sizes in order to generate pages that best communicate his or her ideas. Serif typefaces have small counterstrokes at the end of each main stroke; sans serif do not. With a roman typeface, the characters are vertical, and with an italic typeface, they are slanted.
- The measure of the size of a typeface is the distance from the top of the capital letter to the bottom of the descender. This is measured in points; there are approximately 72 points per inch.
- A typeface in which the characters are allocated only the space necessary for each character (for instance, the letter i would occupy less space than the letter W) is said to use proportional spacing (microspacing).
- The laser printer treats the entire 8½ × 11 page as a single large array of points, 300 points per inch (the resolution of the laser printer is said to be 300 by 300). This provides the versatility necessary to produce professional-appearing publications with a variety of typefaces and graphics.

NEW TERMINOLOGY

The following are important new terms introduced in this chapter; you should be familiar with each of them.desktop publishing

downloaded font
font
font cartridge
footer
halftone
header
italics
kerning
leading
line art
microspacing
monospacing
page layout software
paste-up
pica
point
resolution
roman
sans serif
scanner/digitizer
serif
tracking
typeface

REVIEW QUESTIONS

1. Distinguish between the words *document* and *publication* as used in this chapter.
2. What is the difference between the capabilities of drawing software such as MacPaint and a scanner/digitizer?
3. What is the role of a word processor in a desktop publishing system? How is it related to the role of the page layout software?
4. Of the eight steps in the conventional publishing process, which are affected by bringing the publishing process to the desktop?
5. What are the lengths of the typesetting measures *pica* and *point*?
6. How is the size of a typeface determined?
7. What does the word *font* mean?
8. What are two ways of classifying typefaces?
9. What is monospacing?
10. What is the difference between tracking and kerning?
11. How are tracking and leading similar?
12. What is meant by resolution?
13. What is stored in ROM of a laser printer? Why does a laser printer require RAM?

MATCHING

Match each term in a to h with the most appropriate description in 1 through 8.

a. resolution
b. pica
c. point
d. downloaded font
e. paste-up
f. italics
g. font cartridge
h. leading

1. Provides the means for a laser printer to print text with two or more typefaces.
2. A measure of the number of dots per inch used in forming an image.
3. A measure of the distance between printed lines.
4. Approximately 1/6 inch.
5. A variation of a typeface in which the letters are slanted rather than vertical.
6. Requires RAM in the laser printer.
7. One of the functions performed with page layout software.
8. Approximately 1/72 inch.

TRUE/FALSE

Determine whether each of the following is true or false.

_____ **1.** For some publishing needs, desktop publishing could be done with a microcomputer equipped with a word processor and a laser printer.

_____ **2.** One of the features of page layout software is the ease with which output from other programs such as spreadsheets and graphics can be integrated with text.

_____ **3.** Scanner/digitizers are convenient to use with desktop publishing systems because of the ease with which they can be utilized to make freehand drawings.

_____ **4.** One of the most significant features of page layout software is that it eliminates the need for the design phase in preparing a publication.

_____ **5.** In the publishing process, paste-up is the action of bringing the text and graphics together to form the final page.

_____ **6.** Page layout software can read word processing prepared text together with all formatting codes, thereby eliminating all text entry and formatting with the page layout software.

_____ **7.** Except for certain low-volume publications, the laser printer is not suitable for general printing of publications.

_____ **8.** Type size is measured in picas as the distance from the top of the capital letter to the bottom of the lowercase descender.

_____ **9.** As used with laser printers, typeface and font mean the same thing.

_____ **10.** A sans serif typeface has small counterstrokes at the end of characters' main strokes.

_____ **11.** In an italic typeface, the characters are slanted rather than vertical.

_____ **12.** If you wanted to prepare a professional-appearing publication, you would probably use microspacing rather than monospacing.

_____ **13.** A document with a low leading value would have more lines per page than one with a high leading value.

_____ **14.** Tracking and kerning are the same: the adjusting of space between letters.

_____ **15.** A printer that uses downloaded fonts is likely to have more RAM than one that does not.

ANSWERS TO OBJECTIVE QUESTIONS

Matching

1. g 2. a 3. h 4. b 5. f 6. d 7. e 8. c

True/False

1. T 2. T 3. F 4. F 5. T 6. F 7. T 8. F
9. F 10. F 11. T 12. T 13. T 14. F 15. T

ASSIGNMENTS/PROJECTS

1. Although this book does not include page layout software, a certain amount of layout can be done with the version of WordPerfect that is included. This assignment involves inserting the codes into a document to improve its appearance. The data disk contains the file ASSIGN9.WP1 (Chapter 9, Assignment 1), which is a slightly shortened version of the major section of this chapter entitled "About Typefaces." This is an ASCII text file and includes no formatting codes (you can display it on the screen with the DOS TYPE command). You are to retrieve it with WordPerfect and format it so that its appearance somewhat resembles the corresponding text in this chapter. To this end you should:

Change the margins to 15 and 69.

From the Format Page command (Alt-F8), define a header (option 6). From the resulting submenu, select Header A to be printed on every page. When you are presented with a blank screen, type the header "DESKTOP PUBLISHING."

From the Format Page command, select Page Number Position (1), and then select bottom-centered page numbers for every page.

Use underscore for the main heading ABOUT TYPEFACES.

Use boldface for minor headings (insert blank lines).

Indent the paragraphs that describe serif and sans serif type.

Enter any other formatting codes that you feel will enhance the appearance of the document. Remember that all formatting codes that are to affect the entire document must be entered with the cursor at the beginning of the first line. When finished, save the document (use a new name) and print a copy.

2. You can carry Assignment 2 one step further by using two columns, but this involves some detailed steps not described in Chapter 8. For this, you should start with the original, unformatted copy of the document.

Set the margins to 7 and 77.

Define the header and page numbers.

Define double columns with the Math/Columns command (Alt-F7). From the submenu, select the Column Definition option (4). Respond with Y to evenly spaced columns, enter 4 for the space between columns, select 2 for newspaper columns, and select 2 for two columns. Then, upon returning to the Math/Columns option list, select 3 to turn the column feature on (Column On/Off). After that, select 5 for Column Display. When you exit, the text will be displayed in double-column form if you have done everything properly.

Complete the formatting as described in Assignment 1. You will need to experiment with cursor movement.

Complete the formatting as in Assignment 1.

When finished, save the document (use a new name) and print a copy. The WPC notice inserted by the Limited-Use software may print over a portion of a line because of the way it is done by the software. If it happens, it is not your fault but rather a characteristic of the Limited-Use software.

PART THREE

Spreadsheets and Computer Graphics

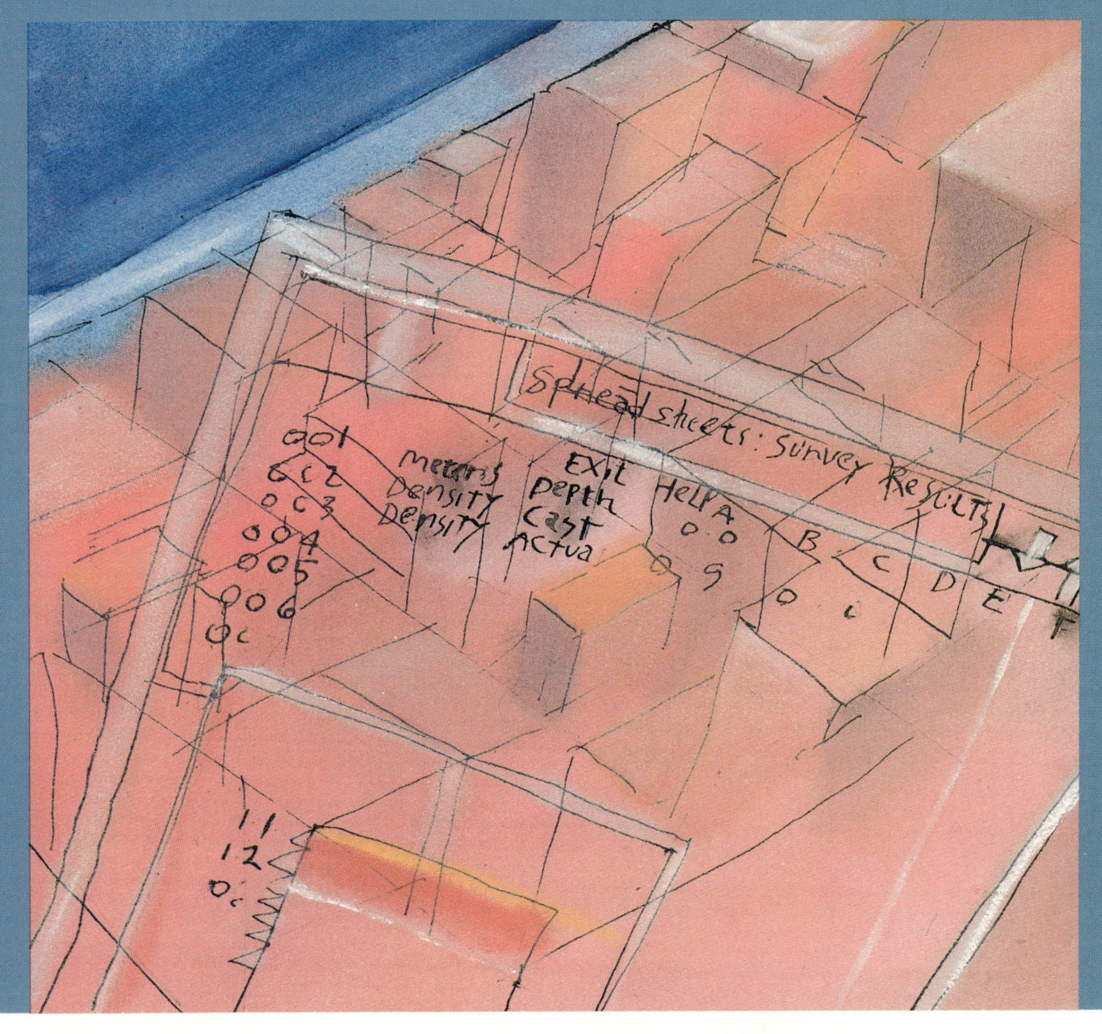

PROLOGUE TO PART THREE

The next of the productivity tools described in this book is the electronic spreadsheet—using the computer to summarize data in a tabular form. Part Three consists of four chapters. Chapter 10 is a generic description of spreadsheets and the features that are found in most spreadsheet programs. In Chapters 11 and 12 you will learn how to use the popular program Lotus 1-2-3. If you have a copy of the commercially available Lotus 1-2-3 program, you can work with it. If not, you can use the JOE spreadsheet program that is available with this book. It's command structure is identical to that of Lotus 1-2-3. Whichever software you use, you will learn basic operations, such as entering and changing a spreadsheet, saving it to disk, and retrieving a previously saved spreadsheet from disk (Chapter 11). You will also learn more advanced operations, such as changing a spreadsheet's appearance and rearranging data in the spreadsheet (Chapter 12). In Chapter 13 you will learn about computer graphics with an emphasis on displaying spreadsheet information in graphics form.

Chapter 10

Spreadsheet Concepts

OBJECTIVES

Chapter 2 introduced you to the nature of the electronic spreadsheet, a program for displaying data in the tabular form of an accountant's worksheet. This chapter describes some of the distinct features of the worksheet and relates them to the electronic spreadsheet. It provides the basis for detailed descriptions of using Lotus 1-2-3 in the two chapters that follow. When you have completed this chapter, you should be able to describe:

- The nature of spreadsheets and the types of problems for which they are suited.
- The general structure of a spreadsheet as consisting of cells arranged in rows and columns.
- The types of information that can be placed in the cells of a spreadsheet.
- The use of formulas through which it is possible to display results of calculations based on information in designated cells.
- Basic spreadsheet commands that allow the user to manipulate data in cells and blocks of cells.
- An organized procedure for solving a problem using a spreadsheet program as a tool.

PREVIEW

Typical Worksheets

The electronic spreadsheet was derived from the accountant's worksheet, a device for arranging and working with numbers using a grid form (rows and columns).

A Cost Analysis Problem

To illustrate the principles of the worksheet, a cost analysis problem for one of the MCT Enterprises offerings is defined. This serves as the basis for studying the nature of the worksheet and how it is used.

Principles of Electronic Spreadsheet Programs

Using the example worksheet for reference, elements of the electronic spreadsheet are examined. Each position of a spreadsheet can contain data or instructions to calculate results based on values in other positions of the spreadsheet.

Processing Data with an Electronic Spreadsheet

As in all data processing applications, electronic spreadsheet programs provide the capabilities of data entry (input), calculation (manipulation), output, and storage and retrieval. Commands are used to manipulate the spreadsheet contents.

Fundamental Steps in Computer Problem Solving

The computer is a useful tool in problem solving. However, it cannot perceive solutions in the creative way that is characteristic of the human mind. We must know how to solve a problem before we can prepare instructions for the computer.

TYPICAL WORKSHEETS

The second of the productivity software tools that you learned about in Chapter 2 is the electronic spreadsheet. Remember that the spreadsheet is patterned after the accountant's worksheet whereby numerical data is organized into rows and columns from which calculations are performed. This type of application is commonplace and most of us have used a worksheet form at one time or another. For instance, consider the four examples of Figure 10-1. The first example is a 3-month expense summary for a student living at home. Summing the columns produces the monthly expenditures; summing the rows produces totals by expense category. The 3-month total is shown in the lower right corner. Notice how this worksheet presents you with both the details and the summary.

The second example summarizes the cost of a trip for two people by three modes of transportation. (Although it clearly summarizes and displays the costs, it does not address the convenience and time factors.)

The third example illustrates how you might tabulate the cost in

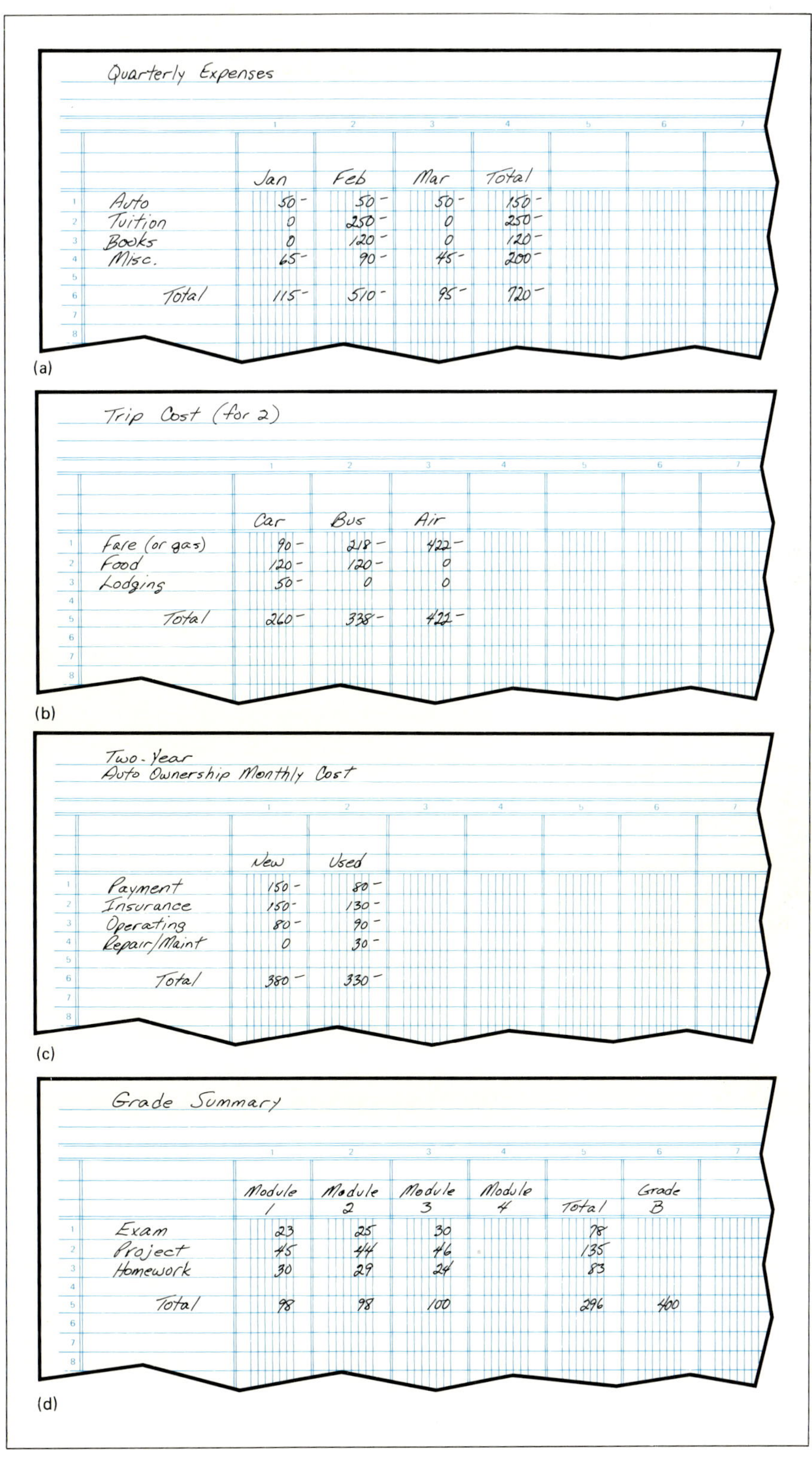

Quarterly Expenses

	Jan	Feb	Mar	Total
Auto	50-	50-	50-	150-
Tuition	0	250-	0	250-
Books	0	120-	0	120-
Misc.	65-	90-	45-	200-
Total	115-	510-	95-	720-

(a)

Trip Cost (for 2)

	Car	Bus	Air
Fare (or gas)	90-	218-	422-
Food	120-	120-	0
Lodging	50-	0	0
Total	260-	338-	422-

(b)

Two-Year
Auto Ownership Monthly Cost

	New	Used
Payment	150-	80-
Insurance	150-	130-
Operating	80-	90-
Repair/Maint	0	30-
Total	380-	330-

(c)

Grade Summary

	Module 1	Module 2	Module 3	Module 4	Total	Grade B
Exam	23	25	30		78	
Project	45	44	46		135	
Homework	30	29	24		83	
Total	98	98	100		296	400

(d)

Figure 10-1
Four sample worksheets.

attempting to decide whether to purchase a new or a used car. By making the necessary efforts to estimate values in constructing a table such as this, you gain a better insight into the total cost. The cost difference between the two methods might end up being much different than you would have expected had you not gone into such detail.

For the last example, assume that you have enrolled in a self-paced learning course in which you aspire to make grade B (requiring 400 points). Your performance in the first three of the four course modules is summarized here. You can see at a glance that you are four points off the grade B pace. You can also see that your exam grades have been improving and that, had you not neglected your module 3 homework, your average would be at the grade B level. This summary clearly shows how you must perform on module 4 to achieve your goal.

Each of these four examples shows us how numeric data can be displayed using the worksheet form. By arranging the data in rows and columns, both details and summaries are displayed in an informative and easily understood form. There is still another aspect of the worksheet: its use as a tool in changing values to reach a desired optimum situation. For instance, assume that the student in the first example has only $650 available for this period. The grand total indicates that $70 must be trimmed from the expenditures. What if it is possible to reduce auto expenses by $10 per month? Changing these entries from $50 to $40 would require that corresponding totals be recalculated (giving $120 for the auto total and $690 for the grand total). Since this is not enough, what if the February miscellaneous expense were changed to $65? This process would be repeated until an acceptable solution was found (or until it was learned that there is no practical solution at all).

Each of the examples of Figure 10-1 uses the worksheet form to organize data in solving a problem. Each includes data and relationships among various data elements; it is a mathematical representation of a real-world phenomenon. As such, it is commonly called a **model.** It is much like the model that a designer builds of a new automobile except that, rather than being a model of something physical, it is a model of something abstract. The model of an automobile illustrates features of the real thing and can be changed quickly and easily to test new ideas. Likewise, the abstract model represents the real world and can be changed repeatedly in an attempt to optimize a solution. In this and the next two chapters, you will learn about modeling using the electronic worksheet. In later chapters, you will learn about modeling using database management software.

A COST ANALYSIS PROBLEM

With this introductory background, consider a specific problem and how to solve it using a worksheet. This will give you a better understanding of how a worksheet is employed and will introduce you to the example that will be used in the next two chapters on Lotus 1-2-3.

The Problem

As a special promotion for first-time retail stores, you, as a partner in MCT Enterprises, decide to offer a "Special Collection Retail Module" consisting of the four basic styles shown in Table 10-1.

Table 10-1 SPECIAL COLLECTION SUMMARY

Garment Style	Your Cost	Quantity	Amount
Style A	13.97	12	167.64
Style B	15.83	12	189.96
Style C	13.42	18	241.56
Style D	14.59	8	116.72
		Total	715.88

You consider this a "foot-in-the-door" package and wish to keep the price below $675 in order to compete with promotions of other companies. However, this summary shows that you will not meet your price objective so you must consider the alternatives.

1. Go with the higher price.
2. Change the quantities offered in order to reduce the price.
3. Evaluate your costs to determine whether any reductions are possible.

As your promotion is to be oriented around the theme "less than $675," you wish to avoid the higher price. The quantities are based on your careful analysis of expected sales demand so you do not wish to change these numbers. The only alternative is to determine whether reductions in cost are possible. Because you wish to cover your costs in offering this deal, you must accurately assess the cost of the various components of the package. To do this, you break down the costs for each garment into three categories: Material, Labor, and Other. (In reality, the cost breakdown

Studies and analyses that would take a prohibitive amount of time without computer spreadsheet programs are made quickly and easily with them.

probably would be in greater detail; three broad categories are used here to illustrate worksheet principles.)

Using a Worksheet for a Cost Analysis

It is essential to see the overall effect of changing each of these factors for each garment. The best way to study something such as this is to create a worksheet model as shown in Figure 10-2. Notice that this is nothing more than a detailed expansion of Table 10-1 but it makes it possible to isolate the factors that contribute to the overall cost.

Now the question is, "By how much is it necessary to change each of these amounts in order to achieve the $675 objective?" Here you must work within ground rules dictated by facts, that is:

1. The Material costs are fixed.
2. The Other costs can be reduced slightly.
3. You might be able to negotiate a reduction with the sewing contractor (Labor) because of the introductory nature of this offer.

After careful evaluation of your costs and a meeting with your contractor, you determine that you can make the following changes.

- Reduce the Labor cost for Styles A, B, and D by the amounts $0.55, 0.60, and 0.70, respectively.
- Reduce the Other cost for Styles A, B, C, and D by the amounts $0.41, 0.44, 0.31, and 0.21, respectively.

The question now is, "Does this meet the price objective?" You can make

Figure 10-2
A cost analysis worksheet.

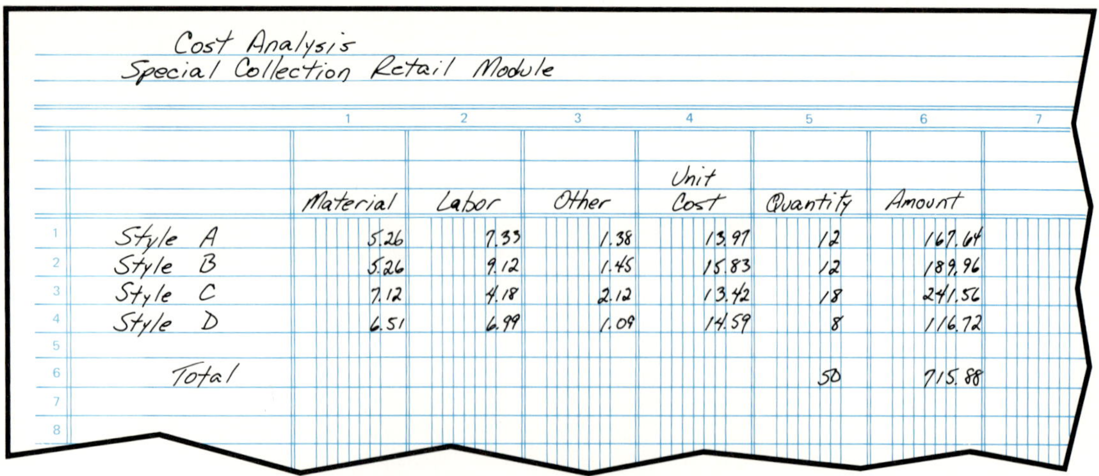

Cost Analysis
Special Collection Retail Module

		1	2	3	4	5	6	7
		Material	Labor	Other	Unit Cost	Quantity	Amount	
1	Style A	5.26	7.33	1.38	13.97	12	167.64	
2	Style B	5.26	9.12	1.45	15.83	12	189.96	
3	Style C	7.12	4.18	2.12	13.42	18	241.56	
4	Style D	6.51	6.99	1.09	14.59	8	116.72	
5								
6	Total					50	715.88	
7								
8								

Material + Labor + Other = Unit Cost

Unit cost X Quantity = Amount

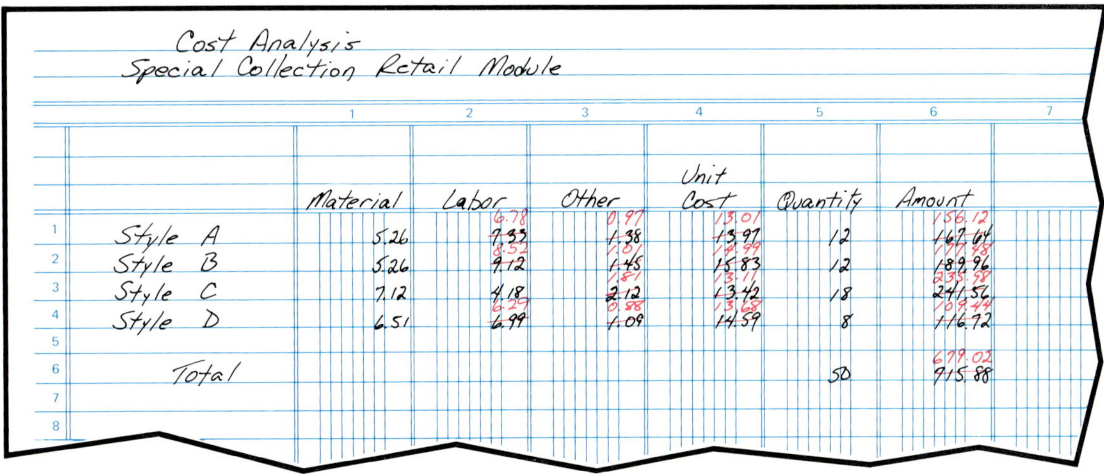

Figure 10-3
Changing the worksheet values.

this assessment by entering new values for Labor and Other, and then recalculating, with the result shown in Figure 10-3. Although close to your $675 objective, it is obvious that further adjustments are needed. You could then examine the details of your costs even more closely to determine whether further reductions were possible. If they were not, you would be faced with the decision either to raise the price or to take a small loss on the promotion in order to maintain the target price. In the end, the worksheet will have proved a valuable tool in presenting information for making a decision.

About the Values Displayed in a Worksheet

From a casual glance at the worksheet of Figure 10-2, we see rows and columns of numbers. However, we know from the description of the example that some of these depend upon others. In fact, we can represent the Unit Cost in a mathematical formula format as:

Unit Cost = Material + Labor + Other

When filling in this worksheet, we enter values for Material, Labor, and Other, and then calculate the Unit Cost by adding their values. Quantity is also a value that we enter. It is multiplied by the Unit Cost to obtain the amount for each style. These amounts are summed to give the total cost for this special retail module. Hence, in this worksheet, we are looking at two different entities: data, and results that are based on computation with that data. Data values are entered, and results calculated according to previously defined rules. If the results are not acceptable, then new values are entered into one or more of the data elements and the results are recalculated accordingly.

In making changes to the worksheet entries, notice that each change produces a "ripple" effect; that is, a change in one position requires calculated changes in other positions. This is a clumsy procedure, especially if repeated changes are made in attempting to determine an optimum configuration. In spite of this, manual worksheets were widely used tools of the businessperson before the invention of the computer because of their effectiveness in displaying data in a way that is easy to understand and manipulate.

Although performing calculations manually in a worksheet might be clumsy and error prone for most people, it is an activity in which the number-crunching capabilities of the computer shine. Let us see how these principles are implemented on electronic spreadsheets.

PRINCIPLES OF ELECTRONIC SPREADSHEETS

In the business world before the introduction of the microcomputer, the word *worksheet* was used to describe the tabular work form. In the microcomputer world, *spreadsheet* is used almost universally to describe this type of application program. That is, VisiCalc, Lotus 1-2-3, and JOE (the software included with this book) are called spreadsheet programs. However, in their reference manuals, many of the software companies, including Lotus, use the word *worksheet*. (In fact, Lotus 1-2-3 includes the Worksheet command to perform certain operations on the worksheet.) Hence, in your reading you will see the words used interchangeably. In this book, worksheet is used when referring to the electronic worksheet and spreadsheet is used in referring to the program (the spreadsheet program or software).

Cells and Their Contents

The electronic version of the cost summary worksheet in Figure 10-4 has the same form as the worksheet in Figure 10-2 in that it displays information in row-column form. Notice that rows are numbered 1, 2, 3, . . . and columns are identified by letters A, B, C, . . . Each position into which an entry can be made is identified by its column letter and row number and is called a **cell.** For instance, the Labor cost for Style A is stored in the cell at the intersection of column C and row 2. This cell is identified by its **cell address** C2. Note that with this addressing scheme, the column letter is first and the row number is second. This is the standard way of addressing cells with spreadsheet systems that use the letter and number method. (Although most spreadsheet programs use letters and numbers, some use numbers to identify both rows and columns.)

We have already observed that the values displayed by the worksheet fall into two categories—those that we select (as data) and those that we calculate using previously defined relationships. With the electronic spreadsheet, cell entries can be either of three general types; for the spreadsheet of Figure 10-4, these are identified in Figure 10-5. The first type of entry, shown in the first row and column, contains the English descriptions that identify parts of the spreadsheet for us. These entries are commonly called **labels,** although in some spreadsheet programs they are called *alpha* data (alphabetic) and in others they are called *titles*.

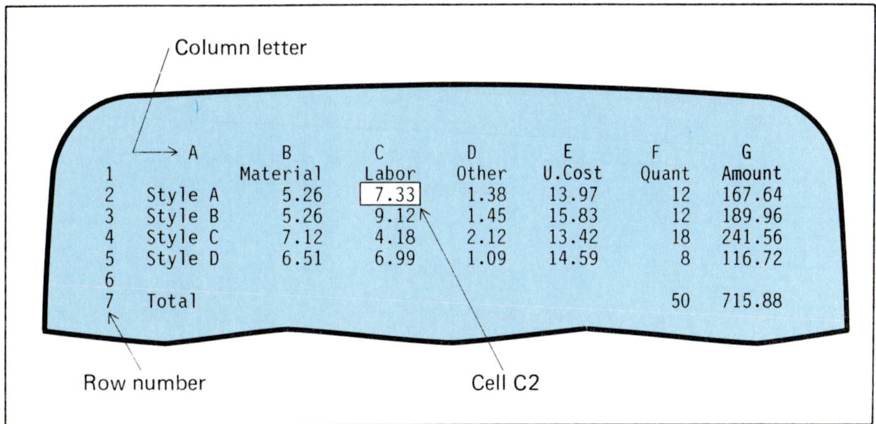

	A	B	C	D	E	F	G
1		Material	Labor	Other	U.Cost	Quant	Amount
2	Style A	5.26	7.33	1.38	13.97	12	167.64
3	Style B	5.26	9.12	1.45	15.83	12	189.96
4	Style C	7.12	4.18	2.12	13.42	18	241.56
5	Style D	6.51	6.99	1.09	14.59	8	116.72
6							
7	Total					50	715.88

Figure 10-4
The cost summary worksheet.

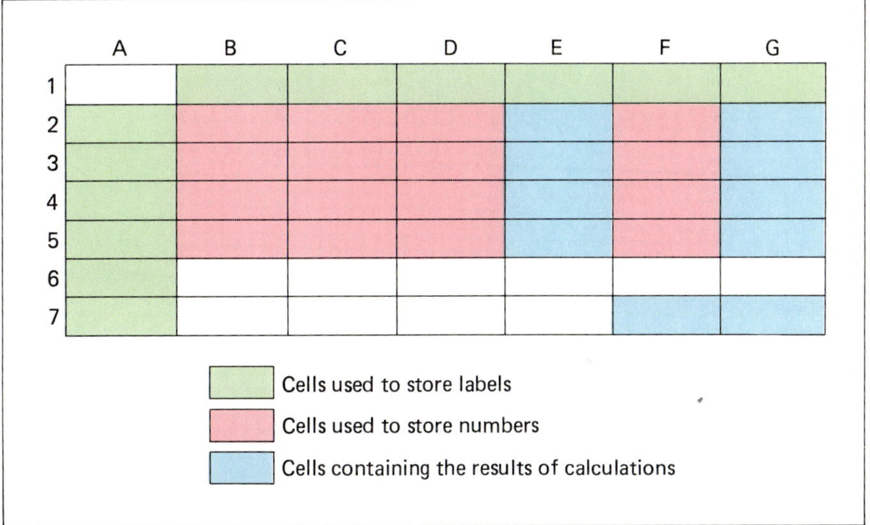

Figure 10-5
General layout of the cost summary worksheet.

The second type of cell entry is numeric data, values that we select and enter in performing the analysis. In Figure 10-5, these cells are shown in pink. In some spreadsheets, these are called numbers, and in others, they are called values. The word *numbers* is used in this book to be consistent with the Lotus 1-2-3 usage.

The third type of cell entry is the value resulting from calculations with quantities stored in other cells, the blue cells in Figure 10-5. When making both label and number entries into a spreadsheet, you type the actual value to be entered. However, for any cell that is to display results of calculations, you must enter the exact instructions for making those calculations. This is called a **formula,** and it is the topic of the next section.

Formulas

For each cell that is to display a calculated value, you must define the data to be used and the operations to take place. For instance, the Unit Cost for Style A would be calculated as follows:

1. Add the values in cells B2, C2, and D2.
2. Display the result in cell E2.

The use of cell addressing as defined in the preceding section allows the language of mathematics to be used, resulting in the following very concise formula.

```
E2 = +B2+C2+D2
```

The portion on the right-hand side of the equals sign is commonly called an **expression.** This expression is then assigned to the cell named to the left of the equals sign, as illustrated in Figure 10-6. When we look at cells of a worksheet containing data, we expect to see that data. When looking at cells with formulas, we do *not* expect to see the formulas; we expect to see the numbers resulting from the calculations performed by the formulas. As you see, the underlying concept of formulas is that they determine the value in one cell based on values in other cells. Once you understand this, you have a basic understanding of how a worksheet is used. After you have a worksheet set up, whenever you enter a new number into a cell, the spreadsheet program automatically recalculates the values for every cell that depends upon the one with the new entry. Thus, with the cost analysis worksheet, you can focus your attention on weighing all of the possibilities represented by your model. You need not be concerned with the details of calculating each time you make a change as the computer recalculates and displays the results. In a matter of minutes, you can try many variations of the cost figures in an attempt to find the optimum cost structure.

Figure 10-6
The concept of formulas associated with cells.

A	B	C	D	E
	Material	Labor	Other	Unit cost
Style A	5.26	7.33	1.38	13.97

E2 = +B2+C2+D2

5.26 + 7.33 + 1.38 = 13.97

Result of calculation is displayed, not the formula.

A Spreadsheet Template

A spreadsheet program such as Lotus 1-2-3 is a tool that you can use to assist you in solving problems. Using it for performing the cost analysis of the preceding sections involves a two-step approach: (1) defining and entering relationships between cells, and (2) entering and changing data values. The first, setting up the worksheet, requires entering all of the labels and formulas. This is sometimes called programming the worksheet. The end result of this phase is called a worksheet **template**: a complete worksheet except that no data has yet been entered into it. As often as not, a given template will be used and reused. For instance, many instructors maintain their student grade records with spreadsheet programs that automatically compute totals and averages. With a template stored on disk, beginning the new semester involves making a copy for each class and then entering the student names. Templates, many of which include highly complex calculations, can be purchased for different applications. Application systems are available that consist of many interrelated templates for performing a particular set of operations. Once a worksheet template has been created, it can be used as an aid to solving the problem for which it was designed.

PROCESSING DATA WITH AN ELECTRONIC SPREADSHEET

Basic Operations of Data Processing

We learned from Chapter 1 that data processing involves the following operations on data:

Input

Calculation (manipulation)

Output

Storage and retrieval

Most of these elements are evident in the example of this chapter. Electronic spreadsheet programs provide these capabilities in a very useful and easy-to-use way. Since the entire concept of the spreadsheet is visual in nature, let consider output first.

	Fall	Winter
Income		
Job	400.00	600.00
Grant	400.00	400.00
Parents	150.00	
TOTAL	950.00	1000.00

Output (Presentation). All of our interaction with a spreadsheet is via the visual output in the form of rows and columns on the monitor screen. The MCT cost analysis example has 7 rows and 7 columns. Many applications, such as product pricing studies or budget analyses, require many more rows and columns. The 256-column and 8192-row capacity of the spreadsheet program included with this book is typical. As you might expect, it would be impossible to display a full-size worksheet on the normal microcomputer monitor. Hence, the screen displays only a small portion of the worksheet as illustrated in Figure 10-7. A portion of the worksheet thus is displayed on the screen in exactly the same way that a portion of a document is displayed. As you will learn, the action of scrolling (moving the view into the worksheet up, down, left, or right) is identical to the corresponding action with a word processor.

Input (Entry). We enter data into the worksheet from the keyboard in much the same way that we enter text with a word processor. The cell into which the data is to be entered is selected (equivalent to positioning the cursor with a word processor) and the data value is typed. This is the electronic equivalent of making an entry into a manual worksheet using a pencil.

÷

+ $(1 + i)^n$

×

Average( )

Calculation (Manipulation). Calculations are performed by formulas assigned to cells. In the cost analysis example of this chapter, we inspected the formula for calculating the sum of the component costs of one of the styles. Worksheet formulas provide the ability to perform all of the basic arithmetic operations (addition, subtraction, multiplication, division, and raising to a power). Most spreadsheet programs have built-in features to perform statistical calculations and common business calculations such as interest calculations. Calculations are performed almost instantly and the results are automatically displayed in the cell to which the formula is assigned.

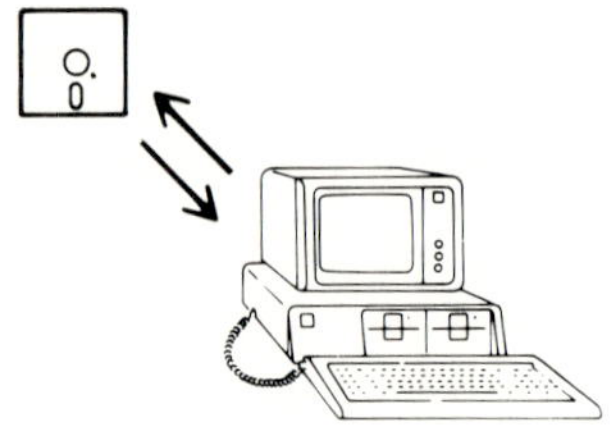

Storage and Retrieval. The value of the spreadsheet program would be very limited without the ability to store worksheets for later retrieval. At any time during the creation of a worksheet, it can be stored to disk as a file. Furthermore, most programs allow a portion of a worksheet in memory to be stored. Worksheets stored on disk can be retrieved from memory, or two or more from disk can be combined to form a third. These actions of storing and retrieving are identical to the corresponding actions with a word processor document.

The Worksheet in Memory and the Screen Display

Figure 10-7 illustrates how the monitor gives us a small view into a portion of the overall worksheet in memory. There is a similar distinction between the contents of a cell in memory (the memory cell) and that which we see in the cell portion of the monitor screen (screen cell). That is, the capacity of

Figure 10-7
A view into the worksheet in memory.

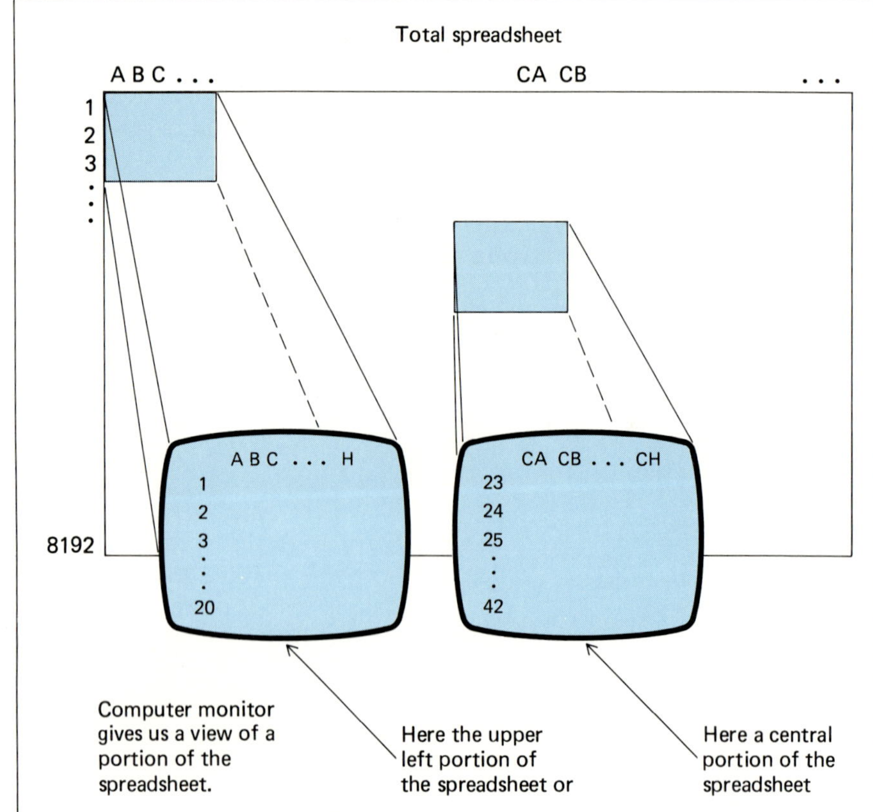

A picture is worth a thousand words. Here the results of a spreadsheet analysis are shown in the form of color graphs.

memory cells is considerably greater than is practical to display on the screen. Lotus 1-2-3 provides a memory cell capacity of up to 240 positions. In contrast, the typical monitor screen is only 80 positions wide. The default Lotus 1-2-3 screen cell width is 9 positions. Thus, a long cell entry might not be completely visible on the spreadsheet screen display. In Figure 10-8(a) we see that a 14-character label has been entered into cell A2.

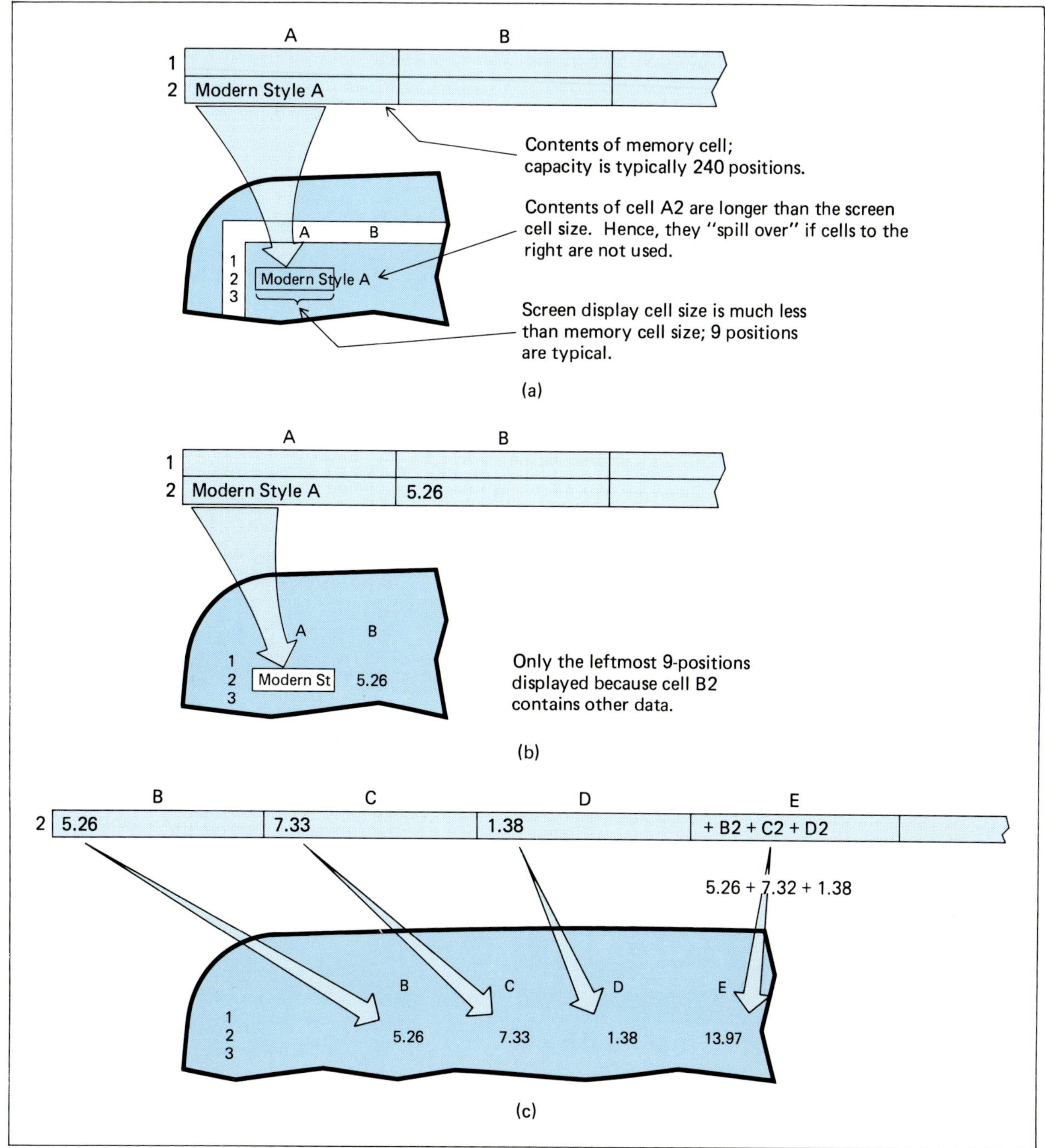

Figure 10-8
Cell contents in memory and as displayed.

Since the cell to the right (B2) is empty, the contents of A2 are allowed by the system to "spill over" into the adjacent screen display area. Even though it appears on the screen that the label occupies both cells A2 and B2, it is stored entirely within memory cell A2, as illustrated in this figure. However, as soon as something is entered into cell B2, the display is truncated and only the first 9 positions are displayed, as illustrated in Figure 10-8(b).

The difference between what we see and the actual cell contents is further illustrated in Figure 10-8(c). Here we see that the formula occupies memory cell E2 but the screen cell displays the number resulting from the specified calculations. For formulas, this is significant because a formula stored in a memory cell is restricted in length to the size of the memory cell.

Spreadsheet Commands

In using WordPerfect, you directed the computer to take actions, such as saving and retrieving a file, changing the format of the document, or moving a block of text from one place in the document to another. Spreadsheet programs are controlled with commands in much the same way. In fact, saving, retrieving, formatting, and moving are all operations that can also be performed on a worksheet through commands. Although spreadsheet programs vary from one software manufacturer to another, certain features are found in most of them. These provide the ability to construct templates and to modify existing worksheets. In general, they are implemented by the use of the spreadsheet program command structure. Following are typical commands that will be found (perhaps by another name) in most spreadsheet programs.

Insert allows you to move all rows from a designated row downward in order to create one or more empty rows. Insert also works on columns to create an empty column by moving columns to the right. Additional information (labels, numbers or formulas) can be entered as needed.

Figure 10-9
The Insert command.

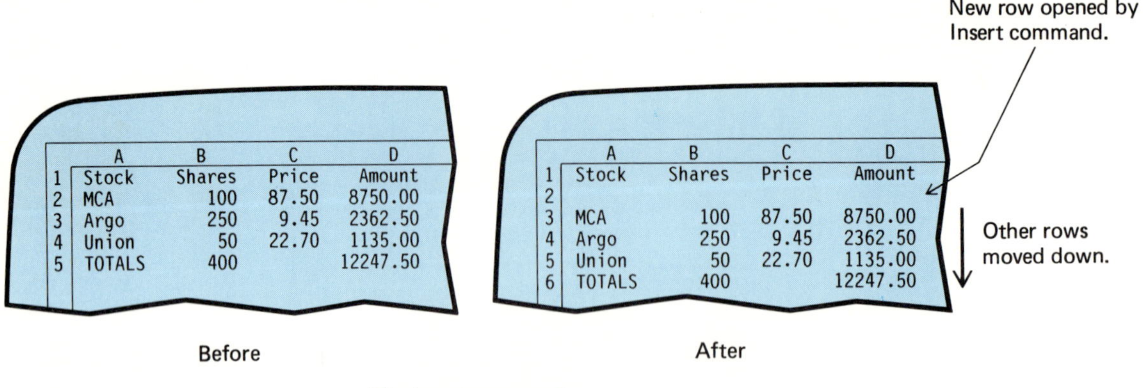

Delete is the reverse of the Insert command. It moves all rows from a designated row upward, or all columns from a designated column to the left. In doing so, anything in the portion of the worksheet being deleted is lost. This command commonly is used to eliminate portions of a worksheet that you no longer need.

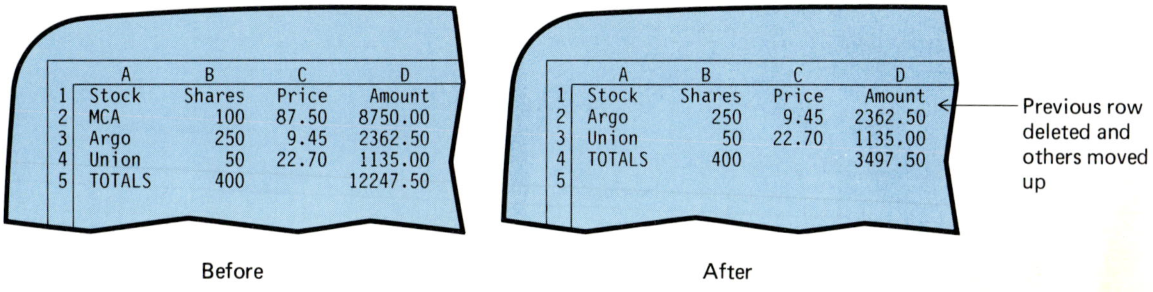

The Delete command

Figure 10-10
The Delete command.

Copy allows you to copy the contents of a cell or a group of cells into another cell or group of cells, or to duplicate the contents of a single cell into many cells. You can even copy cell contents from one worksheet into another worksheet. This command reduces much of the tedium of entering repetitive data.

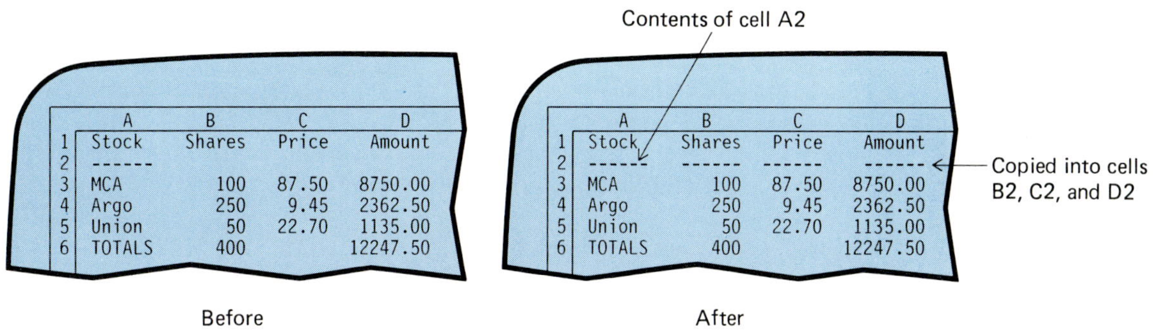

The Copy command

Figure 10-11
The Copy command.

Replicate is a form of Copy that duplicates formulas. For example, the formulas to calculate the Amount in these examples (Shares times Price) are:

```
D2=+B2*C2
D3=+B3*C3
D4=+B4*C4
```

Notice that these have exactly the same form; they differ only in the row number that they address. Entering each of these would be tedious, especially if the stock summary consisted of many more than just three items. However, with the Replicate command, you can enter the first one, and then replicate it into the other cells. The action performed in the following example by the spreadsheet program is to make a copy of the formula after the appropriate cell address changes have been made. For instance, in copying +B2*C2 to cell D3, both of the row addresses would be changed from 2 to 3, thus giving +B3*C3. In some spreadsheet programs, Copy and Replicate are two separate commands. Lotus 1-2-3 does not include a separate Replicate command since the Copy command can be controlled to perform the replication process when used with formulas.

Figure 10-12
The Replicate command.

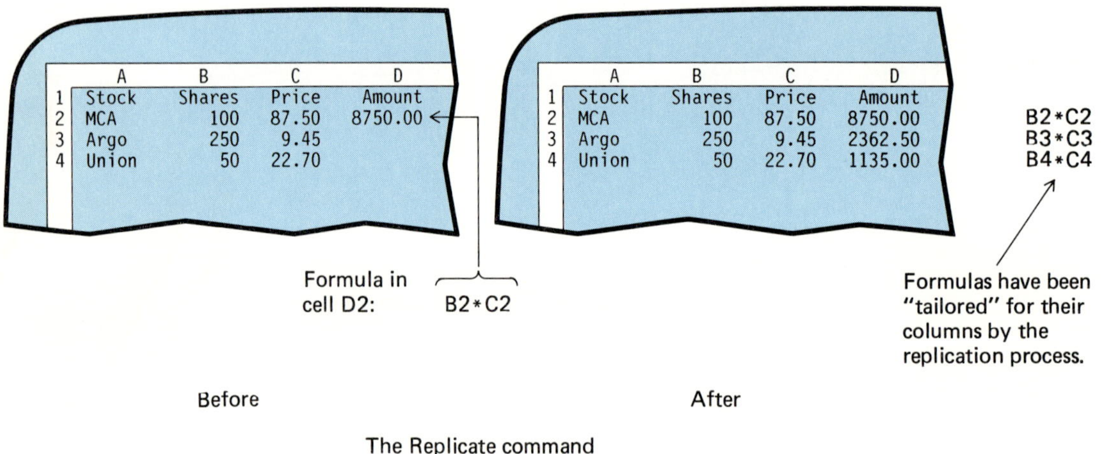

Move is similar to Copy except that no copy is "left behind." That is, the contents of a cell or group of cells can be moved to another portion of the worksheet. The contents of the original cell or cells will be empty. This is especially convenient if you want to add more information to a worksheet or to reorganize the arrangement of existing information.

Figure 10-13
The Move command.

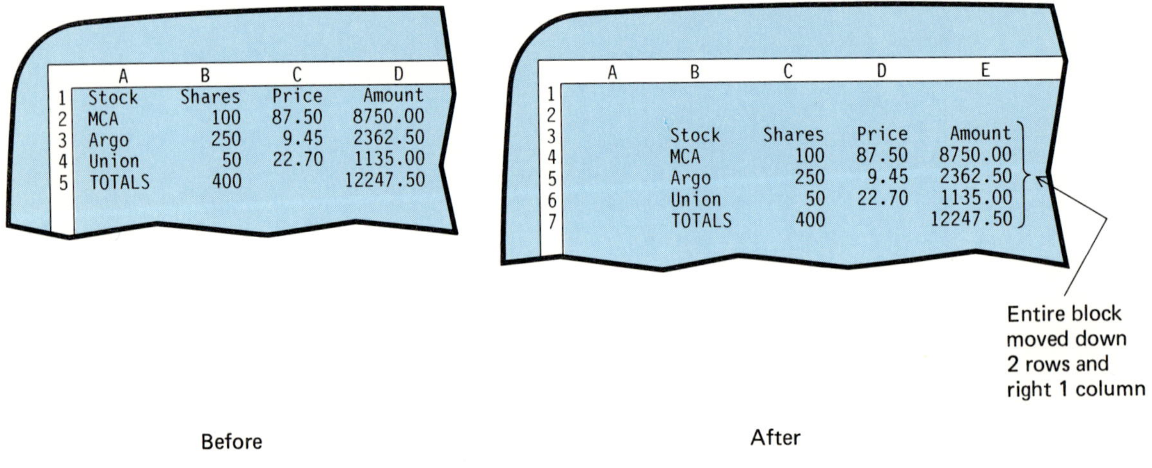

Erase erases the contents of a cell or a group of cells. Note that it does not affect the contents of adjacent cells except to the extent that formulas may use the contents of erased cells.

Figure 10-14
The Erase command.

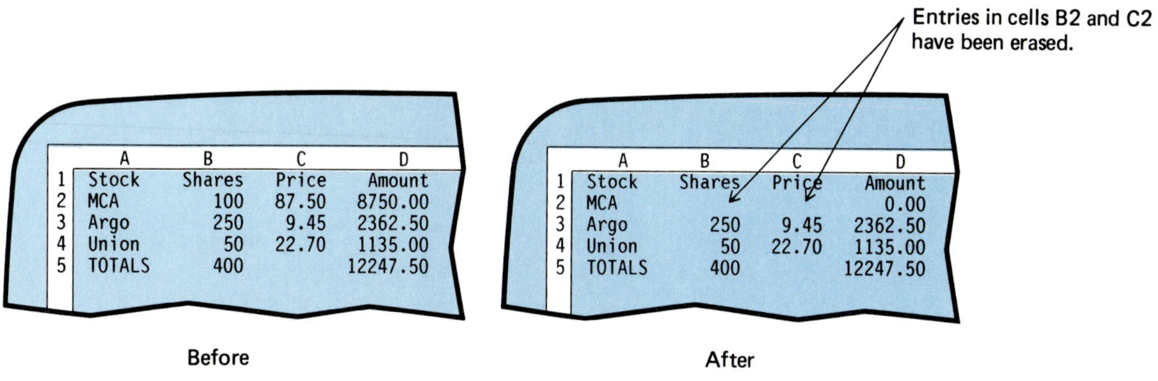

Format allows you to control the way in which a cell or a group of cells displays data. You can specify the justification of the data (left, right, or centered), the number of decimal places displayed, and the inclusion of commas in large numbers. You can also change the display width of cells on the screen to handle large label or data display.

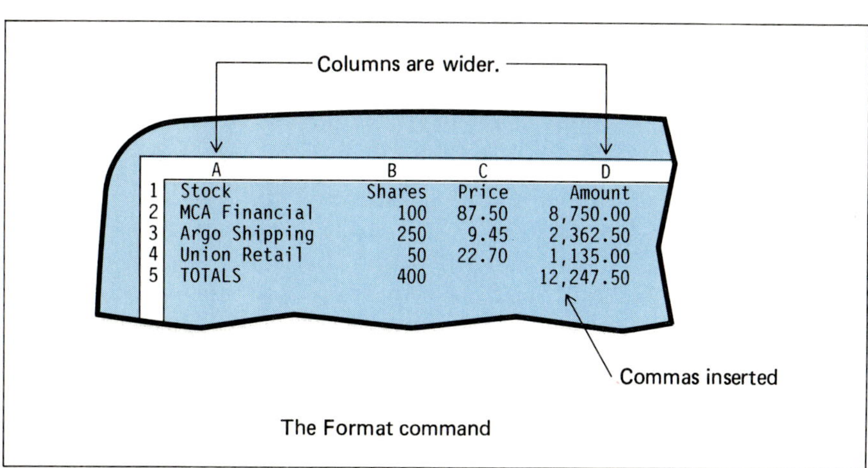

Figure 10-15
The Format command.

Sort allows you to rearrange data in the rows (or columns) of a worksheet into a desired sequence. The sequence can be alphabetic (based on cells containing labels), or it can be numeric and based on cells containing data or the results of calculations from formulas.

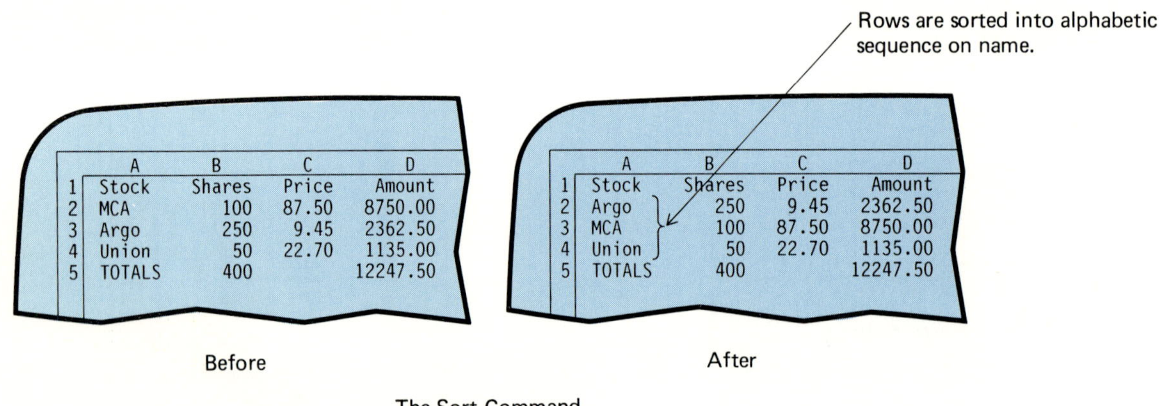

Figure 10-16
The Sort command.

FUNDAMENTAL STEPS IN COMPUTER PROBLEM SOLVING

Word processing programs such as WordPerfect provide a powerful tool for managing documents. The other two productivity tools described in this book, Lotus 1-2-3 and dBASE III, are significantly different in that they are tools of analysis. They both include such provisions for performing operations as:

- Manipulating both numeric and nonnumeric data.
- Performing mathematical computations based on forms that are similar to those of algebra.
- Carrying out actions on a conditional basis depending upon the relationship between two quantities.

To utilize these capabilities, the user must prepare appropriate instructions describing the exact actions to be taken under the conditions to be considered. This is called *programming*. Although the term is most commonly associated with preparing sequences of statements to solve a problem using a conventional programming language, it is equally applicable to problem solving using spreadsheet and database programs.

Without a doubt, the single biggest difficulty the beginning student encounters is to sit down at the computer to solve a problem without thoroughly understanding what is to be done or how to do it. The "instant gratification" generated by the computer responding is usually short-lived and superficial. The computer can only do what we tell it to do; it cannot define a problem or tell us what formulas to use. In preparing an application (such as the cost analysis) for computer solution, an organized approach is essential. Following is a straightforward set of steps to use in preparing computer solutions.

1. *Define the desired results.* Analyze the problem to see what useful results (or output) are required. Decide exactly what information

you wish to come out of the computer. In the case of the cost analysis worksheet, you wanted the ability to vary the data values and observe how the total cost changed.

2. *Analyze the input data.* Does the data contain everything that is needed to produce the desired results? If the needed data is not there in exactly the desired form, is it possible to combine some of the data quantities to produce the desired output? If the answer to one of these questions is Yes, you can go ahead. However, if the answer to both is No, you do not have the necessary input data to produce the desired output. For the cost analysis, the input data was the individual cost items and the quantity. Had you, for example, been unable to determine the Other cost element accurately, the analysis would have been of little value.

3. *Devise an overall plan for the solution.* The objective of a computer solution is to obtain the desired results from the input. The operations necessary to do this must be clearly defined. They commonly include such things as specifying calculations to be carried out and conditions under which various actions are taken. The calculations for the cost analysis were relatively simple. However, what if your evaluation had shown that some of the cost items would decrease with increased sales? Then it would have been necessary to devise a relationship between these cost items and the sales.

4. *Express the solution in a form that can be communicated to the computer.* For a spreadsheet program, it includes defining formulas describing calculations to be performed.

5. *Test the solution.* Once the solution has been entered into the computer, it should be tested thoroughly. One of the lessons that the programmer learns very early in her or his training cycle is the importance of thoroughly testing a program. Frequently, output generated by a computer is accepted as correct simply because it is produced by a computer. This is unfortunate. For instance, consider a formula to apply a discount to a customer purchase, in which the discount is added rather than subtracted. The computer, knowing nothing of the context of this task, will calculate as directed and customers will be overcharged. Errors such as these are detected and corrected by preparing and entering test data.

Because of the interactive nature of productivity software and the microcomputer, it is easy to fall into the bad habit of skipping over the problem planning and solution and immediately to sit down at the computer. Although this might be adequate for your first, relatively simple tasks, the results are usually poor for tasks that are more complex. Do not slip into that habit.

SUMMARY

This chapter has given you your first exposure to the electronic spreadsheet and how it is used to assist us in problem solving. It has described some of the basic features of spreadsheet programs and has defined an application that will form the basis for your first studies of Lotus 1-2-3 in Chapter 11. Summarizing, the important items from the chapter are:

- A worksheet is a display of data and calculated results in the form of a table (consisting of rows and columns).
- Each position of a worksheet formed by the intersection of a row and a column is called a cell.
- Three types of information can be assigned to a cell: labels, numbers, and formulas.
- The formula allows the contents of any cell to be determined from calculations using data from other cells.
- A worksheet template is a worksheet into which labels and formulas have been entered but no data has been entered.
- Spreadsheet programs include the basic operations of data processing: input, output, calculation, and storage.
- Commands are used to perform operations on worksheets such as inserting and deleting rows or columns, copying, moving, erasing, and changing the format of data.
- Computers do not solve problems; people do. The computer and associated software serve as powerful tools in assisting us. The steps in problem solving using the computer are: define the desired results, analyze the input data to ensure that it is sufficient to produce the desired results, devise a plan for the solution, and express the solution in a form that can be used with a computer.

NEW TERMINOLOGY

The following are important new terms introduced in this chapter; you should be familiar with each of them.

cell
cell address
column
expression
formula
label
model
replicate
row
spreadsheet
template
worksheet

REVIEW QUESTIONS

1. What is the basic difference between the numbers in column 2 and the numbers in column 5 of the worksheet in Figure 10-2?
2. What is a worksheet cell and what is it used for?
3. What is the worksheet address of the cell at the twelfth row and fifth column?
4. Name the three types of entries found in worksheets.
5. Define the formulas that are to be associated with the following cells (refer to Figure 10-2):

   a. G2 through G5
   b. G7

   For this exercise, you need to know that multiplication is indicated by the * (asterisk) character. For example, to multiply the value in cell B6 by the value in D7, the form is B6*D7.
6. What is displayed on the screen in a cell that has a formula?
7. What is a template?
8. How do the actions of the Copy and the Move commands differ?
9. How do the actions of the Close and the Delete commands differ?
10. What is the action of the Replicate command?

MATCHING

Match each term in a to h with the most appropriate description in 1 through 8.

a. model
b. command
c. formula
d. label
e. replicate
f. worksheet
g. cell address
h. template

1. For instance, B3.
2. Cell contents that cannot involve numeric calculations.
3. Determines the value displayed in one cell based on values in other cells.
4. Contains formulas but no data.
5. Is essentially a copying operation in which some cell addresses in a formula can be changed.
6. A mathematical representation of a real-world phenomenon.
7. The manual equivalent of the electronic worksheet.
8. Provides the user with control over spreadsheet actions.

TRUE/FALSE

Determine whether each of the following is true or false.

_____ 1. When entering data into a worksheet, care should be taken to avoid errors because once a data value has been entered, it is difficult to change.

_____ 2. The cell address of the cell at the fourth row and third column is D3.

_____ 3. There are three types of cell entries: labels, numeric data, and alphabetic data.

_____ 4. A formula uses values from other cells to determine the value displayed in the cell to which it is assigned. The values from the other cells can be either data or numbers resulting from another calculation.

_____ 5. When a data value in a cell is changed, the worksheet automatically recalculates and redisplays the new value for all cells depending on the value in that cell.

_____ 6. A template is a worksheet into which entries have been made into all cells of the worksheet.

_____ 7. The formula B2+C2 could be assigned to any cell in the worksheet except B2 and C2.

_____ 8. Referring to the worksheet of Figure 10-2, the expression A2+A3+A4+A5 would probably produce an error.

_____ 9. The single biggest shortcoming of spreadsheets is that they cannot be saved to disk.

_____ 10. Scrolling a worksheet is much the same as scrolling a document using a word processing program.

_____ 11. Although spreadsheet programs are useful for experimenting, their computational capabilities are severely limited because they are capable of only the simplest arithmetic operations.

_____ 12. It is possible to copy the contents of the cells in one worksheet into another worksheet.

_____ 13. If you issue a Delete command for column C, then all columns to the right of C will be moved left one column and the original contents of C will be lost.

_____ 14. Once a formula has been assigned to a cell of a worksheet, it cannot be moved to another cell.

_____ 15. The way in which data is displayed on the screen can be changed with appropriate commands.

ANSWERS TO OBJECTIVE QUESTIONS

Matching

1. g 2. d 3. c 4. h 5. e 6. a 7. f 8. b

True/False

1. F 2. F 3. F 4. T 5. T 6. F 7. T 8. T
9. F 10. T 11. F 12. T 13. T 14. F 15. T

Chapter 11

Using Lotus 1-2-3 and Joe Spreadsheet

OBJECTIVES

From Chapter 10, you learned how spreadsheet programs can be used to assist you in solving problems. In this chapter you will have the opportunity to use some of these features by learning to work with the popular spreadsheet program Lotus 1-2-3. The vehicle that you will use in learning these basic spreadsheet principles is the MCT cost analysis spreadsheet that you studied in Chapter 10. When you have completed this chapter, you will be able to:

- Identify the parts of the 1-2-3 screen: the worksheet area, cell address border, control panel, information line.
- Save a worksheet that you have created to disk as a file.
- Retrieve a worksheet from disk.
- Terminate running of the 1-2-3 program, thus ending a work session.
- Move around on the worksheet to select the desired cell for action, such as entering data.
- Enter labels, numbers, and formulas into cells.
- Use the worksheet as a tool in attempting to adjust individual costs to achieve the cost goal set for the Special Collection Module described in Chapter 10.
- Edit the contents of individual cells.
- Print a worksheet.

This chapter is like Chapter 5 (DOS) and Chapters 7 and 8 (WordPerfect) in that you need to read *and* do. That is, read the chapter first, and then do all of the described actions for yourself at the computer. When reading, do not attempt to memorize exact keystrokes necessary to carry out the different actions; simply learn about the actions. When you try them on the computer, things will fall into place much more quickly. If you wish to try some hands-on activity before finishing the entire chapter, read at least to the section entitled "Moving the Cell Pointer" before going to the computer.

PREVIEW

Getting Started

To follow the examples of this chapter, you need spreadsheet software. This section describes running the software on either a floppy disk or hard disk computer.

The Display Screen

The 1-2-3 spreadsheet screen display includes rows and columns of cells and the control panel from which activities are monitored.

Saving and Retrieving Worksheets Using Commands

As with a word processing document, a worksheet is created and manipulated in memory. For permanent retention, it must be stored to disk using a conventional DOS filename. At any time, it can be retrieved from disk and loaded into memory.

Moving the Cell Pointer

One of your first needs in working with a spreadsheet program is to be able to move the cursor from one cell to another. The currently selected cell is the cell into which data is always entered from the keyboard.

Entering Labels and Numbers into the Worksheet

Labels and numbers are entered into a cell by moving to the cell and then typing the desired entry. The entry of labels and numbers is illustrated by entering those for the cost analysis spreadsheet of Chapter 10.

Formulas

Formulas define the calculations to be carried out. They are assigned to cells of the worksheet in much the same way as labels and numbers are entered. The formulas for the cost analysis spreadsheet are entered.

Rules for Building Formulas

The arithmetic operations that can be performed with formulas are addition, subtraction, multiplication, division, and raising to a power. These are used in accordance with the precedence rules of mathematics.

About Worksheet Errors and Correcting Them

A worksheet should be carefully checked to ensure that all formulas are correct before using it. Erroneous formulas can be corrected through the Edit command.

More About Commands

Most of the spreadsheet operations are carried out by commands. Descriptions of commands and other operations are available from the program in the form of Help screens.

Printing a Worksheet

The Print command allows all or a portion of a spreadsheet to be printed directly to a printer or to a file for later printing.

GETTING STARTED

About the Software

Since this chapter involves learning by doing, you will need spreadsheet software. If you have access to a copy of Lotus 1-2-3, then you can use it. If you do not, then you can use the JOE spreadsheet that is included with this book. The appearance on the screen as well as the command sequences are similar. In descriptions in this book, reference will almost always be to Lotus 1-2-3, but the remarks apply equally to JOE. In cases where the screen displays are significantly different, displays from both Lotus 1-2-3 and JOE are included.

Before you can begin to enter a spreadsheet, you must load the Lotus 1-2-3 or the JOE program into the computer's memory. Once loaded, control of the computer switches from DOS to Lotus 1-2-3 or to JOE. Let us consider this loading start-up process.

Running 1-2-3

To work with 1-2-3, you will need the Lotus 1-2-3 system disk or the JOE disk that accompanies this book, a DOS disk for booting the computer, and a formatted data disk (the data disk that accompanies this book can be used). Note that the DOS and data disks are those that you should have prepared in Chapter 5. If you have not already prepared the data disk, then you should refer to Chapter 5 and prepare it before proceeding. To run 1-2-3, carry out the following sequence of operations.

Floppy Disk Computer.

1. Boot the computer with a DOS disk in the A drive.
2. Remove the DOS disk from the A drive and insert the Lotus 1-2-3 or JOE disk.
3. Insert the data disk in the B drive.
4. To load and run the spreadsheet program, type the following.

   A> JOE (for JOE)

   A> 123 (for Lotus 1-2-3)

Hard Disk Computer. *Note*: The following instructions assume that JOE or Lotus 1-2-3 is stored in the subdirectory named JOE or 123 as described in Chapter 5. If it is not, then you must modify these instructions accordingly.

1. Boot the computer from the hard disk (leave the door to the A drive open).
2. Change to the spreadsheet program subdirectory by typing:

   C> C\JOE (for JOE)

   C> C\123 (for Lotus 1-2-3)

3. To load and run the spreadsheet program, type the following.

   C> JOE (for JOE)

   C> 123 (for Lotus 1-2-3)

Whether you are using a floppy disk or hard disk computer, an announcement screen will be displayed. Striking the Enter key will cause this screen to be erased and the main worksheet screen to be displayed. For users of JOE, the first time that you run the program, you will be prompted to identify the type of monitor connected to your computer. When you do so, this information will be stored on the JOE disk and you will not be asked again.

THE DISPLAY SCREEN

Once the spreadsheet program is running, your screen display will appear as shown in Figure 11-1(a) for JOE and as shown in Figure 11-1(b) for Lotus 1-2-3—see page 302. (Note: The highlighting for cell E14 will not be displayed on your screen.) Although some details are different, the general layouts of the two are identical. The screen can be considered as consisting of the following four components:

- The worksheet area.
- The cell address border.
- The control panel.
- The information line.

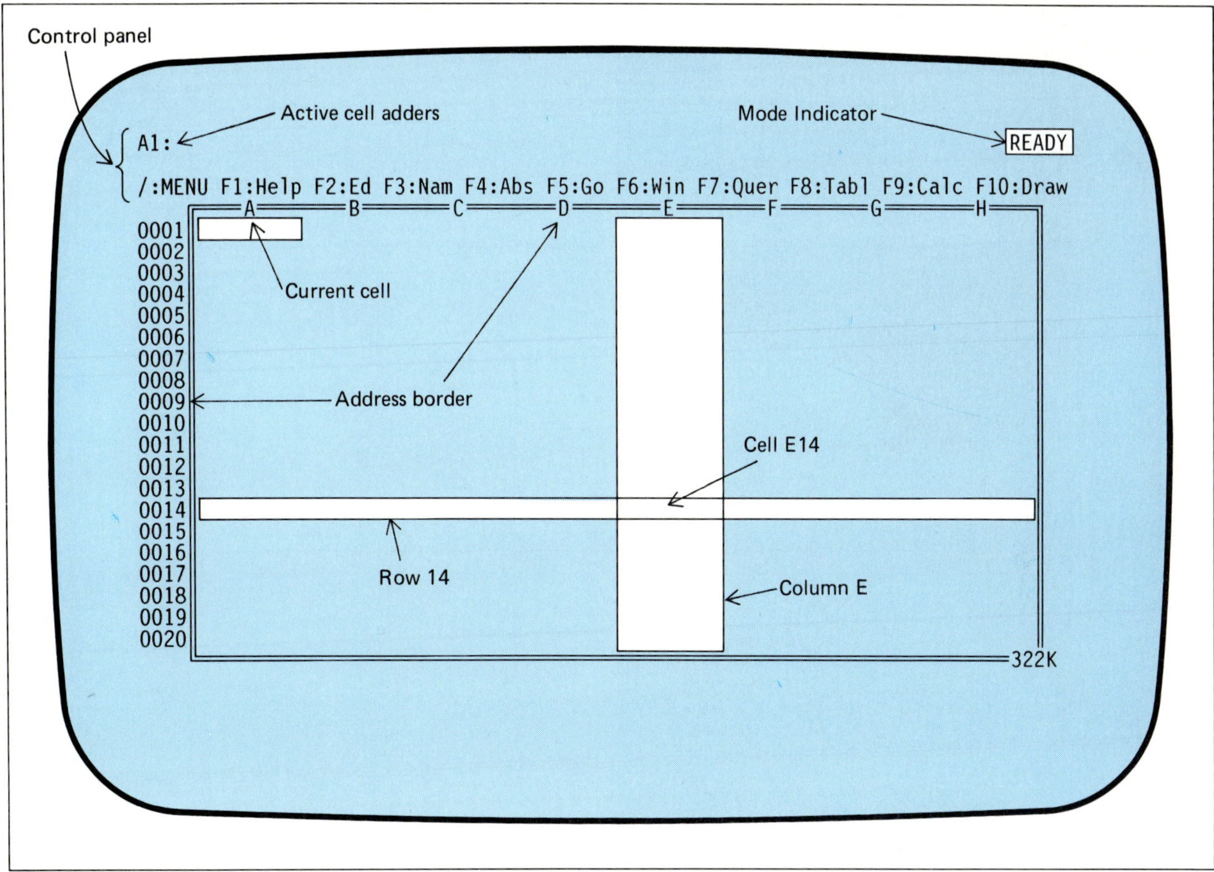

Figure 11-1
(a) The JOE Spreadsheet screen.

The Worksheet and Border

As you know from Chapter 10, the worksheet is made up of columns and rows, with the columns identified by letters and the rows by numbers. In Figure 11-1, the main portion of the screen is taken up by the worksheet itself. The cell address border clearly identifies each screen row (1 through 20) and each screen column (A through H). The intersection of each row and column represents a 1-2-3 cell. For instance, Figure 11-1 shows cell E14, the intersection of column E and row 14. Although only 20 rows and 8 columns are displayed here, the full worksheet consists of 256 columns named A through IV. The first 26 are A through Z, the next 26 are AA through AZ, then BA through BZ, and so on up to IA through IV. The number of rows depends upon the particular version of the software. In Lotus 1-2-3, Release 1A has 2048 rows and Release 2 has 8192 rows; later releases have more. JOE has 8192 rows.

The **cell pointer** is the highlighted area on the worksheet (in this case, cell A1) that indicates the **current cell,** the cell that is the current focus of 1-2-3's attention. For instance, to enter data into a cell from the keyboard, that cell must be the current cell. One of your first activities will be learning how to move the cell pointer.

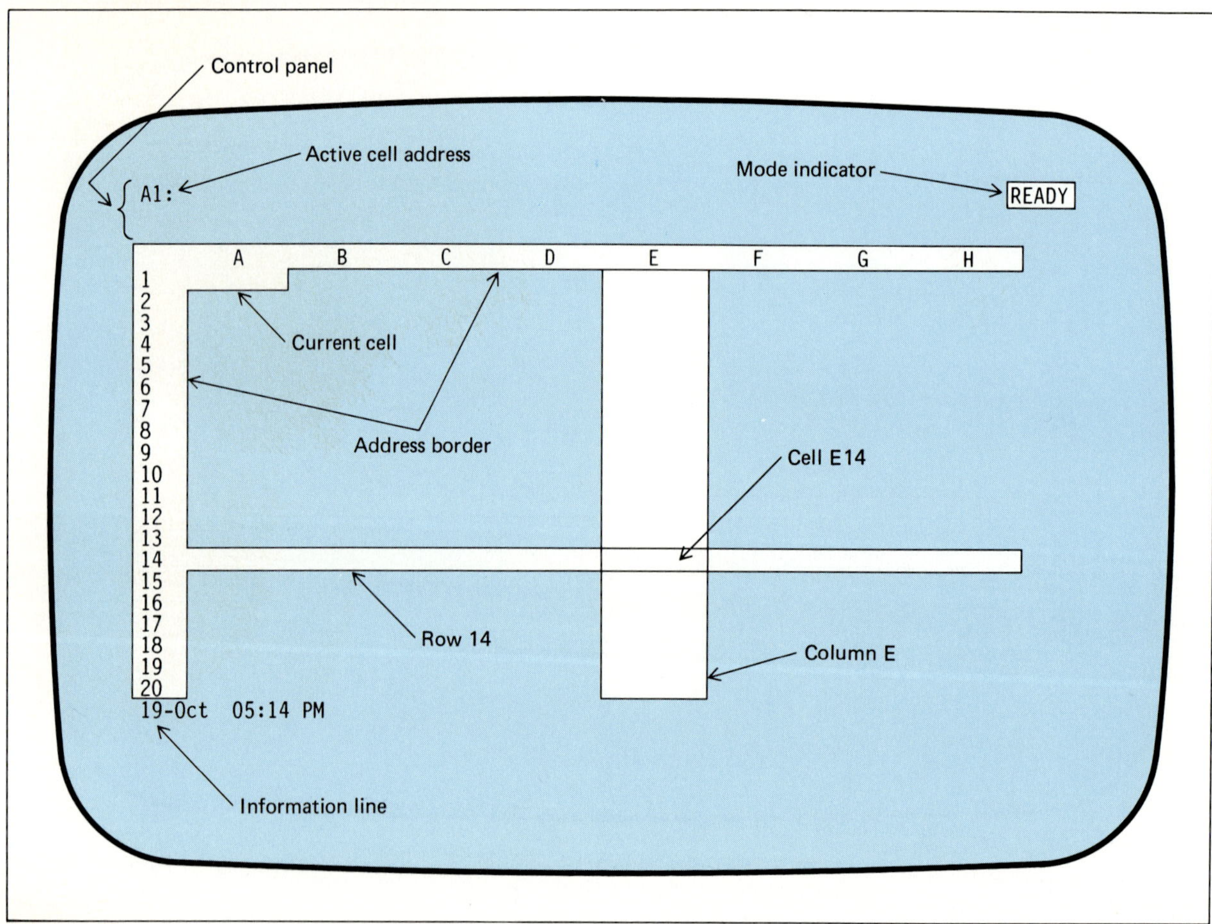

Figure 11-1
(b) The Lotus 1-2-3 Spreadsheet screen.

If you look at your screen display carefully, you will see that the screen width of each cell is 9 positions. This is the default display cell size set by the program. You will learn how to change this value in the next chapter.

Terminology

The word *worksheet* is commonly used ambiguously. That is, it is used to describe both the entire collection of cells in computer memory (for instance, 256 columns by 8192 rows) and the portion of cells into which entries have been made (for instance, the cost analysis spreadsheet of Chapter 10 would occupy columns A through G and rows 1 through 7). Usually, you will know which is meant by the context. In some cases with examples that follow, the latter is identified as "your" worksheet, meaning the rectangular block of cells into which you have made your entries.

The Control Panel

The **control panel** consists of the top three lines on the screen and describes most of the 1-2-3 activities. Information displayed by the control panel includes the following.

- The cell address of the current cell. In the example of Figure 11-1, we see that the cell pointer is at cell A1.
- To the immediate right of the cell address, 1-2-3 displays the contents of the current cell. In this case, nothing is displayed because the current cell is empty; however, you will see how this works when you enter values into the worksheet.
- To the extreme right is the mode indicator, which indicates the current mode of operation of 1-2-3. For instance, when 1-2-3 is first loaded, READY is displayed, indicating that 1-2-3 is ready to respond to a request. When you enter a label into the spreadsheet, LABEL is displayed, indicating that 1-2-3 is ready to accept a label.
- Lines 2 and 3 of the control panel display information that depends upon the particular operation you are performing. Notice that JOE uses line 3 to tell you the actions produced by each function key. You will learn about some of these in later sections of this chapter.

The Information Line

The bottom line of the screen provides three items of information. In Release 2 (and higher) of Lotus 1-2-3, the date and time are displayed. In place of the date and time, JOE displays the name of the worksheet file that is currently loaded. The second item of information displayed on this line is the status of the toggle keys of the keyboard. For example, if the keyboard has been shifted to uppercase by striking the CapsLock key, the word CAPS is displayed. Similar displays appear for the Numlock and Scroll Lock keys. The third information item displayed on this line is error messages. If an error occurs during a worksheet operation, the mode indicator is changed to ERROR and a short description of the error is displayed.

SAVING AND RETRIEVING WORKSHEETS USING COMMANDS

Before you start learning how to enter values into the cells of a worksheet, you should know how to save a worksheet to disk as a file and to retrieve the file from disk. Then you will be able to stop your activity at any point, save your work to disk, and return later to resume where you left off. Saving and retrieving are done with 1-2-3 commands as described in Chapter 10. Although there is much to say about commands, for the moment we will be concerned only with the bare essentials needed to save and retrieve files and to terminate the program.

To get to the command menu from the READY mode, you must strike the slash key (/). When you do this, your screen will appear as shown in

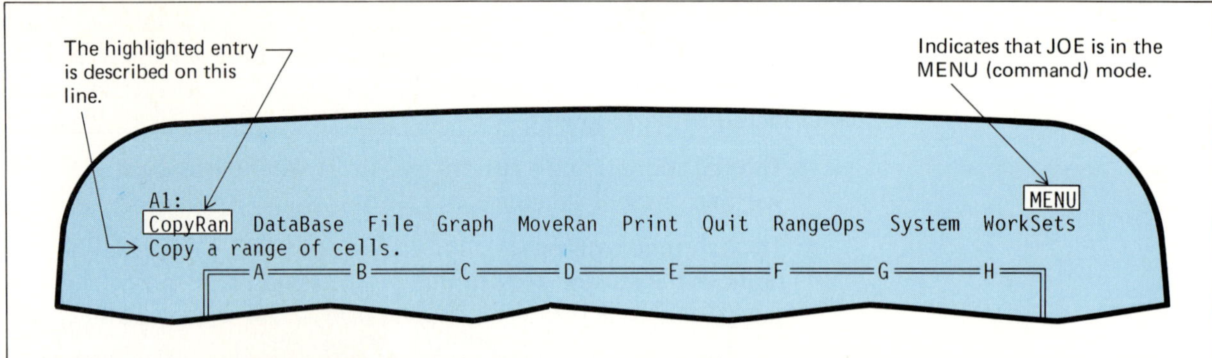

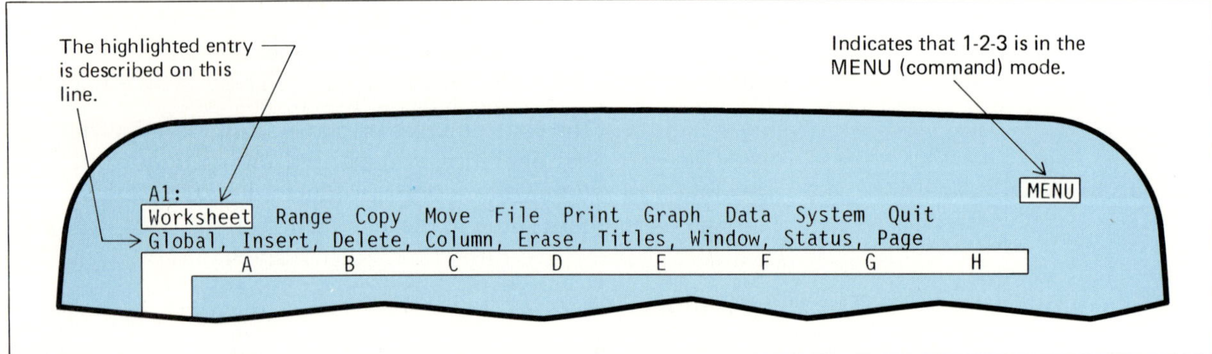

Figure 11-2
(a) Command menu for JOE.
(b) Command menu for Lotus 1-2-3.

Figure 11-2; note that the READY indicator in the upper right has now changed to MENU. In both control panels, the second line contains a list of commands. (Although the command names and the order in which they are listed are slightly different for Lotus 1-2-3 and JOE, the first letters of corresponding commands are the same. This is a key point.)

About the Escape Key

As you will learn in working with 1-2-3, you control actions of the program through keystrokes. Some keystrokes move the cell pointer, others enter different types of data, and still others bring up commands. When you are first learning, it is easy to strike the wrong key, with totally unexpected results. Often the program is awaiting a response from you and will not continue until you respond properly. If that happens, then you should strike the Escape (Esc) key one or more times. This key is somewhat of a "back up one step" key and will usually get you out of trouble.

Initial Setup for the Data Drive

Your first action is to define for your software (Lotus 1-2-3 or JOE) to which disk drive files are to be written. If you are using a floppy-based computer, this is the B drive. If you are using a hard disk computer, it can be the C drive and the same subdirectory as your software (Lotus 1-2-3 or JOE).

Without being concerned about the details of what happens as a result of the following command sequence, carrying out the sequence will change the default data drive to B. Be certain that the disk you plan to use as a data disk is formatted and in drive B.

DO THIS NOW 11-1 **Setting the Default Data Drive**

For this, you must carry out the keystroke sequence exactly as listed in the following steps. For instance, strike the W, then the G, and so on. The descriptions to the right tell you which JOE/Lotus 1-2-3 command is being executed or the action being taken. If you make a wrong entry, strike the Escape key to return to the READY mode. Depending upon the action you have taken, you may have to strike it two or more times. When you are back to READY, you may start over. If you are using a hard disk computer, the entry at step 6 must be different from the one shown here; see the description that follows. Remember, in the following sequence, type the letter W (either upper- or lowercase), then type the letter G, and so on.

1. Type a W	Worksheet/WorkSet command
2. Type a G	Globals/Global command
3. Type a D	Defaults/Default command
4. Type a D	Directory/Directory command
5. Press the Esc key	Erase the current default
6. Type B:\	Enter the new default drive
7. Press the Enter	Accept the entry
8. Type a U	Update/Update command
9. Type a Q	Quit menu/Quit command

If you are using a hard disk as described in Chapter 5 (software and data in a single subdirectory), then at step 6 you must enter:

C:\JOE (For JOE)
C:\123 (For Lotus 1-2-3)

After entering the letter *Q* (the last step), you will be returned to the READY mode. The default data disk is now permanently stored on your program disk; you need not run this sequence again unless you want to change the value.

Saving a Worksheet to Disk

After entering a worksheet, you might be a bit unhappy if, upon turning the computer off, the worksheet were to disappear. In fact, this is exactly what will happen if you do not save it to disk. (The relationship between information stored temporarily in memory and permanently on disk is illustrated in Figure 3-2.) Both saving a worksheet to disk and retrieving one from disk are done through the File command. Even though the worksheet currently on the screen is empty, it can still be saved to disk. Although an empty worksheet on disk is of little value, the exercise will show you how to carry out the operation.

DO THIS NOW 11-2 **Saving a Worksheet to Disk**

1. Switch to command mode by striking the / key; the mode indicator will be MENU and the menu of Figure 11-2 will be displayed.

2. Strike the letter F for File. This will produce the File submenu of Figure 11-3.

Figure 11-3
(a) The JOE File submenu.
(b) The Lotus 1-2-3 File submenu.

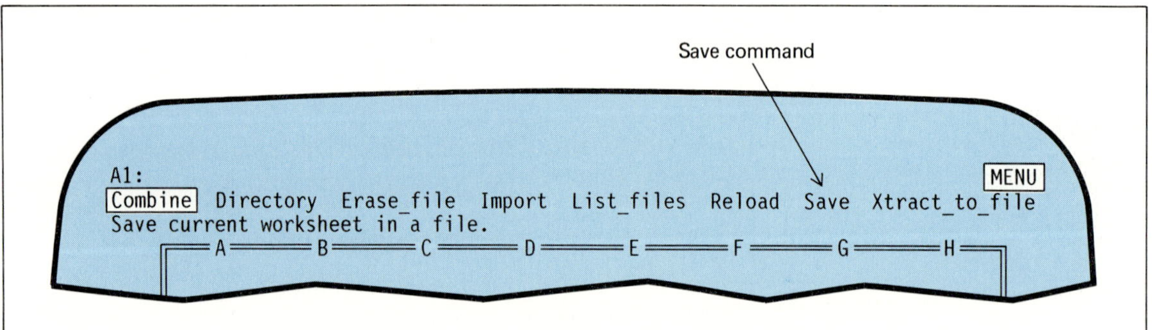

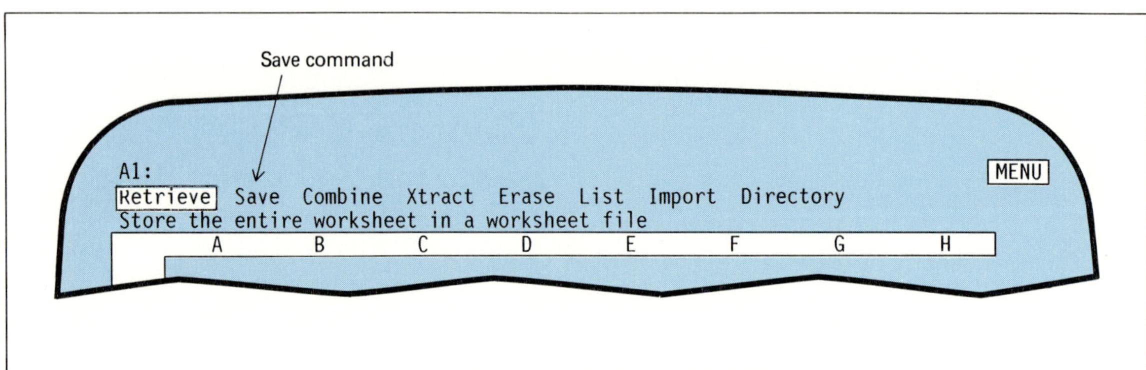

3. Strike the letter S for Save. This will produce the prompt of Figure 11-4. Note that the system shows the drive B (or your hard disk

Figure 11-4
Saving a worksheet as a file.

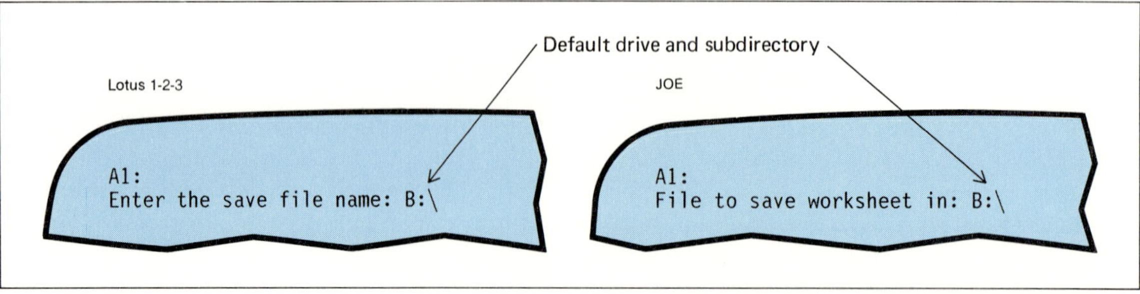

subdirectory) as the default disk drive for saving the file (assuming that you carried out the procedure to set the default in DTN 11-1).

4. You must now type the name by which you want the worksheet stored on disk. Remember, the worksheet name is a DOS filename and therefore is limited to 8 characters. To be consistent with example procedures that follow, type COST for the filename and strike the Enter key.

When the file is saved, a predetermined extension is automatically attached. If you are using JOE, the extension will be WKQ. If you are using Lotus 1-2-3 Release 1A, the extension will be WKS; if you are using Release 2, it will be WK1. Hence, this worksheet will be saved as COST.WKQ, COST.WKS, or COST.WK1, depending upon the software you are using.

As you know, everything in memory is lost when the computer is turned off or if there is any kind of electric power failure even though momentary. Think of how unhappy you would be if the electricity were to go off after you had just completed entering a complex worksheet. The solution to the loss of a large amount of work is to save the worksheet frequently (this is no different than working on a document with a word processor). If you have saved a worksheet while working on it, the next time you execute the File Save command sequence, the filename will be listed as a default in the prompt of Figure 11-4. Then you need only strike the Enter key and the worksheet will be saved again.

Ending a Work Session

Whenever you complete a work session with any piece of software, you should terminate the program with the appropriate command (for most software, it is QUIT or EXIT). This terminates execution in an orderly fashion and returns control to DOS. Then, if you are all finished, you can turn the computer off. Turning the computer off while your software program still controls the computer is poor practice. Some software performs cleanup activities when you terminate; they will not be performed if the computer is simply turned off. Also, if you have not saved your latest changes, most software warns that work will be lost if you terminate, a warning you would not get by simply turning the computer off.

DO THIS NOW 11-3 **Terminating Execution of the Program**

1. Switch to command mode by striking the / key; the mode indicator will be MENU and the menu of Figure 11-2 will be displayed.

2. Strike the letter Q for Quit.

3. The prompt on the control panel asks you to confirm that you indeed wish to quit. Striking the Y key (for Yes) returns control of the computer to DOS.

With JOE, whenever you terminate processing, if any changes have been made to the worksheet since the last save, you will be warned. If you override the warning, the most recent changes will not be on the disk copy.

Retrieving a Worksheet from Disk

Upon returning to work on the worksheet at some later time, reading it from disk back into memory is every bit as easy as saving it. For instance, assume that you have entered a portion of a worksheet and have realized that you cannot finish it now. You would then save as much as you have entered with the intention of completing it later. At some later time, upon bringing the spreadsheet program (Lotus 1-2-3 or JOE) up on the computer, you would be confronted with an empty worksheet screen. The first thing to do would be to load the worksheet so that you could continue your entry or editing tasks. This process is almost identical to that of saving. If you performed the sequence of DTN 11-3 properly, you will be at the DOS prompt; start your spreadsheet program.

DO THIS NOW 11-4 **Retrieving a Worksheet File**

1. Switch to command mode by striking the / key; the mode indicator will be MENU and the menu of Figure 11-2 will be displayed.
2. Strike the letter F for File, then strike the letter R. In the submenu of Figure 11-3, note that it means Reload for JOE and Retrieve for Lotus 1-2-3. These are different names for the same thing.
3. In the resulting screen of Figure 11-5, you have two options for selecting the worksheet to be retrieved from disk. Since you know that you want to retrieve the worksheet file COST, simply type in the name (the extension is not required) and strike the Enter key. Your worksheet will be retrieved from disk. If there is no worksheet file with the name you enter, an error message will be displayed.

Figure 11-5
Retrieving a worksheet file from disk.

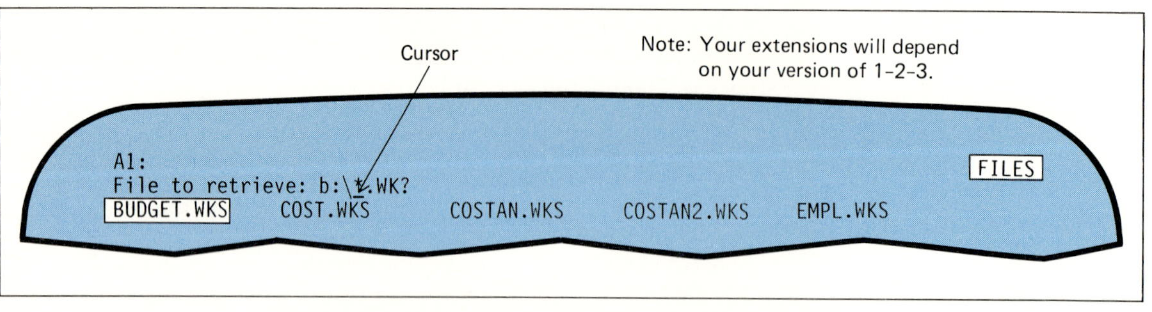

Referring to Figure 11-5, notice that the third line of the control panel includes a list of the worksheet files stored on the data disk. (They are listed alphabetically.) The file to be retrieved can be identified either by typing the name as in step 3 or by selecting from this list. To select from the list, you must move the highlight with the right arrow key to the desired worksheet name, and then strike Enter. If you have more than five files on the disk, the one you desire may not appear on the screen. If you continue to strike the right arrow, the list of names will scroll. When the desired name is highlighted, strike Enter.

Options for Starting JOE

As you know, you start JOE simply by typing JOE and striking the Enter key. You can also specify a worksheet file to be loaded when starting, thus causing JOE to be loaded and run *and* a worksheet to be retrieved from disk. The following examples illustrate this.

`JOE /L`	Retrieves the last worksheet that was saved from the previous JOE session.
`JOE /FCOST`	Retrieves the worksheet COST.WKQ (WKQ is the JOE default extension).
`JOE /FCOSTAN.WKS`	Retrieves the worksheet COSTAN.WKS (created with Lotus 1-2-3, Version 1A).

The /L is a code representing "Last" and /F is a code representing "File."

Do you long to get out into the open while you are working in your computer laboratory on a pleasant spring day? Buy a protable computer and get some sun while you are doing your spreadsheet homework.

MOVING THE CELL POINTER

From the earlier discussion of the screen, recall that cell A1 is highlighted when the spreadsheet program is first run (see Figure 11-1). Remember, the highlighting is called the cell pointer (the cell address is displayed in the upper left corner of the screen); the cell pointer identifies the current cell. Since all keyboard entries are placed in the current cell, the action of entering labels, numbers, and formulas involves first moving the cell pointer to the cell into which the entry is to be made, and then making the entry.

Using the Arrow Keys

Moving the cell pointer is done with the group of four arrow keys on the numeric keypad portion of the keyboard shown in Figure 11-6. (Note: The enhanced keyboard described in Chapter 5 includes a separate set of arrow keys.) In this book, these keys are referred to as the Left, Right, Up, and Down keys. To move the cell pointer to, for instance, cell B6, you would strike the:

Right key one time
Down key five times

This is illustrated in Figure 11-7, where the cell pointer was originally in column A, row 1 (A1). There is nothing magic about this particular sequence. That is, the cell pointer could have been moved from A1 to B6 by the following actions:

Down key five times
Right key one time

In moving the cell pointer, the arrow keys will automatically repeat if you hold them down. This is convenient for moving up or down several rows. When moving to the left or the right, be careful because the movement is very quick.

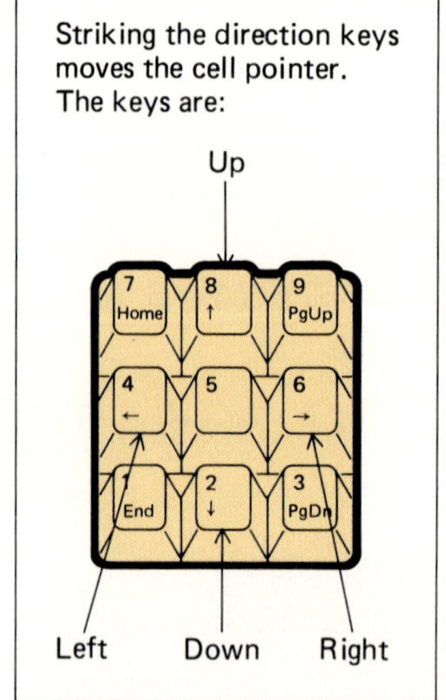

Figure 11-6
The numeric keypad.

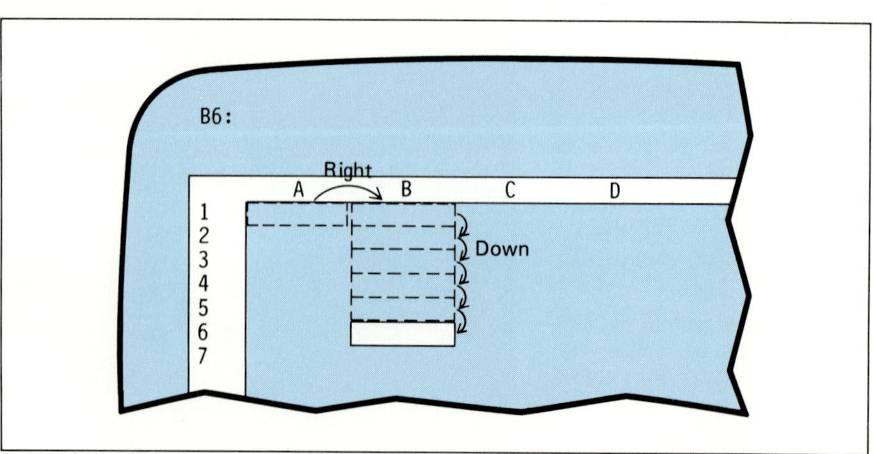

Figure 11-7
Moving the cursor.

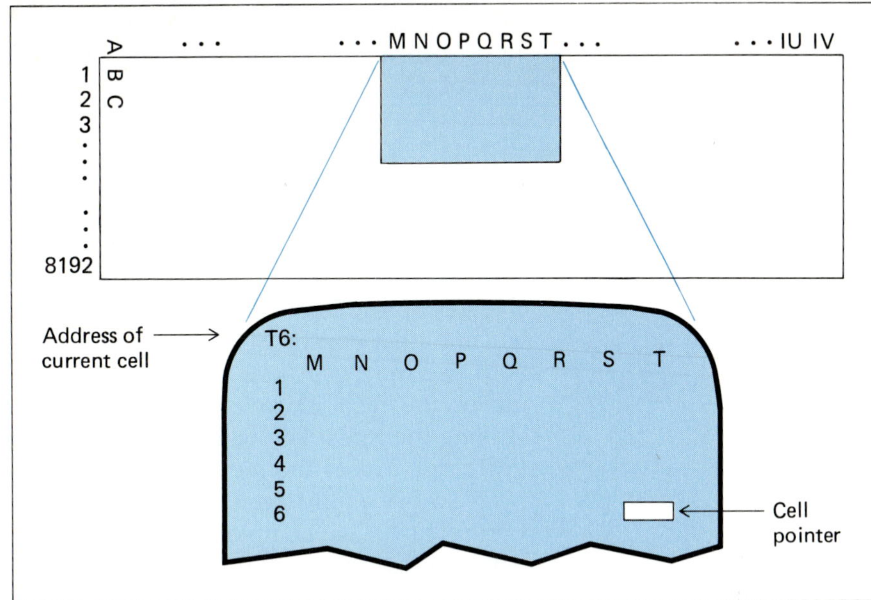

Figure 11-8
Scrolling the spreadsheet.

From Chapter 10 you learned that the screen provides you with a view into a portion of the total worksheet area stored in memory. (You see 8 columns and 20 rows on the screen of the total 256 columns and 8192 rows in memory.) If you try to move beyond the rightmost column (or the bottom row) displayed on the screen, it causes your "view" into the worksheet to move to the right (or down). What you see on the screen is that the cell pointer stays at its current position on the screen but the worksheet columns move to the left (or up). For instance, starting from cell B6 (Figure 11-7), the result of successively pressing the Right key after reaching the right border is as illustrated in Figure 11-8. This action of moving your view of the worksheet is called **scrolling.** You should try these actions.

DO THIS NOW 11-5 **Moving the Cell Pointer**

1. Make certain the cell pointer is at cell A1.
2. Strike the Right key one time and the Down key five times; this moves the cell pointer to cell B6.
3. Hold the Right key down and observe the empty worksheet scroll. Release the Right key when the active cell is T6. If you go beyond it, use the Left key to move left.
4. Move to cell T50 by holding the Down key down. If you go beyond cell T50, use the Up key to back up.
5. To move the cell pointer back to cell A1, you could hold down the Up key until reaching row 1. (You will hear a beep if you continue to hold the Up key after reaching row 1.) Then hold down the Left key until reaching column A. However, a quicker way is to strike

the Home key; it is on the 7 key of the numeric keypad (see Figure 11-6). This immediately moves the cell pointer to cell A1 regardless of its current location.

Other Cell Pointer Movement Actions

Assume that you have just retrieved from disk one of your worksheets consisting of 40 rows and 20 columns and that you need to make some changes in row 30. One way to get there is simply to hold down the Down key until that portion of the worksheet scrolls into view. A simpler method is to use the PgDn key (see the numeric keypad of Figure 11-6), which moves the next 20 rows into view. Thus, if rows 1–20 are displayed, striking the PgDn key will cause rows 21–40 to be displayed. Striking the PgUp key causes the view to be moved up 20 rows.

To move a full screen (8 columns) to the right or left requires use of the Control key. That is, holding down the Ctrl key and striking the Right key will progress from columns A–H to columns I–P. Correspondingly, holding down the Ctrl key and striking the Left key moves to the 8 columns at the left. Keystroke actions in which one key is held down while another is struck are represented in this book by separating them with a hyphen. For instance, Ctrl-Right means hold down the Ctrl key and strike the Right key. (This is the same as with WordPerfect.)

In DTN 11-5, you moved the cell pointer to cell T50 using the arrow keys. If you must move the cell pointer to a specific cell that is not currently on the screen, you can use the GOTO command, which is invoked by striking the F5 function key. In response to the program prompt asking you the desired cell address, you would type it and then strike the Enter key. (For instance, type T50 and then strike Enter.) The view will be moved

SUMMARY OF CELL POINTER MOVEMENT KEYSTROKES

Keystroke	Action
Right	Move current cell right 1 column.
Left	Move current cell left 1 column.
Up	Move current cell up 1 row.
Down	Move current cell down 1 row.
Ctrl-Right	Scroll 8 columns to the right.
Ctrl-Left	Scroll 8 columns to the left.
PgUp	Scroll 20 rows up.
PgDn	Scroll 20 rows down.
Home	Make cell A1 the current cell.
End	Make the cell at the last row and column used by your worksheet the current cell.

to the portion of the worksheet surrounding the requested cell and that cell will be made the current cell.

One other positioning key that is sometimes convenient is the End (see Figure 11-6). Striking this key causes the lowest, rightmost cell used by your worksheet to be made the current cell.

ENTERING LABELS AND NUMBERS INTO THE WORKSHEET

Now that you know how to position the cell pointer at any cell in the worksheet, you need to know how to make entries into the cells. You will learn how to do this by entering the cost analysis example of Chapter 10. From Chapter 10 you know that there are three types of information that you will enter:

- *Labels* (descriptive titles).
- *Numbers* (numeric data).
- *Formulas* (for calculating values from numbers that have been entered).

When you make an entry into a cell, 1-2-3 determines the type of entry by inspecting the first keystroke. This principle of 1-2-3 reacting to a keystroke is not new; for example, you have already experienced the following.

Keystroke	Action
Arrow key	Moves the cell pointer.
/	Changes from READY mode to MENU mode and awaits a command.
F5	Changes from READY mode to POINT mode and awaits the cell address of the cell to be made the current cell.

Other keys on the typewriter portion of the keyboard are interpreted by 1-2-3 to indicate whether a label, number, or formula is being entered. For instance, if the first keystroke from the READY mode is a letter, 1-2-3 assumes that a label is being entered. If the first keystroke is a digit, it assumes that a number is being entered. A partial summary of the first keystroke actions and the keys that trigger them is shown in Figure 11-9.

Simple Label Entry

For your convenience, the cost analysis worksheet that you will be entering is repeated here as Figure 11-10.

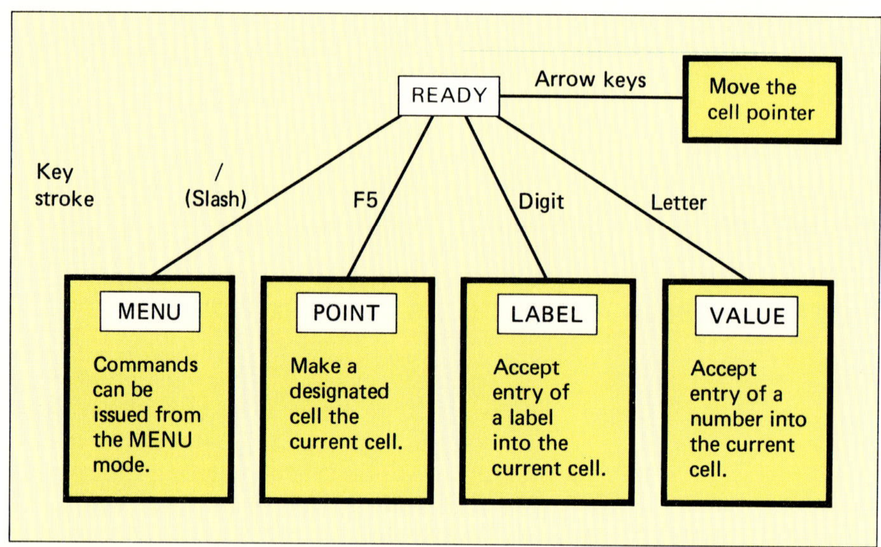

Figure 11-9
The effect of keystroke actions from the READY mode.

Figure 11-10
The cost analysis worksheet.

	A	B	C	D	E	F	G
1		Material	Labor	Other	Unit Cost	Quantity	Amount
2	Style A	5.26	7.33	1.38	13.97	12	167.64
3	Style B	5.26	9.12	1.45	15.83	12	189.96
4	Style C	7.12	4.18	2.12	13.42	18	241.56
5	Style D	6.51	6.99	1.09	14.59	8	116.72
6							
7	Total					50	715.88

DO THIS NOW 11-6 **Entering a Label Into Cell A2**

1. Move the cell pointer to A2 by striking the Down key.
2. Strike the letter *S* (in *Style A*) to begin the entry; this will produce the following screen display.

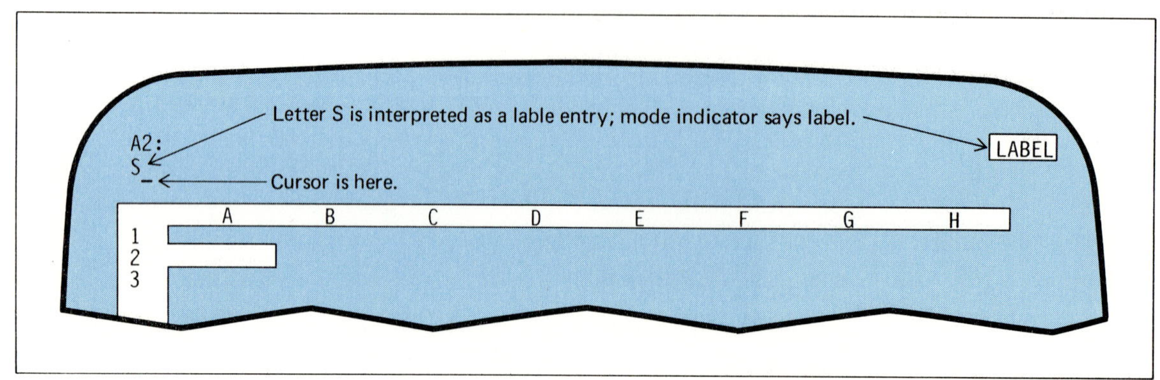

Notice that this keystroke has caused two things to happen. First, 1-2-3 switched to the label mode, as indicated by the word LABEL in the mode indicator. This tells you that 1-2-3 is in the LABEL mode, accepting the entry of a label from the keyboard. Second is that 1-2-3 accepted this first keystroke as the first character of the label; in doing so, 1-2-3 placed it on the second line of the control panel.

3. Type in the remainder of the label. As the label is being keyed in, notice that it is entered into the second line of the control panel as follows:

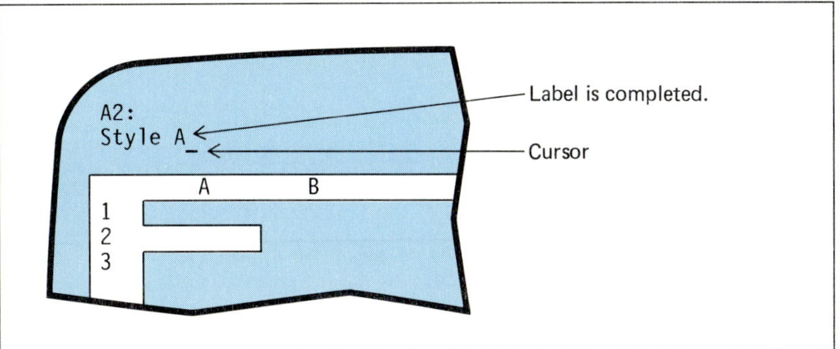

4. As with most computer programs, you must "tell" the computer that you have finished an entry. Do this by striking Enter and your final result will be as follows (for the moment, ignore the single quote that is displayed following the cell address):

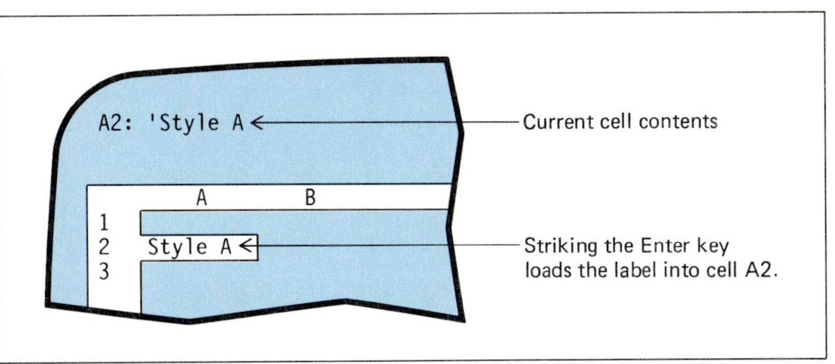

In the preceding example, you caused 1-2-3 to place your entry in the current cell by striking Enter. However, there is another way that is usually more convenient. That is, if you strike *any* of the direction keys, the entry is completed *and* the cell pointer is moved. In the preceding example, had you pressed the Down key, the entry in cell A2 would have been completed and the cell pointer moved to cell A3, ready and waiting for the next entry.

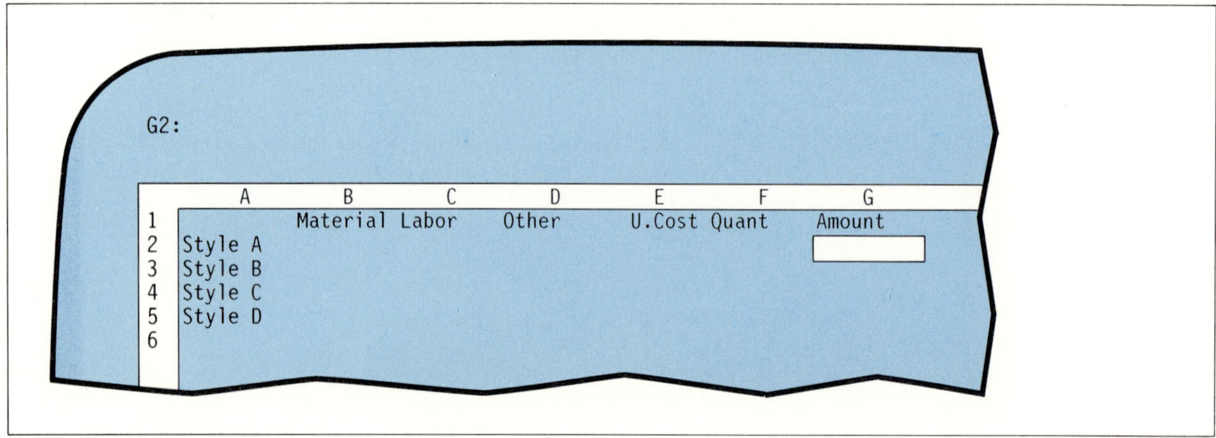

Figure 11-11
The worksheet labels.

You should now proceed to enter the rest of the labels in column A. Then move the cell pointer to cell B1 and begin entry of the top row of titles. When you are finished, your screen should appear as shown in Figure 11-11. Check your worksheet on the screen to ensure that all entries are correct. If you have made any errors, you can correct them simply by moving the cell pointer to the cell containing the incorrect value and reentering it. The new entry will replace the current one. In other words, it makes no difference whether a cell is empty or contains something else (another label, number, or formula) when an entry is made. The previous contents are always replaced by the newly typed quantity.

Positioning of Labels in the Cell Display

Perhaps you noticed when entering the labels that they are positioned to the left in the cell. Left alignment is the default. In contrast, numbers are positioned to the right, or right-aligned. For this worksheet, the default position will give you a result in which the labels are positioned poorly over the numbers they describe. Fortunately, you can override the default left alignment of labels.

Move the cell pointer to any label cell on the screen and you will see the label displayed on the second line of the control panel preceded by a single quote ('). This is one of three characters that indicates a label to 1-2-3; the other two are the double quote(") and the caret(^). The single quote is the default value and is automatically used when you strike a letter key from the READY mode. In addition to identifying an entry as being a label, the label indicators also designate the positioning of the label within the display cell as follows:

' (single quote)	Label left-aligned
" (double quote)	Label right-aligned
^ (caret)	Label centered

DO THIS NOW 11-7 **Entering a Label Left-Aligned**

1. Move the cell pointer to cell C1 (it contains the label *Labor*).
2. Type a double quote. This switches 1-2-3 to the LABEL mode, enters the double quote, and causes 1-2-3 to await the entry of the label (see below).

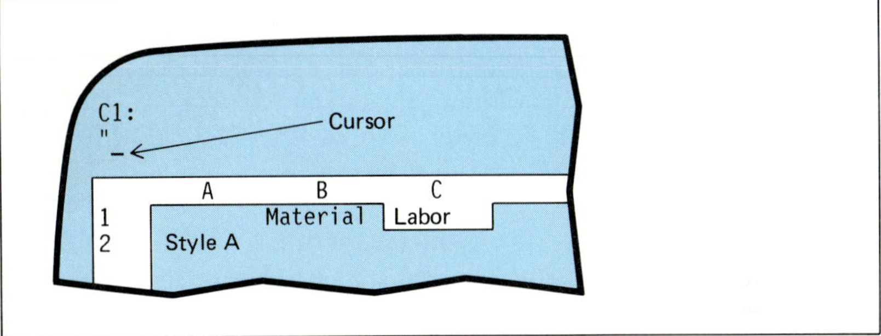

3. Type the label (Labor) and strike Enter. The label will be entered into cell C1 and the screen display will be as shown in the following. Notice that the double quote is not displayed in the screen cell but is included in the corresponding memory cell.

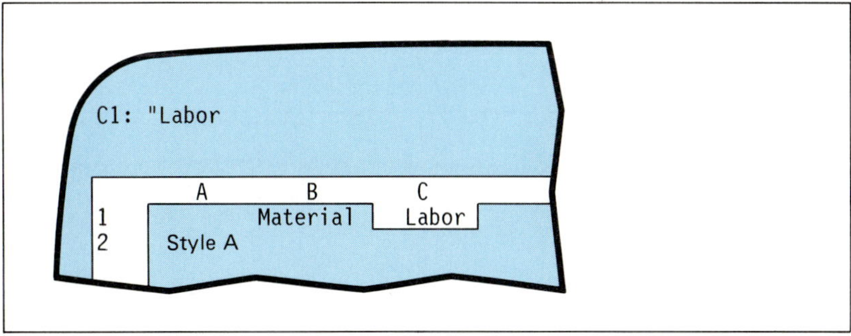

4. Reenter the rest of the labels in Row 1 so that they are all right-aligned.

Entering Numbers

If you were creating a template for the cost analysis, you would enter the formulas next and save a copy without data. Then, for your cost studies, you would enter data values and observe the effect on total cost. However, for this learning sequence, you will learn how to enter numeric quantities next. Remember that this data will be used by formulas in performing the calculations. Hence, each cell entry must be identified as a number when it is entered.

Numbers take a variety of forms; for instance, the number 125 might appear in a worksheet in any of the following ways.

125	–125
12.5	+125
.125	$125.00
0.0125	

Consistent with these needs, any of the following characters causes 1-2-3 to switch from the READY mode to the VALUE mode and accept the entry as a number. (As you will learn in the next section, the VALUE mode is used to enter both numbers and formulas.)

Any digit 0–9	Plus sign (+)
Decimal point (.)	Dollar sign ($)
Minus sign (–)	

You can now proceed to enter the data into your worksheet.

DO THIS NOW 11-8 **Entering Data into the Worksheet**

1. Move the cell pointer to cell B2, the cell into which the material cost for Style A is to be entered.
2. Type in the number 5.26. Notice that when you strike the digit 5, the mode indicator displays VALUE. Your screen should appear as shown below.

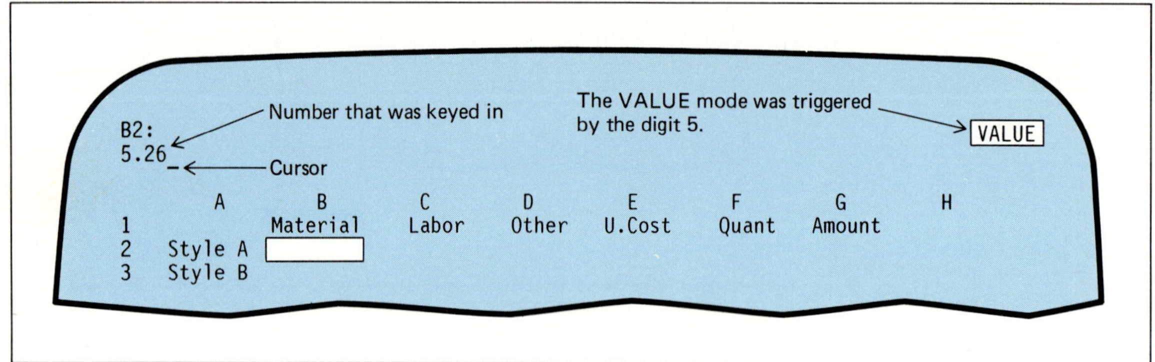

3. As with labels, you can enter this value into the current cell either by striking the Enter or one of the direction keys. In this case, strike the Down key in order to be ready for data entry into cell B3.
4. Enter the data for the rest of the worksheet.
5. When data entry is complete, check your values to make certain they are correct. For any that are incorrect, reenter the correct value in the same way that you corrected label entries.

Perhaps, as you entered your numbers for this worksheet, you accidentally entered an amount ending with a digit 0. If you did, you noticed that it was displayed as, for instance, 5.2 rather than 5.20. The default display for 1-2-3 is not to display digits to the right of the decimal point that are not significant. You will learn how to control this in the next chapter.

More About Entering Labels

Since 1-2-3 inspects the first character to determine whether a label or number is about to be entered, perhaps you have wondered about entering labels with default left alignment such as the following.

```
97 Print
--Tax--
```

Here, the first character you enter will cause 1-2-3 to change to the VALUE mode, not the LABEL mode as desired. In cases such as this, you must first type a single quote, thereby switching to LABEL mode, and then proceed to type the label. If you use centering or right alignment, you will have no problem.

FORMULAS

Chapter 10 describes how formulas in spreadsheets automatically calculate and display values in cells based on the contents of other cells. For example, the formula

```
+B2+C2+D2
```

directs 1-2-3 to add the values stored in cells B2, C2, and D2. If this formula is assigned to cell E2 (the Unit Cost cell in the cost analysis), the sum will be displayed in that screen cell. Completing the cost analysis worksheet requires that you enter formulas into the cells of columns E and G.

About the VALUE Mode

In the preceding descriptions, you used the VALUE mode for entering numbers into the worksheet. Actually, the word *value* has a much broader implication in 1-2-3: it means that the cell contents will be a numeric quantity. The quantity can be a number that has been entered into the cell, *or it can be the calculated result of a formula assigned to the cell.* Hence, when a keystroke changes the mode to VALUE, 1-2-3 is ready to accept either a number or a formula.

Entering Formulas to Calculate Unit Costs

The first group of formulas that will be entered are those for calculating the Unit Cost (column E) shown in Figure 11-12. As the first character in the formula

```
B2+C2+D2
```

is a letter, 1-2-3 will automatically switch to LABEL mode rather than VALUE mode. To avoid this, you must enter the formula as:

+B2+C2+D2

In the following example, you will enter the formulas into the Unit Cost. If the basic format of the formula is wrong (for instance, you enter +B2#C2 instead of +B2+C2), the computer will beep and switch to the EDIT mode. Working from the EDIT mode is described in a later section of this chapter. For now, if that occurs, simply strike the Escape key twice to return to the READY mode. Then you can reenter the formula.

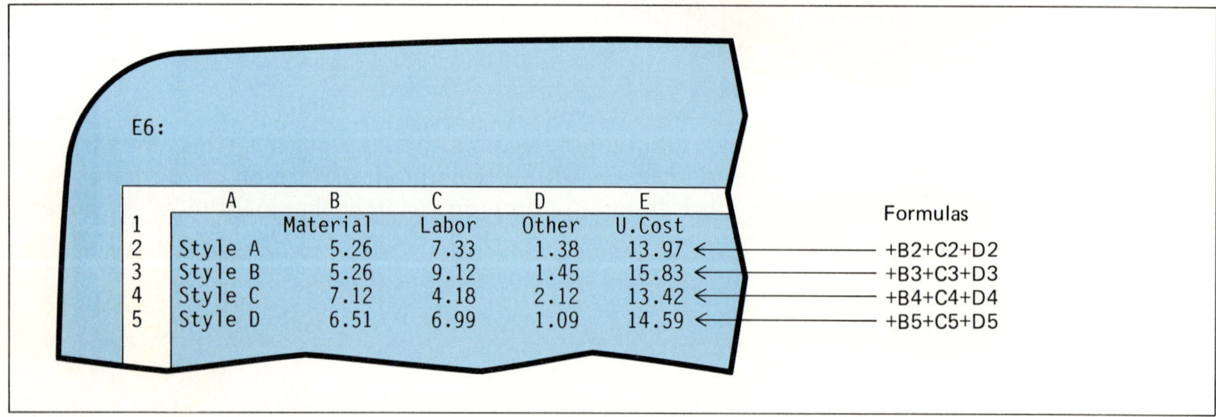

Figure 11-12
Formulas for column E.

DO THIS NOW 11-9 **Entering the Unit Cost Formulas of Column E**

1. Move the cell pointer to E2.
2. Type a + sign to switch to VALUE mode. The upper portion of your screen will appear as shown below.

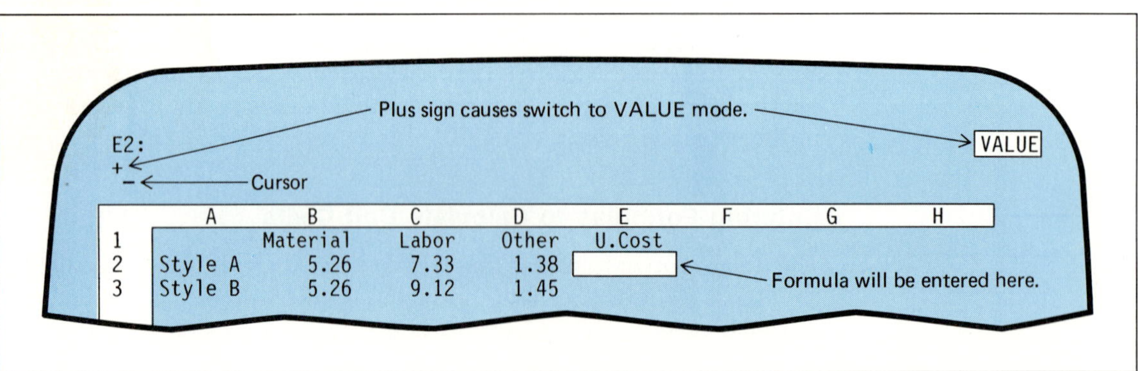

3. Type in the formula. Check it before striking Enter. If it is not the same as the following display, correct it.

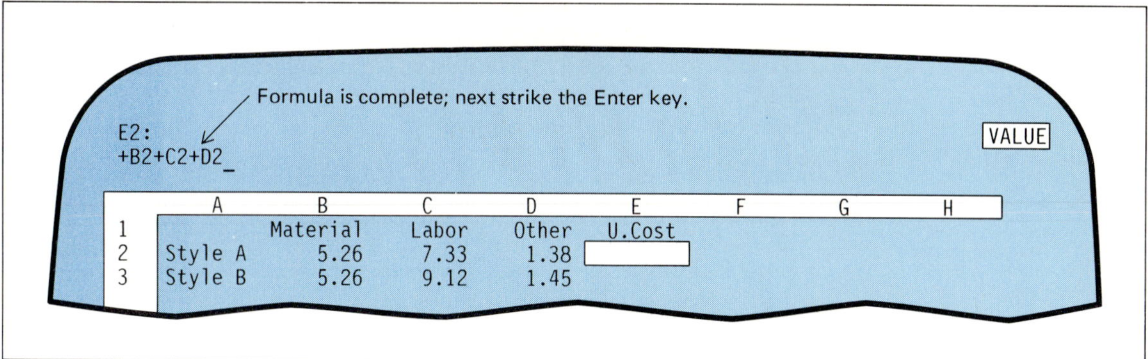

Make needed corrections by striking the Backspace key, which backs up the cursor and deletes as it goes. For instance, if you observed that you had entered

+B2+C1+D2

you would use the Backspace key and erase until you had

+B2+C

Then you would complete the entry.

4. Although you can complete the entry of this formula with either an arrow key or the Enter, strike the Enter key so that your screen will be as exactly as follows:

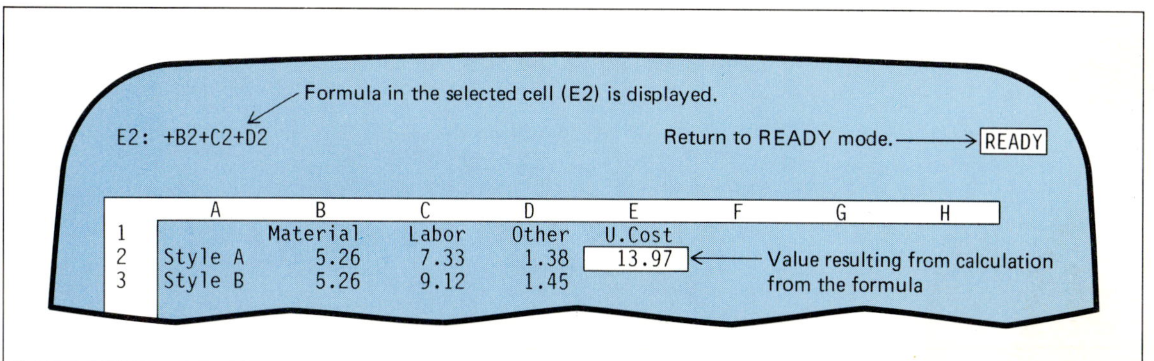

5. If the displayed result in cell E2 is different from the preceding display, something is wrong with your entries. First, check the numbers in cells B2, C2, and D2. Reenter any that are different. If the value in cell E2 is still incorrect, then check your formula. Notice that the formula of the current cell is displayed on the first line of the control panel. If the formula is incorrect, then reenter it just as you would a label or number.

If you forget to begin a formula with a +, you can see it because the mode indicator will say LABEL. If you do not notice this while typing the formula, it will be quite evident when you strike the Enter because the formula rather than the calculated result will be displayed in the cell. If this happens, simply reenter the formula properly.

Creating Formulas by Pointing

There is another way of entering formulas that many users prefer. The method is called *pointing* and involves moving the cursor to the cell to be included in the formula. To illustrate, let us create the formula for the cost of Style B (B3+C3+D3). In the following sequence of steps, the appearance of the appropriate portion of the screen is shown below the description.

DO THIS NOW 11-10 **Entering the Formula Into Cell E3 by Pointing**

1. Position the cell pointer to cell E3, the cell into which the formula is to be entered.

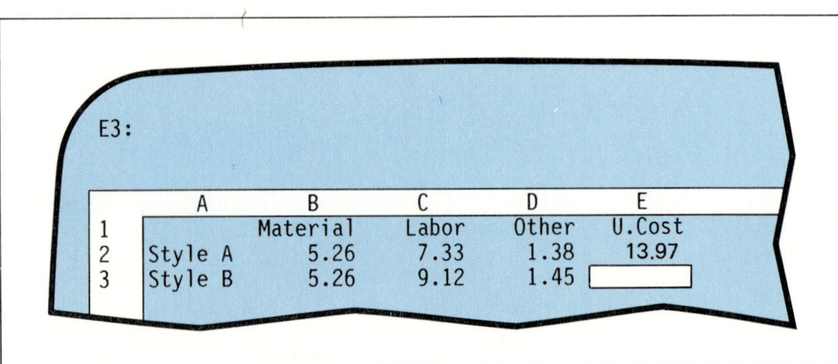

2. Enter the plus sign (+) to indicate that a value entry is to be made.

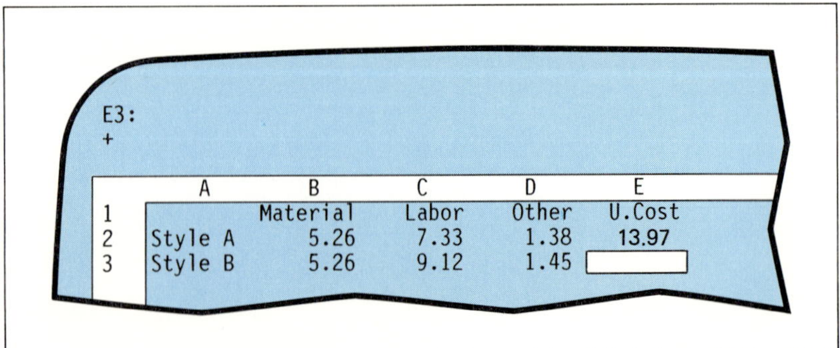

3. Strike the Left arrow key three times, thus moving the cell pointer to cell B3. This is the first cell address required in the formula. Note

that the corresponding address has been entered into the formula that is being constructed on the second line of the control panel.

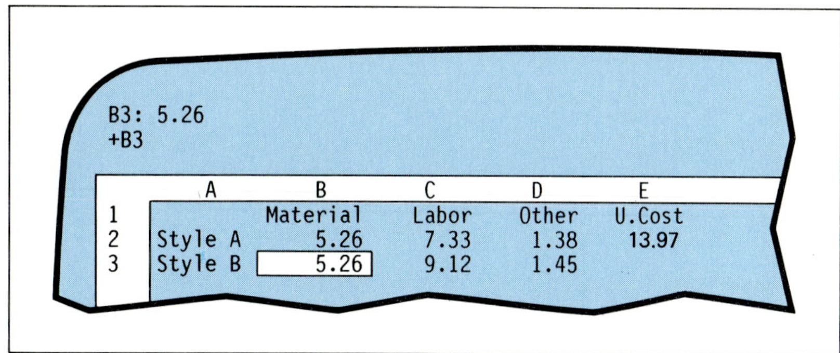

4. Enter a + sign, the next part of the formula. Notice that it has been added to the emerging formula in the control panel.

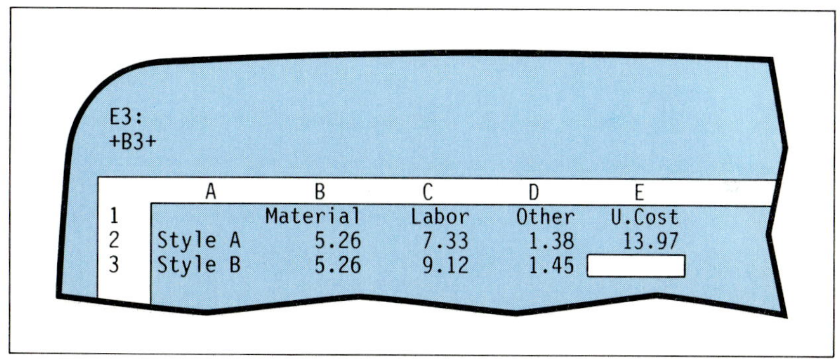

5. Move the cell pointer to cell C3, causing the next element of the formula to be displayed.

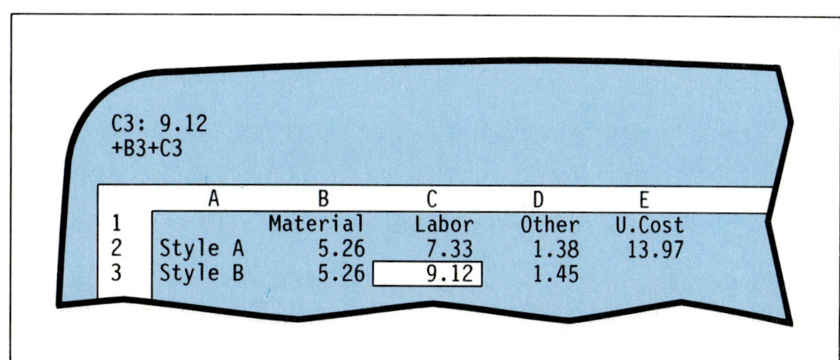

6. Enter a + sign, the next part of the formula.

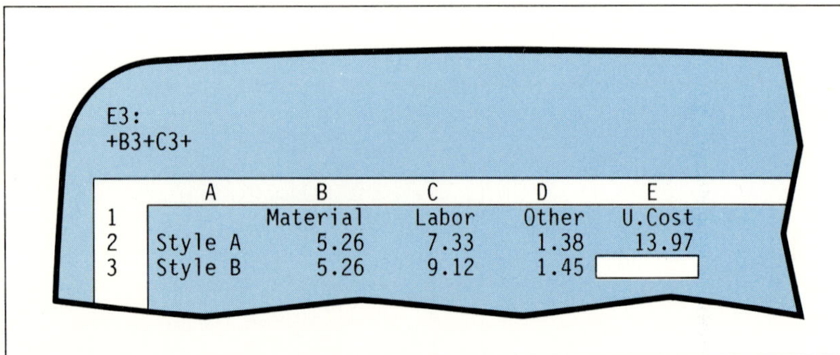

7. Move the cell pointer to cell D3, causing the final element of the formula to be displayed.

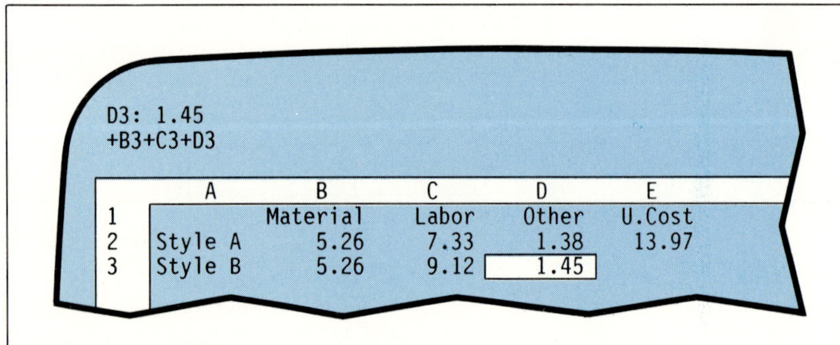

8. As the formula is now complete, strike the Enter key to enter it into cell E3.

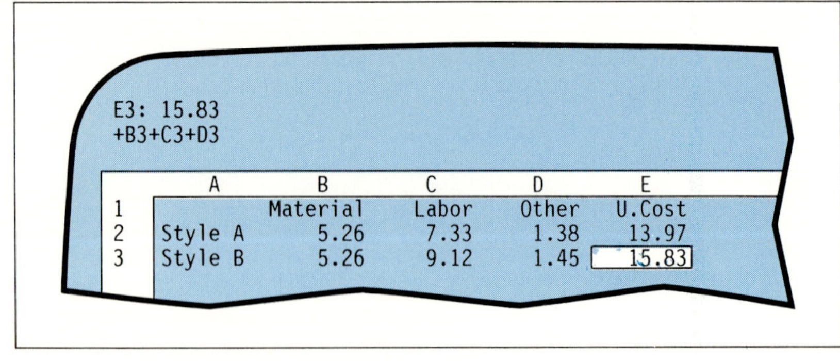

At first, this method for entering formulas may appear to be slower and clumsier than simply keying them in. However, once you get the knack of it, the process is reasonably quick. Most important, it reduces the chance for error. That is, it is much easier to overlook the address D3 keyed in as D2 than to make the corresponding mistake with the visual operation of positioning the highlight to the desired cell.

To complete this portion of your worksheet, you must enter each of the formulas for cells E4 and E5. You may either type the formula or use pointing.

Entering the Remaining Formulas

To complete the cost analysis worksheet, you must enter the remaining formulas summarized in Figure 11-13. Using cell G2 as an example, notice that the Amount value for this line is calculated as the contents of cell E2 times the contents of cell F2. Using the asterisk for multiplication, this formula must be entered as:

```
+E2*F2
```

You should proceed to enter the formulas into your worksheet, thus completing all entries. Do not forget the plus sign to indicate that a value entry is being made. The formulas for cells G3, G4, and G5 are identical except that the row designations differ as appropriate. The final formulas (in cells F7 and G7) are the totals of the values above them in the worksheet.

There is a subtle point about formulas that is illustrated by this worksheet. The formula of, for example, cell F7 uses the contents of cells F2 through F5, all of which contain numbers. However, the formula of cell G7 uses the contents of cells G2 through G5, all of which have formulas associated with them. In other words, the calculated value displayed by cell G7 is the result of the contents of cells G2 through G5, themselves calculated values. This is quite valid and, in fact, is very common in worksheets.

Figure 11-13
The remaining formulas.

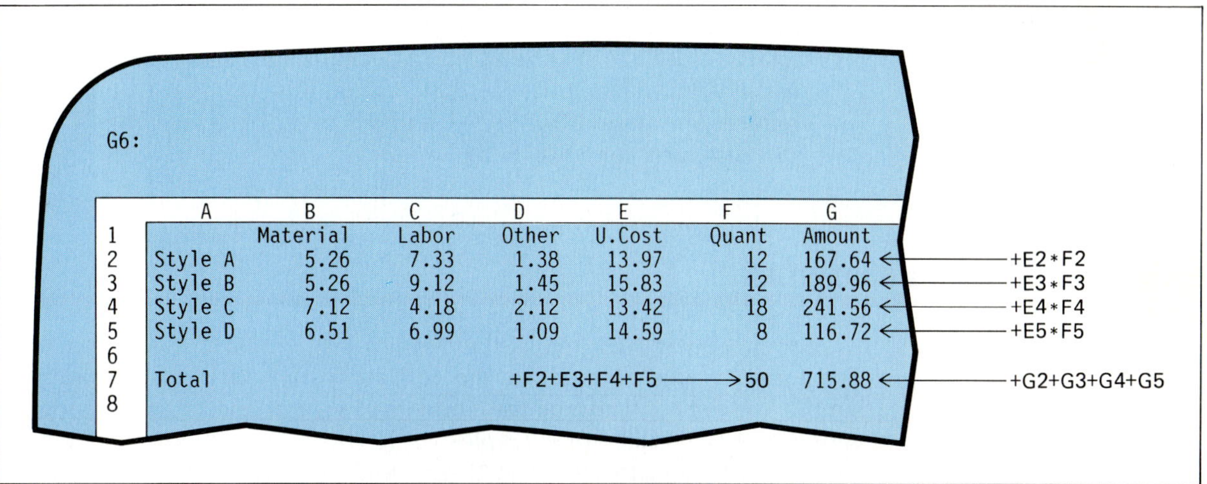

Using the Completed Worksheet

When you have completed your worksheet, you should carefully check each cell display to ensure that it is correct. Then save it to disk; you will need this worksheet for later examples. Note that a copy of it is also available to you on the data disk that accompanies this book under the name COSTAN.WKS.

You can now proceed to experiment by changing the data in the worksheet in order to achieve the desired $675 cost total.

DO THIS NOW 11-11 **Changing Data Entries in the Cost Analysis Worksheet**

1. Change the values of items identified for cost reduction in Chapter 10; that is, incorporate the following reductions in your worksheet.

Labor Reduction		Other Reduction	
Style A	.55	Style A	.41
Style B	.60	Style B	.44
Style D	.70	Style C	.31
		Style D	.21

For instance, the Labor cost for Style A is to be reduced from 7.33 (refer to your worksheet on the screen or to Figure 11-13) to 6.78, which is a reduction of .55. As you type in each new data value, notice the "ripple" effect it has on the Unit Cost, Amount, and Total. When you have completed these changes, the new total should be 679.02. If it is not, check all of your values.

2. Make additional small changes to these data values and bring the total as close to 675 as you can. In deciding how small (or large) to make your changes, notice that a change in Unit Cost of 1 cent reduces the amount for Styles A and B by 12 cents, for Style C by 18 cents, and for Style D by 8 cents.

RULES FOR BUILDING FORMULAS

The formulas you entered for the cost analysis worksheet are relatively simple, consisting of adding the contents of several cells or multiplying the contents of two cells. For examples yet to come, the calculations are more complex. In order to construct them, you must know the rules used by 1-2-3 when performing the calculations.

Operators and Their Precedence

Consider the simple arithmetic expression:

```
24+7x3
```

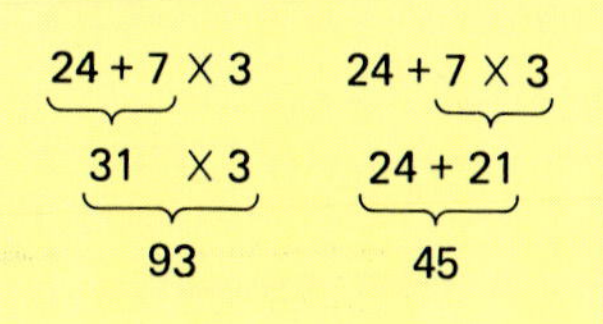

Which of the two sets of calculations to the left is correct and how do we know which form to use?

The answer is that the multiplication must be performed first (as on the right) because the rules of mathematics say that multiplication takes precedence over addition.

This example involves two of the basic arithmetic operations of mathematics; in all, there are five:

Raise to a power.

Multiplication and division.

Addition and subtraction.

They are listed here in their order of **precedence,** that is, the order in which the operations will be carried out in a calculation sequence. Notice that multiplication and division have the same precedence level as do addition and subtraction. These precedence rules are illustrated by the following examples.

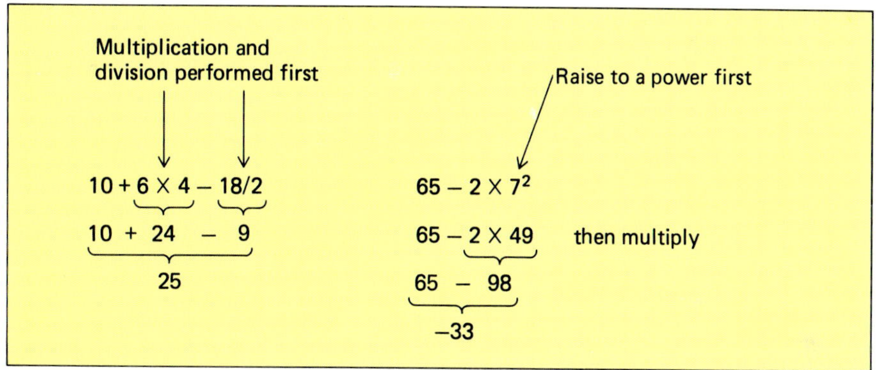

As in algebra, parentheses can be used to group items and change the precedence. That is, when parentheses are used, calculations are performed first on those elements within the parentheses, as illustrated by the following set of examples. In the right-most example of those that follow (representing a compound interest calculation for $100 at 8 percent for 3 years), the addition within the parentheses is performed first. Then the resulting quantity is raised to a power.

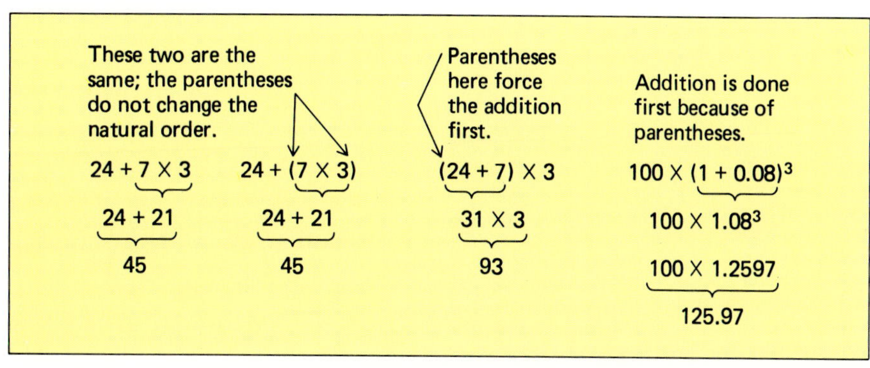

Formulas in 1-2-3

These precedence rules illustrated here with numbers also apply to 1-2-3 formulas. (In fact, they are used almost universally in computing.) In 1-2-3, formulas are constructed by relating variable quantities (for instance, B2, C2, and D2) and numbers with the following **arithmetic operators.**

^ Raise to a power
* Multiplication
/ Division
+ Addition
– Subtraction

The following examples illustrate the major points of constructing 1-2-3 formulas.

Formula	Explanation
+C3+D3–E3	Add the contents of cells C3 and D3 and then subtract the contents of E3.
+F4*F5+23	Multiply the contents of cells F4 and F5 and then add 23 to that result. Note that numbers can be used in forming formulas.
+23+F4*F5 +23+(F4*F5)	Both of these perform exactly the same operation as the preceding example. Note that the rules of precedence are applied: multiplications and divisions are done first and then additions and subtractions. In the second form, parentheses are included. This has no effect on the operation carried out in this case. However, you can use parentheses to make the sequence clear to you.
+C5+C6/4	Divide the contents of cell C6 by 4 and add the result to the contents of cell C5.
(D3+D4+D5)/3	Add the contents of D3, D4, and D5 then divide the result by 3. Parentheses are necessary in this case in order to force the desired sequence of operations.
+D10*(1+D12)^C3	This is the 1-2-3 version of the interest calculation in the last precedence example. Here the value 1 is added to the contents of cell D12 before raising to the power (the number in cell C3).

Most people tend to think of the spreadsheet as a business tool. Although it is widely used in business, it is hardly confined to solving business problems; it is also used to solve problems in many areas of science.

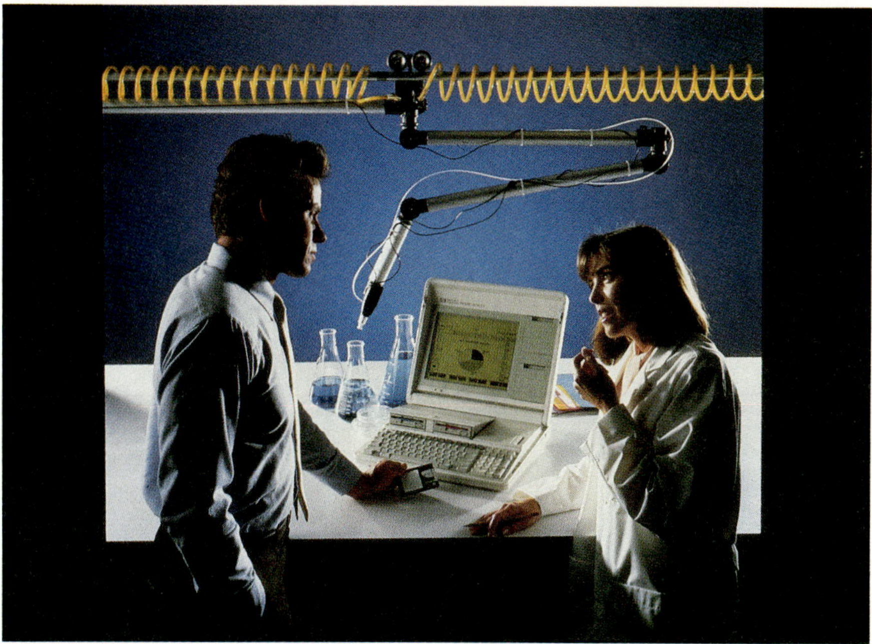

Notice that none of the preceding examples include any spaces within the formulas. If you have studied a programming language such as BASIC, you know that spaces in formulas are ignored and hence can be inserted to make the forms more readable. This is not true with 1-2-3, which *does not allow spaces anywhere within formulas.*

The earlier examples of entering numbers illustrate most of the initial characters that cause 1-2-3 to switch to the VALUE mode (for entry of a number or formula). Following is the complete set of characters that can be used to start a value entry.

```
1 2 3 4 5 6 7 8 9 0 . + - ( @ # $
```

Note that the open parenthesis, used for grouping in a formula, is also valid as the first character.

ABOUT WORKSHEET ERRORS AND CORRECTING THEM

In the preceding exercises, you were instructed to make entries and then to check to ensure that they were correct. For your check, you compared your worksheet with the sample in this book. When preparing your own worksheets, you must do the checking. In this section, we will consider a version of the cost analysis worksheet that includes an error, and will learn how to detect errors and how to correct them. For this example, you will be using a worksheet from the data disk that accompanies this book. Hence, if your cost analysis worksheet is still on the screen and you wish to save the current version, you should do so before continuing.

Errors in Worksheets

For this example, you must retrieve the worksheet named COSTAN2.WKS from the data disk. In your resulting screen display, which should match Figure 11-14, you can see that this is a cost analysis worksheet with an entirely different set of data values. At a glance, it appears to be alright. However, let us experiment with it.

Figure 11-14
The worksheet COSTAN2.WKS.

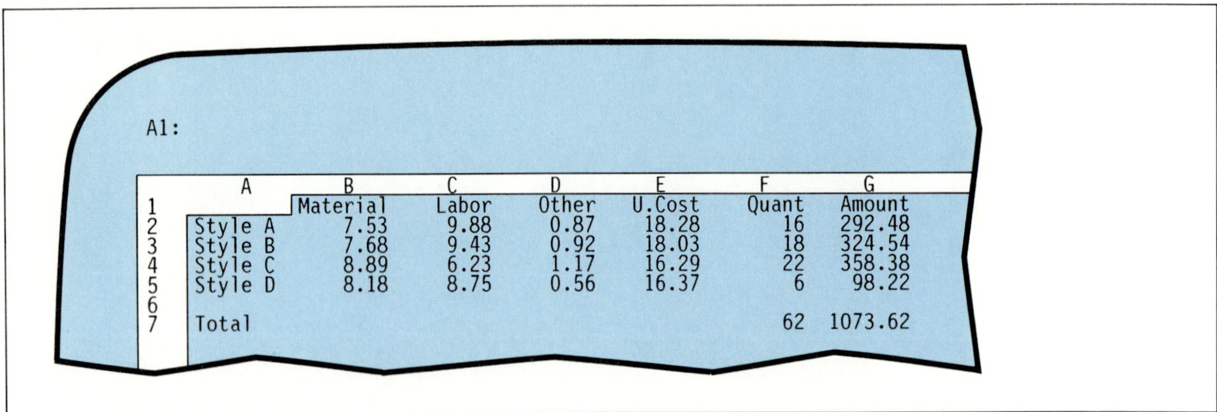

DO THIS NOW 11-12 **Finding an Error**

1. Increase each of the Other cost values by 10 cents (for example, change the Style A Other cost in cell D2 to 0.97).
2. As you make each entry, observe the change in each of the computed cells. Pay particular attention to Style D. Notice that when you increase the Other amount, the Unit Cost *decreases*. This is a distressing fact.
3. Manually add the three component values for Style D and you will see the discrepancy of Figure 11-15. It would appear that something is wrong with the way in which 1-2-3 is calculating this sum.

Figure 11-15
Suspicious results from the worksheet.

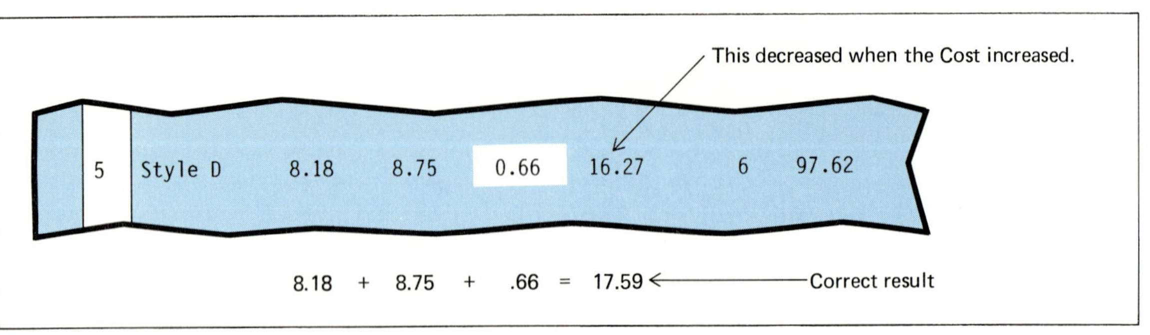

4. Move the cell pointer to cell E5 so that you can inspect the formula. Your screen display should correspond to that in Figure 11-16 in

which the formula has been incorrectly entered with a minus sign. This is easily corrected by reentering. However, do not change it as this formula is used in the next section to illustrate editing.

Figure 11-16
An erroneous formula.

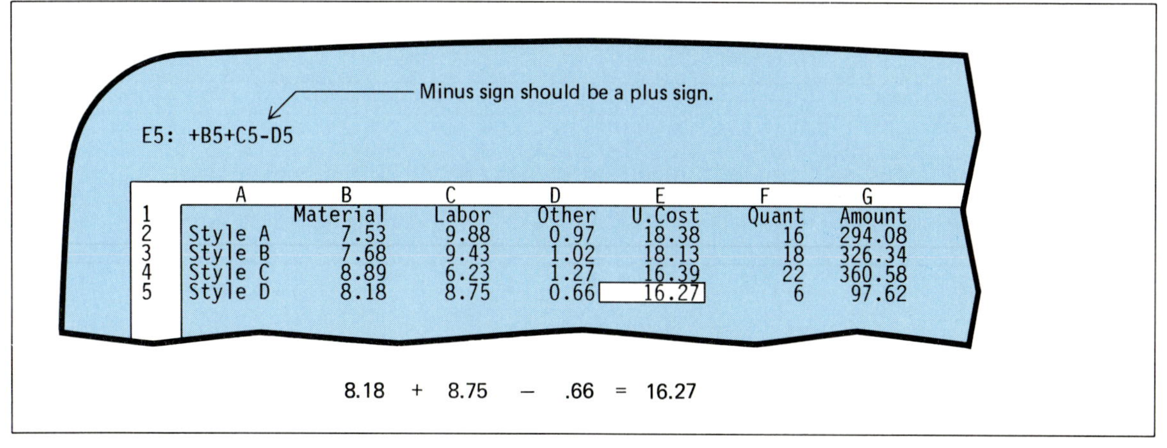

This example illustrates an extremely important factor when working with the computer. That is, never assume that the output from any type of program (and your template represents a program) is correct without double checking. Whenever you create a worksheet, check the value displayed from each formula by performing the calculations manually and comparing them to the displayed results. Once each formula has been checked in this way, it is safe to proceed with manipulating data values in the optimization process. Any businessperson who bases decisions on worksheets that have not been properly checked might find it difficult to stay in business.

The EDIT Mode

As you know, you can change the contents of any cell simply by reentering; this applies to formulas as well as numbers and labels. However, reentering an entire formula (or a long label) is a nuisance if only one character is incorrect. To simplify this process, 1-2-3 allows you to perform editing operations on any cell entry by switching to the EDIT mode. Switching from the READY mode to the EDIT mode is done by striking the F2 key. (If you are using JOE, the third line of the control panel displays F2:Ed as a reminder. If you are using Lotus 1-2-3, then you should have a template that fits around the function keys that tells you the action of each.) To illustrate editing, let us correct the error in the formula of Figure 11-16.

DO THIS NOW 11-13 **Editing a Formula**

1. With the cell pointer at cell E5, strike the F2 function key. The control panel of your screen will appear as follows:

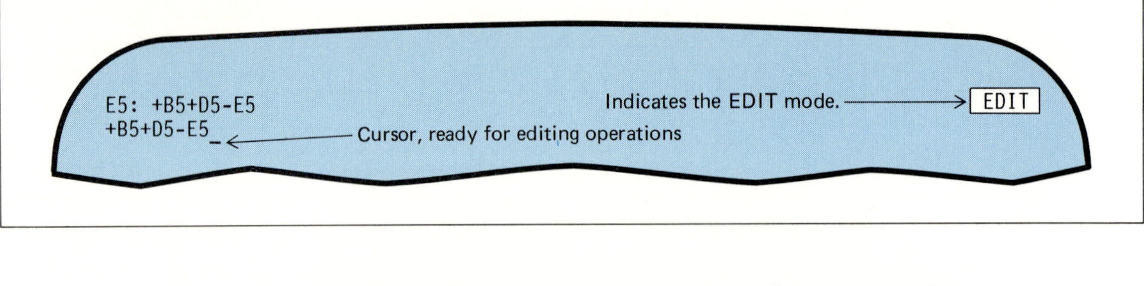

2. Move the cursor to the position of the minus sign.
3. Strike the Del key to delete the minus, producing:

   +B5+D5E5

4. The cursor will be positioned at the E in E5, so enter the desired + character. The result will be:

   +B5+D5+E5

5. Strike the Enter key to complete the operation.

The keys to be used during editing operate in exactly the same way as they do with word processing. Summarizing, you can use them as follows:

- *Left and Right arrows.* Move the cursor to the left or the right.
- *Backspace.* Delete the character to the left of the cursor.
- *Del.* Delete the character at the position of the cursor.
- *Ins.* Toggle between Insert mode and Overtype mode (the newly entered character replaces the character at the position of the cursor). The edit begins in the Insert mode. If the Ins key is used to switch to Overtype, the bottom line of the screen displays the letters OVR.

If you attempt to enter an invalid form into a cell, 1-2-3 beeps and then automatically switches to the EDIT mode without placing anything in the cell. For example, assume that you accidentally keyed in the formula for cell E2 as follows:

B2+C2#D2

When you strike the Enter or an arrow key, the computer will beep, the mode indicator will change to EDIT, and the cursor will be positioned for editing the formula. When you have corrected it, you can strike the Enter and continue.

MORE ABOUT COMMANDS

You received your introduction to worksheet commands at the beginning of this chapter so that you could save and retrieve worksheets and terminate a work session. The approach at that point was, "Do it because it works." Let us consider some more details of 1-2-3 commands.

Basic Principle of Commands

From the READY mode, striking the slash key (/) causes 1-2-3 to switch to the MENU mode, thus producing the control panel of Figure 11-17. (This is repeated from earlier in the chapter.) Although the command names and their order are slightly different for JOE and Lotus 1-2-3, the first letter of corresponding commands are the same. This is important because, as you recall, you can execute a command by typing the first letter of the command name. When the MENU mode is first entered, the first command is highlighted, as we see in Figure 11-17. The third line of the control panel contains a brief description of the highlighted command. If information regarding any of the other commands is desired, the highlight can be moved from one command to the next by striking the Left or Right keys. The description changes with the changing highlight. Try this and you will see how the third line display changes.

To issue the Save, Retrieve, and Quit commands, you have been typing the first letter of the command name. There is another way of issuing a command—by moving the highlight to the desired command and striking the Enter key. This is identical to the method for selecting the

Figure 11-17
(a) Command menu for JOE.
(b) Command menu for Lotus 1-2-3.

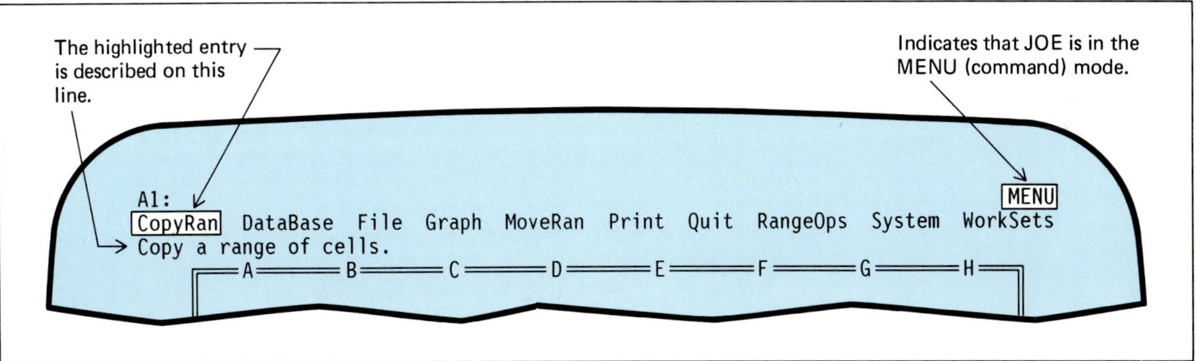

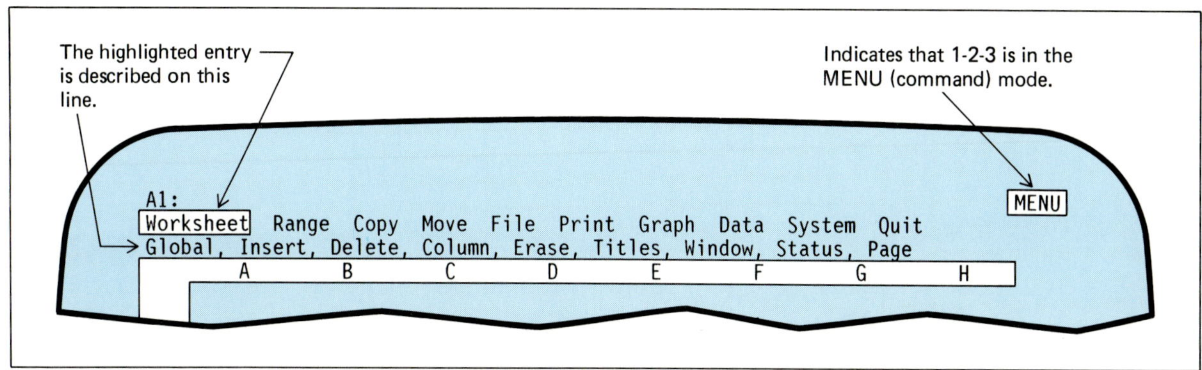

name of a worksheet file to be retrieved. In general, issuing a command by striking the first letter is quicker than moving the highlight.

The execution of some commands produces a submenu of commands from which an option must be selected. You are familiar with that from the File command that produces the submenu shown in Figure 11-3. If you set your default data drive as described earlier in this chapter, you probably noticed that you had to work through several levels of menus.

Getting Help

It is difficult to remember everything about the commands, especially if you do not use 1-2-3 on a regular basis. If you need more information about a command (or many other possible 1-2-3 actions) while working with 1-2-3, you can get assistance from the program. The F1 function key is called the Help key; striking it from the READY mode switches to the HELP mode. To illustrate its use, let us see what descriptive information is available for the File command, one that you have already used in saving and retrieving worksheets. To get a feel for using the Help, you should carry out these actions.

Help with JOE. Striking the F1 key from the READY mode will cause your worksheet to be replaced with the general Help screen shown in

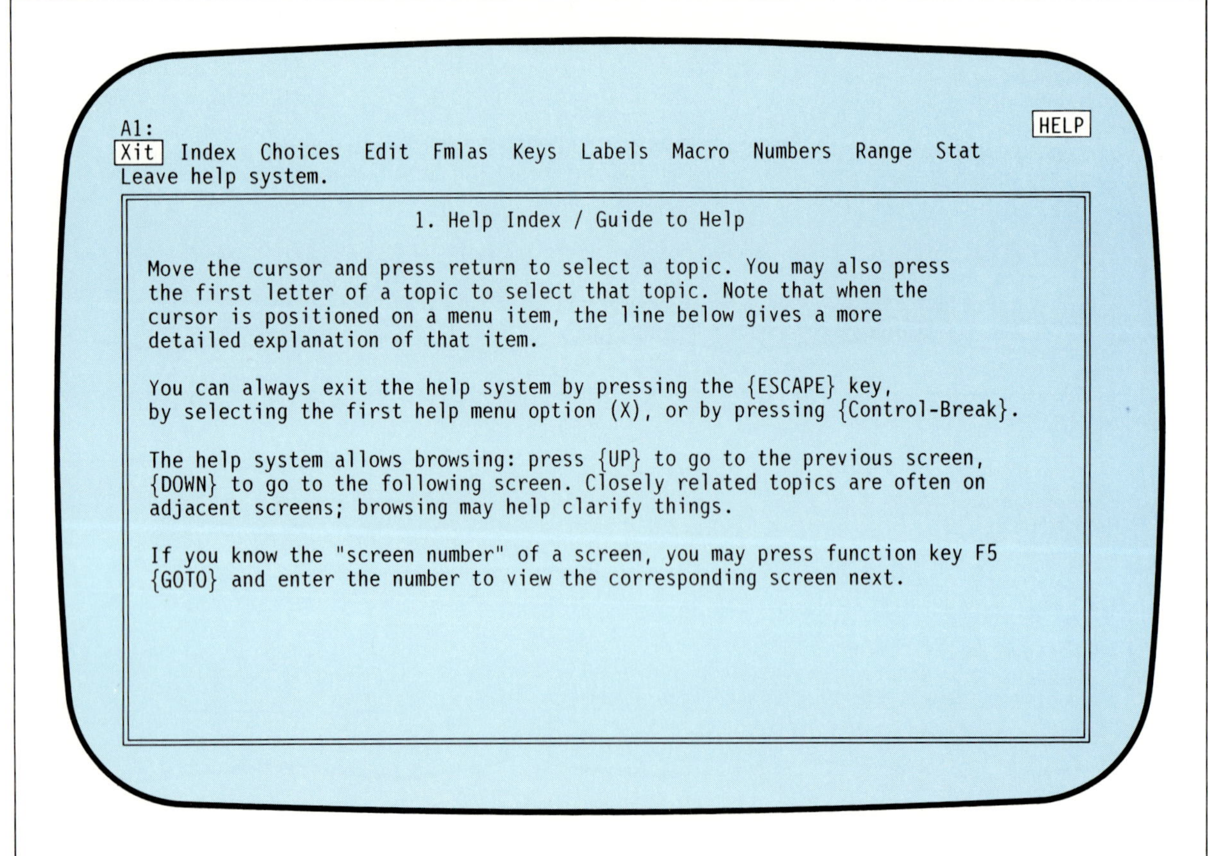

Figure 11-18
The general Help screen for JOE.

Figure 11-18. This gives you a capsule description of how to use Help. The selection menu at the top lists the various categories. Selecting the Choices option (striking the letter C or moving the highlight to Choices and striking Enter) produces the following menu in the control panel.

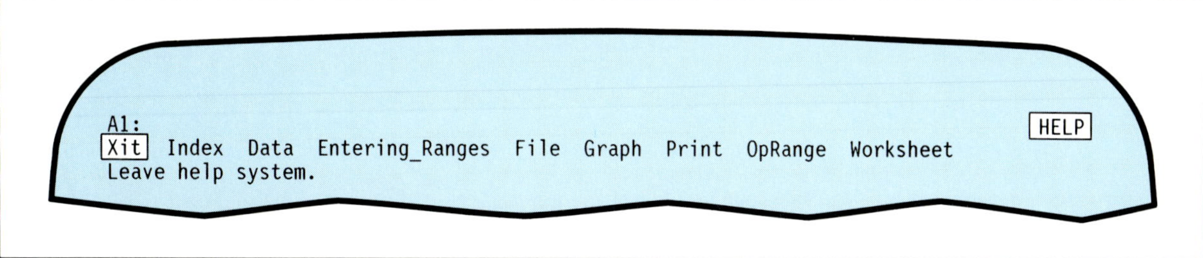

Since we are interested in the File command, type the letter F (for File) or move the highlight to File and strike Enter. Your initial Help screen will be replaced with the File help screen shown in Figure 11-19. Here we see a brief description of each of the eight File commands. Although the descriptions may seem too short to be of much value, remember that they are designed as an aid to users in recalling how JOE features work. They are not designed specifically as learning tools. To get a feel for using the Help

Figure 11-19
The File Help screen for JOE.

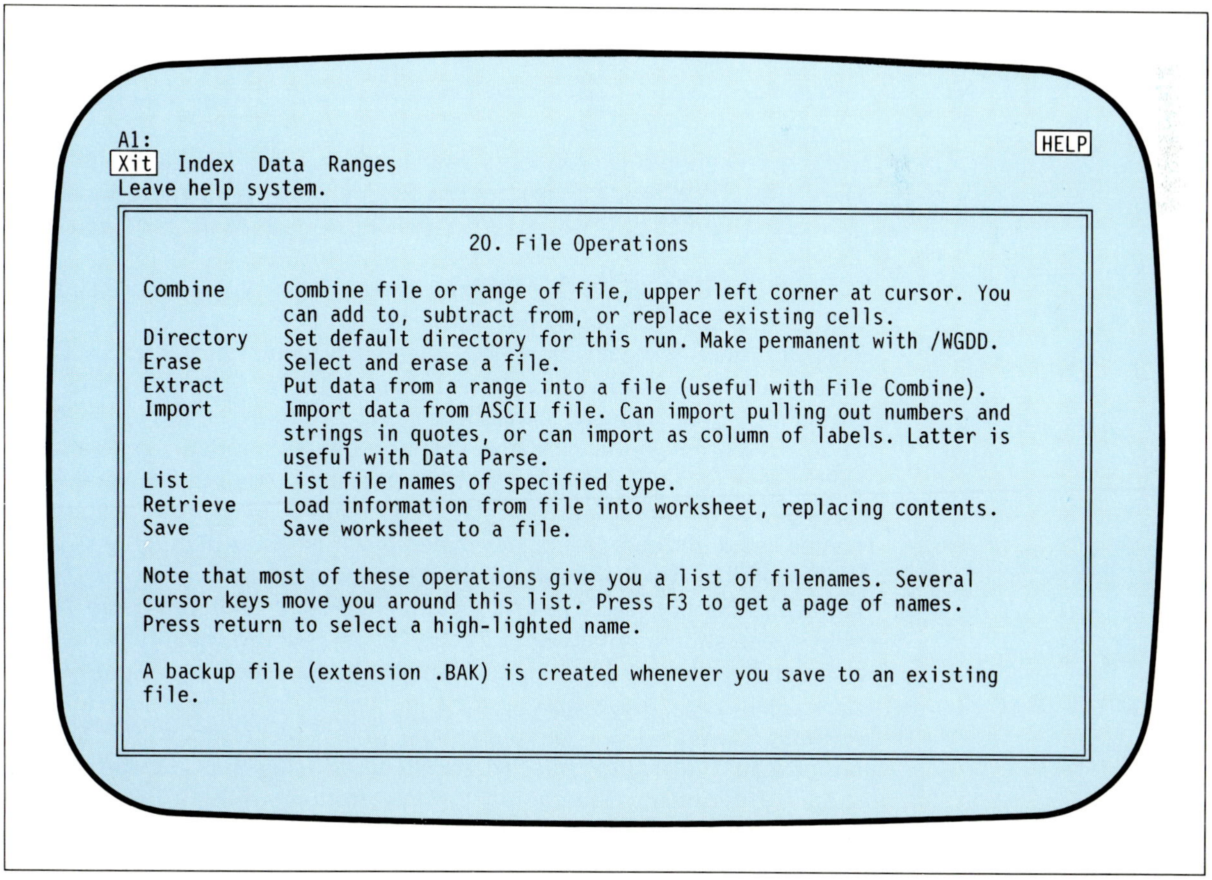

```
A1:                                                                    HELP
Xit  Index  Data  Ranges
Leave help system.

                        20. File Operations

Combine     Combine file or range of file, upper left corner at cursor. You
            can add to, subtract from, or replace existing cells.
Directory   Set default directory for this run. Make permanent with /WGDD.
Erase       Select and erase a file.
Extract     Put data from a range into a file (useful with File Combine).
Import      Import data from ASCII file. Can import pulling out numbers and
            strings in quotes, or can import as column of labels. Latter is
            useful with Data Parse.
List        List file names of specified type.
Retrieve    Load information from file into worksheet, replacing contents.
Save        Save worksheet to a file.

Note that most of these operations give you a list of filenames. Several
cursor keys move you around this list. Press F3 to get a page of names.
Press return to select a high-lighted name.

A backup file (extension .BAK) is created whenever you save to an existing
file.
```

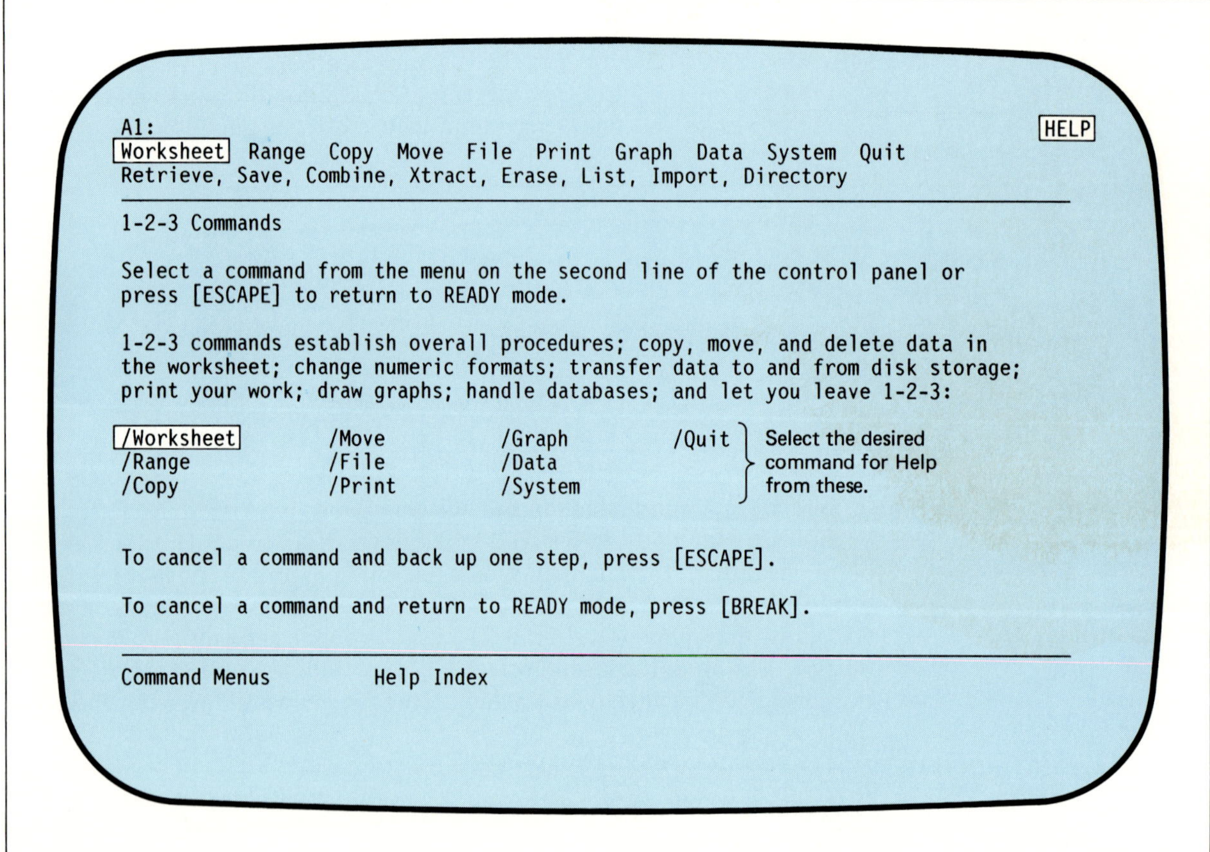

Figure 11-20
Command Help screen for Lotus 1-2-3.

feature, you should experiment. You cannot get into trouble while in the MENU or HELP modes; striking the Escape key one or more times will always get you back to the READY mode.

Help With Lotus 1-2-3. Striking the F1 key from the READY mode will give you an abbreviated summary of actions you can take from READY. Since we are interested in the File command, first switch to MENU mode (strike the / key), and then strike F1. This will cause your worksheet to be replaced with the general Help screen shown in Figure 11-20, which gives you a brief description of commands in general. (The Help screens of this section were obtained using Lotus 1-2-3, Version 2; the screens for Version 1A are similar.) To obtain help for any of the commands listed in the center of the screen (/Worksheet is highlighted), move the highlight to that command with the arrow keys and then strike the F1 key again. Moving it to /File and striking the F1 key again produces the File help screen shown in Figure 11-21. If you wanted information on the Save command, you would move the highlight to /Save and strike the F1 once more. Although these descriptions are useful in helping you to recall features of Lotus 1-2-3, remember that they are designed for reference rather than as learning tools. To get a feel for using the Help feature, you should experiment. You cannot get into trouble while in the MENU or HELP modes; striking the Escape key one or more times will always get you back to the READY mode.

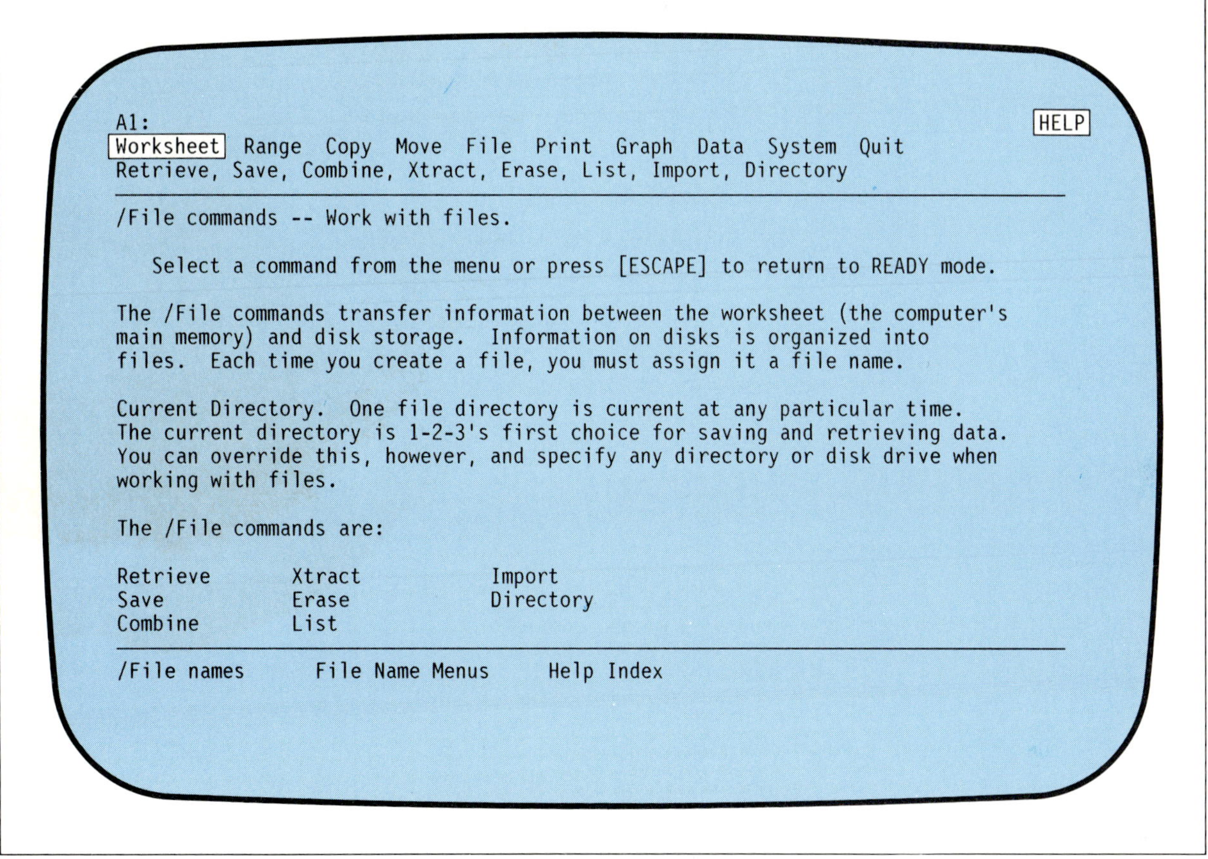
A1: HELP
Worksheet Range Copy Move File Print Graph Data System Quit
Retrieve, Save, Combine, Xtract, Erase, List, Import, Directory

/File commands -- Work with files.

Select a command from the menu or press [ESCAPE] to return to READY mode.

The /File commands transfer information between the worksheet (the computer's main memory) and disk storage. Information on disks is organized into files. Each time you create a file, you must assign it a file name.

Current Directory. One file directory is current at any particular time. The current directory is 1-2-3's first choice for saving and retrieving data. You can override this, however, and specify any directory or disk drive when working with files.

The /File commands are:

Retrieve Xtract Import
Save Erase Directory
Combine List

/File names File Name Menus Help Index

Figure 11-21
The File Help screen for Lotus 1-2-3.

PRINTING A WORKSHEET

About Printed Output

The final action that we will consider in this chapter is printing your worksheet. When printed from 1-2-3, the printed page is the same as the worksheet portion of the screen display (row numbers and column letters are not printed). Your first thought about the Print command is probably that the output goes directly to the printer. Actually, 1-2-3 allows you to send the output either to the printer or to a file on disk in a standard text file (ASCII) format. At first thought, sending the "printed" output to disk might seem a little strange. However, there are several reasons for doing this. One is that the worksheet file in this form can be incorporated into a word processing document. For instance, a worksheet summary of projected sales might be included as part of a letter to sales representatives intended to spark their enthusiasm for emphasizing the products of MCT Enterprises.

As you will see, 1-2-3 allows you to print the entire worksheet or a portion of it. You also have other options, such as inserting special information just for the printout and defining word processing types of options. However, for this example, you will simply print the entire worksheet. In doing so, you must deal with the concept of cell range, a topic discussed in great detail in the next chapter.

Using the Print Command

If you do not have the cost analysis worksheet on your screen, you should retrieve it so you can carry out the following steps.

DO THIS NOW 11-14 **Printing the Worksheet.**

1. Strike the / key to switch to MENU mode.
2. Strike the letter P for Print. This causes a submenu to appear, which gives you the option of sending the output to the printer or to a file.
3. Strike the letter P for Printer output. This produces a menu of several options for controlling the printing.
4. Strike the letter R for the Range to print (that is, the portion of the displayed worksheet that you want printed).
5. Move the cell pointer to cell A1 if it is not already there; the second line of the control panel should say:

    `Enter print range: A1`

6. Strike the period key (.) to set the beginning of the range of cells to be printed; the second line of the control panel will now say:

    `Enter print range: A1..A1`

7. Successively strike the Down arrow key and then the Right arrow key until the entire worksheet is highlighted (rows 1 through 7 and columns A through G), as shown in Figure 11-22. (This is the

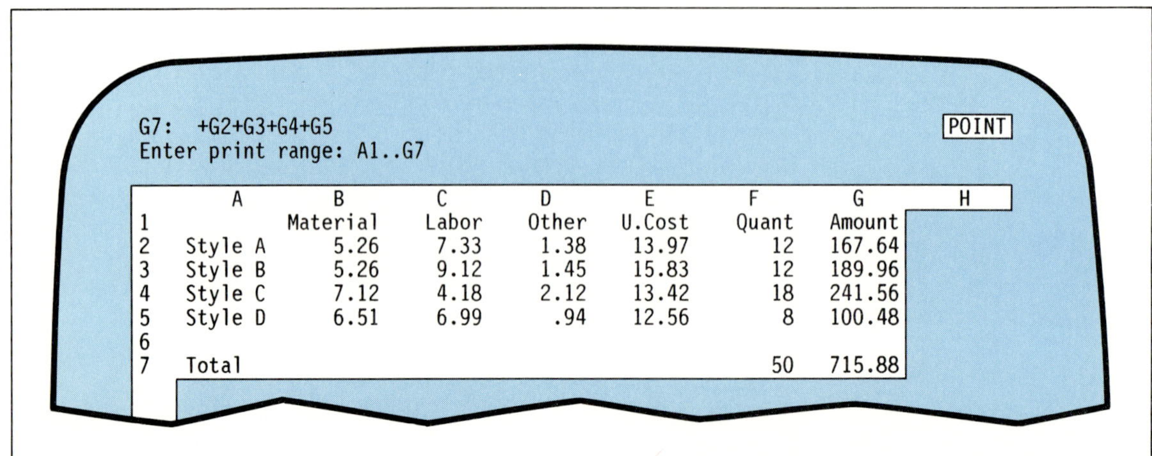

Figure 11-22
The selected print range.

display for 1-2-3; the display for JOE is identical except that the borders are different.) Notice that as you move the cell pointer, the size of the highlighted area is increased. If this does not happen, you have done something wrong and you must try again. Strike the Escape key; the sequence will back up one step for each time the Escape key is struck.

8. To record this range, strike the Enter key and control will be returned to the printer submenu.

9. Check your printer to make certain that it is turned on and ready. Strike the letter G (for Go to printing) and your worksheet will be printed.

10. When the printing is completed, strike the letter Q for Quit and control is returned to the READY mode.

Your printed output will look exactly like the worksheet area of your screen. You can now proceed with other worksheet activities or terminate your session.

SUMMARY

This chapter has provided you the basic tools for using 1-2-3. Through the cost analysis worksheet, you have learned how to create a worksheet consisting of labels, numbers, and formulas; to change the data values in using the worksheet as a tool to achieve an objective; to save the worksheet to disk; and to print a copy of the worksheet on the printer. Summarizing, the important items from the chapter are:

- The 1-2-3 display screen comprises four components: worksheet area, cell address border, control panel, and information line.
- The cell pointer identifies the current cell; this is the cell into which keyboard entries are made.
- The control panel is the center of many of the 1-2-3 activities. Information displayed by the control panel includes the cell address of the current cell, the contents of the current cell, the mode indicator, and command menus.
- The mode indicator tells you the current operating mode of 1-2-3. The principal modes under which you have operated in this chapter are:
  - READY Default mode
  - MENU For execution of commands
  - LABEL Allows entry of labels into cells
  - VALUE Allows entry of numbers and formulas into cells

- The MENU mode (for entry of commands) is activated by striking the / key.
- Saving a worksheet to disk and retrieving one from disk are done with the File command.
- A 1-2-3 work session should be terminated with the Quit command. This returns control of the computer to DOS.
- The cell pointer can be moved a cell at a time, or a screen at a time, or to the beginning or ending of your worksheet.
- Entry of information into a cell is done from the READY mode. The first keystroke signals to 1-2-3 the type of entry (label or value).
- Formulas are constructed by relating cell contents and numbers by the arithmetic operations:

  Raising to a power

  Multiplication and division

  Addition and subtraction
- The preceding arithmetic operations are listed in the order that calculations are carried out when evaluating a formula. This is called the precedence of operations.
- The Edit command, invoked with the F2 function key, allows you to edit the contents of the current cell.
- By striking the F1 key from any point in 1-2-3, you can display a Help screen, which is a written description of a command or concept.
- The Print command, which is executed from the MENU mode (strike / key), allows you to print all or part of the worksheet on the screen. The worksheet can be directed to either a printer or a disk for later printing or inclusion in a word processing document.

NEW TERMINOLOGY

Many of the spreadsheet terms introduced in Chapter 10 are used in this chapter. The following are additional new terms; you should be familiar with each of them.

arithmetic operator
cell address border
cell pointer
control panel
current cell
help screen
mode indicator
operator
precedence
scroll

REVIEW QUESTIONS

1. What is the control panel and what information does it contain?
2. How many rows and columns are visible on the screen?
3. How would you refer to the cell in the third row and sixth column?
4. What is the purpose of setting the default data drive to B?
5. Why is it important to save a worksheet at intervals while working on it rather than waiting until it is all finished?
6. You have just turned on the computer and brought 1-2-3 up. You enter the sequence /FR. What will you see on the screen?
7. What is meant by scrolling a worksheet?
8. The following labels are to be entered into a worksheet with positioning as indicated. In each case, which key should be struck first?

   a. March (centered)
   b. Points (right aligned)
   c. Summer (left aligned)
   d. -TITLE- (left aligned)

9. As you type the first few digits of a number, you realize that the cell pointer is at the wrong cell. How do you cancel this action?
10. After entering a number into a cell, you realize that it is the wrong value. How can you correct the contents of the cell?
11. To enter the formula into cell E2 of Figure 11-12, a user carries out the following sequence of steps.

    a. Move the cell pointer to cell E2.
    b. Key in the formula B2+C2+D2.
    c. Press the Up key to enter the formula.

    What is wrong with this sequence and what would happen?

12. A user gets carried away and enters the following formula into cell E2 of Figure 11-12. What is wrong and what do you think will happen?

    ```
    +A2+B2+C2+D2
    ```

13. Assume that the contents of cells are as follows:

    A1 = 6, A2 = 14, A3 = -5, A4 = 20

    What value will be stored in A6 as a result of each of the following formulas?

    a. A2–A3+A4
    b. A4–A1*A2
    c. A4+A1–A2/2
    d. (A4+A1–A2)/2

14. What action is necessary to get to the EDIT mode in order to edit a formula?

15. Of the three types of cell entries (labels, numbers, and formulas), which can be edited using the edit function?
16. What action is required to place 1-2-3 in the MENU mode.
17. What happens when the F1 function key is struck?

MATCHING

Match each term in a to h with the most appropriate description in 1 through 8.

a. READY mode
b. precedence of operations
c. Help
d. control panel
e. VALUE mode
f. LABEL mode
g. cell pointer
h. MENU mode

1. Striking the letter E while 1-2-3 is in the READY mode causes this.
2. Results from striking the F1 function key.
3. Allows you to enter commands.
4. Important when constructing formulas.
5. Necessary in order to move the cell pointer with the arrow keys.
6. Identifies the current cell.
7. From this, it is possible to enter a number or a formula into a cell.
8. Includes the mode indicator.

TRUE/FALSE

Determine whether each of the following is true or false.

______ **1.** The cell pointer must first be positioned at the cell into which a keyboard entry is to be made before the entry is typed in.

______ **2.** If the program is in VALUE mode, striking the / key causes it to switch to MENU mode.

______ **3.** Saving a worksheet to disk is done through the File command.

______ **4.** The Ctrl-Right key sequence entered from any of the operating modes will cause the display to scroll right 8 columns.

______ **5.** The positioning of a label within the screen cell is determined by the first key struck when entering the label.

______ **6.** Both numbers and formulas are entered from the VALUE mode.

______ **7.** To enter

++++

into a cell as a label would require more than four keystrokes.

______ **8.** If a cell is included in a formula, then the only type of entry that can be made into that cell is a number.

______ **9.** The precedence rule defines the order in which the user enters labels, numbers, and formulas into the worksheet.

______ **10.** If you were in the LABEL mode and struck the Escape (Esc) more than one time, execution of the spreadsheet program would be terminated and control returned to DOS.

______ **11.** If the contents of cells B3, B4, and B5 were 24, 16, and 8, respectively, then the following formula would give a value of 19.

```
B4+B3/B5
```

______ **12.** Both parentheses and spaces can be used in 1-2-3 formulas to make them more easily understandable.

______ **13.** From the EDIT mode, which is invoked with the F2 key, it is possible to edit the contents of the current cell whether a label, number, or formula.

______ **14.** From the MENU mode, a command can be invoked either by typing the first letter of the command name or by moving the highlight to that command and striking Enter.

______ **15.** One shortcoming of the Print command is that it is not possible to print only a part of the worksheet displayed on the screen.

ANSWERS TO OBJECTIVE QUESTIONS

Matching

1. f 2. c 3. h 4.b 5. a 6. g 7. e 8. d

True/False

1. T 2. F 3. T 4. F 5. T 6. T 7. T 8. F 9. F
10. F 11. T 12. F 13. T 14. T 15. F

ASSIGNMENTS/PROJECTS

1. This assignment involves making changes to the cost analysis worksheet, so you should make a copy and work on the copy. You must add Style E to row 6. Data for this style must be:

Labor cost: 5.88

Other cost: 1.04

Quantity: 10

Material cost for Styles B, C, D, and E are to be based on the Material cost for Style A as follows:

Style B Equal to that of Style A

Style C Equal to 1.22 times that of Style A

Style D	Equal to 1.09 times that of Style A
Style E	Equal to 0.94 times that of Style A

2. In planning for a school year, a student creates the quarterly budget worksheet shown in Figure 11-23. Based on the descriptions of the labels and the values displayed, the formulas should be evident. For this assignment, you are to enter this as a 1-2-3 worksheet with appropriate formulas for the two Total lines and the Balance line. When you have completed it, print a copy. Notice that due to the auto insurance in the fall quarter, the expenses exceed the income. The insurance company will allow this to be paid in two $435 installments (fall and spring), or four quarterly installments of $237. Make these changes to determine the effect on the Balance line.

Figure 11-23
Budget worksheet for Assignment 2.

	Fall	Winter	Spring	Summer
Income				
Job	400	400	400	2000
Grant	400	400	400	0
Parents	150	0	200	0
Total	950	800	1000	2000
Expenses				
Auto ins.	800	0	0	0
Auto exp.	200	200	200	300
Tuition	300	300	300	0
Books	100	120	120	0
Misc.	150	300	200	400
Total	1550	920	820	700
Balance	-600	-720	-540	760

Fall Income Total – Fall Expenses Total

Fall Balance + (Winter Income Total – Winter Expenses Total)

3. You decide to create a payroll worksheet for the employees of MCT Enterprises. Entries in the respective columns are to be as follows:

Column	Information
A	Employee last name (assume names no more than 9 characters)
B	Hours worked
C	Pay rate
D	Total deductions
E	Formula: Pay = Hours times Rate minus Deductions

The data to be entered is the following.

Name	Hours	Rate	Deductions
Finch	40	9.60	26.15
Baker	36	8.50	31.07
Zener	44	8.00	33.28
Sparks	40	11.35	44.57
Olson	48	9.60	43.98
Peters	20	9.60	13.84
Ito	40	8.50	27.77
Mier	37	9.60	21.89

Rows 1 and 2 should be used for descriptive headings; leave row 3 blank and enter data beginning with row 4. Directly under the Hours column (column B), enter a formula to calculate the total hours worked by all employees so that this number will be displayed directly under the hours worked by the last employee.

Chapter 12

More on Lotus 1-2-3 and Joe Spreadsheet

OBJECTIVES

From Chapter 11 you learned how perform some of the basic spreadsheet operations described in the general descriptions of Chapter 10. In this chapter, you will learn how to use the other features of spreadsheet software described in Chapter 10. When you have completed this chapter, you should be able to:

- Insert new rows or columns into a worksheet with the Worksheet Insert command sequence.
- Change the default column width from 9 to any needed value. Also, change the width of selected columns.
- Copy the contents of one or more cells from one place in the worksheet to another, and recognize the effect on formulas of the copy operation.
- Format the display of cells displaying numeric quantities defining the number of decimal places to be displayed, and include punctuation such as commas and dollar signs.
- Erase the contents of a group of cells.
- Move the contents of a group of cells from one place in the worksheet to another.
- Use functions to compute the sum and average and to determine the largest and smallest values from a group of cells.
- Use relational operators that allow you to compare the values in different cells and display results based on such comparisons.

- Prepare a worksheet so that it can be incorporated into a word processing document.

These concepts will be introduced with an expansion of the cost analysis worksheet, an employee retraining progress worksheet, and a sales summary worksheet.

PREVIEW

A Task and the Needed Tools

The expansion of the cost analysis worksheet will include adding more information. This includes adding 2 columns so that the cost breakdown can be expanded from three cost components to five. Column widths are also changed and formatting of displayed cell contents added.

Changing the Size of Your Worksheet

The worksheet size can be increased by inserting blank rows or columns at any place in the worksheet using the Worksheet Insert command. The size also can be decreased by deleting rows or columns.

Changing Column Widths

The default cell display width is 9 columns. You can reset the default width as needed with the Worksheet command. You can also set the widths of individual columns. This gives you the capability to set column widths to display your worksheet entries better.

Correcting a Formula and Copying It

With the addition of two new cost components, the Unit Cost formula must be edited. The Copy command allows you to duplicate it into other cells without retyping it for each one.

Formatting Displayed Values

Formatting allows you to control the appearance of numeric values in the display. Using the Format command, it is possible to include such punctuation as decimal points, commas, and dollar signs.

Other Commands

There are two commands not illustrated by the cost analysis worksheet: Erase and Move. With the Erase command, you can erase the contents of cells. With the Move command, you can move the contents of a group of cells from one place in the worksheet to another.

Basic Principles of Functions

A function is a predefined procedure for performing a particular operation. Some of the functions used in this section perform the following actions on a group of cells: summing the values, counting the number of nonempty entries, calculating the average, and finding the smallest and largest values.

Conditional Operations Using Functions

Relational operators in 1-2-3 allow you to compare quantities and define actions to be taken depending upon the results of the comparison.

Absolute Cell Addresses in Formulas

When copying a formula from one cell to another, 1-2-3 automatically adjusts the cell address references of the formula to conform to the new location. In some instances, this is not desirable. Absolute cell addressing allows you to specify certain cell addresses as being fixed.

Combining a Worksheet with a Word Processing Document

You can send the printed output of a worksheet (or portion of a worksheet) either to the printer or to a disk file. Once it is stored on disk, you can insert the worksheet into a word processing document.

A TASK AND THE NEEDED TOOLS

Problem Definition

In the preceding chapter, you used the File command to save and retrieve worksheet files. In addition to these basic operations, commands give you the capability to change a worksheet to adjust to your changing needs. This ability is essential because, when you use a worksheet to analyze a problem, the process of setting it up and experimenting with values provides more insight into the nature of the problem. As you perform "what if" studies with a worksheet, you will find that often subtle (and sometimes major) modifications will make it more effective. Such changes can include expanding the worksheet to include additional data or more calculations, and deleting unneeded portions.

Assume that this has happened to you with the cost analysis worksheet. In order to pinpoint costs more precisely, you have broken labor costs down into two components: labor costs and contracted services. Furthermore, you have separated overhead costs from the other costs. Also, you have decided to improve the appearance of your worksheet. Its final form is shown in Figure 12-1.

To convert your original COST worksheet to this form will require that you know how to do the following.

- Insert empty rows and columns into a worksheet. Three blank rows

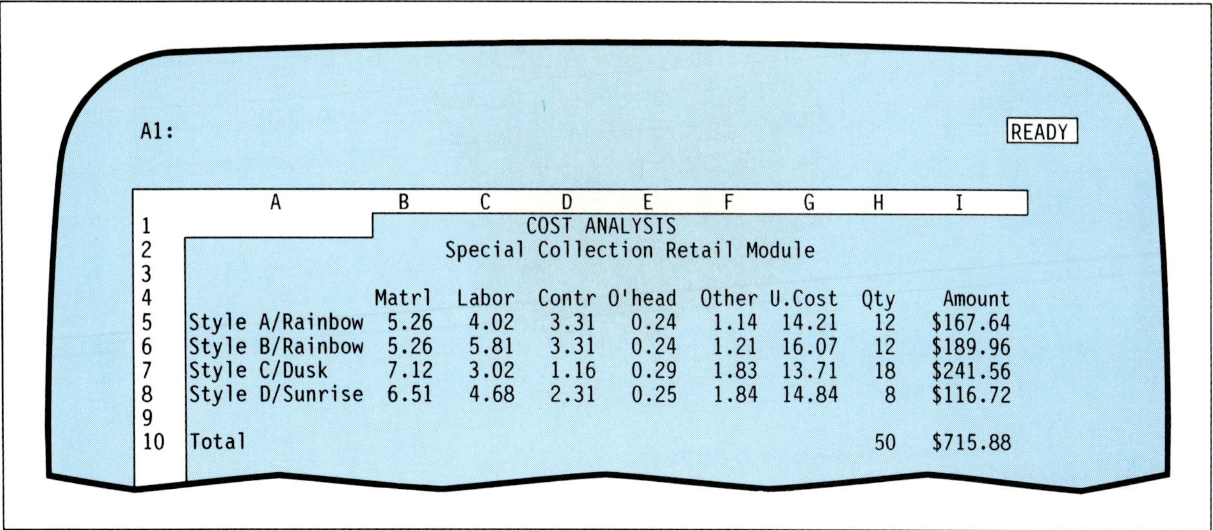

A1: READY

	A	B	C	D	E	F	G	H	I
1				COST ANALYSIS					
2			Special Collection Retail Module						
3									
4		Matrl	Labor	Contr	O'head	Other	U.Cost	Qty	Amount
5	Style A/Rainbow	5.26	4.02	3.31	0.24	1.14	14.21	12	$167.64
6	Style B/Rainbow	5.26	5.81	3.31	0.24	1.21	16.07	12	$189.96
7	Style C/Dusk	7.12	3.02	1.16	0.29	1.83	13.71	18	$241.56
8	Style D/Sunrise	6.51	4.68	2.31	0.25	1.84	14.84	8	$116.72
9									
10	Total							50	$715.88

Figure 12-1
The expanded cost analysis worksheet.

must be inserted at the top of the worksheet for the headings, and 2 blank columns must be inserted for the additional cost components.

- Change column width. Column A must be made wider to accommodate the wider headings. Also, the width of other columns is reduced in order to conveniently display the entire worksheet on the screen without scrolling. Notice that Figure 12-1 displays 9 columns.
- Include format descriptions for the display of values. The amount column includes the $ symbol. Also, all dollar and cent amounts are printed with two digits to the right of the decimal point even if the digits are 0.
- Copy the contents of a cell into other cells. A new formula entered into cell G5 will be copied into cells G6, G7, and G8.

Command Nomenclature

To save your worksheet file in Chapter 11, your sequence of keystrokes was:

/ To switch to MENU mode.

F To invoke the File command from the main command menu.

S To invoke the Save command from the File submenu.

Example descriptions in this chapter detail your step-by-step actions in performing the necessary steps. However, all key sequence actions will be summarized in a concise form. For instance, the preceding sequence of command invoking keystrokes will be represented as:

/FS

As each command is first introduced, the following form will also be used.

/ **File Save**

Note that only the first letter of each command is printed in boldface; these are the only letters to be keyed in to select the command. Since striking the first command letter (F in this case) leads to a submenu in which another option is to be selected, you may wish to inspect each level of the menu as you enter the sequence.

Your sequence of keystrokes in saving also included typing the filename and striking the Enter key. The complete sequence will be indicated as:

```
/FS filename {Enter}
```

where *filename* means that you must type the name to be used for the file and {Enter} means to strike the Enter key.

Ranges of Cells

When you printed your worksheet in Chapter 11, you had to designate the group of cells, or **range,** to be printed. Many 1-2-3 commands operate on a range of cells (this includes commands for column width change, format, and copy that are required to achieve Figure 12-1). A range is any rectangular portion of a worksheet, as illustrated by Figure 12-2. Not only can a range comprise many columns or rows, but it can also consist of a portion of a single column or row. Technically, even the current cell is a range. You may think that a single cell does not fit the definition of a *range of cells.* However, we must be able to designate a cell as a range because many range commands operate on single cells. The key notion is that a range can only be a *rectangular* collection of cells.

To that end, a range can be pinpointed exactly by two cells located at the corners (at opposite ends of the diagonal), as illustrated in Figure 12-3. In this case, the range is specified by the upper left cell, B2, and the

Figure 12-2
Worksheet ranges.

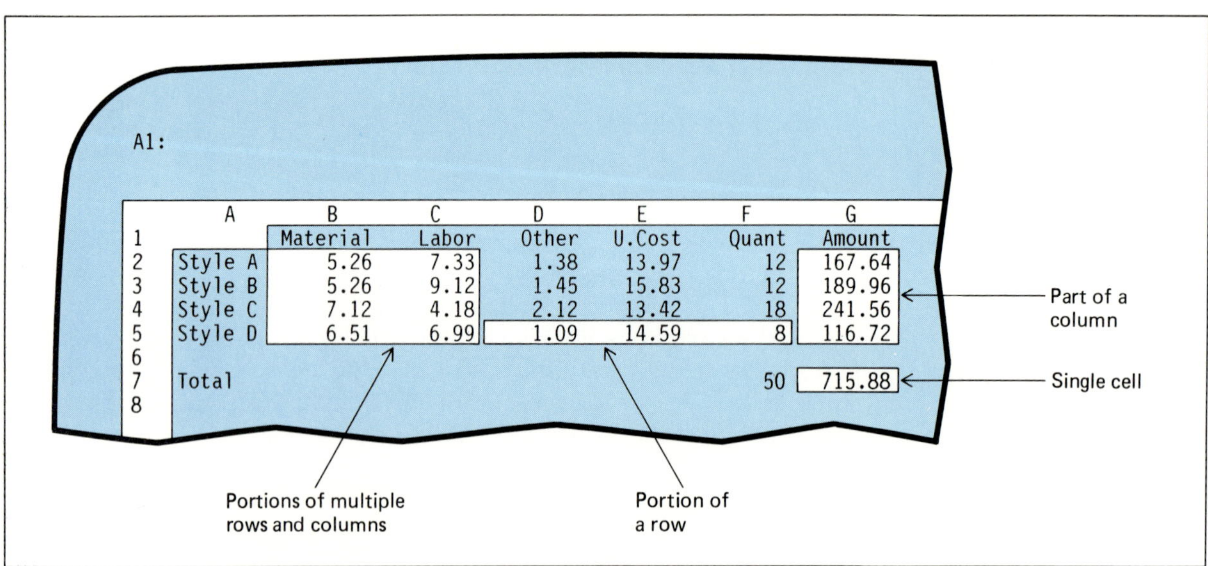

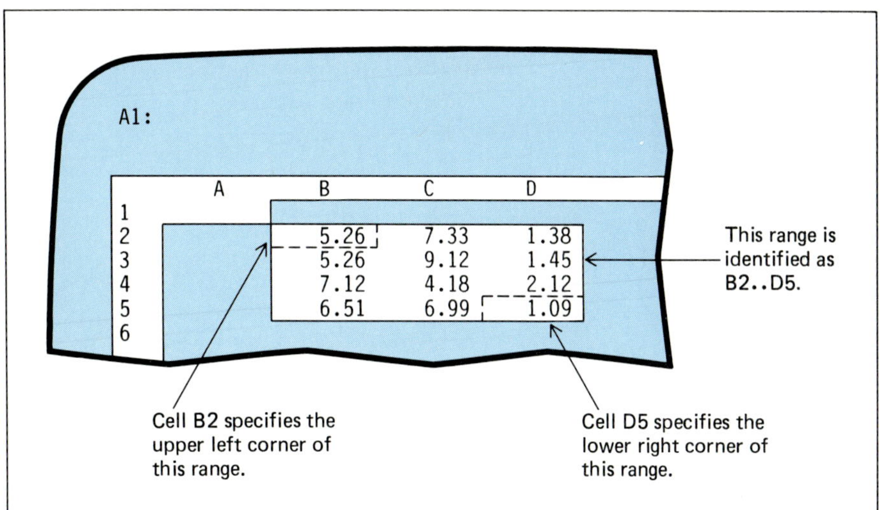

Figure 12-3
Specifying a range by cell addresses.

lower-right cell, D5. The standard method for identifying a range is by the upper-left cell address, followed by two periods, followed by the lower-right cell address, as in Figure 12-3. The sample ranges of Figure 12-2 are:

B2..C5	Rectangular area consisting of columns B and C and rows 2 through 5.
D5..F5	A portion of row 5.
G2..G5	A portion of column G.
G7..G7	The single cell, G7.

CHANGING THE SIZE OF YOUR WORKSHEET

The Insert Command: Inserting Rows

All spreadsheet programs allow the user to open up new (blank) rows or columns anywhere in the worksheet. Existing cell entries are not disturbed other than being moved either down or to the right. To modify your worksheet to the form in Figure 12-1, you must insert 3 new rows and 2 new columns. Let us first insert the 3 blank rows. Since you will be working with the original cost analysis worksheet, you should retrieve either your copy that you saved as COST or the copy COSTAN.WKS included on the data disk. Then proceed with the following.

DO THIS NOW 12-1 **Inserting 3 Blank Rows**

1. Position the cell pointer at cell A1 (for row insertion, it can be anywhere in the first row).
2. Switch to the command mode by striking the / key.

3. Strike the W key for the Worksheet command; this will produce the following Worksheet submenu.

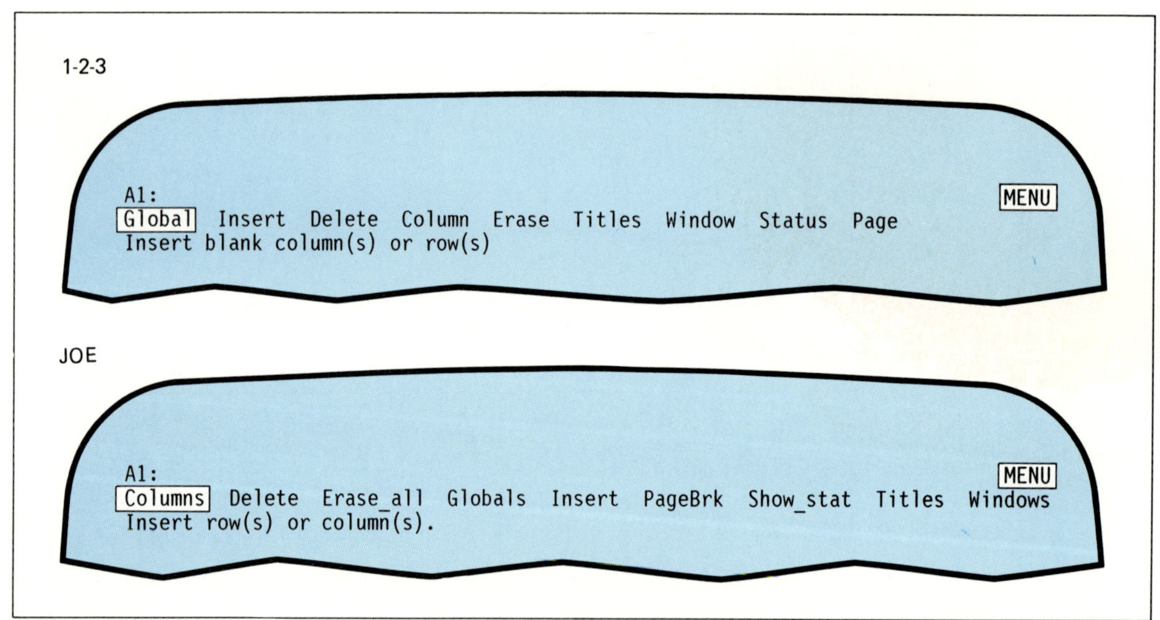

4. You want the Insert command so strike the letter I (or move the highlight to Insert and strike Enter); you will be given your choice of inserting columns or rows.

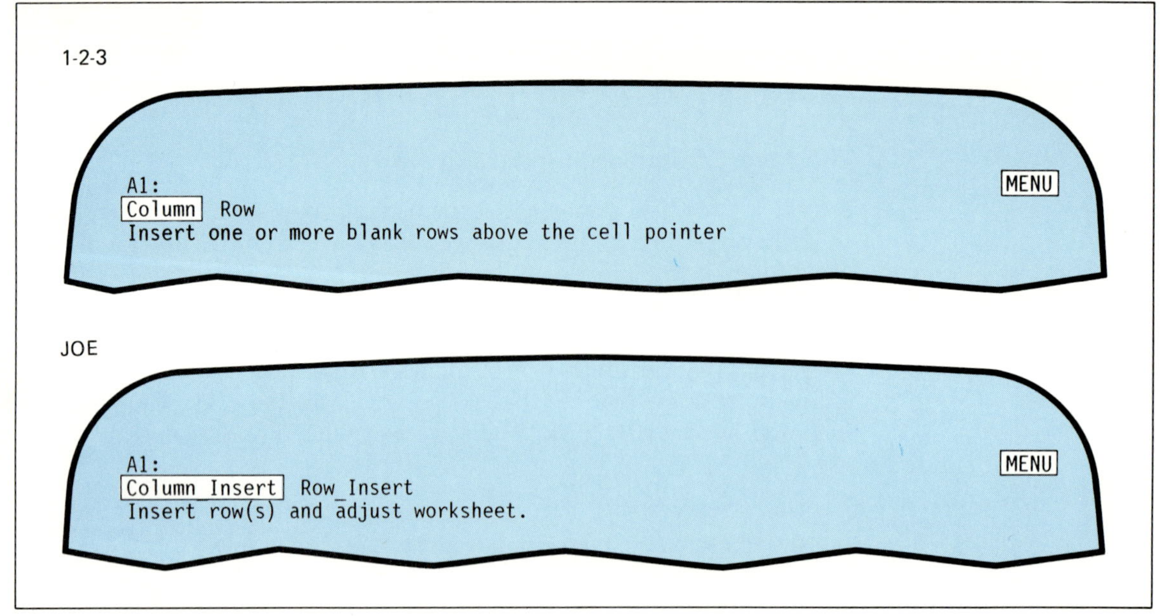

Strike the letter R for Row; your control panel will change to:

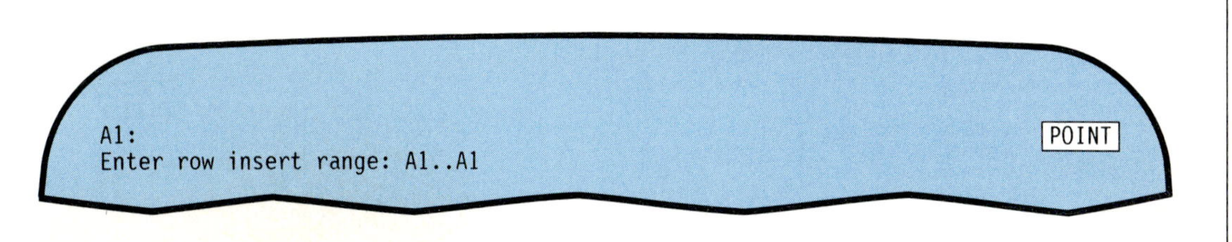

The current range of rows into which blank rows will be inserted is the current cell, or A1..A1.

6. Strike the Down key twice to define the range A1..A3, as shown in the following.

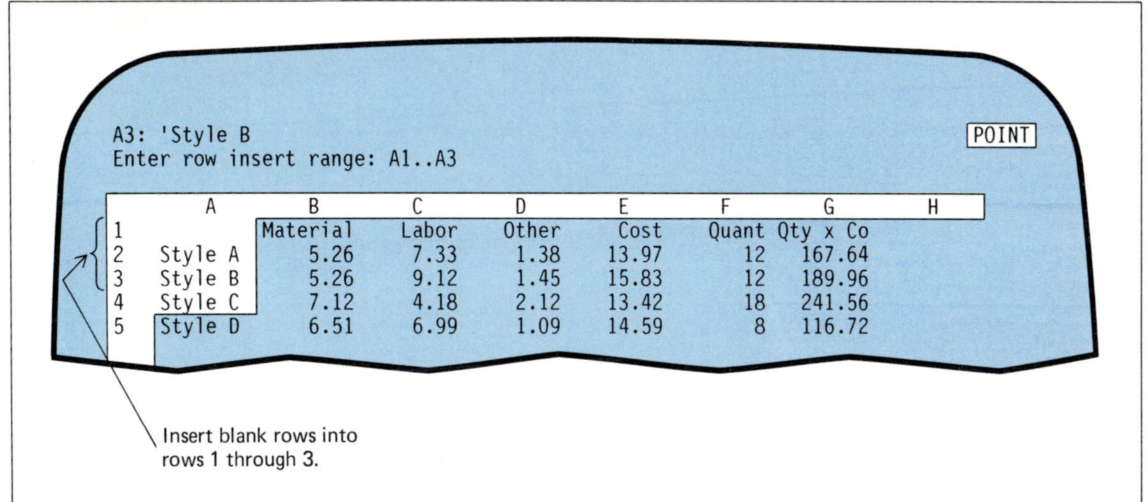

This range specifies that new rows are to be inserted from row 1 through row 3. Note that it is possible to move the cell pointer to the right; for instance, the selected range could be A1..D3. Additional columns in the range have no affect on the insert operation.

7. Strike Enter to carry out the insertion operation. The resulting worksheet is shown in Figure 12-4.

Summarizing, the keystroke sequence necessary to insert these three blank rows is as follows:

```
/WIR {Down} {Down} {Enter}
```

The command sequence is:

```
/ Worksheet Insert Row            (Lotus 1-2-3)
/ WorkSet Insert Row_Insert       (JOE)
```

Although this example involves inserting rows at the top of the worksheet, row insertion is not so restricted. That is, rows can be inserted anywhere in the worksheet.

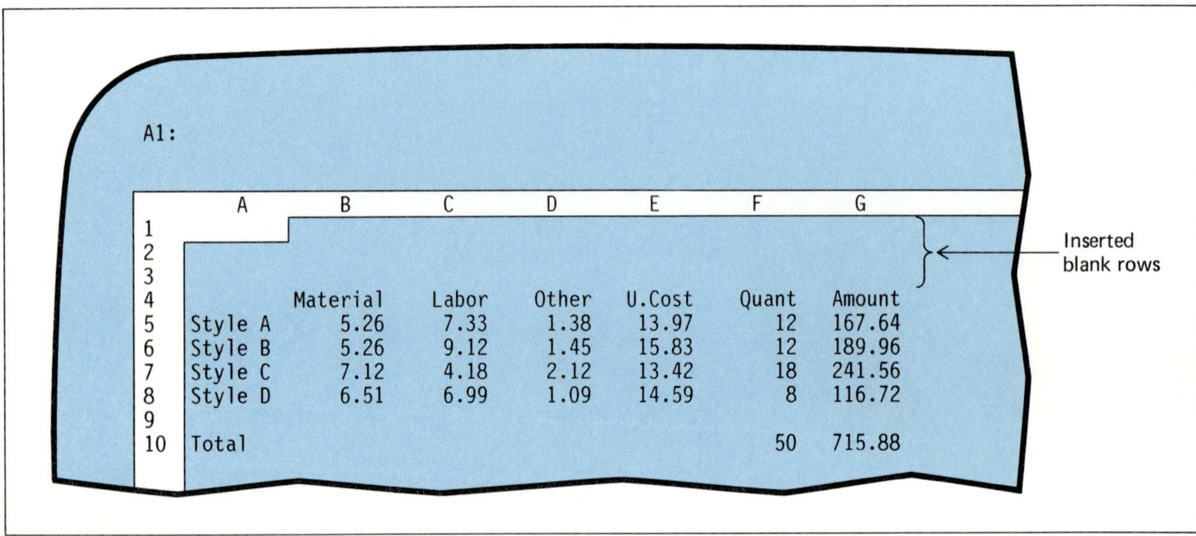

A1:

	A	B	C	D	E	F	G
1							
2							
3							
4		Material	Labor	Other	U.Cost	Quant	Amount
5	Style A	5.26	7.33	1.38	13.97	12	167.64
6	Style B	5.26	9.12	1.45	15.83	12	189.96
7	Style C	7.12	4.18	2.12	13.42	18	241.56
8	Style D	6.51	6.99	1.09	14.59	8	116.72
9							
10	Total					50	715.88

Figure 12-4
The inserted blank rows.

The Insert Command: Inserting Columns

The next step in modifying this worksheet is to insert 2 additional columns for the further breakdown of cost components. The column insertion procedure is almost identical to that for inserting rows.

DO THIS NOW 12-2 **Inserting 2 Blank Columns Into Columns D and E**

1. Position the cell pointer at cell D1 (actually, any cell in column D will be adequate).
2. Enter the following keystroke sequence.

   /WIC {Right} {Enter}

   The control panel sequence will be similar to that of DTN 12-1. If you wish to observe the changing control panel, pause after each keystroke. The cell range in the last step will be D1..E1.

At this point, the previous contents of column D (the Other cost) and everything to the right have been moved 2 columns to the right, leaving columns D and E blank as shown in Figure 12-5. Notice that the Amount column is now scrolled off the right edge of the screen.

The Effect of Row Insertion on Formulas

Before continuing with the modification of your worksheet, let us consider the effect of row and column insertions on the formulas. For example, remember that the Unit Cost for Style A previously stored in cell E2 was computed with the formula:

+B2+C2+D2

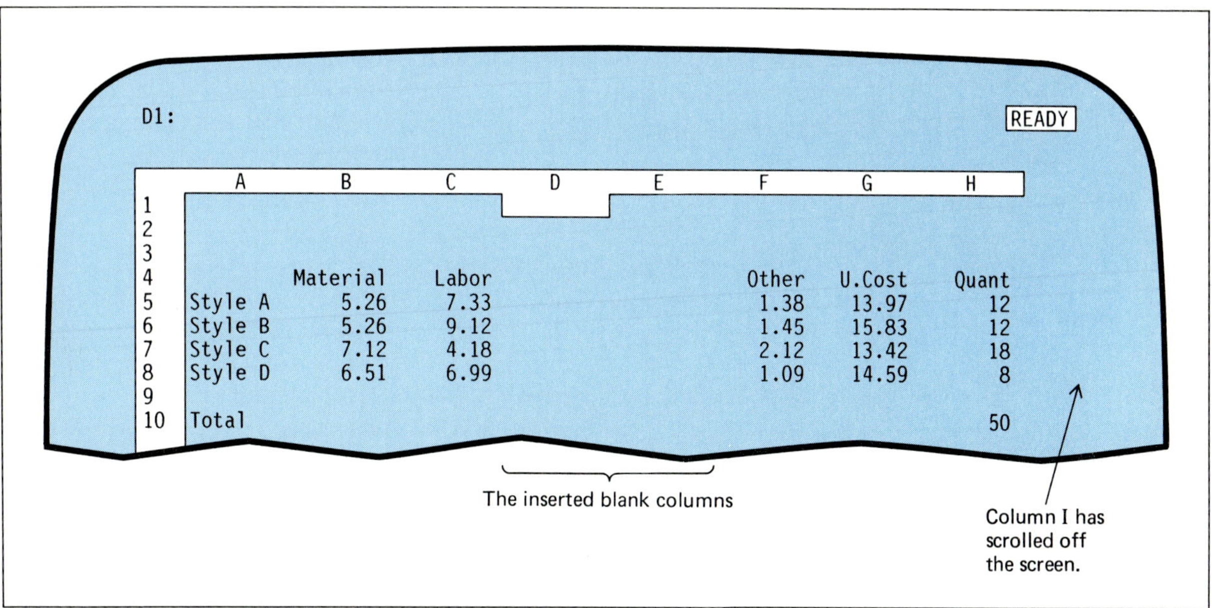

Figure 12-5
The inserted blank rows and columns.

Since this item is now in cell G5, move your cell pointer to that cell and you will see the following formula displayed in the first line of the control panel.

```
+B5+C5+F5
```

Notice that 1-2-3 has adjusted the cell addresses of this formula consistent with the repositioning of the data cells resulting from the insertions. Also note that the cell addresses D5 and E5 (which will be required in the new form) are not inserted automatically into this formula.

Entering Data Into the New Rows and Columns

You can now proceed to make the necessary changes and entries to the labels and numbers so that your worksheet will have the same values as those in Figure 12-1.

DO THIS NOW 12-3 **Entering New Labels and Numbers**

1. For the descriptions in column A, use the EDIT mode and it will not be necessary to retype. For instance, position the cursor on cell A5, strike the F2 key, type "/Rainbow", and then strike Enter.
2. Position the cell pointer at cell D1 and enter the label COST ANALYSIS. Then enter the label Special Collection Retail Module into cell C2.
3. Change the column headings in row 5 so that they are the same as those in Figure 12-1. Shorter headings will be necessary when the column width is decreased.

4. Enter the new data values and change others that need changing. When you make the entries into columns D and E, you will notice that the Unit Cost does *not* change. Remember, that these cells are not yet included in the Unit Cost formulas. You will change these later.

When you entered the titles in the first 2 rows, you may have been surprised that the entire labels (which are longer than the cell width of 9) were displayed on the screen. Recall from Chapter 10 that a distinction was made between the screen cell and the cell in memory. Although each screen cell has a default size of 9 positions, each memory cell can hold up to 240 characters. Just as the screen provides us with a view of a portion of the worksheet in memory, so does the screen cell provide us with a view of the contents of a memory cell. On your screen (as in Figure 12-1), you see that 1-2-3 uses additional cells to the right for displaying long labels (if those cells are not used for something else). Even though the label in row 2 is stored in memory cell C2, its screen display spills over into cells D2, E2, and F2.

Before proceeding further, you should save this version of the worksheet; use the name COST3.

Deleting Rows or Columns

Sometimes, in reorganizing a worksheet, you will need to eliminate rows or columns. You do this with the Delete command, which is the opposite of the Insert. Note that this command does *not* simply erase the contents of cells; it eliminates rows or columns and moves those that follow up (or to the left). In other words, it is the opposite of the Insert command. Although the modification necessary to expand your cost analysis worksheet to that of Figure 12-1 does not require deletion, you should try the command so that you will be familiar with it. For the deletion exercise, you will be using the worksheet that you have been modifying, *so be certain that you have saved it to disk.*

DO THIS NOW 12-4 **Deleting Rows 6 and 7 of the Figure 12-5 Worksheet.**

1. Position the cell pointer in cell A6 (actually, anywhere in row 6 is acceptable).
2. Enter the following command sequence:

```
/WDR
```

That is:

```
/ Worksheet Delete Row              (Lotus 1-2-3)
/ WorkSet Delete Row_Delete         (JOE)
```

3. Strike the Down key one time to define the range A6..A7. These are the rows to be deleted.

4. Strike Enter to carry out the delete operation. The selected range will be deleted and the previous contents of rows 8 and 10 will be moved up.

When the action has been completed, notice that cell H8 (the total of the cells above it) now displays the letters ERR. If you move the cell pointer to this cell, the formula displayed in the control panel will be:

```
+H5+ERR+ERR+H6
```

Since elements from the 2 deleted rows were used in this formula, 1-2-3 did not know what to do. Hence, it replaced them with the error code ERR. You can proceed to correct this formula through the EDIT mode. That is, strike the F2, and then delete them as you would any other unwanted entries in a formula. You will see that the display of cell H8 changes from ERR to the computed value.

This completes the exercise on deletion. You should now retrieve the copy of COST3 from disk. When you do so, JOE will warn you that changes have been made to the worksheet on the screen and that they will be lost. Do not save the screen version of the worksheet.

CHANGING COLUMN WIDTHS

The 9-position default column width is a good compromise for both labels and numbers. However, in many instances, it is convenient to make one or more columns wider to display longer labels or larger numbers. Also, if a worksheet is to contain numbers consisting of only a few digits, using narrower columns allows more of them to be displayed on the screen or printed on a single page. There are two ways you can change column width. One is to change the default value, which will change the screen cell width of every column in the worksheet. Any change to parameters (such as column width) that affects all elements in the worksheet is said to be **global.** The other way of changing column widths is to change individual columns one at a time. If you make a global width change after changing one or more columns, the columns that were changed will *not* be affected by the global change. If, when you change the width of a column, a displayed number is replaced with a row of * characters, then the cell width is not adequate to display the number and the width must be increased.

To better fit the data of the revised cost analysis worksheet in Figure 12-1, the column widths have been adjusted. These widths, which you will use in your copy of the worksheet, are:

Columns	Width
A	15
B..G	7
H	5
I	10

Since most of the columns will have a width of 7, let us first make the global change to 7, and then proceed with the column changes.

DO THIS NOW 12-5 **Changing Column Widths**

1. Enter the following command sequence.

```
/WGC
```

That is:

```
/ Worksheet Global Column-Width          (Lotus 1-2-3)
/ WorkSet Globals Column-Width           (JOE)
```

2. You will then see one of the following prompts.

```
Enter global column width (1..240): 9    (Lotus 1-2-3)
Default column width (1..240): 9         (JOE)
```

Enter the new value of 7 to replace the default value of 9 and strike Enter. The cell width of all cells on the screen will change to 7.

3. To change the width of column A to 15, position the cell pointer at cell A1.

4. Enter the following command sequence.

```
/WCS
```

That is:

```
/ Worksheet Column Set-Width             (Lotus 1-2-3)
/ WorkSet Columns Set_column_width       (JOE)
```

5. You will then see one of the following prompts; note that the newly defined default is now displayed.

```
Enter column width (1..240): 7    (Lotus 1-2-3)
New column width (1..240): 7      (JOE)
```

Enter the new value of 15 and strike Enter. Note that the first line of the control panel now displays [15]; this indicates that the cell width for this column has been set to 15. Move the cell pointer to A5 and you will see that the contents are displayed after this width code.

6. Repeat steps 3, 4, and 5 for column H using a cell width of 5.
7. Repeat steps 3, 4, and 5 for column I using a cell width of 10.

This completes the task of changing column width; check to ensure that all width values are set properly and that your screen display is the same as that in Figure 12-1. Correct any differences. To ensure that you do not lose this latest round of work, save your worksheet to disk.

CORRECTING A FORMULA AND COPYING IT

Editing the Formula to Sum the Cost Components

The next step in modifying this worksheet is to correct the formulas for calculating the Unit Cost. Remember, when you inserted 3 new rows and 2 new columns, 1-2-3 adjusted these formulas; for instance, that for Style A was changed to:

```
+B5+C5+F5
```

With the addition of two new cost components, the formula should be:

```
+B5+C5+D5+E5+F5
```

You can easily correct this with the Edit command.

DO THIS NOW 12-6 **Correcting the Formula in Cell G5**

1. Move the cell pointer to cell G5.
2. Strike the Edit key (F2).
3. Insert +D5+E5 into the formula and strike Enter.

The next step is to make the corresponding correction to cells G6, G7, and G8. However, rather than edit each of them, let us use the Copy command, which is specifically designed to simplify the task of entering repetitive information.

Copying the Contents of a Single Cell Into a Range of Cells

In Chapter 10, you learned that spreadsheet programs allow you to copy the contents from cells into other cells. This includes formulas as well as labels and numbers. However, when a formula is copied, the program automatically adjusts cell addresses. (In some spreadsheet software, this action is called replication.) For instance, when the formula

```
+B5+C5+D5+E5+F5
```

in cell G5 is copied to cell G6, the row numbers must be changed, producing:

```
+B6+C6+D6+E6+F6
```

In 1-2-3, this is done with the Copy command.

DO THIS NOW 12-7 **Copying the Formula in Cell G5 Into Cells G6, G7, and G8**

1. Position the cell pointer at cell G5.
2. Execute the Copy (Lotus 1-2-3) or CopyRan (JOE) command with the sequence:

   ```
   /C
   ```

   In the following control panel display, note that the prompt requests that you specify the range of cells to be copied (the FROM range). The range consisting of the single current cell appears as the default.

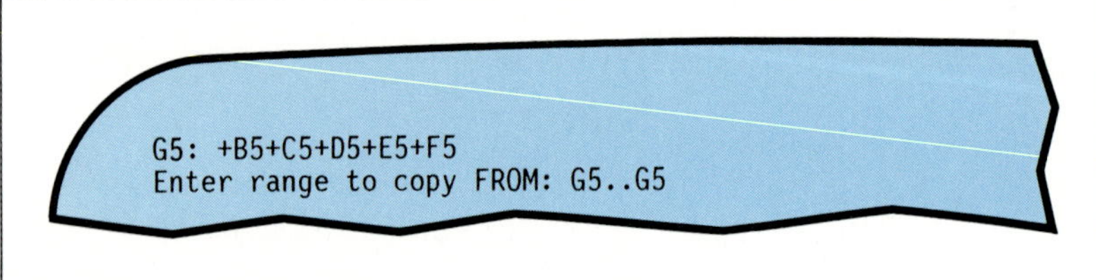

3. Because you want to copy only one cell, strike Enter. The prompt now requests the range of cells into which the FROM range (single cell, in this case) is to be duplicated.

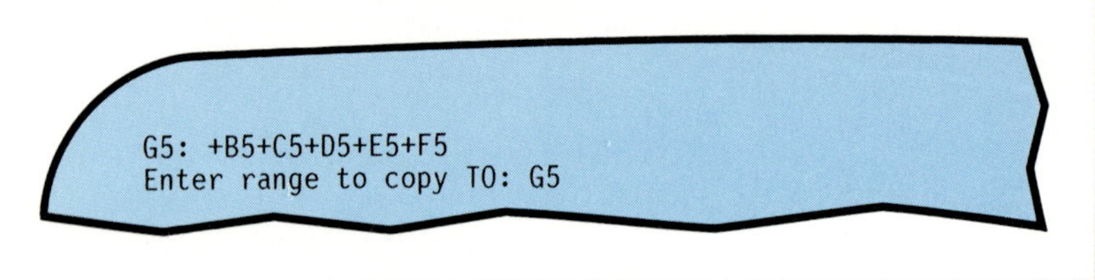

4. Move the cell pointer to the beginning of the range to which the duplication is to occur, This is called the **anchor cell** because it is the "anchor" point from which the range is to be defined. In this case, move the cell pointer to cell G6.

5. Strike the period key (.) to anchor the range.

6. Move the cell pointer to the end of the range; in this case, move it to cell G8.

7. Strike Enter to complete the command. The contents of the FROM cell (the formula in this case) will be duplicated into each cell of the TO range. These new formulas will change the values displayed for these cells. You should compare the values displayed with those of Figure 12-1 to ensure that they are correct. You might also move the cell pointer to each of these cells and inspect the new formulas.

The preceding detailed sequence of steps makes copying seem more tedious than it really is. However, when you master the steps, you will find that the actual process is quick and relatively simple.

The Copy command is not limited to copying the contents of a single cell into other cells. For instance, if for your studies, you decided to copy the range of cells B5..F8 to another portion of the worksheet, the sequence of steps would have been almost the same as the steps of DTN 12-7. The only difference would be in specifying the FROM range as B5..F8 and the TO range appropriately.

FORMATTING DISPLAYED VALUES

Displaying Numbers

In Chapter 11 (DTN 11-11), you adjusted the cost entries in attempting to bring the total price to $675. In the process, you probably noticed that the dollar and cent amounts were not always displayed with two digits to the right of the decimal point. For instance, you might have seen 4.8 instead of 4.80, or even 5 instead of 5.00. The reason for this is that the 1-2-3 default number display format prints a decimal point only if there are digits to the right of the decimal. You probably found that the displayed column of numbers in which the decimal points are not aligned is very difficult to read.

Fortunately, just as you can override the default column width, you can also override the number display format of one or more cells. To better illustrate the effect of this formatting, make the following changes to the Contractor costs of your spreadsheet

Current Value	Adjustment	New Value	Displayed
3.31	-0.31	3.00	3
3.31	-0.07	3.24	3.24
1.16	-0.26	0.90	0.9
2.31	-0.24	2.07	2.07

You should notice in your worksheet that some of the entries in the Unit Cost and Amount columns also reflect this column alignment problem now.

You can avoid this problem and control the way in which numeric data is displayed on the screen with the Format command. Following are some of the formatting options of this command.

Format	Description
General	No trailing zeros after the decimal point are displayed; very large and small numbers are displayed in scientific notation. This is the default format. Examples: 5.2 7.55 165
Fixed	A fixed number of places (0 to 15) to the right of the decimal point are displayed. Examples for three decimal places: 165.000 165.230 165.238
, (comma)	Same as fixed except commas are added between thousands and negative values are enclosed in parentheses. Fixed number of decimal places (0 to 15) must be specified. Examples for one decimal place: 3,526.1 48.0 (356.5)

Format	Description
Currency	Same as comma except that dollar sign is included.
	Examples for two places: \$2,561.00 \$1.28 (\$55.06)

The Format is a subcommand of the Range command. Entering the command sequence

/RF

that is:

/ Range Format (Lotus 1-2-3)
/ RangeOps Fmt (JOE)

produces the formatting submenu shown in Figure 12-6. Let us use these formatting capabilities to improve the appearance of your worksheet to that of Figure 12-1.

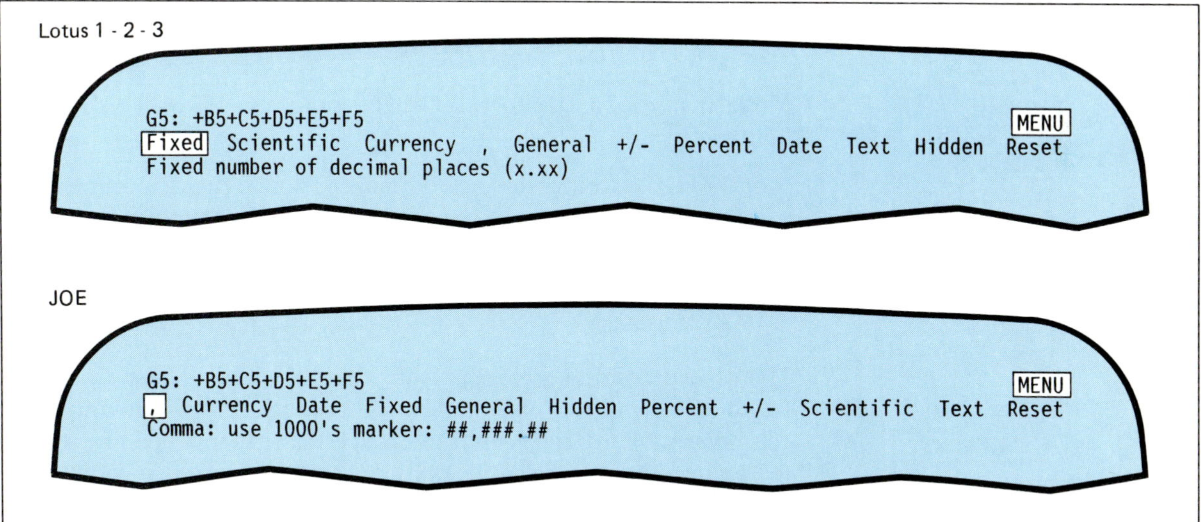

Figure 12-6
Format submenu options.

Formatting the Numeric Data of the Worksheet

Following is the formatting that you need to do for your cost analysis worksheet to complete this modification.

Cell Range	Formatting
B5..G8	Fixed with two places to the right of the decimal.
H5..H10	No formatting required; default is acceptable.
I5..I10	Currency with two places to the right of the decimal.

You should carry out the following sequence of steps to format your worksheet display.

DO THIS NOW 12-8 **Formatting the Cells Containing Value Entries**

1. Position the cell pointer at cell B5.
2. Enter the following command sequence:

   `/RFF`

   That is:

   `/ Range Format Fixed` (Lotus 1-2-3)
   `/ RangeOps Fmt Fixed` (JOE)

3. You will see the prompt:

   `Enter number of decimal places (0..15) 2`

   Note that the default value is 2. Accept this value by striking Enter.

4. You are then prompted for the range with:

   `Enter range to format: B5..B5`

   Move the cell pointer to cell G8; the range B5..G8 will be highlighted.

5. Strike Enter to complete the command. Notice that the numbers previously displayed with fewer digits to the right of the decimal point now include zeros. Also, the first line of the control panel now displays:

   `G5: (F2) 5.26`

   The code preceding the data means that this cell has been formatted to Fixed with two places to the right of the decimal. Moving the cell pointer to any cell within the range that has just been formatted will yield the same code. On the other hand, no such code will be displayed if the cell pointer is moved to column H (Qty) because it still retains the default format.

6. The next task is to format column I to currency. First, position the cell pointer at cell I5.
7. Enter the following command sequence:

   `/RFC`

   That is:

   `/ Range Format Currency` (Lotus 1-2-3)
   `/ RangeOps Fmt Currency` (JOE)

8. Repeat the sequence of steps 3, 4, and 5 using the range I5 to I10.

Your revised worksheet is now completed. If you changed the Contractor entries earlier, you should change them back to their original values. Your worksheet should appear exactly as that in Figure 12-1. If it does not, make the necessary corrections. When you are finished, save this latest version to disk.

The careful formatting of a worksheet is not a matter to be taken lightly. Obviously, unaligned columns make it difficult for even the creator of the worksheet to use it as a tool. We often set up worksheets that others will read. For instance, a summary of needs for a departmental budget will be presented to a manager; projected sales for a new product line will be prepared by an employee for presentation to the management. Each of these is to convey a message—often as part of gaining approval for pursuing a particular course of action. The more professional appearing the information presented, the more successful it will be in conveying your message.

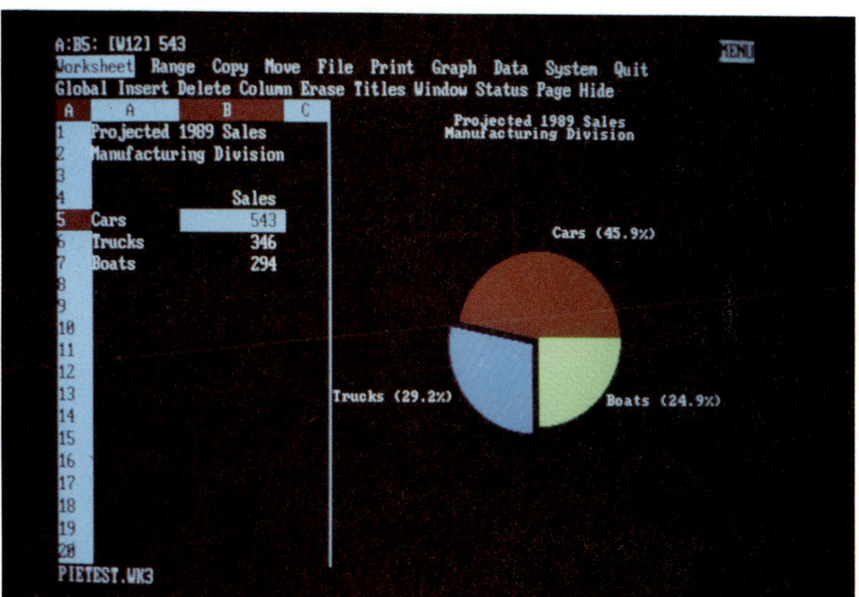

As this photo shows, the inclusion of an appropriate chart alongside your data often can convey the import of your data much more effectively than numbers alone.

OTHER COMMANDS

In addition to the preceding commands illustrated with the cost analysis example, there are a few other commands that are convenient when modifying a worksheet. These include the ability to erase part or all of the cell contents of a worksheet, and to move a range of cell contents from one place to another.

The Range Erase

The Delete command gives you the ability to delete rows and columns from a worksheet, an action that repositions remaining rows or columns.

There is also the need to erase the contents of a range of cells without disturbing the general layout. This is done with the Range Erase. To try this command, first *make certain that you have saved the final version of your revised cost analysis worksheet.* Then with the screen copy, you can use the Range Erase as follows:

DO THIS NOW 12-9 **Erasing the Contents of the Cell Range B5..F8**

1. Position the cell pointer at cell B5.
2. Enter the command sequence.

   /RE

   That is:

   / Range Erase (Lotus 1-2-3)
   / RangeOps Erase (JOE)
3. The following prompt and default will be displayed.

   Enter erase range: B5..B5
4. Extend the range to cell F8. The prompt will be:

   Enter erase range: B5..F8
5. Strike Enter and the contents of the highlighted cells will be erased.

The Worksheet Erase

After completing a worksheet and saving it to disk, you will often wish to begin a new one starting with an empty screen. For this, you need to erase the entire worksheet from the screen. This is done from the Worksheet (Lotus 1-2-3) or WorkSet (JOE) command; the action is one that will affect the entire worksheet as opposed to a selected range.

DO THIS NOW 12-10 **Erasing the Contents of All Cells in the Worksheet**

1. Enter the following command sequence (the position of the cell pointer does not make any difference).

   /WE

   That is:

   / Worksheet Erase
   / WorkSet Erase_all
2. In response to the request for confirmation, enter the letter Y for Yes. All cells will be erased.

Note that upon selecting the Erase command, 1-2-3 asks for a confirmation. If your key sequence was the result of striking a wrong key, you could easily abort the operation by striking the letter N for No.

The Move Command

Sometimes, in revising a worksheet, it is necessary to move the contents of a range from one place in the worksheet to another. The Move command allows you to move the contents of any range of cells up, down, left, or right, as needed. Figure 12-7 illustrates the action of moving the contents of the cell range B3..D6 to corresponding positions anchored at cell F8. The sequence of steps to carry out this operation is almost identical to that for copying. If you wish to try it, retrieve one of your worksheets and try moving the contents of some of the cells. Remember first to position the cell pointer to the anchor point of the range to be moved. Then invoke the Move command with the sequence /M. The prompts will be almost identical to those of the Copy.

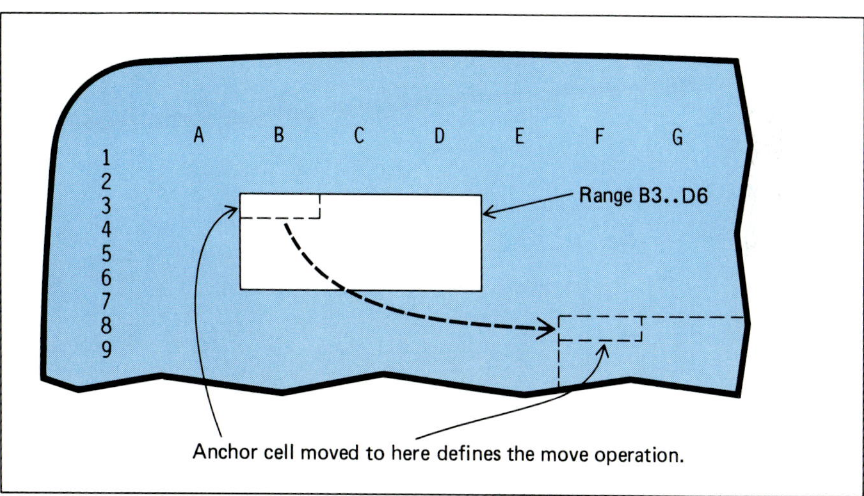

Figure 12-7
Moving the contents of a range of cells.

BASIC PRINCIPLES OF FUNCTIONS

The five arithmetic operators of 1-2-3 provide you with the basic calculating tools. Like most computer software systems, 1-2-3 includes an extensive set of *functions,* which can be thought of as "predefined" formulas. For instance, there are functions to do the following.

- Calculate the square root of a number.
- Sum the values in a range of cells.
- Calculate the average of a range.

- Determine the payment required for a loan given the amount, interest, and time period.
- Compare two quantities in determining an action to take.

The next two examples are designed to give you an understanding of how functions are used in spreadsheet design.

Example Definition

Assume that the management of the company for which you work is in the process of completely modernizing the work facility. An integral part of the modernization is the upgrading of the work force through specialized training units. For training purposes, the employees have been assigned to groups (such as the office group, warehouse group, and so on). For each group, the training consists of a series of units specifically designed to upgrade the skills in the occupational area. One of your colleagues has been assigned to monitor the progress of the different training groups. After a short period of time, your friend is transferred and you are given the task. Figure 12-8 is an example of one of the record sheets that your friend was using to maintain a record of progress manually. As each training unit is completed, the rating for that employee is entered in the appropriate position. After all employees complete a unit, you must calculate the average for that unit. Furthermore, as each unit is completed, you

Employee Name	Unit 1	Unit 2	Unit 3	Total
Anderson, John	68			
Balcer, Anna	79			
Dexter, Howard	69			
Franklin, Benjamin				
Harrison, Albert	48			
Irvin, Shirley				
Knowland, Jeanette	89			
McDaniel, Nancy	89			
Pierce, William	85			
Sutherland, Carol	75			
Thomas, John	81			
Wilson, Raleigh				
Average rating	76			

Figure 12-8
Maintaining a record of employee progress manually.

must maintain a total for each employee. After looking this over, you decide that you could maintain these records much more easily on the computer. Furthermore, you feel that you could provide more information that would be useful in evaluating the performance of employees as well as the success of the training program. To this end, you decide that you will design a spreadsheet that will provide the following.

For each employee:

Total rating for all units completed.

Average rating for all units completed.

For each unit:

Average rating for employees completing the unit.

Number of employees completing the unit.

Highest rating achieved for the unit.

Lowest rating for the unit.

Your expansion of your friend's manual worksheet, as you hope it to appear when all the data entries have been made, is shown in Figure 12-9. Now you need to know how to define the formulas to compute the values in which you are interested. This cannot be done with only the arithmetic operators that you have used in preceding examples. You will need to use 1-2-3 functions. Specifically, typical cell needs for this example are as follows:

Cell	Operation
E3	Sum the values in the cell range B3..D3.
F3	Average the values in the cell range B3..D3.
B17	Average the values in the cell range B3..B14.
B18	Count the number of nonblank entries in the cell range B3..B14
B19	Find the maximum (largest) value from the cell range B3..B14.
B19	Find the minimum (smallest) value from the cell range B3..B14.

For the examples of this portion of the chapter, the data disk includes the worksheet file EMPL.WKS, which is an incomplete version of that shown in Figure 12-9. That is, it includes only the data for the first unit, and none of the needed formulas. You can use it to serve as the beginning point for examples that follow. Thus, you should retrieve that worksheet from the disk so that you can follow the example instructions.

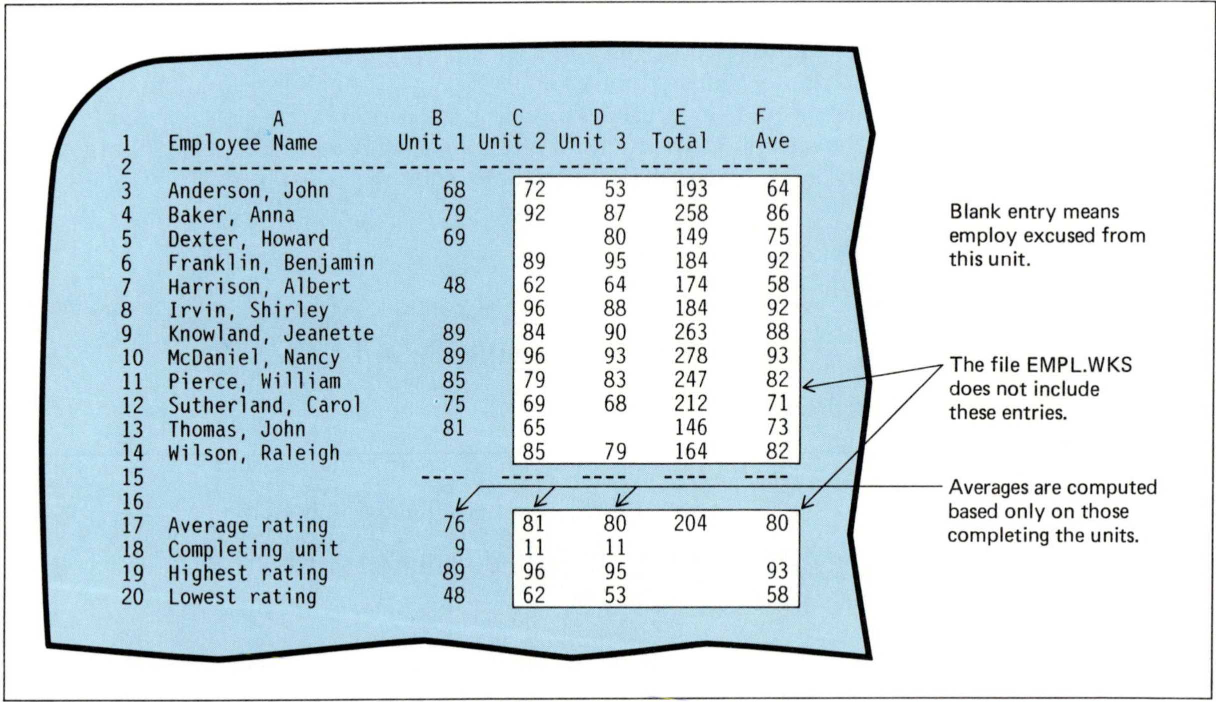

	A	B	C	D	E	F
1	Employee Name	Unit 1	Unit 2	Unit 3	Total	Ave
2	------------------	------	------	------	------	------
3	Anderson, John	68	72	53	193	64
4	Baker, Anna	79	92	87	258	86
5	Dexter, Howard	69		80	149	75
6	Franklin, Benjamin		89	95	184	92
7	Harrison, Albert	48	62	64	174	58
8	Irvin, Shirley		96	88	184	92
9	Knowland, Jeanette	89	84	90	263	88
10	McDaniel, Nancy	89	96	93	278	93
11	Pierce, William	85	79	83	247	82
12	Sutherland, Carol	75	69	68	212	71
13	Thomas, John	81	65		146	73
14	Wilson, Raleigh		85	79	164	82
15		----	----	----	----	----
16						
17	Average rating	76	81	80	204	80
18	Completing unit	9	11	11		
19	Highest rating	89	96	95		93
20	Lowest rating	48	62	53		58

Figure 12-9
Employee progress worksheet.

Using a Function

Let us begin this study of functions with the function to sum the values in a range of cells. In the cost analysis example, you added up, or summed, the values in a range of cells to obtain the Unit Cost using such formulas as:

```
+B5+C5+D5+E5+F5
```

@SUM. The @SUM function provides the following alternative (which is especially convenient if the sum includes many cells).

```
@SUM(B5..F5)
```

Here the name of the function is @SUM and it operates on the range of cells B5 through F5. As you shall learn, all function names begin with the @ character. This signals a function to 1-2-3. Let us enter this into your worksheet.

DO THIS NOW 12-11 **Entering the @SUM Function Into Cell E3**

1. Move the cell pointer to cell E3, the cell into which the function is to be entered.

2. Type the @ character and 1-2-3 will switch to the VALUE mode and the @ will be entered to the second line of the control panel. Continue to type SUM(and the control panel display will be:

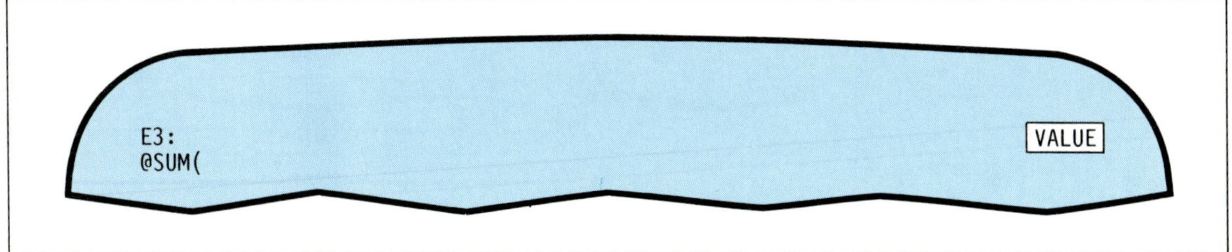

3. Move the cell pointer to cell B3. This identifies the anchor of the range for this function. The control panel display will be:

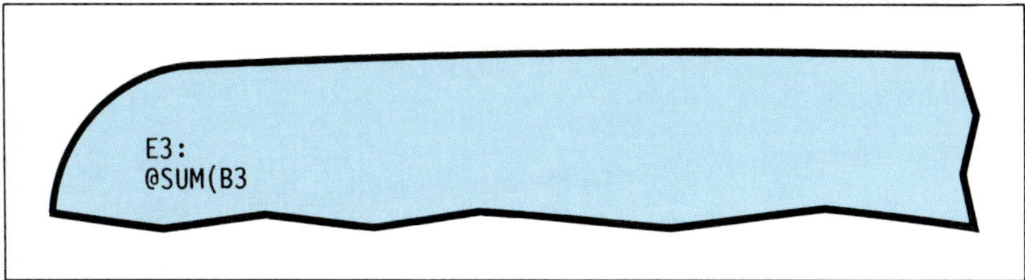

4. Strike the period (.) key to set the anchor for the beginning of the range, giving:

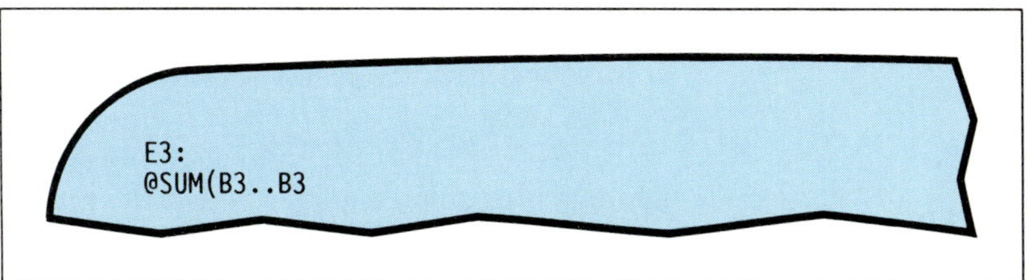

5. Move the highlight to cell D3; this extends the range to cover all cells that you need in the sum, giving:

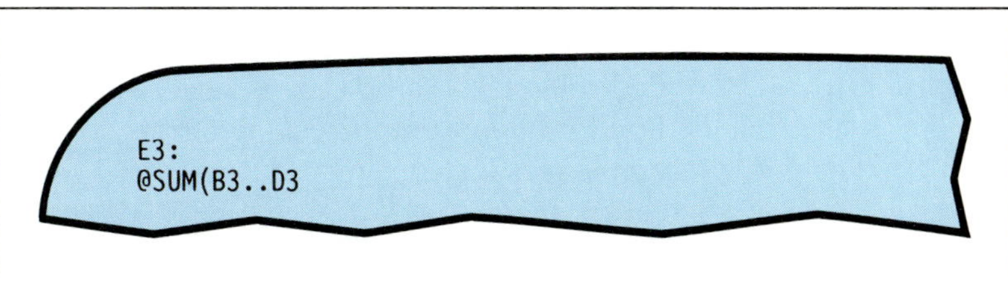

6. Strike the) key to close the parentheses, giving:

7. Strike Enter, thus completing the operation and entering the function into the cell. The value displayed in this cell should be 68, the only unit completed by this employee.

8. Copy this function entry from cell E3 into the cell range E4..E14 using the /C (Copy) command. Remember to position the cell pointer at cell E3 if you have moved it. Then invoke the command. Your FROM range is E3..E3 and your TO range is E4..E14.

In general, since the function yields a single number, it can be used in building formulas as if it were an ordinary cell address or number. For example, the following formula obtains the sum of cells B8 through D8, multiplies it by 4, and then adds 50.

```
4*@SUM(B8..D8)+50
```

Other Statistical Functions

Following is a brief description of each of the functions you need to complete the worksheet of Figure 12-9.

@AVG. This function calculates the average value of a range. The average is calculated as the sum of the numbers in the range divided by the count of entries, with blank entries being ignored. For instance, in Figure 12-9, the average for column B is the sum of all the ratings divided by 9, the number of employees completing the unit. Sample functions for cells B17 and F3 are:

```
@AVG(B3..B14)
@AVG(B3..D3)
```

@COUNT. This function counts the number of entries in the specified cells. For example, in Figure 12-9, rows 3 through 14 contain information for twelve employees. Referring to column B, we see that three of the employees were exempted from Unit 1 (there are no entries for three of the cells). Thus, the entry count for this range is 9. This count would be determined and displayed in cell B18 by the following function.

```
@COUNT(B3..B14)
```

@MAX and @MIN. These functions search the specified range and return the maximum and minimum values from those cells. They are required to obtain the highest and lowest ratings for individual units, as well as for the average. For cells B19 and B20, the functions take the following form.

```
@MAX(B3..B14)
@MIN(B3..B14)
```

Completing the Employee Progress Worksheet

You should now proceed to enter these functions into your copy of the worksheet.

DO THIS NOW 12-12 **Completing the Employee Progress Worksheet**

1. For the average of cells B3..D3, enter the @AVE function into cell F3, and then duplicate it into the range F3..F14. The sequence of steps is the same as that of DTN 12-11 for the @SUM.
2. Enter the @AVE function into B17 for the range B3..B14. Then duplicate it into C17..F17.
3. Enter the @COUNT function into B18 for the range B3..B14. Then duplicate it into C18..D18.
4. Enter the @MAX function into B19 for the range B3..B14. Then duplicate it into C19..D19, and then to F19.
5. Enter the @MIN function into B20 for the range B3..B14. Then duplicate it into C20..D20, and then to F20.

When you are finished, save your worksheet to disk. Then enter the data for Unit 2 (column C) and observe how all of the calculated values change as you are entering. Then enter the data for Unit 3. Check all values to ensure that your calculations are correct.

CONDITIONAL OPERATIONS USING FUNCTIONS

Problem Definition

Owning a sales-oriented company, you and your partner have considered all types of techniques to promote sales. Your latest thought is to promote sales by your part-time sales representatives with a bonus plan. This plan is to be based on the following monthly bonus quotas for your "high season" sales period (the months April through August).

Month	Bonus Quota
April	$4500
May	$5000
June	$7500
July	$8000
August	$6000

Part-time representatives are currently paid 10 percent of their total sales. You propose to change this as follows:

- Each month for which a sales representative equals or exceeds the bonus quota, you will award a bonus point.
- At the end of the high season, the bonus points are totaled. If the total is four or more, a bonus of $1000 is paid.

In deciding whether or not to proceed with this plan, you decide to evaluate its effect using the data you have stored in a worksheet for the sales for the last high season. (A copy of this worksheet, shown in Figure 12-10, is stored on the data disk as SALES.WKS.) Your plans are to expand this worksheet as follows:

- Column I to contain the total bonus points earned.
- Column H to contain the earnings, which is the 10 percent commission amount plus $1000 if the bonus points are four or more.

Figure 12-10
High season sales representative summary.

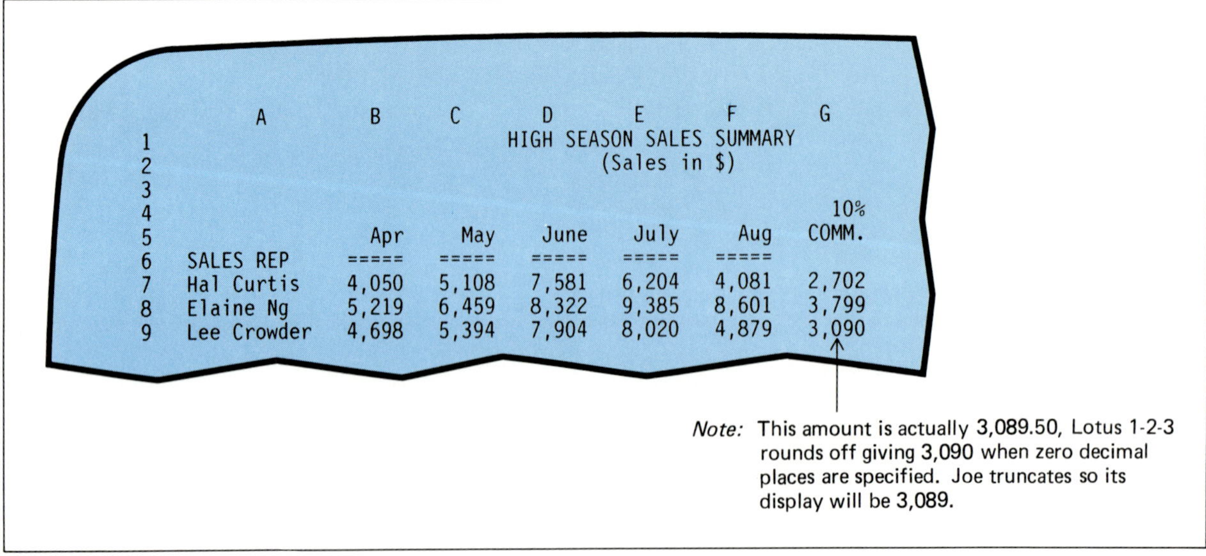

	A	B	C	D	E	F	G
1				HIGH SEASON SALES SUMMARY			
2					(Sales in $)		
3							
4							10%
5		Apr	May	June	July	Aug	COMM.
6	SALES REP	=====	=====	=====	=====	=====	
7	Hal Curtis	4,050	5,108	7,581	6,204	4,081	2,702
8	Elaine Ng	5,219	6,459	8,322	9,385	8,601	3,799
9	Lee Crowder	4,698	5,394	7,904	8,020	4,879	3,090

Note: This amount is actually 3,089.50, Lotus 1-2-3 rounds off giving 3,090 when zero decimal places are specified. Joe truncates so its display will be 3,089.

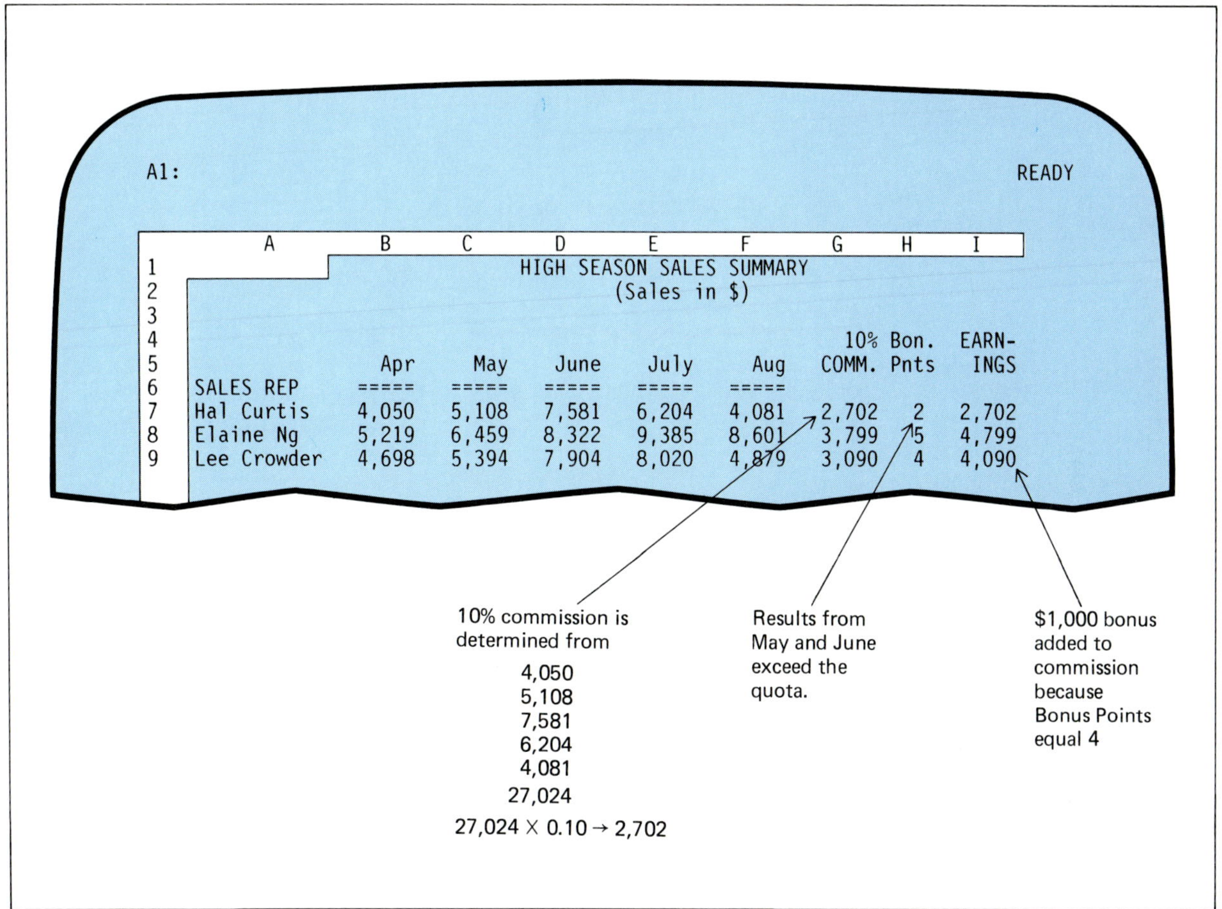

Figure 12-11
The expanded worksheet with bonus calculations.

When you are finished, the worksheet will be as shown in Figure 12-11.

To do this, you need the ability to instruct 1-2-3 to perform an operation on a conditional basis. That is, the amount to be paid to a sales representative must be increased by $1000 if the employee accumulates four or more bonus points. For this, 1-2-3 includes, in addition to arithmetic operators, special operators that allow you to compare quantities.

Relational Operators

We have already learned about formulas built with arithmetic operators (+, -, and so on) that define the arithmetic actions. Similarly, we can create formulas by using the following set of **relational* operators** that define actions in which quantities are compared.

---

*In the Lotus 1-2-3 manual, these operators are called *logical* operators. Since, in general computer use, there is a distinction between relational and logical operators, the term *relational operator* is used in this book.

Operator	Meaning
=	Equal to
<>	Not equal to
<	Less than
<=	Less than or equal to
>	Greater than
>=	Greater than or equal to

In 1-2-3, you use these operators to build **relational expressions,** which allow you to compare two quantities, as illustrated by the following two examples.

Relational Expression	Explanation
D3>8000	If the value in cell D3 is greater than 8000, then this expression is true and has a value of 1 else this expression is false and has a value of 0.
F5=F10+500	If the value in F5 is equal to the value in F10 plus 500, then this expression is true and has a value of 1 else this expression is false and has a value of 0.

Using Relational Operators in Building Formulas

Let us first consider how to use relational expressions in constructing the formula for the bonus points (column H), and then how to use them for comparing two quantities in determining the earnings (column I). Since relational expressions produce numerical values of 0 or 1, they can be used in building formulas. For example, consider the sales of Curtis (row 7 in Figure 12-11).

Month	Cell	Sales	Bonus Quota	Relational Expression	*yields* →	Points
April	B7	4050	4500	B7>=4500		0
May	C7	5108	5000	C7>=5000		1
June	D7	7581	7500	D7>=7500		1
July	E7	6204	8000	E7>=8000		0
August	F7	4081	6000	F7>=6000		0

From this table, we see that each of the relational expressions yields a value of 0 or 1. In this specific case, we get the total points by summing the points for each month. Exactly the same approach is used in 1-2-3, except that we use the relational expressions to build the needed formulas, as shown in Figure 12-12.

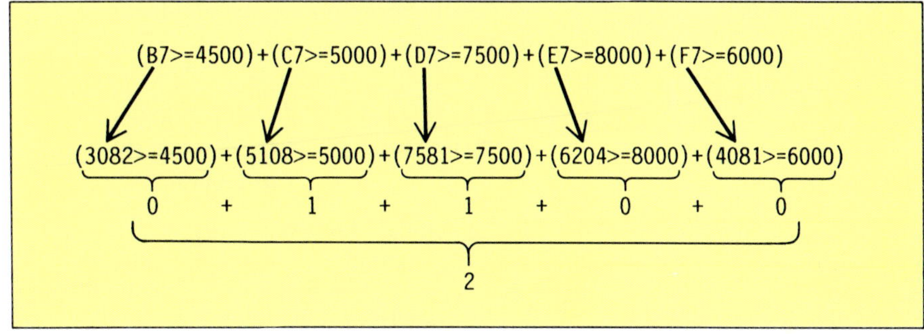

Figure 12-12
Using relational expressions in a formula.

The second expansion to the worksheet is to calculate the earnings for each sales representative. Stated in a form that is consistent with computer representations, the contents of the cells of column I are to be determined as follows:

If total bonus points value is equal to or greater than four,
then the amount of earnings is 10 percent of sales plus $1000,
else the amount of earnings is 10 percent of sales.

To see how this statement corresponds to the features of 1-2-3, consider the illustration in Figure 12-13. In 1-2-3, the conditional form is handled by the @IF function. Notice that it has three components inside the parentheses: the condition, the value to use if the condition is true, and the value to use if the condition is false. The English statement of this function is, "If the value in cell H7 is greater than or equal to four, then return a value that is the sum of the contents of cell G7 and the number 1000; else, return a value

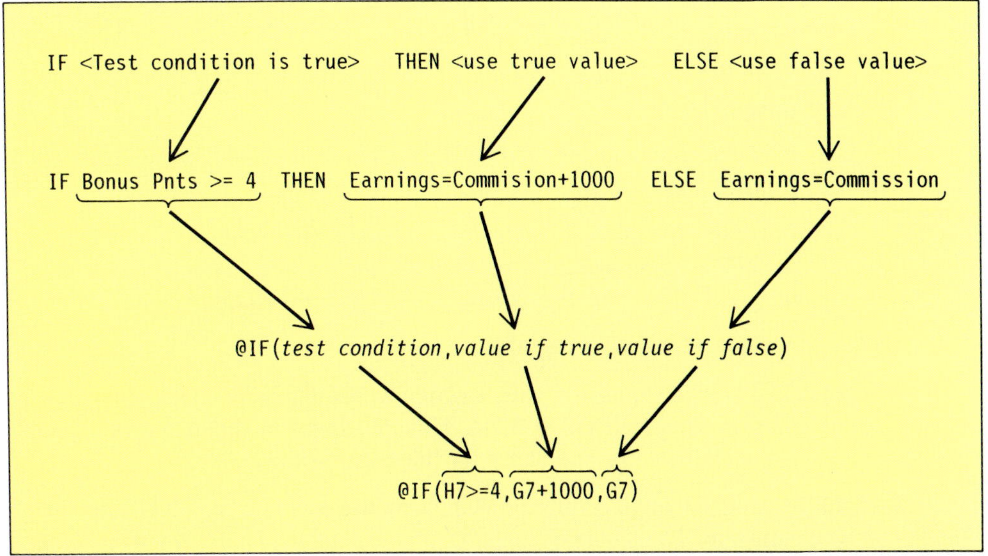

Figure 12-13
The @IF function in cell I7.

equal to the value in cell G7." In other words, add 1000 to the commission if the condition is true.

Completing the Worksheet

You now have the tools to expand the SALES.WKS worksheet to include calculations for bonus points and total earnings.

DO THIS NOW 12-13 **Expanding the Worksheet to Include Bonus Payments**

1. Retrieve the SALES.WKS worksheet.
2. Set the column width of column H to 4 with the command sequence /WCS.
3. Enter the new column headings for columns H and I (see Figure 12-11).
4. Move the cell pointer to cell H7, the cell into which the bonus points formula is to be entered.
5. You must now enter the formula of Figure 12-12. Notice that when you strike the (key, 1-2-3 switches to VALUE mode. When you have finished, line 2 of the control panel should display:

   ```
   (B7>=4500)+(C7>=5000)+(D7>=7500)+(E7>=8000)+(F7>=6000)
   ```

6. Strike Enter to assign this formula to cell H7. Notice that the value displayed in cell H7 is 2.
7. Move the cell pointer to cell F7. Change the sales from 4081 to 6000, the minimum to qualify for a bonus point. Notice that the value now displayed in cell H7 increases from 2 to 3. You just entered a qualifying sales amount for August. Change the contents of cell F7 back to 4081.
8. With the Copy command (/C), copy the formula in cell H7 into the range H8..H9.
9. Next, you must enter the @IF function for cell I7. Move the cell pointer to cell I7.
10. Enter the formula of Figure 12-13. Notice that when you strike the @ key, 1-2-3 switches to the VALUE mode. When you have finished, line 2 of the control panel should display:

    ```
    @IF(H7>=4,G7+1000,G7)
    ```

11. Strike Enter to assign this formula to cell I7. Notice that the value displayed in cell H7 is 2702. This salesperson did not qualify so the earnings are the same as the commission.
12. With the Copy command (/C), copy the formula in cell I7 into the range I8..I9.

As this version of the worksheet is complete, save it to disk as SALES2 (you will need it for the next example).

Testing Your Worksheet

The fact that your worksheet displays values that are identical to those of Figure 12-11 does not necessarily mean that your formulas are correct. For instance, the first relational expression of your formula could be

`(B7>=4600)` instead of `(B7>=4500)`

and your display would still be the same. Errors of this type are usually detected by inspecting the formulas, although such errors are easily overlooked. Similar errors in larger, more complex worksheets are often much more difficult to locate. Hence, before using a worksheet, you should always check all elements with sample data. Each cell that contributes to the results in columns H and I should be checked. A good test would be to change the values in row 8 as summarized in the following.

Test Values					Expected Results		
April	May	June	July	August	Commission	Points	Earnings
4500	5000	7500	8000	6000	3100	5	4100
4499	4999	7499	7999	5999	3099.50	0	3099.50

Concerning this set of values, notice that the first test set consists of amounts that are the exact value at which bonus points are awarded. The second set is a dollar less. The expected results were calculated with a pocket calculator. These values should be entered into row 8, thereby testing a version of the formula resulting from the Copy operation.

DO THIS NOW 12-14 **Test Formulas in a Spreadsheet**

1. Enter the first set of test values into row 8 and check your results.
2. Enter the second set of test values into row 8 and check your results.

ABSOLUTE CELL ADDRESSES IN FORMULAS

Expanding the Capabilities of the Sales Summary Worksheet

After completing the worksheet of Figure 12-11, you decide to experiment with different bonus quota amounts to see whether some other set of

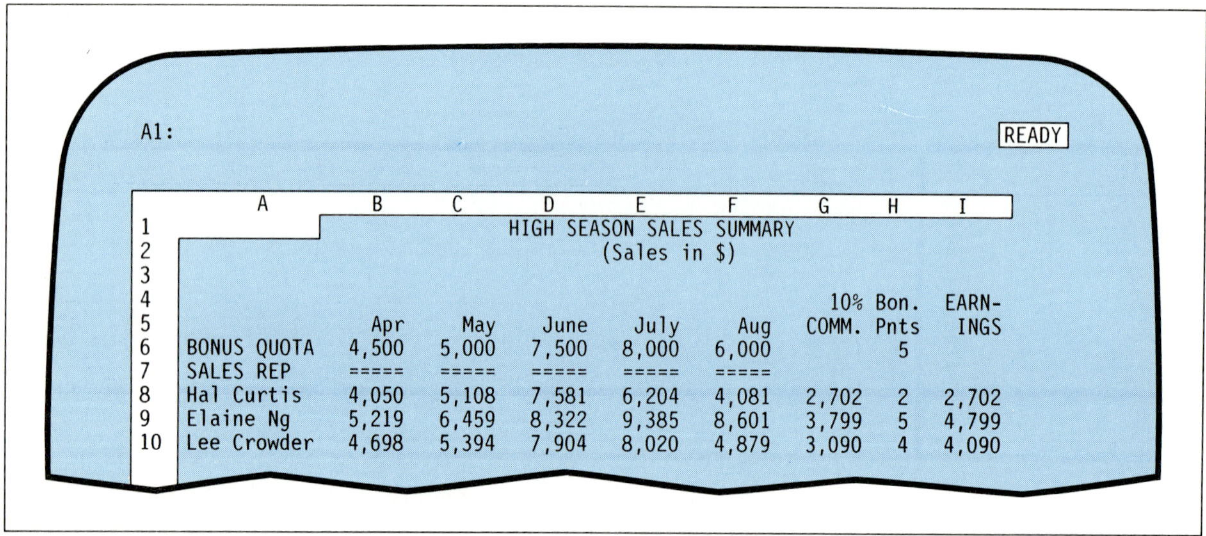

	A	B	C	D	E	F	G	H	I
1				HIGH SEASON SALES SUMMARY					
2				(Sales in $)					
3									
4							10%	Bon.	EARN-
5		Apr	May	June	July	Aug	COMM.	Pnts	INGS
6	BONUS QUOTA	4,500	5,000	7,500	8,000	6,000		5	
7	SALES REP	=====	=====	=====	=====	=====			
8	Hal Curtis	4,050	5,108	7,581	6,204	4,081	2,702	2	2,702
9	Elaine Ng	5,219	6,459	8,322	9,385	8,601	3,799	5	4,799
10	Lee Crowder	4,698	5,394	7,904	8,020	4,879	3,090	4	4,090

Figure 12-14
Including the bonus quota in the worksheet.

values might better meet your objectives. The form that you wish the worksheet to take is shown in Figure 12-14, where a row containing the monthly bonus quotas has been inserted at row 6. To take advantage of these entries, the formula for Curtis that we considered in Figure 12-12 becomes:

```
(B8>=B6)+(C8>=C6)+(D8>=D6)+(E8>=E6)+(F8>=F6)
```

This form of the worksheet serves a double duty for you. Not only are the bonus quotas displayed, but you can easily change them and observe the effect on the earnings.

Unfortunately, there is a subtle problem with this example when you attempt to copy the formula of cell I8 into cells I9 and I10. Remember that whenever a formula is copied from one row to the next, each row addressed is changed to account for this repositioning. Thus, when you copy, the formula in cell I9 will be

```
(B9>=B7)+(C9>=C7)+(D9>=D7)+(E9>=E7)+(F9>=F7)
```

instead of

```
(B9>=B6)+(C9>=C6)+(D9>=D6)+(E9>=E6)+(F9>=F6)
```

To copy this formula, we must be able to designate to 1-2-3 that some of the cell addresses must not be changed when the formula is moved.

Absolute Addressing

In all of the examples that we have considered to this point, 1-2-3 changes cell addresses in formulas when the formula is moved or copied to another cell. This is an automatic consequence of the fact that 1-2-3 determines the location of the addressed cells that make up the formula relative to the location of the cell containing the formula. For instance, in Figure 12-15, the formula in cell D4 that we see as +A2+A3 is actually stored in memory as "the cell two left and one up plus the cell two left and two up."

Figure 12-15
Relative addressing.

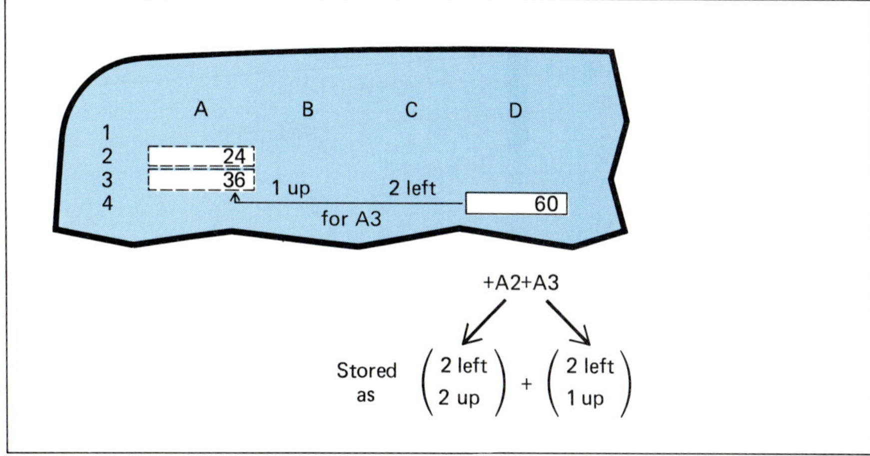

Consequently, this formula can be moved anywhere and we see it displayed with cell addresses that change according to where we have positioned it. This cell addressing is called **relative addressing** because the addresses are determined relative to the location of the formula cell.

For this formula, you need to be able to designate that the 6's in B6, C6, D6, E6, and F6 remain unchanged when the formula is copied. In 1-2-3, cell addressing in which a row or column reference remains unchanged when the formula is moved is called **absolute addressing.** A row or column reference in a cell is designated as absolute by preceding the row or column with the $ character. Hence, the formula must be entered into the worksheet as:

```
(B8>=B$6)+(C8>=C$6)+(D8>=D$6)+(E8>=E$6)+(F8>=F$6)
```

DO THIS NOW 12-15 **Modifying the Sales Summary Worksheet to Include the Bonus Quota as in Figure 12-14**

1. Either reenter the correct data values for row 7 (those that you changed in DTN 12-14) or retrieve the copy of SALES2 from disk.
2. Use the Insert command to insert a blank row at row 6 (/WIR).
3. Enter the label and data values shown in Figure 12-14.
4. Enter the preceding formula (with the absolute row address for row 6) into cell I8.
5. Copy the formula assigned to cell I8 to I9..I10.

Check your display to ensure that it is identical to that of Figure 12-14; if you find any differences, investigate the causes and make needed corrections. When your version of the worksheet is the same as Figure 12-14, save it to disk as SALES3. You will use this version of the sales summary worksheet for creating graphs in the next chapter.

When you use absolute addresses in a worksheet, be careful regarding the operations of moving, inserting, and deleting. Remember, if you perform an operation such as inserting one or more rows, 1-2-3 automatically adjusts the relative address references. However, if you were to insert a blank row at row 1 of Figure 12-14, the bonus quota values would be moved to row 7, but the references in the formula, being absolute, would remain at row 6. On the other hand, this entire worksheet could be moved one or more columns to the right with no ill effects since all column references are relative.

Technically, an address such as B$6 is called a **mixed address** because one part is relative and the other part is absolute. It is equally valid to use an absolute column address if the circumstances require it. For example, in the cell address $K13, the column address K is absolute but the row address 13 is relative. Only if both the column and row designations are fixed—for instance, $B$22, which refers to column B and row 22—is the address called absolute.

COMBINING A WORKSHEET WITH A WORD PROCESSING DOCUMENT

Assume that you decide to send a memo to each sales representative describing the activities of the past season. You decide to include the portion of the worksheet output that lists the monthly sales for each sales representative (columns A through F of Figure 12-10). There are three ways in which you can do this. First (and the least desirable), as the memo is being created on the word processor, simply type in the worksheet table by using a printed copy from 1-2-3. Second, type the letter and leave space for the worksheet table. Then paste in the desired portion of the worksheet as printed by 1-2-3 and make the required copies on a copying machine. Actually, the third approach is essentially the same as the second. The difference is that the pasting is done electronically rather than with scissors and paper.

Your first task is to send the printed output of the worksheet to a file so that it can be inserted into the memo. Referring to Figure 12-10, you will need the range A1..F9.

DO THIS NOW 12-16 **Inserting a Worksheet into a Document**

1. Retrieve the worksheet file SALES.WKS.
2. In order to give the resulting printout a more balanced appearance, move row 1 and 2 headings 2 columns to the left.
3. Position the cell pointer at cell A1, the anchor for the print range.
4. Enter the following command sequence.

   /PF

That is:

```
/ Print File           (Lotus 1-2-3)
/ Print File_output    (JOE)
```

5. You will see the prompt:

```
Enter print file name: B:\*.PRN
```

Notice that the displayed default extension is PRN.

6. Type the filename SALES. When your entry has been completed, this line will be:

```
Enter print file name: B:\SALES
```

Strike the Enter key to complete this action. Even though you do not include an extension, PRN will be used as it is the default. Hence, the file will be stored on drive B as SALES.PRN and the original worksheet file will remain.

7. The following submenu will be displayed. From this, select the Range option (to define the range of cells to be printed) by striking the letter R.

```
Range Line Page Options Clear Align Go Quit  (Lotus 1-2-3)
Align_top Clear Go_print Line Page Option_menu Quit Range_to_print  (JOE)
```

8. You will see the prompt:

```
Enter Print range: A1
```

Strike the period to accept A1 as the range anchor.

9. Move the cell pointer to cell F9, and then strike Enter to complete the range.

10. The submenu of step 7 is redisplayed. Select the Go_print (JOE) or Go (Lotus 1-2-3) option by striking the letter G. This causes the print file to be created.

11. After a few moments, the submenu of step 7 is redisplayed. To complete the operation, it is essential to execute the Quit command by striking the letter Q. If this is not done, the print file stored on the disk will be empty.

Upon completing this sequence, the output will be stored as the file SALES.PRN. At this point, you can terminate the 1-2-3 session and use DOS commands to send it to a printer or display it on the screen. In fact, it is always a good idea to check to ensure that it is correct. Displaying it is done with the following DOS command.

```
A>TYPE SALES.PRN
```

The file SALES.PRN could then be treated as if it were a document created by WordPerfect. It could be retrieved with WordPerfect and edited as required. To insert it into the memo to your salespeople:

1. Create the memo with WordPerfect.
2. Position the cursor at the point in the document at which you wish to insert the text version of your worksheet SALES.PRN.
3. Retrieve SALES.PRN. Remember, if WordPerfect is displaying a document on the screen and another is retrieved, the newly retrieved document is inserted into the one on the screen at the position of the cursor.
4. Insert spacing or otherwise edit the inserted text as desired.

SUMMARY

This chapter has built upon the basic concepts you learned in Chapter 11. Summarizing, the important items from the chapter are:

- A range is any rectangular collection of cells; this includes a single cell, a portion of a row, or a portion of a column.
- If you change the size of a worksheet by inserting or deleting rows or columns, 1-2-3 automatically adjusts formulas. However, sometimes deletions produce results that 1-2-3 cannot resolve.
- The default display cell width is 9 positions. This default can be overridden with the WGC (global) command sequence. Individual column widths can be changed with the /WCS command sequence.
- The Copy command allows you to copy the contents of one or more cells to another portion of the worksheet. If a single cell is being copied into a range, it will be duplicated in each cell of that range. Cell addresses in formulas are adjusted by 1-2-3 automatically.
- The four formatting options described in this chapter are: General, the default; Fixed, in which the user specifies the number of decimal places; Comma, which inserts commas for large numbers; Currency, the same as Comma except it includes a $ character.
- The Format is a subcommand under the Range command; it operates on a user-designated range of cells.
- The Erase command erases the contents of a range of cells. Do not confuse this with the Delete command, which removes rows or columns.
- Functions perform mathematical operations on designated cells. A function is indicated to 1-2-3 by preceding its name with the @ character. (The command summary following this section lists the functions covered in this chapter.)

- Relational operators allow you to construct relational formulas in which two quantities are compared. If the comparison is true, a value of 1 is assigned; if false, a value of 0 is assigned.
- The @IF function gives you a conditional capability. It allows you to assign a formula to a cell that displays the result of one expression if a stated condition is true and another if it is false.
- Addresses in building a formula can be relative, absolute, or mixed. A relative address is one that is adjusted when the formula is moved. An absolute address is one that remains unchanged if the formula is moved. A reference in which one element (row or column) is relative and the other is fixed is called a mixed address.
- To prepare a worksheet for inclusion in a word processing document, use the Print command and send the "printed" output to a disk file.

COMMAND AND FUNCTION SUMMARY

Following is a summary of the various commands and operations described in this chapter.

Command	Key Sequence	Action
Column width	/WGC /WCS	Change the default column width. Change the width of the current column.
Copy	/C	Copy the contents of a range of cells to another portion of the worksheet.
Delete	/WDR or /WDC	Delete rows or columns.
Erase	/RE /WE	Erase the contents of a range of cells. Erase the contents of all cells in the worksheet.
Format	/RF	Format the display of numeric quantities in a range of cells.
Insert	/WIR or /WIC	Insert rows or columns.
Move	/M	Move the contents of a range of cells to another portion of the worksheet.

Function Name	Action
@AVG	Average the values of a range of cells.
@COUNT	Count the number of nonblank entries in a range of cells.
@MAX	Determine the largest value from a range of cells.
@MIN	Determine the smallest value from a range of cells.
@SUM	Sum the values of a range of cells.

NEW TERMINOLOGY

The following are important new terms introduced in this chapter; you should be familiar with each of them.

absolute address
anchor cell
function
global
mixed address
range
relational expression
relational operator
relative address

REVIEW QUESTIONS

1. How many cells are in each of the following ranges?

   a. B5..B9
   b. C6..C6
   c. M23..Q42
   d. F12..E11

2. What is the sequence of operations to insert 3 blank rows in rows 7–9 of the current worksheet?

3. What is the sequence of operations to delete columns F–J of the current worksheet?

4. The following column width changes have been made using the /WCS command sequence: column A to 15, columns E-G to 6, and column M to 10. Then the default width is changed to 7 using the command sequence /WGC. What will be the widths of the columns in the worksheet?

5. Five asterisk characters (*) are to be entered into all of the cells of the first column, rows 5 through 20. What are the steps to do this?

6. How will the values 25, 3669.1234, and -65.1 be displayed with each of the following format definitions?

   a. General.
   b. Fixed with three decimal places.
   c. Comma with one decimal place.
   d. Currency with two decimal places.

7. Is it possible to format part of the cells in a column one way and others in the same column another way? For instance, could cells B3..B6 be formatted as fixed with four decimal places and cells B7..B10 be formatted as currency? Explain your answer.

8. What will happen if the following sequence of operations is carried out?

   Move the cell pointer to cell C6.
   Enter the command sequence /RE.
   Strike the Down key three times and the Right key twice.
   Strike the Enter key.

9. Referring to the cost analysis worksheet, what would happen to the formulas originally in column E if column A were erased? What would happen if column A were deleted?

10. Cell D14 contains the formula @SUM(D3..D12). Four rows are inserted beginning at row 5. In which cell will the formula now reside, and what will its form be?

11. How would the preceding question be answered if 3 rows were deleted beginning with row 7?

12. What changes would be required in the formulas in the worksheet of Figure 12-9 if a blank row were inserted at row 8 to insert the employee Calvin Hobbes?

13. What is the difference between an arithmetic formula and a relational formula?

14. Assume that the following cells contain the indicated values.

D1 -2

D6 135

F6 110

F9 137

What will be displayed by a cell containing each of the following logical formulas?

a. D6>500
b. D6<=F6+25
c. D6<>D1+F9
d. D1*D6<0

15. Using the cell contents of the preceding exercise, what will be displayed by a cell containing each of the following @IF functions?

a. @IF(D6>0,F9,F6+F9)
b. @IF(F6+F9<=D6,F9,F6+F9)
c. @IF(D1<D6,0,D1)

16. What is the difference between a relative address and an absolute address?

17. The following formula in cell H10 is copied to cell H11. What will be the appearance of this formula in H11?

```
+C10-D10*A$10+$K$4
```

MATCHING

Match each command key sequence in a to h with the corresponding action in 1 through 8.

a. /PF
b. /WDR
c. /RF
d. /RE
e. /FS
f. /WIC
g. /RFC
h. /C

1. Provide for the display of very large numbers in the worksheet.

2. Eliminate the second row from a worksheet.
3. Make room for 3 additional columns to be inserted after column D.
4. Save a worksheet to disk.
5. Erase the contents of the current cell.
6. Prepare a worksheet to be included in a word processing document.
7. Duplicate the formula currently in cell D5 into the range D6..G12.
8. Display a dollar sign preceding a numeric quantity.

TRUE/FALSE

Determine whether each of the following is true or false.

_______ **1.** Technically, B4..B4 is not a range because it includes only one cell.

_______ **2.** When new rows are inserted or deleted, the formulas are always adjusted by 1-2-3 to give the proper result.

_______ **3.** If a column width is too narrow to display a numeric value, asterisks are displayed in that cell.

_______ **4.** If the width of column D is set to 22 and the default is column width is changed to 15, the width of column D will not be changed.

_______ **5.** In using the Copy command, the size of the range into which the copy is being made must be identical to the size of the range being copied.

_______ **6.** If a formula is copied to other cells, all addresses in the formula will be automatically changed to account for the location of the copy of the formula.

_______ **7.** The Erase command allows you to erase the contents of the entire worksheet or of only a selected range.

_______ **8.** If the quantity stored in a cell is 1547.6312, it could be displayed by the Currency format as $1,547.63.

_______ **9.** The first line of the control panel displays:

```
G7: (F2) 7.28
```

This means that the formatting of cell G7 is Fixed with a column width of two.

_______ **10.** The following two formulas would produce the same result.

```
B7+B8+C7+C8     @SUM(B7..C8)
```

_______ **11.** The following two formulas will not always produce the same result.

```
(F7+F8+F9)/3     @AVE(F7..F9)
```

_______ **12.** If row 5 is deleted from a worksheet, the following formula would still display the correct result.

```
@SUM(C3..C20)
```

______ **13.** The contents of selected cells are:

```
B3  25    C7  125
B4  30    C8  211
```

The following formula will display a value of 2.

```
(C7>5*B3)+(B3<B4)+(4*B4=C7)
```

______ **14.** Using the cell contents of Question 13, the following function will cause 125 to be displayed.

```
@IF(B4>=B3+5,C7,C8+100)
```

______ **15.** If an entire worksheet is to be included in a word processing document, then the worksheet file itself could be inserted. It is only necessary to print to a file when a portion of the worksheet is needed.

ANSWERS TO OBJECTIVE QUESTIONS

Matching

1. c 2. b 3. f 4. e 5. d 6. a 7. h 8. g

True/False

1. F 2. F 3. T 4. T 5. F 6. F 7. T 8. T 9. F
10. T 11. T 12. T 13. F 14. T 15. F

ASSIGNMENTS/PROJECTS

1. In Project Assignment 2 of Chapter 11 you entered a quarterly budget repeated on the next page as Figure 12-16. For this assignment, you are to expand the worksheet to include a 2-year summary as follows:

a. Add a second year to the worksheet using columns F through I.
b. The year-end balance in cell E16 of the worksheet in Figure 12-16 must be placed in cell F2 and must be added to the fall income in arriving at the total in cell F6. Thus, the formula in cell F6 will be different from those in the other cells of row 6.
c. Reduce the widths of the columns containing numbers so that the spreadsheet will fit entirely on the screen (and will be printed on one page).
d. Insert a description line in row 1 that tells the reader that there are 2 separate years.
e. For the sample data of the second year, increase the first-year values by 10 percent. There are two ways to do this. One approach is to type the new values as a complete new data set. The other is to enter formulas relating them to corresponding first-year entries.

Figure 12-16
Budget worksheet BUDGET.WKS.

	A	B	C	D	E
1		Fall	Winter	Spring	Summer
2	INCOME				
3	Job	400	400	400	2000
4	Grant	400	400	400	0
5	Parents	150	0	200	0
6	Total	950	800	1000	2000
7					
8	EXPENSES				
9	Auto Ins	800	0	0	0
10	Auto Exp	200	200	200	300
11	Tuition	300	300	300	0
12	Books	100	120	120	0
13	Misc	150	300	200	400
14	Total	1550	920	820	700
15					
16	BALANCE	-600	-720	-540	760

Fall Income Total – Fall Expenses Total

Fall Balance + (Winter Income Total – Winter Expenses Total)

2. A stock summary sheet is to be created with the following general form.

Stock	Pur. Price	Sale Price	Num of Shares	Broker Comm.	Profit	Percent Profit
--------------------	-----	-----	-----	-----	-----	-----
Dickerson Computer	25.25	25.80	100	35.45		
Peach Software	8.75	11.30	100	20.55		
HAL Limited	12.85	10.20	100	19.75		
Hardly Peripherals	45.65	75.20	20	34.38		
Slippery Diskettes	32.85	33.05	40	29.87		
Microhard, Inc.	6.25	2.68	200	7.80		
Vaporware Development	11.85	18.65	100	27.65		
Vaporware Development	13.97	18.65	50	15.87		
Tardy Products	14.01	15.63	75	19.56		
Totals			*	*	*	

Analysis:		
	Average Purchase Price	**
	Average Sale Price	**
	Average Profit	**
	Maximum Profit	**
	Maximum Percent value	**

Note that this form represents all label and data entries. The positions into which formulas are to be entered have been left blank. The assignment is to enter this spreadsheet and create the formulas. The Profit and Percent Profit columns are to be computed as follows:

Profit = (Sales Price minus Pur. Price) times Num of Shares

Percent Profit = [Profit divided by (Pur. Price times Num. of Shares)] times 100

Display the result correct to two decimal places.

Totals are to be computed for the columns as indicated by the single asterisks in the Totals row. Special calculations are to be performed as indicated in the analysis portion of the spreadsheet. The computed values are to be displayed in the positions indicated by the double asterisks. Set column widths so that it is possible to get the entire spreadsheet on the screen. Change the column heading descriptions if you feel that is needed.

3. A payroll summary spreadsheet is to be created with the following general form.

Name	Reg Hours	OT Hours	Pay Rate	Reg Pay	OT Pay	Deduct	Net Pay
Arnold Finch	40.0		9.60				
Alice Baker	40.0	6.5	8.50				
John Zener	36.0		8.00				
Howard Sparks	30.0		11.35				
Frank Olson	40.0	13.5	9.60				
Jane Peters	40.0	3.3	11.35				
George Ito	40.0	5.5	8.50				
Ann Miller	37.5		9.60				
Fran Wong	0.0		9.60				
June Frank	40.0	7.5	8.50				
Ed Brister	40.0	4.5	9.60				
Fred Grant	40.0		8.50				
Sue Miller	40.0		8.00				
Charles Inns	40.0	3.0	8.50				
Totals	*	*		*	*		

Average overtime hours: ** Total pay: ***

Note that this form shows all label and data entries. The positions into which formulas are to be entered have been left blank. The assignment is to enter this spreadsheet and create the formulas. The following calculations are required.

Regular Pay = Regular Hours times Pay Rate

Overtime Pay = Overtime Hours times Pay Rate times 1.5

Deductions = 10 percent of the Regular plus Overtime Pay

Net Pay = Regular Pay plus Overtime Pay minus Deductions

Totals are to be computed for the columns as indicated by the single asterisks in the Totals row. The Average Overtime Hours worked is to be computed and displayed in the position indicated by the double asterisks. The Total Pay (Regular plus Overtime) for all employees is to be computed and displayed in the position indicated by the triple asterisks. Use appropriate column widths to get the entire spreadsheet on the screen. If necessary, modify column headings.

4. In the worksheet of Assignment 3, insert another column between the current columns 1 and 2 into which you can enter Total Hours Worked. Then the Regular Hours and Overtime Hours entries are to be calculated using an @IF function.

Chapter 13

Computer Graphics

OBJECTIVES

One of the most dramatic applications of computers is in the area of graphics. With appropriate software, you can do such things as include drawings in printed documents (desktop publishing), use the computer as an art medium, create engineering drawings, transform spreadsheet data into multiple-color graphs, and simulate events with animation. The objectives of this chapter are twofold: (1) to provide you with a broad survey of computer graphics and its many application areas; (2) to give you hands-on experience using 1-2-3 to create business graphs that summarize the data stored in worksheets. When you have completed this chapter, you should be able to:

- Distinguish between business graphics and design graphics.
- Describe the uses of pie charts, bar graphs, and line graphs for displaying data.
- Create the following types of graphs with 1-2-3: pie chart, bar graph, stacked-bar graph, and line graph.
- Save graphs as part of a worksheet.
- Print graphs on a graphics printer.

PREVIEW

About Computer Graphics

Computer graphics is the use of the computer to prepare visual materials. This includes everything from displaying graphs of spreadsheet data to engineering design.

Presentation Graphics

Design graphics programs are used by such professionals as engineers, architects, and interior designers to automate much of their work. For instance, the engineer can enter specifications for a machine into a computer. From this, the computer can display the image on the screen and print detailed drawings.

Business Graphics

Graphs and charts plotted from tabular data are called business graphics. Using spreadsheet data, we can create line and bar graphs and pie charts.

Using 1-2-3 to Create Business Graphs

Data stored in worksheets can be used by 1-2-3 to prepare graphs.

Preparing Pie Charts with 1-2-3

The pie chart illustrates the proportion that each value of a data set represents with regard to the whole. With the Graph command of 1-2-3, you will create a pie chart from the sales summary spreadsheet of Chapter 12.

Saving Your Work

After the specifications for a 1-2-3 graph have been entered, they become a part of the worksheet. Each graph associated with a worksheet must be given a name.

Creating Other Types of Graphs

You will use the sales summary worksheet of Chapter 12 to create line and bar graphs that plot and compare the sales of each sales representative.

Recalling a Graph

Each graph created for a worksheet is given a name and stored with the worksheet. A simple command sequence makes any of these graphs available during a 1-2-3 work session.

Printing a Graph

If a graphics printer is attached to your computer, any worksheet graph can be printed.

ABOUT COMPUTER GRAPHICS

Assume that you work for a manufacturing company and that management has made the decision to install a new software package in your department. Three software companies have made bids to sell you their software: Whizzer, Flash, and Wow. Management is leaning toward Whizzer because it is the most widely used. You and your group have studied each package in detail and have determined that any of the three would do the job. However, on the basis of your evaluations, you feel that Wow is clearly superior. Your manager has given you 5 minutes to present your case at the weekly management meeting. As part of your argument, you have compiled results of studies and testing. Two of the tables to be included in your report showing the superiority of Wow are indicated in Figure 13-1. In the first, you have summarized the time required for each software package to complete a run for each of your four main applications. Inspecting this table shows that Wow is clearly faster for three of the four applications. The second table summarizes how the better speed of Wow and its ease of use would allow your technical people to spend less time programming and testing and more time in creative development activities. These tables will indeed convey your point to management, *if*

Time Test Summary
(Time in Minutes)

Application	Whizzer	Flash	Wow
Doodle	8.25	8.07	5.44
Abbreviate	15.15	13.28	7.50
Consolidate	12.30	13.44	13.50
Terminate	5.55	6.45	1.38

(a)

Technical Staff Time Allocation

Activity	Whizzer	Flash	Wow
Programming	40%	45%	35%
Testing	35%	25%	20%
Development	25%	30%	45%

Development = 100% - Programming - Testing

(b)

Figure 13-1
Tables of data.

Figure 13-2
Graphic display of data.

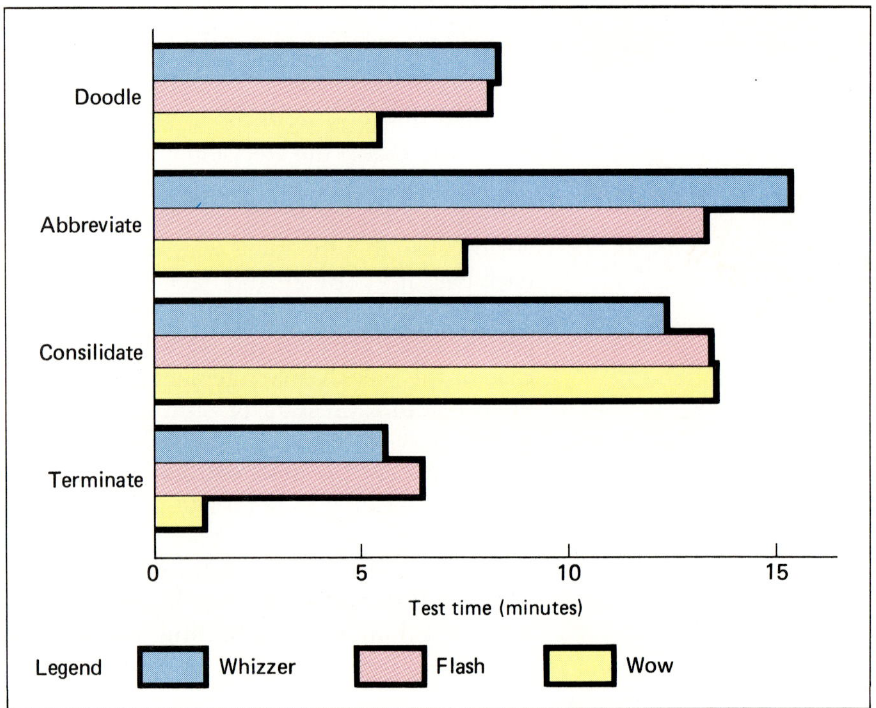

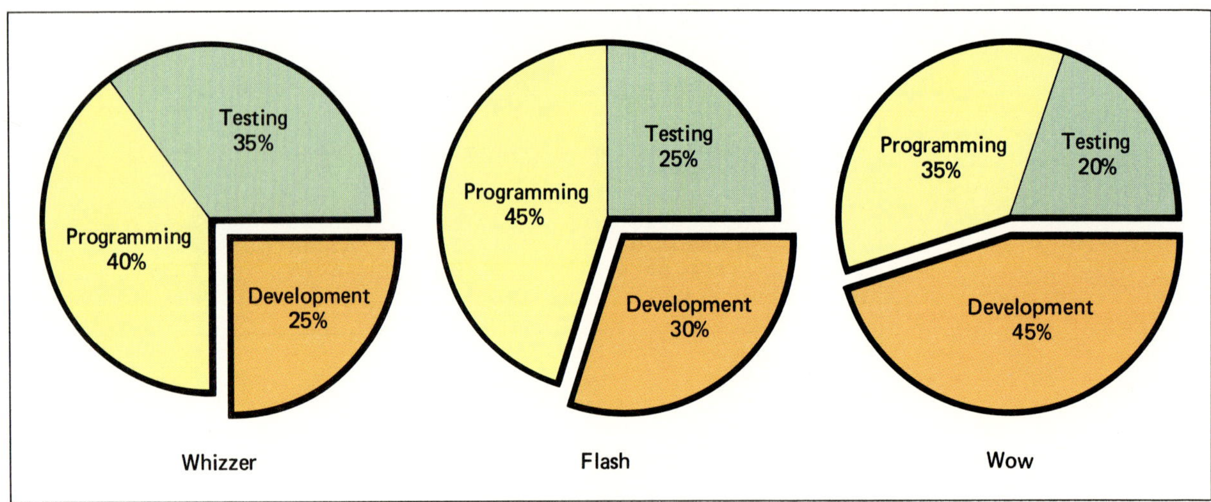

you can get your managers to study them; they do not make much of an impression unless they are studied.

On the other hand, think of the extent to which your presentation would be enhanced if you were to flash the graphic summaries shown in Figure 13-2 on a projection screen. With these, the managers need not study tables of data; the superiority of Wow is clear at a glance.

Graphics such as that in Figure 13-2 can be produced easily using a microcomputer and appropriate software. However, this represents only one small segment of computer graphics. We see examples of computer graphics when we observe special effects in movies and on television.

Almost everyone is familiar with video games. In fact, some of the auto racing games are so realistic that one almost has a tendency to lean into the turn when a sharp curve in the roadway appears. We also see art shows devoted entirely to art generated using the computer as a medium. In industry, engineers use computers to produce drawings for mechanical parts from which specifications can be furnished for automatic machine tools to produce the parts. It is apparent that **computer graphics,** which is the use of the computer to prepare visual presentations, embraces a wide range of activities.

Some applications software has built-in graphics as part of the package. For instance, in this chapter you will learn how to use the graphics capabilities of 1-2-3 to prepare graphic displays from data in a worksheet. Other graphics software is available that allows you to create your own graphic output, much as a draftsperson makes drawings. Some drawing software that allows you to use the computer as an electronic pencil and paper is used both for design and art applications.

The many different types of computer graphics software and applications fall in several categories. For the purpose of description in this chapter, the following classifications are used: presentation or business graphics, design graphics, and graphics for entertainment. The entertainment category is a general one encompassing a variety of applications in animation, education, art, and games.

To use graphics on a computer, both software and hardware are required. In Chapter 2, you learned that before purchasing a computer system, you must evaluate your objectives and applications, select the software that will do the job, and then select the hardware required by the software. If you intend to use a computer for graphics, you must make sure that the hardware you obtain is compatible with the software. The two basic elements are the monitor and the printer, which you learned about in Chapter 4. If you intend to use color, then a color monitor and printer (or plotter) are needed. Other specialized peripheral devices (covered in Chapter 4) are required for different graphics software.

DESIGN GRAPHICS

Engineers and other professionals make wide use of design graphics software in design work. Many design software packages are available, with capabilities ranging from highly specialized to general purpose. For instance, developers using specialized software can do the layout planning for housing developments on the computer and print copies on plotters to present at meetings with appropriate agencies and citizen groups. Changing and adjusting the plan to meet the needs and concerns of all involved can be done on the screen using a mouse or light pen and a new plan can be printed immediately for consideration. Just as spreadsheet software

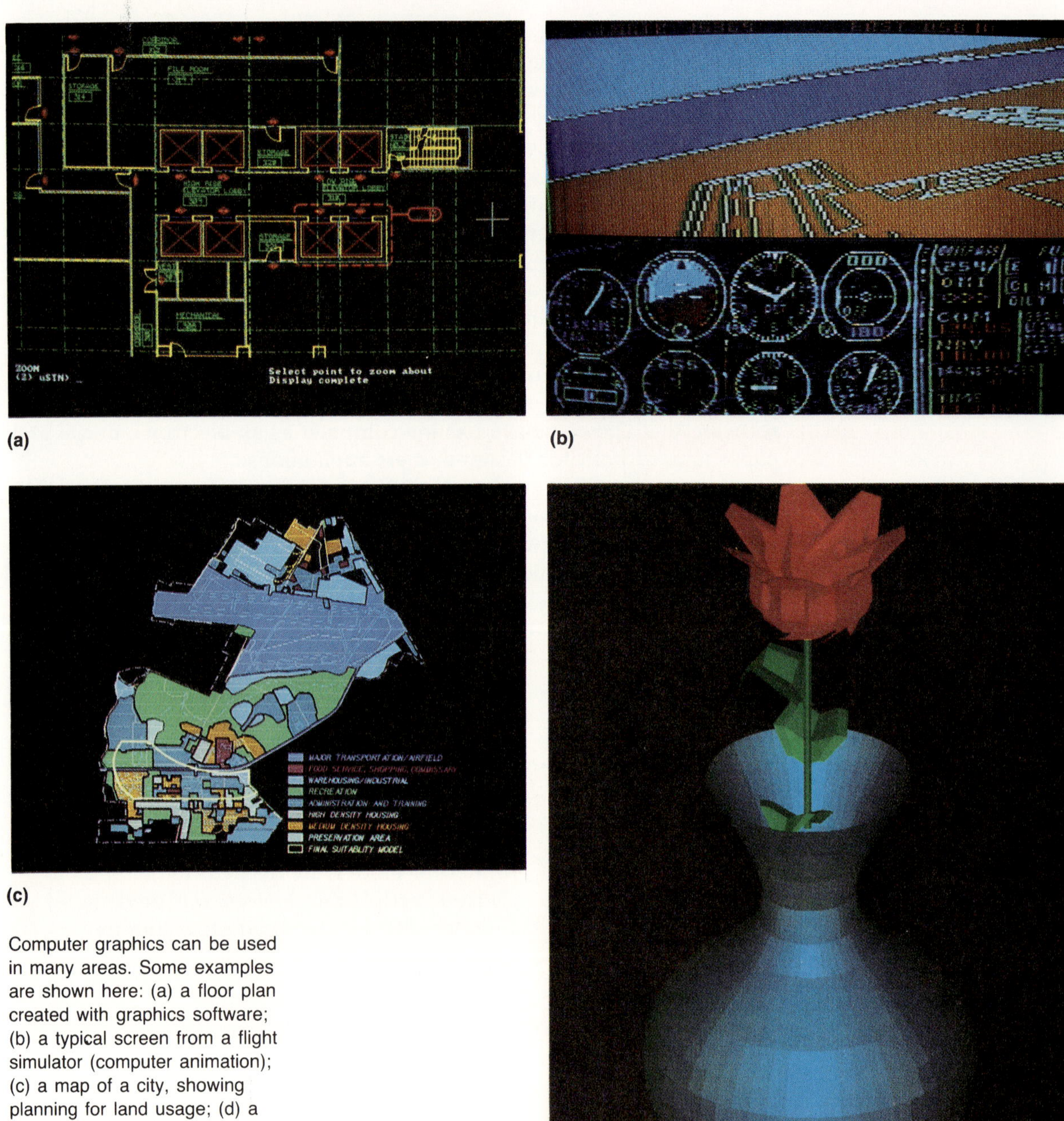

Computer graphics can be used in many areas. Some examples are shown here: (a) a floor plan created with graphics software; (b) a typical screen from a flight simulator (computer animation); (c) a map of a city, showing planning for land usage; (d) a rose drawn by using computer design software.

makes it easy to perform "what if" analyses with data, design software allows the user to perform "what if" studies with graphic layouts. Similarly, architects can prepare plan views and detailed floor plans of homes to be built for clients. A client's request to rearrange fixtures or appliances in the bathroom or kitchen can be met almost immediately and the new version displayed or printed. Even the office manager can work with the interior designer in performing space studies. A careful analysis to make the most efficient use of a facility is critical considering the high cost of office space. In the past, many office layout studies were carried out by making paper cutouts of desktops, file cabinets, and other furniture, and then manually arranging them on a drawing of the room floor plan. With interior layout software, corresponding images can be moved and rotated with ease.

Computer-aided design (CAD) programs are sophisticated software systems that have revolutionized the design of mechanical devices ranging from automobile parts to electrical appliances for the kitchen. For instance, with CAD software, automotive engineers can design a new transmission with all specifications stored in the computer. They can display the transmission housing on the screen in three-dimensional perspective, rotate it to view it from different angles, and explode it to show the parts it comprises. Changes in specifications are easily incorporated into the display. At any time, detailed three-view drawings of all components can be printed.

We constantly read about the extent of automation and use of robot devices in the workplace. All types of factory operations are automated, including electronic circuit board assembly of parts for your computer, welding on the automobile assembly line, and machining operations such as those performed by lathes and grinders. Each automatic device needs a set of specifications defining the exact motions and actions required to do its task; in other words, these tools must be programmed. The logical extension of CAD is to prepare these specifications or programs on the basis of the design information stored in the computer. This is called computer-aided manufacturing (**CAM**); the use of **CAD/CAM** software is revolutionizing the manufacturing industry.

PRESENTATION GRAPHICS

The purpose of presentation graphics software is to turn numbers into pictures of graphs, charts, and diagrams so that they can be understood easily. The tables of data in Figure 13-1 are illustrated graphically in Figure 13-2. These are two of the three commonly used methods for the graphic representation of numeric data: bar chart, pie chart, and line graph. Later in this chapter, you will generate graphs such as these using the graphics capabilities of 1-2-3 operating on data stored in worksheets. This type of graphics is also referred to as business graphics, because it is so widely used to display business data. However, it is not confined to business applications; indeed, the scientist commonly uses these graphic techniques to display scientific data.

Basic Graphics Terminology

Assume that your department manager has assigned you the task of evaluating the expenditures of several projects that have been completed by the department. One of your tasks is to compare actual and budgeted expenditures. Typical of the data you must present is the following table, which summarizes expenditures for the Harcourt project.

	Expenditures	
Year	Budgeted	Actual
1	34,000	39,400
2	34,000	41,100
3	44,000	46,100
4	51,000	57,300
5	48,000	55,500

Here, the expenditures are tabulated by the year. To find the expenditure for a given year, we run down the column on the left to the desired year, and then read across to the columns to the right. Basically, we can say that the expenditures depend upon the year, or in mathematical terminology, the expenditures are a *function* of the year. Business data is commonly represented in terms of time such as this. For instance, sales quotas are designated by the month, company earnings by the quarter, departmental budgets by the year, and so on.

The Line Graph

One way of illustrating this table is with a **line graph,** as shown in Figure 13-3. This uses the conventional coordinate system of mathematics in which two axes at right angles to each other are used to plot data. In this example, the **X axis** (horizontal) displays time in units of a year. That is, each increment of time shown on this graph is 1 year. The **Y axis** (vertical) displays expenditures in units of 1000: each expenditure increment represents $1000. The relationship between the physical entity and the unit of length on the graph is called the **scale.** If the time period were 15 years instead of 5, then a different scale would be used to keep the graph from running off the edge of the paper. Computer graphics programs automatically select the scale on the basis of the range of the data values to be graphed. In the graph of Figure 13-3, the expenditures scale ranges from 0 to 60 (60,000). Since there are no values below 30, the scale can be changed by using a lower limit of 30 and an upper limit of 60, with the result shown in Figure 13-4. Note that this has the effect of accentuating the difference between the two graphs. Scaling such as this is often used to emphasize differences and changes. It is sometimes used to mislead the reader; at a glance, the first-year actual expenditure appears to be twice the budgeted amount.

Using Graphs for Analysis

Anticipating the future is an important part of running a business. For instance, the manufacturer must estimate the sales for a new product in

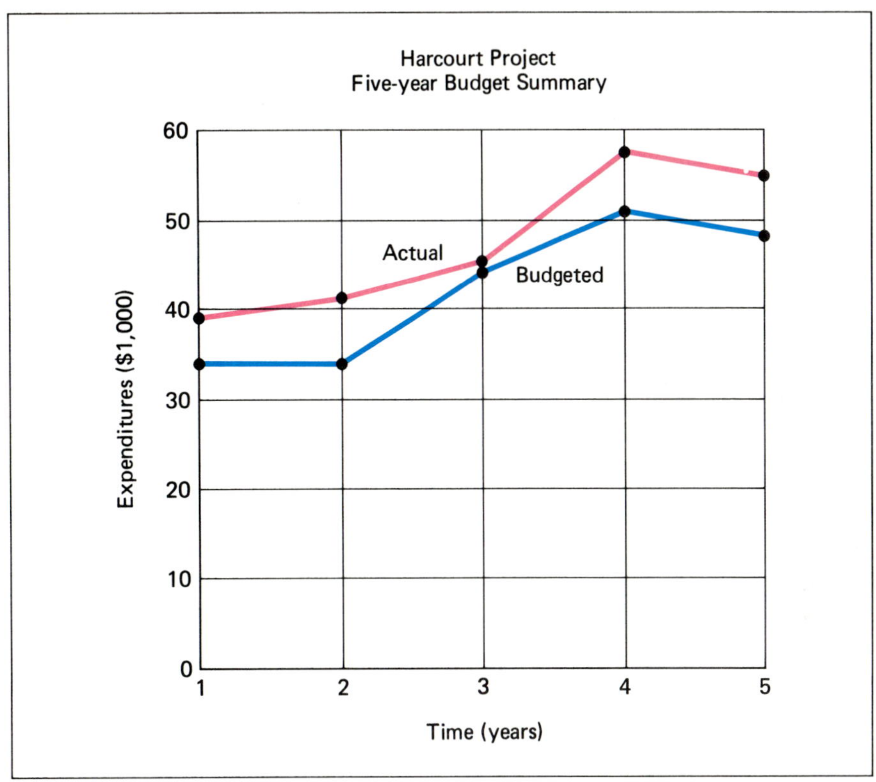

Figure 13-3
Line graphs.

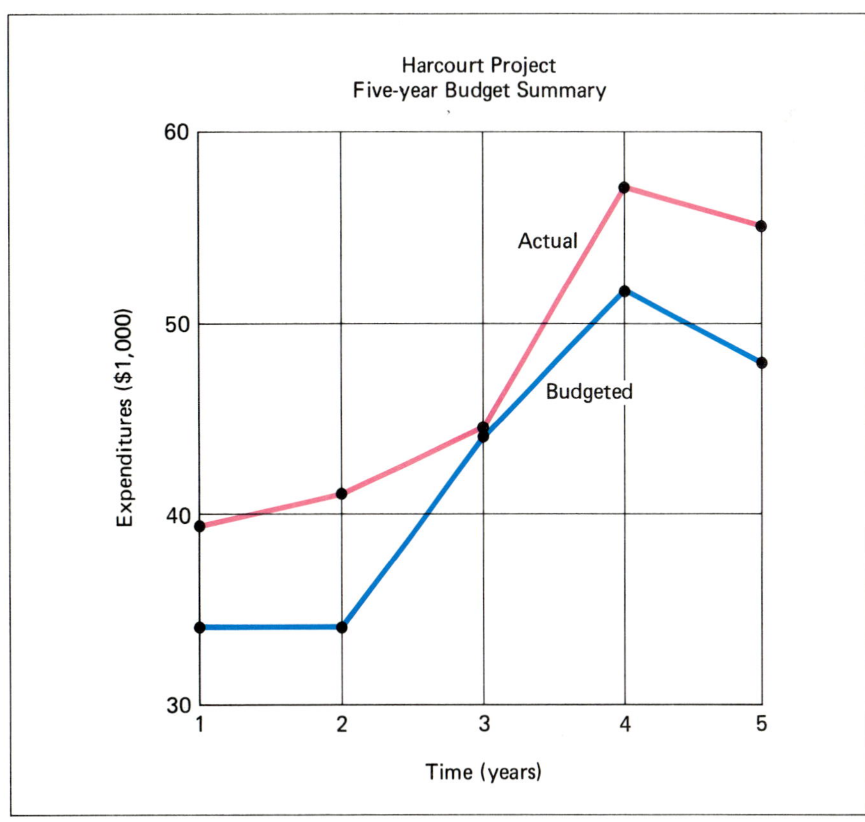

Figure 13-4
Using a different scale for a graph.

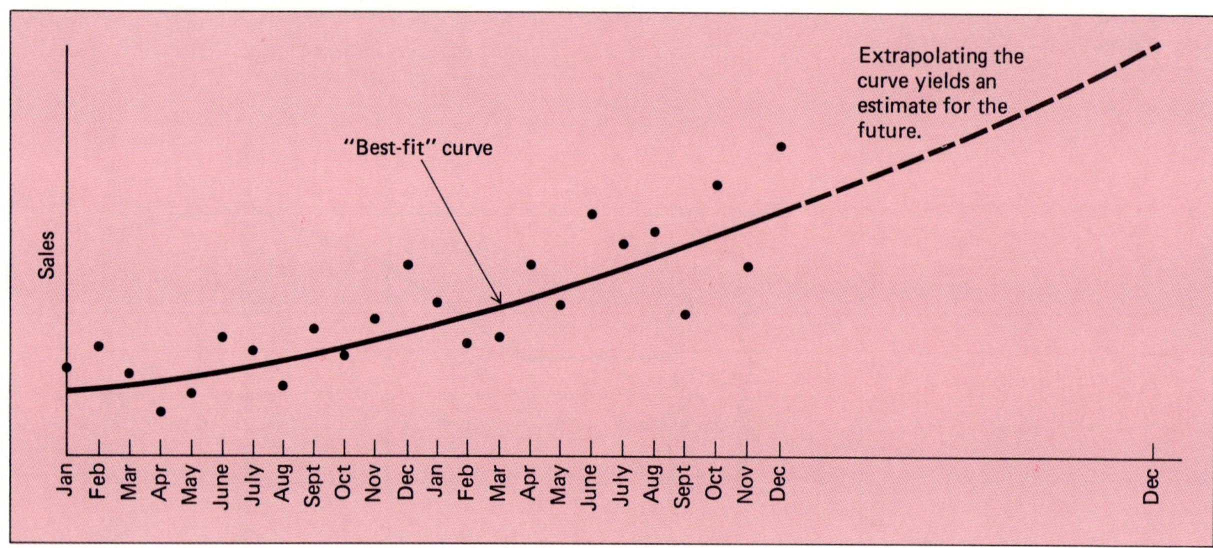

Figure 13-5
Extrapolating a best-fit curve.

determining the price and the quantity to manufacture. Department managers must estimate their budget needs for the coming year. The programming consultant must predict how much time will be required to complete a job. More often than not, such estimates are "educated guesses" based on a feeling derived from past experience. In many cases it is possible to organize past data and to use statistical analysis to extrapolate into the future and predict what will occur. For instance, consider a sales company that has accurate monthly sales data for the past 2 years and wishes to use it to predict the sales growth for the coming year. In Figure 13-5, each of the monthly sales figures has been plotted. Then a "best fit" curve has been drawn that demonstrates the sales growth trend. Extending the curve gives an estimate of the future. Statistical analysis programs are available for analyzing data and producing trends such as this.

The Bar Graph

The **bar graph** is another method of displaying the budget summary data of the preceding table. Bar graphs use rectangles to represent each of the data values, as illustrated in Figure 13-6. Bar graphs, which are also called histograms, are especially useful when there is a need to compare and contrast quantities. They are also commonly used when the X axis does not represent a continuous range. For example, Figure 13-7 compares the performance of three production teams where each team is rated on the basis of an assigned quota, quality control, and cost control. Whether the Auburn team or the Richland team is listed first is of little consequence. However, in the bar graph of Figure 13-6, the X axis represents consecutive years; to list them in any but their numerical order would be confusing.

A different perspective of the data can be obtained by stacking the rectangles to illustrate both the total and the individual components making up that total, as shown in Figure 13-8 (page 404). In this stacked-bar graph, we can clearly see the contribution to the total of each element. The

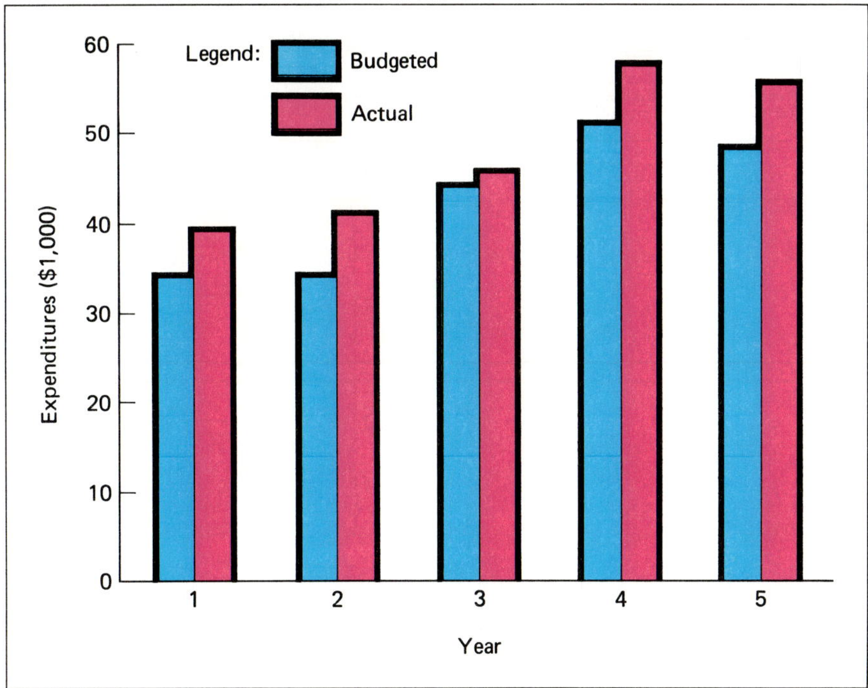

Figure 13-6
A bar graph comparing budgeted and actual expenditures.

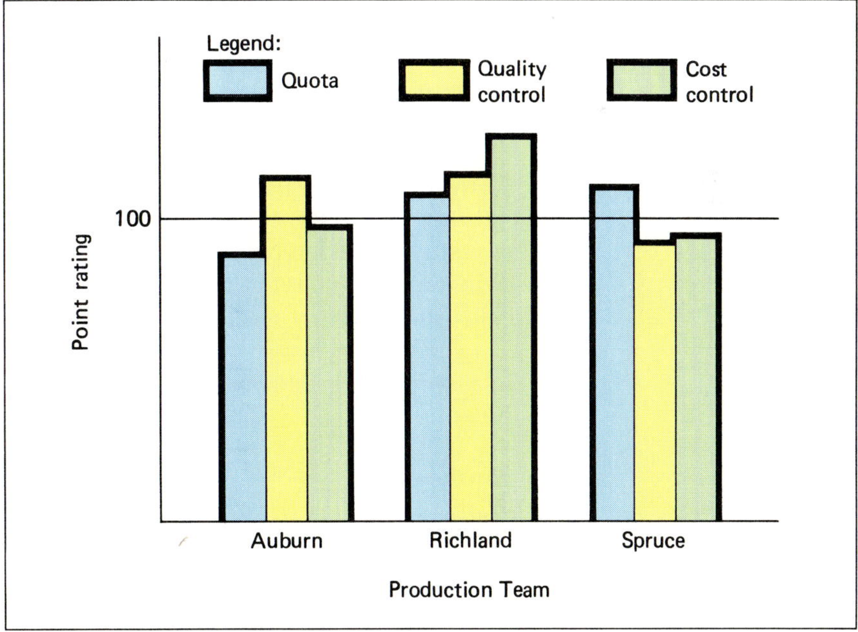

Figure 13-7
A bar graph illustrating the performance of production teams.

expenditures of Figure 13-6 might also be plotted as a stacked-bar graph by breaking them down into individual categories, such as equipment purchase, repair, staff training, and so on.

Sometimes turning the bar graph on its side makes it easier to understand. This technique is used in Figure 13-2(a), which compares the time required for software packages to complete designated operations.

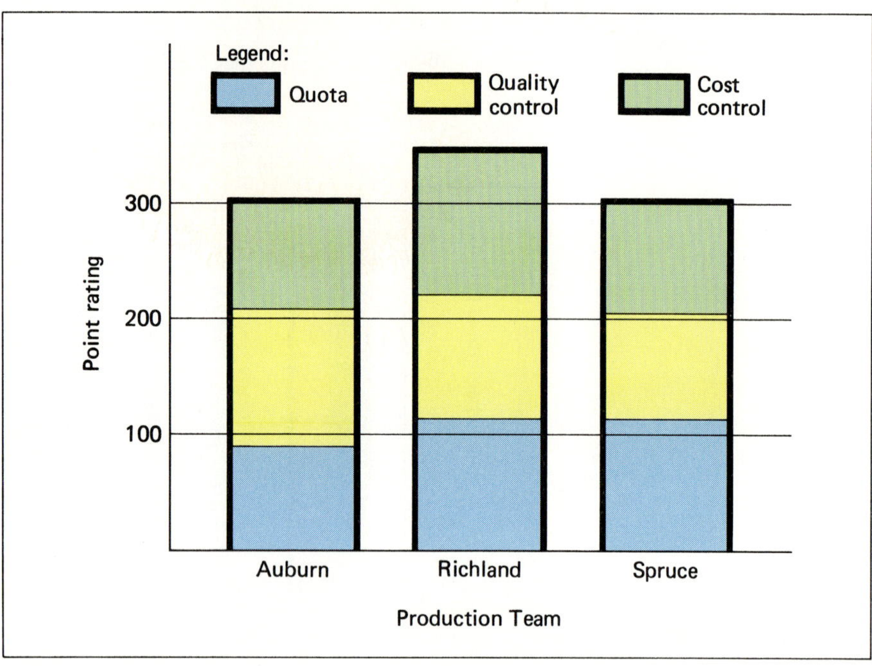

Figure 13-8
A stacked bar graph showing the effect of components on the total.

The Pie Chart

One characteristic of the line and bar graphs is that they display actual data values. The stacked bar chart takes this one step further in that it also illustrates the contribution of the various elements in terms of the whole. The purpose of the **pie chart** is solely to illustrate the percentage that each component contributes to the whole. For example, consider the computer software company that markets the software product Widget. As part of an effort to obtain venture capital for a major expansion, the company prepares a detailed report of all aspects of the product, including market penetration. One set of data that is to be included is the following regional sales summary.

Region	Units	Percentage
Northeast	3,221	29.7
South	2,120	19.5
Midwest	2,703	24.9
Rocky Mountains	1,133	10.4
Pacific Coast	1,684	15.5
Total	10,861	

This data could be represented in the form of a bar graph as shown in Figure 13-9(a) or as a pie chart as in Figure 13-9(b). The pie chart is

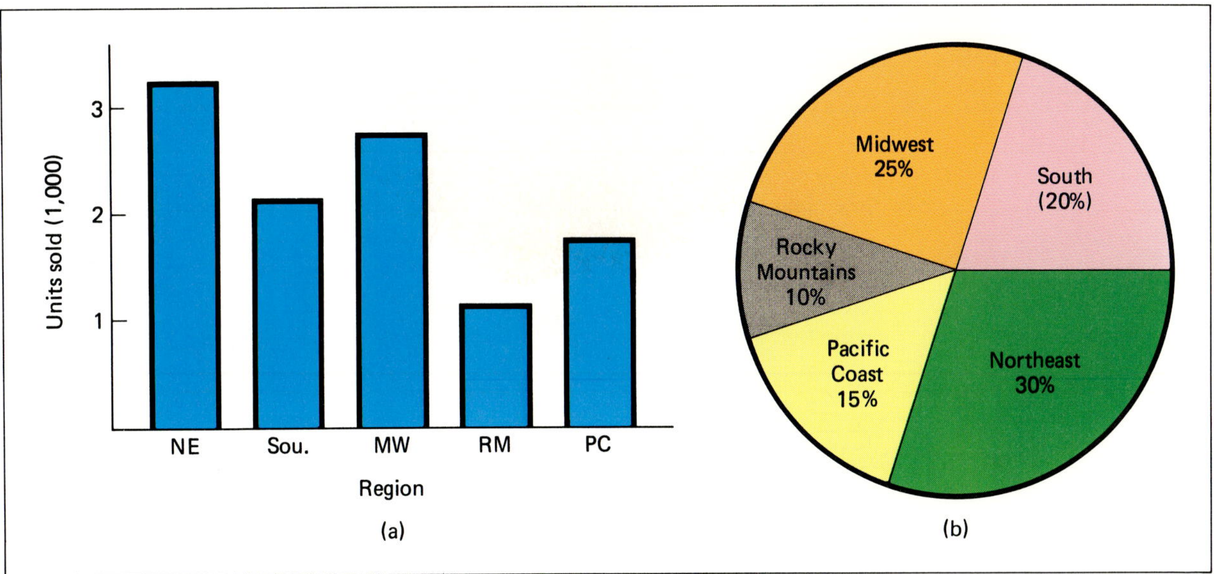

Figure 13-9
(a) Sales information by region.
(b) A pie chart showing proportions.

produced by dividing the units sold for each region by the total units sold, producing the percentage of the total for each region. These percentages are used to determine the "slice" size in the pie. Even though the pie chart does not include an X axis and a Y axis, it still uses two items: a set of descriptions of the data and the data in forming the chart. This will have implications when you create a pie chart with 1-2-3.

Sometimes it is desirable to emphasize one or more segments of a pie chart. This is done by setting that segment or segments apart from the others, as shown in Figure 13-10. The segment that is removed in this way is said to be an exploded slice. As you will learn, with the facilities of 1-2-3 you can easily explode one or more slices of a pie chart.

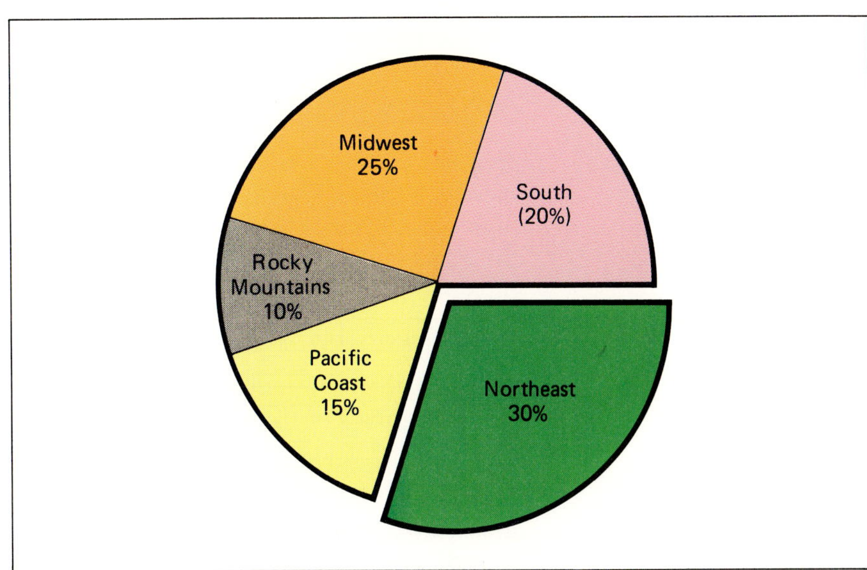

Figure 13-10
An exploded segment from a pie chart.

USING 1-2-3 TO CREATE BUSINESS GRAPHS

The remainder of this chapter is devoted to preparing business graphs from worksheets using the graphics capabilities of 1-2-3. With 1-2-3, you can prepare each of the types that you studied earlier in this chapter: line, bar, stacked-bar, and pie charts. The first type that you will learn to prepare is the pie chart because it involves the fewest parameter specifications and is the simplest to set up. All of the examples are based on the worksheet SALES3 that you completed in the preceding chapter. It is repeated here as Figure 13-11 for convenient reference.

Figure 13-11
The SALES3 worksheet.

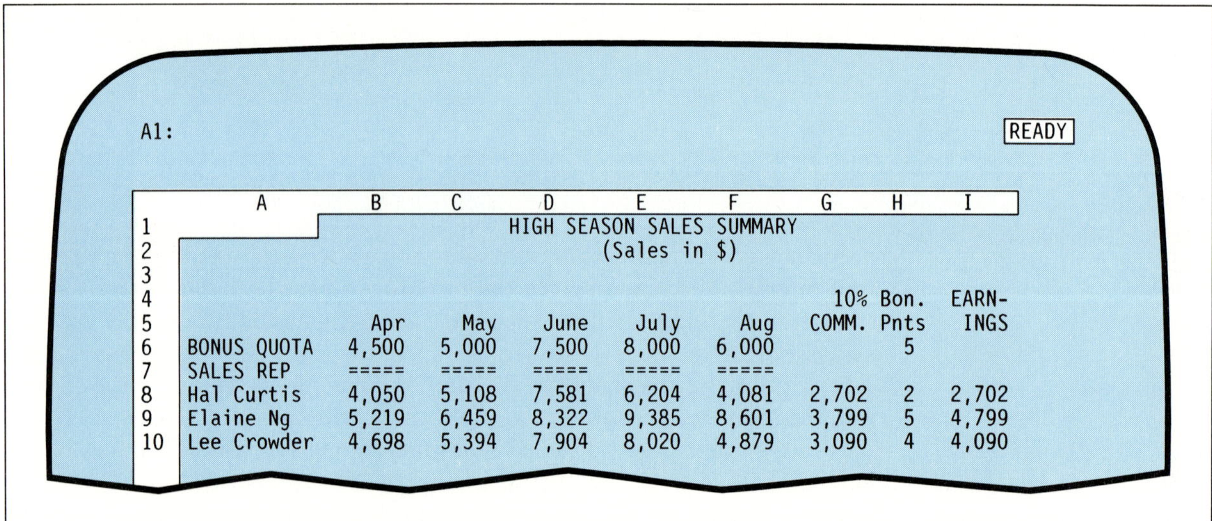

```
A1:                                                          READY

        A           B       C       D       E       F       G      H      I
1                                  HIGH SEASON SALES SUMMARY
2                                         (Sales in $)
3
4                                                          10%   Bon.  EARN-
5                  Apr     May    June    July     Aug   COMM.   Pnts   INGS
6  BONUS QUOTA   4,500   5,000   7,500   8,000   6,000            5
7  SALES REP     =====   =====   =====   =====   =====
8  Hal Curtis    4,050   5,108   7,581   6,204   4,081   2,702    2   2,702
9  Elaine Ng     5,219   6,459   8,322   9,385   8,601   3,799    5   4,799
10 Lee Crowder   4,698   5,394   7,904   8,020   4,879   3,090    4   4,090
```

PREPARING PIE CHARTS WITH 1-2-3

Creating the Chart

As part of your year-end sales summary reports, you decide to include a pie chart that displays the bonus quotas for each of the 5 months of the high season (see row 6 of Figure 13-11). This will present a clear picture of the relative proportion that each monthly amount contributes to the whole. In creating this pie chart, you must:

- Specify the range of data that is to be used in the chart (B6..F6).
- Specify the range of labels that is to be used in identifying each segment of the pie (B5..F5).

You know from the preceding that, unlike the line and bar graphs, the pie chart does not use the conventional X axis and Y axis. As you will see in the following example, the 1-2-3 nomenclature of the pie chart identifies labels as the x-entry; do not be confused as this has nothing to do with an X axis.

DO THIS NOW 13-1 **Creating a Pie Chart**

1. If you have not already started 1-2-3 and retrieved SAVE3, then do so now.
2. From the READY mode, position the cell pointer at cell B5. Although this is not necessary, it will minimize cell pointer movement when you select the ranges.
3. Execute the Graph command with the key sequence /G. This produces the submenu of Figure 13-12.

Figure 13-12
The Graph submenu.

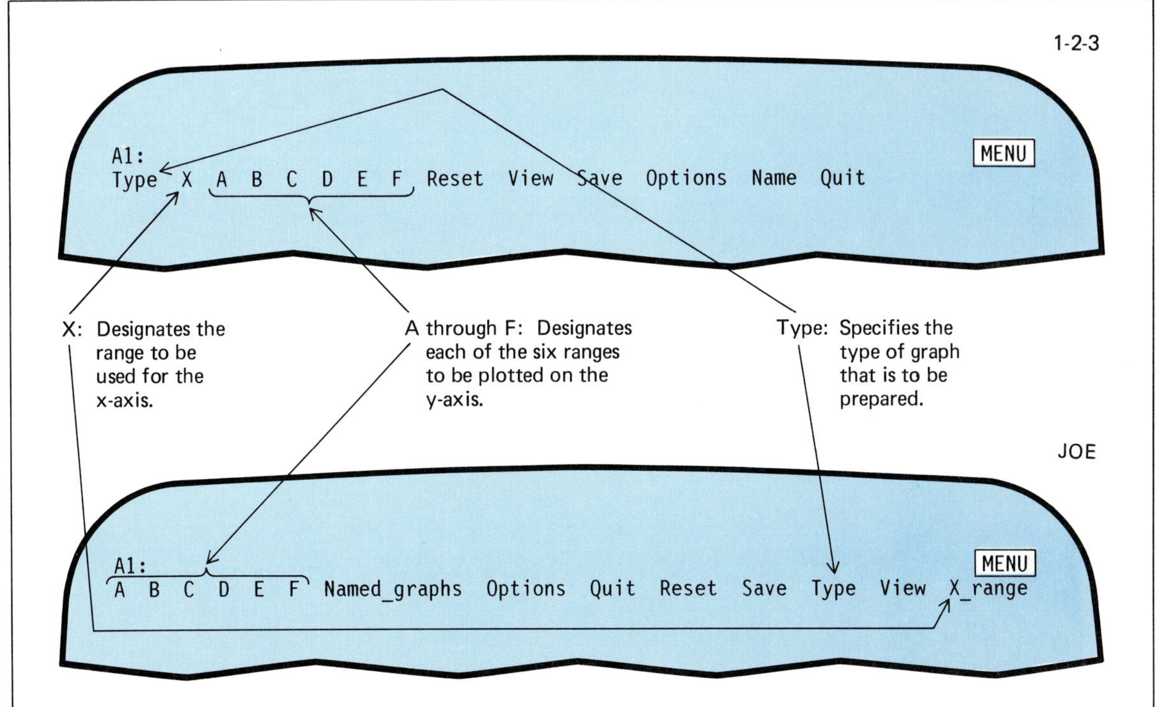

4. Execute the Type command (to designate the type of graph) by striking the letter T; this will cause the following submenu to be displayed.

```
Line Bar  XY  Stacked-bar  Pie                              (Lotus 1-2-3)
Bar_graph  Line_graph  Pie_graph  Stacked_bar_plot  XY_graph   (JOE)
```

5. Strike the letter P for Pie. The Pie option will be selected and the submenu of Figure 13-12 will reappear.
6. The next step is to specify the labels to be used. For pie charts, this is identified as the X range. Strike the letter X; the following prompt and anchor cell default will appear.

```
Enter X axis range: B5    (Lotus 1-2-3)
Enter X data range: B5    (JOE)
```

7. If you did not position the cell pointer at cell B5 prior to the Type command, your default cell address will not be B5. If it is not, then move the cell pointer to B5.
8. Strike the period key to anchor the cell range.
9. Move the cell pointer to cell F5 to complete the range.
10. Strike Enter to identify the range. The Graph submenu of Figure 13-12 will be redisplayed.
11. The next step is to identify the range of the data to be used in determining the number of sections and their sizes. Strike the letter A to enter the first range (the A range). The following prompt and default will appear.

`Enter first data range: B5`	(Lotus 1-2-3)
`Enter A data range: B5`	(JOE)

12. Enter the range B6..F6 (anchor at B6, move highlight to F6, and strike Enter).
13. Upon returning to the submenu of Figure 13-12, display the chart on the screen by striking the letter V for the View command. Your pie chart should look like Figure 13-13. (If you are using Lotus 1-2-3, the pie slices may be oriented differently. However, the proportions are the same.)

Figure 13-13
A basic pie chart.

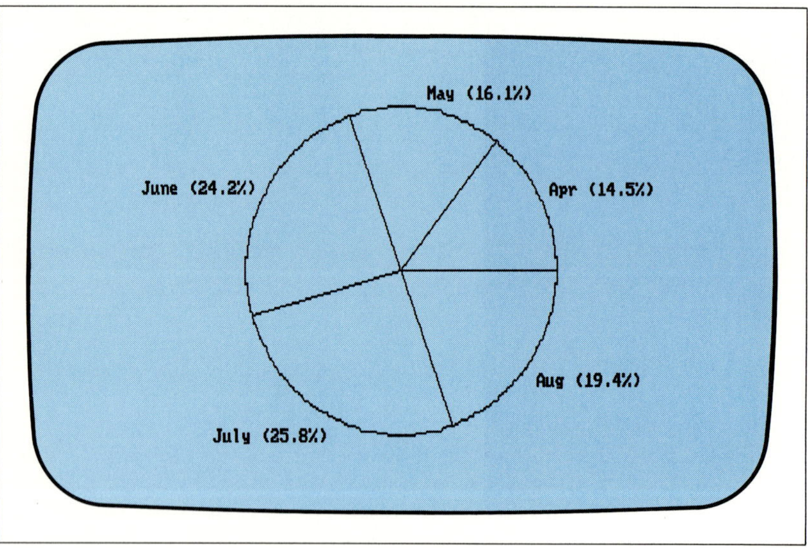

14. Strike the Escape key and your spreadsheet, together with the menu of Figure 13-12, will reappear.

Further Enhancements to the Pie Chart

One of the purposes of creating charts and graphs is to present information so that it is clear and easy to interpret. To this end, they must be complete and self-contained; it should not be necessary to refer to the spreadsheet to interpret the graph or chart. One way to improve the ability of charts and graphs to convey information is to give them titles; 1-2-3 allows you to include two title lines.

DO THIS NOW 13-2 **Entering Title Lines to the Pie Chart**

1. Your screen should still display the menu of Figure 13-12. If it does not, then take whatever action is necessary to display it.
2. For the first title line, enter the command sequence OTF. That is:

   ```
   Options Titles First           (Lotus 1-2-3)
   Options Titles First_Title     (JOE)
   ```

3. The following prompt will appear:

   ```
   Enter graph title, top line:   (Lotus 1-2-3)
   Top title (above graph):       (JOE)
   ```

4. Type the following title and strike Enter.

   ```
   MCT Enterprises
   ```

   You will be returned to the MENU mode and the Options submenu will be redisplayed.
5. For the second title line, select Title again by striking the letter T. Then strike the letter S for Second title line.
6. In response to the prompt, type the following and strike Enter.

   ```
   High Season Monthly Sales Quotas
   ```

   You will be returned to the MENU mode and the Options submenu will be redisplayed.
7. To get back to the Graph submenu of Figure 13-12, strike the letter Q (for Quit) twice. You must back out of two menu levels.

In the earlier descriptions of graphics, all the examples of graphs and pie charts were shown in color. For instance, different colors were used to distinguish one data set from the other in a bar graph and clearly to mark the slices of the pie chart. This same effect can be achieved with the cross-hatching features found in both JOE and Release 2 of Lotus 1-2-3. In order to use cross-hatching with a pie chart, each data value (cell) in the data range requires a corresponding cross-hatching code. There are seven different cross-hatch patterns that can be coded into the display by using the digits 1 through 7; 0 causes no cross-hatching and is the default.

The pie chart of Figure 13-13 is constructed from the data in B6..F6 of the Figure 13-11 worksheet. To cross-hatch each of these five cells, you must specify a corresponding set of five cross-hatching codes. This is done by entering the cross-hatching codes into a cell range that corresponds to the data cell range. For this example, we will enter the codes for the data in B6..F6 in the cell range B12..F12.

DO THIS NOW 13-3 **Designating Cross-Hatching for the Pie Chart**

1. If your screen is not already at the READY mode, then strike the Escape key until it is.
2. Enter the numbers 1 through 5 into the cell range B12..F12. The display for this range of cells will be as shown in Figure 13-14.

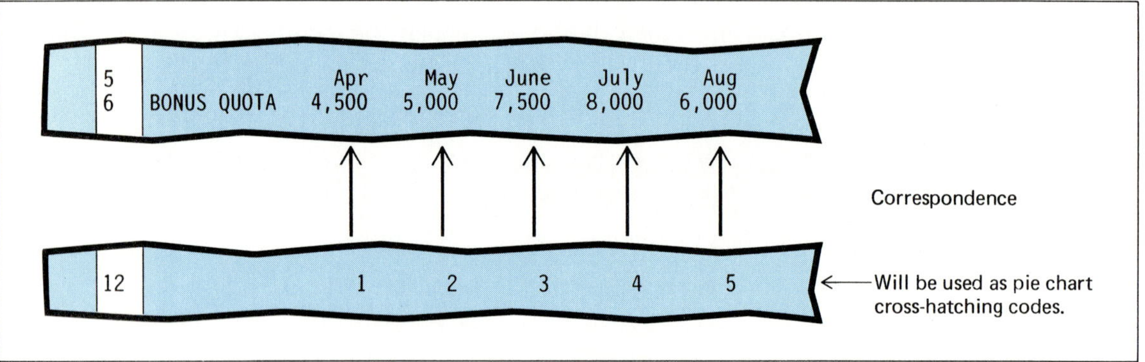

Figure 13-14
Cross-hatch codes to be used with the pie chart.

3. Execute the Graph command with the sequence /G. This causes the submenu of Figure 13-12 to be displayed.
4. When you created the pie chart, you used the A range (refer to the menu) to specify the worksheet data range. You assign cross-hatching codes by selecting the B range. Strike the letter B to select the B range.
5. Designate the cell range by anchoring the cell pointer at B12 and then extending the range to cell F12. When you have the range specified, strike the Enter key.
6. The submenu of Figure 13-12 will be displayed again. Strike the letter V (for View) to display the pie chart shown in Figure 13-15.

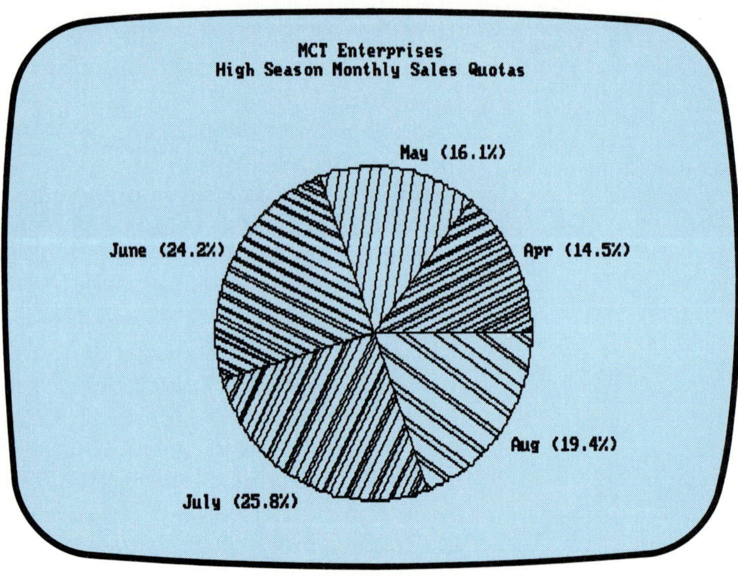

Figure 13-15
The pie chart with cross-hatching.

If you want to change the cross-hatching, you need only return to the READY mode and change the codes in the cell range B12..F12. Although the codes in Figure 13-14 are consecutive integers (1, 2, ···), they need not be in sequence as in this example. For instance, your entries in these five cells could have been 6, 0, 4, 0, and 3. The 0 entries would cause the May and July slices to be displayed without cross-hatching. In this example, the cell range B12..F12 was used for the cross-hatching codes because it corresponds conveniently to the data range. However, this range could have been positioned anywhere (for instance, A11..A15), but it must be included somewhere. The software simply matches the codes defined by the B range to the data defined by the A range.

You can explode any of the slices of your pie chart by adding 100 to the cross-hatching code that corresponds to the data cell for that slice. For example, return to the READY mode and change the entry in cell E12 from 4 to 104, as shown in Figure 13-16. Then invoke the Graph menu (with /G) and display the graph with the View command. The result will be as shown in Figure 13-17.

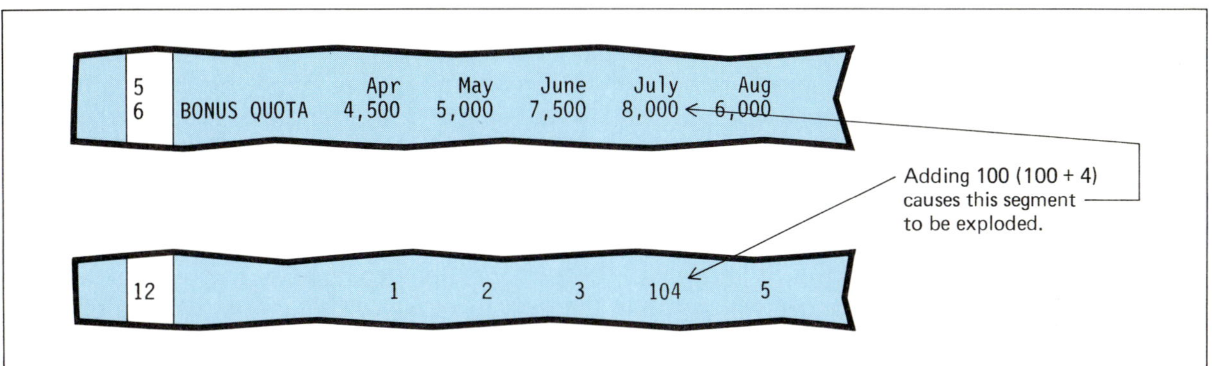

Figure 13-16
Cross-hatch codes to explode the July segment.

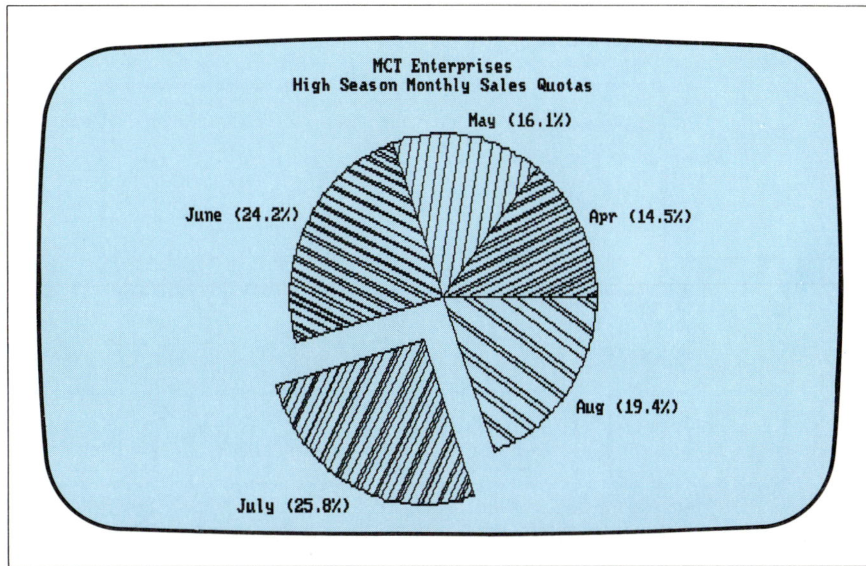

Figure 13-17
Exploding a section of a pie chart.

SAVING YOUR WORK

The Action of the File Save Command

Preparing the pie chart has required numerous, detailed steps. Fortunately, the specifications for this graph are now a part of this worksheet, just as are the formulas. Defining one or more graph specifications for a worksheet involves a change to the worksheet just as does adding a new column or row. Hence, after one or more graph settings have been defined, you must save the worksheet back to disk. In fact, you should issue the File Save command (/FS from the READY mode) to save your worksheet *including the pie chart specifications that you have just entered.* At any later time that you use this worksheet, the graph will be available as if you had never terminated the work session at all. Be aware that the saving operation *is not done with the Save from the Graph submenu* (Figure 13-12). The Graph Save sequence writes a printer image of the graph to the disk for later printing.

Naming a Graph

In preparing graphics presentations from data in a worksheet, you will commonly create more than one graph or chart. For instance, in addition to this pie chart, you will also create line and bar graphs for the monthly sales of the sales representatives. Once they are completed, you will be able to retain all of them as part of your worksheet file (as illustrated in Figure 13-18) and switch from one graph to another. However, in order to create and retain more than one graph with a worksheet, each must be given a name. The graph that you have access to at any time is called the **current graph.** With a simple sequence of 1-2-3 commands, you can make any of the defined graphs in the worksheet the current graph. Before proceeding further, let us use the sequence of DTN 13-4 to give this graph the name QUOTA_PIE so that we might create another.

Figure 13-18
Graph specifications in a worksheet file.

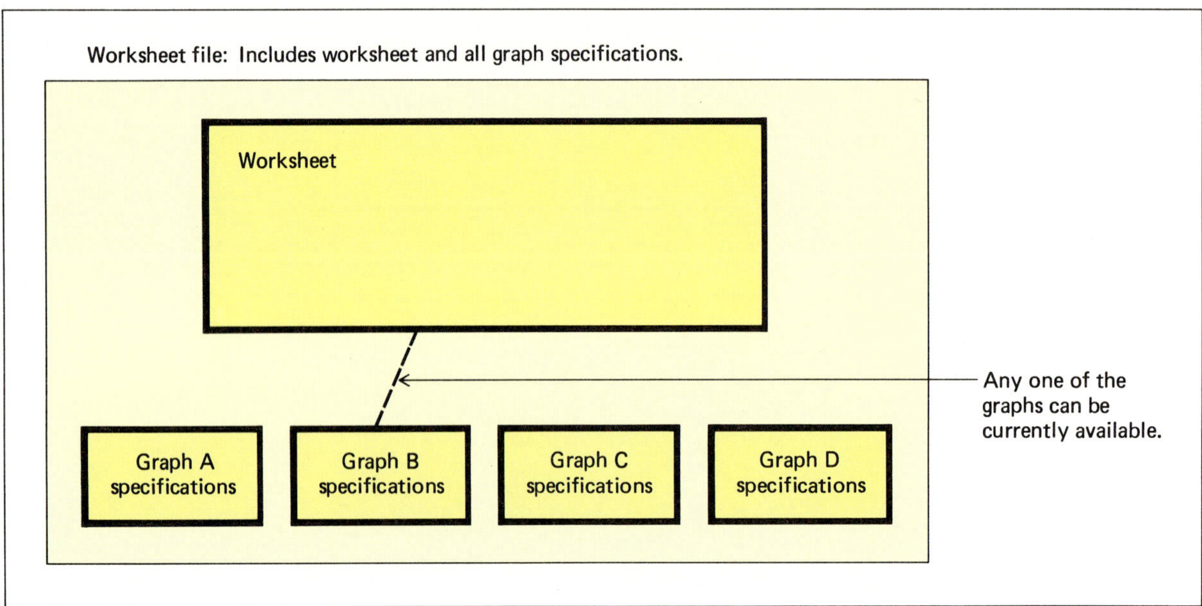

DO THIS NOW 13-4 **Naming the Graph**

1. If you are at the READY mode, use the Graph command (/G) to get the graph submenu of Figure 13-12.
2. From the Graph submenu, execute the Named_graph (JOE) or Name (Lotus 1-2-3) command by striking the letter N. This produces the following submenu.

```
Use  Create  Delete  Reset  (Lotus 1-2-3)
Create_named_graph Delete_one_named_graph Reset_all Use_named_graph (JOE)
```

3. Execute the Create command by striking the letter C. *This does not mean create a graph; it means to create a name for the current graph.* You will be prompted to enter a name. Type the name QUOTA_PIE (use an underscore to separate the two words), and then strike Enter. This gives a name to the set of specifications for this graph so that you can make it current at any time. The name can be up to 15 characters in length (it is *not* a DOS filename).

You must be aware that the action of naming the graph *does not save the worksheet or the graph specifications to disk.* It only makes the appropriate additions to the version of the worksheet currently in memory. To update the copy on disk, you must use the Save command from the main menu.

Resetting Before Creating a New Graph

Now that you have named the current graph, you can proceed to define another. The first thing you must do is to "clear the slate" so that you can enter the specifications for the new graph; remember, QUOTA_PIE is not only safely named and stored, but it is also the current graph. This overall sequence of steps is much like creating a worksheet, saving it to disk, and then erasing all cells to enter another. The following example resets the current graph specifications so that you can begin anew.

DO THIS NOW 13-5 **Resetting the Graph Specifications**

1. From the Graph submenu (Figure 13-12), execute the Reset command by striking the letter R. Note that there is the Reset command in the Graph submenu. Do not execute the Name Reset command or *all* of the named graph definitions will be deleted. The Graph Reset command produces the following submenu.

```
Graph  X  A  B  C  D  E  F  Quit        (Lotus 1-2-3)
A  B  C  D  E  F  Graph  Quit  X_range  (JOE)
```

2. Execute the Graph subcommand by striking the letter G. The graph settings will be initialized, and you may proceed to define the next graph settings.

CREATING OTHER TYPES OF GRAPHS

The pie graph that you created involves most of the basic principles of graph creation. The following overall actions of creating a graph or chart are the same for all types. The details differ from one graph to the next according to the nature of the graph or chart.

- Designate the type.
- Designate the cell range for the X-range. For a pie chart, these cell contents are the descriptions that are placed next to each slice. For bar and line graphs, they are the entries to be placed on the X axis (the horizontal axis of the graph).
- Designate the cell range(s) for the Y axis. For a pie chart, these cell contents contain the data to be used in determining the relative sizes of the slices. For bar and line graphs, they are the values to be plotted on the Y axis (the vertical axis of the graph). With 1-2-3, it is possible to include up to six ranges.

Bar Graphs

For this example, assume that you are preparing a postseason report analyzing the results of the past selling season to go to all the sales representatives. In it you wish to include a bar graph comparing each representative's monthly sales with the bonus quota. In this way, the representatives will be able to assess their performances relative to the bonus quota and to the performances of others.

DO THIS NOW 13-6 **Creating a Bar Graph**

1. You must first designate the graph type (bar). From the Graph submenu of Figure 13-12, set the graph type as Bar by striking the letters TB. The Graph submenu will remain on the screen.
2. Now specify the range of cells that form the X axis by striking the letter X.
3. Enter the X axis range as B5..F5. To do this, move the cell pointer to B5, anchor it, move it to cell F5, and strike Enter. When the action has been completed, the Graph submenu will be redisplayed.
4. The A value range will be used for the bonus quota, so strike the letter A. In response to the prompt to enter the A value range, the first data range is B6..F6. To do this, move the cell pointer to B6, anchor it, move to cell F6, and strike Enter.
5. At this point, if you are curious about the graph, execute the View command by striking the letter V. The bar graph shown in Figure 13-19 will be displayed. Strike the Escape to get back to the Graph submenu.
6. Continuing, the B value range will be used for salesperson Hal

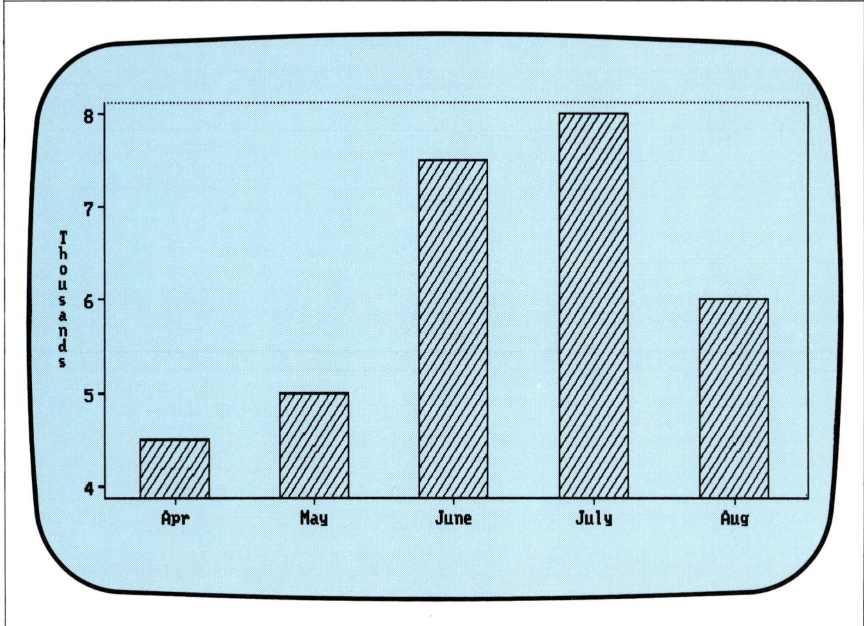

Figure 13-19
The beginning of the desired bar graph.

Curtis. Strike the letter B and enter the second data range as B8..F8, using the same procedure as you did for the A range.

7. Repeat the range definitions with the C value range as the data range B9..F9 and the D value range as the data range B10..F10.

8. Viewing the graph once again, you should have the form of Figure 13-20. This bar graph is rapidly taking form.

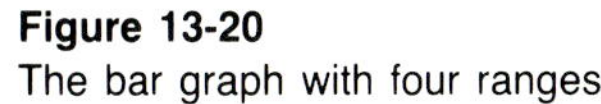
Figure 13-20
The bar graph with four ranges.

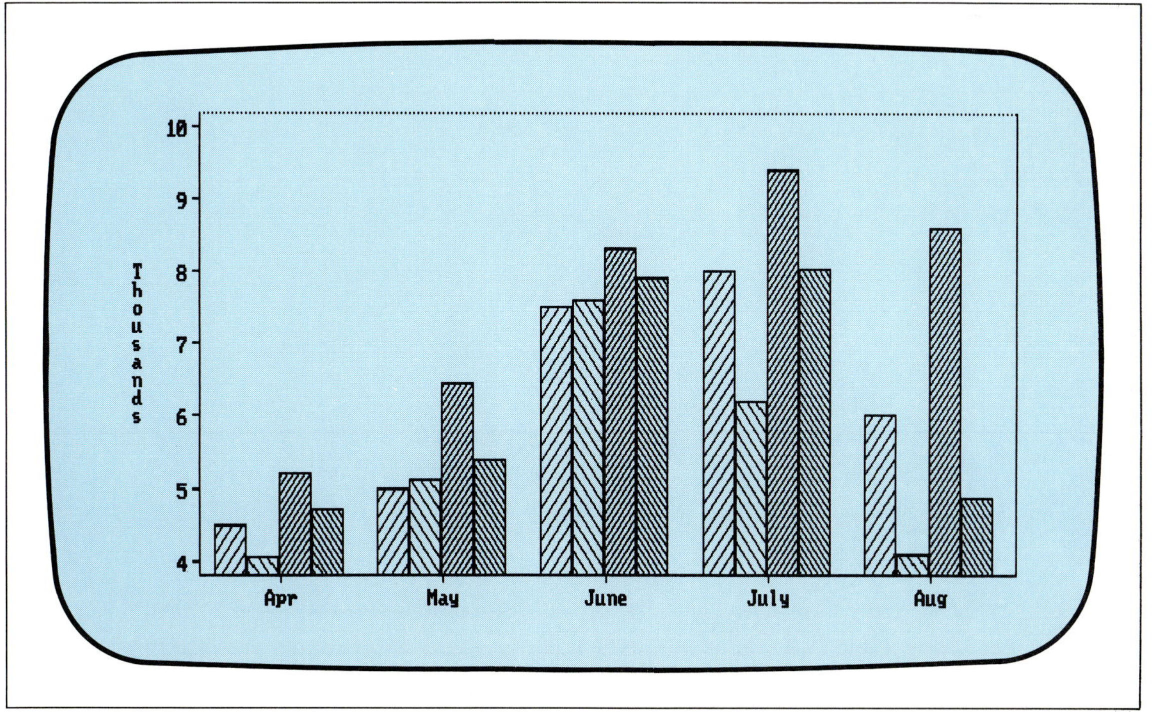

Although this bar graph has a nice appearance, it does not tell us the entire story; that is, we do not know the association between bars and data ranges. Refer to any of the bar graphs from earlier descriptions (for instance, Figure 13-7 or 13-8) and you will see that each color bar is identified by a **legend.** Let us enter a legend into your bar graph.

DO THIS NOW 13-7 **Enter a Legend Into a Bar Graph**

1. From the Graph menu (Figure 13-12), execute the Options and Legends commands by striking O and then L. The displayed submenu will consist of a list of ranges (A through F).
2. To define the legend for the A range (bonus quota), strike the letter A and you will be prompted to enter the A range legend.
3. You can type in whatever description you desire. Since this is the bonus quota, type QUOTA and strike Enter.
4. For ranges B, C, and D, execute the Legends command and repeat steps 2 and 3 using the legends Curtis, Ng, and Crowder, respectively.
5. As this completes legend definition, strike the letter Q to Quit the Options submenu, and control is returned to the Graph menu of Figure 13-12. To view your graph, strike the V and your display should be as in Figure 13-21.

Figure 13-21
The bar graph with legends.

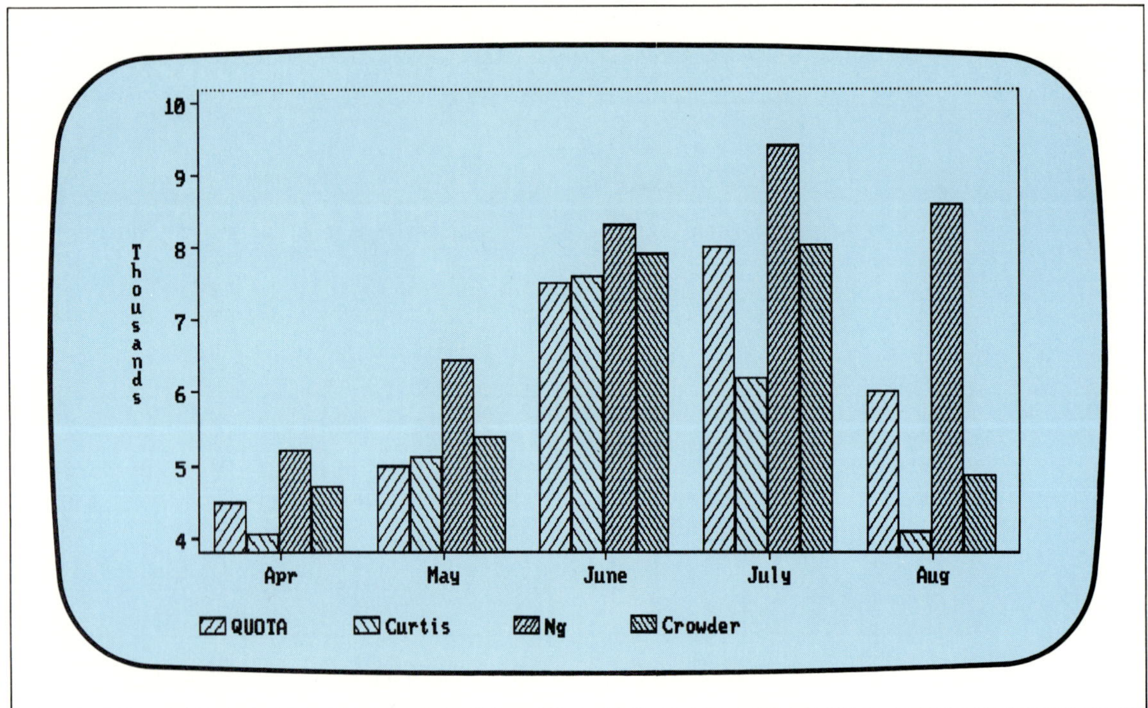

If we wished to include a label, the procedure would be identical to that for the pie chart. To retain these graph settings, use the Name Create sequence.

Changing the Y Axis

Earlier in this chapter, you saw the effect of changing the Y-axis scaling on the appearance of a graph. In Figure 13-3, the range of values displayed on the Y axis was 0 to 60. By contrast, in Figure 13-4 the scale was changed to be consistent with displaying a range of 30 to 60. To simplify creating graphs, 1-2-3 automatically scales to fit the data range. Hence, in your bar graph (Figure 13-21), the Y axis starts at slightly less than 4 (4000), consistent with the smallest data value. In some instances, the form of Figure 13-21 is desirable. However, by starting at $4000 rather than 0, the differences are exaggerated. For instance, at a glance, the August sales of Curtis appear to be only a fraction of the quota. Let us consider how to override the automatic scaling of the program and change the Y-axis display so that it starts at 0.

DO THIS NOW 13-8 **Changing the Y-Axis Range to 0–10,000**

1. From the Graph submenu, execute the following command sequence

   ```
   Options  Scale  Y_scale
   ```

   by typing the letters O, S, and Y. You may wish to inspect each resulting submenu as you go. When finished, the following submenu will be displayed on your screen.

`Automatic Manual Lower Upper Format Indicator Quit` (Lotus 1-2-3)
`Automatic_scale Format_# Indicator Lower_bound Manual_Quit Upper_bound` (JOE)

2. You must first designate that you want to use manual specification of the scale. To do this, strike the letter M for Manual. Do not be concerned that nothing appears to happen and the menu does not change; 1-2-3 has "logged" this change.
3. You can now specify the lower and upper limits of values that you want used for the Y axis. Select the Lower option by striking the letter L.
4. Enter a value of 0 and strike Enter.
5. Select the Upper option by striking the letter U.
6. Enter a value of 10,000 and strike Enter.
7. To return to the Graph menu, strike the letter Q twice (there are two submenus requiring the Quit action).

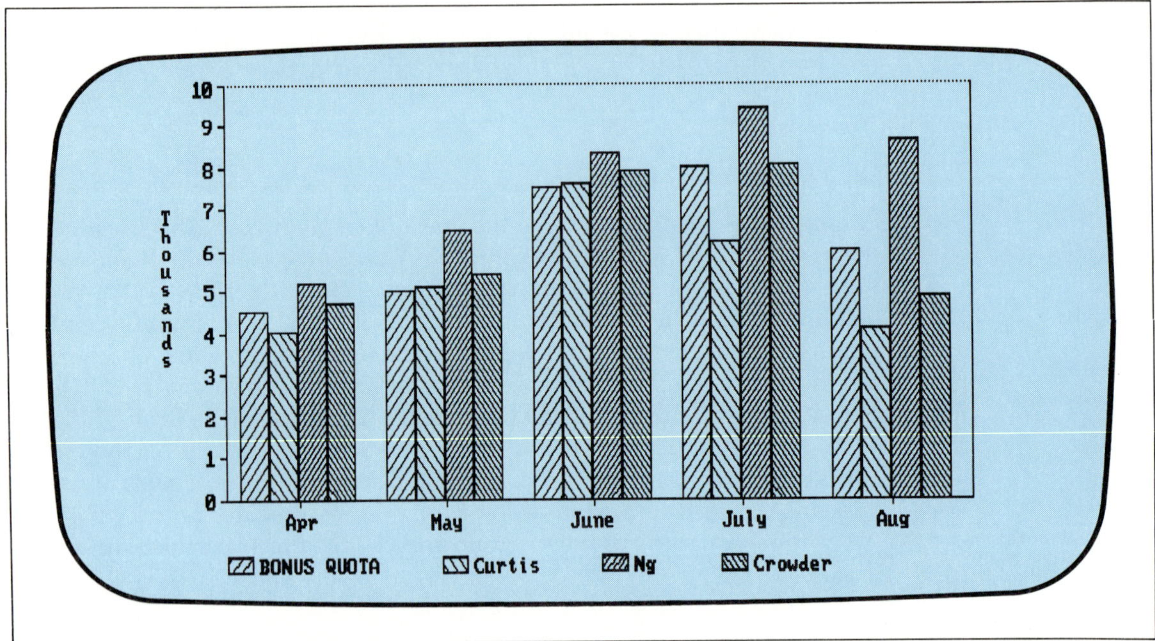

Figure 13-22
Bar graph with a manually scaled Y-axis.

If you view your graph now, it will appear as shown in Figure 13-22. This graph is now complete and so you should give it a name before going on to the next one; you should then save the worksheet to disk. Using the sequence of DTN 13-4, name the graph QUOTA_BAR. Then return to the main 1-2-3 menu and execute the File Save command sequence to ensure that your latest work is not lost.

A Line Graph

Your next step is to create the line graph equivalent of the bar graph for the sales data. Actually, the data requirements and graph specifications for a line graph are almost identical to those for a bar graph. In this case, you can change your bar graph to a line graph merely by changing the type. Do this from the Graph submenu (Figure 13-12) by striking the letter T for Type. From the resulting Type submenu, select the Line graph option by typing an L. If you view the graph, it should look like Figure 13-23. In doing this, you have changed the current set of graph specifications; you have not changed QUOTA_BAR as stored in your worksheet. If you wish to save this line graph as a separate named graph, then return to the Graph submenu and use the sequence of DTN 13-4 to name it. The name QUOTA_LINE would be descriptive.

If you had no bar graph from which to work (the normal situation) and you wanted to create a line graph, then you would need to reset and enter all the specifications. Other than specifying the Type as Line instead of Bar in the first step of DTN 13-6, the sequence of steps is identical to that of DTNs 13-6 and 13-7. However, there is one other specification that determines the appearance of the line graph. Referring to Figure 13-23, notice that each data point is marked by a symbol, and that the points for each

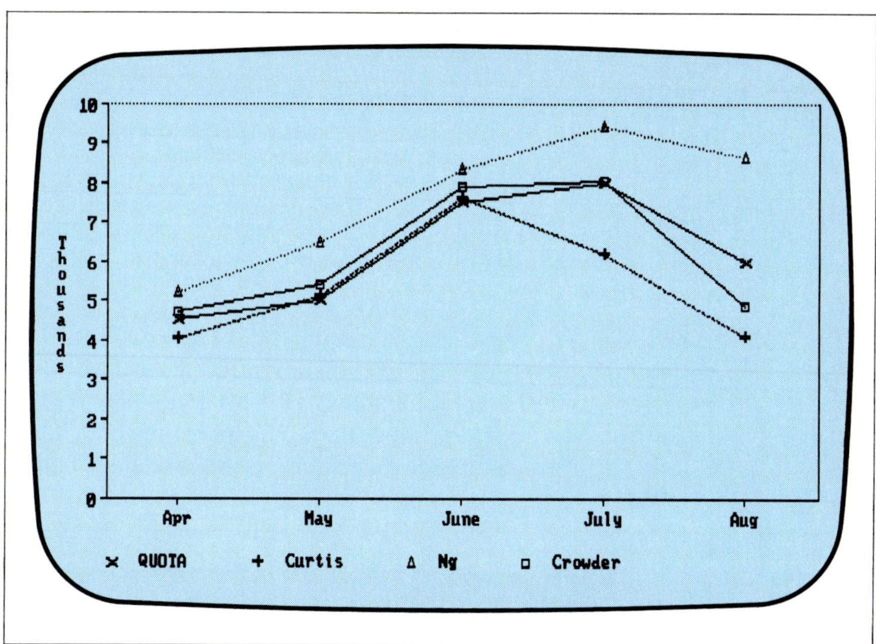

Figure 13-23
A line graph.

data range are connected by line segments. With line graphs, you can specify lines only, symbols only, or both; the default is lines with no symbols. You can change this with the Graph Format command. To see how this works, let us change your line graph so that you have only lines.

DO THIS NOW 13-9 **Changing the Line/Symbol Display of a Line Graph**

1. From the Graph submenu, enter the Options Format Graph command sequence, that is, OFG.
2. The resulting submenu will be:

`Lines  Symbols  Both  Neither` (Lotus 1-2-3)

`Both_lines_and_symbols  Lines_only  Symbols_only  Neither;label_only` (JOE)

   Select Lines by typing the letter L.

3. To return to the Graph submenu, strike the letter Q twice (there are two submenus requiring the Quit action). Then view the graph and you will see that it consists only of the lines.

A Stacked-Bar Graph

The bar graph of Figure 13-22 is a good vehicle for comparing the sales quotas and monthly sales for each sales representative. However, it does not show us total monthly sales. As you recall from the earlier descriptions, a stacked-bar graph displays totals and the contribution of each element to the totals. To create a stacked-bar graph, you must first reset (DTN 13-5), and then enter the graph specifications. The steps are identical to those of DTNs 13-6 and 13-7, with the following exceptions.

- The graph type must be designated by typing S for Stacked_bar.
- The bonus quota has no meaning in the total. Thus, the A, B, and C ranges should be the monthly sales for the three sales representatives.

When you are finished, executing the View command from the Graph submenu will produce the graph shown in Figure 13-24. Note that it is not necessary to designate the scaling, as 1-2-3 defaults to 0 for the lower value of the Y axis. You should now name this graph; use QUOTA_SBAR. Then return to the main menu and save your worksheet using the File Save command.

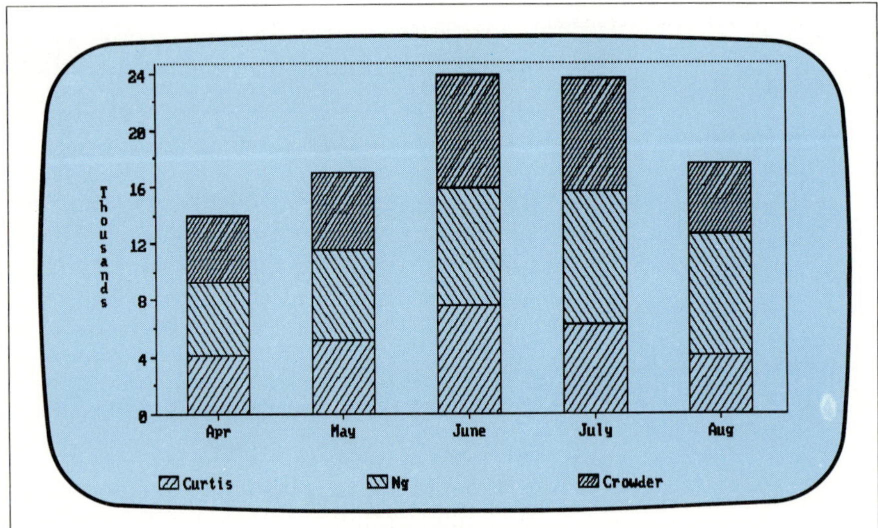

Figure 13-24
A stacked bar graph.

RECALLING A GRAPH

You now have four graph specifications defined for this worksheet (three if you did not name the line graph). Whenever you begin a 1-2-3 work session and retrieve this worksheet, the current graph will always be the one that was current when you last used the worksheet. You can switch from one graph to another at any time; for instance, the following example makes the pie chart (QUOTA_PIE) the current graph.

DO THIS NOW 13-10 **Switching Graphs**

1. From the Graph submenu (Figure 13-12), execute the Name command by striking the letter N; the following Name submenu will be displayed.

```
Use  Create  Delete  Reset        (Lotus 1-2-3)
Create_named_graph Delete_one_named_graph Reset_all Use_named_graph (JOE)
```

2. Execute the Use command by striking the letter U. A prompt will be displayed requesting the name of the graph to be made current. Also, a list of named graphs will be displayed on the third line of the control panel. If you have named all four graphs, it will be:

   ```
   QUOTA_BAR  QUOTA_LINE  QUOTA_PIE  QUOTA_SBAR
   ```

3. Select the graph QUOTA_PIE either by typing the name or by moving the highlight to that name and striking Enter. The Graph submenu of Figure 13-12 will reappear.

You can then display or modify your pie chart as desired. Remember, if you make any changes, you must save your worksheet.

Some computers can even print graphs in full color.

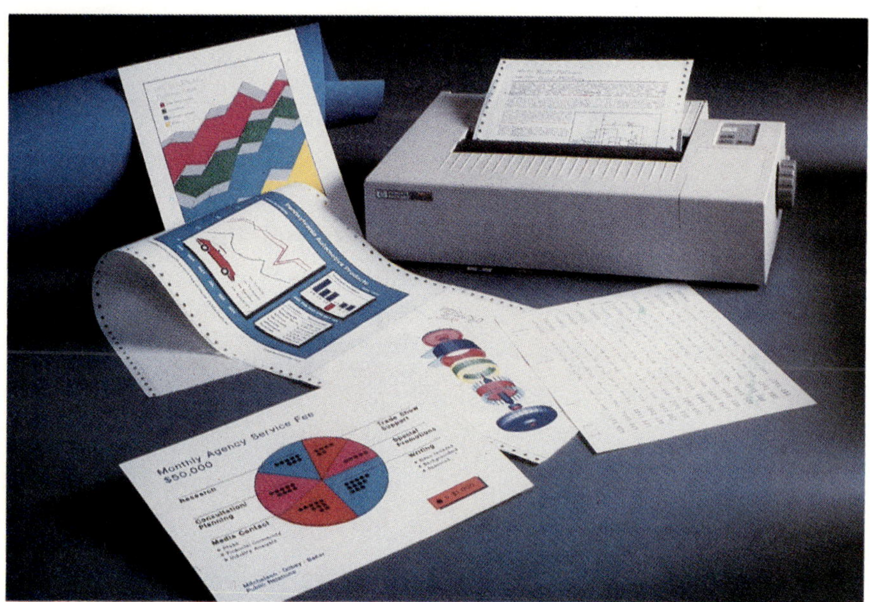

PRINTING A GRAPH

The procedures for printing a graph are different for Lotus 1-2-3 and JOE. Hence, you should read the first of the following sections if you are using JOE and the second if you are using Lotus 1-2-3.

Printer Initialization and Printing a JOE Graph

The first time you ran JOE, the program asked you to enter the type of monitor; this information is required by JOE to produce the correct screen images. In order to print graphics, JOE must be told the brand of graphics printer you are using. You specify this information in much the same way that you specified the default data drive (DTN 11-1).

DO THIS NOW 13-11 **Setting the Printer Type**

1. To avoid possible confusion, return to the READY mode by striking the Escape key as many times as is necessary.
2. Enter the command sequence

   ```
   / WorkSets Globals Defaults Install Printer
   ```

   by typing /WGDIP.
3. A list of printers will be displayed. Select your printer from this list by moving the highlight to it and striking the Enter.
4. Exit this menu by typing Q (Quit_menu). You will be returned to the READY mode.
5. If your printer is connected to printer port 1 (the standard printer port), then you can skip to step 6. Otherwise, you must specify the port with the command sequence

   ```
   / WorkSets Globals Defaults Printer_sets Interface_port
   ```

   by typing /WGDPI. You will be presented with a list of selections 1–8. Select the one that corresponds to your computer configuration by moving the highlight and then striking the Enter. Repeatedly strike the Escape key to return to the READY mode.
6. To save your printer information, enter the command sequence

   ```
   / WorkSets Globals Defaults Update
   ```

   by typing /WGDU. Then return to the READY mode.

This action saves the printer information to the JOE disk so that it will be available whenever you want to print a graph. The only reason to perform this action again would be to designate another printer.

For printing, you have two options: print the current graph or print a graph that you designate. First, check the printer to be certain that it is turned on. Then, from the READY mode, use either of the following key combinations:

`Alt-F10`	Print the current graph.
`Shift-F10`	Print a named graph; JOE will ask for the name of the graph to be printed.

As printing takes place, the graph will be displayed on the screen. When finished, the worksheet will be redisplayed in the READY mode. To cancel a graph printing operation, enter the Ctrl-Break key sequence.

Printing With Lotus 1-2-3

Lotus 1-2-3 consists of several programs; you have been using the worksheet program 123.EXE. To print a graph, 123.EXE creates a separate graphics image file. This file is then printed by the Lotus program PGRAPH.EXE. However, before you can print a graph, you must have specified to Lotus the type of graphics printer connected to your computer. If you are using Lotus 1-2-3, then you should already have run the INSTALL program (from DOS) to specify your computer configuration. If you have not, then do so and specify the graphics printer that you have on your computer.

When this is done, run Lotus 1-2-3 and retrieve the worksheet SALES3, which includes specifications for four graphs. As an illustration, let us print the pie chart.

DO THIS NOW 13-12 **Printing the Pie Chart QUOTA_PIE with Lotus 1-2-3**

1. Make QUOTA_PIE the current graph with the sequence of DTN 13-10.
2. Execute the command sequence

   ```
   / Graph Save
   ```

   by typing /GS. Lotus 1-2-3 is ready to save an image of this graph to disk. The resulting prompt will be as follows (the default drive will be different if you are using a hard disk):

   ```
   Enter you graph file name B:\*.PIC
   ```

3. You must enter a DOS filename; the default extension for graph files is PIC. Type Q_PIE and strike Enter. The graph file image will then be written to disk with the file name Q_PIE.PIC. Note that you cannot use QUOTA_PIE because it is too long for use as a DOS filename.
4. When control is returned to the Graph submenu, terminate execution of Lotus 1-2-3 and return to DOS.
5. Run the graph program from DOS by typing PGRAPH and striking the Enter. (If you have been operating from the Lotus Access System, select the PrintGraph option.)
6. The graph program will display the menu:

   ```
   Image-Select Settings Go Align Page Exit
   ```

   You will also see the full definition of the current print specifications. The Hardware Setup section is a result of the INSTALL program.
7. You must select the graph image file to be printed; do this by typing the letter I (Image-Select). A list of graph image files will be displayed.

8. Select the desired graph image file by highlighting the name and striking the Enter. (Your disk has only one file, so it is already highlighted.)
9. Select the Go command by typing the letter G.

As printing takes place, Lotus 1-2-3 will flash WAIT in the upper right of the screen. When printing is finished, strike the letter E (for Exit) and control of the computer will be returned to DOS.

SUMMARY

The purpose of this chapter has been both to provide you with a general understanding of computer graphics, and to give you specific experience using the graphics features of 1-2-3. By using 1-2-3, you have been able to create, save, and print line and bar graphs and pie charts. Summarizing, the important items from the chapter are:

- Computer graphics is the use of the computer to prepare visual presentations.
- Business graphics is the representation of tabular data in graph form. The three common graphic forms are line graph, bar graph, and pie chart.
- A pie chart is used to illustrate the percentage contribution that each data item makes to the whole.
- Design graphics programs are used by professionals such as engineers, architects, and interior designers to automate much of their work.
- Computer-aided design (CAD) software allows the designer to enter design data into the computer and from that data to display the item on the screen and to print detailed drawings. CAD/CAM software extends this to creating detailed instructions to machines for manufacturing the item.
- All graphics activity in 1-2-3 takes place through the Graph command.
- With 1-2-3, five graph types can be created; the four described in this chapter are line, bar, stacked-bar, and pie chart.
- The overall 1-2-3 steps in creating a graph are:
    1. Designate the type (line, bar, stacked bar, or pie).
    2. Designate the cell range for the x range. For a pie chart, these cell contents are the descriptions that are placed next to each slice. For bar and line graphs, they are the entries to be placed on the X axis (the horizontal axis of the graph).

3. Designate the cell range(s) for the Y axis. For a pie chart, these cell contents contain the data to be used in determining the relative sizes of the slices. For bar and line graphs, they are the values to be plotted on the Y axis (the vertical axis of the graph). With 1-2-3, it is possible to include up to six ranges.

- Graphs can include descriptions, legends, and cross-hatching to better convey their meaning.
- When a graph is created for a worksheet, it becomes part of that worksheet until it is erased (in much the same way as adding a new row to a worksheet). After creating a graph, the worksheet must be saved using the /File Save command if the graph is to be retained.
- If more than one graph is specified for a worksheet, then each must be given a graph name using the /Graph Name command. This command is also used to make any graph the current graph.
- The current graph is the set of graph specifications to which 1-2-3 has access at any give time. It is the graph that is displayed with the View command and is available for modification or for printing.
- Bar and line graphs are automatically scaled by 1-2-3. Manual scaling can by used, which allows you to specify the smallest and largest values to be utilized in setting the X axis and Y axis.
- Graphs can be printed if you have a graphics printer.
- Before a graph can be printed, the printer characteristics must be defined for the program. This is done differently with JOE and with Lotus 1-2-3.
- From the READY mode with JOE, use either of the following key combinations to print a graph.

Alt-F10	Print the current graph
Shift-F10	Print a named graph

- To print a graph from Lotus 1-2-3, a graph image file of the current graph must be created with the /Graph Save command. Then from DOS run the program PGRAPH to print the image file.

NEW TERMINOLOGY

The following are important new terms introduced in this chapter; you should be familiar with each of them.

bar graph
CAD (computer-aided design)
CAD/CAM
computer graphics
current graph
legend
line graph
pie chart
presentation graphics
scale
X axis
Y axis

REVIEW QUESTIONS

1. What is computer graphics?
2. What meant by X axis and Y axis?
3. What is the difference between a bar graph and a stacked-bar graph?
4. Referring to the pie charts of Figure 13-2, do they tell you how much time each employee can devote to the various activities? What information is conveyed?
5. What does it mean when we say that a pie chart is exploded?
6. What do you think would happen to the pie chart display of QUOTA_PIE (see Figure 13-15) if the entries of row 12 were changed to each of the following sets?

a.	**1**	**0**	**2**	**0**	**3**
b.	**3**	**0**	**1**	**0**	**2**
c.	**100**	**100**	**100**	**100**	**100**
d.	**1**	**100**	**2**	**0**	**100**

7. What is the purpose of naming a graph specification?
8. When a graph definition is named and saved, what is the extension used by DOS?
9. What happens to a newly specified graph if 1-2-3 is exited without executing the File Save command sequence from the main menu?
10. How many data ranges can be included in a line or bar graph?
11. What is the purpose of changing the range of the Y axis in the line graph of Figure 13-21 to 0–10,000 (giving the graph of Figure 13-22)?

MATCHING

Match each key sequence in a to h with the corresponding action in 1 through 8.

a. /GNC
b. /GT
c. /GOL
d. /GRG
e. /GNU
f. /GOSY
g. /GX
h. /FS

1. Designate the type of graph.
2. Specify the descriptions to be used for each slice of a pie chart.
3. Enter a name for the current graph.
4. Save the recently created graph to disk.
5. Clear the current graph settings so that a new set of specifications can be entered.
6. Create legends for a bar graph.

7. Change the lower limit of the Y axis from 1000 to 500.
8. Make the graph QUOTA_LINE the current graph.

TRUE/FALSE

Determine whether each of the following is true or false.

______ 1. The X axis of a line graph always displays time.

______ 2. The purpose of a pie chart is to display the relative sizes of quantities that make up a whole.

______ 3. From a CAD/CAM program, an engineer might get a detailed drawing for a part to be manufactured and a set of instructions to machine tools for making the part.

______ 4. One distinction between a bar graph and a stacked-bar graph is that one displays data values but the other does not.

______ 5. In 1-2-3, an exploded stacked-bar chart is one in which some of the elements have been separated from others for emphasis.

______ 6. Even though the pie chart does not have X and Y axes as do bar and line graphs, the X range is used to describe the data range being used.

______ 7. Once the cross-hatching codes have been set up for a pie chart, they can be deleted from the worksheet and 1-2-3 will still retain the information.

______ 8. Any slice of a pie chart can be exploded by adding 100 to the cross-hatching code for that segment.

______ 9. It is not necessary to name a graph if it is the only one to be created for a worksheet.

______ 10. When you name a graph, that set of graph specifications is automatically saved to disk as part of the worksheet.

______ 11. A reason that you might use the Graph Reset command would be so that you could create a new graph for your worksheet.

______ 12. A completely different procedure is used for creating a bar graph than for creating a pie chart.

______ 13. The purpose of a legend on a graph is to identify different sets of data displayed by the graph.

______ 14. Graphs created by 1-2-3 are automatically scaled (by default).

______ 15. The action of making another graph the current graph (using /GNU) requires that an entirely new file be read from disk.

ANSWERS TO OBJECTIVE QUESTIONS

Matching

1. b 2. g 3. a 4. h 5. d 6. c 7. f 8. e

True/False

1. F 2. T 3. T 4. F 5. F 6. T 7. F 8. T
9. T 10. F 11. T 12. F 13. T 14. T 15. F

ASSIGNMENTS/PROJECTS

1. Using your sales analysis worksheet of Chapter 12 (COST3), create a pie chart that shows the portion of the total cost contributed by each of the four styles. Use cross-hatching and include appropriate titles.

2. From COST3, create a stacked-bar graph that shows the unit cost and the five cost components of which it is composed. Include appropriate graph titles and titles for the X axis and the Y axis.

3. Using the version of the EMPL worksheet of Chapter 12 that you completed, create a stacked-bar chart showing the total score for each employee as consisting of scores on each of the three training units. Include appropriate graph titles and titles for the X axis and the Y axis.

4. Using the version of the EMPL worksheet of Chapter 12 that you completed, create a line graph with scores plotted against the three training units. This graph is to include three data ranges: the average rating, the highest rating, and the lowest rating. Include appropriate graph titles and titles for the X axis and the Y axis.

5. Using the worksheet BUDGET.WKS stored on your data disk, make a bar graph displaying the quarterly expenses and income against the quarter. Include appropriate graph titles and titles for the X axis and the Y axis.

PART FOUR

Database Management

PROLOGUE TO PART FOUR

Early in this book, you learned that the computer cannot do anything for us that we cannot already do ourselves. Of course, the computer is much faster and more accurate. In fact, many of the things we do on the computer would be impractical to attempt manually because of the time that would be required. You have already seen how word processing streamlines the entry, editing, and storage of documents, and how spreadsheet programs make "what if" analyses of data fast and efficient. One characteristic of spreadsheet programs is that they provide you with the ability to organize data and to relate data elements (by formulas) to produce useful information. (This is the definition of data processing from Chapter 1: *produce information from data*.) The third of the productivity software tools described in Chapter 2 is the database management system (DBMS); it gives us the ability to manage and manipulate data in files to produce useful information. This is the topic of the next three chapters.

As with the chapters on word processing and spreadsheets, this part of the book on database management consists of a generic chapter followed by hands-on, software-specific chapters. In the generic chapter, you will learn the meaning of *database* and *database management system,* and about many of the capabilities of database management software. In Chapters 15 and 16, you will use the popular database management program dBASE III PLUS. You will learn basic operations such as creating a database file, inspecting data in the file, rearranging the order of records in the file (sorting), and operating on data on a conditional basis. Although the treatments in these chapters are necessarily limited in scope (with only two chapters), they will provide you with a firm foundation in the principles of database management.

Chapter 14

Database Concepts

OBJECTIVES

Chapter 2 introduced you to the nature of database management system (DBMS) programs for managing and using data stored in files. This chapter describes some of the distinct features of databases and the DBMS programs that simplify your task of working with data. The vehicle for this is a database application in which a database is used to monitor the progress of legislative bills in a state assembly. It provides the basis for detailed descriptions of using dBASE III PLUS in the two chapters that follow. When you have completed this chapter, you should understand and be able to describe:

- The data hierarchy of files, which are composed of fields, which are composed of records.
- The principles of database and a DBMS.
- The concept of interrelating two or more data files to obtain information from both for an application.
- The factors to consider in planning a database data file.
- Types of data: numeric, character, date, and logical.
- Creating a database file.
- Entering records into a file and editing existing data in a file.
- Sequential and direct processing of records in a file.
- Rearranging the order of the records in a file by sorting or using an index to a file.

- Principles of file indexes.
- Linking two or more files by the use of an index.

PREVIEW

The Need for Information

The need for information from data stored in computer files is an everyday part of our lives. This section considers some typical examples.

A Manual Data Processing Application

A manual record-keeping system is described for monitoring the progress of legislative bills in a typical state assembly. This system illustrates interrelating data in two files to provide needed information. It forms the basis for describing the meaning of database and the DBMS.

Planning for a Database Application

In setting up a database application, you must first define the results that you require, and then designate the data necessary to produce those results.

DBMS Maintenance Operations

Typical DBMS maintenance operations are those to create new database data files, to enter and edit records, and to delete records.

Accessing Records in a File

There are two primary ways of accessing records in a file: sequential accessing involving one record after the other and direct accessing involving a single selected record.

Reporting

A DBMS includes the means to generate printed reports from one or more files of a database.

Indexing

An index is essentially a directory to a file. Indexes make it possible to change the order in which records are accessed by the DBMS and to access any selected record.

A Business Database Application

Principles of the legislation database application are expanded to a typical business example.

THE NEED FOR INFORMATION

In all aspects of our lives, both personal and business, we see the need for information. Let us consider a variety of examples that illustrate a broad range of applications to provide us information based on data stored in computer files.

To find out the current balance in your bank account, you call your bank and give your name and account number. The clerk types this information into a computer terminal and the computer finds your record among the many thousands in the file and displays it on the monitor. Speed is essential; the information must be located in seconds, *not* minutes. The bank management does not want employees standing around waiting for information, nor does it want you to change banks because of slow service.

As the owner of MCT Enterprises, say you receive a call from a customer requesting the immediate shipment of 200 of your light-blue, Sunset-style jackets. Do you have them in stock? With a computer inventory system, you can enter the stock number and receive an immediate display from the inventory file telling you the exact status of this item. With the computer at your fingertips, the customer need wait only a few moments for you to say (with confidence), "Yes, they will be shipped late this afternoon."

Another of your needs as a business owner is mass mailing, an important part of your business. Periodically, you send sale information and announcements to everyone in a special mailing file. In order to use the bulk mailing rate, the Post Office requires that the pieces be in order by postal ZIP code. One of the functions of data management software is to sort data stored in the file. With this, you can have the computer print address labels in ZIP code order regardless of the order in which the names and addresses were entered into the file.

Where each of the preceding examples involves actions with data in a single file, the monthly preparation of customer bills requires data from three files. The customer's name, address, and current balance come from a customer file. Data regarding purchases comes from the accounts receivable file, which contains data on all sales. Data regarding payments comes from the payments file. All of this must be brought together for each customer in preparing the bill.

For a completely different example, consider the task of keeping records for the issuance of keys to offices and buildings at the institution where you are studying. One or more keys are issued to faculty and staff according to their needs. Some keys open only a single door. Others open doors to several rooms. Still others open the doors to all rooms in an area or building. Now consider the plight of the facilities manager who is faced with the loss of equipment from one of the rooms and wants the names of all key holders with access to that room. First, she would need to determine which keys open the room; then she would have to find out to whom each of these keys has been issued. This may sound simple, but with a large institution, it is a huge and painstaking manual task. Data management software provides the means for getting such information almost instantly.

These are typical data management applications: data in files must be managed to provide needed information. Their descriptions involve concepts and terminology touched on in Chapters 1 and 2. Let us focus on these concepts by considering a typical data management application. In this example, you will consider a problem to be solved and the "commonsense" steps in solving it. From it, you will learn about the storage of data in files and about data management software that make it easy to convert the stored data to useful information.

A MANUAL DATA PROCESSING APPLICATION

Assume that you have taken a job with an organization dedicated to protecting the environment. You have been given the task of monitoring all bills in your state assembly that in any way relate to the environment. This is to be an expansion of a small project begun by your predecessor in which he tracked a few important bills.

The Assembly Bill File

For monitoring the bills, your predecessor had written information about each assembly bill of interest on a 3 × 5 card as shown in Figure 14-1. There are some things about this collection of cards that have direct significance to computer processing of data files. Each card, or record, contains data about one bill. That is, this record comprises the following data items, or fields:

Bill number

Abbreviated title

Author (member of the assembly who is sponsoring the bill)

Date the bill was passed in committee

Date the bill was approved

Comments

The collection of all of these cards form the assembly bill file. Hence, we have the hierarchy of data that you learned about in Chapter 1:

Field A basic unit of data (such as bill number, author, and date approved).

Record A group of related facts or fields of information treated as a unit.

File The organized collection of all records of a given type.

Each field of a record contains information about a given entity, in this case, an assembly bill. The bill number identifies a given bill. The title, author, and other data pertain to that bill. These facts are related and they are relevant to a particular application or group of applications. Notice that the author's name is included because he or she is the author of this

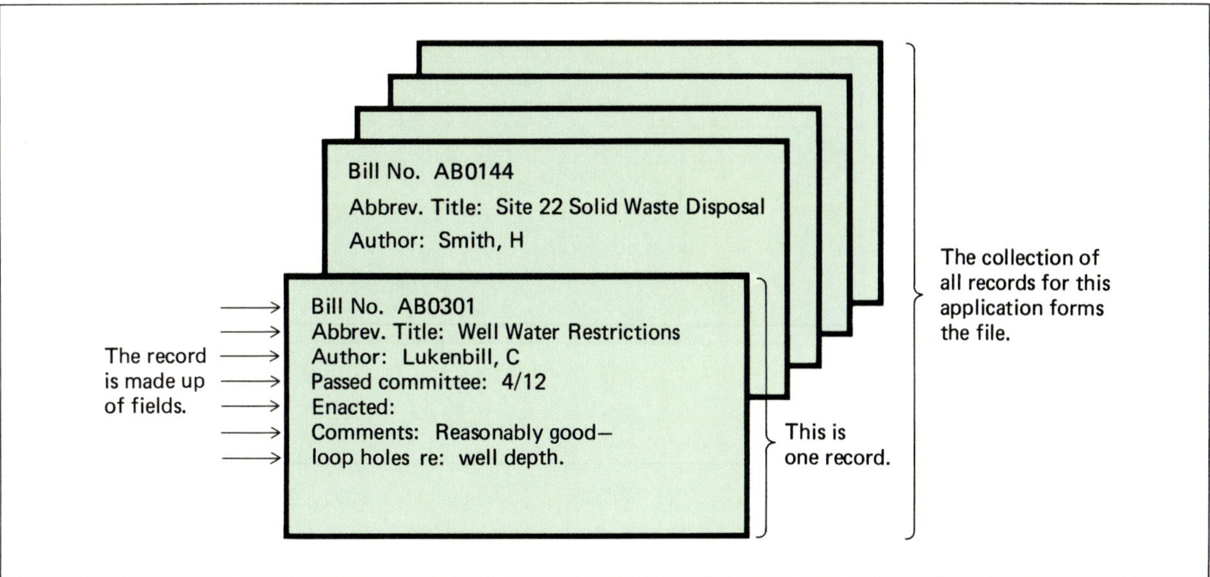

Figure 14-1
A card file containing assembly bill data.

proposed legislation. However, data about the author is not included in this record; the record is for data about the bill, not the author. In setting up files, it is important to maintain this type of distinction.

Your predecessor had certain procedures for working with this file. He had to add a new record for each bill introduced. As each bill left its working committee, he entered the date; as each bill was enacted he entered that date. In using the file, he prepared reports listing, for example, bills that had been enacted, and those that were still being worked on by committee. He also prepared summaries of the bills introduced by each member of the assembly. We can consider these activities in two broad categories: file maintenance and file use. Together they make up a **file management system,** a set of procedures for managing the data in a data file. These manual procedures illustrated in this example are found in file management programs for automating the maintenance and use of data files on the computer.

Interrelating the Data in Two Files

In addition to the assembly bill card file, your predecessor maintained a separate assembly member file, which is illustrated in Figure 14-2. Each card record of this file contains the needed data about a member of the assembly. Together, the Bill and Member files provided the necessary data for your predecessor to do his job. For instance, if he was working on bill AB0301 and needed to address a letter to the author, he would:

1. Find the record for AB0301 in the Bill file and get the name of the assembly member who wrote the bill.

2. Find the record for that assembly member in the Member file to get the address.

Figure 14-2
A card file containing assembly member data.

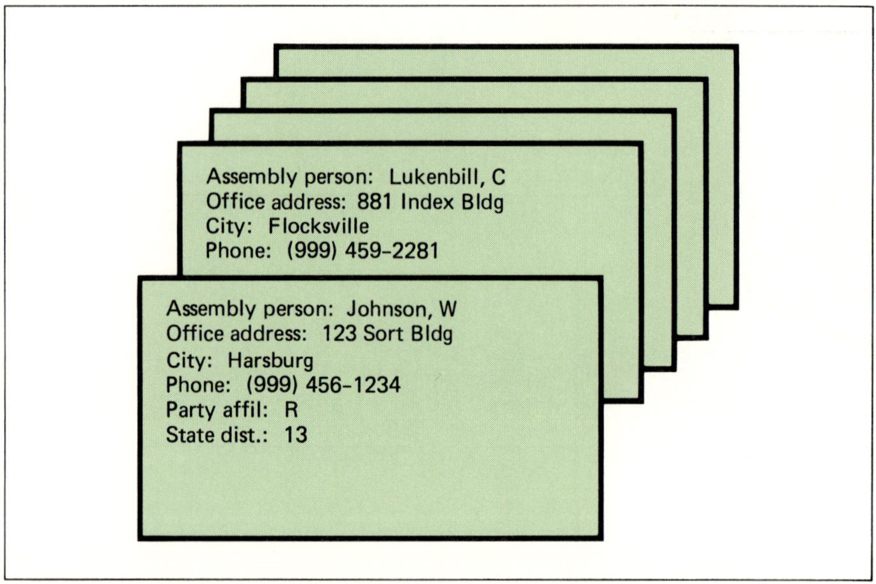

In other words, these two files are used together, as illustrated in Figure 14-3. Note that they are interrelated by a common field: the author of the bill. This has important implications in database processing.

These data files provide information because they are structured and organized. For instance, in the Bill file each record contains the data in the same layout or format: the records are *structured.* Furthermore, the cards are probably arranged in the file in sequence by bill number: the file is *organized.* (The Member file is probably sequenced by assembly member name.) Structure and organization are keys to the usefulness of these two sets of data.

Figure 14-3
Relationship between the Bill file and Member file.

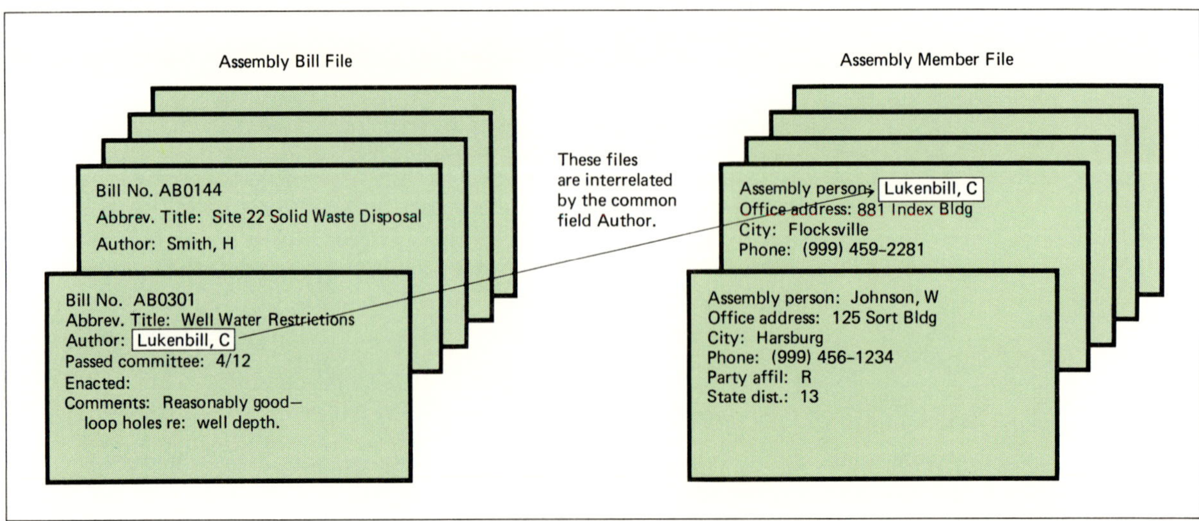

Data from a central database can provide information about your legislators that would be difficult to obtain without a computer.

An Alternative Solution

When someone explains a good solution to a problem, the wise decisions of the problem solver usually appear to be the obvious way in which to handle the problem. However, when solving a problem, the best solution is not always apparent. For instance, at first thought, using the two files of Figure 14-3 appears to be clumsy. Why not simply include the address and telephone number of the author on the assembly bill card of Figure 14-1? Then all the needed data would be conveniently available in one place. For the answer to this, consider the assembly member who has written twelve bills, for which there will be twelve records in the Bill file. The data about the assembly member would be repeated twelve times. This is called **redundant data** because it is repeated needlessly. Redundant data is undesirable because it is clumsy to maintain and creates the possibility of having inconsistent data in a file. For instance, each time a record is created for a new bill, the data for the assembly member must be entered for that record, with the accompanying possibility of entering erroneous data. If an assembly member moves his or her office, all of the records written by that person must be changed. This is a painstaking and error-prone task: a record needing correcting can be missed or the change made incorrectly, as illustrated in Figure 14-4. This is called **inconsistent data** and is made possible because of the data redundancy.

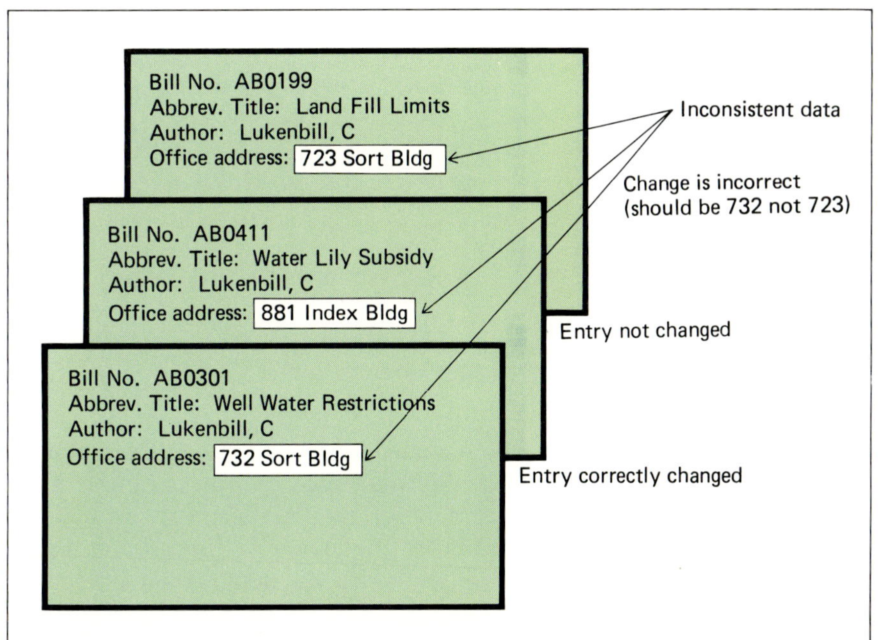

Figure 14-4
Inconsistent data in a file resulting from redundancy.

Database Management

By separating these two collections of data into individual files, you can reduce or eliminate data redundancy and inconsistency. In this application, your predecessor kept information about each bill in the Bill file, and information about each assembly member in the Member file. You are looking at the essence of a **database,** a collection of interrelated files. A DMBS is a program (or collection of programs) that allows you to manage and use data stored in multiple, interrelated files: the database.

In reading computer literature, you will encounter the terms **file management system** and **database management system.** A file management system is considerably less powerful than a DBMS. One of the distinctions between the two is that a file management system cannot interrelate multiple files in the way illustrated by Figure 14-3, whereas a DBMS can. You will also encounter the term *relational DBMS.* There are three broad types of DBMS: relational, hierarchical, and network. The focus in this book is the relational DBMS model. dBASE III PLUS, the topic of the next two chapters, is a relational DBMS.

If you have worked with a programming language such as BASIC or COBOL, you know that writing programs to enter data into a file and edit data already in the file is not a simple task. Furthermore, you know that each file requires its own set of programs. For instance, a program to edit data in a customer file could not be used to perform the same editing operations on data in an inventory file. It would be necessary to write another program. On the other hand, DBMS is designed specifically for managing and manipulating data stored in files. In fact, most of the following actions can be done on a database data file with a few simple database commands.

- Create a new file.
- Enter a new record into a file.
- Change the contents of a record in the file.
- Delete a record from a file.
- Find a record in the file according to some selection criterion.
- Rearrange the records of a file in a specific order.
- Define relationships between two or more files.
- Generate reports consisting of data from the file.

For instance, consider your need for a screen display that includes all data about a bill and the address and telephone number of the author. A DBMS provides the means for you to define linkages between files, as shown in Figure 14-3. Here the Member record is linked to the corresponding Bill record by the name of the author, a field contained in both records. Through the DBMS, data is available to you from both files as if your were working with one.

PLANNING FOR A DATABASE APPLICATION

After careful consideration, you decide to put this application on the computer using a DBMS. You feel that the use of a computer will be essential to accomplishing your goals of maintaining data on all bills that have any effect on the environment, and of storing more data for each bill. Furthermore, you feel that a computer is necessary to get the utmost information from available data. You are faced with devising a computer solution.

Computer problem solving was the topic of the last section in Chapter 10. Similar techniques are used to prepare a computer solution for a problem whether the software tool used is a spreadsheet, a DBMS, or a conventional programming language. That is, (1) define the results you want from your solution, (2) analyze the available data and determine if the necessary data is available, (3) devise an overall plan for the solution, (4) express the solution in a form that can be conveyed to the computer, and (5) test the solution. Let us first consider the results you are seeking.

Capabilities of the Assembly Bill Information System

After careful consideration, you have decided that your assembly bill information system should provide you with the ability to:

- Assign a quality rating (0–100) to each bill and get statistical information based on ratings.
- Classify the bills as having their principal impact on the air, the water, or the ground.
- Designate each bill as regional (you have divided the state into five regions) or statewide, so that you can categorize the bills.
- Assess the performance of members of the legislature with regard to the number and ratings of the bills they write.
- Arrange the records in order based on any of the fields in the file.
- List information for all bills or for those meeting some criterion such as water-related bills with a rating of 90 or greater.
- Display on the screen the entire record for any selected bill plus the author's office address and telephone number.
- List each assembly member and the bills written by the member.

Your next step is to designate the data that you will require to obtain this information, that is, the fields that will make up your record in this file. Your data needs for the Bill file are an expansion of those from the manual system in Figure 14-1.

Bill number

Abbreviated title

Author (member of the assembly who is sponsoring the bill)

Bill type (relates to air, water, or land)

Region to which this bill applies

Rating (0–100)

Recommendation for support (Yes or No)

Date the bill was passed in committee

Date the bill was approved

Comments

You would then detail your needs for the Member file in exactly the same way. For this illustration, assume that you have decided that the data contained in the card file of Figure 14-2 will be adequate for your application. You must now assess each data field and determine the type of data it will contain and its size.

Data Types

Four data classifications are common to virtually all DBMSs: character, numeric, date, and logical. Let us consider each of these relative to the fields of this application.

Character Data. The bill title and author's name are typical examples of character data. Such can consist of letters, digits, and special characters, for instance:

Bill: Restrictions on Insecticide 99-X

Author: Pamella O'Hara

Thus, fields of a data file designated as character fields (often called alphanumeric fields) can contain any character that can be entered from the keyboard.

Numeric Data. The legislation file includes only one numeric data field: the rating, which can have a value of from 0 to 100. Notice that although the first field is identified as the bill *number,* this field is not truly numeric. For instance, one of the sample bill numbers is AB0224. There are many examples of data fields that we refer to as numbers (which contain only digits) that are not treated as numeric data. For instance, your Social Security number (without the hyphens) consists of nine digits. Your account number with VISA, the loan number for your home or automobile, and many other "numbers" consist only of digits. However, almost always these are designated in data files as character fields. On the other hand, fields such as amount owed on an account, number of items in inventory, and score achieved on an examination are designated as numeric fields. These are fields upon which arithmetic operations might be performed.

Date Data. Your legislation file will contain two dates (date passed by committee and date signed into law). You could define these fields as being character and use the standard form month/day/year; for example, 11/18/90. However, your ability to manipulate date fields would be very limited. For instance, arranging records in sequence by date would be very clumsy with normal sorting methods. Simple date arithmetic such as adding 45 days to a date would be difficult. The date-type data found in most DBMSs allows comparing and simple arithmetic operations to be performed on date data almost as if it were numeric.

Logical Data. Most database applications include fields that will contain a yes or no value. For instance, the legislation file includes the recommendation field: the value stored in this field will be either yes or no, depending upon whether or not you recommend passage of the bill. This is commonly called logical data because it can have either of two values: yes or no (or true or false). Although you could use a character field (into which you store Y or N), database management systems include the logical data type specifically for yes/no data.

Field Width

In addition to the data type, the width of character and numeric fields must be designated. This is necessary because a DBMS reserves a specified amount of space in memory (and on disk) for each field of a record. For some fields, the width is predetermined by the field itself. For instance, the bill number consists of two letters and four digits; hence, its width is six characters. On the other hand, the title and author field widths must be selected based on your knowledge of the data. The abbreviated title width should be sufficiently long that each entry is clearly meaningful. Fields containing people's names should be long enough to avoid chopping off the last few letters of the name. Numeric fields must be long enough to hold the largest possible number that will be stored in them. This includes a decimal point if the number can have a fractional part and a sign if it can be negative, as illustrated by the two examples at the left.

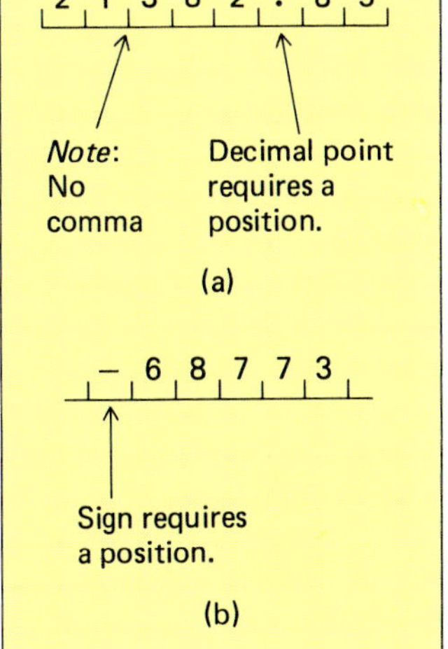

One approach to selecting a field width is: "A width of twenty should be good enough, so I will double it to forty to be certain." This is a poor approach because it results in wasted disk space; for large files, the percentage of wasted disk space can be very significant.

Table 14-1 summarizes the data type and reasonable field widths for the Bill record.

Table 14-1 RECORD DEFINITION FOR BILL FILE

Field	Type	Width	Comments
Bill number	Character	6	
Title	Character	30	
Author	Character	20	
Bill type	Character	1	A—Air W—Water G—Ground
Region	Character	1	1-5—Regions 1-5 9—Statewide
Rating	Numeric	3	0–100
Recommendation	Logical	1	
Date passed in committee	Date	8	
Date approved	Date	8	
Comments	Character	80	

Once all of these characteristics of the fields that make up the file have been determined, the needed data files can be created and data records entered and edited. These are basic file maintenance operations of a DBMS; they allow us to manage the data stored in the data files.

DBMS MAINTENANCE OPERATIONS

Creating a New Data File

One of the characteristics of a database data file is that the file contains information about the data as well as the data itself. That is, when a file is first created with the DBMS program, a detailed description of the record format (Table 14-1) is stored as part of the file. The is called the *data definition.* Only when this definition has been completely entered can the entry of data begin. A typical screen for entry of this information is shown in Figure 14–5 in which a portion of the fields of the legislation data file has been entered. After each field has been defined, the record format is stored to disk and data entry can begin. Note that this process is roughly equivalent to preparing a template for a worksheet in which labels and formulas are entered and the template saved. Then data entries are made to perform the analyses.

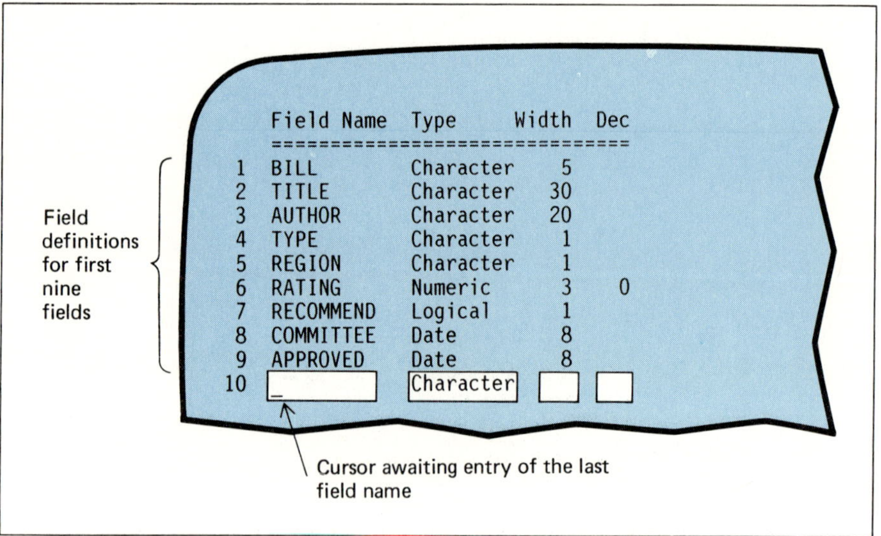

Figure 14-5
Defining the fields of the legislation file.

Entering Into a File

Once the data record has been defined and the file created, data can be entered from a screen such as that shown in Figure 14-6. Considerable care should be devoted to ensuring that the data entry is correct. If the data entered into a file is in error, then results of calculations using that data will be incorrect; in computer vernacular, this is referred to as GIGO, meaning garbage in/garbage out.

Every data file includes restrictions on the data that can be entered into

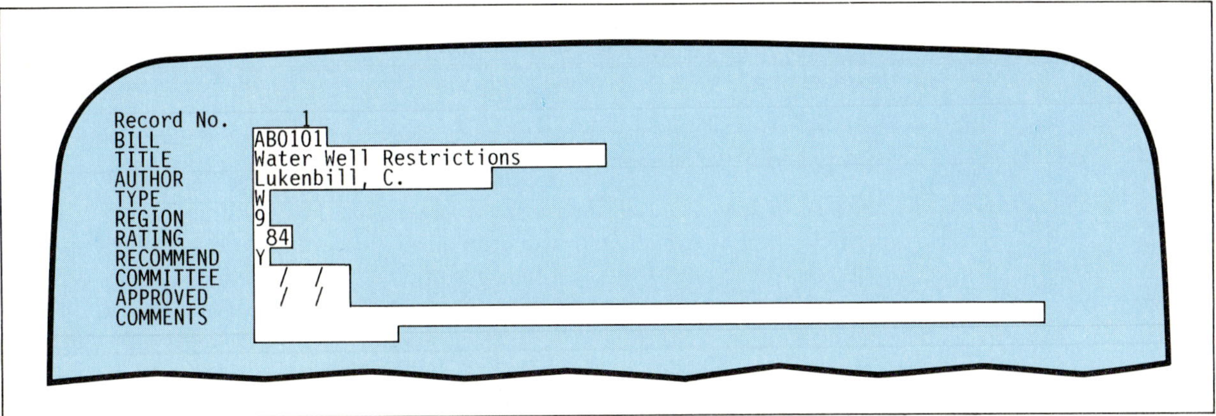

Figure 14-6
Entering a record into the legislation file.

the fields of the file. An obvious restriction relates to field size. For instance, it is impossible to enter a two-letter bill type because the field is only one position in width. Similarly, an attempt to enter ABC for the rating field will be rejected by the DBMS because the field is defined as numeric. These are called **physical constraints** because they pertain to the physical definition of the field. However, physical constraints still allow us considerable latitude for entering incorrect data. For example, although we may not be allowed to enter more than three digits for the rating field, we can enter any value in the range -99 to 999 (three positions). But the allowable rating values for this application are 0 to 100. Some DBMSs provide for the inclusion of **logical constraints** that are user defined and become part of the data definition information. If the rating field were defined with a 0 to 100 constraint, then any value less than 0 or greater than 100 would be rejected. (dBASE III PLUS, the software included with this book, does not provide for user-defined constraints.)

Other Maintenance Operations

Changing the value in a field of a record (editing) is as simple as entering it and can be done through a screen such as that shown in Figure 14-6. You need only move the cursor to the field to be changed and perform an editing operation in much the same way you would do it with a word processor or spreadsheet.

In most DBMS programs the deletion of records from a file is based on the notion that you might change your mind at a later time. Consequently, most delete commands mark the record as being deleted but do not actually erase it from the file. During processing, the DBMS program ignores all marked records so that the user does not even see them. At any later time, any of the marked records can be restored, or they can actually be erased from the file.

ACCESSING RECORDS IN A FILE

File maintenance operations are essential to any database application, but it is the file processing operations that allow us to make that data available in a useful form—as information. Let us first consider the ways in which records read from disk into memory (accessed) are made available for processing.

Sequential Processing

The records of the Bill file are shown in Figure 14-7 in the physical order in which they were entered into the file (physical record numbers are included to the left of the first field for convenient reference). This is called a *file listing* because it is a printout of each field and record of the file. It was generated by a command to access records and print them one after the other from the file in their physical order; the listing task was completed when the end of the file was reached. Reading and processing records in this way are called *sequential processing,* or **sequential access** of the records in the file; sequential access is illustrated by the diagram of Figure 4-8. In

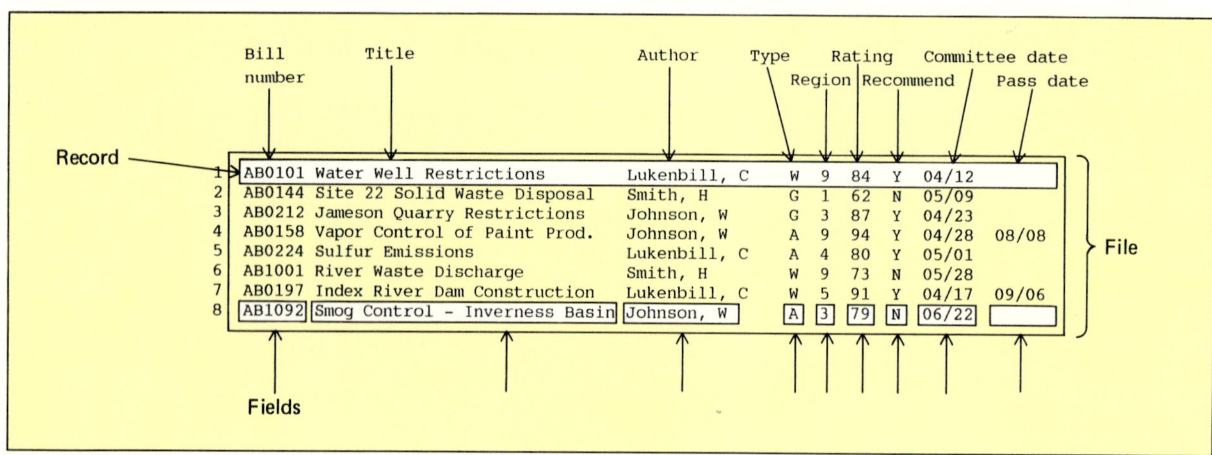

	Bill number	Title	Author	Type	Region	Rating	Recommend	Committee date	Pass date
1	AB0101	Water Well Restrictions	Lukenbill, C	W	9	84	Y	04/12	
2	AB0144	Site 22 Solid Waste Disposal	Smith, H	G	1	62	N	05/09	
3	AB0212	Jameson Quarry Restrictions	Johnson, W	G	3	87	Y	04/23	
4	AB0158	Vapor Control of Paint Prod.	Johnson, W	A	9	94	Y	04/28	08/08
5	AB0224	Sulfur Emissions	Lukenbill, C	A	4	80	Y	05/01	
6	AB1001	River Waste Discharge	Smith, H	W	9	73	N	05/28	
7	AB0197	Index River Dam Construction	Lukenbill, C	W	5	91	Y	04/17	09/06
8	AB1092	Smog Control - Inverness Basin	Johnson, W	A	3	79	N	06/22	

Figure 14-7
Listing of the Bill file.

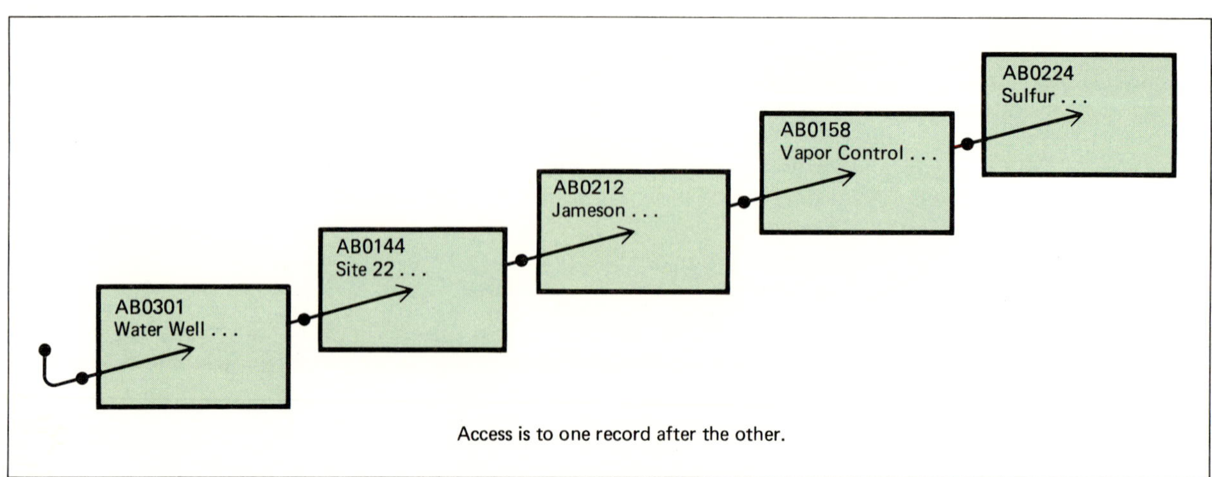

Figure 14-8
Sequential file access.

sequential accessing, the DBMS program always accesses the next record after the current one.

Two of the examples at the beginning of this chapter involve sequential processing of all the records in a file. For example, in preparing mailing labels from the data in the mailing file of MCT Enterprises, the DBMS program must access records and print labels one after the other. One of the features of DBMS programs is that records can be processed in the order in which they were entered into the file (the physical sequence), or in sequence according to almost any field of the record. The processing action of printing the labels involves reading the record with the next higher ZIP code from disk into memory and then printing the address label.

Another facet of sequential processing is that only part of the records in a file might be processed during a processing cycle. For instance, from the legislation file, you might print a report consisting only of assembly bills that have already been approved, or those with ratings lower than 70. In fact, the criterion can be based on more than one field. For instance, you might want those that relate to both air and water, have statewide implications, and have ratings greater than 80. This is called record **selection.**

Changing the Sequence of Records in a Data File

There are two ways to modify the order in which records of a file are made available when processing sequentially. One is to rearrange the physical order of the records in the file based on one or more fields of the record; this is called **sorting.** The other is to construct an index, a topic that we consider in detail later in this chapter. DBMS programs have commands both to sort and to create indexes. Because of the nature of database processing, indexing is much more commonly used than sorting because of its versatility. For sequential processing, both do the same thing: they change the sequence in which records in the file are accessed. In the following examples, the word *sorting* is used, but the principles apply equally to indexing.

Figure 14-7 lists the records of the Bill file in physical record sequence. If this file were sorted or indexed on the rating field, then the sequence of the records would be as shown in Figure 14-9. Here the number to the left

Figure 14-9
The Bill file in sequence by the rating field.

```
2 | AB0144 Site 22 Solid Waste Disposal    Smith, H       G 1 |62| N 05/09
6 | AB1001 River Waste Discharge           Smith, H       W 9 |73| N 05/28
8 | AB1092 Smog Control - Inverness Basin  Johnson, W     A 3 |79| N 06/22
5 | AB0224 Sulfur Emissions                Lukenbill, C   A 4 |80| Y 05/01
1 | AB0101 Water Well Restrictions         Lukenbill, C   W 9 |84| Y 04/12
3 | AB0212 Jameson Quarry Restrictions     Johnson, W     G 3 |87| Y 04/23
7 | AB0197 Index River Dam Construction    Lukenbill, C   W 5 |91| Y 04/17  09/06
4 | AB0158 Vapor Control of Paint Prod.    Johnson, W     A 9 |94| Y 04/28  08/08
```

Records in ascending sequence based on rating field

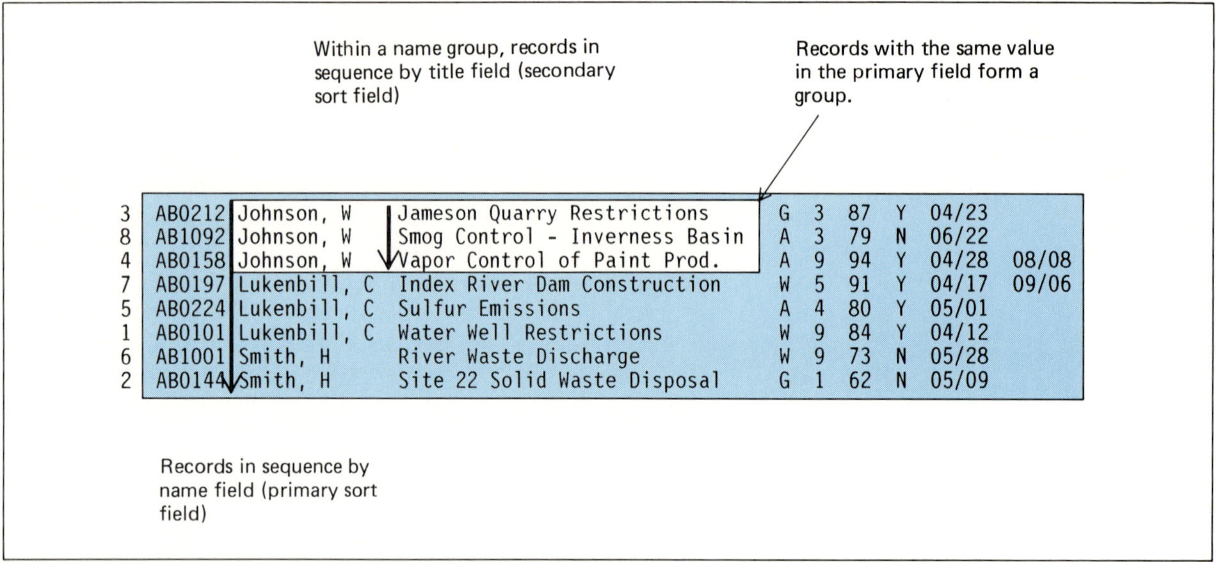

Figure 14-10
The legislation file in sequence by two fields: the author field and the bill title field.

is included to indicate the original order of the records. For instance, the first record listed was the second record before sorting.

Some applications require that records of the file be sequenced on the basis of two or more fields. For instance, you might want to prepare a report in which the bills are arranged by author, and for each author by title. Figure 14-10 shows the result of this type of sorting. Notice that the records are grouped by author, making it convenient to study the productivity of each member of the legislature. Here, the sorting operation involves both fields. The first field is the author and is called the **primary sort field**; the second field is the title and is called the **secondary sort field**. Sorting on a number of fields is necessary for preparing many types of reports, as described in the section of this chapter entitled "Reporting".

Direct Processing

Sequential processing is one way of working with data in files. On the other hand, three of the examples at the beginning of this chapter involved obtaining information from a file for a particular record. For instance, in checking the inventory file to determine if you had 200 light-blue, Sunset-style jackets, you needed information from one record in the file. At that time, you had no interest in any other record in the file. Similarly, with the legislation file, if someone asked you for information on bill AB0224, you would want to display the record for that bill. To obtain this, you would enter an appropriate command that would say, "Find the record with the bill number AB0224 and display it on the screen." This is called *direct processing* or **direct access** of the records in the file because it involves directly locating the single record in which you are interested. (It is also called **random** processing or access.) Direct access is illustrated by the diagram of Figure 4-11. In direct processing, the program accesses whichever record you request.

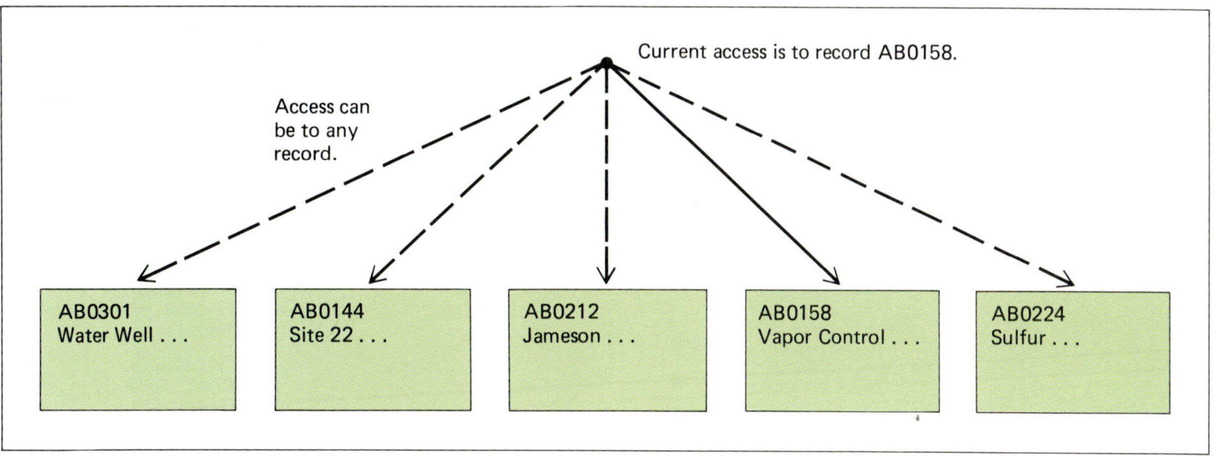

Figure 14-11
Direct file access.

REPORTING

The listings of Figures 14-7, 14-9, and 14-10 are so-called because they are nothing more than printouts of the data stored in a file, one printed line per record. The output of Figure 14-12 is a **report**, and its characteristics are:

1. It is generated using data from two files. Reports can require data from one or from many files.
2. The output data is grouped by assembly member. That is, data for

Some people spend their lives gathering and studying facts about nature. Database software can help scientists organize and analyze those facts. The snow leopard, for example, which is seldom seen, has been studied in detail in an effort to prevent it from becoming extinct. Habitat and life-style patterns are correlated and analyzed using special database software.

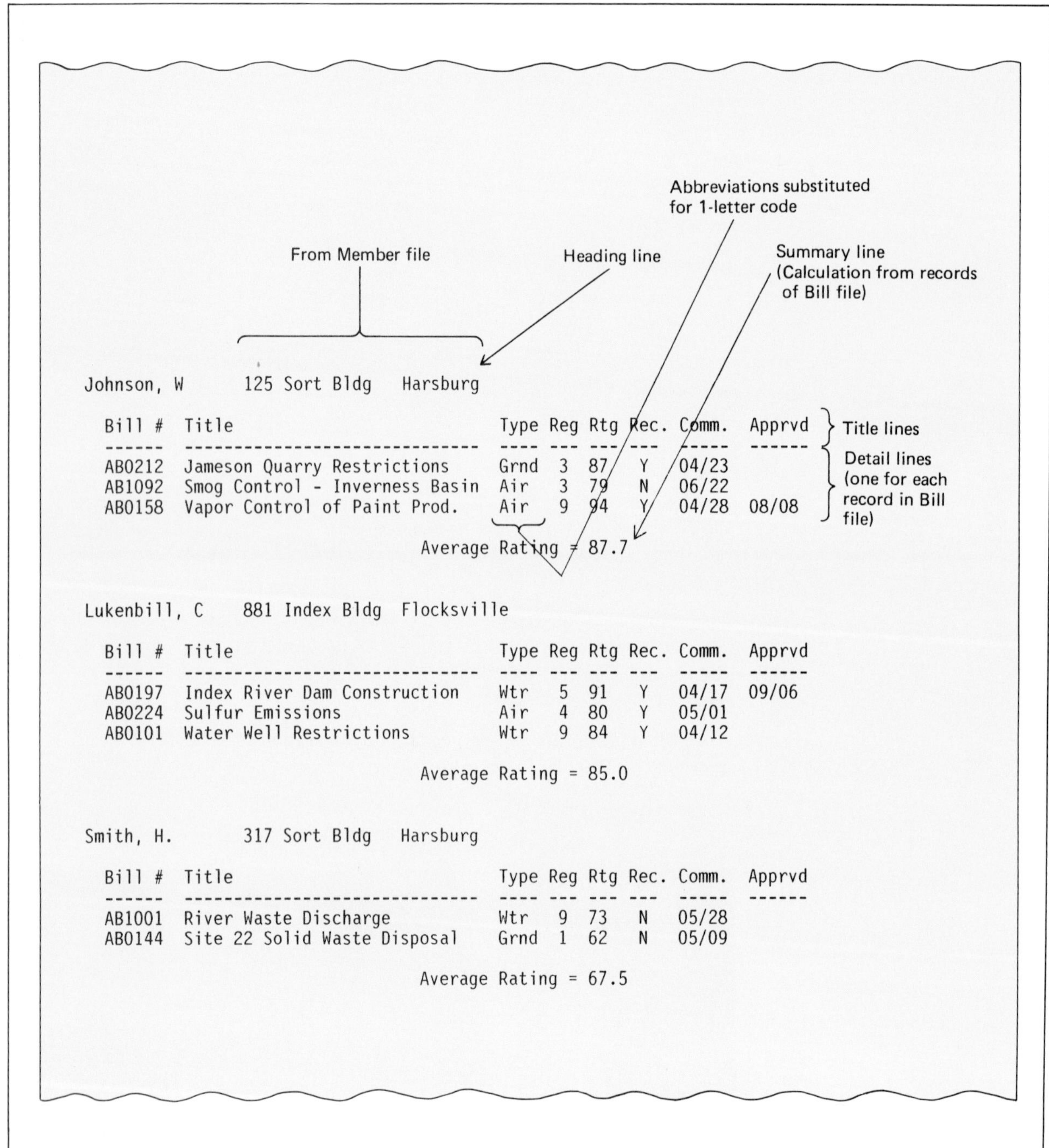

Johnson, W 125 Sort Bldg Harsburg

Bill #	Title	Type	Reg	Rtg	Rec.	Comm.	Apprvd
AB0212	Jameson Quarry Restrictions	Grnd	3	87	Y	04/23	
AB1092	Smog Control - Inverness Basin	Air	3	79	N	06/22	
AB0158	Vapor Control of Paint Prod.	Air	9	94	Y	04/28	08/08

Average Rating = 87.7

Lukenbill, C 881 Index Bldg Flocksville

Bill #	Title	Type	Reg	Rtg	Rec.	Comm.	Apprvd
AB0197	Index River Dam Construction	Wtr	5	91	Y	04/17	09/06
AB0224	Sulfur Emissions	Air	4	80	Y	05/01	
AB0101	Water Well Restrictions	Wtr	9	84	Y	04/12	

Average Rating = 85.0

Smith, H. 317 Sort Bldg Harsburg

Bill #	Title	Type	Reg	Rtg	Rec.	Comm.	Apprvd
AB1001	River Waste Discharge	Wtr	9	73	N	05/28	
AB0144	Site 22 Solid Waste Disposal	Grnd	1	62	N	05/09	

Average Rating = 67.5

Figure 14-12
A report generated from data in the Bill and Member files.

the member is printed on the first line, followed by the detailed lines describing the bills, with one line per bill.

3. After the last detail line for each assembly member, a summary line is printed with the average rating of all bills for that member.

One of the features of this report is that it requires data from both the Bill and the Member files. To achieve this, these files must be interrelated as

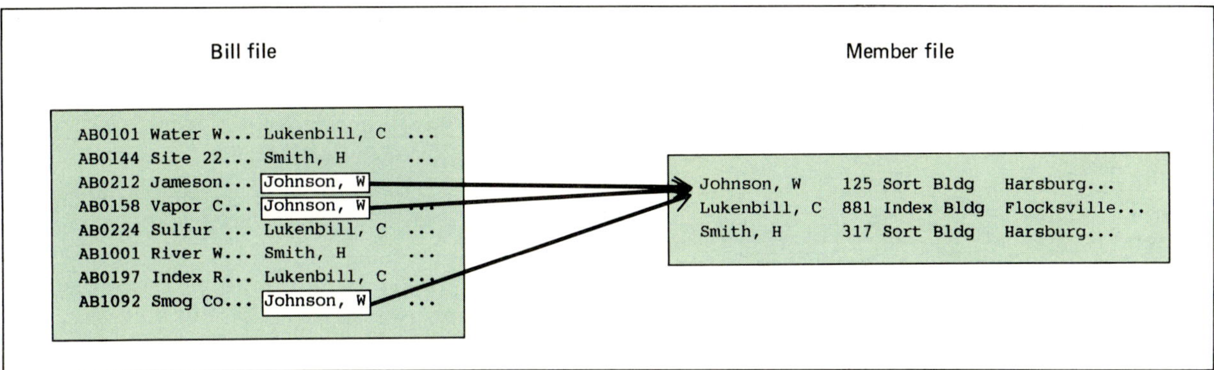

Figure 14-13
Relationship between the Bill file and the Member file.

illustrated in Figure 14-13. Notice that this relationship is identical to that we considered for the manual system in Figure 14-3.

Summary reports such as that in Figure 14-12 are common in business. For instance, Figure 14-14 is a customer bill (one page of the summary report) prepared from data in three files. To generate a report, it is first necessary to specify for the system in detail the exact format of the printed output together with calculations and/or summaries to be performed. The exact way in which these concepts are implemented varies from one DBMS to another.

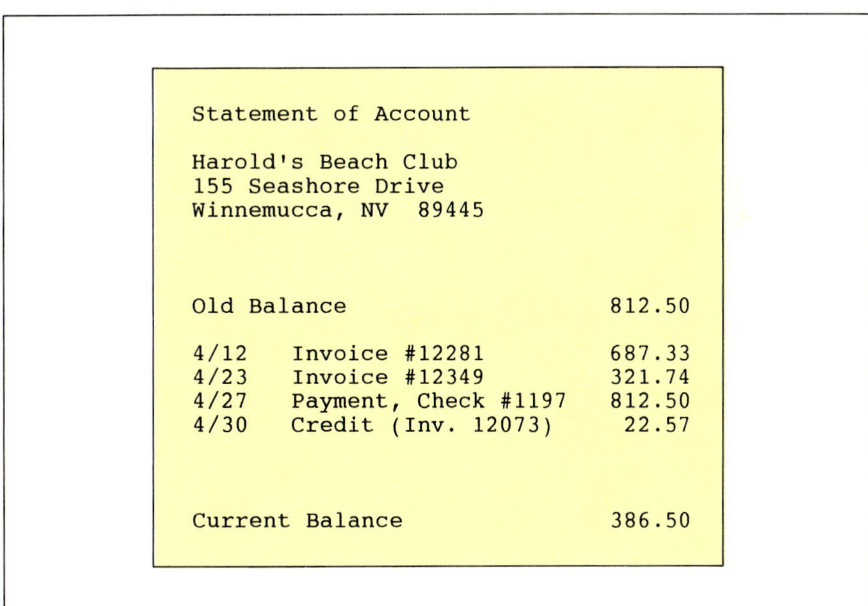
Statement of Account

Harold's Beach Club
155 Seashore Drive
Winnemucca, NV 89445

Old Balance		812.50
4/12	Invoice #12281	687.33
4/23	Invoice #12349	321.74
4/27	Payment, Check #1197	812.50
4/30	Credit (Inv. 12073)	22.57
Current Balance		386.50

Figure 14-14
A customer statement of account.

INDEXING

It was noted in a previous section that the sequence of records in a file can be changed by sorting, but that a better way is by indexing. Sorting changes the physical order of the records in a file. Using an index changes the **logical order** of the records in the file. That is, the physical order is unchanged but the order in which records are accessed by the DBMS program is changed as dictated by the index. Indexes serve two useful functions for file processing. First, they are vital to direct processing, the random accessing of records; and second, they make it possible to process records in the file in an order other than their physical order.

Direct Processing Using an Index

Using an index in everyday life is nothing new. For example, the directory in a large building is an index. It displays a list of the building's occupants in alphabetic order, not in room number order, and makes "direct access" of a particular occupant's room possible. To find the office of Dr. Hargrove, we would look up the name in the directory (index) and read the corresponding office number. Then we would go directly to that room. It is much faster to search the index than to search the building door by door looking for her name. Similarly, the index makes it possible to access a selected record from the file without searching the entire file in the same way that we use the directory in a building.

The indexing principle is illustrated in Figure 14-15, where we see a representation of two files: the data file and a corresponding index file that is based on the bill number. (In this example, a five-record file is used to simplify the illustration.) Notice that each entry of the index file includes only two fields: the data value from the indexing field (bill number in this case) and the physical record number of the data record corresponding to that bill number. Each index entry is said to *point* to a record in the legislation file because it contains the physical record number of that record.

In using this index to access a selected record—for instance, the record for bill AB0224—the DBMS program would:

1. Find the entry in the index for AB0224.
2. Read the physical record number for AB0224, which is 5.
3. Obtain the fifth record from the Bill file.

This process is much faster and more efficient than searching the data file itself for two reasons. First, the index file entries are in sequence based on the index field. This sequence is maintained automatically by the DBMS program, even when records are added or changed, making it possible to use special search techniques that locate a desired record very quickly.

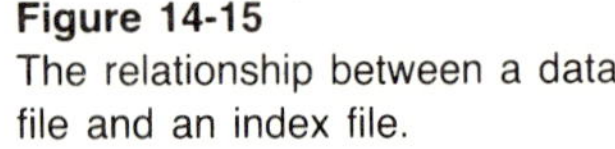

Figure 14-15
The relationship between a data file and an index file.

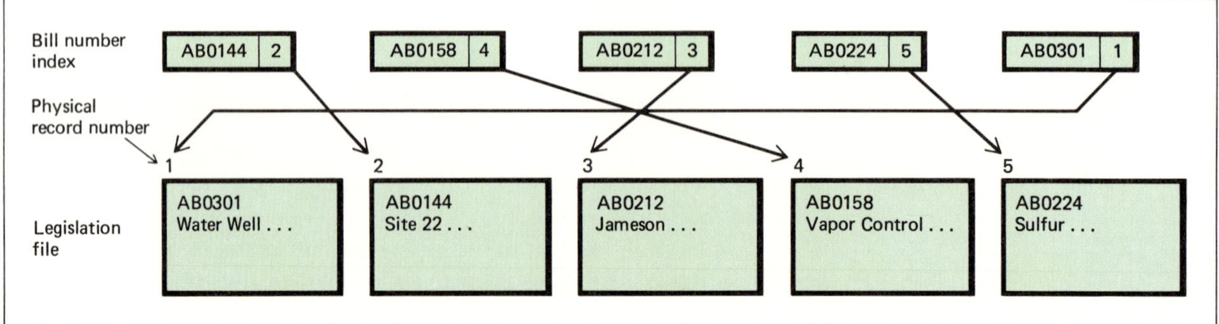

Second, the index is much smaller than the data file so considerably less data must be handled during the search. Sometimes the index is sufficiently small that most or all of it can be kept in memory by the DBMS program during processing.

Sequential Processing Using an Index

While processing a data file, the file can be used with or without an index. When a file is used without an index, the records are available in the sequence in which they are physically stored in the file. However, when a file is used with an index, the records are available in the sequence of the index. For example, to access the records of the Bill file sequentially using the index shown in Figure 14-15, the DBMS program would do the following:

1. Read the first index entry. This entry points to physical record 2.
2. Obtain record 2 from the Bill file, making it available for processing.
3. Read the next index entry, which points to physical record 4.
4. Obtain record 4 from the Bill file, making it available for processing.
5. And so on.

Multiple Indexes for a File

The index based on the bill number gives us access to records of the Bill file in bill number sequence. One of the features of indexing is that you can create an index file based on any field (or combination of fields) of the record. For instance, some processing might require access by bill number and other processing by the bill title. This need is easily filled by creating two indexes, as illustrated in Figure 14-16. During a processing activity, it is a simple matter to switch from one index to the other. Since the index is a separate file, there is no limit (other than a practical one) to the number of indexes that can be created for a file.

Figure 14-16
Multiple indexes.

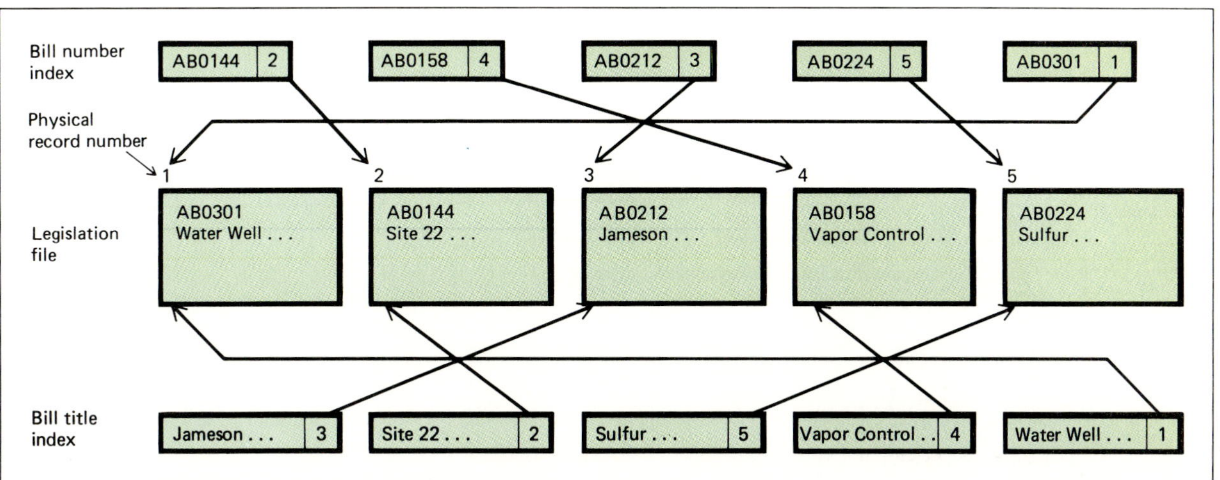

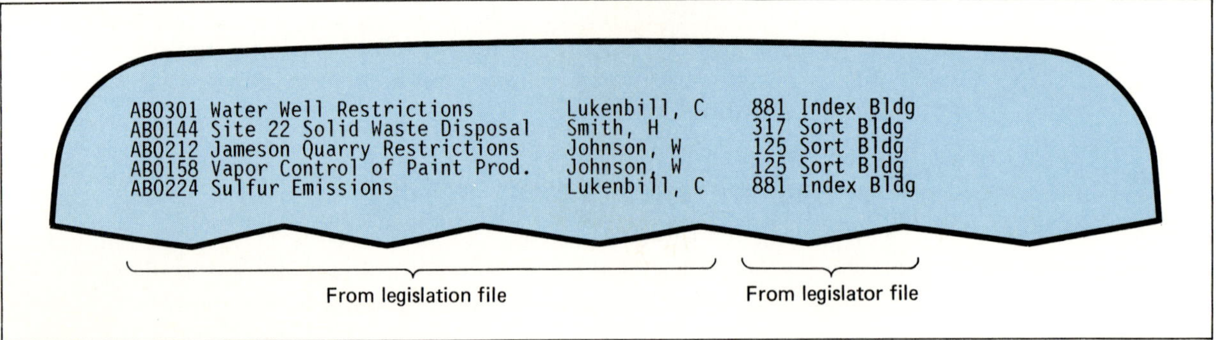

Figure 14-17
A display of data from two files.

The Role of the Index in Linking Files

Figure 14-13 illustrates one of the significant features of DBMSs: the ability to interrelate, or link, files. Linking of two (or more) files is done via indexes. For instance, consider the display of Figure 14-17: This is a physical record sequence display of the five data records shown in Figure 14-15. However, it includes the office number of the bill's author: information obtained from the Member file. To obtain a display such as this consisting of data from two files, the user must provide the DBMS information necessary to define this relationship.

- A primary data file, the Bill file in this case.
- A secondary data file, the Member file in this case.
- The index file that is based on the field of the Member file to be used in linking the two files, the author of the bill in this case.
- The name of the field that links the two files, the assembly member name in this case.

Figure 14-18
Linking two files.

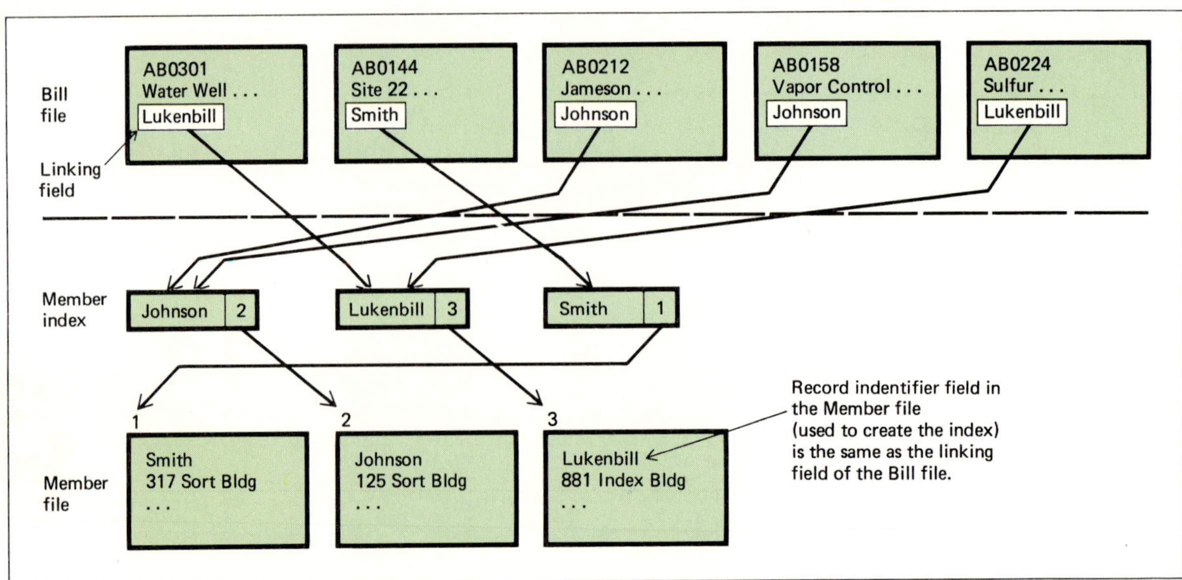

The DBMS program will then set up a linkage such as that shown in Figure 14-18. To generate the display of Figure 14-18, the DBMS program would:

1. Access the first record from the Bill file.
2. Display the needed data from this record.
3. Using the entry from the bill author field (Lukenbill in this case), search the Member index for a matching index entry.
4. Using index entry, identify the desired physical record number (3 in this case) from the Member file.
5. Access record 3 from the Member file.
6. Display the room number from that file.

This process is repeated for each record in the Bill file. Once the relationships are defined, the DBMS program does all of the work in keeping records in step with one another.

Key Field

One of the cornerstones of relational database theory is that any field in a database can be accessed without ambiguity by specifying a data file, and a record in that file, and the field within that record. This has an important implication. That is, for every file, there must be a field (or combination of fields) in the record that uniquely identifies each record. For example, the Bill file record includes the bill number field; no two bills ever have the same bill number—it is **unique**. If, in doing direct access operations, you request the record for AB0212, the DBMS program will locate that specific record for you. This field is called the **key field**. Contrast requesting a record using the key field with requesting the Bill record of bills written by Smith; there is more than one such record so it is not possible to access a particular one in this way.

In the representation of the Bill file, the member name is used as the key field. In an actual application, a name would not be used as a key field because two people might have the same name, for example, there might be two people in the file named Helen Smith. For the Member file, the number of the district represented by the assembly member would be a good choice as a key field. For many applications, the person's Social Security number is used.

A BUSINESS DATABASE APPLICATION

The example of this chapter is a specialized database application; however, it uses principles that are characteristic of database processing. To illustrate, assume that MCT Enterprises has grown and maintains sales outlets in several locations and that its accounting systems include the following four data files (typical fields comprising the records are shown):

Sales Outlet File (one record for each sales office):

Region number

Sales manager employee number

Office address

Regional Sales Manager File (one record for each regional sales manager):

Sales manager employee number

Region number

Name

Home address

Year-to-date sales

Customer File (one record for each customer):

Customer number

Region number

Company name

Year-to-date purchases

Current balance owed

Date account first opened

Accounts Receivable File (one record for each sale to each customer):

Customer number

Invoice number

Invoice date

Original invoice amount

Balance owed

Although each of these files is meaningful and complete within itself, together they form a database in which the information available from the whole is much more significant than that of the individual parts. The relationships among these files, illustrated in Figure 14-19, are the same as that between the assembly Bill file and Member file. They are:

- The Sales Manager file and the Sales Outlet file, related through the region number field.
- The Sales Manager file and the Customer file, also related through the region number field.
- The Customer file and the Accounts Receivable file, related through the customer number field.

Let us focus for the moment on the Customer and Accounts Receivable files. For each customer record, there will be one or more records in the Accounts Receivable file. Furthermore, these files are related by a field that is common to both records: the customer number. These features are identical to those of the assembly Member and Bill file pair. Although the applications are different, the database principles involved are identical.

The Customer and Accounts Receivable files will form the basis for

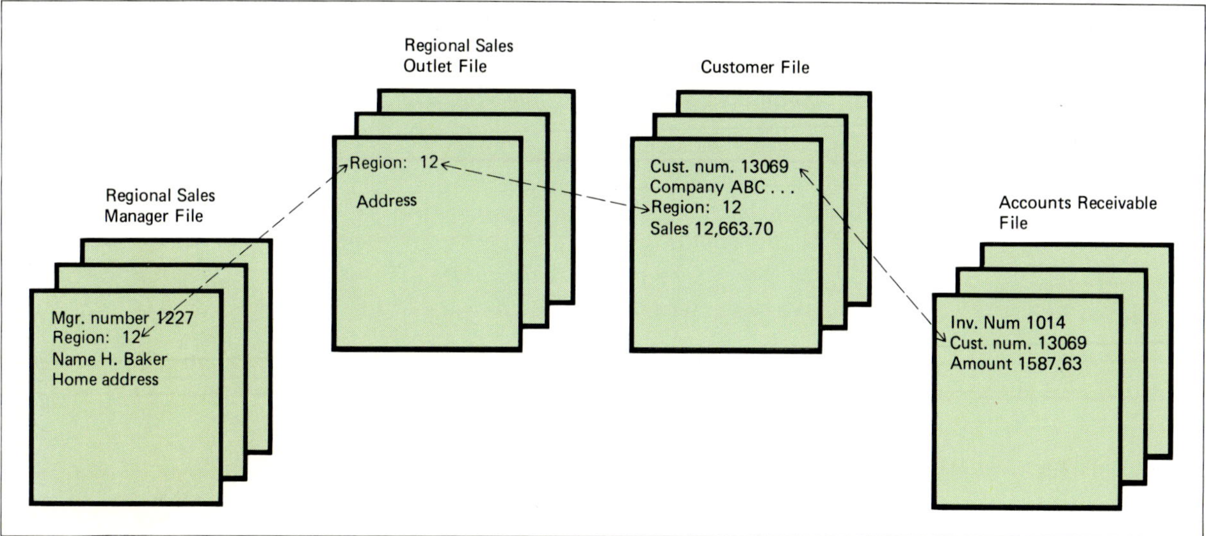

Figure 14-19
Relationships between multiple files.

your study of dBASE III in the next two chapters. In Chapter 15, you will learn how to create a data file, add and edit records, and inspect records in the file. In Chapter 16, you will learn to create index files, to be selective in accessing records, and other advanced topics.

SUMMARY

This chapter has given you your first exposure to database management systems (DBMSs) and how to use them in managing data and converting data into useful information. It has described some of the basic features of DBMSs and has described an application that will be used in your studies of dBASE III PLUS in Chapters 15 and 16. Summarizing, the important items from the chapter are:

- A file is an organized collection of all records of a given type; a record is a group of related fields, basic units of data.
- A database consists of interrelated data files together with index and other files.
- Each file of a database should be set up so that it contains data pertaining to a single entity.
- A DBMS is a program or set of programs for maintaining and using the data in a database.
- The four data types common to most DBMS are character, numeric, date, and logical.
- Designate a field as numeric only if it will contain data on which

arithmetic might be performed. "Numbers," such as an account number or a Social Security number, should be defined as character.

- When a database data file is first created, information describing the exact format of data is made part of the file. This resides in the file together with data that is subsequently entered.
- The two basic types of processing are sequential and direct. With sequential processing, the next record to be processed is the next one in the file. With direct processing, the next record to be processed is whatever one is requested.
- Sorting changes the physical sequence of records in a file. Indexing changes the logical sequence of records in a file by creating a separate index file, giving direct access to records in the file. Indexing is more versatile than sorting.
- In order to link two files, they must have a field in common. The link is from a primary file to a secondary via an index of the secondary file.
- A key field is the field that uniquely identifies any record in a file.

NEW TERMINOLOGY

The following are important new terms introduced in this chapter; you should be familiar with each of them.

character data type
database
database management system
date data type
direct access
field width
file management system
inconsistent data
index
key field
listing
logical data constraint
logical data type
logical record order
numeric data type
physical data constraint
primary sort field
random access
redundant data
report
secondary sort field
selection
sequential access
sort
unique

REVIEW QUESTIONS

1. Describe three situations in everyday life in which information must be obtained from a computer pertaining to you.
2. The following fields are to be included in a data file. Based on your English interpretation of each field, specify which data type should be used for each.

   Driver's license number

   Person's age

Person's date of birth

Automobile type

ZIP code

An indication of whether or not a person is a club member

An indication of whether a person belongs to club A, B, or C

Current mileage of a vehicle to be leased

3. Describe the factors that determine the width that is used for a field in defining a record.
4. What is the difference between creating a database data file and entering records into the file?
5. Distinguish between physical data constraints and logical data constraints. Give some examples.
6. If a record is deleted from a file, what takes place? Explain the rationale of this action.
7. Consider a company payroll database application that handles the payroll processing for all employees of the company. Give an example of sequential processing and one of direct processing for this application.
8. What is the difference between a file listing and a report?
9. Using an index file appears clumsy because accessing a record means reading from two files: first the index, and then the data file. Why not just keep the data file in sequence and forget the index?
10. What is the advantage of using an index with a file when doing sequential processing?
11. Figure 14-18 illustrates linking the Bill file to the Member file through an index of the Member file in order to display the office address of the assembly member together with the bill data. Do you think it would be possible to accomplish the same thing without using an index file? Explain your answer.
12. What is meant by: "A database consists of more files than simply the data files"?
13. Referring to Figure 14-19, what is the primary factor in relating records of one file to corresponding records of another?
14. In Figure 14-19, the Customer file is related to the Accounts Receivable file via the customer number; the Regional Sales Manager file is related to the Regional Sales Outlet file by the region number. These relationships appear to be the same. However, there is an important difference between corresponding data records in these two pairs of files. (It is not explicitly described in the text.) Identify it.

MATCHING

Match each term in a to h with the most appropriate description in 1 through 8.

a. unique
b. index
c. inconsistent data
d. physical data constraint
e. key
f. sort
g. direct access
h. redundancy

1. Could be used to display the records of the Bill file in order by date passed by committee without changing the order of the records in the file.
2. Duplication of data in a file.
3. The unique field in a record that provides unambiguous access to any record in the file.
4. Is the result of the amount of space allocated for a field in a data file.
5. Pertaining to the fact that no two records have the same value for a particular field.
6. Changes the physical order of the records in a file.
7. A process whereby a selected record is read without reading all records preceding it.
8. Can result from redundancy in a file.

TRUE/FALSE

Determine whether each of the following is true or false.

______ 1. File management system and database management system are two names for the same thing.

______ 2. Redundant data in a file is undesirable for two reasons: it introduces the possibility for inconsistent data and it takes up additional disk space because it is duplicated.

______ 3. One of the few disadvantages of a DBMS is that special editing programs must be written for each data file that is generated.

______ 4. Your membership number in a book-of-the-month club would probably be defined in the computer as character rather than numeric.

______ 5. The logical data type is not absolutely essential since a one-position character field could be used to store the same data.

______ 6. A DBMS will automatically adjust the width of each field in a record to accommodate the width of the data value being entered.

______ 7. A database data file contains information describing the exact format of the data record, as well as the data itself.

______ 8. Logical data constraints are restrictions on the data values that can be entered due to the sizes of the fields of the record.

______ 9. In most DBMSs, the action of deleting a record does not actually erase the record from the file.

_______ **10.** In sequential processing, records are always accessed by beginning with the first physical record in the file and proceeding record by record to the last.

_______ **11.** In direct processing, the next record to be accessed can be any record in the file.

_______ **12.** An index changes the logical order of records in a file without changing the physical order.

_______ **13.** An index can be used only with direct processing; it cannot be used with sequential processing.

_______ **14.** In linking two files using an index, it makes no difference if the index is to the primary file or the secondary file so long as it is generated on the common field.

_______ **15.** In Figure 14-19, the Regional Sales Manager file is linked to the Regional Sales Outlet file, therefore, it cannot be linked to the Customer file.

ANSWERS TO OBJECTIVE QUESTIONS

Matching

1. b 2. h 3. e 4. d 5. a 6. f 7. g 8. c

True/False

1. F 2. T 3. F 4. T 5. T 6. F 7. T 8. F 9. T
10. F 11. T 12. T 13. F 14. F 15. F

Chapter 15

Creating and Using Data Files

OBJECTIVES

From Chapter 14, you learned how a DBMS can be used to assist you in managing data. In this chapter, you will use dBASE III PLUS to create the customer file of Figure 14-19 and add records to it. You will also use the Bills file that served as the basis for descriptions of Chapter 14. When you have completed this chapter, you should be able to:

- Create a new database data file by defining the record format.
- Make changes to the record format of your data file.
- Add records to a data file.
- Display on the screen or print the contents of a data file.
- Display on the screen or print the record format of a data file.
- Terminate a dBASE work session.
- Use the dBASE Assistant, a simplified menu form for carrying out dBASE operations.
- Make a copy of a data file from within dBASE.
- Sequentially access records in a data file.
- Directly access records in a data file.
- Edit records in a data file.
- Delete records from a data file.
- Permanently erase deleted records from a data file.

PREVIEW

Getting Started

The procedures to install and run dBASE and the initial screen display are described.

Creating a New dBASE File

Generating a new database data file is a two-step process in which the first step is defining the record format using the CREATE command. Following the examples of this section, you will define the record format for the Customer file.

Adding Records to a File

The second step in generating a new database data file is adding records to the file using the APPEND command. You will enter ten records to the Customer file.

Using the Assistant

dBASE includes a feature called the Assistant, which provides access to the many actions of dBASE commands through a menu system. You will use the Assistant to inspect the records of the file you have created.

Accessing and Changing Records in a File

The primary focus of this section is using the EDIT command to edit records in a file. You will edit all records in a file using sequential file access and edit selected records using direct access.

Deleting Records from a File

Records are deleted from a file with the DELETE command. Each deleted record is "marked" for deletion but not physically removed, and can be ignored during processing. Deleted records are physically removed with the PACK command.

The Browse Command

The BROWSE command provides the ability to display on the screen records of a file (inspect the data), to edit records, and to delete records.

GETTING STARTED

Since this chapter involves learning by doing, you will need DBMS software. If you have access to a copy of dBASE III, dBASE III PLUS, or dBASE

IV, you can use it. If you do not, you can use the special Limited Use Educational version of dBASE III PLUS included with this book. The primary difference between the commercial and Limited Use versions of dBASE III PLUS is that you can have no more than thirty records in a file with the Limited Use version. If you will be using this version, then read the following section for setting up.

Setting Up for Using dBASE III PLUS (Limited Use Version)

The Limited Use version of dBASE III PLUS is stored on two disks that accompany this book:

dBASE III PLUS Sampler Demo Disk #1.

dBASE III PLUS Sampler Demo Disk #2.

Once installed, it can run on a computer with any of the following four computer configurations:

256K of memory and two floppy drives.

More than 256K of memory and two floppy drives.

256K of memory, one floppy drive, and one hard disk.

More than 256K of memory, one floppy drive, and one hard disk.

To run this version of dBASE III PLUS from a floppy-based computer, the system disk that you use to boot the computer must contain a special start-up file. Fortunately, the dBASE disk contains a program to write this file to a system disk that you use to boot the computer. (If you need to format a disk as a system disk, Chapter 5 describes how to create a DOS system disk.) Whether dBASE III PLUS is to run from a floppy or a hard disk, it is necessary to carry out the following installation procedure.

1. Boot the computer up with a normal DOS system disk.
2. Insert the dBASE III PLUS Demo Disk #1 into the A drive.
3. If you are using a floppy-based computer, insert the system disk that will normally be used into the B drive. This is not necessary if you are using a hard-disk-based system.
4. From the DOS A> prompt, type in the following command

   ```
   INSTALL
   ```

   and strike Enter.

The INSTALL program will give you instructions. When the process is completed, dBASE III PLUS will be ready for use. If you are using a hard disk computer, the install procedure will create a subdirectory named SAMPLER on the C drive. All the components of the dBASE software from the Demo Disks #1 and #2 will be copied to that subdirectory. You can use your data disk as is, or you can copy all of the data files to your hard disk. Note that these setup procedures need be carried out only once; it is not necessary to do so each time you use dBASE III PLUS.

Throughout the book, continual reference is made to dBASE III PLUS by name. In the interest of brevity, the word dBASE is used. In all cases, you should interpret dBASE to mean dBASE III PLUS, the software made available with this book. (Note that most of the descriptions and commands are equally applicable to the predecessor, dBASE III, as well as the successor dBASE IV.)

Running dBASE

Activating dBASE (or bringing the program up) involves a slightly different sequence for a floppy disk system than for a hard disk system.

Floppy-Disk System.

1. Insert the system disk in the A drive. Reboot the computer by holding down the Ctrl and Alt keys and pressing the Del key.
2. After the booting operation is complete and the A> prompt displayed, remove the system disk from the A drive and insert dBASE III PLUS Sampler Demo Disk #1.
3. Insert your data disk in the B drive.
4. From the DOS A> prompt, type the following command.

```
DBASE
```

5. Press the Enter key.
6. After about 30 seconds, you will be prompted to remove Demo Disk #1 from the A drive, insert Demo Disk #2, and press the Enter key. Do so.

Hard-Disk System.

1. Change to the appropriate subdirectory by typing the following command sequence from the C> prompt.

```
CD\SAMPLER
```

2. From the C> DOS prompt, type the following command.

```
DBASE
```

3. Press the Enter key.

When dBASE first loads, it will be in the ASSIST mode; to exit ASSIST, strike the Escape (Esc) key (you will learn about ASSIST later). The bottom of your screen will be as shown in Figure 15-1. The first of the last three lines on the screen is called the **status bar**; descriptions in this chapter will refer to it frequently. Note that the cursor is positioned following a period. The period is used as the dBASE prompt (much like the DOS prompt A>), and is commonly called the **dot prompt**. When using the Limited Use version, the dot prompt will be preceded by (DEMO), as shown in Figure 15-1. At this point, dBASE is ready to accept a command.

If the entry on the status bar following the words Command Line is <B:>, then the system is ready to go. If it is not, then you must indicate to dBASE the default location of the data disk. To this end, enter the following and strike the Enter key.

```
SET DEFAULT TO B
```

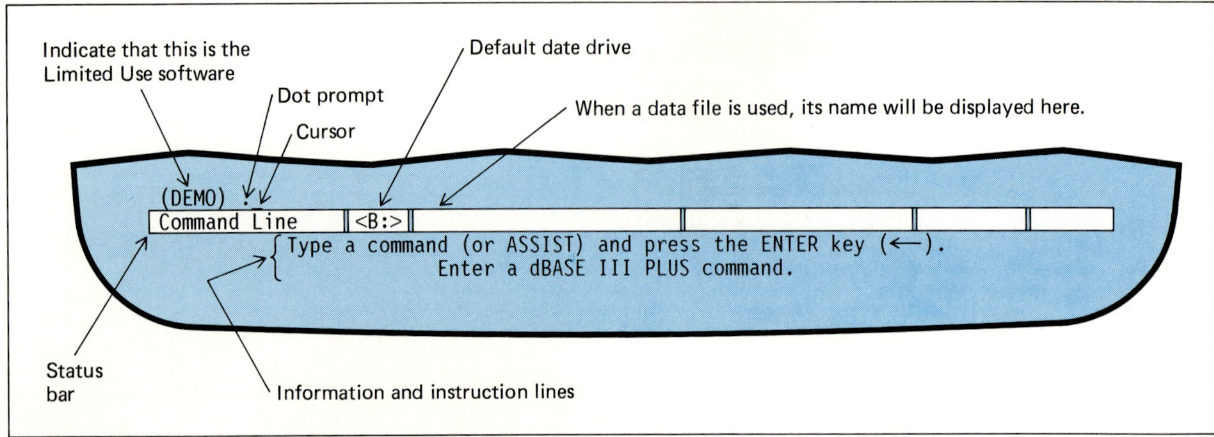

Figure 15-1
The dBASE III PLUS announcement screen.

If you are using a hard disk computer, then use the letter of the drive where your data files are located (A if in the A drive and C if together with dBASE in the SAMPLER subdirectory).

dBASE Commands

dBASE is a DBMS: a programming system that allows us to manipulate files that make up a database. To that end, dBASE includes commands to perform a wide variety of operations on files. For instance, you will use dBASE commands to create a new data file (CREATE), add a new record to a file (APPEND), create an index (INDEX), and change the contents of a selected field in every record of a file (REPLACE). These commands (of which there are over 100) can be executed through a menu from the dBASE Assist mode (described later in this chapter), or from the dot prompt mode (Figure 15-1) by typing the command name and striking Enter.

Getting Help

Most quality software includes *on-line help* that provides the program user with instructions or explanations. For instance, assume that you cannot remember the form of the various options of the LIST command. You can obtain the description from information stored in a special file on the disk with the command HELP followed by the keyword for which you need help. (*Keywords* are words with special meaning to dBASE.) For instance, type the following from the dot prompt and strike Enter.

```
HELP LIST
```

The result will be the screen display of Figure 15-2. Here, you see a syntax description (the structure of a command is called its **syntax**) and a brief description. Many of the dBASE commands have a variety of optional parameters that can used. Each command is designated by an action word followed by its permissible options. The syntax convention uses both angle <> and square [] brackets. The angle brackets indicate that you must insert something (as described by the words enclosed in the brackets). The square brackets indicate an optional item. Words shown in uppercase must

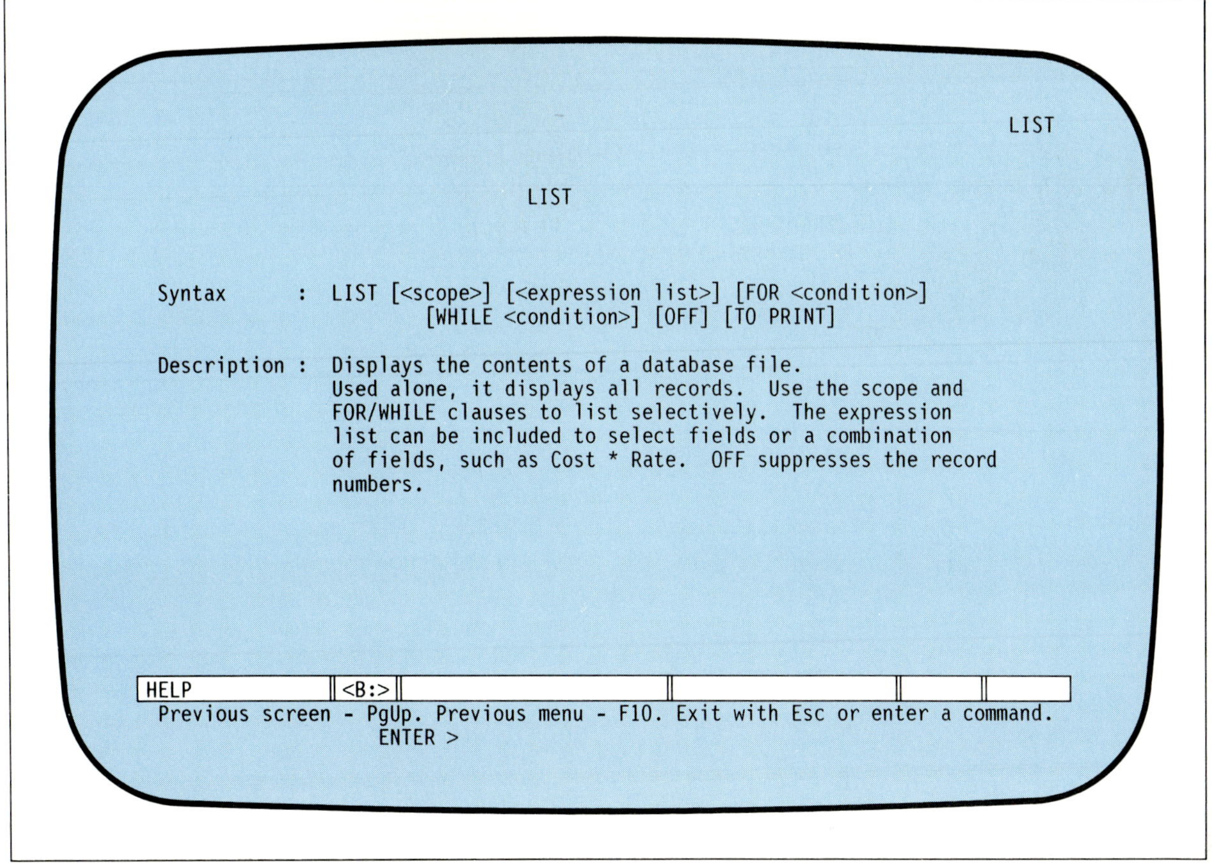

Figure 15-2
Description of the LIST command from Help.

be typed exactly as shown if that portion of the command is used. Based on this syntax definition, the following examples of this command are valid.

```
LIST
LIST TO PRINT
LIST FOR BALANCE>LIMIT TO PRINT
```

Note that you must not type the angle or square brackets when entering a command. To return to the dot prompt from the Help, strike the Escape (Esc) key.

CREATING A NEW dBASE DATA FILE

Figure 14-19 shows some of the many data files that would make up the MCT Enterprises database. To learn how to create and work with a new file, we will focus our attention on one of these: the Customer file. We will assume that all of the planning and design has been completed and that you are ready to create the data file. Remember from Chapter 14 that the process of entering a new file requires two steps: (1) Create the data file, which involves defining each field of the record, and (2) Enter data records into the file.

Record Requirements

During the planning phase of creating a database application, details of each data file are spelled out. Assume that this task has been completed and that the exact record format of the Customer file is as summarized in Table 15-1.

Table 15-1 CUSTOMER File

Field Description	Field Name	Type	Length	Decimal Positions
Customer number	CUSTNUM	Character	5	
Sales region	REGION	Character	2	
Customer company name	COMPANY	Character	27	
Year-to-date sales	YTDSALES	Numeric	8	2
Current unpaid balance	BALANCE	Numeric	7	2
Date account opened (anniversary date)	ANNIV	Date	8	

As you can see, the record is relatively small, consisting of six fields requiring a total of 47 bytes. This is well within dBASE limits of 128 fields and 4000 bytes per record for a database file.

Field Names

As you know, each file stored on a disk is given a unique filename by which we can retrieve the file at any time. Similarly, within a database data file, each field must be given a name by which we can refer to that field. Each field name should be selected so that it describes the field that it represents, as illustrated by the names that have been selected in Table 15-1. As with DOS filenames, you must follow dBASE rules for field names.

- Names are limited to 10 characters. Note that this size restriction applies to the field *name.* It has nothing to do with the length of the data value that will be stored in that field.
- The first character must be a letter.
- Succeeding characters may be letters, digits, or the underscore character. You *cannot* use the hyphen.
- No two fields in a data file can have the same name. (The same name *can* be used in two different data files of a database.)

The underscore is commonly used to separate words as the space is not allowed. In that respect, an alternate to CUSTNUM would be CUST_NUM.

(The underscore is used sparingly in this book *only* because it can easily disappear from view in various printed illustrations.)

Using the CREATE Command to Define the Record Format of a Data File

Your first exercise in this chapter is to create the CUSTOMER data file. If you do not have dBASE running on you computer, you should bring it up now. Do not forget to set the default data drive. If your screen shows the ASSIST mode, then switch to the dot prompt by striking the Esc key.

DO THIS NOW 15-1 **Creating a New Data File Named CUSTOMER**

1. From the dot prompt, type the following command and strike Enter.

```
CREATE CUSTOMER
```

This places dBASE in the field entry mode with the screen shown in Figure 15-3. Ignore the boxed area at the top of the screen for now; you will learn about it after you have entered the field

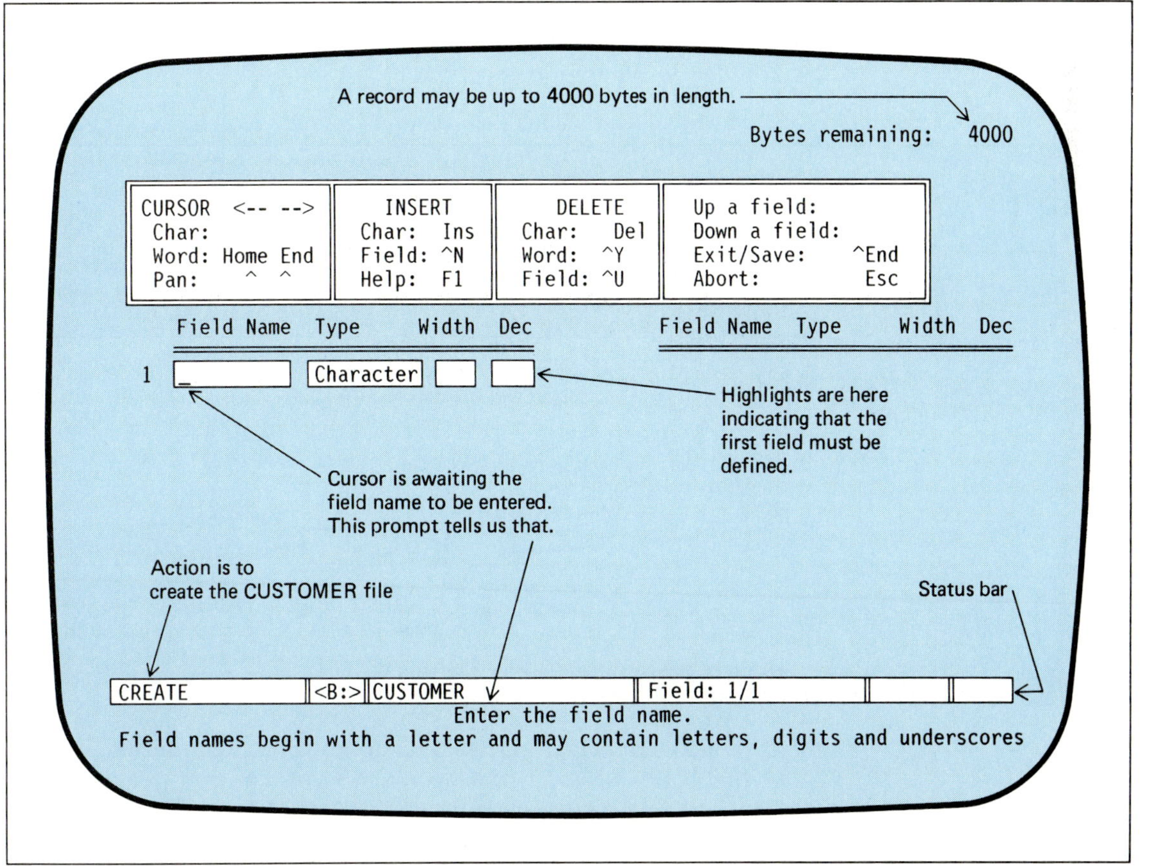

Figure 15-3
The data file creation screen.

definitions. The highlighted line is numbered 1. This line will define the first data field of the record, in this case, the customer number.

2. In entering the field definitions, you must use the record layout of Table 15-1. Type the name of the first field in the record, CUSTNUM, and then strike Enter; this portion of the screen will appear as shown below. (When typing a field name, it makes no difference whether uppercase or lowercase is used; the name is displayed in uppercase.

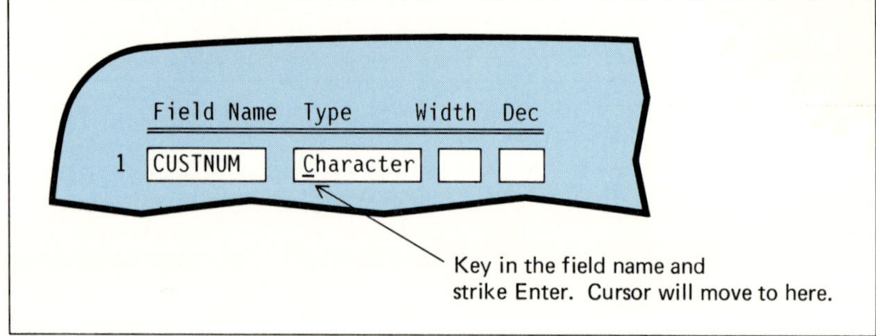

If, after completing an entry, you notice that you entered it incorrectly, do not worry, as you will learn how to make corrections when you have finished.

3. dBASE is waiting for you to enter the type of field that this will be. (Remember from Chapter 14 that fields can be character, numeric, date, or logical).. Since Character is offered as the default, strike Enter to accept it and the cursor will move to the Width highlight.

4. The width of the CUSTNUM field is 5 (see Table 15-1), so type the digit 5 as shown below.

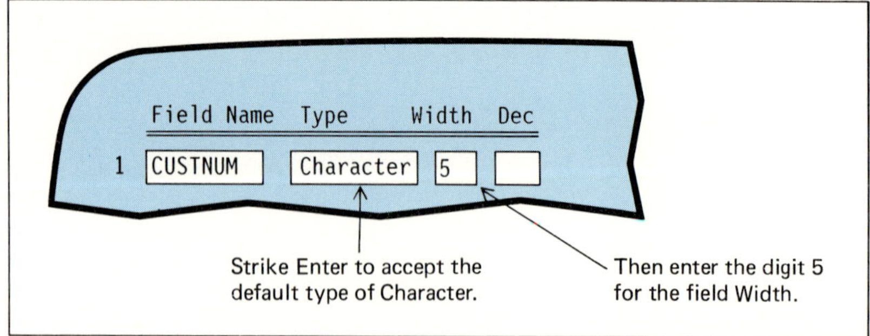

Notice that no attempt is made to position the number within the highlighted area. Knowing that this is a number, dBASE automatically positions it after you strike Enter.

5. Strike the Enter and this portion of your screen will appear as shown at the top of the next page.

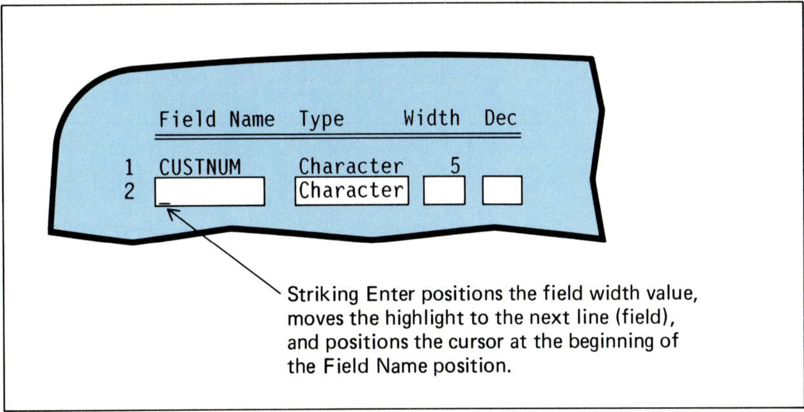

6. Enter the REGION and COMPANY fields in the same way as the CUSTNUM field.

7. The fourth field YTDSALES is numeric. For the Type entry, strike the letter N, which will cause Character to be replaced with Numeric. Then enter a width of 8 and strike Enter. Your screen will now appear as:

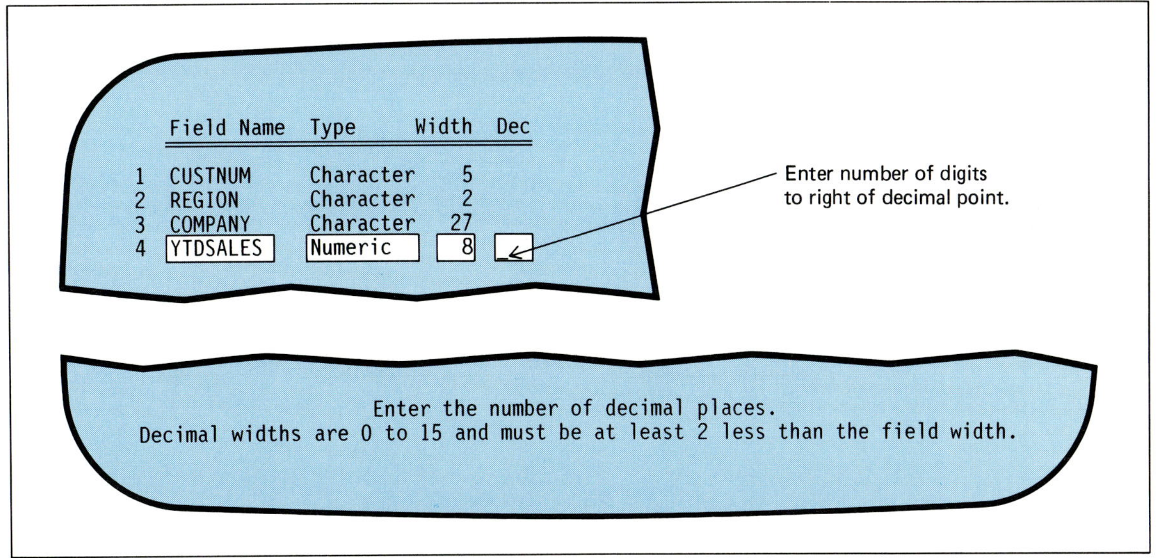

The cursor is awaiting your entry of the Dec (Decimals) value. Since this is to be a dollar and cent amount (two places to the right of the decimal), type 2 and strike Enter.

8. For field 5 of this record, enter the BALANCE field definition in the same way as YTDSALES.

9. The last field definition is the date the account was opened (ANNIV). Type the name, strike Enter, and then strike the letter D (for Date) for the Type. A value of 8 will be entered automatically for the Width and the highlight will progress to line 7.

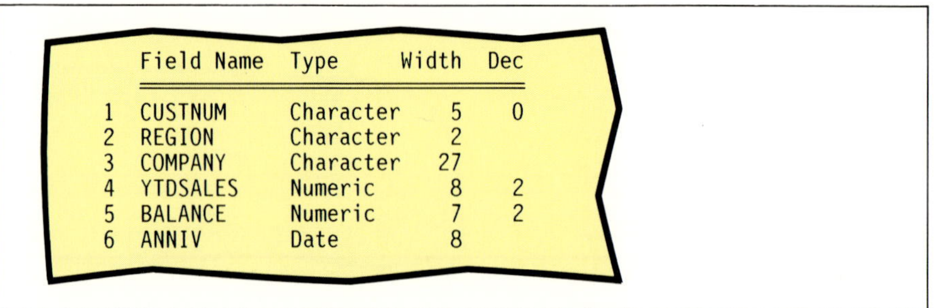

	Field Name	Type	Width	Dec
1	CUSTNUM	Character	5	0
2	REGION	Character	2	
3	COMPANY	Character	27	
4	YTDSALES	Numeric	8	2
5	BALANCE	Numeric	7	2
6	ANNIV	Date	8	

Figure 15-4
The completed record definition.

The completed record definition is shown in Figure 15-4. You should check your screen contents to be certain that your entries are correct. If you made an error while entering information, you can correct it easily as described next.

Making Changes to the Record Structure

The boxed areas in the upper portion of your screen (refer to Figure 15-3) is called a **Help** window and summarizes all of the key sequences to be used for editing record definitions. (If your screen does not display the boxed areas, then strike the F1 key; the display is toggled on and off with this key.) Most of the key actions for editing a file structure are described in Figure 15-5. To illustrate making corrections, assume the following.

Figure 15-5
Editing actions of CREATE.

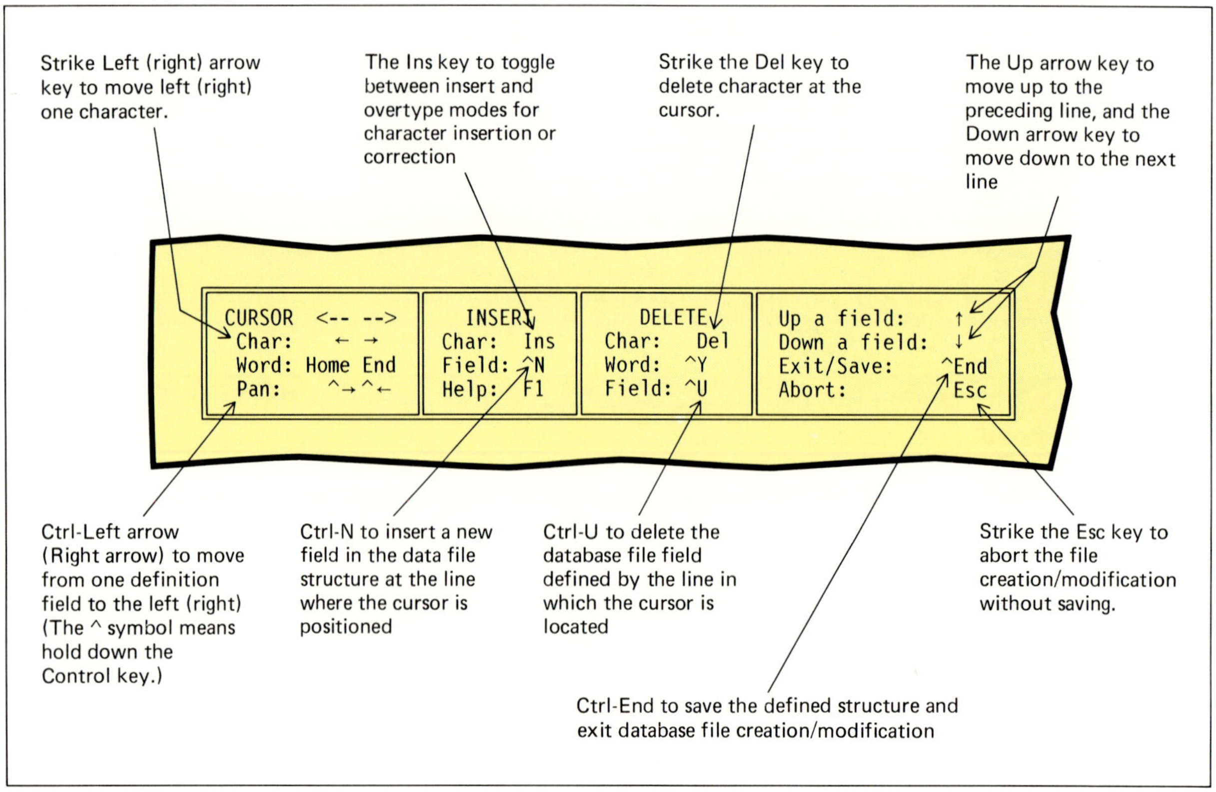

Strike Left (right) arrow key to move left (right) one character.

The Ins key to toggle between insert and overtype modes for character insertion or correction

Strike the Del key to delete character at the cursor.

The Up arrow key to move up to the preceding line, and the Down arrow key to move down to the next line

```
CURSOR  <-- -->   |   INSERT     |   DELETE     | Up a field:    ↑
  Char:    ← →    | Char:  Ins   | Char:   Del  | Down a field:  ↓
  Word: Home End  | Field: ^N    | Word:   ^Y   | Exit/Save:   ^End
  Pan:    ^→ ^←   | Help:  F1    | Field:  ^U   | Abort:        Esc
```

Ctrl-Left arrow (Right arrow) to move from one definition field to the left (right) (The ^ symbol means hold down the Control key.)

Ctrl-N to insert a new field in the data file structure at the line where the cursor is positioned

Ctrl-U to delete the database file field defined by the line in which the cursor is located

Strike the Esc key to abort the file creation/modification without saving.

Ctrl-End to save the defined structure and exit database file creation/modification

- The Field Name of the first field must be CUSTOMER rather than CUSTNUM.
- You entered the field REGION as numeric rather than character.
- You entered the length of the field COMPANY as 37 rather than 27.
- You forgot the BALANCE field.

Even if your record definition is correct, carry out the steps of the following example so that you will be familiar with the actions.

DO THIS NOW 15-2 **Changing the Record Definition**

1. Using the arrow keys, move the cursor to the Field Name entry of the first field (this will be CUSTNUM, if you entered it correctly). Position the cursor on the letter N in CUSTNUM.
2. Strike the Del key three times, leaving CUST.
3. Type OMER to make the name CUSTOMER, and then strike Enter. You have changed the name of this field. Now repeat the process and change it back to CUSTNUM.
4. Move the cursor to the Type definition of the REGION field using the arrow keys. The current definition is Character.
5. Change the field to Numeric (you will change it back after this) by striking the letter N. dBASE will make the change.
6. Change it back to Character by repositioning the cursor and striking the letter C.
7. Move the cursor to the Width entry for the third field COMPANY. Type 37 and strike Enter. Reposition the cursor and change it back to 27.
8. Move the cursor to line 5 (the BALANCE entry).
9. Delete this field definition with a Ctrl-U (hold down the Ctrl key and strike the letter U). The entries of line 5 (BALANCE) will be deleted and the ANNIV field will be moved into its place.

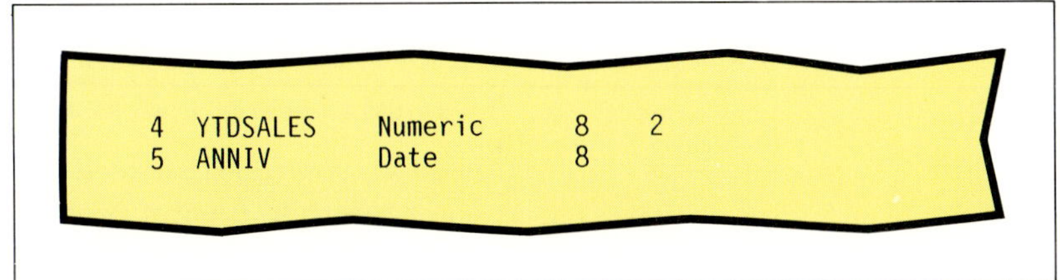

10. You must now insert the BALANCE field to restore your record definition to its complete form. Enter the Ctrl-N sequence to

insert a new field. The ANNIV field will be moved down one line and line 5 will blank as shown below.

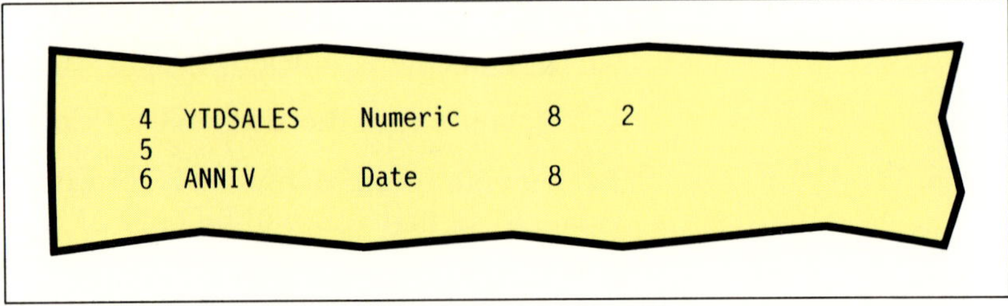

11. Type in this field definition.

This completes the definition of our CUSTOMER data record structure.

Terminating a CREATE Session

There are two ways that you can end a CREATE session. If you decide at any time during the session that you do not wish to proceed and do not want any of your work saved, then strike the Esc key. dBASE will ask for a confirmation that you wish to abort. However, you will usually want to save your work and have dBASE complete the action by creating the empty data file you have defined.

DO THIS NOW 15-3 **Saving the File Definition and Exiting CREATE**

1. Enter the Ctrl-End sequence (hold down the Control key and strike the End key). In response, dBASE displays the following message.

```
Strike ENTER to confirm.  Any other key to resume.
```

2. If, upon reflecting, you realize that you are not finished, strike any key (for instance, the space bar) and the exit will be aborted. You can then continue entering or editing field definitions.

3. Since you are finished, strike Enter. This will cause dBASE to write a new, empty file to disk. When the action is complete, the following prompt is displayed.

```
Input data records now? (Y/N)
```

4. At this point, you could proceed to enter data into the file (respond with Y) or return to the dot prompt (respond with N or any other key). Return to the dot prompt by striking the letter N.

When this action is complete, your data disk will contain the data file CUSTOMER.DBF. Notice that dBASE automatically adds the extension DBF (meaning database file).

ADDING RECORDS TO A FILE

The Contents of a Data File

The contents of your newly created file CUSTOMER.DBF are illustrated in Figure 15-6(a). In addition to the defining information about this data file, it includes a special "marker" called an EOF, meaning end of file. As records are entered, dBASE moves the EOF so that it is always positioned after the last record; Figure 15-6(b) illustrates a file containing two records. The EOF is always positioned to indicate to dBASE the physical end of the file. The process of adding records is called *appending* and is done with the dBASE APPEND command.

Figure 15-6
(a) An empty data file.
(b) Two records in a data file.

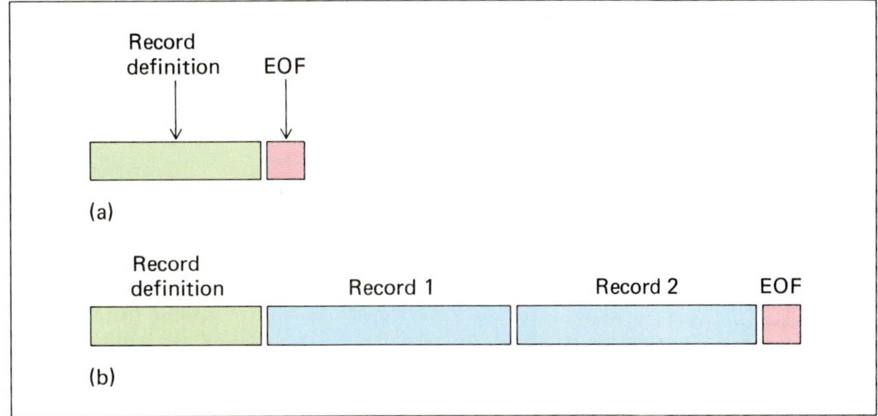

The USE Command

In using WordPerfect and 1-2-3 in the earlier chapters, you accumulated word processing and spreadsheet files on your data disk. To work with one of them, you first had to retrieve it from disk. Somewhat the same is true of working with a dBASE data file. You must first designate to dBASE the name of the file that you want. This is called *opening* the file; it causes dBASE to find the file on the disk and set aside memory for making records available to you. The dBASE command to open a file is USE followed by the filename:

```
USE CUSTOMER
```

Notice that the extension DBF need not be included because dBASE assumes DBF as a default in the same way that Lotus 1-2-3 uses a default of WKS (or WK1). Once opened, the file remains open until it is closed by opening another file, by entering a USE command without a data file name (USE by itself), or by terminating processing with the QUIT. The QUIT is described later in this chapter.

The APPEND Command

You can enter records using the APPEND command at any time whether the file is empty or already contains records. For this data file, you are to

Record#	CUSTNUM	REGION	COMPANY	YTDSALES	BALANCE	ANNIV
1	13069	12	ABC Retail Outlet	12633.70	248.88	06/13/86
2	12573	23	Boardwalk Sportswear Sales	8003.46	1280.22	06/24/86
3	12626	12	Mr. Casual, Limited	8933.48	0.00	08/19/87
4	11882	37	Harlicorn Operations	1012.66	1012.66	06/06/89
5	12292	23	Coast Concepts	5990.86	0.00	06/12/87
6	13312	37	Paradise Leisure Clothing	14889.83	2701.73	04/22/86
7	12272	12	Grand Times	7932.82	876.33	02/28/88
8	13189	37	Crow Canyon Casual Wear	19833.22	2912.29	03/28/86
9	13117	23	Blue Ridge Sport & Casual	1788.29	448.98	09/22/87
10	12217	12	Falcon Ridges Enterprises	5880.10	0.00	04/02/86

Indicates the order in which the records are to be entered

Figure 15-7
Input data for CUSTOMER file.

enter the ten records shown in Figure 15-7. (This is a listing of the CUSTOMER file that was entered during the writing of this book.) First, you will enter the first two records and terminate the append. Then you will issue the APPEND command again and enter the rest of the records.

DO THIS NOW 15-4 **Appending the First Two Data Records to the CUSTOMER File**

1. Open the CUSTOMER file with the command:

   ```
   USE CUSTOMER
   ```

   The file CUSTOMER is now available for use. Note that, in this instance, the USE was not necessary because, when the CREATE was completed, dBASE had left this file open. However, this is the general sequence that you will use: you will create a given file once but you will use it many times.

2. From the dot prompt, you must issue the APPEND command by typing

   ```
   APPEND
   ```

   and striking Enter. You will be presented with the entry screen of Figure 15-8. At the top of the screen is a record number counter indicating that dBASE is awaiting entry of record number 1. Notice that the fields are listed in the same order as they are defined in the record. Furthermore, the highlighted area designates the space allocated for each field. The boxed display describing keystroke actions is similar to that of the CREATE screen (Figure 15-3). If you want to get rid of it, strike the F1 key.

3. Type the customer number for the first record (13069). dBASE will cause your computer to beep, indicating that the field is full. Strike Enter to progress to the next field.

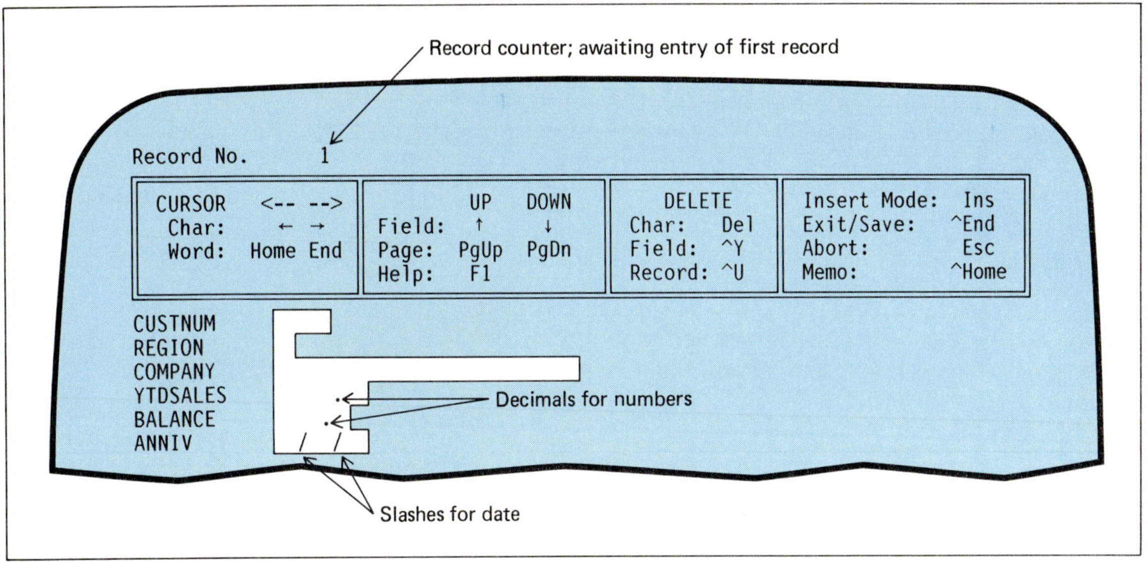

Figure 15-8
Data entry screen.

4. Enter the values for REGION and COMPANY in the same way.
5. For the YTDSALES field, attempt to enter a letter and notice what happens. Then enter the correct values for both YTDSALES and BALANCE (from Figure 15-7).
6. Make an incorrect entry of 16/13/86 for the year. As you enter the digits, notice that the cursor jumps over the slashes. When you strike Enter, an error message will be displayed. Strike any key to continue. Without striking the Enter key, when you finish typing the correct data, type the correct entry over the incorrect one. Your screen should appear as shown below.

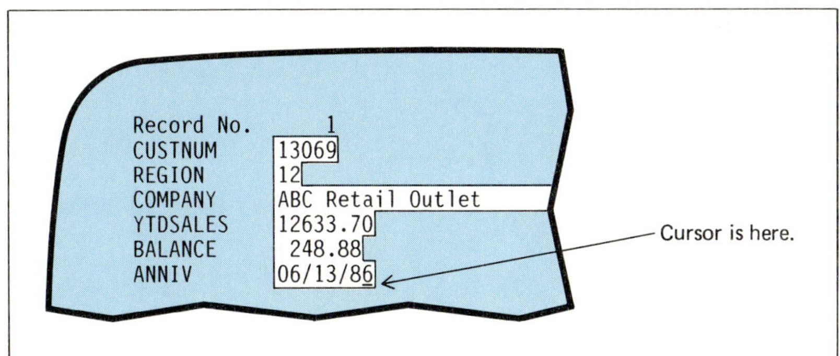

7. If you have any errors, correct them by using the arrow keys to move the cursor (the same methods you used in correcting the record definition in DTN 15-2).
8. If you have moved the cursor to another field entry, move it back to the ANNIV field (the last one) and strike Enter. The highlighted data entry portion of the screen will be cleared and the record number will be increased to 2.

9. Type the values for the fields of the second record in the same way you typed the first. However, since you wish to terminate after this record, *do not strike Enter after typing the date.*

10. With record number 2 still on the screen, use the Ctrl-End key sequence (hold down the Ctrl key and strike the End key). This saves the newly entered record *and* terminates the APPEND mode, returning control to the dot prompt.

When entering a number of records, striking Enter after each field is almost automatic. If you strike Enter after the last field of the last record, then a blank screen appears. *Do not use Ctrl-End at this point.* If you do, a blank record will be written to the file. You can avoid having a blank record added to your file by striking the Escape key to abort the append. Then the append operation will be terminated without the blank screen being saved to disk as a blank record.

Changing the Environment and Continuing Data Entry

As you entered data, dBASE beeped when any field became full. Some people find this distracting; it is especially annoying if a number of people are working with APPEND. There are various working environment parameters that dBASE allows you to change. This is done with the SET command. You have already used this command to set the default data drive to B (if you are using a floppy disk computer). You can also use it to turn the beep (called the bell in dBASE) off by typing the following command from the dot prompt.

```
SET BELL OFF
```

To turn it back on, use the word ON instead of OFF. You may turn it off or leave it on, whichever you desire; it has no effect on the entry of the data. You must now enter the rest of the data records.

DO THIS NOW 15-5 **Entering the Rest of the Data Records from Figure 15-7**

1. Return to the APPEND mode by typing the command:

   ```
   APPEND
   ```

   You should be presented with the data entry screen of Figure 15-8; the record number should be 3. If it is 4, you have entered a blank record into the file. To fix that, strike the PgUp key and the record counter will be reduced to 3.

2. Enter the data for each of the remaining records listed in Figure 15-7. Remember to use Ctrl-End, *not* Enter, after the last field of the last record.

FINISHING UP

Listing the Contents of a File

Before terminating this session, you might want to display or print a copy of your work; this is done with the LIST command. To get a complete display of your data file, you must type

```
LIST
```

from the dot prompt and strike Enter. dBASE will display the records of your file as shown in Figure 15-7. Notice that the field names are used for column headings and the physical record number is printed. If you do not want the record number, use the OFF option with list; that is:

```
LIST OFF
```

If your record is so large that not all of the fields will fit on a single line, you might want to list selected fields. For instance, LIST followed by the word FIELDS and a list of fields (called the *expression list* in the general form of Figure 15-2) could take the following form.

```
LIST FIELDS CUSTNUM, COMPANY, BALANCE
```

This will produce a display consisting only of the listed fields from the records of the file. (Note: You can omit the word FIELDS.)

If you have a printer attached to your computer and would like a printed copy, then use the TO PRINT option of the command and enter it as:

```
LIST TO PRINT
```

Your file contents will be printed to the printer and also displayed on the screen.

Listing the Structure of a Data File

When working with a data file, you will occasionally need to check the record format. You can get this with the following variation of the LIST:

```
LIST STRUCTURE
```

or

```
LIST STRUCTURE TO PRINT
```

The display (or printout) will be as shown in Figure 15-9. One thing to notice about this display is that the sum of the field widths is 57 but the total given is 58. This number will always be one higher than the sum of the field widths because dBASE adds an extra position for its own use.

You probably noticed that your listings caused the contents of the screen to scroll upward, leaving the previous display on the upper half of the screen and yours on the lower half. The CLEAR command will remedy this; just type CLEAR and strike Enter to clear the screen and position the cursor at the upper left screen position. Then enter the LIST or LIST STRUCTURE command.

Figure 15-9
Structure of CUSTOMER.

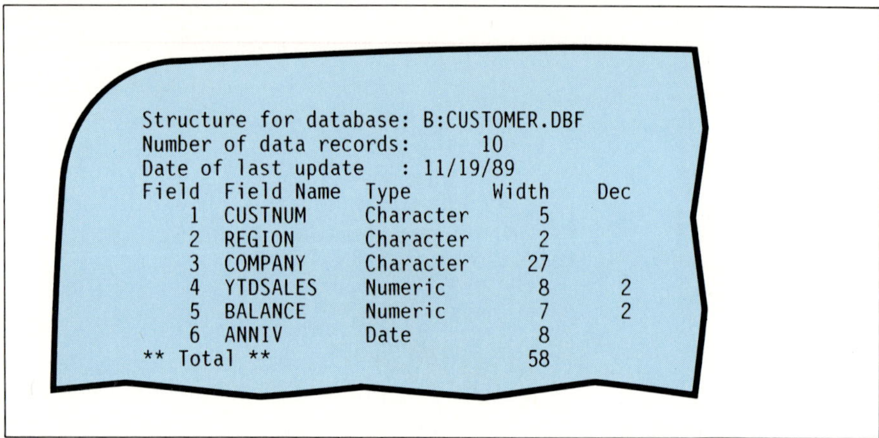

```
Structure for database: B:CUSTOMER.DBF
Number of data records:       10
Date of last update   : 11/19/89
Field  Field Name  Type       Width    Dec
    1  CUSTNUM     Character      5
    2  REGION      Character      2
    3  COMPANY     Character     27
    4  YTDSALES    Numeric        8      2
    5  BALANCE     Numeric        7      2
    6  ANNIV       Date           8
** Total **                      58
```

Terminating a dBASE Work Session

As with WordPerfect and 1-2-3, a work session must be ended by terminating execution of the dBASE program. This will ensure that everything needed for your data file is properly stored on disk.

DO THIS NOW 15-6 **Terminating the Work Session**

1. Terminate by typing, from the dot prompt, the command

```
QUIT
```

and striking Enter. You will be returned to the DOS prompt.

You will recall from WordPerfect and 1-2-3 that before terminating the program you saved your latest work because all additions or changes during the session are in memory, not on disk. With dBASE, as each record is entered during the APPEND (or during editing, which you will do later), it is written to disk. When you terminate execution of the dBASE program, dBASE saves to the file a count of the number of records in the file and then closes it.

USING ASSIST

When you first bring dBASE up, you are presented with the ASSIST screen shown in Figure 15-10. (You got out of this by striking the Esc key.) The purpose of ASSIST is to provide the occasional user with easy access to all commands and their forms through a menu system; the dot prompt mode is not used. Some people prefer ASSIST; others consider it clumsy and prefer working from the dot prompt. In this section, you will learn how to open a file (USE) and to list selected fields using ASSIST. To activate ASSIST, it is only necessary to type in the ASSIST command and then press Enter.

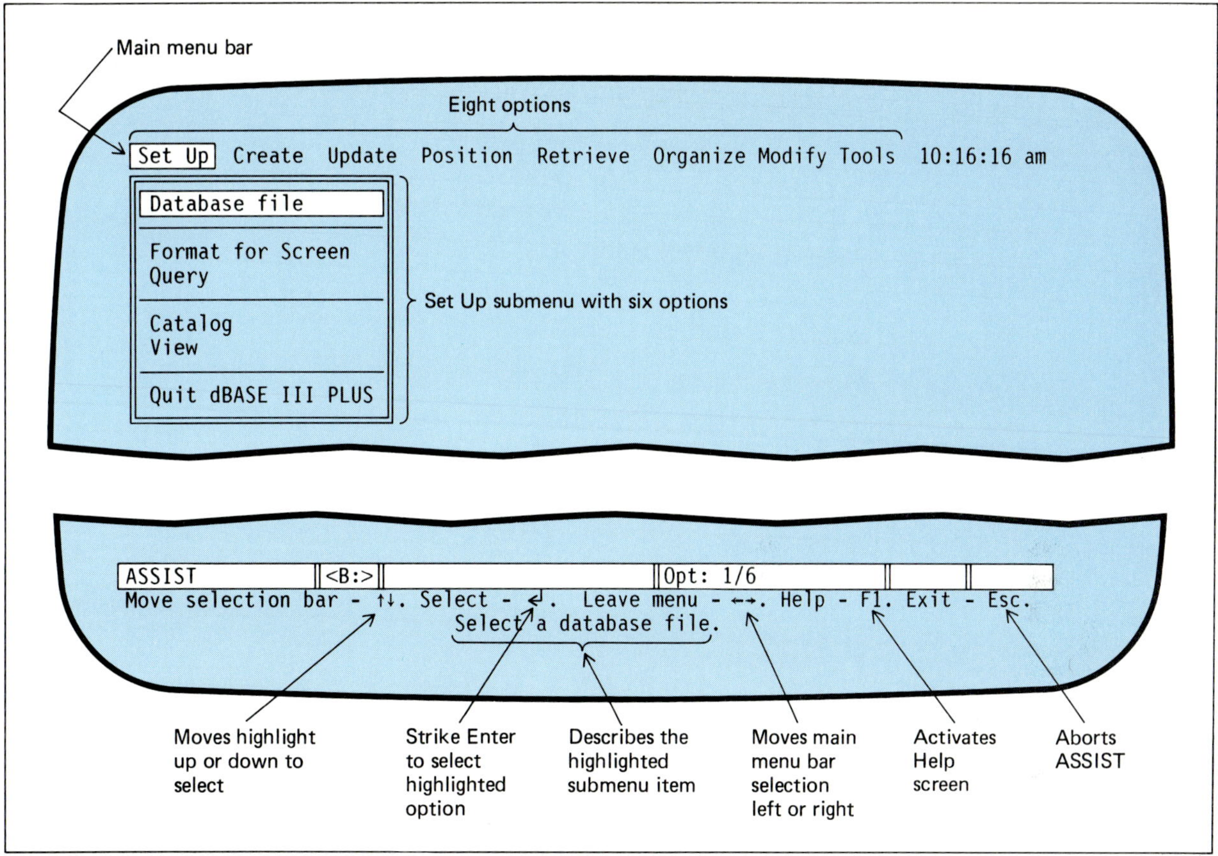

Figure 15-10
The ASSIST screen.

Menus

Across the top of the screen is a *bar menu,* which represents the first-level options. The highlighted entry (*Set Up,* in this case) is the currently selected menu item. Directly beneath is the *Set Up* submenu; it includes six options. At the bottom of the screen are three lines. The first is a general information line; you will see how its contents change as you use ASSIST. The second describes the actions you can take regarding selecting a menu item or switching to another menu. The third line is a brief description of the nature of the highlighted menu option.

In general, the four arrow keys are used to "navigate" the menu structure. At the main bar menu level, the left and right arrows move the highlight to the adjacent menu option. The up and down arrows move the highlight up or down in a submenu. For instance, if you were to press the down arrow key one time, the highlight would move from *Database File* to *Format for Screen* (Figure 15-10).

As the highlight is moved across the main menu bar with the right (or left) arrow key, dBASE displays successive submenus on the screen. Their appearance is similar to that of the *Set Up* submenu shown in Figure 15-10. Figure 15-11 shows each of these. These are the dBASE commands that you can execute from ASSIST. For instance, under *Create* you can create a

Figure 15-11
The ASSIST submenus.

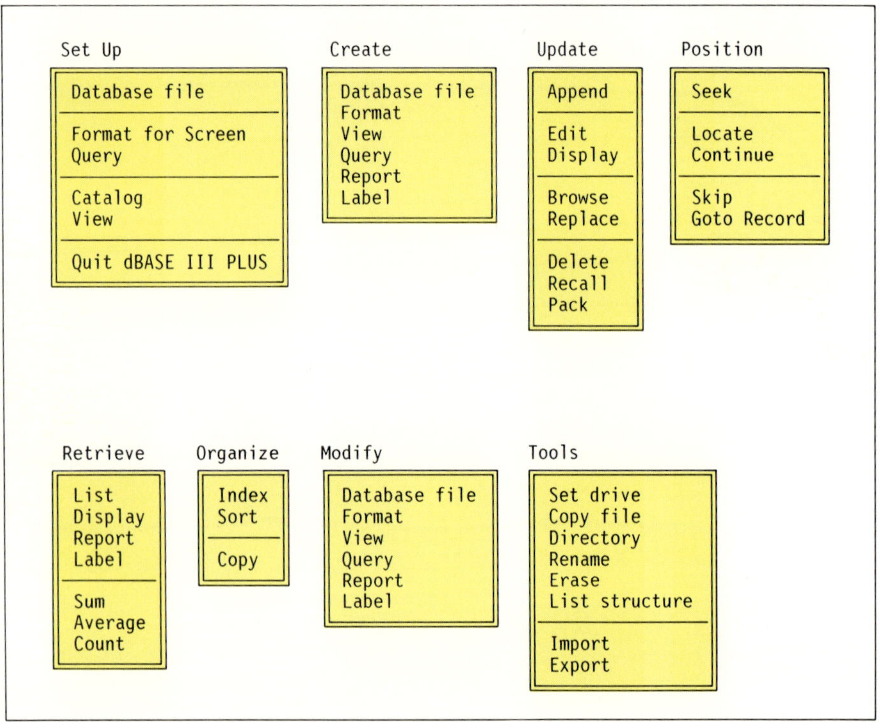

Database file. If you were to select this, you would be placed in the create mode exactly as if you typed the CREATE command from the dot prompt. Similarly, the *List* option of the *Retrieve* submenu represents the LIST command.

Opening the Data File and Listing Records with ASSIST

To illustrate using ASSIST, let us perform the equivalent of the dot prompt command sequence of opening the CUSTOMER file and listing part of its contents.

DO THIS NOW 15-7 **Using ASSIST**

Execute the following command sequence from ASSIST:

```
USE CUSTOMER
LIST CUSTNUM, COMPANY, BALANCE
```

1. Your first action, opening the database data file, is done from the Set *Up* option of the main menu (Figure 15-10). Here, you see that the currently highlighted items allow you to select a database (the bottom line of the screen). To make this selection, strike Enter, which produces the display at the top of the next page. Notice the fourth line from the bottom of the screen entitled *Command;* ASSIST is "building" the USE command (necessary to open the file).

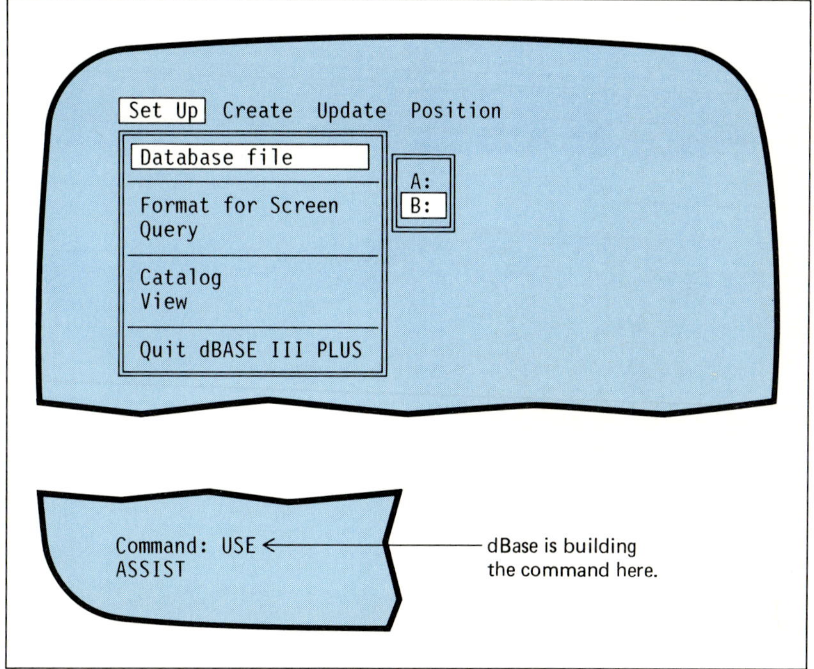

2. Select the disk drive that contains the desired file by moving the highlight to it and striking Enter. (The drive highlighted by ASSIST is always the default drive.) dBASE will then display a list of data files on your disk as follows (notice in your display that the *Command* line now shows the partial command as USE B:).

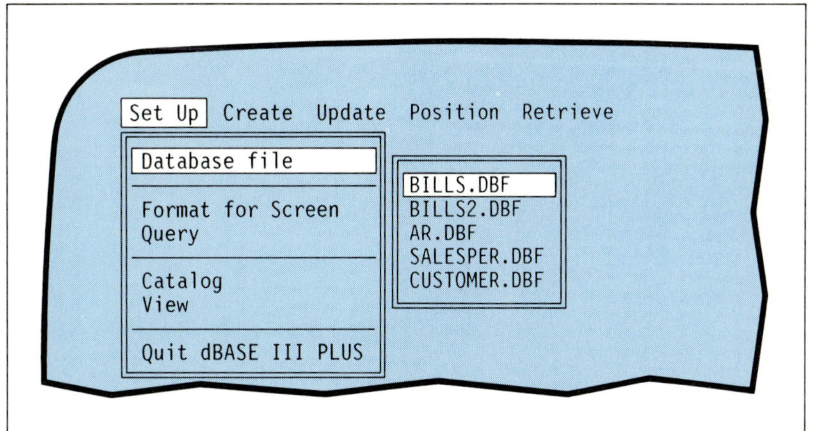

3. To select the CUSTOMER file, use the down arrow key and move the highlight with CUSTOMER.DBF, and then strike Enter. The command at the bottom of the screen will now be

   USE B:CUSTOMER.

   The query

   ```
   Is the file indexed? [Y/N]
   ```

   is also displayed.

4. If you wanted to use an index with this file (indexing is described in the next chapter), then you would respond with Y and be presented with a list of index files. Since you do not intend to use an index with this file, type the letter N. ASSIST will execute the USE command as if you had entered it from the keyboard and the screen display will return to that of Figure 15-10. You can now proceed to build the LIST command.

When "building" a command from ASSIST, be careful to make the proper selections because *it is not possible to undo a mistake.* Had the wrong file been selected in the preceding step, its name would have been appended to the USE command. The only way to correct such an error is to press the Escape and start over again.

5. Referring to Figure 15-11, we see that the List is a subcommand under Retrieve. Move the main menu bar selection to *Retrieve* with the right arrow key. This produces the following submenu.

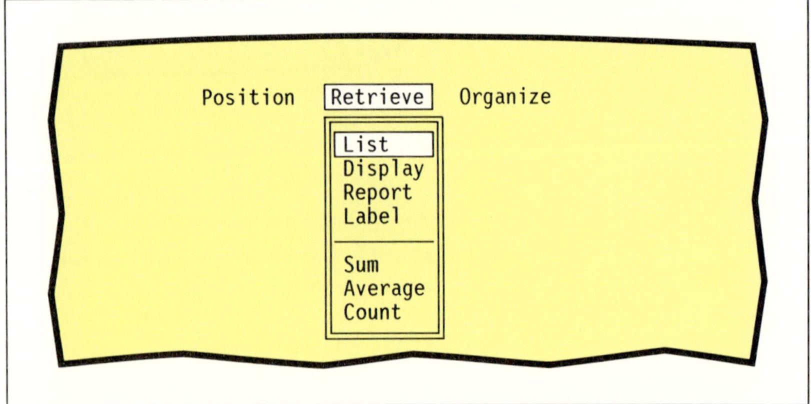

6. Since *List* is already highlighted, select it by striking Enter. This produces the following set of actions that can be taken under the List.

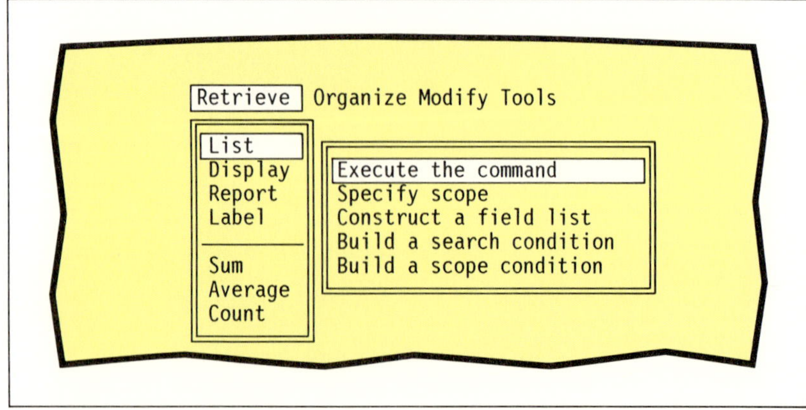

7. You must now designate the fields that you want listed. Do this by moving the highlight to the *Construct a field list* option and striking Enter. One of the convenient aspects of ASSIST is that it displays the fields that make up the database file, as you can see here (and on your screen). Furthermore, details of the highlighted field are also displayed.

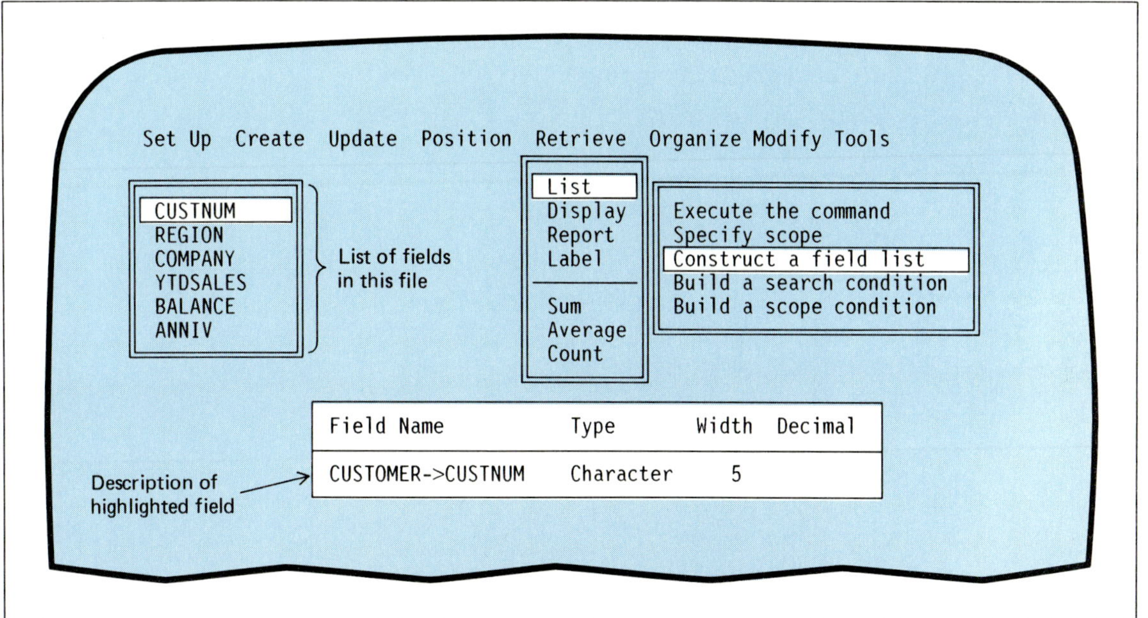

8. Since the CUSTNUM field is highlighted, select it for listing by striking Enter. This will cause the highlight to move to the next field (REGION), the display of the name CUSTNUM in the field list to be changed so that you can tell it has been selected, and CUSTNUM to be added to the command. The *Command* line will now be:

   ```
   LIST CUSTNUM
   ```

9. Move the cursor to COMPANY with the Down key. Be careful not to strike Enter for fields you do not want. Once one is selected, it cannot be removed. Select COMPANY, and then BALANCE. Your *Command* line will now be:

   ```
   LIST CUSTNUM, COMPANY, BALANCE
   ```

10. To exit this field selection mode, strike the Right key (see the prompt on the message line at the bottom of the screen). This returns control to the List submenu of Step 7.

11. The command is now complete and you may execute it. Move the selection to the *Execute the command* option and strike Enter. You

will be asked if you want your output printed. Respond with Y if you do and with N if you do not.

12. When the listing is complete, strike any key and the ASSIST menu is redisplayed.
13. Terminate ASSIST by striking the Escape key.

For someone using dBASE on a regular basis, ASSIST is slow and somewhat clumsy. However, for the infrequent user, it does offer some advantages. If you find it helpful, then use it. If you are comfortable with the dot prompt, then continue typing your commands.

The optical scanners that are at grocery store checkout counters read the bar codes on products. By searching a product database, the computer can locate the record for any item and immediately transmit pricing information back to the checkout register.

ACCESSING AND CHANGING RECORDS IN A FILE

In Chapter 14, you learned about the principles of DBMSs using a legislative bill application as an example database. One of the example files, BILLS.DBF, is included on the data disk that accompanies this book and will be used to illustrate the remainder of the topics in this chapter. If you followed the instructions of Chapter 5 for preparing your data disk, then you should have a copy of it on your data disk. For convenient reference, a listing of the records in this file is shown in Figure 15-12. (The printed listing has been edited so that it would fit on a page.) This is identical to the listing of Figure 14-7 except that the logical field RECOMMEND values are displayed as .T. (meaning true or yes) and .F. (meaning false or no); dBASE displays logical data in this way.

```
Record#                                                        REGION RECOMMEND
    BILL   TITLE                          AUTHOR       TYPE    RATING  COMMITTEE APPROVED

  1 AB0301 Water Well Restrictions        Lukenbill, C  W  9    84 .T. 04/12/90   /  /
  2 AB0144 Site 22 Solid Waste Disposal   Smith, H      G  1    62 .F. 05/09/90   /  /
  3 AB0212 Jameson Quarry Restrictions    Johnson, W    G  3    87 .T. 04/23/90   /  /
  4 AB0158 Vapor Control of Paint Prod.   Johnson, W    A  9    94 .T. 04/28/90 08/08/90
  5 AB0224 Sulphur Emissions              Lukenbill, C  A  4    80 .T. 05/01/90   /  /
  6 AB1001 River Waste Discharge          Smith, H      W  9    73 .F. 05/28/90   /  /
  7 AB0197 Index River Dam Construction   Lukenbill, C  W  5    91 .T. 04/17/90 09/06/90
  8 AB1092 Smog Control - Inverness Basin Johnson, W    A  3    79 .F. 06/22/90   /  /
```

Figure 15-12
The BILLS file listing.

Making a Copy of a Data File

Three of the next dBASE commands that you will be learning in this chapter change the contents of data in the files. You will be making these changes to the BILLS file. (You may also wish to experiment with CUSTOMER or with other files that you create.) So that you do not destroy data that you want to keep, you should make a copy and use the copy. You can do this with the DOS COPY command or from dBASE using the dBASE COPY TO command.

DO THIS NOW 15-8 **Making a Copy of the Data File BILLS.DBF**

1. From the dBASE dot prompt, enter the following command.

```
USE BILLS
```

2. With the dBASE COPY TO command, make a copy of BILLS (the open file) and call it BILLS9:

```
COPY TO BILLS9
```

   If there is already a copy of BILLS9 on your disk (the result of a previous COPY command), you will get a warning message. Tell dBASE to replace it with the new copy.

3. Open the new file BILLS9:

```
USE BILLS9
```

The action of the COPY TO command is to create a new file on disk from records in the currently open file. As you will learn in the next chapter, you can copy all or part of the fields of the file and all or part of the records in the file. Notice that, in this example, the file duplicate has been named BILLS9.DBF; you should adopt some type of naming convention so that you can easily recognize such copies when you want to delete unwanted files from your disk. Whenever you create the copy for experimenting, do not forget to open it with a USE command; remember, opening a new file also closes the one previously open (BILLS in this case).

Accessing Records

When you open a data file with a USE command, dBASE does the following.

1. Reserves an area of memory into which records from disk can be placed during processing; this is called a **record buffer.**
2. Reads the first record from the file, places it in the buffer, and makes it available to you. The record available to you at any time is called the **current record.**
3. Displays on the status bar (as shown in Figure 15-13) the name of the file, which record is the current record, and the number of the records in the file.

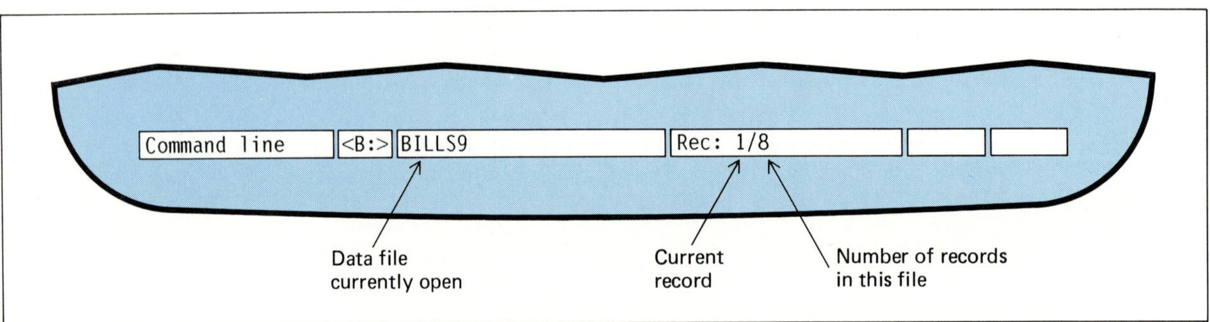

Figure 15-13
The status bar.

At any given time, dBASE gives you access to one record from the file. In Chapter 14, you learned about the two methods of accessing data from a file: sequential access and direct access. With sequential access, records are read one after the other in the order in which they are stored in the file (or as indicated by an index). With direct access, a single record is accessed without regard to which record was accessed previously or where in the file it is located. The LIST command is a sequential access command because it begins with the first record in the file, and then reads and displays the records one after the other. You may have noticed on your status bar after you listed CUSTOMER that the record number indicator displayed EOF/10. dBASE was telling you that it had reached the end of the file and that the current "record" was the EOF.

One way to change the current record is with the GOTO command. With it, you can make any record in the file the current record. For instance, if you wanted to make physical record 5 the current record, you could do it with the command:

```
GOTO 5
```

Try this and you will see the current record number on the status bar change. In addition to positioning the pointer by designating a record number, it is possible to position it to the first or the last data record available. (As you will learn in the next chapter, these will not necessarily be the first and last physical records of the file when an index is used.) These GOTO forms are:

```
GOTO TOP
GOTO BOTTOM
```

The TOP causes dBASE to position to the first record of the file, and the BOTTOM to the last.

Let us now consider the EDIT command to make changes to records in a data file. With this command, you can access records for editing either sequentially or directly.

The EDIT Command

Changing the contents of a record is done via a screen that is identical to the data entry screen (see Figure 15-8 for the CUSTOMER data entry screen). To illustrate, assume that the values for RATING in BILLS9 must be increased by three for all records except records 6 and 8 (bills AB1001 and AB1092). For this, you will need to process records of the file sequentially.

DO THIS NOW 15-9 **Editing BILL9 to Increase the RATING Field Values by 3**

1. If record 1 is not the current record (check the status bar), then go to the top of the file with the command:

   ```
   GOTO TOP
   ```

2. Issue the EDIT command:

   ```
   EDIT
   ```

   The resulting screen display will be as shown in Figure 15-14.

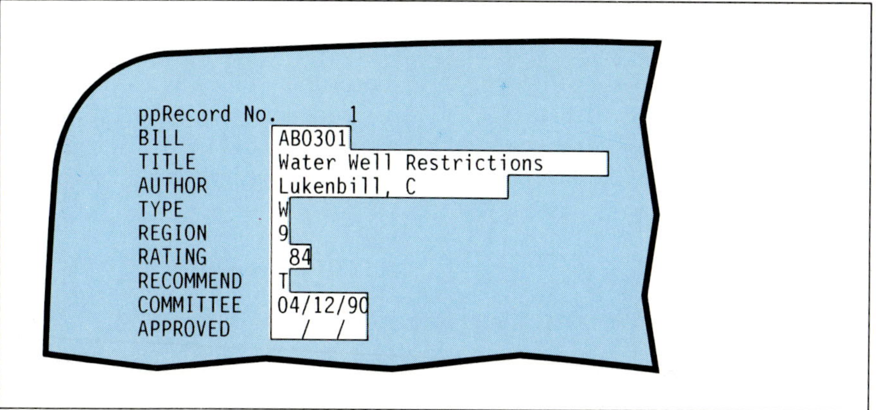

Figure 15-14
The edit screen for BILLS9.

3. Move the cursor to the RATING field, and type the corrected value of 87, and strike Enter.

4. The first record is corrected, so progress to the next by striking the Page Down (PgDn) key; the second record in the file will be

displayed. If, during the editing process, you must back up to the preceding record (for instance, you accidentally strike the Page Down twice), use the Page Up (PgUp) key. In other words, it is possible to move from record to record with these two keys. If you strike the Page Down key when the last record in the file is on the screen, an end-of-file condition occurs and you are returned to the dot prompt. If you strike the Page Up key when the first record is displayed, you are returned to the dot prompt.

5. Correct the RATING field in the same way as with the first record.
6. Repeat this process for records 3, 4, and 5.
7. After editing record 5, strike the Page Down key to progress to record 6; since this is not to be changed, strike the Page Down again.
8. Correct the RATING field for record 7.
9. You have completed the editing task. Terminate editing with the Ctrl-End key sequence.
10. To check your work, you should list this file. However, because of the length of the record, the lines wrap on the screen, making reading it difficult. To avoid that problem, use the following form of the LIST.

```
LIST FIELDS BILL, TITLE, AUTHOR, RATING
```

11. Compare your display with Figure 15-12.

If your values of RATING are not three greater than those in Figure 15-12 for all records except 6 and 8, you will need to make appropriate corrections.

The preceding example illustrates a situation in which most or all of the records in a file must be edited. However, what about the situation in which you must edit only one or two records in a file consisting of several hundred records? Clearly, progressing from one record to the next until you find the desired ones would be impractical. Let us consider the direct access capability of the EDIT command by changing RATING of record 6 from 73 to 79.

DO THIS NOW 15-10 **Editing Record 6**

1. Make record 6 the current record with the command:

```
GOTO 6
```

The status bar will tell you that record 6 is the current record.

2. Issue the EDIT command:

```
EDIT
```

The edit screen will appear and record 6 will be displayed. Note that the EDIT command with no options always edits the current record.

3. Change RATING from 73 to 79.
4. Return to the dot prompt with Ctrl-End.

Actually, the GOTO and EDIT can be combined to gain access for a single record for editing. For example,

```
EDIT RECORD 6
```

makes record 6 the current record and switches to the edit mode. Using this form, either Page Down or Ctrl-End will return you to the dot prompt. Note that Page Down does not progress to the next record because you have asked to edit the single record 6.

If you made any errors in DTN 15-9, use this method to edit those records now.

DELETING RECORDS FROM A FILE

The DELETE Command

You can delete records from a file with the DELETE command. Like EDIT, DELETE alone deletes the current record; DELETE RECORD deletes the designated record.

DO THIS NOW 15-11 **Deleting Records 2 and 6–8 from BILLS9**

1. To delete record 2, enter the command:

   ```
   DELETE RECORD 2
   ```

   dBASE will delete this record and respond with the message:

   ```
   1 record deleted
   ```

2. To delete records 6–8 (the last three records in the file), enter the command sequence:

   ```
   GOTO 6
   DELETE REST
   ```

   dBASE will delete all records from record 6 to the end of the file (the REST of the records) and display the message:

   ```
   3 records deleted
   ```

3. List your file with the command:

   ```
   LIST BILL, TITLE, AUTHOR
   ```

   If you performed the delete actions properly, your display will be identical to that shown below. Note that each of the deleted records is flagged with an asterisk.

```
Record#  BILL   TITLE                         AUTHOR
      1  AB0301 Water Well Restrictions       Lukenbill, C
      2 *AB0144 Site 22 Solid Waste Disposal  Smith, H
      3  AB0212 Jameson Quarry Restrictions   Johnson, W
      4  AB0158 Vapor Control of Paint Prod.  Johnson, W
      5  AB0224 Sulphur Emissions             Lukenbill, C
      6 *AB1001 River Waste Discharge         Smith, H
      7 *AB0197 Index River Dam Construction  Lukenbill, C
      8 *AB1092 Smog Control - Inverness Basin Johnson, W
```

4. Enter the following command.

   ```
   SET DELETED ON
   ```

5. Repeat the preceding LIST command and note that your display does not include the deleted records.

Remember from Chapter 14 that deleting a record does not physically remove it from the file, but only marks it for removal. There are two factors that the dBASE designers took into account with the DELETE command. The first is that there is commonly a need to "remove" a record from a file but to have it accessible in the event that circumstances change and it must be made available again. For instance, you might decide to remove from current processing the record of any customer who has not made a purchase for the past 12 months, and yet have the record available if that customer orders again. Second, actually erasing a record from a file is fatal for that record; once it is gone...

In DTN 15-11, you used two forms of the DELETE. The following examples illustrate each of the forms that you can use.

Command	Action
`DELETE`	Delete the current record.
`DELETE RECORD 12`	Delete record 12.
`DELETE NEXT 3`	Delete current record and the next two (a total of three).
`DELETE REST`	Delete all records from the current one to the end of the file.
`DELETE ALL`	Delete all of the records in the file.

Recalling Deleted Records

This method of deleting records is of limited value if you cannot get them back again. For this purpose, dBASE includes the RECALL command. It has the same forms as the DELETE: one or more records can be restored with execution of the command. For instance, the following will recall deleted records as indicated.

Command	Action
`RECALL`	Recall the current record.
`RECALL RECORD 12`	Recall record 12.
`RECALL NEXT 3`	Recall current record and the next two.
`RECALL REST`	Recall all deleted records from the current one to the end of the file.
`RECALL ALL`	Recall all of the deleted records in the file.

DO THIS NOW 15-12 **Recalling Records 6 and 7**

1. Make record 6 the current record with the command:

   ```
   GOTO 6
   ```

   Check your status bar to be certain that record 6 is the current record.

2. Recall the next two records with:

   ```
   RECALL NEXT 2
   ```

   dBASE will recall (remove the delete flag) records 6 and 7 and then display the message:

   ```
   2 records recalled
   ```

3. List your file with the command

   ```
   LIST BILL, TITLE, AUTHOR
   ```

   and you will see that these records are now displayed.

Permanently Erasing Records

Since deleted records remain in the file, they continue to occupy disk space, which can be a problem if you have limited storage. Also, as a file becomes larger, file processing activities take longer. There commonly comes a time when you must remove deleted records from a file. This is done with the PACK command as shown in the following.

DO THIS NOW 15-13 **Packing the File**

1. To pack the file, type the command:

```
PACK
```

If you have performed the delete and recall actions of the preceding examples, after the packing operation, dBASE will display the message:

```
6 records copied
```

The record counter on the status bar will display 1/6; your file now has only six records.

2. List your file with the command:

```
LIST BILL, TITLE, AUTHOR
```

Notice that the records for bills AB0144 and AB1092 are gone and the records have been renumbered; for instance, AB0212 was record 3 but it is now record 2.

THE BROWSE COMMAND

The last command that we consider in this chapter allows us to inspect records in a file and make changes: it is BROWSE. To illustrate its use, let us inspect BILL9, delete the bill AB0224 record, and change RATING for bill AB1001.

DO THIS NOW 15-14 **Using the BROWSE Command to Inspect and Change BILL9**

1. Type the command:

```
BROWSE
```

Your screen display (Figure 15-15) includes all the records in the file. If you do not have the Help window, strike the F1 key. In the display, the first record is highlighted; it is the current record. Since the screen is not wide enough to display the entire record, only those fields that will fit on the screen are displayed (six fields, in this case).

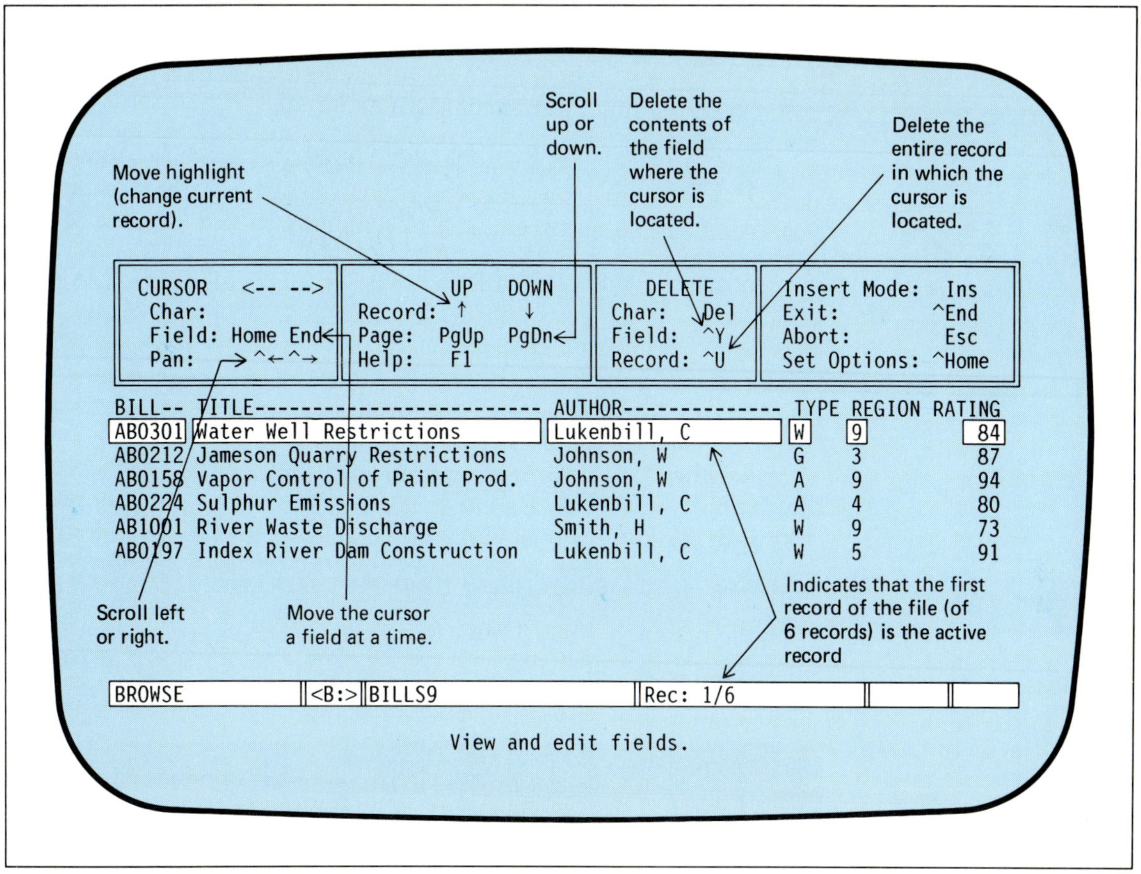

Scroll up or down.

Delete the contents of the field where the cursor is located.

Delete the entire record in which the cursor is located.

Move highlight (change current record).

```
CURSOR    <-- -->  |        UP    DOWN |    DELETE    | Insert Mode:   Ins
  Char:            | Record:  ↑     ↓  | Char:    Del | Exit:         ^End
  Field: Home End  | Page:   PgUp  PgDn| Field:    ^Y | Abort:         Esc
  Pan:      ^←^→   | Help:    F1       | Record:   ^U | Set Options: ^Home

BILL-- TITLE---------------------------- AUTHOR------------- TYPE REGION RATING
AB0301 Water Well Restrictions          Lukenbill, C         W     9       84
AB0212 Jameson Quarry Restrictions      Johnson, W           G     3       87
AB0158 Vapor Control of Paint Prod.     Johnson, W           A     9       94
AB0224 Sulphur Emissions                Lukenbill, C         A     4       80
AB1001 River Waste Discharge            Smith, H             W     9       73
AB0197 Index River Dam Construction     Lukenbill, C         W     5       91

BROWSE          ||<B:>||BILLS9         ||Rec: 1/6         ||      ||

                       View and edit fields.
```

Scroll left or right.

Move the cursor a field at a time.

Indicates that the first record of the file (of 6 records) is the active record

Figure 15-15
The BROWSE screen.

2. To scroll right (bring other fields into view), use the Ctrl-Right key sequence. Enter Ctrl-Right twice to produce the following display of your data.

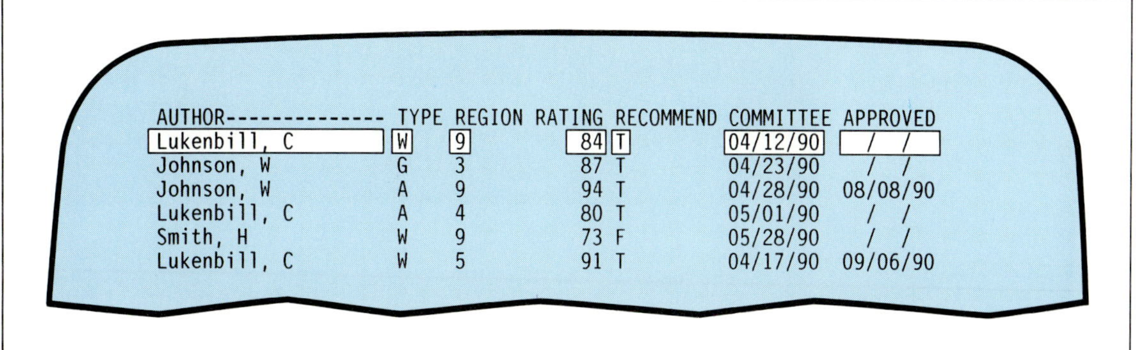

AUTHOR--------------	TYPE	REGION	RATING	RECOMMEND	COMMITTEE	APPROVED
Lukenbill, C	W	9	84	T	04/12/90	/ /
Johnson, W	G	3	87	T	04/23/90	/ /
Johnson, W	A	9	94	T	04/28/90	08/08/90
Lukenbill, C	A	4	80	T	05/01/90	/ /
Smith, H	W	9	73	F	05/28/90	/ /
Lukenbill, C	W	5	91	T	04/17/90	09/06/90

3. Use the Ctrl-Left to scroll back to Figure 15-15.
4. Move the highlight to the fourth record (AB0224) with the Down key.

5. Delete this record with a Ctrl-U. Notice that the word Del now appears on the status bar.
6. Move the highlight to the AB1001 record.
7. Successively strike the End key to move the cursor field by field to RATING.
8. Type 74 and strike Enter.
9. Terminate this BROWSE command with Ctrl-End.

Whenever you enter a BROWSE command, the current record is displayed at the top of the screen. To scroll upward (toward the beginning of the file), strike the Page Up key.

Like the LIST command, you can display selected fields with BROWSE. For example, assume that you wished to scan the date fields for records in the file. For this, you might use the following form of BROWSE.

```
BROWSE FIELDS BILL, TITLE, COMMITTEE, APPROVED
```

From the resulting screen, you can proceed to inspect the records, making corrections to the displayed fields or deleting records. The BROWSE is a convenient and versatile command.

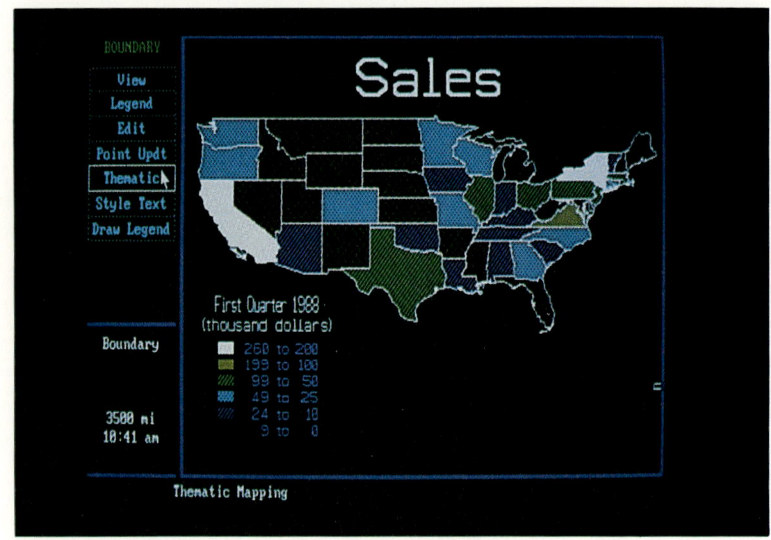

The MapInfo (tm) system allows data in databases (such as dBASE III PLUS) to be displayed geographically using maps that can range in scope from a local neighborhood to the entire United States. Boundaries can be those of a state, city, county, or as defined by the user. Computerized street maps of over 300 cities are available for use with the system.

SUMMARY

This chapter has provided you with the basic tools for generating and changing data files using dBASE. Through the Customer file, which you created and entered, and the Bill file that you edited you have learned how to define a record structure, enter records into a file, edit records in the file, delete records from the file, and display and print the contents of a file. Summarizing, the important items from the chapter are:

- Creating a new database file is a two-step process: first the structure must be defined, and then records may be added.
- The CREATE command is used to define the structure of a new database file.
- Field names for a database file may be selected at the discretion of the user but within the following limitations.
    - The name length is limited to 10 characters.
    - The first character must be a letter.
    - Succeeding characters may be letters, digits, or the underscore character.
- Once a file structure is created, records can be added immediately or at any later time.
- The APPEND command adds a blank record to the end of a file and then allows for data entry.
- After entering the last field of the last record when appending, do not strike Enter; use Ctrl-End or else a blank record will be added to your file on disk. If you must terminate appending from a blank entry screen, then use the Escape key.
- The USE command opens a specified data file. If another file is already open, it will be closed.
- If a file is open when you issue the QUIT command to terminate a dBASE session, that file will be closed without loss of data before dBASE is terminated.
- The LIST command allows you to display on the screen or print to the printer records from a file; you can print all or part of the fields of the record.
- ASSIST allows you to perform dBASE operations from a sequence of menus. This is helpful for occasional users of dBASE. To activate ASSIST, type the ASSIST command from the dot prompt.
- With the EDIT command, it is possible to make changes to the current record or to any selected record.
- The GOTO command has the ability to position the record pointer to any desired record or to the first or last record in the file (make it the current record).
- The DELETE command marks records for deletion but does not actually eliminate them from the file.
- The command

    ```
    SET DELETED OFF
    ```

will cause dBASE to act as if deleted records do not exist.

- The delete status can be removed from deleted records with the RECALL command. Records that have been recalled are unchanged from what they were prior to their deletion.
- The PACK command is used to physically remove deleted records from a file. The physical records numbers are changed corresponding to the records deleted.
- With the BROWSE command, it is possible to view, edit, and add records to a data file.

COMMAND SUMMARY

The following commands have been used in this chapter. Each is shown in its general form. Remember that <> enclose a description of something you must enter and [ ] enclose an optional item. Words in lowercase describe the entry you must make and words in uppercase must be entered as shown if that portion of the command is used. Some of the forms included in this summary are incomplete. Examples of this chapter have not illustrated all of the forms summarized here.

APPEND
Adds records to the end of a database file.

ASSIST
Switches to the ASSIST mode.

BROWSE [FIELDS <field list>]
Allows full-screen display and editing of records.

CREATE <filename>
Allows for the definition of a new file structure.

DELETE [<scope>]
Marks the specified records for deletion.

EDIT [<scope>] [FIELDS <field list>]
Permits changes to database file contents.

GOTO <record number> or GOTO TOP/BOTTOM
Positions the record pointer to the specified record.

HELP <keyword>
Displays dBASE command and function Help screens.

LIST [[FIELDS] <field list>] [TO PRINT]
Displays the records from the active database file.

LIST STRUCTURE [TO PRINT]
Displays the active database file structure.

PACK
Permanently removes records marked for deletion from a data file.

RECALL [<scope>]
Reinstates records marked for deletion.

SET BELL ON/OFF
Turns the bell on/off during data entry.

SET DELETED ON/OFF
Hides/Does not hide records marked for deletion.

USE [<filename>]
Opens the designated file (if no filename is included, then closes the current file).

NEW TERMINOLOGY

Many of the database terms used in Chapter 14 are also used in this chapter. The following are additional important new terms introduced in this chapter; you should be familiar with each of them.

current record
dot prompt
eof
help
record buffer
status bar
syntax

REVIEW QUESTIONS

1. Each of the following is to be used as a field name in a base file definition. Identify those that are not valid as field names and give the reason.
   a. DISCOUNT
   b. CREDIT_LIMIT
   c. LIMIT4
   d. X
   e. 25_QUANT
   f. MAX AMNT
   g. STUDENT#
   h. DISC-RATE
2. After creating a data file, you enter exactly ten data records and then terminate. The next day, when you execute APPEND to add more records, the record number at the top of the screen is 12 rather than 11. What is the most likely reason for this? What would you do to correct this problem?
3. Consider this scenario. Yesterday, you created a new data file, entered twenty records, and terminated. Today, you appended ten more, and immediately opened another file to work on without telling dBASE to close your first file. What will happen to the newly entered ten records of this file?
4. If you set the bell off during entry of records in a data file, how will this affect the entry of data?
5. What is the purpose of the record buffer?
6. What is the difference between the following?

```
GOTO 7
EDIT
```
and
```
EDIT RECORD 7
```

7. When editing, you may progress from one record to the next by striking the PgDn key. There is another key stroke action that will cause the next record to be brought up on the screen. What is it?

8. A file contains twenty-two records and the current record is number 14. How many records will be deleted by each of the following?

    a. DELETE
    b. DELETE NEXT 3
    c. DELETE NEXT 12
    d. DELETE REST
    e. DELETE ALL

9. What is the difference between LIST and BROWSE?

10. For this and the next question, you will need to use dBASE. Create a data file that includes at least one record with each of the four data types. While you are making your entries, determine the answers to each of the following questions.

    a. What is the maximum allowable length for a character field (look at the screen when the cursor is in the Width definition field)?
    b. What are the restrictions on a numeric field regarding both the maximum field width and the decimal definition?
    c. What happens if you attempt to change the length of a date field to something other than 8?
    d. What happens if you strike the Escape key while defining the file? What do you expect will happen if you complete the Escape operation?
    e. Do the following after completing definition of this file. Move the cursor to the second field that you have defined. Strike the Ctrl-N sequence. Strike the Ctrl-U sequence. What do these two Ctrl sequences do?

11. The BILLS file includes eight records plus the EOF. Open this file and describe what happens when you attempt to GOTO each of the following record numbers:

    a. 9
    b. -10
    c. 100

MATCHING

Match each of the commands in a to h with the most appropriate action in 1 through 8.

a. LIST STRUCTURE
b. GOTO
c. CREATE
d. HELP
e. SET DELETED OFF
f. ASSIST
g. PACK
h. USE

1. Permanently get rid of unwanted records in a file.
2. Check the general form of the DELETE command.
3. Find out the width of each field of a data file.
4. Enter field names.
5. Temporarily make certain records unavailable for processing.

6. Open a data file.
7. Make record 20 of a thirty-record file the current record.
8. Enter commands through menu selection.

TRUE/FALSE

Determine whether each of the following is true or false.

_______ **1.** Each time you run dBASE, you must first run the INSTALL program.

_______ **2.** The syntax of the LIST command is the number of fields that can be printed when the command is executed.

_______ **3.** CUSTOMER, PRES_NAME, Q5, and MAX_AMOUNT are all valid for use as field names in a dBASE file.

_______ **4.** If you terminate the CREATE command after defining the last field, your newly created data file will contain no data records.

_______ **5.** If you have just completed working with the file CHECKS and wish to work with the file ACCOUNTS, you must first close CHECKS before USEing ACCOUNTS or data that you have entered into CHECKS could be lost.

_______ **6.** In adding a record to a file, you have just typed the last field and not yet pressed Enter. If you strike the Escape key, that record will not be saved to disk.

_______ **7.** The LIST command displays the contents of a data file on the screen; the PRINT command prints the contents of a data file on a printer.

_______ **8.** ASSIST can be used to enter dBASE commands through a menu system. However, new files must be created through the dot prompt as it is not possible to perform the CREATE function through ASSIST.

_______ **9.** The record buffer is a memory area set up to hold the values being typed in for a new record during the APPEND operation.

_______ **10.** If you issued the command EDIT from the dot prompt, the current record would be displayed on the edit screen.

_______ **11.** The GOTO is a direct access command.

_______ **12.** The command DELETE REST could delete one record or it could delete many.

_______ **13.** The command SET DELETED OFF permanently erases deleted records from the file.

_______ **14.** The RECALL command cannot recall records that have been physically removed from a file.

_______ **15.** One disadvantage of the BROWSE command is that you cannot view all fields in the record because of the narrow screen width.

ANSWERS TO OBJECTIVE QUESTIONS

Matching

1. g 2. d 3. a 4. c 5. e 6. h 7. b 8. f

True/False

1. F 2. F 3. T 4. T 5. F 6. T 7. F 8. F 9. F
10. T 11. T 12. T 13. F 14. T 15. F

ASSIGNMENTS/PROJECTS

1. The BILLS2 file is identical to BILLS except that it includes several blank records. You are to do the following to this file, and when finished, print a listing that includes the fields BILL, AUTHOR, TYPE, REGION, RATING, RECOMMEND, and APPROVED.
   a. Permanently eliminate all blank records.
   b. Enter today's date for APPROVED for bills AB0212 and AB1092.
   c. For bill AB0212, change RATING from 87 to 79 and RECOMMEND from True to False.
   d. Change REGION for bill AB0224 from 4 to 9.

2. A group of bike racers maintains a database file of their progress. You are to create a data file to store the following racing data.

Field	Type	Width
Last name	Character	10
First name	Character	10
Birth date	Date	8
Club name	Character	12
Bike make	Character	10
Best placement	Numeric	2
Earned points	Numeric	3

Following are the first five records that you must enter into this file.

Name		Birth			Best	
Last	First	Date	Club	Bike	Finish	Points
Pratt	Janet	03/22/66	Quicksilver	Cicco	10	20
Nickazy	Eva	05/20/67	Quicksilver	Schwinn	1	55
Sovin	Dorothy	04/19/64	Quicksilver	Lotus	8	25
Damir	Monica	10/07/68	Felines	Cicco	6	38
Lee	Amy	01/04/65	Quicksilver	Cicco	1	101

In addition to these, there are nineteen other records for this file. To simplify your task, these nineteen records are included on the data disk that accompanies this book in the file BIKERS.ASC. They are recorded in a special ASCII format to be compatible with your database data file. After you have typed in the preceding five records, you can append the remaining nineteen by typing the following command from the dot prompt.

```
APPEND FROM BIKERS.ASC DELIMITED
```

For this to work properly, you must have defined your record format as described in the preceding table. After the APPEND, list your file and check to ensure that the values loaded are reasonable.

3. Create a database data file for an automobile leasing agency. The record format must be as follows:

Field	Type	Length	Remark
License number	Character	6	
Make	Character	10	
Year	Character	2	
Size code	Character	2	CO (compact) MI (midsize) LU (luxury)
Lessee acct. number	Character	4	
Lessee name	Character	18	
Lease expiration date	Date	8	
Lease type	Character	1	Q (quarter) Y (year)
Monthly lease rate	Numeric	7	Two decimal places

Following are the first five records that you must enter into this file. Note that no values are listed for the lease expiration date. You must fill in these entries with current values.

License	Make	Year	Size	Lessee Number	Lessee Name	Lease Type	Lease Rate
ABX108	Ford	90	MI	2199	E Z Insurance	Q	194.66
DIJ155	Ford	90	MI	2701	Hart Construction	Y	183.82
EEF908	Chevrolet	90	MI	2001	JP Designs	Y	180.72
EEF921	Chevrolet	90	CO	2001	JP Designs	Y	164.97
BQJ063	Chevrolet	90	CO	2001	JP Designs	Y	164.98

In addition to these, there are twenty other records for this file. To simplify your task, these twenty records are included on the data disk that accompanies this book in the file VEHICLE.ASC. They are recorded in a special ASCII format to be compatible with your database data file. After you have typed in the preceding five records, you can append the remaining twenty by typing the following command from the dot prompt.

```
APPEND FROM VEHICLE.ASC DELIMITED
```

For this to work properly, you must have defined your record format as described in the preceding table. After the APPEND, use EDIT to fill in the lease expiration dates. Then list your file and check to ensure that the values loaded are reasonable.

4. A software evaluator decides to computerize records of productivity software evaluations by creating a database. The software is grouped in four major categories: word processing (WP), spreadsheet (SS), file management (FM), and graphics (GR). The following fields are to be included in the database. Study this list and decide upon appropriate field widths and types. Then create the data file and enter twenty-one records evenly divided among the three software types.

Field	Sample Value
Software product	Beginner's Word Processor
Company name	Supersoft, Inc.
Category of software	WP, SS, FM, GR
Price	999.99 (maximum)
Typical discounted price	999.99 (maximum)
Date of evaluation	
Software rating	1 through 9
Recommended	Y or N

Chapter 16

More on dBASE III PLUS

OBJECTIVES

Chapter 15 provided you with the ability to perform basic maintenance on database data files: creating a file, adding records, deleting records, and editing. The focus in this chapter is on using the data to provide information by creating indexes to give record access in a desired sequence, selecting records based on conditions you specify, and generating reports. When you have completed this chapter, you should be able to:

- Generate an index based on any field in the record of a file.
- Limit access to records of a file to those with data values satisfying a condition that you specify.
- Directly access a desired record in a file based on the value in any field of the record.
- Interactively obtain the sum or average of any field in a data file.
- Use the dBASE report generator to specify the format of a report using data from a data file.
- Prepare reports in which common records are grouped and subtotals are calculated for designated fields.

PREVIEW

Principles of Indexing

An index provides access to records of a file based on a sequence determined by a designated field in the file. Index files are not created automatically when a data file is created; each needed index must be created using the INDEX command. dBASE can maintain index files automatically when the corresponding data files are changed.

Conditional Operations

Relational expressions allow you to compare quantities and to control actions taken by dBASE depending upon the results of the comparison. Used with the FOR command option, you can limit your access to records in a file to those meeting a designated condition.

Obtaining Information From a File

Indexes provide the means for fast direct access to any record in a file based on a data value (as opposed to a record number as in Chapter 15). Statistical commands allow you to obtain the count of the number of records meeting a specified condition and to compute the sum and average of specified fields of a file that satisfy a stated condition.

Report Generation

The LIST command allows you to generate a list of the records in a file. The CREATE REPORT command allows you to specify the exact format that printed output is to take. You can designate that totals for selected numeric fields be computed for all records of the file and subtotals on groups of records with a common field entry.

Using Two or More Files

With dBASE, you can interrelate two or more files to generate reports consisting of data from both files.

PRINCIPLES OF INDEXING

In Chapter 14, you learned that records of a data file are commonly processed in order based on the contents of one or more fields of the file. For instance, a printout of customers and their purchases might be in sequence based on either the customer number or the customer name. Printed labels for mailing advertising information would be in sequence based on the customer ZIP code to take advantage of bulk postal rates. There are two methods to accomplish this: sorting the records of the file thus putting them in the desired sequence; or creating an index that gives access to the records in the desired sequence. In most database processing applications, indexing is used because a separate index file can be created for each field on which sequencing is required. Furthermore, the index provides direct access to records in a data file.

Creating an Index File

In order to use an index with a file, you must first create it; indexes are *not* created automatically when a data file is created. In creating one, you must:

1. Open the data file that is to be indexed.
2. Designate the field on which the index is to be built.
3. Provide a name that dBASE will use for the index filename. Remember: dBASE builds the index as a separate file and uses the extension NDX.

To illustrate this process, let us use CUSTOMER; the following fields make up its record.

CUSTNUM	Customer number
REGION	Sales region
COMPANY	Company name
YTDSALES	Year-to-date sales
BALANCE	Current account balance
ANNIV	Anniversary date

Assume that your processing actions require indexes on the four fields CUSTNUM, COMPANY, YTDSALES, and ANNIV. From Chapter 14, you know that the customer number is the key field—the unique field for which no two records have the same value. Almost all data files in a database application have an index file based on the key field.

In contrast, there can be two or more records with the same value for the year-to-date sales and anniversary date fields. In such a case, the index will cause records with the same values to be grouped together (refer to Figure 14-10).

Although dBASE does not include a naming convention for index files, it is recommended that one be used. In this book, the following guidelines are employed.

- The index file associated with the key field of the data file is always given the same name as the data file.
- Names are selected for other index files so that they indicate both the data file to which they correspond and the field to which they are related. For instance, an index file for CUSTOMER based on the COMPANY field might be named CUS-COMP. Here, the first three letters represent the data file and the last four the field on which it is based.

DO THIS NOW 16-1 **Creating Index Files for CUSTOMER**

The following files are to be created.

CUSTOMER.NDX	Based on the customer number (CUSTNUM)

CUS-COMP.NDX	Based on the company name (COMPANY)
CUS-YTD.NDX	Based on the year-to-date sales (YTDSALES)
CUS-ANNV.NDX	Based on the anniversary date (ANNIV)

1. Open CUSTOMER with the command:

```
USE CUSTOMER
```

2. Create the index CUSTOMER.NDX with the command in Figure 16-1.

Figure 16-1
Creating an index file.

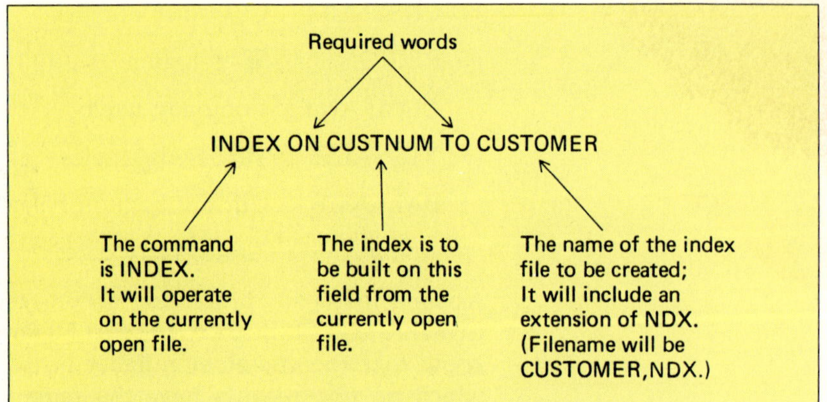

When the indexing action is complete, dBASE will display a message indicating the number of records indexed.

3. The index just created is stored on disk and is now active; confirm this by listing the file with the command:

```
LIST
```

If your index was created correctly, the records of your file will be listed in sequence based on the customer number.

4. Create the index CUS-COMP.NDX with the following command.

```
INDEX ON COMPANY TO CUS-COMP
```

5. You now have two index files for this data file: CUSTOMER.NDX and CUS-COMP.NDX. The one just created is the active one; confirm this by listing the file. Note that the records are now displayed in sequence based on the company name.

6. Create the index CUS-YTD with the command:

```
INDEX ON YTDSALES TO CUS-YTD
```

One index, CUS-ANNV, is yet to be created. That one will be created using ASSIST in the next section.

Before dBASE creates an index, it checks to see if there is already an index with that name. For instance, in creating CUS-YTD, had your disk contained a file name CUS-YTD.NDX, dBASE would have given you the option of aborting the index command or proceeding, thus replacing the existing file with a new one.

Creating an Index File Using ASSIST

You can also create an index file from ASSIST. This is helpful in that ASSIST will display a list of the fields making up the record, from which you simply select the field for indexing from the list.

DO THIS NOW 16-2 **Creating the Index File CUS-ANNV Using ASSIST**

1. Get into the ASSIST mode by typing the command ASSIST.
2. Open the CUSTOMER file from Setup by striking Enter, with *Database File* highlighted on the Setup menu.
3. Select the data drive, and then the file CUSTOMER.DBF.
4. Respond with N to the question of whether or not the file is indexed; you do not want to use an existing index.
5. With the Right key, move the bar menu highlight to *Organize.*
6. Select the *Index* option. dBASE will respond with the query:

   ```
   Enter an index key expression:
   ```

7. You may type the name of the field or strike F10 for a display of the fields in this record. Strike F10. The fields composing the CUSTOMER record will be displayed.
8. With the Down arrow, position the highlight on the field ANNIV and strike Enter. The field name will be entered in response to the dBASE query for the field name.
9. Strike Enter to signal dBASE that you are ready to continue. dBASE will query you regarding the disk on which to write the index file. As the default data drive is highlighted, select it by striking Enter.
10. You are then requested to enter the name of the file (the index filename). Type CUS-ANNV and strike Enter. The index will be created.
11. You may return to the dot prompt by striking Escape.

As with other actions, you should use whichever you find the simplest: command entry from the dot prompt or from ASSIST.

Opening a Data File That Has Indexes

Your data disk now includes four indexes for the CUSTOMER file. Whenever you wish to use the file, you can open without an index (USE

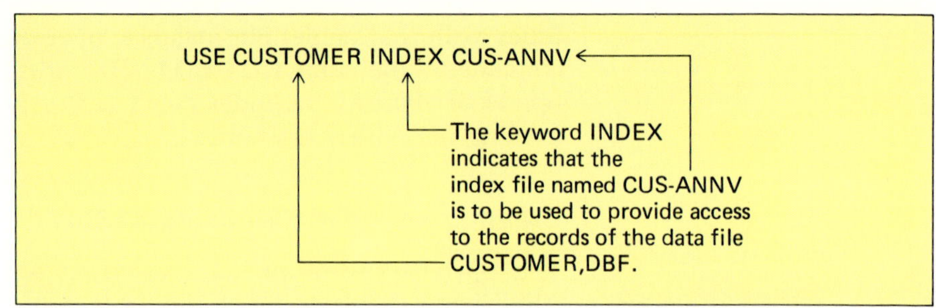

Figure 16-2
Opening a data file with an index.

CUSTOMER, as you have already done), or open it with any of the indexes. Obviously, only one of these can be activated at any given time. That is, you can see the data based on the sequence of CUS-COMP or of CUS-YTD, but not both at the same time. Although a variety of methods can be used in switching between indexes, descriptions in this book will be limited to specifying the needed index in the USE statement. For example, to open CUSTOMER with the CUS-ANNV index, you would enter the USE command in the form in Figure 16-2. This causes dBASE to open both the

Figure 16-3
Using different indexes.

```
USE CUSTOMER INDEX CUS-COMP
LIST CUSTNUM, COMPANY

Record#  CUSTNUM COMPANY
      1  13069   ABC Retail Outlet
      9  13117   Blue Ridge Sport & Casual
      2  12573   Boardwalk Sportswear Sales
      5  12292   Coast Concepts
      8  13189   Crow Canyon Casual Wear
     10  12217   Falcon Ridges Enterprises
      7  12272   Grand Times
      4  11882   Harlicorn Operations
      3  12626   Mr. Casual, Limited
      6  13312   Paradise Leisure Clothing
```

```
USE CUSTOMER INDEX CUS-YTD
LIST CUSTNUM, YTDSALES

Record#  CUSTNUM YTDSALES
      4  11882    1012.66
      9  13117    1788.29
     10  12217    5880.10
      5  12292    5990.86
      7  12272    7932.82
      2  12573    8003.46
      3  12626    8933.48
      1  13069   12633.70
      6  13312   14889.83
      8  13189   19833.22
```

```
USE CUSTOMER INDEX CUS-ANNV
LIST CUSTNUM, ANNIV

Record#  CUSTNUM ANNIV
      8  13189   03/28/86
     10  12217   04/02/86
      6  13312   04/22/86
      1  13069   06/13/86
      2  12573   06/24/86
      5  12292   06/12/87
      3  12626   08/19/87
      9  13117   09/22/87
      7  12272   02/28/88
      4  11882   06/06/89
```

data file CUSTOMER and the associated index file CUS-ANNV. At any time in your work session, you could open CUSTOMER again with another index. Remember, the USE statement always closes any open data and index files first. (This is true only to the extent that we will use dBASE in this book; dBASE does include procedures for having more than one data file open.) The USE and LIST sequences of Figure 16-3 produce the corresponding record listings.

The Effect of Data Changes on Indexes

Any command that will change the contents of a data file can potentially affect indexes created for the file. For instance, assume that you must make the following changes to CUSTOMER.

1. Change the customer number of record 7 from 12272 to 32272.
2. Append a record using a customer number of 11133.

To avoid changing your copy of customer, you can make a copy (call it CUSTOM9), and then perform the operations on the copy. Since CUSTOM9 will be identical to CUSTOMER, you can use any of the index files that you created for customer.

DO THIS NOW 16-3 **Editing Record 7 and Appending a Record to CUSTOM9**

1. Begin by closing CUSTOMER with the command:

```
USE
```

2. Make the CUSTOM9 copy with the dBASE command:

```
COPY FILE  B:CUSTOMER.DBF  TO  B:CUSTOM9.DBF
```

   Be certain to type this command exactly as shown; do not omit the extension DBF from either filename.

3. Open CUSTOM9 with the command:

```
USE CUSTOM9
```

4. Bring record 7 up in the edit screen by entering the command:

```
EDIT 7
```

5. Change the value of the customer number field from 12272 to 32272. Return to the dot prompt with a Ctrl-End.
6. Use the APPEND command to add the new record; the customer number must be 11133 and the company name *Direct Sales*. Make up your own values for the other fields. Be certain to avoid striking Enter after typing the last field; use the Ctrl-End sequence so that the append operation will be terminated without adding a blank record.
7. From the dot prompt, list the file (LIST command). Your screen display will be as shown in Figure 16-4. Notice that record 7 has been changed and that the new record is displayed as record 11.

Figure 16-4
The modified CUSTOM9 file in physical order (no index).

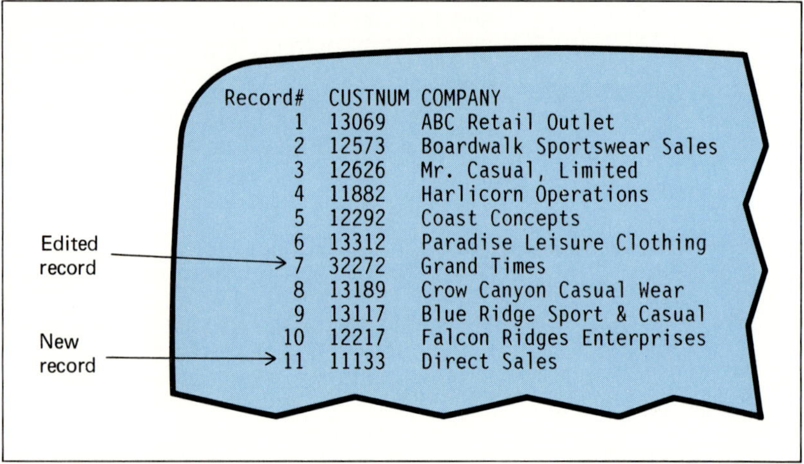

8. Open CUSTOM9 with the index file CUSTOMER.NDX as follows:

```
USE CUSTOM9 INDEX CUSTOMER
```

9. List the file once again and you will see the display of Figure 16-5. Notice that record 7 is out of sequence and the newly added record 11 is missing.

Figure 16-5
The modified CUSTOM9 file as displayed with an obsolete index.

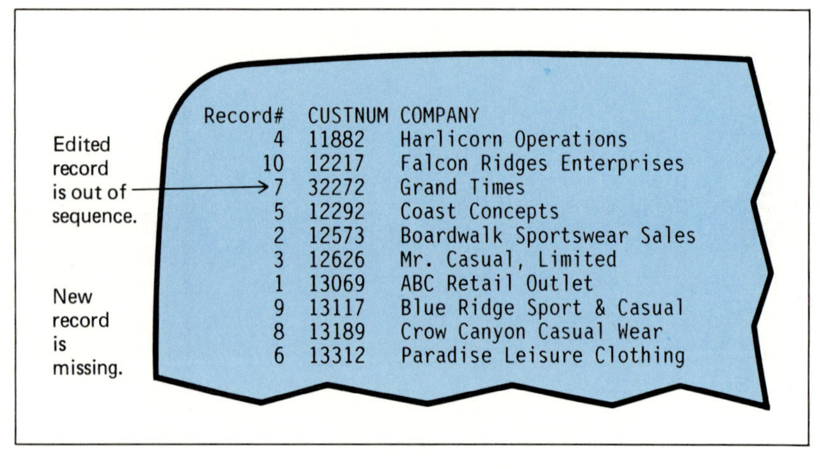

The problem here is due to the fact that the index file is independent of the data file. Since the index file was not open with the data file when the preceding changes were made to the data file, *the index file was left unchanged.* Even though the file was changed, the index file contents remain as shown in Figure 16-6(a), and the file is thus inconsistent with the data file. When subsequently used with CUSTOM9, dBASE used as the record entries records 4, 10, 7, and so on, to access the records sequentially from the data file. When using indexes in conjunction with data files, it is important to remember that *only the indexes designated with the data file when*

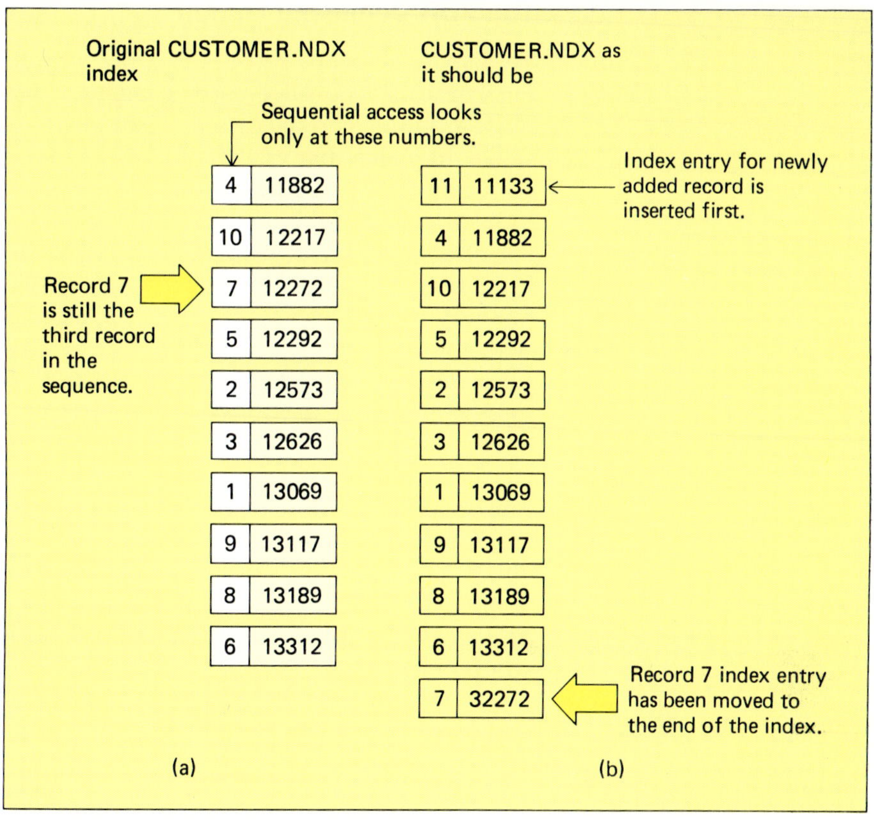

Figure 16-6
(a) Entries of the original CUSTOMER.NDX file.
(b) Entries of an updated CUSTOMER.NDX file.

the file is opened will be modified when the data file is modified. This means that had the file been opened with the command

```
USE CUSTOM9 INDEX CUSTOMER
```

before making the changes, then the index file CUSTOMER.NDX would have been adjusted automatically, as shown in Figure 16-6(b).

If several indexes have been created for a file, only those designated in the USE will be updated automatically. For instance, DTN 16-1 involves four indexes for the CUSTOMER file. It is possible to designate all of them in a USE command as follows:

```
USE CUSTOMER INDEX CUSTOMER, CUS-COMP, CUS-YTD, CUS-ANNV
```

Here, although the CUSTOMER.NDX index is the only one that is active (effects access to the file), the others will be modified as appropriate when changes are made to the file. There are numerous methods for working with multiple indexes that you would learn about in a course devoted solely to dBASE.

CONDITIONAL OPERATIONS

Indexing a file allows you to change the order in which records of the file are presented to you. This is only one of the many database processing needs; another is the ability to be selective about available records. For this, you need conditional capabilities.

The FOR Command Option

To display all of the records in a file, you have used the LIST command. Furthermore, you have used it together with some of the available command options. For instance, in Chapter 15, you used the FIELDS option to select the fields that you wanted displayed. There are also cases in which you want to see only those records that meet a certain criterion—you want to be selective of the records. For instance, you might want to generate a list of all customers in the CUSTOMER file who have made more than $10,000 in purchases so that you can offer them a special discount on quantity purchases. Selecting records according to some condition is done with the FOR command option. For instance, the following form of the LIST will display all customers for whom the value of the year-to-date sales field is greater than $10,000.

```
LIST FOR YTDSALES > 10000
```

This is a *conditional action;* a record will be selected only on the condition that the value stored in the YTDSALES field is greater than 10,000. The ability to select records or, more generally, to perform actions conditionally is fundamental to data processing. This is an essential element of DBMSs, as well as all programming languages, or even the machine language of the computer itself.

In this example, the condition is specified with the FOR option. As we will learn, the FOR can be used with many commands. Its general form is

FOR <*condition*>

where *condition* is a comparison form that can be either true or false. Let us learn how to set up these forms.

Relational Operators and Expressions

In programming languages, comparisons are made using **relational operators.** They are so called because they indicate the relationship between two quantities. For example: "Is the amount owed larger than the credit limit?" "Is the sales region equal to 12?"

As do most programming languages, dBASE includes the following six relational operators for operating on numeric as well as character data.

Comparison	Symbol	Examples
Less than	<	CHARGE < LIMIT
Greater than	>	YTDSALES > 10000
Equal to	=	AGE = 21
Less than or equal to	<=	QUANT <= BREAK
Greater than or equal to	>=	PRICE >= 17.95
Not equal to	<> or #	GRADE <> "A"

The examples shown are called **relational expressions;** they are essentially comparisons between two quantities. For instance,

```
YTDSALES > 10000
```

compares the value stored in YTDSALES with 10,000. If YTDSALES contains a value of 15,000, this relationship will be true, that is,

```
15000 > 10000
```

(15,000 is greater than 10,000) is indeed true. However, if YTDSALES contains 5000, the relationship will be false, that is,

```
5000 > 10000
```

is false. In general, the result of evaluating a relational expression will be either true or false.

When used in conjunction with a command that processes a file sequentially, each record is evaluated to determine whether it meets the condition. For instance, in executing the LIST command

```
LIST FOR YTDSALES > 10000
```

dBASE reads each record from disk and compares the value in YTDSALES with 10,000. If the comparison is true, the record is displayed; otherwise, it is ignored.

Arithmetic Expressions

Assume that you have decided to pay a special bonus to all sales representatives who have sold at least twice the sales quota amount. Your relational expression would then take the form:

```
SALES >= 2*QUOTA
```

The form 2*QUOTA is called an **arithmetic expression** and is virtually identical to expressions of 1-2-3. It says, "Multiply the value in QUOTA by 2." Although large, complex expressions can be formed in dBASE, examples and assignments in this book will require only relatively simple forms, such as adding two quantities or dividing one by another. These will be constructed using the four **arithmetic operators** illustrated in the following examples.

Operator	Example	Description
*	2*QUOTA	Multiply 2 by QUOTA.
/	TCOST/QUANT	Divide TCOST by QUANT.
+	MATERIAL + LABOR + OTHER	Add MATERIAL, LABOR, and OTHER.
–	AMOUNT – DISCOUNT + SHIP	Subtract DISCOUNT from AMOUNT, then add SHIP.

Unlike 1-2-3, spaces can be inserted in an expression to make it more readable. In the preceding examples, spaces are included around the + and – signs but not around the * and /; dBASE ignores all such spaces when performing the calculations.

In setting up comparisons, the quantities on each side of the relational operator can be constant values, field names, or arithmetic expressions such as those illustrated in the preceding set of examples.

Using Relational Operators with Character Data

In addition to comparing numeric data, you can use relational operators with character and date data types to form relational expressions. For instance, Assignment 3 in Chapter 15 requires creating a data file for an automobile leasing agency. One of the fields is a two-position size code in which CO means compact, MI means midsize, and LU means luxury. If you wanted a display of all compact vehicles (those with a CO for the SIZE field), you would use the form:

```
LIST FOR SIZE = "CO"
```

Notice that the CO is enclosed in quotes. If the quotes were omitted, then dBASE would interpret CO as the name of a field in the data file and would give an error message that no such field (or variable) exists. Quoted quantities such as this are called **literals.**

If the character field to be compared contains numbers, do not forget the quotes. For example, if you wanted to display all customers (from the CUSTOMER file) in region 12, you would use the LIST in the following form.

```
LIST FOR REGION = "12"
```

In this case, if the quotes were omitted, dBASE would interpret the quantity 12 as type numeric and would indicate an error because REGION is a type character. The data types on each side of the relational operator must be the same.

Although examples in this book use the double quotation marks, you can use either single or the double quotation marks to specify a literal. Note that the single and double quotes are on the same key of the keyboard.

Testing Logical Variables

Remember that the BILLS data file of Chapter 15 includes the logical field RECOMMEND; it can have a value of true or false (yes or no). If you wanted to display the bills and their titles that have been recommended, then you would want all of the records for which this field is true. To test these, you must not use a relational operator; for instance, the following LIST produces the desired display.

```
LIST FIELDS BILL, TITLE FOR RECOMMEND
```

If you use the form FOR RECOMMEND = .T., dBASE III PLUS will indicate an error.

Logical Operators

Frequently, situations arise in which your selection criterion is based on the values of two or more fields. For instance, you might want to initiate a special promotional effort with customers in region 12 with year-to-date sales of $8000 or more. The English form of the condition is:

REGION value equals 12 *and*
YTDSALES value equals or exceeds 8000

With this form, the overall expression will be true only if both parts are true (because of the *and*). The dBASE form is almost identical to this English form, as we see when it is used with the LIST.

```
LIST FOR REGION = "12" .AND. YTD SALES >= 8000
```

Notice that the .AND. operator, which is called a **logical operator,** includes a period before and after the word AND.

The companion logical operator is .OR., which allows either of two conditions to be true. For instance, assume that you are working with the BILLS data file of Chapter 15 and a special study must be made of bills that are water oriented or pertain to region 3. The English form of the condition is:

TYPE value equals W *or* REGION value equals 3

In this form, the overall expression will be true if either part is true (or if both parts are true). Used in the LIST command, the condition takes the form:

```
LIST FOR TYPE = "W" .OR. REGION = "3"
```

Hands-on Examples

The preceding sections describe numerous examples of using conditions. Let us try each of these on the computer to confirm the results.

DO THIS NOW 16-4 **Using Conditionals**

1. Open the CUSTOMER file with the command:

   ```
   USE CUSTOMER INDEX CUSTOMER
   ```

   Notice that the file is opened with the index CUSTOMER.NDX; conditional forms are completely independent of whether or not the data file is opened with an index file.

2. List the records with YTDSALES greater than 10,000 with the command:

   ```
   LIST FOR YTDSALES > 10000
   ```

   Your screen display should consist of records 1, 8, and 6.

3. List the REGION 12 records with the command:

   ```
   LIST FOR REGION = "12"
   ```

Your screen display should consist of records 10, 7, 3, and 1.

4. Attempt to list the REGION 12 records with the command:

```
LIST FOR REGION = 12
```

dBASE will respond with the error message:

```
Data type mismatch
```

5. List the REGION 12 records with YTDSALES equal to or exceeding 8000 using the command:

```
LIST FOR REGION = "12" .AND. YTDSALES >= 8000
```

Your screen display should consist of records 3 and 1.

6. The next two examples use the BILLS file. Open it with the command:

```
USE BILLS
```

7. List the bills that have been recommended, that is, have a value of true in the RECOMMEND field. Use the command:

```
LIST FIELDS BILL, TITLE FOR RECOMMEND
```

Your screen display should consist of records 1, 3, 4, 5, and 7.

8. Attempt to list the recommended bills with:

```
LIST FIELDS BILL, TITLE FOR RECOMMEND = .T.
```

With dBASE III PLUS, you will get the error message:

```
Invalid operator
```

9. List the bills that are water oriented or pertain to region 3 using the command:

```
LIST FIELDS BILL, TITLE FOR TYPE = "W" .OR. REGION = "3"
```

Your screen display should consist of records 1, 3, 6, 7, and 8.

For the purpose of illustration, all of these examples have used the FOR in conjunction with the LIST. However, you should not conclude that the FOR option can be applied only to LIST; indeed, it can be used with a number of dBASE commands, as will be seen with some of the examples that follow.

Using ASSIST to Build a Condition

In step 9 of the preceding set of exercises, you used the .OR. operator in the LIST command. Let us see how this is done using ASSIST.

DO THIS NOW 16-5 **Using ASSIST to Execute the Command:**

```
LIST FIELDS BILL, TITLE FOR TYPE = "W" .OR. REGION = "3"
```

1. Enter ASSIST by typing the command:

```
ASSIST
```

2. The BILLS file should still be open from the preceding exercise. If you closed it, then reopen it from the *Set Up* option of the ASSIST bar menu.

3. With the Right key, move the highlight to the *Retrieve* option of the bar menu. The submenu *List* option is highlighted; select it by striking Enter. The resulting List submenu shown in Figure 16-7 will be displayed.

Figure 16-7

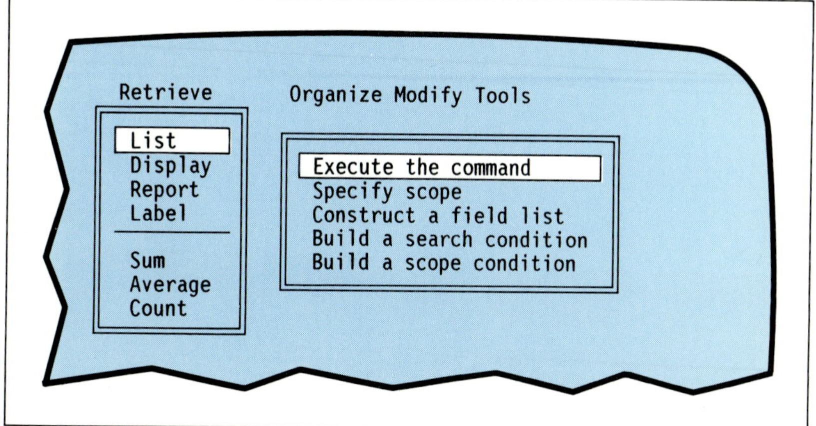

4. The first action is to specify the fields to be listed. Move the highlight to the *Construct a search condition* option and strike Enter. The list of fields composing this record will be displayed (Figure 16-8).

Figure 16-8

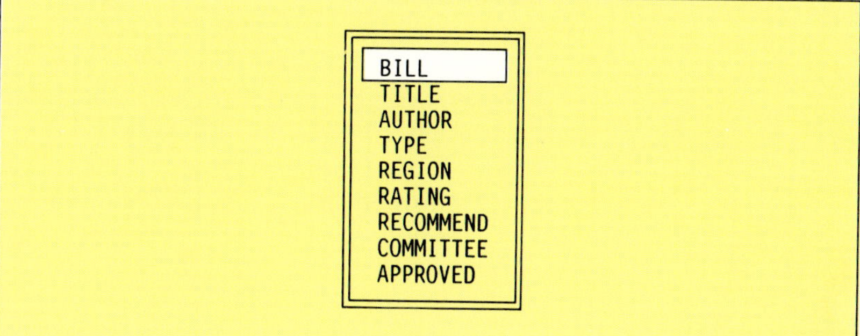

5. You want to display the fields BILL and TITLE. Since BILL is highlighted, strike Enter. Notice that the command is being assembled at the bottom of the screen. It is now:

```
LIST BILL
```

ASSIST does not include the optional word FIELDS in assembling this command.

6. The highlight is at the TITLE field; select it by striking Enter.

7. As you have completed the field selection, strike the Right key to get out of this portion of the menu.

8. You must now define the first of your conditions:

```
TYPE = "W"
```

Do this by selecting the *Build a search condition* option of the menu in Figure 16-7. You will again be presented with the field list of Figure 16-8.

9. Select the field TYPE by moving the highlight to it and striking Enter. This produces the following set of relational operators.

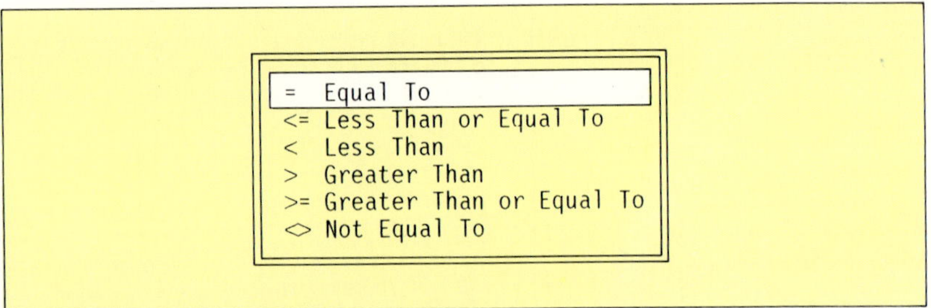

10. You want the *Equal to* operator; since it is highlighted, strike Enter. The following prompt is displayed.

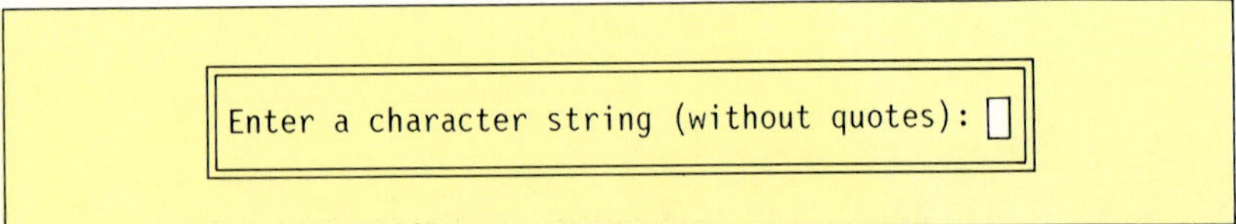

11. As the field to be compared (TYPE) is only one position in width, ASSIST only allows a one-position field to be entered. Enter the letter W (do not forget to use uppercase), and then strike Enter. Notice that the command being build at the bottom of your screen now includes this FOR condition. You also have the following options.

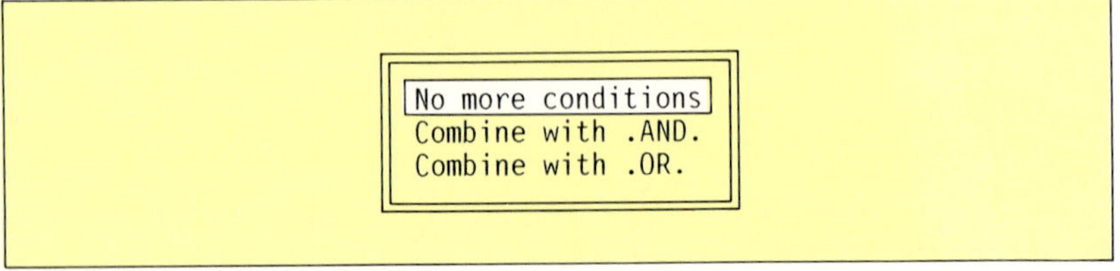

12. Since you must use .OR. with another condition, select the *Combine with .OR.* option.

13. You must then repeat steps 9, 10, and 11 for the

```
REGION = "3"
```

portion of the command.

14. Select the *No more conditions* to return to the submenu of Figure 16-7.

15. As the command is complete, select the *Execute the command* option and the list will be displayed.

This sequence of steps in using ASSIST might appear to be tedious but it goes quickly once you are familiar with it. The principal advantage is that dBASE is continually prompting you, especially in listing the fields from which you must select.

Computers help make law enforcement more effective and safer for police officers. Here an officer is using a keyboard device to enter information that will be used to search a large database and provide the officer with up-to-the-minute information.

OBTAINING INFORMATION FROM A DATA FILE

Direct Access Using an Index

Indexing allows us to access records of a file in a desired sequence (sequential access); it also allows us to locate a desired record quickly (direct access). For instance, assume that you must edit the record of customer number 13189 of the CUSTOMER file. Using the record number to edit a record as you did in Chapter 15 is clumsy because the record number is not a meaningful number to the end user. You need to be able to say to dBASE, "Find the record with a customer number of 13189." You can do exactly this if you have opened the file with the index on the customer number field (CUSTOMER.NDX). Let us try this form of direct access.

DO THIS NOW 16-6 **Using an Index for Direct Access of Customer 13189**

1. Open CUSTOMER with the command:

```
USE CUSTOMER INDEX CUSTOMER
```

2. Enter the FIND command in the following form:

```
FIND "13189"
```

   dBASE will indicate on the status bar that record 8 is the current record.

3. To confirm that this is indeed the desired record, enter the EDIT command. Record 8 (Crow Canyon Casual Wear) will be displayed on the screen.
4. Strike the Escape key to return to the dot prompt.
5. To illustrate what happens if there is no such record in the file, enter the command:

```
FIND "13198"
```

   dBASE displays the message

```
No find
```

   and returns to the dot prompt. Note that the current record is listed as EOF.

In using the FIND command, follow the keyword FIND with the value of the index field that you want dBASE to locate. Because the index is arranged in sequence on this field, dBASE can use special techniques to locate the desired record very quickly.

You could also use the FIND if you needed to locate the record based on the customer name. For instance, assume that you are working on some customer records and you do not have the customer numbers readily available. However, you do know the company names of the records you need to access. For this, you can use the index built on the COMPANY field.

DO THIS NOW 16-7 **Using an Index for Direct Access of Crow Canyon Casual Wear**

1. Open the file with the index CUS-COMP as follows:

```
OPEN CUSTOMER INDEX CUS-COMP
```

   Remember that this closes both the data file and the index file previously opened before opening.

2. Enter the FIND command in the following form.

```
FIND "Crow Canyon"
```

dBASE will indicate on the status bar that record 8 is the current record. In this example, notice that the entire company name is not required (the name is Crow Canyon Casual Wear). For a search such as this, dBASE uses only as many characters as you specify in the FIND statement when doing the comparing.

3. Enter the FIND command in the following form:

```
FIND "CROW CANYON"
```

You will receive the *No find* message because the characters must match exactly; uppercase and lowercase are *not* the same.

Accessing a Selected Record Without Using an Index

Relational expressions and the FOR command option allow us to select records from a file (sequential access); they also give us the means for searching the file for a record satisfying a particular condition. There are frequently situations in which you want to find a particular record based on the value of a field for which there is no index. For this, dBASE includes the LOCATE command, which searches the data file beginning with the first record. For example, assume that you would like to check the bill (in the BILLS file) that pertains to sulfur. You remember that the first word of the name is Sulfur but you do not remember the bill number. You could find the desired record with the LOCATE command.

DO THIS NOW 16-8 **Use the LOCATE Command to Find the Sulfur Bill**

1. Open the BILLS file with:

```
USE BILLS
```

2. The name of the field on which you must do the search is TITLE (see Figure 15-12). Enter the LOCATE command as follows.

```
LOCATE FOR TITLE = "Sulfur"
```

The message

```
Record =     5
```

is displayed and the current record will be indicated on the status bar as record 5.

3. You may inspect the record with the EDIT command. When finished, strike the Escape key.

Note that this form of the LOCATE command includes the FOR command option in exactly the same form in which you used it when listing records in a previous section.

In general, the LOCATE is much slower than the FIND because it must search the data file record by record until it finds the desired one. In doing these exercises, you probably did not notice any difference in speed between the FIND and LOCATE. This was so because of the small size of the files. Had the files consisted of several thousand records, the LOCATE would have taken a considerable amount of time.

Tabulating Data in a File

Data processing was defined earlier in this book as the converting of data to useful information. Thus far, in using dBASE we have inspected selected fields and records from a file but have done no processing. To get an idea of how easy it is to process data with dBASE, let us consider three commands that perform statistical operations on all or part of the records in a file.

COUNT	Counts the number of records in a file that satisfy a stated FOR condition.
SUM	Totals the values of a selected numeric field for all or part of the records of a file.
AVERAGE	Computes the average of the values of a selected numeric field for all or part of the records of a file.

To illustrate, assume that you, as the person responsible for the BILLS file, receive a telephone call from your supervisor, who urgently needs to know the average rating of all bills in the file and how many bills in the file have a rating value of 85 or greater. For a large file, a manual count would be time consuming. With dBASE, it can be done in a matter of seconds.

DO THIS NOW 16-9 **Computing the Average Rating Value and Counting the Number of Bills with a Rating of 85 or Greater**

1. Open the BILLS file with:

```
USE BILLS
```

2. Count the number of bills with a value of the field RATING that is 85 or greater with the following command.

```
COUNT FOR RATING >= 85
```

dBASE will check each record in the file, counting those that meet the specified FOR condition. Upon completing this action, it will display the message:

```
3 records
```

3. Determine the average of the field RATING for all records with the following command.

```
AVERAGE RATING
```

4. dBASE will total the values from the field RATING of each record in the file and then divide by the number of records. Upon completing this action, it will display:

```
8 records averaged
RATING
81
```

5. Upon giving these figures to your supervisor, she tells you that she wanted the average rating of only the water-related bills. For this, you only need add the FOR option to the AVERAGE command as follows:

```
AVERAGE RATING FOR TYPE = "W"
```

6. dBASE will select only those records meeting the FOR condition. The result will be:

```
3 records averaged
RATING
83
```

REPORT GENERATION

In Chapter 14, you learned the difference between a listing and a report. That is, a listing is a file printout consisting of one line per selected record from the file. Although this has been adequate for learning about dBASE, businesses require much more information—they require reports. Reports commonly include more extensive headings, the numbering of pages and column headings on each page for reports longer than a single page, summary lines that display totals of portions of the output, and often data from more than one file. In dBASE, the process of preparing reports is simplified with a special component of the dBASE program called the report generator. To illustrate how the report generator works, we will use the Accounts Receivable file (named AR) of Figure 14-19. The record format of this file is shown in Figure 16-9. Characteristics of this file are:

1. It contains one record for each customer sale.
2. The key field is the invoice number; there will never be two records with the same invoice number.
3. A customer will have one record for each purchase. For instance,

```
Structure for database: B:AR.DBF
Number of data records:       16
Date of last update    : 05/23/88
Field  Field Name  Type       Width    Dec
    1  INVNUM      Character      4
    2  CUSTNUM     Character      5
    3  INVDATE     Date           8
    4  ORIGAMNT    Numeric        7      2
    5  INVBAL      Numeric        7      2
** Total **                      32
```

Figure 16-9
The structure of the AR file.

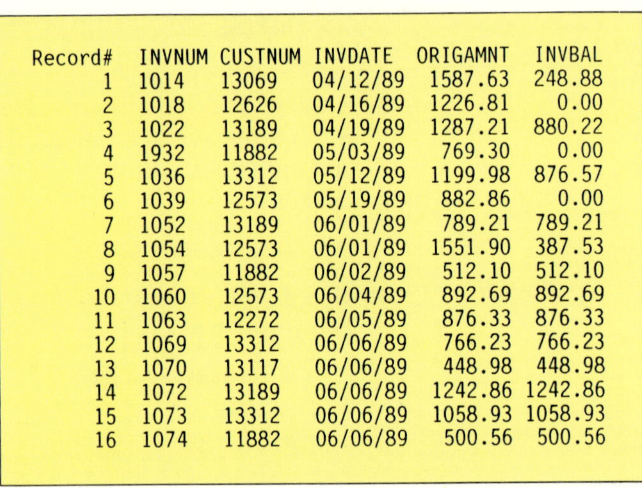

Record#	INVNUM	CUSTNUM	INVDATE	ORIGAMNT	INVBAL
1	1014	13069	04/12/89	1587.63	248.88
2	1018	12626	04/16/89	1226.81	0.00
3	1022	13189	04/19/89	1287.21	880.22
4	1932	11882	05/03/89	769.30	0.00
5	1036	13312	05/12/89	1199.98	876.57
6	1039	12573	05/19/89	882.86	0.00
7	1052	13189	06/01/89	789.21	789.21
8	1054	12573	06/01/89	1551.90	387.53
9	1057	11882	06/02/89	512.10	512.10
10	1060	12573	06/04/89	892.69	892.69
11	1063	12272	06/05/89	876.33	876.33
12	1069	13312	06/06/89	766.23	766.23
13	1070	13117	06/06/89	448.98	448.98
14	1072	13189	06/06/89	1242.86	1242.86
15	1073	13312	06/06/89	1058.93	1058.93
16	1074	11882	06/06/89	500.56	500.56

Figure 16-10
The AR file.

referring to the file listing of Figure 16-10, notice that most customers have more than one record. However, the invoice number is different for each.

4. As payments are received, the payment is credited against the invoice.

5. As part of the month-end processing, reports are prepared using data from this file. These include a summary report of all customers and their balances due, and a statement of account for each customer. Records with 0 balances are deleted from this file at this time.

A Simple Report

For our first exposure to the report generator, we will use it to print the report shown in Figure 16-11. Notice that it includes a *page heading* and *column headings* that are much more descriptive than the data file field names. It also includes a page number. The dBASE report generator allows us to specify the number of lines to be printed per page. When the page becomes full, dBASE causes the printer to position the continuous-form printer paper to the top of the next page, where the column headings are printed again, together with the page number. The main part of the report is made up of *detail lines,* with each line representing a record from the input file. The last line of the report is a *total line,* which includes the total for the original amount and current balance fields.

The report of Figure 16-11 was generated from a report specification generated with the dBASE report generator and stored on disk as a separate report specification file. That file is not included on your data disk; in fact, you will learn how to use the report generator by creating this specification file. In doing so, you will need to designate:

1. Information about the printed page (for instance, number of printed lines per page) and the report heading.

Figure 16-11
A simple report.

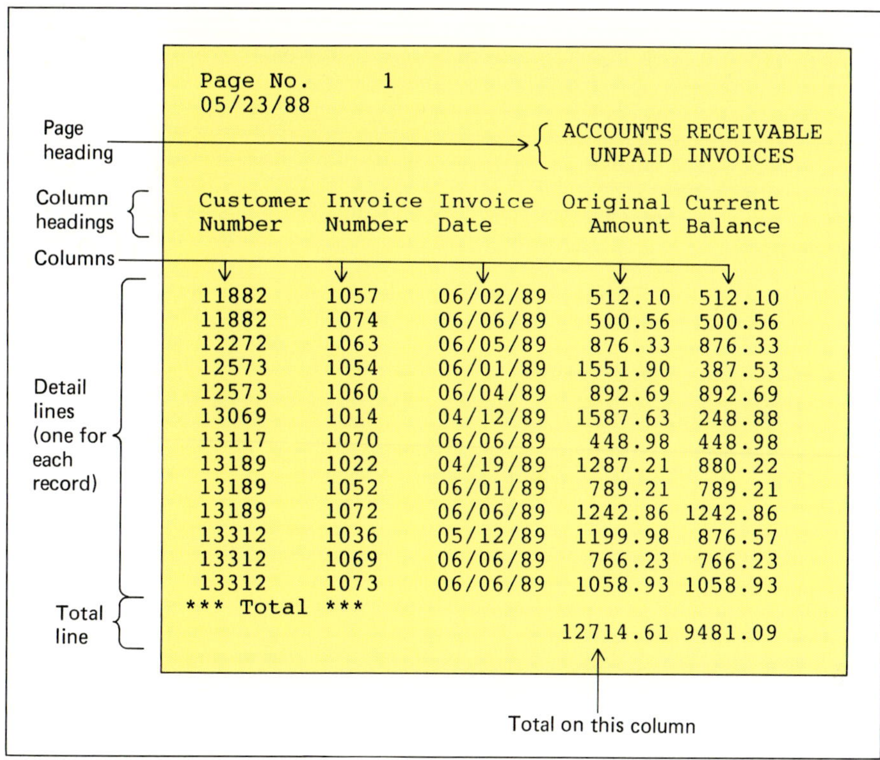

Page No. 1
05/23/88

ACCOUNTS RECEIVABLE
UNPAID INVOICES

Customer Number	Invoice Number	Invoice Date	Original Amount	Current Balance
11882	1057	06/02/89	512.10	512.10
11882	1074	06/06/89	500.56	500.56
12272	1063	06/05/89	876.33	876.33
12573	1054	06/01/89	1551.90	387.53
12573	1060	06/04/89	892.69	892.69
13069	1014	04/12/89	1587.63	248.88
13117	1070	06/06/89	448.98	448.98
13189	1022	04/19/89	1287.21	880.22
13189	1052	06/01/89	789.21	789.21
13189	1072	06/06/89	1242.86	1242.86
13312	1036	05/12/89	1199.98	876.57
13312	1069	06/06/89	766.23	766.23
13312	1073	06/06/89	1058.93	1058.93
*** Total ***				
			12714.61	9481.09

2. Each field to be printed (each column of the report) and the column heading.

3. The format of each numeric field (number of decimal positions to be printed).

4. The numeric fields to be totalled for the total line.

The report specification is created using the CREATE REPORT command and, once created and stored to disk, it can be used whenever needed for preparing the report. Let us now create this specification.

DO THIS NOW 16-10 **Creating a Report Specification to Generate the Report of Figure 16-11 from Data in the AR File**

1. Since this report specification is to use data from the AR file, that file must first be opened with the command:

```
USE AR
```

2. To create the report specification, enter the command:

```
CREATE REPORT AR1
```

AR1 will be used as the name of this report specification file: AR to signify the AR data file and 1 to indicate that this is the first of two that you will create. Your screen display will be as shown in Figure 16-12. The *Options* submenu allows you to specify page characteristics. The default values are for standard 8 1/2 × 11 paper but you easily can change them to suit the needs of the particular report.

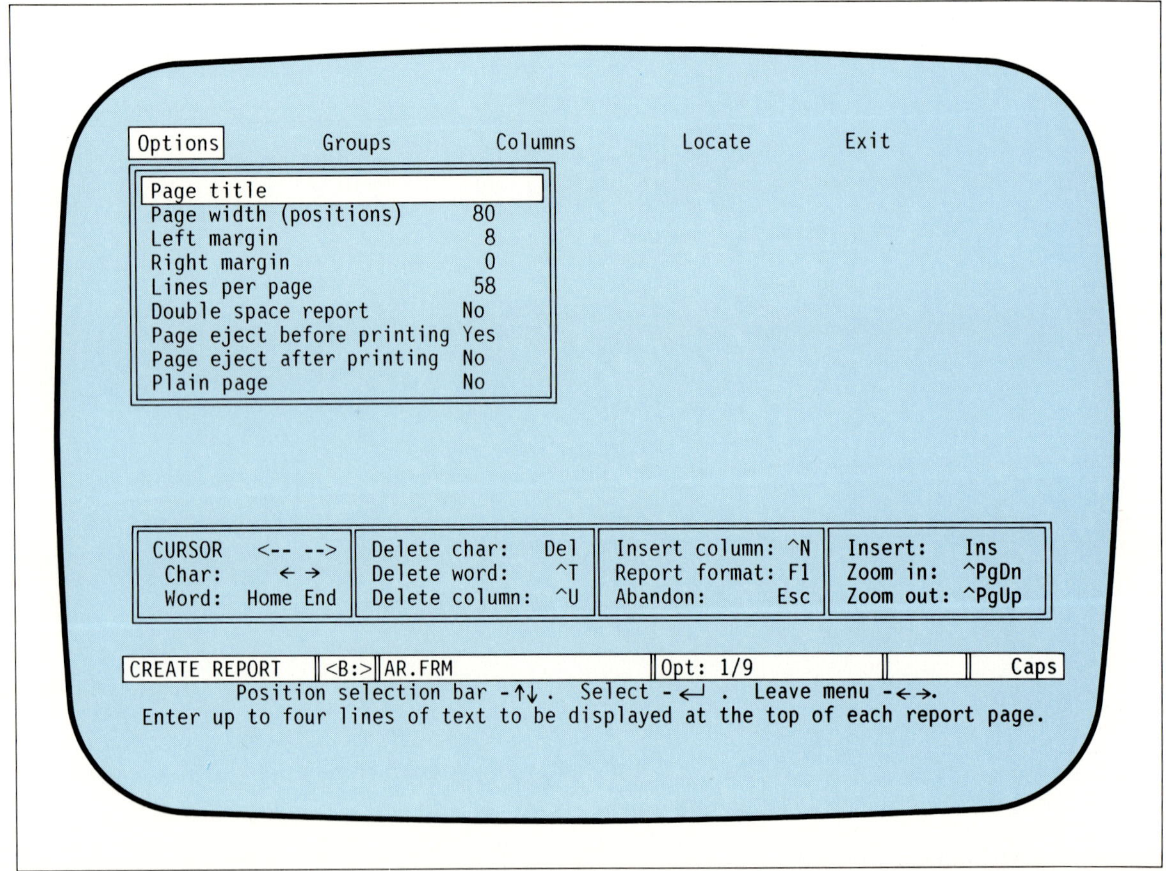

Figure 16-12
The CREATE REPORT Option submenu.

3. The *Page title* option is highlighted; select it by striking Enter. The window of Figure 16-13 will be displayed on your screen with the cursor awaiting entry of the report title. The small triangle (arrowhead) on the *Page title* line indicates that this menu option has been selected.

4. Type the following two report title lines:

   ```
   ACCOUNTS RECEIVABLE
   UNPAID INVOICES
   ```

   The page title can consist of up to four lines.

5. Terminate report title entry with the Ctrl-End sequence. Your screen display will be the same as that of Figure 16-13 except that the first part of the title will be on the *Page title* line.

Next you must specify the data fields to be printed. For each column of the output report (refer to Figure 16-11), you will need to designate the field to be printed (the column contents), the column heading, the number

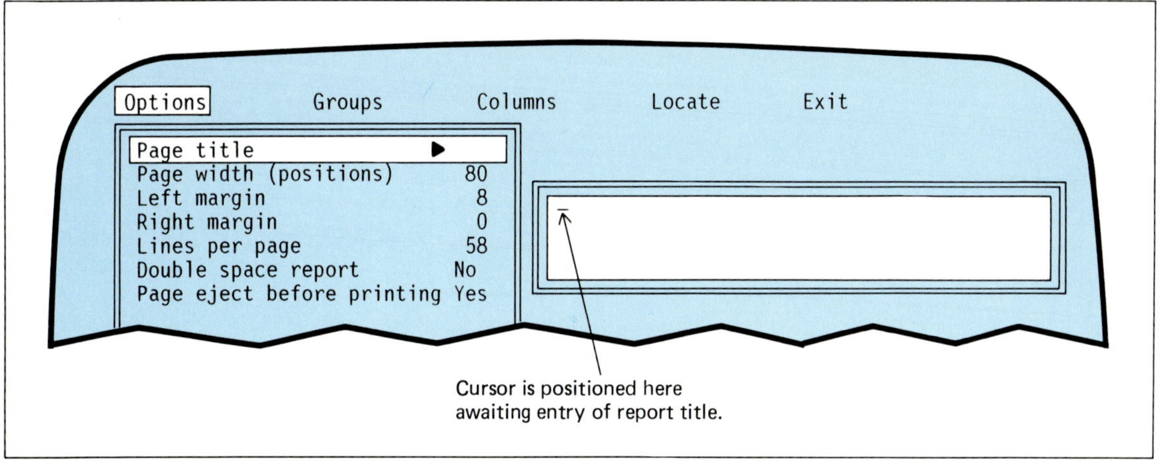

Figure 16-13
Entering the main heading.

of positions to allocate on the printed page, and the number of decimal places for numeric data.

6. With the Right key, move the menu bar selection to *Columns;* this will produce the screen shown in Figure 16-14.

7. Select the *Contents* option by striking Enter. A small arrowhead

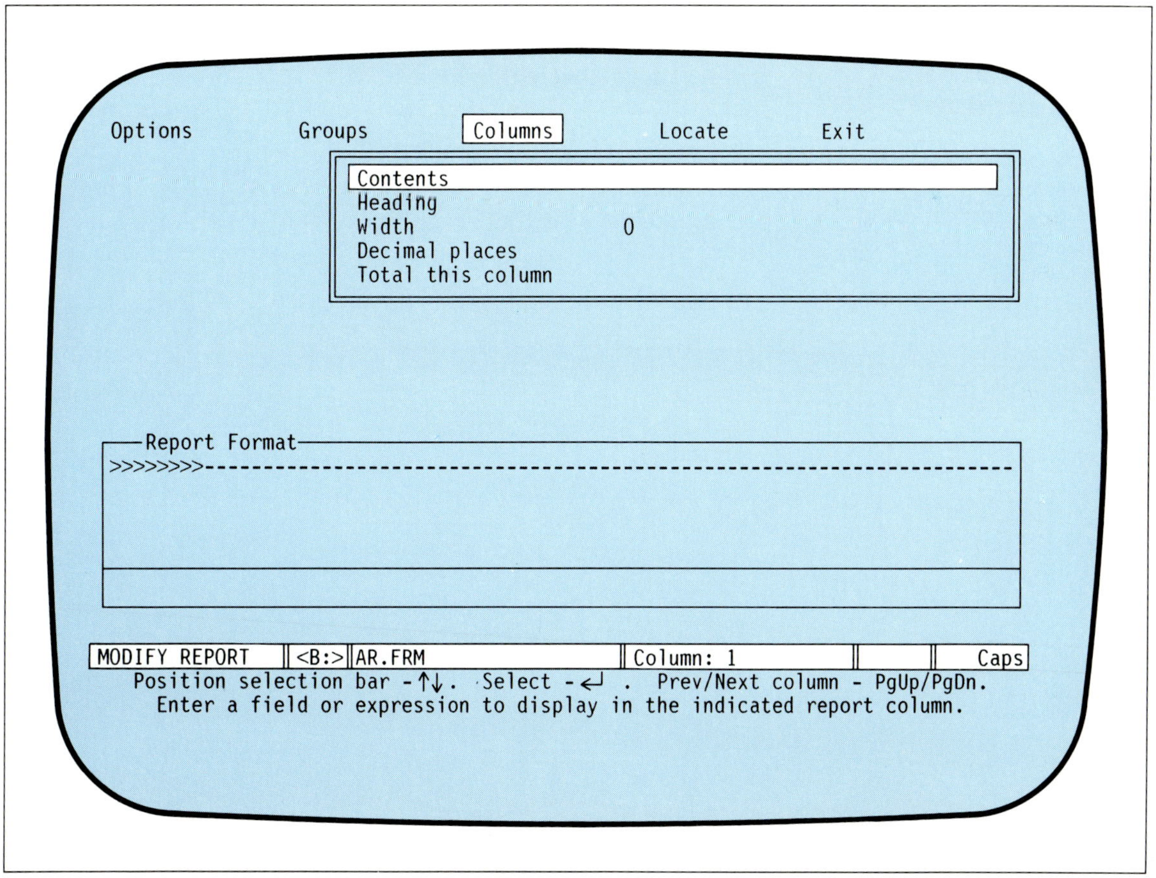

Figure 16-14
The Columns submenu.

```
Options          Groups          Columns          Locate          Exit

                           Contents
                           Heading
                           Width                  0
                           Decimal places
                           Total this column

  Report Format
>>>>>>>>-------------------------------------------------------------------

MODIFY REPORT  <B:>  AR.FRM                 Column: 1                 Caps
  Position selection bar - ↑↓.  Select - ↵ .  Prev/Next column - PgUp/PgDn.
    Enter a field or expression to display in the indicated report column.
```

will be displayed in the highlighted area, indicating that you must enter the name of the field whose values are to be printed in this column.

8. You can type the field name (or an expression), or you can obtain a field list of the data file by pressing the F10 key. Strike F10 to obtain the display of Figure 16-15.

Figure 16-15
Data file field display.

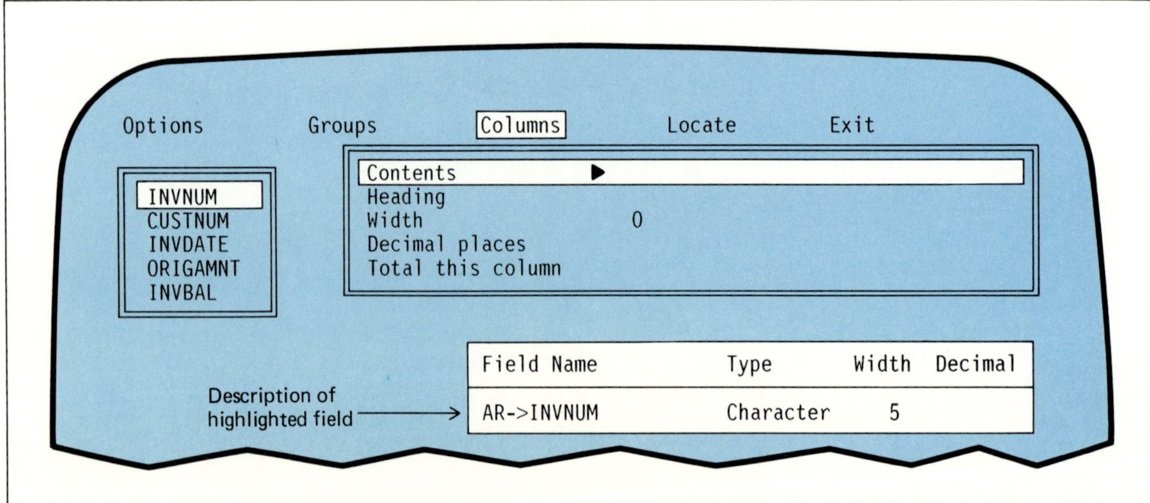

9. Since the customer number is to be in the first column of the report, move the highlight to CUSTNUM and strike Enter to select it. CUSTNUM will be displayed in the *Contents* line; strike Enter to tell dBASE to accept it.

10. Strike the Down key to highlight the *Heading* option, and then strike Enter to select it. Your display will be as shown in Figure 16-16; dBASE is awaiting entry of the heading for this column.

Figure 16-16
Entering column headings.

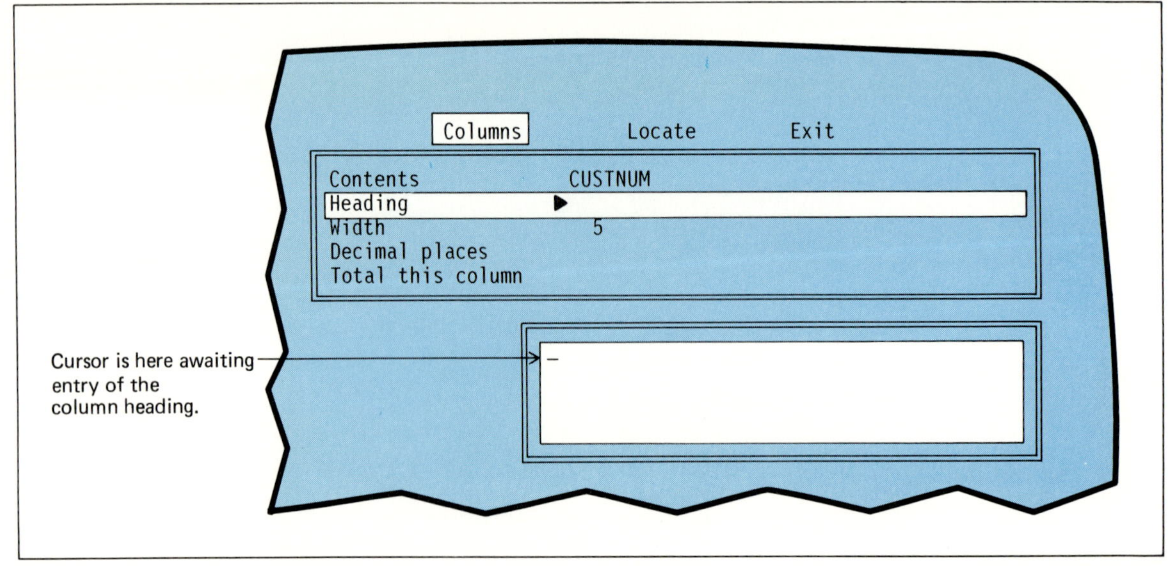

11. Type the two-line heading:

```
Customer
Number
```

Complete this action with the Ctrl-End key sequence. Your screen display will be as shown in Figure 16-17. The box entitled *Report Format* displays the current form of the output line. Notice that the margin, heading, and number of remaining positions on the output line are indicated in the upper portion of the box. In the lower portion of the box, the location of the field (CUSTNUM) is indicated by XXXXX. The uppercase letter X indicates a character field.

Figure 16-17
The Columns screen.

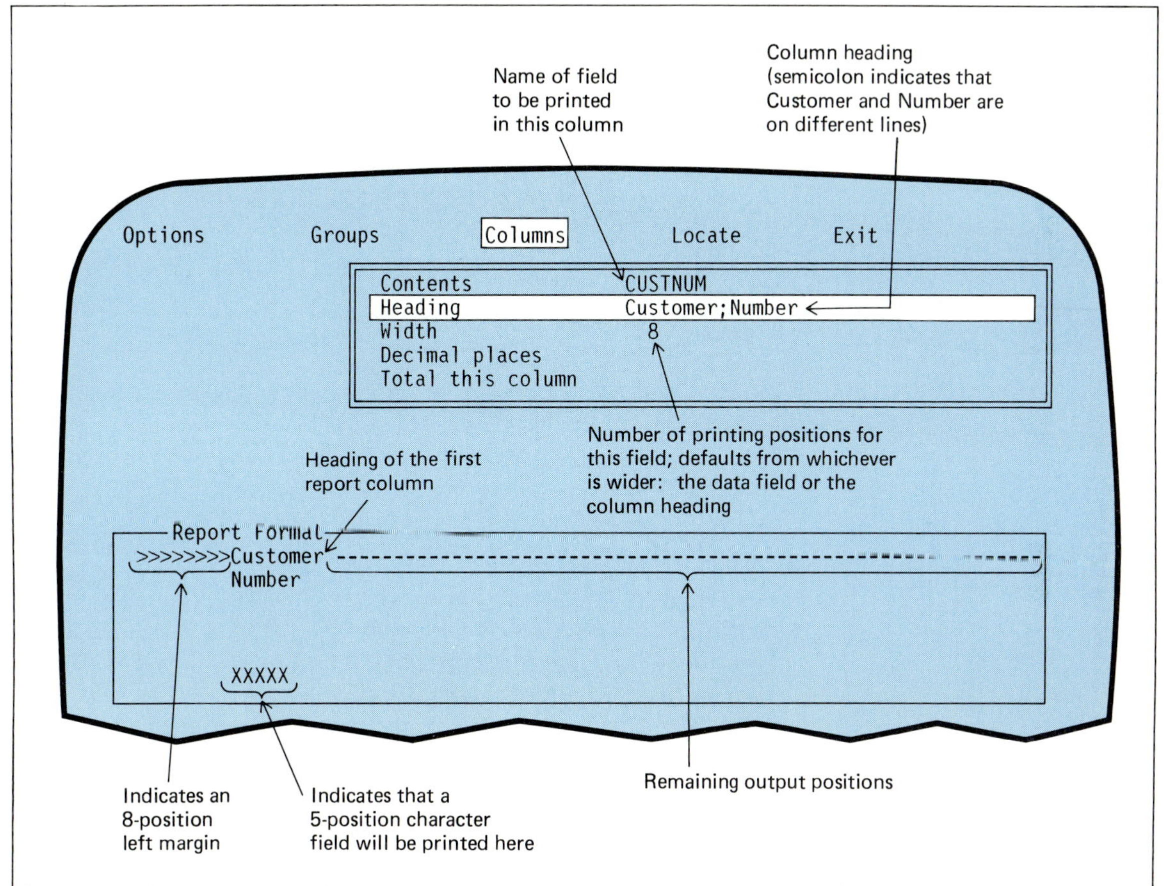

12. Strike the PgDn key to complete the first column; the blank *Columns* submenu of Figure 16-14 will be displayed again.

13. Repeat steps 8 through 12 for the second column, using the field INVNUM, then for the third column, using the field INVDATE. The column headings are to be:

```
Invoice   Invoice
Number    Date
```

14. Repeat steps 8 through 11 (do not strike PgDn when finished) for the fourth column using the field ORIGAMNT. Use the column headings:

```
Original
Amount
```

Your screen should appear as shown in Figure 16-18.

Figure 16-18
Defining a numeric field in a report.

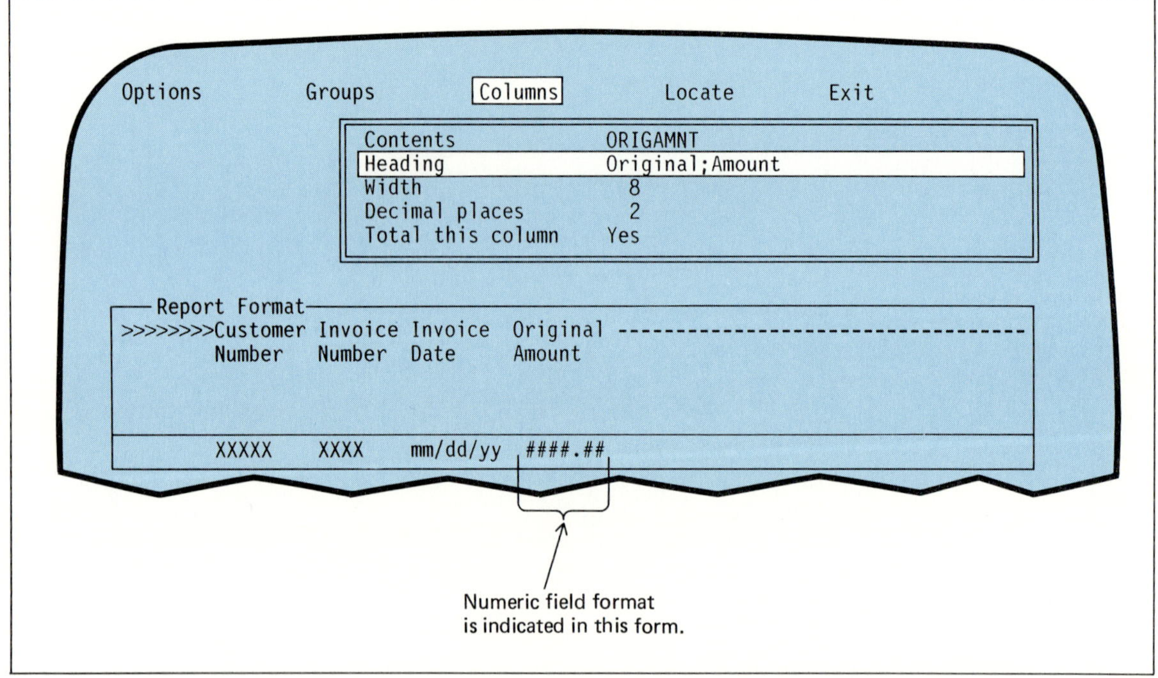

In your line format, you can see that the numeric output is indicated by ####.## where the # character indicates a digit position. The largest number that could be displayed is 9999.99. In this case, the report generator uses as a default the field width and decimal places from the structure of the data file.

The last menu option, *Total this column*, defaults to Yes for each numeric field. This will cause dBASE to calculate and print a total for this column (refer to the report of Figure 16-11). When a column is to be totaled, you should keep in mind that the total will require more digits than any component value. Hence, you must designate a field width for that column large enough to display the largest possible total. In this example, the report generator set the width as 8 to accommodate the heading. If the total of this column were to exceed 99999.99, then you would need to set the width at 9. If you did not want a total on this column, then you would change the Yes to No.

15. Complete the specification for the ORIGAMNT field by striking the PgDn key.

16. Enter the specification for the INVBAL field as you did with ORIGAMNT. Use the following column heading.

```
Current
Balance
```

17. Check each of your column specifications by moving from one field to the next with the PgUp or PgDn key. Correct any error by selecting the same way that you did when entering.

18. When you have checked everything, move the bar menu highlight to the *Exit* option; highlight the *Save* suboption and strike Enter.

Your report specification will be saved to disk using the name AR1 (that you designated at the beginning) and a default extension of FRM; the full name will be AR1.FRM. When the saving action has been completed, you will be returned to the dot prompt.

Printing the Report

Now that the report specification has been stored as a file, you could immediately generate a report, or you could terminate the dBASE work session and generate a report at any later time. As with a listing from the LIST command, you can have the records accessed in their physical file order or in order based on an index. In Figure 16-11, the records are in order by customer number. Notice that this causes all records for a given customer to be grouped together. The data disk contains the index file AR-CUST, which is based on the customer number field. You will use this in the following sequence.

DO THIS NOW 16-11 **Generating an Accounts Receivable Report Using AR1.FRM**

1. Open the AR file with the index AR-CUST as follows:

```
USE AR INDEX AR-CUST
```

2. Generate the report by entering the following command.

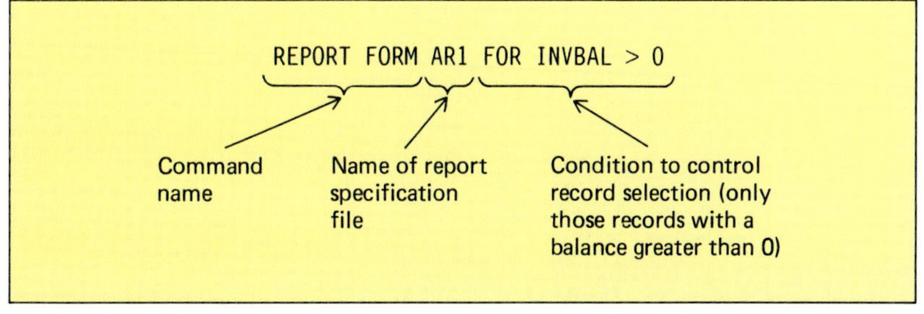

The report displayed on your screen should be identical to that of Figure 16-11.

In the REPORT FORM command, you may select records using the FOR option exactly as you did with the LIST command in the preceding section. Also, if you want a printed copy of the report, you need only include the TO PRINT option, that is:

```
REPORT FORM AR1 FOR INVBAL > 0 TO PRINT
```

For a report in which the records are in invoice number sequence, you would create an index on that field and open the AR file with it.

Control Groups

Figure 16-19 is a portion of the report produced by AR1. Since the records are in order by the customer number field, all records with identical customer numbers are grouped together. Each group of records with the same customer number is called a **control group;** the field on which they are grouped (customer number in this case) is called the **control field.** Each control group represents a semi-independent element of the report. As such, the report becomes more useful if it includes a summary for each control group.

With only some minor additions to AR1.FRM, we would be able to generate the report of Figure 16-20. Here, we see that the customer number is not repeated for each record of a control group; it serves as a heading for that group. Furthermore, the total for each control group is included following the last record of the group. These are commonly called **group totals.**

Generating a Report Specification with Group Totals

The creating of a report specification that gives group totals requires one additional step beyond that of creating AR1.FRM: you must identify the

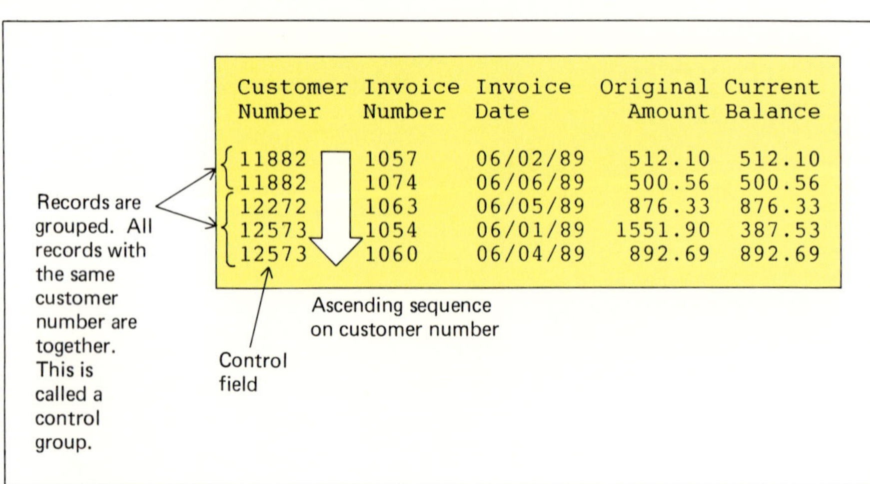

Customer Number	Invoice Number	Invoice Date	Original Amount	Current Balance
11882	1057	06/02/89	512.10	512.10
11882	1074	06/06/89	500.56	500.56
12272	1063	06/05/89	876.33	876.33
12573	1054	06/01/89	1551.90	387.53
12573	1060	06/04/89	892.69	892.69

Figure 16-19
Groups of records.

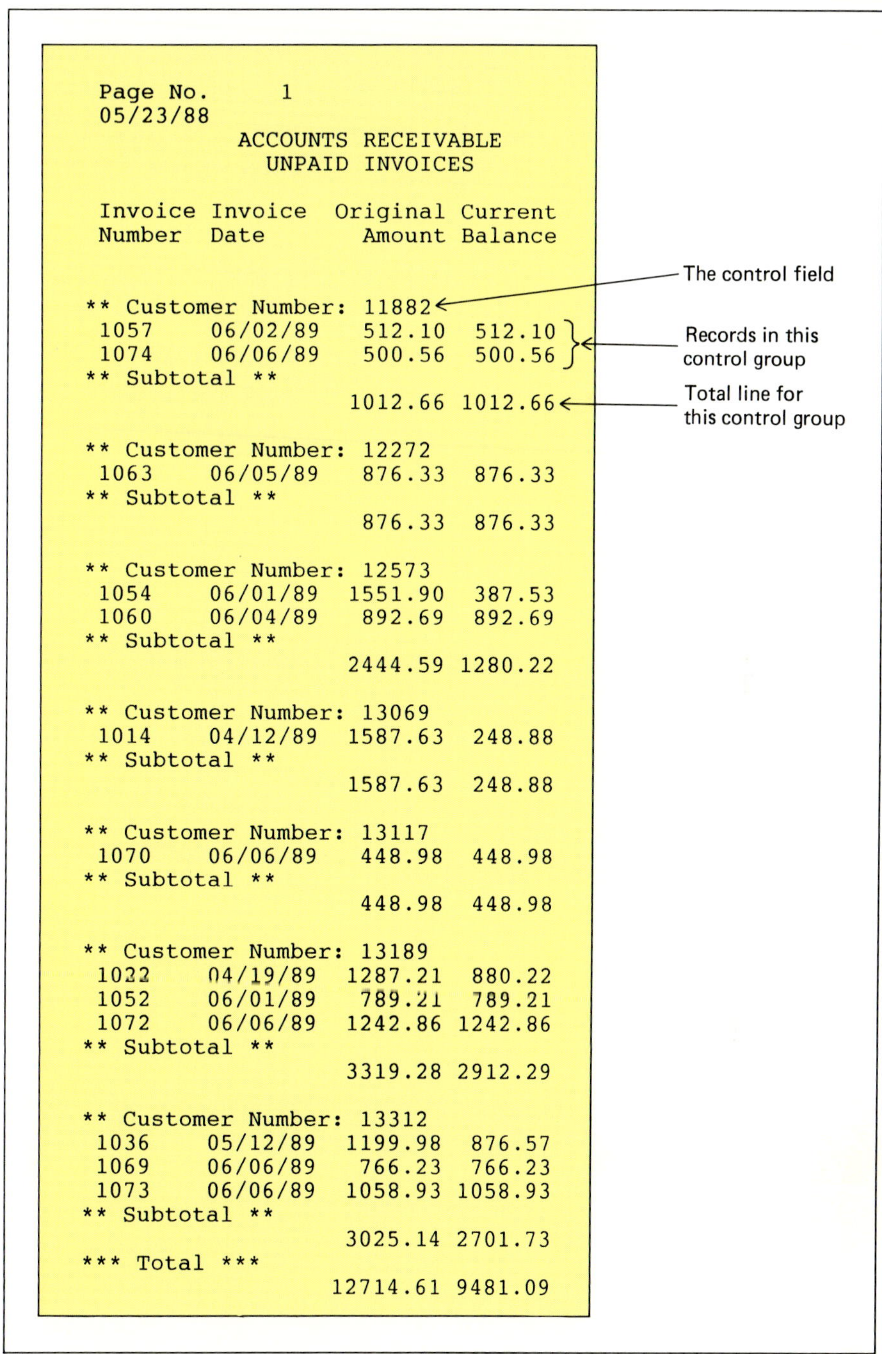

```
Page No.     1
05/23/88
           ACCOUNTS RECEIVABLE
             UNPAID INVOICES

Invoice Invoice  Original Current
Number  Date       Amount Balance


** Customer Number: 11882
1057    06/02/89   512.10  512.10
1074    06/06/89   500.56  500.56
** Subtotal **
                  1012.66 1012.66

** Customer Number: 12272
1063    06/05/89   876.33  876.33
** Subtotal **
                   876.33  876.33

** Customer Number: 12573
1054    06/01/89  1551.90  387.53
1060    06/04/89   892.69  892.69
** Subtotal **
                  2444.59 1280.22

** Customer Number: 13069
1014    04/12/89  1587.63  248.88
** Subtotal **
                  1587.63  248.88

** Customer Number: 13117
1070    06/06/89   448.98  448.98
** Subtotal **
                   448.98  448.98

** Customer Number: 13189
1022    04/19/89  1287.21  880.22
1052    06/01/89   789.21  789.21
1072    06/06/89  1242.86 1242.86
** Subtotal **
                  3319.28 2912.29

** Customer Number: 13312
1036    05/12/89  1199.98  876.57
1069    06/06/89   766.23  766.23
1073    06/06/89  1058.93 1058.93
** Subtotal **
                  3025.14 2701.73
*** Total ***
                 12714.61 9481.09
```


Figure 16-20
Group totals.

group. The easiest way to do this is to use the MODIFY REPORT command that will bring up the screen of Figure 16-12. Then you can continue working on this specification as if you had never terminated the CREATE REPORT work session. To preserve the original, you will make a copy, and then modify the copy. The changes that you will make will be both to improve the appearance of that which you already have and to add subtotals. The modifications will be:

- Change the left margin and page width to center the heading better.
- Specify the group field (CUSTNUM).
- Remove the customer number from the column output because the group heading will include it (see Figure 16-20).

DO THIS NOW 16-12 **Making a copy of AR1.FRM and Modifying It to Include Group Totals**

1. From the dBASE dot prompt, make a copy of AR1.FRM using the dBASE COPY FILE command as follows:

```
COPY FILE B:AR1.FRM TO B:AR2.FRM
```

2. If the AR file is not still open from DTN 16-11, then open it with a USE command.
3. Enter the command:

```
MODIFY REPORT AR2
```

   The resulting screen will be that shown in Figure 16-12.
4. The first step is to change the page width and margins to center the report better. For this, select the *Page width* option (move the highlight to it and strike Enter). Type in the value 60, and then strike Enter to register the new value.
5. Select the *Left margin* option and enter a value of 20. This completes the page setup changes.
6. With the Right key, move the highlight to the *Groups* menu bar selection. Your screen will display the submenu shown in Figure 16-21.

Figure 16-21
The Groups submenu.

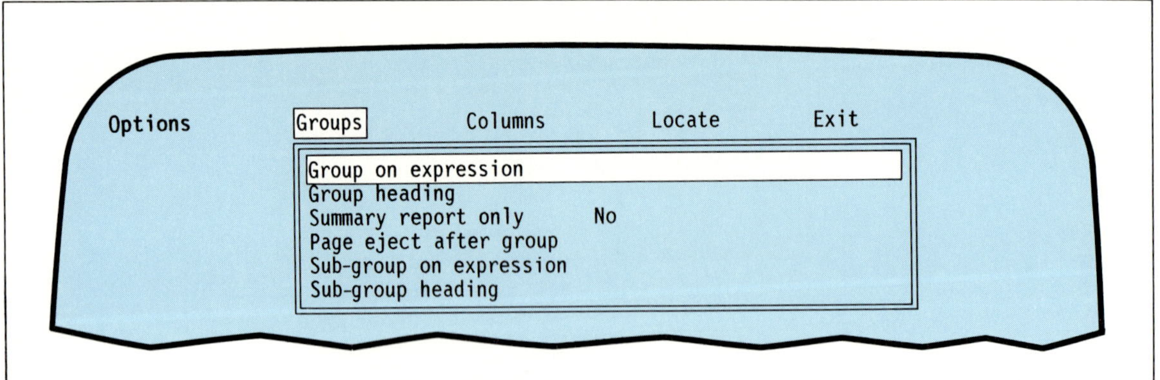

7. The first option, *Group on expression,* is used to specify the control field; select this option by striking Enter.
8. The cursor will be positioned following the arrowhead on the *Group on expression* line. Type CUSTNUM, the name of the control

field, and then strike Enter. (Note that you could display the field list by striking the F10 key.)

9. You must now describe the heading that is to precede each group. Strike the Down key to move the highlight to the Group heading option then strike Enter.

10. Type the group heading

```
Customer number:
```

and then strike Enter. Your screen will be as shown in Figure 16-22. This completes the group designation. The remaining items are left at their default values.

Figure 16-22
Entering the group heading.

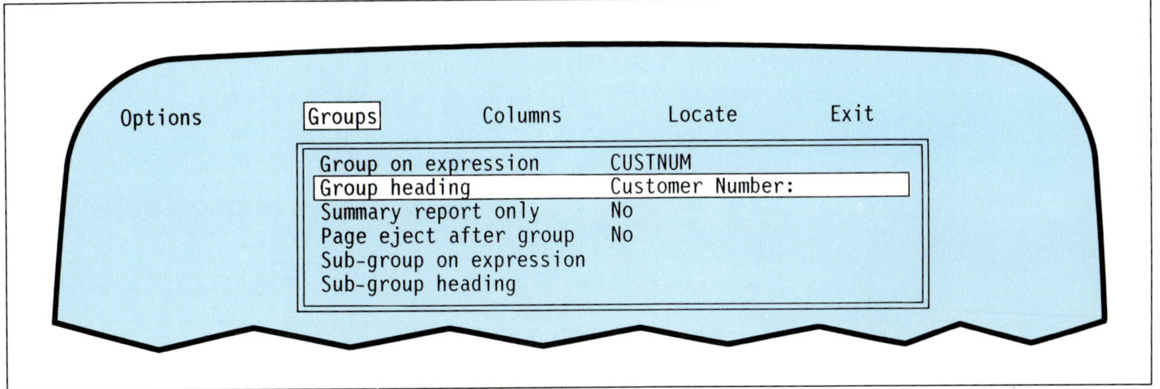

11. To remove the CUSTNUM field from the column specifications, move the highlight to the *Columns bar* menu option. The description of the CUSTNUM column will be displayed.

12. Strike the F1 key to display the Help frame shown in Figure 16-23.

Figure 16-23
Deleting a report column.

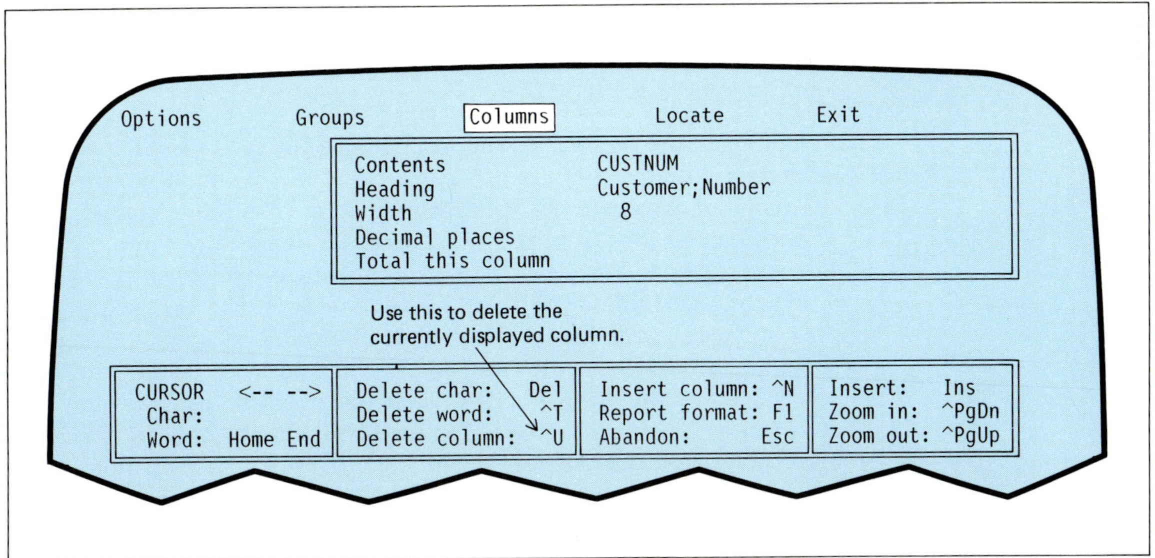

Upon inspecting this, you will see that a column can be deleted with the Ctrl-U sequence. Hold down the Control key and strike the letter U. This causes the currently displayed column (CUSTNUM) to be deleted from the report.

13. The task is complete. The final step is to highlight the *Exit* option and select the *Save*. You will be returned to the dot prompt.

You now have two report specification files on your disk: AR1.FRM and AR2.FRM. To generate a report with AR1, you must first open the AR data file. If you do not specify an index when opening, the records will be listed in their physical file order. Designation of an index upon opening will cause the records to be listed according to the index. On the other hand, AR2.FRM does group totaling using the customer number as the group control field. Hence, if AR is not opened with the customer number index, the printed group totals will be meaningless.

DO THIS NOW 16-13 **Generating the Group Total Report Using AR2.FRM**

1. Open the AR file with the command:

```
USE AR INDEX AR-CUST
```

2. Generate the report with the command:

```
REPORT FORM AR2 FOR INVBAL > 0
```

Your output should be identical to that of Figure 16-20.

USING TWO OR MORE FILES

In looking at the group total report of Figure 16-20, we see that each group is identified by the customer number. However, it would be convenient if the name of the customer were printed as well as the customer number. Unfortunately, the AR record includes only the customer number and not the name. Remember from Chapter 14 that one of the objectives of a DBMS is to avoid redundancy of data (the same item of data being duplicated in two or more files). Hence, to include the name as well as the number would create redundancy; the name of the customer belongs in the Customer file, not the Accounts Receivable file. A DBMS provides the capability to interrelate files (refer to Figure 14-18). In the case of the accounts receivable report, the customer name would be available by linking the AR file to the CUSTOMER file. Then, as dBASE encounters a new group and prints the customer number, using that number it could find that customer record in CUSTOMER and obtain the name for the report. This requires that both files be opened and that the relationship between the two files be clearly specified. Then data is available from both files almost as if only one were being used. If you take a dBASE course, you will spend considerable time and effort working with interrelated data files.

SUMMARY

From this chapter, you have learned some of the basic methods for turning data into useful information. The three broad areas covered in this chapter are indexing, which allows you to change the sequence in which you access records; selecting records by using conditional forms; and report generation. Summarizing, the important items from this chapter are:

- An index can be created on any character, numeric, or date field of a data file record.
- Access to data in a file is controlled by an index file only when the file is opened together with that index file.
- If records are to be added to a file for which indexes have been created, the indexes will be updated with the addition of records only if they were opened when the file was opened.
- When a file is opened with an index, the FIND command allows direct access to any record in the file based on the value of the field on which the index was built.
- If a data field of a file on which an index is built is changed, then that index must be open when the change is made or else the index file will not be updated.
- Relational operators are used to build relational expressions that compare two quantities. The relational operators are:

<	Less than
>	Greater than
=	Equal to
<=	Less than or equal to
>=	Greater than or equal to
<> or #	Not equal to

- A relational expression can be either true or false.
- The FOR command option uses a relation expression to select records according to the condition designated by the relational expression.
- Compound conditions can be formed using the .AND. and .OR. logical operators.

- Calculations are performed in dBASE using arithmetic operators to form arithmetic expressions.
- With the LOCATE command, you can search a file based on a desired value for any field of a record.
- The COUNT command will count the number of records meeting a specified condition.
- The SUM and AVERAGE commands will sum and average the contents of a designated field for all records or selected records of a file.
- With the CREATE REPORT command, you can specify the exact form that a report will take. This includes page layout, headings, data to be printed, and totals and subtotals of numeric fields. This specification information is stored in a file with an extension of FRM.
- Before a report can be generated from an FRM file, the data file must first be opened. If the FRM computes group totals, then the data file must be opened with the index file created from the group control field.

COMMAND SUMMARY

Following are general forms for commands introduced in this chapter.

AVERAGE <field name> [FOR condition>]
Computes the arithmetic mean of numeric expressions.

COPY FILE <filename1.ext> TO <filename2.ext>
Makes an exact duplicate of the file *filename1.ext* and names it *filename2.ext*.

COUNT [FOR <condition>]
Tallies the number of records specified by the FOR condition.

INDEX ON <key expression> TO <index filename>
Create an index file on the specified fields.

LOCATE [FOR <condition>]
Positions the record pointer to the first record that satisfies the specified conditions.

MODIFY REPORT <.frm filename>
Allows for the creation and editing of a report form file.

REPORT FORM <.frm filename> [FOR <condition>] [TO PRINT]
Displays a tabular report of data.

SUM <field name> [FOR <condition>]
Computes and displays the sum of an expression for database records specified in the scope.

NEW TERMINOLOGY

Many of the database terms used in Chapter 14 are also used in this chapter. The following are additional new terms introduced in this chapter; you should be familiar with each of them.

arithmetic expression
arithmetic operator
control field
control group
group total
literal
logical operator
relational expression
relational operator

REVIEW QUESTIONS

1. In addition to the command COPY FILE, dBASE includes the COPY command that will copy the currently open file to a new file record by record. For instance, consider the command sequence:

```
USE CUSTOMER INDEX CUS-YTD
COPY TO CUSTOM8
```

   This COPY command will cause the records of CUSTOMER to be copied to another file on disk with the name CUSTOM8. Do you think that CUSTOM8 will be identical to CUSTOMER? Explain your answer. You may want to inspect the newly created file. To do so, you must first open it.

2. The customer file is opened with the following USE command.

```
USE CUSTOMER INDEX CUS-YTD, CUSTOMER, CUS-COMP, CUS-ANNV
```

   If the LIST command is executed, what will be the sequencing of the records?

3. Only one index can affect the sequence of the records in a file at any given time. What is the value of listing all of the index files in a USE as is done in the preceding question?

4. What is the maximum number of index files that you think could be created for the CUSTOMER file? Explain your answer.

5. Consider the relational expression:

```
3.2*AMNT>=16
```

   What will be the result of evaluating for each of the following values of the field AMNT?
   a. -10 b. 5 c. 20

6. Prepare a LIST command to list records from the CUSTOMER file according to the following conditions.
   a. Account balances greater than 1000.
   b. In region 12 with zero balances.
   c. Year-to-date sales between 5000 and 8000.
   d. The first two digits of the customer number 12.

7. Assume that you opened the CUSTOMER file with the index on the customer name field (CUS-COMP), intending to open it on the customer number field. Then you attempted to find the record with a customer number of 11882 (this is record 4) with the command:

```
FIND "11882"
```

   What do you think would happen?

8. Both the FIND and LOCATE commands can be used for direct access. What are the advantages of each?

9. What would happen if you entered the following sequence of commands?

```
USE CUSTOMER INDEX CUS-COMP
FIND "C"
```

10. Give the command sequence to obtain the average customer balance from the CUSTOMER file both with and without including the zero balance values. Execute the commands and check the results against the data.

11. What would be the nature of a report generated with the following sequence of commands? Notice that no index file is designated.

```
USE AR
REPORT FORM AR2
```

TRUE/FALSE

Determine whether each of the following is true or false.

______ 1. A data file must first be opened before an index can be created on that data file.

______ 2. As each index is created, dBASE automatically changes the physical sequencing of the records in the data file.

______ 3. Whenever a data file is edited, all indexes associated with that data file must be recreated using the INDEX command.

______ 4. When listing the contents of a data file using the FOR option, it is possible to get no records at all displayed.

______ 5. If a file is opened with an index, it is not possible to use the FOR option in a LIST command.

______ 6. If the following LIST were executed, only records with values in the SALES field that are twice the value in the QUOTA field would be listed.

```
LIST FOR 2*SALES >= QUOTA
```

______ 7. If the following LIST were executed, only records for which the logical field CREDIT is true would be listed.

```
LIST FOR CREDIT
```

______ 8. According to the rules for using relational operators in dBASE, the following would list all records with a value in the field CHARGES between 400 and 800 (inclusive).

```
LIST FOR CHARGES >= 400 .AND. <= 800
```

______ 9. The advantage of the FIND over the LOCATE for direct access is that the FIND is much faster, especially for large files.

______ 10. It is not necessary to use the entire field contents when searching for a record based on the value of one of the character fields of the record.

______ 11. Both the SUM and the AVERAGE commands can be used with the FOR option to restrict records included in the calculation.

______ **12.** The commands COUNT, SUM, and AVERAGE will give different results if the file is opened with an index than if it is opened without an index.

______ **13.** In generating a report, totals can be calculated for numeric fields only if the data file is opened with an index.

______ **14.** Using the REPORT FORM command to generate a report does not change either the report specification file or the data file.

______ **15.** It would be meaningless to speak of control groups with respect to a file that is opened on its key field.

ANSWERS TO OBJECTIVE QUESTIONS

True/False

1. T 2. F 3. F 4. T 5. F 6. F 7. T 8. F
9. T 10. T 11. T 12. F 13. F 14. T 15. T

ASSIGNMENTS/PROJECTS

1. Print a listing in sequence based on the Points field of all bikers (Assignment 2, Chapter 15) belonging to the Quicksilver club with best finishes of 1, 2, or 3.

2. Print a listing in sequence based on the License Number field of all vehicles (Assignment 3, Chapter 15) that are Type MI and are on yearly leases.

3. Print a listing in sequence based on the Date of Evaluation field of all software evaluation records (Assignment 4, Chapter 15) that are type WP or SS.

4. Figure 14-12 is a report generated from the BILLS file and the Member file. Although you cannot generate this, you can generate a report in which records are grouped by the author. Prepare a report specification file that will print a report with records grouped on author and subtotals on the RATING field. Run the report.

5. Create a report specification for the bikers of Assignment 2, Chapter 15. Total only the Points field. Run two copies of the report: one consisting of all records in sequence based on the bikers' last names, and the other consisting of bikers with a Best Finish of 4 or better in sequence based on Points.

6. Expand the report specification of Assignment 5 to group by the Club field. Include a subtotal and total on the Points field.

7. Create a report specification for the vehicles of Assignment 3, Chapter 15. Total the Monthly Lease Rate field. Run two copies of the report: one consisting of all records in sequence based on the License Number field and the other consisting only of vehicles with a Size field of CO or MI with all CO entries preceding MI entries.

8. Expand the report specification of Assignment 5 to group by the Customer Name field. Include a subtotal and total on the Monthly Lease Rate field.

9. Create a report specification for the software of Assignment 4, Chapter 15. Total both price fields. Run two copies of the report: one consisting of all records in sequence based on the Software product name field and the other consisting only of vehicles with a Category field of FM or SS, with all FM entries preceding SS entries.

10. Expand the report specification of Assignment 5 to group by the Category field. Include subtotals and totals on price fields.

PART FIVE

Advanced Topics

PROLOGUE TO PART FIVE

If you pursue your computer training beyond this first course or make extensive use of a microcomputer, there are a number of topics that you will learn about. Part five includes brief descriptions of several of them. For instance, in Chapter 17 you will learn more about how an operating system works and some of the features of other operating systems. Chapter 18 introduces you to programming languages and principles of programming. You will follow through in Chapter 19 by learning how to program using the programming capability of dBASE III. In Chapter 20 you will learn about sharing computer resources through the interconnection of computers to form networks both by direct wiring and through the telephone system.

Chapter 17

More About Computer Software

OBJECTIVES

By now you are familiar with DOS and a variety of software packages and have sufficient knowledge to appreciate some of the finer points of software to which this chapter is devoted. When you have completed this chapter, you should be able to describe:

- The components of DOS and how they interact in controlling actions of the computer.
- The principle of memory management whereby the computer memory is divided into different functional segments.
- Resident programs that can be loaded into memory and be called even while you are running another program.
- Problems associated with using two or more programs including transfer of data from one program to another.
- Integrated software packages in which word processing, spreadsheet, and database management are combined into a single program.
- Multitasking whereby two or more programs can be in memory and executing concurrently.

PREVIEW

Operating Systems

An operating system is a collection of programs designed to manage the hardware resources of the computer. In MS DOS, three operating system programs are loaded into memory when the computer is booted: the command processor, the file manager, and the I/O manager. These control overall actions of the computer.

Resident Programs

DOS allows the user to load programs for performing utility type operations into memory; these remain resident while another program, such as a word processor, is being used. At any time, the user can switch from the word processor (or another program) to a memory resident program to perform needed functions, and then back again

Using Different Software Programs

The user of two or more productivity packages (such as WordPerfect and Lotus 1-2-3) is commonly faced with two problems. First, the command structures are different and keystroke sequences used with one are completely different from those used with another, which can lead to confusion. Second, the file formats are different, making the sharing of data among applications difficult, and in some cases impractical.

Integrated Software Packages

An integrated software package is a single program that includes word processing, spreadsheet, and database capabilities. The problems of using different applications are significantly reduced because the command structure for all components is the same and data compatibility among components is built into the system.

Multitasking

Through a combination of hardware and special operating system software, it is possible to have two programs in memory executing concurrently under control of the operating system.

OPERATING SYSTEMS

By this time, you have had some experience using the MS Disk Operating System (MS DOS) that you first learned about in Chapter 5. You have used DOS commands to format a disk, copy and erase files, and display the contents of a disk. You know that a DOS system disk is necessary to boot a floppy disk computer, that you can format a disk as a data disk or as a bootable system disk, and that a system disk includes special files that are loaded into memory when the computer is started. You also know that whenever you complete an activity, whether the execution of a DOS command or running a program such as dBASE, control of the computer is returned to DOS and the DOS prompt is displayed. On a broad basis, DOS provides overall control of the computer. Its functions are:

- to accept, interpret, and execute DOS commands and commands to load and run programs such as WordPerfect (WP) and dBASE (DBASE).
- to control the efficient operation of all input and output devices.
- to maintain order on disks and provide access files that are stored on them.

Note that these capabilities are not unique to microcomputers; indeed, all computers, both large and small, rely on operating systems to manage their resources.

The descriptions of Chapter 5 provided you with sufficient knowledge to use a PC with the software included with this book. However, if you want to take advantage of the full capabilities of the PC and available software, you need to be aware of how DOS works in conjunction with the computer.

The Components of DOS

As you learned in Chapter 5, you can format a disk as either a system disk or a data disk. The difference is that the system disk contains basic components of DOS that must be loaded into memory during the booting operation. If you have issued a DIR command after formatting a system disk, you have observed that the disk appears to contain one file: COMMAND.COM. Actually, this is one of three files, the other two being IBMBIO.COM and IBMDOS.COM. Their entries in the disk directory are encoded such that these file names are not displayed by the DIR command (for this reason, they are called *hidden files*). Also, they cannot be deleted by the DEL command. When the computer is booted up, this trio of programs is loaded into memory, where they remain to provide the overall control of the computer that you have observed. Let us consider the roles, that each plays.

Command Processor—COMMAND.COM. It is the program COMMAND.COM that displays the familiar DOS prompt (A> or C>) and responds to your commands. Remember from Chapter 5 that there are two types of commands: internal and external. The program code for internal commands, such as DIR, is sufficiently short that these are built directly into COMMAND.COM itself. On the other hand, external commands, such as FORMAT, are separate, independent programs that are stored on disk. This includes programs such as FORMAT.COM and other programs that you might run that are not part of DOS. For instance, the dBASE file DBASE.EXE is the dBASE program that is executed by typing the command DBASE from the DOS prompt. The actions taken by COMMAND.COM in response to each of these commands is as follows.

DIR	This is an internal DOS command. Execution of that sequence of the code within COMMAND.COM causes the directory to be displayed.
FORMAT B:	This is an external command. As such, COMMAND.COM loads the program FORMAT.COM from disk into memory and runs it. If the program is not found, an error message is displayed. When the formatting operation is completed, FORMAT.COM returns control to COMMAND.COM.
DBASE	This is a request to run the program named DBASE.EXE. COMMAND.COM searches the disk for this file, and then loads it into memory and gives it control of the computer. When dBASE is terminated with a QUIT, control is returned to COMMAND.COM.

File Manager—IBMDOS.COM. Recall from Chapter 4 that the basic unit of storage on disk is the 512-byte sector, of which there are 720 on the DSDD 5¼-inch disk. Most of these sectors are available to you as user storage for your program and data files. However, some are used for the directory to the disk (which you can display with the DIR command). Others are used for the **file allocation table,** a map of the entire user area of disk indicating whether or not each sector is currently in use. It is the function of the file manager (IBMDOS.COM) to maintain order on the disk. When you perform any file-related activity, such as saving, retrieving, copying, deleting, or renaming, whether with a DOS command or from a program such as WordPerfect, IBMDOS.COM is invoked and monitors the action, and then updates the directory and/or the file allocation table.

When you first format a disk and begin saving files, the file manager places the files on disk in consecutive sectors. For instance, when the data disk that accompanied this book was prepared, the disk was formatted and then all files were copied. Each was placed in the number of consecutive sectors required by its size. On the other hand, for a disk in normal use, as old files are deleted, empty sectors become scattered throughout the disk. Whenever you save a new file, the file manager uses the first empty sectors it finds. Hence, a file occupying three sectors might be stored in three widely separated portions of the disk (see Figure 17-1); files that do not occupy consecutive disk sectors are said to be **fragmented.**

Badly fragmented files can substantially affect the speed of disk processing, especially with a hard disk with its high capacity. This results from the fact that positioning the disk access arms is the most time-consuming part of a disk read operation and reading from fragmented files requires excessive access arm movement. Fragmenting can be eliminated from a floppy disk merely by using the COPY command to copy all files from a heavily used disk to a newly formatted one. For a hard disk, there are programs available that will rearrange all of the files on the disk so that each is stored in consecutive sectors. If you have a hard disk computer, you should consider one of them.

Figure 17-1
A fragmented file on disk.

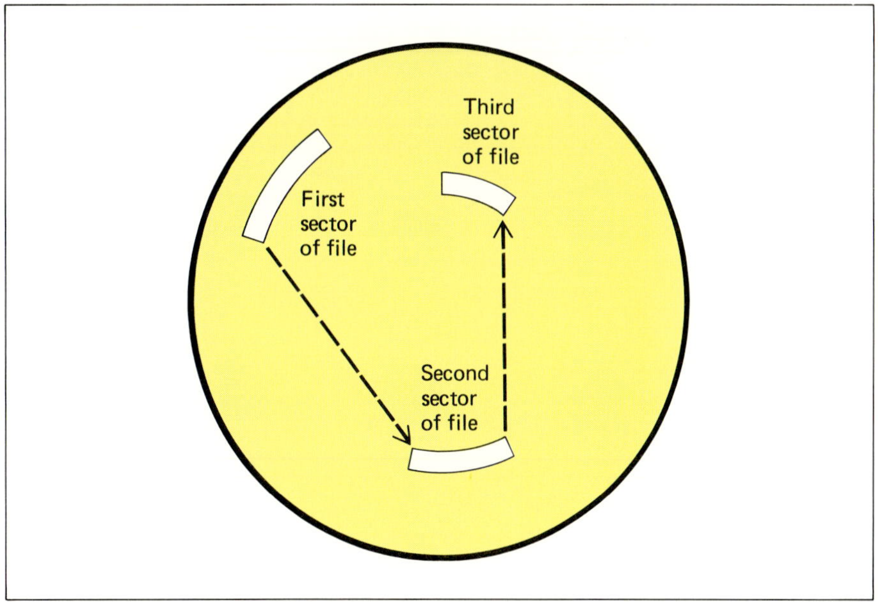

I/O Manager—IBMBIO.COM. All data transfer into and out of the processor from peripheral devices is controlled by the I/O manager (BIO in IBMBIO.COM stands for *B*asic *I*nput/*O*utput). For instance, when you save a WordPerfect document, the I/O manager program writes the file to the sectors indicated by the file manager. When you type a command into the keyboard, the I/O manager reads the character code transmitted as each key is pressed. When it detects the Enter key, it sends the completed command to COMMAND.COM. This is the reason why it is possible to type a command while another is being executed. For instance, while a copy operation is taking place, a DIR command can be entered. When the COPY is complete, the DIR is echoed on the screen and then executed.

Memory Management

One of the characteristics of DOS is the way in which it utilizes the internal memory of the PC. From the hardware perspective, the maximum amount of memory is limited by the internal design of the microprocessor. Because of the number of bits assigned for memory addressing, the Intel 8088 (used in the PC/XT) can address up to 1024K bytes. However, if you have shopped for a computer, you know that the maximum memory available for a PC/XT is 640K bytes. The difference between these numbers is a result of the way in which DOS uses the available memory, as diagrammed in Figure 17-2. Here, you see memory divided into four parts: three used by DOS and one user area. Let us consider each of these.

The last 48K bytes of memory (called **high memory** because it has the high address numbers) consists of ROM: read-only memory that is factory loaded and remains unchanged. Because the original PC was designed to be capable of running without a disk, ROM was essential. In Figure 17-2,

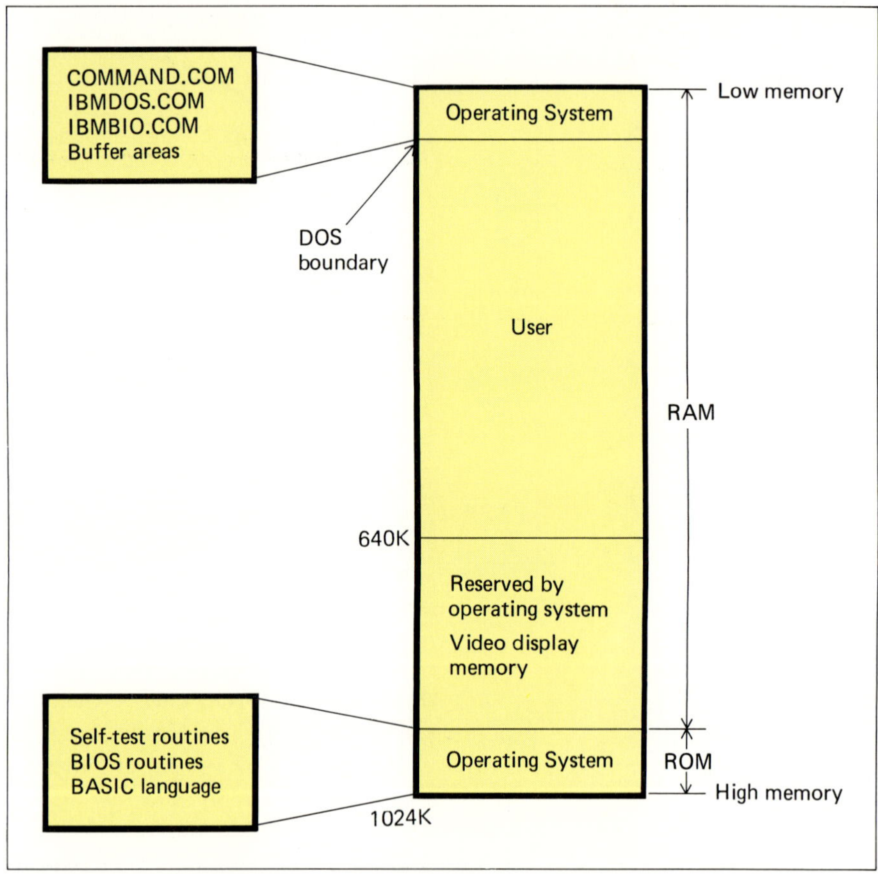

Figure 17-2
Allocation of memory in the IBM PC.

you see that ROM includes three components: self-test routines for testing the computer hardware, the basic I/O system (BIOS), and the BASIC language. (Note that PC/XT Clones are different, in this respect, than their IBM counterparts.) Perhaps you have started an IBM PC without a disk (or a system disk) in drive A. The system boots up from these ROM routines and automatically switches to BASIC, displaying the *Ready* prompt.

From the preceding section, you learned that a system disk contains the three DOS programs COMMAND.COM, IBMDOS.COM., and IBMBIO.COM. When the computer is booted up, a special bootstrap loader program in ROM reads these files from disk and stores them in low memory. The BIOS routines in ROM are supplemented with the more extensive set in the I/O manager IBMBIO.COM. Where the ROM at high memory is a fixed 48K bytes, this low-memory DOS area is not so fixed. In fact, as DOS has evolved through different revisions, the memory required has increased (DOS 3.0 requires approximately 64K bytes and DOS 4.0 requires much more if all its features are implemented). So that user programs will not be loaded over needed DOS routines, the address of the last location required by DOS is stored during the loading process. This is called the DOS boundary (see Figure 17-2) and is referred to by DOS whenever a program is loaded into memory.

In addition to these two memory areas in which the DOS programs reside, the area between the 640K position and ROM is set aside for video memory (for storing the information displayed on the screen) and other DOS uses.

The remaining area of memory, that between the DOS boundary and the 640K position, is available for user programs. This is the area into which programs such as WordPerfect and dBASE are loaded and from which they are run. The 640K mark is commonly called the "DOS 640K barrier" because it limits the amount of memory available to the user. In fact, the full capabilities of the AT computer that uses the more powerful Intel 80286 microprocessor cannot be realized because of this DOS memory restriction. As software has become more powerful and more sophisticated, the memory restriction imposed by DOS has become a limiting factor. Because of the widespread use of DOS, and the huge investment by software companies and users alike, techniques have been developed for expanding user memory of the PC beyond the 640K-byte limit. One such standard was defined by a joint working committee from the major companies Lotus Development Corporation, Intel Corporation (designer of the PC processor chip), and Microsoft Corporation. This standard, commonly called the LIM standard (using the first letter of each company name), involves both software and a specially designed memory expansion board.

One of the important features of IBM PS/2 operating system OS/2 is that this 640K limitation no longer exists. Hence, programs written to be run under OS/2 can be much larger.

Personal Computer Operating Systems

Although most PCs use MS DOS, it is by no means the only microcomputer operating system in use. The Apple Macintosh uses a proprietary operating system designed by Apple specifically for the Macintosh computer. It is considerably different from MS DOS in that commands are executed almost entirely from menu structures, such as that of dBASE III ASSIST. The Macintosh operating system has had a significant influence on the design of software for the PC.

The Unix operating system was developed at Bell Laboratories for use on minicomputers. Because of its power and flexibility, and the fact that it was made available to educational institutions at a fraction of its regular cost, it rapidly became popular in the university environment. It includes such features as: (1) the ability to be modified easily to function with different processors, thereby making it easily adaptable to new computers; (2) a wide array of utilities and software tools, text editors, and communication features; and (3) the ability to run two or more application programs at the same time. Although, at one time, some industry observers anticipated that Unix would replace DOS as the PC standard, this has not occurred.

In 1987, IBM announced the IBM PS/2 and the accompanying operating system OS/2 amid predictions that OS/2 would become the new microcomputer standard because it overcomes many of the limitations associated with MS DOS. Two of the major features of OS/2 are its ability to utilize large memory sizes and to manage more than one program running in the computer at the same time. (This is called multitasking and is described in this chapter.) Although important in many business environments, the multiple program capability is of limited value to the average user of a PC. Hence, there is little incentive for many users to go to the expense and trouble of upgrading to something that will not be of much value to them. Also, extensions continue to be made to MS DOS to circumvent some of its previous shortcomings. The result has effectively been two IBM PC standards.

RESIDENT PROGRAMS

Many software developers have written programs that take advantage of the movable DOS boundary. These utility programs, which enhance the functions of the computer, are inserted between the DOS programs and the user memory. Once loaded, they remain in memory (until the computer is turned off) and can be invoked at any time, even if you are in the middle of a dBASE or Lotus 1-2-3 session. Since they remain in memory, they are called **memory resident** programs. You will learn about three of them in this section: desktop organizers, RAM disks, and memory managers.

Desktop Organizers

A desktop organizer is a utility program designed to help you organize your work with the aid of the computer. These programs typically include a notepad for making and saving notes, a calculator that lets you use your computer keyboard as a hand-held calculator, and an appointment calendar. To illustrate how a desktop organizer works, assume that you are creating a report specification file with dBASE. Halfway through the process, the telephone rings and you are asked if you will be available next Tuesday at 2:30 p.m. for a job interview. Since you keep your appointment calendar in your computer, how do you interrupt the dBASE session in order to refer to the calendar? (Terminating the program and restarting later are a nuisance.) The answer is that you do it with a memory resident desktop organizer program, which can be invoked from dBASE (or other program) without disturbing the current application.

To use it, you must run it (before running your other program) by typing in the name and striking Enter, just as you run any other program. The program is loaded into memory, a message displayed, and control returned to DOS. Note that the desktop organizer is not executed; it is merely loaded into memory as illustrated in Figure 17-3. Repositioning the DOS boundary beyond the memory resident program will protect it from being overlayed by any program that you might load and run. You should be aware that this reduces the amount of user memory you have available for any program you wish to run.

With the desktop organizer loaded and protected by the repositioned DOS boundary, you can run dBASE as if the organizer were never loaded. For instance, referring back to your appointment, assume that you had progressed to the point in defining your dBASE report specification as shown in Figure 17-4(a)—see page 554. To check your calendar, you would

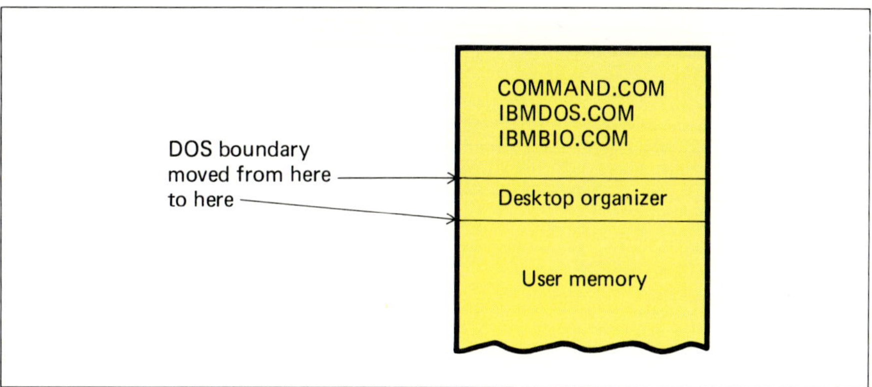

Figure 17-3
A memory resident utility.

strike a special sequence of keys and the organizer would display a window with its menu as shown in Figure 17-4(b). The example shown here is Sidekick, a popular desktop organizer from Borland International. In this case, control of the computer has been switched from dBASE to memory resident Sidekick. Although the computer is now under the control of Sidekick, dBASE still remains in memory. To check your calendar, you would select the caLendar option, which would cause your appointment calendar to be displayed. You could then make your 2:30 Tuesday entry and return to the Sidekick menu. Before returning to dBASE, you might select the Notepad option and make a few notes concerning your thoughts for the appointment. When you are finished, striking the Escape key signals Sidekick to return control to dBASE. Your screen will be exactly as you left it [Figure 17-4(a)] and you can resume as if there had never been an interruption.

RAM Disk

In learning about computers and software, you have worked with relatively basic applications that have not placed heavy demands on the computer. Consequently, you found that each action of the computer took place very quickly. However, for many every-day activities requiring heavy disk access, the time for the computer constantly to read from and write to floppy disk is distressingly long. One way that you can speed disk operations up significantly is to use a **RAM disk.** This is a memory resident utility program that allocates a portion of user memory to serve as a simulated disk drive. Because internal memory operates thousands of times faster than a floppy, a huge improvement in performance results.

For instance, with a two-disk system, in which the floppy drives are A and B, RAM disk software reserves an area of memory and designates it as drive C, as illustrated in Figure 17-5. Once the RAM disk is loaded, DOS sees three drives: A, B, and C. You can use C just as you would use A and B. You can copy software such as a word processor onto the C drive, or you can copy data files, or both. Then access to these files will be at memory speed rather than disk speed.

However, RAM disk is not without its shortcomings. The memory reserved for the simulated disk is taken from the available user memory and subsequently reduces the amount of user memory available for your

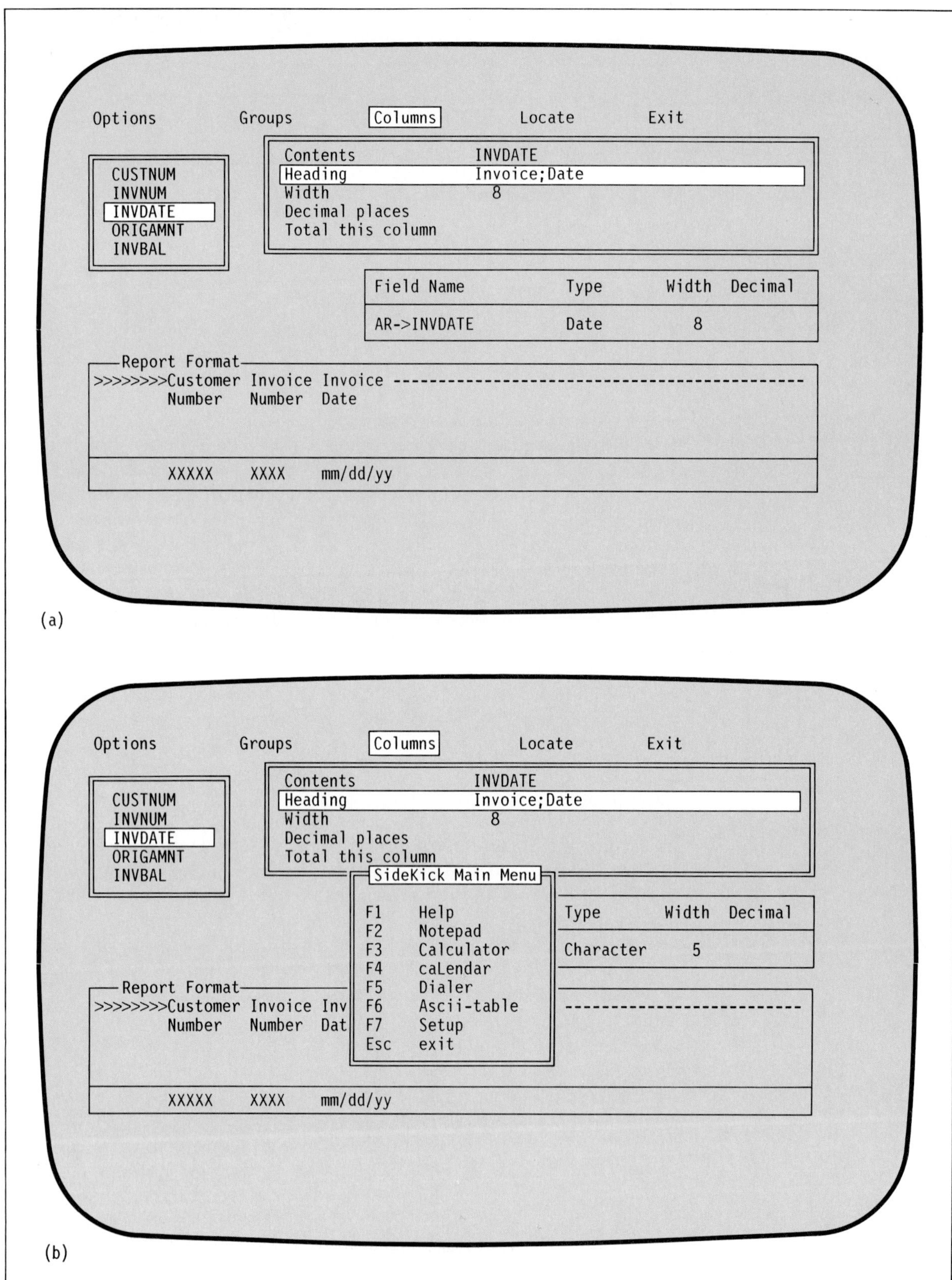

Figure 17-4
(a) The dBASE report specification screen. (b) A window displaying the main Sidekick menu over the dBASE screen.

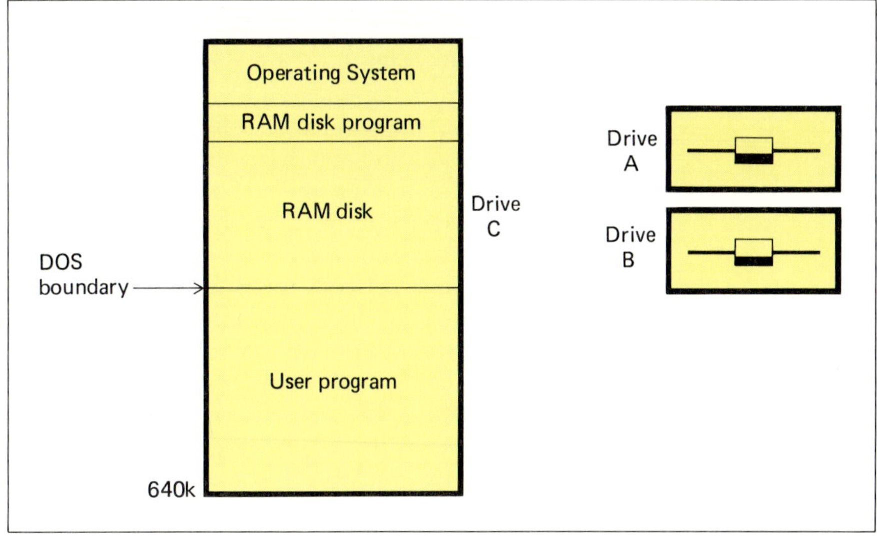

Figure 17-5
Using a portion of memory for RAM disk.

program. This may not be a problem if the memory needs of the program are small. A danger of a RAM disk is that main memory is volatile; that is, if there is a power failure and the computer goes down, everything is lost. Also, it is easy to forget that the data is stored on a simulated disk in RAM and to turn the computer off without first copying the work files from the RAM disk back to the floppy. In spite of these problems, RAM disks are popular enhancements because of the significant speed improvement they provide.

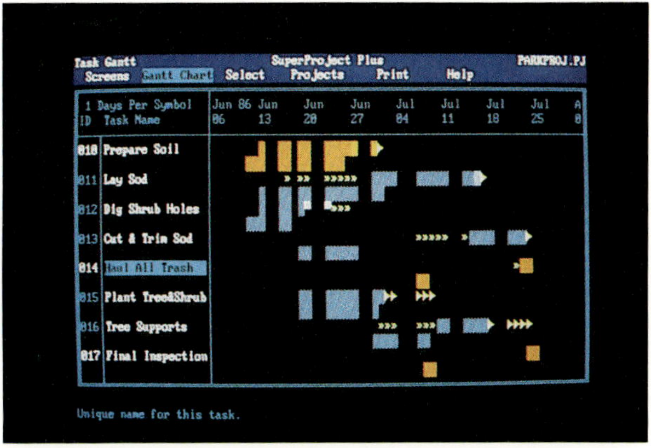

It would be impossible within the scope of this book to describe all of the different types of software available to you. An important category—shown here but not described—is that of project management. Using project-management software, tasks can be coordinated, time tables set, resources summarized, and costs analyzed.

Memory Management Software

You have seen how it is possible to have a utility in memory (the desktop organizer) together with a program and to switch between the two. A memory manager is a utility, loaded in the same way as Sidekick, that allows you to have two or more programs in memory at the same time and to switch among them. For example, assume that you are using a word processor to write a description of how to use a spreadsheet application you have prepared. To describe the details of entering data into rows and columns is difficult to do from memory. It would be much simpler if you had two computers: one into which you typed the directions with the word processor and the other with which you could try each spreadsheet action. The memory management program Software Carousel allows you to do this on a single computer.

Once Software Carousel is loaded as a memory resident utility, you can divide the available user memory into two partitions (or more) and load the word processor into one and the spreadsheet software into the other, as illustrated in Figure 17-6. From the first partition, you can run the word processor and proceed to type your report. At any point, you can switch to the other partition and run the spreadsheet program to check out features that you are writing about in your report. As you switch from one program to the other (done with a simple key sequence), the status of both programs is preserved. For instance, if you use the word processor, switch to the spreadsheet program and perform some actions, and then switch back to the word processor, the word processor is as if you had never left. Although both programs reside in memory at the same time, only one is running at any given time. For example, you cannot have the spreadsheet performing calculations while you work on the word processor. As you will learn later in this chapter, there are hardware/software combinations that do allow this.

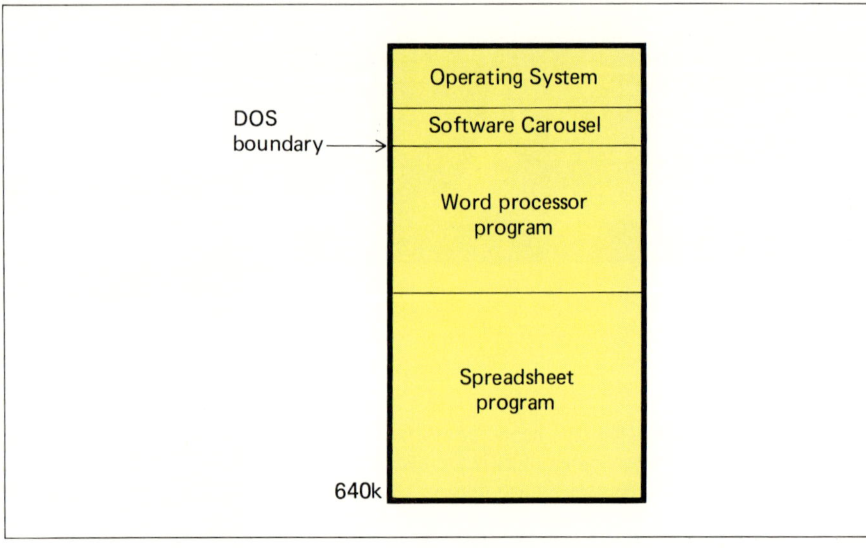

Figure 17-6
Two user programs in memory at the same time.

USING DIFFERENT SOFTWARE PROGRAMS

In the average work environment, many computer users find themselves using two or more different programs for their different processing applications. When these programs are written by different software companies (which is commonly the case), the user is presented with two new problems: differences in the user interface and incompatible file structures.

The User Interface With Software

The way in which a software program communicates with the user and the user enters commands is called the **software interface.** The software interface and command structure for each program are optimized according to (1) the type of program (for instance, word processor or spreadsheet), and (2) the ideas of the designer. For those reasons, we find vastly different command sequences from one program to another, as illustrated by the following tables.

	Command or Keystrokes			
Action	WordPerfect	Lotus 1-2-3	dBASE III	dBASE III/ASSIST
Get Help.	F3	F1	F1	F1
Retrieve a file.	Shift-F10	/WR	USE	Set Up/Database file
Save a file.	F10	/WS	Automatic with QUIT	Automatic with Quit dBASE III Plus

	Resulting Action		
Key	WordPerfect	Lotus 1-2-3	dBASE III
Esc	Repeat a command a selected number of times.	Back up to previous menu.	Abort an action.
F3	Display Help.	Display names of designated cell ranges.	No default action. Any action can be assigned by user.

In learning a software product, it takes considerable practice to become familiar with the command structure and the actual key sequences required. Unfortunately, with the environment illustrated by the preceding tables, knowledge of one program is of little help in learning another. In fact, switching back and forth between these pieces of software can be very confusing as your fingers tend to "remember" the key sequences of the software you use most commonly. For example, if you use WordPerfect most of the time, you might find yourself striking F3 for Help when you are using Lotus 1-2-3 or dBASE.

One of the important user features of the Apple Macintosh system is its user interface. Because the Macintosh interface is an integral part of the operating system design, companies that write software for the Macintosh use this standard interface. Hence, the action of, for instance, saving a file is the same regardless of the software being used. This makes learning a new software product much easier because knowledge gained from interacting with the Apple carries over directly to other software. This is a significant advantage of the Macintosh over the PC.

Exchange of Data Between Programs

The different user interfaces found among programs from different companies is an inconvenience to the user, especially the beginner who is attempting to master complex software packages. However, a much more serious problem is that of sharing data between different packages. For instance, you might need to incorporate data from a database application into a spreadsheet. If the database and the spreadsheet software you are using have a common data file format, you can transfer the data electronically. If not, you must enter it through the keyboard, a clumsy and error-prone process, especially if a large amount of data is involved.

Situations in which data from a spreadsheet or database is to be included in a word processing document are quite common. Version 5.0 of WordPerfect allows you to import (bring into a document) files from a number of software packages, including Lotus 1-2-3, dBASE III, and even graphics programs. To illustrate, assume that you must prepare a broad report describing your business and its projected performance in order to obtain bank financing. To this end, you need to merge spreadsheet data and data from your database with text that you will write using the word processor. Furthermore, in order to summarize data and achieve the desired impact, much of the data will be displayed graphically. The overall concept is illustrated in Figure 17-7. The steps of extracting information from the spreadsheet, database system, and graphics program are entirely separate and independent of the creation of the document. Furthermore, it is necessary that the data be extracted and written to disk in a form compatible with the word processor. WordPerfect can import data from many different software products. However, many other word processors are much more limited in this respect.

This problem is significantly reduced if all software components are written by the same software company. For instance, the Software Publishing Corporation (publisher of the PFS series) designed its productivity software components with some common data file formats. Since the software products of Software Publishing are specifically designed to work with one another, the process of passing information from one product to another is considerably simplified.

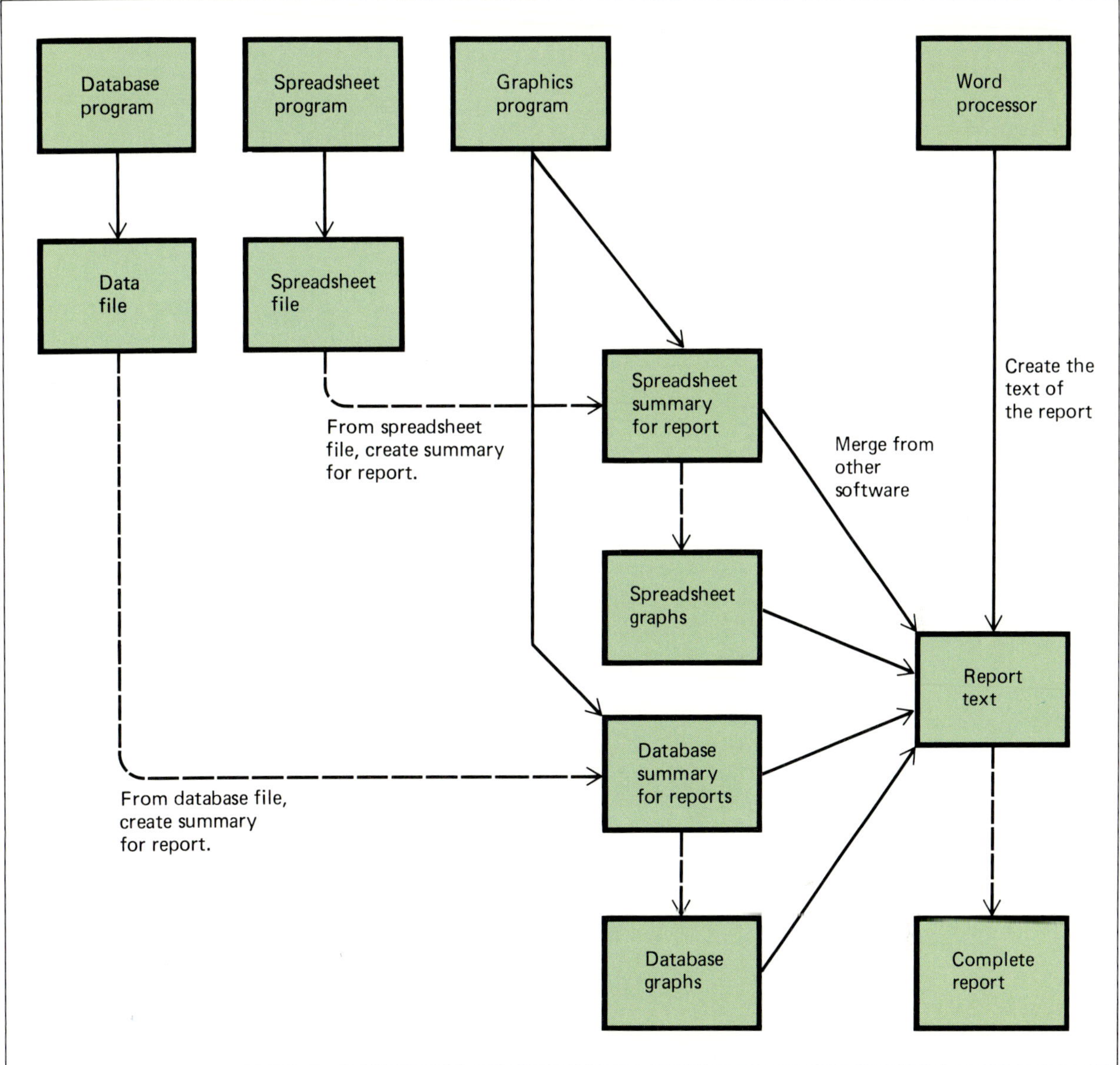

Figure 17-7
Assimilating information from independent software components to generate a report.

INTEGRATED SOFTWARE PACKAGES

What Is Integrated Software?

An integrated software package is one that includes all of the common productivity functions under the control of a single program. Thus, a single integrated package will typically provide the following features.

- Word processing
- Spreadsheet
- File management
- Graphics
- Data communications (this topic is described in Chapter 20)

Such packages feature (1) a common interface with all components and (2) ease of exchanging information between components. Three commonly encountered products are Symphony (Lotus Development), Framework (Ashton-Tate), and First Choice (Software Publishing). To understand how such systems work, let us compare the group of programs you have used—WordPerfect, Lotus 1-2-3, and dBASE III—with Framework from Ashton-Tate, the publisher of dBASE III.

WordPerfect stores a document together with word processing codes on disk as a file; Lotus 1-2-3 stores a spreadsheet together with spreadsheet codes on disk as a file; dBASE III stores a data file together with database codes on disk as a file. Figure 17-8 illustrates how the three products are clearly isolated from one another. If you attempted to retrieve a Lotus 1-2-3 spreadsheet or dBASE data file with WordPerfect, your screen would display a lot of garbage because WordPerfect would not know what to do with the codes of the other programs.

On the other hand, Framework, which has capabilities for all three functions, also stores documents, spreadsheets, and data files as files on disk, each with it own type of codes. However, each type of file is directly accessible from the Framework program, as illustrated in Figure 17-9. The name of the program is derived from the fact that Framework operates on units of information called *frames*. Each word processing document that we

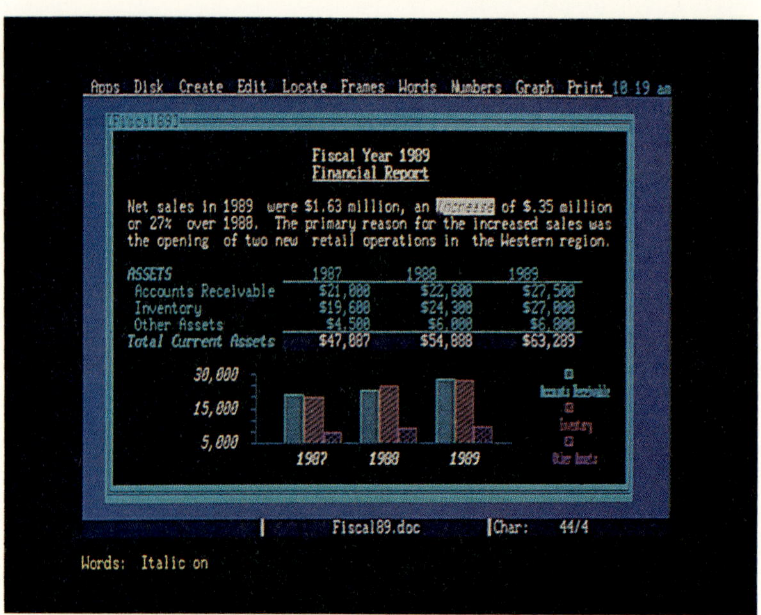

In this photo you see a color screen from Framework, an integrated software package that combines word processing, spreadsheet, file management, graphics, and data communication.

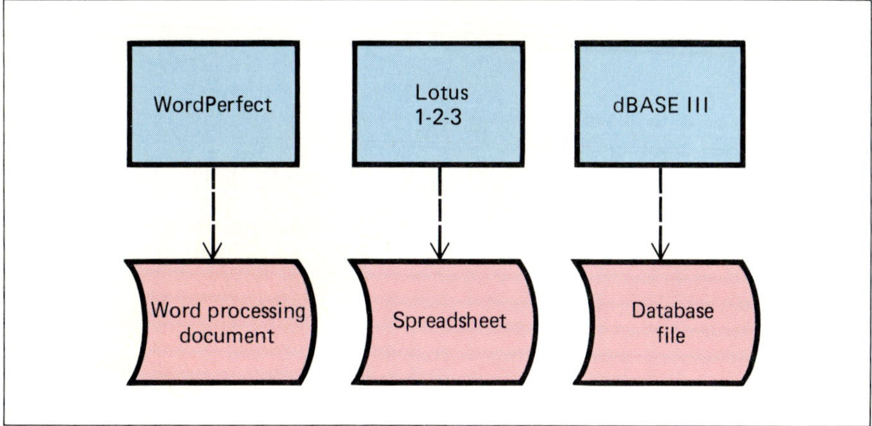

Figure 17-8
Independent software programs.

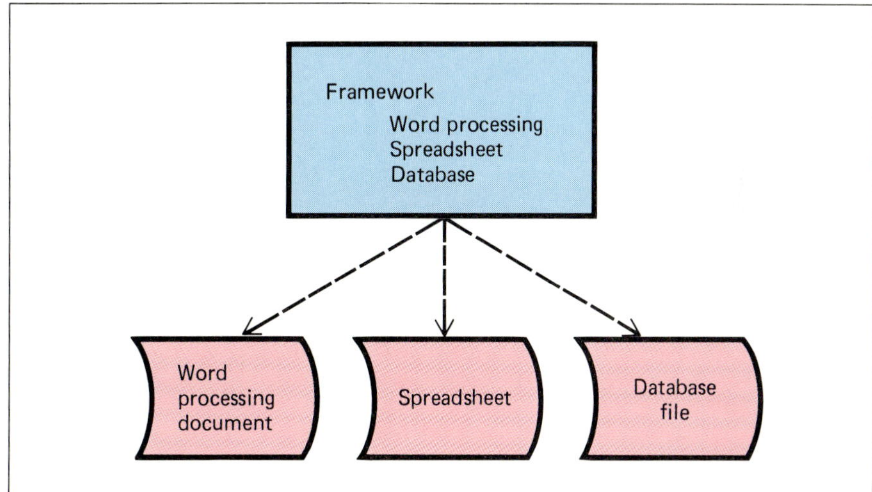

Figure 17-9
Components of Framework.

think of as a file with WordPerfect is called a *word frame* in Framework. Similarly, spreadsheets are stored as *spreadsheet frames* and database files as *database frames*. In addition, graphs can be stored as *graph frames*. Switching from one to another during a Framework session is simple.

To see how Framework integrates these functions, consider preparing the report that is to combine spreadsheet, database, and graphics into a document (Figure 17-7). Framework activities are selected from the bar menu of Figure 17-10, which is used in much the same way as the bar

Figure 17-10
The Framework main menu.

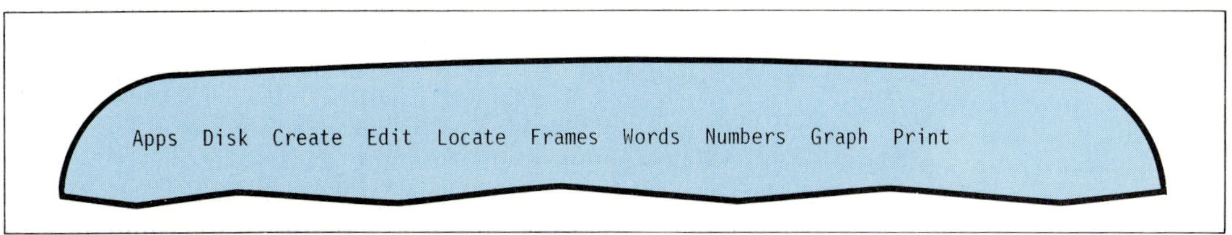

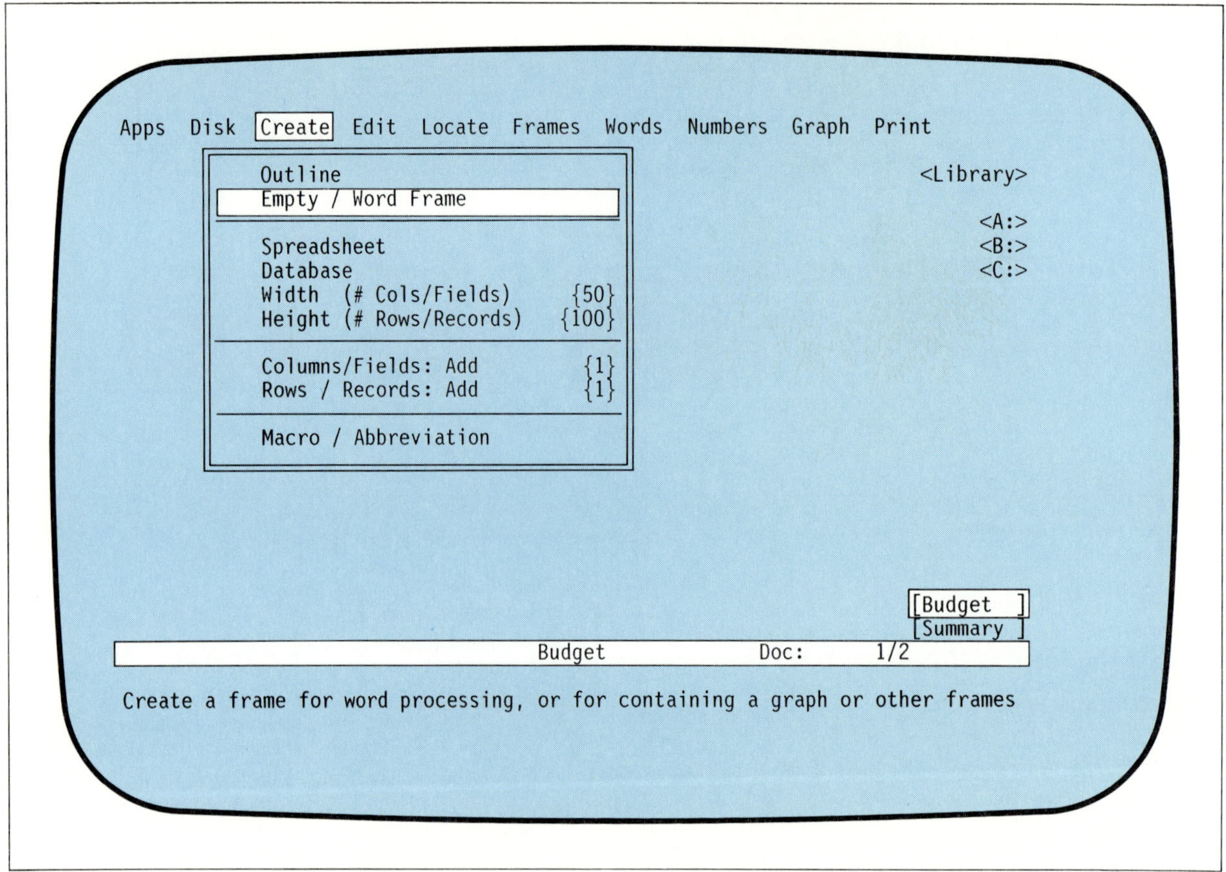

Figure 17-11
The Framework Create menu.

menu from dBASE ASSIST. In Figure 17-11, the Create option has been selected, producing the submenu shown. The highlighted *Empty / Word Frame* option will switch Framework into its word processing mode, from which you can begin entry of your report. At any time while entering your document, you can return to the menu and select a spreadsheet, database file, or graph to work on. You can even display more than one frame on the screen at once; for example, Figure 17-12 shows a screen on which both a word frame and a spreadsheet frame are concurrently displayed. Switching from one to another involves no more than a simple keystroke. Generating a graph frame from the spreadsheet frame is done in much the same way a graph is created in Lotus 1-2-3. Because of the limited size of the screen, Framework overlaps display frames as shown in Figure 17-13, which includes a graph of the spreadsheet data. Whenever you have more than one frame open, Framework allows you to zoom in on any frame on the screen; this causes that frame to occupy the entire screen and the others to disappear temporarily.

It is a relatively simple matter to form larger frames composed of individual frames, such as those on the screen in Figure 17-13. That is, you can combine word processing, spreadsheet, database, and graph frames into Framework *document* frames, from which you can prepare printed

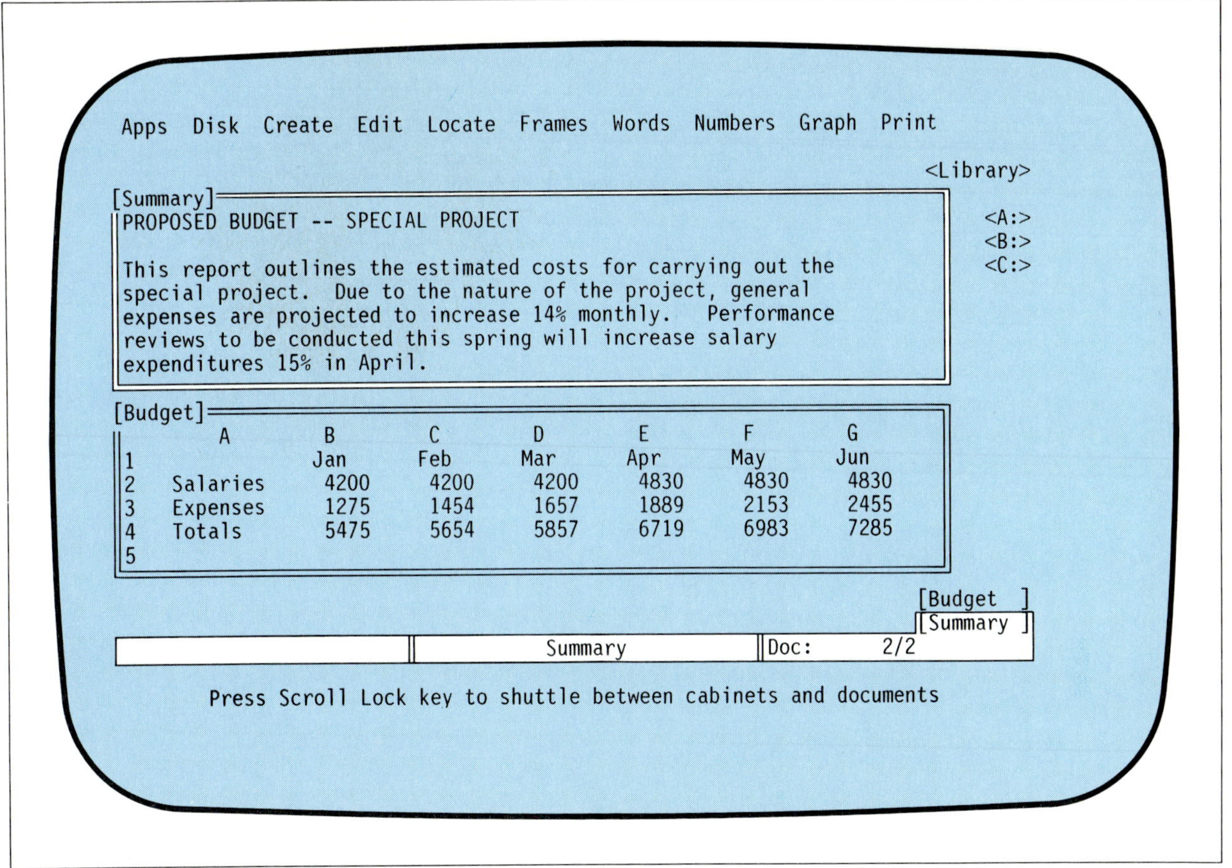

Figure 17-12
A Framework word processing frame and a spreadsheet frame displayed concurrently.

reports. The functions of Figure 17-7 are performed easily with Framework.

Advantages and Disadvantages of Integrated Packages

For the person who must use the three primary productivity tools of word processing, spreadsheet, and database management, integrated software offers the significant advantages of the common interface and file compatibility. However, although the individual components of the package are good, they do not match the top individual programs. For instance, consider the spreadsheet component. In attempting to produce the best possible spreadsheet component, the designers of this portion of Framework were restricted by the requirements of integrating with other components of Framework. The designers of Lotus 1-2-3 had no such compatibility restrictions and could focus solely on optimizing the spreadsheet program.

Actually, advantages and disadvantages depend to a degree upon the needs of the user. For instance, consider the following typical types of users.

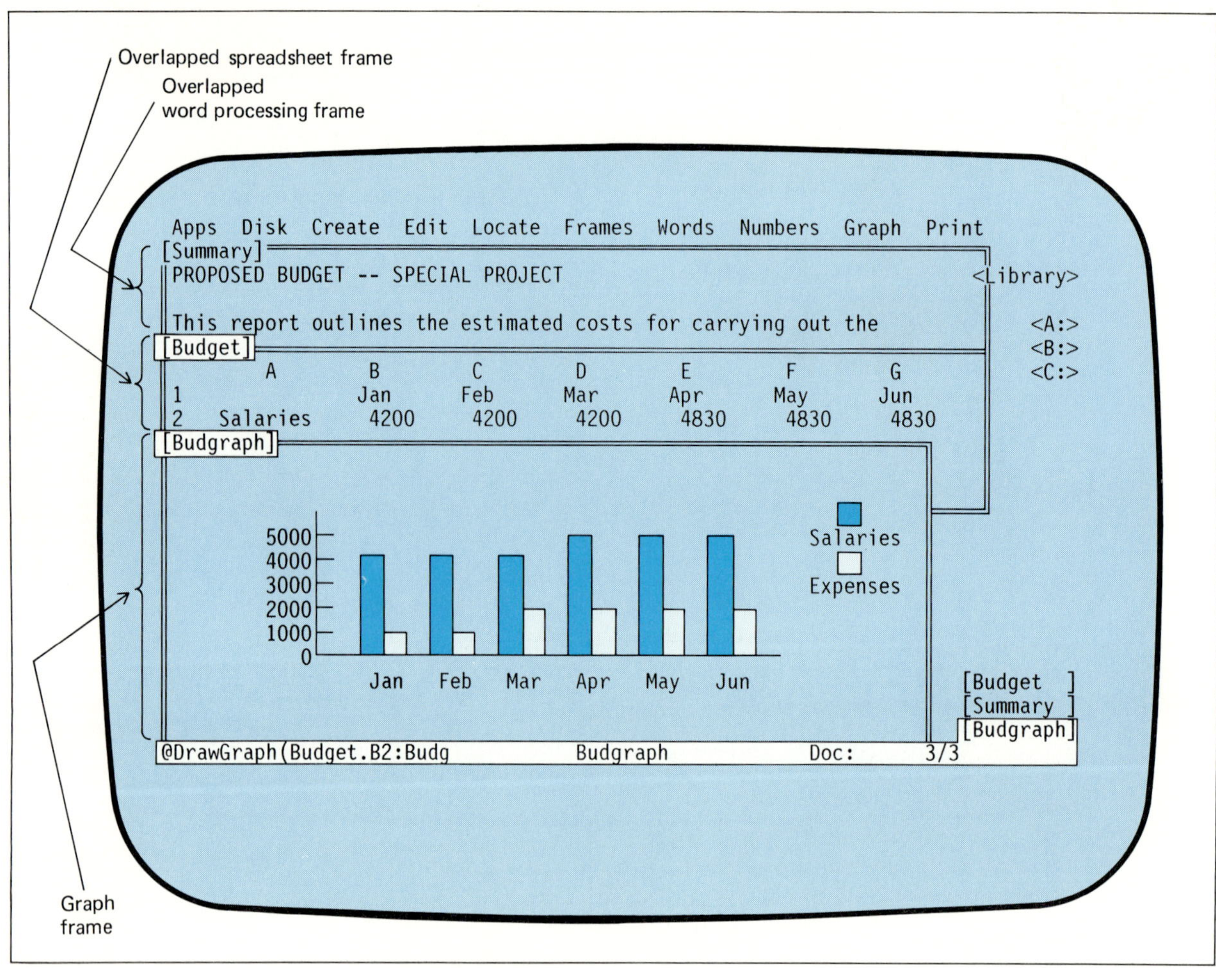

Figure 17-13
Overlapping frames.

- Light user of one program component
- Heavy user of one program component
- Light user of all three components
- Heavy user of all three components with no need for data exchange
- Heavy user of all three components with need for data exchange

Obviously, an individual who will be using only one component (such as a word processor) has no need for an integrated package. A person who makes light use of all three components will find an integrated package convenient because of the common interface. Generally, the heavy user of any software looks for the optimum individual packages for his or her type of work. An integrated package usually does not fill this bill. The inconvenience of totally different user interfaces is nothing more than an annoyance for the person who frequently uses each of the components. If considerable data exchange between components is needed, then individual software packages must be compatible with one another. An integrated package guarantees this and vastly simplifies the process of creating documents consisting of data from spreadsheets, database files, and graphs.

System Integrators

Another way of integrating these software components is with a **system integrator,** a program that controls access to individual software elements as illustrated in Figure 17-14. For instance, in using Microsoft Windows, you would first run Windows. Then you would have access through Windows to programs such as WordPerfect and Lotus 1-2-3 in much the same way that you have access to word, spreadsheet, graph, and database frames when using Framework. At any time, you can switch to another activity simply by loading the desired software into another window. For example, if you needed information from a spreadsheet, you could load the spreadsheet software. Then you could switch between applications with only a few keystrokes. Upon your return to a previous application, everything would be exactly as it was before the change. The overall effect from the user viewpoint is similar to that of an integrated package such as Framework.

Unfortunately, a program such as Microsoft Windows is not the "universal" solution. Not all software is compatible with Windows. Although most software products can be run under Windows, the full features of Windows are available only to those programs specifically designed to interface with Windows. Also, because of its size and complexity, Windows places heavy demands on computer memory and the microprocessor. In fact, most users consider Windows performance on a PC/XT (which uses the 8088 microprocessor) so slow that it is unacceptable. On the other hand, the power of the 80286 and 80386 microprocessors makes them much more amenable to Windows.

Multitasking

Although two or more programs can reside in memory simultaneously, the processor is capable of executing only one instruction at a time. Thus, at

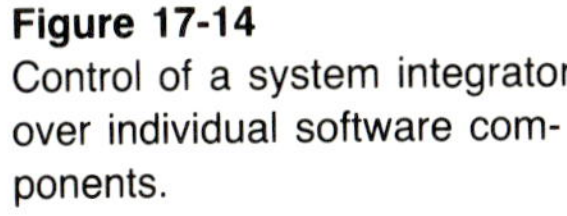
Figure 17-14
Control of a system integrator over individual software components.

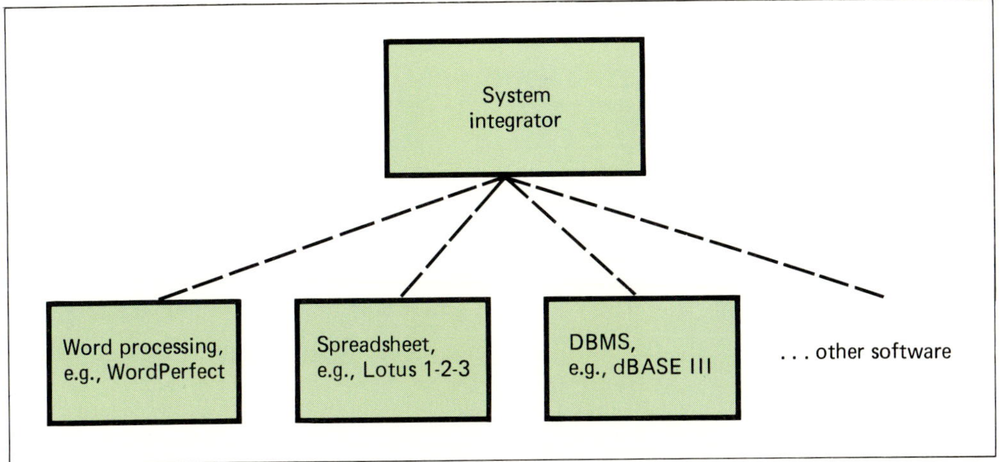

any given time, only one of the programs can have control of the computer and be executing instructions. You are already familiar with this concept from the preceding descriptions of Software Carousel and Windows, where you can manually switch back and forth between applications.

Through the combination of 80386 microprocessor hardware features and special operating systems, this switching back and forth between programs can be done automatically by the operating system so that it appears that two programs are executing at the same time. This is called **multitasking** and each program is called a **task.** One of the features of the IBM operating system OS/2 is that it handles multitasking.

To illustrate multitasking, consider the following scenario. You have a large database file that requires restructuring and updating from data in other files. Once the program to perform these actions is started, it will run by itself; you estimate that the job will take approximately 2 hours. While this program is running, you would like to use the computer to modify an existing spreadsheet. Consider the nature of these two activities.

Database application: Once started, it will run continuously without your intervention. It will involve both processor and disk (I/O) activity taking place at high speeds.

Spreadsheet entry: Your activity of making new spreadsheet entries proceeds only at the rate at which you can operate the keyboard, which is very slow in terms of computer speeds. Responding to your keyboard entry actions will require only a fraction of the microprocessor time; it will be idle while awaiting your keystrokes.

This pair of activities is well suited to multitasking because the operating system can fill in the spreadsheet idle periods with database processing, as illustrated in Figure 17-15. As you can see, the multitasking operating system would give control to the spreadsheet program whenever an entry is made at the keyboard and action is required. However, during the spreadsheet idle periods, control would be switched back to the database application. The transition from one task to the other is performed so

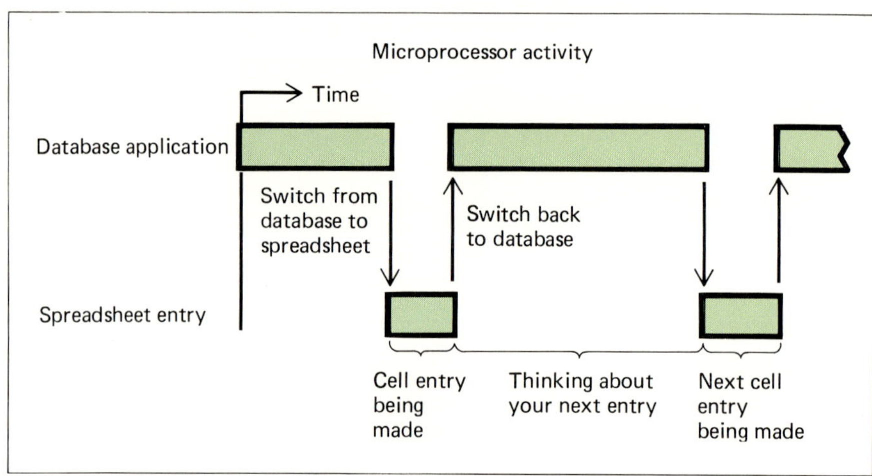

Figure 17-15
Multitasking.

Minicomputers not only allow many tasks to be active in the computer at once but also allow many users working from terminals to use the computer at the same time.

quickly that you would not even notice any delay as you typed your spreadsheet cell entries.

For most of us, the single task capabilities of DOS—supplemented, where needed, by other software—are adequate. However, for certain types of business applications, multitasking provides the means to utilize the resources of the computer more fully.

SUMMARY

This chapter has served to broaden your knowledge of the range of software available for microcomputers. Summarizing, the important items from the chapter are:

- The basic components of DOS are the command processor (COMMAND.COM), the file manager (IBMDOS.COM), and the I/O manager (IBMBIO.COM). When the computer is booted, these programs are loaded into memory, where they perform the following functions.
    - Command processor: Displays the DOS prompt and processes all commands.
    - File manager: Maintains order on disk.
    - I/O manager: Handles all input and output operations.
- DOS divides memory into the following four segments.

- The DOS area: This portion of low memory contains the three program components of DOS together with buffer areas required by DOS as well as memory resident programs loaded by the user. The end of this area is called the DOS boundary, the address of which is "remembered" by DOS.
- Beyond the DOS boundary and up to the 640K address is user memory.
- The area from 640K to 976K is reserved by the operating system. A portion is used for video display memory.
- The last 48K is ROM and contains basic routines necessary to operate the computer without a disk.

A resident program is one that is loaded into low memory (immediately beyond DOS) and remains in memory while the computer is in use. Memory resident programs can be invoked at any time from other software programs with simple key sequences. Examples of memory resident programs are:

- Sidekick, a desktop organizer that includes such features as a calendar and notepad.
- RAM disk, which allows a portion of memory to be set aside to simulate a high-speed disk.
- Memory management software such as Software Carousel, which allows you to have more than one program in memory at one time and to switch between them.

An integrated software package is one that includes word processing, spreadsheet, database management, graphics, and data communications.

The advantages of an integrated software package are a common user interface and file compatibility among components. A disadvantage is that individual components are not as powerful as specialized software programs.

Multitasking allows two or more programs to run concurrently on a computer. This is done under the control of a multitasking operating system that can switch automatically between programs.

NEW TERMINOLOGY

The following are important new terms introduced in this chapter; you should be familiar with each of them.

desktop organizer
file allocation table
fragmented file
high memory
integrated software
memory management
memory resident program
multitasking
RAM disk
software interface
system integrator
task

REVIEW QUESTIONS

1. If you inserted a disk formatted as a system disk into the B drive and typed the command

```
ERASE *.*
```

how much free space would you have on the disk when the erasing was completed?

2. Describe how the actions of the command processor, file manager, and I/O manager are interrelated.
3. A user loads a RAM disk and two other memory resident programs before beginning work with a word processor. How do you think either of the memory resident programs is kept from overlaying the RAM disk in memory when loaded?
4. What is meant by the term *user interface?*
5. Integrated software packages and software integrators both provide the capability for switching between applications (for example, between word processing and spreadsheet) without terminating either session. What is the difference between an integrated software package and a software integrator?
6. A multitasking operating system and a memory management program such as Software Carousel both allow two or more programs to be in memory at the same time. Both provide for switching back and forth between programs. How does a multitasking operating system differ from Software Carousel?

MATCHING

Match each term in a to h with the most appropriate description in 1 through 8.

a. DOS boundary
b. RAM disk
c. fragmented file
d. multitasking
e. command processor
f. system integrator
g. integrated software
h. file allocation table

1. The activity of having two or more programs in memory at the same time with execution continuously switching between them under the automatic control of the operating system.
2. A software package that includes word processing, spreadsheet, and database management.
3. Prevents user programs from wiping out memory resident programs.
4. Speeds up disk operations.
5. Results from the continual addition and deletion of files on a disk.
6. Loaded into memory during the booting operation and remains there during operation of the computer.

7. Used and maintained by the file manager.
8. Allows two or more programs to be used together as if they were part of a single integrated program.

TRUE/FALSE

Determine whether each of the following is true or false.

_____ 1. The command processor (COMMAND.COM) must be in memory at all times that the computer is running under DOS.

_____ 2. The file manager maintains order on the disk but it does not do the actual writing of files to disk.

_____ 3. After the computer boots up and loads the necessary DOS programs, it sets the DOS boundary, which becomes a fixed address that cannot be changed.

_____ 4. Although the 8088 microprocessor can address up to 1024K bytes, DOS does not allow user addressing above 640K.

_____ 5. The user memory restrictions of DOS and OS/2 are the same.

_____ 6. No more than one memory resident program can be in memory at any given time.

_____ 7. With a memory resident program, it is possible to, for instance, be working on a spreadsheet, switch to the memory resident program to make some notes, and then switch back to the spreadsheet as if you had never left.

_____ 8. A RAM disk reduces the memory available to you for running a program.

_____ 9. The primary function of a program such as Software Carousel is to allow you to switch from an application program to a memory resident program and back again without losing any data of the application program.

_____ 10. The user interface is the way in which a program interacts with DOS.

_____ 11. One advantage of the Macintosh over the PC is that the user interface is the same for all software, so that knowledge gained with one software package can be applied to another package.

_____ 12. If a Lotus 1-2-3 spreadsheet file is retrieved with WordPerfect, the spreadsheet will be displayed properly because WordPerfect will recognize the Lotus 1-2-3 internal codes and interpret them correctly.

_____ 13. Framework is called an integrated software package because it combines word processing, spreadsheet, and database management into a single software package.

_____ 14. A system integrator is capable of taking two or more productivity software programs and combining them into a single package so that they become fully integrated.

_____ 15. Multitasking cannot be done with MS DOS.

ANSWERS TO OBJECTIVE QUESTIONS

Matching

1. d 2. g 3. a 4. b 5. c 6. e 7. h 8. f

True/False

1. T 2. T 3. F 4. T 5. F 6. F 7. T 8. T 9. F
10. F 11. T 12. F 13. T 14. F 15. T

Chapter 18

Programming Languages and Programming

OBJECTIVES

In earlier chapters, you learned how to use spreadsheet software to solve certain types of problems and database management software to organize and manipulate data. These software tools are designed to be used for specific types of applications. On the other hand, programming languages are much more general tools, as you will learn in this and the next chapter. When you have completed this chapter, you should be able to:

- Describe the characteristics of a computer program.
- Distinguish between a machine language and a high-level language.
- Recognize the characteristics of the commonly encountered languages FORTRAN, BASIC, C, Pascal, and COBOL.
- Understand the process of converting a program from a high-level language to the computer's machine language so that it can be run on the computer.
- Describe the program design aids pseudocode and flowcharts used by programmers in preparing a program solution to a problem.
- Describe the basic structures of structured programming, an organized approach to problem solving.

PREVIEW

What is a Computer Program?

A program is a set of instructions describing actions to be taken by the computer in processing data to produce desired results. Programming languages provide the programmer with the means for preparing programs.

Low-Level Languages

The computer operates in a machine language that is composed of binary ones and zeros. Ultimately, all directions to the computer must be in this form. For certain applications, the computer can be programmed using a symbolic language that is closely related to the language of the computer.

High-Level Languages

High-level languages are designed to be like English or algebra so that they can be used without a detailed knowledge of how the computer works. Through industry-wide cooperation, some high-level languages have been standardized so that they can be used on the computers of many different computer manufacturers.

Language Translation

The key to high-level computer languages that are independent of the hardware details of the computer is the language translator. A translator is a program that converts programs written in high-level languages to the language of the machine.

The Program Development Cycle

If an application is to be put on the computer, there is a clearly defined set of steps that should be followed: defining the problem to be solved, and then planning, implementing, testing, and documenting the solution.

Program Design

Before a program can be written, a solution must first be outlined: this is the planning or program design phase. Flowcharts, structured techniques, and pseudocode are some of the tools used in program design.

WHAT IS A COMPUTER PROGRAM?

In using Lotus 1-2-3, you entered data into cells, as well as formulas that describe actions for the computer to take in determining the contents of other cells. In a broad sense of the word, you *programmed* a worksheet to perform calculations in order to solve a problem. In using the worksheet, you saw the computer instantly display the computed results when you entered new data. In calculating your results, the Lotus 1-2-3 program converted each of your formulas to a sequence of binary encoded instructions, which the computer used in carrying out the calculations. For instance, consider the following formula, which was assigned to cell E12.

```
+4*B3+D12
```

The English form of a sequence of instructions to perform this calculation would be:

> Get the number from the memory area reserved for cell B3.
>
> Multiply it by 4.
>
> Add the number from the cell D12 memory area to this product.
>
> Store the result in the cell E12 memory area.

The collection of all such instructions resulting from your worksheet forms a program. A **program** is a series of instructions that describe the actions to be taken by a computer in processing data to produce desired results.

All instructions to the computer must be in a binary form called machine language. However, through the use of special software, the programmer can prepare programs using languages much like English and mathematics. These languages include capabilities for the programmer to do the following: (1) specify files to be processed by the program; (2) perform input operations such as reading from the keyboard or disk into memory; (3) perform output operations, such as displaying results from memory on the screen or writing it to disk; (4) move data from one part of memory to another; (5) perform calculations; (6) compare two data values in memory and use the result of the comparison to determine an action to be taken.

There are many ways to classify computer languages; one is by their level. A **low-level language** is one that reflects the hardware characteristics of the computer for which it is designed. A **high-level language** is one that is written to be independent of an individual computer; its instruction forms are similar to ordinary mathematics or English.

LOW-LEVEL LANGUAGES

Low-level languages fall into two categories: machine language, which is made up of the individual binary encoded instructions that control the computer; and assembly language, a symbolic form of machine language used by programmers.

Machine Language

Machine language is the internal language of the computer. It consists of instructions in binary (made up of zeros and ones) to perform operations such as add two numbers, store the result of an arithmetic operation into a memory location, or compare two quantities. Each make of computer has its own machine language; for example, that for the Apple Macintosh is different from that for the IBM PC, which is different from that for IBM mainframe computers. The following are typical examples of machine language instructions for adding two numbers.

00000011000001100000000000001111	IBM Personal Computer
0101101010100000110000000111000	IBM mainframe computer

The binary encoding of these instructions includes information telling the computer the operation to be performed (add in these examples) and where in memory to find the data. As you will learn later in this chapter, all programs must be converted to machine language before being executed by the computer.

Although all actions of the computer are directed by machine language instructions, the average user is seldom aware of the internal actions; indeed, there is no need. Many users of productivity software use their software packages in preparing sophisticated applications without any knowledge of machine language. And users of high-level programming languages often know little or nothing of the details of the machine language of the computer on which they are running their programs.

Assembly Language

Although the computer uses machine language, programming in machine language is quite impractical. Most programming is done with high-level languages that we shall study in the next section. However, some specialized applications require that the programmer work at the machine level in order to take advantage of the specific capabilities of a particular computer. Assembly languages serve this purpose. An **assembly language** allows the programmer to write instructions equivalent to machine language instructions by using symbolic forms. For instance, the preceding machine language instruction to add two numbers on the IBM PC could be coded as follows using assembly language.

```
ADD   AX,ALPHA
```

This instruction tells the PC to add the number in the memory location identified by the label ALPHA to the number stored in the microprocessor's AX register.

Once a program is coded in assembly language, a special translation program is used to convert it to machine language. Because an assembly language corresponds to the machine language of a particular computer, an assembly language program written for one make of computer cannot be used on another make.

HIGH-LEVEL LANGUAGES

What Is a High-Level Language?

High-level languages remove the user from the details of computer hardware. The two most significant features of high-level languages (as opposed to low-level languages) are:

1. They do not rely on details of the computer hardware—they are *machine independent.* For instance, a program written in the COBOL language can be run on any computer that is equipped with COBOL software.

2. The language is "people oriented" rather than hardware oriented.

That is, instructions to the computer are written in mathematical or English form rather than in binary codes or abbreviations.

Like assembly language, any program written in a high-level language must first be translated into machine language before it can be run on the computer. Hence, if you plan to use a high-level language such as COBOL on two different makes of computer (for instance, a PC and a Digital Equipment Corporation minicomputer), then you must have a language translator written for the PC and another written for the minicomputer. To be able to translate your COBOL program to run on either computer, the COBOL language must be standardized. For instance, IBM cannot use the word READ to get a record from disk storage and Digital Equipment use the word INPUT. They both must be the same or programs will not be transportable between computer brands. In this respect, some languages have been carefully controlled regarding standardization. The language specifications for COBOL, for example, were created through the efforts of a large business/government working committee. The original specifications were introduced in 1960 as COBOL-60. In 1968, the American National Standards Institute (ANSI) established a standard version, which was upgraded in 1974, and again in 1985.

On the other hand, the BASIC language was developed privately and has been "enhanced" by each company that has introduced it on its computers. The end result is that no two versions of BASIC are the same (in fact, some are radically different from the original version). Programs of any substance written for one make of computer cannot be run on another without modification; in some cases, such modifications are major. Although ANSI has defined a small set of instructions that form a standard, the standard is generally regarded as too little and too late.

Let us consider some of the commonly used languages: BASIC, Pascal, C, COBOL, and FORTRAN. All of these can be used with a PC. FORTRAN is described first because it was the first widely used high-level language; it finds limited use on microcomputers. In the descriptions that follow, each language is illustrated with a simple program to accept two numbers from the keyboard, calculate their sum, and print them together with the sum.

FORTRAN

During the early 1950s, when all programming was done with assembly languages of individual computers, computer users recognized the need for a machine-independent (high-level) language. In 1954, the idea for FORTRAN (FORmula TRANslating language) was proposed. This programming language, intended primarily for math/science programming, was to be designed around statements that were as near to English and algebraic terminology as possible. This started a major trend in manufacturer-independent languages, leading to a widespread use of FORTRAN by almost all computer makers. However, one problem that quickly became apparent was the tendency of each computer maker to extend its version of the language to make it better than that of the competition. Since most manufacturers had different ideas about the "best way" to do things, the notion of a language in which a program written in FORTRAN could be run on any FORTRAN-equipped computer was jeopardized. The problem was remedied by the standards organization that preceded ANSI. Through large working committees composed of representatives of computer users as well as manufacturers, ANSI has been successful in defining a "standard" FORTRAN to which manufacturers have adhered reasonably well.

Following is the sample FORTRAN program. From the English form of the indented statements, you can surmise what they do. The DO and REPEAT statements cause this sequence to be repeated five times.

```
DO COUNT = 1,5
  READ *, FIRST, SECOND
  TOTAL = FIRST + SECOND
  PRINT *, FIRST, SECOND, TOTAL
REPEAT
```

BASIC

BASIC (meaning Beginner's All-purpose Symbolic Instruction Code) was developed in 1965 by Drs. John Kemeny and Thomas Kurtz at Dartmouth College as a teaching language. It was designed to be used interactively where beginners could use a keyboard to type programs and data directly into the computer and obtain results of processing almost instantaneously. It is available with virtually every microcomputer because it is easy to use and the BASIC controlling program requires relatively little memory. Because of its widespread use in schools and the fact that it is so easy to use, more people know how to program in BASIC than in any other language. Over the years, a number of hardware and software companies have written versions that are much more powerful than the original teaching version. These find use in many professional programming environments, although other languages, such as COBOL and C, are much more widely used by professionals.

Following is the sample BASIC program. You can see that the statements are similar to those of FORTRAN. The FOR and NEXT statements cause this sequence to be repeated five times.

```
100  FOR COUNT = 1 TO 5
110    INPUT FIRST, SECOND
120    LET TOTAL = FIRST + SECOND
130    PRINT FIRST, SECOND, TOTAL
140  NEXT COUNT
```

Pascal

Pascal was first introduced in 1971 by Prof. Niklaus Wirth in Zurich, Switzerland. His aim was to create a language for teaching that would allow programming to be taught as a systematic discipline where the basic techniques of structured programming (described later in this chapter) could be demonstrated. The acceptance of Pascal as a teaching tool in colleges and universities was rapid and widespread. Although the language is powerful and easy to use, its input and output capabilities are not very sophisticated. Furthermore, it has suffered from the lack of standardization, although the expanded version from the University of California at San Diego (UCSD Pascal) is commonly considered a de facto standard. The programming component of dBASE III (which you will use in the next chapter) was derived from Pascal.

Following is the Pascal version of the sample program to sum two numbers. Note that the sequence of statements to be repeated is bracketed by BEGIN and END.

```
FOR COUNT := 1 TO 5 DO
  BEGIN
    READLN (first, second);
    total := first + second;
    WRITELN (first, second, total)
  END
```

C

The C programming language was the third version of a language developed at the Bell Laboratories during the early 1970s. (The previous versions were A and B.) The design objectives for C were many. It was to have the low-level features of an assembly language to simplify the task of writing operating systems and other system software, and yet it was to have the ease-of-use features of a high-level language, be usable on any computer, and include elements specifically tailored to structured programming methods. C is widely used in the microcomputer field for writing all types of system software.

Following is the C version of the sample program to sum two numbers. Note its similarity to Pascal.

```
main()
{int  count, first, second, total;
   for (count = 1; count<=5; count = count + 1) {
      scanf("%d%d%d", &first, &second);
      total = first + second;
      printf("%5d%5d%6d", first, second, total);
   }
}
```

COBOL

COBOL, meaning COmmon Business Oriented Language, was designed specifically to meet the needs of business data processing with its heavy requirement for sophisticated I/O and file handling. It has been estimated that more lines of COBOL code have been written and are still in use than any other language. Its wide use is the result of several factors: it was the first high-level language designed specifically for business; its specifications were prepared by an industrywide committee and it was carefully standardized; and after its introduction, the government required that all government-leased or -purchased computers include COBOL capabilities.

In spite of predictions by many industry analysts that COBOL has died of old age, it is still widely used.

Following are COBOL statements (1985 standard) to sum two numbers. As you can see, the language is much more English-like than the other languages. This is an advantage because COBOL programs are easily readable, but a disadvantage because coding is slowed with so much to write.

```
PERFORM 5 TIMES
  ACCEPT FIRST
  ACCEPT SECOND
  ADD FIRST TO SECOND GIVING TOTAL
  DISPLAY FIRST, SECOND, TOTAL
END-PERFORM.
```

LANGUAGE TRANSLATION

As described earlier, the computer operates only with machine language instructions. Before any high-level or assembly language program statement can be run, it must first be translated into machine language by another program called a language translator. There are two ways of doing this: translate the entire program and then run it, or translate each statement as the program is being run.

The Compiler

Although assembly and high-level languages differ in many respects, both yield programs that must first be converted into the machine language of the computer to be used before they can be run. This program translation phase is done on the computer by special language processor programs that are available from the computer manufacturer and independent software companies. For many high-level languages such as FORTRAN and COBOL, these translators are called **compilers** and the translating operation is termed **compiling;** for assembly language, the corresponding terminology is **assembler** and **assembling.** The process you would follow in preparing and running a program would be:

1. Write the program in the assembler or high-level language and enter it into the computer. The program in this form is commonly called a **source program.**
2. Load and run the translator program, which converts the source program to machine language. The end result is a machine language program, commonly referred to as an **object program.** This translation phase is represented by diagrams in Figure 18-1.
3. Load the object program into the computer and run it. Note that the object program can be run independently of the source program.

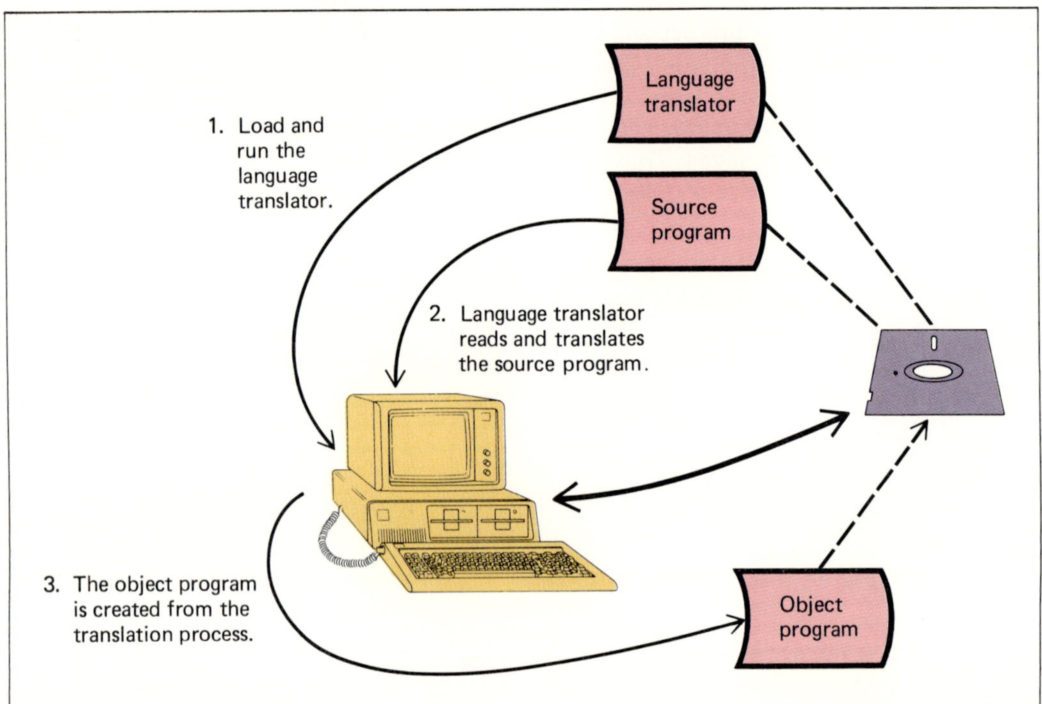

Figure 18-1
Language translation.

Whenever a change is made to a program, no matter how slight, it must be made to the source program. Then the entire program must be translated again to produce a new object program. For large programs, this can be a time-consuming process when a newly written program is being tested and corrected.

The Interpreter

Since BASIC was to be used in schools for teaching beginners so that they could use the computer as a tool, the primary objectives of the BASIC designers were simplicity and ease of use. They desired that there be no separate compiling phase and that the user would continually interact with the computer in entering, running, and correcting the program. To that end, the computer would be under the control of a monitor program from which BASIC source programs could be entered by the user and run without apparent translation. However, when a program is run, the following sequence takes place for each statement of the program (correlate this description with Figure 18-2).

1. The BASIC monitor program (which is controlling the computer) accesses the next high-level program statement.
2. That statement is translated into machine language.
3. The resulting sequence of machine instructions is executed.
4. The executed machine language instructions are discarded.

In other words, each high-level program statement is translated into

Figure 18-2
Interpreting a single statement under BASIC.

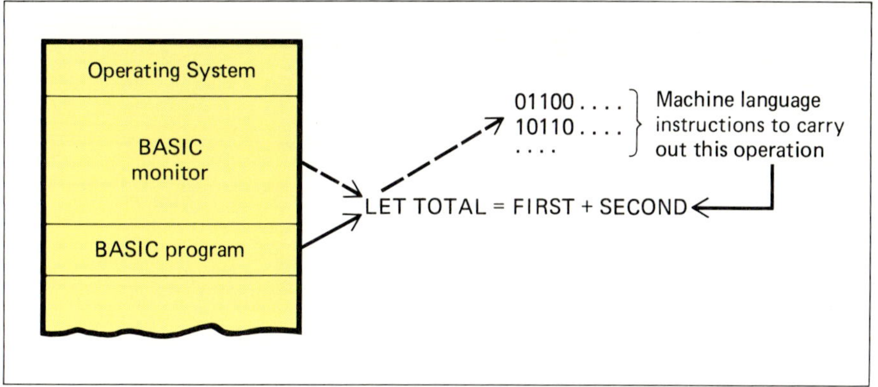

machine language only when it is to be executed. Programming systems that function in this way are called **interpreters.** The interactive design of interpreted languages such as BASIC allows changes to be made easily and quickly and the program rerun. The programmer is always working with the source program; there is no object program with which to contend. Convenience is the obvious advantage. The primary disadvantage is that interpreted programs run more slowly than compiled programs because a given statement of an interpreted program must be translated each time it is to be executed. To yield the best of both worlds, some interpreted languages can also be compiled. Hence, programming development and testing can be done with the interpreter and, when completed, the program can be compiled for everyday use. The dBASE III programming component, which you will learn about in the next chapter, uses an interpreter.

THE PROGRAM DEVELOPMENT CYCLE

In earlier chapters, you learned to use a systematic approach in solving problems with spreadsheet and database management software. A similar systematic approach is critical to using a programming language to solve problems. To this end, the programmer follows a sequence of steps called the **program development cycle,** in which the programmer must (1) define the problem to be solved, (2) design the program (work out a solution), (3) code the program solution using a computer language, (4) test the program, and (5) document the program. (Notice that this sequence of steps is almost the same as the steps described for spreadsheet solutions in Chapter 10 and for database solutions in Chapter 14.)

The average student in a computer software course seldom recognizes the significance of the problem definition phase as problems are carefully defined by the instructor. This is hardly the case in an actual business environment. The programmer is commonly faced with such needs from other departments as, "We require a system to report and perform statistical analyses on student entrance examinations." Before any programming can begin, the exact nature of the problem must be carefully defined,

a

b

c

d

Setting a problem up for computer solution involves a series of steps: (a) facts must be gathered regarding the need; (b) the facts must be integrated, and the general method of solution myst be layed out; (c) the solution must be programmed; (d) the program must be tested and debugged to eliminate errors; (e) finally, the user can utilize the computer output.

e

including the results required and the data available to do the job. Once this is complete, the program design task can begin. The design step (which is often neglected by the beginning programmer) is the focus of the remainder of this chapter.

PROGRAM DESIGN

Developing the overall structure and logic of a program is called **program design.** For programs of any substance, careful design is a critical step because programs can consist of hundreds, or even thousands, of lines of code. Even the slightest error in sequencing statements can cause the results to be incorrect. To aid the programmer in program design, a number of design tools have evolved; let us consider them.

Flowcharts

One of the early tools used for laying out the logic of a program (the sequencing of actions to be taken) is the **flowchart,** which is a logical representation of a problem solution using symbols. For instance, Figure 18-3 is a flowchart that shows the sequence of actions necessary to start a

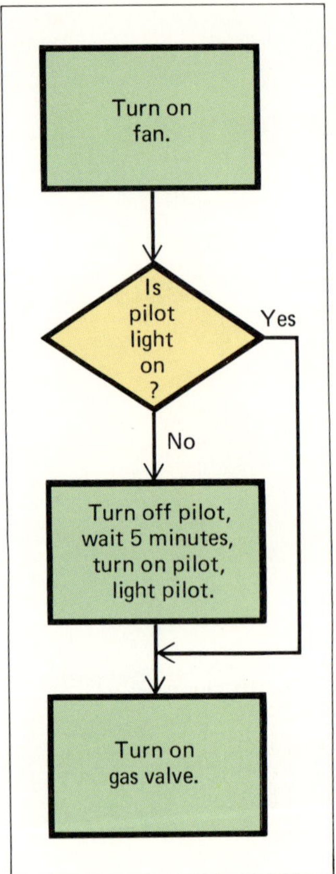

Figure 18-3
A flowchart to light a gas furnace.

gas furnace. Notice that the sequencing of steps, including actions to be taken depending upon a condition, are clearly illustrated. As programming evolved, flowcharting for design became sufficiently important that ANSI published a standard describing standardized flowcharting symbols, with different shapes representing different operations. The flowcharting symbols that are used in this and the next chapter are shown in Figure 18-4.

One of the problems that became apparent early in the evolution of programming was that programmers often focused on details of each flowchart box before carefully assessing the overall logic and needs of the program. The result was commonly a poor program that was "patched" together rather than one that was systematically designed. A more orderly approach to program design came in the mid-1960s when a technique called structured programming was introduced.

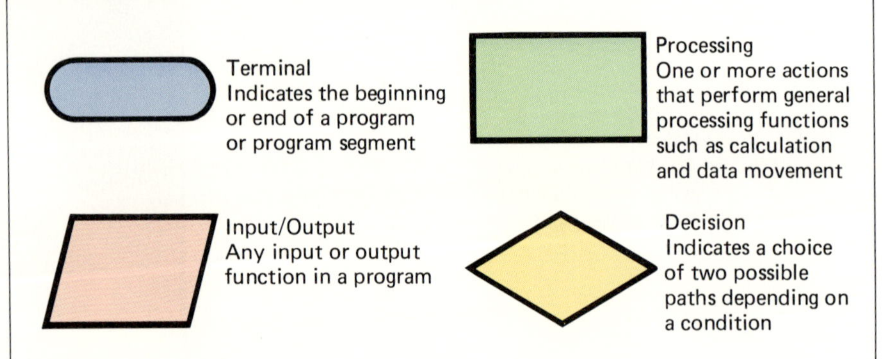

Figure 18-4
ANSI Standard flowchart symbols.

Structured Programming

Structured programming theory is based on the fact that the logic of any program can be expressed using three basic control structures, which provide for sequential actions, conditional actions, and repetition. **Structured programming** is the method of programming that uses only these three structures in preparing a program to solve a problem. Let us consider each of these structures as illustrated by examples.

Sequence. The **sequence control structure** is one in which sets of operations are executed one after the other on an unconditional basis.

EXAMPLE 18-1 **The Sequence Control Structure**

A program is needed to accept a quantity and price entered from the keyboard, to multiply them, giving the amount, and then to display the result.

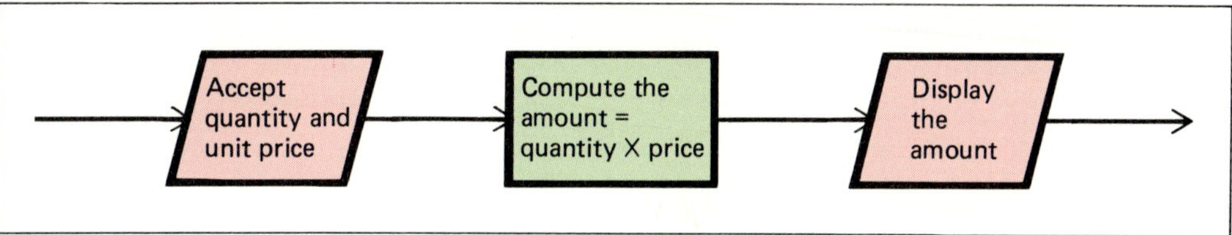

Figure 18-5
The sequence control structure.

This is a sequence of actions, illustrated in Figure 18-5, that must be executed one after the other. Notice that, in this case, their order is significant. That is, the data must be obtained before the calculation can be performed.

Selection. The **selection control structure** provides the capability for performing actions on a conditional basis.

EXAMPLE 18-2 **The Selection Control Structure**

Each calculation of Example 18-1 must be checked. If the quantity is greater than 10, apply a 15 percent discount: that is, calculate the amount as the quantity times the price times 0.85.

In flowchart form, this is represented as shown in Figure 18-6. Notice that it includes a condition to be tested and two possible paths: if the condition is true, the amount is calculated applying the discount; if it is false, the amount is calculated without the discount. Sometimes, a situation arises in which no action is performed for one of the conditions; starting the gas furnace in Figure 18-3 illustrates this special case of the selection structure.

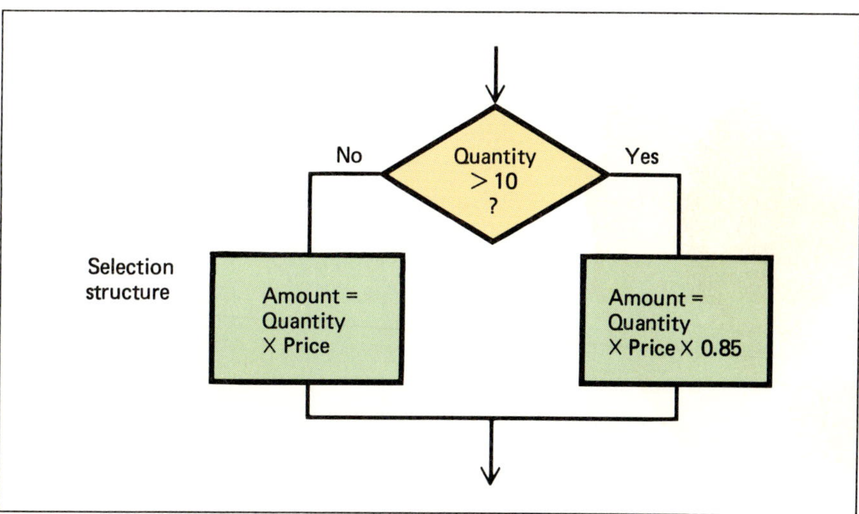

Figure 18-6
The selection control structure.

Looping. The third control structure, **looping,** provides for the repetition of a program or portion of a program.

> EXAMPLE 18-3 **The Looping Structure**
>
> Expand Examples 18-1 and 18-2 to allow the sequence of steps to be repeated until the user decides to terminate.

Repetition of the processing operation is illustrated by the looping structure of Figure 18-7. As long as the condition within the decision symbol is true, the processing will be repeated. Only when the condition is false will there be an exit from the loop. In this case, the condition presumably results from a response by the user. In general, loops are terminated as the result of any number of actions, such as a query by the program to the user, the loop being executed a predetermined number of times, or detecting the end of a data file.

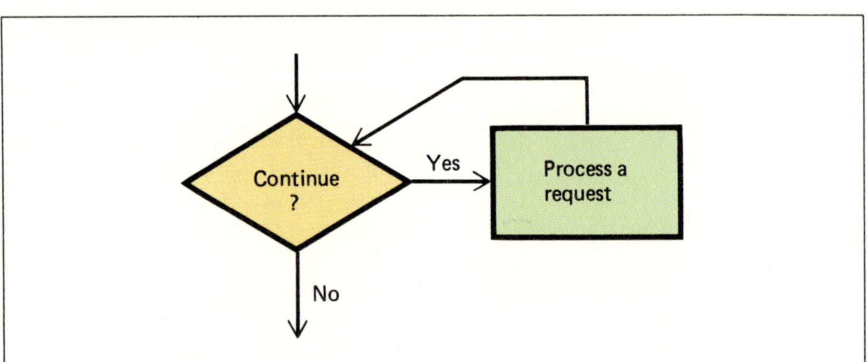

Figure 18-7
The looping control structure.

Sample Flowchart

These three control structures can be used to represent the logic of any programming problem; they form the basis for a systematic approach to computer programming. For example, in Figure 18-8, the three basic forms have been combined to show the logic of the complete version of Example 18-3.

A serious barrier to using flowcharts in program design is that drawing and labeling symbols is very time consuming. Furthermore, changes in logic often require that the flowchart be redrawn. An alternative to flowcharting is the use of pseudocode.

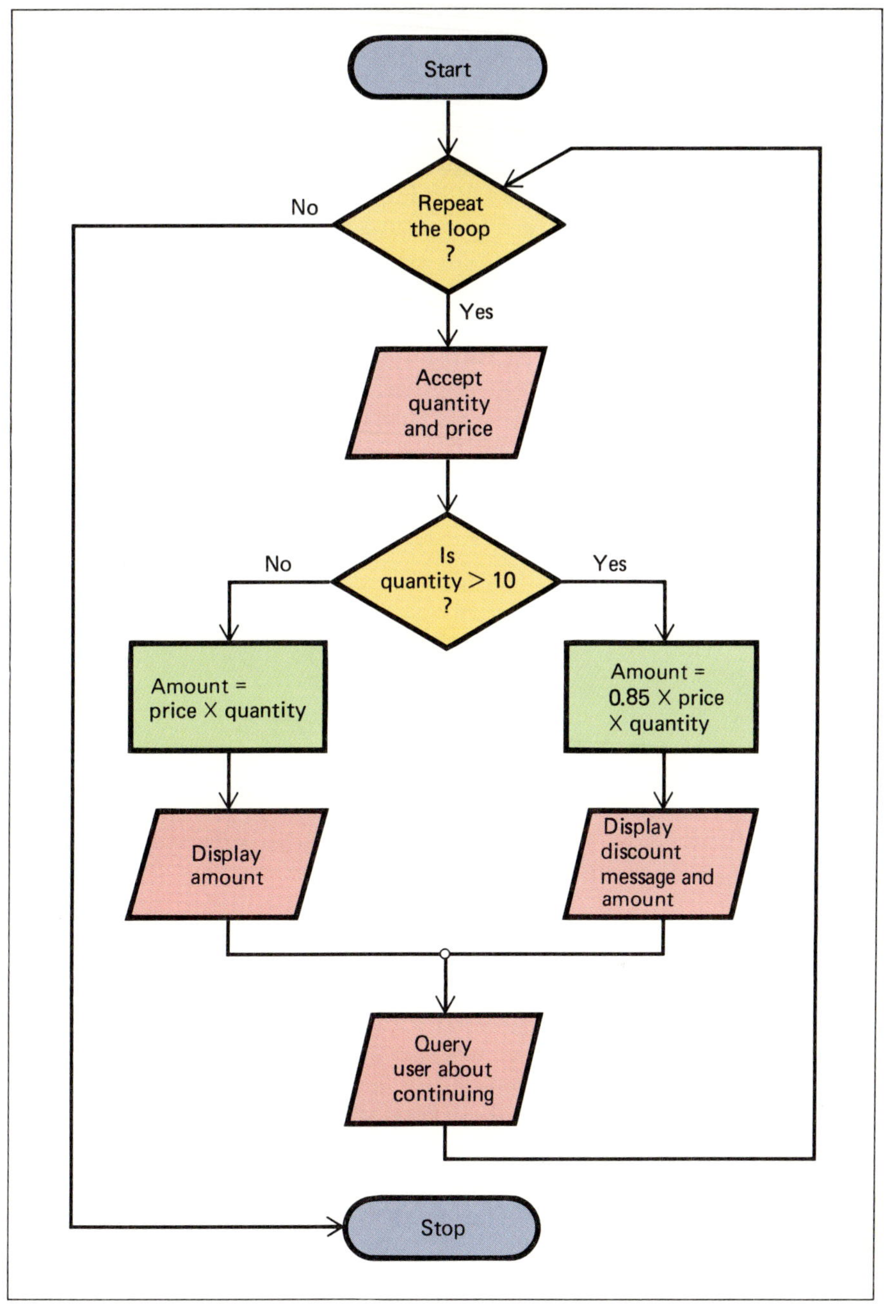

Figure 18-8
Combining structures to form a structured flowchart.

Pseudocode

A **pseudocode** solution to a programming problem is an English description (using structured forms) of the steps to be taken in solving a problem. For instance, in pseudocode, the solution to Example 18-3 takes the form shown in Figure 18-9. In using pseudocode for program design, the broad actions are first specified and then continually refined until a final, detailed solution is obtained. Note that the three structures—sequence, selection, and looping—still form the basis for program design when using pseudocode. In fact, the selection structure is often called the *if-then-else structure,* based on the notion that if a condition is true, then take one action or else take another. Similarly, the looping structure is commonly called the *do-while* because it directs the computer to do something while a condition is true.


```
Do the following sequence while the user wants to continue
   Accept the quantity
   Accept the unit price
   If the quantity is greater than 10
      Compute the amount as quantity times price times .85
      Display a discount message and the amount
   Else
      Compute the amount as quantity times price
      Display the amount
   End of If
   Accept the user response about continuing
End of Do
```

Figure 18-9
Pseudocode for Example 18-3.

One advantage of pseudocode is that the pseudocode solution can be generated using a word processor. As you know from WordPerfect, moving sections of code from one place to another (to handle changes in the logic) is a simple matter. Another advantage is that much of the pseudocode can be included within the program itself as internal documentation describing the program. (All languages provide for the inclusion of comments that are ignored by the compiler or interpreter.) On the other hand, many programmers feel that the program logic is much more evident from the graphic representation of a flowchart than from pseudocode. However, both techniques are valuable program design tools.

Structured Design

With only one chapter in this book devoted to programming, programs that you will write will necessarily be short and relatively basic. However, in the world of the professional programmer (whether the programming is done on a microcomputer or a mainframe), programs are often very large, consisting of many actions to be taken. In fact, some programs are so large and complex that it is almost impossible to envision their detailed logic. For such large problems, a technique called **structured design** is commonly used whereby the overall job is broken down into smaller tasks called **modules.** Structured design is based on the fact that few individuals can grasp simultaneously all of the intricacies and interrelationships of a large, complex program. However, the mind can deal very competently with a small portion of a program or with a large program broken down into a number of small parts.

In using a structured design approach, a large job is broken down into smaller modules. Each module is further broken down until the entire job is represented as an interrelated collection of modules, each performing a basic task. This is a valuable technique that is widely used by professional programmers.

SUMMARY

This chapter has given you a basic understanding of programming languages and program design. Summarizing, the important items from the chapter are:

- Programs consist of instructions to the computer for processing data to produce a desired result.
- Actions of the computer are controlled by machine language instructions that consist of binary ones and zeros.
- Assembly languages allow the programmer to work at a machine level having access to the specific capabilities of a computer but to use symbolic forms in writing programs.
- Assembly language programs are translated into machine language with manufacturer-furnished assembler programs.
- High-level languages are designed to be (1) machine independent and (2) user oriented rather than machine oriented.
- High-level language programs are converted into machine language by compilers.
- A program written in an assembly or high-level language is called a source program. The result of the language translation is another program called an object program.
- An interpreted language is one in which each source statement is translated into machine language as the program is executed. A separate compiling operation is not necessary.

- The following high-level languages are described in this chapter.
  - FORTRAN: Compiler. Designed for math/science use.
  - BASIC: Interpreter. Designed for teaching; similar in form to FORTRAN.
  - Pascal: Compiler. Designed for teaching programming as a systematic, structured discipline.
  - C: Compiler. Includes low-level capabilities for access to hardware features. Originally intended for writing system software.
  - COBOL: Compiler. Specifically designed for business data processing.
- The program development cycle consists of the following five steps: defining the problem, and designing, coding, testing, and documenting the program.
- Commonly used program design tools are flowcharts, pseudocode, and structured programming.
- The three structures of structured programming are sequence, selection, and looping.
- Program design using pseudocode involves describing the step-by-step action to be taken using ordinary English in a structured form.

NEW TERMINOLOGY

The following are important new terms introduced in this chapter; you should be familiar with each of them.

assembler
assembly language
compiler
flowchart
high-level language
interpreter
looping structure
low-level language
machine language
module
object program
program
program design
program development cycle
pseudocode
selection structure
sequence structure
source program
structured design
structured programming

REVIEW QUESTIONS

1. Explain the difference between a machine language and an assembly language.
2. What does it mean when we say that COBOL is standardized?
3. An important feature of writing a program with a high-level language is that the program is portable. What does this mean?
4. For what types of applications are FORTRAN and COBOL designed?
5. The text says that C is a high-level language with low-level capabilities. What does this mean?
6. How does BASIC differ from the other languages described in this chapter?
7. What does it mean when we say that a program must be compiled before it can be run on the computer?
8. What is the difference between a compiler and an interpreter?
9. What are the steps in the program development cycle?
10. Identify and describe the flowchart symbols used in this chapter.
11. Describe the three structures of structured programming.
12. Describe the primary shortcomings of flowcharts for program design. How are they overcome by using pseudocode?
13. The scores from an examination are to be entered into the computer one at a time. The average of these scores is to be calculated by dividing their total by the number of exams. Prepare a flowchart illustrating the logic of this action.
14. Write the pseudocode to perform the actions of the preceding exercise.

MATCHING

Match each term in a to h with the most appropriate description in 1 through 8.

a. assembly language
b. machine language
c. module
d. selection
e. flowchart
f. source program
g. pseudocode
h. object program

1. One of three structures that compose structured programming theory.
2. A visual means for representing the logic of a program solution.
3. The result of compiling.
4. Provides the programmer with access to hardware features of the particular computer for which it is designed but must still be translated.

5. Reads like ordinary English.
6. Must be translated into machine language before it can be run on a computer.
7. A component of a larger program.
8. Consists of binary values.

TRUE/FALSE

Determine whether each of the following is true or false.

______ 1. Computer programs always contain binary ones and zeros.

______ 2. One of the differences between a program written in assembly language and one written in a high-level language is that the assembly language program does not need to be translated to be run on the computer.

______ 3. An assembly language program written for one computer cannot be run on other makes of computer.

______ 4. One of the features of high-level languages is that high-level language programs are machine independent.

______ 5. The FORTRAN language was originally developed for business data processing.

______ 6. One thing that BASIC and Pascal have in common is that they were both developed to be used in teaching programming.

______ 7. The language C provides the programmer with access to hardware features of the computer but is still machine independent.

______ 8. COBOL is generally considered obsolete and is no longer widely used.

______ 9. Compiler and assembler are two words that mean exactly the same thing: a program to convert user-written programs into machine language.

______ 10. Since an interpreter does not translate a high-level program statement into machine language until it is needed, programs run under interpreters run faster than those that are compiled.

______ 11. Flowcharts are used to provide a visual representation of the logic of a problem solution.

______ 12. Structured programming is a method of programming that uses three basic structures: sequence, selection, and looping.

______ 13. Structured techniques are not needed when program design is done using pseudocode.

______ 14. The looping structure is commonly called if-then-else.

______ 15. Structured design involves breaking a large programming job into small, independent modules.

ANSWERS TO OBJECTIVE QUESTIONS

Matching

1. d 2. e 3. h 4. a 5. g 6. f 7. c 8. b

True/False

1. F 2. F 3. T 4. T 5. F 6. T 7. T 8. F 9. F
10. F 11. T 12. T 13. F 14. F 15. T

Chapter 19

Programming in dBASE

OBJECTIVES

The intent of this chapter is to learn the basics of a programming language (using dBASE) and to apply the problem-solving principles of Chapter 18. Although the programming component of dBASE is not designed as a stand-alone language as are, for instance, BASIC and COBOL, it exhibits all of the characteristics of a modern programming language. In fact, it is patterned after the widely used language Pascal. Programs that you prepare in this chapter will utilize many of the principles that you learned in Chapter 16 when working with dBASE. You will use arithmetic operators in building expressions to perform calculations, and conditionals (which you used in the FOR command option) for decision making and controlling the repeated execution of a sequence of commands.

In this chapter, in only the first section (learning to use the dBASE editor) are there hands-on DTNs. After this section, you will be learning the principles of programming in dBASE. Each of the example programs described in the text is stored on the data disk included with this book. You may find it helpful to run the programs after reading the chapter, although they are not intended to be used in a hands-on environment. When you have completed this chapter, you should be able to:

- Use the dBASE editor to enter and edit dBASE programs.
- Understand the use of memory variables in a program.
- Incorporate the following actions into a program.
- Accept data from the keyboard.

- ☐ Read data from a file.
- ☐ Perform calculations.
- ☐ Store a data value into memory.
- ☐ Display results on the screen.
- ☐ Print results on a printer.
- ☐ Repeat a series of statements (the looping structure).
- ☐ Execute a series of statements conditionally (the selections structure).

PREVIEW

dBASE Command Files

Before a dBASE program can be run, it must first be entered and stored as a file. dBASE includes an editor program for doing this. In this section, you learn how to enter a simple program with the editor.

Dissecting the Example Program

The program of the preceding section includes input allowing for interaction with the user, calculation, and output for displaying the results of the calculations.

Program Loops

The looping structure described in Chapter 18 is implemented in dBASE with the DO WHILE command. With this, the simple program of the preceding section is modified to allow repetition.

Using the Selection Structure

The selection structure described in Chapter 18 is implemented in dBASE with the IF command. The IF allows the execution of either of two sequences of statements. The sample program is expanded to include alternative actions.

Processing Data Files

Previous example programs all involved interactive input from the keyboard. Many applications require that data from files be processed. Two examples in this section illustrate sequential processing of the AR data file.

dBASE COMMAND FILES

In Chapter 18, you learned that a program is a series of instructions to the computer to perform a defined task. Furthermore, you learned that when using a high-level language, you must first enter the program into the computer as an ordinary text file. This can be done with any word processor that allows a file to be saved without the word processing formatting codes. Some languages, including dBASE, have their own editors for entering and editing programs; before learning the details of the dBASE language, let us focus on the dBASE editor.

The dBASE Editor

When entering and editing a program, you use the dBASE editor exactly as you would a word processor. (The editor commands were taken from the word processor WordStar.) When you first bring the editor up, your screen display will include the Help screen of Figure 19-1, which summarizes the editor actions. Notice that some of the keys used for editing are the same as those used when editing data in dBASE files, but that others are different. The following summary of key actions supplements the abbreviated help display of Figure 19-1. Those that you will most commonly use are marked with an asterisk.

Cursor Movement

* Arrow keys — Moves the cursor left or right one position, or up or down one line.
* Home — Moves the cursor to the beginning of the current or preceding word.
* End — Moves the cursor to the end of the next word.
  Ctrl- → — Moves the cursor to the beginning of the current line.
  Ctrl- ← — Moves the cursor to the end of the current line.
  PgUp — Scrolls eighteen lines toward the beginning of the text.
  PgDn — Scrolls eighteen lines toward the end of the text.

Deletion

* Del — Deletes the character at the position of cursor.
  Backspace — Deletes the character to left of cursor.

Figure 19-1
The dBASE III word processing help screen.

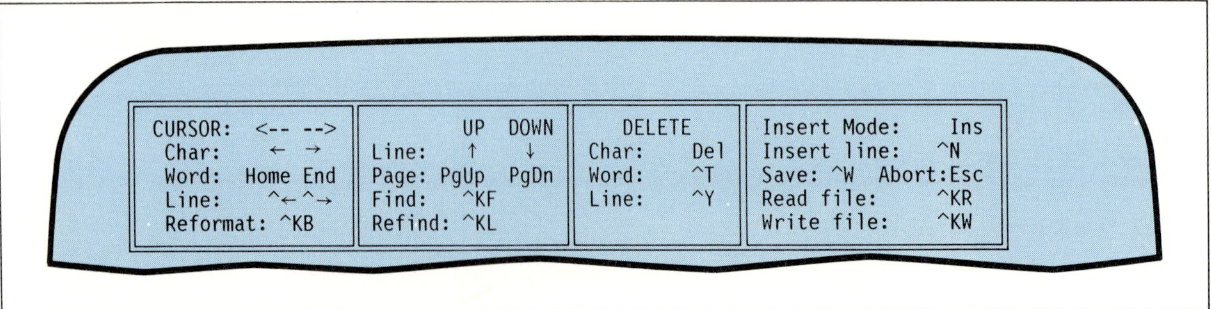

Ctrl-T	Deletes all characters from the cursor position to the beginning of the next word.
Ctrl-Y	Deletes the current line.

Other

* Ins	Toggles between insert and overtype mode. When in insert mode, striking Enter causes a new line to be created at the position of the cursor.
Ctrl-N	Inserts a new line at the position of the cursor.
Ctrl-KR	Inserts another text file at the position of the cursor.
Ctrl-KF	Searchs for a designated string of characters.
Ctrl-KL	Continues the previous search for the next occurrence.

Saving a File and Ending an Edit Session

* Esc	Aborts without saving the file.
* Ctrl-KW	Saves your current work as a file but allows entry/editing to continue.
* Ctrl-End	Saves your current work as a file and returns to the dot prompt (this is identical to the action of Ctrl-W listed in the help frame).

Entering a dBASE Program

dBASE programs that are created with the editor are called **command files** because they consist of sequences of commands. The filename is selected by the user; a default extension of PRG (meaning program) is assigned by dBASE. You bring up the editor with the dBASE command MODIFY COMMAND, followed by the name you want to use for the file. For your orientation to using it, you will enter and run the program solution to Example 18-1. Recall that this example consisted of entering a quantity and unit price, calculating the amount, and then displaying the result (the flowchart for this action is included in the preceding chapter as Figure 18-5). The dBASE program is shown in Figure 19-2. Do not be concerned with what each command does; afterwards you will learn about that.

```
CLEAR
SET TALK OFF
INPUT "Type the quantity: " TO QUANT
INPUT "Type the unit price: " TO PRICE
STORE PRICE * QUANT TO AMOUNT
?
? "The total amount is:", AMOUNT
```

Figure 19-2
A simple dBASE program.

DO THIS NOW 19-1 **Entering the Program of Figure 19-2**

1. From the dBASE dot prompt, enter the command:

```
MODIFY COMMAND TOTAL
```

   dBASE will switch to the editor awaiting your text entry; it will display the Help screen of Figure 19-1. (Delete it with the F1 key if you do not want it.)

2. Referring to the first line of Figure 19-2, type the first command (CLEAR) and strike Enter. Commands may be in uppercase or lowercase. Notice that your action is the same as if you were entering this using WordPerfect.
3. Type each of the other lines. Do not worry about making errors; you can correct them later.
4. Terminate this editor session with the Ctrl-End key sequence. Your program will be saved as the file TOTAL.PRG (the name TOTAL is the one used in MODIFY COMMAND) and you will be returned to the dBASE dot prompt.

If you want a printed copy of your program, then enter the following dBASE command and strike Enter. Do not forget the extension PRG as the TYPE command does not assume a default PRG extension as does MODIFY COMMAND.

```
TYPE TOTAL.PRG TO PRINT
```

Editing a dBASE Program

When you invoke the dBASE editor with MODIFY COMMAND, dBASE searches the default disk drive for an existing command file with the name you specify in the command line (TOTAL in this example). If none is found, dBASE places you in the edit mode with an empty screen as in DTN 19-1. However, if file is found, it will be loaded ready for editing. Let us try this by modifying the command file you just created.

DO THIS NOW 19-2 **Changing the Program of Figure 19-2 to That of Figure 19-3**

1. Invoke the editor and load the program TOTAL.PRG with the command:

```
MODIFY COMMAND TOTAL
```

   The editor Help screen and your program will be displayed and the cursor will be positioned under the letter *C* of *CLEAR*.

2. To insert the first line (beginning with the *), change to insert mode by striking the Ins key. (Ins will be displayed at the top of the screen, telling you that you are in the insert mode.)

3. Strike Enter to insert a blank line preceding CLEAR.
4. Strike the Up key to position the cursor on the blank line. Type the new first line (beginning with the *). Strike Enter, and then type an asterisk, your name, and the date. When you are finished, strike Enter to insert the needed blank line. Blank lines can be inserted at any place in a program to make it easier to read; dBASE ignores them during execution.
5. To insert a blank line following SET TALK OFF, move the cursor to the letter *I* in the first INPUT, and then strike Enter. Since you are still in the insert mode, a blank line will be inserted.
6. In both lines beginning with INPUT, the word *Type* is to be changed to *Please enter.* Position the cursor on the letter *T* in *Type* of the first INPUT.
7. Strike the Del key four times to delete the word *Type.* Then type the words *Please enter.*
8. Move the cursor to the letter *T* in *Type* of the second INPUT. Delete the entire word with the Ctrl-T sequence. Note that Ctrl-T deletes from the cursor to the beginning of the next word; Del deletes only the character at the cursor. Then type the words *Please enter.*
9. Save this file (without exiting the editor) with the key sequence Ctrl-KW. (Hold down the Control key, strike K followed by W, and then release the Control key.) This will save the file with its corrections but leave you in the editor.
10. Compare your program with that of Figure 19-3. Correct any errors.
11. Save the program with the Ctrl-End sequence.

Figure 19-3
Expanding the program.

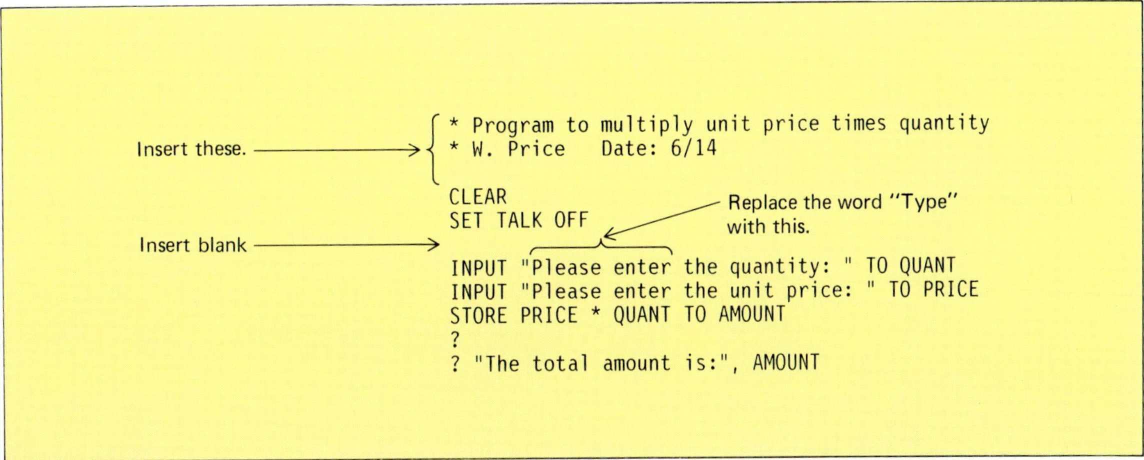

Although you did not see it in this example, the dBASE editor wraps to the next line when the cursor reaches position 66. A long command spread over two or more lines might appear strange on the screen, but it will be perfectly valid. As with interactive commands, a command in a program can be up to 256 characters in length.

Running a Program

Once a program is stored on disk as a file, it can be run from the dot prompt at any time with the DO command:

DO THIS NOW 19-3 **Running the Program TOTAL**

1. From the dBASE dot prompt, enter the command:

   ```
   DO TOTAL
   ```

   This will cause dBASE to load your program into memory and execute it. Remember that each command will be interpreted by the dBASE interpreter (changed to machine language) and executed.

2. Your program will clear the screen and display the prompt:

   ```
   Please enter the quantity: _
   ```

3. Type 13 and strike Enter.
4. Your program will display the prompt:

   ```
   Please enter the unit price: _
   ```

5. Type 22.67 and strike Enter.
6. Your program will display

   ```
   The total amount is: 294.71
   ```

   and return control to the dot prompt.

This completes your sequence of entering, editing, and running the program. Let us now consider the various commands that make up this program.

DISSECTING THE EXAMPLE PROGRAM

From the descriptions of Example 18-1 and from running the program, you can easily guess the function of each command in Figure 19-3. Let us consider the dBASE features that this program uses.

Comment Lines

The first line of the program begins with the asterisk (*) character. The asterisk tells dBASE to ignore that line when the program is executed.

Hence, any line beginning with an asterisk can be used by the programmer to document the program. All future example programs in this book will include at least two lines of documentation: the program identification and the author's name and date. You may include comments at any point in a program; these are valuable in describing the features and actions of the program. You will find them especially helpful if you must modify a program at some later date or use one written by someone else.

Clearing the Screen

The first command of this program is CLEAR. This command causes the screen to be cleared and the cursor to be positioned at the upper left corner of the screen. In this case, you might feel that the CLEAR is not necessary because, when the screen becomes full, previous lines will scroll off the top of the screen as new lines are added to the bottom. However, a clean and uncluttered screen has a much better appearance.

The INPUT Command

The INPUT command, as shown in Figure 19-4(a), causes the computer to display the prompt, stop execution of the program, and wait for the user to enter data from the keyboard. The screen will appear as shown in Figure 19-4(b). After you type in the desired value and strike Enter, dBASE stores your entry in the memory variable listed in the command.

Memory Variables

All programming languages, including dBASE, allow the programmer to define areas of memory for storing data. In dBASE, they are called **memory**

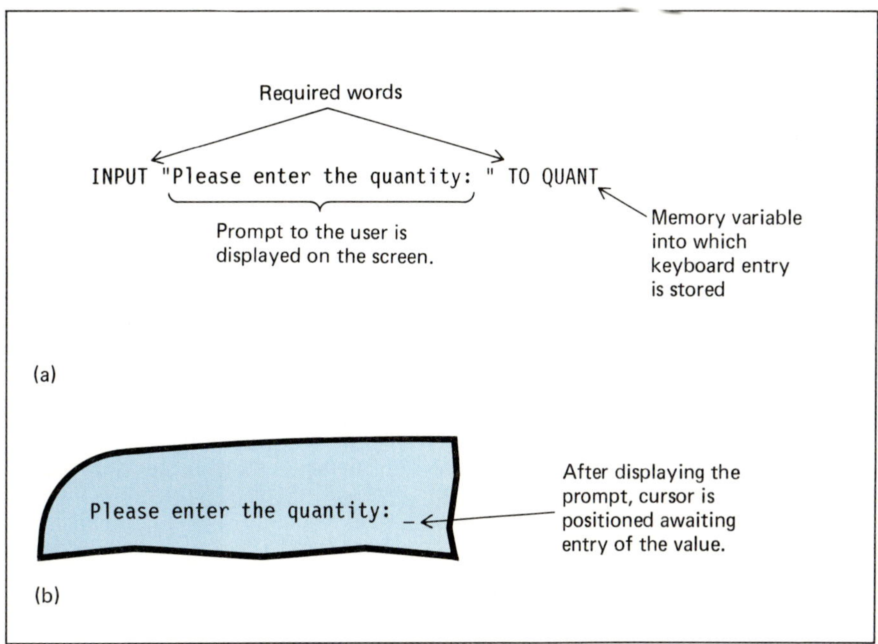

Figure 19-4
The INPUT command.

variables and are similar to data fields in a file except that they are used to hold data in memory rather than on disk. In fact, the rules for selecting memory variable names are identical to those for selecting field names. (If you were to pick up a printout of someone else's program, it would not be obvious which of the data names were database fields and which were memory variables.) Memory variables are automatically created by the interpreter when used in certain commands. For instance, in executing the first INPUT statement of the program TOTAL, the interpreter would automatically set aside a memory area for the memory variable QUANT and store the value you entered from the keyboard in it.

Although command words such as DELETE and INPUT can be used as variable names, you should not use them in order to avoid potential problems with the interpreter. Furthermore, if you are using a data file in a program, you should not create a memory variable with the same name as a field in the record.

Unlike fields of a database file, memory variables need not be declared as a particular data type (numeric, character, and so on). Whenever a quantity is assigned to a variable, dBASE automatically adjusts to the type. Memory variables may be used in almost all of the circumstances in which database fields have been used in the preceding chapters.

The STORE Command

The STORE command allows you to specify calculations to be performed in your program. Like the INPUT command, the STORE command also causes a memory variable to be created and a value entered into it. However, with the STORE command, you can place into memory a fixed value, a value from a database field, the result of any calculation, or the result of a compare. For instance, the STORE command from TOTAL is shown in Figure 19-5(a). In this example, the expression is simply the product of two quantities, PRICE*QUANT). You can use any valid dBASE expression (expressions are described in Chapter 16) in the STORE.

In using sample values of 22.67 for PRICE and 13 for QUANT in this example, dBASE would perform the designated calculations, reserve an area of memory giving it the name AMOUNT, and place the result of the calculation in it. This is illustrated in Figure 19-5(b).

If you refer to the sample programs illustrating languages in Chapter 18, you will see that the STORE operation is performed in most of the languages by:

```
TOTAL = FIRST + SECOND
```

This is commonly called an *assignment statement;* the expression on the right of the equal sign is evaluated and the result stored in the variable named on the left of the equal sign. Note that this form can be used in dBASE as an alternative to the STORE. Hence, the STORE could have been replaced with:

```
AMOUNT = PRICE*QUANT
```

However, this form will produce confusing error messages if you

Figure 19-5
The STORE command.

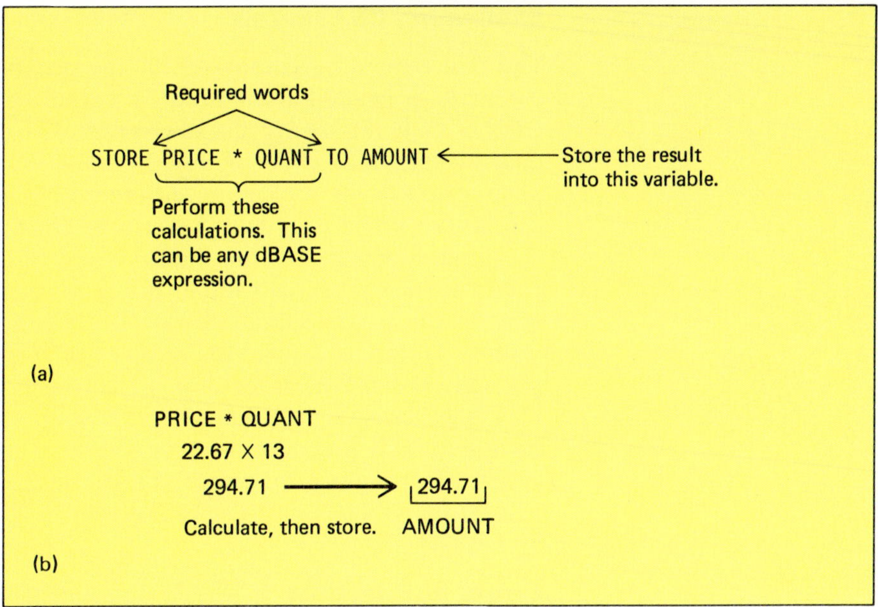

accidentally select a memory variable name that has a special meaning to dBASE. You can avoid this problem by using STORE.

The Display Command

To display messages or quantities stored in variables, you use the question mark character (?) followed by the items to be displayed. The second ? command from the program of Figure 19-3 is described in Figure 19-6. The display code, which is the single ? character, may be followed by one or more memory variables or literals to be displayed. If the ? is included by itself, as in Figure 19-3, a blank line results. In this example, it leaves a blank line between the query lines of the INPUT and the display of the calculated result.

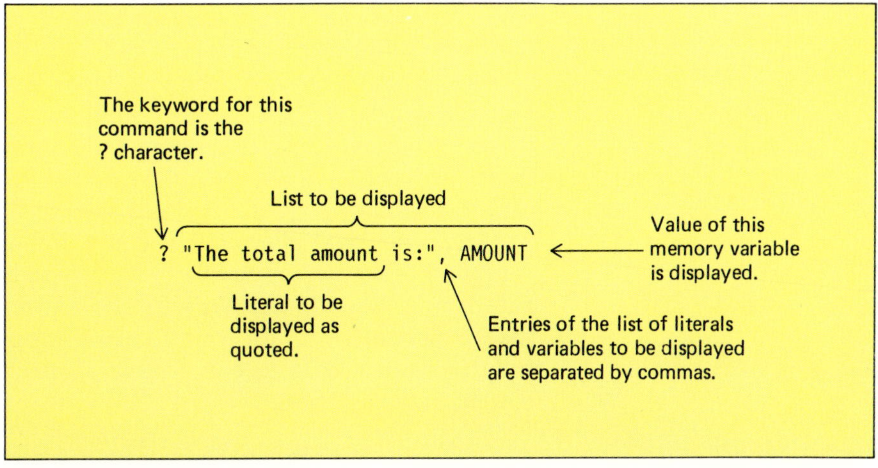

Figure 19-6
The display (?) command.

Eliminating dBASE Talk

The one remaining command in this program is SET TALK OFF. This command is needed in the program because of the way in which dBASE is designed for interactive use. For example, remember that when you indexed a data file, a message was displayed that the operation was complete. The execution of many different dBASE commands causes *talk*, the display of such messages. Talk is produced whether the command is executed interactively from the keyboard or from a program. The STORE command used in this sample program results in talk that displays the stored value automatically unless dBASE is directed otherwise. When you write a program, you normally want to control all screen displays since such unexpected messages can be confusing. The command SET TALK OFF eliminates all dBASE talk; the only screen displays will be those resulting from execution of your input or output commands. If, in the course of a program, you want to turn the talk back on, you can do so with SET TALK ON.

Errors in Programs

There are two broad types of errors that you might make when writing or entering a program. One of them is using wrong forms in creating commands; these are called syntax errors. You are familiar with them from your interactive use of dBASE. When dBASE encounters one during the execution of a program, it stops and displays the command together with an error message exactly as if the command were entered interactively. For instance, if you used the word IMPUT instead of INPUT in the program of Figure 19-3, when dBASE encountered this statement during execution, it would halt and display the following.

```
*** Unrecognized command verb.
       ?
  IMPUT "Please enter the quantity: " TO QUANT
Called from - total.prg
```

At the bottom of the screen, the message

```
Cancel, Ignore, or Suspend? (C, I, or S)
```

would appear. Striking C cancels further execution of the program and returns you to the dot prompt. The I tells dBASE to ignore this statement and continue. The S causes dBASE to suspend execution and return to the dot prompt, leaving all program conditions unchanged. From this, you can inspect memory variable contents and continue execution of the program from the point at which it stopped. Usually, you will strike the letter C to cancel, then use MODIFY COMMAND to correct the program.

The other type of error that you will make is a logic error: telling the computer to do the wrong thing, such as adding two quantities rather than subtracting. You are familiar with these from your study of spreadsheets. Like a spreadsheet, the output of a program must be checked carefully using test data to ensure that all calculated and tested values are correct.

PROGRAM LOOPS

As indicated in Chapter 18, a program consisting of a single sequence executed only once is generally of little value. Example 18-3 describes the looping structure that allows repetition; let us learn how that is implemented in dBASE.

The DO WHILE Command

Remember from Chapter 18 that the looping structure (see Figure 18-7) is also called the do-while structure because it causes a series of actions to be repeated while a test condition remains true. This is done in dBASE with the DO WHILE command which is used in Figure 19-7. (This program includes line numbers to the left of each command. These are for reference in descriptions in this text and are not part of the program.) In this program, you see the beginning of the loop indicated at line 9 by DO WHILE and the end at line 17 by ENDDO. Every DO WHILE command in a program must be paired with a corresponding ENDDO to identify the end of the loop; otherwise, an error will occur.

Details of this pair of commands are shown in Figure 19-8. Notice that the test condition controlling execution of the loop is based on the data value stored in the memory variable CONTIN. Let us consider what takes place during execution of this program.

1. The variable CONTIN is initialized to Y at line 8. The name CONTIN is selected because it reminds the programmer of its function: whether or not to continue. The Y represents Yes.

Figure 19-7
A program loop using the DO WHILE.

```
1   * Program to calculate price times quantity under loop control
2   * TOTAL2.PRG
3   * W. Price   Date: 6/14
4
5   CLEAR
6   SET TALK OFF
7
8   STORE "Y" TO CONTIN
9   DO WHILE CONTIN = "Y"
10    INPUT "Please enter the quantity: " TO QUANT
11    INPUT "Please enter the unit price: " TO PRICE
12    STORE PRICE * QUANT TO AMOUNT
13    ?
14    ? "The total amount is:", AMOUNT
15    ?
16    WAIT "Process another set <Y/N>? " TO CONTIN
17  ENDDO
18  ?
19  ? "Processing finished--goodbye"
```

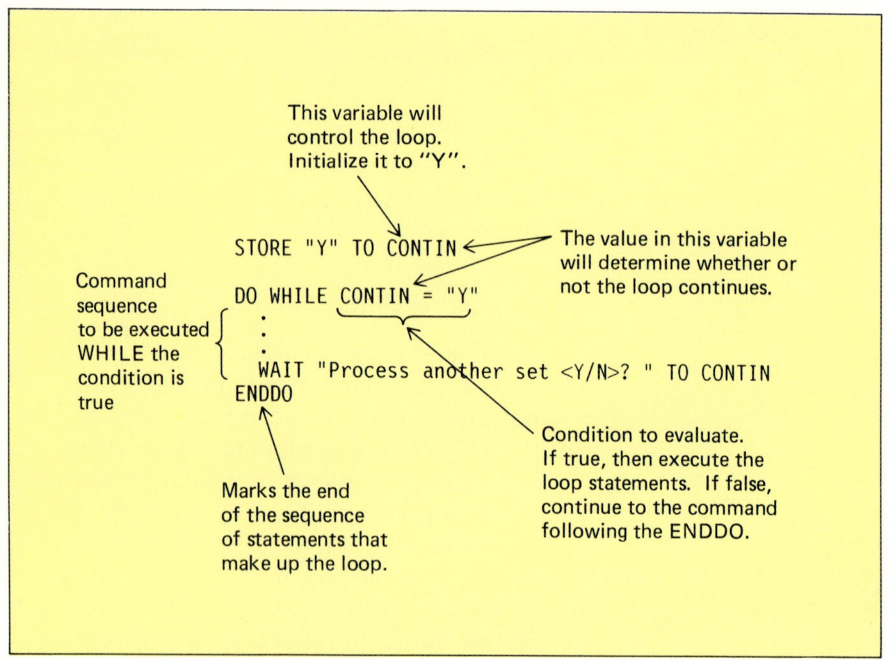

Figure 19-8
Details of the DO WHILE.

2. Upon encountering the DO command, dBASE evaluates the test condition. Since CONTIN contains a value of Y (from the preceding initializing command), dBASE will execute the commands within the loop.

3. Upon encountering the WAIT command (described later in this chapter), dBASE stops and awaits a response from the keyboard, much the same as the INPUT.

4. The user keys in a response, either Y or N, which is stored in the memory variable CONTIN.

5. Upon encountering the ENDDO, control is returned to the DO statement. The condition is again evaluated (does CONTIN contain a value of Y?). If it is true, the loop is executed again. If it is false (CONTIN does not contain Y), execution of the loop is terminated and the program continues to the ? command at line 18, which follows the ENDDO.

Each statement in the body of the loop in Figure 19-7 is indented two positions. The purpose of the indent is to set off the block of statements of the loop and make the overall program easier to read. In this way, the structure of the program in Figure 19-7 is apparent at a glance.

Conditional Forms and Loop Control

In Chapter 16, you learned about conditional forms and building relational and logical expressions. The conditional portion of the DO WHILE is identical to the conditionals in Chapter 16. Notice in this example program that the contents of CONTIN are compared with an uppercase letter Y.

Hence, in order to continue, the user must be certain to hold down the shift key when responding. Any entry other than Y causes the loop to be terminated. You could make this test independent of uppercase or lowercase by using either of the following two forms.

```
DO WHILE CONTIN = "Y" .OR. CONTIN = "y"
DO WHILE UPPER(CONTIN) = "Y"
```

You learned about the .OR. operator in Chapter 16. The UPPER causes any character data stored in CONTIN to be converted to uppercase for the comparison. Notice that the word UPPER is followed by the memory variable enclosed in parentheses. This is one of the many dBASE functions available to the programmer.

Commands that make up the loop must include one or more that change the state of the condition, or else the loop never terminates. In the program of Figure 19-7; this is done with the WAIT, which accepts a keyboard entry and places it in the test variable CONTIN. Figure 19-9 includes two other examples of DO WHILE. In the first, execution of the loop will continue until AMOUNT is no longer equal to or greater than LIMIT. Each time through the loop, the STORE places a new value into AMOUNT. In the second example the loop will execute exactly ten times. It is controlled by the variable CNTR, which is initialized to zero prior to the DO WHILE, and increased by one on each pass through the loop. This is called a *counted loop*. The form of the STORE used here is discussed in detail later in this chapter.

Figure 19-9
Other examples of the DO WHILE.

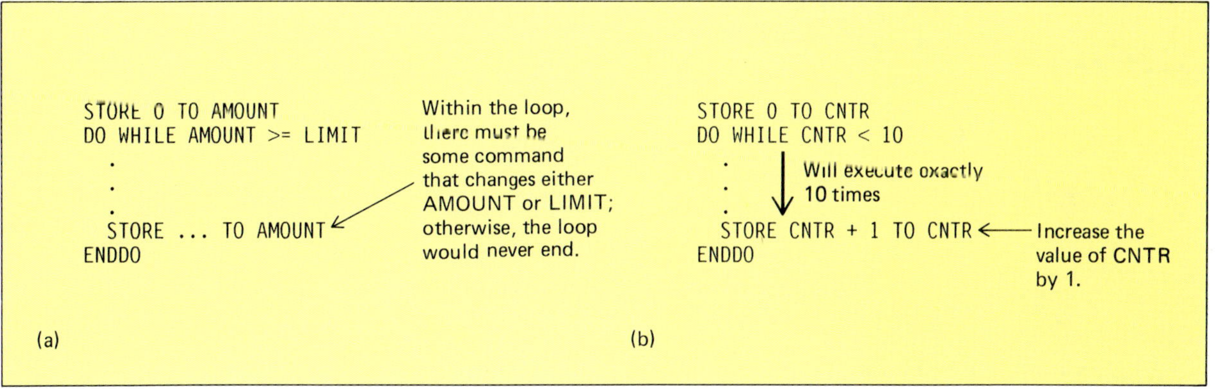

The INPUT, ACCEPT, and WAIT Commands

Input to the program for quantity and price is via the INPUT command (lines 10 and 11). When the user enters numbers in response to an INPUT command, dBASE automatically makes the memory variables into which values are placed numeric. If you had a program in which the user was to respond with a character value, then the value typed from the keyboard would have to be enclosed in quotes. Otherwise, dBASE would give an error message that would appear to have nothing to do with the command.

On the other hand, the dBASE language includes the ACCEPT command, which is identical to the INPUT except that the memory variable created is *always* type character. If, for example, at some point in a program, a person's name was to be accepted from the keyboard, you could use either of the commands:

```
ACCEPT Enter the person's last name: " TO LNAME
INPUT  Enter the person's last name: " TO LNAME
```

However, the advantage of the ACCEPT is that the name could be typed from the keyboard without using quotes.

The WAIT is different from both the ACCEPT and INPUT in that execution halts and waits for *any* key to be struck. This can be the Enter or any other character key on the keyboard; Enter need *not* be struck after a character key. The character entered from the single keystroke is stored in the memory variable listed in the command. In the program of Figure 19-7, the single key response will be stored in the variable CONTIN.

The program of Figure 19-7 is stored on the data disk accompanying this book as TOTAL2.PRG. You may run it by typing DO TOTAL2.

USING THE SELECTION STRUCTURE

The IF Command

The last of the three structured programming structures that you learned about in Chapter 18 is selection—the conditional capability. This was illustrated by Example 18-2 in which a 15 percent discount was applied if the quantity exceeded ten. The following pseudocode taken from the solution of Figure 18-9 describes the action to be taken.

```
If the quantity is greater than 10
  Compute the amount as quantity times price times 0.85
  Display a discount message and the amount
Else
  Compute the amount as quantity times price
  Display the amount.
```

In dBASE, this selection structure is implemented with the IF-ELSE-ENDIF command; it is used in the program of Figure 19-10, which is an expanded version of the program TOTAL2. During execution, when the IF at line 13 is encountered, the value in QUANT will be compared with 10 and the following will occur.

- If the condition is true (QUANT greater than 10), execution proceeds to statement 14 and then 15. Upon encountering the ELSE at line 16, dBASE jumps to the statement following the line 19 ENDIF.
- If the condition is false (QUANT not greater than 10), dBASE jumps to the statement following the ELSE (line 16) and execution proceeds to statement 17 and then 18, and then on to 20.

Sometimes, when preparing a program, you will have an action that is to be taken only if a particular condition occurs (this is the special case of the selection described in Chapter 18). For instance, assume that the

```
1  * Program to calculate price times quantity with discount
2  * TOTAL3.PRG
3  * W. Price   Date: 6/14
4
5  CLEAR
6  SET TALK OFF
7
8  CONTIN = "Y"
9  DO WHILE UPPER(CONTIN) = "Y"
10   INPUT "Please enter the quantity: " TO QUANT
11   INPUT "Please enter the unit price: " TO PRICE
12   ?
13   IF QUANT > 10
14     STORE 0.85 * PRICE * QUANT  TO AMOUNT
15     ? "The total amount (w/discount) is:", AMOUNT
16   ELSE
17     STORE PRICE * QUANT TO AMOUNT
18     ? "The total amount is:", AMOUNT
19   ENDIF
20   ?
21   WAIT "Process another set <Y/N>? " TO CONTIN
22 ENDDO
22 ?
23 ? "Processing finished--goodbye"
```

If this condition is true, then
execute this sequence
ELSE
execute this sequence.

Figure 19-10
Using the IF command in a program.

program of Figure 19-10 is to calculate and display only if the value for QUANT is greater than 10 (otherwise, it is to ignore the entry). Then lines 13 through 19 of Figure 19-10 would be replaced with the following form of the IF that does not include the ELSE option.

```
IF QUANT > 10
  STORE 0.85*PRICE*QUANT TO AMOUNT
  ? "The amount is: ", AMOUNT
ENDIF
```

Using Compound Conditions

In Chapter 16, you used the .AND. and .OR. operators to form complex conditions in the FOR command. You can also use these in the test condition for the DO WHILE and IF commands. For example, assume that the 15 percent discount of the preceding program is to be applied only if the quantity is greater than 10 and the price (amount) is equal to or greater than 25. For this, you would need to replace the IF in lines 13 through 19 of Figure 19-10 with the commands of Figure 19-11. Here, AMOUNT is calculated prior to the test. If both conditions are true, then the statement

```
STORE 0.85*AMOUNT TO AMOUNT
```

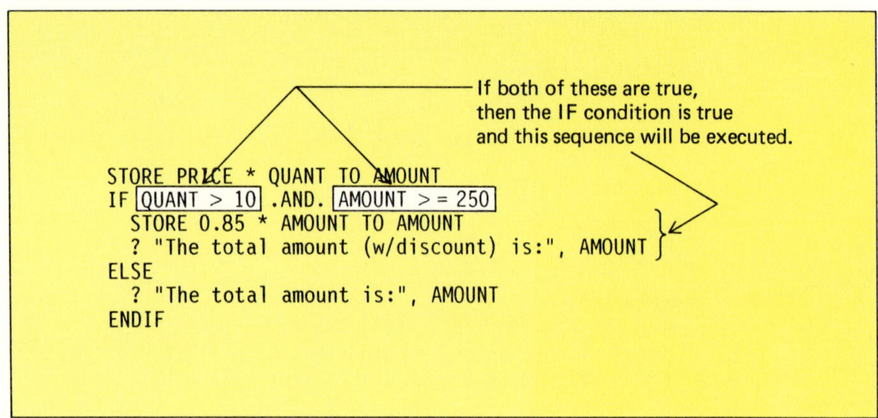

Figure 19-11
Details of the IF.

is executed, causing dBASE to multiply the previously calculated value in AMOUNT by 0.85 and replace it with the new value.

PROCESSING DATA FILES

Displaying Data From a File

The preceding programs that you have studied are interactive whereby input data is entered through the keyboard by the user. Many applications require that data from one or more files be processed. To illustrate using a file for data input, we will study two examples. As you study these examples, you will see that both could be done interactively with a simple dBASE command. However, the purpose of this section is to show you basic programming principles, not to suggest alternative ways of performing operations that you learned about in the earlier chapters on dBASE. Both of these programs use the data file AR.DBF. Following is a definition of the program requirements.

EXAMPLE 19-1

This program is to display each record in the AR.DBF file for which the invoice balance is greater than zero. The displayed output must include the customer number, invoice number, paid amount, and invoice balance. The fields of this data record are:

```
CUSTNUM   Customer number
INVNUM    Invoice number
INVDATE   Invoice date
ORIGAMNT  Original invoice amount
INVBAL    Invoice balance
```

The paid amount must be calculated as:

Original invoice amount – Invoice balance

Program Solution

Like the program of Figure 19-7, this one requires looping, in this case, one that is to repeat until there are no more records in the data file. The general steps in programs processing records sequentially are:

Repeat the following until there are no more records

Get a record

Process the record.

However, in dBASE, the actual program command sequence is slightly different because of the way in which the records are made available by dBASE. That is, opening a file (with the USE command) causes the first record to be made available. Using logic that takes advantage of dBASE features, the solution in both flowchart and pseudocode is as shown in Figure 19-12.

For this program solution, we need only two new principles: how to detect the end of the file and how to progress from record to record. dBASE includes a special function named EOF() that checks the current record (note that the parentheses are required). If the current record is a data record, dBASE sets the value of EOF() to false; if the current record is the end of file (the EOF), dBASE sets the value of EOF() to true. Hence, the form of the DO WHILE becomes:

```
DO WHILE .NOT. EOF()
```

Notice the .NOT. logical operator; it functions exactly as the English suggests. That is, if EOF() is true, then .NOT. EOF() is false; if EOF() is false, then .NOT. EOF() is true.

The other requirement for this program is the ability to access the next record; this is done with the command SKIP.

The program solution for this example is shown in Figure 19-13; you should examine this program (which is stored on your data disk as LIST1.PRG) and observe the following.

1. Before beginning processing, a general announcement is displayed that provides the user with a brief description of the program.
2. The loop is controlled by the DO WHILE at line 17. If the current record is not the EOF, then this condition is true and execution proceeds with the statement at line 18.
3. The IF at line 18 compares the value stored in the field INVBAL of this record with zero. If it is greater than zero, the commands of lines 19 and 20 are executed; otherwise, they are ignored.
4. At line 23, the SKIP command is executed, which causes the next record to be made available.
5. Encountering the ENDDO statement at line 24 causes dBASE to return control to the DO WHILE, which checks the now current record. If it contains the EOF, then execution immediately continues to the statement following the ENDDO (the USE at line 26 in this example), the message is displayed, and processing is terminated.

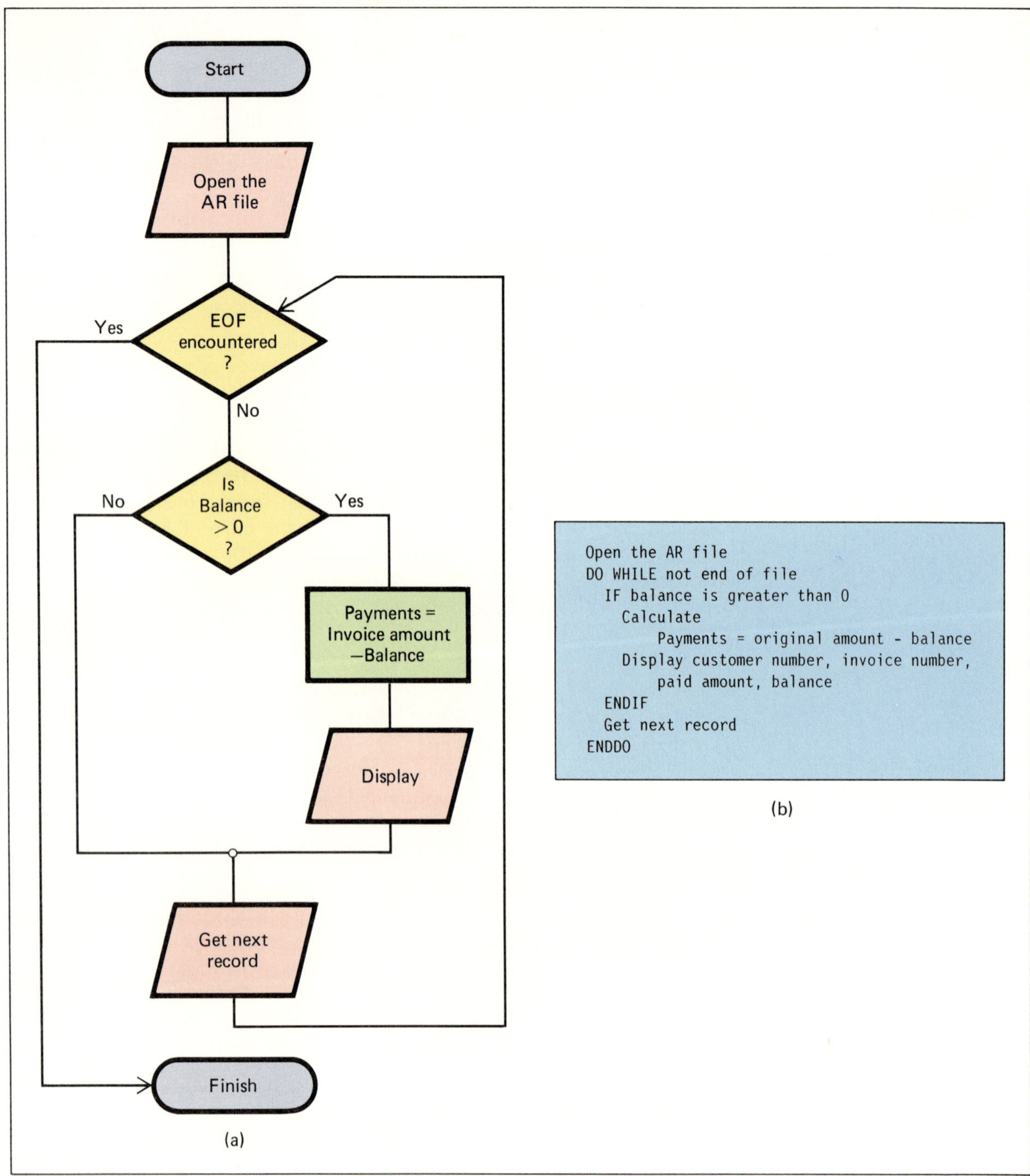

Figure 19-12
Example 19-1
(a) Flowchart solution
(b) Pseudocode solution

Accumulating

The programmer commonly encounters the need to accumulate quantities in a program. This is illustrated by the following addition to Example 19-1.

```
* Program to list records from the AR file with balances > 0.
* LIST1.PRG
* W. Price       Date: 6/14

SET TALK OFF
CLEAR
? "         AR LISTING PROGRAM
?
? "This program lists the amount paid and balance for"
? "each record of the AR file for which the balance"
? "is greater than zero."
?
WAIT "Strike Enter when ready to begin."

CLEAR
USE AR
DO WHILE .NOT. EOF()
  IF INVBAL > 0
    STORE ORIGAMNT-INVBAL TO PAID
    ? CUSTNUM, INVNUM, PAID, INVBAL
  ENDIF

  SKIP
ENDDO

USE
?
? "Processing complete."
```

Figure 19-13
Processing a data file—Example 19-1.

EXAMPLE 19-2

The output of Example 19-1 is to be expanded to include:

A count of the number of records read.

A count of the number of records with zero balance.

The total of the amounts paid.

The total of the balances.

Also, the output is to be printed on the computer printer as well as displayed on the screen.

The needs of this example require no new dBASE principles, only a new technique involving the STORE. As each record is read, values must be accumulated. This is done by initializing a memory variable to zero outside the processing loop and adding the field from the record for each pass through the loop, as shown in Figure 19-14. To understand this STORE, you must recognize that execution of the STORE is a two-step process.

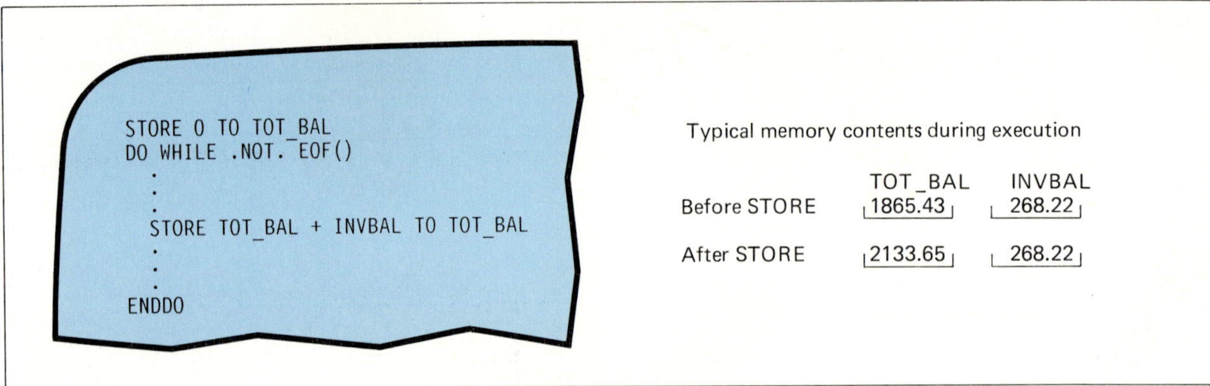

Figure 19-14
Using an accumulator.

First, the expression is evaluated, and then the result is stored in the designated variable. In Figure 19-14, you can see that dBASE adds the current value in TOT_BAL (1865.43) and the value in INVBAL (268.22), and then stores the result (2133.65) in TOT_BAL thus replacing the previous value.

The use of accumulators is the key to the program solution in Figure 19-15; you should examine this program (which is stored on your data disk as LIST2.PRG) and observe the following.

1. Output from the ? command can be directed to the printer as well as the screen with one of the many forms of the SET command. This is done in line 22. Notice that in line 47 the output to the printer is turned off before the program is ended.

2. Four accumulators are needed in this program (two of them are counters). These are all set to zero in the single STORE at line 21.

3. Any record for which the value of INVBAL is greater than zero will be processed by the sequence of lines 29 through 33.

4. Any record for which the value of INVBAL is equal to zero will be counted at line 35.

Printed output from this program is shown in Figure 19-16. In general, formatting output in programs is a painstaking task. In this and the preceding program, the default positioning by the ? command was used. In positioning the output on a line, dBASE does the following: (1) uses the field width for each field to be displayed, (2) separates each printed quantity from the next by a single space, and (3) uses fourteen positions for memory variables. The spacing of the headings in this output (resulting from the program lines 23 and 24) was thus determined. You might find that some experimenting is required to get the correct positioning on programs that you write.

```
* Program to list records from the AR file with balances > 0
* Total and 0 balance records are counted, and
* payments and invoice balance are accumulated.
* LIST2.PRG
* W. Price        Date: 6/14

SET TALK OFF
CLEAR
? "            AR LISTING PROGRAM"
?
? "This program lists the amount paid and balance for each record"
? "of the AR file for which the balance is greater than 0."
? "A summary is included at the end indicating the number of records "
? "read, the number with a 0 balance, the total paid for records with"
? "a balance greater than 0, and the total balance."
?
WAIT "Make certain the printer is ready then strike Enter."

CLEAR
USE AR
STORE 0 TO ZERO_CNT, REC_CNT, TOT_PAID, TOT_BAL
SET PRINT ON
? "Inv.  Cust        Paid    Balance"
? "----- ----        ------- -------"

DO WHILE .NOT. EOF()
  STORE REC_CNT + 1 TO REC_CNT
  IF INVBAL > 0
    STORE ORIGAMNT - INVBAL TO PAID
    ? CUSTNUM, INVNUM, PAID, INVBAL
    * Accumulate the payments and balances
    STORE TOT_PAID + PAID TO TOT_PAID
    STORE TOT_BAL + INVBAL TO TOT_BAL
  ELSE
    STORE ZERO_CNT + 1 TO ZERO_CNT
  ENDIF

  SKIP
ENDDO

?
? "Total records read:          ", REC_CNT
? "Records with zero balance: ", ZERO_CNT
? "Total of payments:           ", TOT_PAID
? "Total of balances:           ", TOT_BAL
USE
SET PRINT OFF
```

Direct output of ? command to printer as well as to the screen

Process this record if the value of INVBAL is greater than 0; otherwise, count the 0 record.

Figure 19-15
Program for Example 19-2.

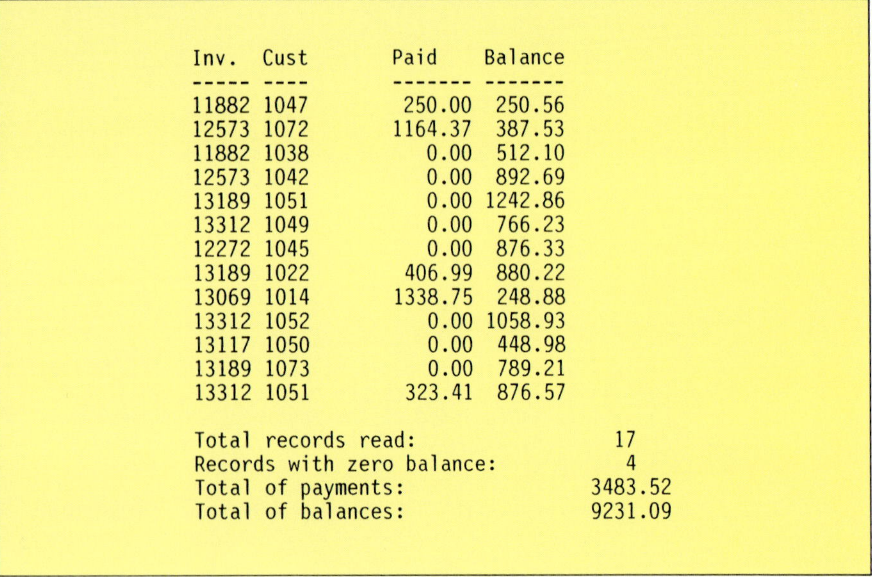

```
Inv.  Cust        Paid    Balance
----- ----     ------- -------
11882 1047      250.00  250.56
12573 1072     1164.37  387.53
11882 1038        0.00  512.10
12573 1042        0.00  892.69
13189 1051        0.00 1242.86
13312 1049        0.00  766.23
12272 1045        0.00  876.33
13189 1022      406.99  880.22
13069 1014     1338.75  248.88
13312 1052        0.00 1058.93
13117 1050        0.00  448.98
13189 1073        0.00  789.21
13312 1051      323.41  876.57

Total records read:              17
Records with zero balance:        4
Total of payments:            3483.52
Total of balances:            9231.09
```

Figure 19-16
Printed output from Example 19-2.

SUMMARY

This chapter has provided you with the basic principles of programming. Summarizing, the important items from the chapter are:

- Before a program can be run, it must first be entered into the computer as a text file. This can be done with a word processor (the file must be saved without formatting codes), or it can be done with the dBASE editor. In dBASE, these are called command files.
- A program is run with the DO command; type the dBASE word DO followed by the name of the program to be run.
- If the first nonblank character in a program line is an asterisk (*), that entire line can be used as a programmer comment and will be ignored by the interpreter during execution of the program.
- Memory variables are used to define areas of memory for temporarily storing data. The rules for selecting memory variable names are the same as for selecting field names for a dBASE data field.
- Messages displayed by dBASE upon completing an operation are called *talk*. Talk can be eliminated from a program with the SET TALK OFF command.
- If an error is encountered during execution of a program, the program is terminated and an error message is displayed in the same way as with interactive execution of commands.
- The looping structure of structured programming is implemented in

dBASE with the DO WHILE command. Each DO WHILE must be matched with an ENDDO to indicate the end of the loop.

- Conditions for controlling loop execution are identical to those used in the FOR command option in Chapter 16.
- The selection structure of structured programming is implemented in dBASE with the IF command. Each DO WHILE must be matched with an ENDIF to indicate the end of the loop. The ELSE option may be included or omitted.
- dBASE data files can be used for input in programs. The file must first be opened with the USE. Progression from one record to the next is accomplished with the SKIP.
- The EOF() function causes dBASE to examine the current record. If it is a data record, EOF() is false; if it is the end of file, EOF() is true. This is commonly used in controlling the loop of a program to process data from a file.
- An accumulator is a memory variable whose contents are increased during repetition of a loop to obtain a total.

COMMAND SUMMARY

Following are the general forms (in some cases, they are partial) for the commands used in this chapter to create programs. Remember from Chapter 15 that <> signifies an entry you must fill in and [ ] signifies an option.

? <list>
Displays a list of values on the next line.

ACCEPT [<prompt>] TO <memory variable>
Allows the entry of a character string into a memory variable.

CLEAR
Erases the screen.

DO <.prg filename>
Causes a program to be executed.

DO WHILE...<commands>...ENDDO
Allows a structured loop in a program. Must be terminated with an ENDDO.

IF...[ELSE]...ENDIF
Allows conditional execution of commands in a program, optionally with an alternative sequence (ELSE). Each IF must terminate with an ENDIF.

INPUT [<prompt>] TO <memory variable>
Allows the entry of a value into a memory variable.

MODIFY COMMAND <filename>
Word processor; allows editing of ASCII text files, including program (.prg) files.

SET PRINT ON/OFF
Sends/Does not send output of the ? command to the printer.

SET TALK ON/OFF
Sends/does not send the results of command execution to the screen.

SKIP
Causes the next record in a file to be made the current record.

STORE <expression> TO <memory variable list>
Stores the result of an expression into one or more memory variables.

WAIT [<prompt>] [TO <memory variable>]
Suspends program processing until a key is pressed.

NEW TERMINOLOGY

The following are important new terms introduced in this chapter; you should be familiar with each of them.

accumulator
command file
memory variable

REVIEW QUESTIONS

1. What will be the data types DATA1 and DATA2 from the following STORE commands?

   a. `STORE "This is it" TO DATA1`
   b. `STORE 25.6*AMNT TO DATA2[a1]`

2. What do you think would happen if the STORE statement at line 8 of the program in Figure 19-7 were omitted and the variable CONTIN were not initialized to Y? Try it on the computer to find out.

3. A user has several sets of quantity and price values to process. After the first set, the user respond to the WAIT command at line 17 of the Figure 19-7 program with the letter *y*. What will happen?

4. Write complete IF statements to perform the following operations.

   a. Accept values for AMOUNT1 and AMOUNT2 if the variable QUOTE contains the letter Y.

   b. Apply a 15 percent discount to the quantity in TOTAL if the variable TEMP contains a value greater than 100; otherwise, apply a 5 percent discount.

5. A program requires that the value stored in the variable PRICE be between 10 and 25 (not inclusive). Can the following IF statement be used for this test? Explain your answer.

```
IF PRICE > 10 .AND. < 25
```

6. What will happen upon execution of the program of Figure 19-13 if the AR file contains no records?

MATCHING

Match each action in a to h with the most appropriate command in 1 through 8.

a. STORE
b. MODIFY COMMAND
c. SET PRINT ON
d. INPUT
e. SKIP
f. DO WHILE
g. WAIT
h. IF

1. Make the next record of a data file available for processing.

2. Accept a numeric data value from the keyboard.

3. Respond to a single keystroke.

4. Place the result of a calculation in a memory variable.

5. Allow a counter to be incremented only if the values in two memory variables are the same.

6. Enter a dBASE program into a file.

7. Read and process exactly ten records from a data file.

8. Obtain a printed copy of the output from running a program.

TRUE/FALSE

Determine whether each of the following is true or false.

______ **1.** dBASE programs stored on disk are called command files.

______ **2.** Since a dBASE program must be entered as a text file, it can be created either with a word processor (saved without formatting) or with the dBASE editor.

______ **3.** Running a program destroys the program; hence, a program must be reentered after each run.

______ **4.** Comment lines in a program are indicated with the asterisk character (*); these are ignored by the dBASE interpreter.

______ **5.** The INPUT command can be used for entering either numeric or character data.

______ **6.** The type of each memory variable (numeric or character) must be declared in the program before it can be used.

______ **7.** The STORE command can be used only with numeric data.

______ **8.** If dBASE encounters a logic error in a program during execution, it stops and displays an error message.

______ **9.** The DO WHILE can be used with or without the ENDDO.

______ **10.** The following loop would execute exactly three times.

```
STORE 10 TO CNT
DO WHILE CNT < 16
  ? CNT
  STORE CNT + 2 TO CNT
ENDDO
```

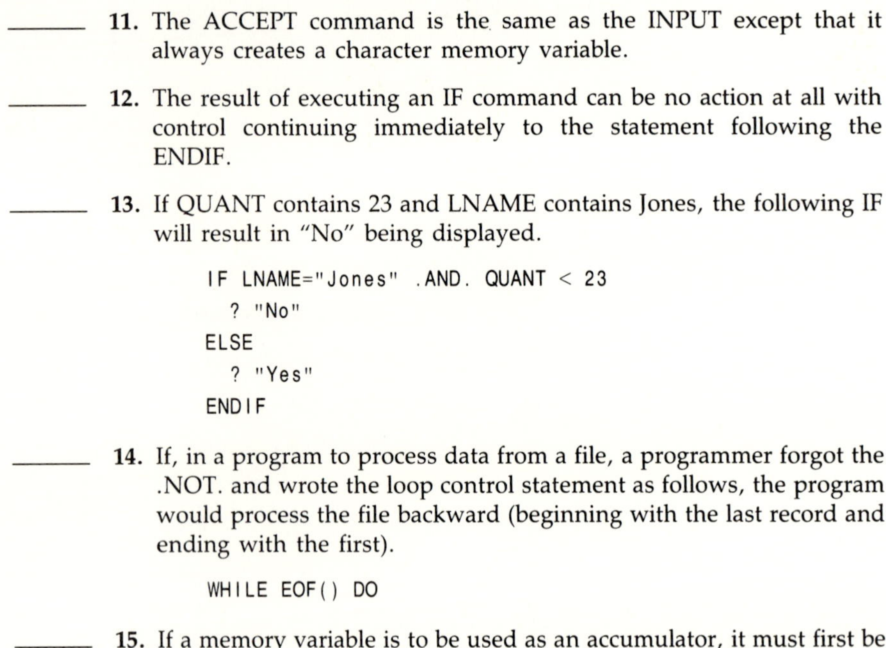

______ **11.** The ACCEPT command is the same as the INPUT except that it always creates a character memory variable.

______ **12.** The result of executing an IF command can be no action at all with control continuing immediately to the statement following the ENDIF.

______ **13.** If QUANT contains 23 and LNAME contains Jones, the following IF will result in "No" being displayed.

```
IF LNAME="Jones" .AND. QUANT < 23
  ? "No"
ELSE
  ? "Yes"
ENDIF
```

______ **14.** If, in a program to process data from a file, a programmer forgot the .NOT. and wrote the loop control statement as follows, the program would process the file backward (beginning with the last record and ending with the first).

```
WHILE EOF() DO
```

______ **15.** If a memory variable is to be used as an accumulator, it must first be initialized.

ANSWERS TO OBJECTIVE QUESTIONS

Matching

1. e 2. d 3. g 4. a 5. h 6. b 7. f 8. c

True/False

1. T 2. T 3. F 4. T 5. T 6. F 7. F 8. F 9. F
10. T 11. T 12. T 13. F 14. F 15. T

PROGRAMMING ASSIGNMENTS

1. Write a program to accept from the keyboard gross pay, tax withholding, and other deductions and compute and display the net pay, which is:

net pay = gross pay – tax withholding – other deductions

Include an appropriate announcement screen. The user is to be allowed to repeat as long as is desired.

2. Modify the program of the preceding problem to display the following message after the announcement screen.

```
Do you want to continue <Y/N>?
```

If the user does not respond with Y, execution of the program should be ended.

3. Write a program to print a table of the powers of two. Output should be:

```
1   1
2   4
3   9
4  16
and so on
```

Terminate processing when the power reaches 16.

4. Write a program to accept a sequence of positive numbers from the keyboard (one at a time within a loop). The loop must terminate when a value of zero is entered. Then print the count of the number of values entered and the largest value that was entered.

5. Using the BILLS dBASE file included on the data disk, write a program to list the following fields for each bill that has received a recommendation (RECOMMEND is true).

BILL

TITLE

RATING

At the end of the report, print the average score of all the bills in the list.

6. Each record in the dBASE data file named SALESPER contains the following information.

Salesperson name

Units sold

Unit commission

Base pay

Bonus point

Bonus

The first thing to do is to open the file interactively and obtain a printout of the structure and data so that you will know with what you are working. Then write a program to calculate the commission (units sold times unit commission) and determine the gross pay for each salesperson as follows:

Base pay if commission less than base pay.

Commission if commission between base pay and bonus point.

Commission + bonus if commission greater than bonus point.

Note that this will require that the ELSE option of an IF command contain another IF statement. Print a report the includes that following for each employee: salesperson name, commission, and gross pay. Include appropriate column headings.

7. Expand the program of the preceding assignment to include printing the total commissions and gross pay at the end of the report.

Chapter 20

Sharing Resources

OBJECTIVES

This chapter is about sharing computer resources, both hardware and software, between computers by interconnecting two or more computers. This can be done by directly connecting the computers or by linking them through the telephone system. When you have completed this chapter, you should be able to describe:

- Local area networks consisting of interconnected microcomputers.
- The hardware and software required for a local area network.
- How files are shared and how access of users to the files of a local area network are controlled.
- The significance of network speed.
- The three types of local area network configuration: bus, star, and ring.
- Gateways that allow a local area network to be connected to a mainframe computer.
- The meaning of data communication: the transmission of computer data over the telephone system without change.
- The function of the modem (hardware) in converting digital data into a form compatible with the telephone system.
- Data communication software that coordinates the exchange of information between two computers connected by a telephone line.
- Services available to the microcomputer owner through the telephone system, including bulletin boards and information services.

- The importance of ensuring that data available through the communications system is secure from theft and vandalism.
- The nature of serial transmission of data as used in data communication.
- The two methods of transmitting data: asynchronously, which is character by character, or synchronously, which is by blocks of data.
- Speed of transmission and factors to consider in selecting speed.
- The distinctions between simplex, half-duplex, and full-duplex data transmission.
- Detection and correction of errors in the transmission of data.

PREVIEW

The Need to Share Resources

In the office that uses two or more computers, there is often a need to share data files and hardware resources among computers.

Local Area Networks

A local area network is two or more computers interconnected to share data and peripherals. Hardware is required to connect the computers and software is required to control movement of information within the network (between computers).

Classifying Local Area Networks

Computers can be interconnected in a local area network in three configurations: bus, star, or ring.

More About Networks

Gateways allow two or more local area networks to be connected, or a local area network to be connected to a mainframe. Mainframe networks consist of computers directly connected or connected by telephone lines.

Principles of Data Communication

Data communication is the transmission of computer data without change over the telephone system. This requires both hardware and software.

Services Through Data Communication

The owner of a microcomputer equipped with communications hardware and software can dial into numerous public and private systems for information. However, the wide access to databases poses the problem of ensuring against loss of data or its unauthorized use.

Technical Aspects of Data Communication

The technical factors of data transmission include transmission speed, method of transmitting the data, and error detection and correction.

THE NEED TO SHARE RESOURCES

From the preceding chapters, you have learned about software and hardware. You have learned to use word processing, spreadsheet, and database software, and how to program. You have also learned the essentials of hardware: for instance, how the hard disk makes it possible to store large quantities of data and how the laser printer allows you to print documents suitable for publishing. Finally, you have learned how the computer and its software are used in the business environment to form the basis for automated processing of data. However, all of these topics have focused on problem solving using a single microcomputer. In fact, the MCT Enterprises case study revolves around a single hard-disk-equipped PC used for word processing, order processing and other accounting and spreadsheet applications. In most small businesses, as the users become more sophisticated, they find that a single computer becomes too limited for their needs. For instance, when one person needs the computer to enter a letter with the word processor, someone else might be using it to process orders. Growing companies usually find that their data processing needs grow much faster then the company. With the relatively low cost of microcomputers, a simple and economical solution is to purchase additional equipment.

To satisfy the processing needs of MCT Enterprises, assume that you have decided to acquire two more hard disk computers, communications capability, and a laser printer. Your first thought is to divide the work load among computers, as shown in Figure 20-1. Unfortunately, by adding equipment to solve the work overload problem, you have created another problem. That is, you now have isolated "islands" of information and processing capabilities. Consider the following typical problems. You must prepare form letters to be mailed to customers. For this, you use the word processing computer since it is the one with the laser printer. Unfortunately, the customer file that you need in generating the form letters is on the hard disk of the accounting computer. The data communications capability of the accounting computer (data communications is described later in this chapter) allows your sales representatives to transmit orders over the telephone line. But occasionally you must use its communication ability to transmit files prepared on the word processor computer to a professional publisher. For some of your spreadsheet studies, you need data stored in the accounting databases. These are all examples of data or hardware on one computer needed to complete a task being performed on another computer.

There is a need to share resources—both hard resources and soft resources. For instance, the laser printer of the word processor computer (a hard resource) and many of the data files in the accounting computer (soft resources) must be available to all computers. Sharing computer resources

Figure 20-1
Multiple computers in a work environment.

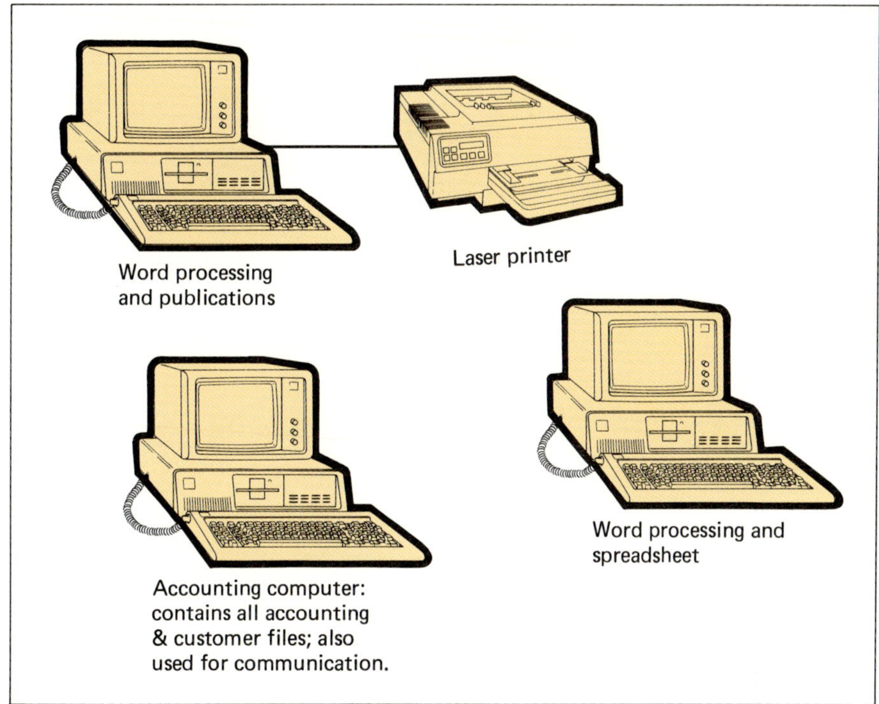

is done by networking, the interconnection of computers, and by data communications, one of the means for connecting one computer to another. These are the topics of this chapter.

LOCAL AREA NETWORKS

In some offices the only need for interconnection of computers is to share a laser printer. For this a simple printer-controlling device such as the Microfazer can be used. Up to five computers can send output to a single printer through this unit. From each computer the printer cable goes to the printer controller, which controls all output to the printer itself.

A **local area network (LAN)** is two or more computers interconnected so that they can:

- exchange data, and
- share peripherals such as hard disk drives and letter-quality printers.

By local is meant that the computers of the network are confined to a single building although they may be located in several buildings, such as on a college campus. The computers are directly connected by cables whose lengths are measured in hundreds or thousands of feet. By contrast, networks in which computers ranging in size from small minicomputers to large mainframes are linked by telephone lines may be miles, or even hundreds of miles, apart. To interconnect two or more computers to form a LAN requires specialized hardware and software. The LAN descriptions that follow are typical of the hardware and software available.

Local Area Network Hardware

The simplest LAN consists of two computers connected by a cable. Most (but not all) networks require that each computer in the network include a

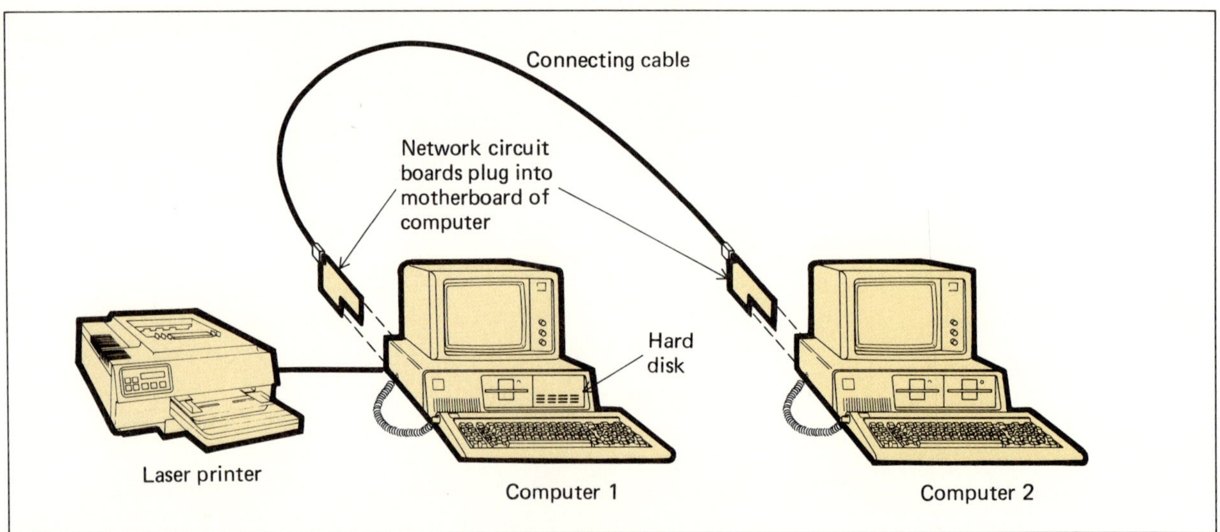

Figure 20-2
A simple computer network.

network card that must be plugged into the motherboard into which the cable connects. This is illustrated in Figure 20-2. With this configuration, both computers have access to the printer and to the hard disk drive in computer 1. With the exception of the network card, these are conventional microcomputers identical to those you have learned about in this book. In fact, you can sit down to one of the computers in a network and use it without even realizing that it is part of a network.

Through the network, you can also use resources elsewhere in the network as if they were actually part of your computer. For instance, working from the two-floppy computer 2 in Figure 20-2, if you addressed drives A and B, you would be referring to the floppy drives in your computer. However, if you addressed drive C, you would be referring to the hard disk in computer 1. If you issued a print command to print a word processing file, your file would be routed through the network cards and cable to computer 1, from which it would be printed.

In this example, computer 1, in addition to responding to the requests of the user at its keyboard, must also perform some functions for computer 2. These are called *network functions,* and in most local area networks are performed by a separate computer called a network server computer, as illustrated in Figure 20-3. Here we see a high-capacity hard disk that serves as the network disk and on which files are stored that are commonly used by other computers in the network. With many network designs, the server is an ordinary microcomputer in the network that has been set up specifically to control the network. In others, it is a computer designed solely for the purpose of network control.

Note in Figure 20-3 that computers of the network have different hardware configurations; each computer can be equipped with the peripherals to meet the needs of the person who will be using it. Some networks even allow microcomputers on the network that do not include any disk drives at all (computer C in Figure 20-3). These *diskless workstations* are identical to the others except that all disk activities channel through the network disk.

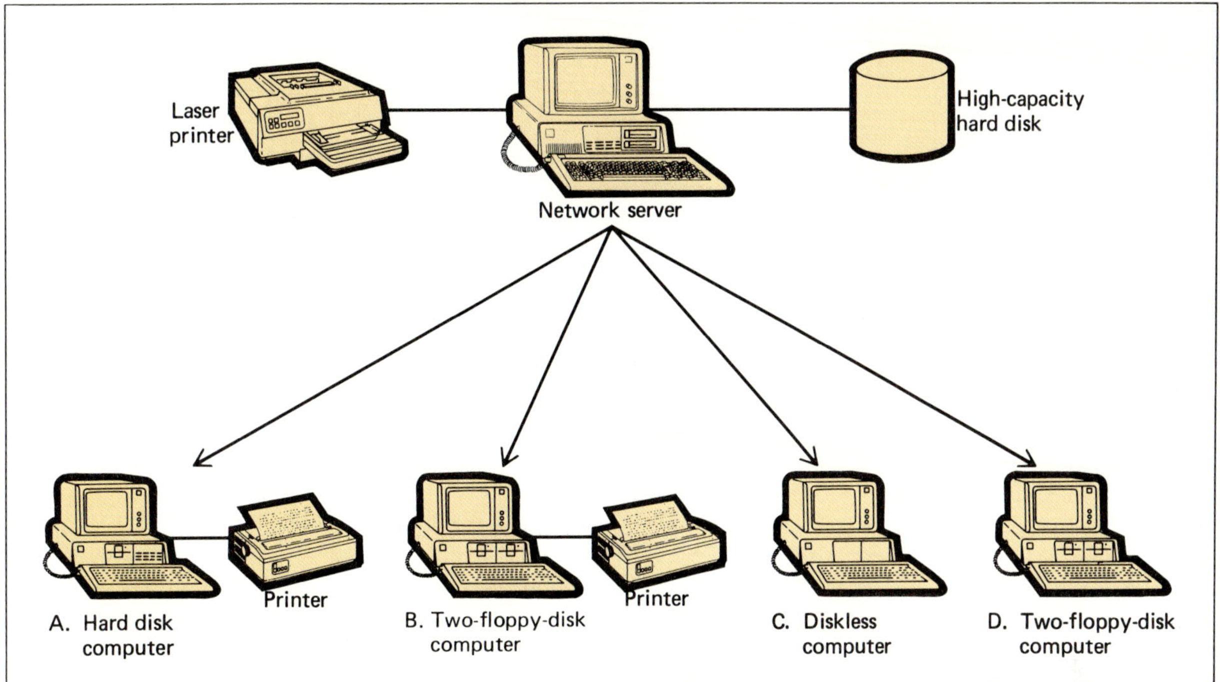

Figure 20-3
A computer network with a file server.

Controlling Access to a Network

When using a computer on a network, you still use an operating system such as DOS in the way you learned in Chapter 5, and productivity software as you learned in other chapters. However, you also use network software that controls flow of data between computers and to shared peripherals. It is easy to envision the need for control of output sent to the laser printer. Without control, if two computers attempted to print at the same time, their output would be intermingled and consequently useless.

Control of access to the network hard disk is a critical function of the network software. Being a network resource, the network disk contains not only your files, but also those of other users of the network, as well as those required by the file server needed for control. Obviously, you would not want someone else changing or erasing your files, nor would you or any other user of the network want the network control programs erased. One method of preventing this is by setting up a subdirectory for each user (done by the system manager, a person who is in charge of the network) and controlling access to the network and to individual subdirectories. (Subdirectories were described in Chapter 5.)

To illustrate how this works, consider a simple arrangement in which a system manager has created three subdirectories with their contents as shown in Figure 20-4. Although these are subdirectories on the network hard disk, the network gives them the drive designations G, H, and I. (DOS allows you to define *logical drives,* which are drive designations given to subdirectories located on the A disk.) There are two types of access to

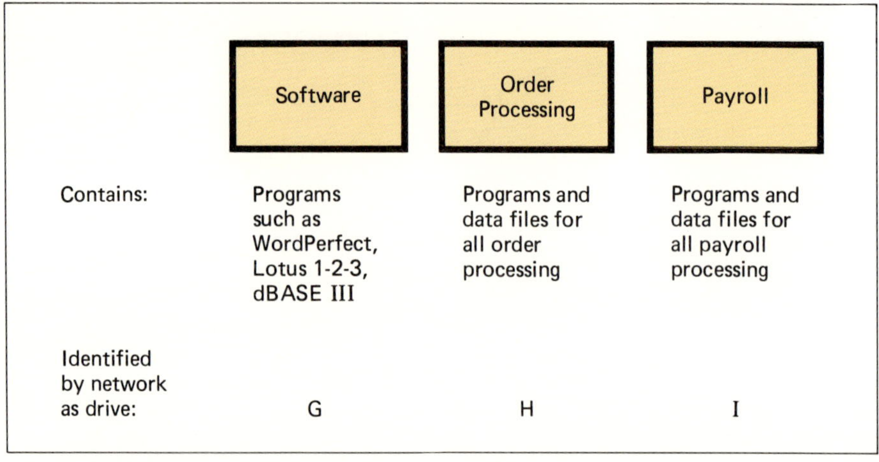

Figure 20-4
Distributing software/application components.

files of a subdirectory: read and write. *Read access* means that a user can read the file from disk. For a program such as dBASE, the user would be able to copy it into memory to run it; for a data file such as the customer file, the user would be able to read records and prepare a report. *Write access* means that a user can change the contents of a file. For the customer file, this could be changing the amount that the customer owed, or even deleting the file. Access to almost all files in a network is designated as **read only,** meaning you can read but not change the file, or **read/write,** meaning you can both read and change the file.

Typical access needs of the system manager and three network users within the organization are summarized in the following table.

User	Function/Responsibility	Required File Access
System manager	Manage the network.	Read/write to all directories.
Jane	In charge of order processing.	Read/write to Order processing. Read only to Software.
Phil	Assist with order processing.	Read/write to Order processing. Read only to Software.
Scott	In charge of payroll; must prepare reports using data in order processing files.	Read/write to Payroll. Read only to Order processing. Read only to Software.
Marion	Write programs for other users.	Read only to Software.

To accommodate each of the users and control access to the files, the system manager would (1) enter the user name and a password into the network-controlled user list and create a subdirectory into which that user could store files; and (2) enter into an access list for each subdirectory of Figure 20-4 the name of each user with access to the files of that directory, and whether the access is read only or read/write.

To illustrate how a user would interact with the system, let us assume that Marion's user name is MARION, that her password is FLASH, and that she attempted to log into the network but misspelled her password. If user access to the network is from the F drive, then her dialog with the computer would be as shown in Figure 20-5. After she realized her error and logged in with her correct password, the network software would identify the directories to which she has access. In this case, she would be given read/write access to her own directory and read access to the software directory, which would be identified as drive G (see Figure 20-4). If she requested a directory listing of drive G, DOS would display the contents of the software directory in the same way it displays the contents of a floppy disk. She would be able to run any of the programs from drive G but she would be unable to write to that drive (she has been assigned only read rights to G). If she attempted to access data from drives H or I (Order processing and Payroll), she would receive an error message because she has not been given the rights to these directories and, to her, these drives do not even exist. On the other hand, when Scott logs in, he would be informed that he has access to drives G, H, and I. For drive I, his rights are read/write, but for drives G and H they are read only.

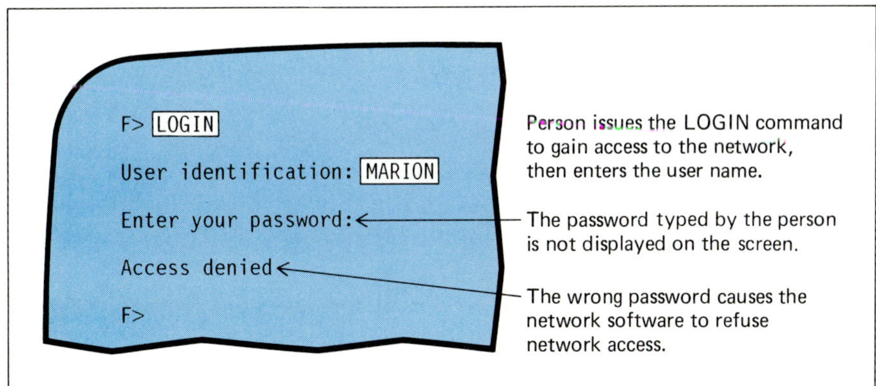

Figure 20-5
A log in failure.

File Sharing in a Network

In the preceding example, both the system manager and Scott have read/write access to the payroll subdirectory; this introduces a potential problem. Assume that Scott is entering weekly payroll information and is about to enter overtime information for employee Charles Dobbins. The system manager is performing maintenance on the file and is about to change the job classification of Dobbins. The action of each of their programs will be: (1) read the record of Dobbins into memory of their respective computers,

(2) accept the entry from the keyboard and change the field in the record, and (3) write the updated record back to disk. If the system manager finishes first, her copy of the record (with the updated job classification) will be written back to disk. When Scott finishes, his copy will be written back with the (overtime information), thus overwriting the newly corrected copy from the system manager.

A simple way of preventing this is to designate such files as *nonsharable,* meaning that two users cannot open the same file at the same time. Although this will prevent such conflicts, it means that two programs using the same file cannot be run at the same time even if they only read from the file. Another way of avoiding this is called **record locking.** This capability is provided by some software, and automatically prevents one program from accessing the same record another program is processing.

Network System Manager

The more hardware and software a user acquires, the more knowledge for using it is needed. Predictably, the hardware and software needs of a local area network are considerably greater than those for an individual collection of computers—enough so that a person trained in using the network should be available. This person, commonly called a *network system manager,* could be one of the users, or might be on the staff as a programmer. The network responsibilities of this person are many and varied, and include (1) performing periodic backup of the network hard disk to magnetic tape; (2) changing the configuration of the network to meet the changing needs of the organization; (3) adding new users to the network and establishing their level of access; (4) adding new data files to the system and deciding where to store them, who has access to them, whether each user has read only or read/write access, and whether or not they are sharable; (5) and coping with daily operational problems, such as a document sent to the network printer that never gets printed or the user is denied access to the network in attempting to log in. There are an endless number of such tasks requiring a good knowledge of the networking software.

CLASSIFYING LOCAL AREA NETWORKS

Two of the ways in which networks are classified are by the speed with which data is transmitted over the network and by the way in which the computers of the network are interconnected.

Network Speed

The speed at which data is transmitted through the cabling of the network from one computer to the other is called **bandwidth.** Speed partially determines how many computers can be using the network at a given time without slowing it down. For example, assume that you are running a program that is constantly accessing data from one of your files on the network disk. Each time your program reads or writes a record, it must travel through connecting wires to the network server. If you are the only person working on the network at the time, file accessing actions will be very fast. However, if there are several users who are also doing heavy disk processing, you will be sharing the network resources and you will notice that file access operations are much slower.

Local area networks have data transmission speeds of 1 megabit (1 million bits) per second and up. This means, in theory, that a 100K byte file could be transferred from one computer to another in slightly less than 1 second. However, in practice, many activities are taking place at the same time on a network and the effective speed of the network is considerably slower than the theoretical. Advertised transmission speeds can be misleading.

Network Configuration

The word **topology** refers to the way in which the computers of a network are physically interconnected by the wiring. There are three common network topologies: bus, star, and ring.

Bus. The computers of a **bus network** are connected by a single cable called a *bus* through which information is transmitted in either direction between computers (see Figure 20-6). In most networks, one of the computers serves as the file server. Since data is moving in both directions, conflicts sometimes arise. There are a variety of methods used to avoid or correct the result of "colliding" data when two computers attempt to transmit at exactly the same instant. Unless the network is overloaded, these work well and the user is not even aware of the actions taking place.

Star. A **star network** consists of a controlling network server that is individually cabled to each computer of the network, as shown in Figure 20-7. All communication is between individual computers in the network and the network server. This type of network is highly reliable because each computer in the network has its own "pipeline" into the network server so there is no simultaneous transmission by two computers over a single line. However, communication from one computer to another must be routed through the file server, placing an unneeded burden on the server. Furthermore, cabling can be clumsy. For instance, if six computers

Figure 20-6
A bus network.

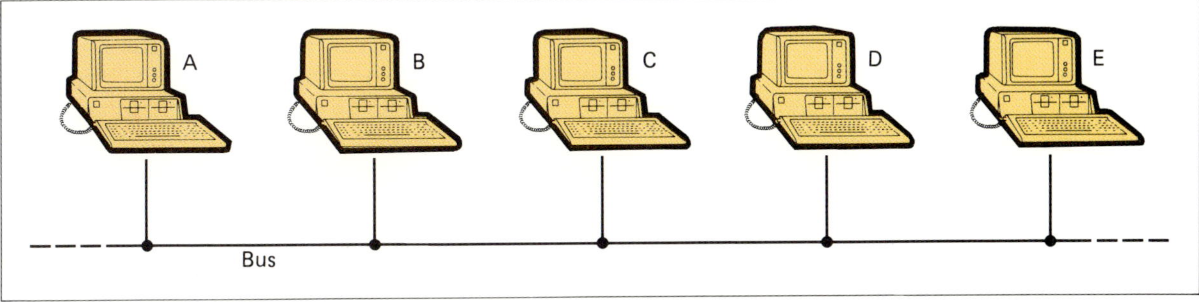

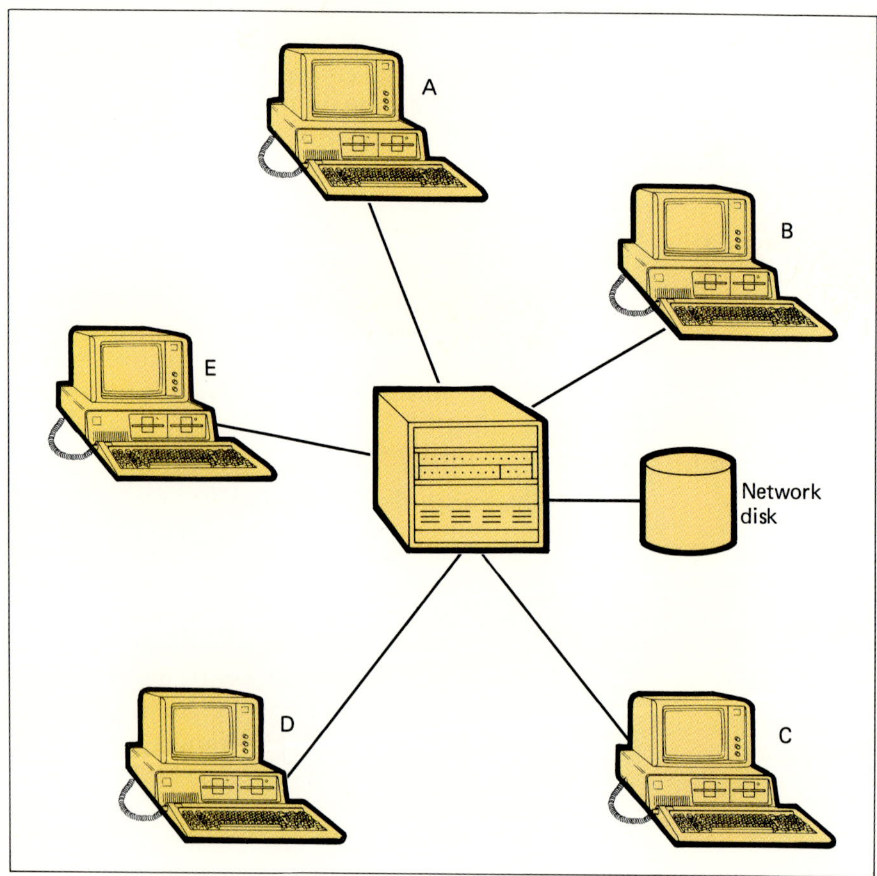

Figure 20-7
A star network.

are located in an office 200 feet from the file server, then six separate cables from the server, one for each computer, will be needed. Contrast this with a single cable for a bus network. The most significant shortcoming is that if the network server breaks down, the entire network is inoperable. However, with the high reliability of modern microcomputer components, such breakdowns are infrequent.

Ring. The **ring network,** as illustrated in Figure 20-8, is like a bus network except that the ends of the bus are connected to form a continuous loop. However, the manner in which the ring works is completely different from a bus. Information flow in the ring is in a single direction. Thus, if computer C in Figure 20-8 is to transmit a file to computer D, it will earmark it for D and send it on its way. In transit, the file will be seen and ignored by computers B, A, and E. It will be processed only by computer D, the computer for which it was originally earmarked. With data flowing in one direction, there is never a problem of data collision as in the bus network. A problem with the ring topology is that the failure of any computer in the ring will disrupt the flow of data in the ring, thus disabling the network.

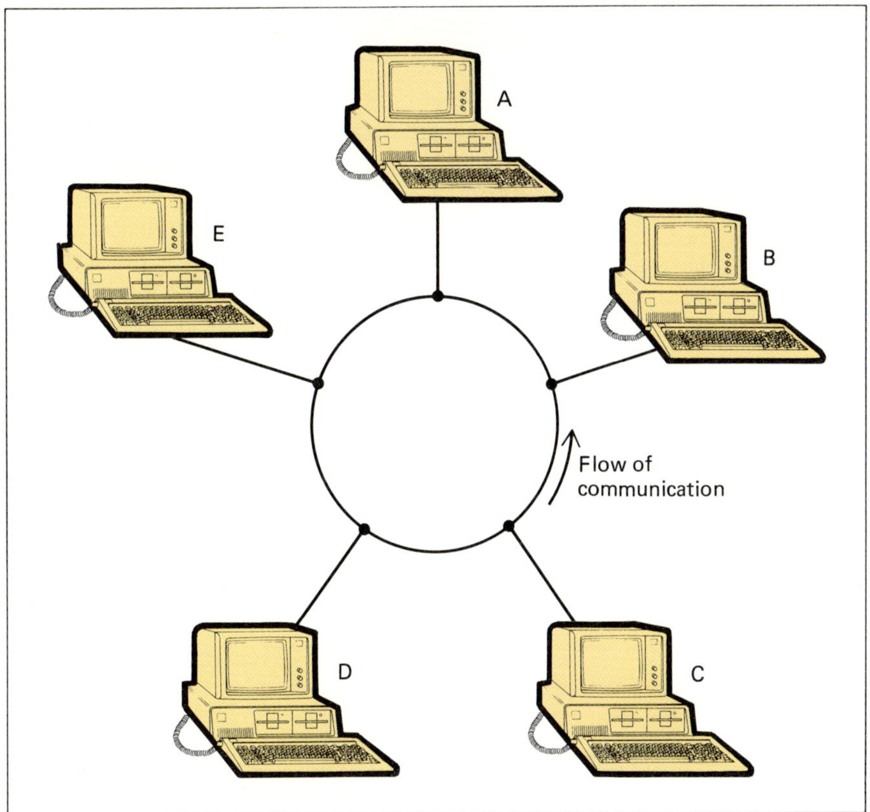

Figure 20-8
A ring network.

MORE ABOUT NETWORKS

Local Area Network Gateways

Local area networks provide a simple means for sharing resources among a number of microcomputers. Some organizations need to share data between two networks or between a local area network and a mainframe. For instance, a large construction company might have two local area networks, one used for accounting and the other for engineering work. For almost all applications, the software and data files are independent of each other. However, for certain applications, users of one of the networks might require access to software or data files in the other. Similarly, a corporation might have a mainframe that handles companywide processing and one or more local area networks for local activities. By copying files or portions of data files from the mainframe to the network, network users can use spreadsheet or database software to perform analyses on the data completely independently of the mainframe. The combination of circuit boards and software that allows two local area networks or a local area network and a mainframe to be cabled together is called a **gateway.**

Mainframe Networks

Networking of computers is not unique to microcomputer systems. Indeed, linking of mainframe computers was common before microcomputers became popular for business applications. Mainframe computers can be linked by direct connection in which the computers are usually in the same room or adjacent rooms, or by very-high-speed telephone circuits in which the computers are separated by hundreds or thousands of miles. Interconnecting of mainframes is done for two purposes: sharing the workload and sharing data. Many companies and governmental agencies use two or more directly connected mainframes working as equals to share a work load. Large computers are commonly directly connected to small computers that take over some of the specialized tasks, such as input and output. In other situations, computers that are linked through the communications system can exchange information easily. For example, the Advanced Research Projects Agency Network (ARPANET) of the U.S. Defense Department interconnects minicomputers and mainframes at over forty university and research institutions in the United States and Europe.

PRINCIPLES OF DATA COMMUNICATION

Introduction

In preceding sections of this chapter, you learned that data can be shared between widely separated computers by connecting them through the telephone system. Indeed, the telephone system was used for transmission of data long before microcomputers became popular. As illustrated in Figure 20-9, through terminals users could dial into computers and gain

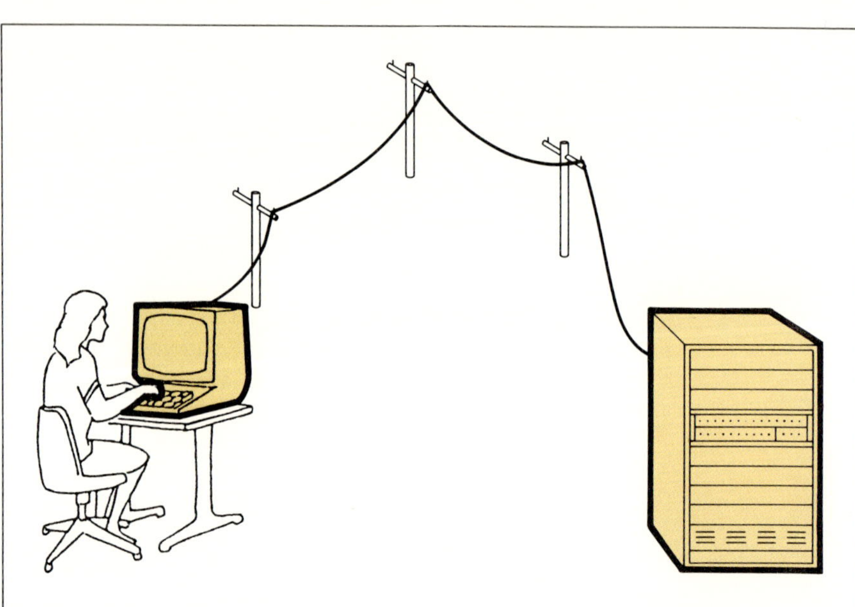

Figure 20-9
Connecting to a computer through telephone lines.

access to the capabilities of large computers as if they were on the premises. For instance, using a portable terminal, a salesperson could insert a telephone handset of any desktop telephone into a special receptacle in the terminal, dial the home office computer, and transmit or send sales information. Using a terminal at home, a professor could dial into the college computer and enter programs. Using terminals at ticket sales offices, airline sales agents could make and confirm airline reservations almost instantly. With the microcomputer of today, these and many other capabilities are available to everyone. In this section, you will learn about how telephone circuits are used for data transmission, and the software and hardware needed. In sections that follow, you will learn about computer communications applications, security considerations, and technical aspects of computer communications.

What Is Data Communication?

Data communication is a type of telecommunication. Telecommunication is the transmission of information over some distance without changing it. (The Greek word *tele* means far, or far off.) A telecommunication system consists of the following three components (which are illustrated in Figure 20-10).

1. A sender (source), which creates the information to be transmitted.
2. A medium, over which the information is transmitted.
3. A receiver (sink), which receives the information.

For an ordinary telephone conversation, the sender and receiver are people and the medium is the telephone circuit. However, in a broader sense, the sender and receiver could as easily be machines; in fact, the first transmission of information over an electrical wire was the telegraph. Our focus of attention is on senders and receivers that are computers (or computer terminals). In other words, a computer (or terminal) "talks to" another computer over the telecommunication network. All processing of data is still performed by the computer; the communications network is simply the means for transmitting the data. Thus, **data communication** is the transmission over the telephone network of computer data without changing or processing the data.

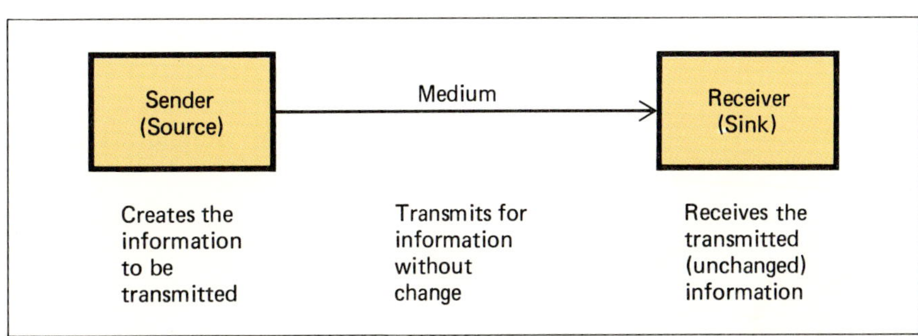

Figure 20-10
Basic components of a telecommunications system.

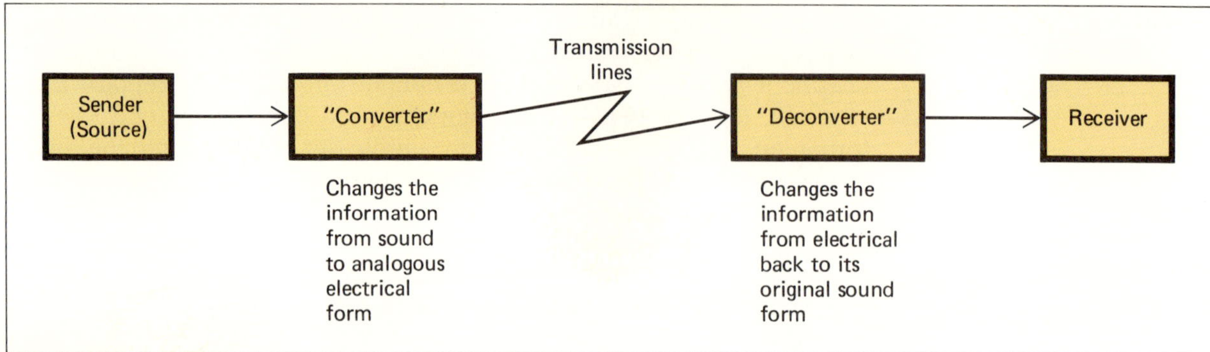

Figure 20-11
Transmission of data through an analog system.

Data Communications Hardware

The sender–medium–receiver concept is not unique to telecommunications. Shouting to another person, in fact, is the transmission of information over a distance via the medium "air," which carries the sound waves. Needless to say, telecommunications increases the possible distance between the sender and receiver. However, in order to do this, the sound (sender's message) is first converted into electric waves that correspond exactly to the sound waves that it represents. This electric signal is termed **analog,** since it is an exact electrical duplication of the sound. Thus, a telecommunication system requires two additional elements, as shown in Figure 20-11. Sound waves are entered into the "converter" and electric waves that are exactly equivalent are transmitted over the medium, the telephone wire.

The circumstances are very similar when the sender and receiver are computers or terminals. Now, however, the computer generates digital signals, which represent discrete values of either 0 or 1 and are not compatible with the continuous analog nature of telephone equipment. Consequently, the converting equipment must change the computer digital signals into the electrical equivalent of voicelike tones, and back again. Electronics people call this *modulation* and *demodulation* of the signal. The units that perform these functions thus are called **modems.** (The name is taken from the first letters of the words *mo*dulate and *dem*odulate.) Their overall role is illustrated in Figure 20-12, which shows two interconnected computers.

Although most telecommunication today uses analog transmission, the microprocessor is changing that. With today's electronics, digital transmission, even for voice, is cheaper and more efficient than analog. In fact, digital transmission has come into use mainly for data use. The change from analog to digital will be a slow one because of the huge investment by telephone companies in installed analog equipment.

Basic Data Communications Software

Like all other computer applications, data communication requires software for the hardware components to function. For instance, if computer A requests a file from computer B, the actions of the two computers must be

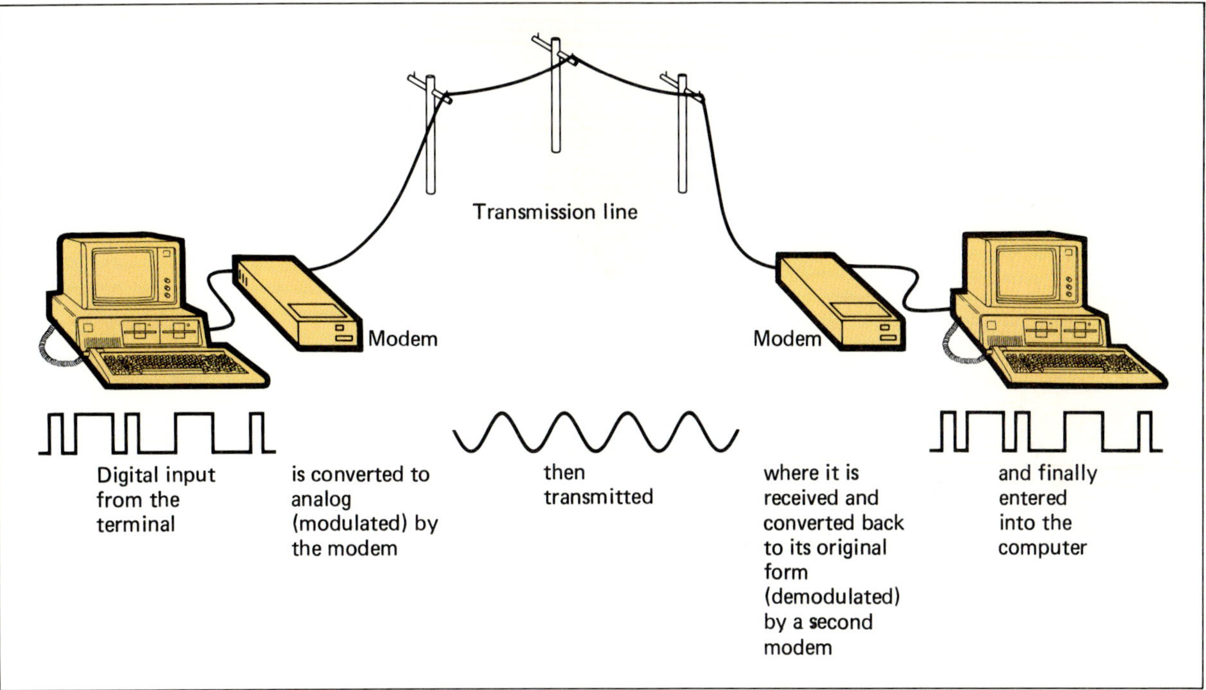

Figure 20-12
Transmission of digital information through an analog system.

carefully synchronized so that B receives and interprets the request from A, and A is ready to accept the file when B begins to transmit. This is complicated by the fact that the computers might be different (for instance, A might be a microcomputer and B a mainframe) and use entirely different operating systems. The need for control is roughly analogous to two people having a conversation; there is a conventional protocol. Assuming that neither is bilingual, they must both use the same language. If one were speaking in German and the other in French, there would be no communication. Furthermore, they must not be talking at the same time, without regard for each other.

As with most other applications, many prewritten communications programs are available for microcomputers. In fact, most of the integrated software packages described in Chapter 17 include communications components. Some functions of basic communications software for microcomputers are:

- To set the communications parameters, including the speed at which data will be transmitted. Other technical aspects of data communication are described later in this chapter.
- To establish the link between the two computers, called **handshaking,** and inform the users that the link has been established.
- To allow the two computer users to communicate with each other through their keyboards and screens.
- To allow for the transfer of files from one computer to the other.

Internal modems (a) are plugged into the motherboard, and external modems (b) sit beside the computer and connect to a serial port. They both do the same thing.

SERVICES THROUGH DATA COMMUNICATION

In using your modem-equipped computer from your own home, there are many computers and computer networks that you can access through the telephone system. Your computer can effectively function as your newspaper, travel agent, library, and so on. Let us consider some of these services.

Public Bulletin Boards

An electronic **bulletin board** is much like the bulletin board in an office where anyone can read the posted announcements or post their own for others to read. Many computer software companies maintain bulletin boards listing information about their software. Such information commonly includes notices of changes, reports of bugs that have not yet been corrected, and tips regarding the use of the software.

Anyone can dial into a public bulletin board (at no charge) and read the announcements. Most have provisions for the user to post notices on the bulletin board. Many bulletin boards are set up for individuals with special interests. For example, a desktop publishing users' group might maintain a bulletin board for anyone interested in desktop publishing. Setting up a bulletin board is a relatively simple matter; it only requires dedicating a modem-equipped microcomputer (with appropriate bulletin board software) and a telephone line.

Most bulletin boards include programs that you can copy and use. This is called public domain software because the authors have made it available free to anyone who wants to use it. However, using it presents a potential danger to the security of the files on your own computer as described in the enclosed box.

Virus: A Real Danger

Unfortunately, there are individuals in all walks of life who seem to thrive on the misfortune of others. Over the years a favorite prank of an occasional programmer has been to imbed a section of code into a program that, when a certain condition occurs, displays an unexpected (usually taunting) message on the screen. Now schemes such as this are jeopardizing the broad access to data in computer networks because a few unscrupulous individuals appear to be intent on causing serious trouble. Typically, a program containing a destructive code will be posted to a bulletin board for anyone to copy. When run, the code will copy itself into elements of your operating system. This code, commonly called a **virus,** can "infect" a hard disk and cause problems, ranging from displaying distracting messages when you least expect them to destroying the entire contents of the disk.

In October 1988 a graduate student entered a nondestructive virus into a computer of the ARPANET system. Unfortunately, it began reproducing itself without control and ultimately infected more than 6000 computers, bringing many large mainframes to their knees. Although data was not damaged, thousands of hours of effort were required to clear the computers.

This incident significantly raised the awareness of the computer community to the vulnerability of our many shared computers. Unfortunately, there is no foolproof method of protecting against a virus or of detecting one before it causes damage.

Information Services

In addition to bulletin boards that provide free access and information, there are many subscription services. Sometimes called *information services,* some of these services offer specialized information for professionals, such as doctors or lawyers, and others offer a general range of information. Of the latter, the most widely used is The Source; the way it functions and its services are typical. You pay an annual subscription fee, and The Source will issue you an account with an identification number, allowing you to dial into The Source at any time you wish. Your use of the service is recorded and you are charged for the time you are logged in. Rates are highest during prime-time hours (7:00 a.m. to 6:00 p.m.); during non-prime-time hours, they are much lower (in the $10–15-per-hour range). Following are some of the services available through The Source.

News. News stories are available from the Associated Press news wire, United Press International Business Wire, *The Washington Post,* and other news sources. A user can view a list of news stories, or limit the scope to, for example, business news pertaining to a particular state. Searches for articles can be conducted based on date or author, or even by keyword.

Research. Over 100,000 pages of financial and market data on businesses, industries, and products are available for researching. For the investor, Standard & Poors Quotes and Prices provide up-to-the-minute stock and bond quotations, as well as financial profiles of companies.

Travel Services. If you are planning a trip, you can use the electronic edition of the *Official Airline Guide* to find comprehensive rate and schedule information for over 700 airlines throughout the world. You can even obtain weather forecasts for your intended destination.

Communications. Bulletin board services, which are available to subscribers, allow messages to be posted for reading by anyone who dials in. Electronic mail service, which is analogous to regular U.S. mail, is available. Each user has a mailbox and can send mail to other mailboxes or receive mail from other users. Unlike bulletin boards, mail for a given user can be read only by that user.

Consumer Services. Special catalog shopping offers discounts on over 200,000 items, ranging from appliances, to computers, to clothing.

Personal Computing. A buyer's guide lists a broad range of computing products and abstracts of reviews. Special-interest groups are supported (such as IBM PC owners or Ashton-Tate software users) for the exchange of ideas.

Data Security

Computer networks and remote access to computers greatly expand the abilities of the individual, business, and government by providing them wide access to a very broad base of data. Unfortunately, this tool, with its potential for so many beneficial uses, provides an equal opportunity for uses that are questionable. Banking systems, for instance, provide the ideal environment for electronic theft of money; central databases are an open invitation to the invasion of personal privacy (see Figure 20-13).

Newspapers and magazines report all types of computer-related crime. Some may appear to be harmless game playing or just snooping; others are clearly fraudulent. The following are some of the typical problems that have been encountered.

- A student figures out the entry code to the university computer system and changes his grades, and those of some friends.
- A systems analyst feels that he has been dealt with unfairly by the company and wants to "even the score." He does this by making subtle changes to critical processing programs, which, over a period of time, introduce garbage into the database.
- A consultant breaks the entry codes to a system and copies pro-

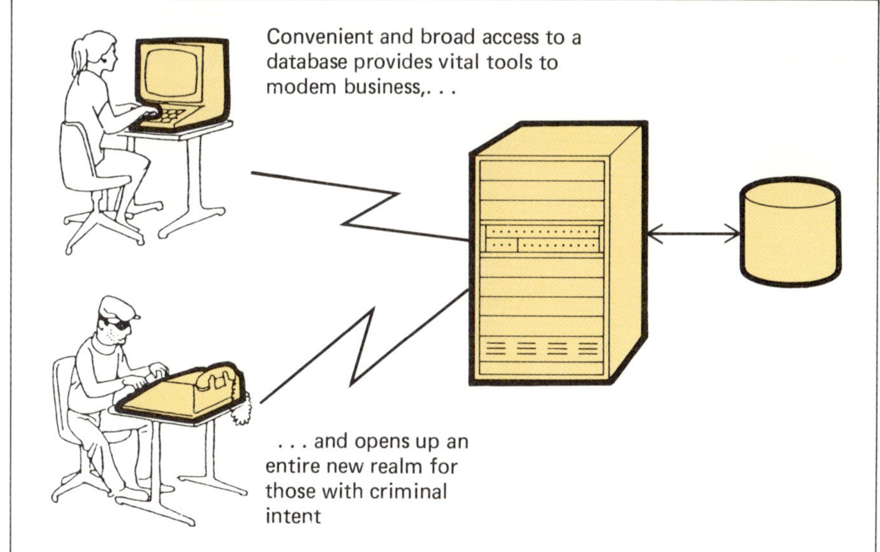

Figure 20-13
Desirable and undesirable access to a database.

When the satellite shown in this photograph is placed in orbit around the earth, it will be capable of relaying thousands of voice and data communications signals from dishes such as the one shown.

grams costing hundreds of thousands of dollars to write. Copies of the programs are sold to competitors.

Most experts readily admit that there is no way to stop the experienced and dedicated intruder from gaining access to a computer system. However, it is possible to use techniques and systems that will make it difficult to steal. A good security system is one that makes it so costly in terms of time and resources to break into the system that doing so loses its appeal. Furthermore, if the security system makes apprehension of the intruder highly likely, its effectiveness as a deterrent increases.

Most on-line computer systems with remote terminals rely on *identification* codes to gain access to the system and files within the system. Such a code may be a simple password consisting of several letters that will permit a user to gain access to the computer for writing programs, or it may be much more elaborate. Some systems require a terminal identification code, a user identification number, and special access codes to various files. The sample log-in dialogue of Figure 20-5 for a computer network is a typical example.

TECHNICAL ASPECTS OF DATA COMMUNICATION

Serial Transmission of Data

In Chapter 4, you learned of the distinction between serial and parallel transmission of data. With a parallel circuit the 8 bits composing a byte are transmitted simultaneously over eight separate wires. With a serial circuit, the bytes are disassembled, and the bits are transmitted one after the other, as illustrated in Figure 20-14. Serial transmission is used in data communications.

Figure 20-14
Serial transmission of data.

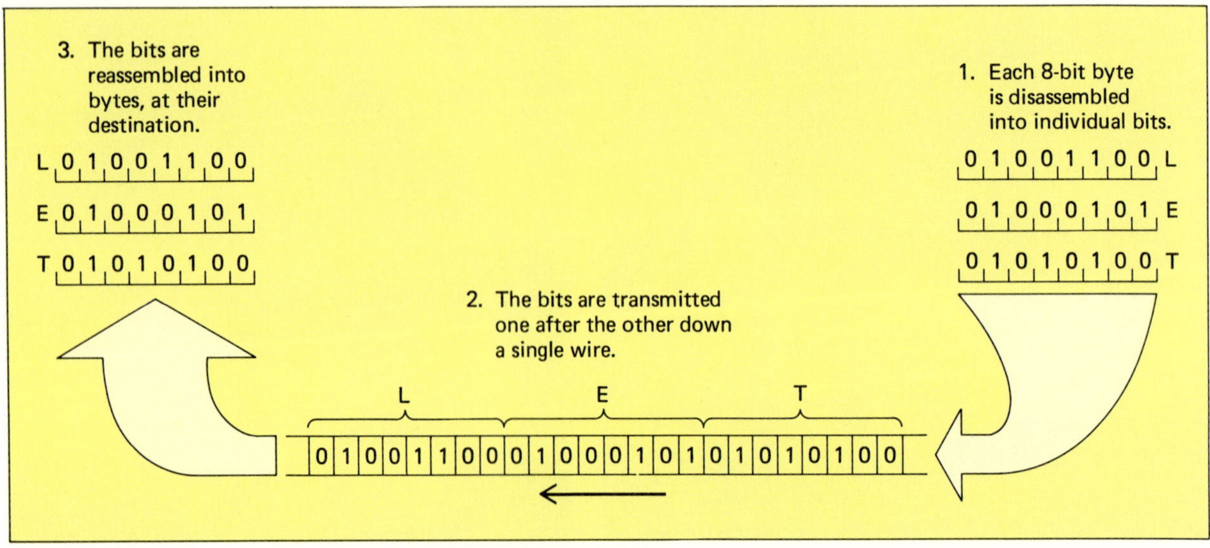

Figure 20-15
RS232 connector.

If different manufacturers are to manufacture equipment that works together in transmitting data (in this case, computer companies, modem companies, and the telephone company), then some industrywide standard is essential. The most widely used standard in the communications industry is that defined by the Electronic Industries Association. Technically, it is called the EIA Standard RS-232-C Interface Between Data Processing Terminal Equipment and Data Communication Equipment. For short, it is usually referred to as **RS232.** This standard defines (1) a standardized electrical connector that includes pins for twenty-five wires—an RS232 connector is shown in Figure 20-15, (2) electrical specifications, and (3) standardized electrical pin assignments, including wires for ground, data, control, and timing. Of the twenty-five lines, one of them is used as the primary line for sending data and another for receiving data. Only a portion of the twenty-five lines of the standard are used with microcomputer modems. Because of the wide acceptance of the connector in the computer industry as a whole, it is commonly used with microcomputers.

When transmitting data serially, it is essential that the modems be exactly "in step" with each other; otherwise, the translation of the received data will be different from the transmitted data. To illustrate, suppose that Figure 20-14 represents data being sent over a communication line and that somehow, the modem at the receiving end "misses" the first 2 bits, as illustrated in Figure 20-16. If it begins reassembling the bits starting with the third bit, then it is obvious that the reassembled message will be garbled. In this example, the 8 bits beginning with the third bit are the ASCII code for the digit 1. This problem is resolved by the modem's use of special techniques to keep in step.

Furthermore, the modems must be set so that they are "talking the same language." That is, the set of parameters that the modems use in converting data to and from transmission form must be the same. This is called the transmission **protocol** and is the subject of this section.

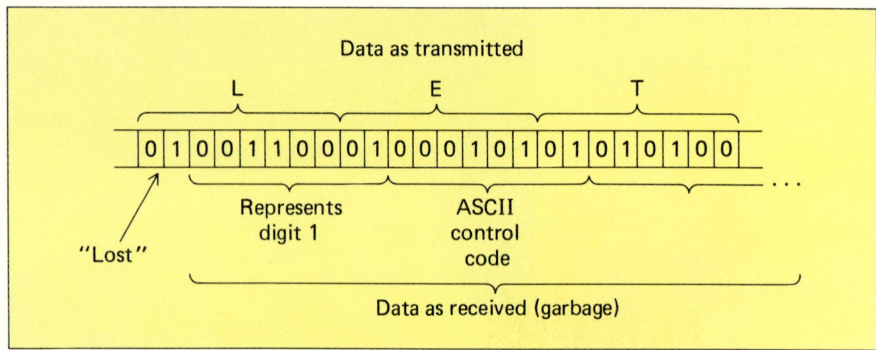

Figure 20-16
The effect of modems being out of synchronization.

Asynchronous and Synchronous Transmission

Most modems transmit data in either of two modes: asynchronous or synchronous. **Asynchronous transmission** is the transmission of each character as it is available. This is suitable for a microcomputer where a person is typing from a keyboard to a remote computer. Although the input from a fast typist might appear to be a continuous stream of data, it is not to the communication system, which transmits data much faster than a person can type. Hence, each character is separated from the preceding character by an indefinite time interval, as illustrated in Figure 20-17. To enable the receiving modem to recognize a character when it arrives, the transmitting modem "frames" each characters. Preceding the character is a start bit and following the character is a stop bit. Thus, the transmission of each character involves 10 bits. (Some techniques use 2 stop bits, in which case, the transmission of each character requires 11 bits.) This type of transmission is also called *start-stop* transmission.

Figure 20-17
Asynchronous data transmission.

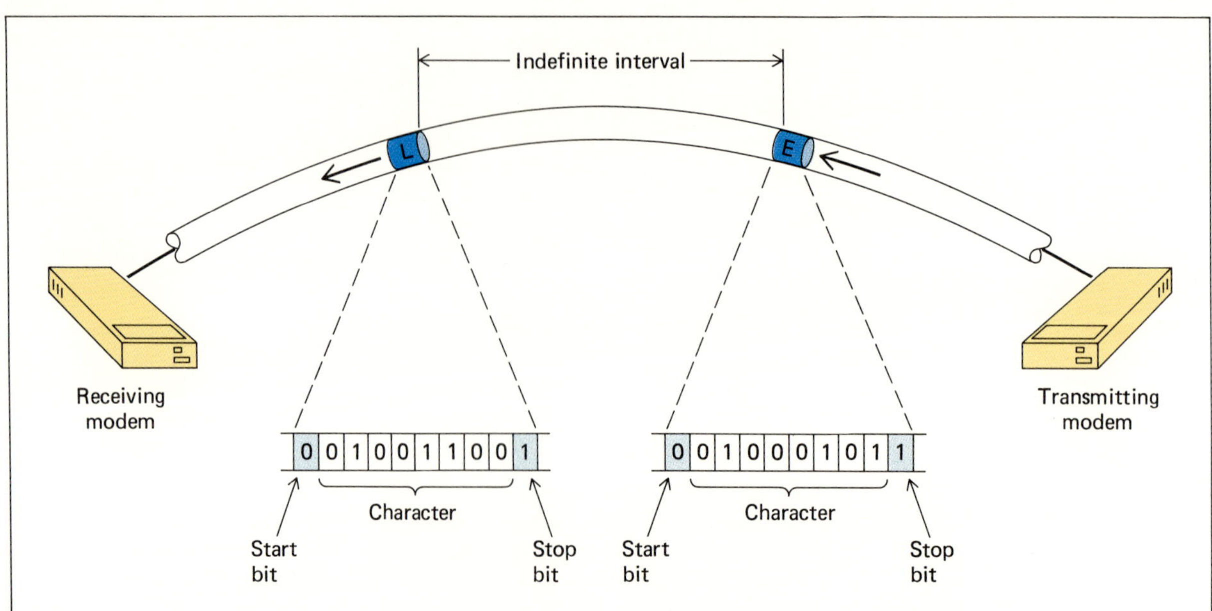

For mini-computer and mainframe data communication in which data files are transferred in a continuous stream from computer to computer, the character-framing feature of asynchronous transmission is not needed. Such applications use **synchronous transmission,** in which many characters are grouped together to form a block of data for transmission. At each end of each block there is identifying information that allows the modems to remain synchronized with one another and to perform error detection.

The primary advantage of synchronous transmission over asynchronous transmission is that it is more efficient. Where asynchronous transmission requires 10 bits per character, synchronous transmission of 7-bit ASCII data requires only the 7 bits for data plus a small overhead for block-framing characters. In general, synchronous modems are more expensive than asynchronous modems. Microcomputer modems are asynchronous, which is better suited for the start-stop nature of transmission from keyboard-entered data. Some microcomputer modems can be operated in either of the two modes.

Transmission Speed

One of the first questions that faces the microcomputer owner when purchasing a modem is that of transmission speed: the rate at which the modem can send and receive data. This is called the *transmission speed* or the *data rate* and is measured in bits per second. Conventional voice telephone lines can handle data transfer at the rate of 9600 bits per second, or 9600 baud.*

Although the communication line is capable of handling 9600 bits per second, the speed at which data can be transmitted depends upon the capabilities of the modem. Modem speeds range from 300 baud (the least costly) to 9600 baud (the most costly). Early modems used with microcomputers operated at 300 baud. As technology has progressed, the cost of higher-speed modems for microcomputers has dropped significantly. In 1988, 1200-baud modems were virtually a standard and 2400 baud was commonplace. Since asynchronous transmission uses 10 bits per character, 1200 baud is equivalent to 120 characters per second.

Although these speeds might seem reasonably fast, consider the situation in which you have signed onto a information utility such as The Source to scan a number of news releases. Each full screen of information that you receive will consist of 80 columns by 24 lines, or 1920 characters. (Actually, it will probably be somewhat less because spaces at the ends of the lines will not be transmitted.) Using the 1920 figure with a modem operating at 300 baud (30 characters per second), the time to fill the screen will be more than 60 seconds. At 1200 baud, the time will be 16 seconds and at 2400 baud it will be 8 seconds. For ordinary interactive use, 1200 baud is a good compromise for speed and relatively low cost. However, a microcomputer owner who must transfer large data files frequently should

---

*The term **baud** is defined as the number of signal changes per second in a transmission circuit. Using sophisticated encoding techniques (not used in microcomputer modems), 1 baud can represent 2 or 3 bits per second. Even though, in common usage, baud and bits per second are treated as equivalent, the common usage technically is incorrect.

consider a higher-speed (and higher-priced) modem. For instance, transmitting the contents of a floppy disk (360K bytes) at 2400 baud would required approximately 25 minutes. Under ideal transmitting circumstances, the transmission would require just over 6 minutes at 9600 baud.

Simplex, Half-Duplex, and Full-Duplex Transmission

Telephone circuits can transmit information in any of three modes: simplex, half-duplex, or full-duplex. With *simplex* transmission, information is transmitted in only one direction. Simplex transmission might be used for a remote temperature- or moisture-sensing unit that transmits readings to a computer.

At first thought, simplex transmission might appear adequate for many applications in which information is collected for remote entry into a computer, whether it be from an unattended sensing device or from a person operating a keyboard. However, almost all data processing applications require communication in both directions. Even for a "one-way" flow of information from a terminal to a computer, the link will be designed to allow the computer to signal the terminal that data has been received. Without this capability, the remote user would enter data and never know whether or not it was received by the computer.

Consequently, almost all applications operate in at least **half-duplex,** which allows information to be transmitted in either direction, but not in both directions at the same time. For instance, consider the sequence of events that might occur when a sales manager, using a portable computer, logs into the central office computer. (1) From the portable computer, the manager sends the log-in information. (2) The portable receives the computer acknowledgment. (3) From the portable, the manager sends a document to be saved to disk. (4) The portable computer receives acknowledgment that the file has been received. (5) From the portable, the manager sends a request for a sales summary file. (6) The portable computer receives the file from the central computer, and so on. To make such transmission possible, the modems must have two electronic circuits: one for transmitting and the other for receiving. The software in both computers is coordinated and causes each modem to switch between its transmitter circuitry and its receiver circuitry as needed.

At first thought, you might think that half-duplex is the only possible way of transmitting data over the single wire of a telephone circuit. However, using special electronic techniques, it is a simple matter to transmit in both directions at the same time: this is called **full-duplex** and is the method used by most microcomputer modems. The simplest example of full-duplex data transmission is the manner in which data entered through a keyboard is transmitted to a remote computer and displayed on the local screen. For instance, in Figure 20-18, each typed character is transmitted through the modem-telephone-modem interconnection to the remote computer. After accepting the character, the remote computer sends it back to the terminal, where it is displayed on the screen. At any given time, characters may be traveling in both directions. Notice that considerable coordination is necessary among the elements of this system. Although using such a system involves a relatively simple sequence of steps, the actions that take place are complex.

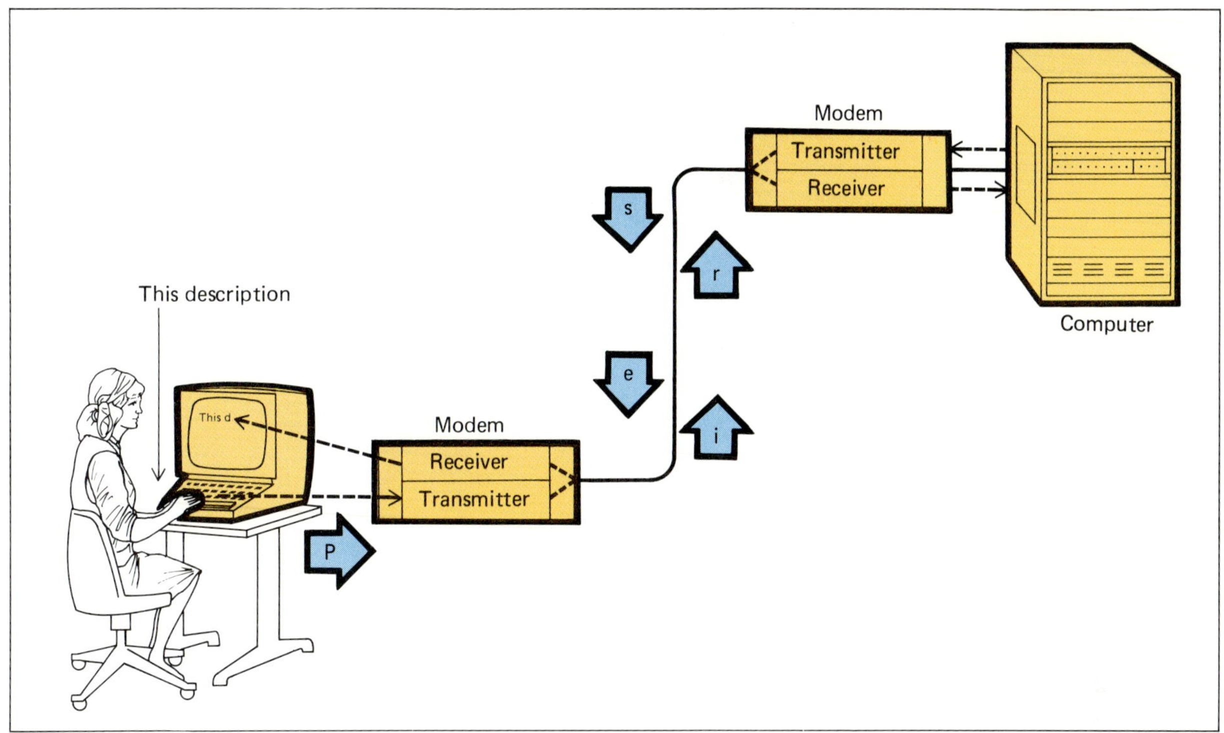

Figure 20-18
Simultaneous transmission of information in both directions.

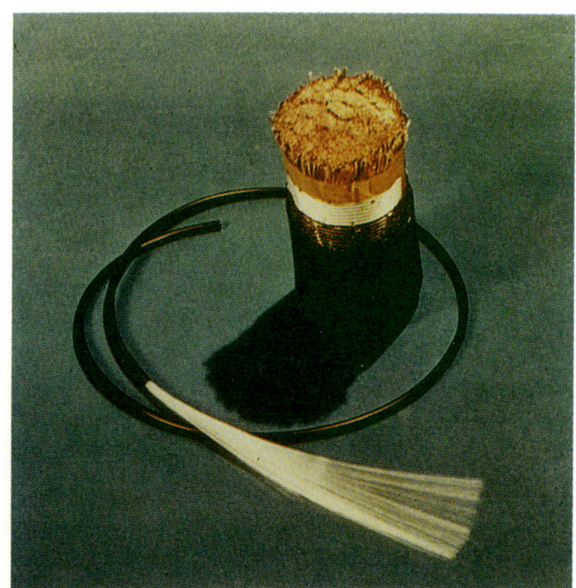

The strands of glass wire shown here can transmit far more information than the corresponding copper cables. Furthermore, the error rate of information transmitted is far lower.

Error Detection and Correction

The detection and correction of errors within the computer are critical to the design of a computer. Error handling is even more significant in data transmission because the error rate is many times higher for a transmission system than for a computer. Whereas voice communication can simply ignore errors, data transmission almost always requires that they be detected and corrected. There are three methods to deal with errors (other than ignoring them):

- Echo check.
- Computer detection with retransmission.
- Computer detection with automatic correction.

Echo checking is used with keyboard-entered data. As each character is entered through the keyboard, it is transmitted to the computer without being printed or displayed on the screen, as illustrated in Figure 20-18. The computer then transmits the character back, or echos it, for printing or display. Obviously, if the user has entered the letter G and the letter A is returned, something is amiss.

In Chapter 3, you learned that each memory byte includes a parity bit that allows the computer to check for errors when data is moved from one place within the computer to another. Unfortunately, parity checking is not adequate for error checking with data transmission because communication systems are many times more error-prone than internal components of the computer. Furthermore, errors in transmission systems tend to occur in clusters, thereby making the loss of two 1-bits in a given byte very likely. (The loss of two 1-bits will leave the parity count unchanged and without error indication.) To counter this, files are transmitted in blocks of characters.

The transmitting computer performs a series of calculations based on the data in the block, and then appends the result of the calculations to the end of the block. Upon receiving the block, the receiving computer performs the same calculations and compares its result with that stored in the transmitted block. If the calculated and transmitted calculations are equal, the receiving computer acknowledges that to the transmitting computer. The next block can then be transmitted. If the calculations are not equal, the receiving computer informs the transmitting computer to send the block again.

Using sophisticated coding methods, the error code calculations can include sufficient redundancy that many detected errors can be corrected by the receiving computer without retransmission of the data.

SUMMARY

This chapter has introduced you to sharing computer resources by interconnecting microcomputers in a local area network and through the use of the telephone system. Summarizing, the important items from the chapter are:

- A local area network (LAN) allows computers that make up the network to share both peripheral hardware devices and files.
- Computers of a local area network are directly connected by wire through a special network circuit board.
- Most local area networks include a computer that functions as a network server. This computer controls all network activities, including access to the network disk.
- Access to a network is controlled by assigning users access codes.
- Access to data files is controlled by defining the files to which each user has access. A user's access to one or more files can be defined as read only (cannot change) or as read/write (can read and change).
- A data file can be designated as sharable, meaning that two or more user programs can process the file at the same time, or nonsharable, meaning that if one program opens the file, no others can use it.
- If two programs are operating on the same file, the software should include some means for ensuring that both programs do not attempt to change the same record at the same time. Otherwise, data will be lost.
- There are three local area topologies (the physical arrangement of computers in a network): bus, star, and ring.
- A gateway is the hardware and software necessary to connect two local area networks, or a local area network to a mainframe.
- Data communication is the transmission, without change, of computer data over the telephone system.
- Modems convert digital signals of computers to analog signals of the telephone system (and back again).
- Data transmission over the telephone system is serial transmission. The RS232 standard defines the characteristics for connecting communication equipment to computers.
- With asynchronous data transmission, used by most microcomputer modems, data is transmitted character by character as it is ready. With synchronous transmission, data is accumulated and transmitted in blocks.
- Transmission speed is measured in bits per second. The maximum transmission speed of a voice telephone line is 9600 bits per second.
- The word *baud* is used to mean the same thing as bits per second. Although equating baud and bits per second is valid for most microcomputer modem transmission, they are technically different and not always the same.
- The modem determines the speed at which a computer can transmit

and receive data using the telephone system. Modems with speeds of 1200 bits per second are widely used for microcomputers.

- Data transmission can be simplex (one direction only), half-duplex (both directions but not simultaneously), or full-duplex (both directions simultaneously). Most microcomputer modems have full-duplex capabilities.
- Error detection is important in data transmission because of the high error rates resulting from telephone transmission. For keyboard interaction, echo checking is used whereby each character is transmitted to a remote computer, and then sent back for echoing on the local screen.
- For transmission of files, calculational methods are used whereby the sending computer determines checking values that are transmitted with the data. The receiving computer can duplicate the process and determine whether or not data loss has occurred.

NEW TERMINOLOGY

The following are important new terms introduced in this chapter; you should be familiar with each of them.

analog
asynchronous transmission
bandwidth
baud
bulletin board
bus network
data communication
data security
full-duplex
gateway
half-duplex
handshake
local area network (LAN)
modem
public domain software
read-only access
read/write access
record locking
ring network
RS232
serial transmission
simplex
star network
synchronous transmission
telecommunications
topology
virus

REVIEW QUESTIONS

1. What is a local area network? What are the advantages to an office of several computers interconnected through a local area network over several stand-alone computers?
2. What is a diskless workstation?
3. Explain the need for record locking in a local area network.
4. Explain the difference between LAN bandwidth and topology.
5. Describe the three types of local area network configurations.

6. If a person in a business environment has a mainframe at his or her disposal, of what value would a microcomputer be?
7. What are the three basic components of a telecommunication system?
8. What function does the modem serve in a data communication system?
9. What are the basic functions performed by communications software?
10. A company uses an on-line system with a large number of remote users. A security expert has installed a very clever sequence of codes and passwords that should be almost impossible to "crack." The company, therefore, feels that the data is secure. Do you agree? Comment.
11. What is meant by "start-stop" transmission?
12. A terminal receives data at the rate of 1200 bits per second. Approximately how many characters per second will be printed?
13. What are the differences among simplex, half-duplex, and full-duplex data transmission?
14. Why is echo checking (for error detection) impractical for use with the transmission of files?
15. What is the purpose of RS232?

MATCHING

Match each term in a to h with the most appropriate description in 1 through 8.

a. baud
b. read-only access
c. RS232
d. bandwidth
e. record locking
f. topology
g. modem
h. full-duplex

1. Changes digital data to analog and analog to digital.
2. A measure of the speed of a local area network.
3. Commonly (but erroneously) used to mean the same as bits per second.
4. Data transmission whereby data is being transmitted over a telephone line in both directions at the same time.
5. Defines characteristics for interfacing computer equipment and telephone equipment.
6. Restricts a user from deleting a file from the network disk of a local area network.
7. Prevents the loss of data by two users attempting to change the same record of a local area network file at the same time.
8. The way in which the computers of a local area network are interconnected.

TRUE/FALSE

Determine whether each of the following is true or false.

______ 1. In a local area network, the computers are either directly connected by wires or through telephone lines.

______ 2. Most networks have a file server, which is a computer to control access of other computers in the network to the shared resources of the network.

______ 3. It is possible to have computers in a local area network that do not have disk drives and yet are capable of disk processing.

______ 4. In a local area network, a file can be set up so that none of the users can delete it from the network disk.

______ 5. Record locking means designating certain records of a file that cannot be changed.

______ 6. In a bus network, there is a separate cable from the network server to each computer in the network.

______ 7. A problem with ring network topology is that the failure of one computer can disrupt flow of data in the network.

______ 8. A gateway is a hardware/software combination that allows two or more computers to share a printer.

______ 9. The purpose of modems in data transmission is to improve the efficiency of transmission by converting digital signals to analog.

______ 10. The term *handshake* used in data communications means establishing a link between two computers.

______ 11. One danger of using public domain software is the possibility of having your computer infected with a virus that can destroy the files on your disk.

______ 12. Using complicated access codes can provide complete security to computer systems that are accessible through the telephone circuits.

______ 13. Most data communication uses parallel transmission because it is faster than serial transmission.

______ 14. Synchronous data transmission is best suited for the transmission of data entered from a keyboard.

______ 15. Echo checking is a method of error detection used with data communication.

ANSWERS TO OBJECTIVE QUESTIONS

Matching

1. g 2. d 3. a 4. h 5. c 6. b 7. e 8. f

True/False

1. F 2. T 3. T 4. T 5. F 6. F 7. T 8. F 9. F
10. T 11. T 12. F 13. F 14. F 15. T

Glossary

Access time The interval between the time at which data is requested from a storage device and the instant when the transfer of data begins.

Alphanumeric (see Character data)

ANSI An acronym for American National Standards Institute, an organization that establishes standards for U.S. business and industry.

Arithmetic/logic unit The unit of a computing system that contains the circuits to perform arithmetic and comparison operations.

ASCII An acronym for American Standard Code for Information Interchange, one of two widely used methods for coding data.

Assemble To convert or translate a computer program from a symbolic assembly language to a machine language.

Assembler A computer program that performs the task of assembling a symbolic program to machine language.

Auxiliary storage Storage that supplements the main memory of a computer. Magnetic disk and tape are commonly encountered auxiliary storage media.

Backup file A copy of a file that is set aside for reference in case the original file is destroyed.

BASIC Beginner's All-purpose Symbolic Instruction Code, a widely used interactive programming language.

Baud The number of signal changes per second in a communications system. Commonly (although inaccurately) used to mean the same as bits per second.

Binary digit In binary notation, either of the digits 0 and 1.

Bit A binary digit.

Boilerplate In word processing, sections of standardized text that are stored as files and inserted into documents where needed.

Booting up The process by the computer of loading the operating format from disk into main memory to make itself ready for use.

Buffer Memory into which data transfers are made during input or output activities; it may be a portion of internal memory or in an I/O device.

Bug A mistake or malfunction in a program or a computer system.

Bulletin board The electronic equivalent of an office bulletin board whereby, through the telephone system, a user can interconnect a microcomputer to send and receive information.

Bus A group of parallel wires (circuits) that provide a communication path between two or more components of a computer.

Bus network A computer network in which computers are interconnected by a single group of wires (a bus) through which data is transmitted in both directions.

Byte A group of eight binary digits operated upon as a unit; the basic storage unit of most computers.

C (programming language) A general-purpose, portable programming language that allows access to features of computer hardware, and yet is high level.

CAD/CAM An abbreviation for computer-aided design (CAD) and computer-aided manufacturing (CAM).

Captured keystroke In word processing, relating to the fact that text that is keyed into the word processor will be saved for later processing and need not be retyped in its entirety.

Cell In a spreadsheet program such as Lotus 1-2-3, a basic unit that can store a label, number, or formula. Cells of a spreadsheet are arranged in rows and columns.

Central processing unit (CPU) A unit of a computer that includes the control unit, arithmetic/logic unit, and sometimes the main memory of a computer.

Character data Pertaining to a character set that contains letters, digits, and usually special characters such as the comma and question mark.

COBOL COmmon Business Oriented Language, a programming language designed specifically for business data processing applications.

Compile To convert or translate a program from a high-level language (for example, FORTRAN, COBOL, and Pascal) to machine language.

Compiler A computer program that performs the compiling operation.

Computer graphics The display of information in the form of graphs or charts.

Control unit That part of the processor that manages overall control of data movement and instruction execution within the computer.

CRT (cathode-ray tube) Referring to a terminal that displays output on a television-type screen.

Cursor The display point on the screen that indicates where the next character entered from the keyboard will be displayed.

Cut and paste In word processing, the operation of deleting text from one point in a document and inserting it at some other point.

Daisy-wheel printer A letter-quality impact printer that uses a printing element consisting of spokelike arms, each terminated with a raised character.

Data A representation of facts or concepts in a formalized manner suitable for communication, interpretation, or processing by humans or by automatic means.

Data communication The transmission over the telephone network of computer data without change or processing.

Data definition file A file that contains formatting and other descriptive information regarding information stored in a database.

Data rate The speed at which data is transmitted from one device to another.

Database A collection of data files integrated and organized into a single comprehensive file system. The data is arranged to minimize duplication and to provide convenient access to information within that system to satisfy a wide variety of user needs.

Database management system (DBMS) The software used for the management and retrieval of the data stored in a database.

Data rate The speed at which data is transmitted from one device to another.

Debug To detect, locate, and remove mistakes from a program or malfunctions from a computer.

Default value In any programming system, a value that is used by the system if the user does not specify some value. For instance, a word processor might automatically use tab stops at every five positions unless the user sets them at other values.

Density The number of useful storage positions per unit of length or area commonly measured in bits per inch.

Desktop publishing A microcomputer system that includes page layout software and a laser printer for preparing near-professional-looking publications.

Diagnostic A statement printed by an assembler or compiler indicating errors detected in the source program.

Direct access Pertaining to a storage device in which the time required to obtain data is independent of the location of the data. Synonymous with random access.

Directory A reference file that is effectively an index of the files stored on a disk.

Disk See Magnetic disk.

Disk drive An auxiliary storage device that houses magnetic disks for the storage of data. The disks can be removable (floppy disks) or fixed (hard disks).

Diskette (see Floppy disk)

Document A data record intended for human use, such as a report sheet or a book; any record that has permanence and can be read by humans or by machine.

Documentation Descriptions concerning the preparation, use, and general nature of a computer program, procedure, or system.

DOS An acronym for Disk Operating System; see also operating system.

Dot-matrix printer A printer that forms characters with a series of dots.

EBCDIC An 8-bit code used for data representation introduced with the IBM 360 and used in IBM and IBM-compatible mainframes.

End-of-line character In word processing, an "invisible character" that is entered with text in order to indicate the end of a text line.

Expansion board A circuit board that is inserted into the motherboard of a microcomputer to provide an additional function—for instance, more memory or additional periperals.

Field A single data item made up of a group of characters; for example, a person's Social Security number.

File A collection of related records treated as a unit. For example, the entire set of customer data records make up the customer file.

File management system A collection of programs to simplify the management of data files. Operations that are normally supported include file creation, record entry and editing, record sorting and selection, and report generation.

File specification In MS DOS, the designator that is used to indicate a file to be processed. For instance, B:CUSTOMER.DBF is the file specification for the file CUSTOMER.DBF located on the B drive.

Floppy disk A thin, flexible magnetic disk storage device. Also see Magnetic disk.

Flowchart A graphical representation for the definition, analysis, or solution of a problem, in which symbols are used to represent operations and logic flow.

Flowchart symbol A symbol used to represent operations and flow on a flowchart.

Font In publishing, the original meaning was the source from which a typeface was generated (for instance, the daisy wheel of a daisy-wheel printer). In desktop publishing, commonly means a single size of a typeface.

Format The arrangement of data in a record.

FORTRAN FORmula TRANslating language, a programming language designed mainly for math/engineering types of applications.

Full-duplex A communication line that allows transmission in both directions at the same time.

Function A predefined set of operations to perform a desired operation. For instance, in Lotus 1-2-3, the @SUM function will calculate the sum of the values entered into a series cells.

Gateway The hardware and software to allow the interconnection of two local area networks, or a local area network and a mainframe computer.

Global Relating to the fact that an action refers to the entire entity under consideration. For instance, a global change of columns in a spreadsheet means that all columns will be affected by the change.

Handshake Referring to the electronic acknowledgment from one computer to another that a communications link has been established.

Hard copy Printed output from a computer device (as opposed to soft copy).

Hardware The physical equipment such as the computer and its peripherals; contrast with software.

Hertz Technically, a measure of radio or electrical frequency; equivalent to cycles per second. When describing computer speed, refers to the speed of the internal clock in the microprocessor; the speed of the original PC was 4.77 megahertz (million hertz).

Hidden code In word processing, any coded character that does not display on the screen. For instance, the tab character causes text to be spaced over to the right and the hard return character causes a line to be ended.

Hidden file A file stored on disk and flagged by the operating system so that its name is not shown on a directory display.

High-level language A programming language whose structure is application oriented and is independent of the structure of the computer; for example, FORTRAN and COBOL.

Icon A pictorial representation of a function to be performed by a computer.

Impact printer A printer that performs its printing action by the impact of a printing element against the paper (or ink ribbon). For instance, a typewriter is an impact printer.

Inconsistent data Duplicated data in two or more files in which a data element in one of the files is different from the same data element in another file.

Indexed file A file that includes an index of records in the file to make direct processing of the file practical.

Input The source data entered into a data processing system.

Input device A device used to bring information into a computer or other data processing device; for instance, terminal keyboard.

Input/output (I/O) Pertaining to either input or output, or both.

Integrated circuit Refers to miniaturization of electronic circuits such that thousands of components are formed on a small chip of silicon.

Integrated software A software package that includes at least the three basic productivity products—word processing, spreadsheet, and data management.

Interactive computing A programming method by which a programmer can "converse" with a computer through a keyboard and receive immediate results.

Internal memory See Memory.

Interpreter A language translator program that converts each high-level statement to machine language as the statement is encountered during execution of the program.

I/O See Input/output.

K When referring to storage capacity, two to the tenth power; 1024 in decimal notation.

Key field A field within a data record to identify the record or to control its use.

Label In spreadsheet programs, descriptive text information that is entered into a cell (as opposed to numbers that may be used in calculations).

LAN See Local area network.

Laser printer A nonimpact printer that uses a laser to form images on a surface that are transferred to a page and printed in the same way as a copying machine prints.

Letter quality Printing in which the characters are fully formed and solid (as opposed to formed by a series of dots).

Local area network (LAN) A collection of computers interconnected such that resources can be shared among them. Usually, the maximum distance between the two most remote computers is relatively short (measured in thousands of feet or less).

Loop A sequence of instructions that is executed repeatedly until a condition occurs to end the execution.

Looping structure In structured programming theory, the structured form that provides for repeated execution of a sequence.

Low-level language A language that is based on the architecture of a computer. Machine language and assembly language are low-level languages.

Machine language A language that is used directly by a machine, thus requiring no translation.

Magnetic disk A flat, circular plate with a magnetic surface on which data can be stored by magnetization of portions of the flat surface.

Magnetic tape A tape with a magnetic surface on which data can be stored by magnetization of portions of the surface.

Mainframe A large computer—often one that performs multiple tasks concurrently and/or serves many users at the same time. Generally considered larger than a minicomputer, but there is no clear line of distinction between the two.

Master file A file that is either relatively permanent or that is treated as an authority in a particular job, for instance, the customer master file. Contrast with invoice file.

Matrix printer A printer that forms characters with a series of dots such as is done with a typical athletic scoreboard.

Memory Pertaining to an internal device into which data can be entered, in which it can be held, and from which it can be randomly retrieved at a later time. Also called internal storage.

Memory resident program A program that is loaded into low memory and remains in memory and is available for use when another user program is loaded and run.

Microcomputer A small computer (often little larger than a typewriter), which, in its basic form, commonly sells for $1000 or less.

Microprocessor A microminiature computer chip that includes the control unit, arithmetic/logic unit, and work registers of the computer.

Microsecond One millionth (0.000001 or 10^{-6}) of a second.

Millisecond One thousandth (0.001 or 10^{-3}) of a second; commonly abbreviated ms or msec.

Minicomputer A relatively small computer that exhibits most of the features of a mainframe computer but on a limited basis. There is no clear line of distinction between the minicomputer and the mainframe.

Modem A device that allows computer digital information to be transmitted over telephone circuits.

Motherboard The principal circuit board of a microcomputer; expansion boards are plugged into receptacles of the motherboard.

Mouse A small hand-held device that a user can move across a surface to control positioning of the cursor on the screen or to select menu options.

Multitasking Pertaining to the concurrent execution of two or more programs by a computer.

Nanosecond One billionth (0.000000001 or 10^{-9}) of a second; commonly abbreviated ns or nsec.

Network In data processing, usually refers to an arrangement of two or more computers interconnected by a communication system. Also see Local area network.

Nonimpact printer A printer that performs its printing operation without striking the paper. For example, an ink jet printer sprays the ink onto the paper and a laser printer uses copying machine methods.

Nonvolatile memory Memory that does not require continuous electric power to retain its stored information.

Object program A fully compiled or assembled program that is ready to be loaded into the computer and run.

Operating system Software that controls the operation of computer programs and that may provide scheduling, data management, and related services.

Output The finished results of processing by a system.

Parallel interface Relating to the electrical interconnection between the computer and peripheral units (for instance, a printer) in which data is tranmitted 1 or more bytes at a time over a group of wires.

Parity check A check that tests whether the number of 1s (or 0s) in an array of binary digits is odd or even.

Pascal A high-level structured programming language.

Peripheral device Any input or output device that is connected to the computer.

Pixel Means picture element and is the addressable unit dot used to form images on the monitor screen.

Procedural language A programming language designed for the convenient expression of procedures used in the solution of a wide class of problems; for example, FORTRAN and COBOL.

Productivity software Software designed for specialized applications whereby the user need know virtually nothing about the computer in order to use it: for instance, word processing, spreadsheet, and file management.

Program A set of instructions or commands to the computer telling the computer what to do to accomplish a given task.

Prompt In an interactive environment (using a terminal or a microcomputer), a brief message that gives the user an indication of what type of response is required.

Pseudocode An "English" version of actual programming statements used as an aid in program preparation.

Public domain software Software that has been made available to computer users at no charge by the author. Public domain programs are commonly available through computer bulletin boards.

RAM (random access memory) Computer memory in which data in any part of the memory can be accessed as quickly as data in any other part of memory.

RAM disk A simulated auxiliary storage device (disk) set up in main memory to improve the speed of disk operations.

Random access The accessing of data without regard to its physical placement in the storage device.

Random processing Processing in which records of a file are processed in random sequence (contrast with sequential processing).

Read-only access Pertaining to data, usually to files stored on disk, that can be read but not changed (not written).

Read-only memory See ROM.

Read/write access Pertaining to data, usually to files stored on disk, that can be read and changed (written).

Record A collection of related fields of data, treated as a unit; for example, the customer record. A complete set of such records forms a file.

Record locking A technique used in file processing where two or more users can be using the same file concurrently but not the same record.

Redundant data In a file or database system, data that is duplicated in two or more different records or files.

Replicate In a spreadsheet system, the process of copying a formula to other rows or columns with automatic modifications to the formula to account for the repositioning.

Resolution A measure of the density of dots or pixels in forming an image with a laser printer or monitor.

Response time With an on-line system, the time delay between a request to the computer for information and the return of that information from the computer.

Right-justify In word processing, spacing the words on lines of a document so that the right margins as well as the left line up.

Ring network A computer network in which computers communicate with one another through a single cable that forms a loop (a ring). Data flows in only one direction.

ROM Read only memory—memory containing computer code or data that is prewritten and cannot be changed.

RS-232 A commonly used, standardized serial interface.

Root directory The base directory of a disk. It can contain other subdirectories.

Scroll The movement of data or text display across the screen (up, down, left, or right)—may result from making additional entries or by some direct user option.

Search and replace In a word processing system, relating to the process of the system automatically searching for specified text and replacing it with something else.

Sector An area of storage on disk; it is the smallest unit that can be directly addressed and hence read from or written to the disk.

Selection structure In structured programming theory, the structured form that provides for execution of either of two sets of instructions.

Semiconductor A material that can be made to conduct or not conduct electricity. Semiconductors form the basis of microminiature computer technology.

Sequence structure In structured programming theory, the structured form that represents the occurrence of one event after another.

Sequential Pertaining to the occurrence of events in time sequence (one after the other), with little or no overlap of events.

Sequential processing Processing in which records are processed beginning with the first and continuing through the last (records processed sequentially).

Serial interface Relating to the electrical interconnection between the computer and peripheral units (for instance, a printer) in which data is tranmitted 1 bit at a time over a single wire.

Serial printer A printer in which characters are printed one at a time in a manner similar to that of a typewriter.

Serial transmission Pertaining to the process of transmitting data through a single conducter, 1 bit after the other.

Soft copy Computer output that is displayed on the screen of a terminal and provides no permanent copy (as opposed to hard copy).

Software A set of computer programs, procedures, and possibly associated documentation concerned with the operation of a data processing system; for example, compilers, library routines, productivity software, and associated manuals.

Sort To arrange records into a predetermined sequence.

Source program A computer program written in a source language such as assembly language or COBOL. Contrasts with object program.

Spelling checker A program, commonly included with a word processor, to check the spelling of all words in a document.

Spooler A program to accept printed output of an application program from the processor at processor speeds, write it to disk, then send it to the printer while the application program continues.

Spreadsheet program A computerized system for entering, manipulating, and displaying information in a table form. Lotus 1-2-3 is an example of a spreadsheet program.

Star network A computer network that employs a central network server computer to which all computers of the network are individually cabled. All data flow is through the network server.

String data Same as character data, that is, pertaining to a character set that contains letters, digits, and usually special characters such as the comma and question mark.

Structured programming An organized approach to programming involving the use of the three basic control structures—sequence, selection, and loop. Characterized by minimizing or eliminating the need for branching instructions.

Subdirectory A disk directory created within another directory that allows the user to view the contents of the disk as collections of related files. This is especially useful for a hard disk that may contain hundreds or thousands of files.

Syntax The structure and coding rules of a programming language.

System A collection of elements to accomplish a specific set of functions. Depending upon its usage, the word commonly refers to: (1) a combination of people, procedures, and machines; (2) computer software; (3) computer hardware; or, (4) the combination of computer hardware and software.

Telecommunications The transmission of information over the telephone system.

Template A prewritten spreadsheet in which all labels and formulas have been entered and the user need only enter the data.

Terminal A device that allows a user to communicate directly with a computer.

Thesaurus A feature commonly included with word processors that will display alternative words (synonyms) for a selected word.

Topology The way in which computers of a network are interconnected—for instance, bus, ring, and star.

Track A circular recording path on the surface of a disk.

Typeface In publishing, a set of characters, numerals, punctuation marks, and related symbols that have been designed with a consistent appearance.

Variable In a programming language, a quantity that can assume any of a given set of values.

Virus A section of machine language code inserted into a program so that it attaches itself to the operating system with the intent of causing trouble, which can range from displaying unexpected messages to erasing a disk.

Volatile memory Memory in which its contents are lost when electric power is turned off.

Window A portion of the monitor screen that is used to display information while other parts of the screen display other information.

Word processing Involving the computerized entry, storage, editing, formatting, and printing of written (text) type of information.

Word wrap In word processing, relating to the fact that the computer automatically moves a word to the next line if it will not fit on the current one as it is being entered.

Worksheet Same as a spreadsheet.

Write protect notch A notch cut in one corner of a floppy disk that must be uncovered in order to write on the disk. If the notch is covered (with a self-adhesive tab), the disk is said to be write protected and data on the disk can be read but not changed.

WYSIWYG An acronym for "What You See Is What You Get." Refers to the screen display of a word processing document being identical to the eventual printed form.

Index

PHOTO CREDIT LIST

CHAPTER 1

Fig. 1–2a: Gabe Palmer/The Stock Market; **b:** Courtesy Intel Corp.; **c:** Courtesy Hewlett-Packard; **d:** Courtesy IBM; **p. 5:** McAllister/Uniphoto; **p. 10:** Courtesy IBM; **p. 12** A. Tannenbaum/Sygma; **p. 16:** Courtesy Hewlett-Packard; **p. 20:** Courtesy Harneschfeger Engineers, Inc.; **p. 23:** Courtesy Sharp Electronics Corporation.

CHAPTER 2

Fig. 2–1: Courtesy Apple Computers Inc.; **p. 28:** Garfield/The Stock Market; **p. 32:** Courtesy IBM; **p. 36 (both):** Ed Linton/U.S. Windpower; **p. 42:** Courtesy Ashton-Tate; **p. 48:** Courtesy Evans & Sutherland.

CHAPTER 3

Fig. 3–3: Courtesy IBM; **Fig. 3–4:** Courtesy Intel Corp.; **p. 58 (top):** Courtesy Harris Corp.; **(bottom):** Courtesy Cray Research Inc. Photo by Paul Shambroom; **p. 63a:** Courtesy Radio Shack, A Division of Tandy; **b:** Courtesy Apple Computers Inc.; **c:** Courtesy IBM; **d:** Courtesy Apple Computers Inc.; **e:** Courtesy IBM; **p. 66 (both):** Courtesy Intel Corp.; **p. 69 (both):** Courtesy IBM.

CHAPTER 4

Fig. 4–3a & b and Fig. 4–5a & b: Courtesy IBM; **Fig. 4–9:** Courtesy Hewlett-Packard; **Fig. 4–12:** Courtesy MSC Technologies Inc.; **Fig. 4–13:** Courtesy Apple Computers Inc.; **Fig. 4–19:** Courtesy Hewlett-Packard; **Fig. 4–20:** Courtesy Seagate; **Fig. 4–21:** Courtesy Radio Shack, A Division of Tandy; **p. 83:** Photo of the Cornerstone DualPage System, Courtesy of Cornerstone Technology; **p. 93:** Courtesy Intermec; **p. 95 (bottom):** Courtesy Hewlett-Packard; **p. 102:** Courtesy McDonnell Douglas; **p. 105:** Courtesy 3M.

CHAPTER 5

P. 130: Courtesy Unison Technologies Inc.

CHAPTER 6

P. 152: Arthur Grace/Sygma; **p. 156:** Courtesy WordPerfect Corporation.

CHAPTER 7

P. 175: Courtesy IBM; **p. 187 (left):** Courtesy IBM; **(right):** Courtesy Radio Shack, A Division of Tandy.

CHAPTER 8

P. 219: Courtesy Texas Instruments; **p. 231:** Microsoft Chart, © Microsoft Corporation, 1986–1987. Reprinted with permission from Microsoft Corporation.

CHAPTER 9

Fig. 9–3: Courtesy Apple Computers, Inc.; **p. 251:** Courtesy The Complete PC, Inc.; **p. 256:** Courtesy Harris Corporation; **p. 263:** Courtesy Xerox Corporation, **p. 267:** Courtesy Aldus Corporation.

CHAPTER 10

P. 279: Jon Feingersh/The Stock Market; **p. 286:** Courtesy Hewlett-Packard Company.

CHAPTER 11

P. 309: Courtesy IBM; **p. 329:** Courtesy Hewlett-Packard Company.

CHAPTER 12

P. 365: Courtesy Lotus Development Corp.

CHAPTER 13

P. 398a: Courtesy Intergraph Corporation; **b:** © Microsoft Corporation. Reprinted with permission from Microsoft Corporation; **d:** Courtesy American Small Business Computers, Inc.; **p. 421:** Courtesy Hewlett-Packard Company.

CHAPTER 14

P. 437: Henryk T. Kaiser/Uniphoto; **p. 447:** © Rodney Jackson/Darla Hillard.

CHAPTER 15

P. 484: Courtesy IBM; **p. 494:** Courtesy Mapping Information System Corporation, Troy, NY.

CHAPTER 16

P. 519: Jose Reyes/Uniphoto.

CHAPTER 17

P. 555 (left): Peter Vadnai/The Stock Market; **(right):** Courtesy Computer Associates International, Inc.; **p. 560:** Courtesy Ashton-Tate; **p. 567:** Courtesy Digital Equipment Corporation.

CHAPTER 18

P. 582–583a: Courtesy Honeywell Bull, Inc.; **b:** Bob Daemmrich/Stock, Boston; **c:** Charles West/The Stock Market; **d:** Gabe Palmer/The Stock Market; **e:** Courtesy Hewlett-Packard Company.

CHAPTER 20

Fig. 20–15: Teri Stratford; **p. 625:** Courtesy Quadram; **p. 638a & b:** Courtesy Everex Systems, Inc.; **p. 641 (left):** Courtesy M/A-COM, Inc.; **(right):** Courtesy General Motors Corporation; **p. 647:** Courtesy Bell Laboratories.